The Swing Era

The History of Jazz

Volume I Early Jazz:
Its Roots and Musical Development

Volume II The Swing Era:
The Development of Jazz, 1930–1945

The Swing Era

THE DEVELOPMENT OF JAZZ
1930–1945

GUNTHER SCHULLER

OXFORD UNIVERSITY PRESS
New York   Oxford

Oxford University Press

Oxford   New York   Toronto
Delhi   Bombay   Calcutta   Madras   Karachi
Petaling Jaya   Singapore   Hong Kong   Tokyo
Nairobi   Dar es Salaam   Cape Town
Melbourne   Auckland

and associated companies in
Berlin   Ibadan

Copyright © 1989 by Oxford University Press, Inc.

First published in 1989 by Oxford University Press, Inc.,
198 Madison Avenue, New York, New York 10016-4314

First issued as an Oxford University Press paperback, 1991

Oxford is a registered trademark of Oxford University Press

Library of Congress Cataloging-in-Publication Data
Schuller, Gunther (1925–   ) The swing era.
(The History of jazz ; v. 2) Includes index.
1. Jazz music. I. Title. II. Series.
ML3506.S36 1986 vol. 2 781'.57 s   87-1664
[781'.57'09043] ISBN 0-19-504312-X
ISBN 0-19-507140-9 (PBK.)

The following page is regarded as an extension
of the copyright page.

4 6 8 9 7 5 3
Printed in the United States of America

For Edwin and George
—and Marjorie

—and in memory of
the incomparable Lawrence Brown

Preface

The die was cast circa 1967, when—perhaps a mite too casually—in my book *Early Jazz: Its Roots and Musical Development* I promised a second installment in a contemplated complete History of Jazz. Little did I realize then what an awesome task I had set myself. Over twenty years, nearly 900 pages of text and over 30,000 listenings to recordings later, Volume II is now, finally, finished— well, almost. As I write this Preface, I am in the pleasurable but time-consuming throes of compiling the over-4000-item Index.

Perhaps my grandest miscalculation in embarking on this book was the assumption that Volume II would take a half a dozen years or so to write, and that therefore I would be able to bring the *entire* history of jazz up to date by the mid-seventies or thereabouts. Work on the book quickly taught me otherwise, for I had quite misjudged—with all of my love and prior knowledge of jazz from the last five decades or so—how extraordinarily rich the Swing Era alone was, quite apart from the postwar developments of bebop, modern jazz, and beyond. Not only was there a vast amount of material to be covered, particularly once I determined that I would include a serious and fairly comprehensive study of the white swing bands (ignored in most jazz histories), but in addition I soon discovered that my prior knowledge of the period was in itself flawed, influenced in that respect by my own previous readings and "accumulated wisdoms" garnered from other jazz histories and the reissue programs of record companies. I soon realized that I would not only have to delve into much more material than I had previously contemplated but also have to redress some major neglects and injustices, and de-mythify a few of the prevailing, long-held jazz mythologies and legends.

In that sense the writing of this book was a fantastic journey of discovery. Rummaging around in many previously neglected corners of jazz history, I was delighted—and privileged—to discover many an artistic gem.

In writing this book, my approach to the subject was essentially simple. I imagined myself coming to jazz without any prior knowledge or preconceptions and beginning, *tabula rasa*, to listen to the recordings—systematically and comprehensively. Although it was not possible in this volume—as opposed to *Early Jazz* with its considerably lesser number of recordings to be dealt with—to adhere totally to the principle of comprehensive listening, the basic premise was still to have heard *every recording* of any artist, orchestra, or group that would come under discussion—and to listen systematically/chronologically in order to trace accurately their development and achievements. This approach obviously led to tens of thousands of hours of listening, much of that to rather pitiful dross (at worst), formulaic redundancy (at best), but thus all the more highlighting the true masterpieces of the art. This kind of systematic/comprehensive listening to the recorded evidence—often the only reliable information the jazz historian has—puts things in true, sometimes glaring perspective—something that selective listening, no matter how intelligent or knowledgeable, cannot provide. As a historian I consider it of paramount importance to discuss—or at least be aware of—the *totality* of an artist's work, if necessary the bad with the good. Even the lesser works can teach us much about an artist.

This kind of comprehensive listening also allows one better to appreciate the interconnections and cross-references between artists, between geographic areas, between periods, all revealing a fascinating and often bewildering web of linkages and relationships criss-crossing the entire field and the entire time period. I have further suggested link-ups with other musical traditions—in particular classical music but also jazz's African heritage—and beyond that occasionally even with other art forms (painting, literature, etc.). No art or act of creativity stands in isolation, self-contained and uninfluenced by its times, its social and cultural environment, and its own history. It is in that sense that I have tried to frame jazz in the larger cultural-historical context. This approach included, quite logically, I think, the isolation and emphasis of certain themes or threads that pervade the entire book, such as the constant threat of and struggle against commercialism, or the pervasive influence of the blues and "blue notes"—such themes also being reflected dramatically in the Index.

I trust that readers will find the many musical examples helpful. There are over 500—some of them fairly extensive—having required many, many hundreds of hours of laborious transcribing from recordings. While not every reader will be able to read musical notation, very often even the visual shape of the musical example, or its relative graphic complexity (to be seen by any discerning eye), will I hope enhance the lay reader's appreciation of the music in question and my textual commentary on it. Musical notation has its inadequacies, of course; it cannot capture tone, expression, subtle nuances and inflections. It is at best a blueprint which has to be fleshed out by the performer's (or in this case the reader's) imagination. But this process will be greatly aided if the reader can combine his reading of the musical examples with hearing the respective recordings. Unfortunately, because of the immense number of records dealt with in this book and the vagaries of record companies' reissue programs, particularly in regard to their retention of reissues in their catalogues, I have dispensed with discographical information or suggested record listings. Records that I listened to, say, in 1976 may long ago have fallen out of reach again.

The period covered in this volume proceeds roughly from the early thirties to the late forties. The book picks up essentially where *Early Jazz* left off, with a few forays back into the 1920s to treat subjects not covered—or inadequately covered—in the earlier volume (e.g. Isham Jones, the Missourians, some of the early Territory Bands, etc.). The book ends with the emergence of bebop, the arrival of Parker, Gillespie, and Monk, tentatively introducing, as it were, the then-new cast of characters of the unfolding drama of jazz history. In the case of some older musicians—Armstrong, Hines, Eldridge—I have taken their achievements more or less through the ends of their careers or lives, to be updated (where applicable) in the context of Volume III.

I regret some omissions, and there may be others that I am not yet aware of. But I wish I could have treated relatively important figures like "Hot Lips" Page or Fats Waller more extensively. They deserve it; but at a certain point I simply ran out of time (and energy), and the book, with flaws and omissions and any other literary warts it may have, had finally to be put to bed.

While I regret the seemingly inordinate length of time it took to write this book, there were certain benefits and advantages. One was that the late 1970s to early 80s turned out to be a period of the greatest, most extensive reissue programs by virtually all the record companies in the history of the music. Many recordings, which for *Early Jazz* I had to laboriously acquire as 78s from record collectors (often at outrageous prices), I could now for the later period obtain in LP reissues. This made life much easier and enabled me to acquire recordings otherwise virtually impossible to hear and study.

Regrettably a number of major jazz figures died during the latter stages of completing the book (e.g. Goodman, Herman, Basie, Williams). Again, time and other practical constraints precluded the kind of updating and rounding out of the picture one might have wished to include.

There is much more to be said and to be done. Jazz did not stop in 1942— or 1948—or 1960, for that matter. I have once again—perhaps foolishly—promised to express my devotion to jazz in a third installment of this history, confirming the view that jazz, as any other creative tradition, is an ongoing process, a continuity which is always changing and in transition, with no predictable end in sight.

I now entrust this volume to you, my loyal readers, in the hope that you will await the next installment with a degree of benign patience.

Newton Centre   G.S.
June 27, 1988

Acknowledgments

A book of this physical magnitude and complexity cannot be written without the help and generosity of many, many individuals and organizations. I owe them all a deep debt of gratitude for making my task that much easier, indeed for making it possible altogether.

Where does one begin, with such a host of generous friends and colleagues? Perhaps with those whose help was the most crucial in allowing me to do the necessary listening and analysis of that prerequisite staple for the jazz musicologist and historian: the recordings. As many records as I already owned, there were so many more in undertaking this history that needed to be acquired, analyzed, and studied. Among those many kind individuals who let me borrow or duplicate their precious and often very rare recordings, or who directed me to sources where I might purchase or otherwise obtain recordings which I felt absolutely obligated to hear (even if I didn't end up writing about them), I would like particularly to single out Tom Tsotsi and Jack Woker. Both were unstinting in their generosity in allowing me access to their substantial record collections over a protracted period of time. As often as I felt I was trying their patience with my never-ending needs, they were always ready to come to the rescue.

Similarly, my very special thanks go to Dan Morgenstern and his staff at the Institute of Jazz Studies at Rutgers University for providing me not only with copies from their vast holdings of rare recordings, but also vital discographical and biographical information which I did not otherwise have access to.

Others who were helpful in supplying me with that one missing side or track that I needed to hear to complete my avowed mission of appraising the *totality* of an artist's work, are Dick Sudhalter, George Hunt, and George Simon. To them I also offer my most grateful appreciation.

But above all, I wish to thank my son, George, who masterminded and coordinated the whole acquisition of literally thousands of recordings, collating them into my Rust and Jepsen discographies, cataloguing them with unfailing accuracy (so that his old man had no trouble in finding them when needed), and finally spending untold hours copying borrowed recordings onto tape. His encyclopedic memory and fine sense of detail were often of crucial help to my occasionally staggered mind.

This is also the time and place to thank those many friends and fellow jazz lovers who over the years have given me encouragement and advice: Martin Williams, Richard Wang, Don Miller, Robert DiDomenica, Stanley Crouch, Frank Driggs, John Hasse, Milton Babbitt and the late John Hammond.

All of us jazz historians must be grateful for the outstanding work and research of those rare hardy souls who compile discographies and the so desperately needed reference books and encyclopedias of jazz. To four of these gentlemen in particular—Brian Rust, John Chilton, Roger Kinkle, and Jorgen Jepsen—I wish to extend my deepest gratitude for ferreting out vital biographical/statistical information, without which, I truly feel, most of us musicologists could not do our work as effectively as we now are occasionally able to do.

My very special thanks to Robert Berkowitz, who so generously provided me with the computer analyses of the element of swing and the representative envelope trace illustrations that comprise Appendix II. His expertise in this field of sound analysis, and his enthusiasm and fascination with jazz and swing, enabled me to fulfill a long-cherished dream of providing an unequivocal technical analysis of that phenomenon, swing, which perhaps more than any other differentiates jazz from other musical expressions.

To my faithful secretary of many years, Beatrice Haines, I am deeply indebted for her tireless typing up of my often unintelligible manuscript. That she could decipher my endless inserts within inserts, arrowed detours through and over piles of yellow-pad pages, is a sign both of Bea's innate intelligence and inexhaustible patience. I am also greatly obliged to Nancy Zeltsman and Jean Hasse who, upon Mrs. Haines's retirement, continued the onerous process of completing the typescript as well as retyping and correcting revisions of parts of earlier chapters—and still more inserts. And to Marilyn Nucci and Andy Hurlbut my grateful thanks for the laborious work of word-processing and alphabetizing the book's voluminous Index.

To Bruce Creditor, my former assistant of many years, I am everlastingly grateful for his efforts on behalf of my book, ranging all the way from typing and incidental research to keeping me supplied with pertinent news clippings and articles, and finally undertaking the last round of proofreading.

At Oxford University Press, Sheldon Meyer has been not only an extraordinarily patient editor, adviser, and supporter of this project, but one who in the first instance encouraged me to embark upon this particular literary voyage. And to Leona Capeless go my grateful thanks for being such a painstaking, gently ruthless, and sensitive editor, helping me to overcome my German-bred verbosity and love of long sentences, and catching the many factual and grammatical discrepancies, invisible to the author but caught by her sharp, well-trained eye.

Also at Oxford University Press, thanks must go to Stephanie Sakson-Ford who, with great patience and sound musical instincts, sorted out the 500 or more musical examples, making sure that they and the verbal text ended up in an appropriately "harmonious" relationship to each other.

And finally I must thank my dear wife, Marjorie, for allowing several rooms of our house to be converted into jazz battle-stations, where for far too long a time great masses of papers, books, records, and tapes related to jazz became the permanent "occupants" of our formerly neat and proper Bostonian home. Without her quiet encouragement and loving support this book would never have seen the light of day.

June 27, 1988   G.S.

Contents

The Swing Era

1

The "King" of Swing

One of the fascinating aspects of civilization and cultures is how certain periods seem to stand out as more memorable and significant than others. Indeed, despite the cyclical ebb and flow of historical tides, and the never-ending fluctuations of action and reaction, there are times when unique or extraordinary events take place that defy the historian's complete understanding. For how can one ultimately explain the Renaissance, or the astonishing creative zenith painting reached in France at the end of the nineteenth century, or the extraordinary wealth of musical invention and innovation in Europe in the decade prior to World War I?

Jazz, too, has had its share of significant historical moments, and the period around 1932 is surely one of these.[1] For we see then not only the end of an explosively creative era, exploring the basic materials and forms of jazz, but at the same time the beginnings of a decade of sustained consolidation and synthesis. Jazz had by 1932 evolved aesthetic, stylistic, technical criteria which were to govern its future for some years without major changes or radical breakthroughs.

The significance of those years can be measured in the achievements of four major jazz figures. Consider, for example, that by 1932 Louis Armstrong had fully developed a new rhythmic language for jazz which he was now in the process of expanding and elaborating. Duke Ellington had achieved the first flowering of his style and had already gathered around him virtually all the personnel that was to play the crucial roles in his orchestra's future development. In Kansas City, Bennie Moten had established yet another concept of orchestral jazz, more blues and improvisationally oriented than Ellington's, and thereby set the stage for a further development of that particular tradition in the hands

---

1. Another period is that of the mid-forties and the birth of modern jazz. Some conservatives, of course, equate the mid-forties with the death of jazz. Even so, they would have to admit that viewed as birth or death, those were uniquely momentous times.

of the Count Basie band, and, eventually, the blues-rooted modern jazz language of Charlie Parker and Lester Young. Last, Fletcher Henderson had by 1932 evolved an orchestral arranging concept, different from either Ellington's or Moten's, which was to expand into the dominant influence on the American popular music scene.

Without a doubt, the Depression figured prominently in these developments. Just as the halcyon days of the early Prohibition era, before the 1929 Wall Street crash, had provided an economic base for the flowering of jazz, so now in the early thirties, with an entire nation tightening its economic belt, widespread unemployment made musicians' and entertainers' livelihoods precarious at best. Jobs became scarce, bands floundered financially, often losing their major soloists, and, in many instances, breaking up altogether. Oddly, though, the early 1930s also saw the arrival of new bands with younger talent. Indeed, the demise of a number of leading orchestras made room for the new ones. Similarly, certain favored cities, like Chicago and New York, yielded some of their pre-eminence to Kansas City, where the Prendergast political regime created an environment that, despite the Depression, provided the kind of economic base there that jazz had enjoyed previously in Chicago.

It is no mere accident that Volume I of this History of Jazz ended more or less around 1932, and that, given the dramatic developments of those turn-of-the-decade years, Volume II deals with the musical developments that ensued from this critical turning point.

It has previously been noted that there occurred in the late twenties a marked stylistic split in jazz,[2] identifiable not only in terms of certain musical stylistic characteristics but in terms of geographic locale as well. We have already seen how two new and basically divergent conceptions of orchestral jazz had emerged by 1932, one centered in Kansas City, the other in New York. History teaches us that, when such stylistic divisions occur, sooner or later one direction absorbs the other. This was to happen to jazz in the latter part of the thirties. In the meantime only the strongest and healthiest musical strains were to survive the economically troubled Depression years. And soon some unexpected musical-sociological alliances were formed, resulting in what has long since been christened the "Swing Era," that remarkable period in American musical history when jazz was synonymous with America's popular music, its social dances and its musical entertainment.

This special identity between a people and its music is perhaps the happiest and most significant aspect of the Swing Era, a quality impossible to recapture now, and, for those who did not actually experience it, difficult to savor in retrospect. World War II and the complex postwar period, not to mention the disunity and strife brought into our national experience since then by a cold war, McCarthyism, the Vietnam war, various crises relating to minority self-identity—all these jagged, craggy lines on the graph of American history have

2. See Gunther Schuller, *Early Jazz; Its Roots and Musical Development* (New York: Oxford Univ. Press, 1968), chap. 5.

effectually blurred our memories of that faraway innocent time of isolationism, political as well as musical.

It has been frequently pointed out by social and art historians that in periods of great financial stress, such as a major economic depression, people tend to turn inward, searching for deeper life values and means of spiritual fulfillment, rather than the pursuit of material acquisition. At such times people readily look to—some might argue "escape"to—music and other cultural or entertainment diversions. Something like this was certainly happening in the United States in the 1930s, in both the "classical" and jazz realm.[3] Despite the Depression—or perhaps because of it—the thirties were for many people a new beginning. For some minorities the period represented another small but significant step up the ladder of social and cultural integration (or what passed for integration then); and, for many blacks, opportunities in music—in jazz, that is—were to open new vistas of economic and social status. In the wake of the initiative begun in the Jazz Age, the 1920s, more black musicians saw jazz for the first time as a profession. And some, perhaps, even dared to see it as an art.

Social historians can also probably account for the generally happy and carefree mood and lack of political/social concern in the music of the Swing Era— political conscience as an integral aspect of music not becoming a priority for jazz musicians until many decades later. But I believe that this very element of diffidence in the thirties can now be viewed with a certain benign tolerance, as characteristic of a bygone era of American political innocence in general. It was for all of that also a remarkable, fascinating period of musical discovery. The language of jazz was veritably bursting at the seams, as creativity and technical innovation drove forward hand in hand. One need only listen to the music of Duke Ellington, Louis Armstrong, Jimmie Lunceford, the Moten/Basie bands, and, later, some of the white swing era bands to realize that jazz was literally exploding in myriad new directions—not only musically and stylistically, but geographically as well.

Whereas jazz had been centered in three or four major cities for a good part of the twenties, in the thirties—through the proliferation of recordings and the growth of the recording industry, the development of network radio and its nightly broadcasts of jazz groups from hotels and ballrooms all over the land—jazz suddenly seemed to be everywhere. By the mid-thirties, jazz had also found the American consumer, black *and* white, and its energies were now directed to satisfying a huge new market. A vast array of musical talent, ranging from genius to the merely competent (or less), was directed toward that effort, and in the

---

3. Along with these developments in jazz and the weaning of American "classical" music from its European ancestry (exemplified in the works of Aaron Copland, Roy Harris, Walter Piston, William Schuman, and others), the thirties also saw the flowering of the two other major American art/ entertainment forms: the Hollywood musical and the American musical theatre, as reshaped by George Gershwin, Jerome Kern, Richard Rodgers, Irving Berlin, Cole Porter, Harold Arlen, Vincent Youmans, Arthur Schwartz, and Vernon Duke. In turn, the American popular song is inextricably and profoundly linked with jazz, the one serving—along with the blues—as the basic melodic/harmonic material on which the other could build.

process a style and aesthetic of jazz were forged which reflected a preponderance of American popular taste. It is undoubtedly the only time in its history when jazz was completely in phase with the social environment, and when it both captured and reflected the broadest musical common-denominator of popular taste in the nation.

The significance of this fact is that to an unprecedented degree a large segment of the American public accepted and appreciated a certain kind of creative jazz, and not merely its more commercial derivatives. By the early 1940s this vast public flocked to hear the big bands, danced to them, or in surprising numbers encircled the bandstands to listen to the music *as music*. At home their ears were glued to the radio during late-night broadcasts. Armstrong, Goodman, Ellington, Dorsey, Lunceford, Basie, Miller, Shaw—all were popular heroes. And although the broad general public tended still to think of musicians as social outcasts, they and their music had a certain daring, irresistible exotic, erotic charm. Above all their music provided an alluring escape from the often depressing real world—into that other romantic world of dancing feet, twirling bodies, and tapping toes.

The broad public may not have been aware—or even cared—that Ellington's orchestra was creating an almost unbroken series of miniature jazz masterpieces; or that the white Benny Goodman had on his road to success appropriated the talents and style of the black Fletcher Henderson. But they danced and listened to all that very good music; and they did so in unprecedented numbers and with unprecedented enthusiasm.

History has crowned Benny Goodman the "King of Swing." Right or wrong, Benny and the majority of the American public accepted that title, unaware incidentally that the black people had their own jazz royalty: *King* Oliver, *Duke* Ellington, *Count* Basie, Earl *Fatha'* Hines and, in a homier, less monarchistic mood, *Pops* Armstrong. It is true that Benny Goodman's popularity[4] epitomized the Swing Era for most people—and still does. His *music* may have been ignored by some (not all) of the leading black musicians, but his *fame* and his skill in assuaging the musical thirsts of a new mass audience certainly were not. Right or wrong, he became the symbol of an era—mostly imitated and admired, at times criticized and crucified. It must be said that the extra-musical elements in Goodman's career have frequently been used to obscure his real musical contributions. Extreme positions have often been taken, reminiscent of the controversies over the Original Dixieland Jazz Band,[5] sometimes seen only in terms of black and white pigmentation—arguments which evade the real complexities of arriving at a fair and true *musical* appraisal.

In a way the story of Benny Goodman really begins with Fletcher Henderson. In 1932 the Henderson orchestra had reached its first great peak of creativity,

---

4. Let it be said here and now that this popularity was not, as some might wish to suggest, altogether separable from his real and prodigious musical talents.
5. See *Early Jazz*, chap. 5.

but this was not matched by any comparable heights in popularity. I agree with John Hammond[6] when he says that the Henderson band he recorded in 1932 and 1933—the two *King Porter Stomp* recordings, *Honeysuckle Rose, Yeah Man!*, etc.—was the best of all the Henderson bands. It had an extraordinary array of soloists: trumpets—Bobby Stark, Rex Stewart, or Henry "Red" Allen; trombones—Claude Jones, Benny Morton, J. C. Higginbotham, and Dickie Wells; reeds—Hilton Jefferson, Coleman Hawkins (in his first prime); bass—John Kirby; guitar—Clarence Holiday (the father of Billie) or Bernard Addison; and Walter Johnson on drums. The band's sound was unique: light, buoyant, airy, loose, and yet remarkably cohesive. And its swing was superb, total and collective in a way that perhaps no other band of the period equaled. Form and content, style and arrangement were truly one. All the parts, from Kirby's bass right up to Russell Smith's lead trumpet, added up to one single cumulative swinging aggregate. Fletcher's band had achieved such a degree of seamless integration, all its parts meshing perfectly with all others, that its momentum carried everything along with it: even an occasional weak solo or ragged ensemble could not afflict this healthy organism.

But, paradoxically, the Henderson orchestra was also by this time a rather demoralized group. Various reasons have been advanced: Fletcher had somehow lost the drive to be a strong leader, after an auto accident in 1928; in the early years of the Depression, recordings of black jazz orchestras were sporadic, as were ballroom and club bookings; and on several occasions auditions for steady engagements were won by newer bands, like Jimmie Lunceford and Cab Calloway. The final blow was the sudden departure of Coleman Hawkins, Fletcher's musical tower of strength for over a decade, who like many players caught in the Depression, was enticed to Europe by a sudden surge of interest there in American jazz.

Despite the loyalty of many of Henderson's musicians and despite a flurry of recording dates in 1934 for the then-new Decca label, Fletcher was forced to disband the orchestra late that year.[7]

At this point Benny Goodman entered Fletcher's life and, through the initiative of John Hammond, an alliance was formed which was to shape the Swing Era and the future of jazz for years to come. For in late 1934, Hammond, realizing that Henderson's own band was moribund, proposed to Benny Goodman that he hire Henderson as his chief arranger. This would obviously help the now unemployed Fletcher financially, but, more importantly, it might provide the young Goodman orchestra with some of the class and excitement which Hammond had so admired in the Henderson band.

Goodman was at this point struggling to establish a permanent orchestra, with

6. John Hammond, indefatigable jazz fan, impresario, recording executive, critic, discoverer and furtherer of most of the major jazz talents of the Swing Era, was unquestionably the most influential (non-performing) individual in the field. His name—and good deeds on behalf of jazz—will run like a constant thread through this entire history.
7. For more on Fletcher Henderson and his later orchestras, see below, Chapter 6; also *Early Jazz*, pp. 272–79.

himself as leader. Several previous attempts since 1931 had failed, and Good-man had always been forced to return to his very lucrative radio and studio work in New York. Goodman has admitted that he was then "in a bad groove men-tally, with not much desire other than to make money, keep the place going for my mother and kids, and have as much fun as possible."[8] To that John Ham-mond adds: "[Goodman] had the idea that real improvised jazz was uncommer-cial, and that you had to have a compromise in order to sell any records. Benny was comparatively out of touch in those days with what was happening in the Harlem world." Goodman had the attitude of a "fairly slick professional musi-cian, one who had lost hope and interest in jazz."[9] It is clear from this, as well as the evidence of his recordings of those years, that Goodman saw little value in the music of orchestras like Henderson's, and no future in white orchestras, like the Casa Loma Band or the various Dorsey Brothers combinations that were emulating the Harlem styles. It is therefore doubtful that Goodman, left to his own counsel, would ever have hired Henderson. It took Hammond to effect this collaboration.

But even before that, Hammond, who was an enthusiastic admirer of Good-man's clarinet, had begun to play a crucial role in Benny's career. Earlier in 1934 Hammond had been instrumental in helping Goodman form his first per-manent band, forthwith securing an engagement at Billy Rose's Music Hall and then, when that engagement was abruptly terminated, a twenty-six-week stint on radio with the National Biscuit Company's now-legendary *Let's Dance* program. One thing followed another. In early 1935 a new recording contract with Victor bore its first fruit in relatively good sales (for a jazz record); the dynamic trumpet player Bunny Berigan joined the orchestra; Hammond persuaded Goodman to hire Gene Krupa on drums, Jess Stacy on piano, and an eighteen-year-old vo-calist by the name of Helen Ward.

But above all it was Fletcher (and Horace) Henderson's arrangements that turned the tide for Goodman. Inevitably, even the finest collection of musicians will remain professionally and artistically shackled without strong material to work with. Of this reality the Henderson orchestra had had abundant proof: every time during the precarious years from 1928 to 1934 when the orchestra did seem to revive with a new spirit, it was because of the stimulus of new arranging and stylistic concepts: Benny Carter's (*Keep a Song in Your Soul*), Horace Henderson's (*Hot and Anxious* and *Yeah Man!*), Fletcher Henderson's (*The New King Porter Stomp* and *Wrappin' It Up*).

Such a revivifying stylistic injection was provided now for Benny Goodman by some of these very same Henderson arrangements. There can be no question that Fletcher's way with pop tunes helped to turn the tide in captivating the public that tuned into Benny's weekly *Let's Dance* broadcast. Fletcher's arrange-ments of current or familiar tunes had a good beat, were smartly orchestrated, cleverly setting off brass and reeds in complementary fashion; and they had just

8. Benny Goodman, *Kingdom of Swing* (Harrisburg, Pa.: Stackpole, 1939).
9. Quoted by Nat Shapiro from a John Hammond article in the English weekly *Melody Maker*, in *The Jazz Makers*, ed. Nat Shapiro, Nat Hentoff (New York: Rinehart, 1957).

enough daring (compared with the "sweet" commercial fare generally prevalent on radio) to capture the listener's ear. Herein, then, lay the uncanny amalgam of success that precipitated the Swing Era: spicing up familiar commercial, popular material with a Harlem-oriented musical seasoning and selling it via a white band for a white musical/commercial audience.[10] This was not the first but certainly one of the more subtle examples of the "exploitation" of black music and musicians in American popular music.[11] For it is an ironic and sad truth that the very style which succeeded finally with Goodman had already existed and flourished for three or four years in precisely the same form with Fletcher Henderson's orchestra. In fact, in a number of instances Goodman took over, virtually intact, the identical arrangements Henderson had already previously recorded and performed for years. With Henderson these performances remained relatively unnoticed (conjecture for a moment what would have happened if Hammond also had not noticed!); with Goodman they became world hits. By the time the Goodman band became an overnight sensation at the Palomar Ballroom in Los Angeles in August 1935, Hammond's formula had begun to produce results: Goodman's recordings of a few of Fletcher's arrangements had caught on and had already created a sizable national following.

Where perhaps Hammond miscalculated was in expecting Goodman's soloists over the long haul to match Henderson's seasoned stars. In a comparison of Henderson's arrangements as played by both bands, not only are Benny's soloists outclassed, but even the ensemble passages lack the collective swing and inspiration that Henderson's men brought to their pieces. Moreover, in the case of *King Porter Stomp*, a head arrangement by artists of Henderson's caliber would in any case be difficult to translate into the realm of painstakingly rehearsed-to-a-fare-thee-well renditions of the kind Goodman fancied, without *some* loss of spontaneity.

To be sure, the element of technical perfection and polish, which Goodman insisted on and got from his players, added a surface sheen that the same ar-

10. While the emphasis here, in the context of this chapter, is for the moment on Fletcher Henderson, it should not be assumed that he was the only arranger of note and of influence. Apart from Don Redman, from whom in fact Henderson had learned his arranging skills, and Benny Carter, both of whose pioneering work I have discussed in *Early Jazz*, other arrangers like Horace Henderson, John Nesbitt, Eddie Durham, Gus Wilson (Teddy Wilson's brother), Jesse Stone and the Casa Loma's Gene Gifford—and, of course, Duke Ellington—had in various ways (and with various degrees of influence) contributed crucially to the development of a truly orchestral jazz by the early 1930s.

11. Hammond would surely argue that Goodman's hiring of Henderson, and taking unto himself the latter's band library, was a fortuitous alliance with great benefits for all concerned: Henderson found gainful employment for his talents with one of the land's up-and-coming bands, while for Goodman it was just the right kind of musical stylistic injection he needed. If one can thus argue that this action was undertaken in good faith, and for the greater recognition of black jazz, it is *after that* that the exploitation factor enters. For very little public acknowledgment was given at the time to Henderson (as well as Goodman's other black arrangers, Edgar Sampson and Jimmy Mundy) for his contribution to Goodman's success. As far as the general public knew, it was Goodman who was to be credited for swing—just as nearly forty years later, a mass public was to credit Marvin Hamlish for music written by Scott Joplin.

rangement may not have had with Henderson. It is the classic battle between, on the one hand, technical perfection at the expense of inspiration and spontaneity, and on the other hand, a freer, looser expression at the expense of ensemble perfection.

This was, of course, precisely the Henderson formula's Achilles' heel. Like so much good wine, it didn't necessarily travel very well; nor could it stand watering down. When the swing bands added the riff[12] to their arsenal of devices, in the end overusing and abusing it, swing as a style and a formal concept was doomed. Its enormous prolonged popular success even well into the forties notwithstanding, swing atrophied rapidly and lost its innovative force. Indeed, its very success presented a most serious dilemma. But that is getting ahead of our story.

Benny Goodman (born Benjamin David in 1909 in Chicago) is a striking product of that unique phenomenon: American urban civilization. His contribution to music, and particularly to jazz, cannot be fully understood except as part of the process of musical acculturation to be found in all large American cities, particularly in their mix of ethnic neighborhoods. Consider these polyglot influences on Goodman: born into a Russian-Jewish immigrant family, taking the mandatory beginner's music lessons at the local synagogue, then studying with a strict German disciplinarian, "classical" clarinet teacher Franz Schoepp by name (who also gave Jimmy Noone and Buster Bailey lessons), as a young teenager hearing the local Klezmer clarinetists, and idolizing and imitating Ted Lewis (himself a first-generation American of German background) but soon progressing to more serious influences like Leon Rappolo, Frank Teschemacher, Volly de Faut, and black musicians like Jimmy Noone and Johnny Dodds.

Even at this early stage one is hard-put to discern specific influences in Goodman's playing. His borrowings from Rappolo, Johnny Dodds (of the King Oliver band), and his fellow Schoepp student, Jimmy Noone—influences which Benny has acknowledged—were so thoroughly assimilated that his own playing was very early on already a composite personalized reflection of them. It is as if he splintered and fractured these influences into the tiniest fine particles, only to reconstruct them into his own unique amalgam. One influence to which Goodman would, I suspect, not readily admit is that of his Chicago contemporary Frank Teschemacher, and yet some of the latter's piercing, jagged high-register excursions and expressive abandon can be heard in Goodman's style, albeit technically far more controlled and smoothed out and emotionally tamed.

Teschemacher (1906–1932), a strangely original, though somewhat obscure and controversial figure, was a prominent member of the Chicago school of jazz, particularly as represented by the famous Austin High Gang (whose nucleus comprised, besides Teschemacher, trumpeter Jimmy McPartland, tenor Bud Freeman, and drummer Dave Tough—with Gene Krupa a later member). Greatly influenced by Dodds's declamatory trumpet-like approach to the clarinet, Teschemacher developed a maverick style uniquely his own. Mostly self-taught, his

---

12. See *Early Jazz*, pp. 28–30, for description and definition of riff.

playing left much to be desired technically—marred by severe intonation problems and a raw, raucous tone—but was overwhelming in its searing emotional
intensity and biting attack. He applied these same qualities to his alto playing,
playing in a hot, strong style, virtually unheard of at that time (as on *Oh Baby*,
for example, with Eddie Condon's Quartet). Goodman, three years Teschemacher's junior, often sat in with the Blue Friars, the Austin Gang's group, but
no two clarinetists could have been further apart in style and temperament: Teschemacher essentially a fervent dilettante, a wild-eyed idealist, musically uninhibited, technically fettered; Goodman the thorough professional, first and foremost the businessman musician, always self-controlled, technically unfettered.
In many ways Teschemacher was the Ornette Coleman of the twenties, a lone
original who, killed in an auto accident on leap-year day in 1932 at age twenty-
five, never had the chance to fully develop his curious art.

I suspect the influence of Schoepp on the young Goodman has never been
taken very seriously by jazz writers and historians. It seems obvious that the
youthful Benny, already a prodigy, acquired in his studies with Schoepp a solid
technical foundation from which he would develop a prodigious, unprecedented
virtuosity as a jazz clarinetist, and this would also enable him later to venture
into the realms of classical music and to hold his own handsomely with virtuosi
in that field. From Schoepp's disciplined tutelage Benny must also have acquired
a deep respect for the value of thorough practice and rehearsal techniques—
indeed, for a *kind* of controlled playing which was basically foreign to jazz (and
often used to be sneered at in jazz circles). But Goodman owes much of his
fame to his abilities as a strict and tirelessly demanding leader, qualities which
did not always endear him to his sidemen, but which men like Fletcher Henderson or would-be leaders, like Bunny Berigan, simply lacked.

Schoepp's influence, it seems to me, is also discernible in Goodman's tone
and his whole approach to the clarinet as a jazz instrument. He was after all the
first major "cool" player in jazz, and this at a time when everybody was trying
to play "hot." His tone was clear and light (although he could at will make it
raspy and "dirty"), his attack controlled, his vibrato well regulated, his technique
fluent—in fact, virtually flawless.

It is remarkable that Goodman succeeded in capturing the popular music
world at age twenty-six, despite an essentially eclectic approach which made him
suppress much of his own musical individuality, generally considered a *sine qua
non* of true jazz. There are no ear-catching, outrageous extremes in his playing,
neither of the "charming" nor the "exciting" variety; he isn't a "personality" or
a "showman." He just makes music, with a lot of talent and matchless control.
His playing has even been called "mechanical" and "devoid of inspiration"—
surely an exaggeration. The fact remains that for many years millions of people
identified instantly with the sound of his clarinet.

These particular and unique technical characteristics of Goodman's clarinet
playing, of course, also account for his ability to play classical music without
embarrassment and without the need to "switch" techniques. And let us not
minimize the importance of Goodman's role in classical music, if only because

he commissioned and caused to be written a classic of twentieth-century literature, Béla Bartók's *Contrasts*. In a sense, Benny was the first Third Stream musician,[13] moving easily in and out of jazz and classical music, from the Palomar
Ballroom to Carnegie Hall, or—to put in another way—"jamming" all night
and then playing Mozart with his viola-playing friend and brother-in-law John
Hammond. If his classical playing clearly shows the influence of his work in
jazz, the reverse is certainly no less true.[14] To say these things is not to argue
that Benny Goodman is *thereby* better than someone else, nor to argue that he
should or should not have been the one to *represent* American jazz in the Soviet
Union on a State Department sponsored tour in 1962.[15] It is simply to call
attention to the uniquely complex position Goodman occupies in jazz, and in
music in general.

Goodman is, of course, not a composer in the sense that Bartók, Ellington,
Jelly Roll Morton, Theolonious Monk, are composers. He is a virtuoso performer and an orchestra leader; and it is in terms of *these* careers that we must
assess his contribution to jazz. His debut on records was made with Ben Pollack,
a Chicago drummer who had played with the New Orleans Rhythm Kings from
1921 to 1923. By late 1924 Pollack had formed his own band in California and,
remembering a twelve-year-old in knee pants back in Chicago who, a few years
earlier, had dazzled audiences with his imitations of Ted Lewis, Pollack sent for
the precocious youngster.[16]

When Pollack moved his band to New York in early 1928, Goodman continued to work and record with him. But in addition he began playing in Broadway
pit bands (for Gershwin's *Strike Up the Band* and *Girl Crazy*, for instance) and
doing all manner of free-lance radio work, as well as embarking on a hectic
round of studio recordings—*hundreds* of them in a virtually unbroken sequence
until 1932. Most of these six hundred-odd free-lance recordings were issued

13. Third Stream is a concept of composing, improvising, and performing which seeks to fuse,
creatively, jazz (and other vernacular musics) with contemporary classical concepts and techniques.
14. Goodman's recording of Debussy's *Rhapsody for Clarinet and Orchestra*, made with the New
York Philharmonic in 1941 under John Barbirolli's direction, stands as a classic performance of the
work to this day. Marred only by a few moments of slightly flat intonation, Goodman's realization
of Debussy's score is hard to fault. Rarely is the solo part played with such a pure liquid tone, for,
when Benny wants to "play pretty," no one can surpass him. His Debussy performance is elegant
and sensitive, and with Barbirolli's help, even captures those moments of mystery which make this
work so special, even in Debussy's canon.
15. Most musicians and jazz experts felt that that honor should have gone to Duke Ellington or
Count Basie.
16. He also sent for a young unknown trombonist named Glenn Miller a few days later. Through
the years many of Pollack's alumni became important musicians in the Swing Era—Bud Freeman,
Jimmy McPartland, Jack Teagarden, Harry James, Charlie Spivak, Yank Lawson, Muggsy Spanier,
and Victor Young, the famous Broadway and Hollywood composer who at one time played violin
for Pollack.
    Pollack is one of those lesser figures in jazz history often overlooked or deferentially treated. But
we owe it to him that, among other things, we can hear what Benny Goodman sounded like at age
seventeen. And the cornetist, Jimmy McPartland, apart from lauding Pollack as a leader, called him
"one of the finest drummers that ever lived." But more importantly, his orchestra served as a professional training ground for countless musicians who were later to acquire fame as soloists or leaders.

under some twenty-five different leaders' names, many of them of fictitious or
farcical pseudonyms, like Whoopee Makers, Mills Musical Clowns, Jimmy
Bracken's Toe Ticklers, and so on. This music was hardly more serious than the
band names. Contracted at first by the saxophonist Gil Rodin, these recording
dates used Pollack men almost exclusively, including cornetist Jimmy McPartland,
trombonists Jack Teagarden and Glenn Miller, drummed Ray Bauduc, and Benny's brother Harry on bass. But soon Goodman made contact with such other
free-lancers as trumpeters Mannie Klein and Charlie Teagarden, trombonist
Tommy Dorsey, guitarists Eddie Lang and Dick McDonough, violinist Joe Venuti, and his fellow Chicagoan, drummer Gene Krupa.

With such a pool of energetic young talent available in a rapidly developing
market for commercial dance music, novelty tunes, and "romantic" ballads,
Goodman soon found himself on a perpetual merry-go-round of studio recording
sessions. The peak years were 1930 and 1931, when Benny actually became a
more or less permanent member of the Columbia house band, led by the violinist-
leader-contractor Ben Selvin. Under the Selvin aegis alone, Goodman recorded
some four hundred commercial dance sides, almost all with appropriately vacuous vocals by crooners of the day.

We needn't concern ourselves too much with these recordings, although they
have their "period" fascinations. But a few points ought to be made about them.
First, Benny developed a tremendous skill and consistency in handling an endless profusion of new tunes, hot off the Tin Pan Alley presses. During the peak
1931 period, Benny was in the recording studio at least once, sometimes two or
three times, a week—churning out improvised solos, testing his versatility, and
further developing his natural gift and youthful precocity. It was an extremely
useful training period and, judging by the recorded evidence, Benny was virtually unflappable in the face of such extraordinary demands.

Second, Benny's unusual technical facility and his relatively good feel for jazz
ensured that he was almost always cast in the role of the "jazz soloist," even in
the most dreadfully commercial potboilers. It should be pointed out that the big
dance-band leaders always liked to have at least one "hot" man around for their
up-tempo numbers, usually to "jazz up" the final chorus or two. This tended to
make the dancers excited, and, before long, whether it fitted musically or not, a
few bars of "hot" jazz became virtually mandatory in any respectable dance-band
performance. Goodman was almost always the "hot" player; and, indeed, on the
hundreds of dance sides in which he participated between 1928 and 1932, the
music perks up noticeably when Benny solos, as an element of jazz is momentarily injected—at times feeble, to be sure (certainly as compared with some of
the great contemporary recordings of Henderson, Armstrong, and Ellington).
Thus, while a good part of each recording was almost purposefully mediocre and
simplistic, so that it might appeal to a larger audience, Benny was usually allowed at least an 8-bar "jazz solo," sometimes even a whole chorus.

The third point is that through this extraordinary series of playing opportunities Benny Goodman was able to consolidate his natural instrumental versatility.
Whether an arranger needed a low-register subtone clarinet or a dirty "hot" solo,
a fast "flag-waver" obbligato, an alto section lead, or (somewhat more infre-

quently) a doubling on bass clarinet,[17] Benny Goodman could be relied upon to do it all. Goodman could function as well on baritone saxophone, as evidenced by his excellent "lead" playing (on baritone) on *Blue* (1928) or his effortless solo on *Room 1411*, sounding for all the world like an early Gerry Mulligan. In 1929 he even recorded several sides with James Melton, the famous light opera tenor (later a regular at the Metropolitan Opera as well)—a challenge which required Goodman to suppress his jazz inclinations totally and to recall hastily the lessons of old man Schoepp seven years earlier.

In listening to Goodman on these pre-Swing Era sides, one is constantly impressed by his uncommon technical skill. Hear the eighteen-year-old Goodman, for example, on *That's A Plenty* (with just piano and drum accompaniment), amazingly fluent, in control of the complete clarinet range and of an already nicely developed full tone. But sometimes even Benny could have problems. Occasionally in the early years his attack or tone seems unnecessarily hard and pinched (*Futuristic Rhythm* by the Mills Musical Clowns, for example), and sometimes he would still be fighting the changes. As late as May 1934 on *Moonglow*, Benny inexplicably plays *a dozen* or so wrong notes—not just poor notes, but *wrong* ones—in something like twelve bars. But perhaps Benny's most embarrassing moment on records came during a Gene Krupa-led date in 1935, on a tune called *Three Little Words*. For some reason—perhaps it was because Jess Stacy laid out during Benny's solo—Benny got completely lost. By the time the first bridge rolled around, he was already a bar or two behind the changes, and never recovered. After a while he just frantically churned out running eighths, just barely staying afloat. Krupa tried to bring him back in by bashing away at rim shots at appropriate junctures, but nothing helped. It was one of the few times the King faltered.

Such obvious flaws were rare exceptions. More often than not one is struck by the fluency of Goodman's musical ideas.[18] Without being terribly original and certainly not profound, they are pleasing, generally in good taste, and, at worse, innocuous. Indeed, on many of the 1929 through 1931 sides, one can already hear the essential Benny Goodman of later years. By the late thirties, with his own band, he had, of course, become even more consistent, technically even more virtuosic. And above all, he had by then constructed a better orchestral framework for himself. But Benny's *basic* style was already fully assembled by the late twenties.

To what extent the titular leader of the different Pollack recording groups could influence their style and content—and how varied the musical contexts in which Goodman and his cohorts were apt to find themselves—can all be clearly heard by comparing several prototypical recordings of the genre. *Makin' Friends*,

---

17. For example, on *Lucille*, by the Hotel Commodore Dance Orchestra, 1931; or, more interestingly, on Red Norvo's re-creation of Beiderbecke's *In a Mist*.
18. It should be noted that his "solos" in the late 1920s are virtually confined to improvisations just paraphrasing the melody, by the nature of these inherently commercial recordings. A truer test of Goodman's conception would have occurred if the recordings had allowed for greater "jazz" freedom. A few sides, referred to below, do give a glimpse of this extra dimension.

for example—a 1929 Jack Teagarden-led session (with Jimmy Dorsey temporarily substituting for Goodman)—projects perfectly the heady, relaxed blues atmosphere for which Teagarden was already famous. One hears this not only in his own trombone solo and drawling vocal but in the whole feel of the piece: the loose-jointed swing of the rhythm section, the somber sonority and texture of the ensembles.[19] Compare this with *Bag O' Blues*, recorded just one month earlier and led this time by Jack Pettis, like Pollack a New Orleans Rhythm Kings alumnus. Despite the title's reference to blues and despite a personnel quite similar to that of the Teagarden date, the whole intent (and content) of the record is different, as well as quite removed from the blues. It is a smartly arranged piece, straddling the fence between jazz and dance music. Although featuring good solo-playing, particularly by the little-remembered trumpet player Bill Moore and an unusual all-low-register Goodman solo, *Bag O' Blues* remains in the end a prim exercise in bouncy two-beat fox-trot dance music.

Proceeding lower down the artistic ladder, compare *Bag O' Blues* in turn to a recording like *To Be in Love*, made only a month later than *Makin' Friends*, this time featuring Sammy Fain, billed as The Crooning Composer(!). This is pop dance music of the day, with the mandatory doubling of the singer by the violin—to reinforce the melody. Here the "improvised" solos had to stick closely to the melody, but at least they were allowed to embellish it mildly and "jazz it up" a bit. The point is that the degree of jazziness was precisely controlled by the leader (or contractor or recording director), establishing a veritable hierarchy of degrees of freedom. Ignoring the melody and just playing on the changes was simply not tolerated. To this dictum there were two exceptions: (1) in obbligato-playing, when the melody was simultaneously stated by someone else; (2) momentarily, as in a break, a fill-in, or a turnback, or in certain brief isolated segments of the tune. Notice, for example, how trumpet player Mannie Klein (in *To Be in Love*, May 1929) hews very close to the melody line for four bars, then for the next four suddenly veers off into a "dirty" blues-inflected free phrase, repeating the pattern in the next eight measures. It is almost as if the leader said to Mannie: "I'll let you play four bars of jazz, if you give me the first four straight." Benny's characteristically fluent obbligato-playing, relaxed and assured, is also heard to good advantage on this side. Survival in these New York studios depended not on how much jazz or sweet style you could play but how well you could fit—on a moment's notice—into the various precisely predefined musical slots.

On the lowest rung of the artistic ladder (and therefore on the highest rung of commercial rating) were the novelty "cornball" tunes. It is sometimes difficult to tell when these were done "seriously"—that is, as a professional obligation determined by the recording director—or when they were done as a put-on. Musicians like Goodman and Jimmy McPartland would often do take-offs on

19. An analogous later example is offered by four 1933 sides under the name of Steve Washington, a black singer. This date produced at least one outstanding performance, the haunting *Blue River*, with its highly unusual minor-key changes and beautiful Goodman obbligatos. It also must have been one of the first recordings on which a black singer was accompanied by an all-white group.

the Original Dixieland Jazz Band and their even cornier imitators. Ironically, the public still preferred the jerky rhythms, the squealing, yelping clarinets, and generally moronic "barnyard hokum" purveyed by the likes of Earl Fuller, Ted Lewis, and Jimmy Durante. And the recording directors, eager for quick sales, pushed such trash—even on committed jazz men like Goodman and Teagarden—whenever possible. Benny was, of course, an expert at this stuff, having started his professional career with imitations of Ted Lewis.

One anecdote, told by Jimmy McPartland,[20] illustrates how tenuous the line between intentional "corn" and readily marketable "novelty" music could be, and how the cynicism of the musicians was on occasion only surpassed by that of the recording director. On one of Goodman's own dates in New York in 1928, after recording three bona fide "jazz" numbers, the players began to kid around, playing as cornily as possible. The recording director rushed out of the booth, shouting, "That's it! That's just what we want!" The musicians acquiesced and, using the chords of St. Louis Blues, made a travesty of all the "barnyard hokum" bands, a performance that stood as a classic of its kind until the days of the great musical satirist Spike Jones fifteen years later. The irony is that this side, entitled Shirt Tail Stomp, outsold all the previously made sides, and in fact, in the eyes of the record company, paid for the session's three jazz sides. Even worse, Shirt Tail Stomp was re-recorded six months later for another label under the pseudonym of The Whoopee Makers, in the hope, one assumes, that it would be an even bigger hit this time.[21]

Most often the dividing line between the outright "commercial" element and the jazzier part (if any) occurred midway in the recording. In the prototypical The Whole Darned Thing's for You (1930), the sweet style—including crooning vocalist and swooning violin—gets its full share. But in the third and fourth choruses, transformed almost in Jekyll and Hyde fashion, a jazz band (of sorts) suddenly bursts forth. Goodman leads the charge in a fine sample of his already fully formed style—increasingly aggressive as the side proceeds.[22] There is also a brief glimpse of Benny's light-toned clarinet-ish alto saxophone.[23]

Even more striking examples of the crass separation between jazz and non-jazz occur on Ninety-nine Out of a Hundred and Let's Drink a Drink, both

---

20. Nat Shapiro and Nat Hentoff, Hear Me Talkin' to Ya, (New York: Rinehart, 1955), p. 279.

21. It is fascinating to contemplate the various levels of professional/artistic integrity that motivated different groups and musicians. "What price compromise?" was a constant question in those days (and, of course, still is). But one can imagine Benny and his studio companions making fun of the commercialism of the ODJB, while others—including, I suspect, a great number of fine black musicians, who couldn't even get into those studios—snubbing their noses at the "commercialism" of The Whoopee Makers—each level of compromise looking down its nose at the next one directly below. To each his own compromise!

22. As an example of how recording directors covered all possible bases, this title (like hundreds of others) was recorded in two versions: one with a vocal for domestic consumption; the other without a vocal, aimed at the Latin and South American markets, and issued as Todo Para Ti, and in the U.S. on a special limited "X" label.

23. Other examples of Goodman's "cool" Trumbauer-influenced alto can be heard on Under Your Window, High and Low, One More Time (all from 1931) and Morning, Noon and Night (1932).

1931 Whoopee Makers titles. These are actually march numbers with the only jazz relegated to four bars (sic) of Goodman on each side. It is curious to hear the $\frac{6}{8}$ ♪ ' ♩ ♪ ' ♩ march patterns arbitrarily break out into two-beat jazz for a few seconds, and then fall right back into the 6/8 meter.

By the end of 1930 Benny Goodman had negotiated a contract with the Melotone Recording Company that featured him as leader. It is surprising, therefore, that these sides are so low in overall jazz content, and even more surprising that trumpeter Charlie Teagarden most often outplays his leader, both in quantity and quality. Clearly, Goodman did not yet have a firm grip on how to create a unique voice with his band. He was still only a good sideman who occasionally was listed as leader on the union contract.

A small step toward stylistic identity was made in February 1931 when four sides were cut under Benny's leadership, employing the services of Glenn Miller as arranger: *When Your Lover Has Gone, Walkin' My Baby Back Home, Basin Street Blues*, and *Beale Street Blues*.[24] The rhythm section is more cohesive, having settled down to the more or less permanent combination of Gene Krupa, Harry Goodman (bass), Dick McDonough (guitar), and Arthur Schutt (piano). Miller's writing for the ensemble, now grown to eleven players, is fuller, with mildly adventurous harmonic touches throughout—particularly the chromatic introductions and tag-codas. Instrumental coloring includes Larry Binyon's flute lead in the first chorus of *Walkin'* and McDonough's sensitively placed guitar tremolos. Also, in the first chorus of *Walkin'*, hear the unusual pattern of syncopated cross-accents between McDonough's guitar punctuations and Krupa's cymbal splashes. But above all, the band is consciously trying to play both "hot jazz" and "modern." The result is something well beyond the normal dividing line between commercial dance music and late twenties jazz. Similarly, as *When Your Lover* progresses, the band moves almost imperceptibly into a latter-day swing era feeling, the "new" Henderson-Redman-Carter arranging influence becoming clearly discernible.

The two *Blues*, recorded on the same day, are at once more purely jazz and yet less "modern," for they hark back to an already older blues tradition, heading in almost the opposite direction from early white swing bands. Again Jack Teagarden, the white blues man par excellence, seems to be in charge, and his brother Charlie produces an impassioned solo on *Beale Street* which would stand unequalled as a fine example of white blues trumpet-playing for many years. Goodman is superb, really getting into the mood with expressive authoritative solos, played with a "dirty" raspy tone, heavily blue-note inflected. Only Krupa nearly ruins things momentarily with a heavy cymbal backbeat (on *Basin Street*), which all but shakes up Jack Teagarden in his solo.

Basin Street Blues was a temporary victory in these jazz musicians' crusade against the commercial establishment. With utter disregard for public prefer-

24. There is little doubt that Miller also arranged the first two sides, issued as Johnny Walker's Orchestra. The two blues, on the other hand, were issued as by The Charleston Chasers, a cover-all name Columbia applied to a number of New York studio groups.

ence, the group daringly started without the mandatory introduction, plunging directly into a verse (rather than the familiar Spencer Williams chorus)—a verse, moreover, which had not existed until Glenn Miller and Jack Teagarden created it the night before the record session. (Their new lyrics were later incorporated in the published sheet music and became a standard part of the song—without credit to them.)

By mid-1931 things were beginning to stir in that New York studio world. Previously, as far as that world was concerned, jazz had gone underground at the end of the Jazz Age, abandoned almost entirely to the Negro bands, who were *a priori* excluded form the white-controlled music business and commercial studios. Perhaps this was their saving grace.[25] But here, suddenly, jazz seemed to resurface temporarily, as these white, mostly Chicago-trained musicians brought real jazz—or at least a form of it—into the Muzak-like world of the New York studios. This momentary confidence in jazz would not last, of course, for the economic bubble was about to burst in 1932, in the depths of the Depression. But 1931 was still a banner year, and Goodman was in and out of the recording studios, as if in a perpetual revolving door.

The temporary surge towards jazz manifested itself clearly in a number of ways, perhaps most obviously rhythmically. Gradually the 4/4 beat, as opposed to the older two-beat style, began to find its way into Benny's recordings, if at first somewhat tentatively. But listen to *One More Time* (issued under the name of Roy Carroll and his Sands Point Orchestra, actually a Selvin house band date). Even the vocalist sings with more rhythmic drive, certainly beyond the typical cloying, crooning legato mannerisms of only a few years earlier. The rhythm section falls into a clear 4/4 gait in the latter choruses, with Goodman leading the group confidently toward a "modern" jazz conception—evidence that he had by now taken the musical initiative away from old Ben Selvin and his violin.

Other interesting examples of this new rhythmic trend are *Poor Kid* (a touchingly sentimental Chaplinesque tune), *Under Your Window*, *I'm Keeping Company*, and *Without That Gal* (all 1931) in the last of which the final chorus vacillates uncertainly between 4/4 and 2/2—as if not quite committed to the new 4/4 beat.

The year 1932 was, as already stated, an extremely lean one in the recording studios. The financial bottom had already dropped out. (Goodman recorded only three times that year, once with Ben Selvin and twice with none other than Ted Lewis.) Benny busied himself with radio work, a new and potentially lucrative medium because it cost the public nothing and did not depend on direct audience outlays of cash—unlike the record industry or the theatre. Goodman also

---

25. To put this in perspective, one should recall that in the same year of 1931 jazz *was* flourishing magnificently in the black orchestras. Ellington was recording *Echoes of the Jungle* and *Mystery Song*, Henderson *Sugar Foot Stomp* and *Hot and Anxious*, Redman his *Chant of the Weed*, Webb his *Heebie Jeebies*—and the white Casa Lomans their influential *Casa Loma Stomp*, *Black Jazz*, and *White Jazz*.

helped to organize a band for the popular singer Russ Columbo, using his old playing partners McPartland, Krupa, Eddie Lang, and Joe Sullivan.

By 1933 work gradually picked up again, and it is at this point that we connect up with our previous narrative, when John Hammond was about to enter Goodman's life.

In late 1933 and early 1934 Hammond set up for English Columbia a series of recording sessions on which Goodman as leader was to feature several objects of Hammond's enthusiasm: Billie Holiday, Ethel Waters, Mildred Bailey, Teddy Wilson, Coleman Hawkins (all black artists but one). For these dates Goodman began to use arrangers more consistently, undoubtedly persuaded by the remarkable success of the Casa Loma orchestra, with its gifted arranger Gene Gifford. Deane Kincaide (who was working for Benny's old boss, Ben Pollack) and Will Hudson (weaned on the arrangements of Don Redman and John Nesbitt with McKinney's Cotton Pickers) and Benny Carter were the first three arrangers to contribute importantly to Goodman's fledgling band.

With such pieces as Hudson's arrangement of Will Hudson's *Nitwit Serenade*,[26] *Bugle Call Rag*, and, particularly, *Music Hall Rag*, the riff cum call-and-response formulas of the Henderson brothers became a fundamental staple of the Goodman repertory. Moreover, in these "flag-wavers," Benny found the ideal vehicle for his own brand of technical brilliance. For the first time the band provided him with a framework that challenged his virtuosity, and at the same time provided him with a platform for a potential starring role. His eighth-note solos on *Music Hall Rag*, played at a murderous tempo of $\downarrow$ = ca. 320, were clearly a tour de force which no other musician of the day could match, let alone surpass. Here, clearly, were the beginnings of a brilliant new virtuoso career.

But had Goodman stopped there, he would have remained a kind of peripheral figure, a category to which some people would still like to relegate him: a mere technical wizard of the clarinet. To what extent it was Hammond's further proddings, as distinct from Goodman's own still hesitant interests in jazz and rekindled ambitions to lead a big band, will perhaps never be precisely sorted out. Nor does it need to be. The fact is that the Goodman band was beginning to savor the sweet smell of success, and was thus easily motivated to keep moving ahead. It was making good professional contacts, finding new performing opportunities, and with that, significantly, a whole new audience—one which the recording companies and commercial dance-band leaders (except for Glen Gray and his Casa Lomans) had until then fairly well ignored: namely the college and high school kids.

Goodman also renewed his search for an individual style which would be recognizably his own. The band discovered the value of dynamics, as in the final chorus of *Down Home Rag*, with its striking *pp-ff-pp* contrasts. It learned

---

26. *Nitwit Serenade* was a bold attempt to emulate and outrival Goodman's arch adversary, the Casa Loma orchestra.

too that you had to find a style for the slower dance numbers as well as the ballads—an area where the Casa Loma band, with its famous *Smoke Rings*, was already well ahead. *Blue Moon* (recorded Jan. 15, 1935) is an interesting early example of Goodman's search for a lyric style,[27] one that he had certainly found by later that year in the hauntingly beautiful *Good-bye*, Goodman's closing theme song.

But the road to artistic success was not without its obstacles and detours. I have often wondered why Goodman's 1935 transcontinental tour, which culminated in the Palomar Ballroom success, was at first such a failure that Goodman almost gave up the band in Denver, just prior to heading for Los Angeles. I suspect that the inroads of commercialism had once again taken their toll. Benny's commitment to the new "swing" music was at this point—before Palomar—still a tenuous one, not yet crowned by economic and popular success. Hammond's Music Hall engagements in New York had flopped; the *Let's Dance* radio-show contract had not been renewed; and the subsequent stint at the Roosevelt Hotel in New York, succeeding Guy Lombardo(!), had been a virtual disaster. Moreover, during the *Let's Dance* tenure, the strongest of the Henderson arrangements had been gradually engulfed by more and more sweet poptunes and vocals. Even Henderson could not always bring life into these tawdry pieces. As Fletcher churned out countless arrangements for Benny in order to help fill twenty-six hours of air time, the Henderson style was ground into a formula. Before long, every arrangement sounded like every other, as Tin Pan Alley tunes and popular standards were simply poured into the arranging mold. The sound of the band never varied (particularly the sound of the sax section), the block-chord harmonies soon became a cliché, and (worst of all) there seemed to be less and less space for solos. This deterioration, I suspect, happened imperceptibly, so that by the time the Goodman band took to the road in the summer of 1935 it had lost much of its initiative and momentum of a year earlier. It was riddled with uncertainty and pressured by the middle-American public taste to play the least adventurous part of its repertory. It became entrapped in a dangerous trend towards playing it—once again—commercially safe.

But the surprising and *not-altogether* explicable success that followed in California at the Palomar saved the band at the eleventh hour,[28] and within a few weeks catapulted it to national fame. The essential message Goodman received

27. To my knowledge it has never been pointed out that the arrangement, probably by George Bassman (the composer of Tommy Dorsey's theme song *I'm Getting Sentimental Over You*), must have been the inspiration for David Rose's *Holiday for Strings* theme. The four bars just prior to Helen Ward's vocal only needed transposition upward and an orchestration in pizzicato strings to qualify for the model for Rose's catchy tune.
Much more mysterious is the striking resemblance of some parts of Bassman's *Blue Moon* to Ellington's *Reminiscing in Tempo*, which was composed many months *after* the Goodman recording!
28. The metaphor of an "eleventh hour" can, in fact, be taken literally, for it was the late-hour broadcast time-slot, which Goodman had occupied on the *Let's Dance* program that was mostly *not* heard by early-to-bed East-Coasters, but *was* heard in California in prime time. When Goodman got to the West Coast, the young dancing crowd had been listening to Goodman's exciting Henderson arrangements for months and were fully ready to meet and greet their new musical hero.

from the young audience that night and in subsequent weeks was that the Fletcher Henderson style arrangements, and Goodman's smart performances of them, had struck home at last. Here was a happy and rare coincidence: a large segment of the public seemed to prefer the best and most advanced arrangements the band had to offer, not, for once, the worst. Incredibly, jazz—at least one kind of jazz—had reached a potentially huge audience. With a new lease on life, the Goodman band rallied and was eventually carried to unprecedented heights of success, reaching an apex in sheer popularity with the famous 1937 Paramount Theatre engagement and the 1938 Carnegie Hall concert.

Before leaving New York for the West Coast in 1935, Benny had already recorded several of Henderson's arrangements. (They were not released until the fall, soon *after* the Palomar success.) The most exciting of these, and perhaps the most exciting recorded performance the early Goodman band ever achieved, was Fletcher Henderson's arrangement of *King Porter Stomp*. It was a near-perfect performance, starting with Bunny Berigan's supremely authoritative introduction, pushing right on across his break into the first chorus.[29] Goodman, too, was in fine form, evidently inspired by the piece, the arrangement and Berigan's pace-setting opening. Berigan's second solo, a working-over of trombonist Jimmy Harrison's original improvisation of 1928 (with Henderson), keeps the momentum high, in the process neatly picking off six high D flats in a row. Only Jack Lacey's trombone, somewhat ungainly and a bit too smeary for the occasion, falls below the general level.

The Goodman/Henderson *King Porter Stomp* already embodied all the stylistic elements the Swing Era was to represent at its peak. For one thing the saxophones here established the basic section sound that literally hundreds of bands were to adopt by the late thirties. Goodman's section could play with bite, it could turn creamy rich, it could play at all dynamic levels, and above all it was superbly balanced and rhythmically unified—all the results of painstaking rehearsing. The brass were similarly well coordinated and featured at least one superior soloist, Bunny Berigan. For another, the rhythm section had learned to play with a steady solid 4/4 beat—not as superbly timed and balanced as the best of the black bands but respectable and in its way exciting nonetheless. Even Krupa, an oftimes annoyingly overbearing drummer, somehow was initially inspired to sublimate himself to the new style. Indeed on *King Porter* he plays with a remarkable variety of touch and dynamics, and even his cymbal backbeats behind Goodman's second chorus are sensitively moderate.

Finally, the *King Porter* arrangement and performance featured a whole new range of contrasts in dynamics, in texture, and in sonority. Notice, for example, what a dramatic effect is produced by the low unison trombones behind Goodman's solo, an ingenious revision of Henderson's original. It is the two-to-three-octave gap between the low trombones and high clarinet that creates an unexpected texture, only partially filled in by the guitar and piano in the accompaniment. Use of varied or contrasting dynamics, as in *King Porter*, was still rela-

---

29. See also, Chapter 6, Part 1, Berigan.

tively rare among jazz orchestras in 1935. (Alas, it was an element which was to be dissipated within a few years, in the "grandstanding" antics of swing bands.)

For me, there is in *King Porter Stomp* a happy synthesis of all these elements. But beyond that the performance remains alive for us today because of its buoyant spirit and expressive energy. It is not merely a well-played musical façade, as with the countless other Goodman performances. And it seems to me that it is precisely the "working so hard at swinging" which generates—this one time anyway—a unique kind of tension, drive, and excitement.

Blue Skies and *Between the Devil and the Deep Blue Sea*, two other Henderson arrangements of the pre-Palomar period, cover much the same ground as *King Porter Stomp*, only not as well (for reasons having to do with the performance, not the arrangement). Each specializes in a particular Henderson trademark: *Blue Skies* with its short pointillistic jabs in the brass (which bands like Les Elgart's were still using to great effect thirty years later); and *Devil*, with its "chains" of sprightly syncopated accents in the out-chorus.

It must have become clear to Goodman rather soon after Palomar that Henderson alone could not keep an orchestra, which was enjoying a success greater than that of any other in the music's entire history, supplied with arrangements. Head arrangements (those created by the band members collectively) would do now and then, but a swing band depended for its repertory and its style on the arranger.[30] Within six months Goodman had acquired arrangements of Spud Murphy (a prolific writer who in the mid-thirties divided his time between Goodman and the Casa Lomans), Edgar Sampson (Chick Webb's chief arranger), Jimmy Mundy (a versatile writer who had won his arranging spurs with Earl Hines), Joe Lippman (later with Artie Shaw), and Deane Kincaide.

These men certainly enriched Goodman's book with some fine additions, but it would be difficult to maintain that they significantly expanded the band's already adopted language: pure Hendersonese. In truth, they all had learned their basic arranging lessons from Henderson and Redman and, like good pupils, honorably upheld that tradition. Goodman's list of arrangers grew in subsequent years: Claude Thornhill, Mary Lou Williams, and Harry James in 1937, in 1939 Eddie Sauter, and in 1941 Mel Powell.

But an arranger is not necessarily a composer. He is rarely *creative* in the full sense that fine composers are. Great composers, whether their names are Ellington or Beethoven, develop and expand their musical language, often to the extent that their late works seem barely traceable to their early ones. With arrangers that kind and degree of creativity is seldom considered desirable. Rather, they are required to be excellent craftsmen, rarely creative *innovators*. (To the extent that one of Goodman's later arrangers, Eddie Sauter, attempted to be innovative and to reach beyond the established Goodman style, his work was largely ignored by the public and, it seems, on occasion by Goodman himself.)

Under these circumstances, any profound innovative developments in the

---

30. Between late 1934 and 1942, when the Goodman band finally broke up, it made over 400 recordings, all requiring some type of written arrangement. This does not include the more than a hundred other numbers that were performed but never recorded.

Goodman orchestral language could hardly be expected. And, of course the band had its audience to satisfy. At best it would remain creatively "static"; at worst it would stagnate. That is why Duke Ellington could in all good conscience pronounce swing "stagnant" in 1939: "Nothing of importance, nothing new, nothing either *original* or *creative* has occurred in the swing field during the last two years" (italics added).[31]

But at first the sheer momentum and excitement of the swing craze enabled the Goodman band to maintain a relatively high level of performance. We are told that the musicians looked forward eagerly to each new arrangement, particularly the so-called killer-dillers—fast up-tempo numbers on which the players could satiate their appetites for virtuosity and—unfortunately in increasing degrees—empty pyrotechnics. Jimmy Mundy's contributions to this genre—*Madhouse, House Hop, Swingtime in the Rockies,* and *Jam Session*—elicited some pretty spectacular performances from the players, almost always highly disciplined ensemble work, and not infrequently some quite respectable solos. New young soloists like Vido Musso (on tenor) and Ziggy Elman (an ex-trombonist who converted to trumpet with Goodman) and, a little later, Harry James, brought fresh ideas and sounds into the band. Elman later became an expert in "schmaltz" (to the evident delight of audiences), but on *Jam Session* (November 1936) one can still hear him at a relatively unsullied stage. His solo is good, if somewhat zany and frantic. But it includes a dazzlingly executed 5-bar descending and ascending glissando (an effect we must remind ourselves Louis Armstrong had previously perfected, and which all trumpet players now tried to imitate), bridging the midpoint of his two choruses in a rather original way. It starts in bar fourteen, rides blithely across the chorus-ending sixteenth bar and ends at the top of measure three of the second chorus. The asymmetrical placement of this glissando "break" sounds absolutely right and "inevitable," in part because Elman also starts his solo two bars late. Since both the beginning of the solo and the "break" are thus shifted two bars over, Elman has preserved the basic 16-bar duration of the chorus, but of course displaced by two bars, and with the harmonies adjusted accordingly.[32]

---

31. *Downbeat,* February 1939, pp. 2, 16, 17. With remarkable wisdom and perception of the issues, Ellington reminds the reader: "It's not very difficult to understand the evolution of Jazz into Swing. Ten years ago this type of music was flourishing, albeit amidst adverse conditions and surrounded by hearty indifference." He warns: "It is the repetition and monotony of the present-day Swing arrangements which bode ill for the future. Once again it is proven that when the artistic point of view gains commercial standing, artistry itself bows out, leaving inspiration to die a slow death. The present dearth of creative and original music is not, I'm convinced, due to a lack of talent."
32. Elman has been much maligned by the jazz fraternity, especially for his "schmaltzy" ballad renditions and overdone *Fralich* style he brought to jazz. And indeed his *Fralich in Swing* (first recorded by Elman with his own recording band and later turned into a hit best seller with Goodman as *And the Angels Sing*) is neither good jazz nor good Klezmer music. But to concentrate only on this occasional aspect of Elman's playing is to miss the point that he could also be (and often was) a dynamic and tasteful jazz soloist. His style was derived, as most trumpet players, from Louis Armstrong (and later he also learned some things from Cootie Williams), but as his twenty or so sides he recorded for the Bluebird label 1938 to 1939 under his own name attest, he molded these influences

Vido Musso also contributes a hot charging solo on *Jam Session* in the best Hawkins tradition, one of Vido's more articulate statements while with the Goodman band. And then there is Benny himself, in a characteristically brilliant, poised, confident solo.

During these years, Edgar Sampson produced some fine arrangements for Goodman, among them *If Dreams Come True, Organ Grinder's Swing,* and one of the band's most popular successes, *Don't Be That Way* (1938), with its much-imitated coda of successively softer "fade-away" repetitions. (An alternate recording, preserved from the famous 1938 Carnegie Hall concert, contains probably the most effective rendition of this "one-more-time" coda, much aided and abetted by the superb acoustics of Carnegie Hall.)

Two of the best arrangements of the entire period were by Harry James: *Peckin'* and *Life Goes to a Party* (both 1937). James had come to Goodman from the latter's unofficial "farm team," Ben Pollack's band—which, as mentioned, in the thirties was still a fertile training center for swing musicians. The twenty-year-old James wrote *Peckin'* originally for Pollack, recorded it for him as a sort of going-away present, and promptly left for Goodman's trumpet section, re-recording *Peckin'* right after joining Benny's band. The young James certainly showed an impressive understanding of the Henderson arranging recipe, particularly as represented by one of the great models of this style, Henderson's *Down South Camp Meeting.*

The last one-and-a quarter ensemble chorus of *Peckin'* displays best the kind of remarkable talent James already had as an arranger. Here the typical 32-bar AABA chorus is divided into four instrumental segments. It begins with a powerfully voiced brassy ensemble of eight bars, a variation on James's initial theme (with James on lead trumpet), then another melodic variant for a contrasting softer saxophone quartet (with sharp brass punctuations) for the next eight, Benny Goodman getting B (one bridge), and back to the initial full ensemble for the final eight, recapitulating the theme in its original form. At that point the piece jumps abruptly from F to D flat major (no modulation) with another contrasting *p* sax ensemble, and it finally goes out with a strong 4-bar coda in which the band is partitioned into four instrumental groups: trumpets, trombones, saxophones, and rhythm section. For good measure, earlier in the piece, James adds a characteristically swaggering solo and employs in the final brass ensemble what is perhaps the first use of the section trumpet "shakes" in a white orchestra—all in all a rather impressive debut.

---

into an excitingly personal style. His recording band (as far as I know it never played club and ballroom dates) reflects very much the better, tasteful, genuinely jazz-oriented side of Elman, featuring a simple nine-piece orchestration of one trumpet (himself), four saxes, rhythm, and no *vocals* (!)—almost all players from the Goodman band. For the greater part of these sessions Elman eschews the "sobbing" turns, scoops, slides, and excessive vibrato of his "Jewish" style, playing instead restrained straight-ahead, unaffected swing-style jazz, well supported by tenor player Jerry Jerome in a Prez-ish mood and Artie Bernstein's swinging, full-toned bass. Elman's own *Zaggin' with Zig, Sugar,* and *Let's Fall in Love* are well worth hearing.

Elman's powerful dramatic solo work for Tommy Dorsey's band in 1941—*Well, Get It, Blue Skies, Swanee*—also should not be forgotten.

Another fine example of Harry James's exuberant arranging skills is *Life Goes to a Party*, an up-tempo "killer-diller." Again the long chains of Hendersonian syncopated brass punctuations, another irrepressibly spirited James solo, and finally a climactic out-chorus in which the last four bars are extended to eight by the simple device of laying a three-beat (3/4) riff figure, repeated seven times (21 beats), over the underlying $5\frac{1}{4}$ bars of 4/4 (Ex. 1).

Ex. 1

Harmonically the piece is rather curious. It is ostensibly in the key of E flat minor, but, through some strange harmonic alchemy peculiar to jazz, it sounds at times simultaneously both major and minor. The emphasis on the blue minor third (in this key, G flat) is so prevalent in jazz, and the ear becomes so accustomed to hearing it against a major key, that here in *Life* one momentarily imagines at several places a split or dual tonality. This odd harmonic ambiguity is underlined in James's own solo when he plays the first sixteen bars in a mixture of minor and major—whether inadvertently, instinctively, or purposely it is hard to say.[33]

It must be said that against this influx of new arranging talent, Henderson's scores held their own very well. So did some of the other older pieces like *Bugle Call Rag* (which Deane Kincaide had done for Goodman back in 1934). There

33. Mention must be made of an experimental oddity in the Goodman catalogue, Alec Templeton's quaint cameo *Bach Goes to Town* (1938). This was arranged by Henry Brant, then a twenty-five-year-old Juilliard graduate and "classical" composer (who in the 1950s became known for his *avant-garde* experiments with heterophony). Templeton's piece gained tremendous popularity in the late thirties on radio variety shows and was one of the first of a whole genre of "swing" pieces which attempted to "jazz up" the classics. Brant's clever arrangement uses only the reed section (four clarinets and bass clarinet) in the opening fugato, accompanied lightly by Buddy Schutz's cymbal beat. Later the whole orchestra joins in one by one, ending up in a typical Hollywood caricature of a big "classical" dominant-tonic cadence. The whole piece was, of course, a tongue-in-cheek parody of baroque clichés, but, as played rather cleanly (if somewhat stiffly) by the Goodman orchestra, it made a lot of friends, not so much for classical music per se, but for the "daring" notion among swing fans that "classical music really might not be that bad." This notion never seems to die and survives into our own day, the Swingle Singers, the early work of the rock group Blood, Sweat and Tears, and the pallid Bach imitations of Claude Bolling providing some relatively recent examples.

exists a performance of this piece from a 1937 broadcast which gives a good idea
of what enormous exuberance the Goodman band could still generate at that
time. A perfect "blowing" piece, with its thrice-familiar IV-I-V-I changes, everybody obviously felt at home in this old standard. Particularly impressive, even
after all these years, are the last two choruses. Taken at a breakneck tempo of
♩= 280, the band races to the finish with the relentless drive of a juggernaut.
The playing in the final brass and reed exchanges is exciting and inspired; it
gives a good indication of the kind of rhythmic complexity bands had by then
learned to master. Listen first separately to the three rhythmic strands of reeds,
brass, rhythm section; then listen again, hearing them as a totality. Whereas the
1934 recording of *Bugle Call Rag* was still played in a somewhat jerky, vertical-
ized rhythmic manner, virtually the same riffs three years later flow in great 8-
bar waves of choruses. Just as the harmonies are horizontalized into an overpowering tonic feeling[34] (with the dominant and subdominant merely rotating
around the key center like smaller orbiting satellites around a sun), so the rhythms
have also been horizontalized from successive quarter-notes (1934) into large
compound units (1937), which one can almost feel as 8-bar entities.

Other stirring performances of the period are *Limehouse Blues* and *I Found a
New Baby*, both from broadcasts (1935 and 1936 respectively), and *Ridin' High*
from 1937. The last is not only remarkable for Jimmy Mundy's "killer diller"
arrangement of what was originally a sedate Cole Porter ballad, but for its rousing battle between Goodman and James, trading eights to a fare-thee-well. *Limehouse*, never commercially recorded by Goodman (except in a Sextet version),
features some superb Berigan and typically fluent Goodman. But it is Spud Murphy's driving arrangement (and Fletcher's for *Baby*) that holds our attention. And
it is often in these vintage standards where Benny does his best playing. For this
is the repertory he grew up with. (*Alexander's Ragtime Band*, Irving Berlin's old
hit recorded in 1936, and Benny's emotional rendition of *Basin Street Blues*,
from a 1935 Palomar broadcast, are other such outstanding examples.) How far
also Goodman's ballad style had developed as early as 1935 can be heard on two
lovely renditions of *Star Dust* (both from broadcasts), still imitated half a dozen
years later in the Miller, James, and Shaw bands. On one of the *Star Dusts* and
on Ellington's *Solitude*, we can also hear Jack Lacey, a fine lyric trombonist of
the period, in excellent early examples of the standard ensemble sound for ballad
theme statements: muted lead trombone over saxophones or subtone clarinets in
parallel harmonies (a concept pioneered also by Ellington and by the Casa Lomans.)

While we can admire all these pieces, even if with some reservations, we must
also remind ourselves (as has the issuing by record companies of untold hours of
radio broadcasts and air checks) that the Goodman band performed a lot of dross
alongside the finer works of Henderson, Mundy, Sampson, and a few others.
Hundreds of recorded vocals—not to mention countless pop/dance tunes of the

---

34. This horizontalization is effected through the many common tones in these chords and in the
particular way they are all contained in Kincaide's harmonized riffs.

day that fortunately were never commercially recorded—were an indispensable part of the Goodman band diet, as songwriters, lyricists, managers, agents, and bookers all tried to grab a piece of Goodman's huge financial pie. Once again these commercial forces increasingly began to control the destiny of the band. In turn this took its artistic toll, as the band's performances became increasingly perfunctory, in many cases downright dull. They were almost always cleanly played, but too often there remained only an empty façade of music, or perhaps an outline of the mechanics of a piece, but with none of the content filled in.

By 1938 the Goodman band had reached an artistic nadir, clearly reflected in its recordings. Of some fifty-odd released sides, very few offer more than an occasional moment of interest: a Harry James-led trumpet trio here, a Jess Stacy solo there, sometimes some real rhythmic ensemble drive (as on Henderson's *Wrappin' It Up*)—this in contrast to the generally listlessly mechanical performances that abound. About the best the band could produce was the lively *Margie* or *Bumble Bee Stomp*, an unpromising jazz title if ever there was one. A flat-footed version of *Flat Foot Floogie* is typical of the band's work during this time. But what provides the real mark of the band's deterioration and drift towards commercialism are the nearly thirty Martha Tilton vocals—empty-headed, coy, and puerile pop songs and performances (sample *What Goes On Here*). What is particularly disturbing is that most of this kind of ephemeral pop tune material came from just-as-ephemeral Hollywood films, a telltale sign of commercial encroachment. And why so *many* Tilton vocals? It isn't as if she were a great singer.

The more "modern" swing style of Goodman's 1938 band aside, there is really little difference between, let's say, these performances and the studio recordings Benny had been involved with in 1931, essentially beholden to the same formula: a bit of jazz here and there, set over a basically dance band beat, and plenty of vocals. The Goodman band here was not much more creative than the Jan Garbers, Dick Jurgens', Kay Kysers, and so on. It is indicative, too, that, like Dorsey and Shaw and others, Goodman kept the real jazz-playing more or less relegated to his small groups—the Trio, Quartet, and (later) Sextet units. Perhaps Goodman deep down—or at least the businessman in Goodman—still did not believe that jazz could make it commercially, his previous successes notwithstanding.

In any ultimate balanced assessment of the perplexing phenomenon of Benny Goodman, his orchestra and its extraordinary popular success during this early period, one eventually must come to grips with his and the orchestra's shortcomings. Apart from the already mentioned problem of the gradual stylistic stultification—a serious problem by late 1938—there was the constant dilemma of the Goodman rhythm section. At the heart of the problem were the bass and drums. Harry Goodman was at best competent but, more often than not, weak. This had two far-reaching consequences: one, that the band's harmonic foundation was weak; and second, that the irrepressible Gene Krupa constantly overcompensated for his weaker colleague. In fact, on approximately half the recordings

Krupa's incessant bass drum pounding completely covers the string bass, leaving the band without any audible harmonic foundation. It is Krupa who drives (or, more accurately, pushes) the band—never Harry Goodman. And certainly we seldom hear the two welded as a unit, in consort with the other rhythm section players. Far too often the bass and drums do not swing; they merely keep time— and this, ironically, in the very band that was perceived as having initiated the swing craze.

It has often been said of the Goodman band that its playing was mechanical and superficial. When this is true—and, excepting for a modest amount of recordings, some recorded broadcasts (particularly those of 1937),[35] and undoubtedly many performances that never happened to be preserved at all, it is true far too often—it is because the Goodman orchestra had a topheavy sound. I mean structurally and harmonically, not dynamically. The depth of feeling and support that a properly functioning rhythm section generates is just not present. The Goodman rhythm section rarely connects up with the rest of the band. A brilliant brass and reed ensemble is constantly trying to support itself on a rhythmically and harmonically weak foundation. This crisp, bright, bottom-less sound was particularly dangerous in a band where the most frequently featured soloist played a high-register instrument: the clarinet.[36] As a result the soloists and section ensembles had simply to proceed under their own steam, so to speak; and how surprisingly well they did this, time and time again! But under the circumstances a complete vertical alignment of the harmonic structure—from the bass up, through the orchestra, to the top lead notes—could never really occur.

How this structural balance might have sounded one can readily hear by comparing any number of Henderson and Goodman recordings. Take *Down South Camp Meeting*, for example. The big difference here is John Kirby on the Henderson recording. He functions fully as an integral rhythmic *and* harmonic element of the entire musical structure. And suddenly we don't mind that the Henderson ensemble is a little ragged here and there, and that the sound of the "horns" is lighter, thinner—at least as recorded—when compared directly with the potent Goodman brasses.[37] Like a tree standing on its roots, an orchestral sound stands or falls on its harmonic/rhythmic foundation. This is something the high register and virtuoso-oriented ears of Goodman never really demanded.

But over and over again, in discussing the early Goodman band, one returns to Krupa. He is a special kind of phenomenon, peculiar to American show business: a perplexing combination of raw talent and exuberant vulgarity. His

---

35. Most recently issued on Columbia CL 820 in 1960.

36. In this connection, it is relevant to note that for the first three years, not until John Kirby was asked to sit in in late 1938, the Goodman Trio and Quartet never used a bass. Interestingly, Goodman never asked his brother Harry; undoubtedly he knew better. Compare all this with Duke Ellington, who *performed and recorded duos* with bassist Jimmy Blanton.

37. Nor is it merely a matter of a recording engineer turning up the bass level; it is a matter of full participation—harmonically, rhythmically, sonically—on the part of the whole four-man rhythm section. In this respect Goodman never did *Down South* full justice until his splendid 1951 recording of Henderson's opus (with Bob Haggart playing bass).

success with the public was primarily visual, kinetic—occasionally purely musical. But his show-biz genius lay in the discovery that rhythm, reduced to its
unsubtlest common denominator, had for a mass public a universal, primitive,
irresistible gut-appeal, a discovery thousands of mediocre rock drummers were
to make again and exploit thirty years later. There are always far too many
people who are impressed by mere energy; and Krupa had plenty of that.

But, as I say, occasionally this energy was converted into real music-making,
and thus one points almost with glee to the sporadic imaginative moments in
Krupa's work. *Swingtime in the Rockies* (1936) for some strange reason abounds
with inventive Krupa touches. First, there is the way he begins the piece with a
crisply controlled sonority and beat, at once cool and hot in feeling; then, on
several occasions during Benny's two solos (particularly the last sixteen bars of
the second solo), how excitingly he "kicks" the rhythm forward; how, in several
full-ensemble segments he effectively uses cymbal and bass drum "bombs," and
still later, after returning to the soft cooled-off opening sounds of the piece, we
hear his ingenious use of that bell-like ring, produced by playing on the crown
of the suspended cymbal. Throughout this performance Krupa displays consummate dynamic control, and through his dynamics helps to delineate perfectly the
form and structure of Mundy's fine arrangement.

Or in *Smoke Dreams* (December 1936): listen to Krupa's sensitive brushwork
as he provides a subtly contrasting undertone of tension for Helen Ward's languid vocal (Ex. 2).

Ex. 2

Hearing these moments of talent and intelligence, one is hard put to also
explain Krupa's often deplorable monotonous drumming in the early Goodman
Trio and Quartet sides, or the horrors of *Sing, Sing, Sing,* or the countless other
examples of Krupa's rigidly relentless pounding (Jess Stacy was wont to call it
"Krupa's banging") or, for that matter, equally inappropriate, the polite or all-
too-pat bounce in pieces like *Anything Goes* and *Stompin' at the Savoy.* (For an
idea of how the latter was *supposed* to sound, one only need listen to Chick
Webb's 1934 recording.) In the end one concludes in bewilderment that Krupa
was one of those singular figures who not infrequently occur in the arts: a combination of genius and showman.[38] (Leopold Stokowski was an analogous example on the classical side.) Krupa was certainly not a dishonest performer;

---

38. The best drummer Goodman ever had in the 1930s was Dave Tough. Paradoxically, some of
Goodman's later drummers (like Buddy Schutz, Nick Fatool, Henry Jaeger), though less offensive
than Krupa, lacked personality and originality. But, then, good drummers have always been hard to
find, and Goodman did his share of looking. That Lionel Hampton was also not the right drummer
for Goodman can be heard on a clutch of 1938 sides when some of the Basie players recorded with
Goodman. Hampton and the famous team of Walter Page and Freddie Green did not jell.

Sid Catlett sparked the band sporadically for a brief four-month period in 1941, and it is fair to
say that the Goodman band never swung as hard or as deeply as when Catlett was at the drums. Roy
Eldridge once said of Catlett that he played with "that weight without ever being noisy," and that it

indeed, his genuine and natural enthusiasm for music of all kinds, but especially jazz, was one of his most charming and captivating qualities. But his lapses of musical taste and—especially during his later Goodman years—his increasing drift towards an unbridled grandstanding showmanship—are hard to condone, and evidently were so for Benny, leading to the final break with Krupa in early 1938, soon after the Carnegie Hall concert.

What is so perplexing about Krupa is that he frequently paid verbal tribute to the fine black drummers from whom he admittedly learned most of what he could do, men like Zutty Singleton and Baby Dodds, and later Chick Webb. He was not averse to confessing that "most white drummers of that day" (the twenties), himself included, "thought drums were something you beat the hell out of," and then he would proceed to do exactly that. There is also no question that for his time Krupa could be considered a quite remarkable technician. But it remains questionable to what musical purposes he sometimes put his technique.

At any rate, an objective historian is compelled to record the fact that, to the large public, Gene Krupa epitomized jazz drumming, while much more creative and technically equally endowed drummers, like Catlett, Webb, and Tough, went largely unappreciated and unheralded, except by fellow musicians.[39]

When Goodman's two major stars, Harry James and Gene Krupa, left his band during 1938, fresh soloistic energy and a new stylistic infusion were clearly needed, if Goodman was to survive the increasing competition from the growing number of swing bands, like Artie Shaw and Tommy Dorsey, with Glenn Miller also about to break through—and, of course, the newest competitors, Harry James and Krupa. Relief came in several manifestations: 1) a great innovative soloist, guitarist Charlie Christian (although Christian was mostly limited to work with the Sextet, only occasionally playing with the full band);[40] 2) two remarkable arrangers, Eddie Sauter and Mel Powell; and 3) on the commercial—as well as musical/artistic—side, two fine expressive singers, Helen Forrest and Peggy Lee. Goodman himself was undergoing a variety of musical and professional experiences that led him to search for newer territories to conquer. The year 1939 was but the first of many periods, observable throughout Goodman's long career, in which some form of outside musical stimulus was needed to keep him from stagnating. For it is in Goodman's nature and temperament that he easily gets bored with people, pieces, styles, and even his own playing. Part of this results, ironically, from the extraordinary levels of perfection he demands of himself and those who work with/for him, and the apparent ease with which he himself

---

was Catlett's powerful depth of sound and spacious beat that not only carried the Goodman band to new swinging heights but corralled its sound into a richer ensemble feeling never previously achieved by the band. Catlett's drumming in effect anchored the Goodman band's playing in a deeper, fuller sound, dramatically different from the airy weightlessness of its early mid-thirties' days. But Catlett was one player Goodman could not control or stare down, and he fired him after only four months.
39. For a further discussion of Krupa as bandleader, see below, Chapter 7, Part 2.
40. See, below, Chapter 6, Part 3, for full discussion of Christian.

maintains those high standards. That kind of ease and facility can become boring, because there are very few challenges which cannot be instantly met. And
Benny needed constant challenges. But where at his level of perfection were they
to be found?

They could be found, but they would be rare. Christian, Sauter, Powell—and
to some extent Cootie Williams later on—were to provide some of that stimu-
lation and inspiration, both in the larger conceptual stylistic sense and in the
smaller-detail form of sparring improvisationally with instrumental equals.

In addition, Goodman was much stimulated by his increasing contacts with
classical music and musicians: Mozart, Bartók, Debussy, Szigeti, Barbirolli, the
New York Philharmonic, the Budapest String Quartet, and so on. These mind-
expanding experiences certainly caused him to welcome, indeed solicit, the more
advanced arrangements of Eddie Sauter—although one must also recall that a
certain inherent conservatism in Goodman (as well as his shrewd business sense)
caused him to block the release of a number of Sauter's more advanced arrangements and to reject others outright.[41]

Nonetheless, the sixty-odd Sauter arrangements Goodman performed and recorded between mid-1939 and the recording ban of 1942 contributed significantly to changing the basic sound and style of the Goodman band. This, in
conjunction with an influx of younger players, eventually combined to produce
by 1941 the finest of the several permanent (i.e. pre-1950) Goodman bands. It
would be wrong to assume, however, that Sauter's contributions simply replaced
the older Henderson pieces. For the best of Henderson's (and Mundy's and
Sampson's) work was retained during the Sauter-Powell years, further enriched
by arrangements by Buster Harding, Budd Johnson, Buck Clayton, and Margie
Gibson. All in all, Goodman's repertory was probably the most varied of any
orchestra's of that time, all the more remarkable for its outstanding quality.

Sauter had been arranging (and playing the mellophone) for Red Norvo's
orchestra[42] since 1936, and had built a considerable reputation as an innovative
orchestrator by the time Goodman hired him in 1939. While many of his scores
for Norvo had explored unusual new harmonic and timbral devices, Goodman's
big band provided Sauter with a much greater opportunity for expanding his
harmonic/timbral palette than the smaller chamber-sized Norvo units could. Those
more limited ensemble situations, to be sure, led Sauter to invent many ingenious instrumental combinations so as to create the illusion of larger and more
varied ensembles. One of his most resourceful bits of orchestrational legerdemain can be heard on the 1936 Gramercy Square (with Norvo's Swing Sextette),
wherein just four instruments—clarinet, trumpet, mellophone, and tenor saxophone—are juxtaposed so adroitly as not only to create the illusion of a larger
ensemble, but a variety of diverse textures.

With the full resources of Goodman's six brass, four saxophones at his beck

41. The list of Sauter arrangements recorded but left initially unreleased is substantial, and includes
among others: How Deep Is the Ocean?, Tangerine, 'Tis Autumn, That's the Way It Goes, Not a
Care, Ramona.
42. See below, Chapter 6 , Part 2, for a full discussion of Norvo.

and call (a fifth, providing the option of a baritone sax, was soon to be added), Sauter was able to enlarge his already highly individual sonoric concept, which was based not on the antiphonal segregation of brass and reeds, as in the Henderson-Redman school, but rather a *blending* of brass and reeds into new warmer timbral combinations and textures. In this regard Sauter drew upon two influences: one, Duke Ellington's scores of the early and mid-thirties, many of which featured precisely such admixtures of timbre and sonority, moreover in highly unusual voicings; and two, that of his leader, Norvo. For Norvo was an astute musician and, judging by the evidence of a piece like *Dance of the Octopus* (1933), a formidable creative talent of great individuality. Norvo was clearly aware of other ways of thinking orchestrally besides those of Henderson and Redman. In particular he was conscious of those of Bill Challis and Lennie Hayton with Paul Whiteman (with whose orchestra Norvo had been featured as xylophone soloist) and, of course, Ellington's. Norvo urged Sauter not only to write linearly and contrapuntally, concepts foreign to Henderson's largely vertical homophonic arranging style, but also to think of individual voicings and voice mixtures, as (again) opposed to Henderson's strictly "choral" approach.

It is these Sauter orchestral concepts that produced such a profound change in—or at least addition to—the prevailing Goodman sound and style.[43] It took a while, of course, for Sauter to get his bearings with Goodman, and he did so most readily with the many Helen Forrest accompaniments he was assigned, starting in late 1939 with *Darn That Dream*. In these vocals Sauter could most completely preserve his own arranging concepts, developed over many years of creating distinctive backgrounds for Mildred Bailey (for her own and her husband Red Norvo's bands).

But Sauter also could, if needed, fit into the established Henderson mode, as shown in *How High the Moon*. In this beautifully relaxed performance, Sauter keeps the brass and reeds discretely and most effectively apart, sounding very much like any other good Goodman band arrangement. There are two tell-tale signs in the score, however, that would not have come from Henderson: one, the brief catchy introduction, featuring staccato reeds and pizzicato bass with clarinet lead (of the kind of texture Willie Smith had used so tellingly in his Lunceford arrangements);[44] the other, the modulation into Forrest's vocal.

I don't think there ever has been a master of harmonic modulation in jazz to equal Sauter. His skill in this respect is certainly equal to Richard Strauss's in classical music, and it has not been matched in jazz in its deftness, economy, and chameleon-like quick-change artistry. In no time one key disappears under one's eyes (and ears), and in an instant one is in another harmonic world. Examples of Sauter's skill in manipulating keys abound in the Goodman (and Norvo) books, and *How High the Moon* is but one of the earlier and, in a sense, "trickier" ones. Sauter finishes the first chorus in C major, and in three short bars

43. Sauter's writing bore even more far-reaching consequences in later years, in that it had a deep influence on both Claude Thornhill and Gil Evans and their respective arranging styles in the mid- and late forties.
44. See below, Chapter 4.

and in what ultimately amounts to one initial ingenious harmonic move, sets the arrangement on its path towards the new key of E♭. The harmonic progression is stated in its simplest outline form in Ex. 3:

Ex. 3

The "initial move" I refer to is the B♭ seventh chord (in a first inversion) in bar 1, for it is there that the die is cast in the direction of E♭. The chords in mm. 2 and 3 are in a sense a spinning out of the B♭[7] tonality through two passing chords (A♭[7] and G[7]) to the B♭-related A♭m[6] chord in m. 3. From here it is only one slight shift of harmonic weight, i.e. through the A diminished chord, and we are on the dominant seventh of the new key. The passing tones/chords in mm. 2 and 3 function in two ways: one, to flesh out the modulation to the expected four bars; and, two, at once to soften the abruptness of the shift to B♭ in m. 1 and consolidate that progression by extending it through a few secondary moves.

The most inventive part of this passage may be the bass notes. Any number of arrangers would have had the bass notes following the harmonic progression downward stepwise (C B♭ A♭ G). However, apart from avoiding stiff-sounding "parallel octaves" which this produces with the upper (melodic) line, Sauter achieves a more interesting bass line. But, even more important, he has the two pivotal Ds (in mm. 1 and 2) function in a *triple* (!) harmonic role. In one role the Ds hark back to the key of C, not quite ready to relinquish that key. They do so because a II-V-I progression—the D being II in the key of C—is about as old as jazz and as basic a function in diatonic tonality as can be. It is one of the most common practices, a progression played by bass players a hundred times a day. The point is that the D is heard and often used by bass players as both the second degree of the scale (always leading melodically back to I) *and* as the fifth in the dominant (G) chord of the key.

In their second Sauter incarnation, the Ds in mm. 1 and 2 take on a kind of subtly anticipatory melodic function, that note being the third of the key of B♭ (to which the passage is heading in m. 4) and the "leading tone" of the new key-to-be, E♭. Lastly, mixed into these two roles, is a third one—functioning harmonically and melodically—of twice lining out the tritone interval, D–A♭, an unconventional and ingenious way of underscoring this particular harmonic progression.

I have dwelt upon these four measures at some length because, picked almost arbitrarily out of dozens of analogous examples, they epitomize the perfection and subtlety of Sauter's modulatory art. And it is the kind of passage the casual

listener might simply pass over, both because it is so subtly, unobtrusively handled and so smoothly and perfectly accomplished.[45]

The Fable of the Rose, Shake Down the Stars, and Franz Lehar's beautiful
melody, Yours Is My Heart Alone, all recorded in early 1940, combine the best
of Sauter's and Forrest's talents. Even more so do the somewhat later When the
Sun Comes Out and The Man I Love (which features in addition some passionately intense trumpet by lead-trumpet Alec Fila). Helen Forrest was, with the
possible exception of Jack Teagarden and Mildred Bailey—and until Sinatra came
along—the finest white singer of the entire Swing Era. She certainly was the
most "human" of them all and could really make you believe in the words and
meaning of a song which, given most of the material she was asked to sing, was
a miraculous achievement in itself. Helen Forrest had impeccable taste; there is
not a single song that she didn't somehow elevate by her uncanny musical sensitivity and fine ear for accurate pitch and subtle nuances. She also knew, more
than any white girl singer of her time, including Bailey, how to use dynamics
and timbre to shade and shape a song, to bring out highlights, to lead from one
phrase intelligently to the next.

Of course, Sauter's linear, essentially lyric approach to composing/arranging
provided a virtually ideal framework for Helen's style. There is a sophistication
and a suppleness in Sauter's writing, both in its sound and its forms, that is the
perfect instrumental parallel to her singing. Theirs was a charmed collaboration,
and its disruption was all the more lamentable for its abruptness.

In the meantime Sauter was really beginning to evolve—within the Goodman
idiom—a more personal style. The first strong examples of this are The Hour of
Parting and Cocoanut Grove, both from April 1940. Both pieces were not only
fine examples of jazz-orchestral writing but a real, partially successful attempt to
make original "compositions" out of tune arrangements. And in both cases the
spirit of Duke Ellington hovered above; indeed, it is clear that Sauter had been
listening profitably to Ellington's Reminiscing in Tempo.

I say "partially successful attempt" to expand arrangement to composition because, insofar as Sauter was working with pre-composed material—Spoliansky's
song The Hour of Parting and Dudley Brooks's instrumental Cocoanut Grove—
he had to respect its basic form (harmony, melody, structure) and work within
certain conventions. (Duke Ellington avoided this problem simply, by rarely
arranging/recording anyone else's compositions; even his "pop tunes" were his
own compositions.) Where someone like Sauter was most free to really "compose" was in the introductions, interludes, modulations, and codas. And yet,
these had to stay relatively within the overall concept of the arrangement, lest
they protrude as mere dismembered segments in the overall form, fragmenting
it. In Parting Sauter's "freest" contribution is its unusual modulation from D to
G♭ midway through the performance. (By 1940 his introduction in parallel whole-
tone chords and muted brass was no longer a very original idea.) A tritone har-

---

45. Other outstanding Sauter modulations or interludes can be heard on The Moon Won't Talk,
Moonlight on the Ganges and, above all, How Deep Is the Ocean?.

monic admixture of D and A♭ allows the trombones to play a descending "whole tone" line of C, A♭, D, C, which suddenly twists off to a low G. This G pedal point is then used as the "lead note" to the key of G♭. The ♭II method of getting to a tonic chord—in effect, the "flat-five" tritone-related substitute for the dominant chord—was in 1940 still a relatively "advanced" and rare harmonic usage.

Cocoanut Grove, a virtually perfect performance, is outstanding Sauter of the simpler sort, in a very Duke-ish vein, and prophetic for its many unison saxophone and brass lines. The very bop-ish unison brass figures, for example, were certainly picked up by Dizzy Gillespie and Billy Eckstine and their arrangers in the mid-forties, while the velvety low-register saxophone unison lines throughout *Cocoanut* must have impressed Gil Evans enough for him to use similar ideas—greatly expanded, of course—later in his extraordinary 1947–48 scores for Claude Thornhill.

In the summer of 1940, when Goodman visited the Mayo Clinic to have a serious case of sciatica treated, Sauter composed a piece called *Benny Rides Again* and arranged *The Man I Love* for the reorganized band's first record date. Exploiting the addition of one more reed player in *Man*, Sauter set Helen Forrest's vocal against a darkly textured background which now included baritone saxophone *and* bass clarinet, plus clarinet, alto and tenor (Georgie Auld). Just as Ellington was wont to do with Harry Carney's baritone sax, Sauter gave the bass clarinet special notes to play within the chords, not necessarily as expected in unison with the bass. For example, in the first four bars of the song the two bass lines split as follows (Ex. 4):

Ex. 4

In the seventh and eighth bars, instead of the standard "turnback" progression, Sauter finds these especially poignant harmonies (Ex. 5).

Ex. 5

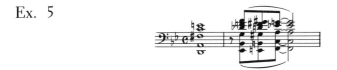

In the second chorus, which begins with a blazing *ff* theme statement in the trumpet (unfortunately played somewhat out of tune), accompanied by the full band with *six* reeds (Benny's high-riding clarinet included), Sauter finds varied harmonizations for each of the three A strains, all of them different from the first chorus. In the bridge, as Helen Forrest returns, freeing herself from the written vocal line in what amounts to the internal climax of the performance, soft saxes intone the following beautiful progression (Ex. 6):

Ex. 6

(in harmonic outline only)

Sauter's *Benny Rides Again* is another matter. Although it has some touching moments—particularly Benny's pretty clarinet over delicate saxophone figures—it is also a flawed work, a piece in search of its form. Indeed, it seems unable to make up its mind between wanting to be a kind of ostentatious *Sing, Sing, Sing* (tom-toms and all) or the bittersweet tone poetry of its second half, which part is, however, not original. It is in fact taken fairly literally from Alexander Borodin's *Dance of the Polovtsian Maidens* (from the opera *Prince Igor*). One also finds the title misleading, expecting a razzle-dazzle tour de force for Benny's clarinet, but getting instead two moderate tempo pieces, not quite welded into one, with Benny idling much of the way.

Another partially flawed work is Sauter's *Superman*. Written for Cootie Williams, the basic piece works well enough, but it was a miscalculation to add an overly long and superfluous slow-tempo coda, not even particularly suited to Cootie Williams's talents.

If such partial failures showed that Sauter was not yet a major *composer*, fully in control of his materials, his arrangements were well-nigh flawless.[46] Hear his and Helen Forrest's *Hard To Get, It's Always You, When the Sun Comes Out.*

Of course, Fletcher Henderson was also contributing all along to the Goodman library with mostly outstanding arrangements: *Show Your Linen, Miss Richardson* (with its, for the time, rather risqué lyrics and an effectively swaggering Ziggy Elman solo), *Stealin' Apples, Frenesi, Henderson Stomp* (with some of the most unbuttoned Cootie Williams playing on record).[47]

By 1939 the Basie band had become one of the two or three leading black bands of the country, and it was beginning to offer competition to all its competitors—particularly in the matter of swing, a subject on which on any given day it could show the "King of Swing" and his band a thing or two. Undoubtedly through the urging of John Hammond, friendly with both Basie and Goodman, Goodman was persuaded to record Basie's *Jumpin' at the Woodside.* As originally recorded by Basie in 1938, *Jumpin'* was a masterpiece of its kind, far outclassing Goodman's 1939 imitation. Still Basie's piece somehow got the Goodman band to produce one of *its* best 1939 performances, generating a deeper fuller sound and avoiding some of the excessively bright clipped staccato style it normally favored. *Jumpin'* also sported an especially spunky Ziggy Elman solo. And one

46. It is worth mentioning at this point that Goodman claimed that Sauter's arrangements were too congested, too full of ideas, and that he (Goodman) had to "take things out" to make them work right. Goodman once quipped: "You could get a whole new tune from what you deleted."
47. Another marvelously uninhibited and inspired open-horn Cootie Williams performance occurred on *A Smo-o-o-th One,* a Sextet date from March 1941.

interesting effect was added by Goodman himself. At the climax the trombones break out into upward glissandos to high F, sounding for all the world like braying elephants. Goodman on the spur of the moment, after hearing two of these "rips," extended each trombone glissando with one of his own—up to the highest B♭ (Ex. 7). It was not only a stunning technical tour de force by Goodman—an effect heretofore unknown to the clarinet—but it gave that climax an added touch of orchestral brilliance.

Ex. 7

But ultimately, for all the band's good intention and talent, such imitations of better "originals" seem in retrospect fairly pointless. I would put Sauter's arrangement of Maurice Ravel's *Bolero* and Toots Camarata's of Serge Prokofiev's *Peter and the Wolf* in the same category: both were well-fashioned in their way, but were of necessity—especially given the time limits of a ten-inch disc—reductions and diminutions of the originals. For example, while it was skillful of Sauter to preserve the 3/4 trombone glissandos of the final measure of *Bolero*, squeezing them into the 4/4 dance tempo, the passage cannot match Ravel's original and is ultimately a pointless exercise.

During this period Jimmy Mundy also produced a number of popular works, mostly solo features like *Solo Flight* (for Charlie Christian)[48] and the outstanding *Fiesta in Blue*, another solo vehicle for Williams. Mundy cast that piece in an ABA form, with the A sections based on the blues. The work is faintly reminiscent of Ellington's *Concerto for Cootie* and, of course, featured Cootie in the plunger-and-growl style in which he was at the time pre-eminent. In the blues sections, Mundy here established for the first time a style of orchestral blues, especially in the use of the saxophones (with the baritone saxophone[49] in the person of Skippy Martin, now a full member of the section and giving a welcome depth and power to the Goodman band's sound), that was to become the prevailing ensemble blues style for the bands of Eckstine, Gillespie, and Gerald Wilson a few years later.

Another arranger, more uneven in her efforts but occasionally contributing some rather fine scores in the Henderson manner, was Margie Gibson.[50] A good

48. See below, Chapter 6, Part 3.

49. The baritone saxophone was a relative latecomer in the big bands. Except for an occasional isolated use of the instrument, only Ellington and Lunceford featured it from the beginning as a regular member of the sax section. Dorsey followed suit in 1940 with the arrival of Sy Oliver as arranger.

50. Born in Baltimore in 1917, Margie Gibson began arranging regularly for Goodman at age 22, free-lancing as well with Harry James, Basie, and Lunceford. It is unfortunate that jazz historians and encyclopedists, including the numerous recent writers on women in jazz, have made little or no mention of Gibson's outstanding work. (I have been unable to find a single source of information as to Gibson's later work or, indeed, as to whether at this writing she is still alive.)

example of her work is *Let the Doorknob Hitcha*, a silly novelty tune (sung rather humorlessly by Cootie Williams), but smartly arranged to contrast the high bright Goodman brass against the warmer darker saxophones, with Davey Tough's drums giving the band a wonderful rhythmic lift. One of the strongest arrangements in the basic Henderson-Goodman mold (i.e. not in the more experimental Sauter vein, and prewar Mel Powell)—was Buster Harding's hard-swinging *Scarecrow*. Relentlessly *f* and featuring strong solos by Goodman and Auld, Harding blended (rather than separated) the brass and saxophones in a fullness of big-band sound that was well ahead of its time, later becoming standard arranging practice and then, alas, much abused in the noisy hectic postwar years.

An original instrumental by Skippy Martin, *Tuesday at Ten*, sparked by Sid Catlett's drums and Mel Powell's aphoristic piano sprinkles, brought, in its riffish way, some more of the Basie style into the Goodman band. But perhaps the most "classic"—and most taken-for-granted—arrangement of those Goodman years was George Bassman's of *Let's Dance*, Benny's theme for the Saturday night radio program of the same name. Recorded on October 24, 1939, *Let's Dance* is a perfect performance, with not a musical hair out of place: everything sparkles, including Goodman's quicksilver tone and flawless execution.[51]

Another major stylistic infusion, in addition to Sauter's, ensued with the arrival in mid-1941 of Mel Powell as pianist (replacing Teddy Wilson) and as arranger. Only eighteen years old at the time, Powell not only left his indelible mark on the orchestra's style and repertory during his one year with Goodman, with a dozen or so brilliant arrangements, but as a pianist he was clearly an inspiration and stimulus to Benny, especially in the Sextet context.

Powell first paid tribute to two of his pianistic idols, Basie and Hines, with *The Count* and *The Earl*. The former starts with an introduction borrowed in overall content from one of Sauter's codas (the one to *Benny Rides Again*) and then launches into a Lou McGarity bucket-muted trombone solo accompanied by saxophones and Sid Catlett's half-open hi-hat cymbal, the latter one of the more delicious aural delights in the annals of jazz percussion, and the whole passage is one of the great moments in jazz altogether. Benny then contributed a brilliant high-riding solo ending with some impossible-to-play altissimo triplets in fourths. Cootie Williams's open horn follows, confident and blues-ish, and Powell takes the piece out with the same kind of full-voiced hard-swinging ensemble Buster Harding had used in *Scarecrow*.

In *The Earl*, Powell the composer/arranger is more on his creative own, even as Powell the pianist pays his deep respects to Hines with a series of the master's most beloved devices, including bouncing right-hand octaves over a long pedal-point left-hand trill. In between we hear brief interpolations of the kind of running clarinet-piano duets and chase choruses Benny and Mel had already worked out in their Quartet and Sextet performances. Besides clean, fine-swinging arrangements of *I'm Here* and 1941's big dance hit, *Jersey Bounce*, Powell also

51. The seeming out-of-tuneness on Columbia CL820, eight bars from the end is an engineering technical flaw, what is called a "pitch-wow," caused in the transfer to LP.

contributed two of the band's most popular successes: *Why Don't You Do Right?* (with Peggy Lee's matchless vocal) and *Mission to Moscow.* The first named, a modified blues, is a swing/vocal "classic," enduringly captivating in Miss Lee's insinuating style,[52] rendered more perfect by Jimmy Maxwell's haunting plunger-muted trumpet obbligato in the last chorus—surely one of that fine trumpeter's most inspired moments.

One may not entirely fancy Powell's march-like introduction and coda for *Mission to Moscow,*[53] but it is admittedly catchy with its $3 + 2 + 3$ Balkan dance syncopations. For the rest it is a typical bright smart-as-a-whip arrangement which not only gave Benny a chance to exercise his fleet fingers, but tantalized the sax section with ensemble passages which at once looked backward to Ellington's *Cotton Tail* (1940) and forward to Jimmy Giuffre's *Four Brothers* (1948).

If Powell to some extent took over the swinging instrumentals from Fletcher Henderson, Sauter continued as the chief arranger for the vocal ballads (now for Peggy Lee) and the solo features for Goodman. Of the latter category *Clarinet à la King* (1941), along with *Clarinade* (1945) by Mel Powell, became very successful showpieces for Goodman. But both works again suffer from various minor blemishes. While Powell's *Clarinade* is certainly the more original and better formed of the two compositions, Goodman's playing is rather stiff and prim, as if trying to point up some hidden "classical" influence in the work. (Goodman even nearly muffs one of the written-out passages—a rare occurrence with him.) This contrasts sharply with the almost incredible ensemble swing of the brass section, particularly in the descending-diminuendo figure in the last two bars of the various A strains. Note also the strong baritone work by Danny Bank, now anchoring the whole sax section.

Sauter's *Clarinet à la King* reverses the problem, in that it elicits fine virtuoso,

---

52. Peggy Lee heard *Why Don't You Do Right?* on a recording by the blues singer Lil Green, and was so taken with it that she begged Goodman to have it arranged so that she might sing it with the band. Goodman agreed reluctantly, never dreaming the piece had the makings of a hit. Much of the credit for that must really go to Lil Green, for Miss Lee appropriated most of the blues singer's style, down to the minutiae of individual vocal inflections and word enunciation, still somehow turning it into her own unique manner.

But the origin of the song goes back even further than Lil Green's recording, where it is credited to the guitarist/song writer Joe McCoy. The resemblance, in part at least, to a 1936 recording by the Harlem Hamfats, called *Weed Smoker's Dream (Why Don't You Do It Now?)*, is unmistakable.

53. Powell had a weakness for such bombastic passages: witness his "Movietone-news" ending to *Darktown Strutters' Ball*, in striking contrast to trombonist McGarity's uninhibited blues-ish true jazz solo.

Mel Powell left Goodman in the fall of 1942 to join Raymond Scott's orchestra and, when drafted in 1943, became a prominent member of Glenn Miller's remarkable Army Air Force band. He rejoined Goodman in 1945, performing brilliantly, particularly in the various Goodman Sextets—Powell and Norvo brought that group to its absolute zenith—but gradually in the late 1940s drifted away from jazz to become eventually one of the leading contemporary "classical" composers of the United States. After a distinguished teaching career for many years at the Yale School of Music, Powell became Dean of the California Institute of the Arts. Although he is a highly respected composer, (indeed one of America's very finest), swing era enthusiasts still lament Powell's defection from jazz.

at times even fervent, playing from Goodman, but Sauter's composition is somewhat of a pastiche. Beginning and ending with a near-quotation of the first four
bars of Brahms's *Fourth Symphony* (albeit in C rather than E minor), it later
lifts a few bars of Wagner's *Tristan und Isolde*—swung, of course. In between,
the piece vascillates between disjointed bits of dissonant harmonies, *a cappella*
muted-trumpet whole-tone progressions, various pedal-point passages (which
hamper the harmonic flow of the piece), and straight-ahead minor-key swing.
Sid Catlett tries manfully to hold all this together, but a steady swinging beat
does not yet a composition make.

In the ballad department Sauter fared much better. Indeed *How Deep Is the
Ocean?* and *My Old Flame*, both Peggy Lee vocals, are near-perfect; and perhaps *My Old Flame* is a masterpiece of the genre. Both pieces are Sauter at his
sophisticated and subtle best and require attentive listening, since many of the
most succulent orchestrational treasures are secreted away in the instrumental
backgrounds. As originally recorded in late September 1941, *How Deep* was
rejected—for reasons not entirely clear, since the performance was in all respects
quite good. Tackling the piece again in early October—this take was also not
released for another four years—Goodman (or Sauter) slowed down the tempo
somewhat and, because of time limitations, was then forced to cut out sixteen
bars of the original first chorus, including a fine 8-bar Vido Musso tenor solo.
As finally issued on a Columbia 78 (36754), the arrangement begins with a rising
figure, which, though not strictly related, seems to have been somehow ingeniously extracted from Irving Berlin's original melody. Rising from the low register in trombones and canonically answered by saxes and then trumpets (each
section in unison and one octave higher than its predecessor), this introductory
material leads organically into Goodman's theme statement. Unison sax lines
continue underneath, but in the second eight Sauter fashions a remarkable poin-
tillistically punctuated background, divided between brass and reeds (Ex. 8a).
Four bars later the saxes return to their sober unison lines, while the brass (Ex.
8b) keep things in motion with a repeated figure which, despite its triplet configuration, has the feeling of double-time.

Ex. 8a

Ex. 8b

(X-headed notes denote "ghost notes")

There follows one of Sauter's most astonishing modulations, leading to the vocal. Beginning with mildly aggressive dissonances, the sound virtually evaporates in a beautifully controlled diminuendo, and suddenly we have slid unnoticed from the original key of Bb to C. Peggy Lee's singing—unemotional, virtually passive—drifts across the song like a slow-moving distant cloud in the sky. Behind her, in veiled tones and downy brass-and-reed hues, Sauter creates an accompaniment that, for all its timbral and rhythmic fragmentation, is pure line. Another deft modulation takes us to the key of Eb for another half chorus, featuring in part Goodman's solo clarinet. A coda, in effect a variant of the introduction, closes the performance in a perfect full circle.

My Old Flame[54] has an even more imaginative introduction than *How Deep*. It is an elaboration of the first three notes of Johnston's melody. By adding one more pitch, to fill out the implied diminished seventh chord, Sauter arrives at the following configuration:

First stated in the saxes and spun out to four measures by an undulating eighth-note phrase, the whole idea is repeated a fourth higher in the brass, leading then directly to Peggy Lee's entrance (in Eb). What is most intriguing about Sauter's introduction is that the first two bars are scored without rhythm section. The three isolated staccato notes in the saxes can thus not be placed in a beat or time frame *except retroactively*, when we discover with the entry of the rhythm section where in fact the beat is. The sense of suspended time thus imparted to this passage—its relative rhythmic "abstraction"—coupled with a sense of keylessness, finds wonderful release in the sudden firm establishment of tonality and beat in the ninth measure with the voice's entrance.

In the accompaniment to the song proper, Sauter draws his inspiration from the original printed sheet-music version of *Flame* by taking up the chromatically ascending counter-line in the left hand (Ex. 9a) and extending it further upward (Ex. 9b). This idea, always given to unison saxes, is used as a unifying thread through all three main sections of the piece: 1) the vocal (Ex. 9b), (2) Cootie's

54. Both *How Deep Is the Ocean?* and *My Old Flame* are among the very finest the American popular song repertory has to offer. The one by the old master himself, Irving Berlin, the other by his protégé, Arthur Johnston, both songs are indicative of the high creative level to which Sauter was attuned. Choice of material, more so even for an arranger than an improviser, is a matter of considerable import, since the basic material—melody, changes, form—must be of some quality to begin with, in order for an arrangement to derive any inspiration from it—unless one wishes to assume that rare exception in which a mediocre piece is simply "recomposed" by the arranger.

solo (Ex. 9c), and 3) Benny's solo (Ex. 9d). During Cootie's solo it is altered to turn back on itself, as it were, descending to the B♮. The third time the counter theme is altered again, not only melodically, but rhythmically as well (Ex. 9d). The ascending figure is now transformed to include all the first eight notes of Johnston's melody (save one, not counting repeated notes) (Ex. 9e). The notes in question are marked *a* through *g* in both Ex. 9d and 9e. The beauty of this passage lies in, amongst other things, the fact that the added melodic variant (mm. 2 and 4 in Ex. 9d) echoes the original melody one bar later and in rhythmically condensed form.

Ex. 9a

Ex. 9b

Ex. 9c

Ex. 9d

Ex. 9e

But there is more. Beginning with Peggy Lee's vocal, there is in Sauter's accompaniment at times a subtle underlying double-time feeling. It is particularly pronounced in, for example, the saxes in mm. 3 and 4 of the song proper: . Even the rocking triplets in the modulation to Cootie's solo are played with a rhythmic inflection that causes the listener to feel *both* rhythmic planes at once: the triplet subdivisions of the large beats and the duple double-time feeling as well, the one explicit, audible, the other implied, only felt .

Then, accompanying Benny's solo, what was rhythmically only momentarily implied earlier is now (Ex. 9d) made explicit in the saxes, the rhythm section incidentally all the while *not* overtly participating in the double-time. But how the double-time feeling has been flowing increasingly (yet always subtly) through the entire arrangement as it proceeds becomes crystal clear when, at mid-point in Benny's solo, the whole orchestra swings into double-time for Benny's solo breaks. And this is then, in turn, magnificently resolved by a sublime series of cadencing chords which Sauter miraculously conjures up (Ex. 9f), ending with a graceful Goodman arpeggio and a pure B♭ chord. But even these final bars are made more intriguing by the striking use of two trombones in unison on the low F and B♭ of the last two measures.

Ex. 9f

On another level, Sauter and the band achieve extraordinary effects through the use of finely controlled timbres and a kind of veiled subtone playing that set the stage for similar sonoric concepts in Gil Evans's hallmark works of the late forties and the fifties. In this connection I must single out the luminous alto saxophone lead work of Skippy Martin—hear him particularly on the modulation to Cootie's solo.[55]

Finally, probably the most important achievement of Sauter's *How Deep* and *Flame* is their total integration of form and content. Whereas even in the most successful of the earlier arrangements (but especially in his own compositions) there is at times a certain unresolved strain between conflicting musical ideas, these two arrangements achieve complete organic unity. And, considering their originality and innovative nature, that is high accomplishment indeed.

When Sauter failed it was generally due to poor material to work with, as in the case of Don Redman's mediocre song *Down, Down, Down* (one can guess what the bass line does in this) or *Birth of the Blues.*

The effect of Sauter and Powell as well as the other mentioned arrangers on the Goodman band was inspiring and wonderfully energizing. During these years of the early forties, the Goodman orchestra—and Goodman himself—played with a dazzling brilliance that was the envy of all the other bands. The emphasis was not on soloists—as with Basie, for example—but on the orchestra, and on jazz *as* arrangement and composition. The more purely improvised jazz was relegated to the Sextet performances and recordings, of which there were any number of outstanding examples: *Limehouse Blues, The World Is Waiting for the Sunrise, After You've Gone,* the 1945 *Rachel's Dream,* and *I Got Rhythm* are

---

55. Another fine, strongly swinging Sauter arrangement, *Tangerine* (1942), despite an excellent performance and a pleasant vocal by Art Lund, was not released in the United States, only on an Argentine Columbia 78—one supposes because of the song's lyrics: "toasts to Tangerine raised in every bar across the Argentine!"

among the best. Here technical virtuosity is one with musical taste and refinement, and an infectious collective exuberance. All these elements clicked into place, especially when Red Norvo, switching to vibraphone, joined Goodman's Sextet in 1945 with either Teddy Wilson or Mel Powell as pianists. The Sextet's best also represents the best of that now long-gone era.

Goodman at this writing is still, of course, very much with us, although a lot less active in recent years.[56] His post-1945 career will be dealt with in another volume of this history, but it should suffice for the moment to note that Benny has from time to time continued to lead fine bands, some of them temporarily assembled for a spate of recordings or an international tour (or various anniversaries of his career) and, of course, the smaller chamber units. His distinguished career has also led him frequently into the classical concert halls, playing concertos with all the best symphony orchestras of the world by major composers like Hindemith, Copland, and Milhaud. He has continued to divide his life easily between Carnegie Hall and the Rainbow Grill.

And yet Goodman's activity on all these varied fronts has been sporadic and seems generally to lack long-range commitment. Perhaps those personal and musical stimuli, so necessary to his professional sustenance, have been harder and harder to come by through the years, especially in view of the fact that Benny is at heart a conservative. And jazz has passed him by several times for developments with which he has had little sympathy, which has left him clinging instead to his swing era ideals. Here personal taste and the ever alert businessman in Goodman converge. Often momentarily intrigued by the experimental, the "advanced," the "complex," Goodman's interest rarely can be sustained in such directions. A prime example of this aspect of Goodman's career was his short-lived and half-hearted involvement with bop in 1948.

In the final analysis, Goodman's ultimate role in jazz history is difficult to assess. As mentioned at the outset of this chapter, he has been at various times over-rated as well as berated (incidentally often for things that were somehow expected of him, but which he never claimed to have accomplished). Goodman is essentially an honest, unpretentious, superior musician, with enormous talents that reside, however, more on the technical side of things. Indeed, Goodman's dilemma—if one can call such a successful career "a dilemma"—is that curious but not uncommon one: that he has in a sense *too much* facility. His many hundreds of recorded performances—and the additional tens of thousands of solos he has played in his lifetime—are, with but rare exceptions, technically masterful. With Goodman, as with so many fine, absolutely respectable musicians—both classical and jazz—the emphasis is on the instrument. He is *ein echter Musikant*, an American transplant of a venerable and ancient European tradition, particularly among certain minorities like the Jews and the Gypsies, for centuries highly gifted musically. The musical instrument is their whole life. It becomes their sole means of expression, and whatever their *persona* is, it is

56. Goodman died in 1986, while this book was in production.

transmitted first and foremost through that instrument. Benny Goodman is not an intellect; his is not a deep creativity. He is not profound in the way we feel Beethoven and Charlie Parker are profound. But he is a *great clarinetist*. And that is, of course, no mean achievement. Indeed, how many untold numbers of clarinetists have failed to achieve even that much?

There are artists in whom the very struggle for technical mastery is converted into an element of tension, which in turn becomes an integral component of their particular artistry. There are others—like Goodman—in whom, because of an overabundance of technical facility, that element of tension is simply missing, perhaps precluded. For this, such artists surely deserve our forbearance, not only our disapprobation. From his late teens on, Benny virtually sailed through every solo and every instrumental challenge ever thrown at him (although less so in his classical repertory, where he had to work pretty hard). Such ease leads inevitably to a certain sameness, even a certain diffidence, a certain casualness. Benny's jazz solos are almost never structurally or harmonically adventurous. They rarely take chances musically, although they often do so technically—at least as viewed by most clarinet mortals. The peaks and valleys one encounters in many fine artists' work are replaced in Benny's case by a vast, high plateau of amazing technical consistency.

Benny has always been utterly true to himself; and in that truth lies a definite originality. For let it also be remembered that Benny Goodman, for all that he has been imitated and caricatured, is a true original. There is no gainsaying his immense influence on jazz, on its musicians, on performers both classical and jazz, as well as indirectly on composers and arrangers. The very length of this chapter is a telling indication of the magnitude of Goodman's impact on the music of his time.

Whatever the final verdict on Benny Goodman as a creative musician will be, one thing is already clear, and that is that in the 1930s he brought American jazz to the attention of his countrymen and to the world in a way that had previously not been accomplished, and rarely achieved since then. If we can say that for one fine moment in American musical history there was an alliance between national popular taste and a creative music called jazz, for that we are deeply in debt to Benny Goodman.

2

Duke Ellington

Master Composer

For Duke Ellington and his orchestra, the 1930s represented a time of intense activity and musical growth, when he perfected the style and sound that he and his musicians had evolved over a period of three years while in residence at Harlem's Cotton Club. It was also a time when Duke and the band began to see a lot more of the rest of the country, and indeed of the world. It was 1932 when the orchestra took to the road, beginning a traveling career that lasted until Ellington's death in 1974. The orchestra's ability to survive the wear and tear of literally thousands of one-night stands, of an endless succession of bus-, train-, and plane-trips, must be counted as one of the minor miracles of human physical endurance. The thirties and forties, moreover, were years of enormous successes, both artistic and economic, not only through the orchestra's personal appearances (seemingly everywhere) but through a consistent flow of recordings, rewarded now and then with substantial popular successes.

The early 1930s also marked the beginning of the Ellington orchestra's trips to Europe and the hobnobbing with European royalty and intelligentsia, something quite agreeable to a sophisticated cosmopolitan like Duke. Hollywood, too, beckoned during these years, while at the same time famous "classical" musicians, composers, and conductors began to take notice of Ellington as a major creator and to treat him as a respected colleague.

Oddly enough, these successes came at a time when the United States was plunged into a devastating economic depression, when many other jazz orchestras were forced to disband or drastically curtail their activities. In reading accounts of the Ellington band's achievements in the early 1930s, it almost seems as if Duke and his men hardly had time to become aware of the Depression.

Musically as well, the Ellington orchestra was in a decidedly expansionary mood. It was in 1932 that the band grew to its full complement of fifteen members—fourteen instrumentalists and one singer. Certainly the major new voice

46

was Lawrence Brown, an extraordinarily versatile trombonist who brought a number of unique musical qualities to the orchestra and to Duke's sonoric palette. I believe the impact that Brown had on the so-called Ellington effect (a term coined by Duke's alter-ego of later years, Billy Strayhorn, to describe the Ellington style and its unique sound) has never been fully appreciated. Not only did the Ellington band become the first to acquire a permanent trombone trio, but Brown was the first trombonist of any major black orchestra to develop a full-blown ballad and lyric style. This was some years before the emergence of players like Tommy Dorsey and Jack Jenney, still a time when the trombone was associated almost exclusively with "hot" jazz, and hadn't quite lost its New Orleans "tailgate" ancestry.

Brown, as leader of Ellington's trombone section, was not only a great lyric player, but his solo style was so unique that it was virtually inimitable. At the same time he was no less of a "hot" improviser, and as a result there was no role (other than the "growl and plunger" technique, handled by Joe "Tricky Sam" Nanton) to which Brown could not be assigned. Such versatility was unprecedented in the 1930s and is still relatively uncommon today.

Nanton, of West Indian heritage, had joined Duke in 1926, virtually a charter member of the Ellington organization. Inspired by trumpeter Bubber Miley, Nanton had early on developed his distinctive "wah-wah" and "talking" style, using a rubber bathroom plunger over a small mute insert.[1] Until Juan Tizol, a Puerto Rican, joined the Ellington orchestra in late 1929, Nanton's "jungle" style (and an occasional somber and robust open-horn solo) dominated the brass section. But Tizol, coming out of a "classical" Italian-style band tradition, well developed in his native San Juan, brought an entirely new voice and perspective to Ellington's brass, a resource that Duke never failed to exploit.

From this one may gather that the three trombonists Ellington now had with the addition of Brown were all totally different from each other in their musical conception: unique individual voices that could, taken together, cover any possible stylistic approach to the trombone. And yet the miracle is that—as proven in countless nights of performances and hundreds of recordings—this trio of uniquely distinctive personalities could, when necessary, blend chameleon-like into a single sonority, of which the discrete component parts were no longer distinguishable.

A second important addition to the Ellington organization of the early thirties was the singer Ivie Anderson. Duke had employed various vocalists from time to time, mostly in connection with his work at the Cotton Club or other shows, and both drummer Sonny Greer and trumpeter Cootie Williams had often contributed vocals. But Ivie Anderson was to be Ellington's first permanent full-time vocalist. Indeed, she was to stay with the Ellington band for twelve years, and she added yet another versatile and special voice to the Duke's musical resources.

Third, Otto Hardwick, Duke's longtime friend and a member of the original

1. An extensive discussion of Nanton's early work can be found in *Early Jazz*, chap. 7.

Washingtonians and other embryonic Ellington groups, returned to the band after a three-year leave of absence as lead alto saxophonist. Thus the band became stabilized not only in its instrumental choirs—six brass (three trumpets, three trombones), four reeds (saxophones and clarinets), the four-man rhythm section, and a girl singer—but also, as things turned out, in its personnel. This stability gave Ellington and his musicians an opportunity to evolve month after month, year after year, towards a common musical goal that ultimately manifested itself in the famous masterpieces of the early 1940s, the creative zenith of Ellington's career.

In Volume I of this History I characterized the Ellington years at the Cotton Club as a "protracted workshop period," during which Ellington developed the basis of his style, and did so in terms of five categories of musical pieces: 1) numbers for dancing; 2) jungle-style and/or production numbers for various Cotton Club *tableaux*; 3) the "blue" or "mood" pieces; 4) pop tunes or ballads; and 5) independent nonfunctional instrumental compositions. The process of refining these musical categories and the techniques attendant to them, continued unabated in the 1930s. But whereas in the early years Duke's own input towards the final creative result was often secondary to that of some of his leading soloists—particularly Bubber Miley—now, in the thirties, Duke's authorship became increasingly predominant. A unique musical partnership, truly unprecedented in the history of Western music, developed in which a major composer forged a musical style and concept which, though totally original and individual, nevertheless consistently incorporated and integrated the no less original musical ideas of his players. No such musical alchemy had ever been accomplished before, with the possible exception of Jelly Roll Morton's *Hot Peppers* recordings of 1926. Miraculously, the Ellington imagination fed on the particular skills and personalities of his players, while at the same time *their* musical growth was in turn nurtured by Ellington's maturing compositional craft and vision. This process of cross-fertilization was constant and, given the stability of personnel, self-expanding.

In this complex relationship each constituent was responsible for certain aspects of the total musical/compositional product. For example, it is clear that Ellington's own influence asserted itself most especially in the realms of harmony, instrumental voicing, and form. On the other hand, timbral or sonority aspects were determined largely by the players, simply by virtue of the fact that their unique tone colors automatically added to any given passage a particular timbral imprint. Yet even here the choices were not totally arbitrary, for Ellington was frequently the final arbiter, and through the years he began more and more to color-coordinate, as it were—to blend and mix like a great painter—the individual timbre ingredients of his musicians into combinations which had never been heard before and which, to this day, have not been surpassed. Almost every player—from Johnny Hodges to Harry Carney, from Cootie Williams and Nanton to Lawrence Brown and Tizol, even Sonny Greer, with his discreet drumming and penchant for using a variety of coloristic percussion instruments, and, last but not least, Duke, with his own powerful rich piano sound[2]—all these players produced such individual timbres on their "horns" that Ellington had almost as many diverse sonorities at his disposal as a ninety-piece symphony orchestra. He certainly made extraordinary use of his fourteen instruments, in a manner and to a degree that perhaps only a handful of composers like Ravel, Schoenberg, Stravinsky, and Webern could have realized.

As one follows the Ellington orchestra's progress towards the great performances and recordings of the early forties, one can hear how Ellington began to use his orchestral vehicle with ever-increasing sophistication and profundity. But it must be remembered that this was a painstaking process which covered a decade or more. And there were failures as well as successes; there were detours and distractions, particularly those resulting from the ever-present commercial pressures. But as it turned out, Ellington's vision of his musical goals was never dimmed, the goals never far out of sight. His musicians, it is reported, at times became frustrated by the increasing control which Ellington seemed to exert on them. But evidently he had a phenomenal instinct for allowing a degree of individuality and creative freedom within the framework of his musical conception, an extraordinary tightrope walk he was able to maintain until the 1940s, when some of his star soloists began to leave him and strike out on their own as leaders.

It will be the burden of this chapter to delineate in some detail the process by

---

2. Ellington's crucial role as pianist of his orchestra is seldom fully appraised. While it is true that Ellington was in style and conception as a player rather uneven (originally a rather average ragtime and stride pianist, but later developing a richly harmonic style of his own), his real forte was as a rhythmic energizer of the orchestra (as a member of the rhythm section) and, above all, as a possessor of the most remarkable piano tone and touch. This was not used to project a soloistic virtuoso style. Indeed, Ellington was not, and had no ambitions to be, a major soloist like Hines or Tatum or Bud Powell. Instead he was a born orchestral pianist and used his amazing tone and rich "orchestral" timbre to project to the orchestra the essence—the sound world—of a given piece, to lead the orchestra, in other words, *from* the piano, to galvanize it rhythmically, to inspire it creatively, and to complement it pianistically when needed.

Perhaps one needed to have stood close to Ellington's piano-playing to fully appreciate the remarkable fullness and depth of his sound. I had that privilege many times, and I can say with total conviction that, with but very few exceptions—one is the remarkable modern Third Stream pianist Ran Blake—I have never encountered a pianist, jazz or classical, who could command at once such purity of tone *and* range of dynamics and timbres as Ellington. He had a way of playing what I call "deep in the keys" to produce the clearest, most controlled impact of the hammer on the strings and, as a result, the fullest purest resonance of those strings. Ellington could play the most forceful piano, matching his entire orchestra at full tilt; and yet I never heard him force or bang, as so many pianists do when they venture into the *ff* range. His tone and projection were such that with one chord or a few fill-in notes he could energize the entire orchestra. And in addition he could combine his basic piano sonority with all manner of timbral sonorities; one heard trumpets, saxophones, horns, oboes, even strings in his playing. Although he rarely featured himself in extensive solos— and although recordings could not fully capture the beauty of his sound—it is well worth paying close attention to Ellington's post-1930 solo passages, particularly his ever more creative solo introductions of the late thirties and early forties, on which he often lavished the most extraordinary harmonic invention.

which the Ellington style developed and coalesced into one of the most splendid creative phenomena that the history of jazz has to offer.

Things began auspiciously early in 1932 with a hit record: the now legendary *It Don't Mean a Thing If It Ain't Got That Swing*, a prophetic piece and a prophetic title. The word "swing," later to be associated in the minds of millions of people with Benny Goodman, had been used by jazz musicians like Jelly Roll Morton and Miley for many years to describe a particular rhythmic momentum and feeling. But apart from Morton's *Georgia Swing*, Ellington was the first to use it in a song title, some years before swing became a household word and ultimately the designation for a whole era in American popular music.[3]

Although by no means a perfect performance, *It Don't Mean a Thing* offered both a quaintly vernacular definition of swing and also (for the time) a pretty good musical demonstration of it. Further, the words of the song have that elliptical and elusive touch that is a trademark of Ellington's verbal language. The text is all the more fanciful in that the response to three of the textual lines is not in words but in the brasses' tongue-in-cheek "doo-wah doo-wah doo-wah,"[4]

> It don't mean a thing if it ain't got that swing
> Doo-wah doo-wah, doo-wah doo-wah, doo-wah doo-wah, doo-wah doo-wah
> It don't mean a thing, all you got to do is sing
> Doo-wah doo-wah, doo-wah doo-wah, doo-wah doo-wah, doo-wah doo-wah
> It makes no difference if it's sweet or hot
> Just keep that rhythm, give it everything you got
> It don't mean a thing if it ain't got that swing
> Doo-wah doo-wah, doo-wah doo-wah, doo-wah doo-wah, doo-wah doo-wah.

Thus Ivie Anderson's debut on records laid it on the line, and in unmistakable jazz terms. Of course, Nanton sets the tone of the piece—after a somewhat shaky Wellman Braud bass and Ivie Anderson introduction—with a typically infectious "talking" plunger solo. Following Ivie's vocal chorus, Johnny Hodges jumps in with florid arpeggio runs, missing, however, a few of the changes; and much of the ensuing ensemble work is stiff and unintentionally ragged, almost pulling the rhythm section apart. But the side is redeemed by Ivie's re-entry with a few

3. It is important to note, however, that Ellington did not hold, in regard to swing, a narrow and dogmatic view—as many jazz musicians and critics did. As much as swing was a crucial element of some of his music, he composed many works that had little or nothing to do with swing. Like the term "jazz" itself, swing was confining and stigmatizing; and Ellington knew that much of his music transcended those narrow definitions.
4. This figure was not new to jazz. Duke had used it in earlier pieces, for example, *Old Man Blues* (see *Early Jazz*, p. 351); and Alphonse Trent's *I Found a New Baby* made prominent display of it. By the mid-1930s *every* orchestra that even pretended to play jazz featured this effect somewhere in its "hotter" numbers, usually as a 2-bar break.

boisterous lines of scat singing (*à la* Louis Armstrong) and a reminder of the song's title. Once again the brass respond with their whimsical *doo-wahs*, fading out into a low register saxophone A♭ ninth chord, capped by Duke's surprise twinkle on the celesta. But perhaps the most felicitous touch on the entire side is Harry Carney's happily lilting baritone obbligato behind Ivie's vocal chorus.

The other side was devoted to Art Hickman's brand new 1931 hit *Rose Room*. Obviously not much time was spent on this polite gesture to popular dance music, probably motivated by Ellington's publisher-manager Irving Mills. The solos by Barney Bigard (on clarinet) and Duke are rather uninspired and listless.

Lazy Rhapsody fares somewhat better, distinguished by a casually relaxed Cootie Williams scat-vocal, almost in the manner of Bing Crosby (who was temporarily working with Duke at this time as a featured vocalist). But in general *Lazy Rhapsody* is rather over-arranged, and with its too-pointed, edgy muted brass it misses the lazy rhapsodic mood its title implies.

Blue Tune initiated a long series of Ellington compositions using that adjective in their titles: *Blue Harlem*, *Blue Ramble*, *Blue Mood*, *Blue Feelin'*, *Blue Light*, *Blue Serge* (and even *Azure* could be included in this list). But unlike some of the later "blue" tone-paintings, *Blue Tune*—while a lovely tune indeed, with Arthur Whetsol's always poignant trumpet—falls short of its promise. Somehow its striking harmonies were not fully exploited, as Ellington had done so masterfully on many other occasions, even as early as *Awful Sad* (1928) and *Mood Indigo* (1930). It is conjecture, but I suspect Ellington hoped that *Blue Tune* might become a popular success like *Rose Room* or his own *Mood Indigo*. But as happened so often in his life, *Blue Tune* was too advanced harmonically and too esoteric melodically for general public tastes. Any song that dared to start with such enriched harmonies as (Ex. 1):

Ex. 1

or, in its bridge, featured these daring melodic contours and highly spicy chromatic harmonies (Ex. 2):

Ex. 2

was several decades too early for Tin Pan Alley consumption and doomed to commercial oblivion.

Much more familiar territory was investigated five days later, when the band recorded two standards even then thrice-familiar—W. C. Handy's (by way of Elmer Schoebel) old 1916 classic *Bugle Call Rag* and Harry Akst's 1925 hit *Dinah*. *Bugle Call Rag* was smartly arranged for the occasion and featured most of the orchestra's soloists in the traditional 4-bar breaks associated with this piece. None is more striking, especially in the context of the other strenuously flashy solos, than Braud's compellingly simple ascending chromatic scale.

For part of the side, *Dinah* is still taken at the comfortable dance tempo in which it was originally conceived. But in the second half its tempo is doubled, almost in the manner in which the piece is now almost always heard, as a fast tempo jam-session staple. The side was poorly balanced and recorded. Perhaps the boys in the band were embarrassed to be heard shouting those inane "Dinahs" every two bars, and Sonny Greer must have felt a bit uncomfortable crooning like some Hollywood tenor. But the side has one extraordinary moment when Juan Tizol lashes into a wild eighth-note break (at ♩= 320!) that surely must be the first bop "lick" ever, long before Parker and Gillespie (Ex. 3).

Ex. 3

A few days later Ellington recorded two jazz classics: *St. Louis Blues*, with Bing Crosby as vocalist, and a remake of Duke's own 1927 *Creole Love Call* in a 12-inch extended version, in which Adelaide Hall's former vocals were transferred to the orchestra—particularly Whetsol's trumpet. In other ways Ellington elaborated upon the original 10-inch version of *Creole Love Call* by making use of the band's expanded resources acquired in the intervening five years. Among

these were Cootie Williams and Juan Tizol. Cootie, as expected, takes over
Miley's old chorus with the plunger and growl, but towards the end of the performance he also breaks into a new role as the first of Ellington's trumpets to
develop a prominently displayable high register. Cootie here contributes importantly to one of those breakthrough musical ideas which turn out to be unique
and unprecedented, not only for Duke but for all music. This occurs in the last
chorus of *Creole Love Call*, a recapitulation of the undulating main theme in
three clarinets. Over this Duke constructs a pyramid of high muted trumpets
that adds a new element of suppressed tension to the music, particularly Cootie's
high E♭. The successive piling up of fourths—static blocks of sound—over lilting

clarinets in triplets, (♩ ♪), while Braud walks in even eighth notes, represents
an entirely new use of jazz instruments and sonorities that must be heard to be
believed. Example 4 reproduces the music in outline.

Ex. 4

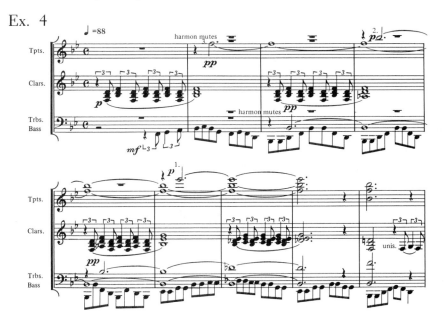

Tizol's special sound and style, which was to be so uniquely exploited a few
years later in *Caravan*, makes an initial appearance here. In the third theme
statement, with the clarinets in the upper middle register, Tizol intones a melancholy counter-melody that is almost hymn-like. But in the last chorus, Tizol,
switching roles, is used as the *bass* instrument, notably in the plagal cadence
with which the piece ends. The reason for this unusual
use of the valve trombone was not only that Carney, who might have played the
bass line, was on clarinet—in fact he took over Rudy Jackson's original 1927
high flute-like solo—but because Ellington had for some years been aware of the

valve trombone's greater agility in the low register (as compared with the slide trombone).

The 1932 *Creole Love Call* is a wondrous example of compositional updating, the kind of thing that is possible with an orchestra of improvising soloists and something that simply cannot happen in classical music (except perhaps in certain works of the John Cage school). It must also be said that, no matter in what version, *Creole Love Call* remains to this day an ageless masterpiece.

Blue Harlem (May 1932), a Bubber Miley composition, features a Cootie Williams chorus without growl and wah-wah which, thus bereft of external sonoric embellishments, shows more clearly his indebtedness to Armstrong. The return of Hardwick to the orchestra is celebrated by a full chorus of saxophone quartet ensemble, and Nanton pays tribute to his mentor Miley with one of his patented muted solos. This is abruptly interrupted by Ellington repeating the introduction, which this time—as if starting the piece all over again—ushers in Bigard with a free-flow wailing New Orleans-style solo. The weakest link of the performance is Braud's rather frenetically unsteady slap-bass stop-time chorus.

On the same day Lawrence Brown made his recording debut as a soloist with Ellington.[5] The tune was a popular eleven-year-old dance favorite, *The Sheik of Araby.* Surely never had this somewhat whiney standard been so utterly transformed. Each of the four choruses presents the tune in a quite unexpected guise. There is, first of all, Brown's solo: jaunty, debonair, eloquent, topped by a graceful lip trill on a high $B\flat$, as effortless as if played on a flute. Its casual air belies the fact that Brown, by his own admission,[6] carefully planned out this solo, for it sounds fresh and improvised, in a style that combined lyricism, "hot jazz," swing and consummate technical command in a synthesis that no other trombonist at the time could muster.

The next (second) chorus of *The Sheik* makes a startling juxtaposition of the saxophone section (led by Hardwick with a typically "watery" dance-band vibrato) and a bumptious jabbing muted solo by "Tricky Sam" Nanton. The rough-hewn Nanton and the sweet saxophones don't mix, of course, but the friction between the two produces an unusual, albeit slightly unsettling, effect.

In the third chorus the melody travels over to the muted brass while being embellished in roving garlands of sound by Hodges's soprano saxophone. Once again—as in *Blue Harlem*—an exact recapitulation of the introduction serves as a transition to the last chorus; and here the Ellington surprise consists of using the entire brass section in clipped repeated 4/4 quarter notes, as if they were playing a banjo part. A brief "tag" coda (alas, rather badly muffed) ends this startling jazz transformation of a tune which is otherwise, even to this day, considered the more or less private domain of bands like Guy Lombardo and Lawrence Welk.

Two days later the band recorded *Blue Ramble*, a clear example of how Ellington's influence as a composer was beginning to assert itself. With this piece

5. For a discussion of Brown's earlier pre-Ellington work, see Chapter 8, below.
6. Barry Ulanov, *Duke Ellington* (New York: Creative Age Press, 1946), p. 102.

Ellington moves determinedly away from the world of tunes or dance numbers towards pure orchestral jazz composition. The improvised solos have become more incidental, more integrated into the fabric of the composition. Moreover, *Blue Ramble* is not merely a 32-bar song structure but a bi-thematic piece, cast in an over-all ABA form consisting of a full 32-bar A section (with the usual bridge or release) and a 12-bar B section. In fact, the piece has no melody as such, certainly not in the traditional sense of a popular tune. Instead the main motivic material in the A section consists of parallel chords, while the B section emphasizes long sustained trumpet tones of 4-bar durations—hardly great melodic invention. Indeed, the most striking *thematic* effort occurs in the repeat of the B section when the unison saxes play a riff (Ex. 5), part of which curiously surfaces again, years later, as the thematic line in Parker's *Cool Blues*.

Ex. 5

The orchestration, too, shows signs of Ellington's personal intervention. Whereas in many earlier performances one has the feeling that Ellington's *musicians* determined to some degree the voicing of chords, in *Blue Ramble* the tight well-balanced harmonizations (in the A sections, for example) are not likely to have resulted from a head arrangement. Uniquely Ellingtonian is the placement of Carney's rich baritone sax on the ninth of the chord, but at the bottom of the harmonic pile (Ex. 6)—a favorite device which, as I pointed out in Volume I of this History, Ellington used as early as *Tishomingo Blues* in 1928.[7] But quite apart from that touch, even the ten-part voicing of such chords (six brass and four saxes) was still quite innovative in 1932.

Ex. 6

Similar to the unorthodox use of the baritone sax is Ellington's positioning of another highly individual voice: Tizol's valve trombone. In measures 7 and 15 of the recapitulation of the A section, where the changes resolve to the tonic of C major, Tizol plays a low sustained A, the sixth of the chord. Any proper harmony teacher would automatically forbid such a voicing. But then Ellington was not going by the rules of traditional harmony books. Tizol's low A certainly gives that return to the tonic an oblique, slightly eerie sound, and in fact prevents it from completely resolving. Furthermore, it works so well because that low A is preceded by a *high* sustained A in the trumpet, three octaves above, and acts as a kind of musical pendant to it.

7. *Early Jazz*, pp. 336–37.

This kind of experimentation with what may appear to be minutiae often constituted the essence of Duke's style, and we shall encounter it frequently in subsequent Ellington scores.

In contrast to *Blue Ramble*—a full-fledged *composition* eschewing the "chorus" principle of basic jazz—*Slippery Horn*, recorded the same day, is a reworking of the well-known jazz staple *Tiger Rag*. It is a total recomposition of those ancient harmonic changes, analogous to the kind of thing that bop musicians did with standards in the mid-forties. The end result, coming as it does from a totally different and peculiarly Ellingtonian point of departure, is in its net effect an Ellington *composition*.

Part of the transformation is the result of dropping the traditional frenetic tempo of *Tiger Rag* to medium speed and, in general, relaxing the whole mood of the piece. Undoubtedly the most startling novelty in *Slippery Horn* from the vantage point of mid-1932 was its opening trombone trio, probably the first ever in jazz.[8] But what really set musicians to talking was Lawrence Brown's sustained high F at the end of the first chorus. This trombone trio is a perfect example of the earlier-mentioned point that, when required, these three remarkable heterogeneous players could blend into one homogeneous single color.

From this point on, *Slippery Horn*—the title an obvious reference to Brown's trombonistic agility—proceeds on the basis of the traditional chorus-variation principle: Barney Bigard, Cootie Williams, and Brown in order. These three soloists, just by being themselves, ensure the element of contrast and variety so indigenous to the Ellington orchestra. Bigard roams the field in wide-ranging arcs, Cootie in a jocular mood, Brown suave, elegant, and ever the romantic.

But the principle of contrast is invoked at other levels of composition as well. For example, against Cootie's airily punching muted solo we have the contrast of Carney's dark-timbred baritone, repeating in riff-like fashion a descending chromatic eighth-note motive which always comes to rest on a melancholy seventh of the chord (marked x, Ex. 7). It is like the dialogue of two people, one happy (Cootie), the other unhappy (Carney). Another element of contrast, although not as original, is the use of *sustained* brass chords, played with crescendo swells as a background to Bigard's *florid* solo.

Ex. 7

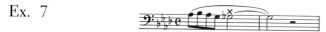

But compositions are built not only of contrast and variety. There need to be unifying elements as well, and these too, Ellington ensures. Note, for example, that the staccato quarter-note triplets heard in the trumpets in the introduction reappear in the fifth through eighth bars of the trombone trio, and again in Carney's baritone—the latter time played more legato, in *contrast* (!) to Cootie's jabby playing (mm. 23 through 30 of Cootie's chorus).

8. Don Redman, who had begun to use a three-man trombone section with his own big band formed in 1931, started to feature trombone trios around the same time Ellington did, notably on *I Got Rhythm* and on the 1932 Harlan Lattimore sides *I Heard* and *Reefer Man*.

The Ellingtonians were back in the recording studios four months later, this time with another "blue" piece, *Blue Mood*; a catchy humorously slanted quasi-novelty dance number, *Ducky Wucky*; a Benny Carter work entitled *Jazz Cocktail*; a pop ballad, *Stars* (only released in France and England); *Swing Low*, a typical show number in the genre of *Old Man Blues* or *Double Check Stomp*; and finally, an interesting Ellington composition, *Lightnin'*.[9] The last indicates the way Ellington's whole development must be seen as a process, a continuity. *Lightnin'*, like a link in a long chain, connects to the past with its harmonic references to the earlier *Blue Ramble*; and at the same time—as a forestudy in many respects of *Daybreak Express*, recorded a year later—projects into the future.

While interesting as a compositional stepping-stone, in both its conception and execution, *Lightnin'* contains a number of miscalculations. Foremost among these is the arbitrary insertion of an entirely anachronistic stride-piano solo that lodges raw and undigested in the middle of the piece. Bigard's solo is ordinary and played out of tune. Perhaps a more interesting miscalculation is the harmonic one (in both Nanton's and the last full ensemble choruses), when two alternate but incompatible versions of the same basic root chord are played simultaneously. Nanton, for example, holds to the original melodic line, which can be seen in Ex. 8a, Nanton's notes appearing in the upper staff. The saxophone quartet, however, plays another version of the same chord. The two together (as can be seen in composite form in Ex. 8b) clash in a manner that is simply inept and does not, as played, even have the virtue of calculated dissonance. A simple repositioning of the saxophone chords (as shown in Ex. 8c) could have corrected the situation, retaining the minor-ninth harmonies.

Ex. 8a

9. Whereas most jazz bands recorded at most one or two *types* of pieces in a typical session (or series of sessions), it is fascinating to see Ellington persistently pursue four or five categories concurrently in each spate of recording dates—from novelty to dance numbers, from romantic ballads to advanced original compositions. Undoubtedly this broad-gauged approach had its origin partly in the theory that, sooner or later, in one or the other of these categories, the band would catch a hit. But it is also a measure of Ellington's versatility and creative breadth.

Ex. 8b

(The white notes represent the four
saxophones, the black notes Nanton)

Ex. 8c

Ducky Wucky, with its carefree, bouncing, rocking two-beat dance tempo, reminds us that in the early thirties the prime function of a band, even Ellington's,
was to provide music for dancing. Still *Ducky Wucky* is, in addition, a real jazz
composition (in this case an Ellington-Bigard collaboration), albeit of the light-
hearted divertimento kind. Brown in his most dapper dancing style delivers a
remarkable 32-bar chorus, which includes among many artful touches an "impossible" one-octave glissando (from high C to middle C) spread over one entire
bar. Interestingly, Williams, one of the other two soloists, seems to rebel a bit
against the touch of "casual silliness" the piece emits and, as if trying to bring it
back to the more serious realm of jazz, charges in with a bold assertive blues-ish
solo. Later in the third chorus, however, Williams comes to grief on the high
notes of the bridge, including a strained, barely squeezed out high E♭. This
final chorus is on the other hand distinguished by a superior saxophone ensemble, led with great style and elegance by Hodges's creamy soprano sax.[10]

   Next, around the turn of the year (1932–33) came a series of recordings with
the well-established singers Ethel Waters, Adelaide Hall, and the Mills Brothers,
all performing selections from the successful all-black revue *Blackbirds of 1928*.
But the more significant recordings were two nostalgic pieces, one of which in
particular, *Eerie Moan*, was a distinguished addition to Ellington's mood-piece
catalogue. It anticipates in conception and essence such later masterpieces of the
genre as *Delta Serenade* (1934) and *Dusk* (1940). Interestingly, though, neither
Eerie Moan nor its original Brunswick coupling *Any Time, Any Day, Anywhere*
is composed by Ellington but by Victor Young. Thus both songs are once again
transformations into pure Ellingtonia of basic popular song material, although
in this case of superior quality. *Eerie Moan* is most notable for its bittersweet
theme statement by Whetsol, and the first appearance in jazz (to my knowledge)
of bitonality: in the opening chord of Ellington's introduction (Ex. 9).

   In February two recording sessions produced two titles that Ellington was to
re-record later and better—*Merry Go Round* and *Sophisticated Lady*—plus an
improved remake of *Slippery Horn*, an Ivie Anderson vocal, another *Blackbirds*

---

10. *Ducky Wucky* was later included in Ellington's score for *Symphony in Black* as the section called
Dance.

Ex. 9

Medley (this time *sans* vocals), and one artistic gem, *Drop Me Off in Harlem*. The high point of this last named, uniformly well-played and easily swinging side is another one of those eloquent Carney-Williams dialogues. Carney, in baritone register, states the melody, while Cootie comments in wry pointillistic fashion. It is also very modern in its exquisite economy. As Example 10a shows, Carney can elicit only eleven shy little spurts of sound from Cootie in the first eight bars. In the second eight Cootie is more generous, but only in the bridge (Ex. 10b) does he favor us with a full-blown "growl" solo.

Ex. 10a

(o = open, ⊕ = half closed, + = closed)

Ex. 10b

   The rest of the side provides a fine accounting of the multi-talented orchestra—a generous parade of uniquely individual voices: Whetsol, Freddie Jenkins, Brown, and Hardwick's lead alto. Even Fred Guy, who about this time switched from banjo to guitar, is discreetly audible.
   Before making his first trip to Europe in June 1933, Ellington cut three more Ivie Anderson vocals: a great blues known alternatively as *Bundle of Blues* or *Dragon's Blues*, and a pair of popular hits-to-be, Harold Arlen's *Stormy Weather* and the Ellington-Hardwick-Brown perennial *Sophisticated Lady*. The three Ivie vocals and *Stormy Weather* were all tunes from the successful "Cotton Club Parade of 1933," with lyrics by Ted Koehler and music by Harold Arlen. Only *Stormy Weather* swept the nation, but fortunately for Duke and Toby Hardwick, people turned to the flip side and discovered *Sophisticated Lady*, which then became Ellington's first big popular song hit. It is one of the few sides on which Hardwick's rococo alto can be heard to good advantage.
   Bundle of Blues is well named because it is just that: a bundle of blues choruses.

Cootie's pedal-point introduction and coda are reminiscent of his pointillistic *Drop Me Off in Harlem* solo, while Brown sounds like a suave "modern" extension of Armstrong's *West End Blues* choruses. But it is this dapper elegance of Brown that began to provoke the first negative criticisms of the Ellington band. Critics like John Hammond and Spike Hughes regarded Brown's playing as a compromise with "the true jazz spirit." They felt that Brown was "out of place" in the Ellington band, but in saying that they were unconsciously prejudging and delimiting the scope of Ellington's music. In years to come not only Brown's playing but Duke's reluctance to be typecast as a "jungle-istic" or "low-down" blues band earned him the sneering critical epithets of "arty," "pretentious," and "not jazz."

Much of this kind of controversy was elicited during the Ellington orchestra's visit to England, where Spike Hughes, himself a prominent bandleader and respected musician, played a curiously dictatorial role in trying to arbitrate British tastes in regard to Ellington. One might wish to admire Hughes's purist attempts to draw public attention to the "real Duke," but the trouble was that what he (and John Hammond in America) regarded as the "real Duke" was based on a particular, quite personal view of jazz, which Ellington had long ago transcended.

The visit to England (and France in July) was in general highly successful, some quibbling critics notwithstanding.[11] Ironically, Spike Hughes, as well as other British jazz orchestras, like Lew Stone's Stonecutters, later succumbed completely to Ellington's charismatic influence. Even while protesting his "artiness"—like Debussy raging in anger against Wagner while succumbing to the influence of his *Parsifal*—Hughes and his cohorts wrote their *Airs in D Flat*, *Pastorales*, and *Nocturnes*, all in an unmistakably Ellingtonian vein.

Ellington recorded four sides while in London, of which *Harlem Speaks* was the best, a typical array of "hot" solos (the way Spike Hughes liked them), ending with an all-stops-pulled-out ensemble chorus, replete with riffing brass, torrid Nanton growls, and surging Bigard obbligatos. (The London version of *Harlem Speaks* is superior to the August New York recording, especially regarding Braud's and Nanton's contributions.)

On the same date, Duke recorded Fats Waller's *Ain't Misbehavin'*, by then an established jazz standard. The side features typical dicty Freddie Jenkins and one of those quintessential polished Brown solos, set against lazily rolling sax figures. But the most unusual moment occurs in Bigard's chorus in a descending 2-bar passage for saxophones. Harmonically it consists of nothing more than parallel triads, but rhythmically it is cast in quintuplet quarter notes (Ex. 11)—certainly a first in jazz.[12] The whole performance, including Cootie's "dirty"

11. Ulanov, *Duke Ellington*, chap. 10.

12. Quarter-note quintuplets had, of course, occurred before in jazz, but only in improvisations; and it is not likely that such soloists (Armstrong or Morton, for example) knew—or cared—that they were playing quintuplets. What distinguishes the example in Ellington's *Ain't Misbehavin'* is that it is the first attempt to use consciously quintuplet quarter-notes in an arranged ensemble.

Ex. 11

growly solo and Duke's chromatically enigmatic ending, is uniquely Ellingtonian—another striking example of the "recomposition" process.

Returning to America after their European visit, the Ellington band committed to wax one of the numbers they had featured on tour, the Hendersonian *Jive
Stomp*, and an interesting recomposing of an old 1905 Van Alstyne ballad, *In
the Shade of the Old Apple Tree*. This simple tune, Duke told Stanley Dance,
"was the first popular song I ever remember hearing as a child." The transformation into Ellington jazz this time occurs progressively, in stages. The tongue-
in-cheek first chorus deceives the listener into expecting a typical dull-toned
saxophone rendition that could have been played by any one of a thousand
American hotel bands. But soon Cootie begins to mutter some strange growls in
the background, which the sax section ignores. Now trumpeter Freddie Jenkins
prances in and tries to arouse the dead-pan saxes with some fancy footwork,
including an excerpt from the "Lone Ranger" theme. At the next stage, Nanton
raises the jazz temperature measurably by embellishing the tune with "plunger
and growl" moans, this finally goading the saxes into a modicum of swing.
Hodges moves still further into jazz with a free harmonic improvisation, and in
the final stage muted brass ensembles and a clarinet trio become the springboard
for Bigard to break out into a full-blown out-chorus. The humorous ending tells
us it was all a kind of loving parody.

Inspired with a zest for travel by the European trip, Ellington decided to
invade the South, thus becoming the first Negro band to play a tour of interstate
theatres in Texas and Missouri. The event was later celebrated in the Chicago
Victor studios on two recordings, *Rude Interlude* and *Dallas Doings* (September
1933). *Interlude* fascinates with its eerily brooding stomping rhythms and unique-
to-Ellington tightly knit muted brass voicings (harking back to *Mystery Song* and
forward to *Delta Serenade*); *Dallas Doings*, though a spirited performance, is cut
of much lighter cloth: some borrowed thematic material from *Rockin' in Rhythm*
and some less than inspired riffing.

Dear Old Southland, the old 1921 standard "composed" by Turner Layton—
actually it was just a reworking of two spirituals, *Deep River* and *Sometimes I
Feel Like a Motherless Child*—was arranged as a vocal vehicle for trumpeter
Louis Bacon, undoubtedly in an attempt to emulate Armstrong's formidable 1930
success with the same piece. Successful it was, particularly with black audiences,
but musicians flipped—figuratively and literally—over the other side, the astonishing, virtuoso tour de force *Daybreak Express*.

The musical depiction of train rides and the countless nostalgic references to
train whistles in blues and other black music can be traced back well into the
nineteenth century and was virtually a staple of 1920s' blues recordings.
Other aspects of railroad lore are depicted in Scott Joplin's *Crush Collision*

March of 1896, a relatively early example (in a long-standing tradition) of musical programmatic writing, with the inevitable dissonant frantic train whistle and "daring" seventh chord marking the collision; and in blues boogie-woogie pianist Wesley Wallace's famous train tour de force, *No. 29*. And later many such pieces found regular use as accompaniments to the hundreds of train chases in the early silent films.[13] But *Daybreak Express* transcends the merely programmatic and functional. Though quite literal in its descriptive approach, it is above all a superior example of Ellington musical *composition*.

Inevitably perhaps, the introduction of *Daybreak* depicts the train gradually gathering momentum in a 14-bar *accelerando* of heavy parallel chords, underscored by engine-imitating snare-drum rolls (Ex. 12). Once the train, and the orchestra, hit express speed ♩=ca. 288), an A♭ pedal point supports a variety of locomotive imitations, from the click of the tracks and chug of the engine to the wailing train whistle. As the train flies across the landscape, mighty parallel

Ex. 12

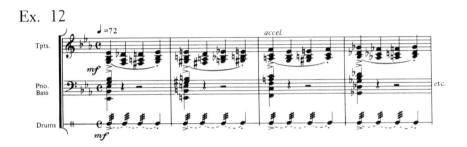

chords, filled out with Cooties's growls and Bigard's high-note wails (Ex. 13), lead to a chromatically descending progression which Hodges embellishes with breathtaking cascading eighth-note arpeggio figures. At this point the whole sax section, over the changes of *Tiger Rag*, launches into a virtuoso ensemble chorus that must have represented the ultimate in technical sophistication at the time (Ex. 14).

Now Ellington modulates to D♭ and the whole band, replete with fancy plunger work in the brass, sax section trills and shakes, screaming lead trumpet, and a daring 2-bar break in the brasses, surges ahead at full throttle. Inevitably the next train station heaves into sight, the train slows down—with Sonny Greer manning the engine's bell—and comes to rest, exhausted, on a G♭ minor-sixth chord in the low saxophones. Jenkins's half-valve cadenza, emulating the wheezing of the steam engine as it sits at the station, and a powerful D♭ ninth chord complete the musical picture. (See also Fig. 1, p. 64.)

13. While the American public is undoubtedly more familiar with Glenn Miller's *Chattanooga Choo-Choo*, *Daybreak Express* (along with Ellington's later *Happy Go Lucky Local*) represents in the field of jazz the zenith of this kind of program music. Honegger's *Pacific 231*, Villa Lobos's *Little Train of Caipira*, and—although not about trains but about a 1904 boat disaster—Ives's *General Slocum* are other well-known symphonic examples of this programmatic genre.

Ex. 13

Ex. 14

Fig. 1

Intro	A	B	C	D
(train gathering speed)	(train whistle, sounds of train in full motion)	ascending parallel chords	descending parallel chords	sax ensemble (Tiger Rag changes in A♭)
14	11 + 13 + 7	12	12	32

D¹	D²	Coda		
full ensemble (Tiger Rag changes in D♭)	full ensemble (Tiger Rag changes in D♭)	(train slowing down)	trumpet cadenza ⌢	final chord
32	30	9	1	1

Daybreak Express was a landmark not only as a technical performance tour de force but as a stunning lesson in the capacity of the jazz medium to equal or better anything that was being done in classical program music—and in Ellington's case with an orchestra of only fourteen!

The most striking thing about Ellington's *Delta Serenade* is its date of composition: one finds it hard to believe that it was composed as early as 1933, for it sounds so much like the great 1939–40 compositions. This is another way of saying that *Delta Serenade* represents a major stylistic/conceptual breakthrough in Ellington's *oeuvre*. It means further that, being advanced even for Ellington, this melancholy serenade was in its way years ahead of anyone else in jazz. Indeed, one can go still further. It contains moments of timbral and harmonic inspiration which had never been produced before by *any* composer, including Ravel or Schoenberg (as the two most likely early-twentieth-century inventors of unique timbral and harmonic flights of fancy).

Actually the harmonies, taken by themselves, are not so novel. By 1933 composers like Stravinsky and Schoenberg had ventured far beyond Ellington's harmonic vocabulary of the time. But it is these harmonies in conjunction with extremely close voicings (Ex. 15a and 15b) and tight muting that produce a truly unprecedented sound,

Ex. 15a

or right after Duke's brief piano solo in the bridge of the second chorus.[14]

Ex. 15b

14. These tight voicings and mutings are a would-be transcriber's nightmare, but Ex. 15b represents a close and likely notational rendition.

This type of backdrop was, of course, the perfect foil for soloists like Bigard, Carney, and Brown, whose poignant improvisations set forth in pure distillation the simple call-and-response patterns of the melody.

Delta Serenade represents a sort of mid-point in Ellington's development, a point at which he found the balance between asserting his own creative imagination and at the same time exploiting the unique instrumental capacities of his players.

There is an exciting new spirit also in *Stompy Jones* (likewise recorded in January 1934), this time in the realm of rhythm. The rhythm section appears to be energized with a new momentum, and the side swings with a cohesive rhythm sound that makes one think of the four-beat drive of the Swing Era and of Kansas City bands like Basie's and Moten's. Freddy Guy's steady chording, now on guitar (also better recorded than previously), and Braud's occasional walking bass in the manner of Walter Page[15] are the main reasons for the new feel of this side. Greer's sizzling cymbal punctuations in the final chorus are a further new sonoric/rhythmic element in the Ellington spectrum. Also new for Ellington is the "bolero" idea of very gradually building up dynamically to a climactic final ensemble chorus. (In this regard *Stompy Jones* was a forerunner of *Crescendo in Blue*, which was to come along three years later). Starting from the subdued tension of Bigard's first chorus, the side builds steadily, making good use of the momentary presence of a fourth trumpet, Louis Bacon (although this was offset by the temporary absence of Tizol). One of the finest moments of this record is a sequence of clipped brass syncopations (in the fifth chorus), answered by interpolations from Ellington and Braud.

As if recording *Daybreak Express, Delta Serenade,* and *Stompy Jones* within a month's time were not enough, Ellington topped off his January 1934 dates with another "blue" piece, *Blue Feeling,* and a solid popular hit, *Solitude.* It was not Duke but Benny Goodman who was to turn out the real moneymaker on *Solitude,* although Ellington tried often enough. Ellington's premiere version is excessively sentimental, setting off Williams and Brown solos against rather trite backgrounds. But by the following September, Ellington had rearranged *Solitude,* alas again without any pronounced popular success. The second version is notable for its strange juxtaposition of the *Mood Indigo* sound of vibrato-less muted brass and low-register clarinet against a saxophone-quartet chorus absolutely dripping with a heavy saccharine vibrato. Poor intonation and balance also plague this performance. But near the end the side is almost saved by a magnificent rising sax figure topped by a sensual Hodges wail, seeming to cry out against the somewhat strait-laced treatment of the song.

After January's effusion of creativity, it is disheartening to find Ellington and his men wasting their time on trivia—like *Cocktails for Two,* but, even worse, because of its absurd pretensions, something called *Ebony Rhapsody.* Unfortunately this pastiche—it all originated in a movie, *Murder at the Vanities* (Earl

15. For a fuller discussion of Walter Page's crucial role in developing the "modern" post-1920s conception of jazz bass, see Chapter 4, below, the Basie section.

Carroll's, that is)—was 10 percent "ebony" and 90 percent Hollywood-Hungarian; a jazzed-up rehash of Liszt's *Second Hungarian Rhapsody*.[16]

Three Ivie Anderson vocals followed suit, of which *I Met My Waterloo* had at least the distinction of a moving Whetsol-Carney duet—always an unforgettable combination—and a snappy Cootie Williams double-time bridge near the end of the side.

Apart from the already mentioned second version of *Solitude*, a September 1934 date produced three interestingly diverse sides, something for everybody. First there was *Moonglow*, the fine Will Hudson tune of the same year. It was not entirely accidental that this piece appeared on the other side of *Solitude*, for Eddie de Lange, the lyricist who had put words to *Solitude*, was also the co-author of *Moonglow*. Furthermore, Hudson had fashioned his melody for *Moonglow* on the chords of Ellington's earlier *Lazy Rhapsody*. Undoubtedly it was hoped—and one can see the shrewd managerial hand of Irving Mills at work here—that a triple-threat combination of Hudson-de Lange-Ellington on *Moonglow*, coupled with *Solitude*, which had climbed since January to the "top hit" lists, would produce a bonanza record that would successfully compete with Benny Goodman's recordings of the same two tunes.[17] To Ellington's surprise it did.

Ellington's recording of *Moonglow* should not be passed over just because it was a commercial success. It is crammed with excellent Ellington touches and is important innovatively because it is one of the first jazz recordings—since Morton's heyday in the *Hot Peppers* series—to make telling structural use of dynamics. Indeed the whole performance is striking, starting with a harmonically shifting introduction, which reappears later in diminution in the second chorus (in m. 8 of the bridge), and, incidentally resurfaces five *years* (!) later as the opening measures of Duke's *Serenade to Sweden*. The reappearance of this progression in the second part of *Moonglow* is a typical example of Ellington's ability to integrate compositionally what may at first appear to be incidental material. As heard in the introduction, the phrase sounds as follows, ingeniously orchestrated as a timbre-melody (Ex. 16a). In the second chorus the same ma-

Ex. 16a

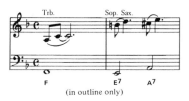

(in outline only)

16. The inordinate 1930s' fascination for Liszt's famous Hungarian *Rhapsody No. 2* is hard to appreciate nowadays, when that rather tawdry pseudo-Gypsy potpourri is not even played at pop concerts any more. But it certainly impressed musicians and listeners in the thirties and forties, and as a consequence runs through the jazz repertory in fearful abundance. There is hardly a band that did not quote or steal from its famous themes.

17. Goodman, who was fast on the rise at this time, and who had previously employed Will Hudson as an arranger, had recorded *Moonglow* in May 1934. His *Solitude* was waxed one day before Duke's own second version, just a few blocks up the street from the Brunswick studios Ellington frequented.

terial functions as a "turn-back," i.e. leading back to the final eight bars of the chorus. But, of course, a turn-back is also a kind of introduction to a reiterated set of changes. Thus the phrase retains part of its original introductory character. However, for that to happen in *one* measure, the material had to be compressed ("diminution" is the technical term) to half its original duration (Ex. 16b). Fi-

Ex. 16b

F   E7   A7   Aaug   B♭6

(in outline only)

nally, the originality of this technical "trick" has the sleight-of-hand effect of covering over and of welding together the joint where the bridge (B) meets the last eight bars (A²) in the typical A A¹ B A² 32-bar song structure. Most musicians in the 1930s were quite oblivious of the structural sectionalization that this four-times-eight-measures format induced. With but few exceptions it was not until the days of Parker and Gillespie that musicians began to improvise lines that veneered over these 8-bar seams. Here, in *Moonglow*, Ellington is again years ahead by producing not only a seamless 12-bar phrase (starting at m. 5 in B going through A²), but does so with a refreshingly sweeping melodic gesture. Obviously the G in m. 1 of A² (Ex. 16b) and the descending phrase it initiates are not part of Hudson's original melody. But that in itself is not so remarkable, for composing new lines on previously composed changes was not an entirely new technique; indeed Hudson's *Moonglow*, as already mentioned, consisted of just that. But what makes Ellington's superimposed 12-bar phrase so satisfying is that it forms the compositional climax of the entire performance. And it all started with those two simple bars of introductory material (Ex. 16a).

I have mentioned Ellington's use of dynamics in *Moonglow*. To put this in context one must realize that dynamics have always played a minor role in jazz, even to this day. Thousands of jazz musicians and tens of thousands of performances, many of them perfectly acceptable in all other respects, have made no use whatsoever of dynamics either to achieve contrast or to use as an expressive or decorative device, and least of all, have they been used as a means of delineating structural aspects of a piece. Much of this disregard of dynamics resulted from a lack of technical instrumental control. Some of it represented a general unawareness of the multiple ways in which dynamics can function in music. Indeed I am certain that dynamic differentiation was considered by many jazz musicians as contrary in spirit to the hell-bent spontaneity of "hot jazz." It was considered somehow effete and intellectual to control and modify expression through dynamic differentiation. It was considered "arty" and "pretentious," and— "worst of all"—derivative of classical music.

Typically Ellington ignored such narrowing injunctions. He saw no reason for an embargo on dynamics, and *Moonglow* is but one fine example of how even a popular tune could be enriched by the deft use of dynamic variations.

In the second chorus (with Hodges as soloist), the background is richly adorned

Ex. 17

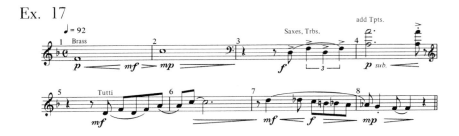

with dynamics (Ex. 17). Particularly unusual were the rather abrupt swells in m. 4. Also notable is the way Carney boots the ensemble with his big tone in mm. 3 and 7, leading the full ensemble from below, as it were. But an even more striking example of the structure-delineating use of dynamic levels can be heard in Cootie Williams's solo chorus, as described below (see also Fig. 2).

And then there are the inimitable soloists, Hodges and Williams. Williams delivers one of his most perfectly conceived—and least heralded—solos, serving as a model for a kind of easygoing relaxed manner that players like Bobby Hackett and Billy Butterfield were to turn into a formula years later. Cootie is very sparing with the growl and wah-wah, all the more so that we may clearly hear his superb choice of notes. Furthermore it is one of those solos—apparently "simple" in structure—which has its own integral logical form. The first eight bars are a kind of exposition of the basic ideas, including the lovely phrase-turns in Ex. 18, and ornamented in the second eight with growls, wah-wahs, and blue notes.

Ex. 18

(only leading melodic notes are indicated)

The temperature rises a mite in the bridge as the saxes have four bars of ensemble. When Cootie returns in the fifth bar he is in his high register, and for the "turn-back," straining against his tight mute, reaches for a couple of climactic high Ds, all the more exciting for the effort they obviously required. In the final eight the tension subsides, at first partially maintained for two bars and then, with a slightly embellished variation of the lyrical phrase of Ex. 18,

Fig. 2

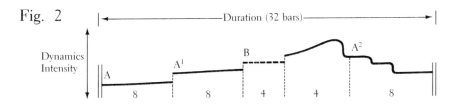

Cootie gracefully bows out—the thematic recapitulation closing the circle of the solo, as it were. The overall form of the solo, presented diagrammatically (Fig. 2), shows the correlation between the 32-bar song structure (read horizontally) and the twin elements of dynamics and intensity (read vertically). Thus we have an exposition A, its embellished restatement A^1, a development section with climax B, and A^2, the varied recapitulation of A.

Sump'n 'bout Rhythm and *Saddest Tale* are from the same date as *Moonglow*, the former a rather sophisticated swing number featuring Duke's piano, the latter composition, choice Ellington, notable for one of the earlier appearances on jazz records of an extended solo for bass clarinet (here played by Carney) and for Duke's lugubrious spoken lines: "The saddest tale (that's) told on land or sea, is the tale they told when they told the truth on me"—intoned in a laconic down-and-out voice, matching anything Bogart ever delivered. It is also notable for an eloquently lyrical Williams solo and, by contrast, the most bitingly bitter low brass harmonies.

The *Saddest Tale* is, not unexceptedly, a blues, and a fine early example of blues-chord substitutions, as each chorus trots out a different set of alternate changes. And it is a pensive, mournful piece. One way in which Ellington achieved this cheerless mood was by scoring for the trombones in the low bass register. This was a new idea at the time—before the days of bass trombones in jazz. Tizol's valve trombone had to make do on low Fs and Gs, but his thin-ish penetrating sound gave those harmonies a peculiar tint, to which Ellington was to return frequently through the years.

Here again, Ellington was conceptually far beyond writing a mere jazz or dance tune. *Saddest Tale* was a somber, almost macabre tone poem; and the wonder is that Ellington could extract such astonishing sounds from only a fourteen-piece orchestra.

Also at about this time personnel changes in the orchestra were beginning to cause some concern. What had been an unusually stable situation for many years was beginning to fluctuate, as illness and various kinds of dissatisfaction began to plague the band. Hardwick and Bigard were often absent; Whetsol, one of Duke's irreplaceable mainstays, was suffering from tuberculosis and left the band in 1935. To compensate for these losses, Rex Stewart, a formidable personality and a veteran of both McKinney's Cotton Pickers and the great early thirties' Fletcher Henderson band, joined Ellington around Christmas 1934 on cornet.

Duke had in recent years felt some dissatisfaction with Wellman Braud, his bass player since 1927, who at age forty-four was now the oldest member of the band. As Ellington's music became more sophisticated harmonically and rhythmically, and particularly as the new 4/4 swing feeling crept into the band's style, Braud's inadequacies became uncomfortably apparent. But Ellington's genteel nature and basic loyalty to his men, then as later, prohibited him from firing any player. Duke took the expedient alternative of hiring a second bass player, Billy Taylor, also a McKinney alumnus. (When Braud eventually left the band, Duke liked the musical possibilities with two basses so much that he replaced

Braud with Hayes Alvis, and for some three years the Ellington orchestra boasted a bass section of two.)

Rex Stewart made his Ellington record debut on a small-band date, *Tough Truckin', Indigo Echoes* (1935), the first an Ellington group had had since 1930. Various sextets and octets featuring Ellington soloists were to contribute to the band's repertory from the mid-thirties on, but in 1935, with the trend definitely in the direction of bigger orchestras, paring down to a sextet was uncommon— particularly one that featured *two* bass players.[18] The titles *Tough Truckin'* and *Indigo Echoes* are average Ellington, but they did serve to introduce Stewart's strange world of elliptical bent notes, sliding twists, half-valve mutterings, and witty asides.

On the same session the full band produced another virtually unrecognizable transformation of an old 1920 hit, *Margie*. If the record was intended to make money, its unusual treatment of a standard certainly mitigated against that.

In point of fact things were suddenly not going well for Ellington. Was it the instability of the orchestra's personnel and the constant rumors of more leave-takings? (George Frazier in *Downbeat* magazine even had the band breaking up altogether.) Was it the growing nagging criticism by some of the jazz writers? Was it the inroads made by "swing music," by bands like Goodman and Dorsey, the growing profusion of commercial dance bands? Was it the consistent inability of his potentially popular successes—*Sophisticated Lady, Solitude, In a Sentimental Mood*—to break through the Tin Pan Alley machinery? Was it the relentless pressures and frustrations inherent in a white-controlled market? Or was it his mother's illness and her imminent death?

Perhaps all of these factors commingled to produce a crippling and depressing uneasiness that manifested itself in Ellington's productivity. Between January 1935 and January 1936 the orchestra made twenty-four sides, of which nine were never issued—something that had never happened to Ellington before, at least not with such a high rejection rate. Three of the issued sides were remakes, a few others were indifferent (like the rather bland and over-arranged Ivie Anderson vocal, *Cotton*), and one—*In a Sentimental Mood*—destined to become a perennial favorite, became a big hit for Benny Goodman and Ozzie Nelson in 1936, but not for Duke in 1935.

It is easy to see why Goodman and Ozzie Nelson sold more copies of *Sentimental Mood* because Duke's version of his and Hardwick's tune is turned, once again, into a fairly uncompromising orchestral *composition* which, in its substance, goes far beyond the perception of the typical 1935 early swing era audi-

---

18. The great success of the Goodman Trio (and Quartet) sides, starting in 1935, initiated a counter trend which eventually led to the espousal of the small combo as the main vehicle of jazz expression. By 1936 and 1937 Ellington's sidemen, especially Bigard and Hodges, began to record in smaller combos, septets and octets. Though very few of them attained the caliber of Ellington's large ensemble recordings, they constituted a more personal outlet for these players, who at times felt constrained by the yoke of Ellington's awesome creativity. There are, however, four quartet sides (under Rex Stewart's titular leadership) recorded in Paris in 1939, with guest artist Djanjo Reinhardt on guitar, that are amongst the most priceless gems in the entire history of chamber jazz. These performances are discussed in Chapter 9, below.

ences. First of all, *Sentimental Mood* had nothing to do with "swing." Secondly, it was arranged in such a sophisticated manner that the emphasis was not on the tune but on the individual soloists' treatment of it, the timbral/textural variety Ellington could cram into this three-minute seven-second side, and the harmonic invention with which Ellington enriched the basic changes of the song. Thus there is a virtual parade of Ellington soloists in a succession of 8-bar solo statements, a much more fragmented way of presenting a ballad than was current in the mid-1930s (Fig. 3).

Fig. 3

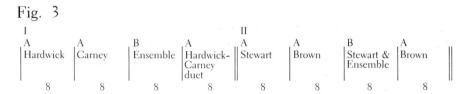

I				II			
A	A	B	A	A	A	B	A
Hardwick	Carney	Ensemble	Hardwick-Carney duet	Stewart	Brown	Stewart & Ensemble	Brown
8	8	8	8	8	8	8	8

The two ensemble sections—the bridge in both choruses (*B* in Fig. 3)—contain the most extended expansions of the basic material, using all the resources of the band. In the third and fourth bars of the last bridge, for example, Ellington divides the orchestra into layers of timbral choirs. Bass saxophone (played by Hardwick) and baritone sax in octaves plus both bassists, playing *arco*, anchor

Ex. 19

down the bass notes with a rich heavy sound. The rest of the saxes supply the middle-register harmony. Further up in register, muted trumpets and trombones play chromatically moving harmonies, while above *them* (in open trumpet) Williams is heard. Example 19 gives these measures in outline form. Surely no "jazz" composer had ever used such a fascinating collection of diverse sonorities. To the audiences of 1935 this could only have sounded "weird" and unintelligible.

Showboat Shuffle is a catchy Ellington piece full of sophisticated "dicty" licks and breaks; three modulations, one of which is ingeniously prepared by a jauntily swinging Rex Stewart and leads into one of his happiest recorded solos; and finally a fadeout ending by electronic means, a device being newly explored in the mid-thirties. Apart from *Truckin'*, a very hot hard-swinging vocal by Ivie Anderson, also featuring an early Ben Webster solo (rather more tense and harried than his later work), and *Accent on Youth*, which marked the temporary return of Whetsol for one of his most hauntingly moving performances, there were two other major efforts: one, the recording in March 1935 of a nine-minute film short, *Symphony in Black*, the other the remarkable extended piece *Reminiscing in Tempo*, composed in the summer months of 1935.

Symphony in Black was not only an early extended work of Ellington's but also a direct forerunner of *Black, Brown and Beige*, perhaps not so much stylistically as programmatically and in overall concept. The programmatic content and narrative structure, of course, derived from the film scenario, conceived and directed by Fred Waller. *Symphony in Black*, moreover, is a touching, highly atmospheric, ambitious quasi-documentary, portraying Negro life in the 1930s in the urban centers of America; it was subtitled "A Rhapsody of Negro Life." It is also remarkable for its very moving pantomime acting and dancing, its complete absence of spoken dialogue and, substituting instead, a fully integrated musical score by a major composer (Ellington). The film won an Academy Award as the best "musical short subject" of the year 1935.

For the four episodes of the film—I. *Introduction* and *The Laborers*; II. *A Triangle*, with sub-sections *Dance—Jealousy—Big City Blues*; III. *A Hymn of Sorrow*; IV. *Harlem Rhythm*—Ellington adopted three earlier pieces (*Ducky Wucky, The Saddest Tale*, and *Merry-Go-Round*) for *Triangle, Blues*, and *Rhythm* and composed new material for the remaining scenes. It is a shame the complete work is not available on records[19]—none of the discographies list the film soundtrack recording—for it contains some of Ellington's most affecting music.

Introduction depicts the fast-paced, nervous, noisy stridency of modern city life—a music that in its boisterous clang and clatter (and use of the timpani for dramatic impact) very much resembles the opening of *Black, Brown and Beige*.

19. To my knowledge the only complete performance on records of *Symphony in Black* is a re-creation of the work, as transcribed from the film's sound track, by the Smithsonian Jazz Repertory Ensemble (conducted by the author) on the Smithsonian Collection of Recordings. Ellington used abbreviated versions of the three existing pieces. The account of the work given here (below) is of the *entire* "Symphony" (really a Suite), that is, as if Ellington could have used the *complete* scores of the three previously extant pieces, as well as all the new "film" material.

Other similarities between the two extended works are *Symphony*'s next section, *The Laborers*—which has its counterpart in *BBB*'s "Work Song" section—*Big City Blues*, a vocal piece like "The Blues" in *BBB*, and *Hymn of Sorrow*, a sacred music whose counterpart is the famous "Come Sunday" theme in *BBB*. *The Laborers* features Hodges intoning a heavy-laden theme over some of the most grimly despairing low-register brass (and tom-tom) music Ellington ever conceived. *Dance* (i.e. *Ducky Wucky*) relieves that fearsome mood briefly enough, before the *Jealousy* episode breaks in. Strident full ensemble harmonies and a haunting Ellington piano interlude lead to *Big City Blues* (i.e. *The Saddest Tale*), sung here—even the Ellington connoisseur may be surprised to hear—by none other than Billie Holiday, only a year after her record debut. Billie also appeared in the film, playing on screen the role of "the other woman" in the triangle. Here the earlier woebegone mood of the film returns as Billie sings her mournful blues in matchless style, preceded by an anguished moaning Nanton plunger solo, and followed by twelve bars of melancholy Hodges supplications, Whetsol's poignantly forlorn muted trumpet, and Carney's gloomy bass clarinet. As depressing as this scenario may sound in description, the music somehow expresses hope. It is what we can observe so often in black music, especially the blues: the pathos of grief and despair expressed without self-pity and sentimentality, without whimpering. The music, though inexpressibly sad, nonetheless radiates inner beauty and nobility. Conversely, it is hard to think of any music in a *major* key (B♭ major here) which is so disconsolate and tragic.

As if this were not enough, the next episode is even more moving—*Hymn of Sorrow*, intoned on softly muted trumpet by Whetsol over organ-like saxes and bowed bass (Ex. 20). Once again the "Ellington effect"—basically unnotatable— here is achieved by a subtle coalescence of harmony, timbre, texture, and melody, all at the service of this hauntingly beautiful lament. There is not much in jazz that can equal it, and one has to turn to Mahler and early Schoenberg (*Gurrelieder*) to find passages of comparable sublimity.

The doleful atmosphere is finally lifted with *Harlem Rhythm* (in *Merry-Go-Round*), this time apparently for good. Good times prevail in Harlem once again.

Ex. 20

Cootie, Bigard, bubbly loquacious Hodges, Brown—brash and outgoing (he bursts in with a rattling lip trill)—exuberant Carney, guffawing trombone trios, sprightly trumpet trios—all these and more parade through this wonderfully effervescent musical merry-go-round finale.

From a slightly earlier film date comes a curious recording with a singer quite the opposite of Billie Holiday: namely, Mae West. *Belle of the Nineties* starred West and also featured—rather incongruously—the Ellington band. Going from Billie to Mae might appear to be going from the sublime to the ridiculous , but Mae actually holds her own rather well as a singer, particularly in her boisterous, inimitably "vulgar" *Memphis Blues*. In a piece that is more ragtime than blues, West extols the virtues of a certain (fictitious) Memphis band—which features not only a "hot cornet," a "ragging piano man," but inexplicably, a "big bassoon" (*sic*). West's other brush with the Ellington band, *My Old Flame*, also comes off well, mainly because the Ellington men manage somehow to adopt instrumentally to her rather corny vaudeville vocal style.

Before we can engage in a musical-analytical discussion of *Reminiscing*, we should assess its general place in the history of jazz, and beyond that, of black music. I have previously mentioned that from the outset Ellington resisted the stigmatization of his music as jazz, or more correctly, as *merely* jazz. Similarly, he resisted—not always successfully—the constant pressures to commercialize his art, to level it off to some pre-ordained mold of easy marketability, i.e. to identify himself with the expected stereotypes. At no time was this pressure, always implicit and frequently explicit in his professional-managerial contacts, stronger than in the mid-thirties, when swing, as epitomized by Goodman, captured the nation. Suddenly Ellington's musical primacy was threatened, not on artistic terms but on the terms by which an essentially commercially oriented society judges success: mass sales, financial rewards, mass popularity. Suddenly Ellington found himself called "outmoded" (because his was not a swing band) by the very same tastemakers who, ironically, had never caught up with Ellington's art in the first place. Suddenly Ellington found himself pressured to declare himself a "swing" musician.

Conscious or unconscious—it matters not—his response was unequivocal and definitive. And that response was contained in *Reminiscing in Tempo*—not in some specific social message or programmatic content,[20] but rather in its form and *musical* content, which burst the pre-set molds established for jazz once and for all. Gone was the 10-inch 78-rpm three-minute time limitation, imposed by pragmatic commercial considerations and prejudice; gone were the 32- or 12-bar jazz forms imposed by similar concerns as to the limitations of mass public taste; gone were the obligatory 8-bar phrases, the pop-tune mentality, the many other simplifications and implicit restrictions imposed by an industry interested primarily in selling records, not creative content. Thus, whatever failings *Reminiscing in Tempo* may have in the view of its critics, these must be seen against a background of the gigantic forward strides that the composition, performance, and recording of this work represented, not only in jazz but in the history of black music in America.

Actually, *Reminiscing* is one of the most successful of Ellington's extended works, not only for its time but even as measured retrospectively against his numerous other major creative efforts through the years. *Reminiscing* was innovative not only in its duration—some thirteen minutes stretched across four 10-inch sides—but in the way its several themes and episodes were integrated into a single unified whole. Nothing quite that challenging had ever been attempted in jazz composition—and with a jazz orchestra. Indeed, perhaps the most remarkable achievement of the work is the way composition and orchestra interact, and cohere in a way that was new even for Ellington—at least on such an extended scale. This is also the subtlest aspect of the work, and it is small wonder that the critics of 1935 failed to hear the thematic coherence of the work or the initmate relationship between the musical content and the orchestra for whom it was exclusively written.

It is a point well worth dwelling upon. For the substantive interaction between composer and performer had, to my knowledge, never been so completely explored and tested—in this case on three levels: 1) the music of *Reminiscing* was specifically composed for a *jazz* orchestra, one—we should not forget—that had its primary function as a dance orchestra; 2) it was written for a specific and limited group of instruments (brass, reeds, keyboard, and rhythm); and 3), even more importantly and precisely, it was written for a *specific* collection of individual players with highly personal stylistic and sonoric traits. It is hard to think of any work in the classical literature that is so uniquely—and so successfully—geared to a specified group of players: not any Beethoven string quartet, any Mahler symphony or Strauss tone poem, nor any Brahms, Rachmaninov, or Prokofiev concerto. Another way to put it is to say that Duke's music for *Reminiscing* is as much inspired by the players and instruments of his orchestra as by his own creative imagination. This is so even at the level of, say, melodic or harmonic invention, not to mention instrumentation and timbral color. Elling-

20. In this connection, I believe that Ellington's reaction to his mother's death as influencing the composition of *Reminiscing* (similar to the case of Ravel and *La Valse*) has been overstated by some biographers.

ton is here writing on his thus far grandest scale, not for a trombone, a muted trumpet, an alto saxophone, but for *the* trombone of Lawrence Brown, *the* muted trumpet sound of Arthur Whetsol, *the* alto sonority of Johnny Hodges. The obverse of that condition is that the work cannot be played by other players (and was not meant to) *except* by careful emulation of those specific sounds and sonorities. In this sense alone, *Reminiscing* is a very special composition, exploring further in a more complex extended format the special relationship Ellington's music had begun to have with his players, from *Black and Tan Fantasy* and *East St. Louis Toodle-Oo* through *Mood Indigo* and *Creole Love Call* to *Drop Me Off in Harlem* and *Delta Serenade*.

But beyond this creative chemistry, *Reminiscing* demonstrates a degree of formal control which Ellington was hard put to equal, let alone better, in later years. This is due in great part to the fact that Ellington restricted himself in *Reminiscing* to one primary theme (theme A in the thematic chart Fig. 4), a contrasting secondary theme (theme B), two brief transitional passages (one modulatory, the other based on a pedal point), and a harmonic vamp on which the main theme is built. As the thematic outline shows, theme A appears fourteen times in six different keys, mostly melodically unvaried, while theme B appears only three times. Transition A is used twice; transition B three times. It should be further noted that the A theme is stated in different lengths, from as short as four bars to as long as ten. The longer durations are achieved in some instances (mm. 81-90, for example) by expanding the basic theme variant of 6½ bars with a 3½-bar extension. What imparts structural logic to this thematic extension is that it is derived from the undulating eighth-note figure which accompanies the main theme (mm. 9–16 in saxes, mm. 21–26 in the trombrone). Another use of this sinuous eighth-note line occurs in the D-major recurrence of theme A (mm. 149–53) in Carney's low-register clarinet.

As noted, extensive development or variation upon the material plays only a minor role in building the work. Only the third, sixth, and thirteenth returns of the theme, for example, are varied. The other recurrences adhere to straight repetition, albeit transposed in different keys and registers and, of course, subjected to subtle harmonic alterations as well as diverse instrumentations. All in all this produces a fine architectural balance between the expected and the unexpected, between repetition and subtle variation. Such variants are combined with different textures, densities, dynamics, and harmonizations, thus fully exploiting the many interacting sonoric variables Ellington had at his command in his orchestra. Consider, for example, the contrast between the light airy texture of version 2—with Hardwick's flute-like alto over Tizol's weaving trombone— and the massive chordal structures and imperious theme statement in version 9. Moreover, whereas in many Ellington late-period extended works one is left with the feeling that particular sections and episodes merely follow each other, haphazardly shoved together, in *Reminiscing* one invariably feels the inner flow of the work; ideas, themes, restatements, all evolve logically, without strain, from one to the next in a virtually unbroken continuity.

The flow of the piece was greatly aided by its single tempo throughout, barring

Fig. 4   DUKE ELLINGTON   77

* Related to two eighth-note accompanimental figures in Vamp, Pre - Theme,
Theme A:

a few ritardandos and Ellington's own out-of-tempo piano preluding. What gave many critics of the day, accustomed to the straight-ahead uptempo swing of Fletcher Henderson, Benny Goodman, or Jimmie Lunceford, an impression of "disjointedness" in *Reminiscing* was the fact that Ellington included several brief passages without benefit of rhythm section. There were four or five of these on the first record side alone. In any case, Greer's drumming, always the epitome of discretion, was not designed to bowl over the average listener with a barrage of rhythm, especially in a slow tempo piece—slow for jazz, that is—like *Reminiscing*, another factor that irked the jazz fans who were probably looking for another Casa Loma-type flag-waver.

This impressive control of thematic material, played out against the full coloristic resources of the Ellington orchestra, gives *Reminiscing* a cohesion and conciseness many later extended works lacked. One notes with pleasure that there is very little extraneous material in *Reminiscing*, and, except for Duke's own meandering piano interlude that closes side two (surely the weakest section of the work), one never has the sense of something being thrown in as a filler. The few non-thematically related passages—they total only some twenty measures out of a total of nearly three hundred (not counting the piano cadenza)—all function logically and organically.

If Ellington held a tight rein on his musical materials in *Reminiscing*, he did so at a price—one that he was certainly willing to pay. The decision to eschew improvisation was one which he did not regard as a serious failing. Indeed, why *must* there be improvisation—even in a jazz piece—as certain critics were suggesting (and still are apt to do). Ellington was composing *music*, not jazz necessarily. In *Reminiscing*, more than ever before, he was trying to break out beyond the narrow categorizations of the commercial world which by an accident of fate he was forced to inhabit. He was determined more than ever before, to avoid the trap into which the market place and the obsession for labeling were trying to lure him to.[21] And if to achieve those higher goals improvising had to be forfeited, so be it. Moreover, as fine as Ellington's musicians were, there can be little question that they could not have improvised successfully *within* the daring musical framework Ellington had conceived in *Reminiscing*. The creative distance between him and them was too great to expect fully integrated extemporized solos. Ellington substituted *composed* solos for improvised ones, leaving the players free to embellish their solos with their own personal, primarily coloristic touches and giving only Hodges (in two brief appearances) a little more free rein.

In view of these realities, Ellington's creative choices and decisions were not only absolutely on target but inevitable. Each "solo" perfectly fits its interpreter,

---

21. To what extent the stigmatization of categories was rigidly maintained in those years, against all logic, is demonstrated, for example, by the fact that Columbia Records labeled all four 10-inch sides of *Reminiscing in Tempo* as a "fox trot," an idiotic appellation in view of the work's true intent and essence.

and vice versa. Furthermore, he left no one out. Everyone has at least a brief solo outing (although Nanton just barely made it with a 2-bar contribution).

Ellington was also chastised by the critics for the work's "lack of swing." Again the question arises: *must* there be swing? By what doctrine and ordination must a jazz piece be forced to swing? The answer, of course, is that it doesn't have to, not then and not now. The only possible criterion by which one can judge such matters is on the basis of a work's premise. Needless to say, if a work *is* based on a premise of rhythmic swing—as most jazz-as-dance music, certainly in the thirties, claims to be—then its failure to do so is clearly a matter for criticism. But, as I have suggested, Ellington's *Reminiscing* was based on no such premise—although it certainly has by the very nature of his music a certain subtle relaxed swing—and therefore the judging of it by such prejudicial criteria is irrelevant, and unfair.

Beyond the structural unity of *Reminiscing* there is the warmth and richness of the music itself, expressed in its melodic and harmonic beauty. There is once again, as in the best of Ellington, an exquisite balance—one might say creative intertwining—of harmony and melody: the one is inconceivable without the other. Indeed, there can be little question that in Ellington's best themes, melody and harmony arise simutaneously from the same inspirational source. Such is certainly the case with the opening theme of *Reminiscing*: a simple poignant melody intertwined with a sinuous undulating counter-motive over a chromatic bass line (Ex. 21).

Ex. 21

When Lawrence Brown is given the theme some thirty bars later, Ellington provides a new even more ingeniously poignant harmonization (Ex. 22).

Ex. 22

As noted so often in this chapter, it is never the harmonies *per se* but the way they are voiced and then sonorically blended that gives that inner glow to the "Ellington effect." With Hodges and Bigard enfolded between Hardwick's luminous lead tones and Carney's darker baritone voice, the effect of these blendings is ravishing. In fact, in 1935 nothing quite like that had ever been heard in music, *any music*. A similar instance of the special use to which Ellington could put Carney's baritone occurs a little later, during the last four bars of side one (Ex. 23). Ninety-nine out of a hundred arrangers would have given the baritone a C in m. 2, and put the B♭ in the octave above, Ellington gives the chord its special dark-warm color by placing Carney on the seventh of the chord, *below* the tonic or root, as it were.[22]

Ex. 23

Another passage of striking harmonic invention occurs near the end of side three (version 9 of the main theme). In its textural density, powerful polytonal harmonies striding across the theme in unison brass, and anchored by two basses grinding out deep parallel fifths, the passage is overwhelming in its dramatic intensity. It is hard to believe that it is played by an orchestra of only fifteen (Ex. 24).

22. This may seem to be a small point to the casual reader, but I strongly suggest that this passage be heard and compared with the notation above, for it is revelatory (albeit one simple example) of Ellington's harmonic language and scoring techniques. It is a key to his special sound world; an understanding of it without appreciating these methods is not likely.

Ex. 24

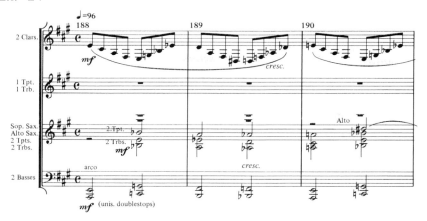

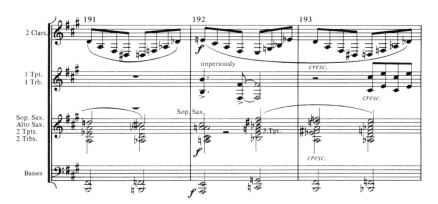

One other notable aspect of *Reminiscing in Tempo* is its scoring for two basses. As much as any other instrumentational coloring, Ellington's use of two basses, mostly bowed and often in double stops, gives the work its special, at times sombre, cast. A most amazing sound and harmony are produced when the two bassists' lines diverge, producing four-part bass lines as in m. 21-22

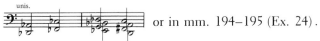 or in mm. 194–195 (Ex. 24).

The harmonic richness in *Reminiscing* is at times overwhelming, as expressive as any one might find in such other heady harmonists as Delius, Ravel, Rachmaninov, and Scriabin. This is by no means to imply that Ellington imitated those composers' chromaticism, for he is totally original in this respect and as different from them as they are from each other. Furthermore, what one finds in Ellington's use of, say, advanced bitonal harmonies is a confluence of two traditions which those other European composers could not have seen—or, with the possible exception of Ravel, certainly chose not to see. For what flows together in Ellington's music—and *Reminiscing in Tempo* is the first composition where these tendencies are given free rein over a prolonged period of time, some thirteen minutes—is the chromaticism of the blues as typified by the "blue notes"[23] of the blues scale and the chromaticization of European/Western harmony as manifested in the increased use, starting around the beginning of the twentieth century, of the upper extensions of triadic harmonies. To put it another way, the major/minor ambivalence found in the blues and jazz had its counterpart in the major/minor harmonies that composers like Ravel, Scriabin, the early Stravinsky and Milhaud—and later Gershwin—began to explore in the early decades of our century. The points of origin for these harmonic elaborations, however, were quite different, both traditions arriving at the same juncture from quite opposite directions.

Whereas the blue notes in the blues (an intrinsic element of jazz from its beginnings) were of *melodic* origin, the European developments were arrived at by a process of extending *harmonic* structures upward. In jazz a blue note—say an E♭ (minor third) in a C major seventh chord—would be the result of a flattening of the major third, in other words, a *melodic deviation*, the result of pitch inflecting. In the European version the E♭ was arrived at by a gradual process (which took centuries) of building chords upward from their roots in thirds. Example 25 shows the process in a simplified form: starting with the third and fifth, the seventh was added (in the sixteenth century), while the ninth came along in the eighteenth century, at first sporadically and only under certain voice

Ex. 25

23. For a full discussion of this subject see *Early Jazz*. chap. 1. See also the related discussion of bitonal harmonic usages in this volume, Chapter 5, below, the Kirk section.

leading conditions, and then late in the nineteenth century as an *autonomous* harmonic extension. But soon composers began to realize that there were three different altered ninths possible within the triadic-dominant system. In addition to the regular ninth found in the major scale of the key (D in our example), there was the minor ninth (D♭), used with great effectiveness since Bach's time, and the somewhat later discovered "raised ninth" (D♯). (Further building upwards in thirds led to the inclusion eventually, in our century, of elevenths and thirteenths.) As indicated in Figure 3 of Chapter 5, below, these upper harmonic extensions led to the development of a whole network of interrelated and to some extent interchangeable dominant harmonies.

Bop musicians heard these relationships and incorporated them in their harmonic/melodic language. For the old blues-derived flatted fifth, the very symbol of bop and early modern jazz, was none other than the classical musicians raised eleventh. But Ellington brought these two traditions together years before the boppers, and nowhere in early Ellington is this confluence of harmonic traditions more explicitly expressed and more consummately realized than in *Reminiscing in Tempo*.

For all its compositional craft and structural unity, it is the loveliness of its themes, its contemplative reminiscing mood, the sensuous, insinuating harmonies, the gentle warmth of its instrumental colors, that make *Reminiscing in Tempo* a memorable musical experience. It should be in the repertory of every jazz orchestra and be known to every American, for it is one of Ellington's greatest master strokes.

Reminiscing in Tempo received a mixed reaction. The work annoyed and confused those who were hopping onto the new swing bandwagon. At the same time most "serious" composers were still unaware of Ellington, and a thirteen-minute tone poem that wasn't in the acceptable twelve-tone or neo-classic styles of the period was not apt to arouse much attention among the "classical" intelligentsia. The jazz critics, led by John Hammond, generally dismissed the work. Hammond, in a scathing review for the newly founded jazz magazine *Downbeat*, severely criticized the work (essentially for not being what it was never intended to be). He continued his barrage of denunciations, once limited to Lawrence Brown but now expanded to include Ellington as well, and the latter's alleged "pretentiousness" and lack of "true jazz spirit."

Despite the many disappointments of the year, Ellington clung to his musical ideals and goals. Indeed, as the months passed these became more defined, more precise. The categories, the *types* of pieces I have previously referred to, became more sharply differentiated, and at the same time the "pure composition" category was developed into a substantial autonomous musical expression, yet indigenous to jazz.

Reminiscing in Tempo represented the vanguard of this effort. But soon there were interesting successors, for one, a series of "concertos" for individual players in the orchestra: *Echoes of Harlem (Cootie's Concerto)*—not to be confused with the 1940 *Concerto for Cootie*—*Clarinet Lament (Barney's Concerto)*, *Yearning for Love (Lawrence's Concerto)*, and *Trumpet in Spades (Rex's Concerto)*.

Taken as a group, these four pieces were notable in a variety of ways, but in retrospect their most remarkable collective attribute was their structural contextual clarity. In this regard they heralded a new direction in jazz composition/improvisation. They were models for many Ellington and Billy Strayhorn pieces of the early 1940s in which, almost miraculously, form and content were fused into an organic whole, stripped of all non-essentials, of all extraneous musical ballast. The point is that when we first heard pieces like *Ko-Ko*, *Warm Valley*, *Cotton Tail*, and *Blue Serge* forty years ago, it wasn't quite as "miraculous" as we then thought. For the four less known "concertos" of 1936 were the harbingers of this trend—even in spite of the considerable qualitative differences amongst them—not only as *concertante* pieces *per se*, but as simple vehicles for bringing compositional clarity and individuality into jazz form.

The point has been made that the concerto form, showcasing a single player, is antithetic to the essential spirit of jazz as a collectively improvised form of musical expression. There is some truth in this assertion, and the relegation of all but one player to secondary assignments was certainly not part of the original New Orleans concept of jazz. But by 1935 that narrower definition of jazz was no longer tenable—certainly not as a reality, although perhaps still as a historical and nostalgic point of reference. In fact it was inevitable that the increasing technical skills and musical sophistication of an Armstrong, a Cootie Williams, a Hodges, a Coleman Hawkins—and yes, a Harry James, an Artie Shaw—would lead to the notion of highlighting those skills in a specially composed setting, an exact parallel to the movement which led to the invention of the European concerto form in the eighteenth century. However, the concerto idea requires a *composer* to provide the setting, a kind of composer who has always been rare in jazz—understandably so, since formal composition was never the first premise of jazz. But Ellington was (or became) that kind of composer, and he had in his orchestra that kind of soloist. It is significant that the next major revolution in jazz, the bop movement, did not feature a concerto approach to virtuosity and the "solo" concept but instead returned essentially to the string-of-choruses format, i.e. an improvisatory, non-compositional approach. Ellington's embrace of the concerto idea is but another striking example of how, while encompassing all of the inherent principles and attitudes of jazz, he also frequently transcended them and expanded upon them. That this occurred precisely at a time when the rest of jazz was moving into the strait-jacket of the riff-cum-"call-and-response" swing formula, whose prime executor was the *arranger*, not the *composer*, and which eventually suffocated even the soloists, is another measure of Ellington's originality and vision.

Of the four mini-concertos recorded in 1936, certainly Cootie's *Echoes of Harlem* is the most significant and the most successful. The least of the four is *Trumpet in Spades*, a rather empty display piece for Rex Stewart, based on the old *Tiger Rag*. With its mindless virtuosity, akin to the florid cornet solos popular in concert band park concerts, it manages to stumble upon almost every cliché of the genre. It is no wonder André Hodeir called it "detestable".[24] Besides, the pun in the title is truly unforgivable.

Yearning for Love is at least a fine ballad-type piece with a conventional 32-bar AABA structure. And Lawrence Brown was, as ever, masterful in negotiating the twists, slides, and turns which were the intent and content of the piece (something that could not even be said for Stewart's effort). But Brown, Ellington's most versatile soloist, deserved at least a three-movement concerto to showcase his varied talents properly. Indeed, Barry Ulanov states in his Ellington biography that in live performances *Yearning* was much longer, and its recorded version of one and a half choruses—with a tacked-on too-theatrical ending—represents a truncated form of the piece.

Bigard's concerto, *Clarinet Lament*, is more successful in every way. Appropriately it draws upon familiar New Orleans materials, allowing the New Orleans-born Bigard to more or less improvise the whole performance, in contradistinction to the other three "concertos." First, there are the familiar flourishes with which the clarinetists of the old marching bands would start off a tune. Second, harmonically *Clarinet Lament* is based on *Basin Street Blues*, with its two-part form of a 12-bar blues and a 16-bar verse. On this well-trodden course Bigard makes all the right moves and several masterful strokes. The band accompanies respectfully, particularly in the final blues chorus, with its ingenious cycle-of-fifths harmonic substitutions.

But Ellington's "concerto" approach reached a temporary apex in *Echoes of Harlem*. Cootie was in perfect form, producing a well-constructed solo brimming with melodic invention and immaculately played. Of the many felicitous moments this performance offers the listener, I would single out Cootie's use of "blue notes." In the key of F the traditional "blue" notes would be the minor third (A♭), the minor seventh (E♭), and the flat fifth (C♭). But *Echoes of Harlem*, cast in an ABA form, has as its primary tonality the key of F-*minor* in the A sections, while the B section is in the close relative key of A♭ major. In F minor A♭ is no longer a blue-note alteration, the minor third being already contained in the key. Similarly the seventh (E♭) has lost its pungent "dominant" function. In other words, in F minor both notes, A♭ and E♭, lose their "blue" quality, leaving only the C♭—"blue" in *both* keys, F major and F minor. Notice, then, how Cootie uses the blue flatted fifth as a building block in structuring his solo. In the first eight bars, the C♭ appears once, in the second eight three times, and in the beautiful 10-bar transition that leads to the B section a dozen times.

This latter emphasis on the flat fifth produces a striking side effect at one point. When the key of A♭ major finally arrives—significantly neither Ellington's melody at this point nor Cootie's later improvisation on it contains any C♭s—the "major" quality of the key seems all the more emphatic. The whole previous transitional passage, with its reiterated C♭s, acts as a gigantic 10-bar

---

24. *Jazz: Evolution and Essence*, New York, 1956 This epithet is contained in a penetrating though somewhat argumentative discussion of *Concerto for Cootie*, according to Hodeir, Ellington's "*chef d'oeuvre.*"

upbeat leading-tone, resolving to the C♮ embodied in the key of A♭ major. Since those C♭s were not in the original Ellington composition but were *improvised* by Williams, the effect just described, not uncommon in nineteenth-century "classical" masterworks, is a striking example of how the collaboration between composer and player can work.

When the piece returns to F minor (after the A♭ episode), Cootie also returns to his blue flatted fifths (four times). The effect of this coda is thus not only that of a form-closing recapitulation, but a return to the nostalgic blues echoes of Harlem. Another unifying element here is the loping bass line played by Ellington and his two bassists in unison. In the final bars (Ex. 26) the piece comes to rest on a solemn "Amen" (F⁷-D♭⁹-Fm) cadence.

Ex. 26

No Greater Love is one of Isham Jones's most successful ballads, and in 1936 Ellington used it as a vehicle to compete in the ever-more crowded swing market. Despite some Lombardo-ish sax ensembles and a sentimental trumpet solo of the kind that was first coming into vogue with some of the more commercial white trumpet players, Ellington remained essentially true to his own style. Hodges, Brown, Hayes Alvis's strong bass (anticipating Jimmy Blanton's work of several years later), intricate ensemble passages played with a disciplined blend—all these were elements well designed to keep the performance firmly within the jazz mainstream. Another vocal, *It Was a Sad Night in Harlem*, features Ivie Anderson in a strong no-nonsense mood. But the performance is even more remarkable for the last half-chorus for which Billy Taylor switches to low tuba (down to the lowest pedal D), in addition to Alvis's string bass. The resultant wide-range depth of sound, from the high clarinet to the *tuba profundo*, gives these final measures an aural grandeur that is even rare among Ellingtonia.

For the rest, in 1936 there were another six pop vocals, intelligently sung by Ivie Anderson with above-average backings by the band, particularly when Brown's trombone was in evidence, which was often. And in September, Duke tried to cash in on the swing craze with three "swing" instrumentals. Even though they featured a pair of Ben Webster solos (this was the latter's second brief stint with the band before eventually joining Duke full time in 1940), some Basie-type stride piano, and some typical riffs—*de rigueur* in a swing piece—they didn't add anything significant to Ellington's creative stature. More attemps at "stepping into swing society" followed in 1937, along with the inevitable pop vocals, plus a couple of re-makes of vintage Ellington.

New East St. Louis Toodle-Oo is unfortunately typical of the latter. Little is left of the haunting 1927 original,[25] and though the harmonies of the A theme

25. See *Early Jazz*, pp. 326–29.

are "enriched" and updated under Cootie's plunger and growl interpretation—he is more respectful of Bubber Miley's original than Ellington is—the performance has an artificial quality about it that even better playing and better swing cannot amend. The arrangement seems crowded at times, and Greer's incessant "clippity-clop" temple blocks and chimes seem entirely gratuitous and foreign to the original essence of the work.

There were, of course, successes as well: pieces like *Caravan, Azure, Diminuendo and Crescendo in Blue*. And even the vocals bore watching. With an aggregation of soloists as formidable as Ellington's and with an arranger as imaginative as Duke, sooner or later there would be an enlivening solo or a briskly paced arrangement, or some highly original orchestrational touches. Take, for example, *Alabamy Home*. Apart from Ivie's sensitive singing and the spirited playing of the orchestra, there are harmonic touches which only Ellington could create, like the unexpected B♮ in the trombone (mm. 3 and 4 in Ex. 27) and the E♮ in the bass sax (mm. 7 and 8).

Ex. 27

Like Morton, Ellington was fascinated by the Caribbean and Latin strains of black music. And in Juan Tizol he had an authentic representative of those musical cultures right in his orchestra. After several previous attempts to capitalize on these talents, Tizol and Ellington collaborated in 1937 on a Latin number. And as recorded in May of that year *Caravan* became a great popular success and one of Ellington's biggest all-time hits.

Because almost no popular tune has been subjected through the years to so much vulgarization at the hands of everything from burlesque pit bands (*Caravan* became a favorite with hundreds of ecdysiasts) to hotel dance bands and muzak dis-arrangements, it is fascinating to contemplate the almost pristine purity of Duke's original rendition.[26]

The special quality of the piece is signaled in Sonny Greer's introduction of tom-toms, Chinese cymbal, Burmese gong, and bass drum, surely a first in jazz history. The composer, on valve trombone, states the sinuous theme, one of

26. If any reader has, like the author, come to shun this tune because of its endless maltreatments, he is urged to listen to the original recording (Col. C3L27); it will be a refreshing surprise.

those melodies which, once heard, cannot be gotten out of mind. What adds to
its haunting quality in this recording is the odd sound of Tizol's timbre and
delivery. As mentioned, Tizol was trained in the Italian concert/military band
tradition, which flourished throughout the nineteenth century in all of Latin
America and survives there to this day. For brass players the main characteristic
of this style is a thin-ish leathery tone and a fast throat vibrato. In *Caravan* it
provides the perfect companion to Greer's exotic drumming.

So discreetly that it goes almost unnoticed, Carney accompanies Tizol with a
simple countermelody (Ex. 28a), a harmonized variant of which is later taken
up by the full sax section in Cootie's choruses (Ex. 28b).

Ex. 28a

Ex. 28b

One of the happiest triumphs of the performance is the way the first three
solos link together into a virtually seamless entity. Notice how imperceptibly
Bigard takes over from Tizol, almost as if it was one player. Similarly as Bigard
fades out, Williams dovetails in with a note that seems to come out of nowhere,
or perhaps out of Bigard's clarinet! Further, there is a remarkable progression—
perhaps accidental (but in art nothing is *truly* accidental)—through the three
solos in the degree of jazz-ness. Tizol's first thirty-two bars[27] are simply an exposition of the theme, almost "classically" stated. In his thirty-third bar (the
bridge) he breaks out into a more jazz-like phrasing. Bigard, when he enters,
adds a few more degrees of jazz temperature, and finally Cootie peaks with a
blues-tinged solo, plunger mute and all. (Again, as in *Echoes of Harlem*, the
piece is in F minor and Cootie makes copious use of the blue fifth, C♭.)

After a sax ensemble, Carney is given ten bars (of the final sixteen), when
Tizol interrupts with a brief cadenza in the style of the initial theme, and the
piece ends on a plaintive quasi-plagal cadence (Ex. 29).

Ex. 29

27. *Caravan* comprises 64 measures (in short *alla breve* meter), the double of the usual 32-bar
structure (in long $\frac{4}{4}$ meter).

What Tchaikovsky's *Arab Dance* from the *Nutcracker Ballet* is to classical music, Tizol and Ellington's *Caravan* is to jazz. It is tragic, in view of of Ellington's lifelong ambition to write large extended works, that no one ever asked him to compose a substantial ballet comprising, like Tchaikovsky's ballets, a number of "exotic" cameo set-pieces, like *Caravan* or *Mood Indigo*.

Azure, recorded the same day as *Caravan*, might have been another movement in such a ballet. Strangely, this uniquely Ellingtonian "blue" piece was only recorded once (discounting for the moment the rather too grandiose reworkings of the fifties and sixties). *Azure* is in the lineage of pastel-colored pieces like *Mood Indigo*, but remarkably advanced (almost to the point of atonality) in its harmonic language. Immediately the mood is set by parallel triads, moving in chromatic half-steps over an undulating ostinato bass (Ex. 30a). The bitonal clash in m. 2 (Bb or A# minor and G major) symbolizes the quintessential color of the entire piece. The instrumentation is that of *Mood Indigo*, with the trumpet and trombone now in close thirds and the clarinet an octave and a fourth below in its chalumeau register (Ex. 30a).

Ex. 30a

Harmonic clashes occur frequently throughout the piece, reinforcing the basic harmonic ambivalence with bitonal spicings (as, for example, Carney's blues phrase in m. 8 of Ex. 30a), or moving further into extensions of tonality, as the weirdly chromatic trombones in Ex. 30b; or the downright *atonal* background

Ex. 30b

Ex. 30c

for Carney's solo, a somewhat remote variant of the opening four bars of the piece (Ex. 30c).[28]

The title of *Dusk on the Desert* leads one to anticipate an Ellington "blue" piece or one of his dulcet programmatic cameos. Instead it turns out to be a blandly arranged swing number, notable only for the indefatigable Carney and for one of the few solo appearances by Wallace Jones, who had replaced Whetsol early in 1937 on first trumpet.

The two-part *Diminuendo and Crescendo in Blue* was one of Duke's most ambitious efforts, again an extended-form piece, and remote from the world of popular tunes and 12-bar blues (even though based on blues changes). Perhaps it was *too* remote for public consumption. One thing was certain: the more complex full-orchestra episodes of *Diminuendo and Crescendo* were at that time beyond the performance capabilities of the 1937 Ellington band, particularly in respect to intonation. Even in the mid-forties the band's performances, though much improved, still did not fully realize the work's full potential.

28. I am intrigued by the information given in all discographies that *Azure* was arranged by Joe Lippman, for it is as Ellingtonian in style and mood as anything Duke—or Billy Strayhorn (more of him later)—ever created. It seems rather remarkable that an arranger, no matter how gifted, should be able to adopt Ellington's mature style so completely in one single opportunity as guest arranger for the Ellington orchestra. Unquestionably, Lippman was a superior talent, arranging for Benny Goodman's "Lets's Dance" radio program as a 19-year old, later arranging and playing excellent piano for Artie Shaw, Bunny Berigan, and Jimmy Dorsey. And his 1949 arrangement for Sarah Vaughan of *Black Coffee* is one of the most moving and dramatic scores ever composed to back a singer. Still, judging by the rather tame and even effete arrangements of Beiderbecke compositions Lippman arranged for Berigan in 1939, it seems inconceivable to me that *two years earlier* Lippman could have conceived an arrangement as creative, as imaginative, as advanced harmonically—in short, as masterful—as *Azure*. I have not been able to find confirmation *or* denial of Lippman's involvement with Ellington's *Azure*, and for me it remains a highly questionable matter.

Although the original performance was issued by Columbia Records in 1941, the work did not attain much currency among Ellington's pieces until 1956, when at the Newport Jazz Festival it became an enormous popular success, admittedly more as a result of Paul Gonsalves's super-charged twenty-seven interpolated choruses than for the composition itself.

Diminuendo and Crescendo in its original 1937 form was, like *Reminiscing in Tempo*, a full-fledged written *composition* with virtually no improvisation. For a jazz piece it was relatively demanding in structure and harmonically, technically complex. Though based on blues changes, *Diminuendo in Blue* featured elongated 14-bar blues choruses with 2½-bar subdivisions (Fig. 5) and modulated

Fig. 5

	A					B							C					
chord progression	I	IV	I	V	I	I	IV	I	V	I	I	VII	I	IV	I	V	I	V
number of measures	4	2½	2½	2	3	2	2	2	2	2	2	2	4	2	2	2	3	1

$$\underbrace{\qquad\qquad}_{14} \qquad \underbrace{\qquad\qquad}_{14} \qquad \underbrace{\qquad\qquad}_{14}$$

(A, B, C show the three types of phrase structures Ellington uses. The last two measures of B constitute a modulation to a new key.)

through a maze of five different keys. Moreover the modulations are often abrupt, startling shifts in tonality which were hard to digest, both for the players and the audience. After the initial key of E♭, the work modulates to G for two choruses, then to C, then to a highly chromatically altered A♭, finally coming to rest on D♭ as the overall *diminuendo* of the piece reaches its quiescent resting point. As a corollary to these somewhat frenetic key changes, the orchestration and phrase structure are unprecedentedly fragmented for jazz. Thematic and accompanimental materials are traded around between choirs of the orchestra in 2- and 4-bar sequences (or even shorter). This is compounded by an analogously abrupt exchange of unison lines with complex harmonic phrases. Whereas in earlier pieces Ellington might have constructed dramatic changes of texture *between* choruses, here he was doing so *within* chorus units, some of which were already complex in asymmetric subdivisions. Such relatively disjunct continuity was virtually unheard of in jazz in the mid-thirties, and it was not exactly conducive to easy finger-snapping listening. Moreover, for the sheer amount of harmonic, textural, and motivic activity in the opening measures of *Diminuendo*, the thematic material was not striking or strong enough to support or justify such complexity. Perhaps "motivic" rather than "thematic" would be a more accurate term to describe what we perceive as the melodic material. The motivic kernels, as show in Ex. 31a and b, are thrice-familiar riff clichés, which can neither be

Ex. 31a

Ex. 31b

identified exclusively with Ellington as composer nor elevated to the status of "theme." Indeed, Ellington does not develop these fragments thematically, although references to the opening motivic cells occur from time to time in subsequent choruses.

Thus the dichotomy between the innocuousness of the melodic-thematic material and the comparatively sophisticated and perhaps overly complex fragmentation of underlying component material constitutes a weakness of the work, although an interesting risk-taking one. The necessary equilibrium between horizontal (melodic) and vertical (harmonic) elements is not achieved. And both critics and audiences were confounded and reacted either apathetically or negatively.

Crescendo in Blue is, of course, the opposite counterpart to *Diminuendo*, starting quietly with a motive whose main ingredient is the melodic cell of Ex. 31a, building inexorably and gradually to a climax, not only in dynamic levels but by exploiting the full textural, timbral, and registral resources of the orchestra. Again there are some 14-bar phrases—really twelve bars plus a 2-bar extension—but this time, in *bolero* fashion, the piece stays in E♭, i.e. no modulations. Interestingly, on the 1937 recording the dynamic pacing of *Crescendo* was handled much better than that of *Diminuendo*, manifestation of a trait common to virtually all musicians in that it seems to be easier to control and pace crescendos than diminuendos. Perhaps this is because crescendos are inherently more exciting—more "goal-oriented"—than diminuendos. Be that as it may, the crescendo build-up was a formula which the more skillful swing bands were to develop into a veritable cliché. The Bennie Moten band of Kansas City had already successfully experimented with the crescendo form (as in *Blue Room* or *Prince of Wails*). That, plus the riff pieces which were coming out of Kansas City—particularly via the Basie band (Moten's successor)—were likely stimuli in Ellington's mind for his *Crescendo in Blue*. He was to perfect this idea and re-create it in an even more interesting way in *Ko-Ko*, the 1940 Ellington masterpiece. Thus *Crescendo* is, apart from its own merits, an important stepping stone in the direction of *Ko-Ko*.

In *Diminuendo and Crescendo in Blue* we are still dealing with essentially a swing-era riff piece, particularly as performed on the 1937 recording, with its two-beat rhythmic feeling and rather stiffly played figures. By the time of *Ko-Ko*, Ellington had elevated his style and musical conception to a much higher plateau. And that 1940 band, especially with Jimmy Blanton and Ben Webster, had learned to swing in a manner that could do justice to the type of material contained in *Diminuendo and Crescendo*. It had also gained the technical control to perform its configurations more correctly and with better intonation, even if still somewhat stiffly, as recordings of 1940s' Ellington broadcasts of *Diminuendo and Crescendo in Blue* testify.

Ellington began 1938 with a recording significantly entitled *Steppin' into Swing Society*. Indeed, Ellington was succumbing temporarily to the no longer avoidable commercial pressures resulting from the nation-wide swing craze. Swing was making headlines everywhere, and Ellington was simply considered part of the swing movement, whether he liked it or not. His performances were called "swing concerts"; college campuses began to take note of the Ellington band; and as the swing craze invaded Hollywood, Duke and his men were presented as leaders in the field. Suddenly the depressing years of the mid-thirties gave way to a new sense of prestige for Duke. For not only was he considered a leader in the vanguard of swing and jazz but, as a veteran bandleader of a dozen years or more, Duke now found himself garnering a level of respect from audiences as well as colleagues that was new in jazz history.

In truth, *Steppin' into Swing Society* was new not only in name and implication, but in substance as well. There is once again a new spirit in the orchestra, a fresh feeling which manifests itself in a variety of ways. There is the added big-toned voice of Harold "Shorty" Baker in the trumpet section, a new springy lift in the ensemble playing, a confidence not heard in the band for some time and exemplified best by Carney's ebulliently imperious solo, and an overall fresh sense of swing and momentum, nourished by Greer's inspired brush work. It was as if a curtain had been rung down on the agonizing frustrations of the past thirty-six months. The struggle, the torment, and the anguish one hears in *Diminuendo and Crescendo in Blue* and in *Reminiscing in Tempo* (as well as in some of Duke's compositional failures) seemed now to give way to a new clarity and economy, a new creative thrust. The blockage of the past years, whatever its reasons, seemed to have been overcome.

Steppin' sets the tone and level for the entire next period in Ellington's development, leading eventually to the masterpieces of the early forties. One hears in *Steppin'* premonitions of such future classics as *Never No Lament* and *Jack the Bear*. At the same time the performance also contains respectful nods to the past: the quintuplet descending figure of *Ain't Misbehavin'* is assayed again, but simplified into sextuplets; the bitonal harmonic shifts of *Azure* reappear in a new guise (Ex. 32). But perhaps most symbolic of the new forward/upward surge in the band is Billy Taylor's stretching his walking bass lines registrally up to an unprecedented high E♭.

Ex. 32

Steppin' was a piece written for the new *Cotton Club Parade of 1938*. But that show's most stunning orchestral excursion must have been *Braggin' in Brass*, a tour de force of unsurpassed brass virtuosity, still making players today shake their heads in disbelief. The basis for the piece is the old standard set of changes used in *Tiger Rag*, which, we'll recall, Ellington had just revived for the umpteenth time two years earlier to fashion a virtuoso display piece for Rex Stewart. Taking up this general idea once again in *Braggin' in Brass*, Ellington composed a whole new first section which featured his three trombonists in "hocket style" at such amazing speed that one's initial reaction is, in fact, disbelief.[29]

Each trombonist has one note assigned to him in a descending pattern (Ex. 33a), the composite of which (in piano reduction) looks as follows (Ex. 33b). The fact is that this passage was played at a brisk tempo of ♩= ca. 316 and that the triadic groupings form a 3/8 pattern (bracketed ⌐⌐ in Ex. 33b), overlaid on the basic 4/4 meter, this cross-accentuation making the overall result even more stunning. Lawrence Brown's blistering solo later on is another measure of this great artist's near-perfect control of ideas and technique.

Ex. 33a

Ex. 33b

Skrontch (also spelled *Scrounch*) was the Cotton Club Parade's big dance finale, in which Ivie Anderson exhorted everyone to learn this new dance. The song practiced what it preached, featuring an unexpectedly strong accent on the fourth beat (Ex. 34).

Ex. 34

skrontch   on   the   fourth beat;   skrontch

Also written for the Cotton Club show was the fine torch song *I Let a Song Go Out of My Heart*. It was not only a superb vehicle for the artistry of Johnny Hodges, but in its last twelve sumptuously velvety measures, it prophetically predated and presaged a number of other fine moments in subsequent jazz history: Ellington's own 1940 hit *Don't Get Around Much Anymore*; Glenn Miller's *In the Mood*'s fade-away ending; and, much later, the sound that Gil Evans made into the hallmark of the late 1940s' Claude Thornhill orchestra.

When Ellington signed with Irving Mills's new record label, Master, in the

29. "Hocket style" refers to a basically polyphonic concept of performing in which a total pattern is created out of single interlocking notes or note groupings. It is a centuries-old European tradition, going back to the Ars Nova and early Renaissance periods, but exists as well in such diverse musics as Trinidad steel drum bands, West African ivory horn ensembles, and Christian hand-bell ringers.

mid-thirties, part of the agreement was to revive in updated versions some of Ellington's early successes. Accordingly, Duke expanded his 1927 *Black and Tan Fantasy* to two sides for the Brunswick label, fortunately retaining most of its original mood and character, while at the same time taking advantage of the new talents in the orchestra not present eleven years earlier. The major additions were solos by Bigard and Carney, Miley's theme and wah-wah/growl solos having become the exclusive domain of Cootie Williams. Among other new highlights were the somber introductions (to both sides) by the two bassists, Alvis and Taylor, playing in fifths. Miley's first solo was now enriched by the growling of the entire brass section, although in the main Williams preserved the basic outlines of Miley's original work.[30] With more space to stretch out, Cootie added an exemplary chorus which included a long-held swelling high B♭, a standard, but always thrilling attention-getting device, ever since Armstrong first used it in *West End Blues* in 1928. Bigard follows suit a little later with a spectacularly long single-note glissando, stretched agonizingly slowly in one breath—nearly forty seconds long—across ten slow bars, traversing only a major third (D♭ to F). At first immobile for a long time, Bigard slides the note up almost imperceptibly, perfectly fitting the *degree* of glissando to its intended duration.

As unsuccessful (in my view) as the re-composition of *East St. Louis Toodle-Oo* had been ten months earlier, the new *Black and Tan Fantasy* is a remarkable example of Ellington's ability to revitalize an older work with an infusion of new ideas and talents, whilst still preserving the essence of the original. It was also important as an early example of *jazz as repertory*—that is, the idea that certain *kinds* of jazz compositions possess a life beyond their initial moment of creation and can, with judicious respect for the original, be perpetuated in new guises without sacrificing their initial conception.

The next three selections, recorded in February 1938—*Riding on a Blue Note, Lost in Meditation, The Gal from Joe's*—were solo vehicles for Williams, Tizol, and Hodges respectively. Williams in a poised, fairly straight muted solo stretches for the first time to a high F (then considered the new outer range of the trumpet and now virtually mandatory, ever since Armstrong's consistent use of the highest register, starting in 1930).

Lost in Meditation, introduced by Tizol in an impeccably restrained manner to create the appropriate *meditative* mood, features—surprisingly—later in the piece a fully intact version of the famous Glenn Miller 1939 reed section sound (with clarinet lead)—note well, one year before Miller! On the other hand, *The Gal from Joe's* was a minor-key riff number by Hodges, thematically rather weak, but nonetheless easy grist for Hodges's creative mill.

---

30. The solo trumpet passages in *Black and Tan Fantasy* are among the most striking examples in all of jazz of how an original contribution to a piece was played virtually unaltered by a succession of players over a period of many decades. These "solos" were *not* improvised, falling instead into that category deemed to be absolutely integral to the composition, with very little likelihood of improving upon their original. When Cootie left the Ellington band, Ray Nance took over Miley's solos in *Black and Tan*, as did Cat Anderson when Ray Nance left, and so on. The point is that, even as memorized, these solos sounded fresh and spontaneous in the hands of all these fine players.

The next clutch of recordings exhibits again a breadth of style normal for Ellington but very rare for other bands. We have another exotic Tizol-Ellington collaboration, *Pyramid*—a bit of a hybrid this time, in which the sum of its parts did not quite add up to a balanced totality. The "mysterious near-East" is presented by Tizol on muted valve trombone, with Ellington himself playing the rhythmic ostinato on a home-made hand drum. Without preparation Carney bursts into the tranquil scene with a brief jazz statement. A suave trombone trio in shifting D♭ and C major harmonies follows, but that mood is shattered by a tawdry full-orchestra section sounding very much like something left over from some big-theatre vaudeville act. Then, almost as in one of those 1930s' travelogues, with the sun setting over the horizon, the piece fades away into the distance: two muted trombones over Ellington's hand drums, Brown holding a beautifully sustained high C, and Tizol solemnly intoning his winding camel-route theme.

When My Sugar Walks Down the Street is another discreet bow to the pop market of the day, with birds going "tweet tweet" and all. But no matter how ordinary the material, the Ellington band, with its tasteful rhythm section (especially Greer) and array of virtually infallible soloists, always managed to transcend the material's inherent limitations.

Rose of the Rio Grande is one of Lawrence Brown's most distinguished statements. As anyone who heard Brown in person knows, this was one of his memorized solos, perfectly organized and planned out, which became an instant favorite with Ellington audiences. The point, again, is that memorizing a jazz solo is neither bad, as some purist jazz critics have tried to maintain, nor especially good, as has been argued by those who feel the need to "dignify" jazz by equating it with "classical" music, but rather that, *being* memorized—Brown played virtually the same solo when I first heard him in person six years later in 1944—it always sounded like a fresh improvisation.

The light-hearted *Dinah's in a Jam* (April 1938) starts out with Rex Stewart's fleet-fingered exposition, as a proto-bop small-band piece of the kind that Goodman's small groups, Shaw's Gramercy Five, John Kirby's Sextet, and Roy Eldridge's Quintet were popularizing in the late thirties and early forties. Even though the performance does not fulfill all its early promise, it remains a fetching Henderson-style riff number, notable for its economy. Although for full band, the many unison lines, the avoidance of massive block harmonies, and the light two-beat bounce, all contrive to keep the performance in an essentially small-group conception.

To represent the pop-song/novelty-tune category, Ellington tossed off a not particularly inspired nor successful update of the old vaudeville hokum-and-jive routines, but this time playing on a swing-conscious generation's awareness of the black musicians' "hip" lingo. "*You Gave Me the Gate, and I'm Swingin'*," proclaims Ivie Anderson. Its compromises with tried-and-true popular-success formulas show even in Rex Stewart's (perhaps tongue-in-cheek) rendition of a typical Harry James type of solo, the kind with which the Goodman band was burning up the countryside about this time.

How deeply expressive a vehicle the romantic ballad had become for the Ellington orchestra is exemplified in *A Gypsy Without a Song*. A fine tune, the result of a three-way collaboration between Mack Gordon, Duke, and Tizol, it is finally Ellington and the players' contribution that makes *Gypsy* a masterpiece of period nostalgia. The fascinations begin almost immediately, when in the first chorus Ellington, like a master illusionist, extracts subtleties of color from his orchestral palette that very few (if any other) musical imaginations have envisioned. The melody in the first sixteen bars is split between two trombonists: Tizol on valve trombone, Brown on slide—but so similarly muted that on a perfunctory listening one would assume the presence of only one player.[31] This sleight-of-hand trick is managed by interpolating two bars of open-horn trumpet by Cootie Williams (in a decidedly unballadic mood) between the two trombonists, thus neatly disguising the seam where Tizol's and Brown's 8-bar phrases join. Further, the subtle intensification of melancholia that Brown achieves by his refined use of the slide (over Tizol's "straight" version) not only exploits in a perfectly disarming way the basic idiomatic difference between the two types of trombones, valve and slide, but uses this physical difference as a subtle variant in expression. It also seems to me that Ellington creates the illusion of having extended his instrumental resources by conjuring up a muted French horn (Tizol) and the soulful *portamenti* of a cello (Brown), even through obviously neither of those instruments was present in Duke's orchestra.

This wizardy is maintained in the bridge (mm. 17 through 24), where unique saxophone voicings (with Carney, as always, contributing most of the uniqueness) serve not only to fully exploit the reed timbres but to generate a further intensification of mood. By scoring the four saxophones in their uppermost register, a plaintive quality is achieved which functions as the perfect foil for the return to the A part (of the standard 32-bar song AABA form).

This amazing bit of musical legerdemain, achieving as it does a maximum of contrasting subtleties with a minimum of means, is as good an occasion as any in this study to point out what a master of form Ellington was. The above-described first chorus of *Gypsy* can serve as a perfect illustration. The degrees of intensification already alluded to can be graphically presented as in Figure 6 (omitting, for purposes of simplification, Cootie's brief interjections at the end of A and A[1]):

Fig. 6

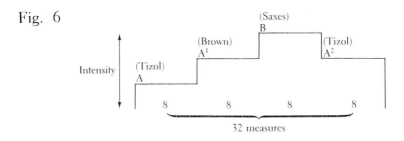

31. Indeed, in Stanley Dance's notes for the Volume II reissue of Ellington Columbia records (C3L39), that very assumption is erroneously made.

But this four-part form with its three strata of intensity is a perfect jazz analogue to classical music's sonata form. A corresponds to the exposition, A^1 to
the second subject (sometimes derived from or related to the first), B corresponds
to the development section, and A^2 to the recapitulation.[32] We perceive the
gradual rise through A^1 to B and the corollary return to A^2 in exactly the same
manner in which a sonata form proceeds from the tonic through an intensified
development section to the dominant, which then resolves—relaxing from the
accumulated tension—back to the tonic.

Moreover, in Ellington's casting of *Gypsy*, this form perfection operates on
two levels: the small form, i.e. the chorus structure (as in Fig. 6), and the large
form, i.e. the entire piece—the one contained within the other. For if we take
the first chorus as analogous to a classical exposition (calling it A), then Hodges's
sovereign solo, representing by virtue of its improvisational character both an
embellishment and intensification of the original material, is the A^1 of our overall form, a clear step upward in the ascent towards the climactic "dominant"
phase. But note how even here, *within* Hodges's solo—so economical, so self-
contained, and yet so moving—there are two strata of intensity. His first eight
bars are basically restricted to the lower octave and a half of the alto saxophone's
range, the highest note being g^1 with only a momentary foray up to b^{b1} in the
fifth bar. But his second eight bars reach well into the upper range (g^2), thus
providing a secondary plateau of intensification on the climb towards B.

The bridge of the second chorus is given to Cootie Williams. Three elements
contribute to make this the entire composition's highest point of tension, from
which the final resolution must then flow. These are 1) that the trumpet represents an inevitable acoustical intensification over the alto saxophone; 2) that from
the point of view of harmonic analysis the bridge in a traditional 32-bar song
comprises the maximum point of harmonic/functional intensification, i.e. the
point most removed from the tonic and therefore crying for a return to it; 3) that
Cootie in this particular instance, perhaps intuitively sensing the form implications here pointed out, delivers a cornerstone solo of only eight bars which is
remarkable for its inner power and depth of expression—the perfect statement
for that "dominant" phase of the overall form (Fig. 7).

Fig. 7

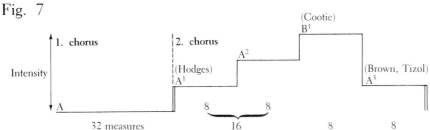

32. The fact that Ellington was probably totally unaware of such an analogy to classical form in no
way makes the point less valid. That which exists—whether by conscious effort or some other partly
or wholly innate process—is a proper subject for analysis. What counts is the phenomenon itself,
since we do not as yet know enough about the anatomy of the creative process and what combinations and degrees of consciousness, as opposed to unconscious or subconscious factors, produce the
final result.

From this point on the piece can only resolve back (and down) to the tonic. But even here Ellington's imagination is still not exhausted. He now draws into service *both* trombonists in duet: Brown on the melody, with Tizol weaving languorous embellishments around it, as an ingeniously subtle variant of the A sections in the first chorus. And how wondrously the tension relaxes at the return of the A^2 section! Here the specific harmonies of the song play an important functional role. In relation to the basic key of G major, the bridge—consisting of a repeated sequence of F^7 and D^{-9} (the latter in first inversion)—sets up what is called "in classical" terminology a "secondary dominant.' The $E\flat$, contained in both the F^7 and D^{-9} chords, gives the bridge a decidedly minor tonality (which Cootie's fine ear exploits magnificently). When A^2 returns with its unequivocal G *major*, lifting, as it were, the minor "curtain" temporarily lowered during the bridge, the effect is one of complete relaxation of all tension. The music literally smiles. (This effect can be expressed in simple harmonic terms in the following scheme, Ex. 35, with the cross-relationship between the $E\flat$s in chords *a*, *b* and the B in *c* defining the essential progression.

Ex. 35

It has often been said that "form *is* content." And perhaps, among the hundred or so Ellington illustrations of this axiom, none is more felicitous than his rendition of *A Gypsy Without a Song*. It provides a glimpse into the composer's workshop and shows how, with consummate instinctive ease, a composer like Ellington solved the riddles of form *and* content. For the one serves the other. *Gypsy* can hardly be relegated to the realm of mere intellectual form constructivism, for its expressive contact is indisputable. It provides an unequivocal demonstration of how a perfect form and the highest level of expressivity are not only not incompatible, but are necessary concomitants to great art. Like children's toy boxes, the small parts of the form of *Gypsy* fit into the larger parts, until the whole structure is fully accomplished. That is mastery of an order that transcends style and idiom, and—as Ellington and a few others have shown—is as attainable in the realm of jazz as in the sacred precincts of eighteenth- and nineteenth-century classical music.

The next two years (mid-1938 to mid-1940) constitute an interesting period in the development of Ellington and his orchestra. Though recording fifty-odd sides during this time and acquiring the services of Jimmy Blanton, Ben Webster, and Billy Strayhorn, the Ellington band settled into a period of relative creative stasis. It was a generally stable period, during which the swing craze reached its peak— epitomized for the general public by Goodman's 1938 Carnegie Hall concert and the emergence of the Glenn Miller band in 1939—and even Ellington was held in the grip of swing's pervasive influence.

This took some strange forms. Before the two years were out, Cootie Williams was to be seduced away in late 1940 by the blandishments of Goodman's success and by what is known among sidemen as the "bandleader fever." But even before he departed, Cootie's work had begun to sound more and more like the leading white trumpet stars idolized by millions: Harry James and Ziggy Elman. In self-defense Ellington turned increasingly to his other major trumpet soloist, Rex Stewart.

Almost as if to counterbalance Cootie's departure and to ensure the element of swing as an integral component of the band's rhythmic language, Blanton and Webster were acquired. Blanton and Taylor worked together a while, but in late 1939 Taylor left; while Webster, who had worked with Ellington sporadically as early as 1935, brought the sax section up to five-man strength.

As mentioned, the Ellington orchestra seemed to be in a kind of stylistic holding period, for, with some notable exceptions (like *Blue Light, Subtle Lament*), the compositions and arrangements catered to the dicta of the Swing Era. In pieces like *Buffet Flat, Old King Dooji, Pussy Willow, Weely, Tootin' Through the Roof, Way Low*—as well as the numerous Ivie Anderson vocals (*La De Doody Do*, for example)—Ellington appeared to have restrained his creative energies somewhat, content to husband his resources and to ride out the competitive commercial pressures exerted by the sudden mass proliferation of swing bands and the American public's embrace of swing as its national music. Ellington's swing/riff pieces, appropriately decked out with all the latest swing stereotypes of unison sax lines (*Old King Dooji*), repetition-laden arranged ensembles (*Dooji, Pussy Willow, Way Low*); overplaying of the drum parts (*Way Low, Weely*) perhaps to deal with a public reared on Gene Krupa's exhibitionism; the final trumpet duets of *Tootin'* designed to outdo Glenn Miller's *In the Mood* flourishes—all these reflected the constraints of the marketplace. It is therefore all the more startling to find Ellington's muse erupting in early 1940 in a creative surge, which was to sustain itself for at least four years—from *Ko-Ko* and *Cotton Tail* to *Black, Brown and Beige*—in a burst of creativity unprecedented in Ellington's career and probably in jazz altogether.

Sometimes the tie-in to the marketplace was quite direct and unmistakable. For example, in 1938 a host of dancers, song-pluggers, and music publishers tried to import to America a Cockney dance step, the Lambeth Walk. As one writer put it, the dance "died on its feet," Ellington's *Lambeth Walk* remaining as the only testimony of its existence.

While this and other Ellington ephemera of the period—like *Hip Chic*, the peppy *Jazz Potpourri*, the rather patched together *T.T. on Toast*—represent the valleys and low foothills amongst a number of creative peaks, we constantly are reminded that even Ellington's lesser efforts are superior to most of the better work of his contemporaries. His are very high-lying valleys in a creative range from which one views the others well below. For no matter how second-rate the material, either by Ellington or by others, he and his players always find at least one distinctive or exciting element to contribute, transforming such material into unmistakable Ellingtonia. Whether it is Hodges or Carney or Brown (indeed the many types of Brown's trombone) or Duke's harmonically exotic and ever more daring piano introductions and codas (hear, for example, *Mighty Like a Blues*), there is always a transforming and elevating touch. Most revelatory in this regard is Cootie Williams. All he has to do is burst in with his tightly muted plunger and growl (as on *Lambeth Walk*), and any Brill Building trifle is instantly transfigured into pure Ellington.

Mighty Like a Blues (September 1938) was jazz critic-writer-encyclopedist-entrepeneur-pianist-composer-arranger Leonard Feather's first compositional effort to be recorded in America. It is to the English-born twenty-three-year-old Feather's credit that he captured Ellington's special "mood" piece style so tellingly. It is a "pretty" piece, featuring low-register Bigard against warm saxophone colors (such as only Ellington's orchestra could produce), and a Williams open-horn solo that rises out of the velvety saxophones like a beacon light in a misty fog. Ellington contributed a brief intro and coda (thematically related) of the distinctive type he was contributing to virtually every piece during this late 1930s period. They were often harmonically spicy, peppered with dissonances that must have struck audiences as disconcerting. In the intro and coda to Feather's opus, Ellington's dissonances derive from a clash between the blue minor third, vigorously projected in the left hand, with the major third in the more softly played right hand—again a creative touch that simply no one else in jazz (even Earl Hines) would have produced, here lavished on a "mere" 2-bar introduction and tag ending.

As mentioned, Ellington began to favor Rex Stewart with more and more solo space, obviously keen on exploiting Stewart's totally individual and exotic way of playing the cornet (not the trumpet). Since the mid-thirties Stewart had been experimenting with his own updating of the old King Oliver "freak" trumpet style. But unlike Oliver, Miley, and Cootie, who all used various mutes and plungers to mutate the trumpet's (or cornet's) normal sound, Stewart often did it without mutes, by using various half-valve positions unique to piston-operated brass instruments. Although in later years Stewart's use of these effects became excessive—often mere caricatures with which to titillate audiences—when used creatively and integrally, they could be a striking enrichment of the orchestral palette. And Ellington knew how to seize such an opportunity.

Stewart debuted this technique in late 1938 with a piece originally called *Twits and Twerps*—a fair onomatopoetic rendering of Stewart's unorthodox sound world—later retitled *Boy Meets Horn*. It became Stewart's big solo vehicle, lasting well into the 1940s—light fare which audiences just ate up. It could have been called "Concerto No. 2 for Rex" to follow the other "concertos" of 1937.

By the same token, *Slap Happy* could have been called "Concerto for Carney." Brightly orchestrated to contrast with Carney's dark baritone and loping triplet configurations, and peppered with unusual harmonic twists and turns, it also featured a great Nanton solo—a player who for some reason had not been soloistically heard from on records for almost a year.

Ellington's "mood" or "serenade" type of piece was represented several times during these years, most creatively in the magnificent *Blue Light*, *Subtle Lament*, and *Serenade to Sweden*, less so in *Stevedore's Serenade* and *A Blues Serenade*.

Prelude to a Kiss, one of the high moments in the 1938–39 period must be counted as one of Ellington's finest ballads, although too sophisticated in its weaving melody and chromatic harmonies to gain wide public acceptance. Curiously, Ellington recorded it not with its lyrics but in an instrumental version which features typically sentimental celloistic trombone statements by Brown, a slightly uncertain Wallace Jones, and Duke (along with a few of his favorite fluttery arpeggio piano clichés) in some surprisingly daring out-of-context harmonic diversions.

It is ironic that Ellington's success as a writer of popular songs was curiously limited, though hardly for lack of trying. Indeed, starting with *Sophisticated Lady* in 1932, Ellington attempted time and time again to write hit songs, popular ballads that might compete with the Gershwins, Berlins, Kerns, Cole Porters, Victor Youngs. And in fact Ellington did contribute tellingly to America's popular song literature: one need only think of *Sophisticated Lady, In a Sentimental Mood, Solitude, Prelude to a Kiss, Do Nothin' Till You Hear from Me, Don't Get Around Much Anymore, I'm Beginning To See the Light, Don't You Know I Care, I Got It Bad (and That Ain't Good), Satin Doll.* However (with the possible exception of the last named), these songs never achieved the popularity of a *Star Dust,* a *Summertime, Body and Soul, Tea for Two,* perhaps not even that of a *Jersey Bounce* or *Chattanooga Choo Choo,* clearly much lesser creations. The reasons are several-fold. One, Ellington was not by the nature of his talent a natural melody writer the way Berlin, Kern, and Gershwin were. By that I do not mean that Ellington could not (did not) write some superb melodies, for he certainly did, but rather that writing tunes was not his primary calling, not his real forte. That lay more in his superior harmonic and timbral sensibility. With one or two exceptions, Ellington had to work fairly hard to achieve his best melodies. Moreover, Ellington's melodies were almost always shaped and profoundly influenced by his harmonic ear. Unlike, say, an Irving Berlin or a Vincent Youmans, who could punch out tunes that could virtually stand alone *as pure melody,* regardless of their harmonic underpinning, Ellington's tunes generally arose out of their harmonies. Indeed, often enough they are the top notes of a harmonic progression, then filled in as the need arose with passing tones, or altered through octave transpositions.

Secondly, his predilections in the melodic realm lay in the direction of sinuous, large-interval, wide-ranging lines, that took a certain sophistication and skill to sing *and* to appreciate. Not every singer can negotiate the twisting, winding contours of *Prelude to a Kiss,* for example:

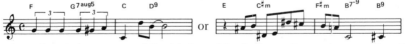

Nor does the pitch content of *Sophisticated Lady* lie easily on the ears, bereft of its harmonic base:

The initial F moving to G$^\flat$, a minor ninth higher, then descending to a G *natural* (!)—this does not constitute the kind of simple conjunct triadic melodic

motion that makes for easy mass appeal. In short, Ellington's melodic imagination was too searching, too sophisticated to settle for some simplistic step-by-step
tune. But by ranging further than most tunesmiths could possibly venture, Ellington almost automatically cut himself off from a certain kind of immediate
popular appeal. His finest songs are much more in the realm of art song than
pop tune, their jazz antecedents notwithstanding.

Thirdly, even when Ellington's tunes themselves were simple enough for mass
consumption, he would invariably support or adorn these melodies with such
sophisticated harmonies that, again, the average listener would be left aurally far
behind.

It is paradoxical that, save for *Satin Doll*, Ellington's greatest "popular tune"
successes with the general public—*Mood Indigo* and *Take the A Train*—were
two *instrumental* pieces, originally without lyrics, in other words not really *songs*
in the truest sense; and one of these, *A Train*, was not written by Ellington but
by Strayhorn.[33]

One approaches a title such as *Battle of Swing* with some trepidation, but this
late 1938 swing exercise rises above the norm—and its title. Indeed, it points
brightly to the future: 1) to bop—with its unusual zig-zag figures, perky brisk
tempo, and translation of the 12-bar blues into a distant stylistic world; and 2)
to Ellington's own *Cotton Tail*, with its daring unison lines. Like so much of
Ellington, it also looks back, this time to the baroque *concerto grosso* concept. A
solo quartet of clarinet, alto sax, cornet, and valve trombone is pitted against the
ripieno orchestra, the former always in harmony, the latter virtually always in
unison (or octave unisons). Of the many delights this performance offers, perhaps the most striking are Rex Stewart's pixie-ish solos[34] and, in the fifth chorus,
Tizol's leaping *Till Eulenspiegel* figure (Ex. 36).

Ex. 36

In another vein, there is the lovely *Serenade to Sweden*, composed in the
spring of 1939 during the Ellington orchestra's second European tour. Here
Ellington is at peace with the world, his fantastic reception by Swedish audiences
having seen to that. And all is at peace within the work: melody, harmony,
rhythm, timbre, all flow together into an amalgam that is at once uniquely
Ellingtonian and yet so indebted to the equally unique contributions of his players. In fact, rendering the theme in notation (Ex. 37) reveals that it consists of a
lovely, quite original harmonic progression, supporting an unpretentious se-

33. For a further discussion of Ellington as song writer, see Alec Wilder's fine account in *American
Popular Song* (New York: Oxford University Press, 1972), pp. 412–16.
34. Stewart's playing on this and other sides of the period, and the whole bop-ish cast of *Battle of
Swing*, make one think that the young Dizzy Gillespie must have been listening. This is neither to
downgrade the influence of Eldridge (Dizzy's idol) in his 1937 records nor of his friend Charlie
Shavers (with the 1938 Kirby Sextet), but merely to suggest that Dizzy's clownish trumpet humor
may not have been entirely unaware of similar traits in Stewart.

Ex. 37

quential melody. But it cannot begin to give an idea of the true feel of this music, which results—as in all great jazz—much more from the *interpretation* and individual realization of the notes than the notes themselves.

It is worth reminding ourselves that the first four bars of *Serenade* were first conceived and used by Ellington in 1934 in the introduction to his version of *Moonglow* (see earlier). In the tradition of Bach and Handel who, like Ellington, were extraordinaryily prolific composers and for most of their lives composing on command, Duke frequently borrowed from his own earlier works. Sometimes this would take the form of direct lifting from previous compositions, or—as I have pointed out in numerous cases—the reworking and refining of previously initiated ideas or concepts. Ellington's *Moonglow* arrangement not only furnished part of the melody for *Serenade to Sweden*, but it also provided the coda for *Concerto for Cootie*. What is fascinating is how the somewhat innocuous introduction to *Moonglow* is turned into one of Ellington's most felicitous melodies. It is as if a master carpenter were to begin a new cabinet with some previously discarded scrap of wood found lying on his workbench and transform it into a work of art.

This time (on *Serenade to Sweden*) Wallace Jones is in fine mettle, followed by Cootie's controlled almost purring growls, and the ever-reliable Carney adds his husky embellishments. But it is Brown who most abundantly captures the essence of the piece in a ravishingly sentient solo, which defies notation and possibly description as well.

One of the happiest and most exuberant of the 1938–39 recordings is *The Sergeant Was Shy*, another reworking of the old *Bugle Call Rag*. *Sergeant* is justly celebrated for its virtuoso succession of "breaks." Bigard is the first to burst in with a high-register flourish, as shrill as any early morning parade-ground drill whistle. Later the trombones and trumpets, answered by unhappy sax moans, deliver two successive breaks which are the epitome of brash, brassy drill-sergeant rhetoric (Ex. 38a, b). And finally Nanton does a hilarious but subtle take-off on a bad-mouthing oafish sergeant.

These bits of "program music" are firmly contained within Ellington's well-structured overall form, neatly enclosed between interrelated introduction and coda. The introduction is a good example of Ellington's sure compositional hand. Walking bass and unison clarinets begin in B♭ minor, drums and trombones are

added after four bars (with raised seventh chords ), muted

Ex. 38a

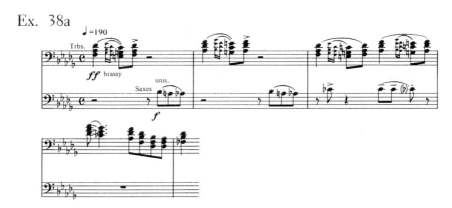

Ex. 38b

trumpets are piled on top of that , and in mm. 13 to 16 a 4-bar clarinet trill is added. (Figure 8 provides a graphic outline of this introduction.)

Fig. 8

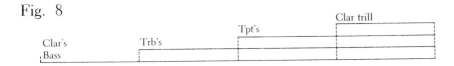

Subtle Lament (March 1939), another exploration of the *Mood Indigo* vein, was at the same time an unmistakable forerunner of the hauntingly beautiful 1940 *Dusk*, trombone trios, harmonies, and all. The orchestra had by now edged very close to the quality of the great 1940s' works. The "Ellington effect" was in full flowering: every harmonic touch, every daub of color, every timbral nuance used to maximum expressiveness. Stewart is ready with a disarmingly simple solo, poignant, longing, questioning—as he fluctuates between the major and minor seventh (mm. 3 and 7 of his solo) (Ex. 39a). His final four bars are indescribably beautiful using the simplest of means—only three notes—but heightened in their expressiveness by Stewart's half-valve colorations.

Bigard, at his best in these "mood" settings, washes his supple liquid tone against muted sustained brass backgrounds. The pungent harmonic clashes that result are a perfect realization (Ex. 39b) of the work's title, as is the "lonely

Ex. 39a

Ex. 39b

wandering" of Taylor's bass. Moreover this bass line and the harmonies it supports turn out to be a blues, but surely one of the most ingenious and beautiful variants these traditional changes have ever undergone (Ex. 39c).

Ex. 39c

Ellington's mastery and fertile imagination are such that he finds additional interesting ways of varying these already striking blues changes in each of the four successive choruses. The second chorus takes up the 2-bar structuring of the theme and divides the twelve bars into six 2-bar phrases, alternating Duke's piano and the trombone trio. Each of the three trombone passages reaches for a successively higher top note: F in the first, F♯ in the second, and finally a resolving G in the third. (Ex. 39d). One hears this both as giving each phrase its individual characteristic ("minor" in the first, "major" in the second, and a pure triad in the third), but also as an overall across-the-twelve-bars ascending progression.

Ex. 39d

How ingeniously Stewart's succeeding solo, toying with these same notes F and F♯ (Ex. 39a), develops and complements the second chorus! But even that doesn't seem to have exhausted Ellington's capacity to explore the subtle harmonic ambiguities of his theme further. For in the fourth chorus, given over (again) to a trombone trio, the vacillating quality of the harmonies is pushed still further, even affecting the bass, who now teeters and totters on A♭s and F♯s, teasingly encircling the tonic G which our ears so badly want to hear. All—trombones and bass—finally resolve to a bright G major, leading then to the already mentioned major/minor (again that harmonic ambiguity) of Bigard's solo.

There are several fascinating and not entirely explicable mysteries connected with the two takes of *Subtle Lament*. To begin with, until very recently it was not even known that a second take existed and that one of the two takes contains a horrendous gaffe by Bigard in his last side-ending solo. Columbia Records' two-volume six-LP archive series on Ellington, as well as Rust's discography, list only one master (11-998-1). But the Smithsonian's 1938–40 survey of Ellington contains an "alternate take" of *Subtle Lament* (marked by them as 11-998-x). To heighten the mystery (and confusion), the Smithsonian's take 1, presumably issued originally on Brunswick 8344, is the one with Bigard's error, while their take x, "previously unissued" according to them, is in fact the recording most of us have known and enjoyed for years (and included in the aforementioned Columbia set).

What is, of course, even more perplexing is the specific nature of Bigard's transgression and how it could have happened in the first place. (James Patrick, the annotator for that segment of the Smithsonian's Ellington collection, incidentally says not a word about Bigard's clinker, indeed commends his solo as "striking and original," an integrated "melodic surface of the collective sound.") A bit of aural sleuthing reveals, in fact, that Bigard played completely wrong changes or in the wrong key, and did so for a full twelve bars! Example 39e renders in notation what Bigard played. A glance at the underlying chord symbols reveals that the clarinet's notes clash virtually at every point. However, transpose those same notes down a perfect fourth and every note of Bigard's fits the changes. I can only conjecture that Bigard (or Duke) had written out a "suggested" solo, at least in outline, but had done so in a wrong transposition.

Ex. 39e

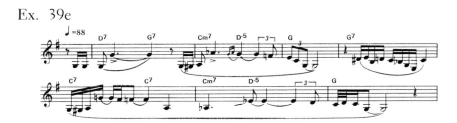

Furthermore, the lovely muted brass half-note accompaniment behind Bigard mysteriously (and mistakenly) stops in the eighth measure, leaving the last four bars of the chorus empty. This was evidently fixed on the real second take by reducing Bigard's original 12-bar solo to eight measures, and substituting the 4-bar primary motive (Example 39c) for the chorus's last four.

This all points to several interesting conclusions: 1) that the piece was not previously rehearsed, and was not even given a run-through at the record date prior to take 1; or 2) that the arrangement was not finished and was finalized only after the abortive first take; and 3) that Brunswick 8344 contains not take 1 but take 2 and that the Smithsonian reissue takes should be listed as (in their sequence) takes 2 and 1 respectively.

One is hesitant to read too much of Ellington's personal life into his music, but listening side by side to the buoyant inner resolve of *Serenade to Sweden* and the lonely quiet agony of *Subtle Lament*, the latter written just *before* the euphoric trip to Scandinavia, one is tempted to view *Lament* as highly autobiographical, expressing much of Ellington's despondent mood of the time.

The other precious gem from this period is *Blue Light*, surely the most neglected and least known of Ellington's masterpieces. Returning once again to the
Mood Indigo model for inspiration, *Blue Light* has one ingenious *aperçu* after
another, almost out-shining its 1930 progenitor in quality. First, it is one of the
most inventive metamorphoses of the 12-bar blues ever conceived, surpassing
even *Subtle Lament* in this respect. Second, how the oblique three-part harmonies (Ex. 40) intoned in the old *Mood Indigo* trio orchestration—muted trumpet,
muted trombone, and low register clarinet on the bottom—interact with this
particular unique timbral combination must be heard to be believed. (Once

Ex. 40

again notation can only give a hint of the magical beauty of this passage.) To fit
into the blues format, how subtly and simply Ellington solves the problem by
changing chord x to y (for the subdominant phase of the blues chord progression,
fifth bar) and to z (for the dominant phases, ninth bar). The remaining four
chords in each phrase stay the same.

But even before that, Bigard catches your heartstrings (and ears) with a pulsating, quietly dramatic low register solo set against a hushed *pianissimo* of only
bass and guitar and stated in an insistent G-minor. Actually G *major* is the key
and is implied but somewhat obscured by the repeated emphasis of the blue-
note minor third (B♭) (Ex. 41a). Thus Bigard's three phrases dovetail with the
underlying changing chords as ingeniously (Ex. 41b) as Duke's theme. Ellington

Ex. 41a

Ex. 41b

responds to these melancholy clarinet broodings with bittersweet dissonance-in-
flected answers (Ex. 42).[35]

Ex. 42

Later Brown, against harmonium-like harmonies, takes one of his most eloquent solos, mysterious in the way the notes of his theme and melody, worlds
away from the blues, nevertheless merge with the basic blues frame.

Ellington closes the side with a blue-note-colored, richly voiced piano solo
(accompanied only by bass) which returns—rather too soon, I feel—to the material of his introduction. Indeed *Blue Light*'s only fault is that it is too short,
ending too abruptly—the piano and bass duet seem tacked on without the band
being involved—and is over before its substance has barely been exposed. Even
with this minor flaw, *Blue Light* remains one of Ellington's most haunting pieces.

There is for most followers of the Ellington phenomenon a kind of magic
moment by which the advent of the peak years of the Ellington band are reckoned: the almost simultaneous acquisition of Jimmy Blanton and Ben Webster.
The former, a youngster of eighteen when he was asked to join Duke, revolutionized jazz bass playing in a few brief years, before he died a victim of con-
genital tuberculosis. Webster, a veteran in 1939 of over ten years of playing with
some of the greatest black orchestras of the time—Jap Allen, Andy Kirk, Bennie
Moten, Benny Carter, and Fletcher Henderson—was already one of the two or
three leading masters of the saxophone (see Chapter 6, below). Both Blanton
and Webster, moreover, were trained in the blues-oriented Southwest/Midwest/
Kansas City tradition, and brought to the Ellington band a fresh rhythmic drive
and improvisational freedom which, both in style and quality, represented a new
element. This infusion of talent, coupled with Billy Strayhorn's recent arrival as
a major arranging-composing force—almost Ellington's *alter ego*—was crucial in
lifting the band to a new creative plateau, analogous to the effect that the arrival
of Lawrence Brown, Juan Tizol, and Ivie Anderson had had in 1932.

Perhaps of the three 1939 additions, Blanton had the most consistent and
dramatic impact, not only on the Ellington band but on bass-playing and jazz
rhythm sections in general. This was inevitable since the bass is the most indispensable instrument of the classic jazz rhythm section and in most circumstances the most consistently audible and influential. For the bass functions simultaneously on several levels: as a rhythm instrument; as a pitch instrument
delineating the harmonic progression; and, since the days of Walter Page, as a
melodic or contrapuntal instrument. To this Blanton added another dimension:
the bass as a solo instrument, improvising like a "horn" in moving eighth- or
sixteenth-note passages, both bowed and pizzicato (plucked).

35. There should be little doubt that Claude Thornhill, who was soon to make a career out of such
dulcet, velvet-tinged piano embellishments, listened well and often to *Blue Light*.

But it was not only in the expansion of the bass's role that Blanton pioneered. It was the natural acoustical qualities of his pizzicato playing that also set new standards. His tone was astonishingly full, a bigness caused not by sheer amplitude but by purity of timbre and an uncanny ability to center each tone. No one had ever produced such a firm clean-edged sound, at once tensile and supple, powerful and graceful. Most importantly, he was the first to develop the long tone in pizzicato, thereby surmounting a long-standing limitation of pizzicato bass playing: the previously accepted notion that plucked notes can only be short and that variability of duration was unachievable. In truth, bass players before Blanton assented to the idea that a quarter note was about all the length you could get out of a pizzicato note, and that even that duration was normally only partially filled. In notational terms, although one wrote

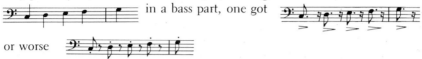

Instinctively players like Walter Page, Israel Crosby, John Kirby, and Blanton's predecessor in Duke's band, Billy Taylor, tried to stretch the duration of plucked notes. But it was left to Blanton to unlock the secret of how to make a bass string vibrate longer and with a fuller resonance.[36] Almost with the uncanny insight of an acoustic scientist, Blanton realized that 1) to prolong the duration of a pizzicato note you need not pluck harder or louder—that only serves to produce an even tighter, shorter sound; 2) that it does very little good to vibrate the string with the left hand since, as in the equation $\text{nothing} \times \text{nothing} = \text{nothing}$, if there is no initial sound substance to vibrate, a post-impact vibrato will be of no help; 3) that, on the other hand, you could maximize the natural resonance of the string by using as much of the fleshy length of the finger as possible—plucking the string with the finger parallel to the string, rather than plucking straight across at right angles; and that 4) you must pluck the string at the point where it sets in vibration the maximum resonance, a factor which varies as to type and quality of strings, the height of the bridge and tautness of the strings, the quality of the bass itself (which is, of course, the resonating chamber), and to some extent the register of the particular pitch. Instead of the usual quick-decay of ordinary pizzicato playing, Blanton could produce whole notes or half notes or other longer durations at will. (An acoustical representation of the two contrasting results is seen in Figure 9.) (See also Appendix.)

The new mobility, firm pitch control, and rock-like swing Blanton brought to his playing acted as an irresistible rhythmic catalyst on the Ellington band. Duke

36. Certainly classical bass players contributed little or nothing to the solution of this problem. Indeed none were even aware of the problem or conscious of a limitation. Until recently the majority of symphony bass players were quite content to produce a dry, lifeless thump on their basses, very similar to the last-cited musical example, invariable in its duration and devoid of any forward momentum, i.e. swing.

Fig. 9

(Horizontal = duration; Vertical = tone amplitude)

himself was so taken with Blanton that he recorded six bass and piano duets with him during the first year of Blanton's tenure—sides that comprise for record collectors and bass players alike one of the special historic moments in the development of this music.

These bass and piano duets were recorded in November 1939 and October 1940 and are for their time remarkable breakthrough performances for the bass. No one had achieved such sustained solo statements—at least on records—as Blanton did on *Blues* and *Pitter Panther Patter* (the latter the best of the six sides, especially in its inspired solo breaks). Blanton's full firm tone, fleet pizzicato technique, and—for the time—advanced harmonic substitutions certainly combine to produce an impressive debut for a young man of twenty-one, playing an instrument which had not yet achieved status as an improvising solo voice. At the same time I think these performances have been rather consistently overpraised and uncritically sanctified. Blanton's legendary impact on bass playing and jazz have evidently blinded most writers to the flaws in these performances, such as the shaky time on *Plucked Again* and *Body and Soul*, the frequent poor intonation, especially in the bowed passages on *Body* and *Sophisticated Lady*. While one may admire Blanton's daring in attempting as much as he does—like the bowed sixteenth sextuplets on *Body* (Ex. 43, m. 28), the parallel fifths on *Lady*, the many adventurous triplet and double-time sixteenth-note runs throughout—overall the execution is far from flawless. Blanton's bowing is especially limited; and this is worth mentioning only because Blanton was not quite the pioneer in this regard as he is often credited to be. Everybody seems to forget that Slam Stewart, another first-rate bass player, in 1938 at age twenty-three had recorded a whole *succession* of bowed bass solos, a year and a half before Blanton's debut recording. Slam Stewart's playing with Slim Gaillard (frequently without his famous upper-octave singing) is quite outstanding, certainly more fluent in bow technique than Blanton's, and considerably more assured in intonation.

Ex. 43

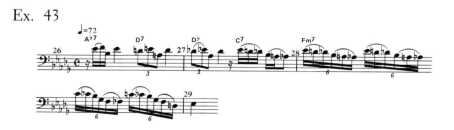

The next three-year period, considered by virtually all Ellington connoisseurs the artistic zenith of his (and the band's) career, was inaugurated in late 1939 and early 1940 by a burst of creative productivity that has rarely been equaled in jazz, let alone surpassed. Ellington's late-1920s Cotton Club period comes to mind as a possible contender. And in some ways, so does the emergence of bop in the mid-forties and the tremendous surge of new young talent—Parker, Gillespie, Monk, the Herman, Eckstine, Kenton orchestras—that sprang forth in those years in wonderful profusion. The difference, of course, is that in the latter example the creative surge was divided among a whole collection of innovative musicians, whereas in the case of Ellington's resurgence we are considering a single individual. One cannot, of course, ignore the crucial role played by his fourteen musicians in this creative explosion, but it is nonetheless clear that Ellington was the primary catalyst here. This is partially confirmed by the fact that, except for the crucial addition of Jimmy Blanton and Ben Webster, the orchestra's personnel during the entire period between, say, 1937 and 1942 was relatively stable. Unquestionably the two newcomers provided an important stimulus to Ellington's creative imagination, but the fact remains that the masterworks that ensued in 1940 were primarily *his* creations.

How then can one explain this remarkable spurt of creativity? The answer lies in the prophetic convergence of a whole series of events which, in combination, lifted Ellington's spirits and freed him from the unease and nagging self-doubts that had plagued him during the previous years. One factor was the extraordinarily successful 1939 European tour, during which Ellington was feted by both critics and public alike, and acclaimed as a serious creative artist in a way that he had not enjoyed in the "swing"-dominated American climate for some years prior.

Secondly, Ellington broke with Irving Mills, his manager of many years. Although Mills, a highly successful lyricist, publicist, music publisher, and entrepreneur, had skillfully guided Ellington's early career, providing immensely important contacts and opportunities for Duke and his orchestra, by 1939 the relationship had begun to deteriorate. Ellington felt the need to extricate himself from Mills's ever-more constraining ministrations and their inevitable commercial ramifications. Freed from these pressures, Ellington's creative juices began to flow again in a virtually uninterrupted stream of inspired productiveness.

Yet another longstanding alliance was also dissolved in 1939: that of his marriage to his second wife, Mildred. Their cooled relationship of recent years had begun to weigh heavily on Duke's mind, and when Mildred gave Duke his freedom, a new beginning in his personal and social life seemed to also give Ellington effectively a fresh start in his work.

Equally crucial in its effect on Duke's creativity—and on the evolution of his orchestra—was the addition, as mentioned, of Blanton and Webster, and above all, Billy Strayhorn. For all three provided an extraordinary infusion of fresh ideas and new orchestral possibilities, which Ellington the composer was quick to explore and exploit. Especially with Strayhorn, Ellington felt he had acquired a creative soulmate as composer and arranger whose musical conception was totally in accord with his own vision. At the same time Strayhorn's contributions partially lifted Ellington's enormous burden for years of singlehandedly replenishing the band's repertory. In time Strayhorn became more than an *aide de camp*—he became Ellington's *alter ego*.

Last but not least in this series of confluent events, the contract with Columbia records ran out in early 1940, bringing to an end an association which had been in decline for some time. The switch to Victor in March of that year precipitated an astonishing flurry of superb recorded performances, and produced within three months such masterpieces of Ellingtonia as *Jack the Bear*, *Ko-Ko*, *Concerto for Cootie*, *Cotton Tail*, *Bojangles*, *Dusk*, *Never No Lament*—to name a few.

All these changes—terminations as well as new beginnings—converging almost simultaneously on Ellington's career seemed clearly to give him a new lease on life, creatively speaking. The uneven, doubting, down years of 1937 and 1938 had quite suddenly given way to a new optimism, a new momentum and a level of inspiration that led in turn to the glory years of 1940–42.

Ellington finished out his Columbia contract in February 1940 with four remakes of earlier Ellington popular hits, three of them vocal versions for Ivie Anderson—*Solitude, Mood Indigo, Stormy Weather*—and an instrumental of *Sophisticated Lady*. Although full of attractive moments, there are also miscalculations. Typical are the disturbing, dully reiterative brass interjections in *Stormy Weather*. Even Ben Webster's obbligato solo behind Anderson is frustrating. It is overly florid, reminiscent of a caged panther nervously pacing the length of his cage, unable to relax or to be free of his confinement. Webster, for all his mastery, stumbles into too many "foreign" notes, which interfere with Ivie's unadorned declamation of Ted Koehler's lyric. Nor does Webster's exaggeratedly sugary sonority (in this instance) couple well with Ivie's more tart and penetrating timbre. The *Mood Indigo* remake is unremarkable, although it provides a rare opportunity to hear lead trumpeter Wallace Jones in a solo, a rather beautiful—I am sure—written-out obbligato line over the main theme. All in all these performances did not add significantly to the Ellington canon.

The new sides for RCA Victor in March 1940 definitely did. *Jack the Bear* with extensive soloing by Blanton, *Morning Glory*, a consummately rendered Rex Stewart vehicle, and *Ko-Ko*, one of Ellington's compositional masterpieces, were a brilliant triple salute to initiate the new decade and the new Victor contract.

Jack the Bear, with its positive exuberant swing, sets the pace. From here on the best of the Ellington band's performance for some years are marked by an astonishing economy, even simplicity of means, a feeling of all non-essentials having been trimmed off, and a sense of inevitability that signifies true mastery. Concise yet varied in form, *Jack the Bear* exploits a full range of Ellingtonian solo and ensemble talents, foremost among these Blanton's buoyant bass. After swooping in with an 8-bar introductory bass solo, which must have stunned musicians and jazz fans in 1940, Blanton is joined by Ellington for a 12-bar exchange (not quite a blues since the subdominant IV-chord is missing). A transitional phrase—*on* the subdominant—in unison saxophones,[37] used twice more in the piece, leads to a 32-bar Bigard chorus over essentially A♭ pedal points. The saxophone transitional theme returns as a bridge to 3 2/3 choruses of blues changes (Carney, Nanton, and call-and-response ensembles). The transitional passage reappears a last time, functioning now as a reverse pendant (see form outline Fig. 10) to its first use, in reintroducing Blanton for his final 16-bar solo. Thus a near-symmetrical form is achieved, the A♭-ostinato chorus of thirty-two bars balanced against the forty-four bars of blues, all of it trisected by the saxophone unison passages and bracketed by Blanton's introduction and coda (Fig. 10).

Fig. 10

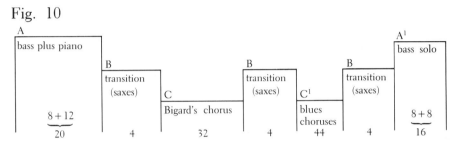

The 4-bar transitional passage works particularly well in its cowelling function because Ellington sets it apart from the other solo choruses by having Blanton double the sax line in unison, two octaves below (Ex. 44a). Thus it not only

Ex. 44a

Ex. 44b

37. It is worth noting that this 4-bar passage functions as a retroactive replacement for the absent subdominant in the preceding twelve bars.

contrasts with the 4/4 walking bass parts in the C sections but makes a smooth transition to the eighth-note coda solo in A^1 (Ex. 44b).

Ko-Ko, a magnificent blues piece in E♭ minor, originally intended for Duke's unfinished opera *Boola*, is a triumph of form and content. It couldn't be simpler: an introduction and coda embracing seven choruses of 12-bar blues. Yet out of these simple materials Ellington built as perfect a "composition" as the three-minute limitation of the 10-inch 78-RPM phonograph record would permit.

Over a throbbing Carney baritone pedal-point, the trombones in parallel triads move through shifting chromatic harmonies which clash (x in Ex. 45) with the prevailing tonality of E♭ minor, a vamping device, incidentally, reminiscent of similar practices in Andalusian Flamenco dance music. Juan Tizol now states

the simple riff theme ![musical notation], to which the saxes in true African

call-and-response pattern answer in kind. If it is true that chance and inadvertent circumstances must be seized upon by the creative artist, then the theme-statement of *Ko-Ko* is a particularly happy example. The leathery, slithery sound of Tizol's valve-trombone makes it the *non-pareil* instrument for the occasion. A saxophone would have sounded ordinary, and on the slide-trombone *this* riff in *that* register and *that* tempo is virtually unplayable.[38] It lies perfectly on the valve-trombone.

Ex. 45

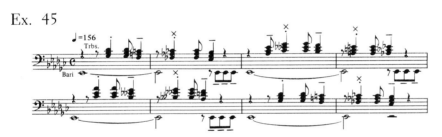

Ko-Ko is cast in the "crescendo" or "bolero" form, each successive chorus building inexorably on its predecessor. In this process of intensification, Ellington uses not only dynamics but other parameters, such as harmonic density, timbral and textural augmentation, and an increasingly expanded range (register). These elements are correlated so as to phase with each other in a steady buildup, one element supporting and complementing the other. (Fig. 11 shows this process in graphic form.)

From the first chorus (A), still relatively calm, Nanton's two succeeding choruses (B and C) begin the upward ascent. His second chorus is on a higher dynamic level than the first and played with a more intense sound (by holding the plunger mute tighter against the bell and forcing the sound against it). While the brass

---

38. On the ordinary trombone the notes B♭ and C♭ ![musical notation] necessitate a move from the first to the seventh position, which requires the hand (and slide) to move a distance of three feet, which even the fastest player cannot negotiate without producing a clumsy slur and unintended glissando.

Fig. 11

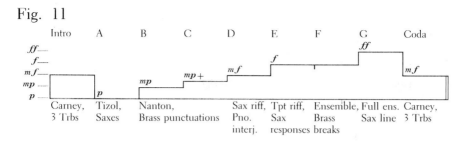

punctuations and unison sax riff remain momentarily the same in Nanton's second chorus, Ellington intensifies his own comping. In chorus *D*, the saxophones move up a fourth, the brass chords also move up and become thicker, while Ellington lifts the piece to a new level of complexity by multiplying his syncopated piano interjections and superimposing "dissonant" harmonies onto the basic tonality in mm. 1 through 4, 7, and 8. These harmonic clashes result in bitonality, i.e. two keys sounded simultaneously. Moreover, the bitonality is of a fairly sophisticated nature. Ellington superimposes a G♭ ninth chord with a

flat five [music notation] over the prevailing E♭ minor seventh [music notation] . Of the upper

chord three pitches are not duplicated in the lower chord [music notation] , these three forming a discrete whole-tone chord. But these three pitches taken together

with an E♭ minor seventh [music notation] make in combination an E♭ thirteenth

chord (with a flat ninth). Which of these three harmonic classifications Ellington actually thought of is impossible to determine, and theorists might readily disagree on what are the proper "spellings" of these chords. My own sense of the passage is that Ellington was simply juxtaposing E♭ minor and G♭ major. This is substantiated by several facts: 1) Ellington alternates between two formula-

tions of these chords [music notation] , the one insistently emphasizing E♭, the

other clearly G♭; and he further delineates the G♭ chord by up-and-down arpeggios (in mm. 2 and 3, 7 and 8). Second, the C♮ in the G♭ chord could be harmonically associated with E♭ minor—it would be the major sixth—*but* the theme in this chorus, as stated by the saxes, includes a C♭ (!), sometimes clashing directly with the piano's C♮ and making a wonderfully pungent harmonic

dissonance: [music notation] .

Two bars of alternating brass and piano jabs prepare the raising of all levels to a still higher plateau of intensification (chorus E). The riff theme rises another third and is now in the trumpets, while clarinet, saxophones, and brass respond

with massive towering chords: .

In chorus E, Ellington divides the orchestra into four choirs: trombones, trumpets, reeds, and rhythm, with Blanton the sole protagonist for the rhythmic section. Miraculously, Ellington finds still another higher level at E and F, again even more brilliant massive chords than at E, and manages to save something for a unison saxophone riff in the middle register. It is hard to believe that Ellington achieved these massive structures with only eleven "horns" and a four-man rhythm section. This last chorus is an extraordinary example—perhaps only Stravinsky has matched it in works like the *Symphonies for Wind Instruments* and the *Symphony of Psalms*—of implying and making us hear more than is actually stated. (In examples of this kind of ingenious and precise voicing, more tones are actually heard than are played, the result in part of sympathetic resonances of the partials in the overtone series that all pitched sounds produce.)

From this climactic zenith the introduction returns and a somewhat abrupt 4-bar coda ends the work. The entire piece is one of Ellington's (and the band's) crowning achievements, triply effective in terms of its music-structural concept, its sonic surface, (i.e. the sheer sounds it produces), and finally, as a powerfully moving, swinging performance. Both intellectually and emotionally it is totally satisfying.

Only nine days after recording *Ko-Ko*—Ellington's "Concerto for Orchestra," as it were—the band was back in the Chicago studios recording *Concerto for Cootie* and Tizol's *Conga Brava*. Both are fine performances and outstanding compositions, notable in part for their unusual structuring. Both pieces feature 10-bar phrases instead of the usual eight. Of course, Ellington had previously used such unusual phrase structures from time to time (for example, *Reminiscing in Tempo* and *Diminuendo and Crescendo in Blue* with their 10- and 14-bar phrases), but he evidently evinced a new interest in such odd-numbered patterns. Interestingly, the common denominator of ten is used in quite different groupings in *Concerto for Cootie* and *Conga Brava*. In the former the conventional 32-bar A A B A song format of four times eight measures is distended to thirty-six in the first chorus, compiled of $10 + 10 + 8 + 8$.[39] In *Conga Brava* the chorus

39. I differ with André Hodeir's contention in *Jazz: Its Evolution and Essence* that A^2 is a "10-bar phrase," as I disagree with many of his assumptions and implications regarding *Concerto for Cootie*. A more precise analysis would be that the first six measures are extended twice, first in mm. 7–8 by an orchestral 2-bar "response" to the solo trumpet's three "calls," and second by a further 1-bar extension (m. 9) to bring the music to the conventional dominant position in m. 10. From there the recapitulation (A^1) of the theme on the tonic can follow.

In the A^2 section, Ellington restates the first eight bars of the theme (six of solo trumpet, and two

consists of a true 20-bar structure. Of the two, I find *Conga Brava* the more interesting, at least in respect to form and *how* this form is expressed, particularly by the main soloist, Ben Webster.

I have pointed out that the A phrases in the first part of *Concerto* really consist of a $6+2+2$ grouping. The phrase in its prime form is more distended than expanded, with a distinct weakening in the *caliber* of the material of the two 2-bar phrases. (This is not true of the A^1 repeat with its fascinating chromatic extension of the theme.) Moreover, the thrice-repeated main motive is really not inspired melody or particularly original. It is, as Hodeir does point out, Cootie's *rendition* of these notes that makes the performance worth hearing—the subtle variations in rhythm, the use of different mutes and colorations, and the use of different dynamic levels.

What happens, on the other hand, in *Conga Brava* is most fascinating and uniquely peculiar to jazz and its African rhythmic antecedents. Tizol's theme comprises twenty bars, divisible into twice ten bars. When used as the basis for two solo choruses by Ben Webster, some interesting things happen. First of all, Webster, essentially a traditionalist raised on the blues traditions of the Southwest, totally ignores the basic ten times two 20-bar metric structure, and pieces together an excellently swinging solo out of a series of 8-, 4-, and 6-bar phrases. Thus a two-tiered structure is achieved (Fig. 12), a distant and drastically simplified relative of those African polyrhythmic, polymetric structures discussed in Volume I of this history. Whether by accident, by sheer instinct, or by design, it is impossible to say, but Ellington at the piano (and to some extent Blanton) clearly aids and abets Webster in his revamping of the two 20-bar choruses.

Secondly, since the harmonic changes consist of I-IV-V chords, the chords of the blues (although here obviously not distributed in the standard $4+4+2+2$

---

of orchestra), and then follows with a different 4-bar phrase which functions both as a conclusion to the first half of the form and a transition to the middle section in a new key.

Curiously, when Ellington's publisher of this period issued the sheet music for *Concerto*, the second A phrase had *nine* (!) bars, corresponding neither to the original nor to the later song version, which became known as *Do Nothin' til You Hear from Me*, in which, moreover, all the A phrases were reduced to the traditional eight.

Although Hodeir's laudatory view of *Concerto* represented for its time (1956) a considerable breakthrough in the state of jazz criticism, some of his argumentation was colored by a casuistry and lack of perspective typical of a certain brand of French intellectualism. It reads as if the very fact that Hodeir considered *Concerto* worthy of praise and extensive analysis made it a unique masterpiece—to the exclusion (one is led to feel) of almost anything else in jazz, including dozens of other Ellington works. Perhaps this distorted perspective was due to some extent to the unavailability in France of the *less* celebrated "masterpieces." But whatever the reason, Hodeir leaves the impression that *Concerto* is an isolated phenomenon, whereas, as I have tried to show, it and other Ellington works are all part of an ongoing continuity of gradual masterly development. Moreover, seen from the vantage point of a longer perspective, one would have to conclude that Hodeir overpraises *Concerto for Cootie*; or conversely, that there are a dozen other pieces (*Cotton Tail* or *Ko-Ko*, for example) on which one could lavish equal or greater praise. It is inappropriate to consider one single Ellington piece as superior to the rest and even to consider it representative of the totality of Ellington's best. His work is much too varied and too prodigious to allow for such a narrow, rather precious view.

Fig. 12

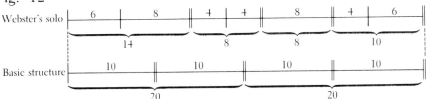

pattern), Webster—like so many blues players, from Bubber Miley to Ornette Coleman—stays very close to the tonic of B♭ major throughout. Whether this was done in self-defense—that is, playing it safe in view of the unfamiliar 10-bar chord structure, or not—ultimately matters very little. The result is a fine solo, remarkable for its economy and concentrated strength. It is also in its way a very modern solo, not only because it is expressed in concise, varyingly elongated phrases which combine into a well-balanced totality, but because—like Webster's more famous *Cotton Tail* solo—it is quite modern for its time, with some unexpected touches of Lester Young and Chu Berry.

Ellington's creative fecundity continued unabated. By May 1940 the band was in the studios twice more recording one astonishing masterpiece, *Cotton Tail*; a near masterpiece in the *Mood Indigo* vein, *Dusk*; two fine musical portraits, *Bojangles* and *Portrait of Bert Williams*; the infectious *Don't Get Around Much Anymore*; and, finally, a lesser number entitled *Blue Goose*.

Even "lesser numbers" by Ellington are apt to be superior to most of the concurrent competition. And *Blue Goose* is not without its distinctive Ellingtonian features. But these are on the side of the performance, the material of the song itself—a pleasant but not outstanding tune done in two-beat fashion for relaxed dancing—being transformed in performance into something quite beyond the reach of most other orchestras. In truth, no other jazz orchestra could boast such major soloists as Hodges, Webster, and Brown, each in his way illuminating the song's melodies in inimitably eloquent fashion. Ellington's restless pursuit of new orchestral colors or voicings is also represented. Witness the bridge of the last chorus with its striking high register reed ensemble.[40] In *Never No Lament* (later known, with lyrics added, as *Don't Get Around Much Anymore*, and one of Ellington's biggest pop hits), the rhythm section moves to the foreground with Blanton and guitarist Freddy Guy in fine mettle. The whole band lays way back in the beat in a manner that most bands in the East had not yet learned to do, but which had become one of the Basie band's specialties. Impeccable solos—at this point in the Ellington orchestra's life, the rule rather than the exception—are contributed by Hodges, Cootie, and Brown, with Brown's "bridge" solo one of his most blistering and a conspicuous contrast to his better known romantic lyric style.

40. As far as my ear can ascertain, Ellington seems to have used the sax section in the following distribution, putting each instrument in its high register: Bigard—clarinet; Hodges—soprano sax; Hardwick—alto sax; Webster—tenor sax; Carney—baritone sax.

The musical portraits[41] are dedicated to two of Harlem's most beloved entertainers: the legendary tap dancer Bill Robinson, nicknamed Bojangles, and the beloved vaudeville comedian Bert Williams. These "portraits" are a kind of parallel to the earlier "concerto" series, and were to be added to in later years with such works as *Portrait of Mahalia Jackson*, *Sidney Bechet*, *Ella Fitzgerald*, *Florence Mills* (the last named actually a reworking of Ellington's 1928 *Black Beauty*).

How accurately and lovingly Ellington caricatures the two entertainers! The "twisted pathos" of Bert Williams's routines, the dignity under the comic veneer, his famous stuttering patter, and the melancholy timbre of his voice are all captured by Ellington and the players, to whom Williams was undoubtedly a revered figure. Nanton's stuttering one-note solo (his second), with its melancholy humor, is one example; another is the eloquent warmth and sobriety of Stewart's opening theme statement.[42] But there is more. Bert Williams's career was at its peak in the first decades of the century, the ragtime era in which minstrel shows, blackface routines, and coon-songs were making the transition into vaudeville. The opening theme of Ellington's Bert Williams portrait is essentially a ragtime figure, *slowed-up* to highlight the whimsy and poignancy of Williams's delivery. Play Example 46a twice as fast on the piano (Ex. 46b) and

Ex. 46a

Ex. 46b

41. An earlier portrait was the 1939 *Portrait of the Lion*—Willie "the Lion" Smith, the stride pianist who exerted a strong influence on Duke.

42. This is another example of the multiple use of the same or similar materials.

Bert Williams:

Concerto for Cootie (middle section):

you have a typical late ragtime or early stride piano piece. Orchestrate it for Ellington's saxophone section and Stewart's poignant horn, slow it up a little, and you have Ellington's master portrait.

Bojangles, as might be expected, is given over initially to Blanton and Ellington in tribute to the art of tap dancing, a rhythmic language executed by the dancer's feet and as such an Afro-American extension of African drum languages. Whereas the rhythm in the *Bert Williams* recording was somewhat thumpy and rigid, *Bojangles* swings with an infectious beat, both pliant and firm. The section ensembles also swing superbly in an updated syncopated Henderson style that roots the music stylistically in the period of Robinson's heyday, the 1930s.

Dusk is another of those haunting pastel-colored three-minute tone poems that Ellington could turn out with such astonishing regularity. Like many of these pieces, *Dusk* too is out of the *Mood Indigo* mold; it is even in the same key and employs an identical harmonic/chordal vocabulary. And yet it has its own entirely unique character. Conjuring up, in its plaintive nostalgic mood, an image of loneliness at eventide, a night of longing about to descend, *Dusk* is clearly one of those pieces that go beyond the confining labels of jazz, dance music, and light entertainment. It is deeply affecting, gently, subtly disturbing, perfect in its utter simplicity. It is music that haunts you—it has haunted me since I first heard it some forty-five years ago, and it *never* fails to move me. Though it pleads and supplicates, it never whimpers; it is never sentimental.

Its form could not be more economical—a 16-bar "*Lied,*" stated three and a half times. The 4-bar bridge must be one of Ellington's most evocative harmonic inspirations (Ex. 47); and again, not only melody and harmony but voicing and timbre come together in an unparalleled musical-poetic statement.

Ex. 47

With the first and the final half-chorus set in *Mood Indigo*'s famous instrumentation, this time with an uncanny touch of eeriness in its wide spacing and plaintive intonation, Rex Stewart follows with a classic statement that captures the essence of the piece as much as Bigard's second chorus solo in *Mood Indigo* did ten years earlier. Indeed I would not be surprised to discover that Stewart's "solo" was composed by Duke and was meant to be an integral part of the composition (Ex. 48). Stewart's velvety cornet sound, vibrato-less yet warm, is the perfect carrier of Duke's poignant message. Note how Stewart prolongs the eerie mood of the exposition with his bitter-sweet half-valve moans and off-balance intonation.

Ex. 48

A trombone trio follows, an imaginative three-voice harmonization of what could have been a Lawrence Brown solo. But it is in the last eight measures of the third chorus that Ellington conceives another one of those special sonoric/harmonic visions that only he could glimpse and realize. Indeed, it is one of the most magical pages in all of Ellingtonia. In these few measures Ellington and his orchestra produce musical sounds that had never occurred before in Western music and have rarely been heard even since then. Again timbre and color combine with harmony and voicing to create this unique blend.[43] Example 49a shows the passage in full score, while 49b offers the same passage in piano reduction (slightly simplified.) Note the unusual bitonal muted-brass voicings, particularly the two lower brass in undulating augmented and major thirds; also Tizol's unique timbre as he alone holds through the end of m. 4 in a chord combining C^{b7} and $F^{aug\,7}$, leading to the tonic B^b in m. 5; and finally the tightly muted brass in dense quarter-note triplets in m. 8.

Other memorable moments of *Dusk* are Lawrence Brown's ravishing solo, Jimmy Blanton's firm beat and clear, well-centered pitches, and the rich low-

43. In all my years of transcribing music from recordings I have never encountered anything quite as difficult to capture in notation as these eight measures in Ellington's *Dusk*. The voicings are so close and dense in texture, the timbral blendings of the instruments so symbiotic—complicated by occasional performance and microphone imbalances—that the individual instrumental parts are extremely difficult to identify with absolute certainty. I cannot claim total accuracy for the transcription in Ex. 49a, but it represents a reasonably authentic rendering.

The astute observer will have noted the similarity at certain points in this excerpt between Ellington's harmonies and those of Delius. The resemblance, however, is most striking when these progressions are played on the piano, for example. For with Ellington's use of certain tightly closed jazz mutes and the unique timbral input of his saxophone section, the harmonies become entirely his own and sound *unlike* any other composer, including Delius.

It is also interesting to note that the here frequently used move to the lowered sixth step (I - bVI - I or I - bVI - V)—a favorite of Ellington's ever since his 1926 *If You Can't Hold the Man You Love* and *Misty Mornin'* of 1928 (see *Early Jazz*, 322, 324)—is the same sublime cadential progression with which Alban Berg concludes his Violin Concerto of 1935.

Ex. 49a

range saxophone voicings throughout of alto, tenor, baritone, and bass sax (Otto Hardwick), blended with Tizol's valve trombone, the two lower saxophones giving the accompaniment an especially dark-rich coloration I don't believe any other band of the time could muster. Ellington's peculiarities of voice-leading, noted as early as the late twenties and always featuring Carney in some unique way, are still adding their singular harmonic color. Note, for example, the second bar of Stewart's solo and how the harmony suddenly darkens, as when a cloud moves in front of the sun (Ex. 50a); or the simple but original voicing in m. 8 of Stewart's solo (Ex. 50b). Even when played on the piano, the special

Ex. 49b

Ex. 50a

Ex. 50b

flavor of this voicing can be heard. Finally, we must note another tiny detail of voicing—one I have never encountered in any other composer's work, again one unique to Ellington. In the second and fourteenth bars of the theme (as well as three bars from the end of the piece) the clarinet plays an E♭ on the last beat. On a G♭7 chord ninety-nine out of a hundred arrangers and composers would have kept the clarinet on F♭ throughout the measure. Only Ellington saw the beauty of the unusual shift to E♭. (Ex. 51 renders the last four bars of *Dusk*.) It is by details such as this, seemingly insignificant at first casual glance, that genius and mastery are known.

Ex. 51

And then there is the stunning achievement of *Cotton Tail*, which among its many virtues must number not only one of Ben Webster's two or three greatest recorded solos, but also a composition that both in its conception and performance was an important precursor of the big-band style of modern jazz. Typically it did so years before anyone had heard of "modern jazz." The jazz avant-garde of the mid-forties all drew upon the ideas in this seminal record: Gillespie in evolving his big-band style, Woody Herman for his catalytic band of 1945 (now referred to as the First Herd), and such now almost forgotten bands as Gerald Wilson's, Elliot Lawrence's, and Charlie Barnet's mid-1940 orchestras.

Cotton Tail's radical stance is established in the first few measures—and never relinquished thereafter. Like Beethoven when he dared to start his First Symphony on a chord other than the compulsory tonic, Ellington flaunts all convention by eliminating any introduction and plunging right in with the theme, and *then* doing so in a most unorthodox manner. First there is the bop-ish theme itself, stated as it became mandatory in the bop era, in unison or, in this instance, in octaves between saxes and trumpets. Second, Blanton starts not on the tonic as expected but appears to be in full gear, so to speak, as if the recording had suddenly picked him up in the middle of an ongoing walking bass line

Ex. 52

(Ex. 52, lower staff). But this unusual opening is not accidental. On the contrary, it serves to underline the extraordinary harmonic components of *Cotton Tail*'s theme. If we look at only the melodic line in Ex. 52 (the upper staff), we might easily consider it to be in C minor or perhaps set in some pentatonic scale 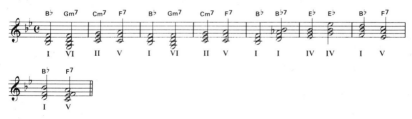 . The E♮ in the fifth bar is, of course, a surprise, but could in the key of C indicate a shift to the major. It isn't until the last note in the sixth measure, however, that the melody reveals itself, retroactively, as having been in B♭ all along. The E♮ turns out to be a flatted fifth, and the whole stance of the melody is harmonically off kilter, at oblique angles to the base harmonies, as it were. These, in traditional form, comprise the venerable *I Got Rhythm* progression (Ex. 53), an initial I-VI-II-V group, once repeated, and then in a descending bass line from a I^7 circling back to the tonic.

Ex. 53

Thus the opening C of the melody turns out to be a ninth, not the usual first, third, or fifth degree with which most diatonic-tonal melodies would begin. And to come back to Blanton, one can see how his notes (Ex. 52) obscure the identity of the tonality even more; or, to put it another way, emphasize the split personality of this remarkable theme and help to disguise the reality that the theme of *Cotton Tail* is one more variant on *I Got Rhythm* changes.

The rest of the work is no less remarkable. The first bridge pits modern sax voicings against Cootie's blistering plunger solo, voicings that musicians like Gil-

Ex. 54

lespie and Tadd Dameron were to turn into a bop convention some years later (Ex. 54). And every time the bridge returns Ellington finds a new variant on this tried-and-true progression.

Then there is Webster's splendid solo, holding back at first but soon erupting in the second chorus bridge into an upward vaulting sequence of diminished-chord figures, stretching to the very top of the tenor saxophone range. These memorable eight bars are all the more striking because they represent a deviation from the expected chord progression (see Ex. 53). Blanton here stays on a pedal Bb while Duke punctuates with powerful bitonal chords embracing both the Bb tonic and its diminished-chord relative. Webster's entire solo, a paragon of logical but intuitively arrived at construction, finds a remarkable balance between a whole world of diverse musical ideas: swinging eighth-note phrases interspersed with long and expressive held notes, some of these embellished with passionate vibratos and shakes, tonal colorations ranging from soft hues to hot and raspy timbres, all a rich mixture of the predictable and the unpredictable.

Miraculously, after Webster's solo—easily expected to be the performance high point in almost any other jazz orchestral context—both Blanton and Greer find even greater dynamic intensity and momentum for the succeeding 16-bar tightly scored brass ensemble—from *what* energy resources it is hard to divine. Then, after eight bars of wonderfully hard-swinging stride piano by Duke, a saxophone ensemble follows which clearly foreshadows Jimmy Giuffre's *Four Brothers* sound of nearly a decade later (although it still uses the alto sax in the lead line). A call-and-response pattern heralds the final chorus, whose bridge logically offers the most dissonant and climactic variation thus far. The final eight bars, by contrast, reduce the intensity and complexity measurably, recapitulating the initial 8-bar theme statement. Ellington's endings tended, even in this period, to be often rather too abrupt—in part a difficult-to-avoid consequence of working in a three-minute time limit.[44] But the purposely abrupt ending of *Cotton Tail*

44. Ellington was certainly aware of his difficulties with endings, although he seems never to have seriously grappled with the problem. Throughout his career, but especially in the last twenty years or so, most noticeably in the extended or suite compositions, otherwise interesting pieces suffered

works perfectly because of the recapitulatory form, its remarkable internal organization, and, above all, the bold counterpoint of the theme statement, so different from the rest of the performance. By their distinctive character the first sixteen bars and last eight function additionally as an *introduction* and *coda*, respectively, framing the entire work in a neatly closed form.

It would not be difficult to devote the better part of an entire chapter to Ellington's *Cotton Tail*—the rewards of such an endeavor would be considerable. Ben Webster's great solo alone deserves detailed analytical attention, for it is in itself an inspired near-perfect composition, all the greater in that it was *not* intellectually, painstakingly composed and constructed; it was an extemporized creative statement. And beyond that single demonstration of the art of improvisation, *Cotton Tail* contains myriad details of both pre-designed and spontaneous invention in melodic, harmonic, rhythmic, orchestrational, textural, and formal terms—and in execution. It is innovative and creative on all fronts simultaneously. It is an inspired work, but obviously it also inspired the players to attain their greatest creative heights. Listen to Blanton and Greer, for example— and it is worth listening to them alone several times—or Ellington's inspired comping throughout; or the foreshortened 4-bar ensemble lead-in to Webster's solo (with its driving brass punctuations and slithering unison sax line beneath); or the perfection of Harry Carney's driving solo, crammed into only eight bars; or the rising and falling sax figures of the last climactic chorus. One could continue at length recounting *Cotton Tail*'s many moments of glory.

But *Cotton Tail*'s ultimate importance goes even beyond such "details." It changed the face of jazz and foretold in many ways where the music's future lay.[45] And it did so at the very peak of the Swing Era. That this event occurred unnoticed by a majority of musicians and audiences does not alter its importance. Some young players and arrangers of outstanding talent *were* listening and were inspired by *Cotton Tail*'s daring and perfection. They also heard a new looseness, a new freedom in the Ellington band. Never before had Ellington opened up a piece for out-and-out blowing on a record date as he did for Webster and *Cotton Tail*. The occasional solo showcase pieces and "concertos" were considerably more pre-planned and determined *by* Ellington as *composer*. The

---

from weak endings, often non-endings. They simply stopped somewhere, unfinished. One often had the sense—and sometimes knew—that in Ellington's hectic schedule time had run out, and compositions due for some particular occasion or recording date would be hastily "finished," some ending or other tacked on—sometimes *at* the record date.

But there is another side to this problem. Ellington and Strayhorn were fond of putting off inquiries about their difficulties with endings by claiming that "they were superstitious of finishing pieces." Another version ran, "some pieces should or could not be finished," because they dealt with ongoing subjects or unresolved conditions. Whether these rationalizations were more of those verbal smokescreens which Ellington could produce with such casual aplomb under a Mona Lisa smile is hard to know. But the fact remains that, intentional or not, many of Ellington's works suffered from this serious flaw.

45. Perhaps it did so not entirely by itself. The Ellington band's *Take the A Train*, *Main Stem*, and—in a different mood—*Chelsea Bridge* and *Blue Serge* were harbingers of the new sounds and concepts about to break forth in jazz.

wind blowing in from the West—through Webster and Blanton—had flown in new seeds which landed on extremely fertile soil. *Cotton Tail* and Webster's solo loosened, ever so slightly, the compositional harness that Ellington had been constructing for over a decade or more. *Cotton Tail*, particularly in its execution, let in a gust of spontaneity, of freshness, of flexibility, which the Ellington band was never to lose again and which offered a whole new way of integrating composition and improvisation.

Remarkably enough, this peak was to be reached (or at least approached) a few more times in the ensuing years—*Take the A Train, Main Stem, In a Mellotone, I Got It Bad (and That Ain't Good), Moon Mist*. But, of course, there were also bound to be lesser achievements, flawed in one way or another. There were the novelty or pop vocals which even the talents of Ivie Anderson or Herb Jeffries could not always rescue. But Ivie's *I Got It Bad* was a triumph of taste and style (more of that later). Herb Jeffries, on the other hand, fared less well, at least on records. One had to experience Jeffries live with Duke to hear the measure of his talent, his recordings—mostly crooned and artificially sweetened—giving a false representation of his real gifts, both musically and vocal-technically.[46]

There were other modest successes—or to put it another way, mild failures—like *Chloe*, with its tastelessly saccharine trumpet solo by Wallace Jones and a quite confused arrangement by Billy Strayhorn; or like *The Flaming Sword*, with its fake Mexicanisms and tacky Latin Quarter production-number routines (much the same can be said for the mindless energy of *Giddybug Gallop*); or the rather ordinary *Sidewalks of New York*, material unworthy of Ellington to begin with.

Even pieces based on better material, like *Harlem Airshaft, Rumpus in Richmond*, and *Sepia Panorama*, are not without blemishes of one kind or another. *Harlem* suffers from a confused (and confusing) introduction, seemingly patched together from odd bits of other unused intros, and the whole piece, including its *In the Mood*-like riff theme, seems to be somewhat of a concession to the swing craze. Its title seems grafted onto the piece or—to put it another way—the music does not fulfill the promise of the title. Cootie's open-horn solo is one of his more ordinary efforts, strained in its unsuccessful reaching for high-note tension. So often in Ellington's work a section's interpolation of some contrasting idea works well, even sometimes heightening the effect, but here the lead-in passages for the saxes serve only to interrupt the flow of the music (and of Cootie's solo). On the other hand, there is an effective swing-style choir-by-choir buildup towards the end of *Harlem*, all the more impressive for its brevity.

Sepia Panorama, interesting for its pyramid form (ABC DD CBA), is blessed with some excellent full-toned Blanton solo work. But starting *sans* introduction

---

46. A much more creative and mature Jeffries can be heard, for example, on his 1946 recordings (on the Exclusive label) with Buddy Baker's *Trombone Octet* in first-rate modern arrangements by the late Paul Villepigue that are well worth rediscovery and study. (The superb trombone choir includes such talented young players as Hoyt Bohannon, Dick Nash, George Roberts, Lloyd Ulyate, Si Zentner, and lead trombone Joe Howard.)

with a phrase more or less borrowed from the third section of *Reminiscing in Tempo*, the piece seems fragmented in its conflicting juxtapositions. Nothing quite leads logically to anything else; the piece lacks the concerted constructive logic of, for instance, *Diminuendo and Crescendo in Blue* or *Ko-Ko*. Even Webster's mid-point solo, so super-relaxed, affable, and pleasant, is too laid back in context and essentially leads nowhere.[47]

Rumpus in Richmond is well named, maintaining a disturbing, restless mood throughout, both in its upward-rising (and never quite resolving) chromatic harmonies and its fine Williams and Brown solos, the former needling and nasty-toned in tight muting, the other brash and brassy, almost angry. Cootie's *a capella* introduction, pretty much borrowed from Armstrong's *West End Blues* opener, seems on the other hand merely tagged onto the work.

The best pieces from late 1940 were *In a Mellotone*, *All Too Soon*, *Warm Valley*, and *Across the Track Blues*. The last named and *All Too Soon* are pure Ellingtonia at its unique best: *Across the Track Blues* via the inimitable talents of Bigard, Stewart, and Brown; *All Too Soon*, one of Ellington's most affecting AABA songs of the period, stated with inimitable sensuousness and taste by Lawrence Brown. It is remarkable how a simplistic two-chorus format—Brown's theme and Webster's luxuriant improvisation on its chords—can in the hands of Ellington and his orchestra add up to so much more. There is in the exposition one of those heady moments worth singling out (happily it comes twice) that is unique to Ellington—which is to say that only with *his* players of this period could its magic have been achieved. I am referring to the third bar in the initial eights. Just as there are optical illusions, there are also aural illusions, and measure 3 contains one of Ellington's best. It results from a mixture of Brown's solo-tone muted glissando embellishments and Hardwick's delicate, sensuously sweet soprano obbligato (Ex. 55).

The actual illusion consists of making our ears believe that Hardwick glissandos up to a high A, when it is actually Brown who slides to that note. The mixture of their sonorities as their notes momentarily intertwine in perfect dynamic balance—Hardwick sounding, by the way, for all the world like some magic violin—causes us to lose track for one moment of who is going where. Indeed, for one split second it appears that Hardwick is also going to gliss upward, but instead turns downward to the D. Only when both players arrive at their destinations do we know how they got there—in perfect contrary motion. Further, we are lulled into this illusion—intended or accidental matters not—in m. 2, where Hardwick *does* slither up a fourth to G, receding via another glissando to the E below, from which our ears now expect him in true sequence fashion to attempt the next note in line, A. What a surprise, then, to hear that in fact the two instrumental lines crossed, rather than going parallel.

Warm Valley is one of Hodges's great solo vehicles. There exist two issued

---

47. Ellington's chorus contains, by the way, a little whole-tone descending figure which perhaps the young Thelonious Monk first heard here and was quite mesmerized by; it was to become Monk's signature cliché.

Ex. 55

takes now: the Smithsonian's three-year survey of Ellington from 1938 through 1940, which resuscitated the originally rejected take 1; and take 4 (recorded six weeks later), which was the only one Ellington lovers ever knew. It turns out that take 1 has many splendid qualities which make its new-found availability all the more welcome. For one thing Hodges is in better form technically, his tone warm and magenta-rich, his intonation secure (whereas take 4 offers a harder tone and some sharp intonation). Similarly, Rex Stewart's solo is more in tune as well as more adventurous on take 1—an opening clam notwithstanding. Listen especially to his probing phrases in mm. 1, 4, and 8 in the last eight of his solo, as well as the astonishing Lawrence Brown-like upward glissando in m 6, virtually impossible on the slide-less trumpet. On the other hand, a harmonically rather overly ambitious passage (the next-to-last eight bars of the piece) was very poorly played: with poor intonation, a considerable lack of blend, and some wrong notes—undoubtedly the reason for its initial rejection.

The well-known take 4, however, also has its virtues and is not to be readily discarded. The "offending" passage near the end was now replaced by a "safer" one, which, however, is more in keeping with the work's languorous mood. In either form it is a performance well worth hearing and one of Duke's most ingratiating melodies, tailor-made for the unique talents of Johnny Hodges.

The perfection of *In a Mellotone* seems to me to depend a great deal on the way background and foreground mesh together into a unified whole. Taken separately, they are considerably less interesting; but put together, they are more than the sum of their parts. The riff theme, for example, although given its spine by Carney's robust tone, is relatively ordinary, one which an Edgar Sampson or even a Larry Clinton or Larry Wagner could have written. But no one else could have provided the trombone-trio background that embraces those riffs.

The same might be said of the playful call-and-response interchanges between Cootie and the saxophone section. A large measure of *Mellotone*'s success can also be ascribed to Blanton's firm clear-pitched bass lines and impeccable beat, a consummate lesson in swing.[48]

The magnificence of Ellington's studio recordings may cause one to forget momentarily that the Ellington orchestra spent most of its time on the road, not in the recording studio. The amount of music the band played in a given year is staggering, measured in the tens of thousands of pieces. For in those days, especially at dances, an orchestra could easily play for five hours, and anywhere from thirty-five to forty-five tunes, mostly in more extended versions than those on the official recordings. In recent decades, tapes and discs of Ellington dances and concerts have surfaced in surprisingly large numbers, many of them now issued on LP. The most famous of these—and one especially recommended to the reader—happens to catch the Ellington band on a night in November 1940, at the Crystal Ballroom in Fargo, North Dakota. Not only can one hear the orchestra as it sounded in its natural habitat, the ballrooms and nightclubs of the land, but these discs, originally recorded by a young engineer and Ellington enthusiast, Jack Towers, happily capture the whole mood and feeling of those evenings with the Duke and his men in that bygone era. (See also pp. 584–86.)

If 1940 was creatively a banner year, 1941 and early 1942 (after which the American Federation of Musicians recording ban broke off all recording) were even more startlingly productive. From *Take the A Train*, recorded in February 1941, through *I Got It Bad, Chelsea Bridge, C-Jam Blues, Moon Mist*, to the mid-1942 *Main Stem*, the flow of creative energy seemed to be limitless and at an unprecedentedly high level. Some of the glory of these achievements must be shared with Billy Strayhorn and, as always, with various members of Ellington's orchestra.

Ellington and Strayhorn's musical collaboration has been unique in the history of music, both in kind and quality. (The only other example that comes to mind in terms of quality is that of Gil Evans and Miles Davis.) But in the case of Ellington and Strayhorn—both were composer-arrangers and pianists—the match is so close that it is frequently impossible to tell with certainty where the work of one ends and the other's begins.

Strayhorn grew up in Pittsburgh and after extensive studies there, primarily in classical music, he came to the Ellington band in 1939 at the age of twenty-four as arranger (and lyric writer). Although his work for Duke was at first rather undistinguished—often limited to arrangements for Duke's singers—Strayhorn eventually absorbed the orchestra's style completely and within two years of his arrival produced one of the band's finest efforts and all-time hits, *Take the A Train*. Other Strayhorn compositions and arrangements from this period include *Chelsea Bridge, Rain Check, My Little Brown Book, Just A-Settin' and A-Rockin'*,

48. It is my theory that, as remarkable as Blanton was, his effect on bass players in particular and jazz in general would not have been half of what it was had he not been so superbly (and consistently) recorded. His strong presence is felt in *all* of the performances he was able to participate in during his short career.

The Kissing Bug, and *Johnny Come Lately*. By 1945, when Ellington was devoting more and more time to longer extended works, Strayhorn did most of the
day-to-day arranging, as well as becoming increasingly involved as co-composer
and orchestrator with the larger works (like *Perfume Suite* and *The Liberian Suite*).

Though jazz critics and writers have generally been mystified by the seemingly
alchemistical process by which Ellington and Strayhorn collaborated and thus
found it impossible to distinguish each one's work, there are nonetheless clear
identifying characteristics that mark Strayhorn's work. To begin with, Strayhorn's
writing tends consistently towards a brighter and leaner orchestral texture. High
register sounds predominate in his work, and his voicings tend to be of the kind
that separate rather than coalesce. Ellington is a great unifier, the ultimate mixer
of colors into new and unheard of blends. Strayhorn prefers generally to keep
colors discrete or at least clear. Where Ellington loves to draw a veil over his
sounds—a parallel is to be found in his general behavior, speech, and use of
language—Strayhorn enjoys, especially in up-tempo situations, illuminating his
sounds with a bright exposing focus.

Second, until the 1945-46 Strayhorn arrangements came along, when the
frantic overblown scoring of the immediate post-war era took over, even in the
Ellington band,[49] there was a marked emphasis on lightweight densities in Strayhorn's work. (*Chelsea Bridge* is a fine example). This lightness—in the sense of
weight—manifested itself in both more transparent instrumental voicings and the
use of subdued dynamics. Ellington's range of dynamics and density, of course,
could run the entire gamut, from the intimate feather-light sounds of *Blue Light*,
say, to the massive structures of *Ko-Ko*. But with Ellington there was always a
fullness of sound throughout the entire range of dynamics and densities, even in
the "lighter" pieces, while Strayhorn's ear generally chose a more thin-textured
sonority.

Third, in faster tempos especially, Strayhorn generally favored a more clipped
staccato style of writing, particularly in his brass writing—again to help focus a
brighter, more pointed sonority (This can be heard to good advantage, for example, in *Raincheck*.)

Last, there was in much of Strayhorn's work an underlying and clearly discernible influence of classical music, especially in the direction of French early
twentieth-century composers like Ravel, Debussy, and Milhaud—and Stravinsky
(virtually a French composer by adoption in the twenties and thirties). Strayhorn's study of these composers was much more conscious and specific than
Ellington's ever was, and at various times Strayhorn not only allowed these influences to guide his writing but actually nurtured them. This extended even to
a keen appreciation of European contrapuntal techniques (an area Ellington
avoided), whose specific influence can be heard in any number of pieces, including, for example, the 1945 *I Let a Song Go Out of My Heart* or *On a
Turquoise Cloud* (not to mention pieces like *Fugue-a-ditty*).[50]

49. Hear *Blue Is the Night, Just You, Just Me, Suddenly It Jumped* in this context.
50. Another conspicuous example of a modern classical influence can be heard in Strayhorn's moody
and often quite atonal *Dirge*, premiered at Ellington's first Carnegie Hall concert in 1943 (but
subsequently withdrawn).

Chelsea Bridge and *Raincheck* must certainly count among Strayhorn's finest achievements in the early forties. The latter is a late-swing era jump number, energized by one of Ben Webster's most ebullient solos, and Strayhorn's fresh, bright-hued orchestral colors and clipped ensemble style.

Chelsea Bridge represents the more Impressionist-influenced side of Strayhorn's writing. Again bright colors and high voicings predominate, but by being stated in softer dynamics their effect is more pastel than vivid. The theme is more a series of harmonies than a real melody, but is nevertheless affecting in its touching simplicity. It is harmonically advanced (at least in the jazz context of the day), although we must remind ourselves that Bix Beiderbecke and Red Norvo were successfully experimenting with similar Debussyan harmonies a decade or so earlier. Bix's *In a Mist*, for example, uses the same harmonic language as *Chelsea*, only in a faster tempo and less serene rhythmic setting.

What Strayhorn exploited in the theme of *Chelsea* is the duality of its chromatic harmonies. The theme is set in its first three bars in minor sixth chords with an added major seventh (Ex. 56). However, Strayhorn causes us to hear

Ex. 56

these harmonies as if they were whole-tone chords. He achieves this effect by two means: 1) through orchestrational and dynamic stressing of the three upper notes (in the right hand in our musical example); 2) by setting these sixth chords in their third inversions. This latter device takes away the rootedness of the harmonies, letting them float, so to speak, more towards the top of their structure. If Carney, for example, had played instead, the effect of this progression would be entirely different, and the whole-tone characteristic, now accentuated in *Chelsea*, would have been considerably de-emphasized. I would add that Strayhorn's more floating "disembodied" use of these harmonies would not ordinarily (or previously) have occurred to Ellington.[51]

Chelsea Bridge stands as a lovely musical vignette, its bright clarinet-led voicings and brief solos by Webster and Tizol offer just enough spontaneous variety to give this short tone poem its "jazz" substance. But it also points to two dangers in Strayhorn's writing and, through his influence, in the Ellington band's style. One is Strayhorn's inability, like Ellington's, to develop material *compositionally* beyond the vignette or cameo stage. This lack of developmental technique was to have serious consequences for much of the extended-work writing of Ellington

---

51. I know of only one other example of such inversions in Ellington's own work, and that occurs in the first movement of *Black, Brown and Beige*.

and Strayhorn in the post-1945 period (it already manifested itself critically in the 1943 *Black, Brown and Beige*). Second, one hears in *Chelsea* the hint of a certain effeteness which was to mar much of Strayhorn's work and, to the extent that much of Ellington's work was intricately intertwined with Strayhorn's, even some of Ellington's work in later years.

Also from Strayhorn's pen at this time came a subtly relaxed swing tune *Just A-Settin' and A-Rockin'*, and *Clementine* and *Johnny Come Lately*, the latter two, vain attempts to recapture the essence (and success) of *Ko-Ko* and *A Train* respectively. Though *Johnny* receives a spirited performance with some hot, brash Brown trombone, it already edges dangerously close to the kind of overly loud and abrasive score that so many swing bands adopted in the mid-forties.[52]

Strayhorn's masterpiece is, of course, *Take the A Train*. Its unforgettable theme line is truly inspired, with, among other things, that fetching augmented chord in the third and fourth bars, and the whole piece has a sense of inevitability that marks the true masterwork. Equally inspired is Strayhorn's saxophone ensemble variation on the theme (after the mid-point modulation), answered by Ray Nance in his best Harry James manner. The second chorus is devoted in its entirety to Rex Stewart who, very tightly muted, delivers one of the most cohesive solos of his career. As so often with Ellington repertory, here too the solo and the piece seem to have been mutually created for each other. For that matter the entire performance, including its beautifully rendered *In the Mood*-like fadeaway coda, seems a near-perfect realization of the work. Conversely, it also seems to me that the *piece*, in itself so clear and uncluttered, elicited quite naturally the kind of superior performance it got—and deserved. It also deserved to become—and became—Ellington's band theme, ushering in thousands of concerts, dances, and club engagements. And, remarkably, one never tired of hearing it. But what other bandleader and composer would have ceded the band's theme spot to another composer?

Strayhorn's role in the Ellington canon will perhaps never be completely or precisely defined, especially in respect to the later years, when the two men's talents and style did merge in a truly indistinguishable manner. Ellington and Strayhorn went to their graves with their secret (as did Hodges and Carney, who might have shed some more light on these matters, but like their leader chose not to). Ellington must have been asked thousands of times by inquisitive reporters, critics, and friends how Strayhorn fitted into the overall scheme of Ellington's and the band's work. Master of the oblique answer and elliptical repartee, Ellington never divulged his true feelings to the outside world. I suspect, however—and the thought will upset some Ellingtonians—that Ellington knew very well the difference between himself and Strayhorn, but was too loyal, as he was to all his co-workers and friends, ever to breach the integrity and artistic intimacy of that relationship.

Much the same can be said in respect to another creative reinforcement that

---

52. Curiously, *Johnny Come Lately* in its original form, called *Stomp*—a counterpart to *Dirge*—was a less intense, more jubilant kind of work, intended as an evocation of the joyous march home after a traditional New Orleans funeral.

was added to the Ellington organization during these early forties' years: the work of Ellington's son, Mercer. But again, how exactly Mercer's composing and arranging interacted with his father's and the orchestra's work, remains obscure and conjectural. Whether Mercer Ellington actually composed and arranged a masterpiece like *Moon Mist* at age twenty-two, or whether he wrote only the composition—certainly no minor achievement—and his father arranged it, or whether the two collaborated as co-composers, or whether Duke wrote and arranged it and merely ascribed it to Mercer as a gift—these and other questions linger on unanswered. Ultimately, I suppose, it matters little who produced *Moon Mist*. After all, Ray Nance (on violin) contributed as significantly to that musical gem as anyone else, although uncredited in the copyright. What counts is that *Moon Mist* exists in all its ravishing beauty and that it emerged, by whatever method or combination of talents, out of the Ellington *ménage*.

And indeed *Moon Mist*, *Blue Serge*, and *John Hardy's Wife* are three major contributions to the Ellington repertory, all officially ascribed to Mercer. While *Hardy's Wife* is not so memorable as a *composition*, its performance represents the best vintage Ellington, starting with the superb melodic-rhythmic swing of Blanton, Greer, and Guy. Brown contributes a vigorous yet lyric rhythmic solo of the kind that Ellington was asking him increasingly to display, while Stewart tees off in Cootie's old role with a searing voluble plunger solo.

But with *Blue Serge* we are on another creative plane altogether, in kind and quality. Structurally it is a fully integrated composition, that is, all its elements are controlled by the composer and not the result of chance contributions by various soloists; and, except for Duke's own second-rate meandering piano interlude, the quality of both the work and its performance realization is superb. *Blue Serge* is a brooding piece, much like the earlier *East St. Louis Toodle-Oo*, and in the same key of C minor. Dark colors predominate, often set in the low saxes, sometimes in low trombones (hear Tizol's unusual pungent low G in the second eight against mellow reed voicings). The three soloists, all in the alto or tenor range, were chosen for their dusky timbres: trumpet, trombone, tenor sax. Even Nance, in probably his most affecting lyric statement ever, is held to the mellow low and middle range of the trumpet. Nanton is quiet and deeply muted; and Webster, although momentarily confused by the shifting harmonies in his first four lead-in bars, recovers to play one of his most expressive solos with Ellington, never breaking the introspective mood of the piece. And the voicings (and instrumentation) of the second and final eights of the piece proper (after Nance's and Webster's solos respectively) are utterly new, even for Ellington—at least in detail if not in concept. Surely these voicings *are* Ellington's, and indeed, I venture to say, they could not have been created by any hand other than Ellington *père*'s.

To produce a *Blue Serge* and *John Hardy's Wife* on a single record date was surely beyond the scope of any other jazz orchestra of the time. But, of course, we must not forget that *Take the A Train* came from the same date (Feb. 15, 1941).

Mercer's *Moon Mist* from a year later is on yet another plane of collective creativity. A more luminous and brighter timbred piece than *Blue Serge*, it was without precedent in music in the particular basic mixture of its musical ingredients, and virtually so even in Ellington's *oeuvre*. (Only *All Too Soon* comes to mind as a possible legitimate predecessor.) For here came together a number of unique talents and musical personalities in a fragile constellation that only the greatest collective sensitivity and taste could bring off successfully: 1) Nance's seductive violin; 2) the heady mixture of Ellington's saxophone section, led by Hodges's creamy alto and anchored in Carney's pulsating baritone (into these were mixed Tizol's gentle valve trombone); and 3) Brown's romantic trombone. Even more astonishing may be the fact that this miracle of a performance was accomplished by only twelve instruments: violin, only three saxes (two altos, one baritone), one trumpet, three trombones, and rhythm section.

Again, an artistic achievement like this could easily absorb an entire chapter by itself. (And indeed *Moon Mist* deserves the most thorough analysis, as much as any Webern *Op. 21*, Brahms *Intermezzo*, or Haydn symphony—or, for that matter, Ellington's *Concerto for Cootie*.) I will limit myself, however, to singling out a few special moments that the casual ear may not immediately catch. To begin with, notice the way Nance frees up the rhythm of the tune, at times lagging behind the beat, at times forging ahead (Ex. 57a, b). Hear also Nance's

Ex. 57a   Ex. 57b

variation on the bridge (his second solo), so idiomatically violinistic: this passage could not (cannot) be played on any other instrument. Notice, too, how here, in what amounts to the climax of the piece, the tension is heightened by Nance's faster rhythms, the harsher colors and stronger support of three trombones and piano in dark low-register chords, and Greer's press-roll brush flutters. And perhaps one of the most remarkable moments of all occurs in the last two bars of this bridge. As Nance rises ethereally into the violin's upper register, two dark trombones, three octaves below, are left to resolve the cadential harmonies.

Last, one must note the beauty of Ellington's piano introduction, economical and pared to essentials, played and pedaled with such sensitivity and refinement. Modern-day pianists might also note the reserve with which Duke resists all temptations to "fill in" behind the instruments. Duke plays not a single note until the sixteenth bar of the composition proper; then, after that one incursion, rests in silence for another fifteen bars. Similarly in the last eight (Brown's solo), Duke *listens*—probably in wonderment—rather than plays, waiting until the final tonic has been reached to add his leisurely closing arpeggios.

Moon Mist was recorded on January 21, 1942. Again such a performance would do most orchestras of the period great honor. But that recording date also

saw the creation of *C-Jam Blues* and Juan Tizol's *Perdido,* the latter a piece
which was soon to become (and remain to this day) a jazz standard. During the
bop era *Perdido* became a fast-paced vehicle to show off the new players' virtuoso
skills. But in its original conception by Tizol it was meant to be an almost stately
and therefore more forceful tune—after all, its title, meaning "lost" or "strayed,"
hardly has a light-hearted connotation—one that in the Ellington orchestra's
original version swings deeply, powerfully, and builds to a grandly sustained
climax. Carney and Stewart are the outstanding soloists here, but while listening
to them one is apt to miss the powerful walking bass lines Alvin "Junior" Raglin
contributes to this performance (Raglin having replaced the ailing Blanton in
November 1941). Raglin is especially inventive in the sixteen bars of Rex's solo,
contouring the bass notes into ingeniously twisting melodic lines, all delivered
with faultless medium tempo swing (Ex. 58).

Ex. 58

Powerful gradual building to a sustained climax is also what motivates *C-Jam
Blues*. Only here the buildup is held back until the five soloists, in direct succession, have all had a chance to present themselves in a single 12-bar blues chorus,
each preceded by a 4-bar solo break. The sequence of solos is piano (Ellington),
violin (Nance), muted trumpet (Stewart), tenor sax (Webster), plunger trombone
(Nanton). The sixth soloist, Barney Bigard, is, so to speak, swallowed up by the
full ensemble which during his two choruses rises up around him like a gigantic
tidal wave. The power of the final stanza is overwhelming, achieved with only
six brass (three trumpets, three trombones), three saxes in unison counter-lines,
a high-riding clarinet, and a steam-rolling rhythm section. In this connection
we should take note of that much underrated drummer Sonny Greer's impeccable monitoring of the solo sequences and absolute control of the final crescendo as he rides the band on to the final crest of the wave, and, once again,
Junior Raglin's perfect bass lines throughout, not only strong melodic/rhythmic
statements in their own right but also making excellent counterpoint with the
improvising soloists.

If *Take the A Train* marked Strayhorn's 1941 breakthrough composition and
performance, Ellington's *Main Stem* formed its 1942 obverse. In structure it
comprises a series of blues choruses (in D major)—in that sense a follow-up to
the highly successful *C-Jam Blues*—with a brief episode in G major providing
solo space for Webster in one of his more raucous statements, and Brown in

what may be the most blistering jazz solo of his recording career (Ex. 59). The remaining parade of stellar soloists includes Hodges, Stewart (who begins his improvisation with a mighty half-valve yelp, unknown to music theretofore), Nance, Bigard, and Nanton. And again it is the amazing rhythm section that sets the tone and pace—right from the start—and never lets up. It is the kind of piece which took the riff-tune idea, then already firmly run into the ground by hundreds of swing bands, and re-elevated it to a very high artistic level.

Ex. 59

There were, of course—even with Ellington—the lesser efforts and required standard fare: more mandatory vocals by Ivie Anderson and Herb Jeffries;[53] two more "Arabian" or "Latin" numbers—they could be interpreted either way for all of their pseudo-"authenticity"—*Bakiff* and *Moon Over Cuba*; minor items like the Basie-ish *Five O'Clock Drag* or the Goodman-ish *Are You Sticking?*. The last title refers to "licorice stick," the swing musicians' nickname for the clarinet. It is a rather too obvious attempt—surely not Ellington's idea, but likely some Victor recording producer's—to cash in on Goodman's renewed popular success in 1941, down even to Bigard's partial emulation of Goodman and Greer's momentary adaptation of Krupa's heavy-handed back-beat drumming. Or perhaps it was all a subtle spoof on Goodman and Krupa. Ellington was not incapable of it.

One final recording in this spate of 1940–42 performances must still be men-

53. One particularly fascinating Jeffries performance is *I Don't Know What Kind of Blues I Got*, for in it we hear *exactly* the kind of timbre and inflection we know from Billy Eckstine in the mid-forties. I am not certain who was imitating whom, although my hunch is that the younger Eckstine was influenced by the older Jeffries. Coincidentally, both singers sang with the Earl Hines orchestra, Jeffries in the mid-thirties, Eckstine in the early forties. What confuses the picture is that Jeffries generally tended towards a kind of contrived crooning in many of his Ellington recordings, but here on *I Don't Know* suddenly came out with a new "voice," whereas Eckstine seems to have been much more consistent and individual over the years with Hines in *his* approach. Perhaps both singers mutually influenced each other at various times. It might also be said that both were not unmindful of Bing Crosby's enormous popularity, even with black audiences—particularly Crosby's success with the ladies for his famous glottal scoops, for which he earned the sobriquet "The Groaner." Both Eckstine and Jeffries worked hard at incorporating this device in their singing styles, although with a black coloration that Crosby did not attain.

tioned. It is Ivie Anderson's sensitive interpretation of *I Got It Bad (and That Ain't Good)*, perhaps the most memorable of all in her distinguished career with Ellington's orchestra. She takes the song's sinuous melody—how Ellington loved those range-stretching melodic ninths in his songs!—

and disentangles it with such economy and warmth of expression, such unaffected simplicity, that the listener is deeply affected, is compelled to be touched. It is quite clear that a few other younger singers (like Woody Herman's Frances Wayne and Claude Thornhill's Fran Warren) also listened hard and were profoundly moved; the essence of their style derives directly from 1940s Ivie.

And how magnificently Hodges escorts her through the song, slithering caressingly through the twisting contours of Duke's tune, with nary a touch of vulgarity. Ellington himself scatters delectable celesta sprinkles over it all. The whole performance is in its simple warmth one of the truly magical moments in all jazz vocal literature.

Although Duke was unable to record in 1942 and 1943, he did not, of course, stop composing. Indeed he embarked on his most ambitious compositional project to date, the fifty-three-minute orchestral suite—he called it "a tone parallel to the history of the American Negro"—*Black, Brown and Beige*. Its premiere took place in New York's Carnegie Hall on January 23, 1943. *BBB* was the centerpiece of an all-Ellington concert, which initiated a series of annual such concerts in that august citadel of symphonic music. And *BBB* was of "symphonic" proportions, a complex work in three movements and innumerable subsections, which the orchestra rehearsed for several weeks at Nola Studios, the rehearsal mecca for all bands in those days.

Although *BBB* was unquestionably Ellington's major effort of the period, its less than enthusiastic reception, especially by the critics of both jazz and classical music, must have been a severe disappointment to him. Even as early as the rehearsals, attended by much of the jazz "intelligentsia," word began to spread that Duke's new composition was "a disappointment," "a failure," "didn't sound like much." The official critical reaction after the premiere was even less kind.

While *BBB* is a work not without blemishes, critical reaction in my view was—as is so often the case—too hasty, impatient, too harsh and, particularly in the case of the "classical" critics, too condescending. These "experts" emphasized the work's weaknesses, rather than focusing on its strengths, which in retrospect are considerable. In looking back on the work in its original form after some forty years,[54] we can see that its flaws, though easy to isolate, are much less significant in the overall work than its virtues.

The critics also failed to note the excellence of the performance *BBB* received

54. Ellington never performed *BBB* again in its entirety or original form, nor did he commit it to records in that form. A glass disc private recording is all that remains of the concert and the original *BBB* performance (recently issued commercially on Prestige P-34004).

that evening back in 1943. Nothing like it had ever been attempted by a jazz band—except perhaps for the Whiteman orchestra's performances of Gershwin works (his *Piano Concerto, Rhapsody in Blue*) and Ferde Grofé's *Grand Canyon Suite*. Given the complexity of BBB by 1940s' jazz standards, especially in respect to tempo considerations and intricacy of form, the performance was almost miraculous. The critics unanimously failed to realize that in a work like BBB— a work rooted in jazz tradition—the essence of *performance* was a much more important factor than some of the technical aspects of composition. They seemed to take Johnny Hodges's soulful rendition of *Come Sunday* (or Lawrence Brown's solos) for granted, whilst harping on the awkwardness of some of Ellington's brief transitional passages.

I believe that BBB is a much more substantial and successful work than anyone realized. It was, as so often with Duke, too far ahead of its time, treated like a kind of sacrificial lamb to progress and future developments in jazz. Unfortunately, Ellington, sensitive to the collective criticisms, lost the courage to perform the work in its original form and, rather than revise its minor shortcomings, broke the work up into a small number of separate shorter pieces, which he then performed regularly and recorded in succeeding years. Oddly enough—and sadly— a still later version of the first movement, *Black*, was recorded in 1958, in which the work's original flaws were unfortunately expanded rather than minimized, furthermore in a harsh sounding and poorly balanced performance. Insofar as that recording also failed to include the *Brown* and *Beige* sections, the recording was an injustice to the work rather than the revival it attempted to be. It is a shame that Ellington was persuaded to lose faith in BBB, because as a result music lost—more or less—a remarkable pioneer work; and, as mentioned, I believe its nonacceptance discouraged Duke from trying similar extended compositional challenges[55]—at least for a while. In crucial ways it interrupted the flow of his creative momentum.

Black, the first movement, is the longest and musically most substantial of the three, and divides into three larger sections. In keeping with its chronological position in the recounting of "the American Negro's history," *Black* is based largely on thematic material relating to work songs and spirituals. Over ominously dramatic timpani beats,[56] an imperious theme rises in unison brass and saxes (Ex. 60a), a heroic transformation of a phrase very much on Ellington's mind in those days, from *Don't Get Around Much Anymore* (Ex. 60b). The main theme has barely been stated when the basic tempo of the music doubles

55. The distinction I am making here is that, while Ellington thereafter wrote many suites and extended works, including the "Sacred Concerts," only rarely did he again attempt the extended complex proportions of BBB. Instead he built his later suites in sequences of single-continuity miniature forms.

56. Although a common enough, perhaps even obvious idea, its effectiveness is undeniable (its potency was certainly not unknown to composers like Mahler and Shostakovitch). But this opening lost a great deal in subsequent translation to tom-toms, where it was reduced to bombast rather than drama.

Ex. 60a

Ex. 60b

Dont get a-round much a-ny-more

in lightly swinging saxes, leading back to the main theme but now also doubled
up (Ex. 60c). In this intensified form it is finally hammered home three times
in canonic succession, first by the trombones, then an octave higher in the saxes,
and finally by high trumpets. This leads directly to the first of the work-song
emulations (Ex. 60d), a surprisingly bright energetic theme in the saxes.

Ex. 60c

Ex. 60d

An *a capella* transition by Carney brings forth a baritone solo in a seemingly
new tempo and key, which in retrospect, however, turns out to be the opening
tempo again and eventually brings back the proud main theme. A trumpet solo,
beautifully played by Harold Baker, leads to a new section featuring Nanton's

plunger trombone in another work song.[57] This section is beautifully extended by Ellington through various transformations of the work-song motive (always featuring Nanton), and by a gradual slowing of the tempo. Nanton's plaintive "yah-yahs" (Ex. 61a,b,c) give this passage an unforgettable poignancy, which unfortunately later Ellington trombonists were never able to recapture.

Ex. 61a

Ex. 61b

Ex. 61c

Episode two, the *Come Sunday* section, follows, introduced by Hardwick's songful alto. The actual *Come Sunday* theme is stated *adagio* by one tightly harmon-muted trumpet over subdued brass. This is one of the work's most evocative sections, a music with echoes of the prehistory of jazz, far removed from the whirl and excitements of the late-swing era. In its serene eventide mood, church bells quietly ringing, it summons up another time and place, the humble origins of the black spirituals and their mood of religious contemplation (and resignation?).

57. In view of the often hinted at but never demonstrated influence of Delius upon Ellington, it is worth noting that the great English composer, who as a young man spent some time on an orange plantation in Florida, used some of the same Negro work song material in *his* works, particularly in his 1902 *Appalachia*.

Lawrence Brown is now given the *Come Sunday* theme, accompanied by profoundly moving harmonies and voicings, which to the best of my knowledge are unique, even in Ellingtonia, and were never used in quite that way before or since. Once again the secret here lies in Ellington's masterful mixing of harmonic and timbral colors: suspended dominant harmonies (in second inversions) cast in the warm vibrant colors of his saxophone section. As Brown continues recalling the *Come Sunday* theme, Ray Nance's violin executes descant obbligatos which gradually assume the proportions of primary thematic substance. (After the Carnegie Hall premiere, Nance forsook these initial bowed figures, rendering them instead in pizzicato. Although technically possible in pizzicato, the passage lost some of its original elegance in that translation.) A brief modulation for piano and muted brass now leads to a restatement of the full *Come Sunday* theme, this time declaimed by Hodges in his truly inimitable fashion.

This melody (Ex. 62) is among Ellington's most sinuously beautiful and original. It is pure Ellington—no other composer of the time could have written

Ex. 62

it—and yet it also fully captures the quality and religious fervor of the Negro spiritual. In Hodges's interpretation in free recitative style, caressing the melody with his famous melting legatos and glissandos, stretching it rhythmically almost to the expressive breaking point, and accompanied by softly palpitating guitar tremolos and somber bowed bass tones, *Come Sunday* emerged as perhaps the most memorable high point of the entire work.

Another *a capella* transition, this time for solo trumpet, leads via some rather tawdry diminished chord arpeggios to the third part of *Black*, initiated by a bouncy but melodically undistinguished jump tune. But even this lesser material is turned into vintage Ellington by the plunger and half-valve manipulations Rex Stewart visits upon it, using parts of the work's main theme as subject matter. Various other work-song motives are then recapitulated by other soloists (including bassist Alvin Raglin and Lawrence Brown) backed by constantly varying instrumental groupings. A four-trumpet *a capella* passage, first heard during Nanton's solo episode earlier in the piece, is also revived. It is here that Ellington, in an attempt briefly to recapitulate most of the previous themes of *Black*, loses some control of the form. Nothing new or important happens to the material, and, with some four or five tempo changes, the continuity and coherence of the work are seriously disrupted. Indeed the final 56-bar section, apparently serving only to bring the movement to a more joyous close, seems tacked on, gratuitous, and thematically unrelated.

Some of the formlessness of the end of the first movement unfortunately extends over into the beginning of movement II, *Brown*. In a profusion of tempos, fragments and snippets of material—some of them quotations of banalities like *Swanee River* and *Yankee Doodle*—Ellington tries to depict various aspects of the Negro's contributions to the nineteenth century, from the American Revolution to the Civil War. There is even a musical bow—via some "Spanish-tinged" passages—to the migration of blacks from the Caribbean to the U.S. and some train music suggesting emigrations to the north. Apart from a lusty plunger-muted brass trio (two trumpets, one trombone), this opening section of *Brown* is a confused and often redundant jumble of second-rate ideas, left undeveloped and only crudely integrated. A mournful (again too brief) saxophone duet in alto and tenor is interrupted by a harshly discordant four-octave rising figure, presumably symbolizing the upheaval brought to the lives of blacks by the Civil War. But this is followed by a joyful "Emancipation Celebration," proclaimed by Rex Stewart's trumpet, joined in due course by Nanton and some happily stomping Raglin bass.

The twentieth century and the blacks' gradual urbanization are symbolized by the Blues, city blues, in a section originally subtitled *Mauve* by Ellington (or Strayhorn). The text by Duke employs an ingenious metrical structure based upon the twin principle of expansion and contraction.

> The Blues . . .
> The Blues ain't . . .
> The Blues ain't nothin' . . .
> The Blues ain't nothin' but a cold gray day
> And all night long it stays that way.
> 'Tain't sump'n' that leaves you alone,
> 'Tain't nothin' I want to call my own
> 'Tain't sump'n' with sense enough to get up and go,
> 'Tain't nothin' like nothin' I know.
> The Blues . . .
> The Blues don't . . .
> The Blues don't know . . .
> The Blues don't know nobody as a friend,

Ain't been nowhere where they're welcome back again.
Low, ugly, mean blues,
The Blues ain't sump'n' that you sing in rhyme;
The Blues ain't nothin' but a dark cloud markin' time;
The Blues is a one-way ticket from your love to nowhere;
The Blues ain't nothin' but a black crepe veil ready to wear.
Sighin', cryin', feel most like dyin' . . .
The Blues ain't nothin' . . .
The Blues ain't . . .
The Blues . . .

The music, of course, reflects this formal scheme, although—like prose or free verse—it does so in a free-tempo unmeasured form. At the premiere *The Blues* was soulfully intoned by the rich contralto voice of Betty Roché (Ellington's singer of the time), accompanied in stark low register chords and dark instrumental colors.

At the words "Low, ugly, mean blues," a shrill atonal chord with turbulent percussion intrusions interrupts the blues, transferred now from the human voice to Ben Webster's eloquent tenor (sounding here more like Hodges). Without transition or benefit of modulation, Ellington then launches into the only orthodox 12-bar blues in *BBB*, stated in bitonal parallel triads by the trombones. (These twelve bars—again too short and undeveloped—were expanded within a year into *Carnegie Blues* and henceforth performed as a separate work, no longer associated with *BBB*.) The voice now returns with the closing stanza, the individual lines shrinking to the final two syllables: "The Blues." A dank dismal chord of ambiguous tonality ends the section, leaving the listener with a disturbing sense of unendedness—and hopelessness.

Beige, the last movement of *BBB*, depicts the history of the Negro in Ellington's own time: the years between the two World Wars. Paradoxically it is the weakest of the three movements. Its formal uncertainty reveals signs of hasty patching together of materials, a trait which was to mar many of the extended works of the later years. More even than in the second movement, Ellington tries to cram too much history into too brief a musical space. The horrors of World War I, the Harlem of the twenties—presumably the gin mills, the false gaiety of the cabarets, the after-hours life (with sly tributes to Willie "the Lion" Smith and Rachmaninov's famous *Prelude* and perhaps to Duke's own party piano), the religious life of Harlem (intoned in a hymn-like passage anchored by Hardwick's sober bass sax), the Harlem Renaissance and its attempts at elegance and social acceptance in a white-dominated world (this portrayed in a suave waltz, beautifully played by Baker in the Carnegie Hall premiere), the worldly sophistication of a Sugar Hill penthouse—all these pass in review in eclectic and disconcerting array.

Gone was the structural unity or controlled thematic unfolding of *Reminiscing in Tempo, Ko-Ko, Cotton Tail*, and *Diminuendo and Crescendo in Blue*. The problem was, I think, not the conceptual one of dealing with all those aspects of contemporary Negro life (although integrating such diversity into a single work of any kind—a book, a painting, a musical composition, a film—could be daunting to any creator), but rather that Ellington failed to realize that such representations reproduced literally and imitatively would at best destroy the work's stylistic consistency and at worst impair Ellington's own creative vision. Whereas so often in the past Ellington had absorbed and transformed various influences, musical and otherwise, subsuming them into a personal language and style entirely his own, here in *Beige* he was misled into duplicating Harlem's musical diversity in a literalistic way that could not possibly assimilate into a single unified work. Like a cluttered living room furnished in too many styles, *Beige* displays its too many undigested lumps of musical bric-a-brac, and instead of prime Ellington we are left with too many handed-down prosaic musical commonplaces.

Beige starts with a discordant, inchoate, and substantively empty music, presumably depicting the horrors of World War I—Ellington was never good at writing noise—and ends with an equally fustian patriotic mélange that sounds thrown together and tacked on. (Some last-minute revisions and cuts were evidently made in the final rehearsals, the scars of which can be readily heard, particularly in Duke's frequent solo piano "fill-in" transitions.) The movement is, however, elevated to approximate Ellington stature by the fine playing of Baker and Brown (in the waltz section), Carney in a relatively rare (and not entirely in tune) appearance on clarinet, and a brief recapitulation by Hodges of the *Come Sunday* theme.

Reactions to *BBB* were, as mentioned, mostly negative. They were also divided along traditional "classical" and "jazz" lines, the classical critics complaining about Ellington's lack of formal control, the jazz critics complaining about the lack of real jazz. There was little sympathy among the classical critics that Ellington was venturing into new and uncharted territory, and that he did not wish to resort to the tried and true symphonic forms to control the work's inherent narrative complexity. He saw, even if they did not, that to pour the unavoidable formal and stylistic diversity of *BBB* into classical molds would be to stifle the music. Given the subject and the nature of the music, it needed to remain free and unbounded. It is better for Ellington to have tried to embrace this formal diversity, even if not entirely succeeding, than to abandon the idea at the outset to begin with and fall back on "safe" formulas and classical schemes.

The failure of jazz critics to recognize that *BBB* attempted—as did all of Ellington's music in one way of another—to go beyond the confines of "jazz" as defined by the critics, was the same that greeted Joplin's *Treemonisha* for not being a "ragtime" opera. Neither Ellington nor Joplin was content to be restricted in their creative visions and imaginations by critical and popular tastes. The jazz afficionados' disappointment over *BBB*'s failure to "comply" with prevailing jazz, i.e. swing criteria, tells us much more about *their* limitations than those they ascribed to Ellington. At the very least, for all its admitted flaws, *Black, Brown and Beige* represented—in Leonard Feather's excellent phrase— "the elevation of jazz to an orchestral art."

Although this is not the place to discuss in detail Ellington's late *oeuvre*, in particular his extended or suite compositions, it may be appropriate to speak in very general terms of his (and Strayhorn's) efforts in this direction and the problems they encountered in these more ambitious undertakings. As a broad generality it can be said—indeed *has* been said—that Ellington never fully succeeded in his almost lifelong quest to express himself in larger, not just longer, forms. This is a more serious issue than may appear at first glance, because Ellington's failure here was not one of simply falling short of achieving certain goals—that can and does happen occasionally to even the greatest composers—but that he never really understood the nature of the problem he was facing in undertaking to write in larger forms.

It is remarkable to see how quickly Ellington in his early years learned from his mistakes. The quantum leaps from *Trombone Blues* to *Black and Tan Fantasy* (with Bubber Miley's help, to be sure), from *Jubilee Stomp* to *Old Man Blues*, from *Creole Rhapsody* to *Reminiscing in Tempo*, from *Reminiscing* to *Diminuendo and Crescendo in Blue*, and from there to *Ko-Ko*, are clear evidence of the extraordinary path of his creative growth.

But, as I have pointed out earlier, this process of growth and development—in the earlier years continuously tested in the crucible of daily public performance and through instant application of his ideas to his constantly available orchestra—was broken in the mid-forties. In particular, the lessons that might have been learned from the formal challenges encountered in *Black, Brown and Beige* seemed to have been abandoned. Certainly no further attempts to grapple with conceptually larger forms were forthcoming, and by all evidence Ellington avoided the issue henceforth, specifically by retreating to the comparative safety of the suite form. The advantage of this format—it is to all intents and purposes a non-form (in the large sense)—is that it allows the composer to bypass the basic problems inherent in constructing longer, larger orchestral designs, limiting himself instead to a loose succession of smaller forms. And that is a skill which Ellington, and evidently Strayhorn as well, never were willing to acquire.

There are some talents involved in the art of composition which can be inborn, intuitive, or acquired subconsciously by absorption of a given musical environment. Ellington certainly had an abundance of these talents: a fantastic ear, an incredible gift for harmony, a talent for original melodic invention, an extraordinary sense of color and of fantasy. But other compositional skills have to be learned, usually by some form of systematic study. From this requirement even the genius is not exempt, although obviously he does not need to acquire these in academic or formal settings.[58] Indeed such craft is often absorbed by composers simply through the study of others' works, and these would inevitably have to include the masterpieces of European music of the last three centuries or so.

Of course, there were no precedents available in the jazz field for Ellington to study, had he even been so inclined. He certainly was not inclined to study—and seemed not even particularly aware of—the great works of European musical

58. It is well to remember that even a genius like Beethoven felt the need to acquire certain additional composition-technical training when already a young adult, and thus embarked upon a two-year course of study with Salieri, the most renowned teacher in Vienna at the time.

art. Jazz musicians in general, at least until more recent generations, have been quite uninterested in and unaware of conceptual developments in classical music (although I suspect that the wily Jelly Roll Morton did try to learn a thing or two from certain more ambitious examples of the classical literature: operas, religious music, piano classics).[59]

In addition, it must be remembered that the kind of autodidactic approach many composers take was essentially unavailable to Ellington, who for other good and honorable reasons spent a lifetime on one-night stands, in hotels and on trains, and was continually occupied in resisting the constant commercial pressures urging him and his orchestras to do artistically *less* than they might.

The unavoidable truth is that large forms do require certain developmental, variational, and integrative skills of the composer, and generally impose demands which his natural innate talents alone may not be able to meet.

In response to the general rejection of *BBB*, Ellington sought refuge in the suite format, which essentially allowed the miniaturist in him to continue to operate at full creative tilt. But even here, in many of the extended suite works, Ellington's talents were taxed beyond their resources. However, I am quite certain that in most cases the weaknesses that crept into these works were more the result of pragmatic conditions, which Ellington faced all his life as a constantly traveling musician. The luxury of working at home in relative seclusion over extended periods of time was virtually unknown to him. And after a certain time he did not even see this as a deprivation, or perhaps he just became immune to it. It is well-known that he considered the maintenance of his orchestra as paramount, even to the detriment of his composing, which—so he reasoned—would not be worthwhile without access to a permanent orchestra. The orchestra was "the instrument" on which he performed, but also the instrument of his sacrifice. He gave up much for it, including the leisure of composing away from it.

In the ultimate assessment of Ellington's failure to work successfully in organically larger forms, the reasons just cited may, of course, not be enough. For high art permits no excuses. With but only the rarest exceptions, an art reproduces only that which is put into it; and every decision, be it of the artist's own making or one imposed from without, will in some crucial way affect that art. For Ellington the choice was clear and unavoidable. For others it would have been decided otherwise.

But before we judge Ellington too harshly, we might do well to remember that the whole question of large forms in jazz has not yet been entirely satisfactorily answered by anyone else. And part of the problem—indeed its core prob-

---

59. James P. Johnson, a more astute observer of at least some aspects of the classical piano literature—and in many respects Ellington's early idol and musical mentor—also came to grief in attempting larger forms in his more ambitious "symphonic" works for somewhat the same reason that plagued Ellington: a lack of formal control. In works like *Yamekraw (Negro Rhapsody)*, *Harlem Symphony*, and even his 1939 *Piano Concerto in A flat* (Johnson's most ambitious and successful extended effort), the basic musical ideas, though tuneful and attractive, are not of sufficient substance to permit extensive development. There is in these pieces also no indication that Johnson had the vision to think in larger forms, other than by resorting to repetition and an occasional chromatically "advanced" modulation or interlude between tunes.

lem—is the integration of improvisation and composition. It is significant that improvisation in the truest and most liberal sense is virtually suppressed by Ellington in his extended works. While earlier extended works, such as *Reminiscing in Tempo* and *Diminuendo and Crescendo in Blue*, had simply eliminated improvisation altogether, the later works were written around individual soloists (*Perfume Suite, Liberian Suite, Far East Suite, Suite Thursday*, for example), individual movements featuring specific soloists. But these were more an extension of the concertos of the late thirties, "vignette" concertos, in which the solos were rarely true improvisation, but rather written down and/or memorized solo parts, played essentially the same way each time.

The exclusion of improvisation is all the more regrettable since Ellington had shown in dozens of remarkable shorter earlier pieces how composition and improvisation *could* be merged. Of course, one knows—and I'm sure Ellington knew—the problems such fusings can create and how difficult they are to solve, both on the composer's *and* the improviser's side. For example, it is quite conceivable that in certain of Ellington's more "linguistically" advanced works, such as *Harlem* or the first two movements of the *Liberian Suite*, he did not feel he could entrust individual improvisation to any of his soloists at the time. And he was right, for none of these players could have grasped in improvisational terms the advanced complex language Ellington was himself experimenting with, and even he not always altogether successfully. Even the younger, more modern players like Clark Terry, Britt Woodman, and Bill Berry could not have coped with such material without stylistically going outside of it, for *they* were committed to the harmonic/melodic language of bop, which Ellington had long ago passed through and now moved beyond. Furthermore, Ellington did not often turn to the very young, aurally modern-oriented players. In replacing his original musicians he turned more often than not to "older" already established players whose musical roots lay in the late twenties, early thirties: musicians like Claude Jones, Quentin Jackson, Russell Procope, Hilton Jefferson, all born in the first decade of the century. Britt Woodman, Paul Gonsalves, Oscar Pettiford, and Clark Terry were the exceptional "youngsters."

On the composer's side—even allowing for his experiments with atonality, free counterpoint and out-of-tempo passages—Ellington encountered problems of his own with which his players could certainly not help him, as Bubber Miley had been able to do in the early days. For by the time the larger-form experiments began in earnest, not only with Ellington but in jazz in general, Ellington was inextricably tied to the concept of the tone poem (his term "tone parallel" constitutes only a minor semantic difference). Ironically, the tone-poem concept evolved with Ellington out of the initially pragmatic necessity of providing music for all sorts of *tableaux* and "production numbers" at the Cotton Club. But it was also, of course, crucial in stimulating and exercising Ellington's considerable aural and visual imagination. By working so consistently in the tone-poem or rhapsodic formats, both relatively free-structured forms to begin with and primarily determined by extra-musical considerations (visual, literary, historical), Ellington seemed never able to free himself from the apparent need for musical pictorialism. With the happy exception of *Happy Go Lucky Local*, many of his later works were in crucial ways restrained by these pictorial ties. By contrast *Reminiscing in Tempo, Diminuendo and Crescendo in Blue, Ko-Ko, Concerto for Cootie, Cotton Tail,* were free of such extra-musical allusions; and surely Ellington was on the right track in those works, not to the exclusion, of course, of highly successful pieces in the descriptive genre, like *Daybreak Express, Bojangles, Warm Valley* (which had very little to do with valleys in the geological or geographic sense).

Although both Jelly Roll Morton and Thelonious Monk—to name two other major jazz composers (from two totally different periods)—occasionally gave their pieces whimsical titles—*Grandpa's Spells, Winin' Boy Blues, Shoe Shiner's Drag, Straight No Chaser, Well, You Needn't, Ruby, My Dear*—their music's character and shape evolved out of their personal language, not out of any extra-musical considerations. The same can be said about literally thousands of jocularly and haphazardly titled jazz pieces—titles in jazz have only rarely (and only mostly recently) had any intrinsic connection with the given piece—although it is also true that Monk wrote *Little Rootie Tootie,* a train piece, and Morton wrote musical portraits such as *The Pearls* and *King Porter Stomp.*

Unlike Morton and Monk, Ellington was, for all of his advanced musical visions, in some ways a conservative—most particularly in regard to the fundamental language of jazz. As suggested earlier, he never did make the transition to a language and grammar of jazz capable of producing music *on its own unique terms,* out of its own intrinsic musical-linguistic resources, i.e. without benefit of extra-musical or visual inspirations. And this fundamental difference represents, of course, the dramatic dividing line between the Swing Era and all post-1945 jazz.

If a composer of Ellington's magnitude was unable to bring off a large-scale composition, with or without the integration of improvisation, must we assume that jazz is not capable of achieving such goals? Not at all, although, as noted, the problems have not as yet been entirely and permanently resolved. But one can point to the evidence of a number of individual successful solutions. Even with, in some cases, totally different objectives and methods in mind, such works by Charles Mingus as *Pithecanthropus Erectus* and *Revelations,* George Russell's *All About Rosie,* Tadd Dameron's *Fontainebleau,* Bill Russo's *Image of Man,* John Carisi's *Angkor Wat,* Ornette Coleman's *Free Jazz,* Leo Smith's *Black Fire in Motherland,* this writer's *Variants on a Theme of Thelonious Monk* and *Conversations,* as well as pieces perhaps more in the suite format such as John Lewis's *Comedy* and J. J. Johnson's *Poem for Brass,* all have in common *inherently* larger form conceptions, some admittedly without the use of improvisation, some attempting a synthesis of jazz and classical concepts, others not. Whether these pieces (and others like them) have abandoned the realm of jazz, or place an emphasis alternatively on jazz or classical procedures—or a blend of both, is ultimately insignificant. Such categorizations are meaningless at the higher levels of creativity, for it is the *musical* result, not the stylistic pedigree, which determines a work's validity. The continuous attempts on the part of critics on both sides of the stylistic fence to stigmatize Ellington represent but one unfortunate example of this apparent need to label, classify, and typecast.

It is distressing that Ellington could not (would not) resolve his formal limitations, since the actual thematic content in the late-period Suites was often quite striking. Indeed, on a small scale his melodic and harmonic invention, as well as his use of instrumental color, were often as brilliant as ever. But, as mentioned, larger forms do require that thematic material be developed—in *some* way or other. And here Ellington's lack of technique and formal skills hindered him. He was content to repeat thematic material, mostly with only the scantest of variations (or indeed none), too frequently relying on endless pedal points, on rambling piano interludes filled in by himself, and more often than not simply breaking off arbitrarily, turning to entirely different unrelated material. This lack of direction and lack of thematic unity occasionally led to the most incongruous juxtapositions. But even in their milder manifestations, rarely could one hear the relevance of one section of music to another. At best, themes and ideas simply succeeded each other; rarely did one have that sense of inevitability which marks great art. Even attempts to link movements together by some unifying element—like the minor sixth interval that is used as a motivic cell throughout *Suite Thursday*—failed because the unifying material was not striking or original enough (a descending minor sixth does not in and of itself make strong thematic material) or was subjected to too many disruptive unrelated incursions.

The real tragedy, of course, was that Ellington's lifelong dream was to write a major extended dramatic work, in fact an opera. He spoke of this often with friends, and I myself can recall more than several occasions when he spoke most feelingly of this overriding ambition—in particular one all-night til-dawn session in Quebec in the early sixties. But even then I could sense that *he knew* it was a dream he would never realize. In the end the Sacred Concerts of the later years took over those aspirations in the form of quasi-dramatic narrative works— religious "dramas," as it were.

Despite Ellington's inability to solve the problems of larger or extended forms, it goes almost without saying that, given his enormous talent, there is much of great value and enjoyment to be found in the later works—right along with the frequent dross, bombast, and tawdry passages. One might single out the *Lay-By* movement (with Nance's superbly organized violin feature) of *Suite Thursday*; from the *Far East Suite* the poetic, sensuous *Isfahan* movement (written for Hodges) to celebrate the historic "Pearl of Persia"; the quite advanced *Madness in Great Ones* and *Sonnet for Caesar* from *Such Sweet Thunder* (also known as *Shakespearean Suite*); or the *"Almost Cried"* section from Ellington's film score for *Anatomy of a Murder*.

But still it is in such later short pieces as *Blues in Blueprint* (1960), *Launching Pad* (1959), Strayhorn's *Blues in Orbit* (1958), and the poignant lament *Where's the Music* (1958) for just four "horns" and rhythm section that we hear the true unfettered, uncluttered, unadulterated Ellington at his most quintessential.

As already noted, the 1942–43 recording ban and the critical failure of *Black, Brown and Beige* seem to have broken Ellington's creative momentum. The peak he and his orchestra reached in the first two and a half years of the decade was never to be equalled again, at least not with such consistency. High achievements, more and more sporadic in later years, were surrounded by much routine and even mundane music-making, especially in live concerts. There was never any question that at any given moment in a given locale, especially when touring in far-off exotic places, the orchestra would take inspiration from any number of stimuli and produce electrifying performances—I heard some in Santiago, Chile, and London, England (to name only two), that will forever be indelibly etched in my memory. But that is speaking of the orchestra's performing qualities. Duke's creativity as a composer and arranger, though still capable of extraordinary heights (and still a notch or two above most of his competitors), waned and turned somewhat erratic.

Alongside visionary pieces like *The Clothed Woman* or provocative arrangements like those from the 1962–63 Reprise (and Atlantic) series re-creating two dozen hit themes from the past (especially Hadjidakis's *Never on Sunday* or Kenton's *Artistry in Rhythm*); or the remarkable 1962 date with Coleman Hawkins, or the collaboration with Dizzy Gillespie on *U.M.M.G.* in 1959, one is apt to find trivia like *Blossom*, horribly played to boot; and that ultimate (*unmusical*) travesty, *La Virgen de la Macarena*; or some of the more overblown and vapid sections of his extended suites.

It is ironic that the Ellington band's popularity was at its greatest at a time—the early postwar period—when the quality of its music-making, both in creative and performance terms, had in fact begun to level off. (This is a phenomenon to be observed frequently in the arts: composers acclaimed by the larger public only long after their peak period or, indeed, after their lifetime; opera singers glorified by audiences when they are well past their prime; painters revered long after their finest work has been accomplished and after years of starvation.) By 1946 long-term residencies, such as the one at the Hurricane Club in New York, solidly booked tours, and frequent recordings were some of the material benefits Ellington and his men were beginning to reap. Unfortunately much of what they recorded was of little consequence: remakes of earlier compositions, attempting to capitalize on their new-found fame with the old successes, the obligatory vocals (especially the light-weight novelty vocals of Ray Nance, like *You Gotta Crawl, Kitty*, and *Antidisestablishmentarianismist*), and other inconsequential items like *Boogie Bop Blues*. Worthy exceptions did occur, of course—*Airconditioned Jungle*, Al Hibbler's performance of *Do 'Nothin' 'Till You Hear from Me*, and Joya Sherrill's of *I'm Beginning to See the Light*, and Betty Roché's of *Take the A Train*, and that amazing atonal creative tour de force, *The Clothed Woman*—but they were just that: exceptions. Whereas five years earlier the average and mediocre had been the exceptions.[60]

A major factor in the comparative decline of the Ellington band in the forties was the departure of a number of key players. Cootie Williams had already left

60. Later successes, both artistic and/or popular, include *Satin Doll* (1953), *Kinda Dukish* (1953), *A Tone Parallel to Harlem* (1951), *Drum Is a Woman* (1956), *Such Sweet Thunder* (1957), the 1964 *Far East Suite*; the music for the film *Anatomy of a Murder* (1959), the recording of Ralph Burns's *Early Autumn*, Ellington's and Strayhorn's recomposition of Edvard Grieg's *Peer Gynt*, and *Night Creature* (1955) for large symphony orchestra and jazz band.

in late 1940, to be replaced by Ray Nance. Barney Bigard left in mid-1942, followed by Ben Webster in 1943 and Juan Tizol in 1949, the latter leaving for the greener pastures of Harry James's band. Other virtually irreparable losses occurred in 1945 and 1946 when Rex Stewart and Otto Hardwick departed, and when the uniquely gifted "Tricky Sam" Nanton died, taking the secrets of his inimitable plunger style with him to his grave. The exodus continued in 1949 with Fred Guy's departure—Ellington was thereafter never to use a guitar again—and then in 1951, the biggest blow of all, when three long-time stalwarts of the band left: Johnny Hodges, Lawrence Brown, and Sonny Greer.

Although, measured by any other standards, there were fine replacements for all these departees, none could ever really take their places—for two reasons: the original players were all in one way or another as gifted as any that jazz has known, and, second—and more important—they were unique, "originals." Anybody who followed after them was bound to be to some extent an imitator, at high levels of musicianship and skill, to be sure, but nevertheless an imitator.

The one major alternative to Ellington's replacement policy would have been for him to abandon his existing course and to sail with the prevailing winds into the land of bop and modern jazz. A band which included Charlie Parker, Dizzy Gillespie, J. J. Johnson, Bud Powell, Oscar Pettiford, and Max Roach and led by Ellington might have seemed to some to be the ideal dream band. But, of course, it wouldn't have been, and Ellington knew it. For all kinds of good and profound reasons he had to continue along the path *he* had chosen and followed over so many years.

This fact points to another crucial truism. I have said earlier that Ellington was in the first twenty years of his career creatively beyond and above all his competitors, and to a significant extent apart from the mainstream of jazz. Someone of such striking originality and leadership has either to be followed (as Armstrong was), or, failing that, must stand apart from the pack. In Ellington's case this was not a major issue as long as the leading styles of the day were tangent to Ellington's and as long as his music could on occasion (as in the swing era) be incorporated into the prevailing mainstream. By 1945, however, a distinct rift with the past had occurred in jazz, one that was to lead the music in dramatically different directions.

Ellington really had no choice. The sheer immensity of his creative talent ordained that he could never be a mere follower, and to abandon all that he had achieved—some of the greatest moments in twentieth-century music—would have been absolute folly and, realistically, unthinkable. Indeed, it is to Ellington's eternal credit that, unlike many bandleaders more or less of his generation, Ellington never hopped on the bop bandwagon, an occasional experiment with "modern jazz" notwithstanding. Thus, in the late forties and fifties, Ellington stood ever more apart from the prevailing mainstream of jazz.

But Ellington had in reality always personified "modern jazz"—whether in 1927 or in 1940. His new role as the keeper of an earlier tradition—as well as that of his own unique tradition—was a curious one for Duke, having consistently been regarded by his peers as a pioneer far out on the musical frontier. If it is true that Ellington was, in the early years, always musically, stylistically, creatively ahead of his contemporaries, it was true in the *last* thirty years of his career only in a limited sense or in specific instances. And as I have already suggested, he never made the transition to "modern jazz" per se, although he had helped so crucially to shape that future. (For example, Woody Herman's First Herd represents a most compelling amalgam of Ellington's legacy and bop, via Ralph Burns and Dizzy Gillespie respectively.)

To put it more precisely, Ellington always remained a modernist, especially harmonically, but he did so within his own unique concept, not the basically different directions of bop and modern jazz. This despite the fact that on occasion Ellington could still out-modernize, out-harmonize, out-compose, out-swing any of his younger colleagues (at least in *some* of these respects until Ornette Coleman came along), but that would be in terms of details, not of fundamental concepts. And to say that Duke remained apart from the central developments in modern jazz is not to invoke a criticism, but merely an explanation of what in fact took place. To which one can only add that Ellington's musical concepts were, even in the later years, always grand enough to embrace the work of a John Coltrane (as on the 1962 Impulse date) or a Gillespie (as on the 1959 Columbia *U.M.M.G.* date).

The late forties and early fifties were for Ellington also economically lean years and, as mentioned, years of mostly modest artistic achievements.[61] Indeed, until 1953 when Ellington joined Capitol Records, his recording activity was dramatically reduced: apart from the second nationwide recording ban in 1948, only two dates of mostly vocals in 1949, two dates in 1950 (one of little artistic merit, the other primarily remakes of earlier compositions), and a mere five dates in 1951 and 1952, many of these devoted to more remakes.

During this period, moreover, Ellington's band experienced a veritable parade of transient personnel, in itself precluding the kind of artistic stability and growth the band had generally enjoyed in the two decades before 1945. It was not until many of the band's veterans returned to the fold, one by one, somewhat sheepishly—first Hodges, then Brown and Williams—that the Ellington orchestra regained some of its earlier glory. With these exceptional voices back in place, many of the recordings of the sixties took on some of the orchestra's old luster and uniqueness.

The loss of key personnel around 1950, the rejection and relative failure of his more ambitious compositional efforts, the comparative isolation from the mainstream of jazz, the economic uncertainties of the postwar era—all contributed to a significant loss in Ellington's creative consistency. Perhaps the standards he had set himself, especially in the period between 1937 and 1944, could not have been maintained under any circumstances. Indeed there is no precedent in jazz for such astonishingly consistent life-long creative growth. (One

---

61. The last three decades of Ellington's career will be dealt with in detail in the next volume of this History.

must turn to the great classical masters of the past like Bach, Mozart, Beethoven, Wagner, and Verdi to find such persistent artistic unfoldment.) And it is probably too early to tell whether later jazz figures such as Monk, Mingus, Davis, Coltrane, and Coleman had within them the potential for such enduring growth— if indeed their talent is of the magnitude of Ellington's in the first place.

Nonetheless, despite the unevenness of some of Ellington's later work, what *is* remarkable is that 1) he never stopped creating and experimenting; 2) never succumbed in any prolonged or significant way to the commercial pressures of the popular market (within which, let us remind ourselves, jazz was then firmly located), and 3) maintained his full orchestra to the end of his life, even as other bandleaders were abandoning theirs, and even when he had personally to subsidize his.

Ellington composed incessantly to the very last days of his life. Music was indeed his mistress; it was his total life, and his commitment to it was incorruptible and unalterable. In jazz he was a giant among giants. And in twentieth-century music he may yet one day be recognized as one of the half-dozen greatest masters of our time.

3

Louis Armstrong

"That's my livin' and my life. I love them notes. That's why I try to make 'em right, see?" Those words—Louis's own—are perhaps as good a summation and explanation of that phenomenon called Louis Armstrong as can be found. In some profound sense it is not much more complicated than that. There is, of course, his talent—his genius, if you will. But then Louis always felt, and deepdown knew, that his talent, his ability to put his lips to his horn and produce "all them beautiful notes," was a gift he had been chosen to receive and to exercise in music every day. All pride aside, he saw himself simply as a courier, a bearer through whom music could be transmitted. Armstrong the "entertainer" could not get used to the idea of being portrayed as Armstrong the "artist." Just "getting 'em right" and making audiences happy with his music *was* his life, and the trumpet was the instrumentality through which he expressed himself.

He was much more Scott Joplin's "The Entertainer" than Rousseau's "Noble Savage" or the nineteenth century's lonely misunderstood "Romantic Artist." Armstrong in all likelihood saw himself as an artisan, a craftsman, and perhaps on occasion proudly, as a "professional." That he was the first major soloist in jazz and elevated the music to the level of an art is indisputable, even if such thoughts were alien to him. For a man may be an artist even when he himself doesn't realize it—and even when he is the most popular personality jazz has ever known.

And yet, linking Armstrong to the thirties and forties, the Swing Era, is not without its perplexities and controversy, for the fact is that he was in a sense not really a part of the swing era. Remaining true to his own artistic tenets and the musical revolution he had enkindled in the twenties, he stayed apart from the next two evolutionary waves that propelled jazz forward, even as his music still indirectly animated and informed these developments. It was odd that Louis in effect remained in the background during the swing era, insulated from it—odd because, unlike the other older New Orleanians or for that matter their *epigones*, the Chicagoans, Louis was world famous. After all, you were not offered roles in Hollywood musicals with Bing Crosby or Mae West if you hadn't "arrived," especially if your skin was black.

Part of the explanation for that kind of stardom—a limited stardom, to be sure—is that Armstrong's fame rested in the thirties upon his discovery by European intellectuals and music lovers and by American insiders. But we already know that the large public crowned Benny Goodman "The King," not Armstrong; and swing was where it was at. Like Ellington, Armstrong never really participated in the swing era—notwithstanding the fact, ironically, that he virtually invented and certainly perfected swing.

Curiously, Armstrong seems also to have been oblivious of the fact that the younger players—and some, like Coleman Hawkins, Lester Young, and Roy Eldridge were not all that much younger—were expanding upon his teachings and to some extent overthrowing them. As far as one can tell, Armstrong initially took little notice of the work of his successors, Henry Allen, Eldridge, and Dizzy Gillespie. This is in sharp contrast to Gillespie, for example, who has catalogued with picayune exactitude every minuscule variation on and derivation of his style—or lack thereof—as he found them in *his* successors and colleagues, from Miles Davis on and including even non-trumpeters like Thelonious Monk. It matters a great deal to Dizzy what, in his view, other younger players owe him, whereas, for Armstrong, this was a matter of only the mildest concern—and awareness.[1] He must have known what Gillespie surely could not have known, that in one way or another, superficially or profoundly, every jazz musician— and even most popular musicians—was indebted to him. And perhaps Armstrong also knew, in his wise and lovable way, that style and individuality of language are arrived at gradually, organically in bits and pieces, and by a process of osmosis not always traceable in every detail, especially as the number of a musical style's practitioners multiplies and as its creative stream expands into a delta.

What is strange, and a little sad too, is that, as the swing craze broke, so little recognition was given to Armstrong as its true progenitor. Oh yes, many musicians admired Louis, even revered him, which is not to say that they always understood their indebtedness to him—until years later. I am sure that Hawkins did, and Billie Holiday and Lester Young—and Roy Eldridge eventually too. But I wonder how conscious Fletcher Henderson was of the fact that his arranging style, which became the basis of big-band swing, was itself a child of Armstrong's rhythmic revolution, as initially translated into orchestral terms by Don Redman, Benny Carter, Sy Oliver, John Nesbitt—and more remotely, even Gene Gifford. Certainly Benny Goodman had little or no appreciation of this fact, nor did the great wide public. As entertainment consumers they really did not care

1. It is fascinating in this connection to learn that Dizzy initially did not listen very much to Armstrong, but was instead strongly influenced by Eldridge; nor did Eldridge at first. Typically, the "young turk," Gillespie, at first regarded Armstrong as old-fashioned, and only realized later that he had really been listening to Armstrong all along, but *through* Eldridge, and that Armstrong was the fountainhead from which he too sprang.

where this "new thing" came from. It was enough that it was there. They did not yell "Author! Author!" And Louis didn't seem to mind. His thoughts were on "them beautiful notes" and, increasingly, getting those high E♭s and Fs.

When the thirties broke, Armstrong had already created any number of masterpieces—*West End Blues, Muggles, Weatherbird, Potato Head Blues, Savoy Blues*—and had virtually singlehandedly forged the new rhythmic language of jazz that would in turn be its foundation for decades and set the stage for things to come. He was recognized by most musicians, certainly all black musicians, as the master. A whole generation of musicians fed on his musical imagination, his ideas, technique, and style. In the hands of many of them, they quickly became the clichés and routine devices of the period—that is, until they were rescued and expanded upon in the early forties by a handful of younger originators.

But by that time Armstrong had become something quite different, at least externally, from what he was in the mid- and late twenties: namely a star trumpeter-singer-bandleader. Though his recordings in the twenties had sometimes been labeled "Louis Armstrong and His Orchestra," they were generally, granted a few exceptions, quintet or sextet recordings, follow-ups to the breakthrough success of the Hot Fives and Hot Sevens. But in early 1929 Armstrong began performing and recording exclusively with big-band backing[2]—a state of affairs that, much to the dismay of his small-group fans, lasted unbroken until 1940, when Louis returned, at first reluctantly and intermittently, to a small-band format. This eleven-year exclusive involvement with big-band fronting—Louis recorded over 200 sides during that period—was in many ways problematic, although Louis apparently did not see it that way. There were several problems, some of which have been the source of controversy among critics, jazz historians, and Armstrong fans for decades.[3] First there is the problem that, unlike many other major soloists, Armstrong had no band-leading ambitions as such. He merely wanted to *front* a band. He never thought in other than solo virtuoso terms, and the orchestra was merely a convenient backdrop against which to present himself. By the same token he was not at all interested in the quality of arrangements or even the types of groups that backed him, witness his recordings with the Mills Brothers, various Hawaiian and choral groups. Nor was he interested in the slightest in the kinds of stylistic and compositional questions that one almost automatically associates with an orchestral medium.

2. This was surely as much Joe Glaser's idea, Louis's manager, as Louis's own. Glaser's formula for success was to have Armstrong hawk the commercial tunes of the day in a not-too-advanced band setting, providing backgrounds for his trumpet and vocalizing displays.
3. It is amazing to observe the high level of emotionalism that is aroused by this aspect of Armstrong's career, both in damnation and defense of it. Perhaps the truth, as so often, lies somewhere in the middle. While on the one hand, in the face of Armstrong's uniqueness, it may be futile to pass judgment on his post-1920s' career, on the other hand—precisely because of his pre-eminent role in jazz—one must eventually come to grips with the *totality* of his life and work. This can only be done in a dispassionate way, which also takes into account Louis's personality and temperament, and the social-economic conditions within which he labored.

The second problem is the matter of repertory. Once Armstrong abandoned the small-group format, he also abandoned the repertory associated with it, much of which he had himself created; and in a sharp reversal he turned his attention almost exclusively to pop tunes, show tunes, ballads, and novelty numbers.

The third issue is related to the other two: Louis's playing changed dramatically. Granted that he had long ago abandoned the integrative ensemble work and collective improvisation of his native New Orleans idiom and had, in fact, established almost singlehandedly the improvised "solo" as the principal protagonist in jazz discourse, thereby proposing a radically new concept of jazz.[4] But now his idea of the solo concept took on a specific and, arguably, much narrower interpretation. It had its pluses and its minuses, as we shall see.

Fourthly, Armstrong embraced singing as a full-time commitment, equal in its allocation to his trumpet-playing. And it was as a singer—of songs like *Hello, Dolly* and *Mack the Knife*—that the large public was finally to know Armstrong in the last decade or so of his life. One cannot resist feeling that his genius and art somehow deserved better than that!

In effect the first Armstrong Orchestra recordings were made in March 1929 and were in many ways indicative of the entire ensuing decade-long dalliance with Louis as big-band front-man. The orchestra was not his—it was Luis Russell's band of that time; and the basic formula in stylistic and formal terms, maintained throughout the entire period, is fixed on these initial waxings. They also set the pattern of a usually superior Armstrong, with average or indifferent accompaniments. Certainly there was no attempt to musically integrate Armstrong's solo work with an orchestral conception, or vice versa.

The stylistic gap between Armstrong and the band was wide and clear. What is disturbing is that it was made so by design. And the formal outline, to be repeated with only trifling variations for a hundred or so subsequent recordings, was part of that design: trumpet solo—Armstrong vocal—short instrumental break (allowing Louis to pick up his horn)—and trumpet final chorus, invariably with an out-of-tempo cadenza, topped by a high note. On *I Can't Give You Anything But Love* (March 1929) we see for the first time how the formula works. So that the record buyer might not be made too uncomfortable by Armstrong's improvisations, which—this was another part of the Glaser prescription—progressed from simple embellishment "paraphrase" elaborations of the melody to freer more complex recompositions of it, Teddy Hill had to play Johnny McHugh's tune straight *three times in a row*. In the meantime a listless, swingless accompaniment chugs along not much aided by Pops Foster's slurpy bowed bass lines. J. C. Higginbotham, one of the most consistently inventive trombonists of his generation, handles his allotted half-chorus well enough, but obviously our attention must be directed towards Armstrong's three appearances: opening muted half-chorus, vocal, final open-horn out-chorus.

It is here that we hit pay dirt. Louis is masterful, particularly in the final solo:

4. For a full discussion of this development, see *Early Jazz*, chap. 3.

sovereign, free as a bird, lyrical, with a final ascending phrase to keep you in suspense as to whether he'll make that final high D. He does—just barely. It is a beautifully constructed solo which we only fully appreciate when we realize that, though it is average for Louis—and indeed there are better solos—there were hundreds of trumpet players who could not achieve anything like it even once in their careers, let alone in *thousands* of comparable replications (Ex. 1).[5]

By comparison, *Mahagony Hall Stomp* is a much more unified all-around effort. There is no rift between the band and its leader—with good reason. For the piece, celebrating the most magnificent of the old pre-World War I bagnios in New Orleans, was dear to all New Orleanians—six of the ten players in the band. That included four-fifths of the rhythm section—Paul Barbarin, Pops Foster, Luis Russell (from Panama by the way of New Orleans)—and guest guitarist Lonnie Johnson; Eddie Condon was the lone—and white—"outsider"! Moreover, Armstrong, clarinetist Albert Nicholas, Barbarin, and Russell had all worked together years before in one of the New Orleans district's most famous abodes, Anderson's Annex.

Now, way off in a New York recording studio in a kind of nostalgic reunion, they re-created in *Mahagony Hall Stomp* the warmth and loose, airy textures of New Orleans jazz, particularly as played by the larger 1920s' orchestras. Spencer Williams's sturdy tune is ideally suited to this kind of polyphonic treatment: trumpet in the lead, two saxophones and trombone weaving lacy countermelodies in their designated registers, all on a buoyant bed of rhythm as only New Orleans players could produce.

Louis is in his element and magnificent. Who else in 1929 could have played with such a relaxed wide-open almost-behind-the-beat feeling? And then there

---

5. Jazz solos should be heard and analyzed in terms of their entire accompanimental context, for a sensitive featured player will react to his accompaniments as he is creating, as much as fine accompanists (a good rhythm section, for example) will react to the soloist.

By the same token, notated examples of solos should by all rights contain transcriptions of the accompaniment so that the full musical totality can be seen (and heard). However, this is less critical in two areas: 1) jazz of earlier periods, including most of the swing era, and 2) jazz which is primarily notated to begin with, for instance, arranged orchestral jazz.

The overlap between these two areas must be obvious, for so much of swing era jazz was pre-set, arranged, composed. Less obvious perhaps is the reason for the reduced need to reproduce complete transcriptions of solo passages. But as I will have occasion to point out frequently in this book, most early "solos"—with rare exceptions, and then only by the greatest and freest of soloists (Armstrong, Hawkins)—were not extemporaneously improvised, but were to some significant degree, or even entirely, pre-determined. In the second area—most swing era *orchestral* jazz—the arrangements, especially the arranged backgrounds to solos having been fixed by the arranger, most soloists also felt obliged to "fix" their solos against what was in effect an invariant background. Ironically, however, it was the fixedness and redundancy (and therefore eventually boredom) of late swing-era arrangements that gradually drove soloists to vary their solos in successive performances, particularly as players' technical skills, command of their instruments and musical ideas, and improvisational abilities in general increased. By the late 1940s, with the arrival of modern jazz and the return to small more flexible combos, real instantaneous improvisation became not only the norm but virtually a *sine qua non* of true jazz.

Ex. 1

* G♯ is a note mistake; Armstrong meant to play G♮.

Ex. 2

is one of Louis's specialties: the long single note held for an entire chorus, its pent-up suspense ultimately released into a reiterated pattern of lunging syncopated notes (Ex. 2). Lonnie Johnson contributes a special blues-ish atmosphere with his guitar solo (of the kind that you could still hear in New Orleans back alleys in the forties and fifties), and underneath Louis's solos, gentle wreaths of counterpoint.

Alas, it is bassist Pops Foster, that New Orleans stalwart, who flaws the performance. In the third chorus the piece switches from *Mahagony*'s 16-bar I-IV-V harmonies to blues changes. Foster misses this and is badly at sea for two choruses, playing tonics for dominants and the like. But he more than makes up for this musical misdemeanor by getting together later with Barbarin to provide some hard-swinging pizzicato walking bass, giving the final stanzas a tremendous lift.

Ain't Misbehavin', recorded in July 1929—this time Louis is reunited with Carroll Dickerson's orchestra—became Armstrong's big record hit in New York as well as his show-stopper in the all-black Broadway revue *Connie's Hot Chocolates*. The recording offered a potent mixture of Fats Waller's jaunty air, Armstrong's rich singing tone, some of his spectacular double-time *a capella* breaks, a climactic solo cadenza, a teasing brief quote from Gershwin's *Rhapsody in Blue*—a good gauge of how popular that piece was already, just five years after its premiere—a good-naturedly raspy-voiced vocal by Louis, and, for the old folks, a touch of Dickerson's pure-toned strait-laced sentimental violin. In short, the performance had just about everything.

Two contrasting pieces were cut a few days later, both unusual for Armstrong in different ways. *(What Did I Do To Be So) Black and Blue* is one of those rare occasions when Louis allowed himself to bemoan—in public—the harsh realities of Negro life in America. Andy Razaf's[6] poignant lyrics, crowned with the piteous lament "How will it end? Ain't got a friend? My only sin is in my skin," are sung with genuine pathos. It is a rare example of Armstrong in a profoundly serious and heavy-hearted vocal mood.

That Rhythm Man gives us Armstrong, as the title suggests, in a rare uptempo, sprightly rhythmic mood. His admirers were going to hear very little of this vivacious side of Louis as he concentrated increasingly on ballads and slower

---

6. This gifted lyricist, regularly partnered with Fats Waller, was born in Washington, D.C., as Andreamenentania Paul Razafinkeriefo, descended from Malagasy (Madagascar) royalty.

tempos. His last chorus here is flashy and poised, with another rarity in the coda: Armstrong easing the music on down from its peak to the quiet in-tempo ending over a long-held fermata chord in the band—an ending that Chick Webb and Taft Jordan were still to imitate five years later on *their* excellent *Rhythm Man* version.

Some of These Days is typical of the "annoying" category of Armstrong's output. Like a high-speed train passing through a succession of coastline tunnels, Armstrong's playing intermittently lights up the performance, then it is plunged immediately into inept darkness when the band plays.

Armstrong's technical mastery constantly astounds. On *Rockin' Chair*, now back with the Russell band, he produces a climactic, perfectly executed one-octave upward glissando, accomplished with a half-valve position and sounding very much like the famous *Rhapsody in Blue* clarinet opener. It was a device which Louis was to expand repeatedly through the years, always bedazzling his audiences with it, and one which was widely imitated by other trumpeters, virtually making it into a cliché.

By January 1930 the creepy tentacles of commercialism had begun to exert an alarming degree of stylistic constraint. On *Song of the Islands* we can hear the results. A painful mélange of non-jazz elements intrude upon Armstrong, and he himself does not escape entirely unscathed. And how could he? Even he must have been less than inspired by (although not recoiling from) the deadly combination of three glutinous violins stating the theme, Foster's "voompy" bowed bass, whining wobbly saxophones, vacuous background humming from the band, and Barbarin on Hawaiian-style vibraphone (while Armstrong's valet, reputedly, played the drums!). The point is that, while Louis always manages to rise above his often appalling surroundings, he is nevertheless subtly affected by them. Even he cannot always be entirely impervious to them, and in any case he has to work even harder to overcome them. Time after time in recordings of this ilk, Louis may win the battle, but only at a price. As one studies the artistic/aesthetic ups and downs of Armstrong's big-band career, one cannot fail to notice that the best, most jazz-related accompaniments inspire him to *Himalayan* heights. On the crassly commercial sides he is often reduced to merely *Alpine* levels. Armstrong's performance was all his life on a very remarkable level. But that should not blind us totally to the subtle ravages his compromising—enforced or accepted, it matters not—extorted.

Similar thoughts spring to mind upon hearing Armstrong's 1930 rendition of *Dear Old Southland*. This was, of course, a piece dear to all black musicians born in the South, and one respects its nostalgic sentimental connotations for them. And yet, as performed by Louis and Buck Washington, it also becomes to some extent one of those over-sentimentalized arias of the type that tenors (invariably Jewish or Irish) would sing in vaudeville or burlesque while the girls changed costumes. Louis and Buck are, of course, many cuts above those tawdry standards, but one wonders what impulses required the world's greatest trumpet player to indulge in this type of effort—and unfortunately one knows the answer.

The next band to accompany Armstrong was the Mills Blue Rhythm Band, with which he cut six sides in April and May 1930. The repertory ran the gamut from a new Hoagy Carmichael tune—*My Sweet*—not one of his best efforts—to old standards like *Dinah* and *Tiger Rag*. *My Sweet* is one of those performances in which Louis has to carry the whole huffing and puffing band with him—*behind* him to be exact. In the final chorus one can hear him working, with a touch of desperation, at this formidable task. *Tiger Rag* on the other hand has other problems, these of Louis's own making. By 1930, many years and several hundred recordings after its origination somewhere in the dark ages of jazz history (Nick La Rocca's claim to "composer" credits for *Tiger Rag* is spurious), this old warhorse—truncated and trivialized through misuse—needed something more than what Armstrong was willing to give it. Its sturdy ragtime changes did not warrant gagging it up with no less than three banal quotes, playing for audience titters: an Irish jig, a Sousa march, and *Vesti la Giubba*, the famous *Pagliacci* aria which *everyone* knew because of Enrico Caruso's all-time early hit record. Armstrong touched at least two ethnic groups with this one, throwing in a patriotic salute for all the rest.

(What *could* be done with *Tiger Rag* had already been shown by Ellington the year before in a six-minute two-part version, and would be shown again two years later in his *tour de force* recasting of those venerable *Tiger* changes into *Daybreak Express*.[7] Admittedly, though, the Ellington boys did pick up a few ideas from Armstrong's version, with its train whistle call-and-response effects and reiterated high-note trumpet shakes.)

In the summer of 1930, Louis found himself working in Culver City, California, at Frank Sebastian's New Cotton Club, there accompanied by the Les Hite band, which had Lionel Hampton on drums and a twenty-two-year-old Lawrence Brown on trombone. As a group, the band was not particularly distinguished at this time, but it could provide the functional backings that Louis wanted. The results were predictably variable. The only constant is Armstrong, constantly outshining the band. One winces now at the slap-tongue tenor of William Franz or the baritone of Les Hite, staccato and vertical; and one is much relieved when Louis sidles in, relaxed, linear, melodic, generously reinventing each tune. He also did a lot of "reinventing" of lyrics, as he was now virtually in the habit of forgetting lyrics (on *I'm a Ding Dong Daddy* he happily admits it right on the record), making a virtue out of his memory lapses and filling in with infectious scat trifles.[8] But *Daddy* was otherwise tailor-made for Louis, the master of the break, with its breaks built right into the song.

The ease and naturalness with which Armstrong learned new songs and then

7. See above, Chapter 2, pp. 61–65.

8. It is one of the more cherished legends of jazz history that scat-singing originated with Armstrong when, in a recording of *Heebie Jeebies* in 1926 with his Hot Five group, he forgot the lyrics at a certain point and on the spur of the moment filled in with scatted nonsense syllables. This legend must finally be laid to rest and exposed as spurious. In point of fact, Don Redman in 1924 (on *My Papa Doesn't Two-Time No Time*) and on numerous other "live" occasions had already scatted his way through an entire song, as a matter of fact, of his own composition.

But beyond Redman's priority in this matter of scat-singing, it is safe to assume that what we call "nonsense syllables" had appeared in jazz very early on, since (as pointed out in some detail in *Early*

ad-libbed them into still newer compositions is truly astounding. As per Glaser's battle plan, Louis did indeed over a period of years record all the newest popular songs, hot off the composer's piano bench, often introducing the songs to the world. More often than not Louis infused them with qualities even their authors had not heard in them, and which frequently became indelibly associated with them. It is also to Armstrong's eternal credit that his choice of material was generally exemplary, which is not anything one could say for the hundreds of pre-Muzak studio bands or thirties' swing bands, who literally fed like scavengers off the worst of the Tin Pan Alley efforts. Armstrong's taste was virtually infallible, considering the temptations to be otherwise; and apparently his choices were made rather instantaneously. Over a period of many years he recorded a vast number of brand new songs, mostly within months of their creation. This startling hit parade of titles includes everything from Johnny Green's *Body and Soul* and Carmichael's *Star Dust* (soon after it acquired words in 1930) to *Pennies from Heaven* and *I'm in the Mood for Love*. A partial list of famous songs Armstrong recorded during the years 1930 and 1931, often in their premiere recordings, might include:

1930	1931
Blue Again (McHugh)	*All of Me* (Marks-Simons)
Body and Soul (Green)	*Between the Devil and the Deep Blue*
Confessin' (Dougherty-Reynolds)	*Sea* (Arlen)
Exactly Like You (McHugh)	*Georgia on My Mind* (Carmichael)
I Got Rhythm (Gershwin)	*I Surrender Dear* (Barris)
If I Could Be with You (James P. Johnson)	*Kickin' the Gong Around* (Arlen)
I'm a Ding Dong Daddy (Baxter)	*Lazy River* (Carmichael)
Memories of You (Eubie Blake)	*Star Dust* (Carmichael)
On the Sunny Side of the Street (McHugh)	*Walkin' My Baby Back Home* (Albert)
The Peanut Vendor (Simons)	*Wrap Your Troubles in Dreams* (Barris)
Rockin' Chair (Carmichael)	*You Rascal You* (Theard)
Them There Eyes (Pinkard)	
You're Lucky to Me (Eubie Blake)	

He missed a few in 1930, like Gershwin's *But Not for Me* and *Embraceable You* and Porter's *Love for Sale*—but not many!

Armstrong's uncanny ability to ferret out the best material was matched only by his even more remarkable ability to enhance these songs with his own creativity,[9] often improvising fantastic new melodies on top of the original. Occa-

---

Jazz) African vocal musics and African languages, with their highly imaginative syllabic structuring, are intimately related. Indeed, in many African traditions music is taught through syllabic identification. Scat-singing is therefore a fundamental aspect of Afro-American vocal techniques and as such must have been known in the dawn and pre-dawn of jazz. Redman's recording, however, seems to have been the first introduction of scat-singing on recordings—if we discount the many silly, babbling nonsense-syllable songs that flourished in the early 1920s (such as *Doodle Doo Doo, Doo Wacka Doo, Doo Doodle Oom*) and which were recorded and performed with such alarming frequency in those infancy days of American popular music.

9. Oddly enough, Armstrong was not a great songwriter himself. Evidently he reserved his extraordinary melodic gifts for his trumpet-playing and singing, limiting (a few exceptions notwithstanding) his "writing" to catchy, light-weight jazz numbers.

sionally this went too far, and he would be reminded that the masses wanted to hear the *melody*. Hence his recording of *Body and Soul*, then a brand new song, in which Green's melody in its straight form is ever-present in the arrangement: in the saxes behind Louis's playing and George Orendorff's muted trumpet behind Louis's vocal.

How *Confession'* ever came to be mated by Armstrong with Hawaiian guitar music will probably, fifty years later, remain a mystery. But that is what incongruously introduces Armstrong's vocal, the guitar sounding more like a Viennese zither than the languorous swaying-breeze undulations one expects. (Even more irreconcilable is the tuba lumbering away underneath.) But miraculously in Louis's trumpet half of the side he plays one of his freest, most loosely inventive solos ever, apparently quite oblivious of the stylistic and aesthetic incongruities occurring all around him.

On the same day he waxed a similarly carefree improvisation on James P. Johnson's *If I Could Be with You One Hour Tonight*. Louis's first solo is as remarkable for its melodic invention as for its structural balance (Ex. 3). It is a dazzling lesson in how to mix primary thematic material with purely ornamental passages without ever losing the sense of the overall melody. Its rhythmic variety is simply astonishing: in sixteen short bars Armstrong not only offers every rhyth-

Ex. 3

mic unit, from sextuplet sixteenths to half notes, but assimilates these raw materials into a total design of great beauty. Though by no means symmetrical in
construction, it is perfectly balanced.

This is as good a time as any to re-emphasize that Armstrong's trumpet skills,
both musical and technical, could not be matched by *any* other trumpeter in
his time (except perhaps Jabbo Smith), least of all by any classical player. The
combination of technical agility, note perfection, endurance, power, elegance of
style and grace, not to mention musical invention as in improvisation, simply
was not demanded or expected of classical players. Even superb players like
Harry Glantz in the New York Philharmonic (who incidentally once recorded
with Ben Selvin's dance band in 1920) could not in 1930 have played Armstrong's *Confessin'* and *One Hour* solos, even leaving out of consideration entirely the element of swing. A classical player of Glantz's caliber would have had
to practice such passages for days to achieve anything like Armstrong's ease and
authority. On the other side, Armstrong could not play the opening of Wagner's
Parsifal the way Glantz could. Still, if one dispassionately compares the demands of one category of playing with the other, one must conclude that jazz-
playing at Armstrong's level was considerably more all-embracingly challenging,
especially if one includes the creative improvisatory demands.[10]

There was one category of trumpet or cornet players that *could* match Armstrong both in agility and range, but not in improvisational skill. This was, of
course, the cornet soloists like Herbert L. Clarke and Bohumir Kryl, the American instrumental superstars of the first three decades of our century. Many of
these players posessed phenomenal technical control and agility, but could never
have matched Armstrong (or Bubber Miley or Bix Beiderbecke) in stylistic originality and versatility.

In the meantime Armstrong was working on another more elusive goal, the
extension of his high register—the brass player's Mount Everest and ever-present
challenge. In the brass fraternity this is where heroes are made and where batting
average counts. There is a universal saying among musicians that "you're only
as good as your last performance." As far as the treacherous high register on
brass instruments goes, the same cruel law holds: "You are as good as your last
high note."

In classical music, high notes are imposed by the composers. But in jazz a
player imposes his own goals and limits, and each generation of players extends
the range, as with the four-minute mile or the seven-foot high jump. In the late
twenties the trumpet's high B♭ (concert pitch) was generally considered the upper

---

10. The next few generations of trumpet players occasionally produced musicians who could, if
necessary, function reasonably well in both the jazz and classical areas. One such player was Mannie
Klein, who in the 1940s created quite a stir when allegedly he was asked by Otto Klemperer to fill
in for an ailing classical colleague in Bach's high-range *Second Brandenberg Concerto* (an account I
have been unable to verify; Klein himself could neither confirm nor deny the story). Mannie Klein
did, however, play the solo trumpet part in the first West Coast performance of Shostakovitch's 1933
Piano Concerto. Later players who are comfortable in both areas include Joe Wilder, Doc Severinson, and in our own era Wynton Marsalis.

limit. But with Armstrong in the lead, the upper range was gradually extended over the next few years through C and D♭ to D and E♭ (the last, for example, on Armstrong's *Tiger Rag* and *My Sweet*).

High F was the next target—jazz bands did not play in E major in those days (except Fletcher Handerson's once in a while)—and Louis climbed to that new Olympian height in *You're Lucky to Me*.[11] Like any stunt once achieved, your audience expects *it and no less* from you every time. In a sense, Armstrong was doomed to wrest high E♭s and Fs from his horn for the rest of his life. In later years, however, as he grew older and his embouchure could no longer take the punishment, he eventually had to abandon the high register.

In listening to Armstrong recordings of this period one must sooner or later come to grips with the issue of the saxophone style and the whole fascination on the part of many black musicians with the Lombardo saxophone sound. One automatically refers to it by that name because, as Armstrong is reported to have said (according to the critic Chris Albertson) in speaking about Guy Lombardo's band: "They put that melody there, and it's beautiful. You can't find another band that can play a straight lead and make it sound that good."[12] It was in its way a unique and instantly recognizable sound. Its recognizability was in fact one of the main reasons for its success with the public and conservative musicians.

What is really baffling, however, is why so many of the black orchestras which

11. Here again there are almost exact parallel developments in classical music, only taking place a decade or two earlier. Composers like Richard Strauss, Stravinsky, and Schoenberg gradually pushed the range of the trumpet upward from C, step by step to E♭, a process that took almost twenty years. But unlike jazz players, classical composers stopped at the E♭. Notes above that were written only rarely, while, of course, by the end of the big-band era no self-respecting player was satisfied with anything less than the altissimo B♭ or beyond.

The solo virtuoso cornetists of the Sousa and Pryor band era, of course, broke into the upper range early in the century, but they too stopped around high F. Armstrong seems to have been quite enamored of one of those cornet virtuosos, B. A. Rolfe. Known in Europe as the Boy Trumpet Wonder, Rolfe early in his career led concert bands, playing the virtuoso cornet literature and whirlwind-tempo circus numbers. In the late twenties he led a similar band on a highly successful three-hour network radio program sponsored by Lucky Strike. This is undoubtedly where Armstrong heard Rolfe and became intrigued with his high register pyrotechnics.

12. Quoted in *Louis Armstrong*, in the Time-Life *Giants of Jazz* series. The fascination with Lombardo-ish saxophone sounds and with massive string choirs, both the bane of jazz purists on the left *and* right, runs through black jazz history in a never-ending counterpoint. These were irresistibly seductive elements, in great part because they equated with success, wealth, and economic stability. But there was more to it than that, as Armstrong's defense of Lombardo certainly implies. Whether it was Charlie Parker's recordings with strings (or Hines in one of his more obscure periods) or the occasional espousal of Lombardo's and Sammy Kaye's formulas for success by even the likes of Ellington (early in his career) or, say, Andy Kirk, the temptation to woo assured public success was ever-present, right below the surface—and often above it. There is another side to this coin, however, particularly as concerns the use of string instruments. Unquestionably strings have been mercilessly abused and misused throughout jazz history, especially in the swing era. But jazz purists should be reminded that it is not the medium, not the instrument, but the manner in which it is used that is usually the problem. Rare though they may be, there are striking examples of intelligent, tasteful use of strings in jazz. (A full discussion of this subject can be found below, in Chapter 7, in the section on Artie Shaw.)

did emulate the Lombardo sax section's sound and style, felt the need to exaggerate it so. The next orchestra Armstrong recorded with, put together for him in Chicago by a trumpeter colleague, Zilmer Randolph, was merciless in its emphasis of that whining, whimpering, effeminate saxophone sound. On *Star Dust* and *You Can Depend on Me*, (November 1931) it reaches the dimensions of caricature, even though it wasn't meant to at all.

Armstrong's admiration for Lombardo took a concrete form in the decision to record brother Carmen's *Sweethearts on Parade*, still with the Les Hite orchestra. Armstrong trots out his most slurry, potato-mouthed singing, undisturbed by Bill Perkins's out of tune accompanying guitar meanderings. As usual—but still amazingly, against all rational expectations—in the final chorus Armstrong finds a dashing nobility in this song material that surely no one else could have envisioned. He sails above the song, audacious and magnificent, totally oblivious of his immediate environment. Armstrong was obviously one of those fortunate players to whom a perfectly functioning background or accompaniment was not a requisite, who could most of the time play *his* very best, regardless; and who often enough could play even better in defiance of a poor accompaniment. That is precisely why Louis became the major soloist he was and could remain one for so a long time.

Charlie Parker had that same ability to rise above his accompaniments or to ignore them. Some musicians, in both the jazz and classical fields have that ability; but most do not, and are to various degrees vulnerable to their surroundings. This is a theme which the reader will encounter frequently in this book.

But on *Peanut Vendor*, recorded the same session, even Armstrong gives up. He evidently felt he could add nothing to this tune (which has no changes, being a one-chord G major piece) other than a muted theme statement, which almost anybody could have played, and a scatty vocal with pseudo-Mexican allusions (although he keeps saying "Spanish, Spanish"). It is an interminable song, and very likely there was no time for a full-fledged Armstrong solo; or else he felt he could not function against the background of sloppily, stiffly played castanets and horrendously out-of-tune guitar strumming.

Terrible intonation also haunts the rest of the Les Hite-backed sides (hear *Just a Gigolo*), although here and there Louis manages to extricate himself brilliantly from his background. And on *Shine*, highlighted by one of Louis's perfectly executed half-valve glissando breaks, he at least could enjoy the strong support of Lionel Hampton, both in his flashy drum work and his pioneering obbligato-playing on vibraphone (behind Louis's vocal).

When the Culver City Cotton Club engagement was completed in early 1931, Armstrong headed back to Chicago, formed a new band there with Zilmer Randolph, and recorded rather voluminously with it in the Windy City during the next year. All in all, it was to be for the most part an indifferent period, in which the direst consequences inherent in the soloist-with-mediocre-band concept were fulfilled.

For the Randolph band was truly mediocre. Most of the arrangements were by Randolph himself, proficient at best, but so poorly played that their relative merits hardly mattered. The band was led by Mike McKendrick, a guitarist who acted as "straw boss" leader but who was given to wildly out-of-tune playing. A thumpy-footed drummer named Tubby Hall and John Lindsay, the bass player who had come to some fame as the excellent bass anchor in Jelly Roll Morton's Hot Peppers recordings, completed the section. The Okeh studio in Chicago didn't help matters either. Lindsay, who might have given these recordings a lift, is virtually inaudible on the first half-dozen sides or so. (He finally surfaces in the November 1931 recordings.) Although George James was a classy alto saxophonist, often contributing elegant little 8-bar interludes, this was clearly insufficient to offset the generally coarse-toned, stiff, and insensitive playing of this band.

Armstrong, on the other hand, often called this his "happiest band." It remains unclear as to what he meant by that, possibly their personalities and general uncomplaining attitude. While in many previous recordings one continually admires Armstrong for his ability to rise above his accompaniments, with this Randolph-McKendrick Chicago band one almost is moved to admire *their* intransigent capacity to be impervious to Louis's talent. *That* represents a very special kind of non-talent.

Most of these sides need not detain us long, once we have recognized that Louis is still Louis and even at his most constrained plays and invents at levels many times above those of any of his contemporaries. But the tragedy is that under these circumstances Armstrong could not grow inwardly. Perhaps, as I have suggested elsewhere, his astounding earlier breakthroughs, conceptual and technical, could not be surpassed. His sheer creativity was bound to level off, comparatively. In a way his grand love affair with soloing and fronting a band was essentially a reorientation of his early achievements in a different direction, towards other goals. In that sense the first two years of the orchestrally backed Armstrong represent the first and very high flowering of that reoriented concept. It in turn was also bound to level off; and that is what perhaps we hear happening in 1931, his third year of fronting a big band—at least temporarily.

Clearly, this Chicago-based band was no help in these matters. Even Louis could not always carry the entire musical burden, ostensibly meant to be always a shared one even under minimum professional assumptions. Louis begins to weaken. His solos occasionally bog down; there are intonational slips, heretofore unknown with him; muffed notes; rehashings of earlier successes (such as the *West End Blues* cadenza on *Blue Again*—but muffed at the end). There is also, very imperceptibly, less and less of Louis's trumpet, and more and more of Louis's vaudeville hokum and jive talk. And, above all, more and more of the grandstanding finales. The hardening of the format, which I have already mentioned in *Early Jazz*, really takes hold here. The sequence of events on each performance becomes routine and quite predictable. The worst of the grandstanding—with its inevitable free-tempo capped-by-the-highest-note cadenza—was not the thing itself, but rather the mesmerizing effect it had on younger trumpet players, like Roy Eldridge or Louis's many other imitators.

Yet, in the midst of this desert of divagation and mediocrity (the band's), there would occasionally blossom a flower of superior beauty. A case in point: *Star Dust* (recorded Nov. 4, 1931). Of the three takes made only two have survived, and they offer an interesting insight into Armstrong's creative laboratory. Example 4 shows both solos of both takes, a comparison of which reveals three basic facts: 1) that these were improvised solos; but that 2) the over-all design was worked out beforehand; and that 3) certain phrases, for example the entire stretch from m. 9 through m. 16, were identical. But even more interesting is the extraordinary rhythmic freedom with which Armstrong recasts Hoagy Carmichael's melody (Ex. 4a, 4b).

Ex. 4a   First solo

Though these rhythms look complex in notation, they do not sound that way. They sound completely natural and right, inevitable rather than calculated. Western musical notation simply has no way of representing such free and spontaneous rhythms in an uncomplicated manner. But this very fact helps to point up graphically/visually how remarkably inventive Armstrong's rhythmic vocabulary really is. The quintuplets and septuplets of the musical examples merely *symbolize* the free unfettered way that Armstrong floats above and around the beat. And if anyone ever thought that swing had something to do with metro-

Ex. 4b

Second solo

nomic accuracy and playing only on or with the beat, here is a graphic illustration of quite the contrary. It underscores the point I was making in the definition
of swing[13], namely, that swing is less a matter of accurate vertical placing of
notes than it is their *linear* projection and inflection. Armstrong, who never saw
a quintuplet in his life—who indeed wouldn't have recognized one if he saw it,
and who certainly couldn't have played one from notation—here gives a dazzling
display not only of his own phenomenally rich musical imagination and originality but of the inherent and essential poly-rhythmic nature of jazz, a quality
not found in European/Western music but one indigenous to many varieties of
African music, the root language of jazz.[14]

13. *Early Jazz*, pp. 6–10, and in this volume, Chapter 4.
14. *Early Jazz*, pp. 6–26.

In contrast to Armstrong's *rhythmic* innovations, which radically revolutionized that aspect of jazz language, his *harmonic* idiom was essentially conservative. Although gifted with a fine ear for melodic invention, Armstrong rarely explored new harmonic territories, but was, apparently, content to stay within the established harmonic norms of his time. Indeed, if Armstrong by chance found himself involved with a harmonically advanced or adventurous tune, it was his tendency to simplify, to clarify the changes, to bring such roving harmonies under one simpler melodic/harmonic common denominator. It seems to me that this ability to combine a conservative pitch language with a progressive and energetically propounded rhythmic idiom constitutes the fundamental reason for Armstrong's considerable popular success. For it is simply a matter of record that the large public always relates more instinctively to rhythm, and by the same token it is much less sophisticated and interested in matters of harmony.

Although Armstrong's singing is generally not of as high an order as his playing—or to put it another way, is more a secondary reflection of his trumpet-playing (rather than the reverse)—it is nonetheless unique, save for its legions of imitators. In his *Star Dust* vocal we see him toying with the melody and its underlying harmonies like a cat with a mouse. Teasing, pummeling, baiting the tune, he sometimes simplifies greatly, often for emphasis, as in the opening line, "Sometimes I wonder why I spend such lonely nights"—all on repeated D♭s. At other times a more instrumental approach to singing prompts him to invent new melodic shapes, frequently ornamented with glissandos and word-eliding ellipses.

What is intriguing is that Louis affected a gravel-voiced singing sound, in its "impurity" the exact opposite of his fully centered pure-as-gold trumpet sound. That his rough-textured voice was not necessarily his only voice was demonstrated amply in the mid-to-late-thirties, when Louis, singing more and more ballads, lightened his voice texture and sang with a much clearer voice—sometimes very beautifully.

The art of improvisation provides no guarantees; it is inexact and variable. Every improviser knows that, and the nature of his craft is therefore to bring his capacity for instantaneous invention to such a high level that it is never less than adequate unto the task, all the while hoping for (and occasionally being able to count on) those special days when he is particularly articulate. Armstrong had a run of such days in January and March 1932. His playing on these particular recordings is beyond anything he had previously achieved.

The series begins with two extraordinary takes of *Between the Devil and the Deep Blue Sea*. Here the two performances are even more differentiated in detail than on the *Star Dust* improvisations, although once again the overall outline and basic phrase contours are predetermined. The second take is more ornate; it takes a few more chances, resulting in a number of minor fluffs, which is probably the reason this cut was not released until the LP era (Ex. 5).

In the meantime, the whimpering saxophones persist, at times truly offensive

Ex. 5

in their exaggerations.[15] But the Randolph band did improve over the months of its relationship with Armstrong, and occasionally provided reasonable accompaniments. Louis sometimes had to openly exhort them to "play out," as he does during a particularly dreary saxophone ensemble on *Love, You Funny Thing*. After his admonition the adrenaline level rises a mite. Still, Louis's performance here is uneven, undoubtedly affected by the listlessness of the band. Nevertheless he produces one heroic bridge, full of unexpected twists and turns, and one spectacular roller-coaster up-and-down glissando (Ex. 6). In those eight bars Harry James's style was born.

Ex. 6

A remake of *Tiger Rag* is not much of an improvement over the earlier one, just faster, so that Louis can get in the seven successive choruses he announces. The same dreary quotations reappear, as do various elements from the earlier *Chinatown, My Chinatown* (also a *Tiger Rag*-type of piece, only in another key).

The final side in this spate of recordings—it turned out to be the last for the Okeh label—gives us Armstrong at his most impassioned (*Lawd, You Made the Night Too Long*). He plays with exceptional conviction and fervor. Again there is a break which must be heard to believed. It is virtually unnotatable, not only rhythmically but also because it features a little trick Louis had been working up over the last year of embellishing notes with tiny grace-note scoops from below. This effect is technically extremely difficult to manage, even in moderately paced

15. It is not a question of snobbishness, as some Armstrong fans have suggested, to find these saxophone mewings inferior, nor does one need to be a "higher aesthetician" to be offended by their appalling taste, as some have suggested. Nor does an admiration for the Armstrong Hot Fives and Sevens signify a prejudice against larger orchestras and by extension Armstrong's work with them. (Although be it also noted that Randolph's band consisted of only nine players!) It is after all also a question of a work's artistic integrity. If in evaluating a collaborative work of art we are forced to separate one part from another, we can, of course, do that, and evaluate each part separately. But let us not act as if it made no difference whether the artistic totality is flawed by one or another aspect of it. For, no matter how supreme Armstrong may be, the sum of all the parts of the entire performance finally add up to become *the* work. It is not so much a matter of denigrating the flawed work, as it is of differentiating between those that are flawed and those that are not.

passages. In the *Lawd* break, Louis unleashes a veritable cascade of these flip-floppy scooped notes, in a clear attempt to break beyond the boundaries of even his own formidable technique and conception.

After a trip to England in the summer of 1932, where Louis played to rather mixed reactions, he returned to record, but now for the Victor label. In his never-ending search for an orchestra, he now chose Chick Webb's eleven-piece band. Although Webb's group was not by any means the ideal accompanist for Armstrong, it was a considerable improvement over the Randolph band.[16] Challenged by a number of good soloists—trombonist Charlie Green, saxophonists Edgar Sampson and Elmer Williams, and trumpeter Louis Bacon (excellent in background obbligato)—Armstrong was exultant in his solo work (as on *Hobo, You Can't Ride This Train*, a piece of his own devising). Webb's band had at least a modern conception which was related to and was in fact an offspring of Armstrong's earlier stylistic revolution.

Two weeks later, now with a group of musicians led by the pianist Edgar Hayes, Armstrong found himself recording a couple of medleys of "Armstrong hits," a highly "original" idea for which some Victor official probably received a big bonus. Mostly silly light-weight performances, the orchestra sounding like a theatre pit-band, Armstrong nevertheless manages to produce one soulful solo on *When It's Sleepy Time Down South*—by now Armstrong's theme song—that Bunny Berigan must have memorized and learned a few things from in *his* search for an identity.

In January 1933 Armstrong turned again to his friend Zilmer Randolph, who, this time, finally did manage to assemble a significantly better orchestra. It included the young Teddy Wilson, already a poised and clear-thinking soloist; the twenty-two-year-old saxophonist Budd Johnson (then already a veteran of nearly a dozen bands); his older brother, trombonist Keg Johnson, and a talented clarinetist named Scoville Brown. Randolph, also the chief arranger for the band, had improved considerably and could occasionally produce proficient effective charts which set Armstrong off spendidly. January 26, 1933, was another great day in Louis's calendar, judging by the aural evidence of the records made that day. Whether it is his tender wistful vocal on *I Gotta Right To Sing the Blues* or his sovereign, free-floating solos on *Hustlin' and Bustlin'* and *Sittin' in the Dark*, Armstrong was in fine fettle. He seemed to have simplified his style to some extent, searching more for a pure, less embellished melodic line. But at the same time a new problem crept into his stylistic format, one that had been lurking in the wings for some time. It was the tendency towards showy grandstanding cadenza-endings, imitating the worst of operatic traditions contrived by sensation-seeking divas and prima donnas. It was almost to be Armstrong's ruination.

On cut after cut we hear him pushing for those high notes, *de rigueur* in any

---

16. It is interesting to note that of the six established orchestras which accompanied Armstrong, four—Luis Russel, Les Hite, Chick Webb, Edgar Hayes—played much better on their own than they did with Louis.

cadenza format (imagine ending a flashy cadenza on a low note!). Gradually the
cumulative strain began to take its inevitable physical toll. Armstrong fell off of
final high notes; his tone was occasionally unsteady, the sound sometimes strained
and tight. On the other hand Louis's resilience, his absolutely extraordinary
physical stamina and natural physiological equipment for trumpet playing, stood
him in generally good stead, creating the illusion of invincibility. And indeed
there were some remarkable days on his playing calendar. Hear his jubilant final
solo on *Some Sweet Day*—it *was* a sweet day for Louis (Jan. 27, 1933)—or the
glorious work on *Basin Street Blues*, and, one day later, a stunning remake of
Mahagony Hall Stomp.

Ironically, at this time, while the high note problem was encroaching, Armstrong's tone was at its purest and richest. He seemed to have developed a special
love for the trumpet's low register, and in truth no jazz player has ever matched
him in this domain (even Bunny Berigan). Listen to his fat-toned middle- and
low-register work on *Basin Street Blues* and you will hear what a trumpet sound
can and should be. Note too that Louis borrows one of his most felicitous double-time inspirations from the 1931 *Star Dust* (Ex. 7).

Ex. 7

Mahagony's first solo is also situated more in Louis's sumptuous middle and
low range, a magnificent arching line up to the high Eb near the end of the
performance notwithstanding. Here, too, Louis latches on to a little triple-tonguing

figure ( ) which he was to exploit in coming weeks and months,
often to ingenious effect. Another one of Louis's favorite devices, the chorus-
long single held note, reappears on *Mahagony*, this time to allow a blues-ish
McKendrick solo (finally he is in tune) to be featured. But Louis is not satisfied
to merely sit on a long high note. With absolutely magnificent control (matched
only elsewhere by Johnny Hodges's alto—except that it's much harder on a
trumpet), Armstrong starts one tone below his final destination, Bb, traversing
the distance between Ab and Bb in not one, not two, but *five* bars in a perfectly
calibrated glissando. Arriving at the top, he now holds the tone taut for two
measures and then gradually "warms up" the sound with a vibrato, which in
turn evolves eventually into a shake or trill (Ex. 8). (Armstrong had already tried

Ex. 8

out this idea back in 1932, on *Between the Devil and the Deep Blue Sea*, but not as successfully and as dramatically convincing.) An overall 12-bar crescendo underscores the effect of something growing, burgeoning, like a balloon about to explode. Explode it does when Armstrong tops this already astounding display with five more upward glissandos, stretched equivalently across the next twelve bars, all flawlessly executed.

But Louis's lesson in jazz improvisation was not even ended with that *tour de force*. Earlier, in the twelve bars preceding the long held note, he proceeds to give a lesson in how one swings on regular even quarter notes (Ex. 9), proving that rhythmic complexity and freedom are not the only fertile ground for swing. Anyone wishing to know the meaning—and feeling—of swing needs to listen to these eight bars, as Louis happily romps through this 12-bar variant of the main theme.

Ex. 9

But even this does not conclude Armstrong's magic show. With incomparable legerdemain he pulls another musical rabbit out of the hat, when he fools our ears with yet another astonishing sonic effect. Louis's trotting-along quarter-note solo (Ex. 9) is muted; the end of the high B♭ (Ex. 8) is open. Where did he change? Where did the metamorphosis from muted to open take place? Why, in that long 5-bar half-valve glissando. As it happens, in a half-valve position the trumpet can be made to sound as if muted. Thus Armstrong, quickly taking the mute out in the eleventh bar of his chorus, matched his next sound (half-valve) to link up musically and sonorically with the previous phrase. Ergo, the perfect transition from muted to open horn. Unarguably, Louis's 1933 *Mahagony Hall Stomp* has got to be one of *his* crowning achievements and thus, by definition, in all of jazz.

Swing, You Cats, the last side on that recording session, found Louis a little below his own remarkable level. Perhaps the extraordinary effort needed to accomplish the miraculous feats of *Mahagony Hall Stomp* exhausted him somewhat. Or perhaps it was Randolph's arrangement which interfered. It fights the soloist, crowds him—especially towards the end—with the clatter of its noisy saxophone section trills. Armstrong had intonation problems here, playing sharp— very rare for him—splitting notes, and he seemed to feel generally uncomfortable.

With Armstrong's otherwise stunning playing on these January 1933 dates, one almost forgets the band. Its work, though an improvement over any of Louis's previous bands, was still not entirely consistent. True to form, the major soloists (aforementioned) contributed many fine moments. (I am especially fond of Keg Johnson's soulful open-toned, unfancy solo on *Basin Street Blues*.) And occasionally the band found a real swing groove. But at other times, particularly on the more demanding arrangements, like *High Society* and *Swing, You Cats*, the band struggled and sounded under-rehearsed. As Budd Johnson is reputed to have said years later, "The band was not up to handling the more sophisticated arrangements." Nevertheless this Chicago band can be said occasionally to have risen to the occasion, especially on the January sessions, providing Armstrong with good functional support.

But from this January zenith, perhaps inevitably, Louis's playing and especially that of the band began to decline. Starting with some sessions in April 1933, the same Chicago band sounded disorganized, dispirited, out of tune; and the Lombardo saxophone whine, apparently kept under wraps for a while, came out in full force again in its most exaggerated manifestation (hear it on *There's a Cabin in the Pines*—well, of course, the title already tells the story), here finding its absolute nadir.

Partly this slump can be traced to a definite deterioration in the choice of material recorded. From Reginald Forsythe's old-fashioned, drearily chompy stomp-piece, *Mississippi Basin*, to J. C. Johnson's *Dusky Stevedore*, the material runs the gamut from poor to mediocre. Many disasters result, as when both Louis and the band get completely mixed up in the middle of *Stevedore* or when, in *Don't Play Me Cheap*, a number concocted by Randolph and drummer Harry Dial, Louis forgets the words, rustling the sheet music as he turns the page, so preoccupied he even forgets to scat for the missing text.

And then there were Louis's lip troubles, resulting from his long over-use and abuse of high notes.[17] A grueling tour through half a dozen American cities could not have helped matters. Finally in July 1933, Louis made another trip to Europe, part vacation, part work. This time, presenting himself in his most commercial light, Armstrong found a frenziedly favorable reception with the public, but a decidedly cool response from the European critics, who were convinced Louis had "sold out." His only recordings from this entire period, eight sides cut in Paris, with a dreadful band of American expatriates and a couple of Europeans, rather tell the story. So does the long recording hiatus, stretching (except for the Paris date) from May 1933 to October 1935, although part of this prolonged silence was also caused by contract difficulties with Victor.

In 1935 Armstrong signed with the then new Decca company, with whom he recorded upwards of 120 sides during the next seven years. Alain Gerber, in his sometimes very perceptive liner notes for a series of MCA LP reissues of many of these Decca sides, speaks of "the vanity that encumbered" Armstrong in the 1933 and 1934 period. And indeed the Armstrong that returns to the recording studios in 1935, after almost a year of inactivity, is a changed man—at least at first. His playing is more modest, even cautious, as if trying to test his strengths.

---

17. A graphic account of one of Armstrong's bloodier lip-mangling skirmishes with high Fs can be found in Mezz Mezzrow's autobiography *Really the Blues*.

He shares the solo assignments more generously with others, at times singing more than playing. More crucially, as Gerber puts it, Louis "has internalized his discourse," and this accounts for "the serenity of inspiration and restraint of expression." The pieces still end with cadenzas, but often slower, more contemplative ones. Some *(You Are My Lucky Star)* end on a mere top-of-the-staff G— at that a little shaky. But in the end he can't resist the temptation to climb back to the top, both literally and figuratively; and so in a piece, aptly called *I'm Shootin' High*, he squeezes out a final high F (although not with the force of earlier times) at the end of the obligatory cadenza.

But while Armstrong was wrestling with these problems, much of this more humbly inclined playing brought a new maturity to his art. It was as if he had finally realized that he might not have to prove in every performance that he was the world's greatest trumpet virtuoso: the king of the high notes. Even many of his vocals were now rather subdued and clearer-voiced; and in his trumpet choruses he used the mute much more than in the past. On any number of sides, he displayed this purer, in general more substantive style, particularly on *Got a Bran' New Suit, Falling in Love with You* (a beautiful Victor Young song, which must have touched the ever-present sentimental streak in Louis), and *I'm in the Mood for Love*.

In the meantime, across the land Benny Goodman's Palomar success had broken, and the Swing Era was officially in full swing. To what extent Armstrong took note of these events and whether they consciously affected his playing would be hard to prove or disprove at this late date. But a brief flirtation with an overt swing style can be heard on *I've Got My Fingers Crossed* (Nov. 1935). Probably also spurred on by Pops Foster's hard swinging bass and Paul Barbarin's drums, Armstrong responds with a very modern-feeling solo, that could have come from the horn of a Gillespie or Eldridge or Ray Nance. The notation in Example 10 won't show it all—we have no way of notating feeling and inflec-

Ex. 10

tion, let alone swing—but it should give an inkling of Armstrong's new approach in a more streamlined direction.

In a sense, of course, the world of jazz had merely caught up with the implications of Armstrong's rhythmic revolution nearly ten years earlier, although it caught up with it in a slightly transmuted form via the work of Redman and Henderson and other orchestral codifiers. So perhaps Armstrong was only responding in November 1935 to this coincidental reunion with his own concepts by again sprinting ahead of the pack a few more years. The anomaly here, however, is that his playing on *Fingers Crossed* is one of the rare examples in his entire *oeuvre* of this kind of be-bop playing, a rare moment of "progress" away from his by now settled and about-to-become "conservative" style.

The greater simplicity in Armstrong's playing at this time—also a more moderate use of the vibrato—actually represented a return to his earlier self after the "vanity" years. The showman and pyrotechnical side of Armstrong became in time an inseparable part of his "act." In a society that prefers the instantly accessible and banal to the more challenging forms of cultural expression, be it folk or "high" art, Armstrong's humorous "good-old Pops" act was a means of survival in an essentially apathetic or hostile climate. But it was not his real self—or at least not all of it. He simply bent to the wishes of his audiences, but without losing his essential dignity. (There are "fusion" players today who have done far worse.)

Armstrong was at heart a lyric player. He was not a fast player, as is Dizzy Gillespie (or the latest heir to Louis's throne, Wynton Marsalis) or as Eldridge tried to be. Armstrong was essentially a melodist, albeit with a highly developed sense of embellishment. As a player he preferred moderate or slower tempos, his fast notes being always at the service of ornamentation, of fleshing out between the main melodic note-stations. This was not a matter of technique, of fingers, of embouchure; it was a matter of conception, of the mind. What the mind conceives and the inner ear hears, an improviser will play. For the fingers and embouchure telepathically obey the mind. In his basically lyric stance Armstrong was a conservative, an advanced and highly successful one, as compared, say, with Jabbo Smith, the latter in spirit and temperament a fast-thinking player. Armstrong in his melodic, basically "vocal" approach to music, shows us to which generation he belongs. He epitomizes the early decades of jazz and its essentially vocal-melodic (blues and ragtime) traditions—even when he stands continually at the music's cutting edge.

For an accompanying orchestra at this time, Armstrong turned to his old friend from Chicago and New Orleans, Luis Russell. This choice was not immediately crowned with success. Russell had been leading a sporadically excellent band for almost a decade, and through the years had from time to time produced some above-average records, and two or three outstanding ones with Louis in 1929.

The Panamanian-born pianist, Luis Russell (1902–63), had worked in New Orleans in his late teens, soon moving on to Chicago, where he played with King Oliver's band in the mid-twenties. By late 1927 he was leading his own band in New York, which had in it some of his former New Orleans colleagues, notably drummer Paul Barbarin and clarinetist Albert Nicholas, and the remarkable Atlanta-via-Cincinnati trombonist J. C. Higginbotham. By 1929 the Russell orchestra had converted from an erstwhile New Orleans-style band—the emphasis on collective ensembles with a few interpolated solos—to a New York-style orchestra playing "advanced" arrangements and "originals," heavily featuring its roster of soloists, which, as of 1929, also included Henry "Red" Allen and the versatile reed man Charlie Holmes. Russell's first real claim to fame was a composition he co-composed with Barbarin, *The Call of the Freaks*, a stompy, moody minor-key piece, which must have sounded captivatingly "weird" to listeners in 1929. It allowed for copious solos (over chromatically shifting harmonies) in the "freak" style, but here not limited only to the trumpet. Russell recorded this piece four times (if we include a 1934 remake entitled *Ghost of the Freaks*), once even with King Oliver. But the earliest version on the Okeh label is most representative and best performed.

Russell was a gifted composer and a constantly explorative arranger, rarely content to fall back on established formulas. His arrangements—whether those of his own compositions or others', at least in the late twenties and early thirties—almost always contained interesting things to hear, without ever going outside jazz traditions. Russell's *Feeling the Spirit, Jersey Lightning, Louisiana Swing* are all impressive compositions, especially the last, with its entirely original bridge changes. Russell also appreciated his star soloists and gave them—especially Allen and Higginbotham—plenty of solo space. Though some of the performances have as many as nine and eleven separate and quite individual solos, there is considerable stylistic coherence; and Russell knew how to frame the solos in unifying and supportive settings. Indeed, some of the best early solos by the fiery and at times quirky "Red" Allen can be heard on his Russell band sides: both takes of *Louisiana Swing* (which incidentally are for the most part identical, i.e. well staked out beforehand), *Panama, Dancing Dave* (the same orchestra under Allen's name). The same can be said for Higginbotham, who was uniformly brilliant, remarkably imaginative, and consistent, even more than Allen—and, I find, much more so than Jimmy Harrison during the same period. Hear Higginbotham on any number of performances, but especially *Doctor Blues, On Revival Day*, and *Jersey Lightning*.

Much of the soloists' freedom of invention was made possible by the superbly rhythmic team work of Barbarin and bassist Pops Foster. Though not entirely consistent—especially when Foster used his rather limited bowing technique—they could produce some of the most spirited 4/4 swing obtainable in those pre-swing-era years when the two of them *wanted* to (for example, *Panama* with its "flag-waver" yet buoyant drive; *It Should Be You*—under Allen's name—where we can hear all the essential lessons Barbarin taught the young Krupa (including his famous back-beat, so tastefully demonstrated here by Barbarin).

Unfortunately, Russell's adventurous writing, both in his compositions and such harmonically roving arrangements as *African Jungle* (recorded under the pseudonym The Jungle Town Stompers), eventually disenchanted not only his public but the Okeh recording directors as well, and ultimately some of his own players. The older New Orleanians, like Foster, preferring the traditional polyphonic style, were confused by the demands of Russell's new-fangled arrangements. Hear their performance struggles with *Slow As Molasses*, for example. And when Higginbotham and Allen left Russell—both went over to Henderson's orchestra—the best days of the Russell band were numbered.

But Russell hung on and found work for his band at various major New York dance emporia, until Louis Armstrong in a sense rescued the orchestra by fronting it, starting in 1935. But the Russell band had one more successful fling with recordings before that. The sides cut in 1934 for the Banner and Melotone labels, featuring a number of classy arrangements by Bingie Madison, revived some of the earlier spirit of the band. *At the Darktown Strutters' Ball, Ghost of the Freaks*, and the virtuoso *Ol' Man River* are all filled with aural delights, both in solo and ensemble terms. Rex Stewart was with the band briefly and contributed two remarkable cornet solos: his quite original unorthodox solo on *Primitive*—it is anything but "primitive"—and his hair-raising virtuoso tribute to Herbert L. Clarke on *Ol' Man River*. But while one may admire these records for their undaunted enthusiasm and relative sophistication, one must also note that a goodly number of ideas, both large and small, are borrowed from other orchestras. They range from Henry Jones's eccentric introductory alto solo on *Darktown*, surely trying to imitate Don Redman on *his* opening of *Four or Five Times* (McKinney's Cotton Pickers), to the whole Casa Loma band feel of the latter half of *Primitive*, and on to *Ol' Man River*'s virtual plagiarization of Duke Ellington's *Old Man Blues* of 1930, reminding everyone that Duke's version was itself deeply indebted to Jerome Kern's classic, cleverly transforming its changes into a four-times-faster virtuoso thriller.

Oddly enough though, despite such a generally splendid record of achievement, the Russell band had great trouble finding a style that fitted their renewed role as Armstrong's sidemen. Proof that it was Armstrong that asked for the Lombardo saxophone sound lies in the fact that it shows up immediately on the Russell band's recordings with Louis, whereas in the band's own 1934 recordings, for example, it is absent. But how truly awful the band could sound, often dragging Armstrong down with it, one can hear on *Red Sails in the Sunset, Thanks a Million*,[18] and *On Treasure Island*.

Occasionally the band acquits itself well in ensemble passages, as on *Falling in Love*, or on pieces with solos by saxophonists Charlie Holmes and Greely Walton or trombonist Jimmy Archey (or later Snub Mosley). But these are often offset by Russell himself, who almost never played a piano solo or break without rushing badly. Mention should be made of Louis Bacon, Armstrong's loyal disciple, who frequently played Armstrong-like lead-in solos or muted obbligatos behind Louis's vocals.

---

18. The earlier reissue of *Thanks a Million* on Decca DL 7922 is so hyped up with reverberation and artificial stereo that it successfully covers over most of the band's sins. The later MCA reissue is much more realistic.

But by May 1936 the Russell band had improved considerably, not only in the way it coped with the now more challenging arrangements by Russell or Bingie Madison but also in the way that these arrangements related to Armstrong's playing. There was a real attempt at musical integration, something that until now had always been missing with Armstrong's accompanying units. Louis blossomed under these circumstances once again, his physical playing health also greatly improved by now.

Of course, one must sympathize with the arranger's plight. How do you accommodate an Armstrong's grand and at times monumental art in a three-minute frame and a thirteen-piece band? When Beethoven inherited the violin concerto from Mozart and found it insufficient to accommodate his own grander conception of what a violin concerto could be, he dramatically expanded the form and enlarged the orchestra, daringly even giving a major thematic role to the timpani. And when Wagner found both the orchestras and performing venues of his times wanting in terms of accommodating *his* grand visions of opera, he simply invented additional new instruments and built the most advanced and unique opera house in the world. If black jazz musicians could have had analogous visions in New York in 1936, they would never have been permitted their realization. So one admires the best of the smallish achievements of these musicians, struggling against awesome constraints and conventions, not to mention managerial ministrations for whom questions of musical integration were at best a moot point.

How far this musical integration had progressed can be heard on at least three excellent sides made on May 18, 1936: *Ev'ntide*, *Thankful*, and that amazing virtuoso tour de force, *Swing That Music*. The first two of the three titles are ballads, quite similar in their mood and harmonic changes, the one by Hoagy Carmichael, the other by Sammy Cahn. Both composers had evidently been listening hard to Ellington's *Sophisticated Lady*, with which both songs have some striking similarities. The arrangements (and performances) do justice to these songs, probably fashioned by Bingie Madison. They were both outfitted with side-ending cadenzas, but harmonically more interesting than those of the past.

Louis's playing flourishes in this stimulating environment. On both *Ev'ntide* and *Thankful* he invents grandiloquent and masterful improvisations, his tone purer and bigger than ever. A new authoritativeness exerts itself, as he takes even the relatively complex changes of *Thankful* and invents magnificent new freefloating arching lines over them, great cathedrals of sound. (Ex. 11).

On his own *Swing That Music*, both Louis and the band excel in the kind of "killer-diller" virtuoso piece that was rare in his repertory. Foster, slapping away mightily on his bass, sets the pace (at around $\quarternote = 300$), and after a (for Louis) quite sprightly vocal, the saxophones are hurled into a whirlwind eighth-note chorus of such bravura that it renders inexplicable the same section's miserable playing just six months earlier. Armstrong follows up with four quite overwhelming choruses that were meant to have audiences gripping the arms of their chairs—if they were still sitting. Starting in the middle range with a paraphrase

Ex. 11

solo on the tune, Armstrong gradually works his way upward every sixteen bars or so, until for the final chorus he hammers home forty-two (!) repeated high Cs, thankfully changing their rhythmic pattern as he sails along, resolving in the last seconds to a climactic E♭. This final chorus is, of course, more an acrobatic stunt than great art.[19] But where it might really have been loathsome exhibition-

19. This feat seems to have been topped by a bit during Armstrong's 1933 trip to England where, to the disgust of his critics, he is reputed to have played on one occasion seventy consecutive high Cs—unaccompanied!

ism with many another player, Louis somehow carries it off as at least high-level craft. Technically it was a staggering achievement for its time; nobody could equal it. Nobody could carry it off with such conviction of its validity as a high form of entertainment and skill.

In addition, the musical/stylistic integration I mentioned earlier comes to our aid. For ultimately it is not only Armstrong's forty-two high Cs we listen to—as was so often the case in earlier grandstanding solos. This time there was a band to support it, a coherent context to sustain it. By the time Louis gets to his high C plateau, the band has accumulated, for itself *and* the listener, so much rhythmic momentum that the end justifies itself. It is heard as a totality, comprising four concurrent levels of activity: the break-away rhythm section, churning saxes, brass punctuations, and over it all, Louis.

Swing That Music both reveals and confirms what I have suggested earlier: Armstrong was not a virtuoso in the sense of a speed player. Rex Stewart, for example, in *Swing That Music* would have played his chorus in eighth-notes, as he did so brilliantly with Russell's band on *Ol' Man River* (1934) or with Ellington in *Trumpet in Spades* (1935). Louis plays no eighth-notes at all, and much of the time spreads out with half and whole notes, especially as he climbs into the highest register. This is totally logical within Louis's concept; the longer note-values reinforce the impact of the approaching climax, and—always important for Louis (in a way that it often isn't for modern players)—the audience could follow the action.

I would add that there is an enormous excitement to the kind of four-layered structure the arrangement offers in its final chorus, each strand at its own speed and with its own function, The swirling saxophone ensembles provide the real motoric energy (along with the rhythm section, of course), while the brass provide a different more incisive kind of propulsion. In a sense Armstrong's high Cs just coast along on this rhythmic juggernaut; and the allusion both to high speed trains and Ellington's *Daybreak Express* in particular is close at hand.

Although Louis was to retain the Russell band as his accompanying instrument through 1947, it was not to be an exclusive arrangement. In accordance with Decca's policy of shuffling its various star attractions together in strange alliances—that no *musician* would ever dream of concocting—Armstrong found himself recording with Jimmy Dorsey's band, Bing Crosby and Frances Langford, a Hollywood Hawaiian group, and the Mills Brothers. While one may marvel at the equanimity with which Armstrong takes on all comers, and matches in *his* way the high professionalism these "recording stars" all posessed, one still can't resist wondering whether the time spent with these groups could not have been put to better use.

The encounter with the Jimmy Dorsey orchestra in the summer of 1936 came off rather well, in fact. The band was disciplined—more so than any Louis had ever recorded with—and played with a fine laid-back beat and a balanced homogenized sound. Louis, now almost completely recovered from his 1934 and 1935 physical problems, thrives on the Dorsey sides. His tone is rich and pure;

ideas flow from him with devastating ease as on *Skeleton in the Closet*—that is, once the fake-spooky hokum repartee is done with. The piece itself had a light airy Henderson-style swing, not unlike Ray McKinley's later *Celery Stalks at Midnight* (McKinley was playing drums for Dorsey on these Armstrong sides). A remake of *Swing That Music* suffers by comparison with the original. Louis is not inspired this time to duplicate his earlier heroic effort, while the band, though technically capable, is a bit on the frantic, driven side. Above all, the Armstrong-Dorsey performance lacks the *drama* of the earlier recording.

After Louis's nearly year-long dalliance with assorted Hawaiians and vocal quartets, he returned to the Russell band in July 1937, once again an improved ensemble. There were strong additions or replacements, in the persons of Henry "Red" Allen, J.C. Higginbotham, Wilbur de Paris, and Albert Nicholas. As it was, they didn't get many solo opportunities on the records (although presumably on location they and the others, like altoist Charlie Holmes, would enjoy the benefits of a less constricted format). It is particularly tragic that Allen was given no chance to play other than third trumpet section work, but he was probably too close a threat to the master.[20] Obviously Louis did not remember how generous *his* mentor King Oliver had been with him, when *he* was a twenty-two-year-young potential rival.

Even the better performances of 1937 and 1938 do not add significantly to Armstrong's stature (or to our knowledge of his art). In his late thirties now, Louis had reached his creative peak—some would argue that he had already reached it in the late twenties—and it was going to be up to others to push the musical boundaries further out. And all around him that was in fact happening: Duke Ellington coming into his greatest period, Lester Young and Bill Basie proposing a new kind of clean relaxed swing, Coleman Hawkins and Herschel Evans expanding the expressive range of the tenor saxophone, Benny Goodman and the hordes of slick swing bands that were crowding the field, younger disciples of Louis like Allen, Eldridge, Rex Stewart, and waiting in the wings, ready to move on-stage, Gillespie and Parker—in their ways as precocious as he was when, as a teenager, he (Louis) spent his formative years working with Bunk Johnson and Fate Marable.

Of course, that wasn't a signal to give up. Armstrong was still at the height of his powers in the late thirties. He took better care of himself now, and was perhaps a bit more careful about daily draining his talents, physical and otherwise, to their limits. Hear him on *Jubilee* (Jan. 1938), playing with absolute control, technical and aesthetic, guided by his superb musical instincts. The Russell band also has things well in hand, except for Barbarin's unfortunate tendency now to imitate the worst of Krupa's clichés, his overbearing emphasis of beats 2 and 4. (Hear it even more obviously on *On the Sunny Side of the Street*.) Krupa was by now the most popular and most imitated drummer in the land, and there is a bitter irony in Barbarin's need to parrot Krupa, for the latter

---

20. For a full discussion of Henry "Red" Allen's original and outstanding work, see below, Chapter 6, Part 3.

learned most of what *he* knew as a young man in Chicago from Barbarin, then working with King Oliver.

Jubilee, written by Hoagy Carmichael and Stanley Adams (later a president of ASCAP) for a Mae West movie, was a lively processional piece in which Louis leads a parade band. On the recordings' final choruses, with no lack of bravado, Louis marches right up to a climactic high F.

Similarly on *Struttin' with Some Barbecue*, after a spectacular high-note entry, Armstrong burns his way through the rest of the piece as if there were no tomorrow. Seasoned showman that he was, after endless breathtaking high notes, he saved his most sensational trick for the last few bars, this time not merely a high note, but a series of wildly flapping glissando effects that defy both description and notation. Despite the barrage of high notes, the work has real substance because once again the arrangement, this time by that fine craftsman, Chappie Willet, helps to integrate the performance as a whole. The band does very well with this piece, spoiled only by Madison's painfully flat high notes in his clarinet solo.

As the swing craze really hit in 1938, with the emergence of Basie, and Goodman's Carnegie Hall success, and a veritable avalanche of black and white swing bands, Armstrong was at times forgotten. Most of 1938 was a rather lean year for him, certainly in the recording studio.

His fortunes were to undergo considerable fluctuations in these years, as Armstrong was suddenly perceived by many musicians and swing fans as old-fashioned. In an attempt to shore up his support with his older fans, he began recording remakes of the older repertory, associated with his Chicago years in the twenties. But this ploy didn't work because the old tunes were now being dressed up for a big band, and rather died from orchestrational overweight. *West End Blues* and *Hear Me Talkin' to Ya* received especially diffident or merely imitative performances, while *Savoy Blues* fared a little better, even as Louis matched Holmes's Hodges-styled alto with more than his usual floridity.

Successes and failures appear side by side with some regularity. A beautifully elegant *You're a Lucky Guy* (from late 1939) is followed inexplicably by a grandstanding travesty on *When the Saints*, called *Bye and Bye*. Here and there Higginbotham almost steals Louis's thunder, as on *Wolverine Blues* or *Save It, Pretty Mama*.

Drifting along like this, Louis was persuaded in the spring of 1940 to make some small-band sides, reminiscent of his early days. Except for two not very successful sides with an octet in 1937, Armstrong had not recorded with anything but big bands since 1929 and had spent his talents almost exclusively on current popular songs and novelty tunes.

Although his die-hard small-group fans were undoubtedly relieved to see the master return to his roots, as it were, the four sides Louis recorded with mostly fellow New Orleanians (like Sidney Bechet, Wellman Braud, and Zutty Singleton), the results were in the final analysis disappointing. Superficially true to the style of New Orleans vintage jazz, the records did not reveal its essence. The solos by Bechet and Armstrong were fine enough, and even matched each other, but the old collective spirit wasn't there. It all sounded a bit too comfortable, like a well-worn slipper. Too much had happened in the intervening years. It was a way of making music that those who had left it for greener pastures could not necessarily recapture so easily. That had to be left to the old-timers who had never veered from the old style, and to the young revivalists sprouting up everywhere. For Louis it was difficult, after eleven years of exclusively dominating every performance, to suddenly suppress his soloistic impulses and to become an integrated part of a collective ensemble.

But it was wonderful to hear Louis once again sing some real simple blues, as he did on Buddy Bolden's old number *2:19 Blues*. Yet overall, Bechet with his impassioned clarinet-playing comes off better than Louis, especially in *Down in Honky Tonk Town*.

Further small-band sides in early 1941, but now with a stylistically mixed group, were even less successful. They never found a cohesive ensemble sound, while Prince Robinson's quite modern tenor jostled uneasily not only with George Washington's earlier-style trombone but with the intruding vaudeville routines which returned full force.

When Louis switched back to the big band later in the year, he also switched back to an even more unequivocally commercial style. On pieces like *I Used To Love You*, it could have been Ray Anthony playing. From his normally warm tone Armstrong moved to a more overtly sweet sound, with the band, of course, following suit, indistinguishable from a hundred other sweet or dance bands of the period. To leave no doubt about his intentions, Louis recorded (for the third time) his theme song *When It's Sleepy Time Down South*, this time in pure sweet band ballad style. *Sleepy Time* surprisingly had no vocal, just Louis's "golden" trumpet; and *Leap Frog*, Joe Garland's fine riff tune,[21] had *neither* an Armstrong vocal *nor* a trumpet solo. It was a straight swing instrumental (unheard of in Armstrong's book), undoubtedly a gift to Garland, a versatile player and arranger (composer of *In the Mood*) who had taken over the musical directorship of the band from Russell in mid-1940. It was snappily played by the band in Garland's tidy arrangement, who also provided the bass saxophone's final pedal A$\flat$, with Louis perched four and a half octaves higher on his highest E$\flat$ (virtually his only contribution to the piece).

Garland had dramatically tightened up the band's playing and had transformed it into a modern, well-groomed swing band. Herein, ironically, lay a new problem for Louis. Whereas in the past the problem had been finding a band that could come up to Armstrong's level, if even only at a discreet distance, now the band was often more interesting to listen to than Armstrong was. The band and the arrangement began to attract attention in a way that probably Armstrong had always feared, and had managed to prevent. Just in terms of the allotted three-minutes-plus of a recording, there were so many fascinating things that a modern swing band could now do that Louis found himself more and more

---

21. *Leap Frog* (not the same as Charlie Parker's 1950 recording) eventually became Les Brown's theme song.

crowded out, either by less solo space or by the increasingly more sophisticated and showy band, even competing *during* Louis's solo with busy compelling backgrounds. Moreover, Louis's playing was now decidedly anachronistic in relation to the Garland band's style and its other soloists, especially Robinson (who was busy listening to new players like Don Byas and Ike Quebec).

Louis was at odds once again. When sometimes, in the mid-thirties, Louis was fronting the Russell band at its hotel-bland worst,—say, on *If We Never Meet Again* (1936)—he protruded by his very excellence. Even at *his* least, he wasn't innocuous enough; he was too commanding. Now in 1941 and 1942, it was the reverse. The new swing styles, urged forward by an unprecedentedly competitive field, had passed Louis stylistically by. His sustained singing solos and ever more cautiously played "big" endings could not compete with the faster moving and louder arrangements that were now the vogue. Besides, younger trumpet stars, like Harry James and Ziggy Elman, were stealing Louis's thunder, even as their adulating crowds were quite unaware of the fact that they (James and Elman) were just lesser direct descendants of Armstrong.[22]

In performances like Louis's *Coquette* (April 1942) and *Grooving* (August 1944), we can hear the warring elements unable to adjust to each other. It is clear that, in terms of what Louis *really* wanted to play, the modern big band had become unnecessary ballast for him. He kept a big band going, under Joe Garland's leadership, until he disbanded in early 1947, in the meantime alternating on records with smaller groups, variously called Hot Seven or Dixieland Seven.

Some of these sides offered pretty ordinary Dixieland stuff, as on *Where the Blues Were Born* and another remake of *Mahagony Hall Stomp*. Others, like *Sugar* and *I Want a Little Girl*, were excellent, Louis playing superbly, abetted by the incomparable Vic Dickinson (at his sardonic, wittiest best), Barney Bigard, and a nicely swinging rhythm section of Zutty Singleton, Red Callender (bass), and Allen Reuss (guitar).

In 1947 Armstrong returned full time to the small-group format, with Jack Teagarden, Barney Bigard, Earl Hines, Cozy Cole, and Arvell Shaw as the more or less permanent personnel, the group called the All Stars.

Here, with musicians of like mind and formidable talent, Louis found a compatible musical format which he was to enjoy for many years. It was a kind of renaissance for Louis; and because he was the creator of the style this renaissance celebrated, it was an authentic reminder to the hundreds of younger New Orleans revival groups that had sprung up in the meantime, of how much life and joyous spirit there was left in the old classic style. At a time when bop was battering down the last defenses of swing, Armstrong's return to his New Orleans roots was welcomed by many traditionalists with a sigh of relief. Indeed, many mainstream music-lovers, alienated by bop and modern jazz, in a sense rediscovered Armstrong and accorded him a popularity he had not even enjoyed during his big-band fronting days. In *Rockin' Chair* and *Pennies from Heaven*,

---

22. And when years later the big record companies wanted mood music with a trumpet in front of a sultry sounding string section, they hired Bobby Hackett or Billy Butterfield, not Louis Armstrong.

from the 1947 Town Hall concert which more or less launched the All Stars, we can hear Louis in top form, both singing and playing, the less pressured format of the older style an obvious boon to his playing.[23]

By the same token the return to a more traditional idiom clearly signaled the fact that the days of Armstrong innovations lay in the past. Through the years, especially after Teagarden, then Hines, and finally Bigard left the group, Armstrong turned more and more to singing, entertaining, clowning, and, as Billie Holiday used to put it, "Uncle Tomming." Ironically, it was in his last twenty years that Louis was to achieve his greatest mass popularity. White America even discovered Louis—at least a certain side of Louis—without ever knowing the real greatness of the man.

Louis Armstrong died July 6, 1971—seventy-one years and two days old. Until the very end he kept on performing, and somehow he generated enough stamina to continue the punishing schedule of world tours—perhaps his greatest personal triumphs occurred on a West African tour in 1960, "the return of the native"— festival concerts and recording schedules. His playing eventually became frail and cautious, his upper lip long ago permanently remolded by the constant pressure of mouthpiece and rim. As he once put it: "It's been hard goddam work. I blowed my chops off." His performances consisted more and more of clownng, mugging, less and less of trumpet-playing; and, of course, more singing—with an ever wider and uncontrollable vibrato but retaining to the end his remarkable control of continuity, of form, of the beauty of logical melodic construction. But whenever he was counted out—rumors that he was dying or *had died* were a common recurrence—Louis always sprang back with extraordinary resilience— the great entertainer to the last.

Dealing with Louis's last years is not easy. One wants to remember, always, his incalculable influence on the history of jazz, as the first major artist and soloist, as the revolutionary who first fully assembled the rhythmic language of jazz. In these respects his heritage permeates all of jazz to this day, even if the traces of his genealogy are now blurred by four or five decades of further evolution. But the seeds Armstrong sowed are still bearing fruit and, in myriad lesser or larger ways, all that we may hear today has been touched by his genius.

But the end was not what it should have been. Nat Hentoff once suggested that Louis should at least have been elected to the American Academy of Arts and Letters, or been accorded a Pulitzer Prize in music. Or better yet—my suggestion—as America's unofficial ambassador to the world, this country should have provided him with an honorary pension (as Finland did with Sibelius) to live out his life in dignity, performing as and when he might, but without the need to scratch out a living as a good-natured buffoon, singing *Blueberry Hill* and *What a Wonderful World* night after night.

As it is, our memories are beclouded by recordings of a sixty-three-year-old Louis singing *Hello, Dolly!* against a cheap brassy Dixieland sextet (over a soggy string section yet), and straining for one more quivery high C. A more touching

23. For more on the All Stars, see below, Chapter 6, part 4, under Teagarden.

aural memory is that of Louis with Ella (Fitzgerald), his playing infirm and short-breathed, no longer in tune, but the Oscar Peterson Trio and Buddy Rich lovingly carrying the old man along on the firm youthful shoulders of their magnificent beat.

As many have said many times about Armstrong: "He paid his dues." And we are his beneficiaries. For our lives have all been touched by his genius and spirit, whether we realize it or not.

4

The Quintessence of Swing

While the orchestras of Ellington and Goodman represent two quite different peaks of achievement in the thirties and early forties—the period now called the Swing Era or the Big Band Era—it will come as no surprise that there was in addition a considerable number of other superior bands who contributed significantly, and in some cases even uniquely, to the development of jazz. These orchestras were Ellington's and Goodman's chief competitors, commercially and artistically, in a field teeming with talent and opportunities. The rivalries between the major orchestras and the famous "battles" between bands that were staged at ballrooms like the Savoy in Harlem were but one outward manifestation and symbol of a period of creative ferment, perhaps never equaled in sheer excitement and productivity, even in such other rich periods as the bop period of the late forties or the "modern jazz" explosion of the early sixties.

It seems quite clear today in retrospect that the Depression years and their aftermath were culturally and artistically the richest this nation has experienced in this century. With financial and material acquisition virtually at a standstill, those lean years forced most Americans to turn to themselves—to rely upon and appreciate more their own creative imaginative instincts and impulses. Self-expression, whatever personal form it might take, became almost of necessity more important than commerce and career. Substantial federal subsidization and the creation of alternative opportunities by such agencies as the WPA helped to stimulate and support productivity in the arts. Even though jazz was not to benefit directly from such social-legislative efforts, being far from sufficiently accepted as an established viable tradition, it nevertheless caught much of that fever of discovery and excitement, that sense of a new beginning, of a kind of renaissance.

For most jazz musicians, of course, with or without benefit of society's support, it was neither a matter of choice nor one of promulgating a new musical order; it *was* one of survival. As Duke Ellington once put it, speaking about those earlier days: "We weren't out to change the world musically. We wanted to make a living and get as much self-satisfaction out of our work as we could."

And the climate of the times was right for just that; the artistic soil was prepared to allow those earlier seedlings sown in the late twenties to grow and flourish. Those tender musical sprouts—the embryonic development of an orchestral style of jazz (through Henderson and Ellington); the simultaneous development of improvising virtuoso soloists as well as skilled technicians and trained (reading) musicians—those seeds and their young plantings, at once fragile and tenacious, successfully wintered the Depression years. Indeed, by the end of the decade, jazz had not only survived, but had succeeded in becoming the nation's virtually sole popular music.

That perception was accurate, of course, only in its broadest, most all-inclusive interpretation. Much of what was called jazz was, by some stricter definition of that term, merely "dance music" or "popular music." Indeed, in a country where jazz, even to this day, is still roundly ignored by the vast majority of its populace, the finer distinctions between real jazz and its many derivatives are considered rather academic. Guy Lombardo, Lawrence Welk, and Liberace are considered by the general public to belong to the same class as Shaw and Goodman and Basie, who in turn are not all that different from the Beatles, Meatloaf, Madonna, Springsteen or for that matter Dolly Parton, Helen Reddy, and Kenny Rogers. In that vast panoramic landscape of commercially successful performers, where the entertainment quotient is considered much more important than any real artistic content or stylistic individuality, where success is measured by the position "on the charts" and by financial statistics, the endless parade of television superstars—in earlier days it was radio—exist primarily to feed a mass market and what has been called, quite aptly, its "industry." Whether the one musician or singer improvises and the other doesn't, whether one is black and another white, whether the one dresses in funny outfits and the other doesn't, whether one musician knows only one or two chords and another is a creative genius—these are all distinctions that unfortunately seem to matter very little in the larger public arena. Determining real quality and musical talent is of little consequence for the great unwashed public while determining one's *favorites* in the realms of "life-style" and "image" seems a much more urgent concern.

But in looking back to the jazz of the thirties, especially in terms of critically assessing its *artistic* achievements, we must make just such distinctions. For when the "swing" styles reigned supreme, it was the swing music of Goodman, Miller, and Shaw, not Ellington and Lunceford, that became the popular music of the land. Perhaps even truer, it was the safer, more commercial dance bands—the Kay Kaysers, Orrin Tuckers, Wayne Kings, and Sammy Kayes—that were the *real* beneficiaries of the swing craze. In a more critical time and with a more discerning audience, these countless mediocre dance bands would not have flourished, certainly not in such numbers. They plagiarized and trivialized the musical innovations and styles of the leading black musicians, reducing the content to a banal, lowest common-denominator of accessibility.

But that was of little concern to the average swing consumer. It also escaped the average American's notice that those white bands who *did* care about playing authentic creative jazz hired black arrangers. So did the fact that the greatest creators of jazz could only rarely be heard on popular radio programs, such as "Let's Dance" or New York's "Make Believe Ballroom," and that one of the greatest of jazz artists—some would argue *the* greatest, Louis Armstrong—did not become a household name until long after his prime, when he happened to stumble onto a hit called *Hello, Dolly*.

The vast majority of even the initiated audience for jazz was indifferent to it as an "art." Then also there were, of course, those—both black and white—who openly opposed jazz as a "degenerate," "sinful," and "vulgar" music. Much of the audience that did go to dances and to ballrooms to hear their favorite bands were young, possibly in love or courting, attracted by both the novelty of jazz and its somewhat "disreputable" aura. They were attracted more by that contagious mixture of anti-parental rebellion and a desire to appear "hep" than any serious concern for the content of what they were hearing.

These depressing ruminations are, alas, a necessary prelude to a deeper consideration of the music of the Swing Era. For they necessitate, unfortunately, the segregating of that history into black and white chapters. This is not to perpetuate the racial social biases that divide black and white musics, then and now, and that were present at the birth of jazz, indeed were even the roots and cause of its birth. On the contrary, it is rather the historian's way of documenting what is in fact a reality—one which black musicians know only too well, for they live with it day in and day out—while the average American suppresses and ignores it. For the historian and the serious student an objective analytic approach to this music must include recognition of the basic facts: 1) jazz was/is created and innovated by black people; and 2) every manifestation of their creativity—from minstrel music (mid-19th century), ragtime (turn of the century), jazz (first half of the 20th century) to rock and roll (the 1950s through the 1980s)—has been taken from them and commercialized by whites. Fortunes and careers have been made on the commercialization of these styles, while the black in each instance has been left to forage for a new form of expression. The last time, however, blacks had had enough, and in the "free jazz" and "creative music" of the sixties and seventies created a music which most whites could not (or did not care to) imitate and which, in any case, did not lend itself to commercialization.

But back in the early thirties in Harlem, when the black self-identity movement had not yet developed the refined technique of actually withholding a music from the white establishment, musicians like Ellington and Lunceford and Henderson and Armstrong could think only of giving, of sharing, and of thereby somehow integrating into the white establishment, of becoming accepted and acceptable. And how generously they gave of their talent and enriched our American music!

By giving, they could in turn receive what small rewards society was willing to bestow on them. For the "successful" ones, especially those who could compromise a little and take the "rough edges" off their music, there could be a certain limited acceptance into the culture and a degree of economic stability.

Jazz musicians, both black and white, were still regarded as mere entertainers and musical "mountebanks"; and you wouldn't want one to marry your daughter or even to have one in your house for dinner. But they were useful in that they could on occasion supply you with some entertainment, a few moments of escape when you could forget the cares of the day, and while the great black orchestras of the thirties could identify and communicate effectively with most of their own black audiences, especially in urban areas, white audiences took much longer to be won over to the new music. It wasn't until jazz had been thoroughly sterilized and sanitized by the white imitators that what we now call swing music really could take hold. By that time, of course,—the late thirties— swing had itself become a commercially formularized music. As Duke Ellington put it in 1939: "Swing is stagnant."

In the early thirties true black jazz was bursting at the seams with creativity and new discoveries, especially in New York.[1] For blacks, who had very few national leaders or heroes to look up to, the new recruits to jazz filled that gap very handsomely. With their penchant for proclaiming royalty, blacks crowned the new leaders of jazz—Duke Ellington, Chick Webb, Jimmie Lunceford, Cab Calloway, Fats Waller—later Count Basie—as the reigning "kings" of their music. It was not always clear at any given time who was *the* king, but in Harlem each band had its loyal subjects. The regular "cutting sessions" and "battles of the bands" were an exciting ritual—like those of the jousters and knights of old— to determine who was the true leading sovereign.

Arguments raged then (and still do today) about who was "the best" among the big five top bands—Ellington, Calloway, Lunceford, Webb, or Basie: for most people and for a longer period of time, it seems to have been Lunceford. But then one night when Chick Webb, who enjoyed an unswervingly loyal following for many years at the Savoy Ballroom—the major battleground for these contests—beat Goodman, Lunceford, *and* Basie, *he* became for many the undisputed champ.

JIMMIE LUNCEFORD

It is not easy to trace the origins of a style as eclectic as the Lunceford band's, particularly when the only reliable evidence—the early recordings—is sparse, and when various participants in the very creation of that style offer wholly contradictory explanations of it.[2]

One of the real problems in trying to analyze the so-called Lunceford style is

---

1. As pointed out elsewhere, jazz, after "moving up" the Mississippi River from New Orleans to Chicago and settling in there in the 1920s, had moved again in the late twenties to New York. This was not only related to the increasing urbanization of the music and the greater supply of talent available in New York, musically the "first city," but also because the major record companies and booking agencies were headquartered there.

2. Of the several accounts of this controversy involving conflicting statements and opinions by Edwin Wilcox, Sy Oliver, Willie Smith (Lunceford band members), and Eddie Barefield, the clarinetist-arranger, the one given by Albert McCarthy in his *Big Band Jazz* is perhaps the best.

that there wasn't a single style but several. There may have been, especially in later years, a "Lunceford beat" or a "Lunceford tempo," but the band's very versatility would almost by definition preclude a single stylistic approach. Moreover, it is a crucial factor that the Lunceford band—this applies as well to Webb, Calloway, and several other of the major black orchestras of the thirties—was not a *composer's* orchestra, like Duke Ellington's, but an *arranger's*. The significant difference between the two is that a composer's creativity, particularly that of an outstanding one, goes deeper and encompasses the totality of a musical creation—from its inner content and essence to its exterior surface expression; while an arranger's creativity, no matter how skillful and sensitive, falls some degree short of that totality. An arrangement is by definition a reworking of some other creator's original material, and only in rare instances, when an arranger really *re-composes* the material in such a fundamental way that it results in a new compositional totality, can it achieve the authenticity of full creation.[3]

Thus it is the single thread of Ellington's *compositions*—beyond the superb individual contributions of his orchestra's players—which over an extended period of consistent cultivation forged an absolutely unique style and sound. In Lunceford's case the variety of functions which were served—music for dancing, sentimental ballads, novelty tunes, and virtuoso "flag wavers," *combined* with the parceling out of these various categories amongst three or four arrangers—led to a less unified musical style, even though there was on occasion some overlap between the various arrangers' work.

Indeed one of the miracles of the Lunceford band was that its performances had as much cohesiveness as they did, a cohesiveness second only to that of Ellington's and Basie's. And that unanimity, one feels, was not imposed from above by the leader, Lunceford, but came more out of a mutual respect among the chief arranger-architects of the band: Sy Oliver (trumpet), Edwin Wilcox (piano), and Willie Smith (alto sax). Indeed, it is amazing how they all learned from each other—and how quickly. But that is a phenomenon observable in all of jazz. It is astounding how quickly new ideas spread in jazz, how quickly new norms are established and immediately assimilated by others. The desire to learn and improve, particularly in the early thirties, was so powerful that new ideas, small and large, were gobbled up and digested in no time, everyone eager to push ahead to still newer discoveries.

There is one other rather special element in the Lunceford band's temperament and constitution that had a consolidating effect on the three main arrangers' contributions, and that was the fact that Lunceford was an exceedingly well-trained, partly classically oriented musician who valued discipline and structured organization—and rehearsing. Lunceford's pianist-arranger Wilcox had a similar background, training, and predilection. And while one other member of the triumvirate comprising the original nucleus of the band, Willie Smith,

3. The complete transmutation of one musical form into another is extremely rare. I will cite several widely divergent examples: Ellington's arrangements of Hadjidakis's *Never on Sunday* and Kenton's *Artistry in Rhythm*; Gil Evans's and Miles Davis's *Porgy and Bess*; André Kostelanetz's metamorphosis of *Tea for Two*; and Charlie Mingus's and Eric Dolphy's transformation of *Stormy Weather*.

probably had less of a "classical" background (he majored in chemistry at Fisk University), he was a well-trained musician and, like Lunceford, one who insisted on disciplined playing and rehearsing.

When Lunceford's family moved to Denver from Missouri, the high-school-aged Jimmie came into the hands of a remarkable teacher and mentor of many musicians, Wilberforce J. Whiteman, the father of the more famous Paul. The senior Whiteman was head of music education in the Denver public schools. Not only Lunceford but Andy Kirk and that outstanding Denver band leader George Morrison studied with the elder Whiteman.[4]

Paul Whiteman in his biography *Jazz* writes of his father that he was "the best-balanced man" he ever knew—"He never had a drink until he was fifty-five and never smoked until he was sixty"—and he added that he was always "keen on athletics." That happens to be also a perfect description of Lunceford.[5] After taking a bachelor's degree in music at Fisk University, followed by graduate work there and at New York's City College (while working with the bands of Elmer Snowden and Wilbur Sweatman), Lunceford went to Memphis and taught music and athletics *(sic)* at Manassa High School. Here he met Wilcox and Smith, and when they went on to Fisk for further study, Lunceford followed them, and became an assistant professor of music at Fisk. By the time Wilcox and Smith graduated, the band, conceived back in Memphis, developed further at Fisk, and having added in the meantime two outstanding rhythm men—Moses Allen (bass) and Jimmy Crawford (drums)—had already acquired a considerable reputation throughout the South.

It is clear that Lunceford tried to emulate his teacher, Whiteman, Sr., in the same way that Wilcox and Smith at heart regarded Lunceford as *their* teacher and emulated his sense of discipline and exacting musicianship. Lunceford in fact was in some ways a black Paul Whiteman—down to leading his band with a long white baton.

But the similarities go further. Like the Whiteman orchestra, Lunceford's band carried a whole retinue of arrangers; he insisted on painstaking rehearsing to achieve the highest possible technical and musical proficiency; he insisted fur-

4. Readers of *Early Jazz* may have wondered why I devoted so much space there to a rather "obscure" Denver musician named George Morrison. One reason was that he was typical of hundreds of black musicians of that turn-of-the-century generation who never made the full transition to jazz. Even though many of them were obliged to learn to play some jazz and did so at various times in their careers, more often than not they made their primary living in dance and society orchestras.

The other reason for dwelling on Morrison's career was that his orchestra, which not only toured Europe in the early twenties but as a roaming territory band played as far south as El Paso, Texas, was a kind of local "conservatory" for black musicians. Like the Chicago orchestras of Doc Cooke, Charlie Elgar, and Erskine Tate (the latter two led by violinists like Morrison, the former featuring no less a soloist than Louis Armstrong), Morrison and his orchestra played a great variety of music ranging from the classics to popular songs to "syncopated" music like ragtime and jazz. More to the point, in the early twenties Morrison's orchestra had in it such fine musicians as Lunceford and Andy Kirk, classmates from the student years with Whiteman, Sr.

5. Lunceford's teetotaling disposition was immortalized by Sy Oliver in 1935 in the delightful *Hittin' the Bottle*. The last words of the tag ending, after cataloguing the ubiquitousness of the bottle, mischievously adds: "Everybody—except Jimmie—hits the bottle."

ther on playing a wide variety of that music most favored by audiences, developing among other things, like Whiteman, a superb *dance* orchestra. Lunceford also stressed in the band's on-stage behavior—as John Lewis was to do with the Modern Jazz Quartet twenty-five years later—that music was a profession to be respected and that, if musicians wanted to be considered respectable, they might begin by treating their music and their profession with respect. This was in startling contrast to the conduct ascribed to jazz musicians, then—and, alas, even now[6]—as rather vulgar gin-guzzling inebriates, disreputable Don Juans, and worthless spendthrifts.

Lunceford would have none of that attitude in his band and cultivated a quite different image. As Wilcox said of Lunceford: "He didn't like anything done sloppily, and that carried into his music."

I am aware that for many jazz fans to link a musician to classical and "serious" training and, worse yet, to portray him as a disciple of Paul Whiteman amount to absolute anathema. But that is another myth that jazz in its maturity might finally dispense with. The notion that a black musician "tainted" by formal training of one kind or another is thereby inherently less of a jazz musician reveals a special inverse racism, as deplorable as its opposite. The theory of pedigree in jazz is simplistic at best. A man, a musician, is what he is; and what he produces as a musician is the sum total of all his talents. A musician's antecedents and heritage neither guarantee nor preclude talent and quality, although they certainly may define and predetermine some of its characteristics. It is precisely those specific personal, intellectual, emotional, and psychological qualities in Lunceford's makeup, influenced by his background and early training, that determined to a very large measure the quality of the Lunceford band's music-making—its strengths as well as its weaknesses. That it was for some years one of the very finest jazz orchestras of its time is undeniable; and we cannot rewrite history in order to reconcile it with some preconceived premise. Not all white influences on black music are automatically negative in impact—starting with the early black ragtime and jazz musicians' assimilation of white European harmony.

As mentioned earlier, recorded evidence of how the young Lunceford band sounded is quite sparse. It was known then as the Chickasaw Syncopators, and evidently featured as one of its main attractions the vocal "preaching" of Moses Allen. These early records are quite primitive in outlook and performance, except for Willie Smith's already quite modern and sophisticated alto solos (on *In Dat Mornin'* and *Sweet Rhythm*, 1930). But perhaps they already reflect the basic Lunceford tenets of embracing wide stylistic diversity. These early performances are odd unalloyed mixtures of orchestral ragtime, southern blues and quite authentic black church preaching, Whiteman's sweet style, and Smith's

---

6. This myth unfortunately is perpetuted to this day—with very little justification, one might add. Rare is the time when, for example, the fine, highly trained and disciplined musicians of the Tonight Show orchestra are not caricatured as buffoons, hop-heads, and weird outcasts of society. To musicians that is surely the oldest, most boring, and falsest of stereotypes.

"hot" Hodges-like alto. In embryo this anticipates and personifies the Lunceford band's mature "style": the preaching, replaced later by humorous novelty vocals and crooned love ballads: the syncopated ragtime rhythms giving way to the smoother two-beat dance feeling of "swing"; the sweet saxophone ensemble sound never completely abandoned; and an improvised jazz furnished by a number of fine soloists like Joe Thomas (tenor), Sy Oliver (trumpet), and Eddie Durham (guitar).

A four-year gap to the next Lunceford recording date makes it very difficult to trace the interim development of the band's style(s). But a test recording made for Columbia in 1933 (originally rejected but issued recently on LP)[7] shows the original Lunceford formula intact, the saxophone section enlarged and better balanced, and a much more cohesive rhythm section. At a fast tempo of $\quarter = 240$, the precarious syncopations for the full orchestra (Ex. 1) in the last chorus of *Flaming Reeds and Screaming Brass* attest to the band's increasing ensemble precision, and show Wilcox's arranging ability in handling the "locked-hand" block-chord writing that Don Redman and Fletcher Henderson had previously popularized. But more telling is the band's reluctance to concentrate on one

Ex. 1

approach alone. Half of *While Love Lasts* is played in a sugary sweet style, including the brass, whereas the second part alternates between a better jazz style and an early form of dance-band swing—thus covering all stylistic bases.[8]

One is thrown a little in following Lunceford's course only through recordings—a risky procedure at times—by the next two sides, the first big hits for the band, their commercial success all the more remarkable for being instrumentals: *White Heat* and *Jazznocracy*. The difficulty here is that, although they are exciting virtuoso performances of striking arrangements (and compositions) by Will Hudson, they are at odds with the already well-formulated Lunceford approach. Will Hudson is a white musician, unfairly ignored in jazz-writing, who co-led (with Eddie DeLange) a quite respectable swing orchestra for some years in the mid-thirties. Of importance for the moment is that Hudson was brought to Lunceford by the publisher and impresario Irving Mills, who in turn had brought Lunceford to New York's Cotton Club. Mills undoubtedly thought of Hudson as having two major assets: 1) he was a gifted composer and arranger, an earlier Morton Gould; 2) with his particular arranging talents, honed and refined with McKinney's Cotton Pickers and Cab Calloway, Hudson had a particular flair for the fast riff instrumentals popularized by the Casa Loma band, especially in their first hit, *Casa Loma Stomp*. Mills, a shrewd businessman, felt that what Lunce-

7. The records were undoubtedly not released because of one of Willie Smith's few stumbles as a soloist (in *While Love Lasts*) and Tommy Stevenson's abortive trumpet solos.
8. This was, of course, a concept well-favored by late twenties, early thirties white commercial dance orchestras, who reserved their "hot" jazz soloists for the middle or latter half of their recordings. (See above, Chapter I.)

ford needed was a couple of "hot" instrumentals à la Casa Loma in his repertory. Indeed the Casa Loma's success in the early thirties had a widespread effect to which no band was impervious. There is little of this particular style in Lunceford's earliest or later repertory, and it was certainly different from the style Wilcox and Smith had initiated in the early thirties and the one Sy Oliver was to create beginning in 1934. These arrangers allowed considerable space for improvised solos, while Hudson's predilection was for a totally arranged, full-orchestra sound, blending all the choirs into one sonority.

This "wall of sound" effect can be heard working well in *White Heat*. But, still, it seems unlikely that *Casa Loma Stomp* was the only model for *White Heat*. Ellington's *Daybreak Express* and Moten's hair-raising, exciting *Toby* were certainly known to all the black musicians of the day (and to Hudson). In its performance momentum and authentic rhythmic energy, *White Heat* is ultimately closer to Ellington and Moten than to the Casa Lomans.

White Heat and *Jazznocracy* were in effect a momentary stylistic detour, for where the Lunceford band was *really* heading was in the direction set by Sy Oliver, who had come over from Zack Whyte's band in Cincinnati.[9] Wilcox's claim that he (Wilcox) and Willie Smith had already set the Lunceford band's style simply does not stand up to close scrutiny. They had set *a* style, one that not only survived as one of several within the band's overall approach, but also one that Oliver absorbed in part into his own writing. The reciprocal influence of Oliver on Wilcox (and later Durham) and Wilcox on Oliver was typical of that period of jazz. As previously suggested, it was in many ways a time for new beginnings and new opportunities, culminating eventually in the big band explosion of the late thirties. Like genetic cross-breeding, it generated a tangled network of influences and counter-influences, innovations, and borrowings of all sorts. This process occurred not only in the broader arena of jazz but could be observed in microcosm *within* certain bands, foremost among these Lunceford's. It is this fact and the resultant eclecticism (of a very high order) that makes it so difficult to disentangle the history of the Lunceford band's early development. Its evolution did not proceed in a simple straight line. Ellington's did; so did Chick Webb's; and once he got going in the mid-thirties, so did Benny Goodman's. But with Lunceford the various arrangers' influences and the somewhat inconsistent levels of performance over the years make a description of this complex situation quite difficult. As an arrangers' orchestra it tried many things, even within a single arrangement, and it took a while to pull these diverse elements together into a recognizable identity.

In the end these stylistic questings were all to come to very little—say, by early 1936—when the band settled into a more or less *single* style, a tame amalgam of both the Oliver and Wilcox-Smith formulas, and when it began to experience a certain amount of creative burnout.

But in the meantime, in the band's early heyday, there is for me no question that Sy Oliver was its major catalyst and chief stylistic architect. From early 1934

9. *Early Jazz*, p. 310.

on, for almost two years, Oliver produced a series of arrangements that really set the Lunceford band apart, and gave it a sound and performance style that at its best could compete even with Ellington's. That Oliver was infatuated with many Ellingtonian features is evident in almost all of his work at some point or other, but to overemphasize the fact would be to unfairly detract from Oliver's own remarkable originality. Certain traits, clearly identifiable with Oliver, appeared in his work the moment he joined the Lunceford band, traits undoubtedly already present in his arrangements for Zack Whyte (which unfortunately were never recorded). Foremost among these was a full-bodied, deep-voiced, full-ensemble sound (hear it towards the end of the early *Leaving Me*); his love for transitions, breaks, and modulations without benefit of rhythm section, usually in highly chromatic harmonic passages (things he may have learned from that earlier master of the break and other orchestral surprises, Jelly Roll Morton); and, above all, his natural feeling for a type of syncopation that lies way back in the beat. This soon became the Lunceford band's most irresistible trademark, perfect for dancing. Whereas almost all the swing bands, black and white, played very much on the beat, indeed on top of the beat—as did the Lunceford band when it played Wilcox's or Durham's arrangements—under Oliver's coaching the band played with a behind-the-beat feeling that at first no one else could imitate or master (except Louis Armstrong, who was, of course, the pioneer in this kind of "open-beat" playing).

Oliver was also imaginative in his use of varied timbres and in combining unusual instrumental combinations, as witness the short bridge for one lead trombone, three saxophones, and bell chimes (no bass or rhythm) in *Chillun' Get Up*, otherwise an update of one of Moses Allen's old "preaching" pieces.

But in *Breakfast Ball* and *Swingin' Uptown*, both recorded in late March 1934, along with many excellent moments, one can hear a problem that Oliver was never entirely to solve. It is a tendency to overload the arrangements with too much background activity and fancy figures, combined with a penchant to over-fragment—what some critics have called Oliver's "mosaic technique." This "weakness," the result of a hyperactive musical imagination, Oliver did manage to control most of the time, sometimes totally (as we shall see). But at other times the temptation to astound with complex continuity was too much to resist. *Swingin' Uptown* does feature one remarkable ensemble passage, one of the first of its kind, a four-part block-chord ensemble chorus for one trumpet (lead) and three saxes. Eddie Tomkins's uncanny ability to blend with the saxes and to play with the same linear fluency natural to saxes at a bright tempo of $\downarrow = 260$ not only betokened a talent (Tomkins's) quite far ahead of its time, but also an effect that could not have been achieved without many hours of rehearsing.

In September 1934 Lunceford returned to the recording studios (having switched at midyear from Victor to Decca) and emerged with five memorable sides. Three involve Duke Ellington compositions, another was *Rose Room* (composed in 1918 by Art Hickman and in the thirties a much favored "standard") and, most astonishing of all, a startlingly innovative (and so far roundly ignored) composition by Lunceford himself, called *Stratosphere. Rose Room,* and *Mood Indigo* are outstanding arrangements by Willie Smith, evidence not only of his own fine talent but of his thorough assimilation of some of Oliver's arranging traits. *Mood Indigo* is particularly interesting for its daring departure from Ellington's own versions. Previous commentators have either ignored or dismissed these Lunceford performances of Ellington, probably because they did not fit their own prior notions of how Ellington pieces should be played. But Willie Smith's *Mood Indigo* is great *precisely because* it dared to depart from any preconceptions regarding Ellington's first great instrumental hit, and moreover because it did so in superb fashion. The originality of the first chorus is startling: the well-known theme stated very discreetly in muted brass while, virtually as foreground, clarinet and saxophones in three-octave unisons escort the theme in a totally original bouncy staccato passage. After a fine lyric solo by Tompkins, Oliver intones the main theme in plunger-growl style (with Bubber Miley much in mind), accompanied by five saxes and pizzicato bass in staccato chords in stop-time. The excellent ensemble and balance of the saxes and bass, accompanying Oliver's understated muted theme, create a breath-taking effect. This is due in part to the striking sonority contrasts, but also to the fact that Ellington's plaintive theme, which moves mostly in single-step-wise fashion, is here set off against rich chromatically shifting chords in the saxes. This performance also has a modern feeling that is decades ahead of its time; without identification one might easily assume it to be performed by a band of Basie's caliber in the fifties or sixties.[10]

Indeed, the style and sound Willie Smith adopts on *Rose Room*, at a leisurely dance tempo, is one that survived well into the sixties, especially as emulated by the Les Elgart band. And Smith's low-register clarinet in the opening chorus was long ago appropriated by younger players like Pete Fountain. Again the ensemble is superb and the two-beat swing infectious. A special moment occurs when Earl Carruthers's big-throated baritone sax is followed by a brilliant downward-zooming clarinet run: the contrast between low saxophone and high clarinet being in context a stroke of genius. *Sophisticated Lady*, another Smith arrangement, was less successful. Along with some fine moments—such as the velvety-smooth muted brass punctuations behind Smith's theme statement—there are other passages that seem out of place in the arrangement, e.g. the heavy staccato sixteenth notes in the saxes and later an overly saccharine saxophone ensemble bridge.

Around this time Joe Thomas, a most consistently brilliant tenor player, emerges as one of Lunceford's main soloists. His gutsy style contrasted well with Smith's florid alto. Where Smith was "hot" but clean in his playing, Thomas was "hot" and much "looser" in phrasing. He loved to run notes together and slur through phrases in a free and loose manner, quite different from Smith's impeccable clarity. It is a credit to Smith's famous insistence on sax sectional rehearsals that Thomas could be tamed to blend so perfectly in section ensemble work.

One of the most unusual works in the Lunceford catalogue is his own com-

10. One unsolved mystery is what sounds like a marimba being played on this side. It is not Crawford, for he was playing brushes on snare drum throughout.

position *Stratosphere*. By no means an unflawed work (or performance), it does, however, contain some startling modernisms that sound for all the world like the Boyd Raeburn band of 1946. Basically in D minor, Lunceford's piece takes some surprising harmonic turns that threaten several times to suspend the key center altogether. Most unexpected is a strident sustained two-note "cluster" in the brass (Ex. 2a), followed by a quick move through quartal harmonies in D♭ to a chain

Ex. 2a

of parallel flatted-fifth ninth chords. Later we hear a rhythmic break on timpani (*sic*). There is also an ingenious repeated-note effect in the trumpets (Ex. 2b),

Ex. 2b

some bitonal harmonies (D minor and G major), quick shifting, colliding parallel chords (Ex. 3);

Ex. 3

and finally a wild almost *atonal* ending.

    Stratosphere's main weakness is that it lacks a strong theme or melody; it is a rather simplistic riff-piece (but if that were enough to condemn it to oblivion, more than half the swing era repertory would have to be sent along with it). While *Stratosphere* doesn't entirely jell, it shows us a side of Lunceford's musicality rarely seen. Obviously here he was in a searching, experimental mood. One must assume that the piece didn't have a chance of acceptance, being far ahead of its time and out of place in the popular market. As its title *Stratosphere* suggests, it was too "far out there." Perhaps fifteen years later, in the Stan Kenton era, it would have been acclaimed a "breakthrough masterpiece" by *Metronome* magazine.

    Sy Oliver's respectful treatment of Ellington's *Black and Tan Fantasy* provides another splendid example of the former's almost limitless orchestral imagination, not to mention his uncanny ability to elicit top-notch performances from Lunceford's players. He himself contributed two excellent solos, matched in quality by Joe Thomas's warm Hawkins-like tenor.

The magical way in which Sy Oliver could blend harmony and instrumental color with his own unique brand of relaxed swing is shown to perfect effect on *Dream of You*, for 1934 a remarkably sophisticated arrangement and composition. Everywhere one hears the mark of a masterful craftsman, of the artist sensitive to every minute detail. Listen to the perfection of voicing and balance in the four-way blend of pairs of trumpets and trombones behind Oliver's vocal [11], or at other times the haunting quality of the low sub-tone saxophones. There is nary a false move in the entire performance, and its perfection is heightened by the utter uncluttered simplicity of the arrangement.

Stomp It Off, another fine Oliver effort, is more complex and in some ways more like Henderson's style of the time, especially in its happy blending of light texture and a hard-driving 4/4 beat—the latter always a rarity in the Lunceford band, which had a virtually exclusive hold on the two-beat feeling, already considered old-fashioned by most bands in 1934.

That Lunceford hadn't forgotten the enormous success of Whiteman's Rhythm Boys in the late twenties (including Bing Crosby) is shown by the frequent use of a vocal trio from the band: Henry Wells, Willie Smith, Sy Oliver. *Rain* and *Since My Best Gal* are excellent examples of their expert style. We also see how the more "popular" entertainment side was almost always skillfully handled and at the same time balanced with real jazz, in the case of *Rain*, with one of Willie Smith's most authoritative solos.

The difference between Oliver's and Wilcox's work at this time, both in quality and style, is clearly demonstrated in a number of Lunceford recordings of this period. Wilcox's *Jealous* and *Rhythm Is Our Business* are pleasant but uneven efforts, lacking Oliver's originality and attention to detail. Wilcox's *Star Dust* is well played but ordinary. One also misses the integration between solo and ensemble that Oliver achieves so often. In Wilcox's arrangements it is not unusual for the individual solo to be on a higher level than the rest of the performance.

Perhaps Wilcox's greatest strength was his arranging of saxophone ensemble choruses. There are numerous examples of this in the Lunceford library, but none finer than the one on *Sleepy Time Gal*. Such saxophone ensemble writing was, of course, not new, having been developed years earlier by such arrangers as Don Redman, Benny Carter, and Duke Ellington. By the mid-1930s every big band prided itself on these virtuoso saxophone passages. Wilcox's contribution to the genre in *Sleepy Time Gal*, great as it is, is outmatched by the *performance* the sax section gives it. No modern "Super Sax" group can equal or top its hair-raising roulades and careening twisting turns. The last chorus offers an

---

11. Indeed more than one commentator has mistaken this background for only trombones, most notably Albert McCarthy in his *Big Band Jazz* (p. 253).

early example of the entire orchestra in well-balanced eight-to-eleven-part block harmonies, a seemingly obvious idea but nonetheless at the time still little used (except by the Whiteman orchestra and its arrangers, Ferde Grofé and Bill Challis). Everyone clung to Redman's old technique of dividing the orchestra into its two (or three) constituent choirs. I believe Sy Oliver was the first to use the integrated full-band sound in the Lunceford band, although Wilcox may also have experimented with it. In any case by the mid-thirties, the Lunceford band had mastered this technique to perfection, and it is a feast for the ears to hear the band bounce through those marvelously buoyant syncopations in eleven-part voicings, balanced so well that one can rarely distinguish trumpets from saxophones from trombones.

Since the band had done so well earlier with three of Ellington's compositions, it comes as a disappointment to note the poverty of invention in two other Duke pieces, arranged jointly by Wilcox and Eddie Durham (the trombonist/guitarist who joined Lunceford in early 1935): *Bird of Paradise* and *Rhapsody Junior* (both items, incidentally, never recorded by Duke himself). Durham loved to use three trombones in unison in the low register, an effect which, unless used very judiciously, can sound terribly heavy-handed and pretentious. The same may be said of the parallel whole-tone progressions which some arrangers considered very "modern." For nothing dates more quickly than whole-tone writing—being essentially circular, i.e. unable to progress anywhere. Even Debussy could not entirely avoid this failing. *Rhapsody Junior* has an embarrassing number of these going-nowhere whole-tone passages.

The band recovered partially from these lapses in *Four or Five Times* (with an infectious Oliver vocal) and *Runnin' Wild*, a good Smith arrangement but not played with the usual high Lunceford performance standards. Indeed both trumpet players, Tompkins and Webster, badly muff the high-note ending. The band redeems itself further in *Babs*, an ingenious Oliver arrangement, full of interesting details and surprises, one of which included probably the first use of an extended passage for three unison trombones in the very high upper register.

At this point two developments occurred: one was the emergence of Eddie Durham as a new arranger voice and the other the merging of the various arrangers' styles into more or less *one* Lunceford style. From here on out it became increasingly difficult to differentiate Durham from Oliver and the latter from Wilcox. It is as if, all having listened to and learned from each other, they now decided to share each other's discoveries. Durham contributed a fine composition and arrangement in *Oh Boy*, especially ingenious in its use of the versatile five-man sax section (which was sometimes enlarged to six by the addition of Lunceford himself on alto). The section now could field four altos (five, if needed, with Lunceford), four clarinets, and two baritones. Durham took advantage of the latter availability in the opening chorus of *Oh Boy* when he used the two baritones not only in unison but in harmony. In fact he builds up the section gradually, adding the tenor after a few bars, and finally the two altos. Later on there are some very fast switches from saxophones to clarinets that add immeasurably to the sonoric variety, the illusion still further heightened by using the reeds in all their different registers: high soft saxes, low clarinets, high wailing clarinets, low somber saxes. Along with plenty of varied textures and colors in the brass, this offers a wide range of contrasts of the kind that Oliver excelled in and Durham here used as well to best effect. To suggest, as Max Harrison does [12] that Durham found it hard to absorb Oliver's style in *Oh Boy*, is unfair. It was in fact as much an assimilation as possible without becoming mere *imitation*.

By mid-1935 the Lunceford band's creativity began to level off. This was due in part, I think, to the increasingly commercial material it was asked to record, and to a certain degree of creative burnout. Also, as I have already indicated, the two or three styles set forth by the various arrangers had now coalesced into a single style, still embracing all those several categories—dance, novelty songs, sentimental ballads, straight instrumentals—but also losing something in originality in the process of merging the arrangers' individualities. An element of compromise and accommodation had crept in, and the result was a more uneven quality. Moments of imagination and invention alternate with the most ordinary passages. Somehow in honoring the many practical and ideological commitments the band (or at least its artistic leader) espoused, it had trouble finding a unifying qualitative common denominator.

Erno Rapee's *Charmaine* (with its vacuously crooning vocal, imitating the worst of the successful white sweet bands); *Swanee River* (where tawdry chime arpeggios in the piano and overly cute muted brass exist side by side with fanciful and beautifully played sax ensembles; Elmer Crumbley's "yah-yah" trombone and Oliver's pungent growl trumpet, which was getting for some reason more and more vociferous and "nasty" in tone during this period); *My Blue Heaven* (with its attempt to re-create violinist Joe Venuti and Whiteman's Rhythm Boys); the dull and feeble *The Best Things in Life Are Free* (wherein the previously crooning tenor voice of Dan Grissom suddenly takes on more of a Bing Crosby baritone quality)—all these represent the nether side of the Lunceford band's efforts at this time.

A little more successful, surprisingly, were some of the "novelty" tunes, which brought out the often cool pixie-ish humor of men like Sy Oliver and Willie Smith. Not only that, but many of these tunes, with their generally rather clever lyrics, were about the subject of music. Substituting music for religion, they are the early "preachin' " pieces updated and geographically relocated in urban Harlem. It is as if the Lunceford organization was trying to teach its audiences something about melody (*The Melody Man*), about modern music (*I'm Nuts About Screwy Music*), and especially about rhythm (*Rhythm Is Our Business*, *He Ain't Got Rhythm*). These and other numbers like *Hittin' the Bottle*, *Running a Temperature*, *Slumming on Park Avenue*, and *The Merry Go-Round Broke Down* (with its calliope imitations) stimulated not only the arrangers' musical imaginations, often directly inspired by the lyrics, but also brought a welcome element of humor and wit. And this was one of the important ingredients

12. In *Jazz Retrospect* (Boston, 1976), p. 63. "First, others found it hard to imitate his [Oliver's] style, as Eddie Durham's *Harlem Shout* and, even more, his earlier *Oh Boy* show."

that made the Lunceford band such an entertainment delight. It is not a paradox that the band lavished some of its best talents on this genre; it was intrinsic to their overall purpose of being at once the best musical group and the best entertainment package in the land.

Hittin' the Bottle features on the plus side good Durham electric guitar, inventive Oliver growling, a spectacular high concert F on Smith's alto (a note considered unplayable in those days), Joe Thomas's raspy clarinet solo, while on the minus side Durham's arrangement is too fancily sectionalized, its modulations strained and pretentious. But *Rhythm Is Our Business* shows how well catchy lyrics, improvised solos, and ensembles could be integrated into a musically satisfying and nevertheless thoroughly entertaining whole.

I'm Nuts About Screwy Music has been condemned by most jazz writers as inane. And, of course, compared with Michelangelo's Sistine Chapel and Beethoven's *Eroica* and Shakespeare's *Othello*, it undoubtedly is. Nor would one want to compare it with Ellington's *Ko-Ko* or, for that matter, Charlie Parker's *Ko-Ko*. On the other hand, it is just too easy with the benefit of hindsight and changing viewpoints to sit in patronizing judgment on the musicians of the thirties. One can no more chastise the Lunceford band for its showmanship than one can criticize a leopard for having spots.

In the United States of the thirties, black musicians were given very few options for professional survival. One aspect of survival was artistic, moral, aesthetic; but another, equally real, was economic and social. Both exerted their pressures, with some people succumbing to economic temptation, others—rather few—overcoming them. It seems quite unreasonable (and untenable) to ascribe more importance to one side of that survival equation than to the other—particularly on the part of someone who did not have to experience those pressures. As reaction to some strains of avant-garde jazz has shown, a music which cannot attain and then *maintain* an audience also cannot survive. I'm afraid that question never arose—or *could* arise—in the Lunceford band's collective mind—or for that matter in Ellington's or Basie's. The choices were narrowed down to minor differences, precisely those we can detect among, let's say, Ellington, Lunceford, and Basie. They were ultimately not aesthetic differences but ones of style and personality. They all made their peace with compromise of one kind or another. Thus the real and only valid criterion of judgment is *to what degree* economic and commercial pressures made inroads on artistic/aesthetic decisions—*not whether, but how much*. And in that regard I think the Lunceford band, at least in its early days and perhaps through the 1930s, could hold its own with any of its contemporaries. As previously stated, the Lunceford formula—his and his soloists' and arrangers'—was to serve up a diversified musical menu for a variety of appetites. This was intrinsic to Lunceford's purpose and philosophy, and it is as silly to, when evaluating their work, criticize him and his musicians for what they weren't, and never wanted to be, as it is to ignore the social context in which they existed. It is like criticizing a ballad for not

being a blues or, similarly, evaluating a blues while ignoring the social environment that generated it.

The big bands of the 1930s provided the major musical entertainment for
millions of Americans through their tours—and nobody toured more than
Lunceford—and through radio. Inevitably much of what these traveling troupes
played was not pure jazz but various lesser related forms, catering to a demo-
cratic variety of tastes. The real miracle is that the great black bands played *as
much jazz as they did*—not that they didn't play enough, according to someone
else's purist standards.

Viewed as musical entertainment, *I'm Nuts About Screwy Music* is an example of rather high achievement, perhaps more appreciated if one ponders
what it might have been in, let's say, Kay Kayser's hands. There is certainly
abundant proof of that in the tens of thousands of recordings by hordes of "sweet"
and "Mickey Mouse" bands that roamed the land or occupied the hotel ballrooms of the nation.[13] Wilcox's way with *I'm Nuts* may be tongue in cheek, but
at the same time he doesn't neglect to fill his entertainment package with delightful musical trinkets. The introduction tells us right away how "screwy music" is going to be defined, in this case jerky, fragmented, whole-tone chords in
muted trumpets (Ex. 4). Willie Smith's Teagarden-like vocal is then echoed and

Ex. 4

illustrated by 2- and 4-bar instrumental insertions which illustrate the *particular*
kind of "screwy music" referred to. Thus the usual 8-bar phrases are expanded
to fourteen (or 16) bars by these humorously "modern" interjections. One is
surprised to find, however, that the mention of flute and cello in the lyrics did
not elicit a bit of word-echoing flute music from Lunceford himself (one of the
instruments he played).

In August 1936 the band recorded a single side, which turned out to be a
minor classic of its kind: Sy Oliver's arrangement of Will Hudson's *Organ Grinder's
Swing*. In its basic simplicity and imaginative use of dynamic and timbral contrast, it is Oliver at his best. The introduction and coda are in E♭ and, like the
covers of a book, enfold the main body of the piece (in G major)—a most simple
yet original scheme. Oliver's economy extends to the instrumentation as well.

13. A nadir in this genre of recording must have been reached already in May 1922 when the Elite
Dance Orchestra recorded the following three titles: *Deedle Deedle Dum*, *Oogie Oogie Wa-Wa*, and
Coo Coo!

The E♭ sections are played by that haunting trio combination of soft cup-muted trumpet, trombone, and clarinet (with which Ellington had made history in *Mood Indigo* in 1930), accompanied solely by Crawford's temple blocks. Then, in the ninth bar Oliver adds a burly baritone, his own growl trumpet, and light daubs of rhythm section. These fetching colors are then exchanged abruptly, at the point where the piece moves to the key of G, for solo celesta in hymn-tune simplicity, accompanied by the temple blocks' klippity-klopp. And now a moment of true magic as whisper-soft saxes and rhythm enter with the simplest of blues-like[14] harmonies, accompanying quietly trembling blues-ish guitar tremolos. Dan Grissom's clarinet takes over for four bars, followed by Paul Webster's boisterous swaggering open trumpet and a pungent growl solo from Oliver. Suddenly we've come full circle, and the arrangement returns to its E♭ coda, a perfect ending to a perfect piece.

Having reached such an artistic pinnacle in *Organ Grinder's Swing*, it was almost inevitable—as if exhausted from the effort—that it would be followed by a variety of lesser efforts, mostly oriented towards dance music. They ranged from infectiously catchy lightweight fare like *Running a Temperature*, Irving Berlin's *Slumming on Park Avenue*, *He Ain't Got Rhythm*, and ballads turned into hard-swinging dance numbers like *I'll See You In My Dreams*, *Honest and Truly*, and *Linger Awhile* (an effective throwback to Bill Challis's Whiteman band style, replete with the kind of trumpet trios which used to feature Beiderbecke) to instrumentals like Durham's *Harlem Shout*, Oliver's *Raggin' the Scale* (Edward Claypole's old 1915 ragtime hit) and *For Dancers Only*, the last (along with Sampson's *Stompin' at the Savoy* and Chu Berry's *Christopher Columbus*) setting the "riff-instrumental" formula for dozens of white swing bands from Dorsey to Miller to Shaw and Les Brown.

But there were also some real surprises in the Lunceford catalogue of late 1936, early 1937. Previously, Sy Oliver had often enlivened ballads by doubling up their tempo (Fred Rose's *Honest and Truly*, for example, was taken at a good "up" dance tempo of ♩= 174, perfect for the Lindy Hop). Now suddenly Oliver took the opposite approach. Johnny Green's *Coquette*, always done at a bright clip, was slowed down to about half its usual tempo (♩= 116) and to wondrous effect, perfect for slow close dancing. Although the overall musical performance suffers from Dan Grissom's pitiable vocal, the instrumental sections swing mightily, much aided by Crawford's powerful Chinese cymbal back-beat bashings. Hearing this, one can well imagine the effect of "the great roar"[15] as Ralph Gleason has recalled, which the band produced when at full throttle.

The Merry Go Round Broke Down is a fantastic bit of musical hokum upon which jazz writers have traditionally heaped much abuse. It's an easy target, of course; it's not jazz, it's not blues, it's not even a straight instrumental. And yet,

14. The Lunceford band was anything but a blues band, a fact for which many jazz writers have never forgiven it. It hardly ever employed blues changes, which, come to think is in its way quite remarkable, and could *not* have been accidental.

15. Liner notes for Decca DL79238. The late Ralph Gleason's lively reminiscences alone are worth the price of the record.

if one has open ears, one can hear some remarkable musical invention lavished on this "novelty" tune. First, one must not take the performance all that seriously, as if the Lunceford band had wanted to create a sequel to *White Heat* or *Organ Grinder's Swing.* They were perfectly aware of what they were about. And that was parody: an outrageous put-on—what Charles Ives used to call a "take-off." It's almost surrealistic bizarreness is in fact its charm, and it was accomplished with much skill. Starting with Wilcox's burlesque-ish piano introduction through Oliver's tongue-in-cheek vocal to the hooting calliope imitations by the band, it is all captivatingly humorous entertainment. But then there are also those radiant ensemble trios, made up of a rare combination of clarinet, high trumpet, and alto sax, and—a sound even rarer in jazz of the thirties—low register electric guitar chords (Durham) along with Al Norris's acoustic guitar.

Willie Smith's whimsical humor comes to the fore in *Posin'* and in Percy Wenrich's 1909 song hit *Put On Your Old Gray Bonnet.* The former features Smith's impish vocal (with one of the great lines in pop lyrics: "position's everything in life") as well as some outstanding Ben Webster-like tenor by that musical stalwart, Joe Thomas. The Wenrich opus, arranged by Smith, is taken at breakneck speed—again a purposely "ridiculous" take-off on a venerated oldie. Sparked by Crawford's bristling drumming, the performance features a hair-raisingly virtuosic trio (in mostly eighth notes (!) at about ♩ = 340) for clarinet, trumpet, and alto, with Tompkins playing the middle voice. The idea for such a trio voicing undoubtedly came from the vocal trios Smith was so often in. That technique, already well established in the twenties and coming originally out of the old barber shop quartet tradition and surviving well into the vocal groups of the forties, like the Modernaires or Pied Pipers, had the tune or melody in the middle voice (in a trio) sung slightly louder than the other two "harmony" parts, one above, one below. Willie Smith simply made an instrumental translation of this idea, giving himself the top part, Tompkins the middle voice, and Earl Carruthers on alto the bottom part. I dare say that very few bands, if any, could have sported such a trio, for there were virtually no trumpet players who could handle such an extraordinarily challenging assignment.

When Eddie Durham went over to the Basie band in mid-1937 (although he continued occasionally to arrange for Lunceford), he was succeeded by Trummy Young, a brash-toned twenty-five-year-old trombonist who had already spent four years with the Earl Hines band and who had an amazingly easy high register. Young was put to work immediately, featured both as trombonist and vocalist in *Margie* and a hard-swinging Oliver instrumental based on the traditional *Annie Laurie.* The latter was a stunning example of how non-jazz material could be transformed into a rocking jazz number. Young's sly vocal and spectacular trombone solo on *Margie*, sounding for all the world like a trumpet (especially when he stretches for high F♯ at the end), helped to make this one of Lunceford's big hits for 1938. In Young the band had acquired its first virtuoso trombone soloist (one who could also compete with Tommy Dorsey in the high-register ballad department), and a new comedic talent—although opinions on that have varied greatly.

But although Durham and Oliver were both still occasionally turning out good arrangements—Durham's strutty *Pigeon Walk*, for example, with its arresting tightly muted brass entrance (after Norris's guitar solo), a *trouvaille* that must be heard to be believed—much of their work was getting listless and routine. Even Crawford's usually impeccably tailored drumming was becoming heavy-footed in the worst of the Krupa manner. Even more unpardonable, pieces like Art Kassel's *Hell's Bells*, with its cornily spooky "cartoon" theme and inane celesta solo, and *By the River Sainte Marie*, with its phonily religious lyrics and appalling Grissom vocal, began increasingly to infiltrate the repertory of the band. Redeeming moments were few and far between—a few measures here, a chorus there.

Even a remake of their 1934 hit *White Heat*, virtually the only 12-bar blues in the Lunceford repertory, turned out to be a rather listless affair. Played at a faster tempo than on the original recording, the piece, at least as recorded, became flighty and shallow; it lost both the juggernaut momentum of the earlier version and the explosive energy with which the soloists had originally imbued the piece. Because of the brighter tempo—an unnecessary decision for an already very fast piece—some of the figures in the final choruses had to be simplified, adding to the "flattened-out" feeling. Unlike Ellington, who virtually *recomposed* such early hits as *East St. Louis Toodle-Oo* and *Black and Tan Fantasy* (in some cases several times), Lunceford simply re-recorded the original Will Hudson chart, which the band had probably played to death in the intervening years. And *Well, All Right* was the kind of riff-cum-vocal-by-the-whole-orchestra piece that every swing band was doing by 1939; it became one of the enduring clichés of the late swing era.

But *Blue Blazes*, a Sy Oliver arrangement, was another matter. Smartly played by the band, it featured some typically energetic Willie Smith and Trummy Young solos (the latter filled with daring rips up to high Fs), and a solid high-note contribution from Tompkins. There is also a spectacular three trumpet break (Ex. 5a) and a quite original ending (Ex. 5b).

Ex. 5a

Ex. 5b

At about this time Sy Oliver left Lunceford to join Tommy Dorsey, where as a black, he was not allowed, to sit in the trumpet section but, invisible, behind the scenes, was allowed to furnish arrangements. The loss to Lunceford was virtually irreparable. Billy Moore, a twenty-two-year-old arranger, took Oliver's place, and, although he was not without talent, his work cannot compare with Oliver's. Moore's first assignment was *Belgium Stomp*, a memento of the band's only European tour (in 1937), a swinging affair marred by some unsuccessful Paul Webster high-note grandstanding and a poor solo by Trummy Young—poor because in its meandering lyric approach it is quite at variance with the intent of Moore's urgently paced arrangement.

Another pair of newcomers to the band managed to re-ignite for a while the fading energies and creativity of the band. They were trumpet player Gerald Wilson, who replaced Sy Oliver, and Snooky Young, who took over the lead trumpet chair vacated by Eddie Tompkins. A measure of their work can be taken in some of the sides recorded in December 1939: Wilson in *Rock It for Me* and *Wham*, and Young in *Uptown Blues* and *Lunceford Special*. The lyrics of the first two just-named titles are interesting in that the former includes the phrase "rock and roll," while the latter offers bop lyrics—"Wham, ReBop, Boom, Bam,"—six years before they became fashionable. The final chorus features a brass riff ♩♩♩ to which one could easily have fitted the famous Gillespie bop motto "Oo Bop She Bam."

Lunceford Special is a typical Durham arrangement that provides ample solo space for four of the band's major soloists and a generally spirited performance. But the real gems in this spate of late 1939 recordings come in the well-nigh perfect performance of the saxophone ensemble chorus (led by Lunceford himself on soprano saxophone) in *I'm Alone with You*—a fine arrangement (and composition) by the little known Bud Estes; and in *Uptown Blues*, the finest record from the post-Sy Oliver years of the Lunceford band. It was also the first real blues recorded by Lunceford, not counting *White Heat* (which is based on blues changes, but is not at all "a blues"). *Uptown* features two remarkable back-to-back solos by Willie Smith and Snooky Young, the latter in his first extended solo opportunity on records. It is a splendid effort, perfectly structured as it moves gradually up in register, discovering some poignantly anguished blue notes on the way, and finally crowned at just the right moment in the second chorus by an exultant altissimo $A\flat$, from which the solo descends three octaves to its starting point. It would be hard to compose a better solo statement, even if given hours to write it.

Another fine blues, *What's Your Story, Morning Glory?*[16], effectively arranged by Billy Moore (his best to that date), reveals that the Lunceford band, like a weary fighter trying to rally in the late rounds of a bout, nevertheless still had a few good punches left.

Exquisitely played, with especially strong solos by Wilson and Thomas, this

16. Strikingly similar to Sonny Burke's *Black Coffee* of the 1950s.

track, as if to underscore the band's by now almost obsessive insistence on variety, is followed by a very uneven *Dinah* (sporting one strikingly original interlocking trumpet-duet), from where the band descends to the absolute depths in an unspeakable arrangement (*derangement* would be a better term) of bits and pieces of Beethoven's *Sonata Pathétique*, a truly pathetic offering.

From now on the band flounders erratically towards its ultimate decline. (It is indicative of the band's stylistic confusion that during the 1939–41 period it had as many as eight arrangers simultaneously on its payroll, mostly churning out more or less forgettable work. Admirable performances (as in Moore's *Battle Axe* and *Monotony in 4 Flats* and Durham's crisply played *Swingin' on C*) stand shakily next to a shallow *Barefoot Blues*, a wretched *Minnie the Moocher* (marking the unfortunate debut of the Dandridge Sisters), a pallid thoroughly sanitized arrangement of Morton Gould's 1940 hit *Pavanne* (from his *Latin American Symphonette*), and Don Redman's *Flight of the Jitterbug*. With both of these last two the band moved far away from any notion of jazz. Even worse is *Siesta at the Fiesta* (1941)—the title already offers little hope—in which even the redoubtable Willie Smith falters badly.

Momentary reminders of a more glorious past occur now and then, as when a new arranger's voice is heard. Gerald Wilson's *Hi Spook* (1941) and *Yard Dog Mazurka* (the opening of which Stan Kenton appropriated lock, stock, and barrel a few years later for *Intermission Riff*) seem to give the band a temporary lift. The slow laid-back swing of Harold Arlen's 1941 popular hit *Blues in the Night* elicits some quite magnificent playing from the band. Willie Smith, sounding more and more like Hodges, contributes one of his most expansive solos; and even Paul Webster, usually by now fluffing high notes, lets loose with a fine hot, growly outburst. But why did this arrangement (which cannot be a head arrangement as is claimed by some) have to be marred by a totally irrelevant and vulgarly scored interpolation of Gershwin's *Rhapsody in Blue?* Could not Lunceford or somebody have stopped that?

That Lunceford couldn't be entirely impervious to Count Basie's growing popular success with an infectiously simpler swing style can be heard in such pieces as *Knock Me a Kiss* (1942) and *Jeep Rhythm* (1944), a typical jump tune of the period which features in Wilcox's piano solo an eclectic blending of Basie and Teddy Wilson. Joe Jones's drumming style, with its steady linear ride-cymbal swish, was beginning to infiltrate Crawford's previously very discreet percussion. One can hear this in Edgar Battle's finely swinging *Strictly Instrumental*.

Within a short time some of Lunceford's best players followed Sy Oliver's example and left the band. The loss of Gerald Wilson, Snooky Young, Trummy Young, but especially Willie Smith, was devastating. The band never recovered its former quality. Lunceford seemed to be unaware of this, for he allowed the repertory of the band to deteriorate totally. The orchestra continued without distinction until Lunceford's death in 1947, co-led thereafter by his two most loyal players, Wilcox and Thomas.

In contemplating the Lunceford band's fate, it seems clear now with hindsight that, its most laudable efforts notwithstanding, it carried within it for many years the seeds of its own demise. What *is* surprising is that the artistic decline came so relatively early. For if one dates that final descent around 1942 or 1943, it came paradoxically at a very exciting time. Orchestral jazz was flourishing economically and artistically, and a new music, bop, was coming to the fore. The big band era, of course, ended for virtually everyone around 1948, but why did Lunceford founder so early and so completely many years before that?

First, there was the virus of commercial pressure to which no jazz orchestra was immune. Ellington resisted it more successfully than anyone else, but even he succumbed occasionally to the demands of the marketplace. At the same time the magnitude of his creative talent was such that it could not be seriously or permanently damaged. Lesser orchestras simply gave up, or were forced to; and others (like Basie) retreated to the relative safety of certain swing stereotypes. And listen to the recorded output unabridged of *any* band of the thirties or forties, black as well as white, and you will find that in all cases the mindless vocal (and novelty) numbers and banal love songs far outnumber the true jazz they were permitted to record. For every jazz instrumental, a dozen inane pop tunes had to be sacrificed on the altar of commercialism. Lunceford was far from immune to these influences.

Second, as I have suggested earlier, the Redman-Henderson (Fletcher and Horace) concepts of orchestral jazz, as formularized in the swing era, led to inevitable stagnation and impasse. Ellington and a few others—the moderns coming up in the late thirties and early forties—recognized that. But the majority simply coasted along on the illusory success of public acclaim: "if it pleases millions of people, it must be good." Lunceford, who evidently became less and less self-critical, was one of the earliest victims of this degeneration. Once Sy Oliver's individualism had been broken down and absorbed by the other arrangers, then simplified and worked around to produce a single Lunceford formula, the end was bound to follow.

Third, I would cite the inherent limitations of the three-and-a-half-minute form to which jazz was limited by the record industry, in turn merely a painfully accurate reflection of the general public's and establishment's lack of regard for jazz. It was in fact perceived only as mere entertainment, not as an art form deserving equal time. The 12-inch disc was reserved for *that*. This is a point rarely raised in connection with the demise of swing. But, although one can perhaps not draw an absolute corollary, that three-minute-plus time limit eventually prevented the development of precisely the artistic expansion the music needed, and which it finally got simultaneously in the LP era and through the new forms of modern jazz. To be sure, pieces like *For Dancers Only* and *Strictly Instrumental* were "opened up" at dances to allow for greater solo expression, sometimes expanding into half-hour performances. But those were exceptions not tolerated on records. And it was unlikely that an arranger would create a 20-minute work which he knew would never be integrally recorded. (Read about the fate of Don Redman's *Cupid's Nightmare* with Cab Calloway elsewhere in this volume.) While one admires Whiteman's ability to record Gershwin's entire

Piano Concerto and Grofé's *Grand Canyon Suite* (the latter spread over eight ten-inch discs!) in tiny three-minute fragments, it certainly is not an ideal way to present such music.[17] And, of course, once again, this exception was granted only because both Gershwin and Grofé were considered on a higher "classical" level, a "mere blues" would not have been accorded such status (except perhaps if sung by Bing Crosby).

Notwithstanding Ellington's extraordinary successes with the small form in his peak period of the early forties—precisely when the Lunceford decline occurred—the further evolution of integrating longer solo improvisations into arranged, predetermined structures was effectively inhibited by the music's inability to break out of its three-minute mold. Ellington happened to be the supreme miniaturist who could move around in that restricted format and still find room for creative maneuverability. The other swing era musicians either couldn't or wouldn't. Mostly they didn't even see any problem.

The problem they didn't see was that, with the enormous proliferation of jazz as a viable popular music, thus attracting literally thousands of fine musicians with ever expanding technical and virtuoso abilities, room had to be made for all this emerging talent. The success of the fifteen-piece big band was only a partial solution; it numerically absorbed most of the fine talent. But once in a band, a fine creative musician needed room to express himself, to grow—hopefully through something more than an occasional 8-bar solo. The potential of this yearning for an expanded format was dramatically demonstrated in one fell swoop by Coleman Hawkins in his masterful 1939 *Body and Soul*—still three minutes in length, but at least all his, and in scope commensurate with his immense talents.

The big band swing formulas went in precisely the opposite direction. As more and more musicians capable of significant solo work crowded into the field, the arranged format—almost in an inverse ratio—became more and more restrictive. But then the ratio of instrumental pieces to popular songs given over to vocalists was, to begin with, about one to ten, a ratio basically antithetic to jazz.

Undoubtedly Lunceford's very success with his public was what prevented him from seeing the danger ahead. He was, of course, not alone in this dilemma. Indeed the whole swing and big-band movement eventually ground to a halt in the mid-forties, giving way to small groups (quartets and quintets) and less formula-ridden styles. But even before that the Lunceford band had lost its leadership position, and had become entrapped in its own popular success. Without the *creative* integrity and determination of Ellington—or on another level, say a Glenn Miller or a Benny Goodman or a Count Basie—Lunceford's (and his team of arrangers') initial vision was dissipated relatively soon. Miller (see below, Chapter 7, Part 2, for more on Miller), though not a major composer but a first rate arranger, and Goodman and Basie, who were neither composers nor arran-

---

17. In this connection one should not forget Ellington's path-breaking 1935 *Reminiscing in Tempo:* 4 sides, 12½ minutes.

gers, all had at least a very clear vision—and a fierce, relentless determination to pursue it—of how they wanted their orchestras to sound. Lunceford didn't seem to have that, or, if he did initially, he had lost it by the end of the decade.

When Sy Oliver left Lunceford, it was like a great chef leaving a famous restaurant (it is always better when the chef is also the owner of the restaurant), for Oliver took with him the orchestra's inspiration and style, its creative force and imagination. And Lunceford, the *ultimate* entertainer, was caught halfway between art and commercial success, slipping eventually completely over to the latter side. In due course he settled for creating the greatest show band, perhaps ever—no small achievement in itself, but one not central to the artistic development of jazz.

But the music of Lunceford's mid-thirties' glory days was, for a moment in time, the very best that jazz had to offer. The Lunceford band, second only to Ellington and for a few brief years even more consistent than his, reigned supreme for a while—until Basie and Goodman came along and, combined with Ellington's full maturing in the late thirties, pushed Lunceford to the sidelines artistically. But the Lunceford band *at its best*—and fortunately in recorded form it is still with us—was something wonderful to admire and cherish, a still timeless music, and a superior, significant part of our American musical heritage.

COUNT BASIE

There is no better way to illustrate the profound rift in jazz styles between the Southwest and the Eastern seaboard, which began to emerge in the twenties and develop into a clearly discernible difference in the thirties, than to compare the orchestras of Basie and Lunceford. For each epitomized a differing concept of jazz in terms of sound, feeling, forms, and even artistic goals. And yet they had one element in common: swing—even though they went about achieving that basic requisite of jazz in quite different ways. Indeed, these two bands proved once and for all that there is not one way to swing but at least two or three and perhaps more—a point that it seems necessary make again and again in response to those who would claim otherwise and who arrogate to *their* particular brand of rhythmic swing some sort of pre-eminent priority. One need only hear side by side Lunceford's *Stomp It Off* or *Lunceford Special* and Basie's *John's Idea* or *Jumpin' at the Woodside* to know that both leaders understood unequivocally that their music was first and foremost for dancing, and that the best way to get those feet and bodies to move was with a beat that swung. Ellington had articulated that idea way back in 1932 with his prophetic "It don't mean a thing, if it ain't got that swing." And among black musicians, from Africa to the Caribbean and New Orleans, from Joplin and Europe to Mingus and Monk, it has always been known and felt that the infectious rhythmic element known as swing was an essential and distinguishing characteristic of jazz—without which in fact jazz was not jazz.

With Lunceford swing could take very subtle forms or occur in highly complex orchestral passages, almost always in the rhythm known as "two-beat." With

Basie, by contrast, swing was almost always set in a blues-rooted 4/4 beat and in structures and textures of the utmost simplicity.

In all of jazz there is no element more elusive of definition than swing. Although it is something that almost all good jazz musicians can do and recognize, and something whose presence or absence almost all jazz audiences can instantly distinguish, it is also something that is extremely hard to define in words. In *Early Jazz* I offered what is in effect a partial definition of swing. But perhaps it is possible now to probe still deeper into the matter by approaching a definition of swing from two points of view: one quite general, experienced as a direct reaction; the other quite specific, analyzed in technical-acoustical terms.

In its simplest physical manifestation swing has occurred when, for example, a listener inadvertently starts tapping his foot, snapping his fingers, moving his body or head to the beat of the music. Rhythm is the most magnetic irresistible force among all the elements of music—harmony, melody, timbre, dynamics, etc.—and one to which human response is virtually universal. In a vast majority of the world's musical cultures, rhythm—and its more specific manifestation, the beat—is the primary, indeed primeval element, to which human minds, hearts and bodies respond. Interesting examples of that fact can be seen in primitive music—be it the truly primitive and undeveloped musical efforts of certain aborigine cultures or the often harmony-less, melody-less but rhythmically obvious exertions of certain modern rock performances. For regardless of whatever other musical elements might be missing or feebly represented, as long as rhythm is functioning, the human physical/emotional response is almost guaranteed, even if that response is also primitive. No such pervasively dramatic results can be achieved with harmony or melody, and even less with the other constituent components that collectively constitute the world of sound and music.

But rhythm or a beat does not in itself produce swing. While a really swinging beat or rhythm will make sophisticated dancers perform quite extraordinary terpsichorean feats, we also know that the vast amount of social dancing in the Western world occurs to the dullest, stiffest unswinging "clomp-clomp" rhythms. Similarly, the good clean rhythm of a superb classical orchestra is not necessarily swing. Indeed, metronomic accuracy and rhythmically regular placing of time points (or beats) do not by any means guarantee swing.

What then in technical terms is this elusive element? There are certain preconditions without which swing cannot occur. One is a regular reiterated beat, a regular pulse, either explicit—as in, for example, the 4/4 beat patterns in bass, drums, and guitar in a rhythm section—or implicit—as in an irregular rhythmic figure which nevertheless adheres to and is rooted in an underlying beat.

Second, these rhythmic impulses—both the notes a musician is actually playing and the pulse underlying those notes, whether in a 2-bar break or a seven-minute improvisation—must be *felt*. They cannot be calculated, counted, intellectually arrived at, and still produce swing. Whatever calculation or study is involved must occur during the learning stages of the process. For a condition of "swing" to exist, any calculating, studying, and practicing must have been translated into a *feeling*. It must arise not from the mind or the brain—although the brain may be involved with its controlling critical capacities by receiving the information conducted to it by the ear—but from one's instincts and natural, at times even unconscious, impulses and feelings. When swing occurs it is innate, not studied. It is free and unhindered insofar as it arises from natural felt impulses; but at the same time it is controlled by the auditory apparati of the ear and mind. It is produced in the not fully conscious realms, but is governed by the conscious mind.[18]

But even when and if these conditions are met—that is, a music which contains a regular steady pulse and which is felt and fully heard—swing may still not occur. More yet is required, aspects which are the result of a highly complex joining of feeling and mental control, as well as a matter of specific technical control of one's instrument. In the first instance I am referring to the ability to maintain a perfect equilibrium between the "horizontal" and "vertical" relationships[19] of musical sounds. This equilibrium occurs when both the verticality and horizontality of a given musical moment are represented in perfect equivalence and oneness. A perfectly beautiful horizontal rendition—let's say of a theme or melody or riff—will not in itself produce swing if the vertical aspects, i.e. the rhythmic (and in most cases the harmonic), are not equally attended to. Similarly, the most impeccably accurate rhythmic timing of notes will not by itself produce swing if the horizontal connections between those notes and the harmonic implications inherent in the vertical structure which modify those notes are not fulfilled. Graphically the situation could be visualized as follows (Fig. 1), with the nodes representing played notes or audible time points, and the arrows depicting the simultaneous integrated flow of performance energies. A part of the brain and the feeling impulses 1) are directed toward maintaining the horizontal flow from note to note. Another element of these energies 2) is involved with the vertical aspects of the music and feeding these up towards the horizontal line. A third part 3) is involved with the opposite: constantly relating the horizontal down towards the vertical. This complicated duct system must be maintained at an even flow and perfect balanced control over whatever period of time the performance is to cover.

But there is yet another aspect of swing which has to be integrated into the above-described performance-energy balance. Swing depends on precisely how a

Fig. 1

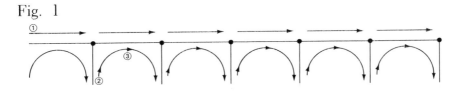

18. I do not believe that emotions as such come into it, at least in the generative stage of swing. Swing may certainly generate emotions, both in the performer and the listener, but emotions are not necessarily overtly involved in the *creation* of swing. And feeling is not identical with emotion. Emotions generate feelings, but are not feelings in themselves.

19. These and other musical technical terms are explained in the Glossary.

given note is entered, i.e. attacked, and how it is terminated; and how each note is linked to every other succeeding note in terms of attack and release. This is an incredibly subtle process which, although audible to the unaided ear, is analyzable only in the realm of microacoustics. A detailed acoustical analysis of this aspect of performance (instrumental or vocal) is so complex and subtle as to go beyond the scope of this book. Nevertheless a few brief graphic illustrations are shown (Appendix, p. 855) which provide convincing comparative visual representation.

Suffice it to say in this part of the text that it is not necessarily a matter of strongly attacked notes swinging better than those that are softly attacked. It is more complex than that, partly because it is to a large extent contextual. The musical context at any given time affects the type of attack needed. Also there is an amazing degree of variety from player to player. Miles Davis's basic "attack" is quite different from Dizzy Gillespie's. Moreover sometimes notes are "attacked," i.e. separately articulated; but at other times they are slurred. Notes at the head of a phrase are emitted differently than those in the middle of a phrase, not to mention that special phrasing phenomenon peculiar to jazz, "ghosted" notes, which are more implied than actually played or heard.

With all these variables, an entire book could be devoted to an analysis of this one aspect of swing—an analysis that would of necessity be highly technical. Furthermore, there are elements of this process which, I dare say, we do not yet fully understand. But happily, though we may not completely understand the techniques involved, we nevertheless can produce them more or less at will, analogous to the creative process itself, which we are far from understanding, and unable to analyze; we are nevertheless able to create, to compose, to invent.

That the Basie band has been from its inception a master of swing could hardly be disputed. It is and always has been a magnificent "swing machine" and in its early days was frequently much more than merely that. It is at present writing the longest-existing jazz orchestra under the same leadership, performing regularly, except for a two-year period (1950–52) when the orchestra was temporarily disbanded and reduced to eight players. For over forty years the Basie band has upheld a particular concept and style of jazz deeply rooted in the Southwest and Kansas City in particular. It draws its aesthetic sustenance from the blues, uses the riff as its major rhetorical and structural device, all set in the language and grammar of swing.

And unlike Ellington's or Lunceford's subtle and complex musical settings, Basie's have always emphasized simplicity of format, simplicity of texture. It is also true that, as in the case of Lunceford, the Basie orchestra's style has always been set by arrangers, sometimes in head-arrangements, but in any case not by composers and certainly not by a composer of the magnitude of an Ellington or a Morton. Moreover, Basie never had any staff arranger with the creative capacity of a Sy Oliver, with the possible exception of Buster Harding. As a result, even in its heyday the Basie orchestra was admirable more for its performance skills than for any creative profundity or innovative compositional contributions.

As I have indicated, this performing skill resided most especially in the band's and, particularly, the rhythm section's ability to swing. Reams have been written about the Basie rhythm section and with good reason, because it is and always has been one of the most consistent and resplendent joys in all of jazz, almost always to be relied upon, almost always living up to expectations. There is a reason for that, and that reason is Freddie Green. For over forty years he has been quietly laying down a steady subtly swinging beat, unifying the rhythm section, providing the harmonic and textural binding in the middle range, and thus furnishing the critical linkage between melody and bass—in short, performing all those horizontal/vertical functions which are the essence of swing era jazz at its best.

But Freddie Green's role in the Basie rhythm section—and by extension that of all guitars in this type of rhythm section—became possible only in the 1930s, as the technical abilities of rhythm instrument players expanded and their functions within the four-piece rhythm section shifted, concurrently becoming clearer and more individual.

As greater technical flexibility developed, it was natural that the rhythm instruments, initially confined to very primitive *rhythmic* functions, aspired to enter the *melodic* realm. And so they did: first the piano with Earl Hines and Morton in the early to mid-twenties, to some extent Fats Waller and James P. Johnson. Next followed the guitar. After replacing the banjo which had been used purely rhythmically in early jazz, the guitar found its melodic voice with players like Lonnie Johnson, Dick McDonough, and above all, with Eddie Lang; and eventually in the mid- and late thirties, with the advent of electric amplification and the arrival of Charlie Christian, the guitar emerged as a full-fledged member of the melodic fraternity. Freddie Green is thus a wonderful anachronism in that he has (almost) never played a melodic solo and seems to be content to play those beautiful "changes" night after night. How many quarter notes that man has played over the years; 250 million would be a conservative figure—and virtually all perfect at that!

Following the guitar, the next rhythm instrument to gain emancipation was the string bass, first when it replaced the tuba and then, within a short time after that, when the bass acquired a quasi-melodic capacity that freed it from providing merely the most rudimentary harmonic and rhythmic functions in the form of root positions and a regular 4/4 or 2/2 beat. The player who more than any other developed the "walking bass" line so endemic to jazz of the thirties and forties was none other than Walter Page, for years the anchor of the Basie rhythm section. As early as 1929 in his recordings with his band known as the Blue Devils—in which Basie was for a while the pianist—we can hear Page's wide-ranging, beautifully balanced bass lines beginning to function on three levels: rhythmic, harmonic, and now melodic. Such bass lines also provided a new contrapuntal element, not in the old New Orleans collective improvisation sense but as a more purely *linear* counterpart, heard with, under, and against the melodic elements in the middle or upper register.

The last member of the rhythm section to be freed for melodic duty was the percussion, the drum set. Here, too, an early leader in this development was Jo

Jones, the drummer in the Basie rhythm section for many years. His earliest recordings with Basie in 1936[20] reveal that the had already transformed the percussion from its earlier, solely time-keeping and mostly vertical-sounding role into a melodic-linear one, in which cymbals, with their ringing capacity and their ability to elongate sound, became a new voice in the horizontalization and linearization of jazz, and with this last innovation swing was finally achievable.

As the four rhythm instruments acquired these new melodic-linear, even soloistic capabilities, they could also discard some of their earlier simpler ensemble functions. And in doing so the rhythm section could merge into a more unified, more sophisticated cohesive ensemble, albeit with four co-equal partners. This cohesion cannot be better exemplified than in the Basie rhythm section.

Most crucially affected by these developments was the piano. As the bass acquired greater melodic and upward mobility, extending frequently into the "tenor" register, and as the guitar settled firmly into its middle-register chordal "comping" slot, it became clear that the left hand of the piano had lost almost all of its earlier harmonic and rhythmic importance. In stride piano, the prevailing piano style throughout the twenties, itself an evolutionary extension of ragtime piano, the left hand played a leaping accompanimental pattern which generally placed bass notes on the first and third beats of a bar, and the harmony notes, one or two octaves higher, on the second and fourth beats (Ex. 6a).[21] But once

Ex. 6a
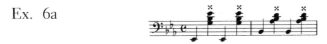

the string bass had acquired its ability to roam linearly all over the lower range, even the bass notes of the piano were no longer necessary and actually were bound to collide and interfere with the bass, obscuring harmonic function and clarity, and producing unpleasant low-register dissonances and voice leadings, as for instance in Ex. 6b.

Ex. 6b

20. A still earlier recording with Lloyd Hunter in 1931 reveals that even then Jo Jones was already breaking away from a merely rhythmic concept of drumming. One hears him composing brief melodic figures on the cymbals, a radical departure from drumming of the period. Other innovators of a more linear conception of playing jazz drums were Cuba Austin, Walter Johnson, and Chick Webb.

21. Tuba parts in early jazz were invariably played in two-beat rhythms, the notes occurring on beats 1 and 3. This allowed the tuba player constant opportunities to breathe—on 2 and 4—in order to fill his 18 feet of brass tubing with air. How limiting this was, can be realized by imagining a three-minute piece with uninterrupted chains of literally breathtaking four quarter notes per bar—a task which for the non-breathing string bass is no inherent problem at all.

Similarly, since the guitar was now playing middle-register chords in constant patterns of either

Ex. 6c

the piano's second and fourth beats (marked x in Ex. 6a) became redundant, an unnecessary duplication of the guitar which muddied the texture and often created terrible intonation problems.

Eventually, when the guitar moved on to become almost exclusively a melody instrument, the left hand of the piano returned to at least part of its former function, i.e. supplying the underlying accompanying harmonies, albeit rhythmically freed up to express itself in irregular or syncopated rhythms (as for example in Ex. 6d)

Ex. 6d

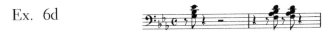

The drum set also was liberated by the bass and the guitar. The bass drum, played at first with four regular thumping beats per bar, would now only obliterate the new moving lines of the bass (a lesson which, for example, a player like Gene Krupa could not seem to learn for a long time). Similarly, a regular reiterated beat on the snare drum could, if not done sensitively, obscure the harmonies in the guitar—although many fine swing era drummers found ways to balance judiciously with the guitar, so as to virtually become a part of the guitar sonority. In the best examples of this kind of dynamic and sonoric blending, the guitar and drum became not two blended sounds but one new amalgam of the two.[22] The cymbal, on the other hand, with its higher pitched overtone-laden sound, was a perfect solution for getting out of the way of the other instruments, riding above them, as it were, in a sonority which had at once the capacity to blend and to isolate.

In the first recordings Basie made in 1936 these developments had already taken place, and the modern rhythm section, four players functioning as a "choir," as an ensemble unit, was already fully present. This is not to say that Basie's rhythm section was unique in accomplishing such a high degree of integration—other rhythm sections (Ellington, Lunceford, Webb, Henderson) in various ways and at various times had by this time achieved as much—but perhaps Basie was more consistently preoccupied with developing this approach as a particular trademark of his orchestra. Perfected to a T in later years, the work of this rhythm section was at times the only redeeming feature of performances which were otherwise totally predictable.

22. No finer examples of that can be found than Sonny Greer's playing on such Ellington performances as *Cotton Tail* (listen to the first 16 bars), or *Echoes of Harlem* and *Blue Light*, or Jones himself on Basie's *Jive at Five*.

The antecedents of this development go back to two earlier Kansas City orchestras: Walter Page's Blue Devils and the remarkable Bennie Moten band of the early thirties. Basie and Walter Page worked in both bands during those years. Representative recordings by these orchestras during that period offer relatively sparse documentation (only two sides by Page in 1929, but without Basie; and ten sides by Moten in December 1932, of which four *(Toby, Lafayette, Blue Room,* and *Prince of Wails)* rank among the very finest orchestral jazz of that entire era).[23] Though few in number, they clearly assert a new rhythmic feeling, as already developed then by these two men. Indeed, Basie and Page worked together almost continuously from mid-1928 through mid-1935, when Basie formed a nine-piece band in Kansas City, including drummer Jo Jones, who had previously joined Moten's band in 1934. The rest of the Basie personnel consisted of three brass (Oran "Hot Lips" Page and Joe Keyes on trumpet, Dan Minor on trombone) and three saxophones (Buster Smith, Lester Young, and Jack Washington). This is the band that John Hammond, the remarkable critic, impresario, and record producer, heard on his car radio and, as his oft-cited account tells, eventually brought to New York in 1936 for an engagement at the Roseland Ballroom.

The Basie band discography begins at this point. Prior to the trip to New York, while the band was playing an engagement at the Grand Terrace in Chicago, John Hammond had arranged a record date for the Vocalion label. Four sides were cut—and in record time, according to Jo Jones, with only one tune requiring a second take, a fact confirmed by the effortless ease and ingratiating light swing of these performances. They were not full-band recordings, but rather a quintet featuring the Basie-Page-Jones rhythm section *sans* guitar, with Lester Young (tenor sax) and Carl Smith (trumpet) as the "horn" soloists. It is clear from the recorded evidence that these players had been adept at this style for some time. How long may remain conjectural, but certainly the simplified continuity and transparent texture heard on these sides did not issue full blown from these musicians on October 9, 1936. Every player knew his role well, performed it with poise, assurance and even a certain simple elegance. In combination, this represented a new kind of jazz, formulated in a very precise way and not easily confused with any other style of that period.

Except for the boisterous, somewhat cluttered opening of *Shoe Shine Boy,* where the bass and left-hand piano frequently collide, the clarity of functions in the rhythm section is startling for its time. Economy, "less is more": these are the ideals pursued. At the same time, within these concepts the ensembles are flexible and diverse. Jo Jones "modulates" deftly from a variety of snare drum effects to all sorts of patterns and sounds on the hi-hat cymbal, always discreetly accompanying the soloist and blending with his rhythm partners. His playing on these four sides alone places him among the very best drummers of the period, for they reveal a degree of taste and sensitivity which few drummers have equalled.

Basie, for his part, also toyed with a variety of pianistic approaches, ranging

23. These fine recordings were discussed at some length in *Early Jazz,* on pp. 293–97, 312–16.

from sequences of full-blown two-handed stride piano (in *Shoe Shine Boy*) to some fine examples of his laconic (single-note) high register manner, with only the subtlest touches of harmony in the left hand (as in the opening of *Lady Be Good*[24]). Also on that same side, under Young's solo, listen to how Basie makes up for the absence of the guitar by ingeniously filling in with lightly swinging middle-register "strummed" chords.

Taken together, the characteristic that emerges most consistently from these sides is their relaxed supple swing, offering a lesson that many modern rhythm players (especially drummers) in these last decades of high-decibel percussion explosions would do well to learn.

The same relaxed swing can be heard in Prez[25] and Carl Smith. Smith, not one of the famous names of jazz, has been poorly treated by jazz writers. He is almost always identified as a poor substitute for "Hot Lips" Page, and in fact, Page had split his lip playing the long, strenuous Grand Terrace show and could not participate in the recording. No doubt Page was a superior soloist and had a much more distinguished career than Smith, who after his brief sojourn with Basie sank into oblivion. But judging by the recorded evidence here, Smith was no mere "surrogate" second-rater. His solo work is fluent, clear in thought and form, at times inspired, as in his exciting entrance on *Shoe Shine Boy*. His solos are interesting in their note choices, fluent and well shaped in overall form.

Another fine Smith solo can be heard on *Lady*, although I sense that here he felt somewhat strait-jacketed by Young's not very inspired riffing behind him. Smith exemplifies the young players who had listened well to Armstrong, learned to swing, and, in the case of the Midwest players, had begun to transform Armstrong's concepts into a more riff-oriented linear style. Roy Eldridge, Buck Clayton, Harry Edison, and soon, the young Dizzy Gillespie were some of the more illustrious trumpet players in this new vanguard.

Of course, the crowning achievement of this 1936 Basie date is Young's solo on *Lady*. Consisting of two choruses based on Gershwin's familiar classic, it is quintessential Lester Young: economical and lean, no fat, nothing extraneous, and masterful in its control of form.

This economy of means can be seen (heard) in four particular respects: 1) compressing the melodic contours into a much narrower range, mostly of one octave and only occasionally reaching beyond that, all the while centering on or circling around one or two central pitches; 2) what I would call the linearization of melodic content; 3) the superimposition of a *single* harmonic zone (to which the melody is then confined) on several chords or an entire chord progression; and 4) the economical use of motivic cells (or gestures), recurring in subtle variants throughout the solo. These compositional characteristics can be viewed analytically in the transcription of Young's solo in Example 7, and then aurally confirmed by listening to the record. All four points, taken together, brought melodic improvisation to a new artistic plateau in that the notes and general

24. The correct title is *Oh, Lady Be Good*; it is misnamed on this and many other recordings of this famous Gershwin song.
25. Prez, a nickname given Lester Young by his musical soul-mate, Billie Holiday.

Ex. 7

shaping of lines was now much more freed from the underlying harmonies. Again, horizontal and vertical had come together in a more symbiotic way, in which both aspects modified and complemented each other.

Starting with my first point, this solo—and most of Young's work throughout his career[26]—reveals to what extent he had already compressed his melodic shapes into a much smaller range and target area. It is as if the up-and-down, wide-ranging arpeggio shapes of earlier times, especially of the Hawkins style of saxophone playing, had been laid on their side or at least scrunched together into a more concentrated space—from ⟋⟍⟋⟍ to ⟍⟋⟍ . In the first thirteen bars of his solo, for example, Young does not range below this D ⟋ , nor above this G ⟋ . Moreover, the entire passage pivots around two pitches, one of them ⟋ , the dominant of the key, acting almost like a fulcrum in mm. 1 through 3 and 8 through 13, the other ⟋ , the tonic, in mm. 4 through 7. Graphically this can be depicted as follows:

Fig. 2

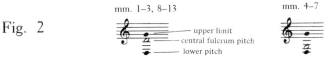

mm. 1–3, 8–13   mm. 4–7

— upper limit
— central fulcrum pitch
— lower pitch

Other similarly concentrated melodic contours can be found in mm. 25–31, mm. 48–52.

Point 2, the linearization of melodic content, can be seen and heard throughout the solo, in that almost all intervallic movement proceeds stepwise or in

26. See also below, Chapter 6, Part 3.

relatively small intervals. Seconds and thirds predominate, while larger intervals and leaps are rare. This stepwise (or conjunct) approach gives Lester's solo its coherence, its simplicity, and its linear fluency. It also leaves ample room for dramatizing special moments in the larger scheme. We can see how Lester achieves a climax of sorts by leaping an entire octave at just the right climactic moment in terms of the overall form.

The bridge of a 32-bar song form (AABA) is always a special juncture, first of all because the *B* part simply *is* different from the A sections, and because it usually contains some harmonic shifts or modulations that contrast with the other three 8-bar segments. The bridge in *Lady Be Good* is especially interesting in the context of the song's overall harmonic structure for it is the only place where the commonplace $\overset{G}{I} \overset{C}{IV} \overset{G}{I} \overset{a}{II} \overset{D}{V} \overset{G}{I}$ progression is broken by a refreshing A *major* seventh (all the other II-chords being *minor*). For all its simplicity it is a startling moment, as if a light had suddenly been switched on or a bright color applied. Lester knew so well how to exploit this special moment. In his second chorus he saves this moment (m. 53) not only for his largest intervallic leap in the entire solo, the aforementioned octave, but also the highest note (C♯) in the solo—in other words, in terms of intervallic usage and range, the climax. In the same place in his first chorus—such is the level of his inspiration and his control of the musical discourse—Lester plays (with one exception) the *lowest* note of his solo!

This ingenious disposition of pitches and intervals is not by any means the only way by which one might argue for the greatness of this solo and Lester Young's work in general. However, just in this respect alone—only one part of a much greater totality—we can measure the magnitude of Young's talent by considering that countless numbers of classical composers, composing a 64-bar structure over a matter of hours, days, or months, would be hard put to produce something as perfectly proportioned. And, of course, Lester was improvising—on-the-spot split-second composing.

Point 3 represents from the vantage point of 1936 an even more remarkable breakthrough—one which was to have far-reaching consequences and implications for later jazz. For it led directly to a harmonic freeing-up of the language of jazz without which Bop, Modern Jazz, George Russell's Lydian Concept, and eventually musicians like Ornette Coleman, John Coltrane, and Eric Dolphy could not have evolved. When we look at this aspect in Young's *Lady Be Good*, we must, of course, remember that we witness it here in a very simple, perhaps even embryonic form.

In looking at Lester's solo in Example 7 again, in addition to noticing that Lester's notes are, of course, not those of Gershwin's melody and that Lester had composed an entirely new melodic structure on Gershwin's frame, we are bound also to notice that all the notes in the first twelve measures, extracted from the underlying harmonic context, could be accommodated in the tonality of G (allowing for some passing tones, upper and lower neighbors, or the like). The first note that clearly could not in 1936 have belonged to a G tonal sphere is the C in m. 13, which here belongs with a Am-seventh chord. The point is that all those G-major figures in the first twelve bars are set on top of a chord progression which includes, besides G chords, some in C major and A minor. This constitutes the art of making one harmonic area (one chord) do, where previously several or many were needed. Naturally, in more chromatic tunes like David Raksin's *Laura*, Johnny Green's *Body and Soul*, or Ellington's *Sophisticated Lady*, such harmonic overlays, as the much simpler chord structure of *Lady Be Good* allows, would not be possible. But that is not to take anything away from Lester Young, who here suggests the foundation for a new technique of threading the fine harmonic eye of a needle.

Another look at the solo, now from a fourth angle, shows us Lester's intelligent use of motivic fragments as building blocks. The passages bracketed under a ⌐————⌐ all feature repeated or alternating notes revolving around one or two common tones. The last of these, starting in m. 40, is the most linear of all, with G as the main pivotal pitch, embellished by upper and lower neighbors and rhythmic shiftings. It is almost a kind of pedal point, a moment of stability between two sequences of wide-ranging more arpeggiated figures (mm. 33–39 and mm. 44–56). Passages bracketed under b ⌐————⌐ represent the other motivic ingredient—descending figures—more often than not starting on the sixth degree of the scale.

Lastly we should note Young's peculiar penchant for occasionally anticipating the notes of the next bar's harmony. These are marked x ⌐————⌐ in the musical example. For example, the last three notes in m. 30 anticipate the G tonality of m. 31; the last four notes in m. 38 sit on a D chord, but appear for all the world to be in G major, anticipating again the G chord of m. 39. Similar anticipations occur in m. 44 and m. 62.[27]

There is, to be sure, more to Young's solo than merely its pitch content, its harmonic/melodic innovations. One could admire as enthusiastically its rhythmic invention, the deft handling of mixing the regular with the irregular, of alternating the expected with the unexpected. But beyond and above the placement of notes, there is Lester's incomparable slightly-behind-the-beat relaxed swing, another innovation with far-reaching consequences for modern jazz. And how can one fail to notice the uniqueness of Lester's tone, with its yellow-ochre burnished tint, lean and vibrato-less (except for the occasional subtle terminal vibrato at the end of longer notes), cool yet somehow also warm and expressive.

Beyond Lester's solo on *Lady* there is, of course, the accompaniment of the rhythm section, the perfect foil for Prez, that aids and abets his every move. Notice, for example, how in Lester's first chorus, Walter Page moves in generally conjunct motion, whereas, as if anticipating Lester's decision to pitch his second chorus at a more intense level (in terms of activity, movement, range, dynamic level), Page, too, moves in greater intervals, even jumping octaves, thus intensifying the rhythmic substructure. When Lester reaches for the climax in

---

27. These characteristics will be encountered throughout Lester Young's work and career, as discussed elsewhere in this chapter and in Chapter 6, below.

the second bridge, Page peaks right with him—in perfect concordance—playing his highest notes thus far. It is worth noting, however, that Page reserves *his* summit for the final bridge of the performance (after Smith's trumpet solo), during Page's own "walking" solo of eight bars.

Throughout these various choruses Jo Jones is the supreme catalyst, adding deft touches of accents: subtle rim shots, cymbal chokes, syncopated cross-accents, sometimes emphasizing a structural feature, at other times reiterating and punctuating a point just made by one of the soloists. Ingenious because Jones's work is always in taste and in balance,it is neither too much nor too little; it fills where filling is needed and otherwise stays out of the way. Would that modern drummers could relearn those lessons!

Some weeks after Basie was safely ensconced at the Roseland Ballroom in New York, he had his first full-band recording session, waxing four sides on January 21, 1937. The band had not been an unqualified success thus far, some criticizing it for its ragged ensemble, others for poor intonation, still others not quite sure what all the fuss raised by Hammond (especially in his *Downbeat* articles) was all about.

It will be well to let the succeeding discussion and narrative tell the story of Basie and his orchestra's development. However, the reader may be forewarned not to expect unqualified praise. Basie's fans around the world are legion. But the argument has been advanced that Basie's formula for success, indeed survival, was extracted at a price. While the Basie band has over the years made thousands of audiences very happy, it has had to forgo initiative, innovation, creativity in the large sense. For these it has substituted a formula for sure-fire commercial success, giving its audiences exactly what they want and expect. That this success has nevertheless been achieved without relinquishing relatively high standards of performance is, in the overall scheme of things, remarkable. To maintain a true and bona fide jazz orchestra for over forty years is high accomplishment in itself. *How* this was accomplished—at least in the early stages—will be chronicled in the following account.

The first four full-band sides (of 1937) reflect the tentativeness that some of the early criticism in New York signaled. Though they are spirited performances, they are also quite uneven. The rough edges in ensemble are not nearly as disturbing as the disparate quality of the solos and the frequent emptiness of content. *Honeysuckle Rose* opens with fine energetic Waller-ish Basie stride-piano—as befits this most famous of Waller tunes—but an inept modulation to Prez's solo and an unwarranted banal overlay of *Tea for Two* on Waller's "changes," plus some further borrowings from Henderson's famous arrangement of *King Porter Stomp*, all contrive to drag the piece down. In *Pennies from Heaven*, though well arranged and played with a pleasant bouncy swing, Basie's piano gets a bit silly, and Joe Keyes's flat trumpet mars the ending. But Jimmy Rushing, the never-less-than-outstanding blues singer, saves the side from complete triviality.

Roseland Shuffle fares a little better. It exudes lots of surface excitement in that fresh riff style, then still somewhat new to New York. But Basie and Young

play cat and mouse with each other—the piece was subtitled *Count and Lester*—
teasing each other (and perhaps "putting on" the audience) with diffident gestures and empty 4-bar breaks, hardly worthy of their talents. It might have all
seemed very humorous at the record date, but decades later the jokes don't stand
up too well. Moreover, *Roseland Shuffle* wasn't much more than a slightly beefed-
up arranged version of the 1936 *Shoe Shine Boy*, but much less good. Surprisingly Lester repeats some of the same licks, now quite a bit staler, from the
earlier session. This, plus the seemingly obligatory *King Porter* clichés in the
first chorus, adds to one's uncomfortable sense that this whole piece was too
hastily thrown together in a "head arrangement."

The only partially redeeming side was *Swinging at the Daisy Chain*, a surprisingly happy sounding piece considering its minor key. Its brightest features
were a beautifully poised, suave muted trumpet solo by Buck Clayton, a wildly
sinuous bridge by Herschel Evans (tenor saxophone) and, in the coda, some
wonderfully appropriate Jo Jones "commentaries" on temple blocks.

A word must also be said on behalf of Coughey Roberts, Basie's lead alto at
the time, a player much maligned by John Hammond. (He actually got Basie to
fire Roberts late that year.) One would not wish to argue that Roberts belongs in
the top ranks of great lead altos (Hodges, Hardwick, Willie Smith, Hilton Jefferson, Hymie Schertzer, Hal McIntyre, and the like), but he actually suited the
Basie sax section rather well. His somewhat pressed cool sound related much
better to Lester Young's and Jack Washington's than Earl Warren's did (Roberts's successor). In terms of timbre it provided an interesting contrast to the
other two choirs, trumpet and trombone, setting off the saxes in call-and-response patterns very neatly.[28] These points can be argued in several directions,
of course, and finally it is a matter of personal taste as to which timbre or
coloration one prefers in a saxophone section. My intent here—as with Carl
Smith earlier—is simply to redress the prevailing uncritically handed-down opinions on some of the lesser lights in jazz.[29]

During the next period, Basie, with Hammond's advice, set about "strength-

28. In this connection it is remarkable how well Herschel Evans, with his opulent, big thrashing
sound, managed to blend so well in the Basie band's saxophone ensembles.

29. It is amazing to find in book after book on jazz, with but rare exceptions, each author redupli-
cating the "accumulated wisdom" on all the famous names, while constantly neglecting the lesser
ones. Minor soloists are discarded with a deprecatory wave of the pen; what goes on behind and
around solos is rarely discussed or appreciated by these ubiquitous "solo hoppers," as if jazz consisted
of nothing but an endless series of improvised solos. Jazz performances are, whether one likes it or
not, totalities that cannot be willy-nilly separated out into one's favorite components at the expense
of all others—not if it is to be considered serious, scholarly, or relevant criticism.
There is also the unfortunate tendency among many jazz writers to concentrate their praise on
those who happened to be well represented on records. But countless musicians, when interviewed,
have confirmed that, especially in the less recorded Midwest and Southwest and in those regions'
territory bands, there were hundreds of superb players who for one reason or another never received
the recognition they deserved. Even if one assumes some of these reports to be "enhanced," or
colored by the "underdog syndrome," and subtracts, say, 30 percent of these claims, it still leaves a
lot of unhearalded talent to be given consideration.

ening" the band. Ed Lewis, a veteran of the Moten and Harlan Leonard orchestras, and Bobby Moore joined the trumpet section, replacing Keys and Smith; Earl Warren came in for Roberts; and, most importantly, Freddie Green joined the band in March 1937, replacing Claude Williams.[30] This latter move, as has been previously suggested, helped to solidify the Basie rhythm section and make it one virtually unparalleled.

But a rhythm section does not necessarily a great orchestra make. Without a composer as leader, a jazz orchestra needs arrangers, and though Bill Basie was working hard to attract some of the best ones, somehow the band had trouble defining its style. A lot of the pieces performed on their recordings and broadcasts were inferior songs or tunes with which even arrangers like Don Redman, Jimmy Mundy, and Eddie Durham couldn't do much. A great part of the work of this period is patchwork, no doubt the product of head arrangements, resorting more and more to repetitious riff sequences, often unevenly performed, occasional moments of quality by Young, Evans, and Clayton notwithstanding. Even Basie seemed at times to lose his composure, as witness his shaky openings on *Boo-Hoo* (a silly Carmen Lombardo song which even the great Jimmy Rushing couldn't rescue) and *One O'Clock Jump*—or for that matter his rather trite cliché patter on *The Glory of Love* and *Boogie Woogie*.

But *One O'Clock Jump* was the Basie band's first big hit, and soon every swing band pounced on it. By 1940 it had been recorded a dozen times. There is a sad irony in the fact that Basie, who is officially credited as the composer, didn't write *One O'Clock Jump* at all. Several fine musicians had a hand in a chain of circumstances that led to *One O'Clock* becoming Basie's theme song. The famous riff with which the piece ends (as recorded) is based on a little motive which Fats Waller stumbled upon sometime in the late twenties. It turned up as the "head" of the Chocolate Dandies 1929 recording of *Six or Seven Times*,[31] arranged by Don Redman with Waller at the piano. Years later Buster Smith, Charlie Parker's mentor, remembered that motive from the Dandies' 1929 recording (although not quite correctly) which was then worked up into a head arrangement by the band. It should also be clarified that all this occurred not in New York in 1937 but rather in Kansas City back in 1935–36, when Basie and Buster co-led the nine-piece band at the Reno Club which John Hammond heard over the radio.

Although inconsistent as an overall performance, the 1937 *One O'Clock Jump* did contain two excellent solos: one of Buck Clayton's finest creations, with its subtly bent and scooped notes, and a bursting-at-the-seams contribution by Herschel Evans.

---

30. A touching account of Williams's involuntary departure can be read in the liner notes to a recent recording by him, called *Fiddler's Dream* (Classic Jazz 135).
31. Ross Russell's account of this thematic metamorphosis in *Jazz Style in Kansas City and the Southwest* (Berkeley, 1971) errs slightly when he states that the riff in question was also used in a recording by McKinney's Cotton Pickers in an arrangement by Redman. There is no such performance.

Not until we get to *John's Idea* (dedicated to John Hammond) do we find a degree of creative and performance cohesiveness that might qualify as both distinctive and truly creative.[32] *John's Idea*, a fine Eddie Durham composition (and arrangement), swings superbly, features some "hot" Evans; strong, clean Jo Jones throughout; and lots of sprightly Basie piano (at moments reminiscent of one of his pianistic mentors, James P. Johnson). The whole performance is charged with splendid energy, particularly in the first entrance by the full band—the kind of effect that jazz writers began to identify as Basie's "powerhouse brass" (even though it involved the reeds as well).[33]

By the fall of 1937 Eddie Durham, who had contributed so creatively to the Moten band with his stunning arrangements for the 1932 recordings, had joined Basie in the triple capacity of trombonist, guitarist, and arranger. His contributions in the last area did help to solidify the band's performance and gave it a more cohesive style, within the basic swing concept set by Basie. Durham's *Time Out, Topsy, Out the Window*, three fine instrumentals, had a salutory effect on the band; and even his arrangements of some of the pop tunes of the day caught more of a jazz spirit. *Time Out* is representative of this period as the orchestra rides freely over a buoyantly swinging rhythm section. Another fine contribution was Skip Martin's arrangement of *Our Love Was Meant To Be*. Martin, a talented clarinetist, playing both with the Indianapolis Symphony and, later in his career, with Charlie Barnet, was a gifted arranger who also wrote and played for Goodman and Miller. His *Our Love* arrangement is a fine example of how a vapid pop ballad could be transformed into a swinging jazz piece.

It was during this period that Billie Holiday, again at John Hammond's instigation, sang with the Basie band. Unfortunately she never recorded with Basie, undoubtedly because Rushing would not readily cede his vocalist priority position to her. Air checks from the Savoy Ballroom and other dance emporia have fortunately rectified that loss. Billie's voice (discussed at greater length elsewhere in this book), firm and virtually vibrato-less, with its taut "marble" timbre, was not only a wonderful vocal parallel to Prez's lean tenor but, by virtue of its extraordinary presence, a welcome contrast to the band's laid-back sound; her voice stood out like the raised foreground in a bas-relief.

Lady Day did not stay with Basie very long. Perhaps she was *too* artistically challenging, too unique. And apparently she did not altogether enjoy working with the band. Her successor a year later was Helen Humes, a fine ballad singer and excellent foil for Rushing's blues shoutings.

At this juncture in the band's development, we can begin to hear the coalescence of the essential Basie style: simple, direct, uncluttered, but creatively un-

32. It is well to remember that during this same mid-thirties period Ellington was producing *Echoes of Harlem, Caravan, Azure, Diminuendo and Crescendo in Blue;* Lunceford *Organ Grinder's Swing, For Dancers Only, Stomp It Off;* Earl Hines *Cavernism* and *Madhouse;* and Chick Webb *Stompin' at the Savoy,* to mention just a few achievements of Basie's competitors.

33. Recently issued airchecks from 1937 and 1938 reveal that the original arrangement of *John's Idea* as recorded soon underwent radical changes, most of which unfortunately cheapened the piece.

innovative, mostly riff-in-blues pieces, with plentiful open spaces for Rushing and the band's major soloists, with that Kansas City swing feeling as the prime selling point and stylistic common denominator. And more and more it became an arranger's orchestra.

Durham hit his stride with a series of well-made arrangements: *Every Tub*, *Sent for You Yesterday* and *Swinging the Blues*—the latter perhaps the most appropriately named title in the entire Basie library. For that's exactly what that band did: swing the blues. In addition, Prez's style became increasingly concise, very "modern" sounding in context. His solos on *Georgianna* and *Every Tub* are the kind that in sonority, shape, and note choices young players like Stan Getz, Zoot Sims, and Allen Eager were to learn by heart and develop not just into a personal style but a whole school of playing (much as what happened with John Coltrane's style in the 1960s). A strong new solo voice was added in the person of Harry "Sweets" Edison, then all of twenty-two years old. Edison's solos were a fresh element, almost always featuring his personal trait of riding on sustained notes (often blues notes) with a wave-like bent-note effect, a trait which Durham immediately picked up and featured in his background ensembles (hear *Now Will You Be Good*, 1938). Edison played with a sense of authority almost imperious at times, a fine example being his solos on *Every Tub* and *Sent for You Yesterday*. Some of these sides also feature Jo Jones solo drum breaks, their inclusion undoubtedly the influence of Chick Webb and Gene Krupa, who were beginning to attract a lot of audience attention with their solo excursions. But notice how tastefully Jones's drum interjections are integrated into the full ensembles on *Sent for You Yesterday*; or the more overt drum breaks on *Swinging the Blues*, never ostentatious, never breaking the continuity of the music.

An anomaly in this spate of early 1938 recordings is *Blues in the Dark*, more Ellingtonian with its growly brass than basic Basie. The performance is unfortunately marred by a gradual slow-down in tempo; and, additionally, it is notable for one of those rare moments when Freddie Green errs, some of his chords under Basie's solo being quite incorrect. On the other hand Rushing's singing is superb, much enhanced by Buck Clayton's muted obbligato. Rushing and Clayton were often teamed up this way, just like Wellman Braud and "Tricky Sam" Nanton had been in Ellington's orchestra. Fascinating to hear Clayton in *Blues in the Dark* recompose and expand upon Armstong's famous *West End Blues* solos.

Rushing's crowning achievement here, however, is *Sent for You Yesterday*—along with his 1941 *Goin' to Chicago* and *Harvard Blues*, one of his very best creations. This is then a good moment to consider briefly his rare talents.

Perhaps Rushing's most memorable asset was his high-pitched intense voice. Its unusual timbre gave a certain urgency to all his performances. Curiously, we tend to hear him as a baritone with all the fullness appropriate to that category of voice; and yet Rushing was really a tenor. He had no difficulty with high G's and A's and was able easily to maintain a tessitura in that upper range. Furthermore he was a well-trained musician who could read music (a rarity in those days among singers) and who had not only studied the violin but played good enough piano to accompany himself in clubs in Texas and on the West Coast before becoming solely a singer.

Born in Oklahoma City in 1902, Rushing joined Walter Page's Blue Devils in 1927 and moved over to Moten's band (along with Page and Basie) in 1931. In his early days Rushing had been mainly a ballad singer, but Basie insisted on his doing mostly blues, even singing pop songs in a blues-ish manner. As Ralph Ellison, also an Oklahoman who heard Rushing in his youth, has pointed out,[34] "one of the significant aspects of his art is the imposition of a romantic lyricism upon the blues tradition, a lyricism which is not of the Deep South but of the Southwest, a romanticism native to the frontier." To be sure, he was not the typical male blues shouter of old: baritonal, untrained, and more declamatory than singing. Rushing's high, clear silver-toned voice and clean execution gave his blues singing a distinctive clarity—one might almost say a certain propriety—that blues shouting had never had before. Remarkably, Rushing's voice was both warm and penetrating, and when he sang/shouted his wailing "Baaaaay-bay, bay-aaay-bay" (as Ellison has transliterated it), the anguish and passion of it were often overwhelming.

The big event in Basie's life at this time was the appearance with Benny Goodman in the famous Carnegie Hall concert on January 16, 1938.[35] Again it was Hammond who persuaded his friend Benny to give the lesser-known Basie a break. And even though only five members of the Basie band—Clayton, Young, Page, Green, and Basie—were allowed to participate and then only in one lengthy jam session on *Honeysuckle Rose*, the concert was instrumental in acquainting many previously unaware people with Basie's music and one aspect of black jazz.

The Basie-ites certainly acquitted themselves brilliantly in such imposing company. The *Honeysuckle* jam session taken as a whole is quite extraordinary, conveying the excitement and spontaneity that improvised, unpremeditated, un-notated jazz can produce. One can well understand the Carnegie Hall audience's enthusiasm in the face of this rousing performance.

The recording of the concert also allows us a fascinating closeup of the essential difference in rhythmic (and swing) conception between Goodman and Basie, more accurately between Krupa and Jones—and one might well argue between white and black jazz.

The rhythm section in this jam session combined the three aforementioned Basie-ites with Gene Krupa. The difference Krupa's addition makes is monumental—really an intrusion. Compared with the relaxed linear swing of the regular Basie rhythm section, the rhythm here is very vertical, even choppy and high-strung[36]—this even though Green's guitar and Page's long-limbed walking

---

34. Ralph Ellison, "Remembering Jimmy" in *Shadow & Act* (New York, 1964).

35. It was the same night that Basie's band was roundly beaten by Chick Webb's in one of the most famous "Battles of Swing" ever staged at the Savoy Ballroom.

36. It would be interesting for others more expert in social dancing than I to pursue the following correlation: it is my impression from viewing films of dancers in the swing era that in fast numbers white dancers were much more vertical in their movements, vigorously bobbing up and down, while

lines are constantly trying to horizontalize and "flatten out" Krupa's influence. But a drum is a powerful instrument, and Krupa's drums dominate, his overuse of the bass drum often completely obscuring Page's bass.

If there remains lingering doubt as to the veracity of the above statements, I invite the reader to listen to the following, most telling evidence of all. By chance, in the midst of this jam session—after the Johnny Hodges solo[37]—the rhythm section was given two choruses *a capella*. For some reason both Krupa and Basie decided to recede into the background—Krupa virtually inaudible, Basie with sparse whisper-soft chordal interjections—placing Green and Page alone in the foreground. The effect is startling: suddenly the flow of beats creates lines and phrases (notice particularly Page's descending line just before the audience's approving laughter). Notice also Green's subtly pulsating accentuation of beats 2 and 4 throughout. The point is that, with Krupa more or less momentarily out of the way, the Basie players transformed the rhythmic feeling into something much more swinging and musical.

As for the rest of the solos, Basie's two sidemen acquit themselves nobly. Young is in top form, in one of his most perfect, fluent, inwardly felt solos. Clayton too plays with consummate control and authority. Only Basie himself is disappointing as he trots out, one after another, all of his favorite licks which were fast becoming the telltale clichés of his simplified piano style. Goodman alternates between diffidence and, when urged on by Krupa, more energetic involvement. But Harry James, in top form, is wonderfully cocky, sparking the proceedings, especially in the prolonged finale, with a seemingly boundless supply of dashingly displayed extroversion.

A midsummer record date (June 1938) was mostly given over to Herschel Evans, who soloed on *Blue and Sentimental* and *Doggin' Around*, also composing and arranging the latter. With his big effusive tone and slippery blues inflections, Evans demonstrates in the span of a few minutes how one player can encompass yearning sentiment *(Blue)* and virile eloquence *(Doggin')*. Both pieces feature an even more pared-down Basie piano, sparse single notes which here still have the freshness of discovery.[38] Another special moment occurs when Lester Young takes up the clarinet at the end of *Blue and Sentimental*. Somehow his thin, elusive, almost disembodied tone—Prez played a cheap toneless metal clarinet—and simple note choices create a perfect (and necessary) foil for Evans's forceful opulence. (The strong clarinet riding atop the final ensemble of *Doggin'* is Evans's.)

---

black dancers were much more horizontal and wide-ranging. This verticality and physical stiffness had its exact corollary in the drumming of most white drummers, until the likes of Dave Tough and Buddy Rich came along.

37. Surprising for such an outstanding artist, Hodges took a while to find himself in this solo. Along with some quite striking moments, Hodges twice nearly erred on the "changes," just barely skating through on sheer good instincts.

38. I wonder why it is that when John Lewis plays "single note" solos critics complain, whereas when Basie does it for forty years, it is found not only acceptable but is made into an unassailable virtue.

Commercialism rears its seductive head on a late August session, resulting in awkward attempts at capturing a popular market with *Stop Beatin' Around the Mulberry Bush* and *London Bridge Is Falling Down*. Matters are more than redeemed, however, with two strong instrumentals: one, the hard driving up-tempo swing of *Jumpin' at the Woodside*, notable for Evans's nagging, nastily squealy clarinet, set over eight frenetic ascending glissandos to high F

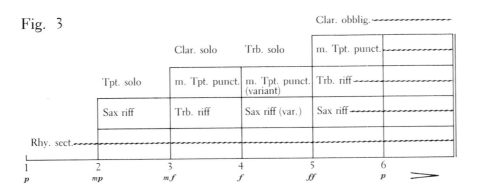

$f\!\!=\!\!ff$ in unison trombones;[39] the other, Evans's own *Texas Shuffle* (Evans was born in Denton, Texas), another fine example of the cohesive ensemble swing the band had by now acquired.

A closer look at how *Texas Shuffle* was put together by Evans reveals something of the simplicity of method and cumulative energy fundamental to one of the better prototypical Basie-style riff arrangements.

The overall format (Fig. 3) consists of five and a half 32-bar choruses, of which the second, third, and fourth are given over to three soloists, respectively Edison, Young (on clarinet), and Dickie Wells (trombone). The performance starts off innocently enough with the rhythm section in a full introductory chorus. Next Edison sets up a single-note riff, embellished with derby fanning, while the saxes start a simple riff, rising always one step to the second (or the ninth) degree (Ex. 8, marked x), thus adding a mild dissonance every two bars. Edison, who at first appears only to be riffing, suddenly breaks out into a full-fledged solo. With an overlapping 2-bar lead-in—as in a relay race—Young now takes over the solo spot (chorus 3). The trumpet section (muted) continues Edison's earlier riff idea with sparse punctuations, while two trombones (open and in unison)

Fig. 3

			Clar. obblig.
	Clar. solo	Trb. solo	m. Tpt. punct.
Tpt. solo	m. Tpt. punct.	m. Tpt. punct. (variant)	Trb. riff
Sax riff	Trb. riff	Sax riff (var.)	Sax riff
Rhy. sect.			
1	2	3	4	5	6
p	*mp*	*mf*	*f*	*ff*	*p*

(The graph does not show that the bridge in the 4th and 5th choruses is played by Evans and the rhythm section, *a capella*, respectively.)

---

39. This effect was retained and added to by Benny Goodman a few years later when *he* recorded *Jumpin' at the Woodside* (See Chapter I).

Ex. 8

take up another very simple riff, well out of the range of the trumpets and clarinet. Again there is an overlap of solos as Wells picks up the soloist's "staff" from Young. The trumpets' punctuations become more intense, while the saxes develop *their* earlier riff into a more rhythmic variant (Ex. 9).

Ex. 9

As the piece builds to its climax in the fifth chorus, the trumpets become even more insistent in their punctuations, the saxes return to their original melodic riff (played *f* now), while the trombones in canonic imitation start a third riff which, however, is simply a variant of the sax riff, reaching for the sixth (degree) rather than the ninth. Above all these layers, Young's clarinet can be heard sailing along in high gear, for all the world like the old New Orleans clarinetists in the final ride-out stanza of a collective improvisation. Indeed the registral distribution of choirs in *Texas Shuffle* goes right back to the early days of jazz: every instrument has its assigned range and function, staying out of each other's way. That is incidentally why the saxes and trombones are one bar apart (Ex. 10a). Since their registers overlap, if both sections played at the same time, their discrete functions would be blurred, the ensemble muddied. As Evans arranged things, they not only avoid colliding but complement each other, fusing—one could hear it that way—into a combined new melodic riff (Ex. 10b). It should

Ex. 10a

Ex. 10b

also be noted that this layering of three competing superimposed riffs would not have been possible had not the basic riff material been so extremely simple, thus avoiding polyphonic chaos (Ex. 10c). The final half-chorus, softly marching off

Ex. 10c

into the distance, is a minor miracle of musical-culinary artistry. Like a great chef, Evans mixes his ingredients into a delicious blend in which it becomes difficult to separate out the constituent parts. Notice particularly how the muted trumpets and clarinet merge into one indescribably beautiful coalescent sound, the acoustical recorded balance here being especially felicitous.

In November 1938 the Basie rhythm section cut the first in a series of ten quartet sides. Unencumbered by the rest of the band, these performances provide an inside look at the motor of the famous "rhythm machine." They are not unqualified successes by any means, but they reveal, as if exposed under a microscope, the inner secrets of these players' symbiotic relationship. The spotlight is most particularly on Basie's piano, beautifully recorded (except for a misbehaving out-of-tune high f‴), with guitar, bass, and drums less present (in that descending order.) The best sides—*Red Wagon, Oh! Red, Dupree Blues,* and *When the Sun Goes Down*—not only swing along impeccably, but they occasionally offer delightful *trouvailles* unique to Basie. In the generally prevailing *mezzo-piano* dynamics—there is nary a loud moment on these ten sides—delicious blue-note dissonances as in *Red Wagon* (Ex. 11 a and b) add a piquant

Ex. 11a

Ex. 11b

touch; similarly the single low pedal F in the third and fourth choruses of *How Long Blues*. In *Sun* Basie displays his most vocal "singing" piano lines. It is as if the piano were human, a talking piano and, like the old blues singers, telling its tale of woe.

But on these sides we also hear, almost glaringly the problem with Basie's style: its clichés and formula solutions. And through the years the mannerisms, which in 1938 were already becoming quite predictable, long since, alas, turned into empty mechanical ciphers, which the fingers twiddle out mindlessly.

But that is getting ahead of the story. These quartet sides[40] are all in all refreshing in their ingenuous simplicity, technically marvels of perfection, balance, refinement (forerunners in many ways of the style and refinement of the Modern Jazz Quartet of some decades later). One must only avoid looking for anything challenging in them.

In late 1938 some big band sides also turn out well. *Shorty George*, composed by Edison and arranged by the somewhat underrated Andy Gibson, is clearly more complex and "modern." The band, particularly Edison and Jo Jones, responded well to these new challenges. Equally exciting is Jimmy Mundy's arrangement of Basie's *Panassié Stomp*, a piece dedicated to the famous French jazz critic whose early books, *Hot Jazz* and *The Real Jazz*, introduced many an American to this music, this writer included. Taken at a very bright tempo, it features excellent solos by Edison, Evans (his last—he died two months later), trombonist Dickie Wells, and, of course, Young. But surpassing even these worthy solos are the final two ensemble choruses, climactically building riff upon riff—except for the last bridge where, with breathtaking effect, the band drops out for eight bars to expose the buoyant soft swing of the rhythm section alone.

Basie, of course, had come to New York in 1936 as a representative of Kansas City jazz. How easternized the band had become in the intervening years can be clearly heard by listening to Buster Smith's moving arrangement of his own composition, *The Blues I Like To Hear*. Indeed the piece shows how much further to the Southwest Buster's Texas-based style was rooted, compared even with the somewhat peppier, "smarter" Kansas City idiom. Listening to this side (and the other Buster Smith arrangements, like *Smarty*, recorded July 7, 1937), one cannot fail to note its distinctive sound and voice-leading, its "crying" blues-drenched harmonies. Clearly, it has a totally different feel: simple and uncomplicated, earthy low-down blues with a heavy rocking beat.[41]

It was around this time that the Basie band acquired its second girl singer, Helen Humes. Her recording debut in a dreary pseudo-jungleistic opus called *Dark Rapture* did not bode well, but Cole Porter's *My Heart Belongs to Daddy* had just the right guileless charm. Marilyn Monroe must have studied this performance—along with Helen Kane's, of course—for her renditions in *Some Like It Hot*.

But Humes's superior vocal from the period is *Blame It on My Last Affair*. Whereas in previous recordings the singer, only in her mid-twenties, had not yet found her own style—one hears touches of Billie Holiday in her *Daddy*, traces

---

40. A few of these quartet records were very successful with Basie's black public. I remember still hearing them on juke boxes, particularly in clubs and restaurants frequented by blacks, in Cincinnati in 1943 when I came there as a young horn player.

41. That Buster Smith retains this particular expressive style to this day (still working in Dallas), I can confirm first-hand. Recent evidence can be heard on a Smith-led date I produced in 1959 for Atlantic Records (Atlantic 1323).

of the young Ella Fitzgerald in *Thursday*—in *Blame* she is definitely a new distinctive voice to be reckoned with. To begin with, the song itself, although reminiscent of Harold Arlen's *Stormy Weather*, is choice material (music and lyrics by Henry Nemo), simply and effectively arranged by Jimmy Mundy. Humes really identified with this song and poured into it an uncommon depth of feeling.[42] Tiny intonational flaws—the voice was not yet fully stabilized technically at this time—detract only slightly from what is otherwise a luminous, emotionally affecting performance.

In early 1939 Basie added a fourth trumpet, Shad Collins. A septet side of *You Can Depend on Me* marks his recording debut with Basie in the company of Lester Young. The latter plays quintessential Prez (Ex. 12)—concise, direct, clean. Unlike Basie's increasingly repetitive piano noodlings, Young's melodic gestures had a way of staying fresh and inventive. They were not mere formula.

Ex. 12

42. Singing with the Basie band, Helen Humes came inevitably to be thought of as a blues singer when in fact she sang virtually no blues with Basie—that was Rushing's domain—and preferred ballads and "torch songs." Indicative of her feelings, she once told the jazz historian Stanley Dance, "Bessie Smith and Ma Rainey were too bluesy for me." Ironically, Humes became a "rhythm and blues" star *after* she left Basie in the 1940s, and achieved her greatest successes late in life after a remarkable comeback in the 1970s.

Insofar as he did reuse certain types of phrases, he always tried to find new places for them: turn-back phrases showed up in the middle of an 8-bar structure, typical opening flourishes popped up at the climax of a phrase, and so on.

Although a not always consistent player, Shad Collins here delivers a fine example of his craft, including his most striking trait, in Jo Jones's words: "popping every note out like he was making spitballs."

You Can Depend on Me also offered a nice example of how interestingly "fours"—in this case in the following sequence: Young, Basie, Collins—divide into a 32-bar structure. In the 4-bar rotation each player finds himself on a different part of the structure (Fig. 4).

Fig. 4

A brilliant, very-fast tempo remake of *Oh, Lady Be Good* introduces a typically fluent Chu Berry, who had by now taken Herschel Evans's vacated tenor position. Except for a gratuitous piano glissando and a few vulgar honks by Prez, the band's superior performance, replete with splendid brass derby-fanning, swings superbly, and is disciplined in a way that Goodman's well-drilled orchestra had set as a standard by now. A fetchingly growly *Evil Blues* provides a rare opportunity to hear lead trumpeter Ed Lewis in a solo spot. Harry Edison's *Jive at Five*, played by a reduced ensemble, is clean and witty in its "jiving" way. It is also an extraordinary lesson in how a great drummer (Jo Jones) can play straight unadorned quarter-note beats on the snare drum throughout—no cymbals whatsoever—and still swing superbly.

Though the Basie orchestra was now well established, developing a solid following of devotees, its musical output—viewed in the long perspective and the highest critical standards—was often undistinguished or at least uneven. Out of thirty-three titles recorded between February 1939 and early 1940, only a half-dozen are worth our attention today. Much of what Basie recorded was made for the juke-box trade and, as with most bands of the period, its repertory was stifled with vocals and pop songs of the day, responding to the pressures to sell the band commercially. It is amazing that no one ever learns the lesson that all that is remembered ten, twenty, thirty years later are the non-commercial, more creative recordings. But eternally, the commercial merry-go-round grinds out its trivia.

The best performances, of course, in this 1939 series of recordings all swing well and feature good solo contributions, notably those of Young and Buddy Tate, who had replaced Berry in March, and who stayed on with Basie for the next nine years. His solo on *Rock-a-Bye Basie* is especially noteworthy, although much in the manner of Herschel Evans, with whom Tate had worked in the Troy Floyd band in the early thirties.

Clap Hands, Here Comes Charlie was a tour de force—one of Jimmy Mundy's "killer-dillers" taken at the fastest tempo the Basie band had yet assayed. It is, to be sure, a piece in an already well-established tradition, going all the way back to Ellington's *Old Man Blues* of 1930, to which *Clap Hands* makes some respectful bows. *Clap Hands* also sports a first-rate Young solo, but then it is marred by terribly out-of-tune trombones and over-formularized final ensemble choruses.

Almost as a counterweight to this virtuosic *Clap Hands*, there is *I Left My Baby*, one of the slowest pieces in Basie's repertory (until *Li'l Darling* and *Shiny Stockings* in the fifties), and also one of Rushing's most moving performances. He is plaintive and sad, underscored by a dramatic, growly arrangement by Andy Gibson. Gibson's work for the band is of a consistently high order, and seems to be one of the strongest elements in the Basie repertory during this period.

Along with these few successes there are plenty of failures, like the totally misbegotten *Moonlight Serenade* (a hastily thrown together arrangement for Helen Humes, obviously trying to cash in on Glenn Miller's earlier hit recording of that title), *And the Angels Sing* (here trying to emulate Martha Tilton's hit record with Goodman), and *If I Didn't Care* (a big seller by the Ink Spots). Humes fares much better on the nicely swinging, soft-spoken, understated *Someday, Sweetheart*.

What might have been a good success for Basie—and indeed was a *tremendous* success for Charlie Barnet a half a year later—was Ray Noble's fine song *Cherokee*. Originally a ballad, Basie was the first to treat this piece as a fast-tempo jazz instrumental. But unfortunately Mundy's seven-minute arrangement, issued on two 10-inch sides, was too long and repetitious in its endless unvaried riffing. The performance, too, was quite mechanical and uninspired, except for Young's tenor solo. Because Young's contribution here is contained on one of Basie's lesser efforts, it has been quite ignored in the Young canon. It ranks, however, as one of the most inventive, prophetic, and tonally luminous solos Young ever recorded during his Basie years.

There is one fine surprise, indeed an anomaly,[43] in this spate of recordings, an instrumental called *Volcano*, attributed in Rust's discography to Count Basie himself—in my view a questionable attribution. For it is virtually the only real

---

43. Another anomaly is *Twelfth Street Rag*, in a totally mechanical rendition of that old warhorse—except for Young's extended solo which, one is happy to hear, mercifully bears no relationship to the original tune.

composition (in the fully through-composed sense) in the entire Basie library, and as such makes one think immediately of Ellington. Indeed, it is worthy of Ellington, a quite remarkable piece, without precedent or followup in Basie's book (and thus far roundly ignored by jazz writers and historians). Based on the standard 12-bar blues progression (in G major here), and set primarily in a Samba or Charleston rhythm (♩. ♩. ♩ |♩. ♩. ♩) , the piece builds through eleven choruses. Actually it builds twice; once through chorus seven, then dropping down to build up again for the ending, which then comes rather too abruptly (the work's only weakness). The building is done in layers, adding instruments successively, much like Ravel's *Bolero* or Ellington's *Koko* which, it should be noted, *Volcano* anticipates by five months. Figure 5 shows this structuring schematically. Jones, with his deft drum work, behaving like a master drummer in an African drum ensemble, is the rhythmic catalyst for the entire piece. Layered over his basic drum patterns are the various riffs, registrally distributed to excellent effect. Hear, too, the thematic/motivic variants in choruses 7, 9, and 11; and how trombones in the full ensemble sequences, mixing with low saxes, rumbling bass and drums, give the whole piece an appropriately volcanic, turbulent character—a splendid miniature jazz tone poem.

Fig. 5

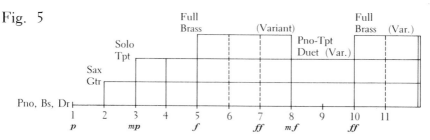

The two most influential pieces from this period were *Dickie's Dream* and *Lester Leaps In* from a recording date by a small Basie group called the Kansas City Seven (Clayton, Wells, Young, and the rhythm section). These performances are justly admired for Young's superior work. Especially *Lester Leaps In* has been hailed as a "classic" for years by critics and musicians.[44] Though featuring a good Young solo, *Leaps* is still, as a totality, marred by serious flaws. The entire performance consists of six choruses of a 32-bar riff theme (by Young), plus a 4-bar intro, as follows:

    I. Ensemble (riff theme)
    II. Young
    III. Young (stop time)
    IV. Basie and Young trading fours
    V. Ensemble and Young trading fours (except for a bridge which goes to Basie)
    VI. Ensemble and Basie trading fours (except for bridge which goes to Basie and last four bars which are collective ensemble).

---

44. Even the astute and highly critical Max Harrison has called it an "authentic *masterpiece*," *(italics mine)*.

At least that is what was intended. As it happened, though, Basie apparently forgot about Young's second chorus and charged in with what was obviously a solo lead-in. He quickly recovered, but evidently still uncertain—at this tempo ($\quarternote$ = ca. 248) the bars fly by at about one a second—tried *twice* more to pick up the solo thread. His third try created fearful dissonances with Prez, who was pressing on undaunted by the mix-ups behind him (Ex. 13). Finally Basie realized his mistake and joined Page and Jones in the originally planned stop-time punctuations.

Ex. 13

For those who would doubt this analysis—obviously a "desecration" of one of the sacred treasures of jazz—I offer the following additional confirmative evidence. Young plays at the beginning of his second chorus exactly the kind of figure typical for a stop-time chorus. So do Page and Jones—in this case one downbeat note every two bars. Secondly, that Basie jumped a chorus is confirmed by the fact that at the beginning of the next chorus he plays a figure almost identical to the one he had to abort earlier.

Then, too, though one would not wish to make a major issue of it, Lester's theme is not his most inspired creation. It is true, of course, that in most jazz the composer (and the composition) are considered of secondary importance, next to the improviser. Granted for the moment. But a great improvisation *and* a great theme could not harm. In addition nothing happens with the theme; there is no organic growth or development. A secondary derived riff is used in the last two choruses, but it too does not lead to any building of the basic material. So that, except for Young's solo—which *is* superb—the piece's overall continuity is rather ordinary, uninventive. The result is a lopsided form in that the three last choruses are anticlimactic.

Young's solo (transcribed in Ex. 14) is worth a closer look, for it not only exemplifies his solo work at its best but also corroborates several interesting traits, some of which I have noted before (recall the discussion on the 1936 *Lady Be Good*). In *Leaps* we hear again the tendency to anticipate phrase beginnings and endings, also Young's penchant for starting phrases on the ninth and sixth degrees of the scale. Here is a statistical breakdown of these occurrences:

Anticipations of phrase beginnings—mm. 40, 125, 160, (162)

Anticipations of phrase endings—mm. 43, 91, (163)

Use of 9th degree—mm. 51, 61, 62, 63, 77, 79

Use of 6th degree—mm. 121, 129, (131)

The parenthesized numbers indicate bars in which the point being made here is perhaps not entirely unequivocal. In any case, as regards the anticipations, the point I am making is not that these are in any sense wrong; on the contrary, they are a fascinating idiosyncrasy of Young's. They give us a jolt, like one of Jo

Ex. 14

Young's first solo chorus in *Lester Leaps In*

(Measure numbers here (and on the previous page) refer to those of the entire performance. Thus Young's first chorus begins m. 37, after a 32-bar "head" ensemble chorus and a 4-bar intro.)

Jones's anticipatory rim shots on the fourth beat, and they make us listen all the more. But at the root of Young's penchant for these anticipations lies a persistent quest for the new, for the asymmetrical. He is constantly trying to break down the binary (2-bar, 4-bar, 8-bar) structures of jazz pieces. He's trying to fit 3- and 5-bar phrases into these forms, often by shifting a whole 8-bar phrase one bar ahead. Similarly, as I have noted earlier, he constantly tries to fit a motive or melodic gesture that was once used in a particular *locus* in the form, into some other spot. So too in *Leaps:* Young's figure in the ninth bar of the second chorus (*his* first chorus, m. 45 in Ex. 14) reappears in variant form in m. 5 of the fifth chorus and in m. 7 of the sixth chorus.

Dickie's Dream, a shorter solo, is even more concise and concentrated in its economic use of motivic material (Ex. 15). The bracketed notes, marked *a* through

Ex. 15

e really tell the whole story. Very little is left unused: melodic ideas and motivic fragments are constantly recycled, reappearing in different contexts and (occasionally) in varied rhythmic guises. Again, Young is always aware of where he is in the layout of the form. Obviously mm. 9, 17, and 25 are crucial structural points in a 32-bar form. Notice how Young reserves these moments for special effects. Measure 9—starting, it should be noted, on the sixth degree—is at once the highest note thus far in the solo and anticipates the same note in an even more important place, namely the seventeenth bar. Hear, too, how Young is harmonically *explicit* precisely where the changes of the song—namely in the eight bars of the bridge with its clean modulating cycle of fifths—contain the most harmonic mobility. Finally, it is beautiful how Young reserves a brand new idea for the final eight bars, starting at m. 25. All this is true compositional mastery.

The Basie style suffers from considerable neglect of dynamics and lack of harmonic invention. True, Basie knows all too well how to exploit the most obvious forms of dynamic contrast, i.e., going abruptly from *fortissimo* full band ensemble to a *pianissimo* rhythm section sequence. Indeed, he uses this effect—invariably the soft rhythm section interpolations occur in the bridge—with mindless regularity. But that's about it for dynamics. A more subtle, variegated use of dynamics, such as Lunceford or Ellington used so creatively, is virtually non-existent in the Basie canon. Crescendos and diminuendos are extremely rare. A more complex internalized handling of dynamics seems to be of little interest, and one suspects that if an arranger had brought in an arrangement which featured more subtly used dynamics, Basie would have suppressed them.

A second flaw is perhaps so intrinsic to the fundamental riff-cum-blues concept espoused by Basie that the criticism may be irrelevant—like criticizing a banana for being yellow rather than red. And yet other blues and/or riff bands *have* dealt with this problem, so perhaps it is an issue worth raising. I am referring to the curious fact that Basie's music is rarely memorable thematically (nor is it in terms of timbre or color).

One may enjoy a Basie performance for its swing, its often exciting call-and-response brass and reed exchanges, and above all its superior soloists. But in all this we rarely remember the themes[45] the way one does Strayhorn's *Take the A Train* and Parker's *Donna Lee*, Monk's *Criss Cross*, Miller's *In the Mood*, Armstrong's *West End Blues*, Morton's *Grandpa's Spells*, Lewis's *Django*, Noble's *Cherokee*, and a host of others.

This goes back, of course, to the basic point that jazz is not in the first line a composer's art (in the traditional sense) but an improviser's art. The material upon which the improvisation is based is less important than the improvisation itself. This conflict—and to some extent contradiction—has existed in jazz since its beginnings. Basie gambles with this fundamental premise, assuming treatment of a given material, either through the work of his improvising soloists or his arrangers, to be more important than the material itself. It is clear, certainly from the aural evidence, that Basie, not essentially a composer, is less interested in compositional/thematic content as such. And yet one knows of many jazz musicians and orchestras where a better balance between these two approaches was struck.

The third failing is in the realm of harmonic invention. From 1936 to 1940 there is not a single example of any even mildly explorative harmonic usage. Chromaticism of any kind was eschewed, and one looks in vain for a rich eleventh chord, even a minor ninth, let alone any bitonal harmonies such as Ellington and Sy Oliver had been exploring for years. Basie's harmonies were simple to the point of triteness. That is why in context Lester Young's use of ninths and sixths stood out almost as harmonically daring.

The first Basie arranger to establish a small beachhead in harmonically "new" territory was Andy Gibson. The March 19 and 20, 1940, recording sessions included several fine Gibson arrangements, one of which—*I Never Knew*—seems

---

45. As one later record album might be inferred to suggest, Basie is a "groovemaker," not a melody-maker.

in the context of Basie's established style to be almost startlingly innovative, although measured by less conservative standards not quite so improbable for 1940. The coda of this wonderfully driving and well-executed arrangement features a striking series of eight chords, played *allargando* (Ex. 16).

Ex. 16

The "exotic" whole-tone or augmented chord modulation to the key of D♭ earlier in the piece is also handled with more taste than was normally accorded this banal device, the bane of thousands of trying-to-be-hip arrangements in the swing era. In addition the performance features a marvelously sure-footed Young solo and an excellent solo by trombonist Vic Dickenson, who had just recently joined Basie.

Dickenson can also be heard to good effect in *Let Me See*, a hard-swinging, bright-tempoed opus (♩=ca. 250) by "Sweets" Edison, again arranged by Gibson. Dickenson's energetic, sinewy style was a welcome antidote to Dickie Wells rather erratic, sometimes billowy, floppy approach to the "slip-horn." In *Let Me See*, *Tickle Toe*, and *Super Chief*, Buddy Tate, much favored by Basie during this period, can be heard to adopt some of Young's traits without relinquishing entirely his more Hawkins/Evans-oriented approach. Tate was barely twenty-six years old (to Young's thirty-one), and it is understandable that the younger player was bound to be somewhat influenced by the "president" and master.

Louisiana was another strong contribution by Gibson to the Basie book, a well-constructed framework for solos by Edison, Young, and Dickenson. Gibson evidently had the chameleon-like ability to adapt himself entirely to Basie's basic concept without being submerged in it. Listening to these excellent arrangements leaves no doubt that Gibson's work was a welcome and much-needed artistic infusion. His full-bodied arrangements spruced up the book, energized the band's playing, adding some harmonic spicing along the way.

Another fresh arranger's outlook came to the Basie band in May 1940 in the person of Tab Smith, a remarkable altoist rather strongly influenced by Hodges. As composer-arranger of *Blow Top*, *The Jitters*, *Platterbrains*, *Moon Nocturne*, and the incomparable *Harvard Blues*, arranger of other fine Rushing settings— *You Can't Run Around*, *Take Me Back, Baby*—Smith brought to the band characteristics not heretofore represented. Smith, for example, *did* know how to use dynamic nuances and chromatic harmonies creatively, as witness his remarkable, sensitive arrangement of *Harvard Blues*. This is one of the early Basie band's very best recordings, a classic of its kind. In the hushed atmosphere of its introduction we can already sense something special is in the offing. The first of several virtually flawless solo contributions is by Don Byas (who had taken over the chair formerly occupied by Lester Young). Perfectly constructed, it is simple and affecting, poignant and languorous. Playing softly with a sense of intimacy not often encountered in jazz, Byas places each of his notes as if they were a series of incontrovertible truths, Jo Jones all the while enveloping these lovely sounds with caressing cymbal swooshes. Listen especially (at the beginning of his second 12-bar chorus) for Byas's anguished moan, followed by a simple downward scale.

The singular almost eerie beauty of this moment derives to a large extent from the use (stated in technical terms) of the Lydian scale, the scale on the fourth degree, imposed here on the tonic (Ex. 17). The effect is heightened by Byas's

Ex. 17

exploiting, un- or subconsciously, the momentary confluence of two diverse musical worlds: the classical modes (which go back to Greek antiquity) and the blue notes of jazz. For the C♭ head-tone of the scale (marked x) is both the blue seventh of the key of D♭ and the fourth degree of the related Lydian scale (of G♭).

It may be interesting for readers to note that: a) this type of melodic/modal playing was used extensively in Sonny Rollins's great 1956 recording, called— appropriately—*Blue Seven*; and b) that the composer-theorist George Russell has analyzed and developed a complete system of tonality based on this and other similar possibilities in our Western tonal system, embodied in his theoretical work entitled *The Lydian Chromatic Concept*.

There now follow three superb choruses by Rushing, in great voice, clear ringing tones and diction. The lyrics, composed by George Frazier, the famous jazz writer of the thirties and forties, are probably the most sophisticated and cryptic blues lyrics ever contrived (including even Joni Mitchell's). It is not clear whether Jimmy Rushing really understood what he was singing, but it certainly sounds convincing. Never was the plaintive tenor cry in his voice more focused; it is as if he were desperately clinging to the words. Behind him, Wells plays the most masterful obbligato of his entire Basie tenure: wordly-wise, sophisticated, elegant—as befits the subject. Meanwhile Tab Smith brings in the saxes in hushed *ppp*, adding soft velvety muted brass in Rushing's second chorus. For the third chorus, the one starting with "Reinhardt, Reinhardt," Smith invents some of the most sumptuous blues harmonies ever composed, worthy of an Ellington or a Gil Evans (Ex. 18).

that's no Har-vard line.___

Notice how tellingly Tab Smith uses dynamics here, not only to create variety, but to accompany Rushing in *p*, and to respond to and punctuate his phrases in *f*.

Tab Smith's artistry as a soloist can be heard to fine advantage on many sides from this period, but perhaps none better than in his pungent, fluent solos on *You Can't Run Around*. Smith's work always manages to be at once fervid and poised.

Another exceptionally fine Rushing performance, *Goin' to Chicago Blues*—in some ways a forerunner of *Harvard Blues*, but not quite on the latter's level—was arranged by Buck Clayton, and introduced by a superb cup-muted solo, full of sorrowful, nostalgic contemplation. All the more startling, then, are the wild double-time outbursts in Rushing's first and last vocal choruses, a harbinger of "things to come" in the Eckstine and Gillespie bands of a few years later.

To complete this trinity of great Rushing blues, there is *I'm Gonna Move to the Outskirts of Town* (from April 1942). Remarkable in itself, i.e., quite apart from any other considerations, it is an important performance because here we hear precisely where Joe Williams learned a goodly share of his blues shouting. The stylistic paternity is unmistakable.[46] Rushing's plaintive "oo-oo-oohs" and

46. Joe Williams's and the author's friendship goes all the way back to 1945, when he was regularly to be heard in several Chicago Southside clubs. Gifted with a magnificent baritone voice, perfectly produced, Joe, then in his twenties, was triply torn between a career as an opera singer (it was, of course, too early for that in those days when the opera houses were closed to black singers), a ballad singer (he was—and is—remarkable in that genre too), or a blues singer. It is pretty clear which won out. Although he is remembered mostly for his work with Basie in the fifties, it is nowadays little remembered that Williams also sang with Jimmy Noone, Coleman Hawkins, and Andy Kirk, among others, in the late thirties and early forties, always returning to his home base of Chicago, a city famous for its blues singers.

Anyone familiar with Joe Williams's singing with the Basie band will be shocked to hear what he sounded like on two recordings with Andy Kirk in 1946, *Louella* and *Now You Tell Me*. Here Joe's voice has little of that fantastic projection for which he is so well known. He sounds rather covered,

voice-breaking cries are a central part of the blues tradition, going all the way back to field hollers and work songs. What is interesting, however—and I must admit (to me at least) inexplicable—is that Rushing never used these devices before or after *Gonna Move*, at least not on records.

Apart from Tab Smith's refreshingly original arranging voice, the Basie band also acquired the writing talents of Buster Harding and its star trumpeter Buck Clayton. These two arrangers, both I believe influenced by Jimmy Mundy's and Andy Gibson's earlier work, gave the Basie band its first wholly consistent *orchestral* style, characterized by a strong fully packed sound, rich section and full-ensemble instrumental voicings, and an uncanny capacity for creating a broadly-paced back-in-the-beat kind of earthy swing. But there was a trade-off. For what the Basie band lost in gaining a cohesive strongly identifiable big-band orchestral style was the marvelously loose, soloistically oriented smaller ensemble concept of the earlier mid-thirties band. Even the length and number of improvised solos was affected, as arranged ensembles occupied more and more space in the performances, at least on recordings. Sometimes the solo still predominated, as in Buster Harding's exceptional 9:20 *Special*, written to feature in its latter half none other than guest artist Coleman Hawkins. Harding's work really comes into its own with this piece and *Rusty Dusty Blues*, another superb Rushing blues. Harding here is one of the first to experiment with full-band double-time figures, which in this slow tempo had a marvelous effect of "loosening up" and enlivening the rhythmic flow of the performance. It was a device which was to spread like wildfire through all the bands, black and white, and by 1945 was a standard feature of all blues or slow tempo pieces.[47]

Buck Clayton's fine arranging style, similar to Harding's, can be heard to good advantage on his 1941 *Down for Double* and *It's Sand, Man!*, the latter with a fresh modern look that begins to anticipate the lean, spirited unison lines of early bop bands (like Woody Herman and Billy Eckstine).

Jimmy Mundy, of course, also continued to work for Basie, contributing such dynamic scores as *Feather Merchant* and *Something New*. His *Fiesta in Blue* was possibly intended as Basie's answer to Ellington's *Concerto for Cootie*. If so, it didn't entirely succeed. Clayton plays his solo part well enough, but *Fiesta* isn't quite as effective a composition as *Concerto*. (Oddly enough, Cootie Williams, by this time with Benny Goodman, recorded *Fiesta* six months earlier to brilliant effect.)

Broadway, a catchy tune by Henry Woode and well orchestrated by him, is notable for two things: one, that rarest of occasions when Jo Jones plays too much, too "busy"; the other, Young's last recorded effort with Basie, one of his most adroit linear solos.

---

in style hovering somewhat uncertainly between Herb Jeffries and Frank Sinatra. On the other hand his diction was at this time already superb, and in several places Joe embellishes the melodies with inventive and technically very difficult variations, glimpses of the extraordinarily vocal virtuosity of his mature years.

47. For more of Harding's outstanding work, refer to Artie Shaw (Chapter 7) and Roy Eldridge (Chapter 6).

For the rest, there were the lesser, more ordinary sides. Some were downright vulgar, like *Down, Down, Down*, almost a caricature of jazz at its most pompous; or the inept arrangement of *Jump the Blues Away*; or silly pieces like *Wiggle Woogie*. And it is amazing to find Basie imitating Glenn Miller's style—and not even tongue-in-cheek—in *You Lied to Me*.

But on the whole Basie's batting average was comparatively high. Out of ninety-two titles recorded between March 19, 1940, and July 1942, when the recording ban began, there are a good two to three dozen performances that are worthy of retrospective consideration (some already mentioned above).

The commercial pressures on the Basie orchestra were as severe and as constant as those for any of the other hundreds of swing bands, major or minor. It was an ongoing battle to find and to insist upon good basic material, whether vocal or instrumental. For with material that is less than inspired, even a good performance is not always enough. But then on some small group sessions with Byas and Clayton in mid-1942, even the performance of the famous Basie rhythm section lagged. Hear their *St. Louis Blues*, and hear one bored, tired rhythm quartet, not at all the "All-American Rhythm Section" proclaimed on the record label.

And then, of course, sad to say, Basie's own pianistic clichés were beginning to mar many of these performances. One loses track of how many times he plays

later, was *still* playing the same dozen "licks." The best of these early forties' performances notwithstanding, there was discernible to the critical ear an encroaching malaise in the Basie band, its chronological appearance a little difficult to pinpoint precisely after so many years. But it seems to me that by the early forties there were too many listless performances, both on recordings and live. A kind of inertia, a lack of energy, had set in, perhaps inevitably the result of too many bookings in which second-rate commercially "successful" material was programmed. There were differences, of course, from night to night, from place to place. And, clearly, when the Basie Band played for black audiences at the local "Cotton Clubs" and "Plantation Clubs," one could hear a marked difference in performance as opposed to dates for white audiences only—something confirmed indelibly from my own unforgettable first encounters with the Basie band in the mid-war years 1943–44. An analysis of programs and air checks reveals quite unequivocally that black bands, including Basie's, were forced or expected to play quite different repertories for different publics. Although Basie prided himself on sticking to one basic repertory—his classic response to the question "What are you gonna play tonight?" was "The same old beef stew"— even he was forced to cater to that whole ménage of managers, publishers, record promoters, tune-pluggers, and the like, particularly on the nightly network broadcasts. Amongst his own public, he could and did play the heart and soul of his best dance repertory.

An interesting corroboration of these observations comes to us in the form of an LP comprising two broadcasts from the Southland Café in Boston, one by Basie in February 1940, the other by Chick Webb in May 1939, barely one month before Webb's untimely death. Hearing these two performance sets side by side, one can easily understand why Webb's band was the victor in the January 16, 1938, "Battle of Swing" and on other "cutting contexts." The sheer energy unleashed by that dynamo Webb, transmitted to the band through his drums, is awesome, against which Basie's more relaxed swing—at times even lacklustre by *its* own standards—cannot stand the test of comparison. Although Basie's band plays with its usual clean (but perhaps somewhat sanitized) ensemble, the excitement of Webb's orchestra is simply electrifying. Moreover, Ella Fitzgerald sings with so much youthful verve, a springy swinging beat and— even in those days—with inventive extemporized flourishes, that Helen Humes was no match for her.

More to the point, Webb plays a better repertory: strong danceable instrumentals and jazzy vocals. I am not aware of Webb ever playing anything quite as abominable as Basie's *Ebony Rhapsody* (which opens the Southland broadcast), a fearful pastiche of Liszt's *Hungarian Rhapsody* and stultified swing formulas which even soloists like Young and Edison couldn't salvage.

It is quite clear that swing music, particularly in its most popular manifestations, had in it from the very beginning the seeds of its own demise. Ultimately the basic arranging and formal devices of swing, becoming increasingly codified and impacted, atrophied. The decline of big bands, though partly economic in cause, is also very much traceable to the fact that the idiom began to exhaust itself creatively. The old formulas were staggering from musical overweight, from malfunctioning parts, creaking joints, blindness, and old age. After a while it was no longer a question of *whether* the genre was going to expire, but *when*.

Of all the famous swing era orchestras Ellington's held on the longest; and one could even put the case that he successfully survived the big-band crash and continued to enrich the medium of orchestral jazz until his death in 1974. Lunceford, as we have seen, collapsed much earlier, in the early forties. Others, including Goodman, Dorsey, Webb, Kirk, hung on a bit longer, while Hines's band got transformed twice into the short-lived Eckstine and Gillespie units, and other bands like Herman's and James's survived the era by adjusting to more advanced styles.

Basie was also a survivor, just barely. He, too, was forced to disband in 1950 and continue sporadically with small groups for a few years. But in 1952 Basie was able to revive his orchestra, adopting a more modern though still essentially conservative style, and was, of course, still successfully active until his death in 1984. New arranging talents came to the rescue in these later years, among them Neal Hefti, Ernie Wilkins, Johnny Mandel, Frank Foster, and Thad Jones.

But even before all that one of Basie's star trumpet players, Buck Clayton, as mentioned earlier, signaled a new era in the Basie history with his first-rate arrangements, starting in 1942, with *It's Sand, Man, Red Bank Boogie*, the very good *Jimmy's Blues, Taps Miller*, and *Avenue C*. Still the transition to a "modern" style took a while to achieve and was not without its awkward moments.[48] Eventually the band found a new form of expression—to the regret of many, who consider the early band as the only true representative one. Even Basie himself is reported to have said in 1950, if he could just have that old band once again before he died, he would leave this earth a happy man. I suppose it comes down to the ancient, often-heard argument that his post-1945 bands had better players, technically more accomplished—and, of course, why shouldn't they be?—but that the old band played with more spirit, more individuality, more spontaneity.

There is truth on both sides of the argument. The old band strove for a kind of lyricism; it preferred understatement; it embraced simplicity and clarity. Basie preferred to withhold a little, rather than to blare it all out, diligently pursuing his stated goal of a small, loose big-band filled with soloists.

But all that has changed now.[49] Although still predominantly a blues-cum-riff band, its playing became in "modern" times much more aggressive, often even strident, but admittedly also more technically polished. I think that Basie lost control of his famous understated approach rather early, I'd say beginning in the mid-forties. When Jo Jones left him, a succession of drummers—Shadow Wilson, Butch Ballard, Gus Johnson, Buddy Rich, and, above all, Sonny Payne—played increasingly louder, driving up the dynamic level of the band in a relentless spiral. Already in the 1944–46 band, one hears a harder, more clamorous brass sound. The band was fast losing its loose-jointed suppleness, turning into an unyielding straight-backed though vertically well-balanced sound, giving the lie to one of Basie's stated tenets: "the minute the brass get out of hand and blare and screech, instead of making every note mean something, there'll be some changes."[50]

True, the blary roughness of the late forties eventually gave way, several bands later, to a more polished balanced sound. Powerful, rich, full-bodied, the later Basie band lost the chill and scream of the band of the early fifties (on Clef Records). Its beauty now lay in its heaviness, its gravity, its density; it was a sound truly built from the bottom up, as Basie once put it, from the rhythm section through the saxes up into the high brass. What this new sound meant— and Basie owed that as much to arrangers Quincy Jones and Frank Foster as anyone—was that the relatively transparent, loose-limbed linear approach of the early Basie band, cushioned and floating on the rhythm section, had been exchanged for a heavier, tight-bodied vertical sound, anchored *in* the rhythm section.

This took a kind of player different from the Claytons, Edisons, Wellses, Youngs,

---

48. Listen, for instance, to the interesting collision between J. J. Johnson's bop trombone solo on *Rambo* and the vestiges of the old Basie style. (Even though J. J. had a hand in fashioning the arrangement, he could not—young as he was and at age 22 lucky to be in the great Basie "swing machine"— affect or transform that well-ensconced tradition overnight.)

49. A more extensive discussion of late post-1945 Basie would go beyond the scope and time frame of this book. The subject will, however, be dealt with in Volume III of this History.

50. *Hear Me Talkin' to Ya* (New York, 1966), 304.

Evanses of old. It is unthinkable to imagine those players in the 1970s' Basie band. But that raises a serious point in itself: whereas we used to listen for Lester Young or Buck Clayton or Herschel Evans in the old band, we don't listen in the same way for Frank Foster or Don Rader or even Al Grey. This was not only because the old band had such superior soloists but also because it couldn't, for many of those early years, find *its orchestral* style—in the way that Ellington and Lunceford did. This was not because Basie couldn't find his Sy Oliver, but, more profoundly, because it took all those many years for Basie and his orchestra to make the transition from a small Midwestern nine-piece improvising group to a big brassy Eastern-style arranger's band. Thus the development of the Basie band can be described in one sense as the loss and decline of its original destiny.

One basic idiomatic problem remained unsolved to the end, namely, the one of melodic/thematic paucity. The pieces in the post-1952 book were mostly without melodic distinction. The riff concept of construction atrophied in the mid-forties, if not sooner, and swing not at the service of good thematic content ultimately bores; it is like a glorious orator reciting empty twaddle. Aside from the occasional creative solo by Thad Jones or Joe Newman or Bobby Plater (or Joe Williams, for that matter), the band gradually offered little more than a resplendent traveling jazz museum, a magnificent "swing machine." It traded any ambitions to remain a creative, innovative ensemble for another three decades of extraordinary popularity.

There is a fascinating parallel between Basie's piano stylings and the band's orchestral rhetoric. Both became utterly predictable, "frozen in perfection" (as the French writer André Hodeir once put it),[51] blissfully non-intellectual, implacably simple—and literally inimitable. Any imitation of Basie's piano or orchestral style is perforce plagiarism. While there are those who would rejoice in that, it also means that Basie's 1950s' style permitted no growth, no development. In its perfected neoclassicism, it was a most glorious dead end.

---

51. In writing about the Basie band of the mid-fifties, Hodeir also likened these players to symphony musicians and "civil servants"—a rather damning condemnation, particularly coming from a Frenchman, since there are more musician civil servants *(fonctionnaires)* in France than any other country in the world.

5

The Great Black Bands

PART 1

EARL HINES

Younger jazz enthusiasts, brought up on LP reissues of earlier jazz, may have to be reminded that the general public in America was only dimly aware of the great black jazz orchestras, particularly in the early and mid-thirties. In the twenties black music was still generally relegated to "race records." Jazz—or "hot music," as it was then sometimes labeled—still had a comparatively small following in the early thirties, while the general public's fancy was caught by the hundreds of dance and "sweet" bands, which also, of course, dominated records and radio. But in late 1935 and early 1936 "hot music" in the form of "swing" suddenly gained national popularity, primarily through the success of two white bands, the Casa Loma orchestra and Benny Goodman's. As "swing" came in, the public discovered some of the bands that had already been around for some years— like Henderson, Ellington, Lunceford, Hines, and Webb—as well as the newer jazz orchestras of Count Basie, Woody Herman, and Charlie Barnet. All in all, however, it was the white bands of Miller, Shaw, Goodman, Tommy Dorsey, Berigan, and James, with their emphasis on a more commercial (and therefore mostly vocal) fare, that attracted the greatest public attention, sold the most records, and received the most radio exposure.

Thus the early work of bands like those of Earl Hines, Chick Webb, and Andy Kirk—the subjects to be dealt with next—though playing outstanding jazz, received minimal recognition. Even a remarkable musician like Earl Hines, surely of genius level, worked in relative obscurity during the thirties—this despite the fact that he had already participated in the widely hailed Armstrong Hot Five recordings of 1927 (and in one extraordinary trumpet-piano duet, *Weather Bird*)— all classics of the Golden Age of Jazz.

Hines's achievements in dramatically extending the role of the piano in jazz—

at times tantamount to creating an entirely new conception for it—would be remarkable enough if they encompassed a lifetime. But the startling fact is that Hines radically transformed jazz piano when he was barely twenty-two years old, expanding upon all previously established piano styles from ragtime to the stride idioms of the early twenties. In Hines's hands the piano's full technical/physical/ acoustic resources were brought into play in a manner that was not only new but was not to be approached, let alone surpassed, until decades later in differing ways by Art Tatum, Errol Garner, Bud Powell, and Oscar Peterson.

Though my admiration for Hines is second to none, I balk at the claims often made on his behalf that he "*revolutionized* jazz piano" (italics added) or is presumed to have *invented* the so-called "trumpet style" and certain other favorite Hinesian devices. Such claims go too far and ignore the extraordinary accomplishments of "Jelly Roll" Morton, Eubie Blake, and James P. Johnson (some would even include "Luckey" Roberts and Willie "The Lion" Smith). That Hines started a new chapter in the history of jazz piano is not to be denied, but to state or imply that Hines somehow began *tabula rasa*, or, worse, initiated a radical break with the immediate past, seriously misrepresents reality. For as with all great "breakthroughs" in the arts, Hines's creativity was both *re*volutionary and evolutionary.[1] His startling innovations were solidly founded on the bedrock of an earlier tradition, to be sure, in its most elevated and advanced form.

Let us examine, for instance, the oft-made claims that Hines invented: the right-hand "trumpet piano style"; the persistent use of right-hand octave doublings; the use of these two devices as accompanimental obbligatos or counterpoints to the main soloist(s). A good listen to any number of Morton performances, including his very earliest ones (in 1923, the same year that Hines also first recorded), reveals that these techniques were intrinsic to Morton's concept of jazz piano and, I would guess, had been so for a decade or more. His upper-register swinging obbligatos *in octaves* can be clearly heard throughout *Muddy Water Blues* and *Big Foot Ham*,[2] but especially behind (and above) the solos by clarinet, alto and trumpet. Like Hines, Morton frequently fills in the right hand octaves with one or two harmony notes, although in this respect Hines's style was generally leaner, more melodic, and less harmonic than Morton's. Moreover, as concerns the left hand, Morton is playing anything but incessant "oomp-cha" ragtime or stride figures. Like Hines, albeit in a manner far less complex

1. It is almost impossible to think of an innovative artist, no matter how radical he may have been deemed by his contemporaries, who along with his revoutionary attributes cannot also be seen as evolving creatively out of his predecessors' contributions: be it Monteverdi, Beethoven, Wagner, Schoenberg, in music; El Greco, Rembrandt, Turner, Picasso, in painting; Shakespeare, Blake, Twain, Joyce, in literature. (Gesualdo and Ives come to mind as possible exceptions, but even their cases are arguable.)
2. Jelly Roll Morton's Stomp Kings, Paramount 12050, recorded no later than June 1923. One of the problems, of course, is that it is quite difficult to hear and therefore fully appreciate all that Morton is doing on these technically primitive 1923 acoustic recordings, particularly with Jasper Taylor's wood blocks banging away in the foreground. On the other hand, Hines's piano obbligatos with Jimmie Noone, for example, recorded electrically five years later, are much more readily audible.

than Hines was to develop some years later, Morton is contantly breaking the regular patterns with cross-accents, syncopations, counterlines, passing tones, and broken tenths.[3]

Nor should we forget Eubie Blake's two-handed virtuosity, broken stride patterns, right-hand octaves and octave slides in his 1921 recording, *Sounds of Africa*, taken at a high speed of ♩ = ca. 210, later to be retitled *Charleston Rag*; or for that matter, James P. Johnson's advanced cross-hand figures in pieces such as *You've Got To Be Modernistic* (1930) and *Carolina Shout* (1921). Indeed, breaks like Johnson's

and

became regular features of Hines's style, almost to the point of becoming a cliché.

There were, of course, specific musical ideas and techniques which Hines *was* the first to use; such as his left-hand upward "glissandos," thereby completely suspending the explicit rhythmic function of the left hand; or his "fantasies," which often transcended the realm of jazz, exploring some previously unchartered Hinesian landscape.

But even these devices were part of a further loosening up of the handed-down piano conventions of the past, a process begun by the likes of Morton and Johnson and Blake.[4]

Hines's individual approach to the piano has most often been described as "the trumpet style." Even if not taken literally, it is somewhat of a misnomer, being both misleading and not entirely accurate. It is misleading because it de-

3. See *Early Jazz*, chap. 4, for further discussion and analysis of Morton's recordings. Hear also Morton's rambunctious fingers-flying solo on the famous Red Hot Peppers' *Black Bottom Stomp* (1926) with plenty of filled-in right-hand octave figures.

4. A striking example of Blake's penchant for surprises and running counter to established conventions was his famous rolling bass, reversed from the expected pattern, in *Sounds of Africa*. Instead of [music notation] Eubie plays [music notation] which on the surface may, to the lay reader, seem not only very similar, but harmless looking. But because Eubie's bassline goes *against* the beat, it is in fact quite unexpected and difficult.

emphasizes the fact that the Hines's style is first and foremost totally *pianistic*. For it is a concept based on the specific and unique properties of the piano: its capacity for multiple sounds (unlike the trumpet's single notes), produced by the fingers (not air); its capacity to embrace simultaneously melody, rhythm, dynamics, *and* harmony; its quasi-percussive qualities; and its ability to render both homophonic and polyphonic structures. But it is also an inaccurate label in that the trumpet, for all its power and brilliance, is essentially a "singing" instrument with the capacity to sustain notes and musical lines, a quality which on the piano, with its automatic tone "decay," can only be approximated. In real acoustical terms there is no pure *legato* on the piano, although great pianists can create the illusion of one. One might just as well have dubbed Hines's a "clarinet style," since he used this concept so frequently as obbligato or descant lines, riding high above an ensemble or a solo, much like the high-register clarinet obbligatos of the New Orleans style.

The term "trumpet style" seems applicable only to the extent that there is something of the lean, cutting sound of a trumpet in Hines's tone and touch, something he conceivably had in his ear throughout childhood from his brass-playing father and uncle, the former a member of a fourteen-piece brass band. Young Earl even played the cornet for a while, but gave it up in favor of the piano. I have a hunch he also found the cornet or trumpet too simple for his fertile imagination and agile fingers—just as he once asserted, "I'm too technical to play the blues." [5]

In the classical field, a player of Hines's prodigious gifts, had he been white, would have had a brilliant concert or solo career. Black musicians in the 1920s knew, however, that such prospects were to all intents and purposes precluded. Nor was a solo career in *jazz* a viable alternative, when virtually the entire field was engulfed by the burgeoning developments in orchestral and ensemble jazz. Inevitably, then, Hines found himself performing in bands, first with Lois Deppe, a local band in Hines's hometown of Pittsburgh, and later in Chicago,[6] not only with Armstrong but with the show bands of Carroll Dickerson and Erskine Tate and with Jimmie Noone's Apex Club orchestra.

Nor is it surprising to find Hines seizing an opportunity to lead a band himself when it was offered to him by a Chicago Southside entrepreneur who had converted a movie house into a luxurious nightclub, called the Grand Terrace. Hines opened the club with a brand new orchestra on December 28, 1928—his twenty-third birthday!

Like all major nightclubs of that era—most such clubs were modelled after New York's Cotton Club (where Duke Ellington and Cab Calloway held forth)—the Grand Terrace required the band to play three shows a night, as well as for dancing. While this permitted only a limited amount of real jazz, it did offer

5. Quoted by Stanley Dance in "Earl Hines," *Giants of Jazz*, Time-Life Records. Mr. Dance's excellent biographical note on Earl Hines is the best brief account available. Mr. Dance's full biography of Hines is another excellent source.
6. It was none other than Eubie Blake who urged Hines to test his talent in the big times, to "get away" from Pittsburgh.

the musicians a wide range of practical experience in a variety of jazz-related musical styles. Although Hines was never to capitalize creatively on these opportunities to the extent that Ellington did in New York, nor to achieve the latter's fame, he reigned supreme in the Midwest, for he held forth at the Grand Terrace until 1939 (when the club folded), in the meantime producing a sizable body of orchestral recordings which must rank high in anyone's view of the Swing Era.

Within two months after the Grand Terrace opening, Hines and his orchestra had their first recording date, which in the jazz field was always a crucial mark of recognition, equivalent to a classical performer's favorable review in the *New York Times* or a composer's première by a major symphony orchestra. Undoubtedly the Victor company, much impressed by Hines's previous recordings on the QRS and Okeh labels and his meteoric rise in general, was banking on a strong success for this recording debut. Unfortunately the band did not make much of an impression on record buyers, who, insofar as they were even aware of jazz, evidently preferred to buy Ellington, McKinney's Cotton Pickers, and, of course, Hines's close friend and collaborator Louis Armstrong, who was beginning to carve out a major triple-threat career as a trumpeter–singer–bandleader.

In truth, Hines's first orchestra recordings were hardly competitive, either artistically or commercially. The band had not yet developed any particular style or identity, and had yet to find the proper format to showcase Hines's unique pianistic talents. Even the best of the ten released sides[7] did not match the quality of Hines's earlier involvements with ensemble jazz (Noone, Armstrong). Nor did the orchestral framework allow him the kind of freedom that his gifts required (and deserved). To appreciate fully such a statement one must first comprehend the immensity of Hines's pianistic talent, not only technically but also creatively. Herewith, then a few examples of his art, as already quite fully developed in the five-year period prior to forming his own band.

We can begin with his earliest recorded solo on his own composition *Congaine*, made on October 3, 1923, with Deppe's Serenaders,[8] when Hines was not yet eighteen years old. Not only does the recording reveal a pianist in full command of his craft, but one who was already straining to reach beyond the then most advanced stylistic and technical achievements. It is fair to say that, even at age seventeen (and we cannot know for sure how many years earlier), Hines was prepared to take up where Morton and others had left off (Ex. 1). Notice particularly Hines's twice breaking up of the regular stride beat with the six successive dotted-quarter rhythms in mm. 15, 16 and 21, 22, a device frequently used by Morton. (See, for example, an almost identical idea on Mor-

7. Six of the sixteen sides made in 1929 were rejected outright by Victor and never released.
8. Gennett 20012, reissued on Milestone 2012.

Lois Deppe (1897–1976) is little remembered today, but was an important early bandleader and singer. Gifted with a beautiful baritone voice, he devoted his talents to classical singing after studies in New York with Enrico Caruso's voice coach, Buzzi Pecci. Later he turned to jazz, leading bands in Pittsburgh and New York, and sang in such famous black Broadway musicals as Lew Leslie's *Blackbirds of 1927*.

Ex. 1

ton's Gennett recording of *Kansas City Stomps*: the last two bars in the repeat of the *B* strain, or the frequent beat-disrupting syncopations in the last ten bars of the final return of the *A* strain.)

By the time Hines was playing with Jimmie Noone and Armstrong in Chicago, as well as recording for the QRS label in Long Island City—all in 1928—he had once again both expanded and crystallized his conception. Any number of fine examples can demonstrate this. Typical of his right-hand obbligato style is *Sweet Sue* with Noone's Apex Club orchestra. Here Hines accompanies Noone's soulful hymn-like "theme" solo with leaping triplet figures, at one point breaking suddenly into lively sixteenth-note cascades—the joyous musical analogue to the wide flashing smile Hines wore all his life while playing.[9]

An example of Hines's penchant for breaking up both the harmonic and rhythmic continuity is contained in the famous *Weather Bird* performance with Louis Armstrong, where in the ninth bar of the last chorus Hines performs some radical surgery on the basic compositional structure (Ex. 2).

Some of Hines's other favorite devices can be heard on the solo piano QRS and Okeh tracks, which in their totality show that Hines had completely absorbed all the lessons to be learned from his predecessors, particularly Johnson and Morton, and had already fully in place the essential elements of his own elaborations of these styles. At the same time they reveal a manual ambidexterity

9. This incidentally, was the orchestra Ravel heard in 1928 during his visit to Chicago and allegedly commented to Noone, "That's some piano player you got there."

Ex. 2

and agility of mind that was unprecedented in jazz piano. Though we can appreciate and analyze the results, we cannot rationally explain how they were achieved. It is for such situations that we reserve the words talent, phenomenon, genius.

This much is clear: Hines's special pianistic devices, allowing him constantly to surprise the listener, stem from his extraordinary mental and digital agility. Any idea that came into his head was instantly transferable to his obedient fingers. Nothing needed to be prepared or practiced: everything was immediately attainable. Thus one of his favorite devices for breaking up the striding rhythmic regularity of 1920s piano was that amazing swirling, careening rush of notes—*roulades* they are called—two stunning examples of which can be heard on the Okeh A *Monday Date* (Ex. 3a, 3b).

In listening to this passage, Hines's off-beat "delayed" rhythms in mm. 5 through 8 (of Ex. 3a) sound as if he had suddenly lost the beat momentarily. But it turns out that he was absolutely on target all the time, the implied beat never wavering under the "stretched out" rhythms—a fact we recognize in mm. 9 and 10 as Hines lands squarely on the C-major chord in m. 11 (the seventh bar of the last "eight" of the tune).

In Example 3b, in exactly the same place in the tune three choruses later, Hines stretches the rhythms *and* harmonies even further out, once again landing in perfect time back in C major at m. 13 (the beginning of the sixth chorus). Notice, too, that in the fourth chorus Hines's left hand plays one beat off in half-note syncopations for an entire 16 bars—an unsettling and nerve-wracking tour de force.

A related "break-up" maneuver is the left-hand ascending run, usually a scale, most often a chromatic scale. (One of the more leisurely examples of this effect can be heard on the QRS *Blues in Thirds*.) Like an arrow shot out of a bow, these runs whizz up the scale, triumphantly hitting their target note somewhere in the middle register, as if it had all been planned and practiced for hours, then merrily proceeding from there as if nothing had happened. [10]

---

10. These amazing runs are often incorrectly called *glissandos*. *Glissando* is an easy and mostly rather banal device which Hines rarely resorted to. Rather, his runs were fingered, at a speed that makes them *sound* like *glissandos*.

Ex. 3a

Ex. 3b

One of the more "advanced" examples of breaking up the rhythmic continuity without, mind you, losing the beat occurs on *Stowaway*, when, in the fourth chorus (of this 18-bar piece—16 plus a 2-bar tag), Hines suddenly breaks into quarter-note quintuplets. The effect of the beat speeding up by one-fifth is disconcerting—the listener is suddenly set adrift from his rhythmic moorings. But two bars later everything is set right again.[11] What is amazing in this "break" is that Hines was not content to play five clear beats per bar, but rather felt the need—and had the ability—to embellish the main notes (Ex. 4).

Ex. 4

Quintuplet speed-ups are, of course, truly of the twentieth century. But most of Hines's other sleights-of-hand had existed in the classical piano literature for at least a hundred years, particularly in the works of Chopin, whose music Hines must surely have studied when, as a young teenager, he was preparing for a concert career under the watchful guidance of his German-born teacher Von Holz.[12] Chopin's nocturnes, mazurkas, and ballades abound with scampering octave runs, zephyr-like roulades, surging swirling bass-register figures, scintillating obbligatos and embellishments. Example 5 provides just one simple comparison. What is especially interesting is that these pianisms and effects in Chopin occur almost always, as in jazz, over a steady beat or rhythmic pattern, usually explicitly stated, sometimes obliquely implied. The only difference is that in the case of Chopin these infrastructures, also all dance-related, were Polish mazurka rhythms, Italian barcarolles, fiery marches, and elegant waltzes.

This discussion of Hines, the innovative pianist, is a necessary preamble to a consideration of Hines, the orchestra leader. Hines has often asserted that he

11. Such "complex" asymmetrical rhythmic configurations were not unknown to Hines's predecessors. One extraordinary example of the right hand taking off in 10-over-8 or 9-over-8 melodic flights, in this case against a steady Habañera beat (♩. ♩. ♩) in the left hand, occurs in Morton's New Orleans Joys (see *Early Jazz*, chap. 4).

12. It is not without significance that many of the greatest jazz pianists—Hines, Hopkins, Hayes, Tatum, Peterson, Garner, Lewis, Tristano, Marmarosa—were quite thoroughly versed in nineteenth-century classical piano literature.

Ex. 5

Chopin—Nocturne, op. 27, No. 2

Chopin—Nocturne, Op. 15, No. 2

was primarily a "band pianist"—strange, coming from someone who is regarded as one of a small handful of musicians able to raise jazz piano to a high and distinct solo art. But I think Hines's assertion has not been correctly understood. It was certainly not false modesty—but possibly true modesty. The statement doesn't really refer to Hines the pianist as such. The distinction Hines was making, I think, was that he was not the creative composer-pianist-leader that Ellington was, or even the soloist-leader that Basie was. He was not a stylist who set and determined a band's style. He was rather, a pianist who, despite his prodigious soloistic abilities, was content to function in the framework of a band, that is, in a larger organism in which he would perform a specific, limited, and preassigned role.

That explains why the style of the Hines band was never determined by himself but by his arrangers, particularly, at its best, by Jimmy Mundy and Budd Johnson. It also explains why Hines allowed so many players in his orchestra to contribute arrangements: besides Mundy and Johnson, Hayes Alvis (bass), Quinn Wilson (bass), Cecil Irwin (tenor sax), Robert Crowder (tenor sax), Franz Jackson (tenor sax), George Dixon (trumpet), Lawrence Dixon (guitar). But having so many arrangers—Henri Woode, Bingie Madison, Buster Harding would be added later to the list—also precluded the Hines orchestra's ever developing a single cohesive recognizable style. What was recognizable was its rhythmic energy, its penchant for lively tempos, its spirit. These qualities emanated from the band's leader, for it was the particular Hinesian *interpretation* of these many diverse arranging styles that brought some degree of unity to the band.

As I suggested earlier, things got off to a rather shaky start with the new Grand Terrace band. The ensembles, though spirited and delivered in a crisp style, were often out of tune, ragged, and disorganized, peppered with wrong notes. In the introduction to *Everybody Loves My Baby*, one of the earliest February 1929 cuts, lead-trumpet Shirley Clay is on the wrong part of the bar for about twelve measures before finally getting it right, just in time for Hines (also a bit shaky) to launch into his first solo chorus. Quick-minded and witty as he is, Hines immediately parodies the shaky beginning during his first bridge with oddly placed cross-accents that give the effect of shifting the beat and misplacing bar lines.

But *Everybody Loves My Baby* did have one basic quality, typical of this band and most of Hines's later orchestras: a snappy, peppy, bouncy energy that never, however, coalesced into a feeling that you could call swing. It was very fast dance music, played in a vertical manner. Actually, it seemed to me that Hines was here trying to emulate the drive of Jelly Roll Morton's Red Hot Peppers performances, especially a piece like *Black Bottom Stomp*. (Even the Hines piano solo breathes of the same air as Morton's on *Black Bottom*.) But whereas Morton is imbued with the spirit of collective improvisation basic to the New Orleans idiom, albeit in a fairly advanced garb, Hines is trying to make an *orchestral* translation, with the aid of devices gleaned from Don Redman and Duke Ellington, like high clarinet trios, syncopated brass ensembles.

In Alex Hill's arrangement of *Beau Koo Jack* we can hear a throwback to the King Oliver Creole Band's famous Oliver-Armstrong trumpet duets, here now arranged, expanded, and stylistically updated and played by Shirley Clay and George Mitchell. On *Blue Knights*, an absolutely dreadful side, the model is Guy Lombardo in a typical hotel-band dance tempo, and sporting an abysmal clarinet solo.

While the band doesn't swing and has no cohesive sound or style, Hines himself is all aflutter with ideas and swings well, even in his more hectic pianistic forays. *Grand Piano Blues* has one of those hurtling openings that only Hines could invent and manage to bring off. Moreover, it is a solo replete with constant harmonic variations, additions, substitutions—truly remarkable for their time.

The singular lack of success of these 1929 Victor sides undoubtedly was one reason why nearly three years passed before the Hines band was invited back to a recording studio. Another was the Wall Street crash, four days after Hines's last 1929 session, and the ensuing Depression. When Hines did return to the studios, it was for Columbia's Brunswick label and with a much revamped and enlarged band—Hines having already dropped the tuba and banjo in favor of the more "modern" string bass and guitar. Certain tendencies had begun to crystallize: a penchant for bright tempos and a hard, clean, urgent ensemble sound, surely a reflection of Hines's own sharply defined, flinty piano sonority. It was a sound world quite different from Ellington's, for example, with its warm colors and fascination with varied timbres.

Sensational Mood is a good presentation of the Hines band's abilities at this time. It is one of those "flag-wavers" which every band from the early thirties on had to have in its "book"—especially since the success of *Casa Loma Stomp*. *Sensational* was composed and arranged by Henri Woode in 1931 for Lloyd Hunter's Serenaders, a territory band that worked out of Omaha. Woode was that band's sometime accordionist and full-time arranger. Hines had hired Woode in early 1932, taking over his arrangement of *Sensational* virtually unchanged.

Hines's tempo was quite a bit faster, probably in order to make room for a full solo chorus by the leader (which he surprisingly muffed by playing wrong changes in the bridge). The performance also featured one of Hines's stalwart work horses, trumpeter Walter Fuller, whose imitations of Armstrong—both his playing and singing—were a great entertainment asset to the band. The later ensemble choruses in *Sensational*, sparked by Quinn Wilson's bass, display the kind of up-tempo rhythmic drive that became the hallmark of the Hines band early on.

That the band was still not very disciplined musically is clear from their first attempt to record another Woode arrangement, *Blue Drag*. Even Hines is caught napping. After contributing some dazzling interjections behind a brief trombone solo, Hines gets completely lost in the fifth through eighth bars of his solo. The clashes between him and Lawrence Dixon's guitar are painful, as Hines fakes his way through these four measures. Then, as if furious with himself, he blurts out a series of angry, sharply attacked major seventh dissonances (Ex. 6). Badly out-

Ex. 6

of-tune whiney saxes and ragged blary brass all point to the fact that the piece was woefully under-rehearsed and indicate why Columbia rejected it. (It was not a particular service to Hines to have it issued in the recent Time-Life *Giants of Jazz* series.)

In 1933 Hines was able to add two strong voices to the band: Jimmy Mundy, tenor sax and chief arranger, and Trummy Young, trombone (whom we have already met in the discussion of Lunceford).[13]

Mundy's *Take It Easy* and *Cavernism*, both recorded in 1933, were significant additions to the Hines band's repertory. Indeed, *Cavernism* represented a major creative breakthrough for the band, determining its future style for many years to come. Firmly in the Redman tradition, developed by the latter with the Henderson and McKinney's Cotton Pickers orchestras, Mundy's arrangements were more sophisticated (and more modern) than any Hines had had access to thus far, without squelching any of the rough excitement and rhythmic energy the band had. Fuller contributed good well-planned solos in the Armstrong manner, while Hines urged the band on with his scampering octave obbligatos and irrepressible solos. An unusual contribution to *Cavernism* is Darnell Howard's violin solo.[14] With Hines for once subdued in the background, the passage sounds for

13. It is interesting to note that Young played brilliant, often gutsy trombone with Hines but was pretty much relegated to novelty vocals and manneristic "humorous" trombone solos in his Lunceford years.

14. The B take, reissued on Epic LN 3223, is much the better of Howard's two improvisations, the A take sounding rather uncertain and quite out of tune. Howard was an interesting, though now unfortunately disregarded, figure in jazz. His fascinating career as a violinist began in Chicago around 1912, continued with W. C. Handy's orchestra (with whom he recorded in 1917) and Charlie Elgar's Creole Orchestra. Taking up the clarinet and alto saxophone (while still retaining the violin),

all the world like one of the early recordings of Bob Wills and the Texas Play-boys. There is little doubt that Wills heard *Cavernism* over the radio, since Hines for many years had a nightly broadcast from the Grand Terrace over a nationwide NBC network hookup, and *Cavernism* was one of the band's big hits.

So was *Rosetta*, a lovely ballad composed by Hines and Woode. It was so successful that Columbia Records had the piece recorded in two versions, one purely instrumental, the other with a Valaida Snow vocal, and then issued all four takes cut at the session. The instrumental version, especially take D, is superior and offers a fine example of the kind of quality the Hines band was beginning to achieve. The arrangement was by Cecil Irwin and featured solos by Fuller, Hines, and Simeon on alto. Hines, who adored this song, is in an exuberant joyous mood, prancing along in one of his more explorative solos. Howard has a full chorus too, abounding with elegant turns and lithe, florid lines. Leading into the bridge, Irwin's gently punching muted brass ensembles jolt the ears with a surprise $C^{\flat5\flat9}$ dominant chord—a harmonic rarity then which even Ellington had not yet broached.[15] But above all it is the rhythm section that comes in for high praise on *Rosetta*. Notice its wonderfully modern swing, particularly after Hines's solo chorus. In Lawrence Dixon and Quinn Wilson, Hines had a fine rhythm guitarist and bassist. Both were superb musicians, also contributing excellent arrangements to the band's book. But above all, there was Wallace Bishop, one of the many unsung drummer heroes of the swing era. His great sensitivity and taste, as well as a buoyant sense of swing, contributed cru-cially to the special rhythmic feel of the Hines band. Bishop was steady as a rock, an absolute requisite for any drummer that would presume to accompany an Earl Hines in his wild rhythmic flights. Here, on *Rosetta*, Bishop supplies a happy bouncing swing using just snare drum and hi-hat cymbal, with but the subtlest of accents on 1 and 3—a figure Jo Jones was to make famous with Basie a few years later.

Two other titles from this period will interest us. *Bubbling Over*, the first arrangement by Hines's guitarist Lawrence Dixon, is a fluent, fast-paced, effer-vescent piece much in the manner of Moten's *Toby*, released about nine months earlier and by then known to all young black musicians and arrangers. Dixon's framework, truly "bubbling over" with rhythmic excitement, is an ideal setting for a series of virtuosic solos, especially by Hines, but also Trummy Young's and Darnell Howard's (on alto). The performance is not a total success, however, partly because Walter Fuller's and Cecil Irwin's contributions (on trumpet and clarinet respectively) are flawed, and partly because, the solos do not—as they

---

Howard then toured with James P. Johnson's Plantation Days orchestra in Europe, and played with Teddy Weatherford (Hines's great pianist rival) in China. After working with King Oliver and most of the busy Chicago theater orchestras, Howard joined Hines in 1931, playing clarinet, alto and violin for him until 1937, after which he went on to lead his own group in the Chicago area. He worked with one of Hines's 1950s' combos, and he died in 1966.

15. This bit of daring harmonic spice was eliminated on the vocal version—undoubtedly considered to dissonant for broader consumption—and also on Quinn Wilson's re-arrangement of *Rosetta* a year and a half later.

do in *Toby*—form a cohesive series of statements that not only relate to each other but to Dixon's compositional frame. But *Toby* was a fine model to emulate, and *Bubbling* helped to point the Hines band in the right direction.

The same can hardly be said for *Blue* (early 1934). This side features two strange anachronisms. One is bassist-arranger Quinn Wilson's odd idea of using his tuba not in its traditional "oom-pah" role, but as a fourth sustained voice with three saxophones, an idea that Gil Evans was to use with great effectiveness in the Miles Davis Nonet fifteen years later. It might have worked if Wilson had blended better with the saxophones, but his vibrato-y imitation of Lombardo saxophones *(on the tuba!)* more or less precluded that.

Even more disconcerting is the vocal contribution by Herb Jeffries—here in his recording debut. The problem is that he is totally unrecognizable. Jeffries, who was later known as a deep-voiced baritone, especially through his hit *Flamingo* with Duke Ellington, here on *Blue* sings in a whimpering crooning style that is a cross between Rudy Vallee and Bing Crosby. Such was the pressure on black singers, especially males, to adopt the prevailing white vocal mannerisms, that they were literally compelled to deny their own vocal identity, distorting it to fit some preconceived popular norm. (Hear also Hines's trombonist William Franklin in the band's 1929 recordings, singing inane popular songs with a purposely tinny, reedy voice, sounding like any one of a hundred early white radio singers.) A similar fate to that of Jeffries here in 1934 befell the young Joe Williams in his recording debut with Andy Kirk's band in 1946, where he too is virtually unrecognizable. The only two black male 1930s' singers who somehow were able to resist these pressures and consistently retain their identity were Paul Robeson and Cab Calloway.

Harlem Lament (also from 1933), on the other hand, is remarkable for one of Hines's most spectacular solos from this period and for Quinn Wilson's exceptional arrangement. Spare and lightly scored in the first part, Wilson contrasts this with an unusually compact, tightly voiced full ensemble in the final chorus, where the admixture of trumpets, trombones, and saxophones is so well blended that one can barely distinguish the various choirs.[16]

Hines's solo for *Harlem Lament* is a dizzying and dazzling virtuoso performance. As remarkable as *Weather Bird* was for its time (and for a twenty-two-year-old), *Harlem* shows us Hines in his first real prime. Since in the coming years Hines's arrangers—apparently with his acquiescence—were to encroach more and more on his solo space (despite the fact that Hines was the star of the Grand Terrace shows), it will be rewarding to look at this glittering example of Hines art in some detail.

For all its speciality, it is typical Hines, particularly in respect to the amount of material presented. Hines compresses more ideas into a 32-bar solo than most pianists can manage in an entire evening. As in a perfectly trained race horse, Hines's capacities are at all times working at maximum speed, double that of

---

16. This was a relatively new concept of jazz orchestra scoring that went against the prevailing Redman-Henderson concept of choir-separating call-and-response orchestration.

most musicians of his generation. This is true not only in horizontal (linear) terms, but vertically as well. For Hines solos are generally operating on several linear—one could almost say contrapuntal—tracks simultaneously. Melodies and themes, counter melodies, harmonies, and of course rhythm, are all amalgamated in a unique symbiosis that sometimes defies belief. One may marvel at Hines's fingers—pianists have a phrase for this: "his fingers are in his elbows"—but ultimately it is his mind which is to be revered, a mind whose imagination and fertility are seemingly boundless, and which is so healthy that it can transmit its galvanic signals to the fingers in perfect synchronization—i.e. his fingers are in his brain!

Hines is one of those jazz artists for whom slowing down is next to impossible. His razor-sharp mind and nimble fingers function best at high velocity. Like many major jazz virtuosos—Milt Jackson, Parker, Gillespie (in his early days)—Hines creates with the fastest rhythmic units available in a given situation. If a piece is slow, these artists will instantly launch into thirty-second-note runs, or play in double time, often doubling up on that. If it is in a medium tempo, they will break into sixteenths. They are most content—as was Hines—when a piece is in a bright fast tempo, in which they can play eighth notes. Such players will rarely slow down to quarter notes or sustained melodic ideas. It is a certain restlessness (and virtuosity) which they, unlike "classical" players who have to play whatever the composer has written down, can exploit and use creatively.

At the beginning of every solo, Hines is—to continue my earlier metaphor—like a race horse ready to bound out of the starting gate, raring to go—and at top speed. Indeed Hines is virtually incapable of being reined in. Rarely does he state the melody in its original simple form;[17] rarely does he state his re-compositions of themes in the simplest available terms; rarely is he content to work on one idea alone. With the total independence of both hands at his command, Hines is constantly engaging both hands in competitive exchanges or vigorous dialogues. His mind (*and* fingers) are continually driven towards complexity—rhythmic and contrapuntal complexity. His mind works so fast and deeply creatively that the "simple" musical statement bores him, leaves him unsatisfied, unchallenged—all this often to the consternation of his listeners. And perhaps this helps to explain the relative modesty of Hines's public success, compared with, say, an Armstrong or an Ellington. I think John Steiner, noted authority on jazz in Chicago, was quite right when he suggested that if Hines, like Armstrong, had developed at a more moderate pace and had allowed audiences to "catch up with him," as it were, he could have had a success equal to Armstrong's. It is fair to say that Hines also lacked Armstrong's superb gift for *melodic* improvisation—perhaps Hines's only weakness. Except for *Rosetta*, which *is* a beautiful tune of haunting elegance, Hines is not remembered for any striking

17. In this respect and in his penchant for creating entirely new, fast (often double-time) lines on top of the original harmonic progressions, i.e. "changes," Hines was about twenty years ahead of his time, foreshadowing the work of Parker and Gillespie in the mid-forties. Apart from some exterior stylistic differences, the only other difference is that Parker and Gillespie wrote *their* re-compositions down and gave them titles, whereas Hines just played them, tossing them off by the hundreds.

melodic invention (of the quality we associate, for example, with Ellington, Lester Young, John Lewis, or Miles Davis). Hines preferred to work with motivic fragments, tiny thematic cells which he used as building blocks in structuring his solos—a talent with but little mass appeal.

If a Hines solo happens not to occur at the beginning of a performance, ever-ready and irrepressible as he is, he will invariably get in full gear during the chorus prior to his own, embellishing it with his distinctive high-register obbligatos. So, too, in *Harlem Lament*. Particularly felicitous are his graceful sixteenth-note runs high above Charlie Allen's simple muted trumpet statement of the second half of the theme (Ex. 7). Hines is ever the superb accompanist,

Ex. 7

selecting the particular type of ornamentation most suited to a particular solo or ensemble. It is as if he always knows what is needed to round out the musical statement. Depending on the register, sonority, density, and relative complexity of the underlying material, Hines will shape his obbligato improvisations to act as the perfect foil. For example, here Allen's straightforward, unembellished, and slightly old-fashioned theme statement elicits from Hines a need to flesh out the passage. Had Allen played a more rhythmic or agile line, Hines would undoubtedly have complemented it quite differently.

Hines's solo chorus incorporates most of the musical and technical ingredients we have come to expect from him: 1) an inventive restatement or re-composition of the theme, usually at a good trot; 2) building the solo towards a climactic high-point, generally in or near the end of the bridge and overlapping into the last eight; 3) lots of right-hand octaves and tremolos,[18] the latter to simulate the vibrato on a "horn," adding expressive intensity to a longer piano note; 4) dialogue exchanges between both hands; 5) vertiginous careening runs somewhere in the solo; and 6) at solo's end a simplification of continuity to ease things back into the band ensemble's next chorus.

Hines's *Harlem* solo has another element, rare even with Hines, and virtually unknown to pianists before him: his use of dynamics to delineate structure, to distinguish between primary and secondary material. In my notation (Ex. 8) of Hines's solo I have indicated primary material in normal size, while secondary or ornamental figures are notated in smaller cue-sized notations. The corresponding dynamic shadings are given as well.[19]

Various jazz historians have argued for years over the relative merits of different periods in the Hines orchestra's history: 1932-34, 1934–37, 1939–40. My ears narrow the peak period to 1934 (leaving aside the very exciting 1943 band, which I heard in person in Cincinnati but which never recorded). The series of performances recorded during two days in September 1934 documents that the Hines band had assumed, along with Fletcher Henderson and Lunceford, a front leadership position in jazz. A year before Goodman, and two or three years before Basie, it helped usher in the Swing Era. For by mid-1934, the Hines band was hitting its full orchestral stride. Out of ten sides cut in September, four were arranged by Mundy, six by Wilson. Oddly enough, much of the material chosen to be recorded was of an earlier jazz vintage, pieces like Joplin's *Maple Leaf Rag*, Morton's *Wolverine Blues*, Lew Pollack's *That's a Plenty* and the early 1920s' standards *Sweet Georgia Brown* and *Copenhagen*. Moreover, these were not only updated in "modern" swing trappings, but they were juxtaposed with Mundy's newest creations, like *Fat Babes*, *Rock and Rye*, and a remake of two earlier Hines hits, *Rosetta* and *Cavernism*.

These pieces and their performances are never less than good; some are outstanding, not only in terms of solo contributions but in the way they are inte-

18. Hines's right-hand octave tremolo was legendary. Although used a great deal in a variety of older piano styles, especially "barrelhouse," "boogie-woogie," and Kansas City blues piano, the right-hand tremolo is difficult to master, to produce evenly, and from the point of view of endurance requires tremendous physical strength of the hands and fingers. Most pianists can manage such octave tremolos only in short spurts. Tatum, Peterson, Garner, and Hines all had the technique to use this effect at will for whatever duration. But I believe Hines took the Olympic crown in this particular arena when, in a concert at Harvard University in 1972, he played a right-hand octave tremolo which lasted an unbelievable two minutes (two full choruses), while the left hand was carrying on for both hands with not the slightest sense of limitation.
19. It is worth noting that much of Chopin's and Liszt's music was notated by those composers in a similar fashion: ornamental passages, interpolated cadenzas, out-of-tempo embellishments were written in small notation (see above Ex. 5). Although it is not unalterably true in every instance, such passages generally carried with them the implication of being played more lightly or in some sense subservient to the main melodic/thematic material, and in a somewhat freer improvisatory manner.
To really appreciate the immensity of Hines's technical virtuosity, piano-playing readers are urged to try Example 8—at quarter-note equals 120!—on their parlor piano.

Ex. 8

grated into the total compositions. Most of all, they swing beautifully. The rhythm section was at this time as good as any; but, more than that, arranger and rhythm section had found each other at last. For there is no example of successful orchestral jazz in which the rhythm section and the compositional or arranging style can be at odds. In the development of an orchestra, either its particular rhythmic style determines the sound and language of that orchestra (as in the case of Basie), or an arranger (or composer—in the case of Morton and Ellington) sets the character of the rhythm section. One way or another they must come to terms. This had not happened earlier with the Hines orchestra, I suspect because Hines, himself a member of that rhythm section, was such a dominant *musical* personality and years ahead of his time, that it took a long period for them all to come together in a more or less cohesive conception through learning from one another. There is internal evidence in these 1934 performances that Hines, without losing any of his soloistic brilliance, gave the arrangers increasing scope in determining the band's basic orchestral conception.

Gone were the faltering, under-rehearsed, undigested readings of earlier years. In their place were smart, cleanly but excitingly executed renditions of both old and new repertories. Interestingly, Wilson's and Mundy's arranging styles, though similar in basic conception, were quite personal in details, say, of voice leading, section balances, harmonic language, and sonority.[20] Mundy, the younger of the two, was perhaps a little more *au courant* with the newer big-band conceptions developing everywhere, from Henderson to Redman, from Durham to Oliver, from Carter to Gifford—and, of course, Ellington. Mundy's superlative *Fat Babes* is solidly located in the Redman-Henderson tradition, which Goodman was to turn into a national popular style within a year. With a bright energetic sound and an irresistibly positive feeling, *Fat Babes* enframes fine improvisations by Mundy himself, Hines, and a superb laid-back trumpet solo by Fuller. The addition of Trummy Young had so strengthened the trombone section, now three players, that Mundy gave a full "hot" chorus to the trombone trio, still a relative rarity in those days. Mundy also has the trombones adding admirably to the final *King Porter*-like chorus by inspired orchestrational touches: first with shakes (or trills) in their tenor-range riffs, and then, heightening the overall intensity, with open growls—a magnificent and original effect.

A similarly inspired treatment is given to *Copenhagen*. Trummy Young contributes another authoritative and spaciously designed solo, beginning with one of those long lip trills (which he had learned from Benny Morton), and then sounding brashly for all the world like one of Stan Kenton's trombonists of ten years later. Meanwhile, Hines is in one of his most unbuttoned exuberant moods.

20. It is one of the miracles of music that great composers using the same basic pitch materials can create works that sound totally different and could never be confused with one another. Compare Brahms, Tchaikovsky, Dvořák and Schumann. The same basic C major chord, for example, will sound quite different in the hands of these composers, as result of different voicings and choices of orchestration. Similarly with jazz arrangers: Wilson and Mundy, for example, working side by side in the same band, achieved quite different sounding results, despite their using the same basic harmonic/melodic language.

Clearly enjoying not only the music but his ability to try almost anything, he jabs and stabs wildly away at isolated *sforzando* notes, with both hands, always finding the right, nay, *inevitable* follow-up phrases: a master in full command of his craft. Mundy generates a crisp hard-swinging ensemble sound that must have delighted Hines, for it was the perfect orchestral counterpart to Hines's piano. Just before the end, Mundy humorously imitates a record on a juke box stuck in its final grooves—a cute idea which in lesser hands might have appeared gratuitous and disruptive.

In the remake of *Cavernism* we hear an even more aggressive Darnell Howard on violin, exploding with a fascinating double-stop passage at mid-point, and a chime-like vibraphone passage in the coda (undoubtedly played by Hines himself).

Quinn Wilson's arrangements match all this exuberance almost note for note. Hear his marvelously rich voicings throughout, and especially the joyous ride-out chorus at the end of *That's a Plenty*, the band "feelin' no pain," and incidentally feeling no loss of swing, even though, interestingly, Wilson is playing two-beat bass against Bishop's four.

Wilson's and Hines's remodeling of *Maple Leaf Rag* represented a complete departure from Scott Joplin's original. It was, of course, a perfect vehicle for Hines, the young master paying his respects to the venerable ragtime king. Wilson's arrangement uses only three of the four original strains, devoting six choruses to the Trio (C) strain. Wilson recasts Joplin's original form of AABBACCDD into AA BB CCCCCC, with no less than four Hines solos scattered judiciously throughout the performance, just to remind us that Joplin's masterpiece was first and foremost written for the piano. Hines is brilliant, retaining the full effervescence of the piece—and maybe a bit more—while creating a veritable glossary of Hines-isms. Played much faster than Joplin would ever have allowed, Hines offers a passing nod to Joplin's A theme. After that, it's all 1930s Hines, culminating in his last solo in a wild encounter with the *Maple Leaf*'s Trio theme. Hines absolutely dared himself to miss notes as he arbitrarily, and almost viciously, stabs with his left hand at various mid-range notes, eventually accumulating a bizarre chromatic counter-theme out of them, while the right hand keeps merrily pumping out syncopated ragtime figures. Hines in the final eight bars completely knocks the beat around, causing pandemonium with the listener, until bars later we realize he knew exactly what he was doing all along. (I have always felt that Hines turned the beat around here—for the sheer joy of creation—but also as a kind of playful cat-and-mouse punishment of Bishop, who had in an earlier chorus mistakenly played right through one of Hines's 2-bar breaks.[21])

Quinn Wilson's way with *Sweet Georgia Brown* and *Angry* is equally persuasive, the former featuring a delightfully quirky tongue-in-cheek George Dixon trumpet rendition of the famous theme, worthy in its humor and taste of a Sy

21. All reference to Hines's *Maple Leaf Rag* relate to the first take (C9463A), most recently reissued on MCA 1311. The other take, also remarkable, features one of his famous "swirling vortex" passages.

Oliver. Men of Oliver's and Dixon's generation could look at this kind of early repertory not merely as corny, but with a certain distance and bemused respect. Hines is in top form, particularly in *Angry*, with a longer-than-usual rambunctiously stomping solo, both hands elatedly splashing about the piano like a little kid in a bathtub. But the solo's ultimate feat is a daredevil ascending run which in its speed almost defies the laws of acoustics: Hines covers virtually the entire range of the piano in one lightning bolt-like scale, this in two bars. At $\downarrow = 208$, that's about 40 notes in 2.5 seconds of elapsed time! Hughes Panassié once wrote that Hines always "intrigues and even worries the listener, never giving him a second's respite"—or two and a half seconds', for that matter. In truth, listening to Hines is always like standing at the edge of a precipice in a heavy wind.

Hines enjoys taking chances. He is among a tiny handful of players[22] who are incapable of playing "wrong notes" because any such note is immediately turned into a "right" note by what they do with it and after it. It is nothing for Hines to let one of his hands leap onto some distant unknown key, and instantly, should it be "wrong," invent a miraculous recovery. Leonard Feather found the most apt cognomen for Hines and his ability to work his way out of his own traps: "the Houdini of jazz piano."

But Hines was apparently less successful in evading the entrapments of commercialism. Until now, much of the repertory that Hines was obliged to absorb into the Grand Terrace programs—inane pop songs and novelty tunes of the day—had only sporadically gotten to discs. But by 1935 second-rate material began to crop up in the recordings, presenting vocal groups like the Palmer Brothers, and ever more frequently Armstrong caricatures by Walter Fuller. The songs themselves were either totally unredeemable, like *Rhythm Lullaby*, or were arranged and played in a lackluster, more commercial way: *Disappointed Love*, for example, with its vulgar bumps-and-grinds drumming, or a remake of *Blue*, with its miserable intonation and Omer Simeon getting lost in the changes. The most telling evidence that something in the band's musical policy had changed is the absence of Hines solos. It is as if he didn't want to be associated with these trivialities. When he did solo, it was usually brief, unspecial, and at times even meandering (as on *Japanese Sandman*). Still, there are moments: Mundy's tenor and Trummy Young's yearning trombone on *Disappointed Love*; the brass section's terrific attack at the end of *Bubbling Over*, urged on by Bishop's fantastic drumming—it was to be his last recording date with Hines—and Howard's burning clarinet wails overhead.

To what depths of repertory the Grand Terrace shows had sunk is painfully audible on a recently issued broadcast air check from this period. The recording directors at Decca must not have been too thrilled either, because after the February 1935 date no recording sessions were forthcoming until two years later. A significant personnel change had taken place in the interim. Cecil Irwin had died in an automobile accident and was replaced seven days later by the talented reed man and arranger, Budd Johnson. Johnson, a Texan, who joined Hines at

22. Dizzy Gillespie, Erroll Garner, Lester Young are a few more.

age twenty-five, had grown up with all the great Southwestern territory bands—
Alphonse Trent, Troy Floyd, Jesse Stone, Terrence Holder, Coy's Happy Aces,
as well as a short stint with Louis Armstrong in 1933. He learned many of his
arranging skills from the versatile Stone, one of the most gifted but little known
musicians in the long history of jazz.[23]

Johnson, in an interview with Frank Driggs,[24] attests to the fact that when he
joined the Hines band it "didn't always seem to click, and they were out of
tune." Moreover, still struggling with repertory problems, the material recorded
in the late thirties was at best uneven, eliciting less than enthusiastic performances from the band, often with a curiously old-fashioned beat and rhythm.
(Hear, for example, the too gemütlich Rhythm Sundae and the somewhat
inspiration-less Inspiration.) Apparently the band was catering to a more commercial dance market. As a leader Hines himself seemed to have lost interest in
the band and to have delegated more and more decisions (of repertory and personnel) to Johnson; and as a player he seemed to have lost a lot of his drive and
inventiveness. Surely the repetitious chain of diminished chords on Ridin' a Riff
is not worthy of Hines, and at the end of Hines Rhythm he bogs down entirely.
Moreover, his solo role was now significantly reduced.

Even a well-constructed solo, as the one on Pianology, is quite conservative
and "held-in," with none of the usual surprises. The record is notable, however,
for an excellent solo by Budd Johnson, who, already an admirer of Lester Young,
was bringing the first influence of that "modern" style to the Hines band. The
Quartet side, Honeysuckle Rose, on the other hand, is marred by the lack of a
bass,[25] and Hines does nothing to compensate for the missing harmonic foundation. Concentrating mostly on the upper range in his right hand, the performance has a curiously unbalanced, top-heavy effect.

All in all, Hines and the band had lost a good deal of their former spirit and
were no longer at the cutting edge of the music. No wonder a Metronome readers' poll in 1938 voted the Hines band seventy-ninth place.

Budd Johnson did not sit idly by. As Hines's surrogate director he worked hard
to raise the band's deteriorated playing standards, as well as the quality of its
repertory. The former was easier to achieve than the latter. If one can judge by
a single broadcast performance, the aforementioned air check reveals that the
band could still play on occasion with a degree of precision and ensemble balance, even if the effect is rather on the mechanical and technical side. Its swing
was of a kind which by then (1938) any number of bands could produce. Solos,
though of good caliber, were generally too brief to make any kind of meaningful
statement. This was a function of the prevailing swing style which was affecting
everybody, with more and more emphasis on arranged ensembles and ever less
room for improvised solos. There are a few exceptions, of course. On the Grand
Terrace broadcasts one can hear good solo outings by Budd Johnson and his alto

23. See below, Chapter 8; also Early Jazz, 288–91 especially.
24. Budd Johnson, Part II; Jazz Review, January 1961.
25. The Hines Quartet consisted only of two rhythm, piano and drums, plus Omer Simeon on
clarinet and Budd Johnson on tenor.

colleague Leroy Harris. Also on *St. Louis Blues* there is an interesting series of "fours," as three of the Hines trumpeters divide two blues choruses among them. The sequence is Harry Jackson (who had temporarily replaced Fuller), twenty-five-year-old Ray Nance (with plunger and growl), and twenty-one-year-old Freddy Webster (with the strange notes). These tracks also show how much Hines as pianist needed to be challenged, either by challenging material or by inventing challenges himself. The very essence of his music-making demanded a high order of complexity; when it was too easy, too simple, he almost couldn't function creatively and fell into clichés.

Under Johnson's watchful care, the band reached one more high period by mid-1939. Although better known for a modest pastiche called *Boogie Woogie on St. Louis Blues*—a hit record that made the 1940 Hines band popular even in the East (in a crowded field now populated by the Goodmans, Millers, Dorseys, Basies, and Luncefords)—the real achievements of the band were centered in a number of fine Johnson compositions and arrangements, recorded in New York in July 1939.

The two most successful pieces were *G. T. Stomp* and *Grand Terrace Shuffle*, the former the result of a head arrangement which Hines and Johnson helped put together and which served as a show finale. Its final inexorable building $B^\flat$ pedal point, ending in a brass pyramid, topped by a high $E^\flat$, was ideal for getting the dozen or so girls off the stage and up the stairs on either side of the bandstand. As Hines once put it, "All that brass behind them really made them jump." A briskly paced riff piece, *G.T.* also featured Hines in a nimble-fingered solo backed by drummer Alvin Burroughs, the newest member of the band. (As an important member of Walter Page's Blue Devils in the late twenties, Burroughs's sharp cymbal work can be heard to good effect on that band's *Squabblin'.*) Hines, in a gay and cheery mood, is wittily accompanied by Burroughs's delightful cymbal chatter, eventually breaking into a full stop-time chorus for the drums, obviously a studio re-creation of the chorus line's tap dancing.[26]

Grand Terrace Shuffle, an even more ambitious piece, was played with clean incisive ensemble swing. For it Johnson composed a 4-bar saxophone ensemble riff so close to *One O'Clock Jump* as to border on the plagiaristic (Ex. 9). But

Ex. 9

(The example represents only the top melodic line)

26. The simple ♪ ♫♫ ♪ ♫♫ figure Burroughs plays behind Hines's solo (on take 1), a figure also much favored by Gene Krupa, is precisely the figure Schubert uses in his great C major Symphony (last movement) in the violins. When played with a crisp rhythm, against Schubert's pizzicato basses and cellos—the closest thing in the early classical repertory to a "walking" bass line—the effect is startlingly like swing era jazz.

Johnson's solo chorus is the major contribution. Economically constructed, somewhat in the manner in which Prez would unfold a solo (although with different note choices, and without Young's special melodic gift), Johnson works with only two or three motivic fragments (Ex. 10), varying them slightly and placing them, like Prez, in different contexts in the phrase structure. The piece ends with chime-like notes in the piano, an idea Hines had used several times before (ever since 1933 in *Cavernism*).

Ex. 10

Even more Prez-like are Johnson's two solos in XYZ, in which Quinn Wilson's old-fashioned slap bass is an anachronistic intrusion on an otherwise "trying-to-be-very-modern" performance.

Piano Man was a Grand Terrace production number featuring Hines in an extended solo spot. Introduced by the players' singing in unison (à la Tommy Dorsey's *Marie* hit), Hines makes this trite device palatable by embellishing it with graceful eighth-note garlands—reminding us (perhaps too much) of Teddy Wilson. But after that, in three successive choruses, it's all Hines. The second is a brilliantly confident excursion in stride piano, the left hand leaping infallibly at the brisk tempo of $\downarrow$ = ca. 276.

Hines was clearly in good form during this visit to New York, which also saw him cut two solo sides for the recently founded Blue Note label. (How he was able to do this while under contract to Victor remains a mystery.) Here we sense that Hines relished his moment of freedom away from the band. He withholds nothing. Indeed, *The Father's Getaway*—and it really was that—is a veritable torrent of ideas. Originally recorded in a 12-inch format, it gave Hines a little more room to stretch out. The carefree Waller-ish opening stanza hardly prepares the listener for the almost zany doings that are to follow. The last two-thirds of the performance are madcap reveling in pianistic and creative virtuosity. The entire litany of Hinesian tricks is paraded before our ears, never missing a beat. At times the performance appears to be on the verge of falling apart structurally. But like Houdini, Hines always manages to extricate himself in the nick of time. Giving cohesion to the overall performance is a pedal-point passage Hines stumbled onto early in the piece, "worrying" it through several times more, until ultimately he develops it into a remarkable 16-bar argument between both hands. The left hand sets up the pedal-point trill, while the right hand launches into a 16-bar chain of arhythmic chord punctuations that actually, one realizes in retrospect, also produce a melodic line, albeit somewhat fragmented. In the coda, Hines finally does tire and, unable to extricate himself from a series of wandering modulations, eventually gives up and with a graceful *ritard* comes to a gentle rest.

We shall remember that trill passage, because in the second Blue Note side, *Reminiscing at Blue Note*, Hines takes up the same idea again, only this time reversing the roles for both hands. Now the right hand sustains an octave tremolo while the left hand punctuates with disjunct tenths. As the title suggests Hines is in a reminiscent mood, the whole piece being a kind of collage of remembered tunes and snatches of familiar pianisms. Fats Waller, James P. Johnson, Clarence Williams, even early Hines, parade before us in a contented and carefree musical kaleidoscope.

But apart from such relatively rare exceptions, the late-thirties period saw Hines temporarily give up his own pianistic identity, opting for a simpler style, one with which Teddy Wilson had gained considerable popularity. The irony of this, of course, was that Wilson had been strongly influenced by Hines. However, lacking Hines's prodigious technical skills, Wilson had settled for a more flowing, simpler idiom. On many Hines sides from 1938 to the mid-forties, we hear him frequently in this Wilson vein—sometimes even approaching the sparser simplicities of Basie, as on *Windy City Jive* and *Swingin' on C*—eschewing both complexity and surprise.

In 1939 the Hines band acquired a musician who was to have a major influence on the future of jazz: Billy Eckstine. He was not only a singer of remarkable vocal endowments, but, as a bandleader, he was to provide a musical haven for quite a number of players who figured prominently in the bop movement. Nine years Hines's junior, Eckstine became a major commercial asset for the Hines band, representing at the same time a younger infusion of talent. Indeed, the Hines orchestra continued to be a training ground for the upcoming generation of players. Hines always had a fatherly attitude towards young talent. Moreover, unlike the more famous and richer Ellington, Basie, and Lunceford bands, with their stable personnel, the Hines band's personnel was more transient. By 1944 it had temporarily harbored a number of future boppers and transitional figures, among them, of course, Dizzy Gillespie and Charlie Parker, as well as trumpeters Benny Harris and Freddy Webster, trombonist-arranger Gerald Valentine, singer Sarah Vaughan, tenor saxist Wardell Gray, bassist Oscar Pettiford, and trombonist Benny Green.

Eckstine was a big success with Hines's black audiences and he provided the organization with at least one major hit record, the 1940 *Jelly, Jelly*. Part of its success must certainly have stemmed from the simplicity of treatment: six uncluttered choruses of blues, three of them vocal stanzas by Eckstine, his young voice richly expressive, backed by guitarist Hurley Ramey's wailing double stops; and to climax the performance broadly sustained full-orchestra blues riffs, urged on by Budd Johnson's magnificent New Orleans style clarinet wails. The performance is marred by questionable intonation in the final chorus and in Scoops Carey's solo, otherwise sounding with its whitish disembodied tone for all the world like a premonition of Ornette Coleman.

This simplified blues style—quite different from Basie's of that time—was pursued in several other pieces, most notably *Stormy Monday Blues* of 1942, another big hit for Eckstine. Skeeter Best's guitar weavings had now replaced Ramey's, and the big-band finale of *Jelly, Jelly* had been expanded to exploit the solid high-note abilities of trumpeter Shorty McConnell. As the band found its blues groove under Eckstine's influence (reflected as well in hard box-office terms), and in general slowed down its tempos and simplified its style, it found a broader audience. Moreover, now freed of its Grand Terrace obligations, it was no longer confined to a show format (often unsuited to non-visual recordings). Its repertory became more that of the typical early forties' big band: jump or swing instrumentals (which more and more people were content to simply listen to, crowded around the bandstand), dance numbers, and, of course, lots of ballads for slow cheek-to-cheek dancing—but in the Hines case with a healthy admixture of blues. Hines's arrangers Bob Crowder and Gerry Valentine found what I have always considered a beautifully congruous accompanimental style for these urbanized blues—the blues elevated to the level of the American art song. Eckstine may have moaned occasionally, but he never shouted the blues; he *sang* them with that rich throbbing baritone voice. This new kind of blues-singing—so different from Rushing's or Joe Turner's, Big Bill Broonzy's and Muddy Waters's—needed a different more sophisticated instrumental background. The Crowder-Valentine formula was quite perfect. From the first days I heard it in 1943–44, it seemed to me the ideal match: warm, sensual, sustained saxophone harmonies, organ-like, under the voice, and in the brass, lean virile unison "responses" to the singer's "call." Above all, it is a poignant sound, which clings to one's memory, a sound which Eckstine perpetuated in his own band of 1944–47, and which Dizzy Gillespie and Gerald Wilson then adopted in turn in their mid-forties' orchestras. Curiously, other mid-forties' bands did not emulate this style, probably because they thought it too simple and its blues orientation too old-fashioned, and preferred instead the new bop virtuosity as championed by Woody Herman's First Herd and Stan Kenton. The style did find its way eventually, though somewhat transmuted, into the Basie band—but that was many years later.

Still, the Hines band's discovery of the blues came a few years too late. While by late 1940 a new Hines orchestra with a revamped younger personnel had in fact emerged, it had also lost its major asset: Hines. The arrangements again seemed to have less and less room for the leader. Further, his solo work had become quite simplified; and while the new orchestra gained in technical skill and precision, it also lost something in expression and depth of feeling. In short, it sounded more or less like a dozen other cleanly playing swing era bands. Its musical arteries were hardening; its musculature, which had once been youthfully taut and lean, was now stiffened and atrophying. Clearly, an infusion of sorts was needed. It came to some extent, as mentioned, with the influx of the younger talent, but apparently a little too late and not fully appreciated by Hines. Though the Hines band, particularly the 1943 version, had a youthful excitement about it, a fresh modern sound, somehow it had lost its overall direction and momentum.

Not having the composer-arranger talent of an Ellington or a Henderson, for example, and lacking the clear vision of how the band should sound that, say, a Basie or a Webb had, Hines failed to exploit the talents of Budd Johnson, who probably had the ability to forge a distinctive orchestral conception, but was never really encouraged to do so (as Sy Oliver had done for Lunceford). Similarly, Hines also failed to exploit fully the creative contributive talents of Parker, Gillespie, and Gray, not knowing how to integrate their special talents into a cohesive distinct style. Thus the band foundered on a lack of overall direction, sparked here and there with remarkable talent but unable to coalesce into a single new voice.

It was in this sense that Hines's realistic, unpretentious appraisal of himself as a mere "band pianist" was so accurate. He could front the band and be its star soloist, but he could not create its style and guide its musical growth.

In the end Hines was not able to hold onto his young turks. Budd Johnson left in late December 1942, while Gillespie stayed in the band only half a year (late '42 to early '43); Parker took Johnson's place on tenor, for the first ten months of 1943, his tenure overlapping briefly with Dizzy's; Wardell Gray came in early 1943, as did Sarah Vaughan (doubling as second pianist); Benny Green stayed until he was drafted in November 1943, and Eckstine himself left a few months before that. Incredibly, for a short time, March and April, they were *all* in Hines's band together.

But by mid-1944 most of them—Gillespie, Johnson, Parker, Gray, Vaughan,

plus Valentine, Pettiford, Freddy Webster, McConnell, and Shadow Wilson—
had transferred over to Eckstine's new band. This mass exodus from the Hines
band resulted in two things: 1) Hines immediately returned to a more conservative approach; and 2) whatever style and character the band had achieved by,
say, mid-1943 was carried on more or less intact by Eckstine's orchestra. Precise
documentation of the Hines band's great switch-around is not available, for it
did not record in 1943 and 1944. When we do hear it again on records in late
1945, it had been cleansed of any burgeoning bop influence.

Its fortunes were erratic in the years of the middle forties—Hines even tried a
twenty-four-piece orchestra with an all-girl string section—and eventually, in
1948, Hines threw in the towel. After three years with Louis Armstrong's All
Stars, a group that included Jack Teagarden, Barney Bigard, and Sid Catlett,
Hines struck out on his own again, heading small groups and eventually settling
in the Bay Area of San Francisco, playing in local clubs like the Hangover and
Black Sheep. Though Hines's playing was unimpaired, his West Coast sojourn
in the fifties and early sixties didn't contribute significantly to his career. But a
series of concerts in 1964, arranged by Stanley Dance at the Little Theatre in
New York City, received ecstatic reviews from the critics and was an overwhelming audience success. This remarkable comeback, in effect, launched Hines
on a second major career, mostly as a soloist accompanied by his old friend
Budd Johnson and the young drummer Oliver Jackson. Hines resumed an active
recording career and enjoyed another decade or so of triumphant tours all over
the world, including command performances at the White House, one on the
occasion of Duke Ellington's seventieth birthday in 1969.

One of Hines's greatest triumphs occurred at the 1966 Berlin Jazz Days, when
critic-promoter Joachim Behrendt organized a highly publicized Battle of the
Pianists. Present were Lennie Tristano, Bill Evans, John Lewis, Teddy Wilson,
Jaki Byard, and Hines. The "battle" had been so arranged that each player would
play one or two numbers alone, then be joined by another player in a duet,
including, of course, exchanges of choruses and "fours." The second player would
then take over alone, only to be joined by the third pianist in duet, and so on
until all had been engaged in duels. As fine as everyone's playing was that afternoon in the Philharmonie, with audiences seated in the round almost as in a
Roman amphitheatre, Hines simply outplayed everybody. The losers' defeat was
almost humiliating. Hines, the last to enter the arena, parodied almost everybody who had previously played while still remaining very much himself, and
commandingly trotted out all the old tricks and daredevil bravura with which he
had astonished the world forty years earlier.

Unfortunately that concert was not recorded. But a selection of recordings
made between 1950 and 1970 (some are contained in the already mentioned
excellent Time-Life *Giants of Jazz* series) gives a remarkably comprehensive picture of the mature Hines. *'Deed I Do*, a trio recording with Al McKibbon (bass)
and J. C. Heard (drums) from July 1950; *Blues for Tatum*, December 1956—
Tatum had died in November; *Brussel's Hustle*, a quartet recording with tenor
sax, bass and drums made in February 1958; *Stride Right*, with a Johnny Hodges-

led group in 1966; *Apex Blues*, a trio performance taped at New York's Village Vanguard; and *Blues in Thirds* from January 1970; and the astonishing *Star Dust* (1973) on Audiophile.

Collectively these performances give us the "compleat" Hines. Not quite as turbulent as in his younger years and perhaps not quite as driven to prove his pianistic prowess, Hines had lost none of his skills: his touch, his incisive attack, none of his ability to handle several musical ideas simultaneously, and none of his extraordinary inventiveness. Indeed Hines's later-period improvisations are apt to touch us more deeply. Their content was more profound; there was more humanity in his playing. Listen to the deeply felt bass lines in *Blues for Tatum*, or, later on, the anguished cries (clusters) in the upper register. Or listen to the continuity of his fifteen choruses on *Brussel's Hustle*. Here form and content have become one. Whereas sometimes in the earlier period, when Hines's more extravagantly inventive solos were in danger of becoming an inventory of ef-fects—good taste almost always saved him, though—the later performances re-flected a mature master's synthesis of technique and expression.

Perhaps most astonishing of all was Hines's ability to keep pace with the ever-evolving language of jazz. His ear had an uncanny ability to absorb new melodic or harmonic trends, keeping his playing in the last two decades astonishingly modern. And his absolute ability to mimic other players' styles, whether Garner or Tristano, Brubeck, or Cecil Taylor, or some anonymous modern player, was never used to ridicule. It was once again that all-embracing joy of spontaneous creation that energized Hines's remarkable career.

If in the end we must conclude that it is as one of the two supreme pianists of our time that we will remember Earl Hines, we must also be grateful for his leadership of a band that for a while was one of the finest of the Swing Era, an era which indeed he helped to usher in.

CHICK WEBB

There is something of the African tribal game-rivalries in the "Battles of the Bands" that used to take place in Harlem's Savoy Ballroom in the thirties. They express the same competitive spirit and need to excel one finds (or used to find) in African village rituals and games. Like its ancestral precursors, the Harlem version was based on traditional, precise, and non-negotiable standards, to which both participants and audience were privy. Virtually a test of manhood, these Harlem rites became, with all their friendly rivalry and mutual respect, a criti-cally important aspect of the development of jazz—constantly honing the cutting edge of the music.

From all reports of that glorious past, Chick Webb and his band, the resident group at the Savoy from 1933 until Webb's death in 1939, was the undisputed victor in most of these battles. And listening to his music decades later one can easily see why. For Webb's orchestra was in many ways extraordinary, and its leader was without doubt the finest big-band drummer of his time.

Webb's career demonstrates once again the painful truth that outstanding music rarely coincides with great public success. Though highly regarded by fellow musicians and by his loyal fans at the Savoy, Webb did not enjoy nationwide prominence until he had acquired a girl singer by the name of Ella Fitzgerald and, in particular, her recording of a dreadful bit of silliness called A-*Tisket* A-*Tasket*.[27] Fortunately the inane ephemera of that day are now long forgotten, while we can today still enjoy the quite remarkable recordings of the Webb band at its orchestral best.

Webb was a precocious talent, not only as a drummer but as a bandleader. Though his earliest work is not voluminously documented, what exists is of such rare quality, already so distinctive and mature, that one can readily believe reports of his early acclaim among leading musicians, including the likes of Duke Ellington, Coleman Hawkins, and Johnny Hodges. While still in his teens Webb began attracting attention in New York with his phenomenal percussion talent. Although he fronted bands at various Harlem clubs and dance emporia, Webb was apparently unable to hold on to his best players. With one exception, appropriately named John Trueheart, musicians always seemed to take advantage of Webb's renowned kindliness, leaving him for more lucrative offers elsewhere. Webb's whole early career in New York was marked by such personnel losses: Ellington took Hodges; Henderson hired Bobby Stark away; Ward Pinkett left with Jelly Roll Morton; and Benny Carter took with him half of Webb's Roseland band in 1928 to start his own orchestra. But Webb, undaunted by these setbacks, continued to regroup, until in 1933 the owner of the Savoy Ballroom, Moe Gale, engaged Webb for a long-term residency. Webb thus became one of three bands which were more or less permanent musical fixtures during Savoy's long reign as Harlem's premier ballroom, the other two being (in earlier years) Fess Williams and his Royal Flush Orchestra, and (in the late 1930s) the Savoy Sultans.

Webb's first issued records—an earlier attempt with his Harlem Stompers in 1927 remained unissued—were made with an excellent group called the Jungle Band. Recorded in June 1929, the two titles, *Dog Bottom* and *Jungle Mama*, reveal an orchestra in some ways startlingly ahead of its time, in other respects still a child of the twenties. As captured by the Brunswick engineers on those two days in June 1929, these recordings are phonographic snapshots of an early jazz orchestra in transition. Thoroughly modern are *Jungle Mama's* uncluttered bright sound, its "hip" advanced augmented harmonies in the introduction and mid-point modulation, its saxophone trios (replacing the traditional clarinet trio formula of the previous half-decade), its fast tempo (around $\downarrow = 215$), its sophis-

27. An interesting corroborating statistic is that, once Ella's popularity had been established, the Webb band recorded only sixteen instrumentals, as opposed to fifty-seven vocals (*not* even counting the two dozen titles recorded under her name and the Savoy Eight). The vast majority of these vocals were by Ella, and of dubious merit. Younger readers, who know Fitzgerald only as a single in the fifties and sixties and a magnificent ballad and scat singer performing real jazz material, will have no idea of the idiotic, often trashy songs she sang in her early career.

ticated tag-endings, and not least of all Webb's own spectacular percussion breaks, scattered all through the performance. More traditional were its basic two-beat rhythmic style (as sonorously projected by Elmer James's tuba), along with that, its basically unsyncopated on-the-beat style, its early 1920s' blues orientation (especially on the other cut, the classic *Dog Bottom*), too great a "reliance on a string of short solos sandwiched in between brief ensemble interludes and modulations,"[28] and the old-timey trombone solos by Robert Horton. Neither modern nor traditional but nonetheless highly original is Webb's remarkably discreet drumming on *Dog Bottom*, especially given Webb's outstanding, irrepressible virtuoso abilities.[29]

What is perhaps most striking is how well these pieces are performed. Ensembles are quite clean and balanced, there is considerable rhythmic precision, and there is even an astute use of dynamics, still a great rarity in 1929. Both pieces seem to have been well rehearsed, underscoring, at least in concept, a basic *orchestral* (as opposed to solo) approach in lieu of the more common string-of-competitive-solos format. But these performances have more than mere technical clarity and discipline; they are moving and expressive in a way that transcends both their style and their time. On balance, they look very much forward and retain a freshness that marks Webb's recording debut as a most auspicious one.

In general, Webb maintained these high standards through the years, perhaps more spiritedly and more consistently than any other band of its time. While Ellington and Lunceford may have attained greater individual peaks at moments in their formative periods, they also wandered in some valleys. Webb may not have had the visionary qualities of an Ellington or a Sy Oliver, but his inspirational drumming and high sense of artistic discipline kept his orchestra on an uncommonly high and steady course.

In early 1931 the Webb band returned to the studios to record a stunning *Heebie Jeebies*, Armstrong's old 1926 scat-vocal hit. Arranged by Benny Carter, the performance is distinguished by a modern, buoyant, more linear swing than was current at the time, sporting in addition well-rehearsed ensembles and (with one exception) satisfying solo contributions. (The exception is Shelton Hemphill's unsteady trumpet in the last two choruses.) Outstanding, although flawed by a few cracked notes, is Jimmy Harrison's solo, notable for its modern relaxed swing. This was the pioneer trombonist's last recording date; he died four months later of a stomach ulcer. Virtually as good, though quite different in style, is Elmer Williams's searching beat-freed tenor solo, quite linearly fluent despite its rangy contours. The three-man saxophone section performed splendidly, its sound tinged with Benny Carter's luminous lead alto. It was a young section, collectively barely totaling seventy-five years in all, in its time what Woody Herman's

---

28. See Schuller, *Early Jazz*, p. 271.
29. Brian Rust's discography errs in failing to list a drummer on *Dog Bottom*. Webb may not have played on it but there is definitely a faint four-beat bass drum present, a pattern for which Webb is known to have had a particular penchant.

"*Four Brothers*" section was in the late forties.[30] Notable also are the richly harmonic contributions by that fine pianist, Don Kirkpatrick, a mainstay of Webb's band until 1936.

Crucial to the steady and systematic growth of Chick Webb's band were the talents of Edgar Sampson, who was to Webb what Oliver was to Lunceford and Mundy to Hines. Sampson entered the Webb picture in 1931 as a composer (*Soft and Sweet, Blue Lou, Stompin' at the Savoy, Let's Get Together,* Webb's theme, and *Blue Minor*) and as Webb's chief arranger and second altoist from 1933 to 1936. Other strong additions to the band in 1933 were Sandy Williams, the great trombonist; Taft Jordan, who delivered the seemingly obligatory Armstrong trumpet and vocal imitations (as Walter Fuller did with Hines); and, most importantly, John Kirby. It is fair to say that Webb could swing any band, all by himself, but in Kirby he had an outstanding ally. Kirby, a veteran of the Fletcher Henderson band, played both tuba and string bass, producing a tone as full and firm on the latter as on the brass bass.[31] Curiously Kirby, whose tuba tone was magnificent and who had tremendous flexibility and endurance on that instrument, retained the tuba well into the thirties—as late as the 1934 *Lonesome Moments*—longer than any other major bass player, I believe.

Together with Webb's Baltimore boyhood friend Trueheart, Kirby and Webb formed a rhythm section which could outswing any other. It was characterized by a more driving, forward-leaning swing pulse, as opposed to the more laid-back Basie variety. And it is, I think, a truism, that there is hardly a Chick Webb side (certainly not until the Fitzgerald era, with its commercial tunes) in which that rhythm section isn't a joy to hear. Most of the credit must go to the incomparable Webb himself, but during Kirby's tenure it was a truly invincible section. Any doubting reader should sample *Stompin' at the Savoy, Let's Get Together, Blue Minor,* and the accompaniment to Pete Clark's clarinet solo on *Darktown Strutters' Ball.*

There were also consistently strong contributions by Sandy Williams, a blisteringly "hot" trombonist who had by 1933 fashioned an individual style out of an amalgam of Jimmy Harrison and Armstrong. Fine examples of his art can be heard on *If Dreams Come True, Stompin' at the Savoy,* and *Blue Minor* (Okeh version)[32]. Taft Jordan took over *On the Sunny Side of the Street,* one of his more majestic efforts, capped by a spectacular 2-bar half-valve glissando break, of the kind Armstrong had already perfected earlier. Jordan can also be heard in

30. My reference here is obviously to the Woody Herman band's "Four Brothers" saxophone section of 1949. In its modernity and sonoric blend, Webb's three-man section had much the same kind of class.

31. Because of the great popularity of Basie's rhythm section in the late 1930s, Walter Page was regarded as *the* pre-eminent bass player until Jimmy Blanton came along. However, such an assessment is quite unfair to at least two other players, Kirby and Billy Taylor, who both in their different ways were also influential leaders on their instrument.

32. It is sad to note that Williams, suffering poor health since 1950, had to give up playing and was forced late in life to eke out a living as an elevator operator.

a more modern and personal manner on *Blue Minor*. Reunald Jones, who in
the fifties used to sit unsmilingly in Basie's trumpet section, one hand in his lap,
nonchalantly picking out altissimo lead notes, was a spirited young man of twenty-
four when he was experimenting in Webb's band with eccentric solos somewhat
in the manner of the early Rex Stewart (on *Stompin' at the Savoy* and *Let's Get
Together*).

In late summer 1934, Webb switched to the then quite new Decca label,
staying with that company until his death five years later. Though soon Armstrong-
vocals by Jordan and pop-tunes by the sixteen-year-old Ella Fitzgerald were to
predominate, there was still at first a healthy balance of instrumentals and vocals.

A superior remake of *Blue Minor* offers robustly swinging Sandy Williams,
while *What a Shuffle* and *Blue Lou* bring back Bobby Stark, who had rejoined
Webb after a six-year stay with Fletcher Henderson. His re-emergence was a
welcome relief and foil to Jordan's Armstrong plagiarisms. Although Jordan and
Stark, like all trumpet players in the generation after Armstrong's, were strongly
influenced by him, it is a measure of Stark's strong musical personality that he
could develop his own vision out of Armstrong's language, while Jordan mistook
faithful mimicking for art.

A fine example of Stark's playing can be heard on *Blue Lou*. Here his sinuous
legato style, one of several musical trademarks, gives his solo more than a touch
of mystery—a rare held-back mood in the otherwise very direct, engaging work
of the Webb band.

One should not overlook Elmer Williams, a consistently creative performer
who back in 1934 already played with some of the raspy heat of the 1940s' Ben
Webster. Hear him on *Don't Be That Way*.

A measure of the distance between Webb's band and Benny Goodman's of a
few years later in terms of swing and rhythmic energy can be gained by comparing Webb's original 1934 performances of *Stompin' at the Savoy* and *Don't Be
That Way* with Goodman's 1938 versions. Goodman managed to make both
pieces nationally popular in a way that Webb could not, but at what a price!
Both use Sampson's arrangement, although *Don't Be That Way* was reworked
to accommodate lengthy solo spots for Goodman and that famous pre-*In the
Mood* fade-away ending. Comparison of both bands' versions affords us a dramatic lesson in how interpretation is everything in jazz. The same arrangement,
the same notes can be exciting or vapid, depending on their execution. The gulf
here between Webb and Goodman was a wide one, the former delivering these
pieces with a raw excitement, rhythmic drive (faster tempos, too), and heated
sonority; the latter with a neatly packaged cooled-off sound, bouncing along in
a safe inoffensive manner.

Alas, a similar foreign element—apart from the encroaching commercialism
of Ella's puerile songs—was beginning to infiltrate Webb's orchestra in the form
of Wayman Carver's flute solos and arrangements. The first of these was an
arrangement of Wilbur Sweatman's 1911 *Down Home Rag*. A period curiosity
at best, which presumably was to be an instrumental counterpart to some of

Ella's more cutesy novelty songs, *Down Home* begins with a "classical" woodwind trio of flute and two clarinets, straightfacedly rendering Sweatman's jerky dotted rhythms. Against that opening setting, Elmer Williams's gutsy tenor and Jordan's modern trumpet rips sound oddly out of place. Though Webb and Kirby tried to enliven the final choruses, Carver's inept arrangement was a formidable hindrance.[33]

Fortunately, the increasingly dominant instrumental personality in the band was Webb's. Always the driving force and inspiration for the orchestra, Webb by 1936 was beginning to assert himself more and more as a soloist—in breaks, introductions, and eventually outright extended solos. *Go Harlem, Clap Hands! Here Comes Charlie, Harlem Congo*, and *Squeeze Me* are but a few of the outstanding examples of Webb's percussion artistry. Indeed Webb is virtually the only swing era drummer on whose recordings one can aurally shut out the other instruments and still have a consistently rewarding musical experience. Webb combined what were for that time exceptional soloistic talents with an impeccable sense of time and, above all, an uncanny ability to articulate with total clarity every sound he produced. Besides the technical skills involved, I think his clarity and control of tone are what make listening to Webb's playing such a

33. More of this type of "novelty" arrangement was on the way. Not only Chick Webb and his Little Chicks, with their childish flute-clarinet duet versions of *I Got Rhythm* and *Sweet Sue* (saved only by Webb's flashy hi-hat stop-time choruses), but other swing bands succumbed to a growing trend to "upgrade" jazz with pseudo-classical morsels. It was the old "symphonic jazz" movement of the twenties all over again, only this time promoted not only in terms of big bands but small chamber jazz groups as well. Hardly anybody stayed clear of this influence, which ironically produced a number of substantial commercial hits in the late thirties.

Actually there were two kinds of classical influences: classics popularized and jazzed up (like Rimsky Korsakov's *Song of India*, Tchaikovsky's *Andante Cantabile* from his Fifth Symphony, Mendelssohn's *Spring Song*, Dvořák's *Humoresque*, Liszt's *Liebestraum*, and so on). The other category consisted of novelty pieces with allusions to classical forms, chamber instrumentations, usually with humorously fancy, aristocratic-sounding titles, such as *Minuet in Jazz, In an 18th Century Drawing Room, Reckless Night on Board an Ocean Liner, Careful Conversation at a Diplomatic Function, Symphony Under the Stars, Eight Letters in the Mailbox, Rehearsin' for a Nervous Breakdown, Beethoven Riffs On, Dodging a Divorce, Bach Goes to Town*, etc. Unfortunately these pieces were generally long (and clever) on titles and short on musical substance. Some of the main practitioners of this *ersatz* fusion were the West Indian composer Reginald Forsythe (who even got Benny Goodman, Gene Krupa, and John Kirby to record four sides for him in 1935); the Raymond Scott Quintette, active from 1937 to 1942; Alec Templeton, whose *Bach Goes to Town* and *Mendelssohn Mows 'Em Down* were big hits on radio in the late thirties; Dr. Henry Levine and His Dixieland Octet of NBC's Chamber Music Society of Lower Basin Street, with "Mademoiselle" Dinah Shore as the singer, a group that had a decided Dixieland flavor; New Friends of Rhythm, featuring clarinetist Buster Bailey with a string quartet and harp in such titles as *Heavy Traffic on Canal Street*; John Kirby's Sextet with Charlie Shavers (for more on Kirby see below, Chapter 9), and finally Alec Wilder, whose octets featuring woodwinds and harpsichord continued the lineage of Scott with pieces like *Neurotic Goldfish, Pieces of Eight, Bull Fiddles in a China Shop, Jack, This Is My Husband*, and *The Amorous Poltergeist*.

This genre represented a nearly decade-long trend which fed on two fairly predictable public reactions: one a pretentious effort to hobnob with the "high-brow" classics and "elitist" culture in general, the other an unfortunate but deep-seated need on the part of a large segment of the public to deride and poke fun at classical music and the "serious" arts.

completely satisfying experience. The clarity heightens the expressivity; and one feels that nothing essential is lacking. With most drummers, even the best technicians of that period, one may hear the gestures, the overall shapes; but often the details, especially in fast passages, are lost in a blur of activity. It is Webb's absolute control of *all* aspects of playing that makes his breaks and solos so exciting.

First, his timing was flawless. Even when played at half-speed on a record player—a speed at which rhythmic flaws show up quite clearly—a Webb drum burst is faultless. Second, he had, even at great speeds, the ability to produce each sound, be it on a snare drum, a wood block, a cowbell, or whatever with the maximum and *equivalent* fullness of sonority: in a sense it was the ultimate "democratization" of the drum set, the individual percussion sounds welded into an equal-partnered ensemble. Furthermore, Webb would spend hours fine-tuning his drums to achieve just the right pitch and timbre. His suspended cymbals hung from "gooseneck" stands rather than the customary bolt-on stands, the goosenecks allowing a much purer and richer cymbal sonority. For an example of his tonal control, listen to his breaks on *Clap Hands* or the magnificent bass drum (fourth beat) accents on *That Naughty Waltz*. Third, his "attack" on any given instrument was so precisely timed and sonorous that it—the attack, that is—already defined the duration of each sound. Sounds are never too clipped or too long; they have just the right amount of time to resonate. Examples 11a,b,c, if followed with the respective recording, will help the reader to appreciate Webb's unique technical skills.

Ex. 11a

Clap Hands! Here Comes Charlie

Ex. 11b

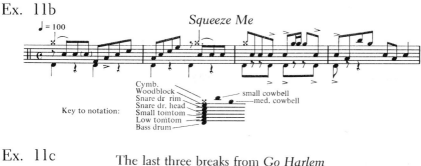

Squeeze Me

Ex. 11c

The last three breaks from *Go Harlem*

Particularly amazing are his solos using a variety of instruments. As can be seen in Example 11b, Webb employs seven instruments—seven timbres—in this short "break": cowbell, cymbal, wood block, snare-drum rim, snare-drum head, two different-pitched tom-toms, bass drum. Not only is Webb moving to each of these instruments at breakneck speed, but each instrument being made of different material—wood, metal, skin—has different response properties. The metal of a cowbell, obviously, has a harder more unyielding surface than, say, a drum skin. That is to say, the drumsticks will rebound from them in dissimilar ways, affecting the attack on the next instrument—one-fiftieth of a second later—unless the player can absolutely control that rebound, *compensating* for the dissimilarity.

This degree of control also enabled Webb to use dynamic nuances and tonal shadings that eluded most other drummers. His crisp yet resonant sound on his instruments, especially snare drum and cymbals, enabled him to generate terrific swing without playing loud, a lesson Krupa, who idolized Webb, never quite managed to learn. Webb could swing lightly, yet with a tremendous inner propulsive energy. And all that, in turn, explains why Webb, although he could be quite the showman (despite his dwarfish crippled appearance), in his own playing at least never needed to exploit showmanship at the expense of musical integrity. Showmanship, to the extent he used it, was but one element among many to be integrated and controlled.

But technique is only one part of the performing totality. In the case of an improviser, there has to be musical invention and a concept of how a solo or a break will fit into the overall work. Here again Webb was unexcelled in his time. He rarely repeated himself, was continually creative, and, most important of all, his solos or breaks never disrupted the overall continuity. One not only feels the

beat pulsating right through them, but the actual figures he chose subtly rein-
forced and amplified the beat; and his breaks flowed in and out of the arranged
ensembles with a seamless sense of inevitability. Webb could also flounder, but
that was very rare (as in the uncertainty at the end of his *Undecided* break or
Spinning the Webb).

Yet even with all these qualities, perhaps Webb's greatest asset, particularly as
the drum-playing leader of a band, was his ability to swing. In countless performances we can hear his inspirational swing feeling, determining, like some great
maestro, the interpretation of the piece, urging the band on to greater heights,
whether in ensemble or solo. Hear his enormous drive especially on *Go Harlem*,
producing a wonderful happy swing feeling on the cymbals; or on *Harlem Congo*
and *That Naughty Waltz*. But sometimes the material defeated even Webb, as
on Larry Clinton's *The Dipsy Doodle* or the "bicycle act" music that is *Sweet
Sue*. In these examples even flawless technique cannot help, because it is superfluous to the content.

By 1937 Ella Fitzgerald, still in her late teens, had become a star of the Webb
band, surpassing even its leader in popularity. Despite the trite material Ella
chose (or was obliged) to sing, her innate talent shone through. Indeed she lifted
these banal songs to heights they did not deserve by her impeccable pitch (ear),
diction, and her even then considerable sense of swing. A song like the 1936 *A
Little Bit Later On* is made almost bearable by Ella's and Chick's combined
talents.

In the main it was the brass soloists who contributed most effectively to these
1937–38 recordings. Again it is Stark who catches the spirit of each piece, as in
his somewhat tortured, growly solo on *Spinning* and his disciplined, well-structured
solos on *Liza*, brilliantly arranged by Benny Carter. Sandy Williams is also still
in top form, especially on *Spinning* and in his lithe swing on *In the Groove at
the Grove*. Meanwhile Taft Jordan had dropped his Armstrong act and was opting for the by now more popular Harry James and Ziggy Elman.

All in all, however, the commercialism that came with Ella's success had
begun to take its toll. By late 1937 a clearly discernible deterioration had begun
to set in. It manifests itself first in the arrangements—especially in the journey-
man efforts of Larry Clinton, Van Alexander, and Tommy Fulford—but also in
the frequently listless performances of the band.

A short-lived positive influence was the fine guitarist-arranger Charlie Dixon,
but I can detect only two of his "charts": the splendid *That Naughty Waltz* and
Squeeze Me. His arrangements are never less than interesting, always exploring
new voicings, instrumental combinations, new textures. *Waltz* is quite unusual
for its emphasis on somber low-register saxophone colors and, in the second
chorus, an uncommon quartet of trumpet, one alto, and two tenors,[34] as well
as many other fine touches.

---

34. I am convinced by the aural evidence of the recording that there were five saxophones on *That
Naughty Waltz*, and that therefore Rust's discography is wrong in not including clarinetist Chauncey
Haughton for the March 24, 1937, date; and that Gabler and Dance on the Decca record jacket are
wrong in excluding Louis Jordan as alto saxophone (Clark being on baritone).

Though the Webb orchestra's recordings lose in quality and rhythmic drive in 1938 and 1939, there is some evidence that its *live* performances continued with undiminished vigor, at the same time featuring mainly its instrumental repertory with only an occasional vocal. Several air checks from 1939 have become available on LP in recent years. They provide telling evidence that the band still could muster a tremendous collective energy, and that Webb himself played with undiminished fervor almost to the day he died. They give some idea of the band's spirit and disciplined energy when they played for a dancing and listening audience, even in wildly jazzed-up versions of *The Stars and Stripes Forever* and *My Wild Irish Rose*. They may also give us some idea how Chick Webb and his band sounded at the Savoy, when they beat *both* the enormously popular Benny Goodman on May 11, 1937, and Count Basie on January 16, 1938.

One of these LPs contains a broadcast taken from the Southland Café in Boston. The date was May 4, 1939. On June 16th the "King of the Savoy," the indomitable "little hunchback" from Baltimore, was dead of tuberculosis of the spine—an incalculable loss to jazz.

MCKINNEY'S COTTON PICKERS

Although the band known as McKinney's Cotton Pickers was already in decline as a major creative force in jazz by the time 1930 hove into sight, it is nevertheless an orchestra whose work in spirit belongs to the thirties and to the Swing Era. Woefully neglected in jazz histories (including my own *Early Jazz*), the Cotton Pickers was one of only a handful of top-notch orchestras during the late twenties, was more consistent than any other orchestra of that time, and in certain respects was not surpassed by any other.[35] Its success can be attributed in large measure to two formidable talents and guiding spirits, Don Redman and John Nesbitt. Until now all the credit for the Cotton Pickers' achievements has been attributed to Redman, but, as the following narrative will show, it was Nesbitt (whose name is virtually non-existent in the jazz literature) who really gave the orchestra its class and artistic consistency. Ellington's compositional gifts and Henderson's unique collection of soloists may have occasionally reached higher peaks of creativity, but for a while at least, they were no match for the MKCP in terms of *consistent* inventiveness and performance standards.

Actually the name McKinney hardly figures in the band's musical achievements, since for most of its existence William McKinney, a drummer by profession, worked behind the scenes as manager and fiscal officer of the orchestra. Although the Cotton Pickers did not begin recording until July 1928, the orchestra's prior history is worth recounting briefly.

It was founded by McKinney and the saxophonist Milton Senior in Spring-

---

35. My own assessment of the McKinney Cotton Pickers in *Early Jazz*, though basically favorable, was somewhat inaccurate because it was based on incomplete aural evidence. Some of the MKCP's finest efforts were not then readily available on recordings—for better or for worse the jazz historian's primary analytic tool.

field, Ohio, around 1923 and initially called the Synco Jazz Band. This name had already been used by another earlier New York group, led by the popular cornetist Jules Levy, and which around 1919 made the transition from primarily ragtime material to a more blues-oriented style. But the name was also similar to that of another group in Springfield, Scott's Symphonic Syncopators, led by the brothers Cecil and Lloyd Scott. When that band left for New York to seek fame and fortune there, McKinney's group suddenly found itself in an uncontested leading position in the Springfield area. As the band grew more in popularity and size, McKinney ceded his drum chair to Cuba Austin, a tap dancer and drummer who was quickly to become one of the band's major musical assets. Having already acquired the services of the very advanced trombonist Claude Jones in early 1925, the band acquired further crucial additions later that year with George Thomas, tenor saxophone (and later the band's most successful vocalist), and the trumpeter-arranger John Nesbitt. In 1924 the band had enjoyed the distinction of playing a command performance in White Sulphur Springs, West Virginia, for the jazz-loving Prince of Wales, the later King Edward VIII of England; and by 1926 the highly successful band leader, impresario, and ballroom owner Jean Goldkette had invited McKinney's Cotton Pickers to fill a long-term residency at the famous Graystone Ballroom in Detroit. Goldkette also had excellent connections with major recording companies, in particular RCA Victor, and in 1928 was able to arrange a recording contract for McKinney's group.

In mid-1927 Don Redman, who had already achieved considerable fame as Fletcher Henderson's chief arranger,[36] was offered the musical directorship of the McKinney band. There is no question that Redman's reputation and skill as a versatile reed man and arranger crucially added to the Cotton Pickers' sense of musical direction and artistic caliber. His seminal work with Henderson had more than prepared him for his new role as musical director. And undoubtedly he found it a pleasure to work with the more willing-to-learn, less temperamental players in the McKinney orchestra.

But the fact that John Nesbitt quickly became the real musical leader of the orchestra is confirmed not only by the evidence of his recordings (as we shall see) but by the account of Cuba Austin. "Nesbitt was making the arrangements and teaching us all how to read."[37] Later in Detroit at the Graystone, where Goldkette had installed "a sort of music school in a locker room," Nesbitt and Redman not only helped their fellow musicians improve their reading skills but also explained and rehearsed their arrangements in almost daily sessions.

The first recordings from July 11 and 12, 1928, are anything but tentative. It is clear that the band had already achieved a distinctive style and concept unlike any other, and within that style a very high performance level, to my knowledge not matched by any other jazz or orchestra of the time. It was a real *orchestra*:

36. *Early Jazz*, 256–67.
37. *Hear Me Talkin' to Ya*, 190.

it had a highly developed sense of ensemble, and in its balanced precision sounded much bigger than its eleven-man personnel would lead one to expect.

Nine sides were recorded in July, and four more in October under the name of the Chocolate Dandies, the arranging chores divided evenly between Redman and Nesbitt. It is quite apparent, however, that Redman, as the titular leader of the band (though it didn't carry his name), was already beginning to concentrate on a more commercial repertory, whereas the instrumentals and straight jazz numbers were Nesbitt's domain. A high percentage of Redman's creative energies was being channeled towards the writing and singing of vocals, novelty tunes, songs which might compete with the big hits of the day (like *Coquette, Nobody's Sweetheart, Four or Five Times*, and *My Blue Heaven*) and established jazz pieces like Morton's *Milenberg Joys* or Spencer Williams's *Shim-Me-Sha-Wabble*. It is to Redman's credit that, at least in the early years, he treated such material with distinction. The wry humor and clownish vocal antics with which he invested these songs, very often in ingenuously disarming "spoken" vocals, were a far cry from the insipid croonings of the period. Nor did Redman and his vocal partners—George Thomas, Dave Wilborn, and Cuba Austin—indulge in the endless Armstrong imitations in vogue then and in the early thirties.

On the other hand, Redman's arrangements are not especially outstanding or imaginative. They are skillful and effective, but rarely original; and then only on the level of small details. Furthermore, since so many of his arrangements here are taken up by vocals, there is little space left for developing arranged ensembles, or solos for that matter. Thus even the best of his work during this period, *Milenberg Joys* and *Shim-Me-Sha-Wabble*, is cluttered and often too fragmented. Despite Cuba Austin's best efforts—and he was a drummer who virtually made it impossible for a band *not* to swing—the ensembles are often disjointed and labored. *Wabble*, for example, is arranged in such a disjunct manner that the band could not maintain any overall continuity. *Milenberg* fares better, partly because longer stretches are devoted to solos (by trumpeter Langston Curl, and Nesbitt and Jones), while other parts of the arrangement exploit Redman's old tried-and-true formula of clarinet trios. He uses these effectively in all three registers of the clarinet, with one especially fetching slidy blue-note low-register break (better played on take 2, the original 78 rpm issue).[38]

Redman's own alto playing vacillated between a stylishly "modern" approach, which he reserved for his intros *(Four or Five Times)* and codas (the closing cadenza on *Some Sweet Day*), and a kind of "vertical" technical style still much beholden to Rudy Wiedoeft and that particular brand of early twentieth-century saxophone virtuosity.

As a composer, Redman's work at this time, excepting his classic *Gee, Baby, Ain't I Good to You* and the Ellingtonian *Blues Sure Got Me* (1930), was embarrassingly plagiaristic. He seems to have been particularly obsessed with Johnny

---

38. This three-clarinet break—or one very similar to it—was to reappear most prominently in Fletcher Henderson's *Down South Camp Meeting* of 1934, a case of the pupil outdoing the master.

Green's *Coquette* and Donaldson's *My Blue Heaven. Cherry* (and the 1930 *Hello*) emulates the former, as *Miss Hannah* ineptly counterfeits the latter. This point needs to be made in view of Redman's rather unfair (because untenable) statement: "Nesbitt was copying everybody else's records."[39] The facts are quite the contrary, at least based on the recorded evidence covering almost three years: Nesbitt was consistently inventive, in his arranging and composing as well as his trumpet-playing. It was Redman who was at this time alarmingly derivative.

As a leader Redman can be faulted for the shoddy material he often had the band record, perhaps due to Goldkette front-office pressures. This tendency, at first moderate and still balanced with fine instrumentals, became a serious problem by 1930, and led not only to the departure of Nesbitt but to a serious decline altogether of the Cotton Pickers. The inevitable commercialism, we have noted with virtually every band, sooner or later was bound to take its toll.

In contrast to Redman's uneven and often only passable work, Nesbitt was astonishingly inventive and consistent. How one wishes that tape recorders existed then, so that even some amateur on-location recording could reveal at least an occasional glimpse of Nesbitt's prior development. All we know about Nesbitt is that he was born in Norfolk, Virginia, around 1900 and, previous to his joining McKinney, had worked with two obscure bands, Lillian Jones's Jazz Hounds and Amanda Randolph's.[40] Where and how he acquired his superior arranging skills, in full cry on these 1929 McKinney recordings, one must leave to conjecture—although I would cite Redman (when with Henderson) and the best of early Ellington as logical influences.

What strikes one immediately about Nesbitt's arrangements is their astonishing inventiveness in the realm of form, both in the large and the small sense, and how economically the various structural elements were integrated. They were not a series of strung-together episodes, but excellent "compositions" in which form and content are blended into one. Moreover, unlike Redman who was quite content to settle most of the time for the standard format of a vocal sandwiched between a first chorus and a cleverly contrived coda, Nesbitt seems never to have used the same form twice. He was constantly searching for and found new ways to juxtapose chorus structures and different types of ensembles and

39. Don Redman (as told to Frank Driggs), *Jazz Review*, Vol. 2, No. 10 (November 1959), p. 10. It is this kind of false "evidence," along with the prevailing wisdom of Redman's virtually unassailable reknown, which also misled me in my discussion of the MKCP in *Early Jazz*. It is true that Nesbitt at first, like most young arrangers, learned his craft by imitating the work of others. But it is also true that he soon began—indeed at the instigation of none other than Don Redman—to create his own arrangements and orchestral compositions.

40. Nesbitt's shabby treatment in the reference literature is quite unforgivable. Neither Feather's *Encyclopedia* nor the usually reliable Kinkle *Complete Encyclopedia* mentions Nesbitt at all. Panassié's *Guide to Jazz* gives him only the briefest of condescending paragraphs. Other books, like Ramsey and Smith's *Jazzmen*, Hodeir's *Jazz: Its Evolution and Its Essence*, Feather's *The Book of Jazz*—to mention only a few among many—also fail to recognize Nesbitt's very existence. Others who do, like McCarthy in his *Big Band Jazz*, or Hsio Wen Shih in his superb essay "The Spread of Jazz and the Big Bands" in *Jazz*, edited by Hentoff and McCarthy, either mention Nesbitt in passing or confuse some of Nesbitt's work for Redman's.

textures, in the process advancing some rather unconventional, even daring, solutions. But what is really astonishing is that his arrangements almost always swung beautifully. The musicians felt comfortable in them. Part of Nesbitt's talent lay in the ingenious way in which he linked and overlapped choruses, the one leading logically to the other, material from the tail end of one providing the connecting link and forming the basis for the next.

Put It There, a composition by the McKinney's pianist Todd Rhodes, Nesbitt's first recorded arrangement, is a brilliant example of his art and craft. The first sounds instantly signal the unusual: an introductory motive which is shifted rhythmically one beat forward, and which is used twice more during the piece as transitional material between choruses (Ex. 12). This re-use of introductory material as a formal concept Nesbitt may have learned from Redman, who often spent much of his best efforts on intros and codas, and who had perfected this device in his three years with Henderson. But Redman never dared to use an off-the-beat intro as in *Put It There*; nor had he ever thought of exploiting the odd rhythmic characteristics of such an intro so efficiently in the body of an arrangement. As Example 12 shows, by shifting the beat forward, the actual third beat of the phrase (or motive) lands on the second beat of the bar. This second-beat accent Nesbitt uses throughout the arrangement, a kind of shifting of the bar line which became a favorite device of Nesbitt's, as we shall encounter it again in most of his other work.

Ex. 12

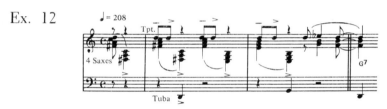

Rhodes's composition is in itself unconventional. It consists of one 12-bar strain in a fairly common progression of V-I-V-I-IV-V-I, but has appended to it—whether by Rhodes or Nesbitt is impossible for me to determine—the afore-mentioned 2-bar introductory phrase, thus making it, as performed, a 14-bar structure. That these two bars may have been an integral part of the composition is indicated by Rhodes's own use of them in his two solo choruses. On the other hand, that they were expendable and not finally an integral part of the piece is argued for by Nesbitt's elimination of them in the fifth and seventh choruses and by something even more inventive. Namely, that the little "intro" phrase is used by Nesbitt in two different configurations: one rhythmic, the other more melodic. Nesbitt alternates these frequently, his choice related either by contrast or by identity to the 12-bar chorus to follow. (See Fig. 1) Nesbitt's use of the melodic intro-variant has the effect of becoming a part of the 12-bar strain, thus subtly elevating what at first appears to be a dispensable brief introductory phrase to the level of the theme itself. Moreover the three appearances of the "melodic" version are themselves subtly varied each time.

Fig. 1

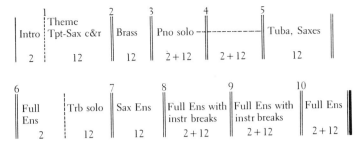

Already this much shows the work of a master, one for whom no detail is insignificant or unworthy of further use or development. But there is much more. The theme distribution (in 10 choruses), as shown in Figure 1, reveals more of Nesbitt's searching imagination. The first chorus is set in the traditional call-and-response pattern, in this case three brass responding to four saxophones. The brass carry the second chorus alone, followed by two unaccompanied piano choruses by Rhodes. A magnificent grace-note harrrumph from Escudero's tuba brings the band back for chorus number five. Here the saxes play a theme variant, while the muted brass punctuate every bar with an accented chord on the second beat. Meanwhile every four bars the second tenor imitates the tuba's harrrumph.

A repeat of the "rhythmic" variant of the introduction now leads to Jones's rhythmically jumpy trombone solo, followed by a contrastingly more linear and chromatically ranging saxophone ensemble chorus. The next two choruses, introduced by the "melodic" version of the intro, are broken up into 2-bar phrases, in the first instance piano alternating with the "horns," in the second a four-way solo sequence: alto, trombone, trumpet and tenor. The last four bars of these choruses are given over to the full ensemble, in each case linking up perfectly with the "intro" phrase. In chorus eight the two bars allotted to the ensemble are further broken up between brass and reeds, providing still more textural and timbral variety (Ex. 13).

Ex. 13

(Note how perfectly the brass elide into the saxophones trilled chords.) Amazingly Nesbitt's mosaic fragmentation does not seem to hamper the soloists and the overall rhythmic flow. Even the brief 2-bar solos link up in some coherent alchemistic way with their successors, thus creating a single musical thought.

The off-the-beat "rhythmic" "intro" variant initiates the final ensemble chorus, again a variation on the main theme, this time with open brass in syncopated punctuations above organ-like sustained saxes.

Even in this synoptic outline one can appreciate Nesbitt's extraordinary imagination and talent. He produces an amazing variety of compositional elements, worthy of the best of Morton and Ellington.

The performance of *Put It There* is, with a few minor exceptions, also equal to the arrangement's demands. The weakest moment is Rhodes's badly lurching and harmonically rather muddy piano solo. Jones's trombone solo is much beholden to Snub Mosley's extravagant style as featured with Alphonse Trent's band in those years. One should note, however, that Jones's chorus is identical on both takes of *Put It There*, indicating a previously worked out, memorized solo.[41] Indeed, all other solo contributions, *except* Nesbitt's, are also identical

41. A brief digression on the subject of "improvisation" in early jazz is perhaps in order at this point. With the issuance of literally thousands of alternate takes on LP in recent years, it has become abundantly clear that, especially in the earlier jazz decades (until the bop period), the vast majority of so-called "improvised solos" were really not improvised at all. That is a point others as well as I have been making for years, much to the annoyance of those who believe that jazz is demeaned by anything less than "pure" and total spontaneity, or by any sort of preparation or previously thought-out plan. The fact is that only the *very* greatest artists in the twenties and thirties could instantly create new and different improvisations, and even then it was a skill only gradually acquired (as we shall see in many instances in the course of this book).

The fact that a solo by Coleman Hawkins or Lawrence Brown was not fully spontaneous in no way lessens my respect for them as creative artists. Nor do I find such an admission to be aesthetically or ideologically disturbing. Certain jazz purists and ideologues do, of course, but their views are based on several misconceptions regarding the real nature of jazz. They are based on an extraordinarily narrow definition of what constitutes (in their eyes) allowable jazz, in turn based on the untenable theory that jazz must be and is by definition fully spontaneous and unpremeditated. That may be an *ideal* to pursue, and spontaneous creation certainly represents the heart and soul of jazz. But by the same token it cannot be made an *absolute* requirement of jazz. There are any number of logical reasons why a solo might not be totally extemporized, especially—I reiterate—in jazz prior to the modern era: 1) the player may just not have been a natural improviser, and may have felt more at ease with a pre-organized solo, particularly in a new and unfamiliar piece (often with familiarity players' solos would "loosen up" and become more truly improvisatory); 2) an arranger or composer may have sought a particular type of solo in terms of content, shape, timbre, range, and dynamic level that would best suit a given piece; 3) a previously worked-out "solo" might have been so successful—as in the case of Barney Bigard's famous clarinet chorus in *Mood Indigo*—that it could not be improved upon and thus would become an integral part of the composition; 4) a fine musician can play even a memorized "solo" with a feeling of just-created spontaneity. There are thousands of such examples in jazz history, as indeed there are in classical music.

For let the reader not assume that a notated solo in a Brahms symphony or the solo part in a Beethoven piano concerto, for example, are necessarily doomed to be played in a stodgy unspontaneous manner just because they are notated. It is in fact one of the distinguishing attributes of a great classical artist that he can render a written work or passage in such a way that, even to ears familiar with the piece, the performance sounds as if it had just been created, had just been improvised, as it were. There are hundreds of such classical artists and it is their gift to create the illusion of spontaneity which separates them from the merely competent.

But such distinctions exist in jazz as well. There are those who can play a prepared solo and make it sound free and spontaneous, and there are those who even while improvising sound uninspired and routine.

I believe that underlying the jazz purists' prejudicial dicta regarding the priority of absolute spon-

on both takes (or virtually so). What is more important, though, is the joyous swing with which the whole performance is imbued. The joy comes in large part from the light, almost translucent sonority the ensembles get. Langston Curl's clear, positive, happy lead sound colors the whole brass section, while Redman's well-defined alto tone provides a spirited lead for the saxophones. But the swing comes primarily from Ralph Escudero (on tuba), Dave Wilborn's powerful banjo, and, above all, Cuba Austin's irresistible rhythmic drive. Although known later for his excellent press roll, Austin at this time was a virtuoso of the small "choked" cymbal. Rarely has anyone used this rather limited instrument to such remarkable effect. His deftly inventive hissing, sizzling cymbal patterns, darting in and out of the ensembles, provide a constant rhythmic counterpoint. While locking the band in an inexorable swing and momentum, Austin punctuates and heightens the continuity with his syncopated accents. And note that these accents usually *complement* the band's figures, rather than paralleling them, as hundreds of drummers in the Swing Era were soon to do. Austin in effect plays the kind of commenting accents that Kenny Clarke developed in the late thirties and forties. Only what Clarke did on the bass and snare drums, Austin here does on the cymbals. This gives the rhythmic infrastructure a unique, at times floating, at times surging flow. Firmly anchored to a swinging beat, Austin nevertheless found a high degree of freedom, passing on some of the time-keeping role to the banjo and tuba in a way that was highly unusual for this period.

Especially dazzling is Nesbitt's next effort, *Crying and Sighing*, composed and arranged by him.[42] Although quite different from *Put It There* in its details of organization, it holds to the same basic precept of constant variation and invention (Fig. 2). *Crying and Sighing* is a 32-bar composition with the standard four-times-eight-bars subdivision and the bridge at midpoint. There are a total of five choruses, broken up by two interpolated sequences: an unusual 16-bar phrase not related to the main theme, and a 6-bar transition before the final chorus.

Let us note in this connection that Nesbitt rarely uses modulations, including those banal whole-tone transitions to which most arrangers were so addicted.

---

taneous creation lies a subtly racist attitude. It is based on a number of often unconscious assumptions and stereotypes regarding blacks: to wit "they can't read music—and aren't they blessed in that?"; to wit "they are wonderfully spontaneous, undisciplined primitives and create out of the uncomplicatedness of their primal instincts, unencumbered by Western civilization"; or "they are not capable of the intellectual prowess of the white man, and therefore they are perfectly suited to that non-intellectual music called jazz," and so on and so forth. It is very much the same kind of thinking on the part of archaeologists and historians that rejected for several hundred years the very notion that certain American Indians had the imagination, intelligence, and skill to build the architecturally extraordinary mound graves of the Midwest and South.

Jazz purists are entitled like any other individuals to their personal preferences. But opinions and preferences do not make facts and realities—remembering also how hard it is to ascertain *unarguable* facts in the arts. I would not wish to deprive any jazz lover of his likes and dislikes; I would only argue that those likes and dislikes ought not to be presented as indisputable facts, to which we are all expected to assent.

42. Probably the title was taken from a line in *Four or Five Times* (recorded the same day): "Maybe I'll sigh, maybe I'll cry."

Fig. 2

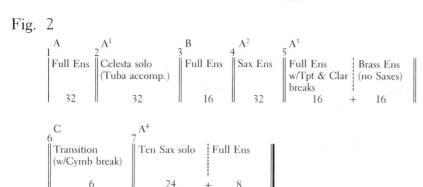

Indeed Nesbitt has enough variation and variety in his arrangements that he rarely sees the need for a modulation to a new key. I suspect he also valued the extra coherence a single key can give a performance.

Crying and Sighing is, like *Cherokee*, a fast-tempo piece ($\quad$ = 252) with the melody set in half notes, underscored by a 2-beat bass. Nesbitt's introduction, highly chromatic and partly in twisting eighth notes, leads smoothly to the "head" statement. Again, as in *Put It There*, the brass with their fine copper-toned burnish sing out the theme, embellished by the more agile saxophones in roving eighth- and quarter-note figures. It is a beautiful theme, moving attractively in step-wise motion over rich ninth and thirteenth chords, a theme which lends itself ideally to the type of rhythmic variation that Nesbitt excels in: rhythmicizing the melody and/or shifting the original rhythmic values into unexpected places. Such rhythmic surprises are scattered throughout the arrangement, with an innate sense of timing as to when and how often they should occur. After teasing us with second-beat accents during the 16-bar insert and following saxophone ensemble, the next chorus shifts to unexpected crash accents on the *fourth* beat, thus creating a hemiola-like combination of 3/4 and 5/4 measures (over the underlying 4/4), which in turn set off "solo breaks" for trumpet and clarinet.

Then, in the second half of the chorus, Nesbitt reserves the brass, who so far had not assumed the lead, for another timbral contrast. The last two bars of the bridge, with its dramatically placed diminished chord, is this time divided into successive virtuoso flourishes between brass and saxes. A superb 6-bar transition in rich ninth chords, firmly anchored by Escudero's deep tuba and sparked by a spectacular Austin cymbal solo, leads to the final chorus. Here the excellent tenor player, Prince Robinson, holds forth for three-quarters of a chorus, easily demonstrating why Coleman Hawkins and other musicians thought so highly of him. Not quite as consistently energetic as Hawkins, he could at times match him in inventiveness. Robinson's solo is remarkable not only for its driving energy but its high tessitura, sounding almost like an alto until the final diminished chord low B. Unfortunately this solo was not as prominently recorded by the Victor engineers, and so it is somewhat overbalanced by the accompanying ensemble. Example 14 demonstrates Robinson's superior sense of structure.

Ex. 14

The next day (July 12, 1928) Nesbitt was ready with two more astonishingly original arrangements, one his own piece, *Stop Kidding* (subtitled *Neckbones and Sauerkraut*), the other, Elmer Schoebel's classic *Nobody's Sweetheart*. Both show that Nesbitt's creative imagination never flagged and that the band must have rehearsed prodigiously, especially to meet the multiple challenges of the very fast-paced *Stop Kidding*.[43] Its highlights are many (particularly on take 1, the better of the two recorded that day) ranging from superior hard-driving solos by Redman (in his best Wiedoeft virtuoso manner), Nesbitt and Jones, through contrasting legato ensemble passages with unusual dynamic inflections to quite astounding sequences of superimposed 5/4 and (later 3/4) measures. Amazingly the band never stops swinging through all these metric permutations: on the face of it a kind of musical obstacle course which bands even ten and fifteen years later would not have been able to master. The 5/4 sequence goes by so smoothly and swingingly that one is apt to not even notice that the normal binary 8-bar phrase structure has in one case been abridged to seven (!) bars and in the next phrase (with superimposed 3/4s) expanded to ten (Ex. 15a, b).

Nesbitt's favorite cross-accentuation, the second-beat accent, turns up in the

---

43. The importance of this and other virtuoso Nesbitt arrangements goes beyond their intrinsic merits, for they were the inspiration for Gene Gifford's early "killer-dillers" with the Casa Loma orchestra, which in turn were so influential on a host of swing era bands from Lunceford to Goodman. (For more on this, see below, Chapter 7, Part 1.)

Ex. 15a

Ex. 15b

(in basic outline only)

saxes behind Jones's trombone solo, again creating a kind of alternating 5/4-3/4 accompanimental pattern (Ex. 16).

Ex. 16

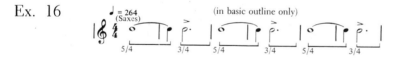

Later in the final full ensemble, Nesbitt pulls one more ace out of the deck when he produces a sequence of legato half-note triplets in the fifth bar (Ex. 17)—a rhythmic/melodic idea, I believe, not used by anyone in jazz prior to Nesbitt.

Ex. 17

Note also how Nesbitt is trying to wean the tuba away from its stereotyped oom-pah role and to use it occasionally instead as a fifth saxophone in legato harmonic passages.

Nesbitt's striving for fresh ideas, for the ideal of "constant variation," also extends to his endings. Any critical listener to jazz will have noticed that each period had its typical cliché endings—when there were endings at all, many performances simply coming to some sort of a stop. Each major arranger— Redman, Henderson, Mundy, Sampson—had their favorite coda devices, which then were imitated on all sides. Nesbitt is his own man once again. His endings are real *composed* endings, usually strong and unequivocal, not lingering, and almost always inventively different. The same can be said for Nesbitt's introductions and transitions which totally avoid in the latter category, as mentioned, those baneful whole-tone modulations which for over a decade seemed to be every arranger's favorite "modern sounding" device.

Nesbitt's *Nobody's Sweetheart* arrangement doesn't quite reach the heights of his previous three efforts (nor those of Lennie Hayton's superb 1930 arrangement for Paul Whiteman, perhaps the finest treatment this memorable tune ever received). But by no means does it fall back on any easy tried-and-true routines, Nesbitt's restlessly active imagination not permitting such creative abstentions. In the first chorus, for example, he eschews the standard saxophone voicing (of alto in the lead) and puts the melody in George Thomas's tenor, *mf* on mike, while the other three (one tenor below and two altos above) play *p* off mike. This was a technique common in vocal quartets since the early years of the century but rarely used (if at all) in 1920s' saxophone ensembles. Nesbitt then maneuvers through three of the most intelligent modulations, featuring twisting and shifting harmonies and other surprises, only to end up back in the original key of A♭ for Thomas's scat vocal, anchored down by Redman's slap tongue baritone bass notes (giving the tuba a rare rest). The last chorus travels far out in its daring re-harmonization of Schoebel's simple changes, topping it all off with one exultant hats-in-the-air second-beat shout by the full orchestra.

Nesbitt's arrangement of *I've Found a New Baby*, recorded nine months later, dispenses entirely with an introduction and plunges into the theme head-on. The performance is distinguished by a strong Nesbitt trumpet solo (in 16 bars of interpolated changes not belonging to the title song), an interesting rhythmic recasting of the bridge for the saxophones (a manner later thoroughly assimilated by Gifford), and more exuberant second-beat brass flares and shakes in the final chorus.

The McKinney Cotton Pickers also recorded in October of 1928 under the name of the Chocolate Dandies, from which date we have two fine arrangements by Nesbitt: *Birmingham Breakdown*, Duke Ellington's composition of 1927, and Hoagy Carmichael's then brand-new *Star Dust*. Both have much to offer. *Birmingham* is especially interesting, because it reveals where some of Nesbitt's influences came from, namely, Ellington.

A comparison of Nesbitt's arrangement of *Birmingham* with Ellington's original conception of the piece (as recorded for the Brunswick label in February 1927) shows that Nesbitt preserved Ellington's original in all basic *compositional* respects, and veered away from it only in those passages which were given over to individual solos. Thus Ellington's piano chorus becomes a Nesbitt trumpet solo; Hardwick's two solos for alto and baritone, respectively, become an arranged ensemble and a striking Cuba Austin cymbal chorus; Miley's trumpet solo becomes a Don Redman alto solo; and the glorious *polyphonic* ensemble with which Ellington closes the piece is turned into a *homophonic* arranged Nesbitt ensemble for brass and high clarinets.

Nesbitt takes a brighter tempo than Ellington, which allows him to interpolate an additional chorus. The McKinney/Nesbitt version is also brighter in sonority, with a more staccato swing than the richer, deeper sound and swing the Ellington orchestra gets.

In Ellington's *Birmingham* we also hear one of those chromatic legato ensemble passages in quickly shifting harmonies that Nesbitt obviously loved and appropriated for himself. But notice how Nesbitt brings textural variety to Ellington's basic riff theme (♩ ♪♩ ♩ | ♩ ♪♩ ♪♩ |) by adding subtle dynamic colorations (♩ ♪♩ ♩ | ♩ ♪♩ ♪♩ |)

All in all, Nesbitt is both loyal to Ellington's work but at the same time brings some fresh ideas of his own to the piece: part arrangement, part re-composition.

Star Dust is interesting because it lets us hear how orchestras used to play this piece in the late twenties, before it acquired lyrics and became one of the most successful sentimental ballads of all time. It was originally a medium-tempo dance instrumental, and is so rendered here by the Chocolate Dandies. It is an adequate but somewhat uneven performance, mostly a series of solos (including one by guest guitarist Lonnie Johnson, whose style does not suit this piece or arrangement particularly well). There is a fine Bix-like Nesbitt solo near the end and a nice warmly-voiced quiet ending.

Plain Dirt, often erroneously attributed in some sources to Nesbitt as composer, in others as arranger—it was composed by C. Stanton, and arranged by Redman—featured not the regular McKinney band but a roster of Redman's friends from the Fletcher Henderson orchestra, and one non-Hendersonian, Fats Waller, unfortunately inaudible throughout. (Waller is heard briefly on three others of the seven November 1929 tracks.) *Plain Dirt* was not an impressive performance, either in its sloppy ensembles or in its diffident solo contributions. Even Hawkins was rather vigorous but mechanical, for undoubtedly he felt crowded in the brief 4-bar spots Redman allotted him and by Stanton's lack of changes.

The performance of *Peggy*, on the other hand, arranged by Nesbitt and recorded on November 7, 1929, is a fine tribute to Nesbitt's leadership and arranging skills. For where Redman seems to have had considerable trouble getting his former Henderson colleagues to play with any degree of discipline, Nesbitt achieves a minor performance miracle with the very same players. Once again the arrangement was totally original in form, different from any others by Nesbitt, and distinguished by many ingenious special moments. Nesbitt seems also to have been listening to the best of Bill Challis's work with Whiteman; perhaps

he was steered to Challis by Nesbitt's good friend Bix Beiderbecke, whom he
knew from Bix's days with Goldkette in 1927. The saxophone voicings in particular have taken on some of the rich warm hues Challis could coax from the
Whiteman section.

The song *Peggy* is obscure and harmonically odd, but its very oddity is what
Nesbitt exploits to brilliant effect. To begin with what normally passes for the
bridge in a 32-bar song is located in *Peggy* in the second eight, not at the usual
mid-point (see Fig. 3). Its form, in terms of thematic material and chord progressions, is thus not the usual *AABA* but ABAC. Moreover, the chorus ends
ambivalently, allowing the option of ending either in the thirtieth bar (unresolved) or in the thirty-second bar (resolved), a feature which Nesbitt seizes upon
by organizing the performance's four main choruses in different lengths: one in
34, one in 30, and two in 36 measures. In addition the different chorus lengths
utilize similar but non-identical chord progressions ("changes") in the latter part
of the chorus. I have marked these two types A and C in the diagram, with C
being a variant of A.

The apparently slight but nonetheless crucial difference occurs in the third

Fig. 3

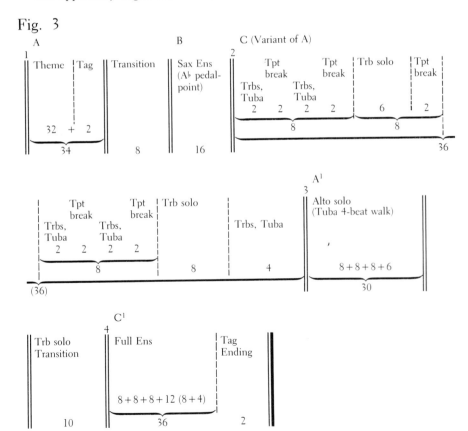

and fourth segments of the chorus structure: in the A type the distinctive move to I^7 and thence to the subdominant (IV) occurs in the song's twenty-first through twenty-fourth bars, whereas in the C type this same move occurs in the twenty-fifth through twenty-eighth bars. In addition to this already complex over-all form, Nesbitt adds two transition passages, one of eight bars, another of ten, as well as one of his own harmonic interpolations, this time a 16-bar pedal point on the tonic chord.

On another level these highly diverse chorus structures—34-8-16-36-30-10-36—are further varied and fragmented, especially so in the C segment (Fig. 3), variously grouping 2-, 6-, 8-, and 4-bar phrases in an amazing variety of textural and timbral contrasts. Considering the complexity of the arrangement, the young trumpeter Sidney de Paris handles his many brief 2-bar solo assignments well, unflappably fitting into the designated slots. Benny Carter is given a full chorus against Billy Taylor's "walking" four-beat tuba. On the other hand, Joe Smith's blary, nasal lead trumpet mars some of the performance, his sound here relating neither to the harmonic texture, nor to the basically warm sonority of all the other players—a strange and inexplicable flaw from the usually reliable Joe Smith.

Nesbitt's creativity extended happily also to his trumpet playing. As in his writing, he was remarkably consistent technically and relentlessly explorative. Moreover, while, like every trumpet player of the time, he had obviously listened to Louis Armstrong, he was no mere imitator. And if he admired his friend Bix, he paid him the ultimate compliment of not aping him. Indeed Nesbitt's playing represents, in a way quite different from Bunny Berigan's, a respectful yet highly personal synthesis of both Louis and Bix. Not as spectacular as Jabbo Smith or as wildly adventurous as Henry "Red" Allen and Bobby Stark, Nesbitt was a more consistent and modest player, and much more the *composer-musician*. His solos are generally marked by a clear design, an easy to follow progression of ideas, and are almost always somewhere during a solo distinguished by a surprise turn or unexpectedly original idea. Nesbitt, unlike many players of the day, never repeated himself, as alternate takes of recordings consistently attest.

Nesbitt's solo on *Nobody's Sweetheart* is typical of his work in its range and rhythmic variety (Ex. 18). Nesbitt liked to combine staccato passages with legato

Ex. 18

runs, the latter usually near or at the end of a solo, thus providing both contrast and balance (Ex. 19a and b). He represented more a composer's outlook on trumpet playing in showing the instrument's greater expressive versatility. In a

Ex. 19a

Nesbitt's solo from *I've Found a New Baby*

Ex. 19b

Nesbitt's Solo from *Stop Kidding* (two takes)

sense Nesbitt played music, rather than the trumpet, intelligently avoiding the stereotypes of that instrument.

An example of Nesbitt in a fiery, spirited mood is provided in *Some Sweet Day*. Other brief outings can be heard on *OK, Baby*, where Nesbitt is in a virtuoso mood, and *Beedle Um Bum*, a triumph of musician over material.

By the end of 1929 the McKinney's Cotton Pickers' decline had become swift and alarming, as Redman turned the band more and more into a "sweet" dance band, virtually unrelated to jazz. Lombardo-ish ensembles, chunky stodgy rhythms, saccharine Joe Smith solos, unspeakable vocals by effeminate crooners like Frank Marvin, Billy Coty, and George Bias abound—even a dreary waltz arrangement by Will Hudson—all demonstrating how low the band had sunk in a matter of months under Redman's titular leadership. The difference between Redman's and Nesbitt's work became ominous. But gradually even Nesbitt could no longer overcome the tawdry material he was assigned, his last good arrangement being of Fats Waller's *Zonky* (in early 1930). Not helping matters at all was Cuba Austin's conversion around mid-1930 to an effect on the snare drum called a "press roll," which he used with relentless monotony on the second and fourth beats in virtually all pieces.

Nesbitt hung on till November 1930 and then left for New York, in the meantime turning out a stunning arrangement of *Chinatown, My Chinatown* for an October recording date of the Fletcher Henderson band.[44] By the end of 1930 the Cotton Pickers band had become totally stagnant. Soon Redman himself left (in mid-1931), the band then electing Benny Carter as musical director—a tenure which lasted less than a year.

Nesbitt's career, alas, came to a premature halt when he began to drift from one band to another—reputedly increasingly alcoholic, dying of stomach cancer in Boston some time in 1935—followed by undeserved oblivion.

CLAUDE HOPKINS

Claude Hopkins for a while led one of the more popular black bands, especially on the East Coast. However, its success was relatively short-lived because ultimately it could not establish a strong enough identity to compete either with more creative black orchestras or the hordes of white swing bands that, whatever their merits or lack thereof, had *some* identifying stylistic hallmark or gimmick. Hopkins and his chief arranger Fred Norman, second trombone in the band, were at once too eclectic in their repertory and redundant in their adopted style. Though Hopkins was a formidable pianist technically, he evidently could not break out of his stride-piano mold, and in later years, after the big-band era, he worked primarily as pianist in Dixieland-style or revival groups, such as those that played at Broadway's Metropole (Sol Yaged, for example) and with "Wild Bill" Davison's Jazz Giants.

---

44. See *Early Jazz*, 275, for a full discussion of this work.

In looking back on his early career, Hopkins himself has pointed to the lack of outstanding soloists in his band as the prime reason for its limited success. Most other observers have chimed in with that viewpoint. I think, however, that that assessment tells only half the story, in that the band's adopted arranging style was in itself both flawed and limited—a stylistic dead end, particularly in clinging tenaciously to a few catchy surface motifs and traits, as Hopkins and Norman certainly did.

But it is best to let the evidence, the recordings made between 1932 and 1940, tell the story. Born in 1903 (like Duke Ellington in the Washington, D.C., area), Hopkins studied both medicine and music at Howard University, actually receiving a degree in the latter. By the mid-twenties he was leading his own groups, and while working in Atlantic City in 1925 found himself quite suddenly engaged as the band with the *Revue Nègre*, which was about to open in Paris, France. There Josephine Baker's nearly nude dancing made history, while on the musical side Sidney Bechet, already known to some Frenchmen from his 1919 tour with Will Marion Cook's Southern Syncopated Orchestra—eliciting a remarkably perceptive critique from the then young French-Swiss conductor and Stravinsky friend, Ernest Ansermet—attracted unprecedentedly wide attention. Shortly, Miss Baker was lured away to the Folies-Bergère, leaving Hopkins, upon the *Revue*'s closing, to scramble for work in Europe.

In the late twenties Hopkins became involved with a band led successively by the pianist Charlie Skeets and the trumpeter Ovie Alston, and he took over its leadership in 1930. Recording began in May 1932, all in all rather auspiciously—although primarily because of the work of an arranger-composer never subsequently associated with Hopkins's band: Jimmy Mundy. Mundy, then playing tenor with the Tommy Myles band in Philadelphia, was selling arrangements to a number of major jazz orchestras, including that of Earl Hines, who promptly hired Mundy as his staff arranger. Who knows: if Hopkins had had the foresight to engage Mundy on a long-term basis, jazz history might now be written differently. But evidently Hopkins's essentially conservative tastes found Mundy's work too advanced. *Mush Mouth*, the work in question, also provided no solo opening for the leader's piano.

Mush Mouth is in fact—especially for its time—an impressive work.[45] Already its form is unusual, albeit in an extremely simple way. Its 32-bar AABA form includes A-segments which happen to consist of 8-bar blues changes (reputedly the older of the two basic blues formats). Later, after two full 32-bar statements, by eliminating the bridge (B) Mundy is able to exploit the 8-bar blues structure—four of these occurs in the middle of the piece—and then finish up with three 12-bar blues stanzas (all diagrammatically represented in Fig. 4).

The solos are quite impressive for their time. Fernando Arbello, like Juan Tizol, a trombonist raised in the Puerto Rican band tradition, delivers a strong blues-inflected tightly muted solo, interrupted in the bridge by a splendidly played trumpet trio, one of the trademarks of the Hopkins band from its Alston-led days.

---

45. Unfortunately, to my knowledge it was never recorded or performed by any other orchestra.

Fig. 4

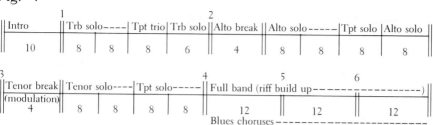

(In later years it unfortunately became one of the band's most redundant and trite cliché features.) Gene Johnson was a quite outstanding altoist, who here bursts in with a wondrously convoluted 4-bar break that might almost have come from the horn of Eric Dolphy or Ornette Coleman, following that up with an agile, adventurous chorus, which pays little obeisance to any of the famous alto players of the day (Carter, Hodges, Charlie Holmes). Indeed Johnson's sound is remarkable for its projection and its full, somewhat dark tenorish sound. Bobby Sands (tenor) follows with a modulatory break and two of the 8-bar blues choruses. Though Sands was very soon to become a slavish and loving imitator of Coleman Hawkins, here in *Mush Mouth* he is still very much his own man: forthright and forceful, experimenting with some curiously wailing bent notes.

Trumpeter Ovie Alston is the other soloist, playing both the open and muted trumpet solo passages. He, too, had a full big sound, rather straight-toned and singing, without evident need of vibrato. He was one of the few trumpet players around who did not imitate or emulate Armstrong. With his unusually smooth legato (in the days of hard-tonguing trumpet players), Alston was much given to chromatically winding (or circular) lines and sported a fine trill, which he used to flashy effect. More remarkably, though, Alston played with a relaxed way-back-in-the-beat swing that was still quite uncommon in the early thirties. Alston was also adept with the wah-wah mute, and he loved repeated-note ideas, which he could spin out with considerable skill.[46]

Hopkins's band had a fine drummer in Pete Jacobs. When partnered with bassist Henry Turner, this team of two—even with Turner on tuba—could produce some amazingly relaxed "modern" swing, as witness the last three riff-building choruses of *Mush Mouth*.

But quite clearly *Mush Mouth* and *Mad Moments* were not the direction Hopkins wanted his band to go. Though it may sound extreme, the first recording session represented an early peak which the band never attained again and from which it gradually slid into oblivion.[47] It never fulfilled its original promise.

---

46. Though I cannot find reliable corroboration of the fact, I am convinced that Alston must have been a major influence on Charlie Shavers, whose work with the Kirby Sextet is but a faster, more fluent example of the kinds of technique and ideas in which Alston excelled.

47. One clear indicator of the band's problems is the fact that, of the twenty sides it cut for Columbia Records between May 1932 and March 1933, *twelve* were never issued.

For one thing it had basic intonation problems which for some reason it never solved, the brass always playing slightly sharp (probably because of lead trumpet Albert Snaer's tendency to play on the high side), the saxes tending towards flatness. For another thing, the sections never worked out their ensemble problems the way, say, Lunceford's or Calloway's bands did. Most of the Hopkins band's ensemble work was ragged. A third problem was Hopkins's stride-piano style which, of course, had to be prominently featured. It was vigorous and incisive, with a strong left hand, but ultimately anachronistic. It soon became an anchor which prevented the band from ever veering far from its conservative moorings.

Its commercial success derived, as with almost all 1930s' bands, from its singers, particularly Orlando Roberson, a falsetto crooner of some skill. But then Hopkins also had Alston, a pseudo-Armstrong-style singer, and Fred Norman, who in a lugubrious halting voice talked his way through depressingly sad though lightweight story-telling pieces, which were a flagrant plagiarism of Don Redman's novelty-hokum approach—except that Redman had a light, high, almost childish voice, whereas Norman's was low and oafish. His Uncle Tom enunciation didn't help matters, although I suppose even that was capable of being considered harmless in those Amos 'n' Andy days, and thus successful.

Hopkins contributed a number of compositions to the band's repertory, sometimes co-authored with Alston (*Chasing All the Blues Away, Swingin' and Givin', Washington Squabble, Everybody Shuffle*).[48] The problem was that they were, both in composition and arrangement, all virtually identical, invariably starting with a pendulant vamp, and usually progressing somewhere along the line to single-repeated-note riffs. They were also not particularly original, being strikingly similar to pieces like Horace Henderson's *Hot and Anxious*. Hopkins's other repertory contribution was a series of older pieces, essentially of ragtime vintage, such as *Nola, Canadian Capers, That's A Plenty, Put On Your Old Grey Bonnet*—more often than not arranged in anachronistic period style, which even musical conservatives were bound sooner or later to regard as corny. The lone exception in this genre was Morton's *King Porter Stomp* (Sept. 1934), of course already well established by then as a *jazz* classic by virtue of Fletcher Henderson's several path-breaking and influential recordings. The Hopkins performance of *King Porter* sports not only excellent solos by Alston and Sands (in his most devoted Hawkins manner), but also by Edmond Hall, along with Gene Johnson, the most gifted and most consistent soloist in the Hopkins band. A kind of black Benny Goodman, Hall had a formidable sure-fire technique, wide-ranging ideas, an urgent, slightly edgy sound and thrusting note articulation (of the kind that Benny would always want to round off and subdue). Henderson's *King Porter* ending, with its famous flaring contrary-motion chords, was imitated widely; it seemed to be part of the piece. But Fred Norman, taking advantage of the band's frequently featured trumpet trio of Snaer, Alston, and Sylvester Lewis,

---

48. The first two pieces named were also known under other titles, *Sweet Horn* and *Aw Shucks*, respectively.

concocted a rather spectacular high-note ending which must have wowed audiences (although admittedly it is not performed to perfection on the Decca recording). Nearly fifty years later, infallible player identification is probably impossible, given the relatively complex interchange of playing roles. But I take the soloist (just before the high-note ending) to be lead trumpeter Snaer, who at the drop of a hat resorted to Armstrong's favorite device of shaking a long high held-note (Ex. 20a). Alston and Lewis then pile in on top of Snaer, who in turn leapfrogs over *them* one bar later, with the piece eventually ending up with a quite spectacular high-voiced D♭ major trumpet chord (Ex. 20b).

Ex. 20a

Ex. 20b

An on-location 1935 performance of *Singin' in the Rain*[49] reveals what a
formidable pianistic technique Hopkins possessed. His long whirlwind triplet-
eighth-note runs, including the spectacular flourish with which the piece ends,
were virtuosic dazzlers, although, as with the similarly endowed Edgar Hayes,
such a technique was essentially classical-ornamental and as such somewhat outside a jazz conception—a problem which even the great Art Tatum sometimes
had to contend with. In any case, these virtuoso piano displays hardly needed
the accompaniment of a thirteen-piece band, which could only interfere and
hang on as unnecessary ballast (witness not only *Singin' in the Rain*, but also
Nola and *Canadian Capers*).

With these tendencies encroaching more and more on the Hopkins band's
repertory and performance conceptions,[50] even Ed Hall and the consistently
spirited though infrequently featured Sylvester Lewis[51]—and in 1934—the arrival of Hilton Jefferson, whose big solo number was *Just As Long As the World
Goes 'Round*, could not arrest the trend of deterioration. Similarly, fine Hopkins
soloists like Jabbo Smith, Vic Dickenson, and Herman Autrey—later in the
waning thirties—could not restrain the band's drift away from jazz, initiated with
arrangements like *Nola* and *Broadway Rhythm*. There was a last fling or two, in
Phil Lang's fine functional arrangement of *Farewell Blues*, which finally achieves
an integration of a major Hopkins stride-piano solo into the overall performance,
and which had one memorable unison saxophone lick, with its pleasing insistence on the seventh degree of the scale (Ex. 21).

Ex. 21

Six sides for the obscure Ammor label in 1940 close out the Hopkins orchestra's discography. Its swing having long ago become overly polite, its repertory
flirting with classical propriety (misunderstood at that), its style hardened into
colorless redundancies, it faded away—and disbanded in 1942, even before the
big band breakups of 1946 and 1948.

49. French Jazz Anthology LP, JA 5156.
50. It is, I think of some significance that Hopkins spent most of the mid-forties arranging for sweet
bands like Tommy Tucker, Abe Lyman, and Phil Spitalny.
51. Hear him playing well on *Hodge Podge*, *Swingin' and Givin'*, *Minor Mania*, and *Farewell
Blues*.

PART 2

FLETCHER HENDERSON

How utterly frustrating it must have been for Fletcher Henderson at the very time when he developed, in such pieces as *Down South Camp Meeting* and *Wrappin' It Up*, a distinctly new orchestral style in jazz, soon to be called "Swing," that his orchestra's fortunes had sunk so low it was forced to disband! Worse yet, this new "swing music" was being sold to a mass public by Benny Goodman, the newly crowned "King of Swing." (If Benny was the "King," what then was Fletcher?) Perhaps, had Fletcher not disbanded, had he held out a little longer and been able to restore a measure of discipline and leadership to his band, he might well have reaped the successes he so deserved. But then again maybe not. For many of his best musicians, who had had enough of lay-offs and unpaid engagements, were "abandoning the sinking ship." Apart from Henderson's fateful inability to manage the band's business affairs, there had also been some severe artistic lapses in recent years that contributed to its ultimate collapse— even though these same "artistic lapses" were undoubtedly desperate maneuvers to find a sustaining public beyond a small coterie of jazz enthusiasts. That is the only explanation of the distressing quantity of trite pop material the band recorded (was forced to record?) in those early years of the thirties. This took many forms but essentially consisted of various attempts to make the Tin Pan Alley pop tunes of the day swing, to transform them into jazz. Like the moth drawn to the flame, Fletcher was compelled by his talent (and that of his players, many of them major stars of the day) to bring to these ephemera the very elements of jazz that, in fact, the public had so far rejected or ignored.

The titles tell the story: *Sweet Music, My Sweet Tooth Says I Wanna But My Wisdom Tooth Says No* (now there's a *classic* title!), *Melinda's Wedding Day, I Wanna Count Sheep Till the Cows Come Home*, all from 1931 and 1932. It is amazing and incongruous to hear one of the most forceful and original and virile soloists of the day, Coleman Hawkins, cheek by jowl in the same performance with some whimperingly puerile crooned vocal,[1] the rest of the arrangements usually emulating white "sweet" (hotel) band styles: Lombardo-ish saxophones, insipidly sentimental brass (both sections' excessive vibratos were alleged to represent *real* sentiment), chunky two-beat rhythm sections—and even unto Edgar Sampson's violin obbligatos, and awful unison saxophones, as on *Poor Old Joe*.

1. The phenomenon of the effeminately voiced crooners in popular music, both then and now, and the appalling taste that spawns it, runs like a constant thread through American musical history. Considering the generally "macho" outlook of the average American male consumer, particularly in earlier decades, it is a phenomenon difficult to explain. Even if one were to assume that it was women who were enamored of these crooners—a risky assumption at best—it would still leave unexplained the mass sales this genre generated, for women were surely not the main buyers of records— especially in the lean Depression years. As a musician I must leave the further explanation of the successes of the Orlando Robersons, Pha Terrells, Dennis Days, Muzzy Marcellinos, Blue Barrons, Tiny Tims, Boy Georges, and the falsetto warbling of thousands of rock groups to sociologists and psychologists.

John Kirby's tuba, an instrument which most forward-looking orchestras of the time had long ago discarded, was increasingly at odds with Henderson's efforts to advance, but, of course, fitted nicely with the aforementioned pop trivia.

Anomalies abound in these sides. For example, *Strangers*, basically a pop vocal for one John Dickens where a few choruses of jazz are surrounded on either side by a sea of watery sweetness, sports one of Hawkins's most astounding solos (See Ex. 2 in Chapter 6, below). On the other hand, in the Henderson band's recording of Gene Gifford's *Casa Loma Stomp*—ineptly trying to emulate the single biggest "jazz" hit of the period—Hawkins cannot even produce a solo equal to the one by Pat Davis, the Casa Lomans' tenor soloist. Then there is the openly parodistic *Underneath the Harlem Moon*, with Rex Stewart pushing his comedic talent to bizarre extremes and Hawkins in his most brazenly ornamented "high-baroque" form.[2]

There are also such anomalous arrangements as Russ Morgan's Duke-ish *Phantom Fantasie*, describable as interesting, experimental—and flawed (especially in its weak non-ending); or Will Hudson's *Tidal Wave*, whose title promises more than it delivers; or the high-speed "bicycle-act" accompaniment music fashioned by Benny Carter in *Happy As the Day Is Long*.

By contrast, there are the many superior performances and arrangements recorded in 1933 and 1934, from the audaciously "modern" *Queer Notions* (Hawkins's avant-garde composition which was so advanced that only he and Henry "Red" Allen could solo on it, and even then in more or less memorized solos) to the breezy, effortless, happy swing of *Rhythm Crazy*, recorded under Horace Henderson's name (Fletcher's brother) in famed Liederkranz Hall (now long torn down), possessor of the finest natural acoustics of any New York recording facility, then and now. The recording allows us to hear how the Henderson band really sounded, an opinion confirmed by Hammond, who produced the recording for English Parlophone. It also reminds us of the significant role Horace Henderson played in his brother's band, both as sometime pianist and, more importantly, as arranger. It tends to be forgotten that an enormous number of the Henderson band's arrangements were by brother Horace, quite apart from the many pieces on which the brothers collaborated and those to which Horace undoubtedly contributed in lesser and officially uncredited ways. There are any number of pieces where one is hard put to ascribe the arrangement definitively to one or the other brother, which is at least as much a compliment to Horace as it is to Fletcher. Later, in the mid-to-late thirties, their work was to decline, both, interestingly enough, in slightly dissimilar ways. Horace tended to be a more pragmatic, less experimental writer; his arrangements "lay well," as the musicians say. He tried to keep riff *cum* call-and-response devices alive longer

---

2. This was the famous record date which must have given young John Hammond, who had set it up, heart seizures; for the last of the players, Kirby, finally arrived two hours and fifteen minutes after the scheduled beginnings of the date. But apparently the men were so chagrined that they recorded three sides in 45 minutes, one of which, *New King Porter Stomp*, is possibly the greatest recording Fletcher's band ever made. (It far outclasses the *King Porter Stomp*, recorded eight months later—not for Hammond). See *Early Jazz*, 277–78.

by minor tonal variations and textural detail. But his penchant for darker colors and simple riff themes, stated preferably in the bass instruments (including trombones and baritone saxophones) eventually also shriveled into a suffocating formula, at least for a while. However, a series of recordings made in 1940 under Horace's own name with his own band reveal not only that he had by then declared his full stylistic independence from his brother, but had created a superb new orchestral language, rich in instrumental color and texture, and quite unlike anything else in jazz at the time. (These recordings will be discussed later, in Part 4 of this chapter.)

Fletcher's arrangements were generally more daring and experimental, also in their use of unusual keys (which the musicians of that era found uncomfortable) and their bright-hued sonority. His more jauntily rhythmic style eventually also atrophied, as he exhausted his stock of swingable rhythmic patterns, relying more and more on previously established stereotypes.

There was one player in Henderson's orchestra who fascinates me particularly, because he seems to have been more responsible for the incomparable swing of the Henderson aggregation in its heyday than anyone else: Walter Johnson, the drummer from late 1930 to 1934, when the orchestra disbanded. Johnson and John Kirby became one of the finest rhythm teams of the thirties, but I feel that Johnson was in effect the real leader of the Henderson band. His drumming was unique in one respect: it sonically enveloped the band; it permeated an arrangement; it penetrated every nook and cranny of a performance. And yet he never seemed to intrude, overpower, overbear. Johnson was especially masterful with the cymbals. He was one of the first to use various-sized suspended cymbals as an ongoing continuity *throughout* an entire piece. Just as he seemed to be unobtrusively everywhere, so, too, he was both subtle and sensitive, yet intense. The intensity came cumulatively from the flow and constantly enlivened continuity of his rhythmic line. And it was a real line: not a series of vertically well-placed time points, but long, large waves of phrases, periods, stanzas. He was one of the few drummers who was aware of the crucial *textural* role a drummer can play. Whereas many excellent drummers supply a good beat and underlying infrastructure, they nevertheless to some extent still play *parallel* to the music. They are under it or along side it, close by. But Walter Johnson was *in* it. And his sound definitively and precisely colored and informed the band's total orchestral texture.

Superb examples of his artistry abound, but one may especially single out—with Kirby at his side—Johnson's work on *New King Porter Stomp*, *Honeysuckle Rose*, *Rhythm Crazy* (co-composed by Johnson), and *Down South Camp Meeting*, the last with Elmer James on bass with not quite Kirby's thrust and Johnson more subdued, no longer on cymbals but confined to the snare drum. Still, it is a superb, precise, buoyant swing.

After some months with Benny Goodman as staff arranger, Fletcher formed a new band in early 1936, this time with high caliber soloists like Roy Eldridge, Chu Berry, and Sid Catlett on drums. Later the very young, gifted bassist Israel Crosby was to succeed Kirby, who left to form his own small band. This Henderson band enjoyed a series of successful residencies at the Grand Terrace Ball-room in Chicago, where Earl Hines was headquartered, and where the always generous Fletcher Henderson was to help out Count Basie's young nine-piece Kansas City band in 1936 by lending it arrangements for the Grand Terrace shows, a type of music with which the Basie band had had no prior experience.

Henderson even had his first big hit record in 1936, Chu Berry's *Christopher Columbus*, as arranged by Horace Henderson. It was the kind of riff swing piece which later other bands—like Goodman, Harry James, Larry Clinton, Les Brown—were to grind into a rigid formula. But in 1936 it still had a degree of freshness. There was also the new-sounding *Jangled Nerves*, co-composed and co-arranged by Fletcher and Roger Moore. Marred by an inconclusive ending and dated pyramids—the "new thing" in the mid-thirties—*Jangled* was an up-tempo piece based on a brief riff snippet as old as jazz itself (and about as original), which nevertheless hung together as an effective vehicle to show off the virtuoso talents of Chu Berry, fleet as an otter, and Roy Eldridge at his youthful exuberant best.

Walter Johnson returned briefly to give the band its former lift on pieces like *Shoe Shine Boy, Sing,Sing,Sing, Rhythm of the Tambourine*, often with a broader, wider, almost behind-the-beat kind of "modern" swing. But the Henderson style was closing in on itself, cutting off its own vital circulation. The band's final demise—except for five more sides cut in 1941 by a temporarily reorganized band—was sad indeed, when one considers that the band could hardly manage even a well-known vintage piece like *Moten Stomp*.

After several more undistinguished attempts to keep a big band going and further arranging stints with Benny Goodman, Henderson settled in at New York's Cafe Society in late 1950 with a sextet. He died, after a series of strokes on December 28, 1952.

CAB CALLOWAY

One of the many missed opportunities in Henderson's career, a scheduled tour of Europe in 1934, was consigned to Cab Calloway, who was at that time en-joying an enormous and long-standing success in New York's Cotton Club. Cal-loway was one of the great musical showmen of the Swing Era, but he also was a remarkably gifted singer. His orchestra was built primarily around his singing and comedic talents but, interestingly, featured first-rate soloists throughout its existence. Though these players often felt frustrated by inadequate solo oppor-tunities—more on records than in clubs and dances, freed from the three-minute limitations of the 10-inch record—they felt somewhat compensated by the good pay that Calloway, as one of the most successful bandleaders of all time, could offer.

Actually the Calloway band's history begins, long before he became its leader, with three previous incarnations: first, in St. Louis as Wilson Robinson's Syn-copators (1923–24); then, in New York as the Cotton Club Orchestra, directed by violinist Andy Preer (1925–27); and third, as the Missourians, directed by singer Lockwood Lewis (1927–30). Preer's Cotton Club orchestra was in fact the group that directly preceded Duke Ellington's orchestra in its famous three-year tenure at that most popular Harlem club.

It is impossible to think of a band that experienced as many dramatic stylistic conversions as Cab Calloway's. In its first two formations (under Robinson and Preer), it was a typical face-less mid-twenties band that had not yet found its direction or style. By the time it became the Missourians, it had turned almost 180 degrees to become an extraordinarily powerful and raucous band of the type that one could readily find in the riverfront joints in St. Louis or Memphis and other smaller cities of the Midwest and Southwest, but not indigenously in New York. Then, under Calloway's leadership, the band changed drastically once again, into primarily an accompanying vehicle for the leader's novelty vocals, but at the same time it became increasingly jazz-oriented and professional in this role, until by the late thirties it had become one of the very finest jazz ensembles in the land.

The twelve sides recorded by the pre-Calloway Missourians are virtually unique in jazz-recording history and contain, in their particular idiom, at least a couple of masterpieces. I fear that I misjudged this band somewhat in *Early Jazz*. While admiring their "elemental, fiery drive," I also suggested that they "worked primarily in clichés." Clichés is probably too strong a word; it might have been more accurate to say that the Missourians repeatedly used the same devices and solutions (the difference between the two judgments being measured, I suppose, by the relative degree of annoyance they arouse in the listener). For it is not entirely clear to me whether the Missourians' redundancy in matters of form and technique was the result of naiveté or a shrewd realization that these devices were so effective as to bear constant repetition. And effective they were. In their rough, unsubtle way, the Missourians produced a brand of exciting, elemental jazz that few, if any, bands could match at that time.

For the music of the Missourians was from the Midwest, St. Louis to be exact. Their musical heroes were Jesse Stone's Blues Serenaders and Bennie Moten's orchestra, both renowned in the Kansas-Missouri territory. Both orchestras, in slightly different ways, had evolved an earthy blues-oriented, strongly rhythmic idiom that gained a lot of its enormous drive from its ragtime ancestry, and in particular that old rousing energizer, *Tiger Rag*. Jesse Stone's transformation of it into *Boot to Boot* is a classic of its kind[3] and, because it was recorded and widely disseminated it served as a "killer diller" model for many territory bands.

The Missourians' *Ozark Mountain Blues* wasn't a blues at all; it was Stone's *Boot to Boot* roughed up a bit, with "freak-style" trumpet solos by Roger Q. Dickerson and blistering hot blasts from trombonist De Priest Wheeler. And where Stone had forsaken the standard roaring tiger imitations, traditionally in the tuba or trombone, the Missourians put them back in—with a vengeance.

The energy level of this band—their bite, their attack, their powerful juggernaut rhythm, powered by Leroy Maxey's drums and Jimmy Smith's tuba—must be heard to be believed. Though they gave their pieces exotic Jazz Age titles

3. See *Early Jazz*, 291.

(Stopping the Traffic, 200 Squabble, Swingin' Dem Cats), they were invariably either based on *Tiger Rag* or blues. They were a powerhouse group with little subtlety and refinement, but in their robust way they could outswing anybody within earshot. (In 1929, in one of the more famous "battles of jazz" regularly held at the Savoy Ballroom, the Missourians soundly beat no less than Duke Ellington's band.)

In listening to their 1929 and early 1930 recordings, one is struck by the riveting, relentlessly sustained energy of the fast pieces. These are usually topped by either a wild collectively improvised final chorus—with all New Orleans gentility driven out of it—or one in which a trio of two high-screaming clarinets and trumpet bring events to an almost unbearable tension (Ex. 1)—the latter a much-used, obviously favorite, sure-fire device:

Ex. 1

(in C major)

Moments of tenderness are rarer, but they do occur. Consider the disarmingly simple muted brass opening of *You'll Cry for Me*, at first bluesy, then suddenly lapsing into quaint medieval three-part counterpoint (Ex. 2).

Ex. 2

One of the most memorable passages in the entire series occurs in *Prohibition Blues*, masterfully declaimed with plunger and wah-wah by Dickerson. (Lammar Wright has the open-horn solo.) Dickerson's second solo is inspired. It is moving and touching in its simplicity, even capturing moments of suspense, an element so rarely heard in the frenetic hustle-bustle of late-twenties' jazz. As Dickerson pauses between phrases, a quiescent calm takes hold, breath-catching in its effect—then resolved seconds later in a beautiful harmonic coda (Ex. 3).

Though the Missourians' approach was simple and unsophisticated—they had no use, for example, for fancy modulations, preferring the straight-ahead unfussy ones—their head arrangements always offered a healthy mixture of solos, trios (brass or reed), and full ensembles—one reason one doesn't find the near-cliché repetitiousness of their technical procedures offensive or boring. The other reason is the band's enormous rhythmic verve.

Listening to Cab Calloway's orchestra, say, in the early or mid-thirties, one wonders how he tamed this wild bunch from St. Louis, and how, in time, with

Ex. 3

many of the players staying right on through the entire decade, Cab's band became one of the most sophisticated and disciplined of jazz orchestras.

Many jazz historians with a purist and pro-instrumental bias have ignored or dismissed Calloway and his orchestra as musically irrelevant. And insofar as others have dealt with the band at all, they have generally picked their way through its several hundred recordings, snobbishly culling only the instrumental solos as being worthy of comment, usually by Chu Berry, Dizzy Gillespie, and one or two others. This is eminently unfair and historically unjustifable on several counts.

First of all, Calloway was a magnificent singer, quite definitely the most unusually and broadly gifted male singer of the thirties. Second, considering his enormous popularity, and therefore the temptation to cater to the basest of mass tastes, Calloway's singing—and even his choice of material (when all is said and done)—is of far higher caliber than any other male vocalist's (with the exception of Jimmy Rushing and some of the great blues singers of the period). Moreover Calloway, amazingly, even in his most extravagant vocal antics, never left the bounds of good taste. It was as though he had a built-in mechanism that kept him from turning corny.

Third, he was a true jazz musician and as such surrounded himself with a real jazz orchestra, something no other band-leading vocalist cared (or managed) to do. In that regard, though he had every excuse to do otherwise, his performances—especially in clubs and dances, as opposed to recordings with their absolute time limits—were always liberally sprinkled with instrumental solos and ensembles, more so the more popular he became (in this respect a deliberate reversal of the usual trend).

Calloway had a phenomenal voice. Its range is extraordinary: from low B to the highest tenor range and, by means of excellent "mixing" and falsetto, even quite beyond that into the soprano range. Like Sarah Vaughan in our time, who also has three voices—soprano, alto, and baritone—Calloway is at once bass, baritone, and tenor, with soprano available when needed. Nor is this merely a matter of range. Calloway can color his voice in the true timbres of those varied registers. His bass and baritone can be rich and deep, or if needed lighter in weight. Similarly, his tenor can take on the fullness of a high baritone or the more high-pitched coloration of a real lyric tenor. But his technique extends beyond timbre to a perfectly controlled coloratura, quite natural and impeccable breath support, and above all incredible diction. Cab's voice in its heyday was as clear as a bell, capable by virtue of its purity of remarkable projection. Given his vivid musical imagination and great comedic and acting talent, it is small wonder that Gershwin composed his inimitable Sportin' Life in *Porgy and Bess* with Calloway in mind (a part which, however, he did not sing until 1952).

To be sure, these astonishing vocal abilities took some time to evolve—a natural tendency with singers, who technically develop slower than instrumentalists, because the voice, unlike a "horn," is a physical part of the body and can only fully mature as the body matures. Calloway's first recordings at age twenty-two reveal a raw vocal talent, at this stage generally a strident high tenor, but with hardly anything one might call a style or a musical conception. The closest he came to that was the occasional allusions to some of Al Jolson's nasal, whining vocalisms. (Jolson was at this time, 1930, along with Rudy Vallee, the most popular male singer-actor-comedian.)[4]

With Calloway at the helm, the Missourians, now called "Cab Calloway and His Orchestra" but *consisting of identical personnel* (except for the addition of two section brass players), was very quickly and completely transformed stylistically. Jimmy Smith was now on string bass instead of tuba, and the band, including the main soloists like Wright, Wheeler, clarinetist Thornton Blue, and reed-man Walter "Foots'" Thomas, now played in a much more subdued, smoother dance tempo and style. In livelier pieces, like the minor hit *Corinne*

---

4. We tend to forget with the passage of time what an overwhelming success Jolson scored with the first part-sound movie, ironically called *The Jazz Singer*—something Jolson was definitely not.

Corinna (1931), the performance still tended to be more relentless than swinging, but on the other hand the playing had become quite clean, balanced, and disciplined. The conversion from a rough-and-tumble Midwestern riverfront band to a sophisticated modern New York swing/jazz orchestra was more than halfway completed.

As a matter of fact, quite extraordinary things go on in these early Calloway recordings. What may surprise the reader, brought up on the generally prevailing view that Calloway was merely a novelty singer, given to "hollering" and "braying," and that his orchestra was no more than a functional band relegated to second-rank accompanimental status, is the fact that from the start Calloway gave generous space to both his soloists and arrangers to feature the orchestra. Indeed, it is surprising how rich and complete most of the Calloway band's recorded performances are, striking an excellent balance between his vocal displays and the orchestra's involvement.[5] This may take a variety of forms: 1) solos interspersed throughout the performance; 2) interesting obbligatos given to soloists *behind* Cab's vocals; 3) integrating instrumental solos and breaks directly into the often especially composed-for-this-purpose song material; and 4) considerable stylistic and formal latitude to the arrangers.

Consider the following facts. Any number of pieces recorded by Cab between 1930 and 1934 (not to mention the later years when players like Eddie Barefield, Chu Berry, Dizzy Gillespie, Jonah Jones, and Milt Hinton were prominently featured) contain a rich sampling of instrumental solos, usually about five or six per side. Excellent examples of this category are *Gotta Darn Good Reason*, (Cab's very first recording date in July 1930), *Some of These Days, Bugle Call Rag, Hot Toddy, The Scat Song, Jitter Bug, Margie,* and *Hotcha Razz Ma Tazz*. In the second (above-mentioned) category, hear the striking background obbligatos on *Beale Street Mama, Evenin', Little Town Gal,* and, again, the early *Gotta Darn Good Reason*, where Andrew Brown plays a highly unusual loping bass clarinet *(sic)* improvisation behind Cab. On *Little Town Gal* and *Evenin'* we can hear guitarist Morris White in two of the many performances on which he broke away from the standard four-beat 'comping, inventing instead complementary countermelodies or graceful arpeggio accompaniments. His sound was very much like that of Freddie Green: clear, delicate but firm. White's lively musical imagination enabled him to be consistently inventive in his accompanimental choices without ever intruding or interfering with the soloists, thereby enriching the texture of the Calloway band's sound (especially that of its rhythm section) in a way that is to my knowledge unique for that time. But White was also a terrific rhythm guitarist, supplying a steady swinging beat in richly voiced chords (as, for example, on *Harlem Camp Meeting, I've Got the World on a String,* and many others).

In the third category I would put pieces like *Bugle Call Rag, Margie, Harlem Camp Meeting, The Scat Song, Jitter Bug,* the last three-named especially writ-

5. Compare this with Armstrong's approach to the same problem. His instrumentalists *really* suffered by comparison, Armstrong usually—and for eleven years—hogging the entire three-plus minutes of his recordings.

ten both in form and lyrics to integrate instrumental solos directly into the pieces. Since Calloway composed and co-authored quite a number of these pieces himself, here is further proof that his notion of band leadership clearly included a sense of the value of having a fine orchestra with superior soloists, and a strong conviction that his vocal offerings should be fully integrated into a jazz *orchestral* concept. Thus we hear his and his band's performances now as total entities. Calloway's vocals rarely obtrude; they are never the stylistic and formal intrusions we hear in thousands upon thousands of crooned novelty or pop vocals of the period.

Nor was such stylistic and contextual integration left to chance. It was something Calloway and his arrangers and musicians worked at all the time, without great fanfare, one might add. There was, I am sure, not even any sense of pursuing some great creative or intellectual achievement; it was simply motivated by the healthy notion that such musical integration made for better musical entertainment.

And here we come to the fourth point, that of the freedom given Calloway's arrangers. Even a minimal sampling of work, such as the 1930 *St. Louis Blues*, the incredibly virtuosic *Some of These Days* and *Black Rhythm, Trickeration, Evenin', Margie, Hot Toddy*, and numerous others (just to stay once again within the pre-1934 period) can give us a sense of the great diversity and breadth of the Calloway orchestra's stylistic range. To this should be added a genre of pieces virtually unique to Calloway which one might call the "moaners," almost always in a minor key and—in Cab's case—most often dealing with the subject of drugs. Indeed, starting with *Minnie the Moocher* (and her playmate Smokey Joe) in early 1931, Calloway began to create a whole cast of mythical characters, populating an imaginary Harlem. The sad truth was that neither the characters nor the place were all that "mythical" or "imaginary." But as long as the reefer-smoking characters were non-Caucasian, the white public that went slumming at the Cotton Club found it an exotic and deliciously "wicked" entertainment.

In retrospect we may find it amazing that an entire body of songs and instrumental pieces was created—and so openly promulgated—on the subject of what we now call "the drug problem." Though most whites and non-musicians didn't know it, songs about "vipers" or "kickin' the gong around" were about marijuana or opium smokers. An entire secret language developed, perpetuated now in the popular song literature of the thirties. Marijuana had innumerable names: "muggles" (the title of one of Armstrong's 1920 classics), "hay," "tea," "shuzzit," "muta," "grefa," "grass," "gunja," "reefer" and, most popular among musicians, "gauge" or "weed." One who smoked "pot"—then an unknown term—was a "viper." And much of this underground lingo found its way into song titles: Armstrong's *Song of the Vipers* and Waller's *Viper's Drag*, Charlie Johnson's *Viper's Dream*, Don Redman's *Chant of the Weed*, Benny Goodman's *Texas Tea Party*, and Cab Calloway's *Reefer Man*, and so on.

Actually, Cab's *Minnie* song saga—to which even the great Harold Arlen contributed twice, collaborating in the early thirties with Ted Koehler in writing for the Cotton Club shows: *Kickin' the Gong Around* and *Minnie the Moocher's*

Wedding Day—derived in type and musical style from a storytelling genre as old as jazz itself, exemplified by the tragic *Frankie and Johnny* and *St. James Infirmary*. These "moaners," which usually told of unrequited love or crimes of passion, were mostly set in minor keys and slow somber tempos. In a way, Cab's *Minnie* songs were the musical counterpart to those other early thirties' American phenomena, the gangster cartoons and the many "Reefer" movies and films about Chinatown opium dens. These pieces invariably borrowed from Ellington's then relatively novel jungle style and featured weirdly growly brass, dark saxophones, lurid gongs, and a heavy ominous beat. Hear Leroy Maxey's ill-boding press roll on *Kickin' the Gong Around*, for example (especially well played and recorded on the second, i.e. 1933, version), or the dank, gloomy atmosphere of *Zaz Zuh Zaz*. The lyrics were often quite graphic and had in their succinctness that power of imagery that the great silent films had.[6]

By now it should be clear to the reader that, rather than being a nondescript accompanimental unit designed to show off the leader's talents, Cab's band was a "musician's orchestra". And for musicians the Calloway recordings are full of wonderful surprises. There is hardly a side which does not offer several musical delights, sometimes tiny, sometimes major. The point is that Cab's arrangers hardly ever repeated themselves. They were always searching, developing, discovering, inventing with a surprisingly sure hand. It will serve us well to sample a few of these musical treats.

In the early days of Cab's leadership most of the arranging assignments went to Walter "Foots" Thomas, who also acted as musical director. Undoubtedly much of the early high quality of the band can be credited to him. The big soloist with the band at the time was Roger Q. Dickerson, a master of the trumpet plunger-and-growl style and a fine representative of the St. Louis school of brass playing. Dickerson's talking/preaching style can be heard to excellent advantage on *Is That Religion?*, affording us a glimpse, incidentally, of how close the relationship was between Calloway's scat singing, developing at this time, and some of the more extravagant expressions of the so-called "freak" trumpet style. Other outstanding examples of Dickerson's work can be heard on the first *Minnie the Moocher* recording, *St. Louis Blues*, and *Gotta Darn Good Reason*.

Like Ellington, Calloway liked to have variety and versatility in his sections. Lammar Wright, a charter member of the Missourians, was responsible for the open-horn or straighter solos. His playing was characterized by a propulsive bullet-like attack (much like Shad Collins's in Basie's band, who also worked during

---

6. Interestingly Calloway developed and pursued other themes in his vocal repertory: for example, the entire *Gal* series, some dozen songs (*Ain't Got No Gal in this Town, Little Town Gal, My Sunday Gal, My Gal, Copper-Colored Gal, Somebody Stole My Gal*, etc.); the *Lady* series (*Lady with the Fan, Eadie Was a Lady*, to which one could add *San Francisco Fan* and *Frisco Flo*); the *Harlem* theme (*Harlem Hospitality, Harlem Camp Meeting, The Man from Harlem*); and, of course, the whole *Hi-De-Ho* group songs. Another song with a remarkable theme was Cab's 1930 *Yaller*, an amazingly outspoken protest song about prejudice against half-castes. Cab sings this virtual "aria" with an anguished, impassioned voice that along with Cab's naturally dramatic voice reveals some of the aforementioned influence of Al Jolson.

three different periods with Calloway) and by well-designed solos which often featured rising scalar or chromatic figures (Ex. 4, from *Nobody's Sweetheart*, Dec. 1930). Wright is also prominently featured on the spectacular *Some of These Days* (both solos after Cab's vocal).

Ex. 4

Wendell Culley was at this time the band's "straight" player.[7] His almost classical concert band style and his clean trills can be heard on the intro and coda of *St. James Infirmary* and *Doin' the Rumba*, respectively.

Similarly in the reed section there was considerable diversity and skill. Thomas played all the saxophones plus flute, Andrew Brown all the saxes plus bass clarinet, and William Thornton Blue lead alto and all the clarinet solos. In this last-named role Blue's shrill, bright, and very eccentric clarinet—not unlike Teschemacher's—can be heard in all its raspy dirty overblown effectiveness on *Nobody's Sweetheart* (Ex. 5).

Ex. 5

7. This is the same Wendell Culley who played with Basie from 1951 to 1959, and played the lovely solo on Basie's and Neal Hefti's *Lil' Darlin'*.

While Brown was not used soloistically very much in the early days (except occasionally on bass clarinet—on which he can be heard to fine effect on *Somebody Stole My Gal (1931)*, for example),[8] Thomas was featured more frequently, especially on alto and baritone. His sixteenth-note break on *St. James Infirmary* (Ex. 6) is indicative of his technical command, as is his extended work on alto on *Six or Seven Times*, already showing the influence of the young Benny Carter and giving evidence of the sensible and elegant contributions Thomas was to make throughout his career with Calloway.

Ex. 6

As Calloway's resident arranger Thomas was also, of course, the chief architect of the band's style(s). If one has been raised on the prevalent assumptions that the early Calloway band need not be taken very seriously as an orchestra, one is not prepared for the many constant surprises and touches these performances hold. Limiting myself to only a few, I would single out *Black Rhythm*, with its solid full-ensemble sound and many excellent integrated solo breaks. Reuben Reeves, who had by now replaced Culley, opens the side with a simple and therefore all the more effective real trumpet-blues solo—after an interestingly unfurling chromatic introduction, arranged, I assume, by Thomas. In the succeeding blues-based choruses Thomas finds not only novel harmonic alterations of the basic "changes," but an interestingly varied series of breaks in the third, fourth, seventh, and eighth bars of each chorus, the ancient traditional places in the classic blues where the instruments "respond" to the singer's "call." Benny Payne has two piano breaks, the brass two more (the second of these a bell-tone pyramid—unusual in the middle of a blues setting), followed by clarinet and Morris White banjo breaks. To top this Thomas reserves his best idea

8. Brown seems to have been the first major black player to seriously take up the bass clarinet. Paul Whiteman and bands that emulated his "symphonic" dance style, of course, also used the instrument for special effects; and there are Benny Goodman's occasional encounters with the bass clarinet (as, for example, in late 1931 on *Lucille* with the Hotel Commodore Dance Orchestra). But Andrew Brown seems to have been the only player, until Harry Carney adopted the bass clarinet, to use the instrument as a real jazz "horn."

Fig. 1

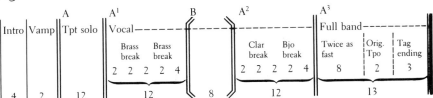

for the final chorus: he doubles the tempo of the first eight bars (not double time, but twice as fast—and short), compensating for this short-footed stanza by repeating the tenth bar twice more, thus almost restoring the chorus to its full intended duration (Fig. 1).

Thomas was a good functional arranger, never less than proficient, often inventive, and not given to repeating himself. His finest early achievement, along with *Bugle Call Rag*, must be *Some of These Days*, amazing to this day for its hell-bent break-away tempo, upwards of 300 to the quarter-note beat. Since the performance is literally peppered with eighth notes, it is—even though not perfect—a staggering technical achievement for its time and, if memory doesn't fail me, the fastest tempo achieved by any orchestra up to that time. It is curious that this tour de force received so little recognition, then and now, particularly when compared with the runaway success of *Casa Loma Stomp* (recorded seventeen days earlier—at a comparatively leisurely tempo of $\quarternote = 240$). Not only does *Some of These Days* offer quite spectacular staccato-style solos by Wheeler, Brown (on tenor), Blue (on alto and clarinet), Thomas (on baritone), but halfway through, the three-man saxophone section wrestles mightily with a flashy parallel-voiced ensemble chorus, almost winning the bout. Wright, as already mentioned, and Culley also soloed, the whole performance ending in a perfect coda of nine punched-out bright C-major dotted-quarter notes (Ex. 7).

Ex. 7

Another splendid coda is contributed by Thomas in *Nobody's Sweetheart*, with its curious trumpet mini-cadenza bumping right smack into an oddly spaced chordal "pyramid."

It is fascinating to compare the early Calloway singing with his more mature period (although we must remind ourselves that his peak successes were achieved before he reached thirty). In the early years his voice appears to have been clearly located in the high tenor range and timbre. Pieces like *St. Louis Blues* and *Nobody's Sweetheart* are full of high Gs, As, and B♭s, consistently holding to that tessitura. But in the first *Minnie* recording (1931) Cab is much more baritonal, somber-voiced. In *Black Rhythm* he sings the first chorus as a light baritone, the second as a bright tenor. In *Six or Seven Times* he sings in a completely convincing female falsetto. His diction and articulation were stunning from the start, but more importantly his improvisational talent was already fully developed early on. Cab could never sing a song the same way twice, and even the first time he had to "recompose" the melody or invent an entirely new one (witness, for example, *Some of These Days* and *Nobody's Sweetheart*). Calloway had such control of his voice, musically and technically, that he could even imitate those crooning tenors that were so ubiquitous in the early thirties. Hear him do so— seriously or as a "put on"?—on *Between the Devil and the Deep Blue Sea* and *This Time It's Love.*

Trickeration (Oct. 1931), another Arlen/Koehler collaboration, is interesting for its sophisticated cohesive arrangement (although a bit rough in performance and in its snappy peppy tempo somewhat under-rehearsed), Cab's great scat singing and impeccable articulation, and Koehler's tricky lyrics. Four months before Ellington's famous swing era proclamation, Cab sings: "Don't mean a thing, this crazy swing; latest thing in Harlem: Trickeration."

Benny Carter's *Hot Toddy*, another fast "flag-waver," which I take to be another Thomas arrangement, is unusual for having no Calloway vocal, being strictly instrumental. It has some of the feel of Moten's *Toby* and *Prince of Wails* (recorded four months later) but not the latter's clarity of execution or incomparable dynamic energy. The fast tempo allows Thomas to cram twelve 16-bar choruses into two and a half minutes and thus a considerable amount of textural and timbral variety, particularly in the later sections, when Thomas turns the piece into an early riff-style number. He combined brass and reeds in a variety of interesting mixtures, e.g. one trumpet, one trombone, two saxes, or in a lower register, two trombones, a tenor, and a baritone.

By now Edwin Swayzee and Reuben Reeves had replaced Dickerson and Culley respectively, both new players brilliantly featured in the late 1931 *Bugle Call Rag* (Swayzee is the muted trumpet). In 1932 Doc Cheatham replaced Reeves, which added to the section a more melodic player whom Cab often used on lyric lead work (as on *I've Got the World on a String* and *I Gotta Right To Sing the Blues*).

Another superior addition to the band was Harry White, a fine trombonist in the Higginbotham tradition, an excellent arranger who now frequently spelled Thomas in the arranging assignments, and a legendary lush whose heroic nonstop drinking bouts were justly celebrated in the 1934 *Jitter Bug*. A superb example of White's talent is his composition and arrangement of *Evenin'* (Sept. 1933). A fine tune, allied to a ravishing set of "changes," its rendition by Cab in White's arrangement is far ahead of its time (with the usual exception of Ellington). It is in fact slightly Duke-ish in its sumptuous harmonies, although the sound of the arrangement and Cab's singing are entirely original.

The song, in the standard AABA format, is basically in a simple poignant minor (the key of G). But it is its bridge, its crowning achievement, that lifts the song far above the ordinary, as it opens up into a soothing G *major*. The three melodic minor-seventh drops (Ex. 8) serve as a balancing contrast to the calmly

Ex. 8

conjunct motion of the A themes. Moreover, as the melody falls, the harmony rises in contrary motion, to the subdominant (in its thirteenth-chord configuration), followed by beautifully shifting ninth chords as the cadencing melody settles back into G minor.[9]

Like almost all of White's arrangements, *Evenin'* creates its own special sonoric atmosphere, in this case a full warm sound, yet loose and airy. The introduction in chromatic harmonies sets the overall basic mood with three low-register clarinets, bass clarinet, bowed bass, and a single-note piano melody by Benny Payne. As the chorus proper begins, with Cab in his best "real singing" vocal style, Payne switches to celesta, adding bright crystalline sprinkles of sound to the otherwise subdued pastel sonority. Indeed, it seems to me that the celesta, which was discovered by jazz musicians in the late twenties, has rarely been used so tellingly, so integrally, as in *Evenin'*—especially in the bridge, (in Example 8), where a countermelody in half-notes adds significantly to the overall beauty of this passage (Ex. 9). Notice, too, Morris White's lacy guitar arpeggios behind both Cab's vocal and Doc Cheatham's elegiac pastel-muted trumpet.

Ex. 9

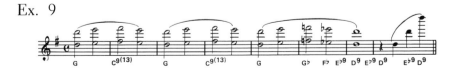

9. Very few of these harmonic and melodic refinements are left in the harmonically rather plain and routine Basie-Rushing version of the same song (1936, Jones-Smith Inc.).

Harry White's imagination and skill are in further evidence in *Harlem Camp Meeting, Zaz Zuh Zaz, Father's Got His Glasses On,* and *The Scat Song,* the first two being his compositions as well. White's arrangements are usually economical and cohesive. In *Harlem,* a humorous evocation of a revival meeting, Harlem style, the repeated "bell-tones" that initiate the basic riff theme reappear throughout in different instrumental guises (high trombone, saxes, chimes, etc.) and function as a thread, tying the different sequences together. But they derive in turn from the four bars of "bell-tone" pyramids in the very introduction (Ex. 10). The fourth introductory bar reappears later as a harmonically daring brass break (Ex. 11).

Ex. 10

Ex. 11

In the meantime Preacher Calloway delivers his scat sermon while his "parishioners" respond in kind: personified in solos by Arville Harris, Edwin Swayzee, the newest incumbent of the growl-and-plunger trumpet chair, and Benny Payne. Notable throughout is the hard-swinging rhythm section.

More of the same, except in a secular setting, occurs in *Father's Glasses,* replete with growly brass, guitar "bell tones," and a fine open-horn solo by Swayzee. Eddie Barefield, the latest Calloway recruit, recently of the Moten band and McKinney's Cotton Pickers, was a strong addition, adding a whole new focus in style and sound to the saxophone section.

Calloway's *The Scat Song* is another White-arranged gem, excellently performed. Here both Cab's amusing scat lyrics—as he calls it "this silly language without any reason or rhyme"—and the answering scat-ish instrumental breaks, are composed right into the song, a brilliant way to give everybody in the band a solo spot. Especially sparkling are Swayzee's and Barefield's contributions, the latter concluding the proceedings with flashy well-executed triplet-note flourish.

To complete these late 1933 Victor sides, there are superb remakes of *Minnie the Moocher, Kickin' the Gong Around,* and Harry White's contribution to the ongoing *Minnie* saga, *Zaz Zuh Zaz.* Once again we are plunged into Smokey Joe's Chinatown underworld, not with silly pentatonic Chinese clichés, but with sinister powerfully gripping, growly minor-key tone paintings. On *Zaz Zuh Zaz,* White gets a deep "inside-the-music" sound of the orchestra, much aided and abetted by Morris White's pungent guitar strummings, while Cab babbles on in

incoherent stupor. The band, chanting in unison as in some ancient tribal ritual, echoes Cab's weird incantations.[10]

The remake of *Minnie the Moocher* is even more graphic and intense than
the original. The arrangement is much enriched by swirling guitar, piano, and
vibraphone embellishments, especially in Cab's final out-of-tempo cadenza: a
whole sound-world new to jazz. Even more unusual is Cab's long downward
glissando starting on a high B and ending 2½ octaves lower, supposedly impossible for a male singer.[11]

Apart from these quite remarkable musical achievements, Calloway's success
can be measured by the fact that, even during the bottom years of the Depression, 1931 and 1932, he and his orchestra were in recording studios about once
a month. Only Ellington and the Casa Loma orchestra could match that. And
as Calloway's popularity grew, instrumental solos and entire instrumental numbers, *sans* Calloway, became more prevalent in the band's repertory. The orchestra grew in size, and, as already noted, one by one some of the original
Missourians were replaced by younger or more "advanced" players. By 1940 only
three of the veteran Missourians remained with Calloway: Wright, Thomas, and
reed-man Andrew Brown.[12] Calloway's penchant and formidable talent for scat-
singing and inventing Harlem jive lingo, skillfully poured into one catchy song
after another, was parlayed into ever-growing popularity. Out of the initial "Hi-
De-Ho" (originally "Hi-De-Hi"), Calloway developed an entire hip hepster's vocabulary, some of it borrowed at first from Louis Armstrong's scat-singing.[13] This
was not an entirely novel idea; after all the Elizabethan madrigalists had their

10. It is a fact, clearly audible on most of Cab's records, that his vocal projection was so powerful
that on all high notes he had to back away from the microphone, lest the results be electronically
distorted.

11. This 1933 version of *Minnie* was not issued until the late fifties, remaining previously unreleased
reputedly because two interpolated Jewish cantoral lines offended the sensitivities of RCA Victor
executives. As Albert McCarthy pointed out, this was in marked ironic contrast to their (and other
recording companies') acceptance of "the most grotesque lyrics referring to black people."

12. Wright's formidable career began with Bennie Moten in 1924 (at age 17), extending all the way
through the Calloway big band years to 1947, and beyond that to free-lancing and teaching in New
York. Perhaps it was also a special pleasure to see both of his sons, Lammar Wright, Jr., and Elmon,
play in the trumpet section of Dizzy Gillespie's big band, Dizzy being Wright Sr's young section
mate in the Calloway band for two years.

13. The "hepster" of the mid-thirties became the bop "hipster" of the forties. If you used "hep" in
1945, you certainly were not hip.

   Both Louis Armstrong and Cab Calloway have avowed that their scat-singing careers began accidentally when they forgot some lyrics, in Armstrong's case on his 1926 recording of *Heebie Jeebies*,
in Calloway's case during a live performance when he quickly filled in with "Hi-De-Ho." (But see
important footnote 17 in Chapter 3, above.) The accidental nature of these events all but confirms
that blacks have a special affinity for free syllabic invention, something that would never occur to a
white singer at La Scala or the Met upon forgetting some lyrics. The fact is that in most African
tribes, speech and song, as well as the use of "nonsense syllables" in their musics, are all intricately
linked, traditions that are virtually non-existent in European cultures. (See discussion of this subject
in *Early Jazz*, 61–62.)

"Heigh Nonny No" and Rudy Vallee had used his "Hi-Ho" salute for years; and any number of pop singers had used other verbal gimmicks as vocal logos.

What is little appreciated, however, is that Calloway's use of this new scat lingo was accomplished at a very high level of inventiveness and ingenuity, not to mention Cab's formidable skill in performance. The point is that these were not the silly old Tin Pan Alley "novelty tunes" with their inane play on words, fit for the mentalities of three-year-olds, but, rather, witty, frequently intricate verbal broadsides that more often than not told a little story. Because these songs were humorous and lightweight—and many are genuinely funny—they have been passed over by jazz historians, little realizing that, even in this curious field, genuine creativity is an appropriate requisite.

The under-side of this point is that most of this material was made for white consumption. Blacks may have enjoyed it, too, but the big market was with the white consumer. And whites in the thirties thought all this jive talk was quaint, amusing, and took people's minds off the Depression or the ominous political rumblings from Europe. There is no question that Cab and Irving Mills, his manager (doubling as publisher-song writer), exploited this factor. Earlier, whites had gone slumming in Harlem to savor the exotic blandishments of the jungle, of Africa. Ellington, Charlie Johnson's Paradise band, and the Missourians had known how to cater to those instincts and prejudices. Now, in the thirties, whites saw black musicians like Calloway and, I dare say, Armstrong and the great tap dancers of the period, as quaint, funny, urbanized mountebanks and entertainers. With Cab and Louis it was no longer "black face" comedy, as in the minstrel and coon-song days, but "black *talk*" comedy—with just enough Uncle Tom-ism left in it to create the illusion of a status quo.

It is not appropriate for a white author to pass judgment on these matters. As a music historian, it will suffice to suggest that the unique quality of Calloway's talent and artistry make such judgments in any case irrelevant. Viewed in a historical context, Calloway's gifts were brilliantly applied to a musical tradition indigenous to blacks and one which he turned into an absolutely inimitable craft. For while one could find any number of Armstrong imitators, instrumentally and vocally, in the thirties there was no one who could successfully imitate Calloway until Sister Rosetta Tharpe and Slim Gaillard came along in the late thirties—although Billy Banks tried often enough. [14]

But, of course, scat-singing and nonsense syllables were by no means the extent of Calloway's art. For it is wrong to typecast Calloway as merely a comedic singer. He had an astonishing, probably unique talent for ballads and straight popular songs. Fine examples of this aspect of his work are *Angeline, I've Got the World on a String, Evenin', Emaline, Long, Long Ago, I Gotta Right To Sing The Blues, I Learned About Love from Her, Afraid of Love, One Look at You, My Gal,* and *I'll Be Around.* What these performances reveal is

14. The tradition of scat-singing did not, of course, die with Armstrong and Calloway. It has been perpetuated to our time through dozens of artists, from Leo Watson and Dizzy Gillespie through Jon Hendricks, Dave Lambert, and Annie Ross to Ella Fitzgerald and Clark Terry, and beyond them right up to those astounding present-day scat virtuosos, Leon Thomas and Bobby McFerrin.

that Calloway had virtually complete technical command of his voice and a fertile imagination to go with it. Indeed in this type of song, he seems to me to be one of the most compellingly expressive singers jazz has ever produced. It is, of course, not what jazz purists will permit to be called "jazz-singing"; and indeed it goes beyond jazz, in the way that Ellington's music or some of Billie Holiday's most profound performances also defy such narrow categorization. Certainly Calloway's vocal technique and the musical imagination that informs it go far beyond the capabilities of the typical jazz singer, let alone your garden variety pop singer.

The disbelieving reader is invited to listen to Calloway's rendition of *My Gal*, a fine but obscure song by an equally obscure writer named Al Bernard (not the same song recorded by Jelly Roll Morton). Though Calloway does not depart radically from the written song, he is nevertheless free in his interpretation, hovering around the melody, inflecting and timing its phrases in completely original ways. Timbre and vibrato are also used as expressive devices, not mere ballast which the voice just carries around. It is singing in which diction and enunciation are an integral part of both the vocal technique and the style. Thus he brings an extra dimension, a sense of drama to the song, which in other hands it would surely not have had.

The handsome arrangement of *My Gal* by Andy Gibson heightens this dramatic effect by setting off Cab's singing against a simple background of soft saxes and muted brass. And like Cab's singing, the arrangement goes beyond standard rhythmic jazz, using instead a pulsating reiterative ostinato as accompaniment. But it also has two blemishes: one, a somewhat ostentatious introduction (with portentous timpani rolls) of the kind that Ellington would sometimes use in his show or film music, later in his extended suites—this one seems to have been borrowed in part from Ellington's 1935 film *Symphony in Black*; the other flaw is its brevity and abrupt, tacked-on C-major chord ending. Undoubtedly the arrangement was cut to fit the 10-inch recording time restrictions.

Calloway's rendition of Alec Wilder's sublime *I'll Be Around* (Feb. 2, 1942) is an even more striking performance (some of its tinges of sentimentalism notwithstanding). Again Cab tugs at the emotions with unexpected vocal inflections and colorations. Here he is a bass-baritone, at times virile, at times mellow as a cello (as he would have quipped). Gibson's arrangement perfectly befits the mood of longing Calloway creates: subtly dramatic and richly colored. An added dimension here is the use of the Cabaliers, a velvet-toned male vocal quartet (formerly called the Palmer Brothers). Gibson uses them in sustained soft backgrounds, both *with* the saxes and in lieu of them. Similarly the introduction uses Ted McRae's bass-baritone-ish lyric tenor against a pastel background of male quartet and celesta—quite a fetching sound.

As we have seen, already in the early thirties in the midst of his scat and *Minnie the Moocher* hits, Calloway was allowing ample solo opportunities for some of his more outstanding players. A major breakthrough, however, on this front, came with the Calloway band's recording of Will Hudson's *Moonglow*, featuring solos by Eddie Barefield (on alto), Arville Harris (on clarinet), and

Andrew Brown (on bass clarinet). It is Barefield's solo that stands out, not only as probably his finest recorded effort on alto—he was usually featured on clarinet with other orchestras—but as a major musical statement of its time. As Example 12 shows, Barefield's solo is a complete re-composition of Hudson's languorous tune. Not quite set in double time (as Parker, for instance, might have done some years later), it is nevertheless a solo in which the available space in the

Ex. 12

beat is rhythmically well filled out. It is a well-constructed solo, probably not completely improvised, which develops or elaborates its materials cogently. Of particular interest are Barefield's four solo breaks (all of which fleetingly flirt with double-time), and all of which contain the kind of flourishes and roulades that precisely anticipate equivalent moments in Eric Dolphy's masterful solos in *Stormy Weather* (in 1960 with Mingus). Indeed in Barefield's last break, not just the notes but the sound, remind one instantly of the mature Dolphy (or is it the other way around?).

The two other solos, while more than adequate, are of lesser magnitude. Arville Harris's clarinet solo is a bit too busy for its own good, while Brown's bass clarinet is essentially ornamentation of the basic melody. Benny Payne adds little daubs of color on piano, celesta, and vibraphone.

The next Calloway soloist to be featured on records was drummer Cozy Cole, who joined Cab in late 1938, replacing the original Missourians' drummer Leroy Maxey, who had served Calloway well through the years. But unfortunately Cole's three solo outings with Calloway—*Ratamacue, Crescendo in Drums*, and *Paradiddle*—are disappointing, both as virtuoso display pieces and as compositional vehicles. *Paradiddle* (1940), composed and arranged by Dizzy Gillespie, is the best of the three. It looks both backward and forward, reminiscent in its winding saxophone theme of Ellington's *Reminiscing in Tempo*, forward in its bold bop-ish harmonies and voicings, especially in the bridge of the head chorus. Sadly, Cole's solo, stuck in endless snare drum triplet patterns, never connects creatively with Dizzy's work.

Around the same time Milt Hinton's bass playing began to be featured soloistically, first on *Pluckin' the Bass* (summer 1939) and then on *Ebony Silhouette* (early 1941).[15] *Ebony Silhouette*, like Blanton's *Mr. J.B. Blues*, featured bowed solo passages. These were at that time still an extreme rarity, simply because jazz bass players had not seriously considered exploring bowing techniques, regarding

15. The Jimmy Blanton–Ellington bass and piano duets fall between Hinton's dates: November 1939 and October 1940. But the real pioneer of arco bass playing in jazz was Slam Stewart, who, after hearing Boston violinist Ray Perry in the mid-thirties play and sing in unison, developed his technique of singing an octave above his bowed bass work. (There is a curious link here in that Stewart's partner Slim Gaillard was a very popular scat and novelty song composer-singer and as such, by the late thirties, Calloway's greatest competitor.) For more on Blanton and Slam Stewart, see Chapter 2 above.

them as a skill best left to the classical symphony musicians. Hinton's and Blanton's breakthroughs were clearly pioneer efforts, unrivaled at the time (except by Slam Stewart), but viewed by today's standards as rather elementary.[16] *Ebony Silhouette* is also a curious non-piece, thrown together by Payne and Hinton, its pizzacato passages unfortunately limited to uninspired scale passages.

Pluckin' was composed by the brothers Eldridge, Roy and Joe, as a fast-tempoed virtuoso vehicle for Hinton. It features an intricate technique peculiar to string instruments—and analogous to one developed on the violin by Niccolo Paganini in the early years of the nineteenth century—which combines plucking and slapping the strings in rapid alternation. (Ex. 13). This side also featured Gillespie's

Ex. 13

Normal noteheads signify pizzicato (plucked)
with stems up = right hand slap
with stems down = left hand slap

first recorded solo with Cab, a fine effort which, though a little tense, reveals in Dizzy at age twenty-two an already distinct and original voice. The distance between promise and mastery, however, is made clear in Chu Berry's immediately following solo, one of Berry's most perfect efforts.

Dizzy's solo on *Pluckin'* was in truth a more successful effort than that on his own composition and arrangement, *Pickin' the Cabbage*. Because *Pickin'* marks Gillespie's debut on records as composer-arranger (and trumpeter) it has retroactively attracted much attention—and has been frequently over-praised. It is, without wishing to make a major issue of it, a minor effort, both in tonality (E♭ minor) and in inspiration. Set over a riff-ostinato in bass and baritone, its theme is catchy enough in typical lightweight swing band riff-tune fashion. Gillespie's solo is fluent, recognizable as his more by its typical Eldridge-type of legato articulation, especially in running eighth notes, than by its choice of notes. Gillespie has trouble liberating himself from the constricting minor-key changes and, I think, confuses the several times recurring C♭ (the minor sixth) with a

16. The real breakthroughs in jazz bass-bowing did not come until the 1960s, with the playing of Paul Chambers in the Miles Davis Quintet and with the arrival of the remarkable Richard Davis.

flatted-fifth move that he had been working on for some time. *Pickin's* best moments occur in the arranged introduction where Dizzy produces four daring parallel eleventh and thirteenth chords (Ex. 14) that were not yet in regular jazz usage with anyone else, except Duke Ellington.

Ex. 14

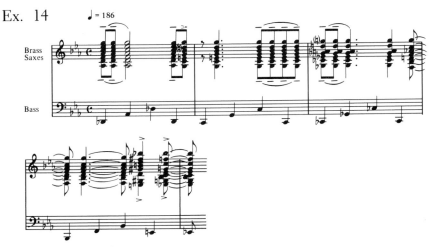

The young Gillespie was still finding himself, and it was a fortunate circumstance that he gained employment for two years with the famous Calloway band, a period during which Gillespie was able to consolidate his style. An uneven erratic evolution delineates his progress, from the circular repetitious solo on *Calling All Bars* to the more confident and fleet-fingered ones on *Bye-Bye Blues* and *Boo-Wah Boo-Wah*. On *Cupid's Nightmare* we can hear Gillespie in an even more experimental mood as he feeds eagerly on Don Redman's highly chromatic harmonies (Ex. 15).

Ex. 15

Cupid's Nightmare is a curiously ambitious piece, much more than a mere jazz tune—or a "fox-trot" as all record labels insisted on calling such pieces right up to the LP era—a real instrumental composition that didn't really belong on a 10-inch record. As the full and much better version available on a broadcast transcription shows, *Cupid's Nightmare* is a slowish instrumental ballad comprising as 48-bar A A B A structure, divided 16 + 16 + 8 + 8 (with the last eight bars a contraction of the first 16). Once Redman has done with the ominously muted brass introduction (whole-tone, of course!), the piece itself begins its long chromatic journey (Ex. 16) in shifting parallel ninths. At a time when stale riff

Ex. 16

figures dominated the field, Redman's piece, with its unanchored harmonies, must have sounded nightmarishly disconcerting to audiences. Some musicians like Dizzy, undoubtedly found it challenging. In the context of a surrounding sea of swing clichés, it might have seemed like quite a daring piece, especially harmonically, but it is ultimately flawed by its lack of real melody and rhythmic contours. [17]

In its original form, *Nightmare* did not fit on a 10-inch disc—at least as long as Redman insisted on also including those later inane riff figures that lead precisely nowhere. [18] So he cut his piece to a truncated ABA format, robbing Gillespie of one of his two solo spots.

Dizzy, always a prankster and cut-up, was finally fired by Calloway, who accused him of throwing spitballs on the bandstand—ironically the *one* time that Gillespie was actually blameless. Much has been written about the ensuing altercation, but the fact remains that Calloway was and remained a strong admirer of Dizzy's. No further proof is needed than the many solo spots Cab gave his

17. Oddly enough, I suspect that Ellington, always an admirer of Redman's, borrowed—as if he needed to—some of *Nightmare's* theme for his own *American Lullaby*, a piece he tossed off in 1939 and presented to Meredith Wilson in 1942 for his radio show, but never performed himself. And perhaps this was in sly revenge for Redman having borrowed the bridge of Duke's *Mood Indigo* for *Cupid's Nightmare!*

18. This same pitch sequence became the ultimate swing era cliché, used by hundreds of bands in hundreds of arrangements in every key, sometimes with minor variations (but not so as to disguise the "original"), usually ponderously punched out by the bass instruments.

young trumpet star, even more so on location than on records. But when Jonah Jones joined the Cab, an occasion celebrated in a similarly titled opus, Dizzy was given less and less solo space. (And that is probably what the spitball incident was really all about—internal band rivalries and jealousies.) Though Calloway was once overheard telling Dizzy not to play "that Chinese music" of his—this from a man who had recorded a piece called *Chinese Rhythm*—he nevertheless seems to have been genuinely, if at times dimly, aware of Dizzy's talent. By the same token, Jones, more firmly established as an Armstrong disciple, was probably "safer" for Calloway, less trouble than the irrepressible upstart Gillespie.

But unquestionably the most featured soloist in Cab's band was the redoubtable Chu Berry. There is hardly a performance on which he did not solo, and several of his major solo vehicles became substantial successes. Among these *Ghost of a Chance* has been often singled out for praise, but my preference is for Berry's *Lonesome Nights*, a Benny Carter composition. In the latter, Berry is much more himself, not quite so bent on emulating Coleman Hawkins in his spectacular 1939 hit recording of *Body and Soul*. Berry had problems with ballads anyway, for he lacked the warm, fully-centered tone that a great ballad player must have—and which Hawkins certainly had in abundance. Berry's was a sound situated halfway between Hawkins's and Lester Young's. That is the reason why Berry became such a successful "speed" player; by playing virtuoso eighth-note solos at top tempos, one can hide one's tone deficiencies. That is also why Berry could secretly admire a player like Freddy Martin who, if he had very little else, had a luscious sound.

Berry's only defense in solo ballads was to play fast notes, often in double time, and to dress up his tone with a wide fast vibrato, in part to simulate the expression the tone itself lacked. But his vibrato was too regular, automated; it didn't come from *inside* the sound, it was merely added to it. On *Ghost* the sound was especially edgy and nervous; and going into double-time exactly on the same comparable place, going into leaping diminished fifths at the exactly same climactic moment as Hawkins did, detracts from Berry's effort. But on *Lonesome Nights*, with a better reed, a warmer tone, and by setting his sights on simpler more personal aspirations, Berry fulfills his potential.

But the real Berry can be heard on *Topsy Turvy*, *At the Clambake Carnival*, *Come On with the Come On*, and on the aforementioned air check.[19] Here, like a fish in water, Berry is in his element, especially on the fast-moving *Limehouse Blues*.[20]

After Berry's death in a car accident in late 1941, his mantle in Cab's band fell eventually to Illinois Jacquet and Ike Quebec, two mighty tenor battlers.

We are fortunate to have Jacquet on some 1943 air checks, made during a period when the American Federation of Musicians recording ban was in effect. (Jacquet never appeared with Calloway on commercial recordings.) After his sensational emergence as an outstanding soloist on Lionel Hampton's *Flying*

19. Alamac Records, ASR 2407.
20. Other fine Chu Berry performances can be heard with his own bands: Chu Berry and His Stompy Stevedores, and Chu Berry and His Little Jazz Ensemble.

Home in 1942, Jacquet, still only twenty-one, played with Calloway almost two years. His playing then, in its elegance and melodic flexibility, still reveals his previous affinity for the alto saxophone, which he only gave up upon joining Hampton. Jacquet's *Body and Soul* chorus with Calloway is elegant and yearning, as he weaves enchanting garlands of notes around the original melody. On the up-tempo *105 in the Shade* Jacquet is in his better-known flamboyant mood, ornately swooping and careening about the swing-riff tune, including a spectacular leap to an altissimo E♭ (concert) , supposedly about an octave *beyond* the tenor's normal upper range.

Jacquet's successor, Ike Quebec, brilliantly upheld this by now famous lineage. On one number after another Quebec displays his firm tone, incisive attack, and melodic logic. *Cruisin' with Cab, Frantic on the Atlantic* (with its bolting, charging entrance, sweeping everything before it, high Gs and all), but, above all, a hard-swinging growly *St. Louis Blues*, all offer superb examples of Quebec's powerful, almost awesome style. His three blues choruses on *St. Louis*, raspy and hot against a growling brass background, provide us with a trenchant glimpse not only of Quebec's art, but the direct power and unremitting swing of this remarkable Calloway band.

As already mentioned, because it was led by a singer, a comedic one at that, the Calloway band has been unfairly ignored or slighted. Even earlier, but particularly from 1939 to its demise in 1948, the Calloway orchestra was never less than thoroughly professional, and often much more, offering well-disciplined ensemble playing and generally first-rate solo work. It played with a consistency and drive that only a few others could intermittently match. The Calloway band's swing was never less than the state of the art permitted; and they never stopped improving.

One large reason for the rhythmic stability and drive of the Calloway band was its bass player, Milt Hinton, with the band from 1936 until it disbanded. No bass player has worked harder and more devotedly at his craft, constantly improving. As we hear the recordings from the late thirties and forties, we can actually see Milt bent over his bass, virtually hugging it, sweating, squeezing that last ounce of acoustic energy out of his instrument. No one has ever seen him give less than his utmost. If Calloway's band outswung most of its competitors, it is largely due to Hinton, aided and abetted, of course, during the band's peak period by two fine orchestral drummers, Cozy Cole and J. C. Heard. On side after side, these players, along with the strong, steady beat of guitarist Danny Barker, created a rock-solid rhythmic foundation that made it virtually impossible for the rest of the band and Calloway not to swing.

Cab always managed to get good arrangements, but in 1940, in Buster Harding, he acquired the perfect arranger to complement both Calloway's pungent singing and the by then clearly developed incisive style of the band. If some of his early arrangements (like *Bye Bye Blues, A Smooth One,* and *Tappin' Off*) made the band sound a bit too much like Benny Goodman, he and Cab and the band soon changed that.

Calloway's band never broke any new ground. Its mature style was more or less that of Fletcher Henderson, regardless of who made the actual arrangements. However, none captured that sound and style better than Calloway's orchestra. And for a singer, who was often not taken very seriously by jazz musicians, Cab surely cared immensely about jazz and maintaining a first-rate jazz orchestra. Would that Henderson and Armstrong had cared as much and provided comparable leadership.

ANDY KIRK

It is fascinating to contemplate the role that geography and chance encounters have played in the history of jazz. Although often giving the impression that "it all happens in New York"—even Basie and his Kansas City cohorts had to go there to really "make it"—it is useful to remind ourselves that 1) there *was* a Kansas City, under a wide-open Prendergast political regime, spawning crucial developments in jazz, including the contributions of one Charlie Parker; 2) that further north in Bismarck, North Dakota, another young man, Charlie Christian, was revolutionizing the guitar, with shock waves of after-effects that, for better or worse, can be felt unto this day in all popular music, even rock; 3) that practically every town in America had a German music teacher and that these provided musical training to the likes of Scott Joplin, Benny Goodman, and Earl Hines, and countless others; 4) that Tatum, Claude Hopkins, Oscar Peterson first studied the classical literature with classical piano teachers; 5) that John Lewis as a teenager in Albuquerque, New Mexico, already heard and knew one of his major influences, Lester Young—not in New York; 6) that it was on the road with the Earl Hines band that Gillespie and Parker first began listening to each other in earnest.

The criss-crossing of bands over the length and breadth of this nation over the decades, with the chance encounters between musicians, has been a factor of virtually incalculable importance in the development of jazz. The long hard tours, the endless one-nighters, though at times painful in actuality, have also played a crucial fertilizing role in the growth of this music. A study of whose paths crossed—and when—would in itself make a very instructive survey of jazz history.

Consider, for example, the fact that Jimmie Lunceford and Andy Kirk both, somewhat by chance, went to Denver, Colorado, to study with Wilberforce Whiteman, Paul's father, and under that remarkable teacher's tutelage both became skillful performers on a host of instruments (brass and woodwinds); further that both played and acquired a certain disciplined professionalism with George Morrison's orchestra in Denver; that the one, Kirk, ended up in 1926 in Terrence Holder's Texas-based band, the other, Lunceford, in Mary Lou Burleigh's band in Memphis, and that she, old enough to appreciate as a teenager in her native Pittsburgh the work of a certain pianist named Earl Hines, soon joined her husband John Williams in Terrence Holder's band, thus becoming with her husband one of the charter members of what in a few years was to be known as

Andy Kirk and His Twelve Clouds of Joy. Thus the lives and talents of the elder Whiteman, three major orchestra leaders, two most remarkable jazz pianists, and one very special woman arranger-composer all intertwine in a scheme of geography and chance.

The parallel between Kirk and Lunceford goes farther in that both gradually gave up their playing roles, turning to leading their orchestras; and both had in their service at least one major creative personality, Mary Lou Williams and Sy Oliver, respectively, who early on set the basic style of their band. Kirk, a modest man, had in 1929 reluctantly taken over the leadership of Holder's Black Clouds of Joy band, while continuing to play tuba and bass saxophone. (Holder was one of the popular early trumpet stars of the Southwest but, apparently because of domestic troubles, abandoned his orchestra in 1928.) Our skein of coincidences continues when, after Kirk had taken over the leadership of the Clouds, George Lee, another important Kansas City band leader, happened to hear Kirk in Tulsa and recommended him for a long-term engagement at the Pla-Mor Ballroom in Kansas City, affording the band some welcome financial stability. In turn, the young Jack Kapp, recording director for the Brunswick label, happened to hear Kirk and asked him to hold a rehearsal in preparation for a recording date. Here again fate interceded in that the regular Kirk pianist, Marion Jackson, failed to show up at the rehearsal. Mary Lou Williams was asked at the last minute to substitute for Jackson. And so Mary Lou Williams became a permanent fixture of the Kirk organization—indeed one of its two stars; the other, in the late thirties, being the remarkable tenor saxophonist Dick Wilson.

The Kirk orchestra's recording history began in late 1929 with two sides cut in Kansas City on the Vocalian label (under the name of John Williams and His Memphis Stompers). *Lotta Sax Appeal* was mainly a vehicle for Williams's baritone sax, played with a gruff tone and a rather stiff, old-fashioned slap-tongue style. The best soloists, however, are trombonist Allen Durham (a cousin of Ed Durham) in two surprisingly fluent, cleanly played choruses, and Mary Lou Williams in a richly chordal, for the time amazingly swinging solo. *Somepin' Slow and Low*, a loosely strung-together series of solos, primitively typical for the period, is notable only for a rather tortured, uncertain violin solo by Claude Williams (later guitarist with Count Basie) and a rather brief two-fisted "advanced" piano solo by Mary Lou Williams, proving that at age nineteen she had already learned her James P. Johnson and Earl Hines lessons very well indeed. At least two of Hines's trademarks are very much in evidence: the breaking up of the "stride" time through displaced chords and disjunct harmonies, and the wandering melodic left hand—all in ten astonishingly self-assured measures.

But even three years earlier, when Mary Lou was only sixteen, she was already an amazingly precocious pianistic talent, as evidenced by recordings she made with her husband John Williams's band. Her solos on *Midnight Stomp* and *Now Cut Loose* (a remake of *Midnight Stomp*) are notable for both their advanced conception and virtuosic execution, second only to Hines and Johnson. Both solos use the same general ingredients—broken "walking" tenths, right-hand octaves and tremolos (à la Hines), stomping shifted rhythmic accents, fleet hand-crossing over-hand cascade figures, and other surprises—but in each instance shuffled around in different sequences.

Two early solo recordings of 1930 further confirm that Mary Lou Williams already had complete command of the full keyboard. They also reveal that she was not an originator but a first-rate assimilator. An exceptionally high grade of eclecticism marks her entire career, from her early days the major influences being Hines, James P. Johnson, Waller, and occasionally Willie "The Lion" Smith, to which she was later to add Tatum and Wilson, and still later Milt Buckner's locked-hands style. In the 1930 *Drag 'Em*, Hinesian right-hand octaves and tremolos, left-hand melodic "fantasies," and other break-ups of rhythmic continuity are combined with strong stompy stride passages. Her playing here is also notable for its refined touch and intelligent use of dynamics (note the delicate calming coda, another favorite Hines device). On the other hand, *Night Life*, a fast stride opus, is spiritually indebted to James P. Johnson, although it too occasionally reminds us of her Pittsburgh heritage. A refreshing twist occurs at the end when Williams ends the piece, essentially in a minor key, with a sudden deft move to the relative major. Clearly, these authoritative, well-structured performances showed that a major talent had arrived on the scene.

Meanwhile Kirk's band, which Mary Lou Williams was about to join fulltime, had begun recording for the Brunswick label. These early efforts show that the band had not yet achieved any particular identity as an orchestra and that it was still in that respect in an early formative stage. Ensemble passages tended to be quite rough and unblended. On the other hand, the very unassimilated diversity of the band makes for some occasionally fascinating eclectic listening in the solo department. At the top of the list, of course, are several more astounding Mary Lou Williams solos. Hear her suspended, bluesily dissonant reiterated minor seconds on *Cloudy*; or her harmonically advanced Gershwin-like solo on *Gettin' Off a Mess*, and the zig-zagging, astoundingly adventurous modulations in and out of the key in *You Rascal You*. (Is there an influence on Thelonious Monk in all this?) But there is also Lawrence Freeman's wildly virtuosic, careening tenor sax solo on *Cloudy*, and Claude Williams's country-ish fiddle solos on *Blue Clarinet Stomp* and *Casey Jones Special*, William Dirvin's quaint single-string banjo solos, and throughout, Kirk's stompy tuba. Though these 1929 and 1930 Kirk recordings are period pieces, they have their period charms, and here and there begin, in the arrangements of Mary Lou Williams, to give a hint of a more cohesive orchestral style to come.

During the next five years, Kirk's Twelve Clouds of Joy were kept very busy in Kansas City's major dance emporia and made two visits to New York's Savoy Ballroom. By the time they recorded again in early 1936 Kirk had ceded his tuba position to the fine bass player Booker Collins and, after having Ben Webster and Buddy Tate successively in the solo tenor chair, Kirk acquired his other major soloist, Dick Wilson. Another addition (in 1931) was the gifted drummer Ben Thigpen.

A true Kansan in spirit, Kirk, like the young Bill Basie, believed in the small flexible band. Kirk had a genuine abhorrence of the brassy Eastern big bands and only succumbed to enlarging his orchestra—yielding to the "fad of having seven or eight brass," all "loud and wrong"—long after it had become *de rigueur.* Kirk's orchestra in the thirties was never overpowering. With its four (later five) brass and three saxophones, it developed a flexibility and unclutteredness that might well have been the envy of the large note-guzzling Eastern swing machines, had they understood the difference.

Of course, by 1936 swing was officially "in." But by not slavishly capitulating to the prevailing dictates, the Kirk band was able to maintain a high degree of individuality, exemplified by an emphasis on improvised solos, buttressed by light-toned flexible arrangements. And arranger Mary Lou Williams, with her light touch and sense of clarity, was the ideal moulder of the band's identity. As things turned out, however, it had precious little time to establish such an orchestral identity, for by 1937 and thereafter, as a result of an immensely popular recording by the band's singer, Pha Terrell, its *jazz* playing days, while not exactly numbered, were certainly threatened.

The reader must recognize this as becoming a very familiar refrain. And in fact, although jazz histories either overdramatize the corruptive impact of Tin Pan Alley or conversely suppress any reference to it, there hardly was a band in the thirties and early forties which did not succumb to its commercial pressures. Virtually every band had—or tried to have—a popular singer who could cater to less sophisticated musical tastes and bring in the dollars at the box office, which in turn would permit the continuance of instrumentals and a true jazz repertory. Indeed many bands' reputations were built entirely or primarily on the success of their singers, which then in turn garnered them more engagements. No one was immune to these commercial pressures. Some, like Ellington and Basie, with Ivie Anderson and Jimmy Rushing, were more successful in resisting the inroads of the marketplace, in part by having better and more jazz-oriented singers. But Chick Webb had his Bardu Ali and Ella Fitzgerald, Andy Kirk his Pha Terrell, Hines his Ida Mae James, Redman his Harlan Lattimore, the Casa Lomans their Kenny Sargent, Goodman his Helen Ward or Martha Tilton, and so on down the line. Of course, some bands, as we have seen, hoped for a successful compromise by having some of their *players* take on the vocal chores: the Armstrong imitators like Walter Fuller or Taft Jordan, the novelty tune dispensers like Lunceford's Trummy Young and Henry Wells and Don Redman, and crooners like Dan Grissom or Quentin Jackson or Earl Warren.[21]

But before Terrell's popularity would finally turn the Kirk band's 7:5 jazz-to-pop ratio around to 4:15, it had an opportunity to show its jazz mettle. That it could swing with an easygoing relaxed beat is indicated in *Git* and *Steppin' Pretty,* while at other times—say, in *Bearcat Shuffle, Froggy Bottom,* or *Chris-*

---

21. Once again the mystery of the male crooners' mesmerizing successes. See footnote 1 of this chapter.

topher Columbus,—the band had not yet found a unified rhythmic identity. In much of the last-named title, for example, the "horns" swing better than the rhythm section, while on *Froggy Bottom*, Mary Lou Williams's old boogie-woogie number from 1929, the typical Kansas City style call-and-response riffs are played in a surprisingly stiff and logy fashion.

Dick Wilson is by far the most consistent performer here, and it is regrettable that—perhaps due to his premature death in 1941 at age thirty—Wilson is so little remembered today. His playing, on recordings at least never less than accomplished, was very often masterly. Moreover, it was highly personal. Although it is clear from his playing that he admired Lester Young, two years his senior, Wilson was very much his own man. It is not unreasonable to imagine his having a significant impact on the next generation of saxophonists had he, like Prez, lived longer and been presented in as favorable a setting as the Basie band.

As in any first-rate artist, Wilson's style was in its totality the integrated sum of all its parts. His lines were sinuous and unpredictable, taking odd, unexpected turns that broke through the usual automated fingering patterns. His solos had a natural organic clarity, executed with consummate control and, for their time, a high degree of sophistication. His tone was unusual in that it was at once imbued with a searing old-style intensity and a subtle "modern" coolness. Wilson's playing has been likened to Chu Berry's, but I find it closer to that of Al Sears, especially in terms of his tone. (It may or may not be relevant that Sears was one of Wilson's predecessors in the Zack Whyte band, whence he came when he joined Kirk.) But it is in that area that I find the one anomaly in Wilson's playing. His sometimes excessive phrase or note-ending vibrato seems at odds with the subtle composure of his idiom.

Wilson had a legato not unlike Berry's, giving him great linear fluency. But unlike Berry's tendency to a kind of run-on breathlessness, Wilson balanced his solos by interposing quick flurries of notes with more sustained phrases. He lacked Herschel Evans's unique sense of drama, preferring to hold his emotions in check, perhaps fearing the danger of sentimentality.

With Lester Young he shared an inventive urge to explore advanced harmonic and rhythmic realms. A fine example of these talents can be heard in Wilson's solo on *In the Groove* (Ex. 17). Notice the unusual, hard-to-play key of B major.

On *Corky* (Ex. 18) Wilson demonstrates his ability to invent concise, compact statements, his relaxed free-floating swing offering a dramatic contrast to Mary Lou Williams's vertically jumpy stride piano, not to mention John Harrington's stiff-tongued theme statement and rather strait-laced maiden-auntish clarinet solo.

Wilson's tribute to uncluttered simplicity on *Scratchin' the Gravel* (Ex. 19), a few well-timed musical *bon mots*, remind me a little of that glorious moment on television's finest jazz hour, the 1957 *Sound of Jazz*, when Lester Young played exactly sixty-three sublime notes on one blues chorus and taught everyone a lesson in beauty. (See Chapter 6, below, pp. 561–62.)

But perhaps Wilson's finest achievement is his extraordinarily concentrated

Ex. 17

Ex. 18

Ex. 19

and fluent solo on *Zonky*.[22] Set in a fast tempo still somewhat unusual for that time, Wilson had both the technique and the ideas to romp through one and three-quarters choruses with the ease of an otter gliding through water (Ex. 20).

One of the major acquisitions of Kirk's band in early 1939 was the guitarist Floyd Smith. His first recorded solo with the orchestra, *Floyd's Guitar Blues* (March 16, 1939), was a strong seller, as much for its novelty of featuring the then very new "electric" guitar as for its intrinsic musical values.[23] For Smith's opus is rather shallow musically, content to exploit the newly-won *technical* capacities of the instrument: its ability to sustain notes in lengthy durations, thereby also enabling the greater use of glissandos—whose wailing and moaning effect Smith overdoes considerably—and, above all, its dramatically increased

22. Both *Zonky* and *Scratchin' the Gravel* were recorded on Jan. 26, 1940, under the name of Six Men and a Girl.

23. It was Eddie Durham, the arranger-trombonist-guitarist, who among jazz musicians apparently first started experimenting with forms of electronic amplification for the guitar. As the size and power of jazz orchestras increased, the acoustic guitar's limited projection came to be seen as an ever greater restriction, especially by arrangers like Durham who were anxious to use the guitar in melodic linear ways. According to an interview with Leonard Feather (in *The Book of Jazz*), Durham began experimenting with a tin resonator while he was with Lunceford's orchestra. He used this "amplified" guitar to marvelous effect on Lunceford's *Hittin' the Bottle* recording of 1935. Durham also claims to have introduced both Floyd Smith and Charlie Christian to a later version of amplified guitar around 1937 when he was touring with Basie—another prophetic on-the-road chance encounter. Durham recorded nine titles in 1938 with this type of electric acoustic guitar (under the Kansas City Five and Kansas City Six names), while during the same year Leonard Ware used a similarly amplified guitar in recordings with Sidney Bechet.

But Floyd Smith's *Guitar Blues* recording was made on an electric *steel* guitar, not the same as the *acoustic* guitar. This was an instrument pioneered (also) by Leon McAuliffe, a major soloist with two early Western swing groups, the Light Crust Doughboys and Bob Wills Texas Playboys. Mc-Auliffe recorded electric steel guitar solos as early as mid-1935, and can be heard to particularly good effect on *Darktown Strutter's Ball*, *Steel Guitar Blues*, and *White Heat*. It should be noted that all three of the above-mentioned players—Durham, Christian, and McAuliffe—were all born in Texas. (Both of these types of guitars are quite different from the Hawaiian guitar which came into use much earlier, in the late 1920s). For a further discussion of these developments, see, below, Charlie Christian, Chapter 6, Part 3.

Ex. 20

dynamic levels.[24] With a sometimes unpleasantly piercing sound, Smith's guitar sounds like a full band, one reason the brass and reeds may have been relegated to the introduction and (rather bombastic) coda of the piece.

On *Big Jim Blues*, Smith is much more musical, playing now the electric *acoustic* guitar, interpolating blues responses very much in the manner of Durham's *Hittin' the Bottle*. *Big Jim Blues* has other virtues as well. Its poignant blues theme composed by Harry "Big Jim" Lawson, lead trumpet of the Kirk band, is turned into a hauntingly beautiful arrangement by Mary Lou Williams, in a manner not unlike some of Ellington's late 1930s' mood pieces. Simple pastel-ish voicings predominate, then are combined in infinitely subtle variants. For only one brief moment is the entire band used; the rest is small-band chamber-ensemble writing, its very economy heightening the understated effect, yet without any mincing or effete aftertaste.

The arrangement comprises an introduction, three choruses, and a coda, with the middle chorus a straight 12-bar blues (Donnelly's trombone solo), while the other choruses offer Lawson's highly unusual 18-bar variant of the blues changes, broken down into the following subdivisions: $7+3+4+2+2$. It is a tribute

$$\text{I} \quad \text{IV} \quad \text{I} \quad \text{V} \quad \text{I}$$

to Lawson's musical instincts that this odd configuration is so natural and organic that the casual listener is not apt to notice anything uncommon at all. The outline in Figure 2 depicts the layout of the arrangement in graphic form.

By dividing the "horns" into one solo trumpet and four pairs of instruments—two clarinets, two tenor saxophones, two trombones, two section trumpets—

Fig. 2

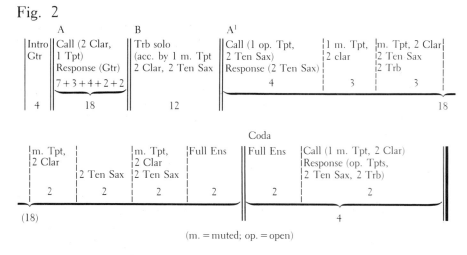

(m. = muted; op. = open)

24. Little did Durham and Smith realize what they were unleashing on the world, unable to imagine the earsplitting decibels and raunchy sonorities of modern rock guitars.

Mary Lou Williams is working like a painter who lays out four or five basic colors, which then can be mixed in various combinations or used in pure discrete form. She could isolate certain timbral duos, combine them into quartets or by adding one extra voice into quintets, and by doing so delineate the basic structure of the piece: timbre at the service of form. A glance at the outline in Figure 2 will reveal that the arrangement uses six different instrumental combinations (not counting the still more timbrally fragmented coda)—all the more startling for the basic modesty of the overall conception. (Incidentally the two tenors were played by Don Byas, who spent about nine months with Kirk, and Dick Wilson.)

There are other delights on these late 1930s' recordings, such as Booker Collins's happy walking-bass chorus on *Zonky*, abetted by Mary Lou's cubistically modern "comping"; or Dick Wilson's tremendous solo on *Tea for Two*; or Earl Thompson's first-rate playing on *Zonky*—his entrance one of those great moments of suppressed excitement that certain trumpet players could coax from their instruments with the aid of jazz mutes. This solo, along with several others and the occasional arrangements which Earl Thompson contributed to the Kirk library, reveals a major talent, equal to anything players like Roy Eldridge, Dizzy Gillespie, or Charlie Shavers could produce at this time.[25] Thompson's solo is technically fluent, well-constructed, authoritative, and a worthy partner for Wilson's (already mentioned) solo.

I'se A Muggin' (March 1936) was one of Thompson's arrangements. Composed by Stuff Smith, the scrappy violinist-leader-comedian, and recorded by him on two 10-inch sides in early 1936, *Muggin'* was a minor jazz-pop hit, and Kirk undoubtedly was eager to piggy-back on Smith's success. The "hep" lyrics, sung by drummer Thigpen, partly in scat, contain the first use on records known to this writer of the term "be-bop." Interesting how Wilson begins his solo, gathering up speed as in a relay race already four bars *before* the end of the lyric. *Wednesday Night Hop* (1937), with its interesting changes, could have been a more successful riff number but for the Leslie Johnakins arrangement, which tediously insists on the lead instrument's playing the same middle E♭ throughout (except in the all the more welcome bridge). On the other hand, it may have been he who made amends by playing that superbly swinging additional (but unidentifiable) percussion instrument during Donnelly's trombone chorus.[26]

Mary Lou Williams is predictably a consistent major contributor to these per-

25. It represents a frequent problem for the jazz historian that certain players (and orchestras) who happen not to have recorded prolifically (or at all), or who died prematurely, or who had peripatetic careers not easily traceable through recordings, are difficult to appraise. Such players are often not listed in any encyclopedias and even the most minimal biographical information is often lacking. Such is the case of Earl Thompson. All that I have been able to glean from discographies is that Thompson played with the great Speed Webb in 1926 and recorded with Paul Howard's Los Angeles-based band in 1929 (see below, Part 4). On the basis of his work with Kirk alone, he should not languish in such historical oblivion.

26. The discographies yield no information on this exhilarating auxiliary percussion effect. It sounds like sleigh bells or possibly stone rattles (or a pebble gourd), but judging by the close microphone placement, it was not played by drummer Thigpen.

formances. But they also make clear that she was essentially a synthesizing, synopsizing stylist, and what one can only describe as an "advanced conservative," contradictory as that may sound. In addition to her thorough familiarity with that great pianistic triumvirate of Johnson-Waller-Hines, she now began slipping in touches of Basie's new, more economical style. This is first noticeable on some of her 1936 trio recordings, especially *Overhand* and *Swingin' for Joy*, although the latter also pays tribute to the special lyricism of Willie "The Lion" Smith. The Basie influence became more dominant in ensuing years—for example, on the 1938 *Twinklin'* or the still later Ellington opus *Ring Dem Bells* of 1941, where Mary Lou plays Sonny Greer's original bell chimes on high-register piano in Basie's aphoristic style—with not quite the same effect, however.

Mary Lou Williams left Andy Kirk in 1942[27] and was replaced by a pianist of formidable talents named Kenneth Kersey. In mid-1942 he provided Kirk with a substantial hit, *Boogie Woogie Cocktail*, which I recall hearing consistently on jukeboxes as late as 1944. Kersey was quite a find. Whereas Mary Lou Williams had taken boogie-woogie, with its murky and somber primitive visions, and given it a more cheerful lacy legato touch, Kersey took the same idiom, tightened its variation structure, energized its rhythms, stylized it and turned it into both a pianistic tour de force and an excellent dance number. It was boogie-woogie cleaned up a bit, efficient, and quite perfect—a miniature boogie-woogie concerto.

As with other orchestras, so too with Kirk, the young up-and-coming modernists were beginning to infiltrate his big band in the early-middle forties. One of these was the first-rate trumpeter Howard McGhee, whose *McGhee Special*, featuring him in a long extended trumpet solo, was also a successful best seller. McGhee is another one of those fine players who has been forgotten in recent years. Admittedly, he didn't have the staying power of a Gillespie or a Hawkins or a Hines, and his frequent enforced absences through the years certainly signify an erratic career. But in his early days McGhee was a leading transition figure in the incoming bop movement.

When McGhee joined Kirk he was just twenty-four and had played with only one other major orchestra, Lionel Hampton's, for a brief spell. It is to Kirk's credit that he recognized McGhee's talent and allowed him to be featured not merely in a brief solo, but in a major recording debut as soloist-composer-arranger. As a composition, *McGhee Special* (recorded July 14, 1942) is harmonically/

27. Mary Lou Williams's post-Kirk career will be dealt with in more detail in Volume III of this History. Like Hines she kept pace with the new developments in jazz and became a prominent member of the bop fraternity, adding to her pianistic repertory such latter-day styles as those of Bud Powell, Errol Garner, and Milt Buckner. But she also composed a number of catchy bop pieces (*Oo Bla Dee* and *Walking*) in the late forties, performed with her trio at Bop City, and had a grand love affair with the bass clarinet, which she featured in almost all of her recordings of the period. But unlike Hines, she eventually retreated to a more preservative position, preceded by several years of musical inaction and a conversion to Catholicism. Extended sacred works followed, teaching, two Guggenheim fellowships, and eventually a return to performing. Highly critical of younger jazz musicians in her later years, she died in New York in 1981.

melodically adventurous beyond the norm of the day. Its rich shifting changes in the key of F major were of McGhee's own invention—not as later in the bop period when players grafted new melodic lines onto previously established "standards"—and it had one particularly interesting feature, namely, a bridge in A♭ major. Whether McGhee realized the implications of this shift to a secondary tonic on the flatted third degree of the key or not, I do not know. Probably not. But what is fascinating about this harmonic move is that on the one hand it symbolizes and presages the gradual drift towards bitonal harmonic combinations which was soon to typify the harmonic language of bop. And on the other hand, the move to A♭ in the bridge was a fresh alternative to the two previously most common bridge sequences, the one (in the key of F) to A major, cycling back to the parent key through steps of fifths (A^7 to D^7 to G^7 to C^7, as in the most common changes of all from Gershwin's *I Got Rhythm*); the other to the relative minor (in our example that would be D minor, a change favored by the way for centuries in classical music); or occasionally to the major of the sixth degree (D major in our case).

A digression of a somewhat technical nature is appropriate here to explain the nature of the expanding harmonic language that was gradually seeping into jazz. Without such an understanding the entire transition to modern jazz and bop is incomprehensible. The brief ensuing analysis describes the foundation, at least in the realm of harmony and melody, that became the basic premise on which jazz of the forties, fifties, and beyond was to operate.

Coming back to the two types of key relationships mentioned above (as suggested by McGhee's composition), in the first instance, the notes of an A♭ chord, in its pure triad form or in its "dominant seventh" version, were the very notes which the young jazz players were soon to combine with those of F major. (It should be understood that the same kinds of relationships and permutations are, of course, possible and used in any and all keys, not just in F major.) This worked so well because by a marvelous quirk of the diatonic system of tonality, as established more or less firmly in the time of Johann Sebastian Bach in the eighteenth century, C, the third of an A♭ triad, is equivalent to the fifth in F major. E♭ (the fifth in A♭) can function as the minor seventh in F major. The tonic A♭ can serve as the minor third or (as jazz musicians heard and used it) the raised ninth of F major, correctly spelled as G♯ but enharmonically equivalent to A♭ (Ex. 21). Finally, the seventh of A♭, namely G♭, was the minor ninth of F major. As long as the A♭ component of a bitonal combination of F and A♭ was superimposed *above* the F fundamental, then a whole network of interconnecting triadic relationships within the broader scope of tonality became available.

Ex. 21

The reverse—or its inversion, i.e. F over A♭—does not work the same way at all. It was rarely used in jazz, and then only with the arrival of atonality in the sixties and seventies.

But the quirk mentioned above extended far beyond the combining of only two keys, related by a minor third. For similar combinations could be achieved with the harmonic relatives of the diminished fifth and the major sixth. In our hypothetical key of F, those would be B major and D major. This meant that, with only slightly varying results, any one of three related keys could be combined with a primary (fourth) key—the analogy to a painter's combining of related colors with a primary one is obvious—and could produce not only very handsome results, but in effect open up a whole harmonic world to jazz musicians in the early forties.

In the second instance referred to above, the relationship between the commonly used "bridge" keys and the one used by McGhee is also symptomatic of the new harmonic thinking, based more and more on "altered" harmonies or "substitutions," as the musicians call them. McGhee's A♭ progression can be seen as a flat third degree (rather than the I Got Rhythm A major) or a tritone (flatted fifth) substitution for the D-major type of bridge.

It should be noted here that these particular harmonic relationships had all been discovered and already developed into a distinctly recognizable new language (syntax) much earlier around the turn of the century by composers such as Debussy, Ravel, Scriabin, the young Stravinsky, Szymanowski, and Schoenberg. And Ellington had used such harmonic relationships as early as the mid-thirties. Figure 3 shows in graphic form how these four so related keys function in very specific ways that other types of key relationships do *not* yield.[28]

Even a not fully comprehending glance at the example will show the myriad note (pitch) relationships indicated by the connecting lines, both solid and dotted.

Thus we can see how an entire new universe of pitch and harmonic relationships came into use, a system in which every pitch could potentially function many times in different keys and in different positions (within the degree ranking, i.e. seventh degree, ninth degree, etc.). For example, the note E♭ (or its enharmonic equivalent D♯) could function in four ways: 1) as the fifth in A♭; 2) as the seventh in F; 3) as the minor ninth in D; and 4) as the major third in B (or C♭). This concept is surely what Charlie Parker had in mind when in later years in an interview he recalled his discovery that he could play "a relative major, using the right inversions, against a seventh chord."[29]

It should be noted that the relationship between these particular keys is a very

28. Because these relationships "travel" both ways, i.e. from F to D or from D to F (from B to A♭ or from A♭ to B), and because therefore such relationships need not be depicted twice but merely as a single "round trip," as it were, the number of lines radiating out from F (our at random chosen primary key) are more numerous than those radiating out from B and (even more so) from D.

29. As quoted by Leonard Feather in *Inside Be-Bop* (New York, 1949), chap. 2.

Fig. 3

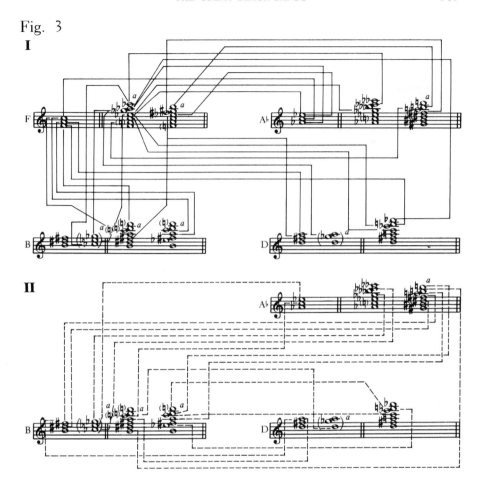

Chords marked with *a* represent enharmonic spellings of the previous chords, designed merely to make the criss-crossing pitch relationships in this example visually clearer to the non-musician. Pitch relationships between F major and the three other tritonally related keys are shown in section I (in solid lines); pitch relationships between B major and A♭ and D are shown in section II (in dashed lines); pitch relationships between D and A♭ are shown in section III (in dotted lines). Connections radiating out from A♭ do not need to be shown as they are already represented (only in reverse direction, for example A♭ to F or A♭ to B).

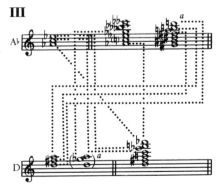

specific one. Other types of relationship would yield entirely different results (which are, even in outline, beyond the scope of this book). The relationship under discussion here is defined and exemplified by the interval of the minor third, the steps F to A♭ to B to D all spanning that interval. However, again by one of those wondrously fortuitous accidents of our Western tonal system, there are two other fascinating aspects to this intervallic network: 1) two minor thirds add up to a diminished fifth (or tritone), i.e. F to B or A♭ to D (see Ex. 22); and 2) the four intervallic stations separated by a minor third divide the octave into four equal divisions; and obviously the compound of two minor thirds, namely, the tritone, divides the octave in half.

Ex. 22

It should also be noted that, for the sake of visual clarity and simplicity, one other common harmonic extension was not included in Figure 3, namely, the sixth degree. But it can be readily seen that the sixth, D (in an F chord), is found again as the tonic in D, the raised ninth in B, and the diminished (or flatted) fifth in A♭. The sixth—D in the following examples—has also been used in jazz, apart from its pure form

in such voicings as   or

or more rarely   .

Though this may sound terribly technical and even mathematical to some readers, they should understand that to the practicing jazz musician and to the composer (*not* necessarily, alas, to the classical performing musician!) these relationships are commonplace, are used on a daily basis, and are fully understood, either aurally or in theory or both. They are, as I have said, the foundation of all post swing-era jazz.

To return to Howard McGhee's *McGhee Special*, its harmonic changes interest us especially because they are prophetic of things to come. The aforementioned move to the key of A♭ in the bridge (in a piece otherwise in F) is in fact the horizontal equivalent—here in its first sampling—of what the boppers within a year or two were going to do vertically, i.e. harmonically, simultaneously. That is to say, whereas in McGhee's piece A♭ and F major succeed each other at a still safe distance, by 1944 and 1945 they were to appear side by side, even simultaneously, synchronized—a progression from mere coexistence to actual cohabitation, graphically, simply depicted (Fig. 4).

So much for McGhee's composition and its implications. But there is also

Fig. 4   1942   1944–45

McGhee's playing, which reveals, and indeed exemplifies, another aspect of the then new incoming language. I refer to his frequent and consistent use of flat sixths and ninths in his melodic invention (Ex. 23).

Much has been made of the use of flatted fifths by Parker, Gillespie, Monk, and Christian in formulating the new modern jazz language. Quite apart from the fact that the flatted fifth is as old as jazz itself, one of the three prime "blue" notes[30] used extensively by earlier blues-oriented players like Bubber Miley, Cootie Williams, and Ben Webster, its use in bop was overemphasized by writers and

Ex. 23

Four excerpts from *McGhee Special*
x = flat sixths; **+** = flat ninths; **○** = flat fifths

30. See *Early Jazz*, pp. 51–52.

press agents. It was made into the "national anthem" of bebop, along with other cliché trappings such as Gillespie's goatee and beret, Monk's sunglasses, and the new bop lingo. The truth is that much more than flatted fifths were involved. What really happened was that *all* the chromatic alterations, previously more or less forbidden, suddenly sprang into common use. And before the flat fives came the flat sixes and flat nines.

In effect, what occurred in the latter half of the thirties was the gradual filling in of those chromatically altered notes that (except for the use of minor thirds and sevenths and lowered fifths *as* blue notes, and except when used as passing tones) had not previously been considered usable as *primary* pitch material. To put it in the simplest terms, the spaces between the white keys of the C major scale were now being filled in by the remaining black keys—E♭, G♭, A♭, B♭, D♭—completing at the same time the full chromatic scale. Historically the notes that were added first were the lowered sixth and ninth, A♭ and D♭ (in the key of C). Readers will recall my mention of this fact in connection with any number of Lester Young solos in the discussion of the Count Basie band. For it was Young—and the outstanding trumpeter Roy Eldridge—who first made that particular harmonic/melodic breakthrough, at least as a consistent element of their improvisations. The filling-in of the gaps in the tonal gamut took nearly a decade to accomplish, with the flatted fifth and raised ninth (the enharmonic twin of the blue-note minor third) coming in last, while the seventh had, of course, already always been in full use.

McGhee's solo displays a copious use of flat sixths and ninths, used essentially in the same way as another trumpeter named Dizzy Gillespie, five months McGhee's senior, was doing at about the same time. The only difference between the two might be a matter of emphasis. While Gillespie was at this time already an even more fluent and facile player and therefore rarely lingering on individual notes, McGhee quite deliberately sits on and points out such "aberrant" notes—"Chinese music" Cab Calloway once called it. The similarities to Gillespie in McGhee's playing extend as well to other aspects, such as the technical fluency—the particular light effortless way in which both men played legato eighth-note lines—the ranginess of their improvisations, easily covering three octaves, and the generally rhythmic speeding up of the subdivisions of the beat: to fast eighth notes and eighth-note triplets. Dizzy with greater technique was the first to break the sixteenth-note sound barrier on trumpet (as can be heard on his early 1942 recording with Les Hite of *Jersey Bounce*).

Finally, there is McGhee the arranger to consider. In this area, too, McGhee showed great promise. Realizing that his solo would need some brief spells to rest his lip, he inventively combined this need with an instinctive sense of building the arrangement to a final climax. Harmonic progression and modulation come to his aid. Starting out in F major, the piece moves to C via one of two slightly pretentious whole-tone modulations, then via a second modulation to the key of D♭, and then, reaching for the climax stepwise, up to D, and ultimately E♭. High notes in the solo trumpet, capped by a high F♯, intensify the climactic ending.

It has not been the intention of the last few pages to detract in any way from Gillespie's priority, both chronological and artistic, in the evolution of the bop style. I have simply tried to establish McGhee's importance as a major transition figure, confirmed, of course, by his later work with Parker (especially on *Relaxin' at Camarillo*, *Carving The Bird*, and *Be-Bop*). If McGhee was not quite on a par with Gillespie, he was certainly not far behind.[31]

Like so many swing era bands, Kirk's reached its peak artistically in the early to mid-forties, enjoying an international reputation. Gradually, however, with its new vocalist June Richmond[32] and a larger heavier brass section, the band's character changed as it catered more and more to a basic rhythm-and-blues market. Kirk disbanded the orchestra in 1948, revived it for a record date in 1956, but for the most part left an active musical career, managing for a time Harlem's Hotel Theresa, and more recently, working as a union official for New York's Local 802.

PART 3

DON REDMAN

Don Redman's role in the history of jazz seems to me to be one of ultimately unfulfilled promise. At times in the 1920s, a major influential figure in the forefront of advanced developments, at other times he seemed, oddly, to falter. His career course was curiously erratic, and his life's work is not marked by the kind of consistent consequent follow-through that so clearly characterizes in different ways men like Ellington or Calloway or Goodman. I have always felt, for instance, that Redman's sudden abandonment of the Henderson orchestra in 1927, departing for Detroit and the McKinney Cotton Pickers, was a strange (and wrong?) thing to do. Its consequences for the Henderson band were certainly dramatic, while the presumed benefits for the MKCP were in the long run mostly illusory. Similarly, the move back to New York, this time to form his own orchestra in 1931, now stranding the McKinney group, did not result in any significant long-term body of work. During the forties, Redman arranged for a great variety of bands—from Paul Whiteman, Nat Shilkret, and Bobby Byrne to Charlie Barnet and Count Basie—without leaving any distinctive impress on those organizations. His general inactivity during the last fifteen years of his life is perhaps another sign of thwarted creative impetus.

By all accounts, Redman was a kindly, gentle, soft-spoken man, a gentleman and a humanitarian, adored by all. It seems significant that this personal side is always brought out in reminiscences of Redman and his contribution to jazz.

31. McGhee spent some time with Kirk, as well as with Charlie Barnet's band, then moved to California in 1945 and was active there for some years, recording with, among others, Parker for Ross Russell's new Dial label. McGhee's later career will be dealt with in greater detail in the next volume.

32. For a brief while in 1946 Kirk had Joe Williams (of Count Basie fame) as the band's singer. (See above, Chapter 5, Part 1.)

Even Duke Ellington, who clearly admired Redman, was moved in his autobiographical *Music Is My Mistress* to laud Redman as someone whom he respected as "tough competition" and whom "everyone loved,"[1]

And yet if we assess Redman's work both as a bandleader (the burden of this chapter segment) and as a composer-arranger strictly on the aural evidence, we find it to be a curiously uneven achievement. Even his earliest work with Henderson, though clearly innovative in helping to establish the basic concepts of orchestral jazz and arranging, is not without certain typically Redmanesque flaws.[2] His tendency towards a certain clutteredness and stylistic waywardness shows up in a number of arrangements for Henderson, especially *Sugar Foot Stomp*, *Whiteman Stomp*, *Rocky Mountain Blues*, and *The Chant*. Brilliant strokes of invention seem always to stand side by side in Redman's work with ordinary or coarse, often pretentious passages. And strangely, his playing, though often fanciful and technical, is generally warmer and more expressive than his writing.

Redman's work with McKinney's Cotton Pickers is discussed in Part 1 of this chapter. Our concern here is with his own orchestra, which began its recording career on September 24, 1931. The major opus here was Redman's own *Chant of the Weed*, his theme song and one of the many compositions in vogue then belonging to the "reefer" genre. Such an association—at least in Redman's mind— called for "weird," "sinister" harmonies. These he supplies in the form of a somewhat ghoulish "atonal" introduction in three unison trombones, bass, and bass drum (the intended effect not aided by the miserable intonation of the trombones),[3] and by a series of parallel whole-tone chords in the first four bars of the A segment of the standard AABA form (Ex. 1a). Permitting little or no variation, except in orchestration (an opportunity which oddly enough Redman does not particularly exploit), this 4-bar refrain wears out its welcome long before its dozenth appearance or so. Furthermore, it hooks up rather clumsily with the remaining four bars of the A segments, one of those slightly awkward juxtapositions which one encounters so often in Redman's work. However, to his credit these latter four bars (and the ensuing bridge) *are* hauntingly beautiful and by themselves among the best things Redman ever conceived, (Ex. 1b).

1. But to put that in perspective, we should also recall that Ellington irresponsibly likened Jelly Roll Morton's playing to that of "high school teachers," adding "as a matter of fact, high school teachers played better jazz."
2. Moreover, the long-held assumption that Redman was the only orchestral innovator in the early days of jazz is probably no longer tenable, or is at least debatable. Quite apart from the extraordinary very early large-ensemble arranging which men like James Reese Europe, Ford Dabney, and Will Vodery pioneered, in Redman's own generation we can no longer ignore the work of Jesse Stone, Gus Wilson, and John Nesbitt (not to mention Duke Ellington). Stone in particular seems to have been a musician much like Redman, not only in his arranging abilities and diverse instrumental talents, but his penchant for teaching his players and helping them improve themselves. (For a discussion of Stone's work, see below, Chapter 8). But Redman happened to have an almost unchallenged influence, in large part because he worked in New York for what was without question the finest and most prolifically recorded black orchestra of the time (the mid-to-late 1920s), Fletcher Henderson's.
3. This introduction was to be echoed some fifteen years later in the Boyd Raeburn orchestra's *Boyd Meets Stravinsky*.

Ex. 1a

Ex. 1b

For the improvisatory section, a kind of gentler "second subject," Redman uses more conventional "changes." Then, before the last chorus Redman inserts an 8-bar meandering transitional passage which sounds for all the world like a modulation—except that, after a few jolting harmonic shifts, it ends up again in the original key of D♭. It is valiantly played by Horace Henderson on piano. In the last chorus itself, Redman plagiarizes—as he was to do again in his 1940 *Cupid's Nightmare*—the bridge from Duke Ellington's *Mood Indigo*. The move here in *Chant* to the flat sixth degree of the scale and the chain of eighth-note triplets in unison saxophones are too close to Ellington to be mere unconscious coincidence.

Of course, *Chant of the Weed* was meant to be "daring" and "sophisticated," representing the latest state of the jazz-tune art. And evidently others, including Duke Ellington, thought so, too. But although one can easily grant the work its conscious modernity, it is upon scrutiny not without serious blemishes, in conception as well as in performance. For the band, including many of the outstanding players of the day (such as Bill Coleman, Henry Allen, Claude Jones, Benny Morton), could not really cope with this material. Intonation is generally uncertain, and most of the piece—especially its whole-tone passages—are played with a harsh, blary up-tight sound. My guess is, too, that Redman was not a demanding rehearser, and fell far short of getting from his players all that the piece required.

A second take from the same date and a performance one year later—with a slightly different personnel under singer Harlan Lattimore's name (for another record label)—fares not much better. On the latter performance, now at a slower tempo and therefore needing to be cut somewhat, Redman eliminates Ed Inge's tortured 1931 clarinet solo (replete with wrong notes). On the other hand, there is inserted a totally irrelevant quote from a famous Irish reel, incongruously pasted onto the end of the bridge; and virtually the entire drum part has now been outfitted, again unfathomably, with vacuous temple-block triplet rhythms. Not until 1940, when on his band's last record date Redman re-made *Chant of the Weed* a third time, did he achieve some of the Ellington flavor of the piece which it needed and deserved all along but never got from his 1931 and 1932 bands. Though the temple blocks are still there in 1940, the offending modulation to nowhere is eliminated, and the *Mood Indigo* bridge is modified so as to sound not quite so blatantly derivative. The tempo is even slower than the 1932 version, but this allows Redman to play some of his best alto work in a warm, florid Hodges manner.

The other piece on which Redman had pinned high commercial hopes was a novelty lyric, written by Harold Arlen for a Connie's Inn show, called *Shakin' the African*. The big laugh and innuendo teaser here was Redman's stressing and separating of the last three letters of the title, colloquially referring to a certain part of the human anatomy. The side is, however, saved by Henry "Red" Allen, who breaks into the coy proceedings with a wild tumultuous trumpet break and solo.

Trouble, Why Pick on Me? interestingly features Earl Hines's old Pittsburgh employer, singer Lois Deppe. Better recorded than on the 1923 Gennett sides, Deppe is here heard to have a rich bass baritone voice not unlike that of Herb Jeffries and another Pittsburghian, Billy Eckstine. The side is also notable for another fine Allen contribution, full of Armstrong-like double-time bits, and an unusual piano break by Horace Henderson. In its unrelated, registrally separated triads it reminds one of Debussy's famous *Etude—pour les Accords* (Etude in Chords)—although it is doubtful that Henderson knew this work. A fetching pentatonic passage in the celesta, of the type frequently used later by André Kostelanetz in his late thirties' and early forties' arrangements, closes out the side.

Like all bands—perceived by the public as entertainment vehicles—Redman's too had to have a ballad pop singer in order to survive commercially. In Redman's case it was Harlan Lattimore (sometimes called "the colored Bing Crosby"), a better than average vocalist. This is faint praise, since the average was by any reasonable aesthetic standards extraordinarily low. But Lattimore seems to have more than earned his keep, recording some sixteen titles (two under his own name) in the first year and a half of his association with Redman. As we have seen in so many other cases, the hard and fast formula for the black bands was to have a balladeer—rarely, by the way, a blues singer, Rushing with Basie and Eckstine with Hines being notable exceptions—plus a novelty-song presenter or two, who delivered (often with the whole band chiming in) Armstrong-mannered vocals or "talking" numbers. These usually were performed by band members: Redman, Fred Norman (with Hopkins), Walter Fuller (with Hines), Sy Oliver and Willie Smith (with Lunceford), the "talking" type being best exemplified by deep-voiced Orville Jones of the Ink Spots. Redman composed and talked his way through quite a few of these humorous "songs," delivered with a boyish pleasantly inflected voice and shy reticence.

In addition, Redman called upon the extremely popular husky-voiced Chick Bullock, who was undoubtedly the most prolifically recorded singer of the entire thirties.[4] Redman also accompanied the tap dancing and singing of Bill Robinson, nicknamed Bojangles, in his big specialty number *Doin' the New Low Down*, from the highly successful *Blackbirds of 1928* (which ran for over 500 performances, outclassed in those days only by Jerome Kern's *Showboat*). The link between Broadway, Tin Pan Alley, and jazz was always a close one—often one of economic survival for jazz—and Redman seemed to know this better than anyone.

But, unlike Ellington, Calloway and Lunceford, and a few other black bandleaders, Redman was not successful (if he ever tried) in balancing the commercial with the creative. Horace Henderson's *Hot and Anxious*, Gershwin's *I Got Rhythm* and *Nagasaki* stand out as tiny instrumental islands in a sea of vocal trifles. But then these three arrangements, all from 1932, were by Horace Henderson, not Redman. Though not impeccably performed by any means, they

---

4. Bullock recorded well over 500 titles between 1930 and 1941. He then faded from the music scene, went into real estate in California. He died in 1981.

have a certain spirit, feature good solos, and occasionally swing rather well. *I Got Rhythm*, for example, has frisky solos by Benny Morton (trombone) and Ed Inge (clarinet), a splendid high-register riff-style trombone trio (one of the first such in jazz history), and a well-swinging buildup in the final choruses, much aided by British Honduran bassist Bob Ysaguirre.

Similarly *Hot and Anxious*—with its famous riff that finally became a hit with Glenn Miller's *In the Mood* (see below, Chapter 7)—was reasonably well performed, indeed much better than the Henderson band's listless draggy recording of the same piece a year earlier. Redman (and Horace) still couldn't get a blended sound out of his players—it is rather hard and brittle—but at least *Hot and Anxious* swings along nicely and contains spirited solos by trumpeter Sidney de Paris and tenor-man Robert Carroll.

Perhaps the best of the three mentioned 1932 sides is *Nagasaki*. Its lively, linearly propelled performance sports two superb back-to-back solos by Claude Jones (trombone) and de Paris, the former including a dazzlingly fast scale up to high F, played as cleanly as if on a trumpet or valve trombone. Towards the end Redman vocalizes the song's clever pitter-patter, interpolating sung responses by the full band of the kind that became so famous in Tommy Dorsey's *Marie* a few years later. Rex Stewart has claimed Redman as the originator of this idea, but he forgot that Cab Calloway had developed it into a virtually prerequisite formula as early as 1930. And even then it was probably not entirely new, for, as Redman once admonished his trombonist friend Quentin Jackson, "there's nothing new in music; it's just played and felt differently."[5]

Redman's 1933 recording of Ellington's *Sophisticated Lady*, though frequently praised and even preferred by some to Ellington's several renditions, cannot in my view really compare. Redman takes a totally different approach to the piece. Whereas Ellington saw his *Lady* as a song *composition*, Redman turns it into a somewhat ordinary *dance* number, robbing it in its too hasty tempo of Ellington's elegance and sophisticatedly blasé languor. Ellington conceived the piece (co-composed with Otto Hardwick and Lawrence Brown) initially as an *instrumental composition*—its lyrics were added a year later—designed as a series of composed solos for some of his players who most embodied "that particular kind of sophistication" (as he might have put it): Lawrence Brown, Arthur Whetsol, Toby Hardwick, Barney Bigard. On the other hand, in Redman's over-fancy arrangement with its chompy vertical rhythm, *Lady* loses these qualities, ironically retaining it only in Redman's own lovely alto solo. Interestingly, in that curious reciprocal relationship that Ellington and Redman had, there are things in this arrangement, particularly those chromatically winding saxophone lines, that Ellington was to remember in his *Reminiscing in Tempo* (1935) and put to much more significant use.

Two sporadic Redman recording dates in early 1934 were followed by a two-and-a-half-year hiatus, by which time the band had seen some personnel changes

---

5. Quoted in Stanley Dance's liner notes for RCA Victor LPV-520, *Don Redman—Master of the Big Band*.

and Goodman's swing revolution had occurred. Vocals and novelty numbers featuring Redman's "swing choir"—actually just the boys in the band—abound. In noting exceptions one cannot really point to complete performances, just parts of some—a good solo here, an arresting countermelody there, an effective ensemble now and then. What adventurousness Redman had espoused in his early days was long gone and had deteriorated into reworking the standard swing-riff clichés (as, for example, on *Shim Me Sha Wabble*) that, ironically, he had helped to generate a decade earlier. But that fact didn't seem to daunt him.

Redman's own playing, notably on soprano saxophone in *Down Home Rag*, Harry Owen's Hawaiian hit *Sweet Leilani*, and *Milenberg Joys* (on alto), is wonderfully fluent and poised. But it was his fate to be active as a player at a time when major personalities like Hodges, Willie Smith, and, of course, Benny Carter were in their prime.

Redman's orchestra was forced to disband in 1940. Except for sporadic short residencies with temporarily formed bands, Redman spent the next decade mostly in free-lance arranging. The new jazz of the late forties and fifties seems not to have touched or interested him, and during the last fifteen years of his life he was mostly inactive, apparently working quietly on a number of "extended compositions" which, however, have to my knowledge never been performed publicly. Redman died in November 1964.

Redman left us an important legacy in his pioneer work with Fletcher Henderson in the mid-twenties, and gave us one fine song: *Gee, Baby, Ain't I Good to You*. The cross Redman bore was perhaps being too diversely talented, as multi-instrumentalist and arranger and song composer. His talents became scattered and diffused, a not uncommon fate in the helter-skelter, unaccommodating atmosphere of popular music.

BENNY CARTER

There are interesting parallels in the careers of Benny Carter and Don Redman. Both are gifted, versatile musicians, multi-instrumentalists, composers, and arrangers. And both were bandleaders whose efforts were not rewarded with sustained success.

Both gave up their orchestral ambitions in the forties, turning primarily to writing—films and television in Carter's case. Here, however, the parallels stop, for, while Redman gradually retired from professional life in the fifties and early sixties, Carter has remained active to this day, both as a writer and a performer. Indeed, some of his finest playing can be found on recordings made *since* the forties and, as a celebrated elder statesman of jazz, on numerous Jazz at the Philharmonic tours and international jazz festivals.

Carter's career is difficult to assess, in part because it is marked by a zigzag course of activities, in turn prompted by his prodigious versatility. Moreover his career falls into two major periods, remarkably paralleling the two major chronological divisions of jazz: the classic and the modern—the dividing line poised on the fulcrum of the mid-1940s. The first period is characterized by Carter's peripatetic life as a performer, arranger and bandleader: the second by a more stationary life in California revolving primarily around composing, a great deal of it for television and other commercial ventures. His life—and his own public observations on it—do not reveal which of the many Benny Carters is the real one. Perhaps there is no single one. Perhaps the diverse elements of Carter's total talent are inseparable and mutually complementary.

At the same time it is this kaleidoscopic profusion of talent which explains why Carter never had the kind of popular success he and his musician colleagues and admirers hoped for. John Hammond, who helped Carter in a variety of ways in the early thirties, felt, in retrospect of that period, that he "was more interested in exhibiting his versatility than in making great music," and, Hammond continued, "this is one reason Benny never became a great band leader."[6] That may be too hard a personal judgment, but there is a kernel of truth in it. Two other alternatives suggest themselves. It is possible that Carter's talent, for all its awesome diversity, was not strong enough to assert itself in the public's mind, in the way that Ellington's, Armstrong's, and Calloway's did—and I have here purposely cited three quite different *kinds* of talents and temperaments. It can be that in our musical society anyone as richly and diversely talented as Carter is to some extent rejected because the public and the music business prefer a single, clearly identifiable marketable personality, not a many-sided marvel who resists being fitted into the standard predetermined professional slots. In the end, I would argue, Carter's problems derive a little from all three causes.

Bennett Lester Carter was born and raised in the San Juan section of New York, also known as The Jungle or Hell's Kitchen, where now stands the city's "Temple of the Arts," Lincoln Center. But in the old days it was the toughest section of town. It was also where Bubber Miley lived, one of Carter's early musical idols. Being a precociously gifted youngster, Carter was already working in small Harlem clubs while still a teenager, graduating later in the mid-1920s to the bands of June Clark, Billy Paige, Lois Deppe, and Earl Hines, as well as two weeks with Duke Ellington. By 1927 Carter had landed with Charlie Johnson's Paradise band, after stints with both Henderson orchestras (Horace and Fletcher); and it was with Johnson that Carter made his recording debut.

It is immediately obvious that Carter was a talent to reckon with, for on *Charleston Is the Best Dance of All* (recorded Jan. 24, 1928) Carter stands out as soloist (on alto saxophone) and as arranger. His solo already has that characteristic poise and neat balance between the expected and the unexpected that characterizes so much of Carter's best playing. His arranger's abilities were also well reflected, although in a somewhat embryonic stage. Notable for a twenty-one-year-old's work was the four-part saxophone ensemble (unfortunately not too well played or balanced) and one daring "pyramid" ensemble break near the end. A short stint later that year, leading the Horace Henderson band (after Henderson had abruptly left it directorless midway through a tour), gave Carter a taste for band leading, a thirst that was not to be assuaged for many years to come.

A peripatetic course in and out of various bands, sometimes as a sideman,

6. *John Hammond on Record* (New York, 1977).

sometimes as a leader, marks the next four-year period. Notable residencies were with Fletcher Henderson, for whom Carter arranged the remarkable *Keep a Song in Your Soul* (discussed at some length in *Early Jazz*, chap. 6), with Chick Webb in 1931 (here he arranged *Heebie Jeebies*) and McKinney's Cotton Pickers, becoming the latter's musical director when Don Redman left them to form his own band. In this period also fall some excellent performances with the Little Chocolate Dandies (Sept. 1929) and the Chocolate Dandies (late 1930 and again in 1933).

With the former group, assembled especially for recording purposes with players from four different orchestras—Henderson's, Johnson's, Luis Russell's, and McKinney's Cotton Pickers'—Carter recorded two tracks, one of which, *Six or Seven Times*, is quite outstanding. It turned out to be Carter's first major solo vehicle on alto, featuring him in three separate choruses: one fully improvised, the second a partially prearranged dialogue with Don Redman scat-singing, the third a written-out solo to which the band, especially the lead trumpet, responded in kind. The tune was by Fats Waller (also pianist on the date) but arranged by Don Redman. This was the piece that contained as introduction and coda an early version of that captivating riff which later became the theme of the Basie band's *One O'Clock Jump*.[7] Why it was tacked onto *Six or Seven Times* is not clear, since it bears no relationship to the tune's actual melody. In any event, Carter's first solo is a model of economy and formal clarity (Ex. 2). Interestingly, almost all his phrases straddle the bar line, ending more often than not on the third beat (marked x in the example)—for that period a novel place to end a phrase. The consistency with which Carter does so gives a certain

Ex. 2

---

7. See above, Chapter 4, p. 237.

structural cohesion to the solo, counterbalancing the otherwise rather rangy phrase contours. The entire solo emanates authority, building gradually through a series of motivically related variants to an agitated apogee in mm. 13 and 14, subsiding quickly yet naturally into the sixteenth measure.

Carter's duet with Redman reworks some of the same motivic material, as Redman imitates Carter's phrases vocally, handsomely taking care of the minute note alterations required by the changing harmonic progression. Carter really teases Redman here, all in good-natured musical camaraderie, resulting in one hilarious moment where Redman is obliged to imitate vocally one of Carter's lightning-fast trills.

Carter seems to have been so enamored of some of his ideas on *Six or Seven Times* that he used them immediately all over again in the next piece, a quite different tune called *That's How I Feel Today*.

A steady, consistent if rarely spectacular soloist, Carter used some of the same motivic ingredients in other solos, even with other bands, as, for example, on *I'd Love It* with McKinney's Cotton Pickers (Nov. 1929). Those cross-accented sixteenth-note figures (in mm. 13–14, Ex. 2) reappear in the form of eighth notes here (in a much faster tempo), and the trills, always a brilliant (and not very difficult) effect on the saxophone, also are used to striking advantage.

Carter's alto playing, especially in his first big-band period, is somewhat enigmatic and elusive. Tonally, he lacks the natural warmth and full-bodied sound of Hodges, or the firm focus of Parker. His tone has more tint than color. Translucent rather than opaque, it backs off, holds back. Though a highly structured improviser who cherishes logic and formal clarity, he skims across the surface of his music, almost too much at ease. Rarely allowing himself an unbuttoned moment, he keeps his emotions understated and on a very short expressive tether. It is more an observation than a criticism to say that Carter found it difficult in his early days to release himself from his intellectual tastes.

Very early in his career Carter had also taken up the clarinet, to which he brought a wholly original tone and style, as yet untried and unheard in the work of, say, Johnny Dodds, Jimmy Noone, Frank Teschemacher, Goodman, or Buster Bailey (Carter's predecessor and sometime partner in the Henderson band). *Dee Blues* (Dec. 1930) is surely one of the early great "classics" of small group jazz, for it not only offered four of the greatest instrumental masters of the time—Hawkins, Carter, Jimmy Harrison, and Bobby Stark—in exemplary solos, but, despite its simple format of a series of 12-bar blues solos, achieved a unity of musical substance which in the new post-New Orleans non-polyphonic style (except for isolated examples in the work of Morton's Red Hot Peppers, Noone's Apex band, and a few early Duke Ellington items), was quite unprecedented.[8]

---

8. An oddity of the December 1930 Chocolate Dandies recordings—five sides on two different dates— is that no drummer was used. He is hardly missed, what with John Kirby's firm bass (mostly on tuba) handling the rhythmic function completely and superbly. There is some question as to the identity of the guitarist, alternatively listed as Benny Jackson or Clarence Holiday. Aural evidence strongly suggests Holiday, who played a number of similar single-note melodic solos on other recordings. His 4/4 comping is rather overbearing, possibly overcompensating for the missing drummer.

Each solo flows logically and empathetically into the next, creating the sense of a well-conceived *composition*, even though the performance is essentially spontaneous.

Carter's clarinet solos—enclosing the performance at either end like the covers of a book—are quite extraordinary. His tone is firm and full with a hue much like that of an A clarinet, and with a slightly edgy thrust in the middle and upper range, taking on the color of both a trumpet and an alto saxophone. In this manner Carter was almost able to match the awesome majesty of Hawkins in *his* brief sweeping "gliding" solo. Creatively both clarinet solos are superior examples of Carter's effortless control of ideas, his always cogent sense of direction. One of the many fine touches is the way Carter takes a four-note descending motive near the end, stretches it in gradually elongating rhythmic values across the last few bars, and then provides a graceful easing down of the entire piece into a "soft-landing" ending.

The ever-restless Carter, always searching for new and different opportunities to apply his diverse talents, remained less than a year as the leader of the McKinney's Cotton Pickers, recording only two relatively ordinary tracks, featuring quasi-novelty vocals by trombonist Quentin Jackson. According to the late Morroe Berger, a close friend of Carter's, the Cotton Pickers, although they had elected Carter their musical director after Redman's departure, found it difficult to assimilate Carter's scores. My guess is that the band, which had deteriorated considerably after its heyday with Redman and Nesbitt, found Carter's explorative arranging style too challenging. Carter, who seems, in any case, not to have been satisfied with *their* work, left in April 1932 to organize his own band.

That got off to a shaky start: one quasi-commercial vocal on an obscure record label (Crown), and in October a rejection by RCA Victor of an entire session comprising three tracks, two of them Carter compositions (*Hot Toddy* and *Jazz Cocktail*) and Will Hudson's *Black Jazz*. *Jazz Cocktail* had been recorded two weeks *earlier* by Duke Ellington, very likely in the same Carter arrangement. Not until March 1933 in a session produced for English Columbia by the ubiquitous John Hammond, by now an active Carter fan, did the products of Carter's months of rehearsing with his new band become audible. Even with a revised personnel which included the young Chu Berry—Carter's bands were always famous for their constantly reshuffled personnel—the results were less than outstanding. Two more sessions in October 1933 and December 1934 yielded somewhat better creative fruits, although the band did not have any measurable commercial success.

Two contrasting views of Carter's orchestras run like a thread through his big-band career: musicians were almost always unanimous in their praise and respect for Carter, while at the same time his bands never achieved much public appeal. This has mystified musicians and even many jazz writers. But the aural evidence of Carter's 1930s' and early 1940s' orchestral recordings, virtually all his own arrangements, bears clear testimony that Carter's music lacked that element of memorability and individuality on which sustained success is built, artistic and/or commercial.

There are distinctions to be made between (ordinary) creativity and creative *originality*, on the one hand, as well as between creativity and memorability on the other. Carter was (is) certainly creative, but he cannot be said to be strikingly original. Perhaps, again, his talents are too scattered to be that singularly unique. Carter was, of course, in the period of the thirties a "superior," quite above-average musician, but not *that* superior so as to stand out like a Hawkins, an Armstrong, or an Ellington, in a field simply brimming with talent. Moreover, Carter was not the flamboyant "entertainer" type that the Irving Millses and Joe Glasers of the world look for and invest in. And though many of Carter's side-men tried to be very loyal to him, in the end they mostly had to seek their musical fortunes elsewhere. The instability of Carter's personnel eventually became a serious liability, for his bands were forever rehearsing—a laudable enterprise, to be sure—but never stayed together long enough to develop and refine a distinctive style.

Carter and his musicians never understood, I think, that producing a well-rehearsed band is in and of itself not enough to impress an audience. What counts is what happens, so to speak, "between the lines," the excitement that collective music-making can generate, and the subtleties of nuances, of blendings and balances, of musical sensitivities and relationships which can be developed and achieved only over a period of time. If one observes with what extraordinary patience and creative stick-to-itiveness someone like Ellington nurtured his orchestra's progress, though often stumbling and learning by trial and error, one can then see the quality that Carter lacked.

Carter disbanded in early 1934 and, after working a while with Willie Bryant, just the kind of showman-singer-frontman Carter was not, he fled to Europe upon an offer to join the expatriate Willie Lewis in Paris. As it turned out Carter stayed in Europe for four years after his stint with Lewis, leading bands in London, Copenhagen, Paris, and Holland. Though he was adored and idolized by the Europeans—and especially by his chief proselytizer Hugues Panassié—his fifty-odd recordings made in Europe, virtually all Carter originals and arrangements, did not add much of substance to Carter's output. For one thing the European players he had at his disposal, although undoubtedly among the best available at the time, could not really do justice to Carter's relatively advanced scores. This was particularly true of the rhythm sections. Then, too, his desire to be pre-eminent in so many areas—saxophone, clarinet, trumpet, composing, arranging, directing—continued to disperse his talent and formidable energy rather than aggregate it.

Among other things, Carter had returned in 1930 to his first love, the trumpet, an affection originally inspired by his boyhood idol Bubber Miley. Under his trumpeter friend Doc Cheatham's tutelage, Carter seriously began to study the trumpet and within a few years became a remarkably proficient soloist on the instrument. Beginning in 1933 (on the Chocolate Dandies' sides) he launched a side-career as trumpet soloist, frequently playing both alto *and* trumpet in the same performance. He was much admired by brass and reed men for his effortless ability to instantly switch instruments and embouchures.

Two fine examples of his trumpet playing may be heard on *Once Upon a Time* (Chocolate Dandies) and *Star Dust* with the Willie Lewis orchestra in

Paris. Both are in the manner and style of Armstrong. Clearly, Carter was hoping that a career as trumpet-playing frontman was an option to explore. Though admired and respected—again that element of "isn't it amazing that he can also play the trumpet so well"—his ambitions as trumpet star were not crowned with popular success.

Remarkable for being as good as it is, Carter's trumpet playing is ultimately and intrinsically limited—although he manages to hide these limitations very well. It is really the lyric aspects of Carter's saxophone style (and tone) transposed to the trumpet. But the trumpet doesn't have the saxophone's innate agility. That is why Carter always limited himself to an essentially ornamental, broadly lyric style, so effectively demonstrated on *Star Dust*. This was, of course, also the basic approach Armstrong took in his band-fronting career; but there it was more by choice than by necessity. Nevertheless Carter obviously found support for his lyric approach to the trumpet in Armstrong's famed presence. It is also uncanny how perfectly Carter could imitate Armstrong's famous upward glissandos (hear Carter on *Once Upon a Time*) and those floppy loose-tongued attacks that Louis invented and used to such expressive effect. Oddly enough, very few trumpet players could manage that effect, and it is therefore a little startling to hear Carter handle it with such casual aplomb, as he does towards the end of *Star Dust*, for example. This recording is also notable for its imaginative arrangement, featuring one of those adventurous near-double-time saxophone ensemble choruses that Carter could toss off with such ease—and which here was played exceedingly well by a section of three American expatriates and one Frenchman.

But one of Carter's finest hours on the trumpet occurred years later in 1939 on *More Than You Know* with his own band of the time. Here Carter's trumpet-playing had become more secure and fluent, allowing a greater amount of phrase ornamentation, as for instance in the second eight of his first chorus (Ex. 3a).

Ex. 3a

♩ = a weighted beat   ◡ = an unweighted beat

Although his phrasing still tended to be a little short-breathed, even a little prim, Carter sometimes perfected the long unfettered line, as in the last eight of his first solo: a ravishing melodic phrase which is equal to anything Armstrong produced in this vein (Ex. 3b).

Ex. 3b

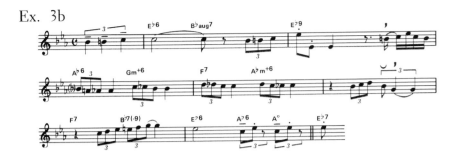

Carter's trumpet playing is marked by lyric elegance and clean technique; in fact it is in a way too clean. It is almost "classical" in its approach, of course with an overlay of Armstrong-oriented jazz characteristics. But in the end it is not *true* trumpet playing, in the sense that Roy Eldridge's or Buck Clayton's or Harry James's is. Carter thinks like a reed man, not a brass player. As remarkable as it may seem to have a saxophonist play the trumpet that well, it is still once removed from natural inborn trumpet playing—with, of course, the inevitable limitations thereof.

It was perhaps predictable that eventually Carter would want to return to the States, if only to hear his music played once again by American musicians. In the intervening years the "Swing craze" had struck and Benny Goodman had been crowned "King of Swing"—which must have had an ironic ring for Carter in view of the fact that, what was now touted as the new jazz, was but a slight updating of the kind of playing and arranging that he and other colleagues like Redman, the Hendersons, Hawkins, and, of course Armstrong,[9] had initiated way back in the late twenties.

Upon his return to America, Carter set about organizing a new band, which, however, didn't debut on records until June 1939. In the meantime Carter kept relatively busy playing with various (mostly recording) groups led by Teddy Wilson and Lionel Hampton, as well as Leonard Feather. On these records he seems to play with a refreshed, renewed energy. On solos like the one on *On the Bumpy Road to Love* (with Teddy Wilson) or *Push Out* with Ethel Waters, Carter played with a rhythmic vigor and clarity of articulation, not quite so consistently present heretofore. Insofar as this and other performances of this period reveal a closer kinship to Coleman Hawkins's mature style, I suspect that the many encounters with Hawkins in Europe— Hawkins worked there more or less the same time as Carter, 1934 to 1939—had a telling effect on Carter's saxophone playing. On *Bumpy Road*, for example,[10] much of the shaping and phrasing is Hawk's, but without the latter's sometime ferocity. Carter brings the

---

9. It is odd—and not entirely accidental, I suspect—that Armstrong's and Carter's careers never intersected professionally.
10. The same can be noted on the 1940 Chocolate Dandies' performance of *Smack*, where Carter plays with a darker, coarser, tenorish sound, emphasizing greatly the alto's lower register (which of course is the tenor saxophone's middle register).

Hawkins larger-than-life ideas and sound back down to normal human size. Whereas Hawkins cared little about boundaries, crossing them all the time, it was in Carter's nature to present things neatly packaged.

When Carter's new big band finally emerged, it was once again to mixed reactions: enthusiastic response from musicians, a tepid reception from the crowds at the Savoy and the Alhambra. Carter's arrangements—his signature tune *When Lights Are Low* (one of his finest compositions) and *Riff Romp* are but two typical examples—were eminently musical, intelligent, and well played. But they also had a disconcerting remoteness about them; they didn't invite you, the listener, in—as Ellington or Lunceford or even Goodman did. There was something mildly antiseptic about Carter's music that might command your respect and admiration, but rarely your love. Did Carter perhaps rehearse too much, and squeeze the emotional content out of the pieces by the time they were recorded? Unanswerable at this late date in any precise way, it is nevertheless a question worth raising.

At this time, 1939, one also begins to notice Carter's adeptness—indeed penchant—for assimilating other styles and conceptions, yet another aspect of his innate versatility. It was nothing for him to adopt Fletcher Henderson's by now all-prevailing orchestral style (as in *When Lights Are Low*) or the sweeter dance styles spreading rapidly through swing land (as in many arrangements: *Slow Freight, All of Me, The Very Thought of You, Cocktails for Two*, to mention only a few). Carter even felt persuaded (in *Vagabond Dreams* and *Love's Got Me Down Again*) to imitate the Glenn Miller band sound(s), down to a Miller/Dorsey-style trombone solo by Tyree Glenn. Nor was Carter impervious to the presence and influence of Ellington (hear Carter's beautiful *Melancholy Lullaby*). In his playing, too, Carter was malleable, one day reminding you of Hodges, as on *Scratch My Back* (with the Varsity Seven), or another day, on clarinet, of Benny Goodman *(Pom Pom)*. Carter's assimilations are, of course, never mere imitations or plagiarisms. Carter's native sense of order and balance is always in the forefront. But at the same time his *band's* style did not stand at the cutting edge of the music, either creatively or commercially. It in no way represented leadership.

At its best the band could be very "impressive." On *O.K. for Baby*, one of Carter's Horace Henderson-type riff tunes, the band gets a wonderfully relaxed back-in-the-beat feeling, not unlike Basie's band of the time. It is a perfect arrangement in that it makes all the right moves at the right time, and is helped immensely by the infectious, springy, linear beat of the drums and bass (William Purnell and Hayes Alvis, respectively), but also by Carter's, as always, propulsive saxophone section writing and a splendidly outgoing trumpet solo by Bill Coleman. Carter's own alto solo reveals that he, in the meantime, was not unaware of one Lester Young. Prez's influence can be heard quite clearly in Carter's solo on *I Can't Believe That You're in Love*, a 1940 Chocolate Dandies recording.

Night Hop was another well-made and well-played arrangement, one in which Carter showed his ability to integrate neatly a variety of improvised solos into an overall arranged structure.

Carter's finest work from this period, I would judge, is *Shufflebug Shuffle*

(Nov. 1939). It is a catchy riff piece (Ex. 4) with (for the time) very "modern" chromatically shifting changes of the kind that would become thrice familiar in the bop period with pieces like Dizzy's *Night in Tunisia* and Pete Rugolo's *Artistry in Rhythm*.

Ex. 4

Carter contributes one of his own loveliest solos, as well as a fetching trombone trio, well played in a clean relaxed manner. On the other hand, Eddie Heywood, Jr.—who had made his recording debut with Carter in mid-1939, and had previously served him well with lacy, nimble-fingered, tasty piano solos (as on *When Lights Are Low* and *Fish Fry*)—here incongruously resorted to some hackneyed boogie-woogie piano, which, although all the rage then with pianists, had nothing to do with Carter's *Shufflebug*. In the end one is left with only Carter's theme, as one of his most memorable achievements.

A glance at the Carter 1939 band's discography shows that there was continuous personnel reshuffling. Things must not have been easy for Carter the bandleader. Every few months saw extensive turnovers in the various sections. Moreover, the commercial pressures, whose effects run like a recurrent thread through big-band jazz history, were bearing down on Carter.[11] That usually meant more singers, more vocals. But despite such "attractions" as Joe Turner, the Mills Brothers, and Roy Felton, a baritone along the lines of Herb Jeffries and Billy Eckstine (and a discovery of Carter's), the band's records sold poorly. The public was listening to Goodman, Shaw, and Miller, and in Carter's own closer musi-

11. The extent to which such pressures could be exerted is recounted by Morroe Berger in the Time/ Life *Giants of Jazz* series on Carter. After recording four instrumentals for Decca in May 1940, the company's executives forced Carter not only to record with the Mills Brothers but to do a boogie-woogie version of Clyde McCoy's anthem of corn, *Sugar Blues*, replete with yelping saxophones and laughing trumpets. When after the record date Carter asked the Decca people not to release the track, they did so anyhow—after which Carter, to his credit, broke off relations with Decca and went over to Bluebird.

cal backyard Count Basie and Duke Ellington were reaching unprecedented pinnacles of success and thus providing insurmountable competition. Worse yet, the band's playing was now uneven at best, deteriorating at worst. Despite Carter's fine reputation as a painstaking rehearser with a sharp ear for intonation problems, many of the 1940 and 1941 performances are out of tune, sometimes badly (*All of Me*, the saxes; *There, I've Said It*, the brass). Carter and the band became increasingly ensnared in the prevailing swing formulas. Occasionally a soloist, like Sidney de Paris on *Babalu* or Carter himself on *Back Bay Boogie*—where he charges into his solo like a colt dashing out of a stall—tries to energize the proceedings. But the end seemed irreversibly in sight. With a piece prophetically called *Ill Wind* and Bluebird's even more painful rejection of a tune named *Tree of Hope* (!), the 1939 Carter band went into the history books.

After a stint on New York's 52nd Street with a sextet that included Dizzy Gillespie and drummer Kenny Clarke—unfortunately the group never recorded—Carter organized yet another band for a cross-country tour that landed him in Hollywood. As the World War II draft robbed him of some of his sidemen, Carter replaced them with younger musicians like trombonists J. J. Johnson and Al Grey, drummer Max Roach (who as an eighteen-year-old had already played with Carter briefly in the 1941 band), tenor men Dexter Gordon and Lucky Thompson, and in 1946 even the young Miles Davis.

Some of this West Coast band's Armed Forces radio broadcasts, which have recently become available on LP, and the band's Capitol sides are quite revealing in that they exhibit once again Carter's ability to adjust to the prevailing stylistic winds. This 1943-46 band was, typical for the war years, brass heavy (four trumpets, four trombones—not to mention *six* saxes), loud and frenetic, generally unsubtle, and definitely well-ensconced in the new bop style. And once again, the results were uneven, although ironically some of the Capitol records achieved some measure of commercial success. We can hear some fine Carter solos on alto (*I Can't Get Started*) and more-daring-than-usual trumpet (a 1944 *Star Dust*), early getting-it-together solos by J. J. (as for example *his* almost double-time solo on the same *Star Dust*) and Miles Davis (*Jump Call*), and a wild Al Grey, like a maddened Trummy Young on a spree (on a 1946 *Just You, Just Me*). But you can also hear some horrendously out-of-tune brass playing—on a regular record date yet—on the 1945 *Prelude to a Kiss*, and Carter with serious reed problems on *Forever Blues*.

No one had tried harder and with so much talent and for so long a time (over 10 years) to make a success of band leading. In the end success eluded Carter, and in 1946 he settled in Hollywood, turning his arranging talents to film scores. As he once put it with bittersweet irony, although "the sweet smell of failure" still attracted him, film work now "interested" him more.[12] He had already had a pleasant taste of this kind of work when he did some arranging and composing (under 20th Century Fox musical director Alfred Newman's watchful eye) for the highly successful 1943 movie *Stormy Weather*, starring among others Lena

12. Cited in Time/Life *Giants of Jazz*, annotated Morroe Berger.

Horne. And Carter's film work led to television scoring and his (as well as TV producers') discovery that he could write music other than straight jazz. His most famous assignments came with the *M Squad* series and the Alfred Hitchcock mystery series, as he became part of that wave of composers like Johnny Mandel, Henry Mancini, and Lalo Schifrin who brought jazz-tinged scores to prime-time television.

Since then Carter has combined the life of a Hollywood fixture with that of a jazz elder statesman. The lure of playing—as opposed to only writing—eventually enticed him back to the alto saxophone, and this in a variety of contexts and styles. As one listens to late Benny Carter and hears the tremendous authority and—yes, even passion—with which he discharges a wide range of assignments, one is tempted to conclude that Benny Carter, the restless ever-searching seeker, has finally found his rightful place (or two) in the sun. His playing as well as his composing and arranging now have a conviction, an inevitableness, and above all a reaching out to an audience, *whatever* audience or audiences— and there are several—in a way that he somehow could never attain earlier. Whether it is the "sexy" mood music settings of *You Belong to Me* and the melodramatic ballad treatment of *Georgia on My Mind*, or the Billy May-type of arrangements then in vogue (1952) of his own *Sunday Afternoon*, or the haunting vocal choir arrangement of *I Wanna Go Home*, or indeed the small-group bop riff-tune *Cruisin'*, it all sits right, as the expression goes.[13] Indeed his own composition *Lullaby in Blue*, with its haunting Ellington-Hodges mood, represents this particular musical genre at its best.

At about the same time Carter was participating in a series of historic recordings organized by Norman Granz that brought together the three greatest alto saxophonists of the first four decades of jazz: Hodges, Parker, and Carter. Though in this awesome company Carter's slightly lesser stature is inevitably exposed, he is still a formidable contender. His playing on *Jam Blues*, for example, is uncurtained: it reaches out, it thrusts itself at you, especially in his last two (of seven) choruses. And with all its bop-ish "diddleyadah" turns and other Parkerisms, it is also still very much essential Carter.

Though Carter, now in his seventies, is still playing well—hear a relatively recent concert recorded in Japan in April 1977 (on Pablo Records)—I should like to leave him with one of his finest moments, the truly magnificent solo on Quincy Jones's *The Midnight Sun Will Never Set* (1961). I've always felt that Carter is first and foremost a lyric player who feels happiest in a slow ballad, especially one in which he can exhibit his formidable talent for meaningful, tasteful ornamentation. This special gift, in which he is most consistent, can be savored throughout his career, from his own early *Blue Prelude* (1933) through *Lullaby in Blue* (1952) and Ellington's *Prelude to a Kiss* (1945) to *Blue Star* (1961). With the recording of *Midnight Sun* to guide us, we can let the music (Ex. 5) have the last word.

---

13. All these diversified assignments were fulfilled by Carter (for RCA Victor) in one late-summer period (in 1952).

Ex. 5

MILLS BLUE RHYTHM BAND

Although no one could really successfully emulate or compete with Cab Callo-way, it was not an untried idea. The gifted singer-entertainer, Billy Banks, not only sang with some of Calloway's panache and style, but invariably used star-studded recording groups with the likes of Coleman Hawkins, Fats Waller, and Red Allen (as in 1932) to back him.[14] The Mills Blue Rhythm Band, fronted by various "entertainers" through the years, was another orchestra that operated in somewhat the same territory as Calloway's. Indeed its repertory was to a large extent identical with and imitative of Calloway's. This was due in part to Irving Mills's titular mentorship (and management) of the band—Calloway and Elling-ton were Mills's two other star clients—and as publisher of Calloway's and El-lington's songs, it was not difficult for Mills to persuade his Blue Rhythm Band

14. Banks had a splendid career, although not strictly speaking in the main jazz tradition. After his own quite successful 1932 recordings, he joined Noble Sissle's band in the mid-1930s, but four years later began a ten-year residency at Billy Rose's Diamond Horseshoe, giving—according to John Chilton's *Who's Who of Jazz*—an astounding uninterrupted 7,151 performances. In the 1950s he worked in variety shows in Europe, then toured Asia and Australia, eventually settling in Japan, where he died in 1967. (See below, Chapter 6, Part 1, fn. 6.)

to record and perform *his* preferred repertory. Calloway's *Minnie the Moocher* saga was, of course, successful in its own right, but secondary bands, like the Blue Rhythm group, helped to keep sales figures high on this and similar Calloway-associated items *(Kokey Joe, The Scat Song, Trickeration)*.

But apart from its Mills-directed, surrogate-entertainer role, the Blue Rhythm Band led a musically distinguished career which has been sadly neglected (or at least minimized) by most jazz historians. for, as with Calloway, the band always maintained a strong roster of fine players and arrangers, and, compared with the millions of pop and novelty items recorded throughout the 1930s by literally thousands of groups, the Mills Blue Rhythm Band's recorded output held to a very high level of musical standards and craftsmanship.

If it did not achieve a distinctive recognizable style, it was undoubtedly because it lacked a leader who could give it a style or an arranger with the originality of a Sy Oliver or a Fletcher Henderson. Edgar Hayes, the band's musical director and chief arranger from 1930 to 1936, was a technically formidable pianist and a fine functional arranger, but not one to give an orchestra a distinguishable personality. Harry White, the trombonist, left in late 1932 to go with Calloway and did his best arranging work with *that* band. Joe Garland, who joined the Blue Rhythm Band around the time that White left, was responsible for a good part of its repertory in the mid-thirties, both as composer and arranger, but left in 1936—*with* Hayes (when the latter formed his own orchestra)—before he could really leave his stylistic imprint on the band.[15]

Other arrangers who worked for the Mills band, like Will Hudson, Benny Carter, Nat Leslie, and Alex Hill, did so on an intermittent basis, again not enough to foster a characteristic permanent style. But the real reason for the relative anonymity and functional approach of the band was that it was designed by Irving Mills from the outset to be a kind of relief band for Ellington and Calloway at the Cotton Club and other major venues where these bands alighted. Above all it was not to compete with them. Consequently the Blue Rhythm Band was led—that is to say more precisely, fronted—by singer-dancer-entertainer-showman types, not necessarily of first-rank star quality. The band worked under quite a succession of these figureheads: Sonny Nichols, Bob Stephens, Baron Lee, Billy Banks, Eddie Mallory (a trumpeter and Ethel Waters's husband), and finally in 1933 Lucky Millinder.

But, as mentioned, the Blue Rhythm Band always featured fine jazz soloists. Moreover, they were given relatively ample space on recordings, as witness pieces like Harry White's *Wild Waves* and *White Lightning*, Hayes's *The Growl* and *Kokey Joe*, and Benny Carter's *Jazz Cocktail* (Mills's band being the third orchestra to whom Carter had offered that composition/arrangement). In most of these sides the rhythm section, always the prerequisite foundation of a clean-playing, swinging orchestra, provided excellent support. Besides the fine team of Earl Hines's former bass player Hayes Alvis (later to play with Ellington) and

---

15. Garland, of course, left a major imprint on several white bands, especially Glenn Miller's and Les Brown's through his *In the Mood* and *Leap Frog*.

one of the better ensemble drummers of the period, O'Neil Spencer, there was Benny James, a first-rate rhythm guitarist, and, of course, Edgar Hayes. His uncommon technique—in a florid and almost classically ornamental style—can be heard on many sides, most notably on *Dancing Dogs* and *The Growl*, the latter featuring a dizzying right-hand run that Earl Hines would have been proud of.[16]

These early Blue Rhythm sides also afford us excellent opportunities to hear Ed Anderson, a much-neglected trumpeter, excellent in both open horn and muted work, whose only misfortune was never to play with any of the top three or four "glamour" bands. But Anderson was a superb musician, playing well within the Armstrong tradition, yet no mere *epigone*. His style was somewhat simpler than Armstrong's in phrasing and melodic invention, but no less expressive. Indeed, his solos on slower pieces like *Wild Waves* and, especially, the 1931 *Moanin'* are hard to match for sheer intensity of expression. His style, concise and essentially "vocal" in conception, was imbued with the feel and spirit of the blues, and with his powerful attack and tone his solos have a way of reaching out to the listener, projecting, remaining memorable. He was, as mentioned, also very adept with various mutes. Hear him in an elegantly poised straight-mute solo on *Sugar Blues* and *Blue Flame* (not the Woody Herman theme song), and growl passionately on *Black and Tan Fantasy* and *The Growl* (1932).

Anderson was eventually replaced by "Red" Allen. The reader will recall that Allen and J. C. Higginbotham had both left the Russell band to join Henderson, hardly anticipating that the latter band would soon fold, as it did in 1934. Both then took refuge with the more financially secure Blue Rhythm Band, along with clarinetist Buster Bailey. This trio of soloists strengthened the already impressive solo potential of the band even more, although by this time Allen had lost some of his earliest fiery drive and uninhibited imagination. Bailey, never a freely creative musician, was nonetheless a superior technician and by now one of the more experienced veterans of the big-band scene, having started out with W. C. Handy way back in the "prehistoric" days of 1917. Unquestionably, he did some of his most exciting work with the Blue Rhythm Band (as, for example, on *Harlem Heat*).

The repertory of the Blue Rhythm Band became ever more varied and eclectic, what with not only Joe Garland and George Washington (a fine trombonist)[17] contributing excellent arrangements and originals, but by also performing

16. Edgar Hayes had been Hines's duo partner in Lois Deppe's 1925 orchestra, featuring *two* pianists—a band that unfortunately was never recorded.

17. George Washington is another one of the many gifted lesser-known musicians jazz has produced. While not a path-breaking major figure, Washington was a consistently inventive soloist whose fine work can be heard not only with the Blue Rhythm Band but with Armstrong's late 1930s' band and Count Basie. The range of his talent can be assessed on, for example, *Kokey Joe* (hot and growly, rangey) or *Harlem After Midnight*. Washington was a well-trained musician, studying with the redoubtable Walter Damrosch at the New York Conservatory, the same Damrosch paradoxically who ranted and raved against the "degeneracy" and "sinfulness" of jazz.

works by the Irish bandleader-composer-arranger and sometime Ellington disciple, Spike Hughes, by Ellington himself *(Drop Me Off in Harlem, Merry Go Round)*, and finally, the ubiquitous Will Hudson.

In *Harlem Heat*, a close relative to Hudson's famous *White Heat* (recorded by Lunceford), Hudson turned out one of his finest arrangements, much aided in its interpretation by the spirited, gutsy playing of the band and the fine solos, especially Higginbotham's (Ex. 6).

Ex. 6

etc.

Interesting, too, is Hudson's wider-ranging use of the reeds, for example, a low-register trio of tenor, baritone, and bass saxophone on the "head"—Joe Garland was also making excellent use of the bass of the family in his 1934–35 recordings—or four high-register clarinets in close harmony for the last chorus.

The Ellington pieces lack the drive and color of the Duke's band. *Merry Go Round* receives a rather "comfortable" performance, its essentially two-beat rhythmic interpretation not really suiting the work. Paradoxically, though, Elmer James plays with much more actual 4/4 beat than Duke's older bass player, Wellman Braud, the whole feeling of Ellington's performance is one of a relentlessly driving, swinging 4/4. This is due not only to the difference between Sonny Greer and O'Neil Spencer, but because the whole Ellington band felt the 4/4 swing so strongly that it transmitted itself across Braud's two-beat bass very persuasively. It is an excellent example of how a strongly felt *implied* beat can be stronger than a less dynamic *explicit* one.

But the Mills band's interpretation of *Drop Me Off in Harlem* was interesting, precisely because it avoided copying Ellington's original. The whole Blue Rhythm Band performance is turned over to Adelaide Hall, who often incidentally guested with Ellington in gutty, growly vocals that hid what a comely soprano voice she really had. Her rendition with Blue Rhythm of *Harlem* is totally original, including some out-of-tempo and stop-time passages which give the performance a kind of elasticity a straight jazz rendering could probably not have achieved. Her singing in a voice of pure velveteen—alternating, however, for contrast with a few moments of her famous growl—is rich with delightful, pert inflections and impeccable diction. It virtually transforms Ellington's opus into an American art song.

By the end of 1936 the Mills Blue Rhythm Band was not only feeling the loss of many of its major soloists—Allen, Higginbotham, Garland, Hayes—but experiencing increased competitive pressure from the big successful white swing bands (Goodman, Casa Loma, the Dorseys, Barnet), not to mention other Harlem bands like Lunceford, Webb, and Basie, who were in their different ways capturing a lot of attention.

In 1937 Lucky Millinder, who had become by now the full-fledged leader of the band, brought in Charlie Shavers and Harry Edison to replace Allen, and Billy Kyle to fill the piano chair—in addition to retaining altoist-arranger Tab Smith, a holdover from the 1936 band—Millinder formed a virtually new ensemble which, however, did not survive beyond early 1938. Even Mills did not offer the band recordings on his own Variety label beyond July 1937.

The year 1938 closed one chapter of the Mills Blue Rhythm Band's history. An interestingly eclectic band with enthusiastic excellent players, not any more variable in its quality than many another Harlem orchestra, it functioned effectively for nearly a decade. Unfortunately it never received from the Mills office the kind of publicity and support Mills's other enterprises enjoyed. When even this limited managerial life-support system was withdrawn, the band was bound to collapse. But during its best days it offered a measure of the extraordinary abundance of talent concentrated in Harlem in the 1930s.

But there is a second chapter to the Blue Rhythm–Lucky Millinder story. Millinder, undaunted by his band's demise, hooked up with Bill Doggett, then a young aspiring bandleader, later a commercially highly successful rhythm-and-blues organist and accompanist. But the Doggett band had no style or format with which to compete successfully in a field that was literally exploding with new but also ever more gimmicky talent. This was the era of the Shep Fieldses, Alvino Reys, Richard Himbers, Frankie Carles, Horace Heidts, Kay Kaysers—each with a ploy or musical gimmick of some kind. Then there were, of course, the many surviving first-rate orchestras like Lunceford, Ellington, Calloway, all in their prime, and the big commercial attractions like the Mills Brothers, the Ink Spots, Bing Crosby, and a thousand lesser others. By early 1939 Millinder was forced to declare bankruptcy. But miraculously he reorganized in late 1940, now fronting a band under his own name (having dropped the Blue Rhythm name), and featuring the singer Sister Rosetta Tharpe. The orchestra harbored at various times during 1941 and 1942 such fine musicians as Dizzy Gillespie,

Sandy Williams, Tab Smith, Lucky Thompson, Stafford Simon, bassists Abe Bolar and George Duvivier, "Sir" Charles Thompson, and drummer Panama Francis.

Rosetta Tharpe (1915–73), primarily a gospel singer, second only to Mahalia Jackson, possessed a remarkably powerful mezzo-soprano voice which she inflected with a biting attack and fiery, swinging rhythmic drive (not unlike that of the later Dinah Washington). In her secular singing a kind of protégé of Cab Calloway, Tharpe provided Millinder with a number of substantial hits—*Rock Me, That's All, Shout, Sister, Shout.* But evidently conscience-stricken over her non-spiritual work, Tharpe left the Millinder band in mid-1942 to return to her religious singing, and then sustained an outstanding career as gospel-folk singer (and guitarist) well into the 1960s.

It took a while for the new Millinder band to find a semblance of a style. Certainly much of the 1941 work is uneven and flawed. Riff-jump tunes (like *Savoy* and *Apollo Jump*), really early rhythm-and-blues numbers, jostle uncomfortably with empty flag-wavers like the remake of "Red" Allen's (Will Hudson-arranged) *Ride, Red, Ride*—the Casa Loma style here anachronistically surviving as a relic of the distant past. Freddie Webster, a trumpet talent regarded by many as an important transitional figure from swing to bop, here as elsewhere on recordings, sounds directionless and unspecial, even inept (on *Savoy*). But on the other hand it is a joy to hear George Duvivier, the bass player, who, along with Ray Brown and Oscar Pettiford, was among the first to extend the revolutionizing legacy left by Jimmy Blanton.

Things took an upturn in the band when Tab Smith exercised his considerable talents in 1942, both as composer-arranger and alto soloist. His *Mason Flyer* and *Shipyard Social Function* are fine functional pieces, perfect for dancing, spiced with "hot" grinding solos (as those by tenor-man Stafford Simon) and all the riffs, blues, and jump ingredients that Harlem ballroom audiences wanted to hear. Such pieces, along with influences from the boogie-woogie style of the late thirties and early forties, represent the basis for the rhythm-and-blues proliferation of the post-war years, which in turn, of course, eventually led to rock and roll and the British rock invasion of the sixties and seventies.

The drift towards R & B in the early forties was not entirely accidental, nor without enormous significance in the field of popular music. As World War II brought millions of blacks to the North or in any case to urban centers where relatively lucrative work could be found in wartime factories operating around the clock, R & B became their special music. But this was merely one branch of a three-way split in styles becoming audible then, the other two directions being 1) the bop or modern jazz idioms; and 2) the increasingly vocalist-dominated and commercially oriented white dance bands. Bop and modern jazz survived, as we know, and indeed flourished, while the white big-bands bogged down in such a morass of commercialism that their demise, as a viable forward-looking *creative* medium, was inevitable—even without the ruinous economic pressures of the postwar years.

Black audiences could no longer tolerate the increasingly insipid and tame dance music of the white bands—they weren't particularly invited into that world anyway—but at the same time many of them could not keep up with the rapid advances in black orchestras (Hines in 1943, Eckstine and Gillespie's *Things To Come* orchestra of the mid-1940s) and the switch to small be-bop combos playing "esoteric," "intellectual" jazz. Or so they perceived it. Rhythm and Blues was the answer for them. And Millinder, who later went completely into the R & B field, along with the likes of Bill Doggett, Earl Bostic, Wynonie Harris, and Louis Jordan, found a musical haven where they could in fact still function professionally. It was, of course, in its way *also* a totally commercial music which permitted no fundamental stylistic deviations or advances. And as such it played no further role creatively in jazz, although it provided often desperately needed employment for many otherwise idealistically motivated musicians.[18]

Of special interest, historically and musically, is the Millinder band's *Little John Special,* since it features one of the early recorded solos of Dizzy Gillespie. It is also a field day for the inveterate "jazz lick" researcher, Tab Smith's arrangement grabbing at any number of riffs that had been floating around black bands for years, most notably the famous "Salt Peanuts" riff which here makes a full-fledged instrumental debut—although bits and pieces of it had shown up as early as Louis Armstrong's *Ding Dong Daddy* and, more recently, in Glenn Miller's *Wham Re Bop* as well as in Basie's *Basie Boogie.* Other public domain riffs—meaning that everybody used them and that they were often as old as jazz itself—appropriated by Smith had been recently heard on Ellington's *Ko-Ko,* Basie's *Boogie Woogie* and *One O'Clock Jump*—and were to appear elsewhere often enough in early bebop and rhythm-and-blues repertories.

That sort of use of black musical vernacular was part and parcel of the creative regression of many black bands, as they fell all over each other to ward off the encroaching modernisms, while clinging desperately to the familiar and colloquial and the ordinary. It is all the more curious, seen in this context, to hear Gillespie's already quite decidedly bop-ish two choruses over a swing band blues, especially against the somewhat chugging stale swing-style rhythm section. Also curious is the midpoint "modulation" which in fact modulates nowhere, ending up right back in the original key of B♭.

Inevitably Dizzy's solo stands out, not only for its style but also for its quality. He is clearly in his own new territory, which a comparison with the three solos immediately preceding and succeeding his own amply demonstrates. The closest to Dizzy's new rhythmic-melodic world is Simon's Young-like tenor solo. And this solo of Dizzy's largely refutes his often self-acknowledged tribute to Charlie Parker, that he (Dizzy) learned his rhythmic feeling from Parker. For one thing, Dizzy's lithe "linear" rhythmic inflection on *Little John* is very much his own

---

18. A partial list of distinguished jazz musicians who worked with Earl Bostic, for example, includes no less than the following: Benny Harris, Blue Mitchell, the Turrentine brothers, Johnny Coles, Gerald Wilson, John Coltrane, Benny Golson, Benny Carter, Don Byas, Tony Scott, Rudy Powell, Eddie Barefield, Buddy Collette, Hymie Schertzer, Al Casey, Jimmy Shirley, Barney Kessel, René Hall, Joe Pass, "Sir" Charles Thompson, Jaki Byard, Cozy Cole, Shelly Manne, Larry Bunker, Teddy Charles.

and not at all the same as Parker's—a much more intensely articulated and somewhat vertically oriented rhythmic conception. For another thing, while Dizzy had met Parker briefly in Kansas City in 1940 and *perhaps* had, by July 29, 1942 (the date of the *Little John* recording), jammed with him at Monroe's or Minton's, all accounts indicate that Gillespie was not especially impressed by Parker *until* they worked together in Hines's band in early 1943. And even then, it was trumpeter Benny Harris who brought the two men together musically. Such accounts—also those of Dizzy's trumpet player friend Buddy Anderson—correspond to the aural evidence of recordings, slim though it is.

Dizzy's solo here clearly shows that at that point in time, say 1940 to 1942, Gillespie's and Parker's musical conceptions were pointed in the same general direction, with some parallels and overlaps discernible (especially in the realms of harmony and tempo), but with some *major* differences as well—differences in part also of those between articulation on a trumpet and a saxophone. Later, of course, their musical conceptions were to converge, each learning from the other in a reciprocal musical union that, considering its impact, was virtually unique in jazz history.

Many of Dizzy's favorite trademarks are already present on *Little John:* the opening descending line starting from a high perched note, the long plummeting lines that swirl around near the bottom before lithely snaking up to a middle-range note, the fast-note flurries here still in eighth-note triplets (in a few-years to be in sixteenths or thirty-seconds). Dizzy's solo is structured so as to reflect and accentuate the basic blues changes (or at least *one* version of how one might relate phrase lengths to harmonic function): a neat eight-plus-four-bar division in both choruses and having the point of departure for the last four bars in each chorus coincide with the dominant (V) chord. Of course, this was still a young twenty-four-year-old Gillespie, who would within a few years invent much more unpredictable and asymmetrical phrasings. And some of *that* he would learn from Kenny Clarke and Thelonious Monk as well as from Charlie Parker.

Gillespie was fired by Millinder—no reasons given. He went on to Hines, Eckstine, and his own bands and became one of the major leaders of the bop revolution. Millinder drifted more and more into rhythm-and-blues, with considerable popular success, and maintained a rather large orchestra straight through 1952, by which time most big bands had disappeared.

In 1942 Millinder had the power to fire Gillespie. Today, we ask: who was Lucius Millinder? The question receives an answer only from the jazz historian.

PART 4

LIONEL HAMPTON

Lionel Hampton made his first recordings under his own name in early 1937, while he was still working with the Benny Goodman Quartet. These were small combo recordings which eventually comprised twenty-three sessions with greatly varying personnel. The series, perhaps modeled on the famous Billie Holiday–

Teddy Wilson sessions (although not of so consistent a quality), was terminated in early 1941. By that time Hampton had left Goodman (in 1940) and formed his own big band, with which he recorded prolifically for several more decades, bridging several stylistic periods from swing and boogie-woogie, jump, early rhythm-and-blues to bop and modern jazz. Hampton is still active today, working now primarily in small group formats.

Hampton has been one of the most successful and enduring multi-instrumentalistis in jazz, obviously one of the few outstanding vibraphone solo-ists, but a drummer and (mostly two-fingered) pianist and talented singer as well. His first big-time professional work was in the late 1920s with the excellent Los Angeles-based Paul Howard orchestra, [1] continued with Howard's successor, Les Hite, and after a year or two of fronting his own band he was discovered by Goodman in 1936.

Even in full consideration of the enormous diversity of major jazz talents in any period of its history, one is tempted to apply the word unique to Lionel Hampton. Certainly no one has outrivaled Hampton in sheer exuberance, phys-ical as well as emotional. Motored by a seemingly limitless supply of energy and stamina, Hampton's playing is known the world over for its relentless physicality, unhampered technical facility (especially on vibraphone), and a seemingly im-perturbable inventiveness. Limitless outpourings of rhythmic energy being al-ways more admired in the popular arena than subtlety or refinement of thought, Hampton's image as the unremitting hard swingster has far outstripped an aware-ness of his considerable lyric and melodic talents.

To be sure, Hampton's approach to music is often unsubtle, uncritical, at times even tasteless. In truth, when he assaults his drums, brutalizes the piano keyboard in his hammered two-finger style, pounds the vibraphone into submis-sion, the perspiration quotient is high indeed, its *in*spiration equivalent often considerably lower. Both in his ability to generate audience frenzy and in his

---

1. Paul Howard's Quality Serenaders was a now-forgotten nine-piece orchestra that deserves at least a footnote in jazz history. Apart from the twenty-year-old Hampton, the band included other tal-ented youngsters like Lawrence Brown, trumpeters George Orendorff and Earl Thompson, and boasted a skillful arranger (and reed man), Charlie Lawrence. In style the band at its best emulated the McKinney Cotton Pickers, particularly some of John Nesbitt's more adventurous scores, although the vestiges of a kind of lingering updated ragtime idiom and the influence of Paul Whiteman's more "sophisticated" arrangements can also at times be heard in their work. In addition, Orendorff was an expert in the "freak" trumpet style and an admirer of Bubber Miley, and Earl Thompson (later doing fine work in Andy Kirk's band) on the other hand was a disciple of Bix Beiderbecke. Thus the band provided considerable versatility, but by the same token had no single cohesive identity. Yet in its finest recordings—like *Charlie's Idea* (really *Tiger Rag*), *Stuff*, *Harlem*, and *California Swing*—there is much evidence of a never less than spirited, inventive music-making, seldom content with just the stock and the ordinary. One is also reminded of the fact that not all the "new" jazz of the period was centered in New York.

Some highlights: Orendorff's side-ending solo on *Stuff* that sounds like it might have been played by Dizzy Gillespie, the "hip" bitonal harmonies in *Harlem*, Lionel Hampton's versatile drum work and scat-singing, and a number of fine Lawrence Brown trombone solos, especially on *Cuttin' Up* and *Gettin' Ready Blues*. The latter provide early evidence not only of Brown's outstanding talent, but of the fact that his unique style was essentially set by 1929 (at age 22!).

own susceptibility to it, Hampton foreshadowed the empty-minded hysteria of today's more outrageous rock singers. Nor is the distance between rock and Hampton's 1940s' early form of rhythm-and-blues all that great, certainly not in respect to its rhythmic, dynamic, and energy levels. What all this unfortunately obscures is Hampton's talents as a balladeer, both as a vibraharpist and a singer, and his equally innate ability to express himself in gentler, more subtle ways.

Hampton's is a natural, uncomplicated musical talent—almost casually inventive—in which the sheer joy of performing, the direct unfurrowed communication to an audience, is more important than any critical or intellectual assessment of it. He is in this sense also not a leader, the way Ellington and Lunceford, for example, were. Stylistic identity and the creation of a recognizable individual orchestral style have never been uppermost in Hampton's thoughts, succumbing instead to a randomness of approach that accounts for much of the inconsistency of quality in both of his own playing and that of his accompanying groups, large or small. Indeed, his ambivalence in these matters caused him, when he contemplated forming a large band, to consider seriously any number of orchestral options, ranging from hot to sweet, from frantic jump to sedate dance, including the use of a large string section. Fortunately Hampton did in the end opt for a more orthodox jazz instrumentation, one which in due course became pre-eminent as a dynamic hard-driving swinging ensemble.

Hampton's Victor small group series is marked by a similar kind of unevenness and ambivalence. Its quality ranges all the way from well-swinging collective efforts like *Muskrat Ramble, Hot Mallets, Down Home Jump* (all with above-average Hampton improvisations), *I Can't Get Started, I'd Be Lost Without You, One Sweet Letter from You* (all with exceptionally sensitive vibraphone ballad work), and the virtuosic Hampton drum showcase, *Jack the Bellboy*, to musical disasters like *Lost Love* (primarily devoted to a crooning Lee Young vocal with an out-of-tune girl trio), the mindless piano pyrotechnics of *Twelfth Street Rag, I've Found a New Baby, China Stomp*, and leaden unswinging affairs such as *My Last Affair* (weighted down by Krupa's vertical chompy drumming) or the very tentative *Shades of Jade*, and a surprisingly listless *Flying Home.* [2] Vacillating between these wildly fluctuating artistic standards is a bewildering variety of contributions by a host of greater and lesser sidemen. Although their names read like a *Who's Who* of swing era jazz, Hampton seemed to exercise very little artistic or leadership control over these musicians. Some played superbly, others certainly did not; some tried to fit into the intended mood or character of the piece or a particular ensemble of players, others did not; some provided an exuberant lift to the performances (like Alvin Burroughs on his 1938 session, or Chu Berry on a number of tracks, King Cole and Oscar Moore on *I'd Be Lost,* Dizzy Gillespie on *Hot Mallets*, Ziggy Elman on *I've Found a New Baby*, Marshall Royal on his sessions). Others dragged the level down or contributed very little.

Although Hampton on these dates frequently engaged intact groups of side-

2. Not the famous 1942 big-band version, but the earlier 1940 smaller group performance.

men from one orchestra or another (Ellington, Goodman, Hines) on the assumption that players accustomed to each other would produce better integrated performances, the results were in fact often quite disjointed and impersonal. Especially striking is the considerable loss of individuality suffered by the Ellington contingent, an often observed condition whenever Duke's men were removed from the context of his orchestra and compositions. Hodges in particular, though still obviously a confident performer, seems only half the artist when not embraced by Ellington's harmonies and enveloped in his orchestral colors.

Although one has to do a bit of hunting for the finer contributions of these sidemen, it is on occasion well worth the effort. Curiously, the brass players fared generally better than the reed men. There are excellent solos by an explorative Cootie Williams (*Ring Dem Bells*), a cocky, irreverent and dashing Harry James (*Shoe Shiner's Drag, Muskrat Ramble*), a precociously brilliant Gillespie on *Hot Mallets*, a typically eccentric and unpredictable Henry Allen (*I'm on My Way*), an "outrageous" Rex Stewart (*Memories of You*); brilliant solos also by Lawrence Brown on *Stompology* and his perfect bee-buzzing imitation—you guessed it—in *Buzzin' Around the Bee*, as well as a romantic burry-toned one on *Memories*; and fine work by J. C. Higginbotham (who, to my knowledge, *never* played a poor solo). Even Ziggy Elman behaved himself musically and delivered a number of tasteful solos, as on *After You've Gone* and *Munson Street Breakdown*.

In addition to Chu Berry's dominant contributions (see below), Hawkins delivers several typically rhapsodic solos, a beautiful romantic one on *One Sweet Letter* and a rocking, raucous one on *When Lights Are Low*. Then there are the fervent Bechet-like clarinet solos by Marshall Royal on several 1942 sides (*Blues in the News, Royal Family*), and the many elegant saxophone section ensembles Benny Carter contributed. Charlie Christian was also importantly present in several roles: as a compelling soloist on *Haven't Named It Yet*, as accompanist—umamplified, by the way—behind Hampton's vocal on *One Sweet Letter*, and as straight-ahead rhythm guitarist. There is also (on the sides with the King Cole Trio) the trio's always inventive, interesting guitarist, Oscar Moore. And, lastly, we should not neglect Ray Perry's unusual contributions on amplified violin.[3] Perry had excellent intonation and developed a style which incorporated much double-stopping, especially in accompanimental situations where he could create the illusion of an entire saxophone section (or at least a pair of saxophones), or all by himself provide swinging harmonic riffs behind a soloist. Hear him to good advantage in these various roles on *Altitude, Bogo Jo, Smart Aleck,* and *Fiddle Dee Dee*.

As I have already suggested, although Hampton hired all these fine players,

---

3. Ray Perry was a Boston-based violinist and saxophonist who in the mid-thirties developed a technique of simultaneously singing and bowing, singing an octave below his playing. Slam Stewart, the bass player, heard Perry and adopted the same technique, except in inversion: singing an octave above his playing. (Perry was forced to leave Hampton because of an illness from which he never fully recovered; he died in 1950.)

Hear him also in outstanding solo work with the Sabby Lewis Sextet (on the Phoenix Jazz label).

he had little actual influence on the outcome of these sessions, for he was apparently oblivious of the varying results and content to unhesitatingly wend his way through vibraphone solo after solo. And though his later big band developed a much more cohesive personality due to the strong talents of some of his arrangers, one has the feeling that Hampton never exercised much artistic and stylistic control there either, except as these were affected by his boundless energy and uninhibited showmanship. It may sound absurd to say it—about someone who has led bands successfully for nearly fifty years—but Hampton is incapable of imposing his musical personality on others, as real leaders almost always do. That reluctance may in fact be a mixed blessing, for Hampton's sometimes questionable artistic taste inflicted on others might have produced even more inconsistent results. As it was, Hampton more often than not responded well to leadership from other directions, be it in the form of his big-band arrangers such as Milt Buckner, Quincy Jones, Bobby Plater (and Benny Carter—on the 1938 small group dates) or the powerful presence of players like Berry, Hawkins, Catlett, or even the young sparkling Gillespie, not to mention Goodman and Wilson in the Quartet settings.

The generally extrovert Hampton can in fact be quite self-effacing. Although he was the titular leader on April 5, 1939, there is no question that Chu Berry moved to front and center, even when not invited to do so (as on *Sweethearts on Parade* and *Denison Swing*), and turning what were intended to be Hampton solos into duets at best, in effect *accompaniments* to Berry. One has the distinct impression that the energetic shuffle rhythm and bright tempo were Berry's idea, not Hampton's; and never did Carmen Lombardo's sugary tune receive such a powerfully swinging treatment. It is an interesting aspect of Hampton's personality, as irrepressible as it often seems, that it can nonetheless sometimes be dominated by the artistry of others of even greater power and depth.

There is an interesting correlation here with Hampton's musical character and artistic predilections. While his popularity rests primarily on his hyper-energetic fast playing in loud riff pieces (*Flying Home, Air Mail Special, Hamp's Boogie Woogie*), his best and most creative playing invariably occurs in ballads, when the tempos are relaxed and the high-tension pressures are removed. At such times Hampton can be a superior melodic improviser, incorporating sensitivity of touch and timbral refinement in his playing. I have already mentioned three ballads from the years 1939 and 1940; to which one could add a 1954 *Star Dust* performance and his 1944 *Million Dollar Smile*.

But superficial excitement and seemingly unrestrained energy are Hampton's most obvious popular trademarks, and they are manifested in a most ostentatious way in his piano-playing. This consists not of orthodox pianism, of course, but rather an essentially percussive mallet technique applied to the upper register of the piano by using two fingers like mallets. The power and rapidity with which Hampton can thus extract sounds from the piano keyboard is in a pure technical sense astonishing—and, like a highly trained circus act, a constant delight for general audiences. It is, however, an essentially purposeless and musically extremely limited technique. It ignores the basic nature of the piano—an instrument not meant to be hammered at—and its great capacity for a variety of tonal nuances and touch. By emphasizing only the percussive side of the piano, this device is self-invalidating, leading only to witless virtuoso displays (as in the aforementioned numbers). One of Hampton's most famous hits using the two-finger technique, *Central Avenue Breakdown*, was only rescued from total artistic failure by the compensating intercessions of second pianist Nat Cole and guitarist Oscar Moore. Pianistic ability of a more orthodox—and productive—sort can be heard on Hampton's *Denison Swing*. The result here, still mostly in a linear single-note style, is much more reminiscent of Basie's sparse piano work than of some mechanical triphammer. *Denison Swing* is a poised, well-conceived musical statement, all the more touching and expressive for its *lack* of digital pyrotechnics.

Great originality and well-conceived solos are, however, not Hampton's *forte*. He is not so much a creator as he is a compiler. His solos tend to consist of a series of remembered or "common practice" motives, which he infuses with his own brand of energy and strings together into a musical discourse. While this method ensures that Hampton is never at a loss for ideas, the solos tend to be based too much on patterns and repetitions, rather than *development* of ideas. Hampton improvisations are more apt to be a collection of riffs. This is especially true in faster temps, whereas in more relaxed contexts his melodic and ornamental gifts are given freer rein. More disturbing even than the reliance on patterns, however, is Hampton's fatal compulsion for musical quotations. Uncritical audiences, of course, love these diversions, delighted to recognize some snippet from the musical public domain and enjoying the improviser's challenge of fitting it into, say, a 2-bar break, a challenge Hampton never fails to meet. The liability of these tactics, however, on a serious level is that they inevitably interrupt the musical argument, rather than extend or develop it. For all of Hampton's inordinate facility, his music-making is often indiscriminate and uncritical.

Hampton is also rarely adventurous harmonically. He may appreciate the "modern" orchestral settings provided by many of his arrangers, but he himself rarely contributes significantly in the way of harmonic/melodic explorations, being generally content to maintain a more conservative stance, well-rooted in the swing language of the thirties.

While Hampton's seemingly uncontainable energy has been a great asset in his public career, one is often left with a sense that all that fervor is not entirely spontaneous. There is something pre-programmed and automatic about Hampton's enthusiasm which, however, when transmuted over to his big band of the forties and fifties, helped to generate a level of sheer physical excitement which no other band was ever able to sustain over such a long period of time. *That* was a dividend of sorts; but there were also some liabilities.

These were not discernible at first, for from the outset it was clear that Hampton and big orchestras were made for each other. There was a natural match between Hampton's energy potential and that of a big band, replete with screaming high trumpets[4] and juggernaut rhythm section. The band began rather conservatively, with a full non-screaming sound and plenty of swing (as *Southern Echoes*, for example, attests). But by 1942 decibel levels in jazz—parallel to the mounting pitch of war frenzy—had risen considerably. With the high-tension *Flying Home*, first written and recorded by Hampton for the Goodman Sextet in 1939, now arranged by Hampton's pianist Milt Buckner, the band had its first big hit, finding the public's fevered pulse with some high-flying trumpet pyrotechnics (by Ernie Royal) and a frantic tenor solo by Illinois Jacquet, which became the model for hundreds of later honking rhythm-and-blues and rock-and-roll tenor players.[5]

As so often happens, the flip side of that 10-inch disc, *In the Bag*, was a much worthier musical achievement—and much less of a popular success. Except for an ordinary Jacquet solo, in which he seems almost to strangle on his own tone, *In the Bag* was the first strong indication of where the Hampton band's real talents lay. It is a hard-punching, driving riff tune (by Hines saxophonist Robert Crowder), excitingly swung and featuring well-conceived solos by trumpeter Joe Newman, trombonist Fred Beckett, and clarinetist Marshall Royal. The latter's passionate playing with Hampton's band is especially intriguing since he rarely sounded like that in all his years as lead alto with Count Basie.

By the end of the 1942–43 recording ban the Hampton band's style had been consolidated, chiefly through Buckner's and trumpeter Joe Morris's arrangements, into a clearly identifiable concept in which power and relentless drive were the principal elements. *Loose Wig* and *Chop Chop* are prime examples of the kind of high-level musical excitement the orchestra could produce and did so consistently. What puts these performances above the level of mere exhibitionistic crowd rousers is the high degree of integration between solo and arrangement, between improvisation and composition. Basic to it all is the down-to-earth uncomplicated drumming of Fred Radcliffe, who, along with his predecessor George Jenkins, set the particular Hampton big-band-drumming style, religiously maintained for several decades by their numerous successors. By 1944 the time sense of guitarist Billy Mackel had been added to this rhythmic foundation, variously amended but never changed in its direction or basic feeling by a succession of excellent bass players, including Ted Sinclair, Charles Harris, Joe Comfort, Monk Montgomery, Charles Mingus, Roy Johnson, and Peter Badie.

Milt Buckner, the other mainstay of the Hampton rhythm section, functioned

4. Hampton once said, in referring to his late 1940s'–early 1950s' band (with 10 brass and 6 saxes), that no trumpet player could get into the band "unless they *started* at high C."

5. It has sometimes been suggested that Jacquet's solo was somehow an amiable tongue-in-cheek parody, beginning with an incongruous quote from Flotow's opera *Martha*. I find it hard to agree with this assessment—the humor escapes me—but in any case even musical parody, often a risky double-edged undertaking, finally must also answer to the highest *creative* standards—an argument I can't make for Jacquet's efforts here. In fairness to Jacquet, although he continued to feature his squealing high-note and honking low-note style through his tenure with Jazz at the Philharmonic, he adopted a less exhibitionistic manner when he joined Count Basie in 1945 and is playing in a fine matured style to this day.

not only as pianist and chief arranger but invented the locked-hands (or block chord) style, appropriated years later and brought to the attention of the public at large by George Shearing. (The remarkable pianist Oscar Peterson has also made brilliant use of this pianistic technique.) It is said that Buckner developed this concept because his hands were so small he had to use both hands to play reasonably full chords—or else be relegated to only linear solos. His use of this technique can be heard as early as 1942 on the "Hampton Sextet" sides,[6] particularly on *Royal Family* and *Blues in the News*.

Other extensive block-chord solos by Buckner can be heard on *Evil Gal Blues* and *Salty Papa Blues* from 1943, performances on which Dinah Washington made her recording debut. Buckner had been arranging for bands since his days with the Detroit-based Earl Walton band in 1931, and I suspect that his chordal style of playing was in fact a translation to the piano of the kind of parallel block-chord writing arrangers, especially Benny Carter, had been consistently using in four-or five-part saxophone ensembles since the early thirties. But Buckner was a richly inventive pianist, with a composer's mind, one who was unwilling to be typecast solely as the block-chord artist. Hear him on *I Can't Believe*, where he enriches Hampton's solo episode with a most remarkable single-line counter melody in the bass-baritone range. That he could play fine fluent linear improvisations is attested to by several recordings, especially *Three Minutes on 52nd Street*, *Kingfish*, and *I Can't Believe*.

Building upwards from the rhythm section, Hampton's orchestra featured a strong saxophone section led by the expressive alto of Earl Bostic (later replaced by George Dorsey), including the powerful rich-toned tenor of Arnett Cobb, and anchored for many years by the gutsy baritone of Charles Fowlkes. The trombones had Fred Beckett, a remarkable player, much admired by J. J. Johnson, whose career was cut short by tuberculosis at age twenty-nine, "Booty" Wood and Al Hayes, both from the stylistic lineage of Trummy Young. Finally, the trumpet section featured such reliable soloists as Joe Newman, Joe Morris, Duke Garrette, Joe Wilder, Kinny Dorham, and a succession of outstanding high-note lead men like Ernie Royal, Cat Anderson, Al Killian, Snooky Young, Jimmy Nottingham, Walter Williams, and Leo Shepherd.

With this calibre of performing talent, all quite young and representing a new breed of players, raised on swing but now already eager to charge beyond that style, Hampton's band quickly established itself as one of the most compelling of the new era. *Loose Wig* and *Chop Chop* from 1944 effectively show the qualities of that band and its versatility. Hear Buckner's block-chord piano and Arnett Cobb's soulful arching tenor lines—there is another eloquent solo by Cobb on *Overtime* and a wonderfully expansive one on Dinah Washington's *Salty Papa Blues*. Hear also the excellent trombone work (on *Chop Chop*) and the spectacular high-note trumpet flourish by Cat Anderson (on *Loose Wig*). This was later carried over intact to the Charlie Barnet band by Al Killian (one of Anderson's

6. It is baffling why this group was called a sextet. It was at least a septet, even if you exclude Hampton in the count. Both the Jepsen and Rust discographies err on the personnel of this group: it did not include Ernie Royal, but it *did* include Ray Perry and baritone saxophonist Jack McVea.

successors). All this was incorporated in well-integrated strongly swinging arrangements that demonstrated the orchestra's unequivocal commitment to a certain kind of hard-driving, deeply swinging jazz.

A quite different piece, unusual in the Hampton repertory, was *Million Dollar Smile*. Although Frank Foster's *Shiny Stockings* for Basie has come to be regarded as the progenitor of a certain kind of very slow-tempo open-spaced jazz piece, *Million Dollar*—twelve years earlier—arranged by Buckner achieved virtually the same results. In addition it offers a fine exchange between Buckner's block-chordal piano and the brass section, solid guitar backing by Mackel, and a fine clarinet-lead reed sound which, however, did *not* sound like Glenn Miller's. At this point Hampton also switched to two basses, playing mostly in unison, providing a potent harmonic foundation for the orchestra's playing.

By 1945 Hampton had enlarged his brass to ten, the tempo and pace had quickened, and the rhythmic overdrive of the band was in higher gear than ever. And now the liabilities began to show: frantic arrangements assuming more and more the main burden of discourse, erratic solos crowded in amongst the frenzied ensembles, increasing time given to witlessly redundant "boogie-woogie" numbers and endless interpolated "classical" quotations. (In a concert performance from this period in only two pieces, one can count eleven such intrusions: Gershwin's *Summertime*, his *Rhapsody in Blue*, Grieg's *Peer Gynt* (twice), the *Gavotte* from *Manon Lescaut*, *Organ Grinder's Swing*, *Holiday for Strings*, and the inevitable *Irish Washerwoman* (twice). The band even lost a lot of its swing, the rhythm section (especially the basses) becoming thumpy and tight, muscle-bound from their collective overexertion. *Flying Home No. 2* and *Slide Hamp Slide* are typical. *Slide* with its frantic riffing and trombone slides in the last chorus, a device which Larry Clinton and a hundred earlier swing bands had long ago run into the ground, could have been taken as a parody of the Mills Blue Rhythm Band's *Ride Red Ride* but for the fact that it took itself so seriously.

Not until late 1946 did some fresh ideas enter the Hampton book, with the arrangements, for example, of Billy Mackel (like *Playboy*) and with the new modern-oriented solo work of Joe Wilder and altoist Bobby Plater (a co-composer of the big 1941 hit *Jersey Bounce*). Indeed it seemed odd that Hampton—who had recorded Dizzy Gillespie in 1939—as late as the end of 1946 was still clinging to a by now rather superannuated swing style, when all the younger bands were switching to a more modern idiom, if not directly to bop. But then suddenly, reverting to a small-group format (an octet) in September 1946 on *Double Talk*, Hampton broke through into the bop ranks. Fluent bop-ish solos by Wilder and Plater, some modern harmonic exchanges between Buckner and Mackel, high range bass lines by Joe Comfort (à la Chubby Jackson of the Herman band) are some of the more interesting earmarks of this new direction for Hampton.

The inroads of bop become more and more discernible in the succeeding months and years—as in trumpeter Kinny Dorham's solos in 1947; Buckner's borrowing *in toto* of the entire trumpet-section lick from Gillespie's *Things To Come* on *Goldwyn Stomp*; the more advanced harmonies, chord substitutions, and bitonal aggregates as on *Hawk's Nest* (Ex. 1)—a slight musical detour via Ellington's jungle style, played with fine authority by "Duke" Garrette on *Hamp's Got a Duke*, notwithstanding.

Ex. 1

Final chord of Hawk's Nest
(D major on top of D♭ +9)

These bop-ish developments reached their apex in Charles Mingus's *Mingus Fingers*, a complex, advanced and not entirely successful composition by the then twenty-five-year-old bass player/composer. Too fragmented and promiscuous in its form—it attempts rather more than it can control—it is nevertheless a striking early example of a new compositional voice struggling to be heard. Many of Mingus's later conceptual and ideological traits can already be heard in this early effort: the caustic biting humor; the wild, dense contrapuntal textures accumulated, so to speak, out of multiple spontaneous lines; the forays into atonality; the use of the flute (played by Plater) and the bass (Mingus himself) in non-jazz ways. The orchestra as a whole did not feel entirely comfortable in this "unorthodox" music, and the performance is less than convincing.

It would appear that this experiment with a kind of radically new (not even particularly bop-ish) language frightened Hampton away from any further such ventures. Hampton's audiences could not have been very enamored of Mr. Mingus's effort either. In any case, Hampton's repertory promptly retreated to a safer fold: boogie-woogie, a sizable leap in the direction of "rhythm-and-blues," novelty vocals (by Sonny Parker), and numerous remakes of *Flying Home*, sometimes under different thematic guises and titles (like *Wee Albert*). The return again and again to boogie-woogie numbers is particularly disturbing. In 1949, for example, the whole jazz orchestral world was going bop crazy, but Hampton was still mining the boogie-woogie lode. The band did, at least, recover its swing potential in the late forties after a period in which the lack of variety in the arrangements had begun to seriously stifle the band's rhythmic vitality and spontaneity.[7]

The orchestra received a strong lift in the early fifties with the work of the immensely gifted arranger Quincy Jones. Only eighteen at the time, he produced *Gabby's Gabbin'*, *Kingfish*, and a virtuosic arrangement of *Oh, Lady Be*

---

7. Particularly interesting is the absence of swing in Hampton's bass section at this time. It was not so much a matter of any individual inability to play with swing, but rather the necessity of both players to play (read) the same bass lines—you couldn't have two different improvised bass lines going on simultaneously—which in the end caused both players to tighten up rhythmically, ensemble considerations having to come first. One bass player would have been much freer, and Hampton, eventually realizing that, returned to the single bass—and a strong one in the person of Roy Johnson (one of the first incidentally to use the then new electric Fender bass).

Good that represented a much-needed infusion of new ideas and a brilliant confirmation of Jones's precocious talent. Another high period for Hampton personally, as well as his band, came during several sojourns in Paris in 1953 (the Paris All Stars date is particularly rewarding), and in Chicago in 1954. An on-location recording made by Columbia's George Avakian at Chicago's Trianon Ballroom catches Hampton and his orchestra at its best and most characteristic. Hampton, himself, apparently in one of his most creative moods, contributes exciting solos as on *Wailin' at the Trianon* and a superb *Star Dust,* its effect lessened only by a few too many audience-pleasing quotes. *Star Dust* demonstrated that Hampton could still be brilliantly inventive when not playing to the gallery.

Wailin' begins with a substantial *a capella* improvisation of (initially) considerable invention, which before it can deteriorate to mere mindless riffing—as so often happens with Hampton—is rescued by a marvelous adroitly timed entry of the rhythm section, a perfect moment of released suspense. Later, Hampton builds intensity again with an amazing sequence of 137 *(sic)* reiterated octave E♭s, as bassist Badie is drawn into the fray, literally impelled into his highest register.

The Chicago recording also features exciting work by Hampton's saxophonists, altos Jay Dennis and Bobby Plater and tenor Jay Peters. Dennis is particularly outstanding in his complex, wonderfully eccentric melodic careenings, usually at breakneck speed. But unlike a lot of modern saxophonists who fill their music out with runs, embellishments, patterns, and other secondary material, Dennis kept his solos highly concentrated and primary—that is to say, melodic—with a keen rhythmic edge in note values which are *inherently* fast. Dennis's sixteenth-note passages, for example, are not filled-in quarter notes but primary melodic/thematic material moving at quadruple the speed of the underlying basic tempo. His playing constitutes one of the more interesting extensions of Charlie Parker's rhythmic premises, and at the same time a link to and forerunner of Ornette Coleman.

Although Hampton never was a creative leader of the magnitude of Ellington, Lunceford, or even Basie, he and his orchestra occupied a varyingly prominent role through the years, never in the forefront of things, but energetically upholding a mainstream line well into the fifties and sixties, even unto this day.

Hampton is what he is, and no amount of latter-day analyzing can—or should—make him into anything else. He is, like Armstrong, one of the old school, where the entertainer role is always prominent, perhaps even primary. And like Armstrong—though certainly not on his creative level—Hampton is a dedicated artist-musician and craftsman, his flamboyance and exhibitionism not withstanding. And perhaps most significantly, Hampton *has* been the keeper of a venerable tradition which, though it stands apart from all recent developments in jazz, is nevertheless a respectable one and one which Hampton, given his age and stature, is well entitled to preserve.

COOTIE WILLIAMS/ERSKINE HAWKINS

Two black bands that flourished briefly in the waning days of the Swing Era were the Cootie Williams and Erskine Hawkins orchestras. Williams, we recall, had left Ellington in 1940 after an eleven-year tenure to join Benny Goodman, but soon got the bandleader itch himself. His own orchestra made its debut in late 1941 and for a few years played an important role as a transitional ensemble halfway between swing and bop, and a haven for many of the younger up-and-coming black players who were unable to find a place in the older well-established orchestras—players like Bud Powell and Ken Kersey (piano), Eddie Vinson and Sam Taylor (saxophone), Joe Guy,[8] George Treadwell, Gene Redd (trumpet), to name but a few. Cootie also fostered the younger composers and arrangers, and he was the first to present Thelonious Monk's *'Round About Midnight* and *Epistrophy*, the former in 1944, the latter in early 1942.

But as a transitional band, Cootie and his orchestra fell prey to the risks and flaws inherent in being caught between two styles. Not fully committed to the incoming bop, and at the same time not quite able to relinquish the safe ground of swing, Cootie, both in his choice of personnel and in the performances of his players, seemed to waver, unable to assume a clear direction. Ken Kersey's big piano solo on *Epistrophy*, for example, didn't at all fit Monk's new language, harking back instead to earlier models, especially the boogie-woogie craze of 1939 and 1940. Right next to Kersey, on the same recorded performance, appeared Joe Guy in a totally different futuristic musical world (Ex. 2a), playing

Ex. 2a

8. Joe Guy (born 1920) was an interesting transitional figure in the 1940s. He was not a great trumpet player, although a capable one, and like Dizzy Gillespie a disciple of Roy Eldridge. As such, a catalyst, he brought the new bop sounds of Harlem to the various bands and groups he played with: Fats Waller, Coleman Hawkins, Charlie Barnet, Teddy Hill, Cootie Williams, and Billie Holiday. A regular at Minton's in Harlem during the incubation period of bebop, when Christian, Parker, and Monk jammed there nightly, Guy spread the new gospel of bebop everywhere.

Ex. 2b

♮ ♭ indicates slightly sharp pitch, played with alternate(false) fingerings

an excellent solo that includes among other things a virtuoso break which Dizzy Gillespie later appropriated and turned into a formula and bop cliché (Ex. 2b).

Similarly, sometimes Cootie's plunger-and-growl solos, a vestige of his Ellington days, seemed anachronistic and gratuitous in arrangements that pursued quite opposite aesthetic goals. When Cootie tried to emulate the reigning sweet trumpet stars, like Spivak, Elman, and James, matters got even worse. And when he took Louis Jordan's hit jump tune *Is You Is or Is You Ain't?* and turned it into a rather saccharinely blues-ish ballad, or when he turned Monk's *'Round About Midnight* into a romantic torch song, the aesthetic/stylistic incongruities were quite severe.

But these and similar miscalculations did not altogether vitiate the band's work. Failure and success often lived side by side on Williams's recordings. He was, like all of Ellington's 1930s' sidemen who struck out on their own in later years, not a real leader and not enough of a composer or arranger to either set a style himself or hire the appropriate arrangers to set it for him (as Goodman had done by hiring Henderson, Mundy, and Sampson). Still, Cootie knew talent when he heard it. We owe it to him that we can hear the twenty-year-old Bud Powell on *Blue Garden Blues* and, eight months earlier, on *Floogie Boo*; and Charlie Parker in early 1945 on the same tune; or the young Eddie Vinson's blues-shouting; or that we can enjoy what surely must be Joe Guy's best solo on records on *Epistrophy*, a tune that Guy, who was much more aware of the new stylistic winds blowing in from Harlem's Minton's and Monroe's Uptown than Cootie, had in fact brought to Cootie.

It is significant that Cootie's later development took him in two ever less progressive directions. His 1945–46 band was a capable, clean playing, well-functioning dance band, with good swing. It had to be, for it worked regularly at the Savoy Ballroom, and anything less than a strong danceable rhythmic beat would have cost the band in popularity and, in turn, employment.

Cootie's band was a powerhouse ensemble, featuring by 1945 six trumpets (including high-note virtuoso Gene Redd), three trombones, five saxes, and rhythm. The orchestra's recording of *House of Joy* is a sample of the kind of exuberant, boisterous riff pieces with which Cootie got the Savoy's customers onto the dance floor. *Salt Lake City Bounce*, based on the changes of Strayhorn's *Take the A Train*, is smartly arranged by trombonist Ed Johnson and features a heavy blues-drenched sound that became the prevailing style of many mid-forties' black orchestras. On the other hand, many of these pieces are ultimately only superficially exciting, essentially loud and brash but rather empty of substance, and in many ways forerunners of the rhythm-and-blues, rock-and-roll bands that began to flourish in the 1950s. When his big band collapsed in 1948, Cootie, too, turned to rhythm-and-blues and led a small r & b group from 1950 to the mid–1960s (when he returned to Ellington's orchestra).

Ironically, while plying the r & b trade, Cootie made some superb big-band recordings in 1958, assembling for these occasions some of the greatest jazz artists of the time in their maturity. Not only was Cootie technically and creatively in top form on such tunes as *Do Nothing Till You Hear from Me*, *Alphonse and Gaston*, *When Your Lover Has Gone*, and the terrific *I'm Beginning To See the Light*, but no less stunning were Coleman Hawkins, Rex Stewart, Lawrence Brown, J. C. Higginbotham, Bud Freeman, Gus Johnson, Milt Hinton. The arrangements by Ernie Wilkins and Joe Thomas set off these stars most effectively, especially in the several exchanges between Stewart and Williams, Higginbotham and Brown, Hawkins and Freeman.

Cootie Williams, as mentioned, finally returned to the Ellington fold, as so many of the original team, tempted by seemingly greener pastures elsewhere, eventually did. He lived out his life, re-creating himself and Bubber Miley in endless one-night stands on the road with Duke. Cootie survived his boss by some years, continuing with Mercer Ellington's band until his death in 1985.

Trumpeter Erskine Hawkins (b. 1914), unlike Cootie Williams, never played under any other leader, organizing his first band as early as 1934 in Montgomery, Alabama. Hawkins, professionally billed as the "20th Century Gabriel," had a much better band than most critics and jazz chroniclers have credited him with. He is little remembered today, and yet his orchestra was one of the most popular for many years (especially at the Savoy Ballroom), and its accomplishments are well worth recalling. Not as spectacular and charismatic, and certainly not as original as Ellington's, Basie's, and Lunceford's, Hawkins's band nonetheless had a distinctive quality very much its own and an admirable consistency of performance in its soloists, ensemble work, and its arrangers. This consistency is attributable in large part to the fact that the orchestra's personnel over a period of a dozen years rarely changed. The band was financially more secure than most and thus able to retain a permanent roster of players. Such financial security was in turn attributable to the band's distinctive yet accessible style, basically "down-home" blues-ish traditional with just enough modern touches and soloistic individuality to retain its essentially black audience.

Hawkins's two chief arrangers, pianist Avery Parrish and trumpeter Sam Lowe, set this blues-oriented, Southern-earthy, sonorically/harmonically rich style in slow and medium tempos that audiences could easily relate to and dance to. Hawkins was for the most part able to dispense with singers—in those days virtually an inescapable requirement—one suspects because he thought of *himself* as "the singer" in the band. Indeed he consistently featured himself in melodic ballad-like trumpet solos and left the "jazz improvisations" to trumpeter Dud

Bascomb. It is obvious that Hawkins thought of himself as another Louis Arm-strong—the Louis, that is, who was fronting a big band—and was in later years not immune to the influence of, say, Harry James or Charlie Spivak. And often enough Hawkins's high-note grandstanding, directed as it was at the less sophis-ticated theater audiences (and not carried out with quite the skill or conviction this actually required), marred many an otherwise interesting recording. But, as we have seen so often in these pages, the temptations of commercial success were never far away in those days, nor are they today. The fusion then of "sweet" and "hot" styles—"commercial" and "creative"—has been replaced in recent years by another fusion: pop/rock and jazz. And then as now, many musicians, under the pressure of economics in what is—we must remind ourselves—essen-tially an "entertainment" field, succumbed to those commercial temptations. For many 1930s–40s' bands a sweet trumpet solo or a couple of singers, or some novelty tunes, were sometimes the difference between survival and demise.

But like Calloway and Lunceford, for example, Erskine Hawkins retained enough true jazz in his repertory—and a fine group of soloists to preserve that jazz element—to leave no doubt where his real allegiance lay.

Indeed, it is interesting to observe that black orchestras, with only the rarest of exceptions, could not go completely "sweet" or "commercial"—for two rea-sons. One, they were not permitted under any circumstances to break into the white commercial market (controlled entirely by white business interests); and, two, whatever *commercial* success might be gained in entertainment music, that was strictly reserved for white bands and musicians. Another way of looking at it is to say that the pressures to go commercial were much greater on white bands than they were on black bands, for the latter were *a priori* ruled out from any such commercial gain.

Second, black audiences generally demanded of their own bands a much higher level of creativity and musical sophistication than white audiences did of theirs. Jazz *was* the black audiences' music; it reflected and expressed *their* lives, *their* social heritage and environment, anecdotally and spiritually. Woe to the black musician or orchestra that strayed too far from that heritage. Whatever tempta-tions to penetrate the larger white commercial market may have been felt, Hawkins, like all of his black bandleader colleagues, knew that ultimately the balance would have to tilt not only towards jazz but to some degree of stylistic individ-uality and creative freedom.[9]

To this end the quality of Hawkins soloists—the two Bascomb brothers, Dud and Paul (trumpet and tenor respectively), Julian Dash (tenor), Heywood Henry (baritone and clarinet), and Avery Parrish (in his role as pianist)—was a crucial element in preserving the band's stylistic identity and popular success with its essentially black audience. (We must remember that white audiences were not

9. Even minor bands like Bob Howard's or Willie Bryant's, about as commercial as black bands could get, still had their roster of jazz soloists and mixed "sweet" sounds, crooners, novelty tunes, jive talk, with a modicum of jazz so as not to embarrass themselves in front of audiences at the Apollo in New York or Howard Theatre in Washington.

listening to bands like Erskine Hawkins; indeed, the vast majority of whites would not have even heard of Hawkins.)

This balance between creative integrity and popular appeal was exceedingly well maintained through the years by Hawkins and his orchestra. Very rarely did they falter in their mission to provide both a solidly functional dance music (Harlem style) and a relatively distinctive musical conception.

Of course, the band's stylistic direction took some time to crystallize. In its early years, say from 1936 to 1938, there tended to be some uncertainty as to what kind of an orchestra the 'Bama State Collegians (as they were called) wanted to be. Typical mid-1930s swing-riff pieces would alternate with sugary sweet pop or novelty tune renditions. I think in part the confusion resulted from not knowing what kind of audience it wanted to play to, or, perhaps more realistically, what kind of audience the band was able to attract. The younger crowd surely would have wanted to hear the "up-to-date" swing tunes (like *Swinging in Harlem, Big John's Special,* or *Uproar Shout*). But the older folks would prefer things like the 1928 *Coquette* or Isham Jones's 1929 standard *I'll See You in My Dreams.* Indeed, Hawkins (and/or the Vocalion recording directors) devoted half a session in 1937 to two songs that were a tailor-made double dose for the "old folks at home": *Way Down Upon the Swanee River* and *Dear Old Southland* (itself based on *Swanee*). This was followed some months later with *Carry Me Back to Old Virginny.* The band's stylistic confusion is further reflected in some of the soloists' work, particularly Parrish: stride piano on *Uproar Shout,* old-fashioned ragtimey piano on *Uptown Shuffle,* a bit like Basie on *Miss Hallelujah Brown,* in a modern "swing" vein on *A Swingy Little Rhythm.*

Interestingly, proof that Erskine's heart was more or less in the right place is the fact that even the "sweet," "hotel band" type of performances turned into jazz soon after the opening or after the vocal had been disposed of. Invariably (as on *Coquette* and *I'll See You*) the arrangements got progressively jazzier as they proceeded, virtually re-composing the pieces, transforming them from mawkish pop tunes into hard swinging jazz. The thrust in the direction of jazz came primarily from Hawkins's three staff arrangers: trumpeter Sam Lowe, altoist William Johnson, and Avery Parrish. Sam Lowe, a great admirer of Sy Oliver and the mid-1930s' Lunceford band, probably was the first to set the Hawkins band's style, but Johnson and Parrish early on fell in line with that conception, so that a more or less unified approach was achieved by 1938.

This was remarkable in itself for, as we have seen, many an orchestra foundered because it could *not* find a single, cohesive, distinctive style in its formative years. Struggles to achieve such stylistic cohesion mark the entire history of swing era jazz. But it is also remarkable because Hawkins himself, not a composer or arranger—and not even a particularly creative soloist—preferred in his own playing a somewhat cloying romantic ballad style (not far removed from what Harry James, Charlie Spivak, and Ziggy Elman were offering their public) and, alternatively, bombastic high-note grandstanding. The fact that Hawkins was neither that secure in the high register nor in full command of his vibrato and intonation did not deter him from these pursuits. In any case, neither of these traits could have formed the basis for a creditable *orchestral* style, and so it is fortunate that Hawkins was content to front his band as "The Twentieth Century Gabriel," do his high-note pyrotechnics, and leave the creation of the band's style to his three arrangers. Obviously, he must have sanctioned that, for the Hawkins band's style was not only allowed to evolve but, more important, Hawkins consistently gave his major players a generous allotment of solo space on recordings. It does leave us with a curious stylistic dichotomy between the erratic playing of Hawkins on the one hand, delineated by his two just-mentioned tendencies, and on the other hand the band's rather solid straight-ahead strictly-made-for-dancing jazz. The two approaches—Hawkins's and the band's—rarely meshed into a symbiotic unity. Still, I suppose an unspoken alliance was struck, one side accommodating the other and vice versa. And as far as the audience at the Savoy was concerned, as long as the Hawkins band kept providing that solid danceable groove, a bit of dubious trumpet-grandstanding couldn't do that much harm.

By 1938, in pieces like *King Porter Stomp, Rockin' Rollers' Jubilee, Miss Hallelujah Brown, Swingin' on Lenox Avenue,* and *Hot Platter,* the Hawkins band *had* found its style, which then, except for a few more or less "cosmetic" embellishments, remained unalterably stabilized for at least a decade.

Hot Platter (1939), arranged by Sam Lowe, is typical of the band's work in those late 1930s' years, for it combines music ideal for swing-style dancing with eminently *listenable* scores. The band was well rehearsed and played with considerable discipline in respect to intonation and orchestral balance. The saxophone ensembles, led by William Johnson, are especially outstanding, revealing both in concept and execution an unmistakable indebtedness to Benny Carter. Excellent solos abound, usually by Dash on tenor, Dud Bascomb on trumpet (hear him on *Lenox Avenue,* for example), and Heywood Henry, as fluent on the high-riding clarinet as on the gutsy baritone.[10]

Dud Bascomb was an especially consistent soloist, equally skilled in open-horn work and plunger muting (both growl and wah-wah). With Hawkins from the very beginning and staying on for ten years until his departure in 1944, Bascomb's consistently fine work can be heard on countless sides. Like the Hawkins band itself, Bascomb was never "spectacular" or "highly original." But on the other hand his playing was almost always inventive, technically fluent, and poised, in an idiom located roughly halfway between Armstrong and Gillespie: lean, clear lines, attractively melodic. Unlike Henry "Red" Allen who suffered the fate of functioning virtually incognito in Louis Armstrong's band for many years,

10. The Hawkins band was in fact one of the first bands consistently to feature a baritone saxophone. That instrument, in the hands of Henry, gave the effect of anchoring the music securely on a solid harmonic foundation, much as in Lunceford's band. Indeed, for many years in the mid-1940s, the Hawkins band had *two* baritone players and used them often, to enrich its lower register. Incidentally, Henry, like Harry Carney, his counterpart in Ellington's orchestra, stayed with this leader throughout the entire existence of the band until it broke up in 1953, all along contributing impressively to the orchestra's excellence.

Bascomb was given solo opportunities by Hawkins and his arrangers on almost every side. Of these many one should single out *Weddin' Blues, Lucky Seven, Midnight Stroll, No Use Squawkin', Bear Mash Blues, Strictly Swing, Gin Mill Special,* and his famous solo on *Tuxedo Junction* (the second trumpet solo on the side)—although in my view during part of this period Bascomb seems to have been too often influenced by Hawkins's use of an overly heavy vibrato.

Dud's brother Paul was another fine soloist stalwart in the Hawkins orchestra. Also one of the original charter members of the band (from the Montgomery days), Paul Bascomb was with Hawkins until 1944 except for a two-year leave of absence in 1938 to 1940 (during which he was replaced by Julian Dash). Playing initially with a fairly light sound in the manner of a cross between Lester Young and Chu Berry, Bascomb returned after his absence with a much more virile, aggressive approach, strongly influenced, I believe, by the Ben Webster of (Ellington's) *Cotton Tail.* His hot, thrusting style also reminds one of the later Gonsalves with Ellington. Paul Bascomb can be heard to best advantage on the altogether excellent hard-driving *Sweet Georgia Brown* (1940), in an extended showcase solo that completely sustains the listener's interest. The same can be said for his *Nona* and the 1941 *Hey Doc.*

Avery Parrish's experimenting with many piano styles in the early days of the band eventually led to one of the Hawkins band's great successes, both musically and commercially: the famous *After Hours* (1940). A showcase for Parrish, it was the kind of simple, effective, moderately florid piano blues (Ex. 3) that was not only ideal for the jukebox trade but eventually penetrated even the larger white

Ex. 3

market, gaining the status of a perennial on all the popular white radio stations, even well into the late forties. A similar success was achieved by the even more fetching *Tippin' In* (1945), composed and arranged by Hawkins's excellent alto player, Bobby Smith. Although indebted in its overall feel and thematic material (Ex. 4) to Ellington, (as in *Don't Get Around Much Anymore*) and in Smith's

Ex. 4

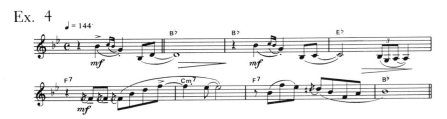

obvious homage to Johnny Hodges, *Tippin' In* nonetheless is a totally captivating piece of work on its own merits. Beautifully arranged and structured by Smith, it features, besides the composed theme statement divided between Smith and Hawkins (with jaunty trombone accompaniments), superbly swinging full ensembles and excellent solos by Julian Dash and Bobby Johnson, an outstanding young trumpeter who had replaced Dud Bascomb in 1944. Johnson plays three-quarters of a chorus—the first sixteen bars in harmon mute, the last eight with plunger-growl—so admirably conceived and executed that, if not previously identified, one assumes the presence of one of the great trumpet stars of the period, not the now well-nigh forgotten Bobby Johnson. He was a worthy successor to Bascomb and contributes brilliantly and consistently to the Hawkins orchestra (as in *Lazy Blues, Hawk's Boogie, Sammy's Nightmare, Fishtail, Coast to Coast*, and many others).[11]

Like all bands during the war years, Hawkins orchestra also grew in size and power, sporting at times as many as ten brass (six trumpets and four trombones)

11. Once again, further information about Bobby Johnson's career, after the breakup of the Erskine Hawkins orchestra, is totally lacking.

and six saxes. But unlike many brass-heavy bands, Hawkins's—always motored by a strong rhythm section—never lost its swing. Indeed, in this department the Hawkins band was virtually *non pareil*, more than satisfying the dance-mad customers of the Savoy Ballroom. In fact, hearing the Hawkins band at full tilt, one realizes that it had command of several ways of swinging, all of them exciting. They could swing hard with a kind of knock-'em-down powerhouse feeling; they could swing in a spirited, lighter, forward-driving manner; and they could swing, at will, with a heavy stomping rooted beat that was the special delight of the Savoy dancers.

Of course, to achieve these varying rhythmic effects, the band did sacrifice something, and that was variety of tempo, dynamic contrast, and anything approaching subtlety of expression. Except for an occasional slow ballad, the Hawkins band held fixedly to one medium-fast dance tempo, upholding a particular tradition so admirably initiated by the Lunceford band in the thirties. As for dynamics, Hawkins seems never to have played less than *f*, and accordingly his arrangers were bound to fashion accompaniments set at relentlessly high-tension decibel levels. Subtlety and variety were not generally among this band's virtues. Eventually, when Hawkins reduced his orchestra to a sextet and in the 1950s turned to rhythm-and-blues, the transition in terms of a heavy rocking beat, loud dynamics, and screaming one-note saxophone solos was not a difficult one.

There were occasional exceptions of moderation, such as the superb, richly voiced *Feelin' Low*—again deeply indebted to Ellington—with exquisite lead alto by Bobby Smith and a blues-ish Ace Harris piano solo that picks up where Parrish's *After Hours* and *Blackout* had left off earlier.

As mentioned, the Hawkins orchestra was never one to venture forth into unknown harmonic or rhythmic territory. Surrounded by a seething sea of stylistic/aesthetic/intellectual turmoil in the late forties, Hawkins's uncomplicated music represented a small island of stability. Still, almost imperceptibly, through the influence of younger players like Bobby Johnson, trombonist Michael Wood (a cross between Trummy Young and J. J. Johnson), and guitarist Leroy Kirkland, the new language of bop was beginning to make its influence felt. Gillespie's and Eckstine's bands, though not commercially successful, made an impact artistically nonetheless, especially on the younger arrangers. One has only to hear *Gabriel's Heater* (1947) (named after Gabriel Heatter, a famous radio commentator of the time), *Corn Bread* (1948), or *Miss Eva* (1949) to realize that even Hawkins could not remain imperturbably oblivious to the onsweep of modern bop.

But even then, the basic conservatism of Hawkins—or was it pressures from RCA Victor executives?—led him to a strange reconsideration and reversal. In 1950—along with 1949 the peak year of bop's final breakthrough to the general public—Hawkins recorded six numbers by W. C. Handy, of all people, from the *St. Louis* and *Memphis Blues* to *Aunt Hager's Blues*, all material that dated from the 1910s. Needless to say, these old chestnuts were dressed up in screaming, moderately "modern" arrangements. Hawkins and Victor were obviously working both sides of the street in the hope of charming customers into buying records on the basis of W. C. Handy's name recognition while not entirely conceding to a more blatant stylistic compromise.

Even so, Handy's music fared much better under RCA Victor's paternalism than Hawkins's own *Tuxedo Junction*, which now, in a re-make, was outfitted with a vocal group singing absurd lyrics and a frenetic brainless Illinois Jacquet-style tenor solo. Such are the malignant ways of commerce.

Still, in following the Hawkins band's course of development over the nearly twenty years of its life, we must appreciate the fact that the really deep inroads of commercialism came only at the very end, shortly before the orchestra disbanded. As we have seen—and as the recorded evidence surely shows—Erskine Hawkins maintained a critical pragmatic balance between artistic integrity and popular success for nearly two decades. That was in itself a formidable achievement.

What finally distinguished the Hawkins band from some of its major competitors is its comparatively lesser artistic vision. By setting its sights primarily to the satisfaction of dancers, albeit very sophisticated dancers, it automatically limited its creative vision. It was thus virtually doomed compositionally to providing an endless supply of riff pieces, melodically innocuous and rhythmically uncomplicated, resisting all temptations to expand its repertory and broaden its stylistic base, as Ellington had done and even, to a large extent, the early Basie band. The Lunceford model, so admired by the Hawkins arrangers as well as his dancing clientele, was in that sense ultimately a dangerous one.

We do not remember the Hawkins band for any memorable melodic or harmonic invention, nor for any marvels of orchestration or new insights in the realm of form and structure. Its single-minded function ass a superior dance band precluded most of that. But it sure could swing and lay down a great beat. What saved the band from total routinization was the quality of its soloists, who maintained that crucial element of spontaneity and free invention so essential to jazz.

HORACE HENDERSON

Horace Henderson is one of the most talented yet most neglected and enigmatic of figures in all of jazz. He had the misfortune of being constantly overshadowed by his famous brother Fletcher. But as composer, arranger, and pianist he need not take second place to anyone of his generation (except Duke Ellington). Indeed, his important role in the development of orchestral jazz in the thirties and forties has been partly obscured by the fact that a fair amount of Horace's work has been erroneously credited to his brother. And somehow his always excellent work as a free-lance arranger for a host of bands—ranging from Goodman to Barnet, from Hines to Redman—has been consistently overlooked in the jazz literature.

Even recordings made under his own name with his own orchestra, representing thus an unequivocal testament to his musical talents, tend to be overlooked (with few notable exceptions, such as Albert McCarthy's *Big Band Jazz*).

Of the nearly twenty sides Horace cut in 1940 (not counting the four with Nat Towles's band) most are of surprisingly high quality, and, as already mentioned, for the most part represent a new direction in Horace's writing. It almost seems as if, no longer riding on his brother's coattails and no longer expected to turn out more riff swingers like *Hot and Anxious* and *Christopher Columbus*,[12] Horace was free to explore other approaches in arranging and composing. The fruits of these endeavors, though shortlived—his 1940 band existed only one year— were outstanding and do not deserve the neglect they have been accorded.

Upon hearing for the first time the recordings of *Shufflin' Joe, Kitty on Toast, Coquette, I Got Rhythm*, and *When Dreams Come True*, one is most of all struck by the totally new sound world these performances create and the marvelous effortless swing on which they ride. One then begins to notice the outstanding soloists, especially trumpeter Emmet Berry, and the matchless precision of the ensemble-playing—a far cry from the rather ragged ensembles of his brother Flethcher's band in many of his early thirties' sides. Next, one is apt to revel in the deep warm sound of the saxophone section, unequaled by any except Lunceford's and Ellington's at their best. One may also suddenly realize that here is not, once again, the tried and true Henderson swing formula of segregated choirs in call-and-response patterns, wedded to interminable riffing, but rather a rich blend of orchestral colors cutting across all the sections of the orchestra, including even the drums and rhythm section. It is rare to hear a rhythmic substructure as so integral a part of the music, where rhythm is intimately meshed with harmony, melody, and tone color in an inseparable union. The discerning listener will also notice the effective use of dynamic shadings, used both as a structural and expressive device, here executed to perfection.

Emmet Berry and tenor Elmer Williams are the two most consistently inspired soloists in the band, although fine work also comes from Dalbert Bright (clarinet), Dave Young (second tenor), and Ray Nance (on trumpet and violin). Berry, a kind of more robust Roy Eldridge—he succeeded the latter as main trumpet soloist in Fletcher's band in 1937—was by this time very much his own man, providing exciting spirited solos with beautiful original arching lines, his driving rhythmic energy in striking contrast to the smoothly running rhythm motor underneath. His solo work on *I Got Rhythm* is but one example of his compelling artistry (Ex. 5).

Elmer Williams, nicknamed "Tone," had indeed one of the most opulent and purest sounds of the many fine tenor players of that era. He not only provided a rich timbral contrast to the other more bright-toned tenor soloist, Dave Young—much in the manner in which Herschel Evans and Lester Young complemented each other in Basie's band—but his almost baritone-sized sound added immeasurably to the dark rich quality of Horace's saxophone ensembles. These have a quite incredible sound and must be heard to be fully appreciated. Williams's fine solo work can be sampled on *Shufflin' Joe, Sultan Serenade*, and *Turkey Special*.

---

12. Horace was never given sufficient credit for his contributions to this major 1936 hit.

Ex. 5

As mentioned, Horace was at this time exploring new sonorities and textures in his arrangements. Some of these are quite novel and yet extremely satisfying and natural-sounding; one wonders why no one discovered them before. They are on a level of—but different from—the most imaginative instrumentations of an Ellington or a Sy Oliver. Two contrasting examples are herewith singled out.

The first is from Horace Henderson's version of *Coquette*. In the bridge of the first chorus, after dividing the ensemble between eight bars of brass (3 trumpets, 2 trombones) and a second eight bars of five brass plus three saxophones in a rich eight-part texture, Horace uses the following astonishing open-spaced reed-voicing (Ex. 6), with a distance of two octaves between the clarinet's top line and the baritone's bottom voice, and the two tenors filling in the inner harmonies. The light transparent sound of this bridge passage presents a fine contrast to the more massive sonorities surrounding the bridge, all this finely etched and precisely controlled by Horace and his players, again making judicious and subtle use of dynamic shadings.

The second example is taken from *I Still Have My Dreams*, where among

Ex. 6

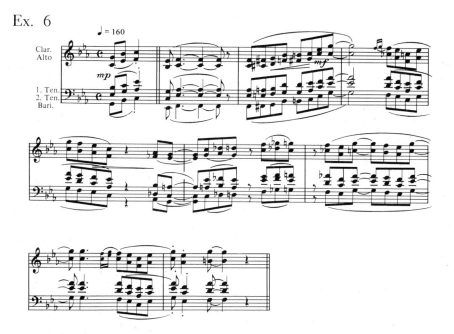

many felicities of scoring we find a beautiful example of Horace's use of low-lying, soft, dark saxophone colors. Whereas Fletcher loved the brighter sound of trumpets and high-pitched saxes, Horace preferred the darker hues and subdued dynamics (reminding one, in another realm, of the two Picard brothers, French explorers, one of whom specialized in flying and balloon ascensions, while the other went into deep-sea diving). Under Emmet Berry's eloquent solo in the second chorus—with the bridge given over to Edward Fant's Lawrence Brown–influenced trombone—Horace sets off the two brass soloists with velvety rich, softly intoned saxophone accompaniments. A combination of one alto, two tenors, and one baritone, of course, lends itself well to such low-pitched scoring, although soft low-register playing on saxophones requires impeccable technical and breath control, as well as soft reeds which will readily produce a softer, darker sonority. This was an art Horace's four reed men had under consummate control, a form of playing which is, alas, amongst most modern saxophone players, intent on a more obviously brilliant and louder projection, virtually a lost art. The effect is most notable in the trombone bridge, where such saxophone

voicings as ♪ provide a whole *series* of contrasts between solo and accompaniment: 1) contrast of texture—a single dominating voice in relief against a thickish close-voiced harmonic background; 2) contrast of color—a fairly bright brass sound against an opaque milky saxophone sonority; 3) contrast of dynamic—a full solo dynamic against almost whisper-soft subtones in the reeds; 4) contrast of register—a clear separation between the alto range of the trombone and the tenor-to-baritone range of the saxophones. This last effect is even more dramatically exploited during the higher-lying twenty-four bars of preceding trumpet solo by Emmet Berry.

A third interesting but not quite as successful example of unusual saxophone writing occurs on *Turkey Special*. Here the section plays a riff countermelody in a three-octave unison (Ex. 7) with the two tenors doubling the middle octave,

Ex. 7

all of which doesn't quite work in one respect because the baritone's E, the sixth in the key of G, lies too low here, obscuring the basic key center, especially since, as luck would have it, Israel Crosby's string bass is badly under-recorded at this point. The too-low voicing has the effect of momentarily turning the harmonies upside down, that is, overbalancing the root bass line; and harmonies can never be heard properly from the top down; they have always to be heard— and played—from the bottom up.

Crosby, by the way, still only a youngster of twenty-one at the time, has a few interesting solo spots on these sides—still a rarity in 1940—one of which, *Flinging a Whing Ding*, however, is much beholden to Jimmy Blanton's famous *Jack the Bear* solos, recorded by Ellington just months before.

One of the most beautiful and satisfying of the 1940 Horace Henderson sides is *Kitty on Toast*, which features the young Ray Nance on both violin and trumpet, just weeks before he was to join Duke Ellington's orchestra and make his spectacular debut there on *Take the A Train*. Nance is as good or better here on *Kitty*, playing an extended violin solo—one of his longest on records: a full two choruses—as well as a brief eight-bar bridge solo on trumpet later on. Nance's solo (Ex. 8) is so interesting because it is so varied and so comprehensive in its exploitation of the violin's idiomatic capacities. Nance's use of double-stops and

Ex. 8

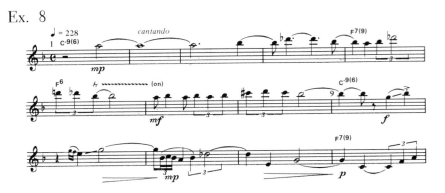

harmonics is especially effective and betokens a level of skill that was beyond most "jazz" violinists of the period. It is for those reasons also truly idiomatic, that is to say, truly violinistic—not, as was so often the case with 1930s' jazz violinists, a matter of rendering trumpet or clarinet licks on the violin.

Part of the captivating quality of this solo—and indeed the entire performance of *Kitty on Toast*—is the composition itself, one of Horace's best and not in the expected riff-tune mold. Its opening changes are hauntingly beautiful and I think quite original (Ex. 9), especially as gently voiced in the four saxophones behind Nance's violin solo.

Ex. 9

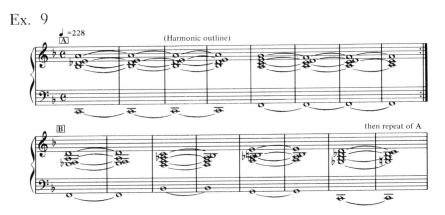

Horace's own playing on these records—his piano is featured on a number of these 1940 sides—is also excellent and contributive to the overall continuity and spirit of each piece. His style here is jauntily rhythmic, with lots of jumping right-hand octaves in a much simplified Earl Hines manner.

Even the pop songs that Horace recorded on these sessions are well worth hearing, for they remain firmly rooted—much more than usual with swing bands (black and white)—in a jazz conception. The scatty vocal treatment by a singer named Viola Jefferson of *I Got Rhythm* and Horace's *Oh Boy, I'm in the Groove* is fetchingly jazzy, more indebted to, say, Ivie Anderson and the young Ella Fitzgerald than torchy "Moon-in June" moaners so prevalent in that era. Indeed, as a total performance *I'm in the Groove* delivers what its title promises; and parts of it "swing like mad." Superior solos by Berry and Fant contribute immeasurably to the overall performance's high quality, as does the constantly swinging, driving rhythm section of Jesse Simpkins, Oliver Coleman, and guitarist Hurley Ramey.

The two ballads—in instrumental renditions—*When Dreams Come True* and *I Still Have My Dreams* are of an equally high order. Many fine moments grace these performances, including a delightfully airy clarinet-led reed ensemble, a fine walking bass solo by Crosby, and exciting contributions by Coleman, including some well-timed bass drum "bombs" (all in *When Dreams*); and a superbly explorative solo on *I Still Have* by Emmet Berry (Ex. 10), clearly the outstanding and most consistent soloist in Horace's band.

Ex. 10

A large part of the success of these Horace Henderson sides must be attributed to the band's superb rhythm section, especially bassist Simpkins (later replaced by Israel Crosby), and drummer Oliver Coleman. They specialized in a simple, unpretentious, relaxed, seemingly effortless, expressive swing that is so nearly perfect one is apt to not even notice it *in particular*. How one *does* notice it is the sense of freedom and ease with which the soloists and ensembles are able to perform on this solid rhythmic bedrock. Indeed that is perhaps the best definition of great swing—like truly great acting: when you don't particularly notice it, when you're not made aware of the craft and effort involved in producing it. The Simpkins-Coleman team could lay down as good a swinging rhythm as, say, the Basie section could, but with quite a different feel. The Basie rhythm section's beat was light, airy, springy, even joyful; Horace Henderson's rhythm section had a full, darker, resonant sound, with a deep throb. And, as with Basie there never was a sense of working at swing; it just was there—inherently, naturally.

Speaking of Basie, I cannot explain how or why the famous refrain from *One O'Clock Jump* got into Horace Henderson's *Shufflin' Joe*. Slightly varied, it opens and ends that side, the first side Horace was to record with his own band and one of his very best.

Finally, these sides provide an interesting and very clear basis for comparing Fletcher's and Horace's arranging styles and orchestral conception. Several of Fletcher's arrangements are included here—*I Got Rhythm, Sultan Serenade*, for example—and hearing them side by side with Horace's scores points up the considerable differences in the two brothers' work at this time. Listen to Fletcher's *Sultan Serenade*, with its call-and-response, clipped rhythmic style—one can almost hear the Benny Goodman band here—and follow it with Horace's *Ginger Belle* or *Do Re Mi*, and one will gain as clear an idea of the two men's contrasting approaches as one could have. It is also worth singling out Horace's *Flinging a Whing Ding*, which, despite its silly title, is in my view one of the few successful intelligent attempts to integrate boogie-woogie into a swing style. It also contains another stunning Berry solo.

With such a good orchestra at his command, the question remains why did Horace abandon it in October 1940 and take over, virtually lock, stock, and barrel, the Nat Towles band, with which Horace then recorded four sides and which he led through December of that year. I think the answer must be that Horace recognized that, as good as his own band was, Towles's was even better. And that is certainly proven by the four sides Horace recorded on October 23, 1940 (which are discussed below, in Chapter 8 on the Territory Bands).

For anyone not familiar with Horace Henderson's 1940 band, these recordings (most recently issued on Tax 8013) will be a discovery and a revelation—as they were for me. And to know Horace's work here and the superior quality of his orchestra, both in ensemble and solo, is to correct an imbalance of perception and a serious neglect of one of the outstandingly prolific and creative contributors to the Swing Era.

EDGAR HAYES

The most curious facts about the Edgar Hayes band are that it existed for only some four years (1937–41) and that after 1941, despite a tremendously successful hit recording of *Star Dust* in early 1938, the band never recorded again (except for a few sides made in Sweden, never released in the U.S.). The brief life of the orchestra is all the more inexplicable since it was a first-rate ensemble with impressive soloists and, in Joe Garland, a formidably talented arranger.

The reader will recall that Hayes had been pianist, arranger, and musical director for the Mills Blue Rhythm Band from 1931 on. His outstanding work there, both as pianist and composer-arranger, contributed significantly to making Mills Blue Rhythm one of the finest of the big Harlem orchestras. When Hayes left the band in late 1936, to form his own orchestra, several sidemen followed him, most importantly Joe Garland. In some two dozen recordings made during less than a year, the Hayes band produced some of the brightest, smartest, most expertly swinging jazz to be found in Harlem.

It is ironic that Hayes's biggest popular success came with his most commercial offering, the aforementioned *Star Dust*, virtually a parody of sweet hotel bands led by Carmen Cavallaro- and Eddie Duchin-type pianists. A florid arpeggio-ornamented piano solo—on a rather out-of-tune piano at that—was accompanied by virbrato-y saxophones and a purposely corny, slidy trombone. Such was the taste of much of the public that this flashy, empty performance, unlike anything else the band had done, sold extremely well, even crossing over to the white radio stations and jukeboxes at a time when such cross-overs were still unheard of.

The band's jazz assets were considerable. Its half a dozen soloists were perhaps not first-level, but nevertheless capable of making consistently fine individual contributions. These included trumpeters Leonard Davis and Henry Goodwin (the latter a most assured swing stylist and specialist in the plunger and growl), trombonist Bob Horton (again covering a wide spectrum of skills, from lyric melodic solos to jaunty swing stylings and the most biting nasal plunger work— second only to "Tricky Sam" Nanton in Ellington's orchestra). In Crawford Wethington and Joe Garland the band had not only two skillful saxophone soloists, but expert doublers. Garland indeed played tenor, baritone, as well as bass sax, and in many of his arrangements featured low-register duets in octaves with himself on bass sax, Wethington on baritone.

But in some ways the most outstanding player in the Hayes orchestra was drummer Kenny Clarke. Twenty-three years of age when he joined Hayes, Clarke was from the beginning an individual, imaginative percussionist who saw no sense in playing in any of the accepted drumming swing styles, including that of Jo Jones with the Basie band. While most drummers were converting to the ride and sock cymbals by 1937, Clarke, a long-time admirer of Chick Webb, remained loyal to the snare drum and bass drum, using both instruments—at first more the snare than the bass—to evolve a new style of drumming that integrated the drums much more into the arrangements and soloists' work. By participating in the orchestra's rhythmic figures as a full-fledged ensemble instrument, as well as injecting independent snare-drum figures increasingly into the accompaniments to soloists, the result was suddenly a true musical dialogue between drums and orchestra, a discourse lifting the drums (at least partially) out of their limited role as a mere provider of rhythmic substructures (and as an occasional soloist in a 2- or 4-bar break). Clarke's drumming on almost all the Hayes sides is exciting to hear, as he alternates between supporting the band in incisive rhythmic figures and laying down a firm, buoyantly swinging beat. Clarke's timing and sense of balance were superb, especially considering that he was pioneering a whole new concept of big-band drumming. The crispness of his underlying snare-drum accents and occasional counter figures is a delight to experience, especially from the vantage point of nearly fifty years of retrospect. For here we have the beginnings of modern drumming.

Although Kenny Clarke, known as "Klook," is today remembered as the inventor of the bass drum "bombs"[13] and as one of the charter members of the Modern Jazz Quartet, his work with the Edgar Hayes band (and a little later

---

13. Kenny Clarke's "bombs," a feature of his playing developed at Minton's in Harlem in the early 1940s in those now famous seminal jam sessions with Thelonious Monk, Charlie Christian, Charlie Parker, and Dizzy Gillespie that laid the groundwork for bop, were bass-drum off-beat accents, actually an extension of his snare-drum work with Hayes. This further freed the drum set from its previous steady four-beat time-keeping function, and in turn passed that burden more squarely onto the shoulders of the bass, with the whole drum apparatus now able to participate fully as a self-contained contributor to the full range of ensemble and texture—and even melodic—considerations.

with Benny Carter) is often overlooked. In the sense that he veered away from
the prevailing mainstream of drumming in those late thirties' years, he is the
Lester Young of the drums. Clarke's outstanding work, even as a first-rate two-
beat swing drummer (for example, on *Queen Isabella*) can be heard on every
Hayes side (except *Star Dust*). But special attention should be paid to *Meet the
Band*, above all the last couple of choruses (with their many ingenious deceptive
endings); the great deep weighty swing of *Laughing at Life* (the first take); and
his solo work on *Edgar Steps Out* and *Manhattan Jam*.

Clarke also was quite proficient with the vibraphone, on which he occasionally soloed (hear him on *Blue Skies* with the Edgar Hayes Quintet). His playing
here formed an interesting bridge between Lionel Hampton and Milt Jackson,
his future Modern Jazz Quartet and Dizzy Gillespie band partner.

I believe that the bright, positive swing and disciplined ensemble-playing of
the Hayes band can in large measure be attributed to Clarke's spirited drumming, much in the same way that Chick Webb galvanized and held together *his*
band. Of course, Garland and Hayes were superior musician-leaders themselves
and saw to it that all musical and performance aspects were well attended to. As
a result everything in the Hayes band *sounds*: ensembles are beautifully balanced, cleanly swung; dynamic shadings are ingeniously exploited for their maximum textural and structural effect; various interesting sonority combinations are
explored, such as unusual mixtures of brass and saxophones or the aforementioned baritone-bass saxophone duetting.

Sometimes the band's two-beat swing, the influence of Lunceford, was a little
too chaste, too politely dance-oriented, occasionally even sounding like some
second-level white dance band. But in general its rhythmic drive and swing
energy were such that the Hayes band could be easily identified with the very
best of Harlem's bands. It's a shame its career was so short-lived.

HARLEM BANDS

Two of the poorest bands to come out of Harlem in the Swing Era were Teddy
Hill's, and Al Cooper's Savoy Sultans. Although they had, according to many
accounts, a loyal following at the Savoy Ballroom, the evidence of their recordings on purely *musical* grounds offers little justification for such a claim, especially in regard to Hill's band. At least the Savoy Sultans were a hard-driving
well-swinging jump-swing band, whose solid beat must have captivated the dancers
at the Savoy. But their playing in the studios on recordings was musically rather
crude and overbearing, oftentimes out of tune, and in its rigid adherence to riff
formulas and cliché phrases—all in the same tempo—suffered from a deadening
redundancy. Its music was made up of 90 percent rhythm, 10 percent melody
and harmony, with nothing accorded to such elements as dynamics or timbre.
Its main soloists, trumpeter Sam Massenberg and altoist Rudy Williams, had a
certain unsubtle effectiveness, trading in melodic invention for motivic repetition, musical sensitivity for a loud forcefulness. And *The Thing* even features
incongruously a bowed bass solo by Grachan Moncur in a lesser imitation of

Slam Stewart's bowed-singing style. But the endless riffing of two- or three-note motives—in the brass with equally endless derby-fanning—led to a stultifying repetitiousness, which undoubtedly motivated dancers not intent on *listening* to music, and which embodied the same limited musical vision which informs so much of today's more mindless, inanely repetitious rock music: music reduced to mere rhythm.

The Teddy Hill band had more or less the same problems and, in most of its recordings, not even the virtue of innate danceableness. Its strident, blary brass and out-of-tune ensembles can be heard on many pieces—try *The Love Bug* or *Would You Like To Buy a Dream?*—or even on thumpy-rhythmed dance numbers like *Where Is the Sun?*, played in a sweet hotel-band style that would make an Orrin Tucker or Blue Barron sound good by comparison. Bill Dillard's vocals are embarrassing, and the *kitschy Twilight in Turkey* and similar "sophisticated" numbers became mostly inadvertent parody. Even soloists like Bill Coleman, Shad Collins, and the often rather over-rated Dickie Wells could not do much to help the Hill band's repertory with the brief solo spots they were given, although Wells does manage one solid, typically extravagant solo statement on *A Study in Brown*. The only remarkable track really worth hearing is *King Porter Stomp*, which features the twenty-year-old Dizzy Gillespie in his first recorded solo appearance—a single bright beacon of creativity in an otherwise ramshackle collection of recordings. It was also the Teddy Hill band's last recording session!

TINY BRADSHAW

A much better band than the Savoy Sultans or Teddy Hill was that of Tiny Bradshaw. Its view of jazz may also have been a somewhat limited one, compared with, say, Ellington or Basie or Lunceford, but at least it was unswervingly committed to jazz, a type of hard-swinging, simple jazz, to be sure, but jazz nonetheless. The Bradshaw band flourished for over fifteen years, although in later years—in the forties and fifties—it turned more or less into a boogie jump-band within an overall rhythm-and-blues style.

Shortly after its founding in 1934—Bradshaw had previously sung with Horace Henderson's Collegians, the Savoy Bearcats, the Mills Blue Rhythm Band, and Luis Russell—the Bradshaw orchestra recorded eight sides for the Decca label. All eight sides are vocals by the leader, delivered in a rather boisterous shouting Cab Calloway style. That may not sound very promising at first, but what is unusual is that Bradshaw's singing is definitely jazz-singing, highly rhythmic and swinging, quite spontaneous, alternating between a loosely sung (or shouted) delivery of the songs proper and scat improvisations. I think it is for the time— 1934—rather amazing singing, worlds removed from the prevailing crooning, effeminate, pretentious warbling that in those years passed for singing in hundreds of bands, black and white, and in its rough-and-ready blues-oriented idiom unequivocally jazz in conception. Moreover, Bradshaw and his band were a rhythmically exciting, hard-swinging group, perhaps not exactly ahead of its time in that respect, but certainly undeviatingly committed to a strong propulsive swing as the essence of jazz—at a time when so many bands could not swing at all or reserved it only for special up-tempo instrumental numbers. The Bradshaw band's limitation, at least on these Decca recordings, was that it played virtually all its pieces—*Shout, Sister, Shout, Darktown Strutters' Ball, Ol' Man River, I'm a Ding Dong Daddy*—at exactly the same tempo, and each performance was cast in an identical structural formula: the "head" sung by Bradshaw, followed by a scatted chorus, then a series of instrumental improvised solos, and closing with a recapitulation of the song.

Within this narrow format, a lot of good jazz managed to occur—although at times Bradshaw's interspersed shouting, presumably exhorting the soloists on to greater heights, becomes rather overbearing. (This shouting was a common practice in many black entertainment bands of the period, providing, I suppose, a kind of superficial excitement and "extra dimension" to performances.) Nonetheless, the band's major soloists were given plenty of room to express themselves freely. What is also striking is how well the solos—and for that matter Bradshaw's *vocal* solos—were integrated into the arrangements, excellently made in detail but, as already mentioned, unvaried in overall structure.

The strongest and most consistent of the soloists was trumpeter Shad Collins, playing both muted and open horn in solos, and wonderfully creative, complementary obbligatos behind Bradshaw. Collins's powerful attack, combined with elegant and well-structured ideas, make very compelling listening.

Happy Caldwell was somewhat uneven as a soloist (on tenor saxophone and clarinet) but could on occasion produce solidly conventional solos in the grand Hawkins style. One of his best is to be found on the *Sheik of Araby*. George Matthews, in later years trombonist with Chich Webb and Count Basie, played with a rough crackly attack and limited flexibility but in this kind of primitive blues-based style could make some very compelling statements.

Eddie Williams was Bradshaw's alto sax soloist [14] and here contributes some rather exceptional solos on *Darktown Strutters' Ball* and *Sheik of Araby, quite* modern for the time, harmonically advanced, and in their freedom and tone color like an early premonition of the young Ornette Coleman. (I must confess that I never heard Procope play anything like this in any of the many other bands he played and recorded with—from Benny Carter, Chick Webb, and Fletcher Henderson to Kirby's Sextet and Duke Ellington.)

Bradshaw did not record again until 1944, and then with a completely revised band and in somewhat updated, swinging jump-band style. *Straighten Up and Fly Right* features a strong tenor solo by "Big Nick" Nicholas, while *Bradshaw Bounce* offers drivingly rhythmic work by trumpeter Talib Daawud and tenor Count Hastings.

This 1944 orchestra was typical of a host of bands and small groups that, with the huge popular success of Louis Jordan, moved more and more into the boogie-woogie and "jump" idioms—Bradshaw still chose to call it "bounce"—and even-

---

14. It is quite remarkable that Bradshaw always had outstanding alto players in his bands: besides Williams, Russell Procope (1934), Bill Johnson (in 1935), George Dorsey (in 1939), Bobby Plater (in 1940), Sonny Stitt (in 1944), Gigi Gryce (in 1946).

tually fully over into rhythm-and-blues, in quite the opposite direction that bop was taking the jazz mainstream. And yet, what is interesting is that—as with Jordan—Bradshaw's music was always infused with the energy and spontaneity of jazz. And of course, behind and at the heart of the sixty or so recordings Bradshaw made after the war until he died in 1958, there is always the blues, both the blues as a form and as a style and a feeling. The jazz elements (as in *Well, Oh Well, Mailman's Sack Boogie, Off and On,* and dozens of other pieces) helped the various Bradshaw bands "to swing harder," as jazz critic Don Heckman once put it,[15] "than any of their more commercially-oriented competitors."

Perhaps the finest tribute to Tiny Bradshaw we can make was that, with jazz and the blues always at his side, he was swinging long *before* swing arrived in full force and long *after* it had disappeared.

15. Quoted from Don Heckman's excellent liner notes to "Rhythm and Blues, from the close of the Swing Era to the dawn of Rock 'n' Roll": New World Records 261.

6

The Great Soloists

PART 1

COLEMAN HAWKINS

It is difficult to think of anyone in jazz who has had a greater influence on his musical contemporaries than Coleman Hawkins. Armstrong and Hines are arguable contenders, particularly the former, since he deeply influenced even Hawkins. But while Hines and Armstrong had countless disciples and neophytes, they did not procreate as many *major* figures as Hawkins. He founded a veritable dynasty of tenor saxophone players, not to mention a number of formidable altoists and baritonists (in particular Johnny Hodges and Harry Carney). Those who came from Hawkins's protean lineage include Ben Webster, Herschel Evans, Chu Berry, Budd Johnson, Don Byas, Teddy McRae, the alas much underrated Lucky Thompson, and in some significant ways much later masters of tenor such as John Coltrane and Sonny Rollins—and, of course, a host of other finer and lesser players. Hawkins's mesmerizing hold on all who followed—except for Lester Young—was overwhelming, permanent, and unquestioned. One very large reason for this pervasive dominance is the extraordinary fact that Coleman Hawkins virtually invented the jazz saxophone, at least the tenor saxophone.

The historian chronicling developments in an art form soon learns that nobody is ever "the first." The moment he declares someone to be "the first," some information is surely to be turned up which makes a still earlier incumbent "the real first." There were, in fact, two other saxophonists, "Stump" Evans and Prince Robinson, who might also have laid claim to such precedence. Evans was senior to Hawkins by one month, but it was his fate to be forgotten by history—for three reasons: he died of pulmonary tuberculosis in 1928 at the age of twenty-four; he played with two orchestras—King Oliver and Jelly Roll Morton—whose conservative polyphonic New Orleans style was being superseded by

426

advanced Harlem orchestras like Fletcher Henderson's (with whom Coleman Hawkins came to first prominence); and Evans played primarily C-melody and alto sax (although he was also adept on the soprano, baritone, and bass of the saxophone family). Evans, like Hawkins, was not only a formidable technician at an early age—hear him in his fantastic breaks and cadenzas with Jelly Roll Morton on *Wild Man Blues, The Pearls, Beale Street Blues*—but also a soulful blues player, which Hawkins never was (until perhaps late in life). Evans was also, of course, a master of the slap-tongue, a technique every saxophonist in popular music of any kind had to learn in those early days. Evans's slap-tongue was remarkably controlled and even delicate, sometimes sounding in its bee-sting precision like a plucked banjo.

Robinson was two years older than Hawkins, and as the latter played with Mamie Smith's Jazz Hounds in 1922–23, so Robinson played with Lillian Jones's Jazz Hounds in 1919–21. Like Evans, Robinson was also a formidable player but *unlike* Evans had a long distinguished career with McKinney's Cotton Pickers, Louis Armstrong, Roy Eldridge, Claude Hopkins, and Henry "Red" Allen, among others. In the mid-twenties he played in one of Ellington's first bands for a while, but Robinson's early work is not amply enough documented on records to make any irrefutable rival claims vis-à-vis Hawkins. Suffice it that we do know of Hawkins's speaking highly of Robinson, which considering that Hawkins was rarely given to complimenting colleagues, probably constitutes very high praise indeed. Moreover, Robinson sounds impressive on such recordings as *Keep Your Temper* (1925), recorded twice with the Gulf Coast Seven and the Blue Rhythm Orchestra,[1] and plays with the same kind of rhythmic drive and energy that marks the early Hawkins.

After sixty years of the saxophone's pre-eminent association with jazz—the general public began in the twenties even to think of the saxophone as *the* personification of jazz—it is difficult to remember that this instrument, unlike the cornet, trombone, and clarinet, was *not* a part of the original instrumentation of early jazz. It was also not used in ragtime, one of the major forerunners of jazz, although it did play a secondary role in the marching bands of New Orleans and the South. The saxophone came to jazz via vaudeville, where saxophone soloists and ensembles became in the teens of the century one of the indispensable features of a good vaudeville show. Though the instrument had been invented by the Frenchman Adolphe Sax in 1840, and although a few composers, mostly French (Bizet, Debussy, Massenet), had written solo parts for it, it was definitely considered a "second-class musical citizen."[2] But in vaudeville and light popular

1. This latter is not the same as the Mills Blue Rhythm Band of the 1930s. It should also be noted that though Robinson later concentrated on the tenor saxophone, on these 1925 recordings he plays alto (with the requisite slap-tongue passages), not tenor, as all the discographies claim. His alto solo on *Hold 'Er Deacon* is an especially good example of his fluent poised style.

2. A deep-rooted prejudice continues even into our time, as the saxophone is, for example, still not a permanent fixture in the standard symphony orchesra. I also know of major music schools that as recently as the late 1960s did not offer a degree in a saxophone major, deeming it not to be a "proper" instrument for such distinction.

music the saxophone began to attract some remarkable talents. By 1914 the Six Brown Brothers, a sextet of saxophones encompassing the entire family, from soprano to bass, began recording ragtime, early printed blues, and "jazz" hits like *Darktown Strutters' Ball*. They played with impeccable intonation and Germanic precision, featuring in the early days the moaning, sliding effects which are produced so easily on the saxophone, and, later, primarily through the influence of their C-melody sax player, James "Slap Rag" White, the novel slap-tongue effect that so delighted our forefathers. But the foremost player of that era was Rudy Wiedoeft. At first (1917) the leader of the Master Saxophone Sextette, he soon branched out as a soloist and as a leader of a highly successful New York dance band in the early 1920s. Rudy Wiedoeft was an astounding technician on the alto saxophone, composing and recording virtuoso pieces that even today are extremely challenging to play.

Stump Evans, I am certain, was inspired in his formative years by Wiedoeft and the other early saxophone virtuosi, translating those technical achievements, however, into the realm of jazz rather than light vaudeville fare. And it is quite likely that in turn Hawkins, born in St. Joseph, Missouri, heard Evans in Kansas City, where the latter was born and was already active in the late teens of the century.

All of this is not to dispute Hawkins's early pre-eminence as the major jazz figure on the saxophone, but it is to remind us that he was perhaps not quite so unique as many jazz historians have led us to believe. It may also help those who find it difficult to believe that their musical hero could play "corny sounding" slap-tongue saxophone to know that, in the context of the early to mid-1920s, not only was there no escaping this effect, but that it never occurred to anyone to think ill of it. It simply was an intrinsic part of saxophone playing.

Like Evans and Robinson, Hawkins was a utility reed-man, playing all the saxophones and clarinet, with the possible exception of the soprano. In his early years with Fletcher Henderson, Hawkins often had to double on the bass and baritone saxophones—in those days Henderson had not yet acquired a bass (string or brass)—and it was only around 1927 that Hawkins was freed of these doubling assignments, except for the clarinet.

But it is clear that he much preferred the tenor saxophone, and the singling out of that member of the saxophone family was undoubtedly unique to Hawkins. It was in fact a strange choice for a musician to make in those days, for the tenor was not even considered a viable *melody* instrument. Melodic and lyric capacities were ascribed only to the alto, C-melody, and soprano (especially in connection with Sidney Bechet). However, here possibly Hawkins's early love for the cello played a role in his picking the tenor over the other members of the saxophone consort.

His earliest recording with Henderson, the 1923 *Dicty Blues* (on Vocalion, Columbia, and Ajax), reveals Hawkins's dynamic energy and unusual command of the instrument, slap-tongue and all.[3] What strikes us additionally is the gen-

---

3. Here again the discographies err. There are three (not two) reed players on, for example, the Vocalion *Dicty Blues*. There is present throughout a clarinet (undoubtedly played by Redman), a tenor (Hawkins), and a baritone sax (possibly Billy Fowler).

erally high tessitura of his playing and his conspicuous control of the highest register of the tenor. This was, of course, his way of turning the tenor into a melodically "acceptable" instrument, and at the same time filling in for the missing alto (for Don Redman in those years with Henderson spent a lot more time on the clarinet than on the alto). In any case, we shall see that Hawkins's early development of the tenor's upper range had long-term consequences in the evolution of his style and sound. Hawkins not only related certain rhythmic inflections to specific tempos, but he ascribed certain registers of his instrument to certain moods and types of pieces. In effect, Hawkins played three saxophones on the tenor: alto, tenor, and baritone. Even though his sound was always huge and projected superbly, he not only could handle the three register ranges of the instrument consummately—these divide roughly into the normal three octaves of the tenor: ⟨musical notation⟩ —but he could shade the *timbre* of his sound to create the impression of an alto or a baritone at each end of the range.

Tracing Hawkins's development both as a virtuoso instrumentalist and as a creative musician to its beginnings, we note both the slap-tongue manner of playing and his intensely rhythmic style in general, initially very rigid and perpendicular, but then changing under the influence of Louis Armstrong (who joined Henderson in late 1924, staying one year).[4] Hawkins's playing at this time was anything but linear/melodic, and certainly not swinging. Armstrong's playing represented a new "modern" jazz style, and his musical and creative superiority to Hawkins at this time is striking. We can hear this on virtually any Henderson side on which they both appear. Of course, we are talking about two musical titans, and as such any comparison of them is inherently at a very high level. We will do well also to remind ourselves that this battle of the titans took place between two very young men, one twenty-four, the other twenty—ages at which nowadays young musicians are just finishing up their studies or are halfway through undergraduate school (respectively), in any case rarely leaders in their field. It is also fascinating to realize that here it was the older player, Armstrong, teaching the younger one, Hawkins, the new, more modern ways. By 1926 we can hear not only a changing Hawkins but one who is applying the Armstrong message in a variety of ways. *The Stampede* is one of Hawkins's finest early recordings and reveals the extraordinary progress he had made since the Mamie Smith days or *Dicty Blues*. The slap-tongue is gone, although a vestige of it lingers and was always to remain a part of his playing in the form of a very definitive assertive attack. But Hawkins certainly learned how to modify and soften his tonguing, especially later in his famous ballads.

But the forceful attack, an articulative parallel to his rich and powerful tone, was always to be an integral component of his style. This was in part a function of the kinds of reeds he used and preferred: very hard and heavy. Most players couldn't even produce a sound on the instrument with Hawkins's reeds—they felt like unvibrating two-by-fours on their lips. But Hawkins was such a lion of

4. See *Early Jazz*, Chap. 3.

a man that not only could he manage such reeds, he evidently needed them to produce the sound and projecting power he heard in his imagination. Since all wind playing consists—to put it for the moment in a rather simplified way—of the instrument's resistance to the air stream being thrust through it (and the reed is part of that instrument and that resistance), we can understand why in Hawkins's case there existed throughout his life that undercurrent of tension and wind energy in his playing. It was based on the principle that the greater the resistance (from the instrument), and the more it can be overcome, the more powerful and dynamic the musical/acoustical result. It was an equation by which he was to live his entire musical life—and to become one of the two dominant leaders on his instrument.

The *Stampede* also shows us the great strides Hawkins had made from a musical/stylistic innovative point of view. A more linear/melodic approach and a less disruptive attack permit him to participate in the light-hearted racy swing of this piece, one of Redman's best early arrangements. Hawkins fashions his solo out of a combination of melodic paraphrase (see Glossary) and arpeggiated chord changes. Notice how he manages to fit into the third "eight" of his solo, within just a few bars, both his then highest note, E♭ , and the tenor's lowest note, A♭ , inserting the latter as a humorous honk. One can take a measure of his forward-thrusting rhythmic energy—he leans into the notes, as if into a strong headwind—by comparing it to the immediately following relaxed, straight paraphrase trumpet solo by Joe Smith. They are worlds apart in energy levels and in inherent swing.

In this period we see and hear Hawkins assimilating the entire conception of tenor-playing which made him *the* master to emulate and which would eventually lead to his most prized and justly famous 1939 *Body and Soul* recording. It took Hawkins considerably longer to find his full mature style than it did, for example, Armstrong, probably because Hawkins was playing an instrument which with him (and Evans and Robinson) was just breaking into jazz. Whereas, of course, the trumpet (and trombone) had already a relatively long tradition of brass-playing to build upon. If one begins with Buddy Bolden early in the century, Armstrong represents the third generation of players, while Hawkins belongs to the first generation of jazz saxophone pioneers.

In 1929 Hawkins recorded with the Mound City Blue Blowers, a novelty group led by Red McKenzie, whose claim to fame was singing into a comb wrapped in paper, producing a sort of raspy muted-trumpet sound. In medium fast pieces like *Hello, Lola*, Hawkins was at this time experimenting with a chugging even-eighth-note staccato style, a not particularly interesting way of playing the saxophone, but one which allowed him to display his seemingly boundless inner drive and penchant for filling out the harmonies of a song in (mostly) arpeggio configurations. Hawkins could at times be an impressive melodist, but I believe that his strongest impulses always came from the harmonic realm of music. It was as if he felt a constant need to embrace the entire harmonic content, mind you, on an instrument that is essentially single-note melodic—as opposed, for example, to the piano, which Hawkins loved to play, played well, but which oddly enough, given his inclinations, he never took up as his major instrument. He really played the saxophone as a combination of the cello and the piano, the two instruments he first learned to play as a child.

Hawkins's *Hello Lola* solo is one long propulsive burst of energy, like a locomotive on a run at full throttle. Only occasional upward rips (to high Ds) interrupt the otherwise steady ostinato-like even-eighth-note runs.

On *One Hour* (on the same Blue Blowers date) we have the first important example of Hawkins as a ballad player, perhaps that aspect of his art which was more imitated than any other. Here, in contrast to *Hello Lola,* in the much slower ballad tempo, Hawkins spreads out rhythmically/melodically in a way that at that time very few players could do or had as yet thought of. Armstrong again would be one such player when he launched into his band-fronting, soloist-playing-the-great-popular-songs-of-the-day career. Hodges over in Ellington's band would be another, as would be Bechet. But I have a feeling that Hawkins never heard much Bechet, primarily because Bechet spent the late twenties in Europe (although he succeeded Hawkins in the Mamie Smith Jazz Hounds in 1923).

Hawkins was a great listener, a great absorber. He could always be found listening to other musicians, standing in the wings at concerts, checking out the other groups, or listening at home to his extensive record collection. But Hawkins also always had to be the first, the best. He could not take defeat easily—and rarely had to. Much of what is referred to as his "originality" really came out of his ability to ingest and synthesize enormous amounts of other musical influences, including, incidentally, classical music, to which he was an avid listener. His musical appetites were as prodigious as his legendary food consumption. He was simply masterful at transferring the best that he heard around him to the tenor saxophone—in the late twenties still a relatively open vessel of an instrument—and then honing all this material to a very personal and technically high-powered idiom.

On *One Hour,* I believe, we hear the influence of Johnny Hodges, who (along with Toby Hardwick) was the first to develop the rhapsodic potential of the saxophone, considerably influenced in this by Bechet, but more modern and cut to the Ellington cloth (which was never far removed from rhapsodizing). Hodges himself had, of course, been strongly influenced—or at least impressed—by Hawkins. But it would not be the first example in the history of music of a "pupil" reciprocally influencing the "master."[5] In any case, on *One Hour* Hawkins is all business, determined to show the world how to produce a major musical statement by essentially re-composing a song in his own image. Already in his first eight bars with which the record begins, Hawkins launches into a full-fledged solo, not a mere introduction. In his 16-bar chorus proper, he reassembles the materials of the song into a new alternatingly melodic and harmonic continuity. The original song is only hinted at; in effect Hawkins reinvents it. The sound and note skeleton is Hawkins; the florid contour-softening ornamentation is Hodges (Ex. 1).

5. Play Hawkins's *One Hour* solo on a 33 ⅓ speed LP at 45 rpm, and you will hear virtually pure Hodges!

Ex. 1

By 1930 the Hawkins reputation was formidable, and there was no dearth of invitations to make guest appearances with other groups or orchestras, especially on recordings, despite the fact that he was still a full-time member of Fletcher Henderson's orchestra. And with whomever he played, Hawkins was almost always the central figure. He also never stopped exploring, sensing innately that musical growth was an endless process and that there were always newer or different ways of interpreting a given set of materials. Like John Coltrane, decades later, Hawkins was always testing, always pushing, always practicing in public (both men's "practicing" being most lesser players' highest art). On the Chocolate Dandies' *Bugle Call Rag* (1930) we hear Hawkins experimenting with melodic downward glissandos—sliding off notes—bending the notes, as it were, to soften the otherwise too jagged outlines. On *Dee Blues*, another rangy solo full of gliding notes, we can hear confirmation that Hawkins was not yet, and not by nature, a blues player. He treats this blues like another ballad.

With Billy Banks's band, on *The Scat Song*, Hawkins offers in three separate 4-bar solos a lesson in how to cram an abundance of harmonic embellishment into a short phrase without effacing the the essential melodic line.[6] On another

6. The discographies are mute on the personnel of some of Banks's finest recordings. Like his mentor Calloway, Banks always hired the best players, and on the May 1932 dates, my ears tell me in addition to Hawkins there is definitely present Henry "Red" Allen, Fats Waller, bassist Al Morgan,

date with the Mound City Blue Blowers (in summer 1931) on *Darktown Strutters' Ball* we hear Hawkins working on another problem, namely, how to linear-
ize in a lively up-tempo his previously staccato eighth-note approach. Here he
was to receive some help, if my ears do not deceive me, from Al Morgan, that
splendid bass player (brother of bandleader Sam Morgan[7]), well versed in the
4/4 rhythmic traditions of New Orleans. Morgan's relaxed linear swing more or
less forced Hawkins into a less rangy, gesturally more contracted, approach. The
usual open spaces provided in a two-beat rhythm style—where the second and
fourth beats are essentially "open" to be filled in—were here closed up by Morgan's 4/4 walking bass, forcing the lower end of Hawkins's range upward and
discouraging him from dipping down into that range with his usual plummeting
arpeggios. Interestingly, Hawkins's eighth notes here are no longer staccato and
flow not in a 4/4 rhythmic stream but in an *alla breve* 2/2 mostly slurred conception. They are not 4/4 eighth notes as in later Swing Era jazz, but more like
sixteenth notes in a slow quarter-note tempo. That is, though played as relatively
fast ♪♪♪♪ ♪♪♪♪ , they feel like ♪♪♪♪ ♪♪♪♪ in a slower tempo. We can hear
the full effect of this in bars 5 through 10 of his solo (not counting his two
introductory lead-in bars). And this is what enables Hawkins to slide so easily
into quarter-note triplets in the thirteenth bar. In feeling they are just triplets in
a "long" beat, rather than cross-accenting triplets across *two* beats—a crucial
musical difference.

What is so fascinating here is how (rhythmically, anyway) Hawkins asserts his
conception over that of the accompanying rhythm section, in fact completely
ignoring it. But Hawkins was famous for this sort of self-reliance. That is why
he could work with literally anybody, regardless of how bad or how good. He
could simply override even the worst accompaniment or rhythm section—or
ignore even a very good one (as in this case of the Blue Blowers' *Darktown*
recording)—creating his Hawkins music in total independence of his surroundings (as, for example, his mid-1930s' recordings with inferior French, Dutch,
and Swiss orchestras attest time and time again). How much Hawkins was here
still steeped in a two-beat rhythmic feeling is shown clearly again by a comparison with an immediately following trumpet solo. This one, first-rate and beautifully poised, is by Muggsy Spanier, firmly settled in a more modern 4/4 swing
conception.

Hawkins's solo on *Strangers* (with the Henderson band, recorded March 10,
1932) is another interesting example of his progress towards a more flowing continuity. Here again (Ex. 2) there is a softening of the still somewhat angular
contours by the use of legato. But even tongued notes are now broadened
rhythmically, not as staccato as earlier, and softer-tongued—all helping to achieve
a greater linearization of his phrasing. The rhythmic *flow* of the solo, set against

drummer Zutty Singleton, and probably Benny Carter (as alto and arranger). These and the August
1932 sides by Billy Banks are outstanding in every respect and do not deserve the neglect that has
been their lot simply because the personnel could not be verified.

7. See *Early Jazz*, Chapter 2.

Ex. 2

4/4 guitar beats and a 2/2 bass, is also maintained by Hawkins's use of only

eighth-note triplets (♪♪♪) and sixteenths. (♪♪♪♪) . This enables him to slightly alter at will the speed of his playing—shifting between first and second gear, as it were—with the sixteenth-note runs teetering on the edge of a double-time feeling (double-time against the guitar, *quadruple-time* against the bass).

The usual burst of Hawkins energy is also evident. However, his usual self-confidence and harmonic authority were momentarily shaken—a rare occurrence—when Russell Procope played some wrong notes in the accompaniment (in bars 11 and 12). Hawkins becomes suddenly uncertain, *diminuendos* almost to silence, but reassets himself in bar 12, pulling the sax section with him. He seems still somewhat disoriented in bar 14, however, where he plays in effect an $E\flat^7$ arpeggio-run against the song's $B\flat^7$ harmony. What is interesting to note is that as the errant sax harmonies in bar 11 hit Hawkins's ears, not only is his melodic thinking disturbed but his otherwise strong rhythmic sense is shaken as well. It is a striking example of how rhythm and harmony go hand in hand in jazz improvisation, and how any disturbance to the one will usually affect the other.[8]

8. This is not to say that the correlation between harmony and rhythm is absolute. Hawkins—and many other players—have been known to run roughshod over wrong "changes" with total rhythmic authority. There is also the fascinating phenomenon in jazz, albeit amongst only the very best players, by which a wrong note (or notes) can be made to sound "right" retroactively by immediately using it again or by deriving a new idea or phrase from it. Dizzy Gillespie, for example, is a master of this technique, turning wrong notes at the head of his famous downward-cascading runs into right ones, simply by choosing the subsequent notes in such a way as to make the first note *sound* right and logical, as if planned that way all the time.

Hawkins's *Strangers* solo, despite its flaws, is a fine example of how a strong-willed improviser can use a limited amount of material to produce, all the more easily, a cohesive and motivically unified statement. The passages marked with brackets can be seen—even by the non-music-reading reader—to be either similar or identical. Hawkins, like Lester Young—another past master at exploiting a limited number of motives and phrases to their maximum economical effect—here uses the same turn-of-phrase six times in sixteen-bars, fitting it into five different chords: Ab, Db, Eb7, F7, and Bb7.

Another way Hawkins had of getting at these rhythmic issues was to break completely free of the beat. Hear him in one of his cockiest, most exuberant free-wheeling moods on *Honeysuckle Rose* (with Henderson in 1932). He is like a great sculptor, working in large arching gestures and shapes. The basic implicit feeling here, moreover, is 4/4, but we hear him constantly trying to break out of those metric bounds, playing between the rhythmic cracks, so to speak (although the notation cannot quite show that precisely.) It is a giant, wrestling with a large problem (Ex. 3).

Although Hawkins was to cavort often in this free gestural, almost rhapsodic style, by 1933 he had discovered another rhythmic device, which became one of his most favored and, in turn, most indelibly associated with him. It was reserved more or less for medium tempos and made almost-even slurred eighth

Ex. 3

Note, too, the remarkable similarities between this solo and Hawkins's solo on
New King Porter Stomp, recorded the same day (see *Early Jazz*, p. 278).

notes sound like loping triplets, by the simple expedient of a strong-weak alternation of every pair of notes.

(s = strong; w = weak)

There were times in his career when Hawkins's use of this rhythm became obsessive, to the detriment of many a solo. But here in 1933 (on *I Wish I Could
Shimmy Like My Sister Kate*, for example) he builds long well-constructed solos
by reserving the loping long-short triplet rhythm for his first chorus, modulating

to full running triplets (♩♩♩) in the second chorus, finally working up to slurred

sixteenths (♪♪♪♪) for a kind of rhythmic high point, returning by the end of the
solo to the original eighths-as-triplets feeling. During this period Hawkins rarely
returned to his former staccato style, although the vestiges of his slap-tongue and
strong-attack approach remain in his slurred playing in the form of an always
pungent, thrusting articulation.

Another example of Hawkins's constantly searching versatility can be heard
on *Donegal Cradle Song* with Spike Hughes, with whom he recorded in 1933.
Here, under the spell of Hughes's Ellington-ish pastel colors and moods, Hawkins draws from his otherwise often purposely hoarse big-voiced tenor the smooth-
est, most velvety, florid playing. The notes are literally caressed out of his horn.

Almost a half-year later Hawkins returned to this rhapsodic ballad style on *It's
the Talk of the Town* with the Henderson orchestra, one of his last recordings
with that band before he left for Europe in the spring of 1934. *Talk* has been
hailed as one of his great ballad efforts, perhaps his finest prior to *Body and
Soul*, and a major follow-up to his *One Hour* performance. But whereas Hawkins in the latter had buried much of the original melody under his own florid
inventions, on *Talk* he is more respectful of Jerry Livingston's nostalgic tune.
Amidst the waves of arpeggios and cresting harmonies, Hawkins allows melodic
fragments to occasionally bob up to the surface, especially those that are the
melody's finest moments (like bars 5 and 6, 23 and 24), which Hawkins must
have felt he could not improve very much. His solo also shows once again his
remarkable control of the high register, tossing off runs in the upper range that

would delight any alto player. By this time high Es and Fs were well within Hawkins's range, but not merely as strained climactic melodic peaks but as fully expressive, fully controlled melodic-harmonic elements. (Hear his ringing high Fs on *Jamaica Shout*). On *Talk*, and many other solos of this period, we can also hear Hawkins's aforementioned ability to play three horns-in-one, the vibrant alto and occasional hoarser baritone trimbres flanking the rich middle tenor.

But *Talk* also revealed a blemish which was in the years to come to turn almost into an obsession, or at least an excessively used cliché: the exaggerated wide vibrato on held notes. Hawkins's use of the vibrato, though admittedly highly personal, was often applied out of all proportion to the rest of a given solo's character. Moreover, it never varied, being of the same width and speed regardless of context. It became the most widely imitated feature of the Hawkins style (one which Charlie Barnet, for example, adopted with a vengeance in those same years).

If Hawkins was a little respectful of *Talk of the Town*'s melody, he was downright deferential in the case of *Heartbreak Blues*. Of course, that may have been because it was his own composition, a hauntingly beautiful ballad, reminiscent of Ellington's 1933 *Drop Me Off in Harlem*. Hawkins was not known as a prolific composer, partly because of his overwhelming reputation as a player. But the fact remains that on occasion he could write excellent pieces, even (in later years) in bop style. In 1933 he wrote one of the most advanced jazz instrumentals of the entire swing era, the kind that Don Redman was always *trying* to write but never could quite manage. Because of its harmonic modernity and eerie whole-tone progressions, it was called *Queer Notions*. And in fact it is a musical oddity, somewhat to the left of the main jazz tradition. Except for Red Norvo's *Dance of the Octopus* and Lunceford's *Stratosphere*, nothing quite like it appeared in orchestral jazz until some of Eddie Sauter's work and the "avant-garde" pieces of the Boyd Raeburn and Stan Kenton bands in the mid-forties.[9] As arranged by Horace Henderson and played by brother Fletcher's outstanding 1933 orchestra, Hawkins's opus was, despite its "queerness," authentic jazz. But it could not have been easy for the musicians to play and hear, and the only players daring enough to tackle "improvisations" on it were Henry "Red" Allen and Hawkins. Two recordings of the piece, cut a month apart, however, show that the solos were not truly improvised; some were identical in both performances, others only slightly varied. But Allen is particularly impressive in his solo, slicing through the whole-tone progressions with almost nonchalant ease. Hawkins reveals an orderly sense of symmetry—rare for him, because he loved asymmetrical phrasings—both in his first solo and in a later whole-tone passage (Ex. 4). Here in the latter the chords descend stepwise, but each of Hawkins's upward-thrusting runs, though locked harmonically into that descending progression, ends on a progressively *higher* note, thus creating a very interesting contrary-motion "fanning-out" effect. This is accomplished simply by enlarging

9. The sometimes rather "modernistic" semi-classical pieces by Reginald Forsythe and Raymond Scott that had a vogue for a while in the late 1930s, do not qualify here for their relationship to jazz is rather remote, nor were they actually all that daring or advanced harmonically/structurally.

Ex. 4

the last interval in each run, a device to which whole-tone harmonies lend themselves easily, and something Hawkins may have studied in his theory classes at Washburn College in Topeka, Kansas, or just may have known instinctively.

By 1933 Hawkins was getting disillusioned with Henderson's inability as a leader to capitalize on the band's extraordinary potential and well-earned fame. Hawkins, a man never beholden to anyone, seized the first opportunity to extricate himself. The opportunity to do so arrived in the form of an invitation by the English bandleader Jack Hylton to come to Europe. Hawkins took a six-month leave of absence from Henderson—never to return to him, as it turned out—and sailed to England on the *Ile de France*.

Although Hawkins had a great personal success everywhere in Europe—he was feted almost like visiting royalty by the British and Continental jazz intelligentsia—it could not have been a terribly stimulating time artistically for him. Granted his awesome ability to play with *anybody* and to play well even in the face of indifferent accompaniments, there were few inspriational moments for him in those five years as a free-lancer, roaming around Europe and finally settling in Holland.[10] Europe was then just beginning to produce native musicians who could grapple with jazz in an elementary fashion, and there certainly was no one who could begin to challenge him. Nevertheless Hawkins recorded prolifically in Europe, especially with a Dutch band called The Ramblers, and much of his own work during his five years in Europe is outstanding.

It was a period of consolidation rather than experimentaion. There wasn't

10. The extraordinary self-reliance of Hawkins as an improviser puts into question the often heard complaints by less assertive players about poor rhythm sections and otherwise "creativity inhibiting" accompaniments. There is another problematic side to this coin, however. In the heat of musical battle, Hawkins was not known for his concern for other players or even the material he played. Hear, for example, how *totally* he ignores Jack Bulterman's lovely Ellington-ish tune *Meditation* (1935), recorded with the Ramblers in Holland. Hawkins's playing was always ego-driven, and every performance was a "cutting contest" which he had to dominate, an approach more personally sensitive or less aggressive players—or for that matter more ensemble-oriented players—did not necessarily share.

much, as I have suggested, that would challenge him to experiment, while on the other hand these musically modest settings in which he constantly found himself, allowed him to perfect and polish the various ideas he had previously developed in the States. He was, wherever he went, the star soloist, automatically given all the room he wanted to display his art. There were rarely, as with Henderson, complex arrangements to fit into and a host of competing soloists to contend with. Of course, Hawkins had that extra dimension that enabled him to exploit these limitless opportunities, whereas a lesser player would simply have been overwhelmed by them.

It is also clear that Hawkins inspired the European musicians he worked with. Listen to André Ekyan and Alix Combelle, at that time the two best jazz saxophonists in France, on *Crazy Rhythm* (1937), playing for their very lives, driven by Hawkins's presence to a level of craft and inspiration they didn't know they had in them.

None of the forty-odd sides Hawkins recorded in Europe are anything less than authoritative. No matter what the material, who the accompanist(s), Hawkins's imagination is never at a loss for the right musical utterance. His incredible ear never let him down. Whether he was exploring a more sensual sound (as in *After You've Gone*), finding new ways of incorporating embellishment as an integral structural ingredient, or, indeed, using vibrato as an ornamental element equal in value to pitch and dynamics (as in *Chicago*), or experimenting with a more advanced 4/4 time feeling as in the great *Honeysuckle Rose* (Paris, 1937, with fellow expatriate Benny Carter on trumpet and as arranger), Hawkins's creative adrenalin seemed inexhaustible. That is not to say that he didn't occasionally spare himself the need to be totally inventive at all times. Hawkins had many clever ways of recycling musical ideas, using the same phrase or gesture in successive takes of a given piece or indeed in different pieces. For example, the beginning of Hawkins's *Crazy Rhythm* solo uses the same lick, merely played a little faster, that he had just used in the preceding side, *Honeysuckle Rose* (in the ninth bar of his second chorus). Indeed alternate takes, for example, from a trio date in Holland (accompanied by the American pianist Freddy Johnson and a Dutch drummer), show clearly that even the great Hawkins at times memorized and repeated sections of "improvised" solos. Listen to *Swinging in the Groove* and *I Know That You Know*, or *Consolation* (with the Ramblers). This is worth mentioning only because many jazz purists have always pointed to Hawkins as the shining example of a musician "who never repeated himself." This is rank nonsense. As mentioned elsewhere, though some of the greatest jazz artists improvised the bulk of their solos, they on occasion would resort to identical statements. And there is no harm in this. It is no shame to repeat and preserve a good musical idea!

One specific idea that Hawkins worked on time and time again during the European years is especially interesting since it became the climactic high point of his famous *Body and Soul* performance of 1939. It is that extraordinary moment in the last eight bars of his second chorus (see Ex. 7, mm. 57–59, p. 443) where Hawkins seems intent on breaking the bounds and range of his instru-

Ex. 5

ment. This magnificent leaping figure haunted Hawkins as early as 1935. On *Meditation* we hear it in its first modest, embryonic form (Ex. 5). It reappears in a similar context in *Well, Alright Then* (Ex. 6).

Ex. 6

Hawkins must have eventually become tired of knocking around Europe playing with inferior musicians. On some of his recordings, like the ones made in Zurich, Switzerland, in 1936, Hawkins sounds especially driven —as if he were trying to compensate all by himself for the lifeless rigidity of the accompanying band. By 1939 Hawkins began to dream of leading his own big band, and he knew that was an ambition he could fulfill only in New York. In addition, war was approaching, and in mid-1939, a month before Hitler's invasion of Poland, Hawkins returned home.

Too much has been written about that triumphant homecoming to warrant elaborate recounting here. Suffice it to say that Hawkins returned to a Harlem teeming with a whole generation of younger tenor talent, eager to challenge the "old master." In the intervening five years of his European sojourn jazz had changed considerably, and the land was in the midst of the swing craze. Harlem ballrooms were dominated by dancers, and it must have given even the self-assured Hawkins a moment or two of pause as to what new developments—and rivals—he might have to contend with.

After holding court in Harlem for several weeks, checking out the new talent, he concluded that there wasn't much to worry about. "I didn't hear a thing that was new," he is alleged to have said. That wasn't quite true, of course. The statement may have carried more bravado than normal in Hawkins's casual condescension regarding other players; and no doubt he could take comfort in the knowledge that all the players yapping at his heels—Chu Berry, Ben Webster,

Don Byas, Budd Johnson, Buddy Tate—were Hawkins disciples in one way or
another. All but one: Lester Young. And while Young's style was still too new
and radical to enjoy a huge following, Hawkins must have known that here *was*
someone to reckon with. If he didn't know it, time would eventually make that
clearer.

Webster had not yet made his path-breaking 1940 recordings (like *Cotton Tail*)
with Ellington. And so for the moment, on those first nights back in Harlem,
Hawkins won the local skirmishes, even though in the end he was to lose the
war. But his recording on October 11, 1939, of *Body and Soul* was an unqualified triumph in every way, even commercially, and was to be a treasure house
of musical creativity for decades to come.

As I have suggested, Hawkins did not return to the American recording studios
unprepared. His travels as a soloist in Europe had given him a unique opportunity to stretch out musically, without the confining restrictions of the more congested riff-beholden big-band swing arrangements. As early as 1934, in London,
Hawkins had recorded two side-filling extended solos, accompanied only by pianist Stanley Black; and on several other occasions he had experimented with
extended three- or four-minute ballad statements. When he opened at Kelly's
Stable on 52nd Street in October 1939 with his eight-piece band, he would often
play an expanded version of *Body and Soul* late at night, a piece he had undoubtedly already explored in a similar fashion while still in Europe. When
Victor's recording director, after recording three arranged numbers, asked Hawkins to record *Body and Soul* as he played it at the Stable, Hawkins was surprised.
But the resulting record made history.[11]

The performance pulled together in one majestic 64-bar improvisation the
various strands of Hawkins's previous stylistic explorations. It is the seamless
inner unity of his *Body and Soul* improvisation that astounds us, even after the
hundredth hearing. And as with all great works of art, we may appreciate its
remarkable unity of content and form intellectually or, in a more casual listening, just sense it unconsciously, instinctively. From the first rich baritone sounds,
it holds our attention and takes us on a melodic/harmonic journey through a
musical landscape without any fault lines.

Starting modestly with a respectful bow to Johnny Green's original melody,
Hawkins gradually moves away from it into a world of his own melodic and
rhythmic invention. By the middle of the first chorus he is entirely on his own
musical cognizance, using only the underlying harmonies as a feeder for his
musical inspiration. With the poised control of a master composer, Hawkins
steadily builds his solo to an anguished climax fifty-seven bars later, using the
various compositional and articulative elements at his command to shape and
guide the line of progression (Ex. 7).

In the realm of pitch, Hawkins locates the first part of his solo—almost the
entire first chorus—primarily in the lower range, conservatively encompassing

11. The annals of popular recordings are filled with instances of a fourth, often "throw-away" side
becoming the unexpected big hit, while the planned prepared numbers had little or no success.

Ex. 7

not much more than an octave. In the bridge (or release), always a high point in the 32-bar song form, he carefully extends the upper perimeter of his melodic line, tentatively saving further expansion of the range for later. In the second chorus, the tessitura is gradually extended still further upward, often in parallel with intensifying dynamics, reaching its melodic apex and dynamic climax in the high F in bar 59. But all along the solo had remained essentially anchored in the lowest "baritone" range, fanning out, as it were, upward towards the climax but never really losing its moorings in the roots of the harmonies. A graphic representation of the overall expanding shape of the entire solo appears in Figure 1. Rhythmically, too, there is a subtle and gradual intensification.

Fig. 1

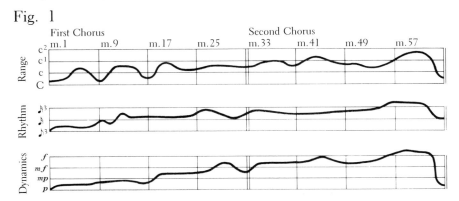

Again starting simply, in single-time, Hawkins makes a progression through the eighth notes of Green's tune to sixteenth notes. Having arrived at that level, he now has an extraordinary inspiration which we hear fully developed in the beginning of the second chorus: namely, to turn those sixteenths (♪♪♪♪) intermittently into double-time swung triplets (♪ ♪♪ ♪) . Both in absolute rhythmic terms and in feeling, the difference is of the utmost subtlety, in a relationship Hawkins shrewdly exploits by shifting back and forth between the two rhythms. As if sitting on a fulcrum, he leans now this way, now the other way, teasing us, and all along delaying the moment of full commitment to the more intense double-time at bar 57. Notice here how Hawkins uses articulation in the form of more vigorous tonguing and accented slurring to underline (along with the other elements) the moment of climax, having previously covered the shifting rhythms under a calming blanket of slurs.

Sonority also figures in the structuring of the solo. Beginning with a warm friendly sound and (for Hawkins) minimal vibrato, he heightens the solo's emotional intensity by gradually applying an ever keener edge to his sound, climaxing in the almost strident bursts of sound in mm. 57–59. And as this level of intensification rises, so do the intensity and width of the vibrato, but within controlled bounds.

One can see from this analysis (Fig. 1) and from the aural evidence of the solo (Ex. 7) how each articulative strand participates in the building of the over-all form, each leading in well-controlled lines of communication to the climax, and then subsiding relatively quickly for the caressive ending. One can almost hear how Hawkins keeps all the strands under control, generally functioning together, and yet occasionally allowing one or the other element to step out of phase to temporarily surge forward, only to be pulled back into line with the others.

Finally, we must note the harmonic substitutions with which Hawkins enriched Green's original. It was the kind of elaboration that only a composer or a very strongly harmony-oriented improviser could bring to the piece. And indeed Hawkins's alterations became, at least for jazz players, ever after an integral part of the song. At one point, however—the climax in fact—these substitutions caused a momentary blemish in the performance. Hawkins had no written-out arrangement of *Body and Soul* for his band and so a hastily put together head arrangement (for the second chorus) had to suffice. In bar 58 two different harmonic substitutions collided, Hawkins playing $E\flat^7$-Daug^9-D$\flat^6$ changes, while the band played the more commonly used $E\flat^7$-D^{-9}-D$\flat^6$ progression. Fortunately, Hawkins was so strong and imperturbable that neither this mishap nor the band's poorly tuned and poorly balanced background detracts very seriously from the overall quality of the performance.[12]

The success of *Body and Soul* was such—it was the first true jazz performance to become a big seller—that Hawkins was virtually condemned to play it literally *thousands* of times during the rest of his career. People requested it wherever he went and were, of course, disappointed when he didn't play it exactly as on the recording. In response to public pressure Hawkins actually tried for a short while to imitate his recording, but quickly rebelled against that compromise. The Promethean Hawkins was *not* one to be chained down, emptily repeating himself. It is not at all unlikely that, in the thirty remaining years of his life, Hawkins played some *Body and Souls* superior to his 1939 recording, very few, naturally, preserved. One such performance, however, was captured in 1959 (in Chicago, at the Playboy Jazz Festival). An amazing creation, this performance vies with and perhaps even surpasses the earlier one. Played with a now tougher, more leathery but just as huge and intense a sound, for all its rhapsodic, florid, baroque ornateness, it is pure substance; every note is virtually inevitable and inexorable. There is hardly anything like it in the annals of recorded jazz.

Hawkins's renewed fame permitted him to form a big band in 1940. But the results were undistinguished in the extreme. Hawkins was a terrible bandleader and devoid of any showmanship. Much like Armstrong, he was interested only in *fronting* a band (rather than creating a real orchestra), allowing him to appear as the grand soloist against its backdrop. The band's personnel was very uneven,

---

12. Although Hawkins's *Body and Soul* would stand for decades as not only a masterpiece of its kind but an intimidating example for others to attempt to equal, Ben Webster's 1944 *Body and Soul*, although less known, is a performance that easily vies for competitive honors. Quite different in conception and format, it too remains a profound but unduly neglected tribute to Webster's art, suffering primarily from the handicap of having been created five years too late.

poorly rehearsed, and musically undisciplined. It was plagued by appalling intonation and never found a sound or style. It was a short-lived venture which Hawkins, the band doomed to strings of one-nighters, abandoned in late 1940 (after one rather dismal record date).

The early forties were a time of transition, for Hawkins as well as for jazz in general. As the younger players associated with the new modern idiom—unhappily soon to be called "be-bop"—came to the fore, it was Hawkins who, to many admirers' dismay, joined ranks with the young turks. The locale for this musical conjunction of new and old was 52nd Street in New York, one of the two breeding grounds for the new jazz. The other was Harlem, where in clubs like Minton's and Monroe's the younger players gathered in jam sessions, experimenting with new rhythms and harmonies, far away from the ever more stultifying world of the big swing bands. The downtown annex, so to speak, of these uptown enclaves was 52nd Street, where in a dozen or so diminutive clubs, many of them former prohibition-era speakeasies, most of the major jazz figures could now be found playing, not in big bands but in small combos. And in this fertile terrain the new and the old met on equal footing. For these were more musicians' hangouts than big money-making night clubs, and if you wanted to hear where the cutting edge of jazz stood, then 52nd Street was the place: "The Street," as it was known. And Hawkins, ever the listener, ever the absorber, working on The Street in 1943–44, heard a great deal that fascinated him. First it was Oscar Pettiford and Shelly Manne; then it was Thelonious Monk, soon Dizzy Gillespie and Max Roach, all of whom Hawkins variously took under his leadership wing by early 1944 either on record dates or in his small working groups.

At this juncture in jazz the choice for an older player—in those years someone aged forty was considered "old" musically—was 1) to move somehow along with the new bop direction; or 2) to resist actively the intrusion of a new style and new players (very often this was nothing more than protecting one's commercial turf); or 3), in such cases when the technical and creative capabilities just weren't sufficient to cope with the new language, try to stand one's ground in the hope that enough of one's audience would remain to be able to continue working. A fourth category, the one most to be admired, felt no need either to resist the new movement *or* openly to join hands with its leaders, but simply to continue growing within one's own established musical vision. Hawkins (and Mary Lou Williams in different ways) belonged to the first category. Countless others, including the entire New Orleans "revivalist" group, chose the second option. Armstrong, well into his forties by this time, represents the third type, while in the fourth genus I would place Hines, Lester Young, Roy Eldridge (after some queasy moments), most of the players with Ellington (including Duke) *and* Ben Webster.

These players in category four remained unperturbed, unthreatened by the new modern innovators. Hawkins's case, it seems to me, was more complicated. While on the one hand, as a jazz elder (who had been around long enough to have "invented" the jazz saxophone—musicians openly called him "the old man"),

Hawkins encouraged the young players and actually hired them to work with him, there was, on the other hand, a sense of being unable to relinquish the lead. His fear of being thought old, either in his personal life (particularly his relationship with women) or as a musician, runs like a thread throughout his later life. He dreaded not being in a front-running, dominating position. But he interpreted that—at least until Ornette Coleman came along—as being always *in* and *with* the young guard. With it all, he preserved enough of his own personality, especially his sound, his attack, and his restless exploratory drive, to be always recognizable as Coleman Hawkins. But he had to try everything, and his musical appetite was voracious.

And so were his digestive capacities. One is amazed at the speed with which Hawkins would assimilate new styles, whether it was that of the mid-forties' boppers or the cooler, more linear jazz of the late forties and early fifties, or even the sounds and concepts of John Coltrane in the early sixties.

All of this is well documented on recordings; and it is a remarkable and often glorious record—until the final physical and musical inner collapse in the mid-sixties. Not that Hawkins's assimilative powers always functioned flawlesly. There are many recordings where he is at odds with his musical surroundings, where his often excessive vibrato or tortured twistings do not fit in with the more streamlined, less heated approach of his musical *confrères*. Or there are times when he is floundering harmonically—his incredible harmonic ear had always been his strong suit—and when he is reduced to "running" the older more familiar changes against the uncompromising mysterious harmonies of, say, Thelonious Monk on *Well, You Needn't* or *Epistrophy* (1957). There are also many sides where Hawkins plays very well, but where he is no longer the star of the show, where players like Tatum, Eldridge, Gillespie, Monk, or—on one occasion—Hines assert themselves in such superior or startlingly dramatic fashion that Hawkins's contribution, good as it is, pales by comparison.

On the other hand, it is not difficult to point to a great number of splendid examples of both Hawkins's art and his adaptibility to the changing musical environment. A fuller discussion of these later achievements will be possible in the next volume of this history, but even a cursory selection would have to include his many fine bop lines (for example, *Voodte, Disorder at the Border, Hollywood Stampede*) or his superb solos on *The Stampede, Stuffy,* and *I'm Through with Love* (all 1945), the last in his best ballad style, now slightly updated and streamlined. Hawkins could still surprise you most any time, not only with his inexhaustible energy but with his mercurial versatility. In successive pieces on the same record date, he could be one moment eloquent and elegant in a debonair spats-and-cane style, a raging bull in the next moment (compare the 1944 *I'm in the Mood for Love* and *Bean at the Met*). Or he could pursue more specific technical goals such as stretching the upper range of his instrument beyond its alleged limit, aggressively invading the upper alto range. The high Gs

of the early and mid-forties soon gave way to B♭s (in tenor saxophone notation), as on *Yesterdays* and *Bu-Dee-Daht*. He also could, when needed, reel off fast eighth-note bebop runs as easily as any twenty-year-old bopper (hear him on the 1954 *Get Happy*). And mention has already been made of his astonishing 1959 *Body and Soul*.

Then there is the remarkable *Picasso*, wherein Hawkins attempts the "impossible"—and succeeds: a solitary soloist *sans* accompaniment of any kind, on a single-note instrument. To my knowledge only James T. Maher,[13] among all writers, has pointed out Hawkins's life-long ambition to create the illusion of harmonic simultaneity in his playing—as Maher puts it: Hawkins's "restive, and impatient, effort to come as close to double-stops as a single-note instrument permits him." *Picasso* is certainly one of Hawkins's major explorations of that majestic goal. A full discussion of *Picasso*, recorded in 1948, will be included in the third volume of this History. For the moment let us simply note—in this summary recital of some of Hawkins's post-swing era achievements—that *Picasso* is one of his most visionary and personal, though also thorny, expressions. Freed from any and all harmonic and rhythmic constraints, Hawkins indulged his creative fancy in keys never played by orchestras (even Hendersons!)—keys like F♯ minor, E major, with side excursions into B major and at one point even G♯ major—and in a free-form, free-association continuity which breaks the bounds of anything previously conceived in jazz. It is possible that, a dozen years later, Sonny Rollins was to bring the art of unaccompanied single-note instrumental playing to an even higher plateau. But once again we are comparing amongst musical giants, and Hawkins unquestionably made the first giant step in this important creative direction.

Finally there is the remarkable encounter in 1962—their first on records—between Hawkins and the Ellington band (at least a nucleus thereof). Hawkins was in excellent form. His *Mood Indigo* solo was masterful, proliferating in its later stanzas into beautiful, strongly articulated melodic thirty-second note runs. But ultimately the glory of the recording belongs to Duke for providing just about the most handsome and refreshingly original settings that any soloist could ask for—and that Hawkins ever enjoyed. But I'm not sure that Hawkins fully appreciated that. I have a suspicion that Ellington's men were more in awe of Hawkins than he was of them, in his usual self-assured way, feeling that such a setting was no more than his due.

But perhaps Hawkins's finest hours came in mid-career in 1949. For reasons that I, not knowing enough of the circumstances, cannot fully explain, Hawkins was at his most creative and poised—and seemingly—happiest when he recorded six sides for the French Vogue label with, among others, Kenny Clarke and Pierre Michelot, the fine French bassist. Maybe it was just Hawkins's pleasure

---

13. Maher's liner notes for *The Essential Coleman Hawkins* (Verve, V6-8568) are brilliant, perhaps the best liner notes ever written. They should be required reading for all Hawkins (and jazz) students. Apart from being deeply insightful and splendidly written, they are light years removed from the usual basking-in-the-glory-of-the-greats approach so often taken by most writers on record jackets, where their own status is embellished by the fact that *they*—and only they—are uniquely privileged to understand the greatness of their subject.

at being back in Europe, the scene of so many of his earlier personal triumphs; or maybe it was the non-competitive nature of the setting: a band in which he was clearly *the* master. Whatever it may have been, Hawkins was inspired— despite French pianist Mengeon's wrong "changes"—but inspired in a more re- solved, mature, less restless manner. We hear a three-way balance of emotion and intellect and technique that even artists of Hawkins's calibre can only rarely command. A brief notated excerpt from *Sophisticated Lady* may provide a pre- liminary glimpse of his mastery here (Ex. 8).

Ex. 8

Hawkins was obviously one of the dozen greatest artists and influences in the first half-century of jazz. With all of his many talents, the quality that perhaps most of all made him virtually unique was the sheer emotional/physical power of his playing. Where his creativity and craft may be sometimes seen as vari- able—what artist's aren't?—the constancy of his musical energies, and the depth and sheer magnitude of his expression were unrivaled. This was not something learned or premeditated; it was an innate and unalterable part of the man. You could never simply ignore Hawkins's playing. It was too powerful; it reached out and grabbed you. In the last analysis it was the combination of his awesome technique and emotional power that made him the compelling artist he was.

But Hawkins paid a price for this incomparable dynamism. There is a rest- lessness, a driven-ness in his playing (with rare exceptions). At times it became compulsive and obsessive. Hawkins *had* to fill all the spaces in the music *all* the time. He hated long notes. He could hardly ever be reflective, musing, playful— as Lester Young or Ben Webster could. (One rare happy such example is his

1954 *If I Had You.*) The motoric energy of his playing was driven by a relentless maximum intensity. At times this could lead to some of his more muscle-bound solos; at other times the performances were skirmishes between a piece and himself—and he always *had* to win. (How fascinating that all this explosive energy was usually hidden under a Mona Lisa smile!)

But those were the exceptions—the human exceptions. The totality of the Hawkins *oeuvre* stands unchallenged and unequaled as a monument to jazz in its highest artistic aspirations.

ROY ELDRIDGE

Most of the musicians celebrated in this chapter resisted long-standing involvements with major jazz orchestras. Nor were any of them famous bandleaders, at least not successful ones. Hawkins, Eldridge, Berigan, Wilson, Young, Webster—all were "soloists" rather than "conductors," performers first, creative leaders and organizers second or third. But interestingly their careers as itinerant soloists, unallied to any particular place or ensemble, intersected frequently and fruitfully. Indeed, as an "elite" of soloists, they tended to gravitate towards each other, musically at least enjoying, and to some extent even needing, each other's artistic company. The recordings of the decade between 1935 and 1945 reveal a veritable network of criss-crossing and overlapping personnels of star soloists—recordings, of course, having the singular advantage of one-time affairs requiring no long-time commitment.

One of the most fruitful and consistent partnerships on recordings was that of Coleman Hawkins and trumpeter Roy Eldridge. Starting with the superb Chocolate Dandies recordings of 1940 (*I Can't Believe That You're in Love with Me, Smack, I Surrender Dear*), Hawkins and the seven-years-younger Eldridge were often found in each other's musical company, in (and occasionally even out of) the recording studios, culminating in the 1950s in a long stint at New York's Metropole Café and numerous tours, American as well as European.

Eldridge has often been described as the link between Armstrong and Gillespie, a summation which, though essentially true, is somewhat oversimplified and should not be taken too narrowly. For it implies that Eldridge's music is some immutable stylistic fixture, predesigned to fit that particular transitional historical slot. Instead, Eldridge, like all great musicians, is a constantly changing and growing artist, defying such easy confining type-casting. Besides, Eldridge was initially quite immune to Armstrong's influence.

Active as a professional musician since his mid-teens (he was born in 1911 in Pittsburgh), Eldridge did not rise to prominence until 1936, when he spent a year with Fletcher Henderson's second band as its major trumpet soloist. By then "Little Jazz," as Roy was affectionately known amongst musicians, had played with a dozen bands—among them Speed Webb, Charlie Johnson, Teddy Hill, and Horace Henderson—and had intermittently even led a few of his own, sometimes as co-leader with his alto-playing older brother Joe.

Eldridge was playing professionally almost a decade before he made his first recording. And apparently his development was not of the quick precocious kind that we normally associate with great creative talent. Eldridge's route to individuality (and success) was apparently a circuitous one, and hard fought for. Eldridge breaks out of the typical trumpet player mold first in the fact that he was *not* initially influenced by Armstrong—although that would happen later—but by saxophone players, especially Coleman Hawkins, and by a few other trumpet players: Rex Stewart and Red Nichols.

One can hear a bit of Nichols's clean, lithe sound in the early Eldridge, although by the time Roy started recording (at age twenty-four) this had long ago been overlayed with a strong patina of Armstrong's wider, deeper timbre. But conceptually and technically even more prominently displayed in Eldridge's playing, virtually throughout his career, is the influence of Rex Stewart, not the Stewart of Ellington days but the recklessly abandoned, uproarious Stewart of the Fletcher Henderson band, say of *Stampede*. Here we hear the model for Eldridge's speed, his bursting energy and rhythmic drive. But the 1926 recording of *Stampede* figured conspicuously in young Roy's life in another rather exceptional way: the fifteen-year-old budding trumpet player had memorized Coleman Hawkins's bristling tenor saxophone solo on *Stampede* note for note, and featured it as his specialty wherever he found work. And to that influence (and undoubtedly to many other Hawkins and Carter recordings), we can trace a new, smoother linear element in Eldridge's style as it coalesced out of several sources in the mid-1930s.

Another trumpet player Eldridge listened to in the late 1920s was Jabbo Smith, vestiges of whose technically explosive and musically wild and explorative style we can also hear in Eldridge's playing.

Eldridge himself has pointed out that Armstrong had absolutely no influence on him until he heard Louis in person in 1932 in New York. And in Armstrong he heard something that neither Jabbo nor Rex had: continuity—what Roy called "telling a story."

It is strange that, at a time when almost every player of significance—and even hundreds of lesser ones—played on recordings by their late teens or earliest twenties, Roy Eldridge's recording debut did not come until he was twenty-four, in early 1935, with the Teddy Hill band, the same orchestra with which Eldridge's disciple, Dizzy Gillespie, was also to make his recording debut only two years later. On these sides and on those with the Teddy Wilson orchestra later that year (primarily providing accompaniments for Billie Holiday), we hear a mostly harnessed Roy Eldridge, generally still holding back—as is appropriate in accompanimental situations. At heart a fiery and even boisterous creative spirit, Eldridge here is a model of circumspect behavior, merging dutifully in collective ensembles or, as on *Sweet Lorraine*, content to merely embellish this fine melody.[14] Like every trumpet player of the period, Eldridge on these early recordings

14. On one occasion, A *Sunbonnet Blue* (July 2, 1935), Roy bursts in with an unceremoniously out-of-context solo that destroys the light, buoyant, almost casual mood Billie Holiday had set for that performance. This and a few other Eldridge mood-breaking intrusions may have led Billie, never one to mince words, to exclude Roy from her list of favorite accompanying instrumentalists.

shows his indebtedness to Armstrong, particularly the band-fronting melodic Armstrong of the 1930s. Eldridge's lines are not as imposing, to be sure; his phrases tend to be shorter and his tone leaner, brighter, poised for a potentially more agile, darting manner. Perhaps it is historical hindsight, but on these early Eldridge sides we seem to hear a spring-coiled tension—in the tone, in the phrasing, in the rhythmic inflection—caged and muzzled. He is clearly not content to merely "sing" long beautiful melodies, leaving unused his abundance of reined-in technique.

But Eldridge was about to set those talents free, and to unleash both harmonic and rhythmic innovations that would clearly separate him from Armstrong and current jazz-trumpet-playing with some dramatically new goals and standards.

The element that was really new in Roy's playing was his inclination to take risks (like Rex Stewart had on *The Stampede* or Jabbo Smith on *Sweet and Low Blues*).[15] Of course, all great innovators, by definition, take risks, break molds, present their contemporaries with the previously unpredictable and unsafe. But Eldridge's risk-taking is that of an exuberant youthful virtuoso performer rather than that of a seasoned master composer. There remained in Roy's performing throughout his playing days a boyish, devil-may-care spirit which in his younger days was fed by an enormous physical energy and technical facility. Unlike Armstrong, Eldridge's risk-taking often got him into trouble. Armstrong by the mid-thirties was taking risks on high notes, to be sure, but in general, even in his younger mold-breaking days, there was always a strong element of poise, of mastery, of maturity, even of planning, that gave Armstrong's playing a unique consistency and stylistic integrity. Eldridge was from the outset much more of a true improviser, rarely planning out his solos either in their general outline or their specific musical ideas.

In the harmonic realm, we catch a glimpse of what new things Eldridge's inner ear was hearing in a late July 1935 recording of *It's Too Hot for Words*, an unmemorable pop tune of the day which Billie Holiday and Teddy Wilson were obliged to record. In just four bars—the introduction to the song—Eldridge calls forth a new melodic/harmonic world that Armstrong could certainly not have envisioned. Nor could some of Louis's other disciples like "Red" Allen, Rex Stewart, Cootie Williams (except, in the last case, perhaps through Ellington's harmonic ears). Melodically/linearly Roy's intro is laden with tritones which fellow musicians at the time found "eccentric" or "weird" (Ex. 9). And in truth,

Ex. 9

15. See *Early Jazz*, 211–13.

not only were they entirely new as melodic or intervallic material, but they landed at odd places in the phrase, creating strange little harmonic collisions and unexpectedly sharp-cornered contours. Even more significantly, they were "flatted" notes, a tendency which Eldridge was to develop into a distinctive hall-mark of his style, and which players younger than Roy, like Howard McGhee and Gillespie, were to take up[16] and eventually develop into an entire tritone-dominated new language. Here with Roy in the mid-thirties it is no more than a dialect, but it opened up new melodic/harmonic/intervallic possibilities that previous improvising ears simply had not heard (or tolerated).

Another breakthrough discernible in Eldridge's early playing is the use of the entire range of the trumpet. We have seen how Armstrong had extended the upper range of the trumpet step by step, stopping, however, at high F. Eldridge, of course, felt compelled to top that—he soon could manage high Gs very com-fortably—but more than that he saw a possibility of using the entire three-octave range in a much more fluid and concentrated way. Whereas Armstrong might separate a solo into three separate octaves or registers, usually building skyward during a solo, Eldridge's daring led him to scale the heights and plumb the depths within a single phrase or even a few bars. Still more spectacularly, he would rummage around in the lowest register and suddenly, almost surprising even himself, jump an octave or two into the highest register, only to come plummeting down again in cascading running figures. He had a young boy's zeal to startle—and to show off. That was a new kind of risk-taking which no other trumpet player had quite dared before in the same way; and, of course, it didn't always work. But we can see how this element of Roy's playing became a musical and technical inspiration to Gillespie, who was really to develop the downhill run, like some incredible musical slalom, first into an art and eventu-ally into a cliché.

We can hear Eldridge exploring the full range of his instrument in one of his most spirited solos, the fast-tempoed *Swing Is Here* with Gene Krupa's Swing Band (February 1936). This is, in conception, already a long way from Arm-strong. Using the trumpet's full range required constructing an entirely different type of melody or line. Indeed it could not, by definition, be as conjunctly melodic as previous playing had been, contained as that was—generally—in one octave or so. Running the gamut from [musical notation] to [musical notation] in a more condensed time frame demanded both a fluency of execution and a more wide-ranging phrase-structuring than had heretofore been contemplated. It invited the upper range in, not as something to be strained for and reserved for climactic high points, but as a normal integrated element of both conception and execu-tion. This, in effect, required a new embouchure, one which was positioned not in the lower middle range, with high notes to be squeezed out when needed,

16. See discussion of these developments in connection with Andy Kirk's *McGhee Special*, in Chap-ter 5, Part 2, above.

but one positioned more in the geographic center of the range, able to lean with minimum effort in either direction, stretching into the upper range or equivalently dipping into the lowest register.

On the same 1936 Krupa date, on *I Hope Gabriel Likes My Music*, Eldridge gives a new and broader significance to high notes. They are now not limited to high points of entire solos, usually coming at the end, but of individual phrases; and they may occur anywhere in a solo.

On these early performances Eldridge does not yet have the full control he was to gain later—Benny Goodman, for example, is masterful here in *his* control of content and execution, stealing the show from everybody on at least three of these four Krupa sides—but one can clearly hear what Roy was striving for: exploring new unprobed territory.

The third element of Eldridge's breakthrough was in the realm of rhythm and tempo. To begin with, he could handle faster tempos with great ease. In fact, he and his friend Chu Berry *needed* and thrived on fast tempos. Their technical abilities, based on faster mental and physical/instrumental execution, operated on a new higher tempo plateau. That's where they felt challenged and stimulated, enjoying the wonderment of their slower-moving older colleagues. But these were not mere pyrotechnical skills. The *musical content* of their improvisation also operated on a speedier wave length. Their fast notes were not embellishments, ornaments, passing tones, larger shapes splintered into small rhythmic units: they were inherently faster, more streamlined ideas, where the small rhythmic units—preferably eighth notes in very fast tempos, or double-time sixteenths in medium tempos—were the very stuff of their musical statements.

Along with this ability, Eldridge cultivated a leaner sound, always vibrant and alive but sharply etched and often punched out rhythmically, that bespoke of a new positive forward spirit in jazz, a reflection perhaps of a society coming out of the Depression. One heard it in all the leading players: in the real speed and ease of Benny Goodman's clarinet, Chu Berry's saxophone, Charlie Shaver's trumpet, Teddy Wilson's piano—and for that matter Cab Calloway's scatting.

There was also an altogether new streamlined fluency in Eldridge's fast slurred runs. They are at once smoother and more articulated. The clear articulation comes not from technical practice alone but, rather, from a greater ability— again a greater speed—to really hear each note as it runs by, to feel it as an important individual unit, crucial to the total musical statement. Every word now counted; there were very few verbal asides. This was an aspect of trumpet-playing—it was a lot easier to achieve on reed instruments, of course—that was truly new, and something that the young Gillespie definitely heard and admired in the playing of the six-years-older Eldridge. Speed and control of high notes are all exemplified in Eldridge's solos on the Henderson *Christopher Columbus* and *Blue Lou*. But perhaps the outstanding example of Eldridge's art in its early pristine form occurs on the April 1936 *Jangled Nerves*—well titled, for it must really have sounded like that to the old-timers. At a hellion speed of $\bemol = 275$, Eldridge charges through his two choruses of fast blues—they follow Chu Berry's smooth-as-an-otter-gliding-through-water solo—with almost nonchalant ease, inventively tossing off new melodic shapes and odd-intervalled harmonies as if they were part of a long established tradition. That Eldridge could now also deal with slower tempos is amply demonstrated by his clear, coherent, and essentially simple solo on *Shoe Shine Boy*.

It was inevitable that Roy's talent would lead, by emulating Armstrong, to fronting bands, smaller groups at first (as at the Three Deuces in Chicago in 1937) or a bigger band in 1939 for various residences in New York. These efforts were generally short-lived but occasionally yielded some fine recordings. Certainly Roy's octet sides of January 1937 are vintage Eldridge, successfully encapsuling his new conceptual and technical innovations: the twisting melodic lines (as on *Florida Stomp*—effectively arranged by brother Joe Eldridge) or the careening, boldly shaped statements on *Heckler's Hop* and *After You've Gone*. Roy is—as brass players put it—"all over the horn." In one 4-bar break on *After*, he begins with a high F and plunges within not too many seconds to a swirling pool of notes centered upon low G. Indeed, Eldridge's control, both of ideas and technique, is breath-taking. And there is a coherence here which, alas, Roy was to abandon often in later years for the sake of more "spectacular" high note effects, what is often called "grandstanding."

But these were good years for Eldridge. He teamed up again with his jamsession buddy Chu Berry in late 1938 to record four outstanding sides which confirmed Roy's leadership position in the trumpet world. *Sittin' In*—especially the faster take two—is a stunning example of Roy's ability to encompass the whole range of his instrument in fleet eighth-note runs that go beyond mere technical skill to make a perfectly balanced musical statement. The last three "eights" of his solo are typical (Ex. 10).[17] No one else could have played that passage at that time—except perhaps Charlie Shavers—but certainly not with Eldridge's drive and swing.

Ex. 10

17. That even a great player like Sid Catlett, the drummer on this date, could stumble badly is shown by his intrusion, two bars early, upon Berry's 4-bar lead-in break to his own solo.

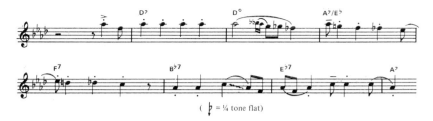

(♭ = ¼ tone flat)

Clearly, Roy was happiest in these up-tempo instrumentals, but on occasion he could also forgo virtuoso razzle-dazzle for beautifully reasoned and poised ballad statements, as on *Star Dust* (from the same 1938 date). Again this was a wholly new way of constructing melodic statements. In addition to those proto-typical figures—mostly ascending—that Armstrong had already imprinted on the song, Eldridge found odd little falling shapes, like sudden downward shifts of wind, that would unexpectedly alter the course of the solo. Even four and a half decades later phrases like mm. 5 and 6 (Ex. 11) still have not lost their surprise element and at the same time their "of-course-it-had-to-go-that-way" inevitability.

Ex. 11

Eldridge's 4-bar introduction—no mere noodling intro—sets the adventurous and serious tone of his intended setting. This was the kind of reshaping of melodic contours (Ex. 12) that Dizzy Gillespie was to develop into an essential personal trademark of *his* ballad style, especially on his famous *I Can't Get*

Ex. 12

Started. Roy's sudden dip down to the low A♭, then snaking his way back up into the middle register, was the sort of thing that would not have occurred to 99 out of 100 trumpet players in 1938.

It is when Eldridge began fronting a big band (his own at first, in 1939) or featured as the "star soloist" (later with Gene Krupa and Artie Shaw) that we begin to hear the occasional lapses of taste, the pyrotechnical "grandstanding," the reaching for unwanted and unneeded high notes. *Pluckin' the Bass,* for example—an odd piece for Eldridge to do, having no outstanding solo bassist at his beck and call—offers one of those wild bursting-at-the-seams solos that, for all its thrashing about, gets nowhere. Indeed it gets downright silly after a while. Similarly on *I'm Getting Sentimental Over You,* Roy starts with a high-register declamatory solo—and a first-note clam—that is totally inappropriate to this song, and might in any case have served better as a climactic ending.

In general the eight 1939 Eldridge Orchestra sides are quite disappointing. They certainly do not fulfill the promise, or even maintain the level, of Roy's earlier work. And the band plays with little distinction, except for an occasional brief solo spot by tenor-man Prince Robinson or Joe Eldridge. The repertory is also ill chosen. Apart from the two above-mentioned pieces, there are two pre-1920s' oldies for which the band shows little affinity, *Muskrat Ramble* and *High Society.* Actually, most interesting in the eight sides is Laurel Watson's singing. By no means great though much beholden to Billie Holiday stylistically, Watson's singing on *I'm Getting Sentimental* is nonetheless rather remarkable for the way she creates a brand-new melodic line, totally ignoring George Bassman's famous melody (by 1938 Tommy Dorsey's theme song for three years), inventing an ingenious free-floating almost stationary line that one would never associate with this song. This invention was probably born of necessity, since Watson apparently could not handle the vocal demands of Bassman's rather rangy tune, encompassing an octave and a half.

Maybe larger accompanimental forces provoked in Eldridge an irresistible temptation to dominate, to exhibit, to overpower. Smaller groups on the other hand, especially when composed of his peers—like Hawkins, Carter, John Kirby, Catlett (on the Chocolate Dandies sessions of 1940)—caused Eldridge to be on his best behavior. All three sides, classics of small-ensemble recording, give us Roy at his very best. His solo on *I Can't Believe That You're in Love with Me,* two full choruses, is a small masterpiece of invention and conciseness. It epitomizes Eldridge's early style in those particular respects which I have previously singled out as being his distinctive contribution in this late-1930s period. A study of his solo (Ex. 13) reveals his easy command of the trumpet's full range—in this solo from high D♭ to low A♭—at a good fast tempo. It also shows us the adventurousness of his ear, spicing his otherwise fluent lines with piquant note ornamentations that even today stand out as original and daring.

It is the song's bridge that especially inspired Eldridge to new heights of creativity. The musical notation does not show his harmonic/melodic surprises as forcefully as the aural experience of hearing them does. But these disturbing notes are clearly stressed and demarcated by Eldridge through dynamic empha-

Ex. 13

sis, shoved forward into the aural foreground, almost as in a sculptor's bas-relief. Especially interesting, for example, in mm. 22–27 of the first chorus, is Roy's use—nine times—of altered pitches (marked *a,b,c,d,x,y*), which mostly rotate around the note E♭, plainly indicating that these special notes were not accidents but rather specific pitch points targeted by Roy for special expressive emphasis.[18] What is particularly fascinating about these note choices is that they are mostly identical (four F♭s),[19] operating, however, in *different* harmonic settings. Thus Eldridge accomplished two rather extraordinary things: 1) he used certain pitches in previously almost never-heard functions in five different harmonic *loci*; and 2), more importantly, he went beyond the three traditional "blue notes" (the flat third, fifth, and seventh) to discover some new ones. For it is as blue notes— more "advanced" and "dissonant" ones, to be sure—that we perceive these various F♭s: *a* begins as a flat ninth, but at the bar line changes to a flat sixth (*b* and *d* are the more common "blue" minor thirds, *c* is a minor seventh), while *y*, E♭♭, is another flat ninth. What is so poignant about these "flatted" notes is, as I have just suggested, that they (F♭ and E♭♭) are only a tone apart and thus modify the note E♭, the one a half-step above, the other a half-step below. Moreover, all of this is no dry academic exercise of Eldridge's—nor of mine in analyzing it. One *hears* both their haunting "flatness," boldly emphasized and leaned on by Eldridge, and their linear/melodic relationship across these five measures, emphasized by reiteration—and, I hasten to add, not evidently worked out on paper but instantaneously *composed* in a matter of seconds.

I have left to the last the four notes bracketed under x, for these are not only more "blues-ish" altered notes (C♭-raised ninth), but, spelled enharmonically as

. With an underlying D[7]-chord substitution (tritonally related), these are the kinds of harmonic alterations which in a few short years the modern jazz musicians would come to use consistently, and which are by now, thirty or forty years later, absolutely commonplace—as complicated as their description here may sound to the lay reader.

Eldridge's *I Can't Believe* solo is also interesting from a larger organizational

18. I have already pointed out Lester Young's somewhat similar use of altered and "flatted" notes in his late 1930s' work with the Basie band (see, above, Chapter 4).

19. F♭ is the same note as E♮ on the piano and fingered the same on a trumpet. But in a tempered system of tuning and in the variable harmonic contexts of this example—five different chords (G♭7, A♭7, D♭7, G♭m6, D♭6) are involved—this note will be *felt* and heard slightly differently, responding to different harmonic functions, and slightly adjusted in intonation. The note E♭♭ (*y* in the example) is the same as D♮ on the piano.

point of view. A cross-referencing of his two choruses (in Ex. 13) shows both an overall consistency and economy of materials and a masterly ability to relate like places in the two choruses either by contrast or by resemblance. Measures 4–7 relate to mm. 61–64 by close identity; so do mm. 12–15 and 44–47. On the other hand identical stations in the chorus structure, like mm. 9–12 vis-à-vis 41–45, or mm. 25–32 vis-à-vis 57–64, are treated in quite different ways. Notice also how Eldridge's phrase-length structuring carries the aforementioned first-chorus bridge passage right across the double bar, well into the final eight bars (mm. 22–27)—in those years still an unusual breakaway from basic 8-bar phrase-designing.

All this demonstrates quite clearly that Eldridge was in full control of his musical materials at all times in this solo, choosing diversity or similarity at will, and having the ability to translate instantly his musical ideas into virtually flaw-less execution on the trumpet.

Later in 1940, Eldridge was back in Billie Holiday's recording orchestra, with its fine rhythm section of Kenny Clarke (drums), Al Hall (bass), and John Collins (guitar). But Roy's work here was once again somewhat restless and inconsistent, ranging from the very beautiful contemplative solo on *I'm All for You*—notice how deliciously he suspends the E♭ in m.6 of his solo (the raised ninth in a C^7 chord), resolving it and its neighbor D♭ in the next measure (F major) with a series of E♮s and D♮s—to *Practice Makes Perfect*, where he is in his own world, too brash and insensitive to Billie's special delineation of this song.

From this same date we do have another Eldridge gem, however: his muted solo on *I Hear Music*. Two brief excerpts indicate how effortlessly Roy played with altered-note conceptions (Ex. 14).

Ex. 14

In the spring of 1941 Eldridge joined Gene Krupa's band as its featured solo-ist, along with vocalist Anita O'Day. It was in this period in which Eldridge became increasingly erratic and even artificial, often playing to audiences for easy effects. His exploitation of high notes and "spectacular" leaping figures became a virtual addiction: the more he indulged audiences, the more they wanted; and in turn all the more he gave them of what they wanted. It was an endless upward spiral, drifting more and more into stunt work and senseless musical calisthenics. *Bolero at the Savoy*, a musical trifle blown up into a bombastic production number by Krupa's tom-toms and Roy's grandstanding, is but the worst example from this period. *Rockin' Chair*, one of Eldridge's most famous solos, occupies the entire side and is actually a strong and at times tremendously moving performance, spoiled only by the opening and closing cadenzas, the latter unforgivably aping the corniest of operatic cadenza traditions. Interesting from a technical/expressive point of view is Roy's application of a raspy, buzzy tone, which enormously heightens his playing's intensity, emotionally and dynamically. It is a way of "forcing" the sound so that the air column actually splits, producing various audible under- and overtones. (These are most clearly heard at the momentarily unaccompanied beginning of the final cadenza.) This device, which took tremendous skill to control, was aptly designed to project over a loudly playing band, literally forcing the listener to take note of the soloist. But as a certain distortion of sound, when overused,[20] it contained the risk of becoming overbearing and eventually, by its sameness, boring. But in *Rockin' Chair* this effect is used to overwhelming expressive power. Hear the almost uncontainable ardor of both first notes in the bridge and the last "eight" respectively (Roy's first chorus). It was also meant to hurt a little, to be disturbing, to express unfathomable stress.

When Krupa's orchestra disbanded in 1943, Eldridge took another fling at band-leading himself. It was a small eight-piece band, featuring himself and a four-man saxophone section (led by brother Joe) and three rhythm. Only four sides were recorded, and one can feel the heavy hand of the Brunswick recording director, no doubt looking for a commercial breakthrough. *Minor Jive* was just that—that is, minor jive—and, along with *Jump Through the Window*, it was trying to get in on the enormous popular success of Louis Jordan's little "Tympany Five" jump band, while *The Gasser* was an attempt to pick up on the embryonic bop language, beginning to spread through Harlem and 52nd Street. *Star Dust*, on the other hand, was another way of looking for a best-seller: to record one of the all-time song hits. *The Gasser* and *Star Dust* are both outstanding, the one featuring a brilliant Roy in a distinctly bop-ish frame of mind, equaling anything that Gillespie and Shavers could offer at that time (late 1943); the other, Roy at his most expansively lyric, a marvelous cross between Armstrong and Harry James (who was making tracks with his ever more popular "sweet" solos).

In early 1944, Roy formed the Little Jazz Trumpet Ensemble, featuring three trumpeters: himself, Joe Thomas, and Emmet Berry. It was not a successful venture. Roy's heart does not seem to have been in it, and Berry consistently outplayed Eldridge with some very handsome, elegant, blues-ish solos (especially on *St. Louis Blues*).

More uncertainty characterizes Eldridge's subsequent attempts to return to the

---

20. Eldridge used this effect frequently, most notably on the 1941 *Green Eyes* with Krupa, and, of course, on hundreds of unrecorded club and dance performances.

big-band format. Roy's work vaccilated between the ostentatious, as on *After You've Gone* and *Little Jazz Boogie*, and the confused, as on *I Can't Get Started*. The latter was especially disappointing, for it had neither the poignant expressivity of Berigan's earlier versions of this tune nor the fanciful imagination of Gillespie's later versions. (Dizzy really took over that piece from Berigan by the mid-forties and made it very much his own.)

Eldridge was in those years desperately fishing for a big hit—like his *Rockin' Chair* with Krupa had been. Another Harry James emulation, *Twilight Time*, sounding like a white dance band, had little success, nor did *Embraceable You*, in which Roy played one of his calmer paraphrase solos, against Will Bradley's muted high trombone. The big hit almost came with *Fish Market*, a catchy riff tune of his own devising. Although Eldridge played well in a sort of "cool" mood, the side was stolen by Sandy Williams's trombone solo, starting with a magnificent long high wail in between-the-cracks microtonal blue notes.

In the fall of 1944, Eldridge was enticed to abandon his own orchestra and join Artie Shaw's big band, with whom he spent the next eleven months. It cannot be said that Shaw's highly eclectic approach to music, ranging from the very modern and intellectual—even quasi-symphonic—to the most traditional, with sweet dance arrangements and pop vocals in between, was the ideal setting for Eldridge's talents. It certainly was not a growth period for him. Except for pieces like *Little Jazz*, composed for him by that fine craftsman Buster Harding[21]— Eldridge is in excellent form, swinging easily—and *Scuttlebutt*, with the Gramercy Five (a sextet from the Shaw band, somewhat in the manner of Goodman's sextets and quartets), there is little that challenged Eldridge in any way commensurate with his formidable gifts. It was a kind of holding period in which he was less the user than the used.

So it was also when Eldridge left Shaw in late 1945 and once again formed a big band, this time with as many as eighteen players. Eldridge's playing was mostly erratic and uncertain, resorting more and more to altissimo screaming and cadenza show-casings. The band was more exciting for Harding's strong, richly voiced arrangements and tenor-man Tom Archia's superior solos than for Eldridge's own contributions. The final session in September 1946 (before reducing the band to combo size) was the least productive of all. For whatever reason, Eldridge was melodically uncertain or actually rambling meaninglessly through the changes, as in *Lover Come Back to Me* and *I Surrender Dear*. A real nadir was reached on the same date in a meandering remake of *Rockin' Chair*, where Roy actually got lost in the changes.

By the late forties as bop and modern jazz really took hold and many of the younger players—as well as audiences and record buyers—began to regard the

---

21. Harding provided many other excellent settings for Eldridge for several 1945 and 1946 Eldridge-led big-band studio sessions—*Little Jazz Boogie*, *Hi Ho Trailus Boot Whip*, *Yard Dog*, and especially *Tippin' Out*. Harding, after fine work for Goodman and Calloway, was here really coming into his own, evolving an exciting, massive, hard-rocking idiom that was well suited to the high-powered big-band styles in the waning wartime years of the Swing Era (see below, Chapter 7, for a discussion of Harding with Artie Shaw).

older musicians with a certain disdain or, worse yet, began to ignore them, Eldridge experienced a crisis of confidence in himself. For some years he seemed quite confused, not knowing whether he should try to keep pace with the new developments—as his friend Coleman Hawkins was doing, almost gleefully—or whether he should continue to play in his own way. To his great credit Eldridge eventually chose the latter path, and so preserved his own unique musical identity.

Eldridge is, as of this writing, no longer active as a player, having developed heart trouble a few years ago. Like most musicians who survived the changing decades, Eldridge has mellowed in the later years. There has been for some time a kind of settled-in maturity in his playing, although that impish impulse to break out into rambunctions flourishes is always present, simmering just below the surface—and often above it. The battle with the high notes—always an irresistible stimulant for Eldridge—continued as long as his embouchure and physical strength permitted. At times it was an agonizing spectacle, hearing the aging muscles still trying to emulate those of a twenty-five-year-old.[22] But that was also always a part of the risk-taking element in Roy's playing.

How seasoned his artistry and creativity often has been in later years can be measured in any number of post 1940s recordings. A random sampling of Roy at his best should probably include his very moving A-major blues on *De-Dar* (from a 1959 Ben Webster date on the Verve label), his two solos on *R & R* (from a 1960 date with Charles Mingus and Eric Dolphy), and his remarkable contribution to *Hanid* (on a 1958 Hawkins–Eldridge Quintet date). Here in one of his most economical and self-contained solos, Eldridge, after a chain of repeated A♭s, unexpectedly removes his mute, producing a huge gaping yawn of a sound on the same pitch. It is both great musical ingenuity and high drama. This performance offers the compleat Roy Eldridge, including, almost as a kind of bonus, several respectful bows to his disciple Dizzy Gillespie—another fine instance of the master momentarily emulating the student.

BUNNY BERIGAN

Jazz loves its legends, especially its alcoholic martyrs. To qualify for such canonization you had to die early, preferably from too much drinking; and it is best that you were white—and played the trumpet. The two BB's—Bix Beiderbecke and Bunny Berigan—were ideal candidates, and they are idolized and romanticized to this day, while Jabbo Smith, Frankie Newton, Tommy Ladnier, and John Nesbitt, who either died prematurely or were forced into early retirement, are allowed to languish in quiet oblivion. On the other hand it doesn't pay to live a long and active healthy life: that will get you very few points in the legend business. Berigan was unquestionably one of the trumpet giants of the thirties. But as one reads much of the jazz literature, especially in its more anecdotal

22. It is painful to hear Eldridge torturing himself with endless chains of high Cs, high Fs (and higher) at the 1975 Montreux Festival. It's even more painful to hear the audience break out into ecstatic gratified applause.

manifestations, one could easily gain the impression that, after Armstrong, there was only Berigan, and that such pre-Gillespie trumpeters as Roy Eldridge, Henry "Red" Allen, Rex Stewart, Cootie Williams, Buck Clayton, Harry Edison, Harry James, Charlie Spivak, Ziggy Elman, Sy Oliver, "Hot Lips" Page, Taft Jordan, Eddie Tomkins, Bobby Hackett, Charlie Teagarden, Mannie Klein, and a host of others simply never existed or were inconsequential peripheral figures.

Such biased writing takes much encouragement from Armstrong's oft-quoted response to a question about his successors: "The best of them? That's easy, It was Bunny." (That must have made Roy Eldridge happy!) Whatever Armstrong's reasons for making that comment might have been—if indeed it is authentic and not taken out of context—the fact is that Berigan, as good as he was, was by no means as unique as his most ardent admirers would have us believe. That he was a superbly talented and in his early years a technically assured trumpet player is beyond argument; but so were all the above-listed trumpet players, some even more consistent or technically spectacular than Berigan. That he was a superior musician with superb musical instincts and a relentlessly creative mind is also unarguable; but so were Eldridge, Allen, Stewart, and Cootie. That he was always a moving lyric player is equally true; but so were a number of others, particularly Cootie and Ladnier, Clayton and Hackett. And while a lyric, singing approach to the trumpet was Berigan's forte, players like Stewart, Newton, and Eldridge could create eloquent lyric statements, as required, *in addition* to other kinds of personal expresions. That Berigan used the full range of the trumpet, exploiting especially the low register, is undisputable; but so did Eldridge and Jabbo Smith, and they indeed expanded the top range much more vigorously. That Berigan took chances in his flights of imagination is also undeniable; but it would be impossible to deny that Eldridge did, and that, in fact, he did so within a more venturesome and complex style, and—it must be said—with greater technical consistency.

Berigan's idolization by certain authors has even led to the deification of his mistakes. A fluff by Berigan is cherished in those circles as some glorious creative moment, which no one else could have dared to imagine. The fact is that, from a brass-playing point of view, many of Berigan's missed notes—discounting the final years when his deteriorating health really affected his coordination—occur not in his technically most daring passages but in relatively ordinary ones. Some of his more spectacular trumpet feats are the result of his most daring conceptions, whereas the more conservative musical ideas are often those which are technically blemished.

All of this is not to denigrate Berigan's talent and achievements but merely to put them in perspective and to demythologize somewhat his position in jazz history. He does occupy an important role in the jazz trumpet's development in that he, more than anyone else, fused elements of both Armstrong and Beiderbecke into a new, distinctive, personal voice.

By all accounts Berigan, like Eldridge, seems to have discovered Armstrong relatively late; and when he did, it was primarily the Armstrong already embarked on a career as a lyric balladeer and bravura soloist. But it would be wrong to assume that Berigan was, even in the early stages of his career, a mere Armstrong imitator. His first recording with the Wisconsin University Skyrockets, Fred Rich, and Hal Kemp (in 1928, 1929, and 1930 respectively) reveal a young Berigan not only with already his own sound and melodic identity but with the ability to create fluent well-structured explorative solos.

These extremely rare Wisconsin recordings are fascinating to hear not only as historic documents of the nineteen-year-old trumpet talent—he had been playing professionally since the age of thirteen (!)—but also as proof of Berigan's precocity and early stylistic independence.[23] His strangely searching solos (on *Slow Beef, Postage Stomp*), neither linearly melodic nor rigidly harmonic, reveal an inventive improvisational talent that was not beholden to any known model. The notes in a solo break from a blues, *It's a Sin*, like:

could not have been played by Armstrong or Tommy Ladnier or George Mitchell in 1928, not even Henry "Red" Allen (who in any case did not record until 1929 and who, as we have seen, was at first rather more closely allied to Armstrong's harmonically conventional style).

Another excellent example of Berigan's abilities at this time can be heard on *Them There Eyes* (with Hal Kemp's band in November 1930). His three brief solos here are unusually cohesive — within themselves, as well as in relation to each other. All three (Ex. 15a, b, c) are based on a motivic idea whose main elements are syncopated repeated notes and the use of the blue seventh, the

Ex. 15a

Ex. 15b

23. It remains a mystery why the Paramount label would record an unknown, virtually student group on its 12000 "race" series.

Ex. 15c

second solo beginning very much like the first, only an octave higher. In his third solo, instead of starting on the fifth degree and moving up a fourth (enfolding the seventh in between), Berigan inverts the idea, starting on the tonic and moving down to the fifth degree (with the seventh again placed in between as a melodic modifier). It is all extremely simple and clear—and quite perfect. Not many twenty-three-year-olds in those early jazz decades could have matched such masterful eloquence.

The solo also gives a brief glimpse of one of Berigan's mature hallmarks, his remarkable fluency in the lowest range of the trumpet, an area Armstrong had begun to explore, but which Eldridge and Berigan were to really make an integral and consistent part of the trumpet's technical/expressive vocabulary. Berigan's famous power and tonal projection, as well as his vigorous technical command, can also be sampled in the second chorus of *Them There Eyes* (with Kemp) in which, muted, he joins three reeds in an agile ensemble chorus that few trumpeters in 1930 could have handled. Berigan plays the melodic lead, while one clarinet plays a top line above him and two others the harmony below—a four-part voicing arranged by Kemp's pianist (and later orchestra leader for Bing Crosby's radio shows) John Scott Trotter, and daringly geared to the natural technical fluency of the clarinet rather than the trumpet.[24]

Berigan played for nearly half a dozen years in the New York studios, very often alongside Tommy and Jimmy Dorsey, Glenn Miller, Benny Goodman, and Artie Shaw, also working for longer periods with the Paul Whiteman and Dorsey Brothers orchestras. In the several hundred sides cut with these varied pickup and permanent groups, Berigan was able to consolidate and refine his style. Hear him with Glenn Miller in 1935 (on *In a Little Spanish Town* and *Solo Hop*, the latter with a final cadenza in the Armstrong manner); with Gene Gifford's orchestra (in a marvelously blues-ish New Orleans mood on *Nothin' but the Blues* and *Squareface*); in a fluent clarinet-like running eighth-note solo on *The Buzzard* (with Bud Freeman's Windy City Five); on Benny Goodman's *Let's Dance* radio program in outstandingly inventive solos on *Star Dust, Limehouse Blues,* and *Honeysuckle Rose,* all from a January 5, 1935, broadcast; with Red Norvo on *Bughouse* (struttingly self-confident) and *Blues in E-flat* (soulful); or with Mildred Bailey (and Johnny Hodges and Teddy Wilson) on a date arranged for English Parlophone by John Hammond.

Berigan's solo on *Keep Smiling at Trouble* with Bud Freeman's band is typical of his work at this time (Ex. 16). Beginning in the low register—Berigan loved

---

24. Richard Sudhalter errs in his notes on Berigan in the *Giants of Jazz* Series of Time-Life Records when he refers to this chorus as being by "the brass." First of all, Kemp had only three brass—this ensemble has four parts—and not even the other trumpet player, let alone trombonist Wendell Mayhew, could by any stretch of the imagination have managed such a virtuosic ensemble passage at this bright a tempo.

Ex. 16

to start his solos low, making his sudden leaps into the upper range all the more startling—in flowing lines that would be equally appropriate on clarinet or violin (the latter Berigan's first instrument as a child), he next fashions a simple bridge by returning three times to its initial pitch and spinning different refrains from it, then ending with a final "eight" of great originality, with oddly spaced notes that come as a complete surprise after so much regularity earlier.

Another outstanding moment, one typical of Berigan's always searching explorative mind, occurs on Gifford's aforementioned *Nothin' but the Blues*. Here (Ex. 17), in his second solo (after Wingy Manone's vocal), Berigan takes the simplest idea, the descending fifth C-F, and expands it upward one tone (to D) whilst adding the blue third, A♭. While this triad (D-A♭-F) functions harmonically in both the F^7 and $B♭^7$ chords (mm. 4 through 6), Berigan ingeniously twists it around rhythmically in repeating and contrasting patterns, squeezing the maximum of motivic invention out of these three little pitches. Later in bar 8, anticipating the V-chord (C^7) scheduled for bar 9, he bends an F down to a plaintive E, giving the whole chorus an anguished pungent quality that captures the essence of vocal-instrumental blues. (Berigan was to return to this wailing semi-tone bent note hundreds of times in his career.) In bar 10 Berigan caps this blues stanza with a very modern up-and-down leaping figure, of the kind that Henry "Red" Allen had been exploring for many years (see Part 3 of this chapter). The whole chorus, one of Berigan's very finest, is typical of the inventive-

Ex. 17

ness of his imagination, of his ability adroitly to combine the expected with the unexpected, and a superb example of his glorious rich golden singing tone.

One of the many musicians who was strongly impressed by Berigan's talent was Benny Goodman. Benny and Bunny had often worked together in the studios in the early thirties in pickup bands (sometimes led by Goodman) and, as mentioned, on the *Let's Dance* broadcast series. When Goodman took his band on its first transcontinental road trip in the summer of 1935, he hired Berigan as his leading soloist. The recordings made by the Goodman band with Berigan are some of the best representations of both artists. Certainly Berigan's two solos on *King Porter Stomp* (recorded July 1, 1935) must count as among his very finest creative achievements. His performance here represents the mature Berigan in full opulent flowering.

Berigan's solo work on *King Porter* exemplifies his unerring sense of form, a virtually infallible clarity of statement. His two solos, one muted, the other open horn, are miniature compositions which many a writing-down composer would be envious of having created, even after days of work. This structural logic transmits itself even to the lay listener in the absolute authoritativeness of his playing.

The ingredients in both solos are really quite simple: great melodic beauty combined with logic and structural balance. Every note, every motivic cell, every phrase leads logically to the next with a Mozartean classic inevitability. And each phrase, whether heard in 2-bar or 8-bar segments, has its own balanced structuring and symmetry. Take, for example, the last eight bars of his first solo (Ex. 18). Starting on the syncopated high Cs, the phrase falls to its midpoint, rests there a moment (in bar 20) and then rises again to the final tonic note. And whereas the first four bars use syncopation as an element of surprise, of swing and of tension, the last four bars lie squarely *on* the beat, providing a wonderful sense of resolution not only to the phrase but to the whole solo.

Something similar happens in Berigan's 8-bar introduction which, after its jauntily swinging opening, settles down to ten repeated quarter-note Cs, clearly

Ex. 18

signaling the beginning of the song proper. This signal is also, of course, given by the harmonies—the arrival of the tonic chord after eight bars of introduction—but Berigan underscores this harmonic function perfectly by stabilizing his improvisation on a single pitch, embracing, as it were, the song-starting double-bar on either side. We see here several layers of symmetry, that is, within both short and longer phrase lengths. The rise and fall of the phrases function similarly, in well-balanced though simple antipodal juxtapositions and contrasts.[25]

Berigan's second solo, following Goodman's, seems almost to be a climactic extension of the latter. It takes up Goodman's ideas where he left off and builds upon them, mostly by means of repetition and mooring each phrase on a high $D\flat$ (see Ex. 19). Again, symmetrical balancing gives the solo a wonderful equilibrium, seemingly a natural gift with Berigan.

But that is not all. As always, there is Berigan's incomparable — and irrepressible — swing. On any given Berigan recording he usually out-swings everybody else (although on *King Porter* Goodman matches him point for point). But Berigan's sense of swing was an innate talent, a given talent, a feeling beyond study or calculation, one that Berigan heard in the playing of both Beiderbecke and Armstrong but which he synthesized into his own personal rhythmic idiom.

Berigan's other great asset was the extraordinary beauty of his tone. Though

25. Benny Goodman, not to be outdone by Berigan, also turns in an excellently balanced solo which, incidentally, also begins with an on-the-beat reiterated single pitch, and in other ways seems to have been stimulated and inspired by Berigan's opening solo.

Ex. 19

technically based on perfect breath support, the purity—and amplitude—of his tone was controlled at the moment of emission by his inner ear, as with any great artist renowned for his tone. Berigan could project in his mind and ear a certain sound, and then the physical muscles (embouchure, breathing, fingers) would, in coordination, produce the desired result.

Like much of Berigan's work, the *King Porter* solos are not innovative break-throughs. Berigan usually operated from a base of traditional logic, rather than radical invention. He was essentially a lyric conservative who, however, within that ideal could on occasion produce some startlingly fresh ideas, mostly unexpected juxtapositions, surprises—but always within a well-grounded established stylistic terrain.

Berigan stayed with Goodman only four months. He performed a similar interim role with Tommy Dorsey's band in early 1937, singlehandedly uplifting the quality of that band and contributing such magnificent solos as the ones on *Marie* and *Song of India*.[26] Indeed these solos saved these pieces qualitatively, keeping them well within the jazz arena, whereas without them both numbers would have been more or less successful well-performed commercial recordings.

With so much talent and success—Berigan was a greater sensation with the Dorsey band than even Dorsey himself—it was inevitable that Berigan would also try his hand at band-leading. The progress towards this goal was gradual and slow. Initially, John Hammond, a great early admirer of Berigan, organized Berigan-led recording dates, starting in December 1935 under the name of Bunny Berigan and His Blue Boys. These performances are vintage Berigan. In pieces like *Chicken and Waffles* (a Berigan tune), *I'm Coming Virginia* (masterfully recorded many years earlier by Beiderbecke and Trumbauer), and *Blues*, we hear a Berigan in full command of every aspect of his playing. Whether it is the beautifully controlled low E♭s in *Blues*—a note below the orthodox range of the

---

26. See Chapter 7, Part 2, below.

trumpet—or the beautiful "shakes" on high B♭s (cleaner and more controlled than those of Armstrong), or the majestically rising figures of his second solo on *Blues* and, later, such marvelous little low-register double-time figures as in the eighth bar of his second chorus, it is pure creative playing where content and technique are inseparable, instanteously feeding on each other and issuing forth simultaneously. So assured and assertive is Berigan's playing on some of these sides—say, *Chicken and Waffles*—that I am tempted to call it "stride trumpet," with a respectful dual bow to its driving striding energy and to Berigan's funda-mentally traditional stance.

The year 1936 saw more Berigan-led record dates including his second re-cording of *I Can't Get Started*,[27] a new Vernon Duke song which Berigan had begun playing at the Famous Door on 52nd Street with a group titularly led by McKenzie and Eddie Condon. Although not as famous as its big-band sequel, recorded a year and a half later, it is nonetheless a beautiful performance, quite original in its design and proportions: eight bars of Berigan theme, a Berigan vocal, a trumpet cadenza, and the final majestic high-register peroration. Most of this material was reused in the famous 1937 version, partly verbatim, partly modified and expanded for a longer 12-inch disc performance, and becoming somwhow even more majestic in the process.

But the earlier sextet version has a pristine freshness and charm all its own. One of its most touching sequences is Berigan's vocal. He was not a singer, of course, but neither, strictly speaking, was Armstrong and a host of other trum-pet-playing Armstrong imitators. Berigan must have felt that he could do as well as any of them, and probably better than hundreds of "professional" singers and crooners. As it turned out, his superb musicianship and taste more than com-pensated for the lack of a trained or natural voice. One is surprised at first by the timbre of the voice, a light tenor quality in a baritone range. It is tender, soft-spoken, with a fast little vibrato that has its own peculiar attractiveness. Moreover his singing is relaxed and rhythmically free—like his middle register ballad trumpet-playing—and totally unpretentious. But I think what ultimately fascinates us, what enables us to hear this vocal rendition (and the later one, too) hundreds of times without tiring of it, is that Berigan's singing is a kind of window into his soul. The voice—particularly the "amateur" voice—is the most personal of all instruments, of course, and it is virtually impossible to hide any-thing behind it, for it exposes all. And what we hear in Berigan's voice—re-fracted through Vernon Duke's poignant melody and Ira Gershwin's bittersweet lyrics—is his human vulnerability, his frailty: I can't get started, indeed. One need not resort to amateur psychoanalyzing to hear in Berigan's singing—and often, for that matter, in his trumpet-playing—the hidden turmoil, the inner aches, the vulnerability that must have been at the root of the alcoholism that was to destroy him.

Equally as fetching—and a perfect instrumental complement to Berigan's vo-cal—is his 10-bar cadenza, an ingenious device to 1) dramatize by anticipation

27. The first recording of *I Can't Get Started* was made ten days earlier under Red McKenzie's leadership, in which Berigan was restricted to a straight (beautifully played) melodic statement.

the final climactic solo; and 2) to modulate via a cycle of fifths to the key of D♭, enabling Berigan to end the performance on his favorite high note, D♭. What is striking about the cadenza is that each of its five stations serves a different purpose and describes a different mood. In its concise and aphoristic way it is like a mini five-movement suite, each episode with its own character; similar to some of Anton Webern's miniature forms, where entire statements that took previous composers minutes to express are condensed into a few seconds (Ex. 20).

The first 2-bar segment establishes the overall tone of the cadenza: simple, affirmative, set in double-time, a device, of course, first used on the trumpet ten years earlier by Armstrong (*Potato Head Blues.*)

Ex. 20

The second stanza, in F, develops this basic gesture in an even more agile and rangy way. Indeed, Berigan is too generous: his second bar spills over into an additional beat, making an unexpected 5/4 bar and causing considerable confusion among the accompanying players.

The third episode, in B♭, brings sudden contrast. It is played in a slightly slower, more relaxed, hesitant tempo, and *piano*—but surprisingly with a touch of raspiness in the tone, as if in suppressed anger. The fourth strophe, in E♭ and in a middle dynamic, explores the trumpet's lowest register, ruminating in that slightly growly timbre that is characteristic of the instrument's nether range. Then suddenly, as if vanquishing all introversion and hesitancy, Berigan leaps up two octaves in the final episode, now in the key of A♭, in single-time, and in clear bell-like tones. The impact of these two final cadenza bars, leading as they do to the new key and Berigan's final in-tempo solo, is all the more dramatic for the controlled, contained manner of the four previous stanzas. It is a masterful and instinctive use of dynamics, of musical characterization, or harmonic progression—in short of drama, of musical story-telling. It probably couldn't have happened without Armstrong's *West End Blues* cadenza, but it was a noble first extension of it. In its emotional directness and lack of pretension, for all its formality, Berigan's cadenza is more than a bravura show piece; it partakes deeply of the essence of Berigan's star-crossed art.

Berigan's majestic final sixteen bars give the whole performance its climactic justification. And even here Berigan surprises us: whereas most trumpet players—even Armstrong, I think—having reached the pinnacle, would have remained at that level of intensity, Berigan gradually takes us down two octaves in a typical "unwinding" passage with a beautifully calibrated diminuendo, where he can then sing out Vernon Duke's song once more in his rich low-register. A return to the upper range and a final resonant high D♭ make as fully satisfying a conclusion to this remarkable performance as one can imagine.

A word must be said about the accompaniment: it is virtually perfect. For example, it is hard to imagine a more fitting accompaniment to Berigan's fragile singing than Artie Shaw's sympathetic clarinet obbligato fill-ins and Joe Bushkins's lacy webs of enveloping piano garlands. More like some great gypsy cimbalom player than a jazz pianist, Bushkin's sensitive backing of Berigan provides an ideal frame in which the singing is set. The same can be said about Mort Stuhlmaker's very special bowed-bass harmonic support. (He changes to pizzicato for Forrest Crawford's tenor solo and the final sixteen Berigan bars.)

But perhaps the biggest surprise on this and many of the other Berigan-led 1936 recordings is the excellent work of Forrest Crawford, an obscure tenor-man whose brief four-year career was cut short by tuberculosis, and of whose activities, after his physical recovery, nothing is known to me. Hear especially his solos on *Swing Mr. Charlie* and *Rhythm Saved the World*, with their full Hawkins-like sound and uncluttered direct expression.

Other Berigan recordings followed with some regularity now, sometimes accompanying Billie Holiday and other singers, sometimes under Berigan's own leadership. Some of these mid-1936 sides were uneven, a degree of uncertainty beginning to creep into Berigan's playing. Some were not much more than loosely strung together Dixieland-style performances, hardly a way to build a mid-thirties swing band. But conversely, Berigan's astonishing 4-bar modulating break on the November 23, 1936, recording of *That Foolish Feeling* is a marvel of musical and technical dexterity.

It was inevitable, given the magnitude of Berigan's reputation, that the next step would be the formation of a big swing band under his direction. The two months he spent with Dorsey in 1937 were intended to be the latter's "paternal" contribution to Berigan's training as a big-band leader. Unfortunately, Berigan was temperamentally unsuited to leading and drilling a band, being more intent on free-spirited playing and on expanding his consumption of alcohol. The band's initial dates and recordings were not too well received. And, in truth, it took the band several months and four record dates to find its musical footing. Although Berigan was mostly in fine form, the band itself was somewhat undisciplined, especially compared with such drilled-to-the-nines orchestras as Goodman's and Dorsey's. Berigan had no conception of how to create a distinctive orchestral style. Like Armstrong, he was merely interested in fronting a band, using it as a vehicle and a backdrop for his solo work. These early Berigan big-band recordings suffered from a stultifying lack of variety in regard to style and format. Moreover, the band had no other major soloists, with the result that arranger Joe Lippman found himself writing mostly ensemble work, rather unimaginative at that. The eighteen-year-old tenor saxophonist Georgie Auld was a peppy, irrepressibly ambitious player, but at this time his almost total adherence to Rudy Wiedoeft's anachronistic vertical staccato style was more an intrusion than an addition.

But by summer (of 1937) the band had lost some of its stiffness, was discovering the virtues of Fletcher Henderson's call-and-response patterns (as preached by Brother Benny Goodman), and above all was learning to capture an infectious light-hearted swing.

In the midst of this period of discovery Berigan decided to remake *I Can't Get Started*, backed by the full band now and expanded to the four-minutes-plus permitted by the 12-inch disc. Issued in the fall of 1937, it was an instant success—with everyone: the public, musicians, and critics.

As mentioned, the expanded version drew heavily upon the earlier arrangement. In fact, its last three segments—Berigan's vocal, the trumpet cadenza, and the finale—were more or less lifted intact with only minor changes. On the other hand, another cadenza was added, this time in free tempo on four sustained chords (C, B^7, Dm, G^7), serving as the introduction to the piece. Rather than seeming gratuitous or redundant, somehow it adds to the grandeur of this performance. Other additional touches are the contrastingly smooth saxophone ensemble, interlarded between Berigan's first theme statement and his vocal, and George Wettling's delicately fluttery brush work behind Berigan's singing, serving the same sympathetic, supportive, embellishing function as Shaw's clarinet and Bushkin's piano had in the earlier rendition.

By late 1937 the band was improving considerably, playing with more polish and swing, and two of its players emerging as much-needed soloistic counterweights to Berigan: trombonist Sonny Lee and the rapidly maturing Georgie Auld. Berigan's playing, although no longer entirely consistent, was often very strong and inspired. At times it became almost swaggeringly assertive—in a manner that the young Harry James, by then in Goodman's band, must have much admired. On other occasions Berigan displayed an almost eerie sense of drama and daring, floating in out of nowhere on high notes—as on *Miles Apart, The Wearin' of the Green*—causing one to think of a clarinet and indeed played with the ease of that instrument. Other solos—like the one on *I Cried for You*—were remarkable for their uncanny ability to combine utterly logical structuring with unexpected surprises. And a fine example of the band's expressive range can be heard on *Jelly Roll Blues*, right after Berigan's solo, in an ensemble passage that sings and throbs in a moving way that many swing bands had by 1938 for the most part already forgotten (or perhaps never learned).

A curious episode in the Berigan band's history is the series of recordings in late 1938 of a suite of Bix Beiderbecke compositions. This was an unusual departure for Berigan in that performing Bix's piano pieces meant transcribing them for instruments and performing them more or less *as composed*. This was a concept of jazz-as-composition and jazz-as-repertory that was far ahead of its time and antithetical to most jazz musicians' views then and, alas, even now. On the other hand, jazz in the form of miniature compositions, especially with catchy nonsense titles, was very much in the air in 1938, especially after the success of Raymond Scott's Quintette with *Minuet in Jazz, Reckless Night on Board an Ocean Liner*, and a dozen other such titles. The trend went all the way back to Red Norvo's remarkable *Dance of the Octopus* of 1933[28] (from a session on which he also recorded Beiderbecke's *In a Mist* on marimba).

Berigan's experiment with Bix's compositions was at best a modest success. Although sensitively transcribed by Bunny's arranger Joe Lippman, the performances the pieces received were mostly pallid and rhythmically mechanical. Beiderbecke's complex, constantly shifting chromatic harmonies need to be fully, i.e. vertically, *heard* by *every* member of an ensemble, when played in instrumental transcription. They do not survive well in a superficial, merely *linear* part-by-part rendering. Moreover the musicians, except for Berigan, seemed to be intimidated by the music—the old problem of trying to get jazz musicians to play slightly unorthodox written parts with the same freedom and drive with which they improvise. That it could be done, even then, was ably demonstrated by Berigan, who was the only one who *felt* the music and played it with the appropriate relaxed swing. It is interesting, however, that Berigan, such a dynamic soloist, was content with a subsidiary ensemble role in these performances.

Another composer in whom Berigan was interested was Juan Tizol. He performed not only the latter's *Caravan* many times, but also Tizol's much less known *Night Song* (written for Cootie Williams and recorded by him and Charlie Barnet, but never by Ellington). *Night Song*, a haunting linear theme out of

28. See discussion of this in Part 2 of this chapter.

Tizol's *Caravan* and *Pyramid* mold, was recorded by Berigan late in 1939, by which time his playing was beginning to deteriorate noticeably. Missed notes were more frequent; intonation and pitch were becoming unsteady; and his vibrato, formerly so pure and controlled, was turning loose and wide, like that of an aged opera singer. Playing Tizol's theme in the highest register with a cup mute, notorious for its distortion of intonation, didn't help matters. That Berigan was, however, not out of commission yet was clear from his very next take, *Ain't She Sweet*, where he was his old self: fluent, swinging, self-assured, ideas and phrases flowing out with sovereign ease.

It was around this time that Berigan declared financial bankruptcy. (It is said that he even lacked the forty dollars needed to *file* bankruptcy papers.) His heavy drinking habits had not only undermined his health—he landed in the hospital in December 1939 in a totally exhausted state—but his reputation as a leader, to such an extent that clubs and bookers were increasingly reluctant to engage Berigan, for they realized that there was very little chance of his appearing on time and sober. On several occasions Berigan had fallen off the bandstand or the stage, one time landing in an orchestra pit with a broken foot and a broad feeling-no-pain smile on his face. As bookings became scarce, Berigan was unable to meet his payroll—when the band broke up, his musicians hadn't been paid in six weeks—and his best men began to desert him. A short stint with Dorsey in 1940 tided him over the spring and summer of that year. Undaunted, he organized another band in September and took to the road in endless one-nighters. But like one of the songs Berigan recorded with Dorsey had said: *This Is the Beginning of the End*.

Berigan and his band, with ever changing line-ups, hobbled along for another year and a half, recording eight sides for the obscure Elite label. Though not in anyway distinctive, the band played its typical swing era charts reasonably well; and as *Skylark*, for example, shows, Berigan could still, on occasion, produce beautifully constructed, highly musical results. But at the same time one can hear the strain in his playing, especially in the upper register. He sounds tired and cautious, his former daring replaced by a wary conservatism, knowing deep down that the physical playing apparatus could no longer be counted on to respond to more spectacular ideas.

Berigan died in a New York hospital on June 2, 1942, with Tommy Dorsey at his bedside. The official cause of death was cirrhosis of the liver. That is how jazz lost one of its greatest story-tellers.

PART 2

ART TATUM

In the long history and development of jazz rarely has a major figure been surrounded by as much controversy as pianist Art Tatum, Jr. While he was deified by his fellow musicians, canonized by most critics and historians—becoming virtually a legend in his own lifetime—Tatum was also the subject of considerable negative criticism, especially in his later years and after his death in 1956. The irony in that is, of course, that Tatum produced his finest and most mature work in his later years.

Whatever the relative merits of these judgments, I believe the divergence of opinion regarding Tatum is also rooted in the uniqueness and solitary nature of his art. Tatum never fitted easily into any of the stylistic slots, as they evolved or were labeled. In a large measure Tatum's art and his career developed parallel to but not really as a part of the jazz mainstream, whether in the thirties during the Swing Era or in later years when bop and modern jazz had evolved as the prevailing styles. For Tatum was artistically a loner, not only in the sense that he spent the major part of his career as a solitary soloist—he performed in ensembles only intermittently and, indeed, seemed more comfortable as a solo player—but also in the sense that he always stood apart from any major stylistic trends. He did not care to follow the dominant styles around him; and while universally admired by musicians, especially other pianists, very few were able or inclined to emulate him. This peculiar isolation has made it virtually impossible to categorize Tatum, and in turn this has made him vulnerable to "criticism" by those who require everything in jazz to fit neatly into definable classifications.

In a way the Tatum controversy revolves around whether he merely stood *aside* from major jazz developments or was all his life actually *above* them. Clearly, his influence in creative terms—and to a large extent even in pianistic-technical terms—was modest. Either musicians were so awed by his prodigious talent that it seemed impossible to emulate him—many were tempted to give up music altogether rather than contemplate such a challenge[1]—or they simply did not regard him as a strong stylistic leader. Insofar as one *can* speak of a Tatum influence, it was usually indirect and stylistically/technically once removed. In a sense Tatum's art was inimitable—except by reduction of its very essence, a fact borne out by thousands of imitative cocktail pianists, playing a much simplified Tatum style.

On one point there is universal agreement: Tatum's awesome technique. But his complete digital mastery of the keyboard—despite the fact that he was 85 percent blind—may also have been his Achilles' heel. For much of what is flawed or of lesser creativity in Tatum's work can be directly related to his extraordinary technical facility. In the earlier part of his career he could rarely tame his nimble fingers and alacritous mind to embrace the simple rather than the dense and garrulous. His was a profuse art, so abundant that its problems were not, as with most players, how to attain greater technical control of his materials but, rather, how to channel his superior gifts into a more deeply expressive and creatively more original language—challenges which, if his career is seen in the long view, he really did not entirely meet, at least in the sense

---

1. Rex Stewart wrote, in recalling his hearing Tatum for the first time (in 1926), that he seriously "toyed with the idea of giving up my horn." Even the great Earl Hines, in matters technical surely Tatum's equal, confessed that he never wanted to tangle with Tatum at after-hours sessions or parties, and all his life avoided an encounter with him.

and the degree that an Armstrong or a Parker did. In the end, for all its brilliance, Tatum's art—craft is perhaps a more apt term—remains eclectic, largely predictable, and surface—of a high order, to be sure, but not one that *compels* others to follow. One could admire Tatum, adulate him, marvel at the technical mastery with which he endowed his musical concepts, but one was not necessarily inclined to follow in his footsteps.

Some did, of course: Coleman Hawkins in his formative years, Oscar Peterson and Milt Jackson in our time. During the thirties and forties a string of "little Tatums" appeared among pianists, but all were definitely inferior, either lacking Tatum's technical proficiency or unable to develop artistically beyond his level, in the sense that Oscar Peterson, for example, *has* been able to do.

The paradox is that Tatum was touched by genius, which manifested itself early on in his career more or less full-blown. We can hear it on his first recordings in 1932 and, judging by accounts of fellow musicians like Rex Stewart, Teddy Wilson, Duke Ellington, and Benny Carter, it was evident much earlier, in the mid-1920s when Tatum was still in his mid-teens. What seems to have been in place from the outset were Tatum's prodigious manual skills and an uncanny ear for adventurous harmonizations, both of these talents much aided and abetted by extremely large hands that could roam over the entire keyboard with ease and span enormous chords not within the reach of most other pianists. Tenths, even twelfths in either the left or right hand, were easy for him, even when filled in with one or two other notes.[2] It was his penchant for chromaticism and extravagant harmonizations that led him generally to shun pieces with simple changes, including the blues (which he played but only sporadically).[3] He much preferred harmonically more complex tunes, and even in such cases did not hesitate to embroider these with "advanced" substitute chords or sometimes even entire substitute progressions.

In these two respects — his incredible speed (all the more remarkable since Tatum was virtually blind, having been born with only partial vision in one eye) and his astonishing harmonic inventiveness — as well as his impatience with the simple, his general creative restlessness, Tatum was much like Earl Hines, who, by the way, also shunned the blues. Hines, who was Tatum's elder by four years, must certainly have impressed Tatum as a youngster, and undoubtedly even influenced him in some secondary ways. But such influence, I suspect, manifested itself more in the form of encouragement and confirmation, for Ta-

---

2. Such chords as or were easy for him to reach, even a whole series of such chords in a relatively fast tempo. Tatum could also do things like trilling with the thumb and forefinger while stretching an octave with his little finger: . This explains how, for example, on *Tea for Two* he could play a tenor counterline in whole or half notes and still keep a semblance of stride going by pumping out bass notes more than an octave lower.

3. In his entire recording career Tatum recorded only a dozen blues, and, except for *St. Louis Blues*, they never were a regular part of his repertory.

tum's technical skills were then already equal to Hines's and, in any case, too similar to offer him either major revelations or inspirations. Rather, Tatum's initial stylistic and creative impulses came from Fats Waller and James P. Johnson, whose early 1920s' piano rolls he memorized and studied.

But another large part of the artistic mix that characterized Tatum's playing had its roots in classical music, which, he formally studied for about six or seven years at various schools in his hometown of Toledo and in Columbus, Ohio. In fact, at least one of his teachers felt that Tatum had in him the makings for a classical career. But this was an ambition not granted black musicians in the twenties and thirties. Nonetheless, Tatum's study of classical literature, particularly that of the eighteenth- and nineteenth-century piano classics from Bach to Chopin and Liszt, left an indelible mark on his playing both technically and stylistically. We learn with interest that Tatum's pianistic skills were much admired by certain renowned classical pianists, Leopold Godowsky and Sergei Rachmaninov among them.[4] This led many of Tatum's more enthusiastic fans to propagate the notion that he was technically superior to the classical keyboard virtuosi of his time. They didn't know that the entire range of Tatum's virtuosic skills, including his lightning-fast arpeggios and runs, are set forth in the middle-to-late nineteenth-century piano literature from Chopin and Liszt to Ravel. Indeed they originated with those composers and other virtuoso pianist-composers like Saint-Saëns, Litolff, Scharwenka, Moskowski, and Albeniz. It is simply untrue that Tatum created his arabesque virtuoso technique out of the blue, and that he was therefore somehow technically superior to his classical brethren. On the contrary, he acquired these skills precisely from the classical literature, albeit at a level of perfection that no black or jazz pianist (except possibly Earl Hines) had ever achieved before. He then transferred this dazzling technical equipment to the field of jazz, originally applying much of it directly and quite unchanged.

Tatum's immersion in classical literature, I believe, also left its mark on his rhythmic language, especially in the early years. Tatum's time was certainly precise, controlled. But it was, in its early stages, also rather too subtle and surfacy to elicit the toe-tapping, finger-snapping beat that a Basie could generate, for example. His playing centered then much more on harmonic elements, allowing rhythm, swing, beat to play a secondary role. His classical training may also explain why Tatum had such a highly developed penchant for out-of-tempo (free-tempo) improvisations. All of this is not to say that Tatum couldn't swing. There is plenty of evidence he could—listen to Tatum on *Mop Mop* and *Esquire*

---

4. However, the long-held myth that Vladimir Horowitz was an ardent admirer of Tatum seems to have no basis in fact. (See the introductory foreword on Tatum to Time-Life's *Giants of Jazz*.) I suspect, moreover, that those classical artists who admired Tatum did so in the generally patronizing way that classical musicians have traditionally viewed black and/or jazz artists, not to mention blind ones. Black musicians earned renowned white classical musicians' admiration only when they were perceived as emulating classical standards and properties.

It is interesting that Tatum's technique was admired by classical musicians in the 1930s and 1940s clearly for its classical leanings and technical perfection, qualities they could relate to. But where were the classical admirers of Thelonious Monk's or Pete Johnson's more "unorthodox" and intrinsically jazz-rooted techniques?

Bounce or *I Cover The Waterfront* (from 1943 and 1955, respectively). It is to suggest, however, that swinging was generally not Tatum's primary concern.

Nor was Tatum an outstanding melodist, as one might speak of Lester Young or Charlie Parker or Thelonious Monk. Tatum's spectacular right hand, while never at a loss for the next note, only rarely could be restrained to state simple themes or motives, at least until his later years. It seemed always in need of exploding into cascading runs and arpeggios, into careening arabesques. What little original truly melodic material might rise to the surface of his performances was more often than not merely the upper lines of the harmonies, rather than intrinsically melodic material. This lack of a personal melodic gift—combined with his restless facility, and unquenchable desire to compress musical ideas, to cram more into a 2- or 4-bar phrase than it could rightly hold—also led Tatum to indulge in an inordinate amount of melodic quotation, most of it classical or at least non-jazz in origin.

To understand Tatum and to retain a balanced view of his achievements, we must remember that he was not a composer, certainly not in the sense that Ellington or Monk were, and, as I have suggested earlier, not even in the sense that Armstrong or Young might be called composers, i.e. creative *improvising* composers. Nor could one think of Tatum as an arranger, even in that special sense that one might call Morton an "arranger" for the piano. One *can* think of Tatum primarily as a re-harmonizer of other composers' popular songs and show tunes. In that role he was brilliant, for he frequently improved upon even fine composers like Gershwin or Rodgers or Berlin. But such a function does not require enormous original creativity, or any remarkable melodic gift. The melodies, the tunes, the themes were always already there, waiting for Tatum to ornament them, reconstruct them, dissect them, elaborate them. As mentioned, it seems to me that "craft" might be a more apt term for such a process than "art."

And this special but limited talent of Tatum's does raise the question of his originality as an artist. To begin with, Tatum never had to create the basic material with which he worked, namely, American popular songs. He simply appropriated that which already existed and elaborated upon it. Second, Tatum cannot be said to be original in the sense of creating new forms of expression, certainly not in the realm of melody or rhythm, and not even in that of harmony—his best suit—since all those spicy harmonies and substitute changes he featured so effectively were already an integral part of the late nineteenth- early twentieth-century classical vocabulary, most especially that of Ravel and Debussy, but also, less obviously, that of such minor but extremely popular composers of the 1920s and 1930s as Cyril Scott, Christian Sinding, Ethelbert Nevin, Charles W. Cadman, Percy Grainger, Eastwood Lane, and Zez Confrey, all of whose works were regularly published for decades in the enormously successful music magazine *Etude*.[5] And, of course, composers and arrangers much closer to Tatum's chosen field, like Ellington, Ferde Grofé, and William Grant Still,

---

5. It is very difficult to gain an idea today of the immense influence *Etude* exerted in America in the early (especially the pre-electronic) decades of our century. Much of its popularity rested on the publication each issue, as a centerfold insert, of some popular or relatively accessible classical piano piece or song, by composers such as those mentioned above.

were also fluently versant in this harmonic vocabulary. What *can* be said is that, along with these last-named, Tatum brought such "advanced" harmonies into *jazz* and made them one of the two most salient and consistent features of his style—not just an occasional touch of harmonic spice.

Third, Tatum's "originality" was undercut by the redundacy with which he used certain harmonic and ornamental devices, and by the fact that he was not truly speaking an improviser. Tatum, far more often than not, worked out his "improvisations" and, except for occasional minor variants, played them virtually the same way over long periods of time. Generally, he did make them sound as if they were improvised, and the average listener would probably not have been able to detect whether they actually were or not. But, as I have already suggested elsewhere, not only is this also true of numerous other major jazz artists—like Lawrence Brown, Coleman Hawkins, even Louis Armstrong, to name only a few—but all really fine classical artists also make the composed music they perform sound spontaneous, as if they were improvising it.

Form was another problem for Tatum. Incapable of approaching form and continuity creatively with a composer's inventiveness, and being unable in any other way to vary spontaneously the form of his performances, Tatum became almost totally locked into an ABA format of out-of-tempo/in-tempo/out-of-tempo sequencing. The only variant of that pattern was sometimes to eliminate the introductory out-of-tempo section and begin immediately in-tempo, especially when he was performing in a trio context. Unfortunately the routinization of larger formal aspects led Tatum in turn to favor patterned and predictable solutions in the smaller formal realm. Invariably, for example, seventh and eighth bars of 8-bar phrases were filled out by some glittering descending run. Or invariably, opening free sections would be set in relatively (for Tatum) relaxed open-spaced timing, whereas closing free sections were almost always compressed in time, rushed through as if the piece had to be gotten through by some imaginary imminent deadline. This was as true in concerts as in the recording studio.

In this connection it must be said, however, that, once recording tape and the LP had been invented—and Norman Granz had the wisdom to let Tatum loose, unfettered, in the recording studio—Tatum's forms and continuity freed up considerably. Tatum suffered from the limitation imposed by the 10-inch three-minute-plus record of the early decades of jazz (in a way that Duke Ellington, for example, did not—for Ellington found ways to overcome or work creatively within these limits). The long-playing record released Tatum from those particular restrictions, enough so that his playing on records then approximated much more his in-concert performing and his even freer after-hours private-party playing, which was universally considered his best playing. In short, a large measure of Tatum's performing concepts relied on European concert traditions: existing compositions—popular songs in his case—which he could "re-compose" and elaborate; a European-based harmonic vocabulary; preset forms or outlines; and an array of standard pianistic devices, rather than intuitive improvisations—all these to allow him to retain full control over his performances.

Tatum's recorded output is, of course, immense—in a twenty-three-year period some nearly four hundred titles (if we include private and air-check record-ings issued on LP)—and it is neither practical nor necessary to comment on most of these. It will suffice to trace Tatum's development in its broadest out-lines, recognizing at the outset that almost everyone of Tatum's performances is from a pianistic-technical point of view a marvel of perfection. Indeed, if there is anyone reading this book who has not heard a Tatum recording, I would encourage him or her to do so forthwith. For his playing must be heard to be believed, and in its technical perfection it is something beyond verbal descrip-tion, at least this author's verbal capacities. The note-perfect clarity of Tatum's runs, the hardly believable leaps to the outer registers of the piano (he is not known ever to have missed one), his deep-in-the-keys full piano sonority, the tone and touch control in pyrotechnical passages clearly beyond the abilities of the vast majority of pianists to merely render the notes in some nominal way—these are miracles of performance which must be appreciated aurally.

It is ironic that Tatum's public popularity was tied to two of his least achieve-ments: on the one hand, his early rather mechanical preset show-piece style (as in *Tiger Rag, Tea for Two*), and on the other hand, his 1940s' trio work. Tatum was above all a soloist. He found ensemble playing confining and often rode rough-shod over other players, wrestling them to the ground with a barrage of technique or, worse yet, seemingly not even recognizing their presence at all. (Listen to Tatum's 1937 recordings with his Swingsters band—actually a Les Hite unit—where poor Lloyd Reese and Marshall Royal are constantly being swamped by Tatum.) He was an "orchestral" pianist; that is to say, he delighted in emulating an entire orchestra on the piano and had the technique to carry it off. He could manage melody, a full range of harmony, bass lines, and rhythm, all simultaneously, emphasizing a full orchestral ensemble sound rather than any individual orchestral colors or timbres. One can then imagine how confin-ing he must have found functioning in an ensemble as, say, only "the pianist" (although he did so brilliantly on the famous 1943 Leonard Feather All Stars Commodore recordings).

Tatum's earliest work has been likened to Fats Waller's; and unquestionably the latter's influence was very strong. But this is discernible primarily in his ballad and popular song renditions which formed the nucleus of his repertory. In stan-dard show pieces like *Tiger Rag* (which Jelly Roll Morton had already turned into a solo virtuoso display piece decades earlier) Tatum relied much more on the hybrid late-ragtime/early-stride/novelty-piano style of, say, Zez Confrey (of *Dizzy Fingers* and *Kitten on the Keys* fame). All three were virtuoso fast-tempo styles ideally suited to Tatum's technical capacities. *Tiger Rag* had been for many years one of his party show-off pieces, and it remained in his repertory more or less in the same format and style for about two decades. That he, too, could have technical problems is shown by his debut in the recording studio—a 1932 recording of *Tiger Rag* which has only recently come to light—in which there are a number of note and rhythmic stumbles, mishaps that were eliminated by the time he re-recorded the piece in 1933. This time, instead of remaining unissued, his performance became a minor hit. Played at a dazzling tempo of around 376 for the quarter note, the beat, that is,[6] with the right hand flying along in eighth notes (sic!) most of the time—and all this by someone known to be virtually blind—the recording of this most popular of numbers was bound to impress an incredulous public, which hardly noticed that the performance was otherwise thin in musical substance. It was a sensational pianistic acrobatic act, and its thrills were just about as ephemeral.

In the 1933 *Tea for Two*, the first of a half a dozen Tatum recordings of this tune, he is in a more spontaneous, less acrobatic form. Even though the performance is replete with Tatum's patented runs and arpeggios, and is in point of fact rather cluttered in its constant effects, it somehow manages to accommodate all this in a typical Waller setting. Even the tempo is unusually relaxed for Tatum, falling into that easy gait that Waller favored so much of the time, and generally striking a happy, carefree mood that perfectly fits Youmans's tune. *Tea for Two*'s ingenious modulations fascinated Tatum, as did the highly chromatic changes of Ellington's *Sophisticated Lady*. But here Tatum's 1933 recording, one of the earliest besides Ellington's own, shows clearly the conflict constant in Tatum's early playing between technique and content, between essence and manner, between substance and ornament. As richly harmonic and chromatic as Ellington's song already is, Tatum could not leave it alone. He loads even more extravagant chromaticisms and chord substitutions onto it and overembroiders Ellington's melody with so many high-register besequined runs and double-time intrusions that Ellington's suavely elegant Lady becomes a garrulous over-dressed flapper.

By the late 1930s Tatum's playing had settled in, gaining in poise and simplicity of expression. A new confidence and control of his materials can be heard in pieces like *Gone with the Wind* or *Stormy Weather* (both from late 1937), although this seems to have been also accompanied by a certain loss in rhythmic drive, audible in his more youthful performances. Both tracks have their explorative moments: *Gone* in a fetching advanced bitonal passage; *Stormy* with a series of expressive blues-ish passages (Ex. 1 and 2).

Ex. 1

6. That beat is comparable to playing sixteenth notes at the medium tempo of ♩ = 94.

Ex. 2

Like Coleman Hawkins, Tatum was an avid listener and absorber, not only in response to a burning desire to learn and grow, but more specifically as a means of keeping tabs on his competitors. And like Hawkins, he was not above integrating another's successful style into his own playing. By 1939, for example, in an attempt—unconscious perhaps—to refine and simplify his style further, he played much more in a Teddy Wilson vein. Wilson had, of course, himself been influenced by Tatum years earlier when he first ran into him in Toledo. Not gifted with Tatum's incredible technique—nor even quite with Hines's, another influence on him—Wilson evolved a simplified fusion of both pianists' more florid and energetic styles, one more readily suited to ensemble playing, in which Wilson excelled, and through which, especially in the Goodman Trio and Quartet and his own small band recordings (many of them accompanying Billie Holiday), Wilson gained a sizable reputation, greater in fact than Tatum's.

Over the Rainbow (1939) is quintessential Tatum from this period (and the Wilson leanings are momentarily less obvious). Set in his favorite free-strict-free format, it features a fine array of scintillating runs and extravagant short-term modulations, which always end precisely on target where and when they are supposed to. The third and fourth bars of the bridge (Ex. 3a) are particularly noteworthy as harmonic variations, increasingly explorative with each return of this section. (One should note, too, how Tatum uses the theme of this bridge as a turn-back phrase in the last "eight" of the second chorus.) Even more adventurous are some of Tatum's single-note lines in the second chorus, pre-bop in their harmonic implications and twisting shapes (Ex. 36). (Nat King Cole was to appropriate some of these lines a few years hence, making them an essential ingredient of his style.)

Over the Rainbow shows a new unity of conception and warmth of expression that bespeaks the mature Tatum of later years. But unfortunately at the very end the mood is shattered by a rather hysterical telescoping of the final ten bars of the song. Tatum gobbles up these chords and measures at breakneck speed, spewing them out in nine seconds flat (instead of the twenty-six they would have taken at his previously established tempo).

Ex. 3a

Ex. 3b

It was during this period, too, that Tatum attracted wide attention with his renditions of "light classics," like Dvořák's *Humoresque*, Massenet's *Élégie*, and yet another pyrotechnical version of *Tiger Rag*.[7] These light-classic offerings, all pre-set in what amounted to re-arrangements, involving a diffusion of their original charm and sentimental values, were creatively on a par with the ever-increasing and irritating use of interpolated quotations. What, after all, has the *Stars and Stripes* to do with Massenet's *Élégie*? Or what are Irish jigs doing in (supposedly) jazz performances? The point, of course, is that these particular Tatum creations were hardly jazz at all, But a gullible public, once again, fell for the irresistible notion of "jazzing the classics."[8]

Equally disappointing are Tatum's (one supposes) intended tributes to Hines, with the latter's song *Rosetta* and his big 1940 hit recording of the *St. Louis*

7. This time, pushing the tempo even beyond his earlier recordings to around ♩= 398, even Tatum could not entirely stay the course, having trouble with a number of dizzying passages.
8. It is strange—and a pity—that Tatum never saw fit to perform or record more jazz-related compositions, like Beiderbecke's *In a Mist* or Red Norvo's *Dance of the Octopus*—or some of Ellington's instrumental compositions.

Blues in boogie-woogie style. The latter Tatum performance unfortunately barely rises above plagiarism; while in the former Tatum all but smothers the gentle beauty of Hines's tune.

With the white public's discovery of boogie-woogie and sanitized versions of barrelhouse piano in the late thirties and early forties (these based, of course, on the standard blues changes), Tatum also turned somewhat more frequently to the blues. His *Wee Baby Blues, Last Goodbye Blues, Battery Bounce* (two of these tracks featured blues singer Joe Turner) with a six-piece band, showed that Tatum *could* simplify and deepen the expression of his playing when he cared to. Indeed, his performances here seem to pay tribute to the superb Kansas City blues pianist Pete Johnson (also co-composer of two of these pieces), the ultimate master of a style that balanced fantastical right-hand embroideries with the depth and down-to-earth power of Southwestern blues.

Although Tatum here moved somewhat closer to the central jazz tradition, the distance he still needed to cover can be measured by comparing his playing with that of the fine trumpeter Joe Thomas (out of the St. Louis brass blues school). Hear the contrast especially in relation to Thomas's superb solo on *Stompin' at the Savoy*, also recorded on this Tatum-Turner date.

A second session six months later (in June 1941) seems to have moved Tatum even further towards the mainstream, at least temporarily. *Rock Me Mama* and *Lonesome Graveyard*, again with Joe Thomas's rich blues trumpet, feature a number of moving Tatum solos, all the more expressive for the radiant beauty of his tone. In one section of *Rock Me Mama* the usually irrepressible Tatum even lays out completely. At the same time he seems no less inventive harmonically when given the opportunity. In *Lonesome Graveyard*, for example, Tatum pits some astonishing, gently clashing bitonal harmonies against Oscar Moore's guitar (Ex. 4) in what was undoubtedly meant to be the latter's solo chorus, but which Tatum deftly turned into a fascinating piano-guitar duet.[9]

A moving Tatum performance of Ethelbert Nevin's sentimental ballad *Mighty Lak' a Rose*, privately recorded in July 1941 by Jerry Newman, gives us a glimpse of the after-hours Tatum. Recorded with Newman's portable equipment in a Harlem club called The Gee Haw Stables (which *opened* when most after-hours places were finally closing), Tatum is in one of his mellowest, most laid-back moods. Indeed his free-time opening chorus is so generously paced, the time frame is so stretched out, that one is instantly reminded of Monk's suspended-time improvisations of the mid-fifties, say, his remarkable *I Should Care*. (It doesn't seem unthinkable that the young composer of *'Round About Midnight*, a regular denizen of Harlem after-hours places, would have heard Tatum on many a night 'round about 7:00 a.m.) Tatum is apparently in a ruminating and experimental frame of mind. He literally teases the harmonies to death, pulling and yanking them to and fro like a playful cat with an overly resistant mouse. At one point he seems unable (or unwilling?) to resolve a particularly recalcitrant atonal chord—and leaves it unresolved (Ex. 5). In another passage (Ex. 6a), just

9. Moore was Nat Cole's trio guitarist between 1939 and 1947, the perfect harmonic foil for Cole's Tatum-influenced lyric variation style. (See Chapter 9.)

Ex. 4

Ex. 5

Ex. 6

before he launches into the fast in-tempo section, Tatum offers us one of those hobbling descending whole-tone runs that have long ago become associated with Monk. Thereafter Tatum suddenly quotes *My Old Kentucky Home* (Ex. 6b), at the same time stumbling onto the most amazing chord sequence, far removed from the song's simple original changes.

These recordings by Newman also captured Tatum in some surprisingly poignant blues singing (especially on *Toledo Blues*). Spontaneously improvised— and now far removed from the formality of the European concert hall to which he generally adhered—Tatum is singing, in a night-weary, sleepy, slurry voice, of lost love and sexual innuendos which would have shocked (and repelled) those "fans" who admired Tatum for his musical discipline and "classical" propriety.

It is during this period that Tatum, always known and admired for his refined piano touch, began to develop a much harder, at times almost ferocious attack, much more suited to swing than his genteel earlier approach, and a style later much emulated by Oscar Peterson, Tatum's most ardent disciple. This more aggressive Tatum can be heard to good advantage on a 1941 *Body and Soul* and *There'll Be Some Changes Made* (recorded by Newman and released on the Onyx label).

In this same period Tatum also developed a propensity for longer lines and more continuous phrases. Though he had always had the technique and the ear for extended structures, somehow he preferred short contrasting phrase exchanges between, say, two bars of a paraphrased melody statement, alternating with two bars of runs or arpeggios. The binary structuring of most 32-bar songs, of course, lent itself readily to such phrase subdivisions. Indeed, the majority of popular songs from the twenties through the early forties generally fall into a pattern of two bars of relatively active melodic movement followed by two bars of more stationary character, four of these 2-bar sets making the standard 8-bar phrase. It is those stationary two bars which Tatum loved to fill out with his spectacular runs. But in the forties we hear him beginning to expand such runs not only to lengths of eight, ten, even fourteen bars but also crossing over the natural boundaries between the 8-bar phrase segments. One such 12-bar dazzler occurs in Tatum's *Lady Be Good*, recorded with trumpeter Frankie Newton in September 1941 (again on a private recording by Newman); another one of ten bars on the Leonard Feather–Coleman Hawkins 1943 date for Commodore; a full 16-bar run in his 1945 recording of Rudolf Friml's popular *Song of the Vagabonds*.

The Commodore Esquire All Stars date was the first time Tatum and Hawkins had worked together, at least formally on records. I have mentioned that Hawkins listened carefully to Tatum and found confirmation for his own playing in Tatum's remarkable harmonic ear and chord-conscious style. During his years in Europe, Hawkins had enlarged and perfected his conception, and in his 1939 *Body and Soul* recording had even created a major triumph of melodic invention and variation technique—something Tatum had not yet achieved at that level. Here they were now on the same recording session, masters of harmonic manipulation and a challenge to each other. With Cootie Williams and Edmond Hall

also aboard, backed by a stellar rhythm section of Al Casey (guitar), Oscar Pettiford (bass), and Sidney Catlett (drums), the recording session was bound to hold
high promise. Tatum was certainly on his best behavior, fulfilling his function
as sideman and occasional soloist brilliantly. His work here, in this embryo-bop
setting, succeeds in being both basic Tatum (albeit leaning in the Teddy Wilson
direction) and linear near-bop. The strong rhythm section, particularly Pettiford's vigorous bass walking, spurred Tatum on to some of his most swinging
playing.

Still I find the date as a whole an oddity. For me (except for *Esquire Blues*)
Hawkins's leonine, overheated playing is incompatible with either Tatum's nimble-
fingered, poised playing or Cootie's superb blues-tinged wailing trumpet, not to
mention Hall's raspy, almost "obscene" clarinet. This curious mélange—typical
of so many "All-Star" recording sessions—almost works, but not quite. To the
extent it succeeds, it does so largely because of the rhythm section, including
Tatum, somehow holding the diverse strands of musical styles together.

In early 1944, Tatum formed a trio with the guitarist Tiny Grimes and bassist
Slam Stewart, which was soon to bring him his greatest public success thus far.
But as is so often the case, that which is popular is not necessarily of the highest
artistic order. Many of the trio's recordings are flawed and except for Tatum's
own playing do not even measure up as trio/ensemble performances to the best
work of the Nat "King" Cole or Clarence Profit trios.[10] Although a fine technician with the bow—still a rarity in those days in jazz—Stewart's solos were here
rhythmically rather stiff, melodically simple-minded, and invariably overloaded
with corny quotations, much less promising than his earlier work with Slim
Gaillard. Grimes improved through the year he stayed with Tatum, but in the
early trio recordings as a neophyte guitarist he was quite limited, technically and
creatively.

Tatum himself confined his playing to a much simplified style, limiting particularly his harmonic imagination. Moreover, most of the trio's repertory was
pre-arranged, leaving very little room for real improvisation, with the result that
most of its recordings have a calculated feeling. They remind us of a kind of
musical façade with not very much depth behind it.

Nevertheless, for less critical ears, bedazzled by Tatum's virtuosity, the trio
was a considerable commercial success. It spawned in turn a number of similar
units, partially or wholly influenced by its style and format, most notably Lennie
Tristano's trio of 1946—hear the relationship in Tatum's *Body and Soul* and
Cocktails for Two, particularly in the more contrapuntal passages between piano

---

10. The Clarence Profit Trio (1937–44) recorded only a dozen or so sides in 1939 and 1940. It was
an eclectic, versatile group which played well-rehearsed, somewhat prim arrangements, featuring the
leader's elegant finely textured piano and guitarist Billy Moore's curious amalgam of Hawaiian guitar
and Django Reinhardt. Their recordings were somewhat more commercially oriented than their club
appearances, and in pieces like *Dark Eyes* and Ellington's *Azure* they distanced themselves rather
considerably from jazz. But at its best—the earlier recordings provide a glimpse of this—this pioneer
trio (along with the Nat "King" Cole Trio) became one of the earliest models for dozens of similar
groups flourishing during the 1940s.

and guitar—and Oscar Peterson's trio (especially in the early pre-U.S. Canadian years).[11] The seeds of not only the Peterson trio's style and its arrangements, right down to specific musical ideas and devices, but also Peterson's piano style in general, can be heard quite plainly on such Tatum trio recordings as *Flying Home*, *I Got Rhythm*, and *Exactly Like You*. The last, a tour de force performance recorded privately in a Milwaukee club (and issued, in part, by the Smithsonian Institution on an album devoted to Art Tatum, called *Pieces of Eight*), sports another one of those afore-mentioned long-line runs, this time an *entire chorus* of virtually straight eighth-note (or eighth-note triplet) motion. This more linear type of invention, not accompanied moreover in this case by Tatum's usual stride left hand, comes quite close to the kind of modern jazz conception then emerging with the younger players like Peterson, and Bud Powell.

Tatum's playing on *Exactly* wasn't quite bebop, for it was still too chord-conscious, given half the time to harmonic arpeggios and thus more ornamental than purely linear/melodic. These arpeggios, especially in the second solo of this cut, were harmonically quite advanced, often related bitonally to the underlying changes (see mm. 6–9 in Ex. 7), thus using the kind of oblique substitutions that musicians like Monk and Eric Dolphy were to develop into a whole new language years later. Again the allusion to bop is tempting to make, but Tatum's at-right-angles harmonies were still firmly anchored to their bass roots, i.e. not really free to develop quasi-independent lines. They were still once-removed from the new bop vocabulary, and the young boppers knew it. They pretty much ignored Tatum, for they sensed (correctly) that he was really not one of them.

It is significant that Tatum did not pursue the more modern direction assayed in *Exactly Like You*. The point needs also to be made that Tatum did not venture into quite such treacherous harmonic waters on any of his commercial records of the time. It may well be that he felt, as he expressed it on several occasions, that audiences would not be able to follow him that "far out." But that again differentiated him from the boppers. They *did* venture forth; they felt they had no choice: this *was* their language.

Although Tatum was to return to the trio format from time to time after the mid-1940s, his finest playing came always as a soloist. We are fortunate that the mature Tatum was recorded both by Capitol and Columbia Records (in 1949), and later in the years 1953-55 by Norman Granz for his Clef label. Actually these postwar years were lean ones for Tatum. Work was scarce, and between 1947 and 1953 there were two periods, one of two and a half years and another of three years, during which Tatum did not record at all. Bop had come in and taken over, and like many "older" players—even though in 1945 Tatum was only thirty-six—he was generally neglected by musicians and audiences alike.

The Capitol series offers at least two masterful performances that may, in fact, be Tatum's crowning achievements: *Willow Weep for Me* and *Aunt Hagar's Blues*. From the brief introductory vamp—which recurs a half a dozen more times as a unifying motive—to the final pixie-ish coda, *Willow* is Tatum at his

---

11. The other major trio influenced by Tatum's was Dave Brubeck's of the early 1950s, the influence centered entirely in the leader's piano style (since his trio had no guitar).

Ex. 7

*1 Tatum's eighth notes are swung in triplet eighths.

*2 The parenthesized whole-note chords above the staff represent the harmonic implications,
   chordally arranged (i, e, in m. 6 F major over A♭ major).

*3 The C major chord in the piano was usually played against G♭ major, but here Slam Stewart
   chose to phase in with the piano in A minor.

most eloquent and concise. Here everything is of a piece. Whereas often in
earlier performances, despite whatever brilliant playing, one can get nervous
with the constant intrusions and deviations of decorative runs and harmonic
detours, in *Willow* every musical gesture evolves organically out of its predecessor. Ann Ronnell's beautiful song is here not wrenched to and fro or inundated
by avalanches of cascading sheets of sound. But rather, Tatum seems extraordinarily respectful of the song itself, including its hypnotically repetitious A sections. This respectfulness extends to his preserving these sections' reiterative
characteristics in his own reworking of them, and even to the extent of adhering
obediently to Ronnell's highly unusual double-time feature in the fifth bar. In
fact, on one of these fifth bars Tatum goes Ronnell's song one better by doubling
up the original double-time!

    After a haunting 4-bar opening vamp (Ex. 8), Tatum's subtle stretching and

Ex. 8

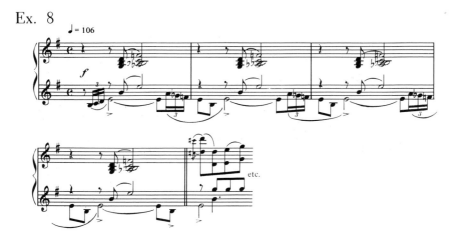

contracting of the tempo in the first sixteen bars already heralds a more considered approach to his fondness for free-tempo variations; and even the pyrotechnics at the end of the bridge are harmonically better integrated. Then, too, when Tatum comes to the last "eight" of the first chorus, he retains the overall character of his two previous A sections. But notice how tantalizingly he rocks the beat and tempo back and forth in the subtlest of rubatos. It is seemingly in tempo, and yet amazingly it is also free within the bar.

Another new element in Tatum's playing at this time, well represented in *Willow* and *Aunt Hagar's*, was a more mature, more clearly delineated use of the chorus structure. From this period on Tatum seemed to have understood the need to give each chorus its special character, even mood perhaps, rather than his more helter-skelter earlier approach of allowing any and all ideas to be crowded into a single chorus at will. In this more discriminating approach, sorting out his ideas more selectively and assigning them carefully to specific episodes in the *overall* structure, Tatum gains a firmer grasp on the "compositional" lucidity of his improvisations.

The fourth appearance of his introductory vamp motive in *Willow* (see Fig. 1) sets up the second chorus, quite different from but nevertheless an elaboration of the first chorus and once again retaining the original unity of the song's A section. But this time Tatum splits all the A sections into twice four bars of newly invented contrasting materials: the first four bars, rich advanced bitonal blues harmonies;[12] the second, totally different perky zig-zagging gestures. Moreover, in the initial four measures Tatum sets up a subtle alternation every two bars between single-time and double-time, which in turn is used as a means of intensification and rhythmic development. This process continues right on through

12. These blues-oriented phrases undoubtedly came readily to Tatum's mind because Ronnell's *Willow Weep for Me* changes are reminiscent of blues changes. Indeed they *are* blues changes but condensed into eight bars as follows: I–IV–V–I - I. The first four or five bars thus can easily give

$$4 \quad 1\tfrac{1}{2} \quad \tfrac{1}{2} \quad 1$$

the feeling of a standard blues.

Fig. 1

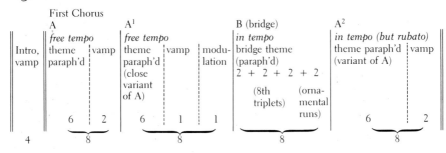

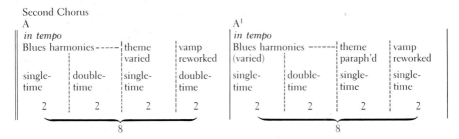

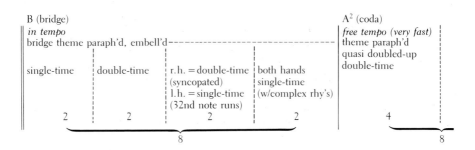

the bridge and begins to build towards some yet-to-come climax. Here in the bridge, Tatum at first prolongs the single-time double-time alteration in two 2-bar phrases and then, in a real stroke of genius, divides it *horizontally* between the two hands: that is, in the fifth and sixth measures of the bridge the right hand plays in syncopated double-time (moreover, harmonically related to the blues harmonies with which Tatum began the chorus), while the left hand is set in single-time *but* filled out with whirling thirty-second-note runs. Through all this the original melody of the tune, though obviously not actually played as such, is nevertheless present in fragmentation or simply by subtle implication.

The last eight of the second chorus and the tag-coda, welded into a single unit, are the real climax of the performance, evolving out of the entire process of intensification begun in the first chorus and, as we have seen, accelerated in the second. Whereas so often in the past, Tatum's frantic *prestissimo* codas seemed arbitrarily, mechanically attached, as if he had an automatic obligation to honor his patented ABA format in this manner, here the suddenly forward lurching tempo of the coda, gobbling up the first four bars in six seconds flat, seems not only appropriate but absolutely inevitable. It works so well this time because, as I have shown, this final forward push of the tempo a) has been prepared for at least three-quarters of a chorus in ever shorter and intensifying segments; and b) it arises in the first instance out of Ronnell's playful toying with time (double-time, that is) in her A phrases. It is a superior example of how a jazz performer may seize upon one apparently minute element and build almost an entire "compositional" conception on it. The "free" coda also works as an ending, because after four bars of very fast super-stride tempo, Tatum relaxes the time almost by half, then relaxes further into a free-tempo return of his opening vamp, thus letting us down gradually whilst bringing the whole performance around full circle and ending with a whimsical chime-like figure, one of Tatum's favorite piece-ending signatures.

The complexity of the process by which this performance is structured can perhaps be best appreciated in diagrammatic form—and by several listenings to the actual performance—represented in Figure 1.

If *Willow Weep for Me* is an example of Tatum working successfully at complex structures, effectively using harmony and rhythm interlocked as organizing elements, *Aunt Hagar's Blues* offers the same level of perfection but in a much simpler and gentler setting. Again, there is a balance of elements, a natural flow in its ideas, whereby the sum total is somehow greater than all of its individual parts. Curiously, this is so despite what, on the face of it, seems like an irrelevant intrusion upon W. C. Handy's blues opus by another totally unrelated song. This was *Black Coffee*, a popular tune of 1949. But Tatum interwove this latter theme so sensitively with Handy's blues that it seems to become, after a few listenings, an integral part of Handy's piece. Even more curiously, Tatum used for his *Black Coffee* interpolations quite specifically the great recording made by Sarah Vaughan in Joe Lippman's superb arrangement issued a few months before Tatum's first Capitol session. I have mentioned that Tatum was an avid

listener and absorber; and he surely listened appreciatively to Lippman's rich
harmonizations, which were in a class and style very similar to Tatum's own.

The overlaying of *Black Coffee* begins, rather daringly, right at the outset of
the performance. Handy's *Hagar's* theme is subsumed into it in chromatically
spicy harmonies. Even more surprisingly, these first four *Black Coffee* measures
sound, at first listening, like an introduction: it is that kind of reiterative ostinato-
like material (Ex. 9a). It turns out, however, to be the first four bars of the blues,

Ex. 9a

not all that different from those blues-oriented harmonies Tatum had just applied in *Willow Weep for Me*, recorded on the same day two titles earlier. It is
also the kind of musical material which, alas, Tatum has on many occasions
turned into pure big-chord bombast. Here in *Aunt Hagar's*, however, he teases
the piano with a delicate refined touch that he obviously has always had at his
command but did not always choose to use. In the fifth bar Tatum disarms the
listener further by spinning out the simplest of unadorned single-note lines, at
first over sustained left-hand whole-note chords and then gradually easing into a
leisurely legato stride bass.

For his second chorus, Tatum returns to the *Black Coffee* material in more
depth, and again in the fifth bar lightens the texture (very much, incidentally,
the way Joe Lippman did in his arrangement for Sarah Vaughan). A chromatic
double-time figure (mm. 19 and 20, Ex. 9b), which Oscar Peterson has appropriated into his copious repertory of Tatum-isms, almost threatens to break the
relaxed spell of the performance. But Tatum pulls back just in time to end the

Ex. 9b

second chorus in old-time lazy blues triplets, sprinkled with an effervescent run or two.

It is only in the third chorus that Tatum deals for the first time seriously with Handy's thematic material, beautifully voiced in widely spaced tenths while alternating major and minor harmonies (see Ex. 9c, mm. 25 and 26). The next two bars are so convoluted—unexpectedly—as almost to shake the music from its rhythmic moorings—it is a rare Tatum example of rhythmic uncertainty— but miraculously Tatum recovers in time to end (in the fifth bar of the chorus) on a mordant flat-five chord, followed just as surprisingly by light, airy high-register blues-ish octaves.[13]

The fourth chorus, sustaining the mood of the latter half of the previous chorus, opens with two bars of high-register blues tremolos which flow imperceptibly into one of Tatum's crystalline right-hand runs—two and a half bars of thirty-second notes over sustained chords and the gentlest of stride. A jocose

13. This passage fits so perfectly Martin Williams's truism, in speaking of *Aunt Hagar's* and *Willow*, that both performances "offer in abundance the Tatum paradox that all surprises quickly assume an inevitability as one absorbs them."

Ex. 9c

episode in minor seconds (mm. 43 and 44, Ex. 9d) almost mars the basic mood of the performance, but again Tatum pulls out just in time to effect a safe landing on more appropriate terrain.

Tatum plays with such authority that what happens next may go by unnoticed except to the most receptive ears. Tatum cuts the chorus short in the tenth bar, inadvertently skipping *a whole beat and part of another*[14] and launches into the coda—which turns out to be none other than our old friend, the *Black Coffee* strain (mm. 47–50) from the opening measures. Tatum brings the performance to a close in the sixth bar of what would have been the fifth chorus—an odd place to stop—on a beautiful resonant D♭ eleventh chord. Apparently Tatum was more interested in the *Black Coffee* material in the first place and quietly ended the performance once he had returned to it.

Despite its minor flaws, Tatum's *Aunt Hagar's Blues* is one of the most balanced, cohesive, and sensitive performances of his career. Along with *Willow Weep for Me* and a few others from the mid-1950s Granz series, it deserves the accolade of "masterpiece."

Except for one moderately successful Trio date in 1952, Tatum did not record again until December 28, 1953. But in those two marathon sessions, plus two others in 1954 and 1955, all for Norman Granz's Clef label (reissued more recently on Pablo), Tatum recorded an unbelievable 121 titles, the heart of his sizable repertory.

Even the least of these belong to Tatum's mature work, and the best of them may be numbered amongst his very finest life-long achievements. Certainly this heroic effort does not deserve the petulant, cavilling, unreasonable, and often incoherent criticism unleashed upon it by André Hodeir in 1955.[15]

It would be impossible within the confines of this essay to comment in detail on these recordings. Of the many cuts worth hearing I would cite *Too Marvelous*

14. Could this be the result of a badly managed tape splice, or is this what Tatum actually played?
15. First published in *Downbeat*, Hodeir's essay was reproduced in *The Art of Jazz*, ed. Martin Williams, Oxford University Press, New York, 1959.

Ex. 9d

for Words (which is almost what one would have to say of this performance); *Somebody Loves Me, If I Had You,* and a remarkable *Embraceable You,* with fine chorus differentiation and a wonderfully imperious horn-like theme in the third chorus (used again in the 1956 collaboration with Buddy DeFranco on *Memories of You*).

Then there are from the so-called *Discoveries* series, recorded at a private party in July 1955, some remarkable performances, issued most recently on the Smithsonian's *Pieces of Eight* tribute to Tatum: *Jitterbug Waltz, I Cover the Waterfront,* a furiously fast Hinesian *Love for Sale,* and an astonishing *Sweet Lorraine.* Two excerpts from the last-named are worth quoting (Ex. 10a, b) as

Ex. 10a

Tatum invests this tune, which he recorded many times and must have played literally thousands of times in his life, with new, sometimes almost harsh harmonizations, with jolting, jagged lines that seem to be trying to break new ground. There is something somber and desperate in his playing here, perhaps reflecting a deep-down realization that he had not much time left to live, something he had known since 1954.

These late performances show that Tatum was growing musically to the very end. For one thing he was extricating himself more and more from the tyrannies of the stride style. He could abandon it altogether or modify it, break it up into new patterns, or on occasion still dazzle with his famous super-stride. This allowed him in turn to play with great rhythmic freedom within a set tempo and an expanded range of expression. It also enabled Tatum to evolve at times a broad open-spaced, behind-the-beat swing which he had been unable to capture in earlier years (and which, again, the loyal Oscar Peterson was to appropriate and forge to perfection as one of the most captivating hallmarks of his style). Hear this open swinging on the 1955 *I Cover the Waterfront* (from the *Discoveries* series), *Lover Man* (with Buddy DeFranco in 1956), to name just a few. (Was this possibly a case of the master being influenced by the pupil—Peterson, who had by now gained a popularity with *his* trio, including the great Ray Brown on bass, a popularity greater than Tatum's?)

Finally, Tatum had by now outgrown the need to interpolate quotations, an earlier tendency which had led to many lamentable lapses of taste. There are virtually no quotations in all these later performances.

In the last years Tatum was also persuaded to make some quartet record-

Ex. 10b   ♩= 104

ings, notably with Ben Webster, Roy Eldridge, Lionel Hampton, and Buddy DeFranco. These may not be among his very best, although any late Tatum is more than worth hearing and is bound to offer many remarkable moments. The old battle between Tatum the unfettered soloist and Tatum the confined ensemble player is occasionally apparent, but on the whole Tatum seems quite accommodating to his fellow soloists, at times even offering remarkable rapport, as with Hampton, for example, on a beautifully reflective *More Than You Know*. The Buddy DeFranco date from early 1956 produced at least one highly successful collaboration, *Lover Man*. DeFranco plays with much warmth, almost entirely in his low-to-middle register, leaving the upper range open for Tatum's ornamentations and complementary descant lines. And Tatum's largely linear (and at times grandly swinging) solo is one of his most inspired.

On his final record date, two months before his death, Tatum was paired with Ben Webster. It is a curious encounter that doesn't quite jell. Both Tatum and Webster were masters of their craft, to be sure, but also musicians with strong and totally different identities: Webster, the arch-romantic, his playing by then a fascinating mixture of lush sonority and almost toneless breathy vibrato, his musical statements variously languid and strong, but always simple; Tatum, near death, quite subdued, a little pale musically, dispassionate, at times mechanical. Again there are moments, but they are mostly Webster's, not Tatum's.

Tatum died on November 5, 1956. Jazz in its modern garb had moved way past him, and many of the younger players had never learned to appreciate Tatum the way they could Charlie Parker, who died a year and a half *before* Tatum. To many of them Parker was a hero and a martyr; but Tatum was at best a puzzling anachronism, an anomaly, who was still standing apart from the mainstream. He was indeed one of the most complex, enigmatic, and elusive figures in jazz—and a phenomenon.

TEDDY WILSON

In many respects one can hardly imagine two pianists, though contemporaries and influential upon each other, as different from each other as Teddy Wilson and Art Tatum. As the previous discussion of Tatum pointed out, the younger Wilson met Tatum in Toledo in 1931—Wilson was all of nineteen at the time— and was certainly more than impressed by him. Conversely there is strong evidence that in the late thirties, when Wilson was becoming a nationally known figure through his work with Benny Goodman, Tatum began to reduce, at least temporarily, his richly extravagant, irrepressible style to the more modest proportions of Wilson's.

Wilson was, of course, like all pianists, also profoundly inspired by Earl Hines, whom he heard a great deal during his Chicago days in the early thirties and even before that on recordings. The Hines influence is clearly audible in Wilson's early work, and some of Hines's favorite stylistic traits became central features, albeit modified, of Wilson's style, particularly the high-register, dancing right-hand octaves.

It is a measure of Wilson and Tatum's greatness that, although they were weaned on many of the same musical sources—Hines, Jelly Roll Morton, classical piano literature—they developed totally individual idioms. A comparison of the two pianists' musical/stylistic conceptions reveals clearly how distinct and diverse were their musical personalities. If there is one domain where these differences are most pronounced it is in the realm of harmony. Whereas Tatum's ear and temperament compelled him to push constantly to the then permissible outer limits of the harmonic vocabulary, Wilson was—to the end—harmonically a staunch conservative. Tatum's harmonic energy is unbounded, whereas Wilson's stays very clearly within well-defined limits. Moreover Tatum's emphasis on harmonic exploration leads him to sacrifice melodic interest, and often rhythmic as well; whereas, of course, Wilson's emphasis on melody and rhythm compels him to sacrifice harmonic invention. Wilson's harmonic/melodic language is essentially triadic, with sevenths and occasional ninths as the most advanced elaborations. Tatum on the other hand was almost incapable of limiting himself to mere triadic formations, for he preferred to play as much as possible on the outer chromatic extensions of the diatonic language.

As I have pointed our earlier, Tatum relied heavily on the melodic/thematic material of whatever song he was performing. In that sense he was one of the supreme paraphrase improvisers. Tatum generally stayed close to the composer's original melody, whereas Wilson was constantly inventing his own. Paraphrase improvisations were relatively rare with Wilson, although he could obviously do them. In that respect Wilson was much more of a true improvising jazz artist than Tatum, and his harmonic reticence was in fact a byproduct of his remarkable melodic gift. It is clear that Tatum took less risks as an "improviser," preparing his performances and, once set, retaining them over long periods of time in their broad outlines and even in many of their essential details. Wilson, on the other hand, by temperament was more the constant inventor, reluctant to play anything the same way even twice, let alone hundreds of times. I doubt very much that Tatum could have, for example, dealt as successfully with the last-minute, loosely spontaneous, instantaneously creative series of small group sessions that produced the Billie Holiday recordings from 1935 to 1937. To be more precise, Tatum could function well enough as a sideman, as the 1943 Leonard Feather All-Star dates for the Commodore label show. But I don't think he could have exerted the musical leadership, taste, and balance that make the Holiday series, and Wilson's own concurrent septet and octet recordings, such a vital contribution to 1930s' jazz.

Staying in the realm of melody but in its more ornamental aspects, Wilson was the master of what I would call "melodic decoration"; that is to say, combining the decorative with the essentially melodic. Tatum's ornamentation, on the other hand, spilled quickly over into pure arabesque, pure embellishment, mostly in the form of arpeggios, runs, patterns in thirds or octaves—all essentially non-melodic "passage work" and embroidery.

Wilson could also play his share of pearly arpeggios and runs, but he kept these ornaments in a better balance within the overall continuity of a performance.

Interestingly, there are even differences in how both men used arpeggios. Some exceptions notwithstanding, Tatum's arpeggios invariably are descending, zooming downward like an arrow, usually encompassing the entire range of the piano from the highest tinkling octave to the lowest forceful bass notes. Wilson's arpeggios, on the other hand, more often than not are both descending and ascending, swooping down *and* up, usually back to their point of origin. Tatum also had a favorite but less-used upward run, which would break off somewhere in the upper middle register and then jump two or three octaves to some altissimo single note, which miraculously he *never* missed.[16] (See above, Ex. 10b).

Melodic ideas, even decorative ones, must be stated in rhythmic shapes, of course, and in this respect there is, again, an interesting difference between

16. There is one superb moment in the 1956 Tatum–DeFranco collaboration on *Lover Man*, where by sheer chance both men start upward fast-note arpeggios, but halfway up DeFranco turns back down while Tatum continues on up to the top, producing a marvelous double configuration

pno. ⌒
clar. ⌒ and a sweeping finish to the phrase.

Wilson and Tatum. Wilson varies his rhythms much more within a given phrase or gesture. His melodic configurations are generally stated in a *mixture* of rhythmic groupings: quarter notes, eighths, triplet eighths, sixteenths, triplet sixteenths, and so on. Additionally, Wilson's phrases tend to be of quite varying lengths. Tatum on the other hand tended to stay with a particular rhythmic unit, say, thirty-seconds, or sixteenths, or—his favorite—triplet eighths. Wilson's mixing up of right-hand rhythms gives his playing an airy, uncluttered texture, as opposed to Tatum's much denser continuity.

Tatum's temperament also demanded an altogether more volatile level of expression. This manifested itself in his wide-ranging dynamics and variety of touch. Wilson, by contrast, was much more conservative in his use of dynamics, staying almost always in a safe middle ground of *mp* or *mf*. Dynamics have only on the rarest occasions played a dramatic or functional, form-delineating role in Wilson's playing. His touch, too, is less varied than Tatum's. It is exquisite, of course, but it does not have—or chooses not to have—the *range* of touch and attack that Tatum commanded: from the most dulcet and *legato* to the brassiest hammer-like attacks, and everything in between. Indeed, Wilson favored a generally crisp, clipped articulation—again in the interests of clarity and an uncomplicated airy continuity.

All of these elements, taken together, tend to give Wilson's playing a modest, at times even placid or sober character. Wilson does not have to dominate, as Tatum almost always did; and Wilson is not as relentless as Tatum. He doesn't mind easing up—on himself, on his listeners, on his fellow players. His basic modesty, as a person and as a player, leads Wilson, the perfect ensemble player, to meet other musicians halfway rather than overwhelm them, as Tatum often did.

If Tatum did not take risks, as mentioned, in the larger formal and improvisatory sense, he constantly took risks in smaller ways. He was generally bent on breaking technical and harmonic boundaries, always pushing himself to the utmost physical limits. Wilson on the other hand stayed within the bounds his taste and sense of musical sobriety set. He is thus outwardly a less arresting performer but one who underneath the calm exterior is perfectly functioning, sensitive and subtle. In a technical sense it is riskless playing; it ruffles no feathers. but it reveals impeccable taste, astonishing consistency, and absolute integrity. It is virtually fail-safe.

To summarize the trenchant differences between the playing of these two keyboard giants, the following point by point comparison (Fig. 2), somewhat simplified in catch-word phrases, should prove helpful.

Like so many major creative talents in music, Teddy Wilson's artistic personality already expressed itself in a highly individual manner in his teen years and, as his early recordings show, was set in all its basic features by the time he was twenty. On his recording debut (with Louis Armstrong in January 1933) Wilson is mostly inaudible and relegated to brief transitional or obbligato passages. But the glimpses one *can* catch of him already reveal his easy relaxed swing, and

Fig. 2

TATUM	WILSON
Harmonically complex	Harmonically simple
Sacrificed melodic interest	Sacrified harmonic interest
Took fewer risks in improvising	Constantly inventive in improvising
Much passage work and ornamental embroidery	Decorative, always substantially melodic
Arpeggios generally descending	Arpeggios mostly descending *and* ascending
Identical rhythmic units in phrases	Varied rhythmic units in phrases
Dense texture	Airy texture
Volatile range of dynamics	Subdued, controlled, limited range of dynamics
Varied touch/articulation	Unvarying touch/articulation
Need to dominate ensembles	Happy to fit into ensembles
Relentless energy	Relaxed energy, able to ease up

his intelligent use of the basic late-twenties' stride style, replete with Hinesian high-register octaves.

Nine months later, recording with the Benny Carter-led Chocolate Dandies, we can hear Wilson more clearly and extensively, confirming that the essential ingredients of his own style were in fact already all in place. Not, of course, as smooth and lucid as later on—even his famous versatile left hand seems a bit thumpy on these sides—but the dancing, bouncy right hand is there, even if limited uncharacteristically to the piano's mid-range (especially on *I Never Knew*).

Even on the rather chaotic Mezz Mezzrow date (sporting an awful Benny Carter vocal as well as Mezzrow's corny arrangements and inept alto playing), and on an orchestra date with Benny Goodman in May of 1934 (*Moonglow*), Wilson still sounds a bit muscular and ill at ease. But hear him a few months later with Red Norvo's Swing Septet. On *I Surrender, Dear* and *Old-Fashioned Love*, Wilson lifts the performances from rather confused, desultory levels to moments of inspiration and high elegance. Given the rhythm section's listless oomp-chah accompaniments, Jack Jenney's rather disappointing, somewhat lugubrious trombone solos, Charlie Barnet's hysterical overwrought tenor, and Artie Shaw's squeaky inept playing (he squeaks twice on *Old-Fashioned Love*), these sides seem doomed to failure. But Wilson and Norvo obviously inspired each other. On *Old-Fashioned*, Wilson comes through with a bright, driving Hinesian half-chorus and, by contrast, on *I Surrender* with a prototypical lacy ornamental solo, filled with that spontaneous rhythmic variety I spoke of before. This is fine, quintessential early Wilson and worth seeing in musical notation (Ex. 11).

The year 1935 was an important and very active one for Teddy Wilson. Be-

Ex. 11

sides working with Willie Bryant and recording with Bob Howard, Putney Dandridge, and Taft Jordan,[17] continuing to work intermittently with Red Norvo and Mildred Bailey, Wilson also made his debut as a leader, both of his own instrumental groups (mostly septets) and of the famous series of recordings with Billie Holiday (see later in this chapter). Furthermore, 1935 marked the creation

17. Bryant, Howard, and Dandridge were but three of a whole collection of song-and-dance men fronting bands in Harlem who emerged after Cab Calloway's enormous success in the early 1930s. In one way or another they all emulated Calloway, although Howard, for example, did more straight singing (in the Louis Armstrong manner) in a voice strangely split between a high milky-sounding tenor and a rather hard-timbred baritone. He also had the unfortunate habit of shouting corny jive talk during and over his star soloists' choruses (as did Bryant). Ironically, these front-men leaders always paid the best salaries, enabling them to attract first-rate players like Wilson, Carter, Webster, Rex Stewart, Cozy Cole, all of whom worked at one time or another with Howard. Billy Banks, discussed elsewhere, was perhaps the most gifted of these singer-dancer-comedian leaders.

Carter, incidentally, besides playing alto and trumpet for Bob Howard, did most of the band's arranging. *I'll Never Change* features a series of trumpet duets in thirds (Carter and Rex Stewart) that surprisingly anticipate the Tijuana Brass of the 1960s.

of the Goodman Trio (later expanded to a quartet with the addition of Lionel Hampton), of which a historic series of recordings made Wilson virtually a household name among swing fans and jazz cognoscenti. Most of these opportunities were, once again, the direct result of John Hammond's indefatigable efforts on behalf of Wilson, whom Hammond had brought to New York from Chicago in 1933 specifically to record with Benny Carter.

July 1935 was a particularly significant period for Wilson since that is when, within a little more than a fortnight, he debuted with both the Goodman Trio and as a leader of his own band. It was in these recordings that the larger public first became aware of Wilson. It heard what it was to hear regularly for five more decades: clean, relaxed, uncluttered playing, cohesive and logical in form, airy in texture, graced by flawless taste and a refined touch not heard on jazz piano since Jelly Roll Morton's finest days, judiciously sprinkled with pearly decorative runs, all set over a marvelously mobile left hand. Above all, it was that happy, positive, even-tempered spirit which Wilson brought to his performing. It represented a new refined classicism, as it were, in jazz, which easily attracted the new swing-oriented audiences of the mid-thirties.

One device of which both Tatum and Wilson were masters was the playing in the left hand of a sustained tenor line, while also keeping the basic stride effect going with staccato bass notes below. Combined with the right hand, this created the impression of a three-handed pianist. It was not, I hasten to add, an effect that could be achieved by using the pedals of the piano,[18] but it obviously required large hands. Wilson used the device regularly as a way of breaking the potential monotony of uninterrupted oompah-striding and also of providing a kind of stabilizing counterpoint to his generally agile right-hand configurations. A fine example of this technique can be heard early in Wilson's career on his October 1935 solo recording of Hines's *Rosetta* (Ex. 12) and the early Goodman

Ex. 12

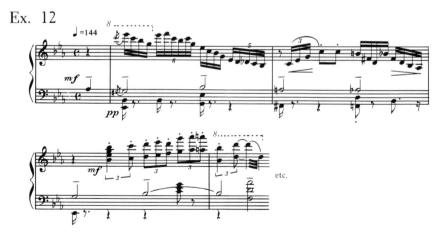

18. Wilson's discreet, sensitive use of pedaling is perhaps one of the least recognized aspects of his playing. Of the many solo recordings where this can best be appreciated I would single out the 1941 *Smoke Gets in Your Eyes.*

Trio recordings, *Nobody's Sweetheart*, for example. The latter is, along with such other Trio performances as *Body and Soul* and *After You've Gone* (from the first Trio session in July 1935), among the finest examples of Wilson's art and, beyond that, an outstanding illustration of the new concept of driving, exciting chamber jazz the Goodman Trio brought to jazz. Wilson is at his sparkling best, but at the same time a model of beautifully balanced, cohesive, improvisational composing.

The same driving spirit can be heard on *Sailin'*, a Teddy Wilson composition, recorded with a septet that included Ben Webster and Benny Goodman. As the title suggests, the performance really sails along, with Goodman in one of his finest solo flights, playing with terrific drive and attack, at times with a "dirty" raspy sound of uncommon intensity. In the last chorus, a series of descending eighth-note runs, instigated by Ben Webster and Jonah Jones and imitated by the other "horns," provides an exciting climax to this impassioned ensemble performance.

That Wilson's playing was not all graceful, decorative, *melodic* improvising is shown by the Goodman Quartet's recording of *The Man I Love*. Here Hampton and Wilson combine to create an organ-like background to Goodman's theme statement. With Hampton playing mid-range whole-note vibraphone chords, and Wilson filling in below with rich low-register harmonies—his lowest bass notes sound like a tuba—the effect is one of dirge- or hymn-like dignity, and a striking departure from the song's usual interpretation as a maudlin torch song.[19]

Wilson has always been one of the most consistent of improvisers. This consistency is achieved, as I have suggested, to some extent by taking very few risks stylistically and technically, by constantly improvising within a limited stylistic compass. Big surprises are rare in Wilson's playing, and in fact there is a certain general predictability about his work. Listening to a lot of Wilson recordings in succession can become somewhat monotonous. Many solos duplicate each other, and the Xerox effect can have a numbing effect. And yet, one is not inclined to use the word "cliché" in regard to Wilson's work, in part because it is, even at its least inventive, always in good taste with ample displays of his refined touch and clean sense of structural balance.

That Wilson was sometimes less than "immortal" can be heard on many mid-thirties' recordings, such as the perfunctory *Liza* (from the same date as *Man I Love*) or a February 1937 *Runnin' Wild* (quite different and much improved on an air-check performance of the same tune a month later). With Mildred Bailey in 1935 we hear Wilson playing rather ordinary stride and simple-minded boogie-woogie (on *Squeeze Me* and *Downhearted Blues*, respectively). Sometimes even Wilson could not rise above the listless playing of his colleagues, as on a goodly number of Goodman Trio or Quartet recordings: for example, swamped by Hampton's wrong chords on *Stompin' at the Savoy*, or Krupa's incessant, overbearing vertical drumming on *Whispering* and *Oh, Lady Be Good*, or on the tired sounding *Vibraphone Blues* and *More Than You Know*.

---

19. The Goodman Quartet's *Tiger Rag* is another welcome and, given the material, remarkably *un*hackneyed performance.

But Wilson's lulls were many another pianist's highs and, in any case, never lasted long. Wilson really hit his stride—the reader will I hope forgive the pun—in 1937. Listening to the solo recordings of *Don't Blame Me* and *Between the Devil and the Deep Blue Sea*, one can hear at once an increased daring and authority in his playing. One suspects that both Tatum's and Hines's increased popularity with the new swing fans had a stimulating effect upon Wilson. One is also compelled to realize (on *Between the Devil*, for example) that technically Wilson could, when he wanted to, do almost anything that Hines could do, but that his innate modesty and even temperament precluded his indulging in excessive displays of technical ostentation. If we consider both takes of *Between the Devil* as being well within Wilson's reach technically, we realize how much he usually held back.

On *Don't Blame Me* we encounter one of those rare occasions when Wilson was willing to expand his harmonic thinking. As the piece's final phrase unwinds in a beautifully paced ritardando, Wilson finds an exquisitely subtle series of chromatic pastel harmonies to bring the performance to a satisfying close. But this was about as adventurous as he ever got.[20]

During these years of the late 1930s the Goodman Quartet often reached extraordinary levels of ensemble perfection and inter-communication. It could create with ease such exciting stuff as *I'm a Ding Dong Daddy* or sophisticated semi-arranged pieces like *Opus ½*. In such a varied repertory Wilson could respond effectively to any mood or style as required, from a lacy blues piano through a tuba-like accompaniment behind Hampton's vocal to some marvelous "behind-the-beat" swinging (all these on the very special *Blues in My Flat*); or, in another context *(Sugar)*, typically iridescent, happily smiling piano. It must also be said that, when Krupa left Goodman, David Tough's sensitive ensemble drumming added incalculably to the group, Tough's more line-conscious playing allowing the other three players much greater freedom and flexibility. When bassist John Kirby joined the group in late 1938, making it the Goodman Quintet, his walking bass lines provided an additional, firmly swinging harmonic foundation, enabling the soloists, including Wilson, to become even freer melodically.

But in April 1939, Wilson suddenly left Goodman, ostensibly to form his own band. But the recorded evidence also shows that Lionel Hampton's success with the public and his increasingly histrionic exhibitionism eventually crowded Wilson into a secondary role. Yet his last date with Goodman (in December 1938) produced at least one excellent ensemble performance: *I Know That You Know*, with a smartly swinging, fluent Wilson.

Wilson had little success with his big band; it lasted less than a year and made a dozen-odd recordings of some quality but insufficient individuality. The band's sound and style were a close reflection of Wilson's own playing: crisp, clean, tasteful, balanced. Most of the arrangements were by Wilson himself, but he also used the services of Edgar Sampson, Buster Harding, and even Ben Webster

20. Other fine examples of Wilson in a harmonically relatively explorative mood are his *Body and Soul* (1941) and the beautiful coda of *These Foolish Things* (1942).

(the last in an excellent arrangement of 71). The band's repertory was geared primarily to dancing, and included many of the period's typical riff-swing numbers, as well as the mandatory girl-vocalist ballads. Though Wilson was always featured, even if briefly—his big show-case number was a fast-paced *Liza*—he also provided solo opportunities for his leading players, especially, of course, Ben Webster, and altoist Pete Clark, trumpeter Karl George (playing in a Harry Edison Basie-band style), a fine little-known trombonist, Jacob Wiley, and occasionally J. C. Heard on drums. But the problem was, as so often in the Swing Era, the solos were sandwiched in between arranged ensembles and usually too brief to establish any lasting personal identity. By taking care of the needs (and desires) of his soloists but, at the same time, not providing varied and individualized orchestra settings (as Ellington did) or at least a linear sequence of loosely strung together improvisations (as Basie did), Wilson was unable to establish a recognizable and memorable orchestral identity.

The band did, however, achieve a respectable balanced and disciplined full sound, and it could on occasion generate considerable ensemble swing. *Wham,* that national anthem of late 1930s' jive-talk—smartly arranged by Harding—is a good example of the Wilson band's capabilities in this respect. Very interesting, too, are the unusual saxophone ensembles, accompanied only by Heard's cymbals, on *Moon Ray* and in the coda of *Sweet Lorraine,* both arrangements by Wilson. A *capella* sax ensembles were not original with him—Benny Carter had previously pioneered this idea—but Wilson here certainly creates some very effective and handsome ones.

At the other end of the quality scale the band also played terrible fake jungle-type tableaux numbers—probably with grass-skirted flame dancers—like *Booly-Ja-Ja,* and "hard-luck" torchy songs like *Lady of Mystery.* One can well imagine that the urbane Mr. Wilson rebelled at such tripe. But unfortunately such pieces, along with the mandatory crooned love songs in slow dance tempo, were the survival fare for swing bands, both white *and* black, in a crowded and highly competitive field. It is also true that Teddy Wilson lacked the showmanship and extrovert charisma that other bandleaders—and much lesser musicians—like Bryant and Howard had.

After the non-success of Wilson's big band, he returned to smaller, more manageable combos, mostly sextets featuring players like trombonist Benny Morton, clarinetists Edmond Hall or Jimmy Hamilton, the last soon to become an important member of the Ellington orchestra, and that fine drummer J. C. Heard. Wilson also found recording work with Mildred Bailey in 1940, but those sides feature relatively little Wilson, being devoted primarily to Bailey's singing and Eddie Sauter's wood-windy, harmonically advanced arrangements. When Wilson *was* allowed to solo, his conservative idiom sounds oddly out of context in Sauter's experimental frameworks.

Wilson's best work during these early 1940s was either in solo performances or with his trio, incorporating J. C. Heard and bassist Al Hall. Indeed, the spate of sides produced in April 1941 must surely represent an apex in Wilson's creative development. Whether in the elegiac, nostalgic mood of *Smoke Gets in*

Your Eyes or the sprightly, airy, light-hearted *Rosetta* (Ex. 13), we are hearing the finest pure mint Wilson.

For me the masterpiece of the series is *I Know That You Know*. Treated as a sort of "perpetual motion" piece, Wilson's hands are all over the keyboard, delightfully swinging figures rolling off his right hand with Mozartean clarity and

Ex. 13

ease. So often with swing era musicians—the first generation to command this level of technical powers—virtuoso solos tended to be rather mechanical, even contrived. But Wilson rarely loses that spontaneity that is the essence of jazz. In *I Know*, taken at a very bright tempo, we can hear a prime example of the extraordinary variety and mobility of Wilson's left hand and how this left hand complements and interacts with an equally diversified right hand. The net result is a dazzling counterpoint of ideas: combining, overlapping, contrasting—variety *in* both hands and *between* them. Especially ear-catching are the bits of tenor lines that creep in frequently amongst the stride, forming beautiful horn-like counter-melodies and achieving a marvelous lightness of texture. Though Wilson, as mentioned before, does not generally do much with dynamics, it is worth noting how impeccably he differentiates the right hand here at a slightly higher dynamic level from his left hand, emphasizing the latter in counter-lines only as needed. The point is that these subtle dynamic manipulations serve musical/structural purposes and are entirely under Wilson's technical and touch control.

A word of caution to the listener/reader is perhaps in order. To appreciate Wilson fully one must listen very intently, following his discourse with undivided attention. Whereas Tatum and Hines are much more dramatic and volatile in expression, literally throwing themselves at the listener, even overwhelming him, Teddy Wilson always holds something of himself back. For all its brilliance, Wilson's is a relatively reserved and subtle art that asks *you*, the listener, to meet *him* halfway.

These peak years of the early forties were followed by a long-ish, more diffuse period, during which Wilson scattered his talents in a variety of not always artistically rewarding directions. Working on Broadway as a member of the Goodman Sextet (in the show *Seven Lively Arts*), playing as a studio or staff musician in New York radio stations, teaching at the Juilliard School, touring frequently in Europe (often in Goodman reunion groups), Wilson lost much of the creative focus of his earlier work. To be sure, gifted with such a fine talent, Wilson could not play badly for any length of time, or play with less than style and taste. But his playing could be—and after the mid-forties did often become—routine, typical, ordinary. "Ordinary Wilson" is still of a high order of craftsmanship and beyond the reach of most pianists. But in Wilson the creative thrust and desire to grow waned after the early forties. Still active well into his seventies, touring and performing on a schedule that would daunt most younger men, Wilson in his later years reached a settled-in maturity that could still provide a wide range of musical delights.[21]

RED NORVO

One of the finest and most consistently creative musicians of the Swing Era—still quite active today, incidentally—was Kenneth Norville, known to the music world as Red Norvo. The fact that Norvo played the xylophone—in later years

---

21. Teddy Wilson died on July 31, 1986, after the writing of this history was finished.

he played the vibraphone as well (or the vibraharp, as he preferred to call it)—in the early 1930s a highly unlikely candidate for a jazz instrument, makes his selection as a major soloist in this chapter all the more remarkable. But the fact is that Norvo accomplished for the xylophone what Coleman Hawkins achieved for the tenor saxophone: he took it from its vaudeville environment and single-handedly brought it into the world of jazz. But Norvo was (is) more than merely a superior instrumentalist. In the thirties he was an influential force as an innovative soloist *and* a creative orchestra leader, that is to say, one who saw the jazz orchestra as something more than a vehicle for him to front, as Armstrong and Hawkins, for example, saw bands. For Norvo, a jazz orchestra was a collective instrument which through its style, arrangements, and compositions could make important contributions to the music. Norvo has been, through the years, an outstanding uncompromisingly creative improviser, and at times a startlingly gifted (though little appreciated) composer.[22]

Something resembling a xylophone, that is to say pieces of wood (or metal)—or in the earliest times even dried bones—beat upon with sticks or hammer-like implements, seems to have been around since virtually the beginnings of man. In our millennium, a great variety of such mallet instruments became established in many regions of Africa as an integral part of its many musical cultures. From this African heritage a simple form of xylophone, as it came to be called in Western music, traveled to America where it functioned occasionally in black minstrel shows as a novelty instrument.[23] By the early twentieth century, the xylophone had, like the saxophone, become an indispensable element of any decent vaudeville show. The saxophone's Rudy Wiedoeft had his xylophone counterpart in George Hamilton Green, a remarkable virtuoso on the instrument and one of the most popular musical entertainers in all America during the 1920s. (Green recorded more than 250 sides between 1919 and 1922 alone.) And the popular saxophone quartets and sextets of the teens and twenties had their counterparts in xylophone and/or marimba ensembles, involving often as many as six or seven players. By 1928, one of these, the Collegians, could claim the twenty-year-old Norvo as its star soloist.

Even though jazz and the blues had more or less driven ragtime to the sidelines by the early 1920s, it clung on in vaudeville for another decade or so, to a great extent as repertory performed on the xylophone—and now rechristened "novelty tunes." Numbers like *Xylophone Rag* by H. H. Booth, *Xylophonia*, *Greased Lightning*, *Canadian Capers* were some of the staples of this repertory,

---

22. Norvo destroyed a whole series of early compositions, similar to his *Dance of the Octopus* (1933), because Jack Kapp, the head of Brunswick Records, in his great business executive wisdom, regarded such music as meaningless rubbish and tore up Norvo's recording contract. Given the calibre of *Dance of the Octopus*, this senseless decision can only be regarded as one of the great tragedies of American music.

23. The xylophone was, of course, also known in Europe, and first used in an orchestral setting in 1876 by the French composer Camille Saint-Saëns in his *Danse Macabre*. Less remembered is the fact that a Polish musician, Michal Guzikov, (1806–37), traveled all over Europe as a xylophone virtuoso—in other words an early Red Norvo—and was very much praised by many famous artists, including Felix Mendelssohn.

as were sentimental songs like *Mighty Lak' a Rose* and *Back Where the Daffodils Grow*, played on the more dulcet-toned contralto of the mallet family, the marimba, replete with heart-fluttering tremolos and multi-mallet barbershop quartet-like harmonizations.

But Norvo was already listening to Louis Armstrong, Bix Beiderbecke, Frankie Trumbauer, Red Nichols's Five Pennies, and, most importantly, Earl Hines.[24] While Norvo greatly admired George Hamilton Green—any xylophonist in the twenties would have had to admire this master of the mallets, at least in technical terms—and was making his living in vaudeville, he was irresistibly drawn to jazz, and via a series of residencies with the orchestras of Victor Young, Ben Bernie, and, in 1931, Paul Whiteman, he eventually landed in New York.

Norvo's recording debut in August 1932 on *Rockin' Chair* with a group of Whiteman musicians, led by violinist Matty Malneck, backing Mildred Bailey (by then Mrs. Norvo), affords a first glimpse of Norvo as an improvising jazz musician. His almost continuous two-mallet double-stop obbligato behind his wife's superbly moving rendition of this song—it was to be associated with her for most of her career—shows Norvo's ability to weave constantly inventive variations in a relaxedly modern poised swing feeling.

On the other hand Norvo's first recording *as a leader* offered much less evidence of his latent jazz skills. *Knockin' on Wood* and *Hole in the Wall* are both vaudeville-style performances. (How could it be otherwise? The aforementioned Jack Kapp would surely not have allowed anything as "uncommercial" as jazz to intrude into his recording precincts.) Both pieces feature flashy arpeggios and runs with tripping embellishments, set over relentless oompah accompaniments. The few attempts at jazz here by clarinetist Jimmy Dorsey and pianist Fulton McGrath are negligible and feeble. But the two sides did establish that the twenty-five-year-old Norvo already had at his command a formidable mallet technique, and that even such relatively simplistic material as these pieces could be played with a degree of sensitivity in touch, sonority, and harmonic hearing.

But Norvo's next record date, on November 21, 1933, represented a quantum leap upward in quality. He recorded a superb adaptation of Beiderbecke's *In a Mist* and his own remarkable *Dance of the Octopus*. He had to do this surreptitiously, because Mr. Kapp would never have approved the waxing of such elitist, esoteric "stuff." Indeed he flew into a rage when he later found out about Norvo's secret midnight session, on which these pieces were recorded. We owe the existence of these two recondite classics of jazz to Mortimer Palitz, who supervised the date (and who was later instrumental in recording Alec Wilder's Octets), and to John Hammond, who somehow persuaded Brunswick to release the recordings in 1934.

Norvo's adaptation of *In a Mist* resulted in what to my knowledge is the most moving and sympathetic performance of that work, including Beiderbecke's own.

---

24. Norvo also recalled listening to Ray Miller, a now little remembered dance band, active in Chicago in the 1920s. It had at various times players like Miff Mole, Muggsy Spanier, and Frankie Trumbauer, outstanding soloists all, for the time. Based on recording evidence, it espoused a more spontaneous, occasionally "hot," more soloist-oriented jazz style than most white 1920s dance bands.

Norvo scored it for xylo-marimba (a five-octave composite of the two instruments), bass clarinet (played by none other than Benny Goodman), bass (Artie
Bernstein), and a guitar (Dick McDonough). And by using the rich lower-middle
range of his instrument in mostly four-mallet harmonizations, with Goodman's
sensitively integrated bass clarinet colorations, Norvo captured perfectly the lonely
bittersweet poignancy of Beiderbecke's composition. Norvo also incorporated a
new, more purely melodic middle section, which Bix had added after making
his own recording, and which Bix's friend, arranger Bill Challis, had transcribed
and notated for the publication of *In a Mist*.

As daring and as unusual as *In a Mist* may have been, one is certainly not
prepared—in a jazz context—for the musical audacities of Norvo's own *Dance
of the Octopus*. It is clearly the most advanced composition of the early thirties,
falling almost outside the realm of jazz, and being in no sense a dance or "entertainment" music. The only pieces of that period that begin to match it in
originality, though totally different in style, are the opening of Ellington's *The
Mystery Song* (1931) and Hawkins's mid-1933 *Queer Notions* (recorded three
months earlier by Henderson, but not released until December 1933).

Norvo's opus, *sui generis* in all respects, stood alone for over a decade, until
pieces like George Handy's *The Blooz*, Pete Rugolo's innovative works for Kenton in 1945, Tristano's atonal Trio recordings of 1946, and Ellington's freely
non-tonal *Clothed Woman* (1947) came along.[25]

Dance of the Octopus is in two parts. Perhaps one and a half is more accurate,
for the piece does end rather feebly and abruptly, not quite fulfilling its initial
promise, nor quite achieving a balanced form. The first part is unrestrainedly
atonal, loosely constructed in a free-form free-associative "abstract" continuity.
Chromatically shifting four-part marimba chords, sinister bass clarinet trills, and
behind-the-bridge pitchless guitar arpeggios combine to set the eerie tone of the
opening section, its deep-sea mood further perpetuated by low, sustained, ominous-
sounding bass notes (Ex. 14). This introductory material sets up Norvo's princi-

Ex. 14

pal idea: floating, freely atonal ruminating figures, moving through inky harmonic regions, occasional contrapuntal tentacles reaching outward and upward—sometimes in contrary motion (uncommon in jazz)—punctuated here and
there by string bass and bass clarinet interjections. Only at the end of the first
part, in a series of bitonal cadencing chords, does the music come to anything
like tonal *terra firma*.

The second part, set in a regular 2/2 meter, features a pleasantly syncopated
motive in thirds. But even this more endearing mood is partially undercut by its

25. Other early tonally ambiguous pieces are Jimmie Lunceford's *Stratosphere* (1934) and Claude
Thornhill's *Portrait of a Guinea Farm* (1941).

constantly shifting accompanying harmonies, not quite atonal, but certainly tonally uncentered. The final ten bars, as mentioned, drift off into a kind of musical dead end, and the piece ends rather innocently and almost apologetically, undoubtedly cut off before the intended ending because of time limitations.

One can readily understand why Norvo, with such a creative mind and an inventive ear, would have picked Eddie Sauter as his musical running mate. Indeed, given a remarkable composition like *Dance of the Octopus*, it becomes clear why it was possible for Norvo to have a strong influence on Sauter and the original direction the latter's arrangements for Norvo (and Goodman) were to take.

But the encounter with Sauter was still a few years off. In 1934, Norvo, under the guidance of John Hammond, began to record with the likes of Bunny Berigan, Teddy Wilson, Chu Berry, Artie Shaw, Charlie Barnet (with whom he co-led a band for a while). Although the eight sides cut for Columbia in 1934 and 1935 were collectively uneven, Norvo's playing was generally exemplary and unequivocally improvised jazz. The series did produce one very moving performance, the classic *Blues in E Flat*, featuring outstanding melodic improvisations by Norvo, Berigan, and Wilson.[26] It is also a fine example of collective music-making and the high level of mutual inspiration a compatible group of creative musicians could generate. Moreover, Norvo's one solo chorus is as eloquent and simple an illustration of his lyric artistry as one will find, and this on an instrument which no one had ever expected to produce eloquence and lyricism. Even great composers like Stravinsky (in his ballet *Petrushka*) or Bartók (in his *Miraculous Mandarin*) had not gone beyond using the xylophone for very special effects, usually macabre or bizarre, or as a coloristic doubling of other instruments. The notion of playing a blues or a ballad on an instrument which had no sustaining ability was really daring, except that one suspects that Norvo alone among men didn't think it was daring at all, but quite natural and inevitable.

Of course, Norvo's ability to make a blues sound "inevitable" on a xylophone—to make that instrument sing, as it were—was based on a remarkable conception of how to defy and overcome the instrument's inherent limitations. And Norvo's *Blues in E Flat* solo affords us an uncomplicated glimpse into how this was achieved.

The basic problem of the xylophone—more so than the marimba and the vibraphone—is that its notes when struck with a mallet have no sustaining capacity. Their natural duration is very short, especially in the upper range, and the xylophone has no sustaining pedal, as does a piano or a vibraphone. To create the *illusion* of a longer note, the xylophonist has to use a tremolo, a rapid alternation of two notes or the same pitch, "rolled" with two mallets. But if you tremolo all the time, it can get awfully boring, for it is an effect that wears out its welcome rather quickly. The xylophonist then has to resort to other devices, one of which is the arpeggio, outlining chords and harmonies in rapid mallet alternations. But constant arpeggio-playing can also get very tedious. And so the

26. See Part 1 of this chapter for a discussion of Berigan's work here.

xylophonist has to be a remarkable inventor of melodies, of motives, of themes which do *not* require an excessive amount of filling out with tremolos or arpeggios. The xylophonist can play double-stops (or octaves), of course, with two mallets simultaneously, or with four mallets, producing full harmonies. Such harmonic effects work beautifully in moderate or slow tempos but are quite limited, purely technically, in fast tempos. Norvo, by the early thirties, had developed a virtually infallible sense of balance among these various devices, steering a narrow course between the instrument's various limitations and his impeccable musical taste, almost never allowing himself to become entrapped in clichés.

Norvo's sensitive and varied use of tremolos is symptomatic of his tasteful approach. On his chorus in *Blues in E Flat*, Norvo uses several kinds of tremolo, in addition varying their speed and attack. One is a major-second tremolo (or roll or trill—all more or less synonomous terms) [musical notation] (in mm. 2 and 9); another is a minor-third tremolo [musical notation] (in mm. 7 and 8); and lastly an octave tremolo [musical notation] (in mm. 10 and 12). Just as common, but by chance not used in *Blues in E Flat*, is the single-pitch tremolo [musical notation] . Norvo can create the *illusion* of a single sustained note by applying a roll or tremolo with a very soft *legato* attack for each stroke, or simulate the vibrato of a voice or a horn by doing a relaxed slow roll. The first two notated examples (above) also create the impression of a vibrato, vibrato being a relatively quick and subtle oscillation between slightly higher and lower pitch variations. With what variety, taste, and sensitivity Norvo uses these technically limited (ultimately) devices is beautifully demonstrated on *Blues in E Flat*.

But Norvo's importance lies not only in his abilities as a virtuoso improviser but in his role as an orchestra creator and leader. It is clear that Norvo had from the outset an original conception of how a jazz orchestra might sound. As already mentioned in Chapter I in connection with Eddie Sauter's work for Goodman, Norvo had early on absorbed approaches to orchestral jazz other than those of Henderson and Redman. His year with Whiteman had made him profoundly aware of that band's original and often experimental late 1920s', early 1930s' orchestrations. Then there was the Chicago-based Ray Miller band, with its relatively sophisticated stylings, plus Norvo listened seriously to Duke Ellington's and Lunceford's orchestras with their unique sounds. And finally he was absorbing the rhythmic and harmonic innovations of men like Armstrong, Beiderbecke, and Earl Hines.

In Eddie Sauter, a Columbia University and Juilliard-trained trumpet and mellophone player and budding young arranger, Norvo found the ideal creative spirit to help him shape his band. Sauter's earliest compositions and arrangements in 1936—for example, *Gramercy Square, Decca Stomp,*[27] *A Porter's Love*

---

27. Many of these pieces, typically *Decca Stomp*, foresee the small-band stylings of the John Kirby Sextet of a few years later.

Song, I Know That You Know—already reveal many moments of originality, while at the same time one can hear that the twenty-two-year-old arranger had listened well to Ellington's unique voicings and instrumental blends, also his odd-numbered asymmetrical structures (as in the 17-bar phrases of *Gramercy*). I have already commented on Sauter's remarkable ability to make four horns sound like many more and in a variety of timbres.[28] Indeed, every arrangement offers some unique moment(s): an original modulation, an interesting voicing, some piquant dissonance (usually supplied by Norvo, as at the end of *Gramercy* or in his xylophone solo on *Decca Stomp*).[29] And throughout there were Norvo's refreshing, sensitive solos and obbligatos. And towards the end of 1936, Norvo's wife, Mildred Bailey, began singing with his band (or alternatively recording with his orchestra under *her* name).

Mildred Bailey was one of the finest jazz-influenced vocalists of the Swing Era. In addition to being blessed with a light, clear, bell-like voice and a fine ear, she had excellent diction and could sing a song with such conviction and warmth that she would make you, the listener, believe in it, no matter how ephemeral it might actually be. She also had a keen appreciation of jazz and always tried to surround herself with the best jazz musicians. Mildred's early influences were Ethel Waters and Bessie Smith, but by the time she recorded *A Porter's Love Song* with her husband Red's orchestra in mid-1936, she had come somewhat under the sway of Billie Holiday, particularly in the use of some of the latter's distinctive decorative inflections. That is not to say that Mildred Bailey was merely an imitator or assimilator of other styles. Rather, she synthesized these influences and developed her own voice and style. Indeed, it can be said that she was the first important white singer, and as such the first really to break away significantly from the essentially all-blues traditions that prevailed before Bailey. Her predecessors (like Bessie and Ethel) were black, and virtually all "jazz" singing in the 1920s was in terms of blues and blues-ish pieces, often with very suggestive lyrics and double-entendre titles. Mildred could sing a fine blues— witness her *Downhearted Blues* (1935) and such blues-flavored songs as *Rockin' Chair* and *Lazy Bones*. But her light voice and wide range of vocal/technical abilities enabled her to explore as well the white popular song repertory, most of it coming from Broadway, turning it into jazz material, all this at a time—the late 1920s, early 1930s—when the crooners, both male and female, had begun to take over the field completely.

Generally speaking, Mildred's best performances occurred in association with a strong and progressive arranger's conception, (She did not function quite as well in loosely strung-together improvisational settings, and certainly not as well as Billie Holiday did, for a true jazz singer to *that* extent Mildred was not.) And, of course, Eddie Sauter represented just such an original arranger's voice. *A Porter's Love Song*, conceived and arranged by Sauter, is an excellent example

28. See above, Chapter 1, latter part, for Sauter's contribution to the Benny Goodman orchestra.
29. These early 1936–37 Norvo sides also provide us with welcome glimpses of fine drum work by Moe Purtill, who was to contribute so importantly to Glenn Miller's success a few years later. (Hear his exciting yet restrained work, for instance, on *A Porter's Love Song*.)

of the kind of integration between voice and orchestra, between song and arrangement-*qua-composition*, that could be achieved.

Red Norvo's particular kind of creative and forward-looking orchestral leadership also had a lot to do with the artistic success of many of these Sauter-Bailey collaborations, as did some of the fine intelligent players Norvo had in his band, like trumpeter Stew Pletcher, clarinetist Hank d'Amico, tenor player Herbie Haymer, bassist Pete Peterson, and drummer Maurice "Moe" Purtill.

Irving Berlin's *Remember* receives a superb Sauter treatment, featuring as its centerpiece a lyrical xylophone solo by Norvo (rather than a Bailey vocal), also a fine d'Amico clarinet solo, with Sauter taking full advantage of Norvo's recently enlarged saxophone section (to four) and continually mixing brass and saxophones in rich, creamy blends never quite attempted before.

Smoke Dreams (January 1937) is by all odds one of the strangest arrangements Sauter ever concocted, especially considering that it was not an instrumental, but a vocal for Mildred Bailey. There have been various stories circulated regarding the reason for Sauter's ultra-modern and, for 1937, extremely "dissonant" score. One is that Sauter was upset with Bailey for some reason and purposely made the accompaniment very difficult. (If this is the case, Mildred—with her excellent ear and intonation—seemed hardly to notice and sang the song effortlessly, despite Sauter's intended obstacle course—although after his "atonal" introduction, she had to have pianist Joe Liss feed her her first pitch.)

A second account, less believable, suggests that Norvo and Sauter were upset with the quality of the song, *Smoke Dreams*, and as a sort of revenge on the publisher decided to write as "uncommercial" and inaccessible an arrangement as possible. It is amazing, regardless of which story is true, that the record was issued at all by Brunswick.

Whatever the true intentions may have been, the recording has been taken very seriously by a number of jazz critics and historians, a fact that must have caused Norvo and Sauter some amusement. For, if we are to take *Smoke Dreams* as parody, then it is not very good parody, and its grim dissonances and stiff performance fail to make clear what in fact is being parodied. As a serious exercise in "polytonality"—as Norvo called it years later—it is hardly more successful, since its bitonal and polytonal layerings are simply pasted on top of each other and hardly ever used in any meaningful functional way. It thus remains an intriguing musical oddity, of which neither its purpose nor its outcome is very clear.

I Would Do Anything for You is Sauter once again in normal form, discovering wondrous orchestral blends and textures. The closest Sauter comes to Henderson's call-and-response technique is when he briefly juxtaposes muted brass and saxes in neat 2-bar interchanges (see Fig. 3).

The Norvo-Sauter-Bailey alliance worked well for another year or so, producing such fine vocals and scores as *Russian Lullaby, Worried Over You, There's*

Fig. 3

muted brass	saxophones	saxophones	muted brass
2	2	2	2

a Lull in My Life, Loving You, More Than Ever, Rockin' Chair (one of Mildred's most moving and heartfelt performances), *Please Be Kind,* and *My Melancholy Baby.* Some of these featured the velvet-toned lead trumpet of Louis Mucci, giving the brass the kind of mellow sound that Sauter preferred and without which he really couldn't blend brass and reeds so successfully. (For example, Goodman's or Miller's sharply etched brass sonorities could never have been successfully used to achieve Sauter's cross-timbral blendings.) Louis Mucci performed much the same kind of role years later in Claude Thornhill's late forties orchestra, as a superb lead trumpet, giving that band its special velvet sonoric patina.

Thanks for the Memory was one of Mildred Bailey's finest and most representative vocals, this time not arranged by Sauter, but accompanied by a septet consisting of a few members of Norvo's band, plus Chu Berry, Teddy Wilson, Allan Reuss, and Dave Tough. The last-named three, along with Norvo's regular bassist, Pete Peterson, achieved an amazing laid-back swing, especially during and after Chu Berry's solo. Allan Reuss in particular demonstrated again that he was one of the very best rhythm guitar players.

Although musicians and critics appreciated the inventiveness and subtle swing of the Norvo band, audiences remained generally unimpressed, preferring the louder, harder-swinging virtuosity of the Goodmans, the more gimmicky and at times pretentious early repertory of a Shaw, and, of course, the powerful Harlem bands like Webb, Basie, Lunceford. In the face of this, Norvo enlarged his orchestra and converted to a slightly more aggressive style, exemplified in such recordings as *Just You, Just Me, Nuances by Norvo,* and *Rehearsin' for a Nervous Breakdown,* featuring the more forceful trumpet work of Jack Palmer and George Berg's booting tenor solos, in what later became known as the "jump style." *I Was Doing All Right,* also with a brighter, more energetic sound, features some most excellent d'Amico clarinet—at the level of a Goodman or Shaw—as well as what must be the first use of harmonics on the xylophone, a very special light-toned effect achieved by striking the bar on the node with the mallet while simultaneously placing a finger lightly on the middle of the bar.

But by mid-1938 various problems had begun to trouble the Norvo organization. There apparently was much dissension within the band's personnel, causing all but Pete Peterson—loyal to Norvo to the end—to leave one by one. Sauter too left Norvo (soon to go with Goodman), and finally in 1939 Mildred Bailey became ill and was forced to retire temporarily. Red and Mildred rarely worked together again after that, and in the summer of 1939 Red disbanded his orchestra.

Norvo made several more attempts to maintain big bands, the last in 1942. Ironically this was, in a purely technical sense, the best band Norvo ever had. But it once again failed commercially, recorded only two sides (two others were left unissued, including Alec Wilder's beautiful *I'll Be Around*), and the band soon passed into oblivion. But on *Jersey Bounce* and *Arthur Murray Taught Me Dancing* we hear the cleanest, most disciplined brass and reed section Norvo ever had, mostly unknown and now forgotten players. The band's weakness was its rhythm section, and competing with the hard-driving bands of the war years (or with the lush orchestras of James and Shaw), Norvo's simply didn't survive.

In one sense it was perhaps fortunate that Norvo was obliged to discontinue his orchestra, thereby forced to work as a single or fronting small groups, this in turn presenting him as the individual soloist he was, rather than as merely a sometime soloist in a band context. Norvo's solo work can be assessed on many of his late thirties' and forties' recordings, most strikingly, for example, on the two-sided seven-minute *Just a Mood* and *Honeysuckle Rose* with the Teddy Wilson Quartet (September 1937). These John Hammond-organized performances brought together not only Norvo and Wilson but trumpeter Harry James, still with Goodman at the time, and bassist John Simmons. For those who remember only the flamboyant and often saccharine James, it would be well for them to listen to his eloquent, superbly authoritative blues playing on *Just a Mood*. James here reflects an extraordinary amalgam of Armstrong, Berigan, and himself. Technically more assured and controlled than either Armstrong and Berigan, but without quite their depth of feeling, James could at his best combine a kind of warm romanticism with the earthiness and stark simplicities of the blues.

The high calibre of Norvo's creative and soloistic abilities can be aptly appraised on *Just a Mood* in direct comparison with Wilson, two masters side by side. It becomes clear that Norvo was even more the *melodic* creator than Wilson, this despite the considerable limitations of the xylophone, a factor which, as I have already pointed out, in a sense forced Norvo, using his great innate talent, to become a *superior* melodist. His three choruses on *Just a Mood* are prime Norvo, a brief 12-bar excerpt of which affirms (Ex. 15) that Norvo was also always a searching melodist, one whose phrases often incorporated harmonic/ melodic ideas well in advance of their time.

Norvo's 1942–44 small band, featuring young players like trumpeter/arranger Shorty Rogers, trombonist Eddie Bert, and clarinetist Aaron Sachs, never re-

Ex. 15

corded commercially because of the American Federation of Musicians recording ban. But their work survives in performances transcribed on 16-inch discs
during a Town Hall concert in New York, June 9, 1945. The band was stylistically—at least on this occasion—at odds with itself, the three horn men plus
special guest Flip Phillips all playing in quite different idioms. But the event did
produce one of Norvo's all-time great solo performances, a quintet version of *I
Don't Stand a Ghost of a Chance*. Although Red played mostly vibraphone
during the Town Hall concert, for this piece and one other *(The Man I Love)*
he switched back to his first love, the xylophone, an instrument on which he
was always most at ease. His two choruses, comprising the entire performance
of *Ghost of a Chance*, are in effect a virtually perfect miniature Norvo *composition*, which happens to use the harmonies of *Ghost of a Chance*. It is a perfectly
constructed improvisation, striking a fine balance between the melodic and the
virtuosic—his sudden thirty-second note bursts are among the solo's high points—
and skillfully avoiding every predictable turn-of-phrase. The solo is full of unusual figures, unexpected twists and turns, and wonderfully logical substitute
harmonies. In its Mozartean clarity and tonal beauty—yes, on a xylophone—
and in its awe-inspiring compositional unity, this is one of Red's most creative
solos.

  The Man I Love exists in two similar versions, one from the already mentioned Town Hall concert, the other from a commercial recording made for the
Keynote label on July 27, 1944. In both instances Norvo sings out in his most
eloquent ornamental ballad style, but after one chorus breaks into an approximately two and a half times faster tempo. It is a brilliant virtuoso display, filled
with dazzling 4-bar breaks and ingratiating sequential patterns (which dexterously
avoid fast-note tedium). What is even more fetching about the performance is
that, while Norvo plays at breakneck speed, the rhythm section devotes two bars
(in fast tempo) to every measure of the original song. Thus a two-tiered effect
evolves, where on one level the speed of the chord progressions of Gershwin's
song in the second half of the performance remains close to that of the opening
section, while the actual tempo of the music has more than doubled. In graphic
form the relationship between the two sections looks as follows (Ex. 16):

Ex. 16

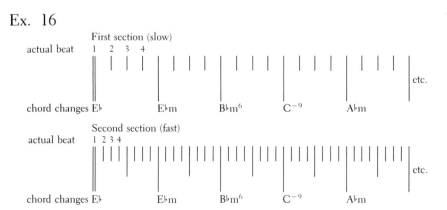

This way of treating an up-tempo rendition of a slow ballad became common practice by the late forties, but I believe Norvo's recording of *The Man I Love* was one of the earliest uses of this split-level device.

It was around this time that Norvo joined Benny Goodman's Sextet, providing that group with a welcome artistic infusion. Norvo here converted to vibra-phone, playing the instrument—in contrast to Lionel Hampton—in more of an ensemble style. Norvo found that playing his favorite, the xylophone, did not work with the Goodman Sextet, the absence of sustained notes being a great handicap. But playing the vibraphone *with* the clean, clear, crisp non-vibrato approach of the xylophone, Norvo found, *did* work. It was then, too, that Teddy Wilson discovered that marvelous three-way combination of piano, vibraphone, and clarinet in close upper-register voicing, one of the joyous never-tiring hall-marks of the group. *After You've Gone, Rachel's Dream*, and *I Got Rhythm* are fine examples of the Goodman Sextet's prowess in those mid-1940s years.

Irving Berlin's *Russian Lullaby* is little known today, but in the Swing Era it was a piece much favored by jazz orchestras. Norvo recorded it twice, once with his 1937 band in an Eddie Sauter arrangement, the second time in 1944 with a septet that included trumpeter Joe Thomas, trombonist Vic Dickenson, and clar-inetist Hank d'Amico. In the earlier 1937 version, taken in a fairly bright tempo, d'Amico happened to play a wrong note in an interlude section preceding Nor-vo's solo. The offending note, a C♯, was part of a turn-of-phrase which d'Amico used often throughout his career—in short, one of his cliché phrases. It just didn't fit too well here. Norvo, who was a master at picking up a previous solo-ist's ideas and developing them—he and Wilson were constantly doing this to each other, their successive solos often sounding like one—and in this case Norvo extended his mimetic skill even to d'Amico's wrong-note phrase. In bars 9 through 12 of his solo, Norvo teasingly incorporated d'Amico's erring C♯ (Ex. 17), un-cannily making it sound right in *his* use of it.

Ex. 17

It is almost unbelievable, but when Norvo recorded *Russian Lullaby* again *seven years later*, this time in a Johnny Thompson arrangement and a much slower tempo and different conception, he reverted to a very similar turn-of-phrase, at the same time imitating a motive Teddy Wilson had just played a little bit earlier (Ex. 18). Could it be that a) Norvo remembered d'Amico's wrong note and his own toying with it in *his* solo all those years, and b) that this

Ex. 18

memory had been jogged by Wilson's coincidentally similar phrase? Norvo's elaboration of this material is reproduced in Ex. 19, the tremolo notes B-E♭-A♭-D♭ all coming after a similar intervallic drop and representing a similar dissonance as the C♯ in Ex. 17, also analogously placed at the end of the motive.[30]

Ex. 19

Norvo was always at the forefront of activities, and it therefore should not come as a surprise that he presided over a record date for Comet Records in June 1945 which included Charlie Parker and Dizzy Gillespie, as well as such (by then) established stalwarts as Teddy Wilson and Slam Stewart. These unusual sides are discussed in greater detail in Volume III of this history, and need detain us for the moment only in respect to Norvo's role in these performances. Norvo was at his brilliant best throughout the date, but perhaps he never played a more soulfully meditative solo than on *Bird's Blues* (also known as *Slam Slam Blues*) (Ex. 20). Playing vibraphone, Norvo here played with a rhythmic freedom that clearly anticipates the ornamental style and subtle swing of Milt Jackson. In his role as the "modernist," Norvo plays an inventively "polytonal" interlude on

Ex. 20

30. Norvo in turn became so fond of this motive—jazz musicians would call it a "lick"—that he used it frequently in later years, ingeniously dropping it into different pieces as, for example, his 1946 *I Surrender Dear* with Woody Herman and His Woodchoppers.

Congo Blues, followed by a break and two amazingly fluent bop-streamlined blues choruses (Ex. 21).

Equally brilliant is Norvo's solo on *Hallelujah*, played with his typically focused energy and drive, occasionally exploding into unexpected cascades of notes.

In 1946, after some years with the Benny Goodman Quintet (and Sextet), Norvo joined Woody Herman's orchestra, not only as vibraphone soloist, but as

Ex. 21

associate leader and composer-arranger for Herman's band-within-a-band, the Woodchoppers.[31]

Just as Art Tatum is remembered mostly for his Trio work, so too Norvo is today remembered for the outstanding trio he formed with guitarist Tal Farlow and bassist Charles Mingus in 1949, the latter two replaced by Jimmy Ramey and Red Mitchell respectively in 1952. On any number of titles—one might single out *Move* especially, but also *I've Got You Under My Skin, Godchild, Zing Went the Strings of My Heart, Farewell to Alms, Sweet Georgia Brown*—one can hear not only the astonishing virtuosity and consistency of these players but a level of close-knit intricate integration, each player functioning in several roles (sometimes simultaneously), that until then had not been achieved in jazz. The Norvo Trio remains in memory as one of the finest small small groups in jazz history, and will be discussed at greater length in the subsequent volume of this History.

If Red Norvo had the misfortune of loving and playing an instrument which is little appreciated by the general public, he nonetheless gained the respect of all musicians who worked with him, as well as those who were not so fortunate to do so. In his absolutely uncompromising artistry, his unblemished creativity and impeccable musical taste, Norvo is among the very best artists jazz has had to offer.

PART 3

BILLIE HOLIDAY

The question persists, it haunts the jazz literature: What is a jazz singer? (More commonly: What is *not* a jazz singer?) Many an astute critic or writer has foundered on this question, rendering their *opinions* as if they were documented, demonstrable, scientific fact. One writer, for example, opined—at least with the modifier "to my ears"—that Ella Fitzgerald and Anita O'Day were not jazz singers but Edith Piaf was. In some loftily esoteric sense that is perhaps an arguable position, but why such narrow defining? And why are such hard distinctions made with singers but not with instrumentalists?

Part of the reason is that singers reputedly (and facetiously)—both in the classical and jazz fields—are often not considered "musicians"—not good ones anyway. The quip that singers have resonance where their brains ought to be is a stock joke among musicians all over the world. Singers are suspect, especially those who are successful. Among popular and jazz singers the taint of Tin Pan Alley is an almost insurmountable barrier towards acceptance by hard-line critics. And Tin Pan Alley and the Brill Building (for many decades the headquarters of the popular music business) are, of course, the all-time favorite whipping boys of jazz critics. It is automatically assumed—with the authority of the Mo-

31. See below, Chapter 7, Part 3.

saic commandments—that songs are "trashy," "puerile," "inane," "insipid," and
that a handful of chosen jazz singers always, or nearly always, "triumph over the
material." It is the most prevalent cliché of jazz-writing, for it gives such writers
the insular security of belonging to a benign exclusive club whose tastes in such
matters are supreme and unassailable.

It isn't that simple, of course. The voice is not only the most personal of
instruments, but it deals of necessity with texts (or—in scat-singing—with syllables that nevertheless have abstract verbal associations). And here personalities
are as numerous and variable as the number of persons that express them. Recognition of even that simple fact would alleviate much of the pontification that
passes for criticism on the subject of singing in jazz.[1]

In my view it is not as thorny a subject as some of the more vociferous writers
would have us believe. A reasonable definition of a jazz singer might include
the following criteria: a singer who is musically creative with the capacity to forge
an original style (not merely mannerisms); one who can and does (but doesn't
always have to) improvise; and one who can reshape the material into something
personal and individual. By such a definition, Sarah Vaughan, Billie Holiday,
Mildred Bailey, Frank Sinatra, Peggy Lee, Nat Cole, Anita O'Day, Fran Warren, and Chris Connor would count as jazz singers, still leaving open the questions of "*how* creative," "*how* good," "*how* individual."

One singer about whom there has never been any question as to jazz pedigree
is Billie Holiday. Although she received her share of criticism—different at various periods of her career—her jazz credentials were never in question. And of
course by the end of her life she had been virtually canonized and become a
legend in her own time, including a fascination that clings to her life and work
to this day and producing a whole Billie Holiday industry.

It is a truism to regard Billie Holiday as one of the great artists of jazz. But
her art transcends the usual categorizations of style, content, and technique.
Much of her singing goes beyond itself and becomes a humanistic document; it
passed often into a realm that is not only beyond criticism but in the deepest
sense inexplicable. We can, of course, describe and analyze the surface mechanics of her art: her style, her techniques, her personal vocal attributes; and I
suppose a poet could express the essence of her art or at least give us, by poetic
analogy, his particular insight into it. But, as with all truly profound art, that
which operates above, below, and all around its outer manifestations is what
most touches us, and also remains ultimately mysterious.

So powerful is the mystery of her art and the fatal attraction of Billie's tragic
life that many writers and critics have been unable to resist reading their own
personal creeds and philosophical tenets into her work. Thus many have seen
only its tragic side, emphasizing the oppression of black artists, racism, the evil
forces of commercialism: "the messenger of misery," as Leonard Feather once

---

1. Jazz-writing and criticism, even more than classical music, is a field rampant with hotly contested
judgments and acrimonious feuding between writers who have staked out territories they possessively
consider their private domains of expertise. Intruders of any kind are not welcome. And nowhere do
the opinions divide more bitterly than on the question of jazz-singing.

put it.[2] Indeed, latecomers to her work, drawn to it—like the non-musical intelligentsia and political left—by her recording of *Strange Fruit* (1939), were bound to see only the gloomy and, to put it plainly, more calculated aspect of her art, being unaware of the infectious joy and optimism of her early recordings.

The harrowing details of Billie Holiday's childhood and adult life are too well known to warrant repetition here.[3] Our account will limit itself primarily to her recordings and will thus begin with the first of these, made in 1933 when Billie was eighteen years old. John Hammond, that indefatigable discoverer of talent, roaming through Harlem and pursuing every lead, sometimes even unto the lowliest dives, had come upon Billie by accident in a club called Monette Moore's.[4] This was but one of the many places, speakeasies all, where Billie found sporadic employment, working mostly for tips: the Log Cabin, the Yeah Man, the Hotcha, Dickie Wells, and many others. Monette Moore's conversion from the blues to a more white-oriented popular song was symptomatic of the times, as even among black people Bessie Smith's fame declined and Ethel Waters became the reigning queen of song. In consequence, the Harlem clubs were filled with hundreds of Ethel Waters imitators. What struck Hammond about Billie was that she was clearly not one of them. She already had the beginnings of an individual style. His efforts to record her, at a time when the American record industry was in its worst Depression doldrums, were finally rewarded when Benny Goodman, in the initial phase of his climb to fame, egged on by Hammond, decided to turn over to Billie the final side on a session otherwise devoted to Ethel Waters. The song was *Your Mother's Son-in-Law*, a quasi-novelty number from the unsuccessful all-black musical *Blackbirds of 1933*.

Understandably, in the awesome presence of Miss Waters, surrounded by mostly white musicians, and facing her first microphone, Billie was scared and nervous. And it shows on the record. Extreme nervousness affects one's blood circulation, which in turn affects negatively not only one's breathing, so absolutely vital to a singer (or a wind instrumentalist), but one's capacity to think, to be freely creative. Dean Kincaide's sophisticated un-Harlem-ish studio-style arrangement, set in too high a key, also could not have instilled much confidence in Billie. She literally gulps for air at the end of each phrase and seems unable to find anything personal to do with the song. She is riding on sheer talent. What remains is one of her greatest assets: the unique timbre of her voice, and a certain gutsy, shouting rhythmic delivery that she had learned from Bessie Smith records. The improvisatory freedom which she admired in Louis Armstrong was yet to be revealed.

2. Feather's notes for Columbia's *Billie Holiday, The Golden Years* (3CL 40), although also very personal, give a well-balanced, beautifully written, objective yet warm, capsule account of Billie's career.

3. However, for the uninitiated, biographical background reading is very much recommended: Billie Holiday and William Duffy, *Lady Sings the Blues* (New York, 1956); John Chilton, *Billie's Blues* (New York, 1975); Melvin Maddocks, *Billie Holiday*, Time-Life Records, 1979.

4. Monette Moore was a much-recorded blues singer in the 1920s but turned to vaudeville and Broadway in the 1930s, frequently understudying for Ethel Waters. It was when Moore was substituting for Waters in *As Thousands Cheer* that Billie appeared at Moore's place.

Billie was given a second chance a week later with an inconsequential item of only eighteen bars' duration, called *Riffin' the Scotch* (by guitarist Dick McDonough with lyrics by Johnny Mercer). Rejected by Columbia, it was remade two weeks later and this time found acceptable. The side is more outstanding for Shirley Clay's[5] and Jack Teagarden's solos, but at the same time we can begin to hear in embryonic form, even in this all-too-brief chorus, Billie's individual way with words and pitches. She twists and bends them to her purposes, giving the song, the first of many in her repertory about unrequited love and dashed expectations, a bouncy devil-may-care joviality. On the level of rhythmic energy alone, her performance must have stood out radically among the otherwise pervasive limpid crooning styles then current.

It would be a year and a half before Billie would re-enter a recording studio, this time teamed up with Teddy Wilson (another Hammond protégé) for what turned out to be a three-year-long fruitful recording association. But even before that remarkable alliance could begin, a most important (but almost always totally neglected) date in Billie's recording history occurred (March 12, 1935): the fifteen-minute film *Symphony in Black* featuring the Duke Ellington orchestra.[6] Billie sings the *Big City Blues* segment—previously recorded by Ellington as *Saddest Tale* (without Billie)—that is part of a four-movement suite Ellington created for this film. It is pure Billie Holiday, in her first full flowering on an electronic medium. All the essential elements of her style are in place: the unique olive-toned timbre, the reshaping (mostly the stretching) of rhythms to press the maximum of expression out of the words; the little dips, scoops, and sags with which she inflects (and thereby emphasizes) particular words and pitches; the strongly felt implicit beat and swing, for all her exterior rhythmic freedom (Ex. 1); the direct, *unsentimental*, all the more poignant delivery.

Receiving minimal distribution, the film and Billie's singing in it made almost no impact, standing as an obscure venture, an unrecognized artistic achievement of rare haunting beauty and technical skill.

Ex. 1

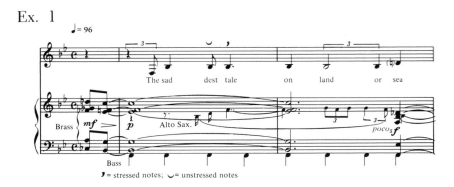

5. Shirley Clay, a fine black trumpeter, was then working with Don Redman's band. His appearance on this date marked the first time Goodman recorded with a black musician.
6. To my knowledge the sound track from this cinematographically and musically remarkable film has never been made available on commercial records (see above, Chapter 2).

A fifteen-minute short about the history of and life among blacks was not, in the 1930s, a viable route to success. Recordings were patently better. And so July 2, 1935, the first of the Teddy Wilson sessions, marking the beginning of a henceforth more or less uninterrupted recording career, became an important date in Billie's life. It also produced some startlingly good recorded performances.

What makes these Holiday recordings so successful—and here again John Hammond's fine hand is discernible—is, above and beyond Billie's singing, the high calibre of the talent with which Hammond surrounded her. It was to become clear years later that Billie thrived best—perhaps only—in the company of great soloists and essentially improvisatory accompaniments. (Some of the arranged backgrounds she was given in the 1940s had a deadly, palling effect on her.) But with the likes of Wilson, Roy Eldridge, Buck Clayton, Ben Webster, Lester Young, and first-rate rhythm sections, she seemed especially inspired, and—the point must be made—in a generally happy frame of mind. Billie's first three years of recordings constitute her finest period with, as Leonard Feather once calculated, twice as many happy songs as sad songs. Most of these 1935–39 recordings, some with Teddy Wilson-led small groups, others under her own "leadership" (but all organized by John Hammond), are classics of jazz, not only because of Billie's unique talent but because of the generally high quality and authentic creativity of the accompaniments. Indeed, accompaniments is a misnomer. Whereas on literally thousands of swing era recordings there is a clear qualitative gap between the vocals and their instrumental surroundings, in the case of Billie's first hundred or so performances, she is an equal among equals. And the joy of these performances is that they are seamless creative entities, not mere instrumental accompaniments for a vocalist, but rather singer and musicians matching and inspiring each other. There is no need to wince or to be tolerant when the vocal comes on.

It is impossible (and unnecessary) to enumerate the individual virtues of these many superior recordings. Though they may vary somewhat in quality, I dare say there is not one that is not worth hearing, that doesn't have some outstanding moments, either vocally, or instrumentally, or both. Some of the sidemen, particularly Wilson, Eldridge, and Young—but I cannot neglect to mention Harry Carney (on clarinet!) and trumpeter Charlie Shavers—did some of their finest work on these recordings, undoubtedly inspired by Billie and by the generally high level of collective music-making.

But Billie's work is our main concern here, and rather than render a blow-by-blow account of each recording's high points, we shall single out a few especially outstanding Holiday performances as ideal representations of her art.

Of the several unique qualities Billie brought to jazz-singing—in some instances for the first time (or at any rate in a more clear-cut form than any other previous singer)—none is more important than her ability to reshape (re-compose) a given song to make it wholly her own. She did this on two levels—almost always simultaneously: on the larger structural level by freely reinventing both the melody and its rhythms, on the smaller level by embellishing these with her own wholly original vocal adornments. *I Cried for You*, a fine 1923 song by Gus Arnheim and Abe Lyman, recorded by Billie on June 30, 1936, is a revealing demonstration of her methods. Example 2 shows both the original song (excerpted) and Billie's reworking of those particular measures. (Note that the orig-

Ex. 2

inal song consists of forty measures, five times eight phrases in an unusual ABACA
pattern.)

Even in her prime, Billie had a limited range. It could be stretched from F
below middle C to the C one octave above, but in general she felt most comfortable between G and A ♪ . As a result she invariably compressed
melodies into that range, often going beyond vocal necessity to the sheer joy
of invention in smoothing out the contours of particularly rangy lines. Note
how in *I Cried for You*, located exactly in the just-mentioned range span,
Billie reduced the number of pitches she sang in the first eight bars to five
♪ , rearranging the rhythms along the way to emphasize the
A and F by means of elongation or reiteration. She retained the downward
octave leap (in her third bar, Ex. 2), undoubtedly because that is the most unusual and captivating feature of the original melodic line, and as such a contour
which she felt *had* to be preserved. The more ordinary shapes in mm. 5 and 6
she felt she could dispense with and recast on a single pitch, but in a new,
fascinating rhythmic configuration.

Another marvelous example of how she could simplify material, paring it
down to its barest essentials, occurs on *One Never Knows* (January 12, 1937),
especially in the bridge of her second chorus. Here again she uses just five
pitches—F, G, C, D, C♯—ingeniously stretched across eight bars. Such extraordinary economy and purity of expression are rare in the annals of jazz, but
Billie's closest soulmate in these respects was Lester Young. Hear him on *This
Year's Kisses* (with Teddy Wilson's group) and, above all, in perhaps the most
heartrendingly moving eight bars Prez ever played: his brief solo on *Fine and
Mellow* during the 1957 television program, *The Sound of Jazz* (not the Columbia recording, but the actual sound track).[7]

Rhythmic values in popular songs, as composed and printed, tend to be stated
in the simplest terms, for maximum accessibility. The more inventive singers,
popular and jazz, have always freed themselves from the printed page and loosened up a song's rhythms. But no one before Billie had gone quite so far in that
direction. Again, Example 2 (mm. 9–16, 20–24) shows with what uncanny
instincts she could transform ordinary rhythms into new swinging patterns.

In these few examples we have seen how Billie was able to loosen up large-
scale structural entities, such as 8-bar phrases. But on the small-scale structural
level, too, her embellishments of single notes added yet another quality uniquely
her own, defying imitation. Although these ornaments degenerated to mannerisms in later years, in her early work they had a certain innocent charm and
freshness. To my knowledge she never spoke about their origin or purpose, but
one possible explanation, besides the influence of Bessie Smith, may be that she
heard them as subtle, necessary adornments to a vocal style that was in essence
very simple. Whereas most singers colored their voices with vibratos, sometimes

7. See also p. 561 below, near end of Lester Young section, which follows.

very heavy, more often than not pasted on to the voice, Billie used vibrato very sparingly and for dramatic emphasis, but most of the time not at all. It may be then that she sensed a voice, so totally unadorned and straight, needed to be occasionally embellished and allowed to unbend. Her use of these scoops, dips, fall-offs, sags, and up-and-down twists was generally in excellent taste and not used to excess—until the later years when some of her performances were more embellishment than substance. But in these early years she used these devices with great subtlety, invariably to punctuate or bring out a particular word or note. They can be found in mm. 1, 2, 14, 17–19, 21–22 in Example 2,[8] and elsewhere scattered throughout her *I Cried* chorus, always subtly varied.

What is perhaps most remarkable about Billie's methods of reworking a given material is that she used all three just described means concurrently—sometimes in conjunction with each other, sometimes in alternation—or simply one at a time. The possible permutations of such variants are, of course, many; and it is fascinating to hear how Billie's musical instincts kept her from over-ornamentation or letting melodic adornments become a merely mechanical device or trick.

All of these techniques Billie learned from Bessie Smith, assimilated, however, and then distilled in Billie's own highly personal way. Bessie, too, had a limited range—indeed, much more so—and became a master at delivering entire blues performances within the range of a fifth without any sense of limitation. Of course, most of Bessie's blues were simple pentatonic pieces to begin with, largely improvised or re-composed with her accompanists. She, too, would reduce entire phrases to one or two pitches, letting rhythm and inflection provide the counter-balancing variety. Undoubtedly Billie Holiday much admired the direct and sturdy simplicity of such an economical, almost recitative-like approach. This in turn went hand in hand with the unsentimentality of both singers' art, reaching in Billie's case at times even a certain coolness and distance from the subject matter.

Finally, Bessie also embellished many of her opening or phrase-ending pitches and words with ornamental scoops, turns, and fall-offs. The only difference between the two singers was that Bessie's embellishments were generally carried out in a tragic, moaning, or wailing manner, slow and heavy; whereas Billie's were surprisingly agile and untragic, even perky. Bessie was, of course, singing exclusively slow-tempo blues, her slower embellishments being therefore in keeping with that genre. Billie, on the other hand was not a blues singer per se, and sang very few blues in her lifetime—even though one might argue all of her singing is colored to some extent by the blues.[9]

If Bessie Smith was one major influence on Billie Holiday, then Louis Arm-

8. Musical notation has no standard designations for such ornamentations, there never having been any need for them until jazz came along. The following four signs are, I believe, reasonable graphic representations: ⌡ = scoop, ⌄ = dip, ⌐ = fall-off (usually quick), ⟍ = longer, sagging fall-offs. In addition Billie loved to use a gracenote and *portamento* combination, notated in our example as ♪ (see mm. 3, 19, in Ex. 2 above).

9. For a full discussion of Bessie Smith's style see *Early Jazz*, 226–41.

strong was the other. It is from him that she evolved the horn-like, instrumental approach to singing in which she was for a while supreme and unique among singers. Not that she imitated Armstrong, either in the specifics of his trumpet style or his singing, but she took over in principle Armstrong's concept of improvisatory liberty and the notion of phrasing like a horn, wherever the words would allow it (or bending the words to that will). That is to say, the primary creative impulse in Billie's singing came not from the printed page and the priority of the text, as with most orthodox singers, but from a basically instrumental conception into which text and original melodic line were subsumed. Other singers would *perform* or *render* a song; Billie would *create* one.

It was her horn-like approach to singing that so endeared her to musicians and that allowed her to fit so seamlessly into an overall performance. Moreover, she was an *ensemble* singer/instrumentalist, not a concerto soloist. That is why so many of her early recordings are so superb—virtually "collective ensemble" creations—and why, conversely, much of her later work in front of arranged block-chord backgrounds fares considerably less well.

Nor should the influence of Louis Armstrong's *singing* on the young Billie be overlooked. That it was a very direct and strong influence cannot be doubted after one hears, for example, Armstrong's vocal on *Between the Devil and the Deep Blue Sea*, released in early 1932—surely a record Billie would have heard (along with other Armstrong hits of that period like *You Can Depend on Me, Georgia on My Mind, All of Me*). Listening to Louis's singing on these recordings, particularly his vocal inflections and text articulation, one hears the essential elements of Billie's style. Listen, for example, to the first sixteen bars of Louis's vocal on *Between the Devil*, especially phrases like "But I hate to lose you" or "I forgive you," transpose them up an octave and to a female voice (and subtract some of Louis's phrase-ending glissandos) and you have the clearest model for Billie's art in its formative years.

What Billie also learned from Louis—and not at all from Bessie—was a terrific, natural, relaxed sense of swing, primarily through the use of syncopation. For Bessie and her 1920s' accompanists (with the exception of Louis) swing was still a largely unknown feeling, particularly in the many slow-tempo blues that were the staples of her repertory. But Louis had shown in his late 1920s' recordings how time, meter, and beat could all be set free through the use of syncopation and double-time and a variety of attack and inflection. The teen-age Billie, growing up on Armstrong records, absorbed these lessons fully, for even on her earliest recordings a "modern" sense of swing is already present.

It is astonishing that, for all her starting at the other end of the process—the instrumental rather than the vocal—Billie was in general very faithful to the lyrics, both in execution, through her superb natural diction, and in conveying their meaning. It is true that Billie sometimes converted happy songs into sad ones and vice-versa. But those were, I believe, matters of momentary mood and external circumstances. On the whole, she resolved the problem of not letting the words (by often less-than-first-rate lyricists) interfere with her singing by instrumentalizing the material at hand, and by alchemizing words and music into a new alloy in which the parts were no longer separable. And if we admire Billie for her constant ability to elevate often mediocre song material to sublime heights, then it is precisely because she was able to make both music *and words* serve her creative purposes.

When Billie was unable to subordinate a text to her musical intentions, she almost could not function. There are such examples[10] where in particular the lyrics are so wordy (and perhaps silly)—and set in a fast patter tempo to boot and therefore so confining—that she could find nothing much to do with them. In such cases she had no improvisatory maneuverability, to stretch or contract the phrases. In general, she preferred stretching the rhythms of the lyrics, as her singing of *I Cried for You* shows so brilliantly. She loved floating long rhythmic values over fast tempos, changing the melodic line—her own or the composer's—when the shifting chord patterns, now out of phase with the delayed melody, demanded it. Her uncanny ear allowed her a high degree of freedom and mobility in this respect. I know of no examples where she was ever trapped between the demands of the "changes" and her melodic improvisations.

The other major and absolutely unique quality about Billie's singing was the timbre of her voice. This was an innate gift, God-given, if you will, certainly one of her natural physical attributes. Even so, Bessie Smith was undoubtedly an influence here too, if only by way of confirming for Billie's young ears the musical validity of such a reedy timbre. For Bessie's voice, though thicker, heavier, larger, and richer than Billie's, did have a certain tart, at times even twangy, country-style coloration. But in Billie's lighter, less opulent voice, the reedy timbre—akin to that of an English horn—became its dominant quality. How she then learned to color it, embellish it as it were, with brighter or darker hues, depending on her mood or the song in question—or (more likely) her interpretation of it—is one of the great fascinations and mysteries of her art.

In some songs (like *I Can't Believe You're in Love with Me*) her voice could be soft-spoken and subdued, like a quietly muted trumpet; in others her voice could get gritty and tart (as in *These Foolish Things* and *What a Little Moonlight Can Do*). At still other times she could take the grit right out of her voice (as in the 1937 *They Can't Take That Away from Me*), singing with a warm gentle timbre, as pure as the driven snow. By mid-1936—Billie was still only twenty-one!—her voice was becoming heavier, hoarser, tougher, although again she could modify, soften, and brighten it, seemingly at will. Often the (at first) slight hoarseness was an enhancing element. It gave a sense of grounding to the voice, as opposed to its earlier buoyant, even giddy-light quality. Later, as the years passed and her drug addiction took its physical toll, the timbre of her voice darkened and became downright acrid. Eventually, in the final decade, the voice became coarse and grating. Strangely, however, even in those years—and this is again an example of the power of her musical/aural instincts—though her speaking voice was shot and her speech slurred, she retained an amazing degree of control, relatively speaking, over her singing voice.

But as with her restructuring of a song's pitches and rhythms, so too in the

10. For instance, *It's Too Hot for Words, A Sunbonnet Blue, Twenty-four Hours a Day, Now They Call It Swing.*

coloration of her voice, it wasn't just one element that she varied. Within the basic timbres described above, she would further brighten or darken certain vowels, certain syllables or words, as the context and the meaning she was trying to impart might dictate to her. She maximized the effect of her already rather broad Southern accent, stretching *i*'s to bright-hued *aaah*'s, for example, and coloring vowels with infinitely subtle shadings and timbral nuances.

But not only vowels were used to highlight words or certain pitches, but consonants as well. No one ever sang the word "love" as she could. (Hear it on *Easy Living*, for example.) But then no one ever had such a lilting, rolling *l*, in speech or song. Listen to her way with the words "little" and "lovable" in *Miss Brown to You*. Such use of consonants, apart from their uniqueness of enunciation, served to flavor and heighten the expression of certain syllables or words almost at will, all part of her instinctive improvisatory approach. Such consonantal emphases also were used as tiny subtle "percussive" nuances, often adding enormously to her rhythmic swing.

Every Holiday fan undoubtedly has his own many favorite moments among her hundreds of recordings. It is best to let the uninitiated reader discover these for himself or herself, but a few additional examples of how Billie combined all these expressive means are perhaps not out of order. For example, in the fifth and sixth measures of *It's Like Reaching for the Moon* (not counting her first pick-up measure), one of Billie's most wistful filled-with-hope performances, notice how subtly she falls off the word "stars," giving an uncanny sense of space to the word; and then stretching the next word, "reaching" as if really reaching for something—love, of course. It is Billie at her most tender and yearning—and most imaginative. As in so many of her 1935–38 recordings, where invariably one fine sideman or another is supplying superb background obbligatos behind Billie, *Reaching* has Harry Carney on clarinet (!) weaving the most amazing fluent, mostly thirty-second note figures. It often happened that, when Billie was stretching rhythms into elongated floating durations, her obbligato partners would complement her singing with agile fast playing, invariably providing a perfect foil to her singing. (Hear Buck Clayton in a similar role on *When You're Smiling* and *If Dreams Come True*, both 1938.)

Unforgettable also is the way Billie sings "I adore you" on *Did I Remember*, a performance which, along with *No Regrets*, is also remarkable for the special musical affinity between Artie Shaw and Bunny Berigan. Listen to their duetting on *No Regrets* and the superb unity of conception on *Did I Remember* by all concerned (except Joe Bushkin).

Billie had an uncanny ability to go way beyond the song material, to mold it, shape it, characterize it in whatever mood *she* happened to be in. Two recordings in mid-1936 demonstrate how totally Billie could lay claim to a song, changing its mood and character. Gershwin's radiant lullaby, *Summertime*, then a brand new song, is turned by Holiday into a moody despairing torch song. The ominous almost menacing quality of the performance derives not only from Billie's relentlessly pessimistic treatment but from Berigan's growly trumpet and Cozy Cole's lugubrious tom-toms, all spelling doom. It is a strange interpretation, and one is puzzled to know whether it was in fact Billie who set the mood or one of the musicians acting as quasi-arranger. Similarly, A *Fine Romance*, originally a bouncy Fred Astaire film vehicle, is given a rather disdainful icy treatment, diametrically opposed to the aims of the composer, Jerome Kern. Conversely, on *I've Got My Love To Keep Me Warm*, one of Irving Berlin's carefree songs and one of Billie's greatest performances, she lifts even the depressing lyrics about winter and icicles into a positive realm, in her final half-chorus exulting in the triumph of "warm" love over cold despair.

Sometimes Billie's ways of appropriating a song could be downright destructive—at least to its original character and mood (even if what one is left with is pure Billie Holiday, which on its own terms could never be less than remarkable). A case in point is her recording of *I Can't Get Started* (1938). Here Billie changes the melody so much that, were it not for the stated title and the lyrics, one would not recognize it as Vernon Duke's famous song. Granted that Billie on many occasions improved certain songs with her improvised emendments. But one wonders what motivated her to flatten out one of the finest tunes of the decade into something much less imaginative than Vernon Duke's original. (No wonder that some song pluggers and Broadway enterpreneurs would not let her near any of their songs.) Similarly, Billie performs major surgery on Fred Ahlert's 1928 hit *I'll Get By*. Instead of adhering to the tune's sinuous lines, she compresses virtually all of it into her middle-upper register, hammering away at no fewer than twenty-six (!) repeated As, which even her ingenious ways with rhythm and timbre could not prevent from becoming overbearing.

But such misfirings were the exception. There are Holiday performances where she even submits to the material, fashioning her own parallel to the original, as on *I Must Have That Man* (1937). While Billie could at times be quite distant from a song's text, here she went along with it, allowing herself considerable emotional play. In her words "crying for heat," embellished with subtle sobbing turns and sagging sighs, she lets the emotion engendered by the lyrics out into the open. I see a corollary between this more overt expression and the performance's absolutely perfect slow-ish tempo: neither pushed by a fast tempo and too many words, nor obliged to stretch two bars of text across 4-bar phrases, she sings the lyrics more or less in step with the original. And I believe that this greater proximity to the original allowed her also to stay in close touch with its intended mood and character. The presence of Lester Young, the great platonic love of her life—she and Prez are definitely playing to each other, Prez with one of his most expressive solos—may also have been a factor in drawing so much overt feeling from her. Much the same can be said about Billie's *Easy Living*, one of her most iridescent and exuberant "in love" songs.

On the other hand, Billie keeps a discreet distance from an intentionally emotional even melodramatic song like *Moanin' Low*, rather coolly gliding across its surface, smoothing out its melancholy lines (musical and verbal). No torch song here for her.[11]

11. I'm not convinced that Billie's treatment serves this song best. Eva Taylor's classic 1929 recording with the Charleston Chasers, aided and abetted by Dave Tough's relentlessly ominous "gallows" press-rolls and Joe Tarto's lugubrious bowed bass, seems to me to come much closer to the heart of this macabre ballad, pedigreed jazz or not.

Sometimes her fellow musicians could be at odds with Billie's interpretation. Take *Why Was I Born?*, for example. Closest to Billie's approach is Buck Clayton, although a bit on the sentimental and commercial side. Billie here is trying to "cool off" the weepy melodramatic approach established by Helen Morgan on this song in 1929, turning its pathos outside-in, as it were, without, however, losing touch altogether with its original mood. Teddy Wilson, on the other hand, is strangely impervious to the song's drama, scampering cheerfully through one of his more elegant "Mr. Clean" improvisations. Benny Goodman is uninvolved, musing, looking for a meaning and not finding it.

Worse things than that have happened in jazz and popular music to be sure. But the point is that at the level of Billie Holiday's artistry questions of compositional unity do arise, especially considering that so often these thrown-together ensembles did manage to find such remarkable coherence. Perhaps performances of songs, above all other forms—because of their unavoidable, predetermined text connotations and mood—demand to be more "of a piece." Ellington knew that and invariably tailored song accompaniments to one specific mood or characterization. (*Big City Blues*, alias *Saddest Tale*, is but one of hundreds of examples.) And the arrangers of the 1940s, when the singers took over popular music with a vengeance, knew it too.

But, of course, Hammond didn't want arrangements for Billie—a laudable and correct premise, but not without its risks. With almost no preparation, quickly fashioned head arrangements, no composing (even in the Ellingtonian sense), no absolute leader in an essentially collective-ensemble approach: given these conditions, it is a miracle that the performances have stylistic integrity as often as they do. In retrospect those risks were worth taking.

Foolin' Myself (June 1, 1937) has a remarkable rhythmically daring moment where explicit time is warped almost to the point of suspension, while the *implied* underlying beat is nonetheless fully preserved (Ex. 3). It should be pointed out that this phrase is in certain spots virtually unnotatable in orthodox notation, for Billie's notes are often behind their own intended beat. The top staff shows Billie's melodic/rhythmic line as she recomposed the melody, the bottom staff shows the actual feeling and intended rhythms of the song as it would have been sung by most non-jazz singers.

Other superb performances from this period, many of them with Billie in her happiest, most buoyant mood, are *Carelessly* (bittersweet), *How Could You?*[12] (laughing off her sorrow and swinging vibrantly *on* the beat), *He's Funny That Way* and *Easy Living* (both quintessential Holiday), *Nice Work If You Can Get It* (perky, completely original, consummate vocal control), and *This Year's Kisses* (classic simplicity).

As one listens to these sides, all from 1937, one is staggered by the realization that we are in the presence of a genius, a twenty-two-year-old girl in full artistic/musical maturity[13]—a girl who had already been a Harlem prostitute for five

---

12. Harry Warren's catchy tune blithely plagiarizes the opening of Fletcher Henderson's *Wrappin' It Up.*

13. Let us not forget that it took (for example) Coleman Hawkins ten years to reach such a similar level of musical maturation.

Ex. 3

years of her young life, drug-addicted, with a chaotic, consistently masochistic love life, a constant witness to the seamier side of the black experience, and more. How such sublime art could flower and flourish in such an abysmal environment is not only a singular tribute to Billie Holiday but to the indestructible power and vitality of jazz itself.

For one not present at Billie's 1930s' recording sessions, it remains mysterious as to how she learned these hundreds of songs—and so impeccably. The question arises not out of mere idle curiosity; it is a valid issue: first, because of the technical perfection of her performances, higher and more consistent than any of her accompanists (including even Teddy Wilson, but possibly excluding some of her rhythm section sidemen—like Kirby and Cole—with, to be sure, much less demanding assignments). Second, it is not possible to so thoroughly recompose and improvise upon that many songs without knowing them completely. You can only intelligently deviate from something—perform variations on it—if you know it deeply. We are told that Billie did not read music. How then did she learn so many songs so well as to make them so completely her own? How, for that matter, did all the other players learn the material that well—Eldridge, Wilson, Hodges, Kirby? A majority of these songs—many of them now well-known standards—were brand-new at the time, virtually brought to the recording studio by the publisher on the day of the session.

Furthermore, the availability of alternate takes reveals that Billie's treatment of a song, once set, did not vary appreciably. She did not *really* improvise, in the truest sense. Her performances were fixed beforehand, not only in overall format and style, but in all significant details. Deviations from a first take will invariably be infinitesimal, cosmetic.

There also remains the question of who chose all this material, when we remember that we are talking about well over a hundred songs, just between 1935 and 1938! As I have already mentioned, it is fashionable for the jazz critics to trash the songs and their composers (with the exception of Gershwin, of course, and a few beknighted others), while praising the jazz musicians for elevating the allegedly wretched material to such sublime heights. But can it really have been all that bad? Can one really maintain, against all evidence, that these songs, words or music or both, failed to inspire Billie Holiday and her musicians? In fact, how bad can a set of chords be? How bad a melody? How bad a set of lyrics?

It seems to me that these musicians, Billie in particular, thrived on this material, personalizing it, to be sure, and—granted—improving it here and there. Unless one wants to assume that all good improvisation is a priori better than, say, the composed song on which it is based, then one must allow at least for the possibility of either qualitative equivalence between the two, or on occasion even the superiority of the original over the improvised version. If that were not so, then automatically all improvisations by a set of musicians on (allegedly) *superior* songs would be better than those on songs deemed to be inferior. Neither Billie Holiday's hundreds of recordings nor those of thousands of other jazz artists can even remotely begin to demonstrate such an assumption. Indeed, as I have already shown, some of the best songs—best by everyone's agreement— receive the least effective (or in any case most problematic) treatment. Billie's *I Can't Get Started* is but one case in point.

No, it isn't all as simple as most jazz writers would have us believe. Billie Holiday, for one, is frequently inspired by the songs she sang. Her need to restructure them was not in and of itself a negative comment on the song; it was rather that it was—by her own admission, defiantly defended on a number of occasions (as, for example, when she was fired by Basie's managers)—the only way she could sing and perform. In fact, an objective view of this situation reveals that only the very worst wordiest songs defeated Billie, which leads to the suggestion that even she could not conquer truly deplorable material and that, therefore, the material she *was* able to work with could not have been all that bad, and indeed must have had enough redeeming value to inspire her. Moreover, Billie seems not to have objected to all this allegedly "bad" material. Even if we assume for the moment that she had no say in choosing the songs she sang—an unlikely scenario—she seems not to have rejected any of them or openly objected to them. This again is unlikely if they were truly unredeemable songs, given her temperament, her strong will, *and* given her increasing successes and fame, which would by 1937 certainly have allowed her to demur occasionally. It is, in short, inconceivable that Billie Holiday would for three years in a row sing intolerable material.[14]

---

14. I suspect that what throws many a jazz critic off is not the supposed inferiority of the songs themselves, i.e. Tin Pan Alley as such, but rather the devastating mediocrity of most popular commercial singers and crooners who recorded these songs in the 1930s. Such critics equate (or confuse) performance with composition, blaming the latter when the performance is really at fault.

In April 1939, Billie Holiday recorded a composition, *Strange Fruit*, which was to alter the course of her career. Its controversial success was also to affect her singing, not so much in style, but in choice of material and type of accompaniment. Two earlier brief and unsuccessful stints in the world of big bands— one with Basie (1937), no recordings; the other with Shaw (1938), one side— had convinced her that her only future lay in a solo career. Part of that decision also stemmed from the realization of, indeed resignation to, the fact that her singing would never be appreciated by the large audiences that were thrilling to even the most mediocre of (mostly white) band singers. When on the advice of John Hammond, Barney Josephson hired Billie Holiday for the opening of his Café Society club in Greenwich Village, Billie seems to have found her niche. Stardom—of a sort—was within her reach. But it was destiny that brought the schoolteacher poet, Lewis Allen, to her at Café Society with his haunting metaphoric poem, *Strange Fruit*. Set to music by Allen and backed by her Café Society house septet (which included her latest paramour, the pianist Sonny White), Billie recorded the work in a manner and dramatic presentation that was about 180 degrees removed from any of her previous recordings.

In its starkness, it was reminiscent of Bessie Smith's late work. In its recitative-like approach and funereal beat, it was like a timeless blues or dirge. But its subject matter—lynchings in the South—had never before penetrated the "moon-in-June" Hollywood/Broadway world of popular song, at least never in such an explicit and graphic form. Left-wing and Park Avenue liberals, as well as Greenwich Village intellectuals and bohemians, loved it. Brunswick Records did not, and declined to record it, but Milt Gabler's newly founded Commodore Records did. American radio stations were wary of it, and the BBC in England actually banned it. Most Middle-America white swing fans never heard it and went on discovering Glenn Miller instead.

Strange Fruit is more than a song. It is a powerful moving document and monument to Billie's artistry—and guts. It is also a fine unpretentious composition in B♭ minor, a key Chopin and other composers knew to use well for their more sombre pieces. The work divides into two basic sections: A (8 bars plus a 2-bar tag/refrain), B (8 bars), all in a simple introduction-plus-A A B B format. Its changes, particularly in the A section, are hauntingly beautiful, exploiting minor-major relationships and a late 1930s chromaticism for startling effect. After a touching muted-trumpet introduction by Frankie Newton, Sonny White states the A strain, the only time the actual theme is heard, in a manner that is almost too gracious for the occasion. But Billie, ignoring the melody, now brings things down to a starker "I'm-gonna-tell-it-like-it-is" level, her voice heavy with sorrow and pain. It is again a mark of the depth and breadth of her artistry that, without any drastic modifications, her basic style embraced this somber opus too.

Once again, it is Billie's pure, un-self-pitying, distilled-emotion approach to this material that haunts our memories. The lyrics, which could have become obvious and maudlin, are treated with cold respect for the awesome facts. The hurt is there, but it is not worn on the sleeve. It never slobbers, Billie's poignant, finely textured voice threading a wary course between the potential pitfalls of pretentious social drama and awkwardly "serious" pop balladry.

On the same date Billie recorded three other pieces—Jerome Kern's *Yesterdays*; her most famous blues, *Fine and Mellow*, and *I Gotta Right To Sing the Blues*. Clearly, something fundamental had changed, had broken the continuity with her past recorded work, because these pieces and many others that followed—*Some Other Spring, Night and Day, Body and Soul*—were all set in uncommonly slow, gloomy tempos. Adding to the sombre mood are the increasingly arranged sustained background ensembles and generally plodding rhythm sections. It is as if the success of *Strange Fruit* and *Fine and Mellow* had hypnotized her into some languorous *adagio* mood, causing her virtually to forget that there were such things as bright tempos and *con brio*. With a great sense of relief one grasps at her performance of *Them There Eyes*, almost the only emotionally bright spot in eighteen months of recording.

Where her voice and carefully honed style had been perfect for *Strange Fruit*, it did not suit her despondent, lost-soul interpretation of *Yesterdays*, with Kern's melodic line obliterated beyond recognition. On the other hand, *Fine and Mellow*, vibrato-less, anguished in tone, emotionally exhausted, narrow in range, was right out of the Bessie Smith mold, and became for the rest of Billie's life one of her most requested numbers.

Strange Fruit had indeed changed her. She now saw herself as a dramatic singer, a "serious" artist. And as she became locked into this new self-image, her style turned into mannerisms. As John Hammond was to put it many years later: "The more conscious she became of her style, the more mannered she became." *Strange Fruit*'s success "was the worst thing that ever happened to her."

By 1939 another "strange fruit" had entered her life: opium, soon to be followed by heroin—and in parallel to those intrusions, two painfully unsuccessful marriages. But at this very same time her fame finally spread to all corners of the land, her income multiplied tenfold and more, and success piled upon success so that by 1946 she could put on a solo concert in New York's Town Hall and more than sell out the house.

Recordings on the other hand were rarer, and in 1942, as a result of the A. F. of M. ban, came to a complete halt. What recordings Billie made tended to be in the new "tragic" mold: achingly slow tempos, melancholy moods, at times depressingly so *(Gloomy Sunday)*. Although the particular ensemble excitement—and the risk-taking—of the 1935–38 sessions was now supplanted by homophonic arrangements, mostly rather dull ones at that, Billie could on occasion rise above these soggy accompaniments to produce some chilling musical experiences. *God Bless the Child* (1941), composed by Billie and her friend Arthur Herzog after a gigantic brawl with her mother, unfailingly goes to the listener's marrow. What in other hands could easily have been maudlin and weepy, becomes profound and strong in Billie's performance. The piece is unpretentiously simple, couched in flowing haunting harmonies, against which Billie's tart unflinching voice stands in pungent relief. And no one else could have handled the falling notes in the bridge with such sensitivity and taste.

Even more extraordinary is her recording (on the same date) of Ellington's *Solitude*. In my view this is perhaps the most powerful—and oddly neglected—recorded performance of her career. It is more than a song; it is more than a musical performance. To hear her sing the words "haunt" and "taunt," stretched to the maximum of intensity, taut and vibrato-less, is to experience the ultimate anguished meaning of those words. The listener is irresistibly drawn into *her* solitude. Each note is straight as an arrow, with occasionally a warming terminal vibrato; and like an arrow, it pierces and penetrates. The mood of utter loneliness is heightened by Roy Eldridge's faraway, faintly audible muted obbligato behind Billie and by Eddie Heywood's wistful solo (with some lovely high-register passages in thirds), almost managing to sustain Billie's unearthly mood.

The performance has one minor flaw: Billie's last note is a little sharp and tight, a fact worth mentioning only because ordinarily her intonation was impeccable. Her ear guided her voice infallibly to the center of each pitch, an achievement all the more remarkable for the fact that she used little or no vibrato. The vast majority of vocalists, including classical singers, tend to cover a multitude of intonational sins with their vibratos. But for Billie the vibrato—as in earlier centuries, especially the late Renaissance and Baroque periods—was not a merely decorative permanent *appliqué* to a voice but an expressive medium, to be used sparsely and to specific meaningful effect.[15] Her ability to hit a note consistently dead-center—without benefit of voice-training, I might add—is one of the more astonishing aspects of her art.

After the recording ban, Billie switched to the Decca label (apart from 12 sides for Commodore). Decca—I am convinced not only with Billie's acquiescence but at her request—began recording her with large opulent-sounding orchestras and arrangements, including strings, by Toots Camarata and Bob Haggart, among others. These sides are fascinating because, contrary to what is usually written about them—deploring the use of strings and lauding her ability to prevail over them—Billie seems clearly energized and inspired by these accompaniments. Although one cannot necessarily take every artist's words of self-analysis at face value, it is worth noting that Billie felt her best singing to have occurred on her recordings with strings. Even if this can be argued not to have been literally true, it is nevertheless a clear indication of how she (like Parker and a dozen other great jazz artists) felt about the use of strings and semi-commercial arrangements.

The evidence of the recordings is unequivocal. The arrangement of *Lover Man*, for example, one of Billie's finest and justly famous recordings, clearly stimulates and animates her. Her last "Huggin and a kissin" is one of the more unforgettable moments in her entire repertory. Her performance here is full of longing, but without the despondency of many of the recordings of the preceding years. The same can be said for *That Ole Devil Called Love*. The instrumentation in these Camarata dates—one trumpet, four saxophones, rhythm, and six violins—is light and transparent enough to allow Billie a certain freedom and

15. In this connection it is also important to remember that African singing is universally vibrato-less, a vocal tradition which traveled with black people to the New World and is most purely preserved in black jazz-singing and, by extension, most modern postwar jazz-*playing*.

mobility, while at the same time she seems to be feeding on the ideas contained in the arrangements. These records, along with others from the mid-forties and early fifties, are also of enormous interest because they reveal the strong influence Billie had on two outstanding young singers of that period: Sarah Vaughan and Dinah Washington (*Lover Man* for the former, *That Ole Devil* for the latter).

But the calamitous jumble of Billie's personal life began to take its toll on her work. It is from the mid-forties that one can begin to clearly measure her decline, artistic as well as physical. In 1946 on Jazz at the Philharmonic performances—lately issued on LP—we hear her struggling to stay on pitch (*Travelin' Light*, for example). In 1947 Billie was arrested on narcotics charges and spent nearly a year in a Federal reformatory. Other arrests were to follow, but somehow Billie always bounced back. As her precarious existence began to ravage her voice, its range, always limited, shrank even more. In addition it shifted downward, gaining a coarse beauty in the low register (where she had always been weak) but losing at the top. Arrangements were now transposed down a tone or a third. Her repertory, too, shrank. No longer able to be a leading creative force, Billie withdrew to the safety of her most "popular" repertory, her concerts and club appearances turning into a "show business" act, albeit still of a relatively high artistic order.

Amazingly, her voice could at times still sound fresh and pure, as on the 1949 recordings with various orchestras (Buster Harding, Sy Oliver, Gordon Jenkins), or as late as 1955 (on *Always*, with Charlie Shavers and Tony Scott). But even when her voice was tired and gritty, her singing could be emotionally overwhelming. Indeed, some feel that the painful disarray of her life added a new dimension of depth to her art. Her singing—and her repertory—seemed to become more and more autobiographical, and not just in pieces like *Ain't Nobody's Business* and *Don't Explain*. Audiences increasingly read the more sensational aspects of her personal life into her performances, clinging to every word as if it might reveal some additional dark secret.

Billie now resorted to a lot of free-tempo recitatives, which allowed her to be even more the dramatic chronicler she in a way always had been, at the same time saving what was left of her voice. By the mid-1950s that wasn't very much. But even with a cracking wreck of a voice, it is amazing how Billie could still conjure up much of her former magic (*Fine and Mellow* on the 1957 "Sound of Jazz" television show, or *You've Changed*, in 1958, with the Ray Ellis orchestra, replete with strings, vocal choir, and J. J. Johnson asides). The end finally came on July 17, 1959—only four months after her friend Lester Young's death. It is said that her bank account held all of seventy cents.

In attempting to assess Billie Holiday's place in jazz history, one is easily overwhelmed by the powerful sway of her art and the tangled tortured tragedy of her life, almost—it is perhaps not too much to say—of epic proportions. She was a haunted creature, with a rage to live. And the raw materials of her life constantly surfaced in her work, often in searing and painful detail. The joy and hope of her early work gave way to the fatalistic despair and angry outcries of the later years: a "slice-of-life" art, parable and metaphor all rolled into one. In the later years it sometimes seemed that only through song could she exorcise her personal demons. Blessed with a unique voice and timbre, of many shades—ranging from clear and scalpel-cold through warm and sultry to harsh and grating—Billie could penetrate popular song material as no one before her (and very few after her). And who can forget, once heard, that exquisite tremor of vulnerability in her voice? Or her capacity to "cry without tears," as one writer once put it? Somehow beautiful, even at its briniest, her voice could imbue even her darkest songs with dignity and tenderness.

For under all of Billie's exterior toughness and harsh street language there must have been an extremely soft and sensitive soul. Her harsh temper sprang from a supreme lack of confidence, her masochistic relations with men but a cruel manifestation of her deep sense of inferiority. And yet, that very insecurity made her—kept her—musically sensitive and somehow hopeful.

In the end, it is not for us to judge her life; after all, we have been fortunate enough to receive the bountiful gifts of her art, which that life produced.

LESTER YOUNG

We have looked at a fair sampling of Young's work in the chapter-segment on Basie. But, of course, Lester also qualifies as one of the great individual soloists, the theme with which this chapter is concerned. And in terms of a revolutionizing and lasting effect on several further generations of jazz players, it is an incontrovertible fact that Lester was *the* most influential artist after Armstrong and before Charlie Parker. What eluded Coleman Hawkins despite his life-long heroic strivings, namely, domination of the saxophone world, virtually fell into Lester's lap. And before his life was a little more than half over, he had not only spawned a whole school of followers but created a completely new aesthetic of jazz—for all instruments, not just the tenor saxophone. The essence of his heritage is that he proposed a totally new alternative to the language, grammar, and vocabulary of jazz, one that broke away from the prevailing Armstrong tradition and did so incisively, unequivocally—and unapologetically.

Many jazz innovators' early development is preserved on records. But Lester Young did not record until 1936, by which time his radically "new" style had already been firmly fixed, probably as many as five or six years earlier.[16] We may well wonder as to its origins. To put the question in another way: How did Lester

---

16. One strong bit of evidence of Young's early uniqueness comes to us in an odd form: the complete rejection by the entire Henderson band of Young's playing, when he was with the band briefly in 1934. Under the pressure of his players—and his wife, who tried to make Lester listen to Hawkins recordings, presuming to convert him—Henderson had to let Lester go. (Ben Webster was his successor.)

Pianist John Lewis, who first heard and met Lester in the late 1920s in Albuquerque, recalls that at that time Lester was already playing in a style "like no one else's—very special ideas," referring incidentally not so much to his tone as to his musical ideas.

elude the omnipresent influence of Louis Armstrong—and Coleman Hawkins?

Lester himself gives us at least one very important clue: *he wasn't listening to Armstrong!* He was listening to Jimmy Dorsey and Frankie Trumbauer—particularly to the latter's *Singin' the Blues* and to his C-melody sax. Nor did he listen much to Coleman Hawkins; and, when he did hear him the first time with Fletcher Henderson's band in Kansas City, he seems not to have been much impressed. Not that he had disdain for his famous colleague, but, rather, in 1933 he was already hearing (and playing) a much different kind of music. For one thing, Hawkins's aggressive robust style was completely antithetical to Lester's nature. Clearly his gentle soul, his shy and introvert nature, his live-and-let-live philosophy of life were bound to reject—for himself, at any rate—the ego-centered, competitive world of Hawkins. But there was more to it than that. Lester could not accept Hawkins's essentially staccato, hard-tongued, vertical, chord-anchored approach to the saxophone. His way of hearing music was the way of the blues—and of telling a story in music.

Lester may have been laconic in his speech, but when he did talk it was often about two subjects: the blues and "soul" (in its primarily musical connotation). He often referred to the blues as a primary, pervasive musical source, and the vast majority of his own compositions are cast in the blues form. We know, of course, that he was a great blues player, not only during the Basie years but right through to the end of his life. Many of his finest moments occur in the context of the blues. And as for the story-telling aspects of the blues, that, too, was a major point of contention with Lester—that is, telling a story in one's music, a concept he extended as well to non-blues materials. He frequently spoke of the necessity of the improvising musician *knowing the words*—the story—of the song, on which he was extemporizing.

But my point is not that Lester Young was such a great blues player—as true as that may be—but rather that it was his blues-permeated musical aesthetic, an aesthetic once again nurtured in the musical traditions of the Southwest (*not* the East), that shaped Lester's music in such special and original ways. For the blues, unlike ragtime, for example, is fundamentally a *linear* concept of playing and singing. It has to be, and it always was. It had to be because it is a narrative form of expression. It is essentially a vocal tradition; it tells a story. And it does so in a simple concentrated form, in its original manifestations as sung and played by *folk*, not by professional musicians. As a consequence, blues in its pure forms has little to do with formal training, with technique (vocal or instrumental), with such matters as virtuosity, developing a wide vocal range, with "proper" harmonies, and even with perfect intonation—attributes most essential, say, to ragtime and various Eastern-seaboard antecedents of jazz. In these latter forms, primarily instrumental, the vertical demarcation of the music—into beats, into meters, into simple, regular and usually symmetrical phrase structures—was primary. It was its *raison d'être*. In Southwestern music, and particularly in the blues, the emphasis is on line, on flow, on phrases and sentences, and to some extent even the acceptance of asymmetry—in short, projecting a horizontal form. (In older country blues, for example, irregular forms like 13-, 11 $\frac{1}{2}$-, and 8 $\frac{1}{2}$-bar structures were not at all uncommon.)

I am suggesting that Lester Young's primarily linear, less harmony-bound and thus rhythmically freer concept of jazz derives from the blues, viewed as a broad generic model.[17] There can be little question that Lester heard the blues all through his youth, both on his own and traveling with his father's family band, whether in Algiers, Louisiana (where he partly grew up), or in New Mexico or Oklahoma (where he spent periods of time as a young musician)—or even in Minneapolis, where his father moved the family when Lester was ten years old (in 1919). Playing first the drums, then switching in his early teens to alto saxophone, Lester finally settled on the tenor around 1928. But he didn't necessarily adopt the standard tenor sound, adhering instead to the alto sonority of his previous instrument and, as mentioned, being quite captivated by Trumbauer's C-melody sound, located about halfway between the alto (in $E\flat$) and the tenor (in $B\flat$).

Indeed, Trumbauer's influence on Lester is both pervasive and precise, no idle anecdotal remembrance on Lester's part. One has only to listen to Trumbauer's solo on *Singin' the Blues* to hear Lester's tone, virtually vibrato-less, his attack, his definite but smooth, gentle cat's-paw way of moving from note to note, even the generally diatonic non-chromatic note and interval choices—in short, his entire special brand of lyricism.[18] None of these stylistic elements are even remotely discernible in Hawkins's playing of the early thirties, let alone 1927, the date of *Singin' the Blues*. The most striking difference between the two concepts is in respect to the attack: Hawkins's hard, propulsive, a vestige of the slap-tongue school of saxophone playing; Trumbauer's firm, refined, tempered, *the attack matching the body of the note*. In fact, in the context of 1920s' jazz, Trumbauer's basically lyric, quite linear approach is perhaps more of a miracle than Lester's of a few years later.

The other element of Young's musical aesthetic derives directly from his *persona*, his nature, his temperament. Almost all who knew Lester well speak of his gentleness of character, his extreme sensitivity, his concern for the underdog and, as a corollary, his distaste for loud, aggressive, noisy ostentation. Not that he was a weak man; but he preferred to express himself in terms of understatement and in highly original, oblique, elliptical manners of speech and dress. He loved "pretty" things and "pretty" music—hence his deep love for fine ballads and his equally profound abhorrence of the extrovert honkings and vulgar bellybanalities of many of his Jazz at the Philharmonic colleagues, catering to the lowest common denominator of audience tastes.

There are several ironies in this tale thus far, especially vis-à-vis Hawkins. One is that Hawkins, as mentioned, had the need to dominate, to lead, to constantly maintain superiority—even over his best disciples. Lester was incapable of leadership in the ordinary worldly sense, and yet *he* became the true leader of a new jazz vanguard, retaining much of his influence even *after* the arrival of Parker. Secondly, it is ironic that Lester's soft-spoken world of under-

17. Much the same can be said about Charlie Christian's aesthetic/stylistic origins, as discussed later in this part.
18. Slow down Trumbauer's *Singin' the Blues* solo to 45 rpm from 78 and the proximity of style of the two men comes even more sharply into focus.

statement should assert itself so successfully against the more competitive, aggressive mode of Hawkins (as well as the enormous popularity of Armstrong). But most ironic of all is that Hawkins came from St. Joseph, Missouri, initially growing up in the Kansas City area, and should by all rights have been a true musical son of the Southwest. But that honor, too, fell to Lester's mantle. Hawkins was seduced into the big-time entertainment world of the East before he knew the difference—and, incidentally, never *really* learned to play the blues.

It is hardly an accident that Lester Young should have ended up with Basie, definitely a Southwestern blues-oriented band. In its linear concept of swing and uncongested (at first) largely unarranged, airy-textured approach, it was the ideal setting for Lester. It was one in which he could flourish and grow—and which, without necessarily wishing it so, he would soon dominate. There were challenges within the band, of course, such as his in-public rival (but in-private close friend) Herschel Evans, a Texan, and yet a charter member of the Hawkins school of tenor saxophone. But the beauty of the early Basie band was its stylistic looseness—*within* an overall concept—which allowed for a considerable amount of individual diversity.

Evans and Young, famous for their tenor battles, rarely soloed on the same piece on recordings. And when they did, they were kept far apart from each other, as on *Georgianna* (in early 1938). The performance is informative not only in letting us hear at close range the deep stylistic gulf between the two schools of tenor playing but also in reminding us that at that time both players were considered equivalent in stature, each with their fiercely loyal following. It has sometimes been suggested that it was Evans's death in 1939 that allowed Young's style to forge ahead in influence and popularity. But that theory ignores the stunning bombshell effect Hawkins's *Body and Soul* recording of 1939 had on the musical world, much greater than any of Evans's work. Could the tide towards Young's style have been stemmed at all, it would surely have been contained by Hawkins's famous solo.

It was at this time that Lester began to appear on other influential recordings, notably the series with Billie Holiday and Teddy Wilson. "Lady Day," so named by Lester, and "Prez," so named by Billie, were obviously musical soulmates and inspired each other on any number of these occasions. *When You're Smiling* (January 1938) is a superior example of their collaboration and of Lester's sovereign work at this time, in its clarity and simple logic much like guitarist Charlie Christian's of a year or so later.

Within the Basie band, too, some small-group jazz was evolving, aided and abetted, once again, by the tireless John Hammond. The Kansas City Six sessions, which he organized for both the American Record Company[19] and the new Commodore label, offered not only prime Kansas City jazz but first-rate Young, on both clarinet and tenor. Because Basie could not participate, owing to contractual restrictions, and because Hammond decided to use two guitars,

---

19. The ARC session was at first left unreleased, and eventually traded over by Hammond to Commodore and issued by them.

Freddie Green (acoustic) and Eddie Durham (electric), these are piano-less performances. Hence the solo arena was left to Buck Clayton and Lester, a fortuitous circumstance since, again, these two musicians were spiritual and musical brethren. There are times when one can hardly tell Lester, on clarinet, apart from Clayton on cup-muted trumpet. The sides contain excellent Young tenor, as his notes waft in and float almost disembodied above the rhythm section, cast in cool almost-even eighths, worlds apart from Hawkins's heated loping triplets or dotted-eighths-and-sixteenths.

But the masterpiece of the session, and one of the real classics of jazz, is *I Want a Little Girl*, with Lester's inimitable clarinet-playing. Lester played a cheap metal clarinet that he picked up somewhere on his travels, but whose tone he loved dearly. On it he could produce some of the most touching and affecting music of his career. Indeed, already the 4-bar introduction to *Little Girl*, rivaled only by some of Ellington's more expressive medium-tempo preludes, signals the advent of a sublime performance. In his beautiful, simply expressed flowing opening line, Lester seems to lay bare his soul. All the gentleness and sensitivity of the man are expressed in those four bars (and his later solo). In his tone and choice of notes we hear a sensibility, indeed a *vulnerability* that most jazz (as distinguished from pure, folk-rooted blues) tended to bury under an overlay of technique and virtuosity, and which very few musicians would dare to expose. These four bars put much jazz—as art and humanist utterance—into critical perspective.

Part of the pathos of these opening measures lies, paradoxically, in a "wrong note" in the first bar. Assuming Eddie Durham's choice of four parallel dominant ninth chords, the last one augmented (F^9—E^9—D^{b9}—$C^{9(+5)}$), to be correct, Lester should have played an E^b as his fourth note. Instead (Ex. 4), he plays an E natural, thereby adding an inexplicable poignancy to the passage

Ex. 4

caused by the momentary "dissonance." (As usual the effect cannot be completely captured in notation, and must be heard to be appreciated fully.) That this "dissonance" was no mere accident but actually intended by Young and Durham is borne out by the fact that both takes of *Little Girl* contain the same opening measures.

Later on, in Lester's solo proper, some delicious "dissonantal" clashes in the two guitars again contribute significantly to the haunting mood of this performance. As Lester lines out one of his favorite melodic contours—in fifths and fourths (Ex. 5)—the two guitarists add to the piquancy of the harmonies by playing an F-*minor* seventh at the beginning of the second measure, instead of

Ex. 5

the expected F major. The major seventh interval that this A♭ forms with Lester's G, adds just that subtle extra touch of harmonic tension and of the unexpected. Curiously, in take two, the guitarists revert to two alternative progressions in bar 1 and bar 9 of Lester's solo, but not quite agreeing with each other (Ex. 6a, b). Whereas they are in accord with each other in m. 1, in the second half of m. 9 they go slightly different ways, Green hearing an Fm⁶, and Durham playing a C-augmented chord! But the A♭ in both players' chords do not jibe with Lester's (correct) use of the A♮ at the end of the fourth beat. Perhaps played by brass instruments or by strong reeds at a loud dynamic level, these "dissonances" would be disturbing and quite wrong sounding. But here, in *p* dynamics, with Lester's pellucid tone and the subtle elusiveness of the soft guitars, the effect is absolutely delightful, precious in the best sense.

Ex. 6a

Ex. 6b

There is in this whole performance (on both takes) a sense of airy weightlessness, especially in Lester's playing. But there is also a feeling of contented serenity that contrasts strikingly with the anguished outpourings of some of Lester's work of his late years. Here, somehow, he still seems at ease with the world.

Lester's clarinet-playing was not always dulcet-toned. It could at times be edgy, spiky—much like Pee Wee Russell's (or Frank Teschemacher's on a bad day). On *I Ain't Got Nobody* (with Basie's Bad Boys), for example, we hear Lester contrast his aciduous clarinet tone with that of his mauve-toned tenor, as clear and cool as a mountain brook.

For a brief period in late 1940, Benny Goodman, discouraged by the loss of

Lionel Hampton in his Sextet, considered abandoning it and leading a Kansas City Six type of group instead. From one of the group's rehearsals for a test recording—the plan never came to fruition—performances have come to light which reveal prime Prez: perfect and characteristically unostentatious on *I Never Knew*; ingenious in his two laid-back breaks—one an inversion of the other—on *Ad Lib Blues*; and a paragon of easy, relaxed, mellifluous swing on *Lester's Dream*. The octave leaps in the middle of earlier solos (as on *Dickie's Dream* and *Let Me See*) have now been expanded into chromatically filled out "rips." "Rip" is perhaps too strong a word, for they are relatively gentle thrusts, more yearning than aggressive and a far cry from those powerful upward wrenchings that Hawkins, for example, discovered in the thirties and exploited for the rest of his playing days. If such a leonine roaring idea could be tempered and becalmed, it was Lester who would find a way to do it.

Goodman probably didn't know it at the time, but Lester was about to leave the Basie band—and actually did so a month and a half later. Like Hawkins, Young had dreams of fronting his own band. But the idea was a non-starter: Lester, without either leadership qualities or the showmanship to impress club owners and bookers, got only one engagement in the first six months and even could not snare a recording contract. In May 1941 he disbanded, lucky to find some recording work with various ad hoc small groups: Billie Holiday, Una Mae Carlisle, and Texas blues pianist Sammy Price. Typical of the cruel ironies that fill the annals of show business, a singer, second-rate at best, like Carlisle could get a record date, while a genius like Young could not. But with Una Mae and Billie he at least made some excellent sides, contributing his special brand of ever-more relaxed melodic improvising. Listen to his sinuous entry on Billie's *All of Me*, his pure distilled melodies and wondrously unhurried swing. While swing bands, both large and small, were playing louder and faster all the time, heating up, as it were, and using increasingly congested and mechanized arrangements, Lester was going in the opposite direction, interiorizing his art—and cooling down. Even on typical riff tunes of the period like *Just Jivin' Around* (with Sammy Price and His Texas Blusicians), Lester's playing is creamy smooth, gliding in on soft-tongued uncomplicated tonic repeated notes. To his penchant for sixths and ninths (see above, Chapter 3, Basie segment), Lester had by now added the major seventh, not as a phrase-starting note, but as one usually forming the apex of his arching lines, either in a scalar approach or in arpeggios (Ex. 7).[20]

It is worth noting in this connection that, paradoxically, Young, fine blues player that he was, generally *avoided* the traditional blue notes, preferring instead—even in blues, let alone in non-blues pieces—the more "open," the more "positive" major steps of the scale. Lester was basically a diatonic player, what musicians sometimes call a "white-note" player. It is one of the alchemistic mysteries of his art that his improvisations rarely sounded bland or harmonically

---

20. The E natural at the beginning of *I Want a Little Girl* (Ex. 4) is a part of this arching, flowing phrase-type as well.

Ex. 7

unseasoned. Compared with a player like Ben Webster, for example, whose playing in his prime was richly ornamented with blue notes, sliding into and out of them, including bent pitches, pitch-modifying vibratos, and shakes, Lester's playing by contrast is almost prim in its diatonic immaculateness. And yet its content is rich; its interior substance is always just below the surface shining upward through it; or, to put it more precisely, the surface and the content beneath are inseparable: they are, in fact, one and the same.

Lester's generally diatonic ear, his emphasis on both the melodic use of fourths and fifths intervals and harmonically on the sixth and ninth steps of the scale, combined with his linear conception of phrasing—all these have had far-reaching influences, even into our own time. For, essentially, the modal playing of the 1960s and 1970s had its inception with Lester Young. So did the whole modern linear melodic approach to jazz improvisation. I would argue that a concept such as George Russell's Lydian Chromatic Concept of Tonal Organization was unthinkable without Lester's prior explorations of such directions. I am referring here not so much to specific types of tonal or modal organization—although Lester can also be seen as the father of such modern offshoots—as to the general concept of freeing melodic design from a rigid relationship with its harmonic underpinnings. The notion that melodic ideas can assume a certain degree of autonomy, independent of any particular harmonic progression, really began with Lester.

In 1942, while co-leading a small band in Los Angeles with his brother Lee, Lester teamed up with Nat "King" Cole and bassist Red Callender for what turned out to be a historic trio session. *Body and Soul* and *I Can't Get Started* are undoubtedly the most successful collaborations from this date. Lester's tone now was darker; the pale yellow of earlier days had turned ochre. It was also larger, apparently more aware of Webster and Hawkins, but calmer, more spacious, and without their intense vibratos. In effect, now out of Basie's band for a few years, Lester had turned from a compelling blues-and riff-oriented swinger, playing mostly for dances, into a romantic ballad player, appearing as a "soloist" at clubs and concerts. Lester's straightforward approach to *I Can't Get Started* is intriguingly complemented by Cole's ornate piano style, harmonically more adventurous and conceptually more linear than, say, either Teddy Wilson's or Basie's—Lester's primary accompanists up until then. Notice, too, how Lester concentrates on those sustained As (in the bridge), neatly fitting that pitch over its four successive chords, A—D—Dm—G: so simple and ingenious and inevitable sounding.

There is so much written in the existing literature about Lester Young's gradual deterioration, both musically and physically, after the early forties that one is left with the impression that his late work, that of the last fifteen years, was consistently undistinguished. On the other hand, liner note writers, promoting some late-dated Lester Young reissue, tend to extol the virtues of those particular recordings beyond their actual value. The reality lies somewhere between these assumptions, and is, in fact, much more complicated. For Lester, a gentle man, unable either to dominate others or effectively fight back when put upon, was extremely dependent on and sensitive to his musical surroundings, whether in terms of those who accompanied him or those who were his audience, or both. He was not a forceful, totally self-reliant player like Hawkins, for example, who could ignore his surroundings and play his best regardless of who accompanied him. Lester needed the right kind of support; otherwise he could not function fully. Audiences, too, affected him. The louder and cruder the audience—as at most of the Jazz at the Philharmonic (JATP) concerts—the more he succumbed to their riotous demands, really despite himself. Like a moth drawn to the flame— or a trained seal reacting to applause—Lester was irresistibly lured into giving the audience the standard tenor saxophone banalities they hungered for: low-note honkings, endless repeated note bleatings, repetition, redundancy, and all the rest.

But put Lester in a more sensitive setting, and he invariably responded beautifully—until the very final years when he simply gave out physically. I think perhaps too much has been made of Lester's traumatic army experiences in 1945, and their aftermath. It has been too simple to classify postwar Young as uniformly lacking in the creativity and inspiration characteristic—so the theory goes—of his early period. I submit as a more reasonable assessment that, with but few exceptions, almost all major jazz musicians reach their creative zenith in their twenties or thirties and then, around age forty, level off to a less actively innovative plateau, and that Lester Young was no different. (Granted that some players—like Earl Hines, Mary Lou Williams, Coleman Hawkins—continued to keep apace with newer developments; but it would be difficult to argue that they were late in life still "innovative leaders.") I further submit that much of Lester's postwar playing was *different*, rather than merely poorer. And last—and most important—the quality of his playing varied considerably depending on who was accompanying him. Thus some of his finest playing, for example, can be found on the sessions where John Lewis was the sensitive accompanist; or, by contrast, when Sid Catlett was the dominating catalyst, eliciting from Young some of his strongest, most forceful playing. Lester was like a feather in the wind, pliant and susceptible—and vulnerable. Let us say then that Lester's creativity in the last third of his life could be likened to a low burning flame, somewhat withdrawn and without the electrifying flash of the earlier years.

Listen to him on *Afternoon of a Basie-ite* (late 1943), driving and aggressive, his tone thicker and heavier, but with the same unique fluency as earlier. As great and sensitive a drummer as Jo Jones was, Catlett—a major creative figure himself—could challenge Lester in a way that his Basie colleague could not; not better necessarily, but differently. At this time, too, we hear Lester take on some of the expressivity and breathiness of tone we associate with Ben Webster (as on *Sometimes I'm Happy*). Lester had lost some of his cool abstractness and replaced it with a certain amount of soul. He was now using harder reeds, producing a more robust sound. The tone was no longer weightless and disembodied but heavier and more projecting, with a new luminous quality in the upper register. His musical ideas were not necessarily different, but the manner of *projecting* them was.

On *Lester Leaps Again*, a blues in G (on a Kansas City Seven date in 1944), we even hear him play with a bite and open sound that makes one think of the big horn of Sonny Rollins in the late 1950s. It is magnificent Prez, roaming, explorative, full of daring leaps, giving a new meaning to this title. Similarly on the second take of *Destination K.C.*

The variability in Lester's playing can be heard on the two final sessions before his induction into the army in September 1944. On a Savoy date with pianist Johnny Guarnieri, Lester participated vigorously in the jubilant, fiery atmosphere of these performances (especially on *Exercise in Swing*), dedicated to the memory and spirit of Fats Waller, who had died only months before. But on a Kansas City Six date with Joe Bushkin substituting for Guarnieri, Lester seems ill at ease. Milt Gabler, the producer of these Commodore records, recalls that Lester was quite remote, unreachable. His work here is redundant, uninvolved, and seems pasted together out of commonplaces.

And yet on his first date after his army stint (spent mostly in confinement in detention barracks), [21] Lester sounds positive and spirited. On *D. B. Blues* (short for Detention Barracks), his tone is a little harder and narrower than before—as one writer put it: with an "ironic edge." But Lester's special brand of plaintive lyricism is also still there, especially on *These Foolish Things*. Lester was now turning more and more to ballads—he is also said to have spent a lot of time listening to singers like Frank Sinatra and Dick Haymes—turning away to some extent from the typical medium-tempo swing/riff numbers associated with him for so long. In a way, standards like *These Foolish Things, I Can't Get Started, Sunny Side of the Street*—to name just three of Lester's favorites—represented relatively new territory for him, an area where he could now more readily ex-

---

21. Readers who wish to acquaint themselves with this appalling and tragic episode in Lester Young's life, can do so in any number of sources: for example, Nat Hentoff's account in *The Jazz Makers*, ed. Nat Shapiro and Nat Hentoff (Rinehart, New York, 1957); or a briefer summation in Time/ Life's recent *Giants of Jazz* collection of Lester Young.

press his originality. Significantly Lester created his own melodic improvisation on *Foolish Things*, dispensing entirely with Harry Link's and Jack Strachey's famous tune.[22] Lester is at his most poignant on this track. There is a pure distilled lyricism and interior beauty—may one say a wisdom?—in his playing here, that it is hard to find (to this extent) in his earlier work. Note the brief examples transcribed here (Ex. 8a, b, c, d), especially the luminous arpeggio-crowning high D in his second bridge (Ex. 8c) and the plaintive, pleading inception of the last eight bars (Ex. 8d, mm. 41–43).

Ex. 8a

Ex. 8b

Ex. 8c

Ex. 8d

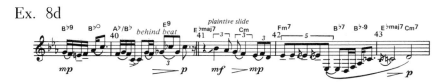

22. Lester had an interesting habit of playing a ballad for a few days or a week, first lining out the composed theme, followed by improvisations upon it; a week later, dropping the theme and beginning with his improvisation of the previous week; the next week with his second chorus, and so on, one by one, moving successive choruses into that opening spot.

With Lester's trusted friend, Vic Dickenson, that much neglected masterful trombonist, at his side and Red Callender on bass (Freddie Green did *not* play on this date as has often been claimed), Lester felt much at ease. Not so a few months later, where we hear him noticeably crowded by Nat "King" Cole's hyperactive pianisms. Cole was, of course, a highly interesting stylist, one about whom I write with great admiration elsewhere in this book (Chapter 9), but his busy, somewhat nervous playing on, say, *I've Found a New Baby*, happens not to be the kind of sympathetic *non-competitive* support Lester needed. I also think that Lester sorely missed the comforting fundament of a walking bass.

The dully arranged ensembles of a date in early 1946 are not much help either. Lester sounds disoriented and weak, treading water, the disorganized endings on all four tracks a tell-tale sign of his lack of interest in the proceedings. (Listen by contrast to the uniformly neat, controlled endings of the 1951 recordings with John Lewis and Jo Jones.)

It was during this period that Lester signed up with Norman Granz's Jazz at the Philharmonic tour. Lester sometimes got caught up in the frantic, emotional atmosphere of those affairs—reflecting the release of pent-up energies in those postwar times. But on the other hand, it is amazing how often Lester seemed to represent, in these frenetic, almost circus-like concerts, a paragon of stability and classicism. Take *Sweet Georgia Brown*—what a crazy hodge-podge of late swing and early bop, played at a frenetic tempo of around 300 to the quarter note. There is Mel Powell recalling the best of the old Benny Goodman Quartet/Sextet days; Willie Smith careening around buzz-toned in chromatic spirals, getting nowhere fast; Dizzy Gillespie getting everywhere, cocky and full of beans; Al Killian grandstanding with altissimo trumpet shrieks; and Charlie Parker, with a bad reed (not in his best form), splashing around in rather insane gyrations. In the midst of all of this, there is Lester, playing his clean, well-shaped "classic" lines. He solos right after Parker, and a comparison of the two is instructive. Lester's time is solid and settled, his ideas so well organized. Parker on the other hand stumbles quite a bit, forcing his tone, getting hung up on note patterns, and falling behind the beat. Of course, to be fair, Parker was trying for much more than Lester, and he was relentlessly battering away at the outer boundaries of the sound barrier. But still, it is enlightening to observe how poised Lester is, in what must have been for him a somewhat unnerving environment. The same kind of Lesterian composure amidst clamorous din can be heard on *I Can't Get Started* (Milestone).

The gently lyrical side of Lester comes even more to the fore on a JATP *Slow Drag*, which he turns into a sinuous yearning blues threnody. On other occasions—frequently on his specialty number, *Lester Leaps In*—he is seduced into a fair amount of audience catering. But on one particular *Lester Leaps In* (preserved on Verve VSP-41) we can hear him trying to integrate these more ordinary mannerisms into an overall statement. His five choruses here are exemplary—their only possible "fault" that they do not tell us anything "new" about Lester—richly spiked with dramatic high points and contrasts, a marvel of formal control. This two-and-a-half-minute solo must be heard in its entirety, but among its most salient features I would single out the marvelously convoluted "noo-dling" at the beginning of his second chorus, the wild false-fingering sliding/slithering opening of the fourth chorus, and its brilliant climactic bridge. All of this is played with a full, thrusting tone that gives the lie to those who used to complain about Lester's "small, lightweight" sound.

An August 1946 date, somewhat miscast between pianist Joe Albany and drummer Chico Hamilton, turned out rather unevenly for Lester. His tone was tight and metallic on *Lester's Be Bop*, but on a languorous ballad treatment of *She's Funny That Way* he seemed to be successfully exploring the "baritone" register of his instrument.

From a date with his own touring group in 1947, we have the superior and very popular *Jumpin' with Symphony Sid* (named after the famous bop disc jockey of New York), his playing sovereign and inventive; and a beautiful *Sunny Side of the Street* and *S. M. Blues*. Both give us relaxed, subtle behind-the-beat play-ing—Lester at his "southern-drawl" best.

On the other hand, young Roy Haynes's rudimentary overbearing drumming and Argonne Thornton's confused unswinging piano-playing[23] on *Movin' with Lester* and *Lester Smooths Out* could not have been much to Lester's taste—with the expected strained, leathery-toned results.

By late 1948 we hear the first consistent signs—at least on records—of Lester losing a degree of physical control, especially in regard to intonation (as on *Something to Remember* and the otherwise touchingly tender *East of the Sun*).[24] His gradual physical and psychological deterioration was beginning to take its toll, and many of his ballads of those years (the late 1940s) have an exceedingly melancholy and mournful mood (see his *I'm Confessin'* and a 1948 *On the Sunny Side*).

But lo and behold, the picture brightens considerably when John Lewis be-comes his regular accompanist (in 1950 and 1951).[25] I am convinced that Lewis was Lester's favorite pianist; and indeed the history of jazz does not offer a more sensitive and intelligent pianist-accompanist. The seventeen sides Lester re-corded with Lewis are to his late discography what rays of sunshine are after days of overcast skies. For one thing, Lester had returned to his "alto" sound. For another, he played here with an airy, buoyant, more syncopated and rhythmi-cally varied swing than in his immediately preceding work. His intonation was generally under control, and his sense of space and structure admirable. Even the sloppy endings were gone, effortlessly formulated by Lester and John in per-fect mutual consent. The mood of *Frenesi*, a new genre in Lester's repertory, is

23. Thornton performed well enough on the earlier *Jumpin' with Symphony Sid* and *No Eyes Blues*. Roy Haynes, of course, subsequently developed into one of the finest of modern drummers and is by now long-ago established as one of the real masters of his craft.
24. That Lester could have problems with intonation from time to time can be heard as far back as 1938 on a number of the performances from the *Spirituals to Swing* Carnegie Hall concert.
25. Lester falters badly in a 1950 session with Hank Jones, Lester seemingly foggy-brained and constantly falling back on dull formulas. Unquestionably, Hank Jones is a fine pianist, but there failed to be sufficient musical chemistry between him and Lester.

sun-lit and charming. The upward rips, a relic of the JATP days, are here light and fluffed-up. *Let's Fall in Love* is "lovely" and pliant.

The key to the success of these records is John Lewis and (on the 1951 dates) Jo Jones. John plays with a Mozartean clarity that enables Lester to float across the rhythmic understructure, spinning out his shapely lines. John never crowds a soloist; he only fills in as needed (at phrase endings, for example), and is at all times truly supportive. Indeed, when Lester gets a little lost momentarily (as on *In a Little Spanish Town*), John "feeds" him right back with a few adroitly placed chords. The miracle of John's accompanying is that it constantly keeps in mind—or makes audible by implication—the melodic outline of the songs. John's balanced classicism is the perfect corollary to Lester's refined art; his clear, crisp, lithe piano touch the ideal foil for Lester's suède-elegant lines.

Nor is Lewis simply a passive partner. Apart from his many fine solos on these sides—Lester gave him lots of solo space—John is often the initiator and stimulator of ideas. Take that joyous romp *Lester Swings*: John keeps turning up the heat with his insistent chordal syncopations, eventually building them into an imperiously rising left-hand bass figure. When Lester runs out of steam (*and* notes) in the end of the third chorus's first eight, John is right there, both hands in full cry, and gets Lester back on track by the bridge. Similarly, in the exquisite but poorly recorded *Slow Motion Blues*, John feeds Lester one of his most poignant lamentations (towards the end of the first chorus). In the second chorus John glides gently in and out of double-time, prompting Lester to do the same, leaning, however, more in the single-time direction. Both men are delicately poised on the divide, balancing one time feeling against the other in the subtlest of rhythmic counterpoints. In the third chorus John initiates a lovely falling blues-in-thirds idea, which Lester five bars later *inverts* in slightly varied form.

This kind of sensitive interplay is what Lester Young rarely got in his post-Basie days. It did occur at least one more time on some fine sides, made with the Oscar Peterson Trio. Most notable is *I Can't Get Started* (August 4, 1952), with Lester in his *I Want a Little Girl* mood (except for the missing clarinet). Peterson accompanies most discreetly, leaving the harmonic backing primarily to Barney Kessel's guitar. But one can also hear Lester's continuing problems with intonation, especially in his upper register, and occasionally notes simply won't speak for lack of air support.

Lester was less and less able to take care of himself physically, drinking to excess and eating little. Only the care of friends on the road, like Peterson, kept him going. Periods in the hospital, without access to alcohol, would also serve to stabilize his physical and mental condition. But increasingly a fumbling, uncoordinated playing along with recycling of old clichés was the rule, while fine sessions like the one with Roy Eldridge, Vic Dickenson, and Teddy Wilson were the exception. This January 1956 date, issued as *The Jazz Giants*, offers anything but that. The soloists (except for Dickenson) all seem profoundly tired and not a little bored, further weighted down by Gene Ramey's rather plodding bass (which even Jo Jones and Freddy Green could not enliven). Almost all the solos are too long, and as a result are filled with rambling, meandering redundancies. Even Wilson seems not to be trying very hard.

And yet Lester occasionally struggles through to some very special and haunting moments, particularly on *This Year's Kisses*, a piece he had last recorded with Billie Holiday and Wilson nearly twenty years earlier. His tone now was outwardly gritty and hoarse, but still somehow illuminated from within with an unearthly radiance. Lester's solo on *This Year's Kisses* is almost beyond endurance in its plaintive, almost lachrymose but at the same time stark mood. Wilson shatters this mood when he follows Lester with an emptily ornate passionless solo. On *You Can Depend on Me* one can almost *feel* Lester struggling to find the energy to play, working so hard—and *making* it. His long singing notes aquiver with a tiny, weak trembling vibrato.

I cannot, of course, pretend to know intimately all the live performing of Lester's final years; and perhaps amidst the pitifully groping, floundering attempts to somehow keep going, there were moments when the light of Lester's art again shone brightly. I *do* know that one such moment occurred on the December 1957 telecast *The Sound of Jazz*, unquestionably the finest hour jazz has ever had on television. How fortunate we are that one of Lester's final and most glorious moments was thus captured on electronic media: his heart-rending twelve bars on *Fine and Mellow*.[26] Whitney Balliett and Nat Hentoff, co-producers of the program, have both spoken eloquently of Lester's sad condition during the rehearsals and performance. Lester was so totally remote and uncommunicative, as well as physically incapacitated, that at one point it was thought necessary to cut him out of the show altogether. But that seemed too cruel, so it was finally decided to limit his involvement to one chorus on Billie Holiday's slow blues, *Fine and Mellow*, in the hope that she, his long-time friend, would provide the one possible stimulus for a reasonable musical participation.

The document of that television show[27] demonstrates the triumph of soul over matter. For Lester, so sick that he could hardly stand, barely able to draw enough breath to sustain even a short phrase, nonetheless rose to the occasion and played a canticle of such overwhelming expressiveness as to put all the other playing into distant perspective. I think that Lester was dimly yet deeply aware of the fact that even some of his best friends and colleagues in the studio had given up on him. But he was to teach them all a lesson—a lesson particularly in economy and what he meant by "telling a story." In his twelve halting, recitative-like bars (Ex. 9) he played a bare forty-five notes (not counting another eighteen embellishmental or passing tones), this about half of Webster's majestic and ornate solo and one-third of Gerry Mulligan's double-time chorus. This was, of course, not some statistical game to see who could play the fewest notes. But Lester showed them, and showed for all times—as he had so often done in the past—that sometimes one single deeply expressed note could say more than a hundred skillfully executed others. Lester was undoubtedly also expressing his feelings for

26. An LP recording on Columbia, made three days before the actual telecast, with a different sequence of soloists, has Lester flanked by Billie Holiday and a vigorous, youthful-sounding Ben Webster. But it is, except for Dickenson's obviously respectful tribute to Billie and Lester, much the lesser of the two versions, among other things, in Lester's case, painfully out of tune.
27. The audio track of *Fine and Mellow* exists on an ESP recording issued in 1973 and is still, to my knowledge, generally available.

Ex. 9

Billie—perhaps he sensed it would be his last chance to do so—and kept his solo, like her singing, pared-down to essentials.

In any case, in Lester's brief solo here we have one of the truly profound moments in jazz. It stands as a monument to the music, beyond categorization and beyond analysis. It was perhaps at once Lester's testament and epitaph.

Billie and Lester—two great tragic figures of jazz—never saw each other again. Little more than a year later, they were both gone; they died within four months of each other.

Like many key figures in jazz, Lester was a phenomenon, a genius, if you will—and a paradox. It could hardly have been foreseen that such a new and radical stylistic and aesthetic alternative to the firmly established Hawkins and Armstrong traditions would come from such a gentle, outwardly unassertive man. It was revolution by understatement. He was in a sense the Gandhi of American jazz, who left us all a heritage that is still very much with us.

CHARLIE CHRISTIAN

It is always a source of surprise to discover in what diverse regions of the country many of the major and lesser figures of jazz were born and/or grew up.[28] In the earliest days, the great majority of jazz musicians were born in and around New Orleans. Later many came from New York. And even though we know that a tremendous geographic diffusion of jazz had already occurred by the second

---

28. A random sampling of surprising name and place couplings might include: Mildred Bailey—Tekoa, Washington; Eddie Barefield—Scandia, Iowa; Count Basie and Elmer Williams—Red Bank, New Jersey; Bix Beiderbecke—Davenport, Iowa; Bunny Berigan—Calumet, Wisconsin; Chu Berry—Wheeling, West Virginia; Jimmy Blanton—Chattanooga, Tennessee; Lawrence Brown—Lawrence, Kansas; Nat Cole—Birmingham, Alabama; Vic Dickenson—Xenia, Ohio; Eddie Durham—St. Marcos, Texas (on the Mexican border); Gil Evans—Toronto, Canada; John Lewis—Albuquerque, New Mexico; Charlie Mingus—Nogales, Arizona; Art Tatum—Toledo, Ohio; Lester Young—Woodville, Mississippi (grew up in New Orleans and Minneapolis).

decade of our century, much of it in the direction of the Southwest, it is still surprising to find so many coming from or being raised in the Kansas-Oklahoma-Texas territory. Such names include Coleman Hawkins, Ben Webster, Budd Johnson, Buddy Tate, Don Byas, Henry Bridges, Tommy Douglas, Earle Bostic (saxophone players all), Jack Teagarden, Jay McShann, Jimmy Rushing, Hot Lips Page, Jesse Stone—and, of course, Charlie Christian, born in Bonham, Texas, and raised in Oklahoma City.[29] Pointing out the geographic centering of Christian's early years in Texas and Oklahoma is not a mere idle statistical exercise. It is in fact at least the partial answer to bandleader and Minton manager Teddy Hill's famous puzzled question about Charlie Christian: "Where did he come from?"

The implication in Hill's question was twofold, one having to do with Christian's almost miraculous bursting onto the New York jazz scene full-blown, as it were, at age twenty-three, musically fully mature; the other relating to the kind of musical origins that could produce such a major innovative talent. The simple short answer is that the Southwest is guitar country and blues country, the Texas blues tradition particularly being one of the oldest indigenous traditions and probably much older than the New Orleans idiom that is generally thought to be the primary fountainhead of jazz. And Christian embraced all of that: a guitarist who brought the Southwestern blues into modern jazz—and more.

To understand the spectacular rise of Christian, we have to recognize, in addition to his obviously precocious, enormous innate talent, a variety of formative influences from the following overlapping musical traditions—the Southwestern blues guitar, classical music, and the highly developed diverse country music of the Texas-Oklahoma region. And once again, we must factor in John Hammond's remarkable enterpreneurial genius in ferreting out major talent. For it was he who brought Christian to the East coast and engineered the coup which persuaded the initially apathetic and resistent Benny Goodman to take Christian into his Sextet in 1939.[30] The rest is history, including the sad fact that by February 1942 Christian was dead of tuberculosis (ironically, almost at the same time and of the same cause as that other remarkable young talent,

---

29. Christian's year of birth has now been established as 1916 (not 1919, as previously given in many sources), according to information recently unearthed by Time-Life researchers in connection with its *Giants of Jazz* anthology of jazz guitar. (John Chilton's always excellent and quite reliable *Who's Who of Jazz* had at least the year correct, as Feather's *Encyclopedia of Jazz* did not).

30. Hammond surreptitiously sneaked Christian onto the Goodman bandstand at the Victor Hugo Restaurant in Beverly Hills. Goodman, thinking to get rid of the gauchely dressed, unpromising-looking intruder, annoyedly counted off *Rose Room*, assuming that Christian would not know that tune. But Christian launched into a forty-five-minute chorus-after-chorus improvisation, producing an overwhelming ovation, and convincing the astonished Goodman not only that Hammond once again was right but that he better hire Christian on the spot.

It is little remembered today that, when Christian appeared on the scene, Goodman had already considered adding an electric guitar to his Quartet/Quintet. To that end he had brought Leonard Ware, another pioneer electric guitarist, into the group on a trial basis. But after the Los Angeles *Rose Room* encounter, Charlie Christian was Benny's unqualified choice.

Jimmy Blanton, the innovative bass player with Duke Ellington, who died in July 1942).

Although Frank Driggs has written brilliantly about Southwestern jazz, especially the extraordinary role played by Kansas City and its musicians in the 1930s, the broader picture of the whole Southwest's musical traditions has yet to be written. When it is, it will be a fascinating study of the cross-cultural influences between and amongst a vast panorama of musics, comprising the troubadour-like tradition of itinerant blues singers and guitarists, the innumerable small Texas blues bands of the 1930s, the whole rich complex of earthy dance musics ranging from the Anglo-American country dances (jigs, reels, schottisches) and crude stompy polkas of the Czechs, Poles, and Germans in the region, to the Mexican and French Acadian dance idioms, the cowboy songs of the frontier, the rural banjo picking tradition—all this intertwined with a ubiquitous fiddle tradition, both white and black.

This incredible amalgam, feeding on all manner of diverse ethnic and cultural backgrounds, was brought into even greater cross-cultural flux by the advent of radio, recordings, and jukeboxes—and not least by the Southwestern oil boom of the 1930s, precipitating substantial population migrations. There can be little question that the young Charlie Christian, as a teenager playing in his father's strolling string band in the non-black neighborhoods of Oklahoma City, played (and heard) a great variety of music. Ralph Ellison, the novelist and essayist, a boyhood friend and neighbor of Charlie's, pointed out that the group's repertory "included the light classics as well as the blues".[31] Anyone who has ever wandered through the back alleys of southern cities and towns knows what a rich Ivesian musical potpourri could emanate from a thousand radios and jukeboxes, all manner of sounds floating through the neighborhoods. (At least this was so in pre-television days.) And thus one can well imagine that young Charlie absorbed, consciously and unconsciously, a great variety of the popular music styles of the time and the region, including, I am convinced, that of the most pervasive Southwestern music of all, especially on radio: the early Western Swing bands, essentially string bands like his father's, who as early as the beginning 1930s featured guitarists playing *improvised single-note lines*. These players also pioneered the electric or amplified guitar[32] but have never, to my knowledge, been given credit in any jazz-writing either for their jazz leanings or their efforts on behalf of guitar amplification.[33] Players like "Zeke" Campbell, Bob Dunn, and

31. No one has written more feelingly and intelligently than Ellison about Charlie Christian and the cultural/social milieu in which he grew up. His beautiful essay on Christian, first written for the *Saturday Review* in 1958, then reprinted in Ellison's collection of writings, *Shadow and Act* (New York, 1964), is mandatory reading on the subject of Charlie Christian.

32. I have written elsewhere on the important role Eddie Durham played in the development of guitar amplification (see Chapter 4, Part 2, Andy Kirk).

33. Bob Dunn seems to have been the first to apply a homemade pick-up and amplifier to the guitar, in January 1935, while playing with the Texas-based Milton Brown and His Musical Brownies. (Eddie Durham's resonator-amplified solo on Lunceford's *Hittin' the Bottle* was recorded eight months later and issued in early 1936.) Dunn tended to feature more the slidy Hawaiian effects, very popular on recordings going back to the late twenties. But Leon McAuliffe and Muryel "Zeke"

Leon McAuliffe were very much in a jazz groove and by the mid-thirties certainly far removed from any of the older guitar, mandolin, banjo vertical "finger-pickin' " country styles.

It seems a reasonable assumption that Christian heard these bands—and dozens of others like them (Roy Newman, The Texas Wanderers, Jimmie Revard and His Oklahoma Playboys, etc.)—both on radio and recordings, and in person, as they roamed around the Southwest territory. This is not to imply, necessarily, that Christian got his style single-handedly from these Texan guitarists, but it is to suggest, at least, that a guitar tradition of the kind he represented and perfected was already of long standing by the time he burst onto the scene in New York in mid-1939.

We shall see momentarily how certain very specific *jazz* influences also played a major role in Christian's early development. But we must not neglect also to note the fact, as Ellison points out so tellingly, that the black youngsters of the Oklahoma City ghetto were not exactly "innocent of contact" with classical musical forms and were, in fact, trained in harmony and had an "extensive music appreciation" course and a varied instrumental program, including concert band and symphony orchestra. Although Christian could not participate in the latter two ensembles, since the guitar was already his chosen instrument at a very early age, he certainly was fully aware of a music other than blues, jazz, and country. As Ellison further so correctly points out, speaking not only of Christian but also of most of the younger musicians of the thirties, "especially those who contributed to the growth of bop," their desire to master the classical technique was linked with the struggle for recognition in the larger society" (read "white"). And the incontrovertible evidence of jazz developments in the thirties shows that, in hundreds of cases, it was the synthesis of two techniques, the one classic and "correct," the other "eclectic and unconscious, which led to many of the technical discoveries of jazz" (Ellison).

Oklahoma City, of course, also had its own vigorous *jazz* tradition. For one thing it was the home of Walter Page's remarkable Blue Devils orchestra.[34] For another it was the home of Jimmy Rushing. It was also a regular stopping place for all the bands of the Mid- and Southwest, including the most famous of them all, Bennie Moten's. But what seems to have really stimulated Christian and set him onto the stylistic path for which he later became so famous was the arrival

---

Campbell (the former with Bob Wills and his Texas Playboys, the latter with the Light Crust Dough-boys) played primarily in a jazz idiom, highly blues-inflected and invariably in a single-note linear style. As the electric guitar took hold, these bands became increasingly dominated by that instrument, to a large extent taking over from and crowding out the fiddle. These bands also turned more and more to a jazz repertory and instrumentation, adding trumpets and saxophones—by 1940 Bob Wills had a seventeen-piece band(!) including two trumpets and three or four saxes—and was recording such older jazz and ragtime material as *Weary Blues, Tin Roof Blues, Milenberg Joys, Darktown Strutters' Ball, Four or Five Times,* and *Gulf Coast Blues,* as well as newer pieces like *I'm a Ding Dong Daddy, Black and Blue, Steel Guitar Rag, Swing Blues, Avalon, White Heat,* even Johnny Hodges's *New Jeep's Blues*—and, most indicatively, *Did You Ever Hear a String Band Swing?*
34. *Early Jazz*, pp. 293–98.

of Lester Young in Oklahoma City, first in 1929, and then again in 1931 for a more extensive stay as a member of the Blue Devils. It seems clear that Young's more linear conception of jazz and of the tenor saxophone,[35] quite different from Hawkins's vertical and chord-conscious style, had a profound and lasting effect on Christian. Such an influence was all the more possible, given the fact that the guitar was much freer of classical technical domination than the other more symphonically established instruments, and that there were already a number of blues-oriented linear guitar players active all around him, offering tacit encouragement in that direction or possibly even representing actual models.[36]

Given the diverse musical environment in which he grew up, it is small wonder then—and I think significant—that Christian, when asked about early influences, never pointed to any in particular—and certainly confounded Teddy Hill. Christian seemed to like everybody and everything musical, and not much more could be prodded out of him.

Unfortunately we have no hard evidence of Christian's playing until he arrived in New York and began recording with Lionel Hampton and Benny Goodman in September and October 1939, respectively. We do have, apart from Ellison's, a smattering of personal remembrances of Christian's playing, going back, however, no earlier than 1937 when various musicians, including Eddie Durham, Mary Lou Williams, Mary Osborne, and Oscar Pettiford, began to encounter Christian in places as scattered as Minneapolis, Oklahoma City, and Bismarck, North Dakota.

Christian seems to have left his father's family string band (two other brothers also played a variety of instruments in it) to travel with Alphonse Trent (Christian played bass with him), the Jeter-Pillars band, and possibly other territory bands like Lloyd Hunter's and Nat Towles's, occasionally also fronting his own small band with one of his brothers in Oklahoma.

That is almost all we know of Christian's brief pre-Goodman career. But what seems clear, nevertheless, is that Christian's innovative style was quite matured some years before his arrival in New York, probably as early as 1935, but certainly by 1937, after Eddie Durham, meeting Christian while on tour with Count Basie's band, had introduced Christian to an early form of electric guitar. It was then that Christian could really express his horn-like conception and riff-based ideas effectively and competitively with other jazz instruments.

Less than a month after Christian's historic initial encounter with Goodman in Los Angeles, he found himself in the recording studio for the first time—with Lionel Hampton and some very distinguished company: Coleman Hawkins, Ben Webster, Chu Berry, the young Dizzy Gillespie, Benny Carter, and a superb rhythm section of Milt Hinton, Cozy Cole, and Clyde Hart. It was to the rhythm section that Christian was relegated, for, whatever the reasons, Christian was not

---

35. See above Chapter 4 on Lester Young with Basie.
36. It would be fascinating to know whether Christian ever heard in his formative years the playing of Django Reinhardt, that extraordinary Belgian-born maverick, who also developed early on an essentially melodic/linear virtuoso style. This, however, came out of French-Spanish gypsy folk traditions rather than any intrinsically American jazz styles, let alone blues.

given any solo space and furthermore was limited to the acoustic guitar. Nevertheless he acquitted himself superbly, contributing brilliantly to the group's strong swing.[37]

But in less than a month Christian recorded again with Goodman, and this time on electric guitar as one of the front-line melodic soloists recording *Flying Home*, *Rose Room*, and *Star Dust*. Here we find all the essential elements of Christian's style: the clean uncluttered lines, often in arching shapes—his favorite phrase contour; his flawless time; his consistently blues-inflected melodic/harmonic language; the structural logic with which he invested form, whether in shorter segments (8-bar structures) or full choruses.[38] Actually there exist more compelling Christian solos than the Goodman Sextet version of *Flying Home* (indeed a "live" performance of that piece from mid-August 1939, issued on an air-check recording, presents an even more substantial and expressive Christian solo); and other Sextet recordings, like *Breakfast Feud*, are certainly more masterful. But the studio-made *Flying Home* is nonetheless a fine example of Christian's innate ability to build a coherent, if unspectacular, musical statement out of the simplest of melodic raw materials.

On *Rose Room*, his famous "Goodman audition" piece, Christian was given a full chorus, about all that could be rescued, as it were, from the audition event, given the time limitations of a ten-inch disc. But what a finely formed, logical *composition* he produced here. Note the splendid triplet eighth-note run in bars 12 and 13 (Ex. 10).

Ex. 10

37. Because of Christian's superiority as a solo-line player, his rhythm playing has been much neglected; occasionally one even reads implications that he was not terribly effective in this area. But if proof of Christian's prowess as rhythm guitarist be needed, we can find it abundantly on such sides as *Hot Mallets* (with Hampton), on some of the tracks from the Spirituals to Swing Carnegie Hall Concert, both with the Goodman Sextet and the Kansas City Six, but above all with the Edmond Hall Celeste Quartet. Hear the perfect buoyant swing of Christian and bassist Israel Crosby—they sound absolutely like *one* instrument—on *Jammin' in Four* and *Celestial Express*.

38. I have purposely not mentioned Christian's tone because, although I believe he had a remarkably pure, bell-like, centered tone, its ultimate realization on the recordings was subject to at least two technical and not always entirely controllable modifiers: the electric amplification of the guitar, still a relatively new technology at the time, and the particular way in which it was recorded in the studio by various recording engineers on different occasions.

Why *Star Dust*, also from the first Goodman Sextet session, was originally not issued[39] is a mystery to me. It is not only outstanding Christian, but it presents him in a *harmonic* vein, a relatively rare treat. It also was well recorded and shows off Christian's full firm expressive tone at its expressive best. How he found those superimposed minor triads with which he begins his solo (Ex. 11a), set in a special blues-ish relaxed swing—on, of all pieces, *Star Dust*—is hard to divine, but obviously a mark of his extraordinary creativity. That this was not an isolated *trouvaille*, just stumbled upon, becomes clear when we see how Christian develops this triadic idea throughout the solo. Notice how a relatively innocent cadential phrase in the seventh bar is reused and developed later on (mm. 17–20, Ex. 11b). Note also that these sliding chordal effects are uniquely gui-

Ex. 11a

39. It appeared only on a Japanese Columbia 78.

Ex. 11b

taristic, achieved by sliding the fingers (three in this case) in parallel formation, the amplification and elongation of the sound (compared with the unamplified guitar) making this all the more effective and expressive. It is a device natural to the guitar, in that the chord voicings lie well in the left hand, corresponding closely to the tuning of the guitar's three upper strings. (Such sliding parallel shapes had, of course, been used to fine effect, either in thirds or triads, by Hawaiian-style guitarists for at least a decade, and eventually became that instrument's ultimate cliché device, whether in Hawaiian-style groups or in commercial Nashville country bands.) Christian carries these parallel triadic harmonies through the first six bars of his solo, doubling up the tempo in the fifth bar with a figure which sounds amazingly like the wolf's theme in Prokofiev's *Peter and the Wolf*, there played by three French horns in parallel triads). After an upward scoop of an entire B♭-ninth chord in the sixth measure, Christian tops off the

phrase with a graceful arpeggio up to high G: . This, too, lies

beautifully in the hand, a figure beloved by guitarists and one which, with its characteristic final leap up a fifth, Christian used in endless variants, both harmonically, as here, and linearly in hundreds of other solos. It might be noted in passing that the contour as well as the actual notes are almost identical to those of the second bar of *Star Dust's* melody (transposed):

The next Goodman Sextet date produced one of Christian's more famous performances, although in retrospect, again, not necessarily one of his best, being somewhat flawed by repetitiousness. Certainly, at the time, Christian's riff on *7 Come 11*—he apparently could conceive such riffs by the hundreds—was an exciting, still relatively fresh idea in jazz, especially as stated here in a four-way unison: clarinet, guitar, piano, vibraphone. The performance as a whole is distinguished by great swing and drive, with Nick Fatool (drums) and Artie Bernstein (bass) inspiring Goodman to some lusty improvising. Hampton, in his solo, also hammers away heartily, at one point thumping out a series of marvelously insistent "wrong note" F♭s (over reiterated A♭ chords).

On the same date (November 22, 1939) Christian made his recording debut with Goodman's big band in a fine authoritative solo on *Honeysuckle Rose*, set over a soft, flowing saxophone ensemble background. It is all too brief due to the exigency of giving other players (like Ziggy Elman and Benny, of course) solo spaces while still leaving room for the band's famous crisp, impeccably played ensembles.

From the aforementioned Carnegie Hall concert, there survive a number of fine Christian solos, incorporating now some new and unusual winding, twisting lines, as for example in the last four bars of *Memories of You* (Ex. 12).

Ex. 12

In *Good Morning Blues* we can hear Christian building a solo gradually from very simple, calm, folk-like materials, mostly stated in quarter notes and eighths, to more rapid excited sixteenth-note runs. But his finest moment came on *Paging the Devil*, with the Kansas City Six. Besides featuring a most eloquently simple Lester Young blues, it gives us Christian, the Texas blues guitarist *par excellence*.

By early 1940, alas, we see (hear) some evidence that of Christian's inspiration is beginning temporarily to flag. He rarely played a poor solo, but, for whatever reason, a fair amount of his work now reached a kind of plateau, featuring typical but often unspecial solos. Pieces like *Six Appeal* and *Boy Meets Goy* are not worthy of Christian's real talent.[40]

It seems to me, too, that the riff-tune idea, brought to the Goodman Sextet by Charlie Christian, was increasingly abused, or at least over-used by that group. It eventually became an end in itself, losing its original function *and* its freshness, and assuming finally a robot-like routinization. At the same time, the very popularity of the riff-line-as-theme, overlaid on top of familiar changes, led, I am sure, in a seminal way to the bop lines and fresh thematic material in modern jazz of only a few years later.

But a set of remarkable performances, both by Christian and the other players in the group, came about in early 1941 under clarinetist Edmond Hall's leadership—his Celeste Quartet, featuring boogie-woogie pianist Meade Lux Lewis

---

40. Recording dates with blues singer Ida Cox (another John Hammond favorite) and the Metronome All Stars produced little Christian of interest, either because he was not given solos at all or because they were all too brief, sandwiched in amongst too many others.

on celesta and bassist Israel Crosby. Here Christian responded creatively, on the one hand, to a different musical environment (clarinet, celesta, and bass—no drums!) and, on the other hand, to the challenge of being confined to acoustic guitar, at the behest of the session's producer Frank Wolf, co-owner of the then new Blue Note label. On *Profoundly Blue*, perhaps a masterpiece of its kind, Christian produces three superb blues choruses, fascinating in their "older" style, showing clearly how far back Christian's roots go in the Southwestern blues tradition, and notable for their pared-down simplicity and sustained, eloquent storytelling mood. His solo is set in the unusual texture of just guitar, celesta, and bass, each in its respective register and role. Memorable, too, is Crosby's playing, functioning at once as harmonic foundation *and* "rhythm section," at the same time weaving fine contrapuntal/melodic lines, especially in his continually reiterated triplet figures.[41]

Meanwhile, Christian kept on recording frequently with Goodman's Sextet, soon expanded to a Septet and an Octet with the addition of Cootie Williams and the young tenor player, Georgie Auld. Of these later performances one must single out Christian's work on *Breakfast Feud* and *I Found a New Baby*, recorded on the same day,[42] January 15, 1941. These solos are prime Christian and became for all forward-looking young guitarists of the time benchmarks to be studied, imitated, and built upon.

Breakfast Feud is especially revealing of Christian's capacities to put the guitar unequivocally on a par with the other major jazz "horns." His five solos are strong, almost stern, no-nonsense in character and absolutely uncompromising in their intent on carving out new territory for the guitar, accomplishing all this with consummate technical control.

If we examine why Christian's best work of this period (as on *Breakfast Feud*) sounds so utterly logical, effortless, and pleasing, we discover certain recurring traits and note patterns that bind his solos into a coherent continuity. We also discover that Christian's idiom is essentially a very conservative one. Like Teddy Wilson, he breaks no new ground harmonically or rhythmically, and there is in Christian's playing a comforting sensibleness. The novelty of Christian's playing lay in the use of what was to all intents and purposes a "new" instrument, a new "sound," which suddenly had broken into the front line of melody instruments.

What makes Christian's solos so engaging is their overall smoothness and

41. Two other sides, *Jammin' in Four* and *Celestial Express*, are equally outstanding, featuring the leader's happy, buoyantly expressive New Orleans clarinet and some fascinating (though often overrecorded) Lewis two-handed blues celesta. Interestingly, when Hall recorded with a quintet in 1944 with Red Norvo (on vibraphone) and Teddy Wilson, the intent seemed to have been to imitate the Benny Goodman Quartet of earlier years. Hall himself had by then more or less capitulated to Goodman's clarinet influence, playing the latter's ideas but with his own liquid tone—an exception being his haunting, stately blues choruses on *Blue Interval*.

42. The "official" issued recording of *Breakfast Feud* on LP includes three Christian solos, the first two spliced in from an earlier December date, originally rejected by Columbia. The Smithsonian's *Collection of Classic Jazz* has gone Columbia one better by putting together a composite "performance" which comprises *five* Christian solos, from both recording dates, presented in consecutive sequence.

seamlessness of structure. There is an inviting regularity in his phrasing—phrase-lengths, phrase-shapes—which only rarely spills over into repetitiousness and monotony. For example, a new phrase will invariably link up with its predecessor by picking up on its last note or two, or at least in that particular pitch and register region. It is exceptional when Christian begins a new phrase in another octave or across some large intervallic leap. Generally, too, his solos are not rangy; they usually function within the range of an octave or a tenth in the upper register of the guitar, subtly revolving around a central pitch axis, usually the third of the tonic key. He may reach above or dip below this pitch fulcrum, but his lines always converge back onto it. This gives his improvisations a wonderful sense of security, of being well-anchored in familiar ground.

Further, the larger contours of his lines are so pleasing to our ears because they consist of a flowing alternation of rising and falling shapes. Moreover, these alternations are generally cast in almost classic symmetrical proportions, very much in the classic sense of *arsis* and *thesis*. A surging rising figure (*arsis*) will invariably be resolved by a relaxing falling one (*thesis*). Examples 13a, b, c depict three samplings chosen almost randomly, all from the five-solo *Breakfast Feud*.

Ex. 13a

Ex. 13b

Ex. 13c

The bracketed figure *a* in Ex. 13a, with its characteristic final interval of the fifth, and its energizing "upbeat" feeling, was a particular favorite of Christian's—it appears about a dozen times in various transpositions or guises in the *Breakfast Feud* solos alone. It was invariably followed by a descending line which more often than not involved a nexus of pitches (shown bracketed under *b*, in all three examples), again in subtle variants. This latter figure, a favorite way of unraveling or ending a phrase, is used no less than *seventeen* times by Christian in *Breakfast Feud*, in various ways, of course. Remember that these solos were originally all on separate takes, recorded, moreover, on two dates nearly a month apart. They afford us, either separately or collectively, a fascinating glimpse of how Christian, by combining congruity and contrast, elaborates upon the basic blues changes with infinite but subtle variations.

Christian's recurrent use of formulaic motivic figures[43] would become quite tiresome if it were not alternated with contrasting passages. Christian provides these as well (Ex. 14a, b).

Ex. 14a

Ex. 14b

Surprisingly, the most compelling solo Christian produced on *Breakfast Feud* is contained on neither the Columbia nor the Smithsonian issues but on a Jazz Archive record (JA 6). Here Christian plays a full *three* and two-thirds choruses (actual, not spliced together), starting with the identical phrase that starts the second of the Smithsonian solos. But this time Christian goes in a quite different direction, producing a solo which it seems to me relates quite clearly to the country blues guitarists mentioned earlier. Not only does Christian emulate the type of twangy slides, scoops, and string-crossings the latter use,[44] but he also uses less syncopation, staying more on the beat and relying a great deal on straight even eighth-note lines. Example 15 reproduces the entire Smithsonian *Breakfast Feud* solo, including the 4-bar ensemble lead-in.

Similarly, on *I Found a New Baby* we see many of the same devices and ideas used, with again a copious use of the previously noted motivic figure *a* (in Ex. 13), here in the key of D minor rather than B♭ blues (Ex. 16a, b).

This type of figure, incidentally, lies well in the hand of guitarists and has in addition to its linear shape a strong harmonic implication, a duality Christian knew very well how to exploit.

Christian was also the author of that neat little ensemble riff-idea which closes *Gone with What Draft*, the second 2-bar phrase being virtually the same as the first, but shifted one beat earlier for a delightful off-center feeling.

43. All jazz players, of course, have such typical motivic figures at hand, ready to use in any given situation. They form, so to speak, the backbone of their style, what jazz musicians call their "bag." The better players know how to vary this "bag" and to intersperse it with fresh, more inventive material. In the hands of lesser musicians these figures tend to deteriorate to the level of cliché.
44. Christian was fond of riffing the same note on alternate strings (hear the repeated B♭s on the Jazz Archive *Breakfast Feud*), thus producing a variety of timbral textures—an effect also much used by Lester Young with saxophone alternate fingerings.

Ex. 15

Ex. 16a

Ex. 16b

These late 1940 to early 1941 Sextet dates offer many other fine musical pleasures, by Goodman himself, occasionally Cootie Williams, and an astonishingly consistent yet perplexing Auld—perplexing because his solos are excellent, authoritatively stated, but virtual plagiarisms of Ben Webster: tone, notes, rhythm and all!

At the same time the evidence of the later Sextet recordings reveals that a certain gradual stagnation of inspiration was creeping into the performances. The earlier freshness that the chamber-jazz concept had generated was waning, and much of the group's playing was taking on a certain mechanical routine quality. In these years the Sextet was only to make a few sporadic recordings, finally to be revived again with changed personnel in 1944. By that time, of course, Christian was long dead, becoming too ill to work in 1941 and consigned to a sanatorium with an advanced case of tuberculosis.

But if Christian's health began to deteriorate in early 1941, his playing surely did not. In fact, judging by the private recordings made by Jerry Newman and others at jam sessions in places like the Nest Club in Minneapolis, Minton's and Monroe's Uptown in Harlem, Christian's playing was taking on ever greater dimensions of depth and originality. Clearly, in the unfettered environment of these jam sessions, often surrounded by equally explorative musical minds like Thelonious Monk and Kenny Clarke, Christian was inspired and challenged to new heights of solo flights.[45] *Solo Flight* was, of course, the name of Christian's showcase recording with the Goodman orchestra, a composition and arrangement fashioned out of bits of Christian riffs by Jimmy Mundy. Although the piece had a considerable public success and was highly touted by younger guitarists (especially Wes Montgomery), it is over-all not a terribly successful affair. The piece is one of those late-swing-era over-cluttered arrangements which hardly leaves the soloist any room to play. Christian fights off the band as best he can, but it is a losing battle. The result is musically mechanical and calculated. Nor does the band's exaggeratedly clipped, cold staccato style relate in any way to Christian's linear, warmer idiom.

Christian practically *lived* at Minton's in the last year of his life, playing night after night in the prolonged jam sessions that would end only at the four o'clock closing and permitted a musician to play as many choruses as he had the imagination or stamina for. There can be little doubt that among the younger musicians who sat in at Minton's, Christian was at the time (1941) the most advanced, the most original, and musically the most mature—even more than Gillespie and Monk.

There exist superior, multi-chorus Christian solos from Minton's which give us a much clearer picture of the man's real talent and technical prowess, certainly more so than the perforce in many ways limited Goodman Sextet sides. At Minton's he was not limited to brief inserts, now and then; and the loose yet

45. On the sessions in Minneapolis, Christian is in brilliant form, playing with tremendous drive and energy (hear his linear, totally original creation on *Tea for Two*, for example). But the accompanying rhythm section, mercifully unknown, is so abysmal that it is a nerve-wracking experience to listen to these performances.

sophisticated atmosphere of Minton's allowed for a much freer kind of explorative creativity. More than that, solos like those on *Stompin' at the Savoy*, *Up on Teddy's Hill*, and *Charlie's Choice* indicate that perhaps Christian was just really coming into his own artistically, his earlier brilliance notwithstanding. His work here seems to me relentlessly creative, endlessly fertile, and is so in a way that marks a new stylistic departure. Indeed, it signals the birth of a new language in jazz, which even Parker did not have as clearly in focus at that time. Its only precedent can be found in the work of Lester Young and Roy Eldridge, but even in the playing of these musicians there remains a certain adherence to older stylistic traditions, what I would call the "romanticism" of the swing era.

Christian at Minton's distances himself from those values in significant ways. His rhythms are more sharply delineated, more incisive, driven by a new, cleaner kind of propulsive swing energy. Moreover, his eighth notes (or sixteenth notes in slower pieces) are played in a much more even manner, very close to the bop rhythms that were to become standard procedure within a few years, and far removed from the loping tripletized eighths of a player like Hawkins, for example. Interestingly, such even-note lines are to be found in abundance among the country-style guitarists like Campbell and McAuliffe. While almost anybody would regard their rhythmic style as more "square" and less swinging, the similarity is undeniable. The point is that Christian (and Young) could take those rhythms and *make* them swing.

Melodically, too, Christian offers a more modern streamlined conception, almost completely linear, i.e. less chained to the underlying chords, and filled out with more chromatic passing tones. At the same time such smoothing-out chromaticisms are regularly contrasted with more angular shapings, making much greater use of melodic fourths and fifths. Example 17 is typical of this type of line, already much explored by Lester Young. I would further point out that at this time Christian appeared to be moving away somewhat from the traditional blues-inflected lines. Not that he ever left the blues entirely behind, but he is clearly, like Parker in *his* later years, trying either to break away from the conventions of the blues or to expand them into a wider vision.

Ex. 17

He seems also to be developing longer single-sentence lines. Much of Christian's early playing tended to be short-breathed, not in an inept way, but merely as a considered element of his style. It seems quite conceivable to me that Christian's guitar playing was not uninfluenced by his work on the trumpet as a youngster in Oklahoma. Indeed, frequently one can hear Christian in his earlier work breaking phrases, breathing, as it were, just as a "horn" player might. At Minton's, in countless hours of experimenting, Christian seems to have shaken off that earlier influence.

The beauty of Christian's late work resides in its poise and maturity, qualities inherent in both his style's traditional roots, that is to say, in its essentially simple folk-like "blues-as-story-telling" concept, *and* in his (by 1941) many years of experience as a constantly developing artist—founded in the first place on a most precocious talent.

There can be little doubt that at the time of his death in 1942 Christian was on the threshold of becoming a major voice, perhaps, had he lived, *the* major voice in shaping the new language of jazz. All the greater the tragedy of his loss, one that has, I believe, not yet been fully fathomed and appreciated.

BEN WEBSTER

After nearly a half-century of listening to Ben Webster, in person and on recordings, it is hard to realize—let alone believe—that one of the greatest balladeers in jazz (some would argue, myself included, *the* greatest) should have started as a buzz-toned, frantic, downright comical, slap-tongue saxophonist. But it *is* true; and the tell-tale evidence exists on recordings, with Blanche Calloway (made in 1931) and even—minus the slap-tongue feature, but the hysteria and congested phrasing remaining—on the great Bennie Moten sides of 1932 (*Toby, Lafayette*). It is also true that, once Webster had assimilated the influence of both Hawkins and Johnny Hodges and found his own voice—not too many years after these unpromising beginnings—he became one of the greatest and most consistent, invincible artists of jazz.

We have seen in the discussion of Coleman Hawkins that the saxophone, particularly the tenor of the family, had to be developed from a buffoon-like vaudeville contraption with no discernible musical values into an expressive lyric instrument, eventually learning to simulate the human voice and soul more accurately than any other instrument, jazz or otherwise. By the time young Webster arrived on the scene the tenor saxophone was not yet quite of age, and even its greatest proponent, Hawkins, was just beginning to break out of its stiffly vertical role as a harmony chaser. In less critical circles the slap-tongue stereotype of the saxophone was still lingering on, and in an entertainment band like Blanche Calloway's the raucous, primitive slappy honkings associated with the instrument for decades were evidently still considered *de rigueur*. Webster at his most unswinging ludicrous worst can be heard on an appropriately titled James P. Johnson piece called *Misery*. From this to Webster's *Cotton Tail* and his famous Fargo, North Dakota, *Star Dust* (both with Ellington's orchestra) is the story of a great musician's emancipation from the clichés and trappings of a formerly misunderstood minority instrument.[46]

It took a while for Webster to understand that the tenor saxophone need not be—and maybe *should* not be—played at breakneck speed, that that was perhaps not its true calling, that instead it could be the "lyric baritone" of the saxophone family. By Webster's own account it was the remarkable and wise Russell Smith, lead trumpet with Fletcher Henderson for sixteen years,[47] who advised him to slow down and use his by then considerably developed tone to more personal effect. Webster's solo work with Moten indicates that this was sound and much-needed advice, for Webster there sounds breathless and confused, even unintelligible. He enters four bars late on *Lafayette*, then plunges into a convoluted busily "technical" solo not enhanced by his exaggerated vibrato. Compared with, say, Hot Lips Page's sovereign work here (or even trombonist Dan Minor's on *Toby*), it becomes clear that the twenty-three-year-old Webster was still in another and lesser league.

By 1934, with Henderson, even though already a bit slowed down and now much more in a Hawkins mold—he was the latter's successor in the by now famous tenor chair—Webster was still apt to falter. His solos were rarely of a piece. *Happy As the Day Is Long* is a fair example of his problems. He starts off well enough, but by the middle of the second "eight" begins to stumble. In the bridge he clings desperately to some old-time New Orleans clichés (of the *High Society* type), ending the solo weakly in a sort of one-foot-up-in-the-air stance. Although now trying to play with more line, when in trouble he reverted to fast razzle-dazzle arpeggio patterns.

But Smith must really have gotten to him because by the end of 1934, recording with Benny Carter's short-lived band, we hear Webster (on *Dream Lullaby*) approach his later mature ballad style with a stately coherent solo. It is, of course, much influenced by Hawkins, Webster's idol, who had by then recorded his breakthrough performances of *Talk of the Town* (1934) and *One Hour* (1929), with Henderson and the Mound City Blue Blowers respectively (see Hawkins section of this chapter). But Webster is not prepared to be just a slavish imitator of Hawkins on *Dream Lullaby*. Already we can note his tendency to round off lyrically the contours of phrases and hold his vibrato in check in a way that Hawkins didn't learn until much later.

We next hear Webster with Teddy Wilson—he was a frequent member of

---

46. It is interesting to note how completely differently Ben Webster and Lester Young evolved, when one learns that not only did both men cut their musical teeth on Frankie Trumbauer's *Singin' the Blues*—how many players were influenced by this seminal recording!—but also that both men were close teen-age friends in Texas and stand partners in Lester's father's traveling band.

47. The career of Russell Smith (1890–1966) fascinatingly encompasses three major periods in the history of jazz. From his early days, still in the ragtime era, with Ford Dabney (1914), Tim Brymn, Jim Europe, and Joe Jordan—four of the leading black musicians of the 1910s—through the 1920s *and* the Swing Era (with Henderson, as well as such bands as Claude Hopkins, Benny Carter, and Cab Calloway), Smith played the role of a stabilizing, anchoring element in the brass players' world for nearly four decades. The respect in which he was held by fellow musicians is indicated by his nickname "Pops"—otherwise accorded only to Louis Armstrong.

Wilson's small bands, including those that accompanied Billie Holiday's celebrated recordings—where he plays in a relaxed loose-jointed manner (say, on
Sunbonnet Blue) that is already some distance away from Hawkins's tighter, harder
style. A fine, gutsy, more vigorous Webster solo survives from this period in a
full chorus on *Truckin'*, with Ellington's orchestra.

The other new tenor player around town (New York) was Chu Berry, much
favored by musicians *and* John Hammond, the most active recording impresario
of the time. Berry also worked frequently in those Teddy Wilson units, and
inevitably we hear touches of Chu's very flowing, linear style creep into Webster's playing—hear him on *The Voice of Old Man River* with Willie Bryant's
orchestra in 1935. Webster's more velvet-glove approach—as compared with
Hawkins's—can be heard also to good effect on *I'll See You in My Dreams* with
Teddy Wilson in late 1936. There is a warmth in his playing here that, once
matured, was to characterize the bulk of Webster's later work. There is also a
surprising bop-ish altered-note phrase in the bridge (Ex. 18), at the beginning,

Ex. 18

and a typical Hawkins "rip" up to high F. Not only is Webster's delivery of these
diverse elements less brusque than Hawkins's in similar circumstances, but we
hear Webster's growing ability to forge logical, balanced, expressive musical
statements. A measure of this new-won ability can be seen by comparing Webster's relatively linear conception with Krupa's choppy, vertical drumming beneath him.

In 1939, after a year with Cab Calloway in 1937, Webster was with Teddy
Wilson's ill-fated big band. By now Webster's tone had taken on the ability to
assert itself, if needed, in a gutsier, huskier voice. We also hear on a number of
pieces (like *Exactly Like You* and 71) specific bits of phrase patterns that were to
play a major role in structuring Webster's first great breakthrough solo, on Ellington's *Cotton Tail*, and one of his most memorable efforts altogether (Ex. 19).

With *Cotton Tail* Webster had truly found his own voice, only rarely to be
confused with that of Hawkins.[48] It is a solo nearly perfect in its overall composition, as well as in its internal details of construction. Webster was fond of
entering a solo with a breathy low-register swoosh. He disliked sudden or precipitous intrusions. An analysis of his voluminous solo work clearly shows that he

48. It is also true, alas, that Webster was to be under-appreciated for many years, viewed largely as
a Hawkins *epigone* rather than a master in his own right, and this fact eventually drove him to
emigrate to Europe, where he lived out the later years of his life in Amsterdam and, then finally, in
Copenhagen.

Ex. 19

 = ghost notes

preferred to enter and exit unobtrusively, flowing in, as it were, on the prevailing tide of the music. His stealthy entrance on *Cotton Tail* is in its subtleness and surprising understatedness one of the all-time hair-raising moments in jazz. It also embodies one of Webster's other favorite devices, a descending chromatic line, usually evenly spaced and often set in cross-rhythms. In mm. 1–4 we hear one of Webster's smoother versions of this configuration; we shall encounter it again later in this solo in a more flamboyant form.[49] In mm. 5–7 a more varied (and concealed) use of the same idea follows, lining out the notes A♭ G G♭ F E E♭ (incidentally almost all of these by chance doubled in Blanton's high register walking bass). More of the same occurs in mm. 13–16, as the G in m. 13 works its way down to the D four bars later.

The next eight bars (the bridge) brings forth a 2-bar phrase, sequentially treated, and intelligently phased in with Ellington's superimposed brass interjections. Webster's second chorus surprisingly ignores the expected *I Got Rhythm* changes in the first eight bars, building instead to a first climax by a rising sequential diminished-chord figure, vigorously supported by crescendoing piano chords by Ellington (Ex. 20) and Blanton's seven bars of reiterated B♭s.

Ex. 20

49. An ascending version of this pattern was also frequently used by Webster, most notably in *Conga Brava* and *Just a Settin' and Rockin'* (with Ellington).

Webster was a master of interspersing fast-moving passages with long-held notes, which he would decorate with a variety of vibratos and shakes (see also mm. 14, 25–26). He was particularly fond of, and often used, a minor-third tremolo (downward) on A♭, which lies very well on the tenor saxophone, here in mm. 43–44 (in his second chorus). Now the aforementioned descending chromatic pattern reappears, this time in the bridge (mm. 49–56). Notice, too, how Webster eases out at the end of his solo, neatly eliding into the upcoming brass ensemble.

In its overall form Webster's solo creates a kind of arch shape, placing a peak of intensity (in register and dynamics) more or less halfway through the solo. The beginning of a second chorus was often with Webster a place for such intensification, and also, as here, a place from which to prolong a plateau of excitation until the calming denouément just before the end, easing on down to bring the solo back full circle to its slithering-in opening.

Ben Webster was, along with bassist Jimmy Blanton, the most crucial addition to the Ellington band of the late thirties to early forties period; indeed, the *last* such crucial addition. He not only augmented the Ellington saxophone section to five but added for the first time a full-time tenor player—and one with an extraordinary tonal range, from warmly lyrical to gutsily forceful. Together, Webster and Carney now gave the Ellington saxes a rich virile sound that no other section of the time could match. Webster also brought to the Ellington band (along with Blanton) that bluesy, earthy rhythmic feel that came from the Southwest and particularly Webster's hometown of Kansas City, what might best be described as a "linear pulse," otherwise known as Swing.

It is important to note that Ellington's orchestral vision was broad enough to accommodate the new thrust and authority of Webster's conception. Indeed, Webster seems to have been the one to open up Ellington's imagination to the notion of liberally expanding his players' solo contributions. Except for the occasional showcasing of a particular soloist, solo spaces before Webster's tenure in the band were allotted very cautiously under Ellington's watchful compositional eye, sparingly and precisely placed in controlled amounts. When Webster first joined the Ellington orchestra, he was given only brief, interpolated episodes—but what a magnificent and sinuous four-and-a-half bars Webster contributes on *Solitude*, his first solo with Duke (not counting his work during his previous brief spells with Ellington in 1935 and 1936). Compare this with the lengthy statements on *Conga Brava* and *Cotton Tail*, just months later. Webster, in musicologist Larry Gushee's excellent phrase, gradually "managed to lay claim to large tracts of Ellington's turf," and became for a while the band's most prolific soloist. Of his nearly three dozen recorded solos with Ellington in a three-and-a-half-year period, all were superior, quite a few masterful. Among the latter I would single out (besides *Conga Brava* and *Cotton Tail*) *Stormy Weather*, *Bojangles*, *All Too Soon*, *Chelsea Bridge*, *C-Jam Blues*, *Perdido*, and *Main Stem*.

A remarkable performance of *Star Dust*, though not recorded commercially, is preserved on records through the efforts of Jack Towers, a great sound engineer now living in Maryland, then a very young jazz enthusiast working in North

Dakota. The occasion was a dance at the Crystal Ballroom in Fargo, in one of the aforementioned showcasings, that were also designed to give the rest of the band a breather. It is an especially interesting performance since it catches Webster at his best, but at the same time (in this number at any rate) still rather beholden to Hawkins, in particular the Hawkins of *Body and Soul* fame. The latter title, the reader will recall, was the big jazz hit of 1939, also marking the return of Hawkins to the United States after five years of self-imposed "exile" in Europe. Of enormous influence on all musicians, but especially tenor saxophonists, it was inevitable that Webster, who modestly still considered Hawkins *the* master, would be unable to escape its influence altogether, given its breakthrough qualities *and* its extraordinary popularity.

The similarities between Webster's *Star Dust* and Hawkins's *Body and Soul* are mostly structural, not only in what he plays but *when* he plays it (Ex. 21). The first chorus (of which the initial twelve bars are missing on the recording, because Webster started before Towers could switch discs in time) is mostly melodic paraphrase, with Webster's warm tone especially buoyant and alluring. But then, just as Hawkins works gradually toward double-time figures, so does Webster in his second chorus. The climax of Hawkins's solo came near the end; Webster places it earlier, as is his wont, near the middle of the performance, but for it he uses the same type of up-and-down leaping figure in fourths and fifths (m. 15) as Hawkins had, followed a bit later by a "rip" to a high F. Also adopted from Hawkins's masterpiece is Webster's more frequent use than usual of altered harmonic substitutions in mm. 56 and 62, for example (not included in Ex. 21).

Webster also follows Hawkins's format in his overall expressive continuity, building to ever higher levels of intensity, expressed both in the expanding range and increasingly higher dynamics, as well as an increasingly raspier, thrusting tone. The only difference in those respects is that Webster relaxes the built-up tension earlier than Hawkins, coming to an at-ease position in a more measured fashion. (In this regard, Webster's *Star Dust* is typical of the form his solos generally took.) Although it is a broad generalization, subject to some exceptions, the shape and design of both players' improvisations throughout their mature years as a rule take the following form, graphically depicted (Fig. 1a and b).

Beyond the points indicated above, Webster is very much his own man. The particular note-configurations (with the one exception already noted) are entirely

Fig. 1

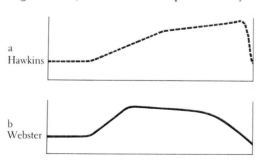

a
Hawkins

b
Webster

Ex. 21

of his own devising. And above all, the tone, warm and pliant at first, virile and raspy later on, is unmistakably Webster's. We should note how the gently rocking double-time figure which initiates the second chorus (Ex. 21, motive *a*, mm. 21–22) re-emerges twice more, in mm. 37–38 and (in the third chorus) mm. 71–72, a fine example of motivic variation. Also hear the magnificent, majestic upward-rising figure in mm. 23–24 which also reappears twice more, at the end of the second chorus (mm. 51–52) and still later in the third chorus, not notated here (in m. 70), this time combined with motive *a*.

These are but some of the more obvious structural links that bind Webster's *Star Dust* into a coherent whole. The entire solo is inspired by a logic and an inner balance that causes each note, each phrase to proceed infallibly to the next. In it we recognize what we always perceive in a masterpiece: a sense of the inevitable.

We cannot leave Webster's Ellington period without referring to what was undoubtedly his second greatest musical influence: Johnny Hodges. Hodges and Webster sat next to each other in the Ellington orchestra, and there is little question that Webster learned a great deal from the great altoist. Indeed, Webster often gratefully credited Hodges with showing him "how to play my horn." Hodges's influence upon Webster—in terms of the former's tone, the subtle blending and inflecting of pitches (of which Hodges was surely the ultimate master), and in general Webster's whole ornamental style with its complete assortment of musical enbroideries, tendrils and frills—kept growing through the years, pulling him more and more away from his original inspiration, Hawkins.

During his tenure with Ellington, Webster also recorded with Jack Teagarden and Slim Gaillard (hear Webster's strong, perfectly formed solo on *Ra-Da-Da-Da*),[50] and in 1944 he began leading his own small groups. In this context, unencumbered by other competing soloists, Webster could concentrate fully on his ballad playing, of which he became within a few years, and for the rest of his life, the undisputed master, even outclassing Hawkins. His tone, by turns warm and eloquent or forceful and virile, was his greatest asset. Next to Hawkins's somewhat leathery tone, Webster's was pure velvet. But when needed, it could roar and surge—and break with anguish. In time it became the most vocal, the most human of all the great jazz voices of his generation. In that most ancient of black musical traditions, Webster was a storyteller who spoke through his horn. The inner poetry of his playing, swelling with imagery and meaning, was enriched by a constantly growing vocabulary of impressions and expressions.

In due course Webster learned how to use pregnant long notes in fast tempos, like a great orator, pausing, and pacing his statements for greater emphasis—a far cry from the impetuous youth who squandered his musical energies so wastefully with Moten and Henderson. His sense of timing and space altogether became virtually infallible; and at all times there was that warm, soulful, human

50. I am fascinated by the close similarity of Webster's opening measures on *St. James Infirmary* (with Teagarden's Big Eight) to Matt Dennis's beautiful song *Angel Eyes*. The latter was written in 1953, but could it be that Dennis, a fine musician and arranger, knew this recording and was inspired by it?

tone to carry the message. And the shadow of Hodges hovered never far away. But where Hodges, on his own, could be diffident and deadpan, gliding *over* the music, Webster was always reaching out, extending himself, and getting *inside* the music.

Of the innumerable performances Webster recorded between 1944 and his death in 1973, space permits the mention of only a sparse sampling. There is a beautiful *Memories of You*, Eubie Blake's great ballad, with Sidney Catlett's Quartet, featuring Webster's great sound, long lyric lines, and—as high points— one incredible upward wrenching outburst, followed not much later by one of the tenderest high Fs a tenorman ever blew—pure Hodges this, refined through Webster's soul.[51]

Then there is *Conversing in Blue* (1945) with Benny Morton's All Stars, an amazing demonstration of how the most diverse musical objects can be fitted into a choice collection, when assembled by a great artist. Basically a tender, wistful solo, Webster manages to incorporate into it some of his favorite swoops and swooshes, braying tremolos, and breathy ghost-like notes. And the All Stars' last ensemble chorus is in itself a masterpiece, on a par with Webster's playing. In it a delicate counterpoint of musical blues fragments is woven by Morton, Bigard, and pianist Sam Benskin, while Webster intones in airy *pp* subtone sustained pedal notes, at times *below* that of the walking pizzicato bass of Israel Crosby. I am certain, incidentally, that this type of playing by Webster, along with his performance with Red Norvo's Sextet on *Easy on the Eye* (1957), was well absorbed by Sonny Rollins, leading over the years in Rollins's development to the latter's inimitable *Blue 7*.

Skipping a few years, we come to one of Webster's all-time sublime performances, his *Danny Boy* of 1953, backed by the Oscar Peterson Trio (with whom Webster worked well and often). What could have been the ultimate sentimental tear-jerker becomes in Webster's hands a rendition of exquisite taste and control. Feeling no compulsion to throttle the material with suffocating embellishments or to slip into double-time—a virtual mania with younger saxophone players— Webster with serene tranquility and perfect pacing holds the listener breathless. Notice how in his second chorus he gives the original melody, which he paraphrases in the first chorus, just enough ornamental rope to make it his own and yet not to camouflage it beyond recognition for the listener. The second chorus, in the alto range, seems to me to be another subtle tribute to Hodges.

In this performance, too, Webster exhibits to perfection one of his unique trademarks: that incredible breathy sound that has just enough tone and pitch in it to hold it together. And sometimes it is *only* vibrating air, giving the *illusion* of pitch.

On *Easy on the Eye* with the Norvo Sextet, Webster is at his most suave, treading lightly, never shouting the blues, a remarkable example of forceful understatement. It is worth noting in this context that, in Webster's playing, the

---

51. I have already referred to one of Webster's other superior performances, the 1944 *Body and Soul*.

blues and ballads phased so much into each other as to become indistinguishable. If he "approached the blues like a ballad" (Whitney Balliett), he also approached ballads like a blues (the author).

In 1957 the great jazz impresario Norman Granz brought Webster together
on records with Hawkins, in what turned out to be one of the great saxophone
summit meetings in jazz history. What a match! The encounter allows us not
only to hear the two tenor giants together, in duets, in fours, in successive solos,
but to compare them at close range.

With Bill Harris, the great trombonist (also in 1957), we hear Webster, on
Duke's *In a Mellotone*, scoop up whole phrases of notes, swooping in at times
like a tidal wave, or lightly "conversing" with Harris, and at other times parodying the trombonist's halting, dryly humorous idiom. And yet he never loses
sight of his own style—and of Hodges's shadow.

Finally there is a 1959 date bringing together Webster, Hawkins, and Webster's old friend from his Texas days, Budd Johnson. Clearly, Webster is a master
of the situation, even with such formidable competitors. The trio is accompanied
by the deeply swinging Ray Brown, and Jimmy and Jo Jones (piano and drums
respectively), as well as guitarist Les Spann. Whether he is playing with a milky
opaque tone, purring along in some ruminating figures, or letting out great yelps
and swoops of sounds, or—beyond any of those—almost breaking notes asunder
in anguished outcries (these can all be found on *In a Mellotone*), or tip-toeing
pp on high Gs (as on *Time After Time*), or putting together one by one a musical
line out of single, widely spaced, fragmented notes (as on *Budd Johnson*, Ex. 22),
Webster seems in absolute control of his musical materials. It is truly magisterial
creating/playing.

Ben Webster was a giant of the tenor saxophone and one of the great jazz
musicians of all time. How ironic, then, that while still at the height of his
powers he fell into such obscurity in the 1960s in this country that he felt compelled to move to Europe. After some frustratingly inactive years, leading groups
in New York and Los Angeles only sporadically, Webster pulled up stakes in the
U.S. in 1964, moved to Holland, and toured as a respected and renowned soloist
in many northern European countries. He eventually settled in Copenhagen in
the late 1960s and died in Amsterdam in September 1973 on a visit there.

Hawkins, we have seen, hung on in his last years and despite declining health
and alcoholism continued to work in this country until his death in 1969. He,
of course, had had his expatriate period thirty-five years earlier; Webster (and
Don Byas, another outstanding tenor saxophonist who also moved to Holland in
the late forties and died in Amsterdam a year before Webster) followed suit much
later. But the implications are the same in all three cases: the country in which
the music known as jazz was born and which can count these three musicians
among its greatest ambassadors could not, at various periods covering cumulatively nearly four decades, provide the kind of environment in which these fine
creative artists could pursue their art and craft in dignity and security.

In some respects Webster suffered the most neglect. It seems incomprehensible, for example, that no major study of Webster's work has been published,

Ex. 22

that the jazz histories and anthologies are fairly silent on Webster.[52] It is true, of course, that Hawkins retains pre-eminence as the first great master of the tenor saxophone and by virtue of both his talent and his historical position the mentor and inspiriter of all but a few saxophonists in the entire history of jazz—foremost among them, of course, Ben Webster. But it is unfair to conclude from that estimate of Hawkins that Webster occupied some significantly lesser position in the history of the instrument, and thereby deny him the status of an incomparable artist in his own right.

It has become fashionable in certain circles to concede that Webster was a supremely effective balladeer. But that, too, is to miss the real point of Webster's art. He certainly was unequaled in transforming ballads and popular songs into high art by virtue of his improvisatory skills. But it is the range of his expressive powers, the richness of his inventions in their awesome variety, that makes it possible to argue that in some deep human sense Webster may have been the more profound and ultimately compelling artist—at least in the last thirty years of his life. It is true that Webster developed relatively slowly and did not find his full artistic/personal identity until the 1940s. The same can be said of Hawkins as well, although the time frame must be adjusted a half-decade or so earlier;

52. Only Leonard Feather pays brief homage to Webster (in *The Book of Jazz*, p. 100), but partially undermines his tribute by some unfortunate analogies to both Clark Gable and an overly mascara'd and berouged woman, and the "boudoir" school of the tenor saxophone. Such commentaries are not helpful either to an appreciation of Webster's high art or to jazz in general.

and Hawkins did have the formidable task (excuse, if you will) of first having to *invent* the tenor saxophone as an instrument capable of articulate expression. But Webster had in fact the opposite problem: Hawkins's hold over the saxophone was so immense and so comprehensive that anyone following in his footsteps would inevitably face a major struggle in discovering his own identity *within* the basic Hawkins lineage. That incidentally suggests the measure of Lester Young's achievement in founding an alternative school and conception to those of Hawkins. But it is worth noting that Young could do that only by completely abrogating Hawkins's influence from the start. That was a radical choice that Webster evidently would not or could not make. The point is that it is easier, given the basic talent of originality, to find a new identity in another contrasting style rather than *within* someone else's conception.

But that describes precisely the dimensions of Webster's art. For, once freed of Hawkins's influence and confident of the realization that he could create his own mature idiom, Webster and Hawkins could nevermore be confused with each other. And whereas Hawkins eventually and gradually lost his powers towards the last years of his life, Webster seemed to have kept on growing, searching, finding an ever greater range and depth of expression with ever greater economical means.

I think that Webster was a great poet, perhaps one of the few true poets jazz has had. He used notes and melodies, rarefied and precious at the end, like a poet uses words and metaphors, reduced to their quintessence and innermost meaning. As with most truly great art, Webster's cannot be fully explained. And when he played, it didn't need to be.

PART 4

JACK TEAGARDEN

In many ways Jack Teagarden, born Weldon Lee Teagarden in Vernon, Texas, in 1905, was unique and thus deserves a special segment in these chapters devoted to the giants of jazz of the thirties and forties. He was certainly an astoundingly gifted trombonist who single-handedly created a whole new way of playing the trombone—a parallel to Earl Hines and the piano comes to mind—and did so as early as the mid-twenties and evidently largely out of his own youthful creative resources. There seem to have been few (or no) influences from other trombonists, unless it were some early Texas player who never recorded and is therefore unknown to us and forgotten—an unlikely thesis at best. Teagarden seems rather to have drawn his early inspiration from singers, especially blues singers and the vocal music at Holy River meetings in his hometown. As told by George Hoefer, Jr., in an interview for *Downbeat* (March 9, 1951), Teagarden also listened to the recordings of Bessie Smith, from whom he must have learned something about clarity and simplicity of musical thought. Certainly there can be little argument that Teagarden was the first trombonist—even more than Jimmy Harrison and Lawrence Brown, let along Miff Mole—to bring to the trombone an essentially vocal-lyric style. That is not to say a "sweet" melodic style, as any number of trombonists could manage—Tommy Dorsey was, of course, the greatest of these—but a lyric song-like style firmly *within* the jazz and blues idiom. That in itself was a remarkable breakthrough achievement, one by which he was to influence several generations of trombonists to come.

But Teagarden was also a remarkable and wholly unique singer, undoubtedly the best and the only true jazz singer next to Billie Holiday, Cab Calloway, and Louis Armstrong (whom he, unlike dozens of others, did *not* imitate). Moreover, Teagarden's singing and trombone-playing were virtually interchangeable. They not only operated in the same baritone-to-tenor range, but borrowed from each other conceptually, stylistically. Many of his early vocal offerings—especially the wordless or scat improvisations—sound for all the world like a baritone horn or trombone. The trombone's capacity for sliding, bending notes finds its exact parallel in Teagarden's singing in the manner in which he slithered through a song, the way he slurred over consonants, inflecting notes to form seamless lyrical shapes. Indeed, there is a close parallel between Teagarden's basically soft-tongued attack on the trombone—so different from Jimmy Harrison's, for example—and his easygoing almost diffident enunciation of words, which gave his singing its uniquely relaxed character and instrumental feel. As Whitney Balliett once put it: it is as if Teagarden were "trying to abolish consonants in favor of a new vowels-only language."[1]

There is another fascinating link between Teagarden's playing and singing. The pitches on a trombone are produced by a combination of seven positions on the instrument's slide, produced by extending the slide outward from the mouthpiece and what is called in music and acoustics the harmonic series. Figure 1 displays in graphic form the basic potential reservoir of available pitches.

Thus if a trombonist wishes to play, say  he can play it in the following sequence of positions:

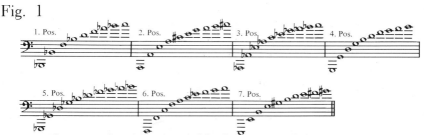

(There are other possibilities but these are the most common and practical.)

Fig. 1

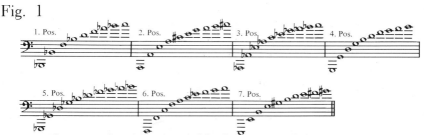

The seven trombone slide positions and their harmonic series. (Some notes in certain positions are insecure and therefore used only rarely)

---

1. Whitney Balliett, *Profiles: Jack Teagarden*, New Yorker, April 1984.

Fig. 2

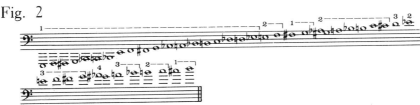

The numbers above the staff indicate the available number of basic positions on which given pitches can be played.

Obviously, as can be seen by comparing with Figure 2, in the upper range of the trombone a player has many more choices for playing a given pitch than in the middle and lower range, and consequently, if a trombonist wishes to play the above same five notes one octave lower, he is much more limited in his choice of positions, namely:

a) III - I - V - III - I
b) III - VI - V - III - VI
c) VII - VI - V - III - I

And still another octave lower there are hardly any choices left:
Indeed one note (marked x) is not available at all.

III-VI- V - x-VI

The above constitutes the basic orthodox approach to trombone-playing. It means, for example, that the note 𝄢♭• can be played, if held to this concept, in only two positions, III and VII. But Teagarden early on seems to have rejected such orthodoxy and found ways to play notes in all kinds of *un*orthodox positions, in effect keeping his playing almost entirely to the first four positions— and not too much of the latter two. This he accomplished by a remarkable lip (embouchure) flexibility and a certain amount of sleight-of-hand (and of-lip) illusion. Jazz trombonists nowadays play, and have for many decades already played, with these so-called "alternate positions," and players like Lawrence Brown and Urbie Green—as well as in recent decades many classical trombonists—are past masters of this technique.

But when Teagarden first initiated this "unorthodox" concept, it was virtually unknown and unused, except by some of the more dexterous concert-band trombonists, like Jiroslav Cimera and Arthur Pryor. By what instincts and inspiration Teagarden arrived at this concise slide technique is hard to say at this late date. He is reputed to have said to various questioners on the matter that he was too "lazy" to move the slide to the lower positions; another time, "Man, I don't like workin' that hard. I just use my lip," as reported by Paul Whiteman's pianist Roy Bargy. It also may have originated with Teagarden as a result of his playing the baritone horn as a youngster, a valve rather than a slide instrument. Certainly the legato smoothness, characteristic of the baritone or euphonium, carried over into Teagarden's trombone-playing. He clearly did not want to hear the slide effect of the trombone, especially prevalent in the early New Orleans "tailgate" style, but preferred instead the clear slide-less articulation natural to the baritone.

In any case, I see in this particular short-hand slide technique another fascinating parallel to Teagarden's vocal style. Just as he short-circuited and suppressed consonants—the main articulation points in any vocal style—in his drawling, nonchalant singing, rounding off the language as it were, so he rounded off and rejected the "correct" articulations of orthodox trombone-playing. Teagarden's essentially unique approach to the trombone, coming primarily out of a vocal tradition, is also what distinguishes him quite clearly from that other early master of the instrument, Jimmy Harrison.

It used to be assumed by many of the earlier jazz writers and historians that Harrison influenced Teagarden. More recently, some writers have allowed that probably both players influenced each other mutually, after they met in New York in 1927. I believe the latter point of view to be true, but only to some minor extent. For the two players' styles remained quite distinct, and, if anything, it was Harrison who in his last year or so tended towards a more linear and lyric style, never to the point of losing his own stylistic profile, however. What might have happened in Harrison's further development must remain conjectural, for unfortunately Harrison died in 1931 at the age of thirty.

The differences between the two players' styles lies in the origins of their respective concepts: Teagarden's in a vocal conception, Harrison's in a brass-playing tradition, particularly through the influence upon him of King Oliver and Tommy Ladnier. Harrison worked with the latter, Oliver's most loyal disciple, for many years in Fletcher Henderson's band. These different origination points manifested themselves in the two players' respective sounds (Teagarden's warm and open, relaxed; Harrison's brassy, somewhat narrow, and intense), in their attacks (Teagarden's clean, rounded off, insinuating, essentially legato in conception; Harrison's rather rough and hard, crackly, direct, and more staccato in conception), and in the way they sustained longer notes (Teagarden well-sustained, linear, singing with a very discreet use of vibrato; Harrison more vertical, and shorter, less sustained, most notes being played with quick tapering diminuendos, and his use of a strong terminal vibrato, often very intense). Another way to describe the last difference is to suggest that Teagarden would "sing" through a note, making it sustain and lead to the next note. Harrison, by contrast, in a basically more punctuated style, used his fast and intense vibrato, usually near the end of a note, to propel that pitch across to the next note.

But the two players also had some musical qualities in common. They certainly were—with the exception of Miff Mole, who virtually defies characterization[2]—the first trombonists to reject the old tailgate style to which the trombone had been relegated thus far, limited mostly to the middle and lower range of the instrument. Harrison clearly wanted to play like the trumpet players and more in their range, not the trombone's barrelly register. They were also the first trombonists to play fast, not only in terms of faster tempos but in

2. See Chapter 9.

rapid passage work. Compare their playing to, say, a Charlie Green's, a fine blues player, but one who clung to the heavier, slow-moving tailgate manner of the pure New Orleans style. Their playing also was cleaner, sleeker, more economical. And above all, their more fluent techniques permitted them to explore a wider range of expression, a wider range of moods.

I feel that Harrison was in the end not as consistent, both technically and conceptually, as Teagarden. But then we have to remember that Harrison was ill much of the last two years of his life, and altogether made only some twenty recordings on which he can be heard as a soloist. And many of his contemporaries say that he is not represented well on recordings: that the spirit and intensity of his playing in a "live" ambiance did not project as well in the recording studio.

As mentioned, in his last years Harrison moderated his style slightly in the direction of Teagarden's, while the latter certainly expanded his expressive range to include a more aggressive, outgoing, punchy Harrison-like approach. But ultimately they retained distinct and separate musical styles, each forging a tradition upon which others would build: Dorsey and Jack Jenney on Teagarden, Dickie Wells, J. C. Higginbotham and Sandy Williams on Harrison.

Although notation of jazz can never capture all the nuances of actual performance, two representative examples of Teagarden's and Harrison's styles can give some indication of the differences between their respective approaches. *Bugle Call Rag* and *Dee Blues* (Ex. 1 and 2) both offer some of Harrison's finest moments on record. They reveal the essence of his punchy style, and its indebtedness to an intrinsically brass tradition and blues players, like Ladnier and Bubber Miley (pre-Ellington).

By contrast, Teagarden's *Bugle Call Rag* performance (Ex. 3) recorded with the Musical Clowns, an Irving Mills-led group, in November 1928, shows him in his typically relaxed mood, a beautifully formed solo with its high point the long wailing note in m. 16.

Teagarden's career as a jazz musician began at age sixteen, working successfully with the legendary pianist-leader Peck Kelley, also the Southern Trumpeters (with whom he traveled as far south as Mexico) and Doc Ross's Jazz Bandits. It was the latter band that took Teagarden to New York in 1927. There, after jobbing around rather sporadically, he eventually landed a job with Ben Pollack in the summer of 1928. His recording debut as a sideman soloist, however, occurred a few months earlier with Roger Wolfe Kahn's band, when he substituted for Miff Mole, the then reigning wizard of the trombone in New York. The tune was a long forgotten pop song of the period, *She's a Great, Great Girl*, which Teagarden could not have known before. But here we hear him, now twenty-two, almost a seasoned "veteran" of six years, completely at ease (except for one missed note) in his own already essentially well-formed style: relaxed, fluent, and poised. Less "spectacular" technically than Mole's work of the period, but on the other hand warmer and more lyrical in conception, and yet truly jazz, Teagarden's unprecedented trombonistic display must have startled

Ex. 1

and later

Ex. 2

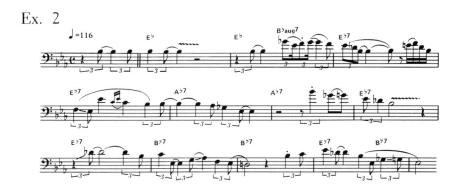

Ex. 3

the musicians in Kahn's band. It was soon to become known as Teagarden's style, one on which hundreds of trombonists in the next decade would try to build their careers.

By October 1928, Teagarden was recording with an Eddie Condon group, a septet featuring also cornetist Jimmy McPartland and clarinetist Mezz Mezzrow. On *Makin' Friends*, one of two titles recorded that day, Teagarden made history with two unexpected contributions: his first vocal and his first use on records of a water glass substituting for a mute, a device for which he duly became world famous. Teagarden had discovered this effect years earlier while touring with Peck Kelley's band. It was achieved by removing the flared bell of his trombone and holding a water glass over the open end of the tubing, thereby producing a slightly buzzy, stifled, plaintive sound that had a distinct vocal quality, especially in the trombone's upper register, where it sounded like a female blues singer. It also sounded a bit like Red McKenzie singing through his kazoo.[3]

Teagarden clearly dominates the entire recording. After his dirty, bluesy, somewhat wayward opening statement and a McPartland-led ensemble passage and Mezzrow clarinet solo, Teagarden, to everyone's surprise, launched into a vocal. Drawled in his later famous and inimitable fashion, its lyrics slurred through with a barrelly baritone voice, the words are barely comprehensible. Urged on by a delighted Mezzrow, Teagarden follows with a roaming loping scat vocal that manages at once to sound like his trombone and as if he had a hot potato in his mouth. There now follows Teagarden's water-glass-muted chorus in its fairly high-register setting, sounding for all the world like a trumpet. Indeed when, after his first chorus, McPartland enters with a low-register phrase, it sounds momentarily as if the two instruments' roles—trumpet and trombone— had been registrally reversed. Teagarden's solo in his best quietly wailing blues style, discreetly embellished with subtle vocal melismata, is unfortunately marred by Condon's incessant insensitive clanking on the banjo, not to mention innumerable wrong changes.

After Teagarden's unexpected outing with Roger Wolfe Kahn, word got around that a new trombone wonder had arrived in town, and it wasn't long before Teagarden was hired by Ben Pollack, whose Chicago-style band was making quite an impression in New York, featuring, as it did, Benny Goodman, Jimmy McPartland, Glenn Miller, Ray Bauduc, and, on the commercial side, a string trio with the versatile flutist-saxophonist Larry Binyon. Teagarden stayed with Pollack for nearly five years, participating in nearly thirty recordings. Although many of these Pollack recordings are ultimately of minor importance, Teagarden's contributions to them are almost always standouts, particularly noteworthy being *Futuristic Rhythm*, *Keep Your Undershirt On*, and especially, *My Kinda Love* and *If I Could Be with You* (1930), the last named in Teagarden's then emerging blues-tinged ballad style.

During this period Teagarden contributed to many other fine jazz recordings, notably with various Irving Mills bands, some Red Nichols groups, numerous Goodman-led studio dates, one of these with Bix, from which we have Teagarden's *Strut Miss Lizzie* (see Ex. 8), the Mound City Blue Blowers, Joe Venuti, and Eddie Lang's All Star Orchestra, and occasionally, starting in 1930, under his own leadership.

It is the early part of this period that intrigues us the most, for it was here that Teagarden honed and perfected his style, not only on the trombone but as an ever more impressive vocalist. On *Diga Diga Doo* (with one of Mills's bands), one of the sillier tunes of the day, Teagarden produces a hot, blistering jazz solo, surely unprecedented on the trombone in its well-sustained interest and continuity, its clarity of form, its technical assurance, and ranginess (from low F to high D) (Ex. 4). It is also enlivened by a low-register snarl at the beginning

3. See below, the Mound City Blue Blowers, in the Hawkins section of Chapter 6, Part 1.

Ex. 4

of the second "eight," that not only comes as a total surprise but in the way he gets out of it seems retroactively to have been the most logical invention.

I think all in all Teagarden's *Diga* and *Bugle Call* solos are better solos than any that Harrison had created up to that time, at least on records.[4] But on the other hand Teagarden seems to have been in some special ways influenced by Harrison, particularly the latter's *Oh Baby* solo (Ex. 5) (with Henderson, recorded April 6, 1928).[5] Harrison's flutter-tongue snarl also comes in his second "eight" and in general features quite a few figures also used by Teagarden, particularly the descending ones (bracketed in Ex. 3 and 5).

Oh Baby was, I believe, Harrison's most extensive solo to date. It is also one of his most cohesive, although here too, as is so often the case, notes get away from him, and there is, unlike with Teagarden's sure-footed direct solos, something elusive in Harrison's work. Whereas Teagarden sounds relaxed, even casual, exuding an air of casual inevitability, Harrison's more intense approach reveals subtle signs of struggle, as if his concept was a little beyond his technique.

4. Nor can they compare ultimately with Teagarden's famous expansive, explosive solo on Armstrong's 1929 *Knockin' a Jug*.
5. Teagarden was working during early 1928 with the Scranton Sirens at New York's Roseland Ballroom, opposite the Henderson band. He had occasion to hear his friend Harrison virtually every night.

Ex. 5

Interestingly, a fine 2-bar break Harrison plays near the end of Henderson's *Feeling Good* has the relaxed casual swing of Teagarden. The exchange of ideas between the two men during this Roseland period must have been lively and constant.

In one respect Harrison was clearly superior to Teagarden, and that was in regard to collective ensemble-playing. Harrison, trained in the King Oliver Creole Band school of New Orleans polyphony, was a past master at fitting in and contributing significantly to such improvised ensembles. But Teagarden felt generally constrained in that style. For one thing he seems to have been solo-oriented from the beginning, probably under the influence of the Texas solo blues-singing he grew up with. For another, he seemed uncomfortable about bumping into the trumpet line with his well-developed easy high register. Third, collective polyphonic improvising was associated with the "tailgate" school of trombone playing and as such was intrinsically restricted to certain limited gestures and moves. It was clearly not a solo concept, and Teagarden was from the outset after something more individualized.

A second recording session with Eddie Condon (in February 1929) produced more vintage Teagarden on *That's a Serious Thing*. It is Teagarden at his most elegant and a perfect foil for the fervent, passionate playing of trumpeter Leonard Davis,[6] the other main soloist on the session. It is also Teagarden in already a very modern stance: concise, economical, fluent, ornamented with lots of tricky bop-ish turns. It shows us Teagarden in a concept which was to sustain him (and others) well through the late thirties and into the forties.

His performance on *Serious Thing* also reveals that, unlike many jazz musicians of that era, Teagarden was a true and indefatigable improviser. He copies himself only in exceptional circumstances, and constantly reinvented his solos. He was fond of saying that he always felt each solo could be improved upon and, in any case, it was against the true spirit of jazz as a creative music to repeat oneself.

Here are Teagarden's solos from the two known takes of *Serious Thing*, notated directly one below the other, for easy comparison (Ex. 6a, b). There are dramatic differences between the two solos, produced within minutes of each other, not the least of which is the fact that take two is primarily set in double-time, an intensification of expression over the first already excellent solo.

A curiosity of take one is Teagarden's entry on a phrase which is almost identical to the melody of *Stormy Weather*. That Harold Arlen song was, of course, composed four years later. It is entirely possible that Arlen heard the Condon-Teagarden record, for he was at this time—just at the beginning of his song-writing career—not only a steady habitué of the major jazz and night clubs but also very active in the New York recording studios as a singer, pianist, and arranger. (Arlen's arrangement for Hendrickson's Louisville Serenaders is an excellent, highly professional piece of work.) The matter must remain conjectural, of course, but the similarity between Teagarden's opening phrase and the beginning of *Stormy Weather* is too enticingly close to assume mere coincidence.

Futuristic Rhythm, a Jimmy McHugh song, had a great success as a pop hit in late 1928. It had enough bounce in its syncopated rhythms and "dicty" lyrics to be attractive to both recording executives and jazz musicians. It was recorded frequently in those days, before it became a forgotten relic of the 1920s' jazz era. Teagarden alone recorded it four times within a three-week period (with various Benny Goodman-led Mills and Pollack groups), each solo totally different and with great swing.

Another of Mills's bands, recording under the name Gil Rodin's Boys, produced another unusual Teagarden first: the great trombonist featured on trumpet—where he was less than "great" but nonetheless passably professional. Indeed his poor, thinnish trumpet tone in *It's So Good* fully detracts from his excellent choice of notes in a decidedly bluesy Armstrong vein. But what makes this record a kind of classic is Teagarden's singing. In his (here) slightly reedy vocal timbre, slurred-over lyrics, and casually free rhythms, Teagarden sounds

---

6. Leonard Davis was a product of the St. Louis school of brass playing (dealt with in Chapter 8, below, on Territory bands), and played with many famous black bands, including Charlie Johnson's Paradise Band, Louis Armstrong, and Edgar Hayes. This was one of the very first racially mixed recording dates.

Ex. 6

like an itinerant Texas blues-shouter, suddenly transported into the New York studios. Take away Rodin's band and imagine a simple four-string guitar accompaniment instead, and the listener is transported right back to central Texas blues country. Whether by choice or by accident, Bud Freeman's harshly guttural tenor and, later, thinnish, amateurish clarinet underline the strange primitivism of this performance. Without knowing the record, one would assume it to have been recorded on location in San Angelo, Texas, at 2:00 a.m.

Five days later Teagarden was again in the studio, this time recording one of his favorites (and one with which he was to be associated all his life): *Basin Street Blues*. His most memorable rendition of this Spencer Williams classic was to come two years later, when he and Glenn Miller fashioned lyrics for the piece[7]

7. See above, Chapter I.

for a Benny Goodman record date. That recording stands as classic early Goodman and superb Teagarden, both on trombone and vocal. But the earlier performance here mentioned does not fall too far behind, having as it does not only
a fine Armstrong-like trombone solo in his best "vocal" style—the solo is once
again a mirror of Teagarden's singing—but also one of Pee Wee Russell's most
extraordinary musical statements (among many).[8]

Another vintage Teagarden performance from this period was *After You've
Gone* (with Red Nichols and His Five Pennies, Feb. 3, 1930), on this occasion
much aided and abetted by Glenn Miller's arranging talent. Here we can hear
again how in his vocal Teagarden reshapes, rounds off, and simplifies Turner
Layton's famous melody, all in the interests of a more personal linear conception
(Ex. 7). It is the same melodic resourcefulness that Billie Holiday also knew so
well, and I suppose in both artists there was the element of accommodating to a
voice with a limited pitch range. And as with Billie, so with Teagarden, it was
rooted in an underlying urge to "instrumentalize" the songs they sang, a need
to bring voice and instrument together under one common musical impulse, at
the same time rendering them more individualized. In Teagarden's case, the

Ex. 7

8. See later in this chapter for more on Pee Wee Russell.

rounding off of melodic lines, the slurring together of words, the de-articulation of consonants and rhythms were in addition an innate reflection of his calm, unagressive, relaxed personal manner, one which was to make him a unique jazz musician, but—later on—a very poor bandleader and businessman.

A fine example of Teagarden's relaxed, modern, almost "cool" style exists on a 1930 *Strut Miss Lizzie* recording with Irving Mills's Hotsy Totsy Gang (Ex. 8).

Ex. 8

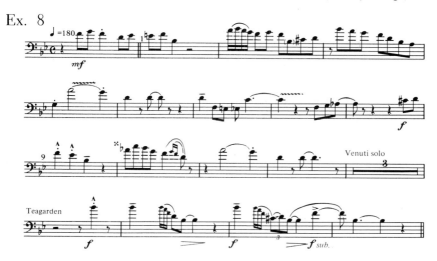

Teagarden's solo here captures all the elements of his style: simplicity and economy of structure, elegant Bixian phrasing (Beiderbecke was also on the date), remarkable technical ease (he sounds almost like a plump-toned cornet) with absolutely no strain in the high range, effortless natural swing. But even more striking is the modern *linear* feel of the solo, even though, as Example 8 shows, the lines move up and down quite a bit.

As Teagarden took up singing more and more, at the urging of fellow musicians and audiences, his enunciation took on greater clarity. This trend is already noticeable on *If I Could Be with You* (1930) and can be traced in an incremental chronological line through Teagarden's sublime vocal masterpieces *I Gotta Right To Sing the Blues, Texas Tea Party, A Hundred Years from Today* (all from 1933), *Stars Fell on Alabama* (1934), *I Hope Gabriel Likes My Music* (1936), and on into the years when he led several big bands and became rather popular, as much for his ballad singing as for his trombone playing. From this last period—July 7, 1941 to be exact—comes one of Teagarden's greatest vocal accomplishments, the beautiful *Nobody Knows the Trouble I've Seen*. In the understated intensity of its feeling, the inner radiance and genuine soulfulness, it ranks with the very finest jazz-singing offered through the years—from Bessie and Billie to Calloway, Sinatra, and Rushing.

In the meantime the trombone was not neglected. In performance after performance, his ways firmly set by now, Teagarden's trombone is never less than compelling. Each solo is a brief Teagarden composition, clear and seamless in form and line, genuinely felt, exquisite in taste, whether florid as in A *Hundred Years*, warm and amiable as in *Moonglow*, happily swinging as on *I Gotta Right To Sing the Blues*, boisterous and out-going as on *Jack Hits the Road*, or brilliantly virtuostic as on *Lover*. Only occasionally, particularly in the period when Teagarden was with Whiteman (from 1934 to 1939) and with his own band, is there a degree of predictability in his work—the inevitable result of the tedium and fatigue of endless road trips and one-night stands.

Once again we must be grateful to John Hammond for having the foresight to bring Jack Teagarden to his now legendary 1933 Goodman sessions for English Columbia, in which he rescued Teagarden briefly from a few days of one-nighters with Mal Hallet's Boston-based dance band. Teagarden had temporarily sought refuge with Hallet after the break-up of his second marriage and accumulating alimony payments. If anyone had "a right to sing the blues" it was Teagarden, and he did so with a vengeance on October 18, 1933, in that song title. He sings with a wonderful intensity, almost a sense of desperation. Listen to the plangency and ardor of his vibrato, the pleading in his voice at the word "misery," the urgency of the two upswept "me's," and the unsentimentally affected "sit and cry."

Hammond was also responsible for Teagarden's involvement in two other recording sessions, both prophetic in their distinct ways: Billie Holiday's first and second debut dates, and Bessie Smith's last. Ironically, Billie's second session, the more successful of the two, took place only six days before Bessie's last appearance in a recording studio. It was as if the elder singer was handing the crown over to the younger one, with Hammond as the intermediary. Teagarden performed brilliantly on Billie's date—she needed all the help she could get[9]— while his role was by the nature of things rather circumscribed on Bessie's date. For, although no longer the great commercial success of a decade earlier, Bessie, who could still belt out a mean blues when called upon, needed to dominate a recording session completely.

Another Hammond session one year later, when Teagarden was already with Whiteman, brought him together once again with Goodman (who was just now forming his finest permanent big band) and Teddy Wilson, Hammond's (then) twenty-one-year-old pianist find. Wilson already reveals his own distinctive voice in a well-formed, typically clean chorus, but it is Teagarden who ultimately dominates the performance—a fact that even Goodman realized by ceding not only a major solo but the closing ensemble to Teagarden. It is one of his solos that seems to contain in it most of the trombone music one was to hear in the bands of others for the next decade or so. *Moonglow* seems to have particularly affected Jack Jenney (his section mate in the Hallet band), just as a solo like *That's What I Like About You* (1931) already presages much of Bill Harris's spectacular work with Woody Herman of fifteen years later.

Stars Fell on Alabama was another Teagarden winner. A kind of maverick,

9. See Part 3 of this chapter.

Teagarden was not beyond putting together unusual instrumental groups. He was one of the first leaders to incorporate French horns in his big band in the early forties, and here in 1934 on *Alabama* he featured the great harpist Caspar Reardon, alongside Trumbauer's C-melody sax and one of his old pianist-band-leader bosses from 1920, way back in the dawn of jazz, Terry Shand. Reardon's impeccable crystalline harp accompaniments provide a sensitive setting for one of Teagarden's gentlest and most lyrical vocal performances. With Goodman weaving delicate obbligato lines and arpeggios around the harp and Teagarden's vocal, the whole performance exudes an aura of refinement that is refreshing and anything but effete or pretentious. Nobody is trying to prove anything, and the odd mixture of instruments coalesces into a wonderfully low-keyed, re-laxed—as one critic put it—"amiable" effect, not unlike some of Bing Crosby's or Perry Como's best efforts.

The years with Whiteman kept Teagarden quite busy. Whiteman really appreciated the jazz talents of the Teagardens—Jack and his brother Charlie[10] (as he had Bunny Berigan and Bix Beiderbecke before them)—and the solid swing-ing rhythmic capacities of bassist Art Miller and drummers Herb Quigley and Larry Gomar. Not only the Teagardens' presence in the Whiteman band but the recordings it made in the mid-1930s should remind us of the fact that White-man's commitment to jazz and his band's capacity to honor that commitment was far from negligible. This can be sampled on such performances as the two tributes to Harlem—*Fare Thee Well to Harlem* and *Christmas Night in Har-lem*—*Darktown Strutters' Ball, G Blues, Itchola*, and numerous others. Indeed some of these sides—or portions thereof—swing as well as many another white (or black) band, otherwise blessed by some of the jazz-writer fraternity.[11]

With Whiteman, who always paid high salaries and represented financial se-curity—a rare commodity in jazz, even on its more commercial fringes—Tea-garden was able to put his personal life somewhat in order. With his typical

10. Charlie Teagarden, the younger brother of Jack by eight years, nicknamed "Little T," was one of the Swing Era's better jazz trumpeters. Blessed with a full, well-centered tone (like his brother Jack's), Charlie was effective in ballads as well as jazz solos. Unduly overshadowed not only by his brother but by the likes of Berigan, Spivak, Eldridge, James—even Wingy Manone—Charlie was nonetheless a consistent contributor to quality jazz. He always played with taste and integrity, and I have never heard a bad solo by Charlie. His considerable talent can be sampled on such recordings as *Beale Street Blues* (with the Charlestown Chasers, a Benny Goodman group, in 1931), *Someday Sweetheart* (with Venuti and Lang, 1931)—he was just barely eighteen on these recordings—*Junk Man* (with brother Jack, 1934), *Farewell Blues* (with Whiteman, 1935), and *I Hope Gabriel Likes My Music* (with Trumbauer's orchestra, 1936).

11. Whiteman continues to be maligned by most "jazz aficionados." It is unfair to claim, for ex-ample—as one writer did as recently as 1979—that Teagarden was only allowed "one eight-bar solo" with Whiteman between 1936 and 1938. True enough; but the writer conveniently forgot to mention three items: 1) that in an earlier period from January 1934 to late 1935 both Teagardens soloed on at least 20 sides; 2) that Benny Goodman and his Palomar Ballroom success in 1935 turned the whole country into a swing-crazy commercial juggernaut, against which Whiteman honestly felt he could not compete (the likes of Shaw, Lunceford, and Armstrong did not at various times react any less ingenuously); and consequently, 3) Whiteman embarked upon a project of recording five of the major works of George Gershwin with his "concert orchestra."

unpretentiousness and humility, he always looked upon the Whiteman period as excellent training with a big band, with an eye towards the day when he would be able to lead his own permanent orchestra.

Towards that end Teagarden also kept trying to "improve" his singing—and diction. One becomes aware of the ever greater clarity of enunciation, as in his light-hearted vocal on *I Hope Gabriel* (on a Trumbauer date, 1936), or on *Serenade to a Skylark* (a Commodore Jam Session date in 1938), proving once again—if proof were needed—that he was the finest white blues singer. His trombone-playing was not neglected either. Witness the bursting, crackling solo on *I Hope Gabriel*, the whimsical and somewhat mournful *Diane*, the amazing second solo on *Jack Hits the Road* (with Bud Freeman's orchestra, 1940).

As mentioned earlier, Teagarden was not much of a bandleader. He did not have the authoritative leadership personality or business acumen the best leaders had (or were able to acquire, as in the case of Ellington through his manager, Irving Mills). Teagarden thought, naively, that good music well played, attractively presented, would suffice to bring relative commercial success. And he saw all his colleagues one by one going into band-leading—Goodman, Dorsey, Miller, Berigan, Krupa, James, Will Bradley, Herman, and so many others—that he felt almost compelled to do likewise. He launched his first band in 1939, with Charlie Spivak as a business partner and assistant leader, but, unable to cope with the payrolls and schedules, by the end of the year he was $46,000 in debt. Somehow he re-formed a second band in early 1940, which lasted in one form or another despite personnel erosion by the draft during World War II, until late 1946.

Though the Teagarden Orchestra's work was uneven, often dreary—and, like all bands of the period, it had to play a lot of pop-song dross—it also was capable of making fine music. I have already mentioned the poignant, spiritually rich *Nobody Knows the Trouble I've Seen*. And there were others, featuring not only Teagarden's trombone and vocals but excellent solos by Spivak (later it would be Lee Castle), saxophonist Ernie Caceres, that master drummer Dave Tough, and a fine young clarinet player by the name of Clint Garwin. The arrangements, mostly by Red Bone, Hub Lytle, and Fred Norman, were, like Teagarden's tone, full-bodied, rich, and colorful. Fine examples of all these combined talents abound: *Octoroon, Swinging on a Teagarden Gate, Somewhere a Voice is Calling, Harlem Jump, I Can't Get Away from the Blues, The Mole, Mr. Jessie Blues*. And on many an occasion the band could swing as well as most any. True, Teagarden's orchestra did not break any new ground, and it was disappointing to see Teagarden, under the pressure of audiences, managers, and agents, trying to play sweet solos in the manner of Tommy Dorsey—not quite Teagarden's cup of tea, both conceptually and technically. In the end both Teagarden and the band began to sound like any dozen other typical swing bands; it had lost the creative passion. In its desperate efforts to remain financially afloat—which meant playing hundreds of college dates, society dances, and proms along with the normal ballroom gigs—it operated in a kind of strange isolation from the forefront of jazz, which was heading towards bebop and the small combo revolution and the demise of big bands.

Along with a sizable number of famous bandleaders—Herman, Goodman, James, Dorsey, Les Brown—Teagarden threw in the towel and disbanded in 1946. He returned to the place where jazz musicians always went when in trouble: The Street—52nd Street, that is, in New York, bustling with jazz clubs, in those days the mecca of jazz.

In May 1947 Teagarden was invited to perform in a concert in Town Hall with his old friend Louis Armstrong. Not only were the concert and the recordings that resulted from it a great success—especially Teagarden's superb rendition of *St. James Infirmary*—but it led to the formation of Armstrong's All Stars, a sextet which included Earl Hines, Barney Bigard, and Sidney Catlett. The All-Stars gave many of these musicians a new lease on life. Armstrong was in particularly fine form during these years, as one can hear on *St. James* or *Jack Armstrong Blues*, or the Boston Symphony Hall concert. Indeed, as brilliant as Teagarden's playing was, on many an occasion Armstrong was still *the* master of the traditional style, and sometimes, as in the joyous *Jack Armstrong* romp, more creatively adventurous than any of his (younger) All Star colleagues.

It was both touching and paradoxical to hear such great traditional jazz in those late-forties' years, in the midst of an otherwise seething sea of bebop frenzy. Although out of step with the new jazz of Parker, Gillespie, J. J. Johnson, Bud Powell, Thelonious Monk, Armstrong's All Stars survived as well and as long as they did by the sheer quality and authenticity of their music making. This was something quite beyond the New Orleands-Dixieland revival movement. Indeed it wasn't part of the revival at all: it was simply a number of the world's greatest jazz musicians filling out the chapters of their roles in the greater continuity of jazz history.

Like all good things, the All Stars, virtuosi of great artistry but also of highly individual temperaments, came to an end, lasting only a few years. Catlett was the first to leave, followed by Hines and Teagarden in 1951, Bigard in 1952. With Teagarden it was more a reawakened desire to once again "get a band together." With brother Charlie and sister Norma Teagarden (as pianist), and old friend Ray Bauduc on drums, Jack formed his own "All Stars," an ensemble which in various guises and personnels—one group was co-led by Earl Hines—survived until Teagarden's death in 1964. He was by then the "dean" of trombonists, "Big T," beloved by his more tradition-oriented fans, and, unlike other elder statesmen of jazz, not entirely ignored by the younger generation. Indeed many—Gerry Mulligan, Bob Brookmeyer, Jimmy Giuffre—admired him and learned from him. That he could in most ways keep pace with the "moderns" was proven on many an occasion.

It is perhaps appropriate to here bid Teagarden farewell by letting his music speak for him: an excerpt from an extraordinary *tour de force* performance of Richard Rodgers's *Lover*, recorded with pianist Charlie LaVere's group in 1950 (Ex. 9). It is a stunning two-minute display of Teagarden the trombonist, the

Ex. 9

consummate musician: effortless sovereign technical mastery, richness of tone, a total lack of exhibitionism even in this basically virtuosic setting, and above all, the need to "sing" on the instrument, no matter what the context. "Big T," indeed.

PEE WEE RUSSELL

Finally, two other musicians must be included in this chapter: clarinetist Pee Wee Russell, a close associate and lifelong friend of Jack Teagarden, and trumpeter Henry "Red" Allen. Russell (1906–69) was one of the most original figures in jazz history; he never did quite fit into any of the established stylistic molds, and he maintained his unique identity throughout a long career, covering at least three major periods in jazz. I think the Dixielanders like to claim Russell as one of their own, but in fact he was well beyond that kind of narrow categorization.

His earliest recordings, made in 1927 with Red Nichols and His Five Pennies, show as yet little of the true Russell character and unbridled individuality. If anything, these recordings—often heralded as "legendary" Russell masterpieces—seem rather groping and unsure, filled with odd and often poor note choices. (The miracle of the later, mature Russell was that he could always make "odd" note choices sound right!) Nor does he display here any of that quirky, scratchy sound for which he was admired in later years. Russell's playing on *Ida, Sweet as Apple Cider* and *Feelin' No Pain* sounds nervous and jittery—and why not? It was his first session on records. His phrasing is short-breathed; he stumbles over notes—listen to his E♭ in measure 13 over a B♭ chord—although his high-riding obbligato in the final jammed chorus is much more spirited and at ease. On *Riverboat Shuffle* Russell's solo is more poised, albeit (except for the last eight bars) rather conventional. He plays with a pleasant warm sound and restrained rhythmic feeling, in "properly" rounded-off phrases and simple step-wise progressions, not the spiky gestures of Russell's later years.

But by 1929, on two different recording dates—one legendary, with the Mound City Blue Blowers and Coleman Hawkins, the other with Jack Teagarden—the quintessential, unclassifiable, maverick Russell quality was beginning to emerge. On *One Hour* with Hawkins, Russell presents us for the first time with a clear example of his skewered tone and penchant for flatted fifths (and other "odd" notes), which in the context of this particular performance offered about as dramatic a contrast to Hawkins's ebulliently grand style as one could imagine.

A few months earlier, Russell's solo on *Basin Street Blues* had attracted even more attention or, in the case of some musicians, created considerable puzzlement. And, indeed, it was for its time as odd a musical statement to come out of the still developing, relatively young jazz language as had ever been heard. At first hearing one of these Russell solos tended to give the impression of a somewhat inept musician, awkward and shy, stumbling and muttering along in a rather directionless fashion. It turns out, however, upon closer inspection that such peculiarities—the unorthodox tone, the halting continuity, the odd note choices—are manifestations of a unique, wondrously self-contained musical personality, which operated almost entirely on its own artistic laws. What appears at first glance (see Ex. 10) to be a complete ignorance of the laws of orthodox voice leading or melodic construction, is really the expression of a musical vision which goes quite beyond such orthodoxies, supersedes them in highly personal and imaginative ways, and creates its own new alien landscape. But stranger still is the fact that even in this remote terrain, Russell's musical ideas are almost always unpredictable, either in the large or the small form. And it is this element of the constantly unpredictable that is the most remarkable measure of his talent and uniqueness. To which one needs to add, for those uninitiated into the special world of Pee Wee Russell's music, that he was not just some intriguing, freak, oddball eccentric: he was also one of the most touching and human players jazz has ever known.

The really intriguing question—and ultimate mystery—in regard to Pee Wee Russell's conception is the question of its musical-stylistic antecedents. We know in his adolescence he admired Leon Rapollo, Jimmy Noone, Johnny Dodds, and Jimmy Lytle, but Russell didn't sound like any of those players, at least not tonally. The only close stylistic relative is in fact Frank Teschemacher, but it is not likely that it can ever be unequivocally demonstrated who influenced whom. For Teschemacher and Russell were the same age, born two weeks apart (in Missouri, although one grew up in Chicago, the other in Oklahoma), and their paths as young clarinetists did cross in Chicago in 1926 and 1927. There are striking similarities in their playing of those early days: the spiky, generally piercing tone in the upper register; the throaty underdeveloped low-register sounds, the off-center imprecise attacks in soft or medium dynamics, and overly edgy attacks in *fortes* and *fortissimos*. But such similarities soon dissolved as the two players matured, Teschemacher becoming more and more controlled and conventional in his playing (before his untimely death in 1931), Russell on the other hand developing quickly into one of the few totally *sui generis* musicians jazz has known.

Example 10 provides a good first glance at Russell's strange musical world—at least as regards pitch and phrase structure[12]—a world once aptly described by critic John Wilson as "Chicago surrealism." But again, while the notation can partially track the vagrant mercurial course of Russell's *Basin Street* solo, only a hearing of it can confirm that these little bits and odds-and-ends of phrases ultimately form a coherent whole.

Ex. 10

By 1932, on one of his next record dates, this time with the Billy Banks orchestra, Russell had molded his personal vision into an even more characteristic style and assured technique. On *Oh Peter* he exhibits his famous gritty low-register tone while stating the song's theme, and later contributes a simply structured solo, mostly in conventional 2-bar phrases. The real hero of this side, however, was Henry "Red" Allen, who inspires—even drives—Russell to some heroics of his own in the last two ensemble choruses. On *Bald Headed Mama* an even more confident Pee Wee enters in a growly, angry mood, settling down a bit later to a good blues solo. Again Allen is magnificent, but we can hear here another early sign of Russell's fully matured later style.

On *I Would Do Anything for You* of two months later (still with Banks) we find Russell on tenor saxophone, matching his clarinet-playing of the time with a rough, raspy, forced sound that nevertheless is anything but gratuitously harsh. Russell turns the song into a blues solo, punching out a string of blue-note

---

12. Russell's unorthodox tone and elusive tonal inflections can, needless to say, not be rendered in musical notation.

minor thirds and flat fifths with an insistence that very few white players of the time could have appreciated, let alone managed to bring off.

When Pee Wee wanted to play "pretty," as on *Tennessee Twilight* (October 1933), his tone would turn inside out, as it were, and take on a funny off-kilter oval shape, like a not quite convincing wry smile. Always full of surprises, Russell sticks to Alex Hill's tune for the most part, but then suddenly launches into one of his quirkily askew double-time breaks, replete with fuzzy tone.

Russell was not by birth, or by nature, a blues player, as for example King Oliver, Tommy Ladnier, Jack Teagarden, and Charlie Parker were, and his clarinet-playing contemporary Barney Bigard could be when he wanted to be. And yet many of Russell's blues are amongst the most heartfelt and striking jazz has known. However, this identification with the blues took a while in developing. I have the impression that at first Russell found the blues and its form somewhat confining; and while he could from the outset play havoc with popular standards, teasing and dissecting them, pummelling them into submission, he respected the blues too much to dominate them, at least in the earlier years. Instead he settled on a kind of safe standard blues chorus which he more or less resuscitated whenever the occasion arose. Hear, for example, the fond similarity between his blues solos on *Madame Dynamite* and the earlier *Bald Headed Mama*, also with *Home Cooking*, where Russell plays a soft, gentle, elusive, mostly low-and-middle-range improvisation. Still, just to show that he can still be master of the occasion, he later offers in the final ensemble chorus some weird, piercing, never-before-heard lip-shaking obbligato effects, along with an overblown growly tag-ending.

One almost gets the impression that by the mid-thirties Russell had taken on—or had been forced by popular acclaim to assume—the role of the maverick, the oddball, the sad-faced clown, the wistful court jester. Behind the wry smile, however, he seemed often to be wracked with pain, barely managing an occasional anguished grin, an ironic aside, a bitter joke. Russell's imagination was irrepressible, his ideas totally unpredictable. Once he had found his special stylistic niche, he seemed never to falter, to veer from it, even though *within* this larger conception its myriad details could be (and mostly were) constantly fluctuating and alterable. Like "Tricky Sam" Nanton or Thelonious Monk or John Lewis, he used his technical limitations to creative advantage, turning what would be unorthodox and "inept" ideas in others' hands into compelling personal statements.

Russell was one of the great storytellers in jazz, an Edgar Allan Poe, a Wilhelm Busch, and Charles Schulz all rolled into one. You could never *quite* pin down what he was saying, but you knew he was saying something—something no one else could or would ever say. He had a thousand different little offbeat stories to tell, and evidently, judging by his considerable recorded output, seemed never to tire of telling them. Nor could one tire of hearing him.

Of the dozens and dozens of mostly extraordinary solos it is possible here to single out only a select few. Suffice it to say that in general there never was in Russell's output a bored or boring solo, and there never was a moment of playing that you could have foretold. Russell was about as free of formulas and clichés as any jazz musician I can think of. The closest he came to a cliché were his beloved blue-note flatted fifths (which he would stick in in the oddest, most unexpected places), and his sudden octave leaps out of one clarinet register into another. But even these ideas, discernible to the careful listener in much of his work, always seemed somehow fresh, invariably appearing in an unusual or unexpected context.

Russell had many tone qualities at his command, almost all of them unorthodox, often raspy, dirty, scratchy, shrill—a timbral zoo of sounds that could *never* have come out of a conservatory clarinet studio. And yet, unbelievably, this *ménage* of tonal aberrants almost always produced a great deal more than some gratuitous distortions. On the contrary, the *sound* of his playing formed the substance, the guts of his musical vision as much as the notes and melodic lines themselves. *Love Is Just Around the Corner*, recorded under Eddie Condon's name in January 1938, is a prime example of his tone (in this case "scratchy" and "raspy"), unusual note choices, and unorthodox form-building, combined to make a unique Russell statement. His insistent reiteration of $C\flat$s and $A\flat$s, flatted fifths and minor thirds in F (the parent key of the piece), over twenty-four bars of the 32-bar song is the kind of idea that even in 1938 very few musicians could have brought off or ever would have dared—or wanted—to bring off. Nor was it usual to build an improvisation downward, as here in *Love* and innumerable other Russell solos. Unlike many soloists who build solos upward from a relatively quiet beginning to a climactic high point—Coleman Hawkins's (1939) *Body and Soul* is a prime example of this technique—Russell frequently started high (in range and intensity) and gradually or abruptly wound down his solos, often with the intention of exiting quietly to make room for the next solo player. On the face of it this type of reverse form-building seems contrary, even perverse, but once again Russell had a way of making it work to his and the music's advantage.

Another example of tonal eccentricity, producing nonetheless extraordinary expressive music, occurs on *Baby, Won't You Please Come Home* from 1938, under Pee Wee's own leadership, on the HRS label). The strangled, boxed-in sound Russell gets here was surely never heard before on a clarinet—even in the days of the clarinet-comedians (like Wilbur Sweatman, Fess Williams, Ted Lewis). It was unusual even for Russell, and I suspect that James P. Johnson's rather rigid and domineering stride-piano accompaniment here forced Pee Wee, the ultimate individualist, to assert himself in the most unorthodox manner he could find at the moment.

As individualistic as Russell was, he was nevertheless one of the best ensemble players ever. Time and time again, in final collectively improvised ensemble choruses, Pee Wee, after some outrageously personal solo statement, would come back into the ensemble fold, riding high over the other instruments in tried-and-true New Orleans clarinet tradition, staying out of the way of the trumpet (an ability much appreciated by all the trumpet players who ever worked with Russell), all the while energizing the whole ensemble with inspiring rhythmic figures or high-riding wails and glissandos. The final ensemble chorus of *Tappin' the Commodore Till* (with Budd Freeman and His Gang) is a striking example of Russell's abilities in this realm.[13]

Russell was, of course, not always Peck's bad boy, musically speaking. Listen to his simple, affecting, heartfelt playing on *Friar's Point Shuffle* (from August 1939 with Eddie Condon and his Chicagoans). True, his tone is strangely opaque—it seems to be colored a dirty blue—and his notes are oddly inflected, bent and twisted, sliding between the cracks; but it is all done in such a disarming manner that the net effect is surprisingly warm and humble.

On *It's All Right Here* (an old Mamie Smith song from 1920), again with one of Eddie Condon's recording groups, we hear an entirely different Russell personality. Here he is once again totally unfettered, cockily strutting through his ten bars of solo, as if at the head of some imaginary parade. It is a superb example of how rhythmically free (and *unpredictable*) Russell could be and yet maintain a solid stomping swinging beat (here wonderfully supported by the often much underrated drummer George Wettling). It is as if his playing can be parsed into two rhythmic layers, the one given over to a spontaneously created superstructure, fleshed out with myriad tiny rhythmic variations and deviations, the other a substructure (inherent in the underlying composition and therefore *predictable*) where the larger spans of time, the deeper rhythmic/metronomic momentum, are maintained.

A recording from July 1940, *Shim-Me-Sha-Wabble* (with Bud Freeman), provides another example of Russell's unique rhythmic and linear invention. Here the improvised lines zig-zag in apparently illogical twists and turns. When we expect a line to move upward, Russell suddenly turns it downward or sideways. It is uncanny—even a bit eerie—how in retrospect, as one's ear follows Russell's notes at close quarters, what at first seems misjudged and even inchoate, suddenly becomes coherent.

Another Condon date on November 11, 1940, produced four sides on which we can hear not only other characteristic aspects of Russell's personality but how these were influenced (at least sometimes) by the other players in the group or by the particular song material used. On *Pretty Doll*, for example, Russell brings forth his prettiest tone, colored by a most delicate vibrato. On *Oh, Sister! Ain't That Hot?* we find Russell in a happy, bouncing, buoyant mood, undoubtedly inspired by Fats Waller's infectious piano romping, both in his own solo and in his backing of Russell.

On *Jig Walk* (under his own leadership in a group called The Three Deuces) made in 1941, we hear another Russell, this the one who throws all caution to the wind, plunges into his solo recklessly, with complete abandon, turning "wrong" notes that he fell upon into "right" ones, at times daring the music to feed him an outlandish idea he can't tame, a bad note he can't twist right.

13. It is interesting to note that in respect to ensemble-playing, Pee Wee and Jack Teagarden, Russell's partner on dozens of recording dates, were complete opposites. Both were mavericks, creators of totally individualistic styles; yet Teagarden had to work hard to suppress his soloistic abilities enough to submerge into improvised ensembles, while Russell seemed to delight in the relative anonymity of ensemble-playing and the clarinet's special traditional role in it.

On *The Last Time I Saw Chicago* we have Russell in one of his truly great slow-tempo blues performances. In some ways it is *two* performances, his two choruses being totally different from each other, clearly demarcated at mid-point by every musical device that one player and a clarinet can muster. Russell's first chorus is set in the low chalumeau register of the clarinet. Starting with one of his famous "muttering" double-time figures, he twists and turns it, seemingly uncertain of direction until it eventually lands on an F, a note which in this B♭ blues functions as a fifth, a second, and a tonic on the three basic I-IV-V harmonic positions of the blues. Starting in the fifth bar, Russell takes that F, bends and twists it in quarter tones: this over the E♭ chord, the flattened F, almost an E♮, producing some anguished dissonances with Joe Sullivan's piano background. Russell continues to worry this note to death, irreverently pulling and tugging at it like a cat playing with a mouse. Adding to the slightly uneasy effect are Sullivan's soft tremolo accompaniment and Zutty Singleton's somber, mournful drum press roll, the contrast heightened by Russell's insistent agitated double-time over the accompaniment's rather more serene single-time.

As mentioned, all this changes abruptly at the second Russell chorus, when he shoots up into his high register, settling into a broadly rocking single-time. The more subtly throaty quality of tone of the first chorus is now exchanged for a hard, raspy, piercing, jabbing sound which carries its own peculiar anguished eloquence.

There is one feeling that binds the two halves of the solo together, however, at least for this listener. Despite the disparity between the two choruses and the instrumental ranginess of the musical ideas, there is something inherently vocal about Russell's performance. It is as if clarinet and human voice—some remarkably extended voice, to be sure—are welded into one. The inherent lyricism of the human voice and the clarinet meet here on common ground. Russell didn't hear that *Last Time* blues primarily or exclusively on the clarinet, but in some alchemistical way as a *vocal* expressed *through* his clarinet. Compare this with Buck Clayton's blues on the 1960 *Englewood* (with Russell's Quintet), wonderfully logical in line and structure and in its own way perfectly realized. But is is a completely "instrumentalized" blues, or, better, "trumpetized." It is at once an idiomatically perfect *trumpet* blues and a pure example of the gradual absorption of the blues by instrumental jazz. Russell's solo on *Englewood*, on the other hand, growly and hairy-toned (like *The Last Time* or the 1950 *Three-to-One Blues* [with Condon]), clings to the freer earlier vocal tradition of the blues. And for me, therein lies the greater humanity of Pee Wee's late blues-playing; it never got caught up too much with only the clarinet.

One of Russell's strangest and most inexplicable solos occurs on a 1946 recording of *Since My Best Gal Turned Me Down* (with his own Jazz Ensemble). Here in a bright-tempo Dixieland setting Russell, ignoring the prevailing buoyant mood, sneaks in with a quietly plaintive falling phrase, made up of nine subtly sliding long notes (Ex. 11). Most players having stumbled onto such an "aberrant" idea, especially upon hearing the rhythmic section happily and unperturbedly chugging along, would now have tried to correct course, as it were, and get back into the appropriate prevailing mood. But not Russell. Having

Ex. 11

summoned up this strange little phrase-child, Russell remains stubbornly committed to it. Over the next twenty-eight bars he twists and bends it to fit the
subsequent upcoming harmonies, varying the phrase rhythmically (although never
breaking out of the original 4-bar duration) and adding little embellishments to
it, but never undermining its original form and shape. It was highly unusual in
1946 to lay nine asymmetrical notes over a 4-bar (16-beat) phrase; it was even
more unusual to carry this "ugly-duckling" idea further and develop it into a
beautiful swan.

Between 1946 and 1956 there was a prolonged hiatus in Russell's recording
activity. The interim period was eventful enough, including as it did the separation from his wife, a marked increase in his drinking and, as a result, a general
physical deterioration that reduced his weight to less than seventy-five pounds
and brought him to a near-fatal illness in 1951. But after several operations and
months of recuperation, Russell recovered and resumed playing and recording.
One of the first recordings of that period was made in 1956 with George Wettling's Jazz Trio—two sides, *Old Folks* and *I Would Do Anything for You*, were
especially felicitous examples of Russell's late-years work—and here we hear indeed a new Pee Wee Russell. He is not quite so quirky as in earlier times, the
ideas seem simplified and perhaps less adventurous, but no less strong, and the
tone has mellowed and warmed in some respects. But it has also become breath-
ier, less overtly projecting. These new recordings, along with the aforementioned

Three-to-One Blues, I'd Climb the Highest Mountain, and *Muscogee Blues* (the latter two from a 1958 date with Russell's Quintet), the 1961 *Mariooch* on Candid, reflected this gentler, more orderly sound world. I cannot fully explain the change: it may have been the result of Russell's physical tribulations; it may have resulted from a whole different psychological-mental attitude about playing and the kind of music he wished to project; it may just have been age—he was fifty in 1956, an age when jazz men are alleged to have already lost (or are beginning to lose) their original creative thrust and energy (as we have seen, not always a viable assumption).

But what is more interesting is that a much younger colleague, Jimmy Giuffre, after a now legendary encounter between Russell and Giuffre at the Music Inn in Lenox, Massachusetts, in 1956, adopted a breathy low-register sub-tone clarinet style very much like Russell's of that period.

At the same time Pee Wee, who had never enjoyed the stigmatization of himself as a Dixielander (or, after the many years at Nick's in New York, as a "Nicksielander"), began to be discovered by some of the modern jazz musicians and record producers. Recordings with the likes of pianist/arranger Nat Pierce, pianist Tommy Flanagan, trombonist/composer Bob Brookmeyer, drummers Jo Jones and Osie Johnson—some of those from a particularly outstanding session with Coleman Hawkins, organized by the critic Nat Hentoff for the then new Candid label in 1961—became fairly common for Russell. Not that he now became a bebopper; Russell was much too independent and individually creative a player to simply hop onto the nearest stylistic bandwagon. But his ear and his musical ideas were—and always had been—expansive enough to be unclassifiable in the standard stylistic stereotypes or, now, to jell comfortably with post-swing-era jazz idioms. As an example of his *compositional* gifts in the modern direction, listen to his Monk-ish *28th and 8th,* recorded on the aforementioned Candid session. On the other hand, precisely because Russell remained true to his own peculiar identity, I think it is wrong to make Russell into a born-again bopper, as several critics have tried to do. He was from the beginning to the very end in 1969 beyond easy categorization, and in that sense alone, he defined and exemplified what it is to be a true jazz musician.

HENRY "RED" ALLEN

There are some interesting cross-references between Pee Wee Russell's and trumpeter Henry "Red" Allen's playing, even though they came from quite different backgrounds and pursued in the main very different careers. Both were highly individualistic players, with a pronounced penchant for odd, unpredictable melodic constructions, and late in life both came to be very much accepted by modern jazz players and critics. Indeed, they held their own creatively very well against musicians in many cases two generations younger. In fact, it can be easily demonstrated that both musicians moved along with the times and advancing jazz styles without in the slightest abdicating their own distinctive musical personalities; and both did much of their finest work in their later years.

Despite this, they suffered the common fate of being too often—and erroneously—lumped with the two main traditional jazz styles: New Orleans in the case of Allen, Dixieland in the case of Russell.

Allen was born in Algiers, Louisiana, a suburb of New Orleans (in 1908), and grew up in the heart of the Crescent City's musical life. His father, Henry Allen, Sr., was the trumpet-playing leader of one of the town's most famous brass bands. (Two Allen uncles were also well-known parade-band musicians.) His father's band rehearsed in the Allen home, and as a result the youngster at one time or another got to hear all the players who passed through Allen, Sr.'s band: such men as Buddy Bolden, Oscar Celestin, Bunk Johnson, King Oliver, Louis Armstrong, Kid Rena, Sam Morgan. Even Sidney Bechet, who in the early days occasionally played trumpet in Allen's band, frequented the Allen home. It was almost inevitable that young Henry would become a musician, initially playing violin and, a bit later, alto horn. At age ten he was "graduated" to trumpet and soon became a full-fledged member of his father's band.

Then, after gigging with various local groups (including work on the Mississippi riverboats with trumpeter Sidney Desvignes), the nineteen-year-old Allen entered the big time in New York by playing for a few months in 1927 with King Oliver's band at the Savoy Ballroom. After a brief return to New Orleans, working this time with Fate Marable on the S.S. *Capitol* (and subsequently turning down an offer from Duke Ellington), Allen returned to New York in mid-1929 to record under his own name for Victor Records, at the same time joining Luis Russell's orchestra.

His earliest solo work from this period reveals a young twenty-one-year-old who had (like everyone else) come under the spell of Louis Armstrong, particularly the Armstrong of *West End Blues*, *Savoy Blues*, and other Hot Seven and Hot Five recordings. His tone was a bit leaner than Armstrong's, the vibrato less luxurious, but many of his ideas, melodic turns, phrasings, and articulations came from Louis. Inevitably, Allen—eight years Armstrong's junior, after all— had by 1929 not reached the degree of maturity that already marked Armstrong's work of the late twenties. Though Allen was well trained and blessed with a solid technique, plenty of fire and spirit, a buoyant sense of swing, most of his early improvisations have a quirky, erratic, restlessly searching quality about them. He was not to find his completely personal, consistent voice until some years later, around the time he was working with Fletcher Henderson.

Nonetheless, the early Allen recordings reveal a very special talent with a burgeoning capacity for original expression. He may have been mesmerized by Armstrong's introductory *West End Blues* cadenza—particularly its final downward turn and cadence; he may have picked up from Louis the quick terminal vibrato on held notes; he may have borrowed from the master the dramatic upward, wailing half-valve glissando with which to start important phrases. But along with these borrowed devices, we can already hear Allen's *own* stock-in-trade ideas: the sudden odd turn-of-phrase; the asymmetrical rhythmic construction; the strange abrupt mixing of double-time flurries—almost an obsession at first—with sudden long held-notes; the love of landing on the sixth of any chord;

the use of fourths (and fifths) in his melodic construction—rather than a more conjunct step-wise invention; the use of contrasting dynamics; the rapid attention-getting alternate-fingering trills on a single note; his love of fast octave jumps—all these were in elementary and embryonic forms already discernible on Allen's earliest recording: *It Should Be You, Feeling Drowsy, Dancing Dave* (under his own leadership) or *Jersey Lightning, Doctor Blues, Louisiana Swing* (under Luis Russell's name.

On *Jersey*, which was recorded in September 1929, we can hear the first use of Allen's rapid octave jumping in a wild break near the end of his solo

 . It was an idea which in one form

or another was to fascinate him (and his audiences) for most of his life, and we will encounter it time and time again, without somehow getting annoyed or bored with it. Allen had an amazing gift for keeping his devices and formulas fresh-sounding. This was, as with Pee Wee Russell, largely a matter of contextual placement, that is, a quirky unpredictability by virtue of which one could never tell *when* Allen would spring one of his favorite ideas onto the listener.

Perhaps Allen's best early solo occurs on the May 1930 *Louisiana Swing* with Luis Russell's band. Whereas Allen would in this period often charge into his solos with a burst of energy, a wild flurry of ideas, but then be unable to sustain the creative momentum, here on *Louisiana* there is a remarkable coherence, a rare maturity of invention—not only for Allen but any trumpet player of the time (except Armstrong). It is the longest of his early solos—a healthy one-and-three-quarters choruses—and played with a relaxed sustained poise that contrasts markedly with his more fidgety, restless work of the time. However, it must be noted that Allen's *Louisiana Swing* solo was not totally extemporized that May day in the studio. The two separate takes issued from that session reveal that Allen had previously worked out this beautifully constructed "improvisation," for the two recorded performances are in most ways very similar, in many ways identical.

It is also possible to detect in this solo a mild influence of Bix Beiderbecke. Although Allen is not known to have ever acknowledged such an influence, the aural evidence—revealed in the lithe buoyant rhythmic swing and certain lyrical melodic turns—is such that it is at least a reasonable assumption or question to consider. (We note at the same time that Beiderbecke's style, too, derived in large part from Armstrong.[14])

Allen was not by inclination and musical background (the brass bands and lively collective ensembles of New Orleans) a natural ballad player. His strength lay more in vigorous, rhythmically exciting, declamatory statements rather than long lyrical melodic lines, as is evident on his first ballad recording, *Roamin'*, from July 1930. Here we can hear a vast difference between Allen and Arm-

14. See *Early Jazz*, pp. 187–194, for a full discussion of Bix Beiderbecke's work.

strong, the latter having launched by then what was to turn into a ten-year career of fronting a band as the supreme instrumental balladeer of the 1930s. Allen's tone did not possess the opulence of Louis's; nor did he have until much later in life the repose and purely melodic imagination needed to pursue this particular art form. Allen's *Roamin'* is capable enough in delineating the tune's melodic outlines, but ultimately it lacks the warmth and ease—and tonal beauty[15]—that all really great lyric players have in common.

On the other hand, a fast-paced number like *Panama* (with Russell's band) really challenged the best in Allen. It is a wonderfully assured solo, consistently interesting, and full of excellent phrases Louis Armstrong would *not* have played.

Allen's lyric gifts were in fact best expressed in the blues, a form and language much more in his blood and musical genes than the pop songs of Tin Pan Alley. Hear his wonderfully reasoned blues discourse on *Stingaree Blues* with King Oliver's band (in September 1930). Allen's two-chorus solo is interestingly parsed out into two quite distinctive and contrasting statements, the one solidly traditional, the other bursting with new-found invention (Ex. 12), including at the

Ex. 12

15. Compare this with Allen's beautiful solo on *Heartbreak Blues* in 1933 with Coleman Hawkins or his glorious lyric performance in 1957 on *I Cover the Waterfront* (with his own All Stars).

same time a number of Allen's favorite devices. Note how he both begins and ends the second chorus on his favorite harmonic interval, the sixth (somehow never cheap or maudlin with Allen); note also the several sixteenth-note falling phrases, and—in this case a new Allen idea—the rising spiraling diminished-chord arpeggio. Then there are also the magnificently expressive, subtly inflected blue notes in mm. 5 and 6 of the second chorus. But his crowning achievement here is the strikingly original phrase starting in m. 2 (2nd chorus), elegantly cascading downward in a way that would not be found in Armstrong's vocabulary.

Allen was *the* outstanding soloist in Russell's orchestra, and it was during his tenure with that group that his work attracted national attention. Indeed, during much of this period RCA Victor was featuring Allen (under his own name) as a young trumpet star in the hopes of finding a worthy competitor in popularity to Armstrong (on the Okeh label). This effort did not succeed, presumably because in the end Allen's talents were not quite of the grandeur and calibre of Armstrong's—although that assumes more discriminating discernment on the part of the public than experience leads one to expect. In addition, Allen was nowhere near the charismatic entertainer-showman that Armstrong had learned to be by the late twenties-early thirties. Allen was less career-ambitious than Louis—or less than Louis's wife Lil allowed Louis to be!—content to be able to play his music at a high professional creative level and make a decent living from it. One remarkable proof of Allen's innate modesty and pragmatic sense of perspective is that for three and a half years he played in Armstrong's orchestra (1937–40) virtually incognito in the presence of the master, who would not allow others in his band to be featured, let alone a potential rival like Allen, all common familial and youthful New Orleans bonds notwithstanding.

This is the place to single out, however, one other member of Russell's band, and one of Allen's most constant musical companions: the great trombonist J. C. Higginbotham. The two men played side by side not only in Russell's orchestra (for two years) but also later successively in the Fletcher Henderson, Mills Blue Rhythm, and Armstrong bands. When in 1940 Allen organized a sextet, J.C. was the trombonist, a tenure that lasted seven years, and which was renewed again in the 1950s during Allen's famous long-run residency at the Metropole in New York.

Higginbotham was two years older than Allen but not quite as fully developed a stylist when he joined Luis Russell in the late 1920s, a year before Allen. This was not for a lack of innate talent, but rather that the trombone was, as compared with the trumpet, simply not yet as elaborately developed as a jazz solo instrument. It took a long time for the trombone to lose its very specific New Orleans tailgate functions, and, of course, it had no brilliantly innovative model to follow as the trumpet did (in different ways) in Oliver and, above all, Armstrong. Indeed Higginbotham can be considered as one of the early style originators on the trombone, breaking away from its limited role in collective ensemble jazz towards a more fluent, versatile, trumpet-oriented solo conception. Early on, influenced by Kid Ory and other New Orleans trombonists, it was Jimmy Harrison's pioneer work, again Armstrong-influenced, that pulled Higginbotham toward the new solo-virtuoso direction. In the end, by the early 1930s, Higginbotham actually surpassed Harrison in skill and imagination (while we note that by then, sadly, Harrison was in a state of physical deterioration and by 1931 dead from a severe stomach ulcer). Higginbotham retained much of the robust sturdiness and broad "bass" sonority of New Orleans trombones, at the same time building a whole new world of technical and expressive fluency on that venerable foundation. His range was for the time extraordinary, which allowed him among other things to differentiate strikingly registral layers and easily negotiate dramatic two-octave leaps in his solos. His commanding full-bodied tone and attack had enormous presence and projection. His lip trills, ornamental turns, and generally clean, agile slide technique served to give him an exceptional expressive/imaginative range and allowed him to create long flowing phrases. One of the most consistent trombone players in the history of jazz (along with Lawrence Brown, Vic Dickenson, and, of course, Teagarden), Higginbotham's outstanding work can be heard on almost every one of his recordings. But let us especially single out (with Henry Allen) *It Should Be You, Swing Out, Sugar Hill Function, Got Rhythm in Your Feet, Roll Along, Prairie Moon*; (with Russell) *Feelin' The Spirit, Jersey Lightning, Doctor Blues, On Revival Day*; (under his own name) the great 1930 classic trombone-blues recording, *Higginbotham Blues*;[16] and later on three great blues recordings in 1939 for the Blue Note label: *Weary Land Blues, Basin Street Blues*, and *Blues for Tommy*.

Interestingly, Higginbotham came somewhat under the influence of Lawrence Brown in the mid-1930s—indeed to such an extent that it is occasionally difficult to tell the two players apart. But even more interestingly, Higginbotham, one of the all-time greatest blues players on trombone, kept his powerful earthy blues-style quite distinct from his more elegant Brown-influenced playing. A fine example of this latter Higginbotham approach occurs on the 1936 *Lost* (with Allen's orchestra).

But to return to our main subject, Henry "Red" Allen left the Russell orchestra in late 1932. Previously he had participated in a series of first-rate recordings under the leadership of Billy Banks, who, through the efforts of Irving Mills, was able to hire a remarkable all-star aggregation of musicians that included at various times not only Allen, but Coleman Hawkins, Fats Waller, Pee Wee Russell, Tommy Dorsey, drummer Zutty Singleton, Pops Foster, and that other strong New Orleans bass player (and disciple of Foster), Al Morgan. Allen is

---

16. *Higginbotham Blues* is also notable for one of the rare and earliest examples of exceptionally well-played bowed bass, in this instance by Pops Foster, the first and greatest of the pioneer New Orleans bassists (1892–1969). A player of extraordinary power and rhythmic energy, Foster energized many a jazz ensemble in his long life, in particular Luis Russell's orchestra (with which he played eleven years) and most of Henry Allen's groups.

Higginbotham Blues offers a stunning translation of Armstrong's *West End Blues* idiom onto the trombone, and it ends with a powerful recitation of the famous *Organ Grinder Swing* theme,

ample proof that this ancient chant, going back to the earliest days of jazz and Storyville, was part of black musicians' staple repertory long before Will Hudson fashioned it into a song in 1936 and Sy Oliver turned it into a hit for Jimmie Lunceford.

outstanding on all these sides, twenty-four in all (including alternate takes recently issued), contributing first-rate solos and sparking the many collective ensembles with his spirited lead playing. And it is wonderful to hear the two mavericks, Allen and Pee Wee Russell, working together, alternately challenging and complementing each other. Hear them, for example, on the incredibly exciting *Bugle Call Rag*, both masters locked in duet embrace, playing for their lives (listen especially to the fourth blues chorus and the final 16-bar collective finale). The twenty-three-year-old Gene Krupa is also very effective here, driving the ensemble with clean incisive swing. And it is a rare pleasure to hear on these Banks sides Pee Wee Russell on tenor saxophone, as he transfers much of his hoarse, scruffy clarinet tone to the tenor, playing at times with an astonishing vigor, at other items with the relaxed swing and pale sound of early Lester Young.[17]

An interesting recording date in May 1933 under the leadership of British bandleader, bass player, composer-arranger, Spike Hughes, produced still more resplendent Allen work, although in a rather different kind of setting. Hughes had brought with him to America a number of jazz compositions, very much in the style and image of Duke Ellington—a refined orchestral sound world which Allen had not yet encountered as a player. Moreover, the band that Hughes hired was Benny Carter's, which included not only Dickie Wells (some of his very best work is to be found on these sides), Chu Berry and Sid Catlett but, as an extra, the great Coleman Hawkins. This was formidable company indeed, but Allen held his own very well. Although no one could have topped the sheer magisterial grandeur of Hawkins's sweeping, all-embracing solo on *Sweet Sorrow Blues*, Allen acquitted himself nobly in an unusually expressive solo, filled with florid double-time explorations and rhythmic surprises.

At around this time Allen joined Fletcher Henderson's great orchestra and thus was able to participate in some of the most important historic and seminal orchestral recordings of the decade (many of which, as we know, were to exert a tremendous influence on future developments in jazz). After Rex Stewart's departure in 1933, Allen inherited the major solo trumpet chair in the Henderson band, an opportunity for which he was now, at age twenty-five, fully ready

---

17. On Billy Banks's last date in 1932—after which he reputedly returned to his family's shoe business in Cleveland *(sic)*—he not only recorded Ellington's brand new *It Don't Mean a Thing If It Ain't Got That Swing* but was able to bring into the studio another all-star band including Allen, Tommy Dorsey, Pee Wee Russell, Fats Waller, Foster, and Singleton. On *Who Stole the Lock?* Dorsey plays a 16-bar trombone solo which consists almost entirely of a long 8-bar lip trill—the best and fastest ever recorded in jazz!—and a single-note reiteration which somehow, despite such a simplistic conception, turns out to be by contrast with the other solos in context a remarkably inventive solo.

Incidentally, the discographies are void of personnel identification for Banks's recording dates of May 10 and August 18, 1932. My ears tell me that the first date *definitely* had on it Allen, Hawkins, Waller, Al Morgan or Pops Foster, and Zutty Singleton. (Personnel for the second date is mentioned above.) In any case, Banks always surrounded himself with first-rate players, and his recordings—sadly neglected, I suspect, because most jazz historians think of him as a Calloway-type of entertainer not worthy of consideration (although with almost as remarkable a voice as Calloway's)—deserve much more attention than they have received—if only for the work of his remarkable sidemen.

and eager to seize. Allen's solos with the Henderson band are characterized by a tremendous sense of authority and at the same time a feeling of wild abandon, a kind of wonderfully controlled disorder. Allen charged into each solo at full tilt, brimming with energy. But now, unlike in earlier days, he was able to *sustain* the intensity, harness his fertile imagination, maintain full control of his ideas, bizarre though at times they may have sounded to his contemporaries. Even at his wildest Allen seemed to be fully in charge. And that is precisely the point: without giving up any of his unorthodoxy, Allen had by now found ways of channeling his ideas in a more coherent and directed manner. One can hear this on all his major solos with Henderson—*Wrappin' It Up, Down South Camp Meetin', Big John Special, Hotter Than 'Ell, Hocus Pocus, Nagasaki*—but perhaps none reveal "Red" Allen, the adventurer, more quintessentially than his solos on *Queer Notions* and *King Porter Stomp*. Both pieces are discussed in full elsewhere in this volume.[18] Suffice it therefore to concentrate here on Allen's solos.

The so aptly named *Queer Notions* is a "modernistic" piece which no other trumpet player I can think of from that era (except maybe Jabbo Smith or Peanuts Holland) would have felt comfortable improvising upon. But these "strange" harmonies and "peculiar" whole-tone progressions were perfect grist for Allen's creative mill. Indeed he had been playing solos that fit just such a piece for at least four years. If *Queer Notions* can be described as a piece in search of a soloist, it had found one in Allen. All his previous experiments with flat fifths, minor sixths, and minor ninths were now going to really pay off.

In some ways his solo here is his greatest—at least from this period. Played for the most part with a straight vibrato-less tone and in derby, producing a slightly muted, veiled, "remote" sound, Allen's solo negotiates the harmonic rapids like a happy salmon cavorting upstream. Allen twists and darts easily in and out of the changes in ways that even the composer, Coleman Hawkins, could not quite accomplish in *his* solos. In Allen's final eight bars, after what passes for a bridge in this piece (played by Hawkins), he tops even his previous efforts by pushing the initial idea with which he began his solo (Ex. 13a) even further out into a harmonic no man's land (Ex. 13b). This latter passage clearly anticipates in its sound, its articulation and advanced pitch language, the Dizzy Gillespie of fifteen years later.

Allen's solo on *King Porter Stomp*, though more conventional than *Queer Notions*, has its adventurous moments and is a prime example of Allen's ability early on to break out of the confinement of 2- and 4-bar phrasing, in general to break the tyranny of the bar line, a matter that was otherwise not fully resolved by jazz players until well into the bop era. The first twelve bars of Allen's *King Porter* solo (Ex. 14) show how the phrase, beginning in m. 7, is extended *over* the structure-delineating double-bar into the twelfth measure of the chorus. The kind of chromatic substitutions (mm. 6 through 10) Allen uses here were by

18. See Part 1 of this chapter; and Chapter 5, Part 2.

Ex. 13

Ex. 14

then no longer the exclusive domain of Allen. Hawkins, Higginbotham, Benny Morton, and a few other players were by now exploring this device energetically. But the point is that Allen had been doing this since his very first recordings five years earlier. In the intervening years many a musician—and listener—had accused Allen of playing "peculiar" music, of having "a weird ear." Another five years later, and all the young players were appropriating this device as standard equipment.

That Allen could play simple, perfectly constructed non-experimental solos is shown readily on his 1934 *Rug Cutter's Swing*, one of those proto-typical riff tunes that Horace Henderson was so good at turning out. Playing the head (in cup mute) in smooth eighth-note style, Allen sounds exactly like the young Charlie Shavers, of a few years hence, when with the John Kirby Sextet. Allen, until he joined the Mills Blue Rhythm Band, rarely used a mute, even a straight mute. He once explained that he preferred to play the trumpet "open and clear." "With a mute you can cheat"—how many modern trumpeters have taken advantage of that fact! "Play the horn wide open; you cannot lie."

Allen's solo proper on *Rug Cutter* is a model of economy. In keeping with the repetition-prone riff nature of the tune, Allen constructs an entire 56-bar

Ex. 15

motives e) and f) are related to c) and b) respectively

solo out of a mere six brief motives, riffs in effect (marked *a* through *f* in Example 15).[19]

Here was the perfect answer to those of his critics who saw in him only an erratic, overly complex player.

One of these "critics" evidently was Roy Eldridge, who ironically took over the solo trumpet chair in 1936 in Fletcher Henderson's band, a chair previously held by Allen. And in truth, Eldridge was a logical successor to Allen and the even earlier incumbent of that position, Rex Stewart. For in many respects Eldridge combined in his playing some specific traits of *both* Allen and Stewart. Oddly enough, though Eldridge was quite content to acknowledge his early admiration for Stewart, he was less charitable—and I think less honest—in regard to Allen. He is known to have denied any influence from Allen, for he claimed that the latter played too many "wrong notes."

We have to remember, of course, that Eldridge was in his younger days one of the most pugnaciously competitive spirits that jazz has ever known, and that he denied not only emulating Stewart and Allen but even Armstrong, who, he said, did not at first impress him terribly much. Impressed or not, Eldridge learned not only from Armstrong but Stewart and Allen as well, with a bit of Jabbo Smith thrown in for good measure.

It is to rewrite history a bit to make Eldridge the sole link between Armstrong and Gillespie, as if Allen and Stewart and Cootie Williams and Bunny Berigan and Bix Beiderbecke and Jabbo Smith had never existed. Eldridge's influence on Gillespie and modern jazz was, of course, enormous and quite direct. But I suspect that that was for some very specific reasons, namely, Eldridge's speed and spectacular high register. For those two aspects are first and foremost what youthful brass players work for and are impressed by. I can attest to this as a brass player myself, and the 1930s and 1940s were marked by extraordinary technical advances in the United States on the part of brass players—jazz as well as classical—dedicated in large part to playing ever faster and higher. Indeed in a somewhat superficial and technically oriented view, the entire history of trumpet and trombone playing in jazz could be described as one of "progress" in continually extending speed and range limits upwards (and I have taken some pains to delineate that progress in this book, where appropriate).

Eldridge was driven by these same urges and, although he eventually had much more to offer than speed and high notes, the players younger than he were impressed by his technical feats and virtuosity, in a way that they were not by Allen's playing.

Allen had a limited high register; high C (concert) was about the limit for him—I know of only one high F in his *entire* recorded career, and that was a fluke accident—and while he had a virtuosic technique, he was not at all interested in dazzling his peers or listeners with exhibitions of fast technical displays. His experiments lay in an entirely different direction, much more difficult to

19. Thelonious Monk's composition *Raise Four* of 1968 shows a striking similarity to Allen's *Rug Cutter* improvisation. Its main melodic feature, the tritone $B\flat$-E, is used even more prominently and consistently than in Allen's solo.

grasp (literally) or appreciate. Interestingly, there are no direct imitators of Allen because, I think, he was too unique, too adventurous, but in ways that did not interest fellow musicians as much: asymmetrical forms, uncommon melodic/ harmonic experiments, oddly shaped lines.

In those respects Eldridge, only three years Allen's junior, was basically a much more conservative player, and more narrowly a *trumpet* player, a *brass* player, rather than a musician who played the trumpet. If we compare Eldridge's and Allen's playing in the mid-thirties, we will learn some very interesting comparative facts. Eldridge, for example, was much more given to producing relatively short phrases in essentially symmetrical 2- and 4-bar constructions. (He, too, like all jazz players, learned to create in much longer and metrically looser, freer flowing lines later on.) Eldridge's melodic motion is essentially linear and conjunct, much less harmonic than Allen's. His obsession in the early days with technical fluency almost *prevented* him from lingering long enough to turn the odd phrase, to explore figures that did not lie readily in the fingers and embouchure, to sing out on a long plangent note. Again, all of this he certainly learned to do within not too many years. But in the mid-thirties, when his style was not yet entirely formed or matured, the emphasis was on technically out-playing, out-"virtuosoizing" his rivals.

By the same token, he was then still very much listening to Allen, his denials thereof notwithstanding. One need only compare Eldridge's work on, say, *Here Comes Cookie* (with the Teddy Hill band) or *Wabash Stomp* and *Florida Stomp* (under his own leadership) with Allen's work of the period (1934–35) to realize that Eldridge was not entirely impervious to Allen's influence. The opening of *Florida Stomp* (Ex. 16), for example, is not typical Eldridge at all in its pitch choices and melodic contouring; it *is* quintessential Allen.

Ex. 16 $\quad \downharpoonright$=120

When Henderson's orchestra disbanded in late 1934, Allen moved over to the Mills Blue Rhythm Band, reunited once again with his old friend Higginbotham (who had come to the Mills band earlier that year). During the same period Allen was also in the midst of a multi-year contract with the American Record Company, which had in 1934 acquired Columbia and thereby become one of the three major record companies in the country. Allen had started out in early 1933 in a partnership with Coleman Hawkins and, given the prodigious talent of these two artists, the Allen-Hawkins partnership could have developed into one of the most important and enduring alliances in jazz history, like Hines and Armstrong, Parker and Gillespie, John Coltrane and Miles Davis, Milt Jackson and John Lewis.

But it was not to turn out that way. In the first place, the ARC recording executives were interested only in grooming Allen as a commercial competitor to Armstrong. To aid and abet them in this scheme, they had various publishers provide Allen and Hawkins with the latest pop songs, hoping somehow to capture a major hit with these trivia. Second, ARC was little interested in Hawkins, for they took him along in the bargain as long as Allen would sing their songs on every recording, again an attempt to cash in on Armstrong's success as a singer. And sing on every side Allen did. He was never a great singer, although he enjoyed it and certainly avoided the worst of the croonerisms of the thirties. He had too much integrity merely to imitate Armstrong's singing. And yet a rough similarity was apparently unavoidable, which in turn left Allen with no alternative to develop his own distinctive vocal personality. His singing was, even for black audiences, neither original nor plagiaristic enough.

Although Hawkins comes off best on the ten sides he cut with Allen—before he left for Europe—and Allen manages well enough with both his singing and playing chores, the performers were rarely able to triumph over the material the way Billie Holiday and Teddy Wilson were able to do a few years later, under similar publisher-dominated circumstances. [20]

When Hawkins quit, Allen continued as sole leader of the recording group, waxing another seventy-two sides—*all* with Allen vocals. It is hard to say whether it was the influence of these commercial pressures, or the different creative climate of the Mills Blue Rhythm Band—on a considerably lesser level than either the 1933–34 Henderson band or Luis Russell's in its turn-of-the-decade heyday—that wrought a change in Allen's playing. When he joined Mills he took to a more simplified style, losing in the process much of its creative cutting edge; and in deference to the band's arrangers (who tried to create a sort of milder surrogate Ellington jungle band) Allen began using all sorts of mutes and jungle-istic growl effects.

The stay with Mills did not add much to Allen's stature nor to his further development as a soloist. He did have one major popular success as a composer, with his famous *Ride, Red, Ride*. Composition is stretching the word a bit, of course, for it is another one of the hundreds of pieces based on the simple changes of *Tiger Rag*. But played at an incredible tempo of $\flat = 370$, the piece made a tremendous impact on audiences out for a rousing good time. Occasionally lurching back into half-time from its frenetic tempo, the piece has a frustratingly unsettling quality about it. In the end, with its rather empty excitement and pyrotechnical exaggeration, by no means perfectly played, *Ride, Red, Ride* became a caricature of itself, an uneasy encounter between a band and a fast tempo.

As mentioned, Allen in 1937 became submerged (and virtually inaudible) in

20. See Holiday and Wilson sections, respectively in parts 3 and 2 this chapter.

Armstrong's big band. His own solo work (continuing exclusively under his name) during this period was also affected and became on occasion rather uneven and ordinary. *Really* wrong notes began to creep into his playing, although it would have been foolish to count Allen out of the running. On *Canal Street Blues* in 1940, for example, or with Zutty Singleton's band on *King Porter Stomp* and *Shim-Me-Sha-Wabble*, or with Billie Holiday and Teddy Wilson in 1937 on *You Showed Me the Way*, and with Lionel Hampton in 1939 on *I'm on My Way*, we hear Allen play with his old gusto and vivid imagination, his slow blues *(Canal Street)* warm and passionate, his solo with Billie beautifully disciplined. *I'm on My Way* is especially striking, a paragon of control and economy. The old telltale trademarks are all there: the sudden octave descents, the double-time spurts, the spiraling arpeggios, and the tight intense vibrato, except that now they are set in bold pared-down contours, lean and modern, prophetic, and looking well into the future.

In 1940 Allen formed his All Stars sextet, including Higginbotham, saxophonist Don Stovall and that excellent drummer (already excellent as a teenager with Walter Page's Blue Devils and the Alphonse Trent band), Alvin Burroughs. Starting out as a Dixieland group, Allen's All Stars was immediately thought of as part of the great New Orleans revival of the early 1940s. But to everyone's surprise, except Allen himself, the sextet had by the mid-forties adopted a much more wide-ranging and in many respects quite modern stance. Indeed, Allen's recordings from 1946, particularly such items as *The Crawl, Buzz Me, Get the Mop*, reveal a considerable transformation from when we last heard Allen. The sextet was a kind of bebop jump band à la Louis Jordan, and Allen's playing had begun to absorb more than a touch of bop phrasing. This is not meant as an adverse criticism, nor does the statement really imply some major stylistic transformation on Allen's part. For his playing—in its free asymmetrical phrasing, its faster tempos, and its eager embrace of running double-time figures, its purposely "misplaced" anticipatory cross-accents, its modern pitch choices—had all along looked forward to the innovations of bop. In some sense the music had now caught up with Allen.

Recorded evidence of his work from 1946 to his death in 1967 is relatively slim. But two recording dates from the late 1950s testify tellingly to the fact that Allen never stopped growing musically, and in fact in the last fifteen years of his life regained fully his earlier creative potency. In some ways his playing with Coleman Hawkins in 1957 (their first encounter in 24 years) and with Kid Ory in 1959 was the finest of his entire career. What it had lost in some of the early youthful brashness, it had now gained in seasoned maturity. *I Cover the Waterfront* is one of the most magnificent extended trumpet solos of that or any other period. It brims with interesting bold, contrasting ideas, draws continually upon his lively creative imagination, is alternately gently ruminative and passionately expressive, and is played with a new rich, husky, breathy, singing tone. And if in this performance he can sound at times like a richly endowed Bobby Hackett or a wise, matured Miles Davis, or on his *I Got Rhythm* (with Kid Ory's Creole Jazz Band) like a fluent Joe Newman or a dashing Dizzy Gillespie, it is again a tribute to the largeness of his original talent in that, by just a little extension in this or that direction, as the years passed, Allen could embrace other styles without really ever going outside of himself.

It must have been gratifying to Allen that his late work—at the Metropole or on recordings like *Let Me Miss You, Baby, Love Is Just Around the Corner,* and the fourteen sides he cut with Kid Ory—brought him a recognition and admiration from critics and audiences that had often been denied him in earlier years.

7

The White Bands

PART 1

THE CASA LOMA ORCHESTRA

The Casa Loma Orchestra is generally cited as the band that set the stage for the Swing Era, the first white band consistently to feature jazz instrumentals and pursue a deliberate jazz policy, and thus the most influential white big band of the early 1930s until Benny Goodman's breakthrough success of 1935. There is much truth to these claims, even if they require some qualification. How strange it is, therefore, that the Casa Lomans have been so skimped in jazz histories, and—in many cases—dealt with quite disparagingly or ignored entirely.[1]

The Casa Loma Orchestra represents in fact a complex, fascinating example of a musical paradox: an orchestra whose impact was at once enormous and yet negligible (or at least short-lived), whose work was full of contradictions and enigmas, and whose musical origins have never been thoroughly examined. It seems to me that the many questions the work of the Casa Loma band raises are of vital enough interest to be seriously addressed, particularly considering the band's chronologically pivotal position in the history of jazz.

The questions are many, and their answers are not entirely easy to trace some fifty years after the fact. Where, for example, did the style of the Casa Loma Orchestra originate? Why was it so popular with young white college audiences? Why did it fail to impress jazz critics and musicians (although its great popular success was certainly appreciated and even noted with envy)? Why were so many prominent black (and white) orchestras and leaders impressed by the Casa Loma band? What precisely were its artistic qualities? Was it as bad an influence on jazz as its detractors suggest, or as important a catalyst as its supporters claim?

---

1. The only author who has tried to seriously assess the role of the Casa Loma Orchestra and to present a balanced picture of its impact is Albert McCarthy in his *Big Band Jazz* (New York, 1974), pp. 189–93.

632

Did (could) the band swing or not? And perhaps the most intriguing question of all: how is it that an obscure white guitar and banjo player, Gene Gifford, could create in *Casa Loma Stomp* (1930), seemingly in one musical stroke, the full-blown progenitor of hundreds of swing-style offspring—in effect tantamount to the national anthem of 1930s' jazz?

The answers to those questions must of necessity be found in the band's recorded work. At least it is the only more or less unequivocal evidence extant at this late date. The band first recorded in late 1929, having begun life a few years earlier as one of the numerous dance band units under the Jean Goldkette banner,[2] originally called the Orange Blossoms and led by one of Goldkette's assistants, Henry Biagini. In 1929 the Orange Blossoms band was scheduled to inaugurate a new nightclub in Toronto, the Casa Loma, and when the club failed, the players decided to rename their group the Casa Loma Orchestra—in the club's memory, as it were. Soon, thereafter the band dismissed frontman Biagini and reorganized as a cooperative orchestra and a corporation—the first of its kind—with one of its saxophone players, Glen Gray, as its president and the rest of the band as its board of directors and stockholders. Gray continued to play in the sax section, while their violinist Mel Jenssen was asked to front and "conduct" the band.

But the man who has been credited with setting the style of the Casa Loma band was neither Gray nor Jenssen but Gene Gifford, a banjoist and guitarist who had joined the Orange Blossoms in 1929, after he had played with a number of bands in the South and Southwest, most notably the Blue Steele Orchestra out of Georgia and Memphis. At one point he had even led his own band in Texas. While there is no incontrovertible proof that Gifford arranged for any of these orchestras, it is very likely that he did so, in particular for his own Texas band. What is certain is that he became very active as arranger in Detroit in early 1929 for a number of Goldkette's orchestras. And when the Orange Blossoms band metamorphosed into the Casa Lomans, Gifford remained as its chief arranger.

It is clear from the band's early (1929) recordings that Gifford was by then already a capable arranger, writing scores that were both technically and musically challenging, obviously demanding long hours of meticulous rehearsing. However, it may be stretching a point to assume that Gifford created this style single-handedly out of his own imagination and talent. Gifford's idiom can be traced to a number of sources including the Blue Steele and Jimmy Joy orchestras, the latter a very successful jazz-oriented, Texas-based dance band which recorded prolifically in the mid-1920s and which Gifford must surely have known and heard, both on recordings and on his travels in Texas.

But an even stronger influence on Gifford's arranging style may have been that of John Nesbitt, the outstanding trumpet player and arranger of the McKinney Cotton Pickers in the late twenties. I have dealt with Nesbitt's work in considerable detail in Chapter 5. Comparative listening and analysis of Gifford's

---

2. See above, Chapter 5, Part 1, on the McKinney Cotton Pickers.

1930 scores for the Casa Loma band and Nesbitt's 1928–29 arrangements for the McKinney group can leave little doubt that many of Nesbitt's most innovative ideas rubbed off on Gifford and were, in modified ways, taken over by him. The similarities are too striking to be merely coincidental or to be ignored. Since both men were working in Detroit for Goldkette-managed bands, and since Nesbitt's scores precede Gifford's by (in some cases) two and a half years,[3] it is at least a supposition for further research that Gifford must have been strongly influenced by Nesbitt's work.

There are several layers and types of influences discernible. In the most general way there is the basic notion of creating outright jazz instrumentals, of turning songs and tunes into jazz numbers, as opposed to "arrangements for dancing," with or without the usual hot or semi-hot jazz interpolations. The latter approach was, of course, what 98 percent of those late-1920s' orchestras who had at least *some* jazz pretensions were providing. The idea of a jazz-instrumental composition *not* created for the primary purpose of dancing—like Nesbitt's *Crying and Sighing* or his remarkable version of *Chinatown, My Chinatown* (recorded by Fletcher Henderson in October 1930, two months *before* the *Casa Loma Stomp*)—was at that time still a rarity.

As we shall see below in some detail, Gifford's *Casa Loma Stomp* reveals too many similarities with Nesbitt's arrangements of 1929 and 1930, especially *Chinatown*, to be ignored or dismissed as mere coincidence. As to the question of how Nesbitt arrived at his unique arranging conception, I have suggested earlier (see above, Chapter 5, Part 1) that he unquestionably learned much of his arranger's craft from Don Redman, not only by hearing the latter's work for Henderson but by working side by side with Redman in 1927 when Redman became the McKinney Cotton Pickers' chief arranger and musical director. But Nesbitt must have evolved the faster tempos and numerous original rhythmic figures typical of his own arrangements for McKinney and Henderson on his own, as *his* contribution to the Redman style. For one finds precious little of that particular kind of up-tempo arrangement in Redman's work with Henderson or McKinney.

It must be said that, because of its great popularity with a broad segment of the (mostly white) audience, Gifford's *Casa Loma Stomp* did more than any other piece in the early thirties to advance the idea of jazz instrumentals, at least in the guise of frenetic "killer-dillers," meant to be listened to *as* music, rather than as background for dancing. More importantly, it is not too much to say that the Casa Loma band and Gifford's *Stomp* brought jazz as an orchestral instrumental music (not mere *dance* music) out of its previous exclusively black

3. For example, Nesbitt's major works *Put It There*, *Crying and Sighing*, and *Stop Kidding*, and *Birmingham Breakdown* were recorded as early as July and October 1928, while Gifford's *San Sue Strut* and *China Girl* came along in February 1930, and *Casa Loma Stomp* not until December of that year. By the way, the suggestion made by some (Marshall Stearns, for one) that Gifford may have been influenced by Eddie Durham's work with the Bennie Moten band in Kansas City is untenable, since Moten's breakthrough recordings of *Toby*, *Prince of Wails*, and *Lafayette* were not made until December 1932, a full two years *after Casa Loma Stomp*.

domain over to white audiences, musicians and record companies—from "race records" to broad white popular support. The Casa Loma orchestra's role in that respect alone, regardless of its ultimate jazz quality, was crucial, pervasive and much greater than that of any other similar pieces or earlier instrumental precursors, whether by Henderson or Nesbitt—or Ellington for that matter. The real market for popular music comprised white audiences, mostly the young college crowd, who unfortunately seldom heard any black music and authentic jazz at all. (I am certain that the meaning of Gifford's 1931 composition, *Black Jazz*, was lost on most of its white audience—quite apart from the fact that the title was a calculated word-play on the previously recorded *White Jazz*, rather than a serious tribute to black jazz music.) Indeed, only a few tunes-turned-into-instrumentals by white orchestras of the period come to mind, most notably Challis's and Hayton's arrangements for Paul Whiteman, such as *Nobody's Sweetheart, Sugar, China Boy,* and *Coquette*. In the sense, then, that for better or worse *Casa Loma Stomp* became a stylistic model for some years for other orchestras, from Henderson and Hines to Goodman and Barnet, its influence and impact are irrefutable. And I believe that at least part of the credit must go indirectly to Nesbitt.

But also, on a more specific level of musical detail, the link between Nesbitt and Gifford is unmistakable in a variety of ways. First, Gifford in general emulates not the basic call-and-response concept of Redman and Henderson, with its clear antiphonal division of brass and reeds, but rather the more homogeneous mixed-timbre sounds favored by Nesbitt. Secondly, when Nesbitt does break up the choirs into separate units, he usually does so in unexpected and unorthodox ways, juxtaposing timbrally diverse groupings or working with rapid alternation (in two or one, even half-bar phrases) of timbres and textures.[4] Gifford often uses the same device and most effectively, particularly in the latter half of his own *San Sue Strut* or the ninth and tenth choruses of *Casa Loma Stomp*.

Third, Gifford uses many of the same rhythmic figures favored by Nesbitt in his arrangements, fast-tempo figures such as: [musical notation] or [musical notation] or [musical notation] or [musical notation] or [musical notation]. Such figures were part of Nesbitt's trumpet-playing style, which in turn was part and parcel of a fairly widespread early brass playing conception, generally favoring a complex staccato, notey, rather vertical approach. Trombonists like Claude Jones in Detroit (with McKinney's Cotton Pickers during this period) and Miff Mole, trumpeters like the young (pre-Ellington) Rex Stewart, and the saxophonist Coleman Hawkins favored this rhythmically energetic style. Although Nesbitt was more of a composer-trumpeter than a trumpet virtuoso and thus more creatively wide-ranging and explorative in his improvisations than most, he did use a fair amount of this *staccato* repeated-note approach; and from his playing this moved over into his arranging. But whereas in Nesbitt's writing these kinds of figures were offset by many other more linear flowing types of ideas, Gifford

4. See my discussion of Nesbitt's work in Chapter 5, above.

seized upon such staccato repeated-note patterns with a vengeance and developed them into the mainstay of his rhythmic/motivic idiom. These devices became almost a fetish with him: the more the audiences liked their flashy razzle-dazzle, the more he adhered to them. Nesbitt on the other hand sensed innately that such patterns were limiting; that they didn't really swing too well and needed to be balanced with other less pitch-static shapes and configurations.

Another specific musical idea Gifford borrowed from Nesbitt is the kind of "wailing" figure heard, slightly varied, in the last chorus of *Casa Loma Stomp*:

. Nesbitt had often used a similar "flaring" gesture before that, most notably in *Chinatown* (with Henderson):

and in *I've Found a New Baby* (with McKinney):
Indeed the 8-bar ensemble phrase in the last chorus of *Baby* (recorded April 8, 1929) also includes Gifford's favorite repeated-note figure:
(see Ex. 1).

Ex. 1

The general as well as specific resemblances between Nesbitt's *Chinatown* and Gifford's *Casa Loma Stomp* are too striking to be ignored. The whole feel of both pieces is similar, even though the Henderson band's rhythmic drive, motored by Kirby's 4/4 bass, cannot be matched by the Casa Lomans' merely peppy approach.[5] The chorus sequence and whole buildup of Gifford's piece is similar

5. In this connection it is interesting to note that both the McKinneys and Glen Gray's Casa Lomans adhered to a basic two-beat rhythm with only the banjo—Dave Wilborn in the one, Gifford in the other—relentlessly pumping away in uninterrupted 4/4 beats. Since many other bands of this period arrived at a similar rhythmic/metric compromise, it is impossible to make any hard and fast claims of a specific influence here in one direction or another. Nonetheless, I find it at least conjecturally interesting and perhaps relevant that the two bands, Gray's and McKinney's, adhered to the same rhythmic approach, rather than a dissimilar one.

to that of Nesbitt's *Chinatown*, including, as already mentioned, the climactic "wailing" figures towards the end. Even the opening theme of *Casa Loma* is cut from the same motivic and rhythmic cloth as *Chinatown* (see Ex. 2) (the latter a venerable standard composed back in 1910 by the Hungarian-born song composer Jean Schwartz and long ago turned into a "jazz instrumental").

Ex. 2

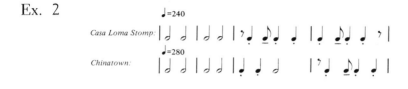

By citing the above illustrations of the younger Gifford's learning from the older Nesbitt, it is not my intention to reduce Gifford to a merely epigonal figure. He was too talented for that. But I do wish to suggest that even exceptional talent rarely issues forth full-blown, unaffected by its predecessors, untouched by earlier sources and influences.

Of course, Glen Gray's Casa Lomans were a young band in 1930, their average age in the early twenties, full of energy and ambition—and some talent, even if this talent tended to express itself in ways more technical than expressively creative. Their commercial assets were considerable: they played in a flashy, externally exciting manner; they rehearsed Gifford's arrangements to near-perfection. They made a very attractive appearance, dressed impeccably in tails and white tie; they gave off an air of optimism, conviction and youthful exuberance that was catching and fascinated the young college generation. Their repertory alternated between snappy jazz instrumentals and seductively arranged slow ballads, ideal for close dancing, a balance of repertory which they were undoubtedly the first to develop into a consistent policy with such a high level of performance skill. There hovered about them some of the spirit, elegance, and technical perfection of the late-twenties Whiteman band, godfather and mentor to so many bands of the early thirties, black and white, willing or reluctant. The Casa Lomans, of course, with but few exceptions would have none of Whiteman's more pretentious "concert arrangements," but the crisp energy of the Whiteman orchestra's finest jazz scores (like *Happy Feet*) and the urbane elegance of its more sentimental song material served as a generic model for their fresher, more youthful approach.

Among the white bands of that period the Casa Lomans certainly carved out a new stylistic niche imbued with the spirit of jazz, even if they missed much of the black essence. By 1931 they had gathered together an impressive front line of jazz soloists: clarinetist Clarence Hutchenrider, trombonist Pee Wee Hunt (his partner Billy Rauch handled all the lyric work in a way that antidated and often matched Tommy Dorsey's), trumpeter Joe Hostetter (later to be replaced by Grady Watts and Sonny Dunham), tenor-man Pat Davis, and a brilliant, technically self-assured drummer named Tony Briglia, much admired by the young Buddy Rich. These soloists were no match for those in Henderson's great band or Ellington's, or Chick Webb's and Cab Calloway's. But they knew the difference between jazz and dance music; they knew that even the smartest arrangements need the leavening of improvisation.

The Casa Lomans also knew about swing. They at least knew it existed and tried very hard to capture this elusive rhythmic element. Perhaps they even tried too hard. Very often their up-tempo performances took on a driven, mechanical rigidity, muscle-bound in its all-too-obvious exertion. But that is only a relative measurement; compared with almost all other white bands, they often succeeded where others did not even try. Further in their defense, it might be said that Gifford's generally technically challenging scores were hard to perform, with or without swing, and took much painstaking rehearsing. Often by the end of a prolonged rehearsal period, all spontaneity had been squeezed out of the performance; a kind of rhythmic *rigor mortis* would set in. Then, too, the particular on-the-beat rhythmic figures which Gifford favored, devoid of the loosening effect of syncopation, did not lend themselves to a deep, relaxed swing. Their swing was more driven and external, with a superficial peppy energy that, again, the college kids thought was just fine, not having ever heard any other.

And yet it seems to me unfair to land too heavily on the Casa Loma Orchestra's problems with real swing. None of the great black orchestras were entirely consistent in this regard either and, of course, often sacrificed clarity of articulation and balance, not to mention intonation, to swing. Moreover, very often individual soloists might swing, but the band as a whole would not find that rhythmic groove. But beyond that, it is simply inaccurate and unfair to characterize the Casa Loma band as uniformly unswinging, as is so often done in writing on the subject. We need only to listen to the February 1930 *San Sue Strut* to hear how forward-looking and adventurous they were in their rhythmic feeling for the time, playing, despite the complexity of the arrangement, with a fine sense of linear-horizontal swing. Even the slower and heavier-paced *China Girl*, recorded on the same date and hampered by a bowed bass, always a swing-inhibiting element, jogs along nicely with a comfortable relaxed beat. Much of this is due to Gifford's own steady but linearly conceived—that is, *non*-vertical—4/4 banjo beat. And there can be little doubt that he *tried* to instill that same long-line feeling in the band's arranged ensembles.

Compare these performances with those of Bennie Moten around the very same time—say, from October 1929 and October 1930. The choice of Moten for comparison is not an idle one. for if it is true that Moten's band was the progenitor of black Swing-Era orchestras, as epitomized by the Basie band in the mid-to-late 1930s, and that in the same way the Casa Loma band is often said to be the precursor of all the white swing bands, then we would by all reasonable reckonings expect the Moten band to be an epitome of early swing. Such, however, is not the case on the sessions mentioned above. Of course, two years later the most startling transformation had taken place in the Moten band, some of its December 1932 Victor sides counting among the greatest jazz masterpieces of their time and clearly heralding a new music to come. But at the turn of the decade Moten's band still knew little of swing, mostly plodding along with an old-fashioned, heavily stomping beat held over from its early 1920s' days. Even Count Basie, making his recording debut with Moten on these sides (*The Jones Law Blues, Small Black, Oh, Eddie*, among others), is far from swinging. So is the rest of the rhythm section of Willie McWashington (drums), Vernon Page (bass), and Leroy Berry (banjo). The latter, interestingly, did not play in a full 4/4 pattern, as did Gifford and Dave Wilborn (with McKinney), but rather with a choppy emphasis on beats 2 and 4. Again, an occasional individual soloist like trumpeter Ed Lewis, guitarist Eddie Durham or singer Jimming Rushing would find a modicum of swing, but this would not necessarily transmit itself to the whole band by any means.

Such comparisons could be made with any number of other bands, both black and white. So the question of the Casa Loma band's alleged inability to swing must be seen in perspective: compared with whom? And when? Seen only through the hindsight of hearing later swing bands, the Glen Gray orchestra can perhaps be dismissed as somewhat deficient in the realm of swing. And compared with the *very best* of Henderson and Ellington, the Casa Lomans are again no match. But even these illustrious black orchestras were far from consistent in infallibly maintaining swing.

The fact is that, as with so many bands of the late twenties and early thirties, Gray's Casa Lomans were no worse than most of their competitors. To put it another way, they were as variable and inconsistent in matters of swing and rhythmic spontaneity as all but the best black bands of the period. I suggest one cannot assess this element properly unless one has listened systematically to all of their recordings. Jazz historians have typically listened far too selectively and prejudicially, picking from a limited choice those favored records that would substantiate their point of view. This is especially easy to do with the Casa Loma band, for their repertory was quite varied, ranging from jazz instrumentals like *Casa Loma Stomp* and *White Jazz* to heady ballads like *Smoke Rings* and light ephemeral dance numbers like *Indiana* and *Do the New York*, my point being that many of these categories of pieces were not even intended to swing.

But beyond that, in the early thirties—indeed, well into the mid-thirties— swing was a quality and style element that very few bands even thought about, let alone achieved and mastered. On any objective and systematic comparative basis the Casa Loma band fares quite well, even if one acknowledges that in their best jazz instrumentals their *kind* of swing was somewhat mechanical and stiff. It rarely achieved that linear forward-leaning quality, the *inner* momentum, the rhythmic spontaneity, that we have taken for granted in jazz ever since the late thirties. The Casa Lomans created the *illusion* of swing with their young audiences—actually hardly anyone was calling it swing as yet, and their audiences would probably not have recognized *real* relaxed swing even if they heard it—by substituting rhythmic energy and precision. And these predispositions led to a kind of *vertical* on-the-beat playing that precluded swing in its highest and most relaxed linear form. It did, however, often bring them close to swinging by the sheer drive and energy and beat-to-beat momentum they brought to their up-tempo instrumentals.

On the other hand, Gifford and the Casa Lomans never really understood syncopation and the true essence of black rhythm. What Gifford took from Nesbitt were some of his specific arranging devices and innovative instrumentational ideas but *without* their intrinsic black musical content. In particular, Gifford and the Casa Lomans shied away from syncopation and rhythmic looseness. Either they did not understand what syncopation contributes to jazz and swing, or else they simply couldn't achieve it. I rather think it was the former. Syncopation *bends* the vertical rhythm into a linear or horizontal feeling. Listen carefully to the Casa Lomans' early recordings and you will hear—even in their improvised solos—an enormous concentration on unsyncopated, straight up-and-down quarter- and eighth-note rhythms.

But for the young white collegians of the early thirties, hell-bent on kicking up their heels, the razzle-dazzle energy and technical virtuosity and precision of the Casa Loma's "killer-dillers" was something new and utterly exciting. They did not, of course, hear Chick Webb or Duke Ellington or Fletcher Henderson or even Jimmie Lunceford until—perhaps—years later, by which time real swing had been introduced to a broad public by the Basie band, Benny Goodman, Charlie Barnet, and quite a few others.

The Glen Gray band—remember it was a cooperative orchestra—ought also be commended for making the transition so quickly from one of Goldkette's flowery, at best semi-hot dance orchestras (the name Orange Blossoms giving a fair idea of Goldkette's intent) into an unmistakable jazz unit. This metamorphosis took less than four months. The band's earliest sides[6] under their own name, at best what used to be called "hot dance music"—meaning an occasional 8-bar "hot" solo—featured sweet, vibrato-y trumpets and saxophones, sugary violin obbligatos, crooning vocals, and a pleasantly bouncing two-beat rhythm. But only three record dates later Gifford had already transformed the band into a *jazz* orchestra with the aforementioned jazz originals *San Sue Strut* and *China Girl*.[7] Apart from the already-cited qualities of these sides, mention must be made of another aspect in which Gifford truly excelled: the daring of his introductions and codas. I have pointed out elsewhere that this was also one of Nesbitt's specialties, particularly his strong definitive endings. But Gifford had his own special way with beginnings and endings. Of the former, *Casa Loma Stomp* and *San Sue Strut* must be singled out as remarkably original and modern in concept as well as execution. Interestingly, whereas in his introductions Gifford loved to separate the brass and reeds into contrasting units, in his codas he preferred to divide the orchestra along registral lines: low instruments against

---

6. In reality the earliest recordings by the Casa Loma band were made under the name of Johnny Burris (for the Gennett label in Richmond, Indiana, in March and April 1929). These sides, although arranged by Gifford, are basically in a sophisticated dance-band sweet style also favored by Paul Whiteman. One track, however, *So Comfy*, goes well beyond that limited goal, featuring a number of improvised solos and some fairly adventurous riffing in the later stanzas and the coda.

7. George Simon errs when he says in his book *The Big Bands* (New York, 1967) that "significantly, all six of the (Okeh) sides were up-tempo jump tunes, the sort that first attracted the collegians." In fact only two of the first seven (*sic!*) sides could be described as "up-tempo jump tunes."

high instruments, often in contrary motion and on separate rhythmic tracks.[8] Perhaps Gifford's most daring ending of this kind occurs on *China Girl*, although badly muffed by the band. (Either they ran out of rehearsal time or simply found it too difficult to play.) As rendered in Example 3 (in outline only), one can well imagine how the players of that time would be disoriented by the rhythmic complexity and instability of these four bars.

(Note that the two instrumental groups are an eighth apart, but that the rhythmic relationship between high and low instruments reverses briefly in the middle of bars 2 and 3 (indicated by dotted lines)—surely a disconcerting break in pattern for the upper-register players.)

Ex. 3

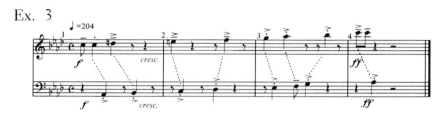

As mentioned, the work of the Casa Loma band was uneven; and much of this unevenness of quality came from the band's very versatility, its penchant to go off in many different directions more or less simultaneously: jazz orchestra, sweet band, dance band, dispenser of sentimental ballads (especially through their expert crooner, Kenny Sargent), deliverer of novelty vocals (with their talented trombonist-singer Pee Wee Hunt), and even "choral" numbers sung by vocal trios and quartets that came close to sounding like Fred Waring's or Lawrence Welk's singing groups.

In the early days "flag-wavers" like *Casa Loma Stomp*, *White Jazz*, *Black Jazz*, *Clarinet Marmalade*, *Wild Goose Chase*, and *Maniac's Ball* alternated with richly scored ballads like *Smoke Rings* and *Blue Prelude*, which featured trombonist Billy Rauch in a lyric style that anticipated (and almost matched) the later work of Tommy Dorsey. Most of the fast jazz pieces had a certain "steamroller" effect and soul-less, empty-headed, mechanical virtuosity for which the ballad pieces with their warm instrumental colors (muted trombones, soft saxes) offered some soulful compensation—as did the plain dance numbers like *Help Yourself*, *Do the New York*, and *Lucky Me*, all in the manner, if not the quality of Paul Whiteman's late twenties' dance style. Gifford and the Casa Lomans were not averse to stealing ideas from others, no more than the other bands

---

8. I believe that Gifford learned about such endings from Marvin Longfellow, Blue Steele's tuba player and arranger, now a forgotten name, but someone who, judging by his well-crafted arrangements interspersed with jazz solos, ought to be better remembered. Pieces like *Sugar Babe*, *I'm Leavin'!* (recorded in Savannah, Georgia, in 1927) give a representative idea of Longfellow's talents and of Steele's band; and note the sophisticatedly original coda. Incidentally, four of Steele's players—Gifford, Davis, singer-saxist Kenny Sargent, and trumpeter Frank Martinez (one of the earliest Beiderbecke disciples)—all ended up in the Casa Loma Orchestra by 1928.

which stole from *them*. For example, much of *Ol' Man River, Chinatown, My Chinatown, Blue Jazz*, and *Limehouse Blues* show direct influences of Duke Ellington—*Old Man Blues, Daybreak Express*, and Duke's amazing version of *Limehouse Blues* specifically. On the other hand, I am quite certain that Eddie Durham and the Moten band did some hard listening to Casa Loma's *Maniac's Ball*, recorded a whole year before Moten's *Toby* and *Lafayette*.

Some of the Casa Lomans' stiffness began to relax by 1932—in pieces like *Black Jazz, Limehouse Blues, Indiana, The Lady from St. Paul*—mostly because the rhythm section, especially bass player Stanley Dennis, was switching more and more away from the tuba to the string bass and a walking 4/4 beat.

Some pieces tried different avenues of approach, away from the Casa Loma's norm: *Blue Jazz* (with its Ellington-ish jungle effects), *Sophisticated Lady* (featuring soft flute and woodwind colors, and a muted violin stating Ellington's theme), and *Washboard Blues*. The last featured Connie Boswell, not only as vocalist but as arranger (at least in collaboration with Gifford) in one of her famous in-and-out-of tempo renditions.[9] Hoagy Carmichael's semi-tragic song, set by Boswell in almost operatic aria fashion, with a formidable array of contrasting tempos, instrumentations, textures, and moods, seemed an appropriately

---

9. Connie Boswell (1912–76) was one of the outstanding singers of the Swing Era. Originally part of the Boswell Sisters, a trio of New Orleans-born girl singers who began working professionally and recording in their mid-teens (in 1925!), Connie worked as a single after 1935 until her retirement in the 1950s.

The Boswell Sisters recorded prolifically in the early thirties—sister Helvetia also played violin, Martha the piano, with Connie sometimes doubling on cello—backed by such jazz musicians as Berigan, Goodman, Joe Venuti, Mannie Klein, the Dorseys, Eddie Lang, and the Dorsey Brothers Orchestra. Although the Sisters' recordings may strike us today with a certain dated period charm, it should be remembered that: a) they were the pioneers of this kind of vocal-group style and technique, influencing other vocal groups such as the Mills Brothers (not to mention the Andrews and McGuire Sisters of later years); b) they were the first to infuse popular vocalizing with a strong element of jazz (including the *instrumental* use of voices); and c) their performances, *heard in context*, are remarkably inventive and intricate, quite beyond anything of their time and even what their host of imitators managed to achieve.

Connie, in addition to being lead singer, was the group's arranger, fashioning not only the vocal parts but the instrumental parts of the arrangements as well. In this respect, she, along with Mary Lou Williams, was the first important woman arranger/composer in jazz. She was also remarkable for her early—and, for a white singer, very daring—absorption of black singing styles, especially the blues-singing of Bessie Smith, into what previously and otherwise generally was a field populated by white crooners, vaudevillians, and barbershop quartets. Connie was certainly a pioneer among white singers in using jazz inflection and phrasing, a "horn"-like approach to singing, a rhythmically spontaneous off-the-beat syncopated swinging style, and even what we might call a black-influenced jazz diction. Equally unusual was the use in her arrangements of frequent tempo changes—sometimes as many as six or seven in one piece—often at breakneck speed. All of this was absolutely unheard of in the early 1930s, and it is astonishing how well the trio and its jazz accompanists performed these complex and unpredictable scores. It should also be noted that Connie influenced a host of fine singers, such as Ella Fitzgerald, Mildred Bailey, and Peggy Lee.

A measure of Connie's outstanding talents and the breakthrough quality of her art can be gained by sampling some of her (and the Sisters') many recordings: for instance *It Don't Mean a Thing, Heebie Jeebies, There'll Be Some Changes Made, Rock and Roll* (sic) with the Jimmy Grier Orchestra, and the quite remarkable *Everybody Loves My Baby*.

lugubrious vehicle for those depth-of-the-Depression years. On the other hand, lacking as it did Boswell's dramatic talent and rich voice, the Casa Lomans' *In the Still of the Night* (1932), which received a similarly somber but stiffly played treatment, remained merely depressing. A real disaster came in the form of *Four Indian Love Lyrics*, a pastiche of fake native tunes, pretentiously scored in a semi-symphonic setting that had no relation to jazz or even dance music.

A standard feature of the Casa Loma band was its trombone duets, bringing together the virtuoso talents of Pee Wee Hunt and Billy Rauch.[10] *I Got Rhythm* and *Wild Goose Chase* are fine examples of this Casa Loma specialty.

By 1935 Gifford's reliability as chief arranger for the band had begun to decline. Among his last efforts were his own 1934 *Stompin' Around* as well as fine arrangements of *Chinatown, My Chinatown* and *Nagasaki* (a song whose intrinsic staccato passages were well suited to Gifford's Casa Loma style). Constant remakes of Gifford's earlier hits, particularly *Casa Loma Stomp*, served only to render those pieces increasingly mechanical and rigid (although the 1937 recordings of both *Casa Loma Stomp* and *Smoke Rings* are exceptions, superbly played and brought successfully into a high-level swing style). By 1935 the band began to drift seriously in its direction, clinging more and more to commercial exploitation of its two main singers: Kenny Sargent, the enormously popular balladeer and crooner (with a superbly controlled falsetto), and Pee Wee Hunt, whose humorous vocals, delivered in a Jack Teagarden-influenced drawl, were a successful foil to Sargent's syrupy confections.

Other changes in jazz and popular music were also beginning to impact on Glen Gray's Casa Loma band. After years of popular domination of the white market by them, Benny Goodman was taking over the lead with a "newer" brand of swing, and the whole field was exploding with young and highly competitive talent. Glen Gray turned to the twenty-six-year-old arranger-composer Larry Clinton, who was followed a year later by the excellent Dick Jones when Clinton left to form his own band, and still later by Larry Wagner, who gave Casa Loma one of its last big instrumental hits, the two-part *No Name Jive*.

The soloists of the band provided the only modicum of jazz continuity during these later years, although they too were often crowded out—more on records than on dances—by pop songs and other commercial ephemera. Apart from Hunt and their capable though somewhat uneven clarinetist Clarence Hutchenrider, the Casa Loma band offered Grady Watts, a most reliable straight-ahead (and unfortunately much underrated) trumpet player; Sonny Dunham, a virtuosically gifted but often overly ostentatious trumpeter (later bandleader in his own right), and tenor soloist Pat Davis.

Davis has been much maligned by jazz writers. He is perhaps an easy target because his playing was inconsistent, eccentric, and at times downright corny. And yet he was in his own peculiar way an original. At his best his solos com-

10. A minor mystery remains in regard to one of the band's earliest trombone-ensemble experiments, the 1930 *Alexander's Ragtime Band*. Here one clearly hears a trombone *trio* (with a more softly voiced trumpet playing a fourth harmony part *above* the trombones), although the discographies list only two trombonists, Hunt and Rauch.

bined great technical command and range with seemingly limitless energy. His originality came from an odd-ball way with musical ideas, analogous perhaps (though not similar) to someone like Pee Wee Russell or Frank Teschemacher. It seems to me that Davis, like Lester Young, was also enamored of Frankie Trumbauer's C-melody, white-ish, straight saxophone sound and transferred it, albeit in a more robust form, to the tenor sax. Indeed, Pat Davis occasionally makes one think of Young in certain notes, certain turns-of-phrases. Davis can be heard to good advantage on *Black Jazz, Stompin' Around, Nagasaki, Ol'Man River,* and the 1937 *Casa Loma Stomp* (on Decca). On the other hand, how inept Davis could be may be heard on *The Goblin Band* and *Jimtown Blues,* the kind of playing modern musicians nowadays make fun of. One can only hope that Davis, too, was being deliberately corny.

Trumpeter Watts is best heard on *Lazy Bones,* on which guest artist Louis Armstrong *sang,* not played *(sic), I Got Rhythm,* and *Chant of the Jungle.* Dunham's often spectacular, brash trumpet can be heard to advantage an *Ol' Man River* (perhaps his best work), *Wild Goose Chase, No Name Jive,* and *Nagasaki,* as well as his popular 1937 hit record of Eubie Blake's *Memories of You.*

Clarinetist Hutchenrider, another Casa Loma stalwart since 1931, was one of the band's most popular soloists. Although somewhat erratic technically, he always managed to infuse his solos with a kind of spontaneous free-spirit energy (best exemplified on *Blue Prelude, Clarinet Marmelade,* and *Dixie Lee*). In later years he modified his style to conform to the prevailing Goodman mode, in both tone and musical ideas. One of his best improvisations, however, was delivered on baritone sax on *I Got Rhythm.* A baritone solo was in itself an odd rarity in those days, and a full two choruses on that "unwieldy monstrosity" (as most sax players saw it) was absolutely unheard of. Hutchenrider acquitted himself well, especially in the nicely swinging second chorus.

A very gifted, highly unusual soloist in the Casa Loma band was the Canadian Murray McEachern, who played both alto sax and trombone. His lyric trombone style (in the Dorsey vein) gave the band *two* such players—the other was Rauch—although McEachern, like Lawrence Brown, could function well enough in more rhythmic jazz settings as well. His fine trombone work is heard on *Moon Country, Star Dust,* and *Boneyard Shuffle,* while McEachern's buoyant alto appears on *Georgia on My Mind.* Together Rauch, Hunt and McEachern comprised one of the finest trombone teams of the time. Hear them, for example, in *Chant of the Jungle, Drifting Apart, Out of Space,* and *Sleepy Time Gal,* the last two in superb lyrical arrangements by Dick Jones.

Such well-crafted, sophisticated arrangements—add those of Joe Bishop's *Out of Space* and Frankie Carle's *Shadows*[11]—managed to temporarily hold back the inroads of commercialism and a virtual takeover of the band's repertory by its vocalist Kenny Sargent. *Out of Space,* with its outstanding trombone choir and

11. Glen Gray recorded Carle's *Sunrise Serenade* with the composer at the piano just two months before Glenn Miller's hit record. Glen Gray's version, probably arranged by Larry Wagner, not only features Miller's clarinet-lead reed sound but a most astonishing quasi-atonal intro and coda, set in woodwind colors dominated by flute and bass clarinet.

Duke-ish muted brass colors, must have been familiar to the young Gil Evans before arranging *Robbins' Nest*, while there can be no question that the arranger of *Shadows* was *very* familiar with Richard Wagner's opera *Die Walküre*, lifting one of that opera's more innovative harmonic progressions straight out of the *Magic Fire Music*.

By the late thirties, Glen Gray and the Casa Lomans *had* learned to swing— in a sort of hard-working way (closer to Goodman than to Basie, let's say). But, of course, by then almost everybody had. The white band that ten years earlier pioneered "swing" was now but one of hundreds, and was struggling to keep up with the rest of the pack. The 1940 *No Name Jive*—as its name inadvertently implies—was an eclectic riff tune which brought together the diverse worlds of Basie (the riff formula), Ellington (the bolero-like build-up of *Crescendo in Blue*), Miller (the false-endings of *In the Mood*), and Goodman (a certain bouncy, bouyant, driving swing). And it was one of the very few pieces the Casa Lomans played that was based on the blues changes.

This brief history of one of the most active and most successful bands of the 1930s has at least, I hope, raised the possibility that the Casa Loma Orchestra will in the future be accorded more than the condescending footnote it has had to be contented with in the past.

DORSEY BROTHERS ORCHESTRA

The Dorsey brothers, Jimmy and Tommy, were prominent in jazz and popular music long before 1935 when each went his separate way to lead his own orchestra. The brothers had come to New York ten years earlier, after playing and touring with the Scranton Sirens and California Ramblers, and then soon established themselves in the burgeoning dance orchestra field as outstanding section players and sometime "hot" soloists. Sojourns with Jean Goldkette (in 1926), Paul Whiteman (1927), and the likes of Roger Wolfe Kahn, Vincent Lopez, and Rudy Vallee were interspersed with prolific recording activities in the New York studios as sidemen.

Here Jimmy was in direct but cordial competition with Benny Goodman, and he often substituted for the latter when Goodman was not available. Tommy's friendly "rival" was Glenn Miller, already trying to carve a niche for himself in musical circles as a trombonist and arranger. Tommy and Glenn were section mates on dozens of dates, learned a great deal from each other, and remained good friends and colleagues even when both led competing bands in the late thirties.

By 1928 Jimmy and Tommy had begun to organize semi-permanent bands of varying sizes and instrumentations, primarily for recordings and special engagements (including Broadway shows, as for example, Sammy Fain's *Everybody's Welcome* of 1931[12]). It was an exceedingly eclectic band for many years. If it did

---

12. This was the show for which the late Herman Hupfield wrote *As Time Goes By*, later to become famous in the Bogart-Bergman film *Casablanca*.

achieve any stylistic identity, it was in emulation of the Whiteman orchestra of the late twenties. And like that organization, which featured not only soloists like Bix Beiderbecke and Frankie Trumbauer but also superbly crafted arrangements by the likes of Bill Challis, Ferde Grofé, and Lennie Hayton, the Dorsey Brothers Orchestra made a point of adhering to a modicum of jazz by featuring such excellent sidemen as Charlie Margulies, Mannie Klein, Muggsy Spanier, Phil Napoleon, later on Bunny Berigan and George Thow, tenor player Skeets Herfurt, violinist Joe Venuti, guitarist Eddie Lang, drummer Ray McKinley, and Glenn Miller as chief arranger. Some of their better singers were Mildred Bailey, Smith Ballew, Bob and Bing Crosby.

Nonetheless, the main emphasis in the early years was on a commercial pop/dance repertory, mostly set in rather overblown, often string-laden arrangements. Just as Beiderbecke sometimes had to struggle to keep the true jazz flame alive in the Whiteman band, so players like Berigan and Napoleon had their work cut out for them when they were given the occasional 8-bar bridge solo or some other brief "hot" episode. The orchestra's ambivalent approach—trying to be all things to all people (including the sales-minded recording executives)—led to some very curious, now in retrospect almost humorous, period pieces like the 1928 *Indian Cradle Song*, *Evening Star*, and *Beside an Open Fireplace* (1930).[13]

The Dorsey Brothers' nearly two hundred recordings between 1928 and 1935 offer ample proof that neither Tommy Dorsey, who fronted the band, nor Jimmy, who was the much-featured prime soloist on clarinet and alto, were true first-calibre jazz players. Tommy's limitations as a jazz improviser were pretty severe. Although technically adroit, his jazzier solos were rhythmically somewhat stiff, conceptually hemmed in, and far from original stylistically or melodically. It was even then what we would now regard as a rather ordinary "Dixieland" approach. To be fair, though, Dorsey knew his jazz limitations and in recognition thereof eventually evolved his ravishingly beautiful romantic ballad style.[14] It is

---

13. Even more incongruous from a jazz point of view are two multi-side recordings made on two occasions by a huge orchestra built around the Dorsey Brothers nucleus, with added woodwind, horn, and string sections, as well as in one case no less than five vocalists: Smith Ballew, Hal Kemp, Nye Mayhew, Saxie Dowell, and Skinnay Ennis. One of these recordings was in fact conducted by the young Eugene Ormandy, who was at that time conductor of the Roxy Theatre orchestra on Broadway in New York. *Was It a Dream?*—a waltz—and Romberg's *Lover, Come Back to Me* (the latter with a 25-piece orchestra) were given lavish treatments of symphonic proportions by one George Crozier, with elaborate *rubato* introductions, modulations, codas, instrumental interludes. These musical extravaganzas were a misbegotten extension of the kinds of "concert" arrangements Bill Challis had been making for Whiteman, and one wonders what the Dorsey brothers had in mind in organizing these recordings. Hollywood films, I would suppose.

Both pieces were excellently played by all concerned, although it is a trifle disconcerting to hear a bit of brash Phil Napoleon trumpet next to a cloyingly sentimental oboe solo. *Was It a Dream?* even contains a brief *Klangfarben* passage—surely a first in popular music—during which a single pitch, F, is reiterated in eight different overlapping instrumental colors. Arthur Schutt, that astonishingly gifted and versatile pianist, even managed to sneak in a quotation from Puccini's *Tosca*: the famous opening chords with which the opera begins. While one may admire the musical sophistication which such a "highbrow" quotation represents, one wonders what it is doing in a quasi-jazz popular song, played by a Broadway dance orchestra.

14. For a further discussion of these matters, see Part 2 of this chapter on Tommy Dorsey.

rather startling, however, to discover that in those early years, in terms of jazz, Tommy was much more at ease, much more spontaneously creative on the *trumpet* than on the trombone. Disbelieving readers ought to hear Tommy's trumpet on pieces like *My Melancholy Baby, Dixie Dawn, Forgetting You* (all from 1928) to become convinced.[15]

It is interesting to follow the course of Tommy's development as a trombonist during these Dorsey Brothers years. His playing was at first basically jazzy in a rhythmically stiff restricted manner, and often projected with a hard leathery tone. To one accustomed to Dorsey as the suavely elegant, lyric trombonist of the later Swing Era, it is surprising to find that this ballad style makes a rather late and then only sporadic appearance on his recordings. It is there briefly, in embryonic form, on *Evening Star* (1928) and doesn't reappear until a whole year later on *Your Mother and Mine*.

Meanwhile, over a period of time Tommy's more rhythmic jazz playing lost some of its initial stiffness, although it also never lost a sense of uncertainty and lack of melodic invention. There is hardly a jazz solo or background obbligato during the 1928 to 1932 period on which Dorsey does not run into some note trouble, what musicians call "fluffs" or "clams." It is evident from the recordings that at some point in the early thirties Tommy decided to give up trying to become the world's best "hot jazz" trombonist and switched more and more to the lyric stylings with which he had experimented intermittently. It is clear that Jack Teagarden's arrival on the scene in New York helped Tommy to make up his mind as to which stylistic direction to pursue with his trombone. This is not to imply that he gave up all attempts to play jazz, but rather that he began to see where his real strengths lay and where, therefore, he could make a break-through success. That he could occasionally oblige with a quite capable jazz-style solo is exemplified by a number of later recordings, beginning with his unusual side-ending *a capella* cadenza on *St. Louis Blues* (1934) and a fine solo on *Tailspin* (1935).

The situation with Jimmy Dorsey was not much different. A great admirer of Rudy Wiedoeft, the spectacularly skillful popular saxophone virtuoso of the early 1920s, Jimmy could never entirely free himself of this influence, and one hears traces of Wiedoeft mannerisms in Jimmy's alto-playing well into the forties. Indeed, in the earlier years of the Dorsey Brothers band and even with his own post-1935 band, Jimmy was fond of featuring himself in flashy Wiedoeft-style solo numbers (like *Beebe, Oodles of Noodles, Dusk in Upper Sandusky*), which were at a considerable remove from anything one might call jazz. By the early and mid-thirties the Wiedoeft influence had been partially replaced by a sincere admiration for Johnny Hodges. But here, too, the playing remained largely imitative—at times, compared with the real Hodges, rather pallidly so—tending rather to the "pretty" and "facile."

As a clarinetist Jimmy was also quite eclectic, technically more than capable, of course, but ultimately beholden (at various times) to other prevailing clarinet

---

15. Jimmy Dorsey was *also* a fairly good trumpet player and can be heard soloing on the 1935 *That Eccentric Rag.*

styles, ranging from Goodman to Shaw and Herman, from Johnny Dodds to Barney Bigard.

I think the real root of the problem with the Dorsey brothers as *jazz* players was that in their formative years they never really heard—or did not hear sufficiently—the great black jazz innovators of the calibre of King Oliver, Louis Armstrong, Coleman Hawkins, Duke Ellington, Bubber Miley, and Bessie Smith. Though Dorsey senior, the boys' original music teacher, was a strict disciplinarian and undoubtedly gave the youngsters a solid technical foundation (and lots of experience in his parade and concert band), I suggest the contact with real jazz at best was intermittent, at worst superficial. Moreover, living and working on the East Coast and touring in Pennsylvania, New Jersey, and Ohio was not quite like working in Chicago, where the young Bix could hear Louis Armstrong every night, or where Benny Goodman could absorb the rich lessons of a Jimmy Noone. The Dorsey brothers, raised in a milieu of hard-working, struggling, unaffluent Pennsylvania coal miners, never lost that drive to hustle for a living, in *whatever* musical ambience or style, so long as it would keep poverty at bay. Somehow neither of them drank long enough at the true fountainhead of jazz. And it didn't take much to pull them away from jazz.[16]

Jimmy Dorsey was, of course, a formidable technician, on both the alto and clarinet; and if one searches for an answer to the perplexing question of why so many saxophonists, black and white—from Hodges to Parker and even Ornette Coleman—admired Jimmy Dorsey's work, one must turn to *that* aspect of his playing. It may come as a surprise to the passionate jazz fan reader with unalterable allegiances and strong musical/ideological leanings that most jazz musicians are not truly purist in their tastes. They will more readily admire an outstanding instrumental *technician*, of whatever stylistic persuasion, than a player who is creatively strong and individual but technically, say, "unspectacular."[17]

Jimmy Dorsey's technical skills did allow him, in turn, to be the versatile, wide-ranging eclectic he was—more than, in these respects, his more limited brother Tommy. While Jimmy was never a creative innovator, he was a gifted assimilator and could perform convincingly in a variety of idioms. Once one has accepted that, one is not quite so startled to hear Jimmy's remarkably beautiful and "authentic" blues-clarinet-playing as early as 1929 on *Praying the Blues*, an expressive tour de force. It is, of course, indebted to Dodds and Bigard and Omer Simeon, but it at least *is* the real thing. The real issue, then, is: if he could produce one such distinguished, convincing true sample of jazz, why not more often?

---

16. It is significant, for example, that after evolving a creditable swing style by the late thirties, Jimmy Dorsey in 1940 took off on a Latin tangent, achieving enormous popular and commercial successes with such numbers as *Brazil, Malagueña, Maria Elena, Six Lessons from Madame La Zonga*—none of them related to jazz in the slightest.
17. This also explains why Louis Armstrong and many black musicians could admire Guy Lombardo's saxophone section, why many black bands—from Duke Ellington across the spectrum—admired the Whiteman and Casa Loma bands. It may also be noted that popular *commercial* success often engenders respect!

Given the Dorsey brothers' eclectic searchings for an identity, both in their orchestra and as individual soloists, it is remarkable that they never succumbed to the widespread influence of the Casa Loma Orchestra. I cannot quite explain this, unless it is, again, a resistance on their part to stay clear of any single identifiable "jazz" style, which was certainly, for better or worse, how the Casa Loma band was perceived. Through the influence of its soloists and arrangers (which included by 1934, besides Glenn Miller, Fulton McGrath, Dick McDonough, Bobby Van Eps), the Dorsey Brothers Orchestra eventually evolved a light, airy, bouncy style in which the arrangement was primary, solos and improvisation secondary and incidental, but which at its instrumental best nevertheless achieved a pleasant danceable kind of swing jazz. Typical of the orchestra's work at that time were pieces like the 1933 *Mood Hollywood* and *Shim Sham Shimmy*, both pieces composed by Jimmy and both featuring solos by Bunny Berigan. (Berigan's very economical, wailing, blues-ish solo on *Shim Sham* is especially noteworthy.)

Rather *untypical* by then was the curious recording of *I'm Getting Sentimental over You*, the song that later became Tommy's theme and indelibly associated with his trombone. Tommy first played George Bassman's song when he was with Richard Himber's band briefly and realized that it would make an attractive ballad feature for himself. He recorded it in September 1932 with the DBO, to a resounding non-success. Though Tommy's ballad-playing was already of a rather high order—the tone perhaps a little slimmer, less mature than in later years—the accompanying arrangement was just short of disastrous. Inexplicably, the arranger set the piece in a lugubrious, dark, sustained organ-like manner (including a gloomy bowed string bass) that dragged the music down into a rhythmless morass. (The baby-ish, inept, virtually voiceless singing of one Jean Bowes did not help matters.) From such a performance it would have been hard to predict that in a few years this song would become Tommy Dorsey's all-time hit and, in its pleasant way, forever identified for millions with the entire Swing Era.

Almost as disappointing were the arrangements Glenn Miller made in the summer of 1934 of a series of older jazz standards: *Milenberg Joys, Basin Street Blues, St. Louis Blues, Weary Blues, Dippermouth Blues*. Although the soloists like George Thow and Jimmy Dorsey managed to maintain the looser, freer spirit of jazz, Miller's arrangements, of his still too experimental kind (see Part 2 of this chapter), were marred by stylistic incongruities—certainly in relation to the venerable "classic" jazz repertory here involved—and a fussy clutteredness that did not serve these simple pieces well. The results were rather mechanical and artificial as the players were caught at cross-purposes with the material.

It is not necessary to plot the highly erratic artistic course of the Dorsey Brothers Orchestra in great detail. It covered a broad spectrum, from the most obsequious commercialism and puerile pop and novelty songs (mostly with singers whose infantile croonings must be heard to be believed) to amiable dance numbers, laced with an occasional bracing jazz solo. It is finally a question of whether one wishes to remember the orchestra for its rare best or its plenteous mediocre.

At its best—as in the splendidly spirited *Fine and Dandy* (sparked by Charlie Margulies's inspired trumpet), *Fidgety* (1933), *Shim Sham Shimmy* (1933), *Stop, Look and Listen* (1934), *Tailspin* and *Dippermouth* (1935)—it contributed significantly to that gathering momentum that eventually led to the full flowering of swing.

JIMMY DORSEY

When Tommy, in one of his famous fits of temper, walked off the bandstand at the Glen Island Casino in New Rochelle, New York, in May 1935, the two brothers remained separated and not in communication for over ten years, until finally reunited temporarily in working together on the 1947 biographical movie, *The Fabulous Dorseys*. While in the wake of this breakup Tommy appropriated one of Joe Haymes's bands as his own, Jimmy simply continued with the personnel of the Dorsey Brothers Orchestra but now called it the Jimmy Dorsey Orchestra. His, and the orchestra's, popular and financial success were instantaneous. Continuing with the "sweet-swing" style the brothers had finally evolved before the big breakup, Jimmy's band managed a fairly broad repertory with taste (for the most part), as well as impressive instrumental skill and ensemble discipline. The many technically challenging arrangements (by Joe Lippman, Larry Clinton, Fud Livingston, Toots Camarata, Bobby Van Eps) were always carried off with efficiency and skill, the result of careful rehearsing. The expressive and emotional substance, on the other hand, was often rather thin, and the light-weight novelty numbers like *By Heck, Dr. Jekyll and Mr. Jibe, Parade of the Milk Bottle Caps* were still always there. But in balance, it was an orchestra which could with some justice regard itself as operating within the jazz arena, at least as jazz was viewed in the Swing Era by most white bands.

Jimmy's outstanding instrumentalist was clearly Bobby Byrne, who immediately took over Tommy's role after the big fight, and at times seems to have been an even more astounding player than Tommy. For one thing Byrne could handle a variety of stylistic assignments, including a fair representation of spontaneous jazz. Under Byrne's leadership, Jimmy's trombone section became the best group in the band and one of the very best trombone sections in the whole country. Whether in romantic ballad settings or in hard-driving, swinging, harmonized riffs, the trombones played with a degree of near-perfection in tonal blend and unity of phrasing that even the best of the rival bands could rarely match.

As for Byrne's solo work it was never less than outstanding, technically, musically. In his lyric solos it is at times easy to confuse him with Tommy Dorsey himself, so absolutely perfect was his absorption of his mentor's style. Indeed, as already suggested, Byrne could on occasion outclass the master himself. He was in fact a more versatile, relaxed jazz player than Dorsey, and more at ease in the uppermost trombone range, a register into which Dorsey rarely ventured. Byrne's jazz solos, cool, free flowing, structurally well-conceived, were in many ways well ahead of their time. He was in this sense—along with Jack Jenney—a transitional figure, looking ahead to the great white trombone virtuosos of a later day (Urbie Green, Bill Watrous). Building on Dorsey's and others' pioneer work, Byrne clearly represented the next generation of trombonists which, among other things—as the new technical and stylistic agility spread through the trombone world in the late thirties—prepared the way for the revolutionary breakthroughs of J. J. Johnson, Kai Winding, and Bill Harris.

Among Byrne's consistently fine work with Jimmy Dorsey, one can single out his beautiful *In a Sentimental Mood, At Your Beck and Call, Deep Purple, John Silver*, and a 1939 *Body and Soul*. To put this kind and quality of playing in a much larger context and perspective, one must say that no classical trombone player of the time could have come even close to matching, for example, Byrne's clean, effortless, elegant work on *In a Sentimental Mood* (1936).

Jimmy Dorsey's discography is much too filled with *Tulip Times, Robins and Roses, Killy-Ka-Lees*, and dozens of other pop ephemera of the time to be able to make a case for this orchestra as a jazz ensemble of first rank or of major importance. There were also far too many repetitious bouncy riff numbers (like *Chicken Reel, Hollywood Pastime, Dorsey Dervish, Mutiny in the Brass Section*), and—worse—those trite voodoo or jungle pastiches (like *Swamp Fire, What Makes Sammy Run*)—noodling clarinet solos over pounding tom-toms and "menacing" low trombones—that were all the rage in the Swing Era.

But Jimmy's band could manage at times to achieve a commendable swing, for example in *Stompin' at the Savoy, Don't Be That Way*, and *Major and Minor Stomp*, along with capable solos by Jimmy, trumpeter Shorty Sherock, tenor Herbie Haymer, trombonist Sonny Lee (who replaced Byrne in 1939), and tastefully supportive drumming by Ray McKinley. In a daring move for the time, Jimmy even hired a black singer, June Richmond, as his "girl vocalist"—although it cannot be said that her work here matches that of her later work with Andy Kirk.

By late 1939, when Joe Lippman came in as pianist and arranger, the Jimmy Dorsey orchestra had achieved a fairly full, rich, well-balanced sound, losing a lot of its earlier lightweight character. In such intelligent pieces as Lippman's *Turn Left, Turn Right, Murderistic, Aurora, Bar Rabble*, and the aforementioned *Major and Minor Stomp*, the band could now rank with the best of the white swing bands. And in the ballad department, Jimmy could easily vie with his competitors—in pieces like *It's the Dreamer in Me* and *Contrasts*, his theme song. Both were composed by Jimmy, the former featuring his very prettiest liquid clarinet tone, the latter (originally the contrasting "romantic" middle section of *Oodles of Noodles*) his Hodges-influenced florid alto.

Still, when in the early forties, well ensconced in the already mentioned commercialized Latin style, Jimmy's band attempted some of the most popular repertory of the day—*Jersey Bounce, Daybreak, Serenade in Blue, I've Got a Gal in Kalamazoo*—it was no match for brother Tommy's band or Glenn Miller's.

As with so many Swing Era bands, the ultimate assessment of the Jimmy Dorsey orchestra falls into that problematic area where commercialism, financial and competitive survival, and the seductions of mass popular appeal combine to undercut much of what the orchestra was actually capable of. It is probably fair to say that under these economic and extra-musical pressures, an orchestra like Jimmy Dorsey's never was able to achieve its full jazz potential. But in its minor way it did cling to that ideal well enough and long enough to earn a modest place in the history of American jazz.[18]

BOB CROSBY

The Bob Crosby orchestra was in its heyday quite special—and for a while one of the very best in the land. Organized as a cooperative by Gil Rodin from the nucleus of Ben Pollack's band after that group disbanded in 1934, the players hired Bob Crosby, the more famous Bing's younger brother, as singer and front man. Bob was also blessed with an excellent baritone voice—similar to brother Bing's but enhanced by an intriguing, attractive, slight quaver—and he had the kind of name recognition the new band needed, having already sung successfully for the Dorsey Brothers Orchestra. Fine singer though he was, Bob was not his orchestra's musical director or stylistic pacesetter. That responsibility fell to the band's arrangers—clarinetist Matty Matlock, tenor sax Dean Kincaide, and bassist Bob Haggart. With four of the band's leading members born and trained in New Orleans, there was present in the Crosby orchestra's original personnel— which also included trumpeter Hank Lawson, tenor sax Eddie Miller, drummer Ray Bauduc—the makings of a first-rate Dixieland-styled band. And there is more than a coincidental connection between the band's cooperative collective structure and its adherence to a collective improvisatory style of music.

By 1935 various bands had "experimented" with featuring jazz standards of an earlier era: Tommy Dorsey, the Dorsey Brothers Orchestra, Hal Kemp, Paul Whiteman—interestingly enough mostly white bands. But no orchestra pursued the rediscovery of New Orleans and early Chicago jazz as consistently and as authentically as the Crosby orchestra; and this right in the middle of the Swing explosion.

In looking back to an earlier repertory and style—a style thought by most jazz musicians and bandleaders of the time to be old-fashioned and obsolete—the Crosby band became in a way the first "jazz repertory orchestra," and the first to recognize that, even in 1935, jazz already had a venerable history and a worthy accumulated artistic tradition. While Armstrong's and Morton's great achievements of the 1920s were long forgotten and being roundly ignored—even by Armstrong himself—these young New Orleans-oriented musicians of the Crosby band remembered, and kept the music of the classic era of jazz current as a living, active music.

18. Jimmy Dorsey's band survived rather well into the 1940s and early 1950s, developing along moderately modern lines, at the same time maintaining—as a precaution—a good Dixieland combo.

After economic pressures in 1953 induced Jimmy and Tommy to reunite, Jimmy joined Tommy's orchestra—in effect reviving the Dorsey Brothers Orchestra —playing with that band until Tommy's tragic death in 1956 (choking to death in his sleep after a heavy meal). Despite ill health, Jimmy led the orchestra for another year, until he, too, was forced to turn the band over to trumpeter Lee Castle. Jimmy Dorsey died in June 1957.

Having said that, one must also note that the Crosby band's musical policy, unique and interesting though it may have been, was a safe and conservative one. It was anything but forward-looking, and it could, of course, count on the support of many jazz lovers, who were not at all sure about some of the new directions jazz was taking in the 1930s. It must also be said that the Crosby band played its fair shape of pop tunes—which was mainly Crosby's department—and typical swing instrumentals, although, at least until 1939, in a much healthier balance and proportion than most bands, including most black bands. Nor did the Crosby band embark upon a Dixieland policy the moment it began recording in mid-1935. After one lone early tryout of the idea in *The Dixieland Band* and *Beale Street Blues*, the next twenty-six sides were devoted to commercial Tin Pan Alley trivia (such as *Eeny Meeny Miney Mo*) and one popular swing instrumental, *Christopher Columbus*.

It wasn't until almost a year later, in mid-1936, when two Dixieland-style performances, arranged by Bob Haggart—*Muskrat Ramble* and *Dixieland Shuffle*—became popular successes, that the Crosby band began to pursue a more or less consistent policy of reviving New Orleans and Armstrong-associated material. Even at that, *Muskrat Ramble* and, a few months later, *Sugar Foot Strut* and *Come Back Sweet Papa* (both pieces Armstrong had recorded in the 1920s) were sneaked in at the end of sessions otherwise devoted to pop vocals by Connie Boswell and Judy Garland.

The eventual success of the Crosby band's jazz repertory with a fairly large public was in fact based on a compromise: a blending of the new big band sound of swing with the freedom and loose-textured spontaneity of small-group Dixieland. Matty Matlock and, especially, Bob Haggart were responsible for this successful stylistic fusion, and many of the most memorable recordings and performances of the Crosby band are attributable to their talent and inspiration.

The recorded titles tell the story of the band's commitment to the New Orleans heritage, ranging from *High Society* to *Milenberg Joys*, from *Wolverine Blues* to *Jazz Me Blues* and *Original Dixieland One-Step* to *South Rampart Street Parade*. The band's many superb performances tell the rest of the story. [19]

For their playing of, say, *Between the Devil and the Deep Blue Sea* or *South Rampart Street Parade* or *Panama* was anything but a drab, polite dusting off— or conversely an overly raucous rehashing—of these old standards. They played these pieces with love and understanding, with a combination of respect and great zest, an exciting spirited rhythmic drive that led to inspired performances and made the pieces sound new and fresh again.

Unquestionably, the Crosby band had just the right complement of players to carry out its various assignments, especially on the jazz side. It was that rare happenstance when a group of players and a style are perfectly and happily

---

19. Nonetheless, it is to revise history and, at best, rather misleading to make the Crosby band look even "purer" than it was, as many of the Decca and Coral reissues have done, by re-releasing *only* the best of the Dixieland pieces. The fact of the matter is that out of the well over 300 titles the Bob Crosby band recorded between 1935 and 1942, a good 280 were pop tunes, sentimental vocals, and a dozen or so swing instrumentals. Fewer than forty sides were devoted to genuine Dixieland jazz numbers.

matched. Indeed, one is amazed in retrospect at the extraordinary consistency of all the main soloists: Lawson, in later years Billy Butterfield; Matlock, in later years Irving Fazola; trombonist Warren Smith, later Floyd O'Brien; Eddie Miller; the three pianists, Bob Zurke, Joe Sullivan, and Jess Stacy; and most outstandingly Haggart and Bauduc, both of them the rhythmic driving force behind the entire band. Bauduc was an inventive, disciplined drummer of the Baby Dodds and Zutty Singleton school, and an important contributing member of the band—although occasionally his playing could become overbearing. In general, all these players set and maintained uniformly high standards, expressively and technically, both in their solos and disciplined well-balanced ensemble work. Indeed, it is difficult to find a bad or mediocre solo by Lawson or Matlock or Miller.

And as for Haggart, he was not only a remarkably gifted arranger but a strong bass player, one of the first to solo consistently on the bass and probably the first white player successfully to "walk" bass lines in the manner of Walter Page. His fine work can be heard on any number of Crosby band performances—and, of course, on his famous 1938 hit record in duet with Bauduc, *Big Noise from Winnetka*. Hardly a masterful composition—indeed it seems to me an only slightly more sophisticated attempt to create a popular hit in the manner of Goodman's *Sing, Sing, Sing—Big Noise* is at least technically quite accomplished. Haggart's use of a variety of pizzicato effects and articulations, including one in which *both* hands alternate in fast string-plucking (an effect Milt Hinton and Pops Foster had been working on for some time), another passage using between-the-cracks microtones, these and his good firm beat keep even this creatively limited opus quite interesting. Shorter "walking" solos by Haggart occur on many records, such as *I Hear You Talking, Run Rabbit Run, Hindustan*, or his beautiful contrapuntal line in *Vultee Special* (Ex. 4) behind O'Brien's tightly-muted trombone solo.

Ex. 4

Another outstanding player was Eddie Miller, and I would guess he was one of the very few tenor saxophonists of that time whose sound and style could have fitted into a Dixieland concept. (The tenor saxophone was not a regular part of the so-called "front line" instruments of traditional early New Orleans jazz.) Miller's lean tone, agile technique, and energetic rhythm were the perfect counterpart to the three other prime "horn" soloists: clarinet, trumpet, and trombone. There are, in fact, numerous instances of a four-way collective improvisation with Miller's tenor as the fourth polyphonic voice, one of the most glorious of these occurring in *Milenberg Joys* (excerpted here in Ex. 5).

Miller's solo work with Crosby—and indeed throughout his career—was of a consistently high order. His statements, whether brief or extended, were almost

Ex. 5

always well constructed, logical, coherent, and above all in concord with the prevailing mood or character of the composition at hand. And yet his playing was never merely submissive or accommodating to its context; it was in fact highly individualistic, particularly in the sense that Miller was one of the very few tenor players who did not succumb to the influence of the major saxophone styles of Hawkins, Webster, Chu Berry, and Herschel Evans. If anything, Miller's playing displayed a close kinship to Frankie Trumbauer and Lester Young. One could not call him an early "cool" player, for he played with much too much intensity and relentless rhythmic drive to warrant such an appellation, but his lean, almost vibrato-less tone was far removed from the "over-heated," "dramatic" styles of the Hawkins school. Oftentimes Miller's streamlined, linear style and lithe tone remind one of early Lester Young and sometimes even, as in *Eye Opener*, of the young Stan Getz. Miller was, to be sure, not as spontaneously creative and rhythmically loose as Young, but he certainly aspired to the same kind of clean, incisive, intelligent, melodically linear approach. Outstanding Miller solos, too numerous to enumerate here, abound on virtually all Crosby band tracks. As one sample, picked at random out of many, the reader might do well to hear his work on *Swingin' at the Sugar Bowl*.

Similar laudatory comments can be made about Lawson and Butterfield, who probably did their finest career work with the Crosby band. Lawson, who played with the band—and in the small Dixieland group within the big band, known as the Bob Cats—during two different periods (1935 to mid-1938 and again in 1941 and 1942), provided a dynamic leadership with his powerful expressive tone and attack and constantly inventive improvisations, albeit in a conservative post-Louis Armstrong style. There is many an exciting climactic final chorus in which Lawson, always energetically supported by Bauduc and Haggart, leads his troops to triumphant joyous victory. To hear the Crosby band at its most brilliant, in full cry, led homeward by Lawson as in *South Rampart Street Parade* or *Who's Sorry Now?*, is to know the incomparable joy and excitement of collective music-making in the hands of a group of highly compatible musicians, led with irresistible fervor by a musician of Lawson's calibre and integrity.

Of the three major pianists that played with the Crosby band over the seven years of its existence, I find Bob Zurke the most interesting and original. Zurke, who died in 1944 at the age of thirty-three, spent almost three years with the Crosby orchestra and the Bob Cats. His sometimes wild, almost undisciplined playing lent to the two Crosby groups a dynamic hurricane-like force, that was light years removed from the polite babbling of most 1930's band pianists. Zurke's playing was often quite "impolite," at times even slightly incoherent, but one always knew when listening to him that one was having some kind of remarkable encounter or experience. It might be a rambunctious, jerkily rhythmic solo that conjured up pictures of a bucking bronco; at other times the astonishing independence of his two hands and ten fingers led him into the most complicated contrapuntal mazes (as in *Little Rock Getaway*), from which he would always extricate himself just in time.

Occasionally the juxtaposition of Zurke and Miller created a kind of irresolvable stylistic friction. There was sometimes no way that Zurke's vertical, stomping, hell-bent playing, with wrong notes that somehow didn't sound wrong, could meet with Miller's controlled, precise, linear playing on any common ground.

Joe Sullivan and Jess Stacy, Zurke's successors in the Crosby band, were more eclectically inclined, less rhythmically compelling. And although they contributed many a fine moment to the orchestra's performances, their work seems to me in its totality less striking than Zurke's.

Of the two clarinetists the Crosby band had—Irving Fazola, also from New Orleans, was added in 1938 and succeeded Matlock as prime soloist a year later, but (like Lawson) Matlock returned to the band in mid-1940—Matlock was certainly the more original and significant contributor, as already mentioned, through his first-rate arrangements but above all through his outstanding true New Orleans-style clarinet-playing.[20] Fluent in all registers of his instrument, Matlock could play with a full, rich, chalumeau, low-register sound; deliver a more assertive middle-register raspy-toned playing (as in *Old Spinning Wheel*); he could "sing" intensely (as in *Gin Mill Blues*), or soar above the orchestra in brilliant high-register flights (as in any number of final out-choruses). The extraordinary *That Da Da Strain* (1942) seems to combine all of these elements in one performance. Matlock and Lawson were a remarkable team in collective ensembles, driving and prodding each other, complementing each other, and ingeniously staying out of each other's way.

Fazola was in general a more easy-going, subdued, less original player and by heritage more out of the Jimmy Noone clarinet school. He used his warm, beautifully rounded tone to best effect in slower numbers, lyric solos and ballads. (Hear him, for example, on *Sympathy* (1940) or *My Inspiration*.) In up-tempo swing instrumentals, he often sounded very much like Benny Goodman. Indeed, in a blindfold test of the spirited *The World Is Waiting for the Sunrise* of February 1939, the most acute ears might be fooled into thinking the clarinetist was Goodman—albeit a less brilliant Goodman. On the other hand, a measure of Fazola's limitations can be taken on his rather mechanical rendition of *Jazz Me Blues*, or that national anthem of New Orleans marching jazz, *High Society*, where Fazola plays the famous traditional clarinet solo more or less "correctly" but without the drive and spirit that the rest of the band gives even this famous warhorse.

Clearly the poorest player in the Crosby band was its guitarist, Nappy Lamare. A fair rhythm guitarist, Lamare too often could not keep his harmonic changes straight. There are many lapses of this kind in his playing, as on *Savoy Blues*, and his attempt at a solo in *Loopin' the Loop* with the Bob Cats is embarrassingly bad.

It must be clear from all of the above that Bob Crosby himself, at least from a specifically musical point of view, had virtually no influence on the jazz aspects of the band's repertory. But as previously suggested, we must not forget—

---

20. This clarinet style survives today, to my knowledge, mainly in the playing of the contemporary New Orleans clarinetist, Pete Fountain.

in our enthusiasm over its brilliant Dixieland work—that, in order to survive, it too had to cater to the nether tastes of swing audiences and recording executives. This is where the handsome, affable Crosby, pleasant and uncontroversial, could satisfy the more pressing commercial needs of the orchestra. But even here, one of the reasons one can admire a large part of the Crosby band's output is that it tried to invest even the silliest pop trivia with a modicum of jazz feeling, jazz rhythm, jazz energy, and jazz creativity. In pieces like *Vieni, Vieni*—or in the "Indian" vogue so popular with late-1930s' swing audiences, *Big Chief De Soto*—the band generally managed to rescue these works from blatant commercialism and bring them back into the world of jazz by high-spirited improvisations and hard-driving ensembles. In better material, like *Coquette* or *Fidgety Feet*, the band fared even better and could achieve real greatness. The band, of course, had to play its fair share of orthodox swing numbers—pieces like *Cross Patch, I've Hitched My Wagon, It's Wonderful*, the rather labored *Tit Willow, For Dancers Only, Christopher Columbus*. When Glenn Miller's new dance band sound swept the land in mid-1939, the Crosby orchestra was not above immediately emulating it—and very well at that. (Sample their pleasant Latin-flavored *Boogie Woogie Maxixe* or *Blue Orchids* and *Ooh, What You Said*.)

The Crosby band experienced two down periods, when its jazz quotient was at a low ebb and pop ballads or novelty tunes threatened to take over. The first was during 1938, when a whole sequence of pieces seemed intent mainly on pleasing an uncritical public. *March of the Bob Cats* and *Big Crash from China*, filled with swing and pseudo-jazz clichés, catered to ever lower audience tastes. *Speak to Me of Love* is a virtually incoherent mélange of tired old Dixieland licks and empty vocalisms (by Marion Mann), which even Billy Butterfield's golden trumpet sounds could not rescue. The nadir of infantilism was reached in the silly lyrics of *Big Bass Viol*, featuring also one of the earliest string bass solos, well played by Haggart but otherwise awful material. As Charles Ives would have said in an analogous context: "This one's for the rubes."

Waldteufel's *Skaters' Waltz*, Gershwin's *Summertime* (in a wooden hotel-band type of arrangement), and the simplistic Dixieland nonsense of *Stomp Off, Let's Go* did not help matters much. The band seemed to have lost its inspiration and sounded tired and apathetic. Only the aforementioned *My Inspiration* and a superb Butterfield performance of Haggart's fine ballad *I'm Free* (later known as *What's New?*) seemed to retain some of the earlier qualities and musicianship.

Spirits seemed somewhat revived—at least temporarily—with the emergence of the velvet-toned Irving Fazola as one of the major featured soloists of the band. It was during this period that arrangers Matlock and Haggart consolidated their fusion of Dixieland and swing, a pleasant hybrid, typified by such pieces as *Washington and Lee Swing* and *Air Mail Stomp*, which seemed to please a wider audience spectrum. A momentary high point was reached with the stunning performances of *Air Mail Stomp* and *Peruna*, the latter one of the Bob Cats' all-time best, only marred by Joe Sullivan's frantic rushing in his solo chorus.

But another decline, mostly in choice of material, hit the Crosby band in late

1939, lasting well into 1940, a period during which the orchestra had replaced the mighty Benny Goodman on Camel Caravan, radio's most popular musical show of the time. Marion Mann's pallid vocals now dominated completely, and even Crosby himself had difficulty in finding a place for his own singing on records. The Bob Cats, supposedly a small-group Dixieland jazz ensemble, spent most of their time accompanying singers. Great artistic achievements (sic) like *I, Yi, Yi, Yi, Yi* and *Chick-Ee-Chick* took priority over even *A Gay Ranchero!*

Eventually even the public had enough of these sillinesses, and the Crosby band's recording activity declined dramatically in 1941. But somehow—sparked by the return of both Matlock and Lawson to the band—the old energy and drive and commitment to jazz were renewed. In January 1942 a spate of recordings, featuring fine pieces like *King Porter Stomp, That Da Da Strain, Brass Boogie,* and *Milenberg Joys,* revitalized the band considerably. But the victory of jazz over pop was short-lived, and after Stacy's charming blues, *Ec-Stacy* (with its gentle echoes of Bix Beiderbecke's *In a Mist*) and Phil Moore's[21] Strayhorn-influenced tributes to impressionism, *Black Zephyr, Black Surreal,* the Crosby band accomplished very little of quality.

The orchestra disbanded in late 1942 when Crosby went to Hollywood to work in the movies. After military service in World War II, he resumed band-leading, but with little success. A variety of film roles, a career in business, and intermittent revivals of the Bob Cats complete the Crosby biography. Lawson and Haggart, along with Butterfield and Miller, on the other hand, in 1968 formed the *World's Greatest Jazz Band*—an obnoxious name—playing the old Dixieland repertory (until 1974) with a spirit and fire which made them the envy of many a much younger player.

The Crosby orchestra was the first big band to develop along pronounced Dixieland lines, and it gave the old repertory new life, which even many of the revivalist bands of the 1940s could not manage. They imbued the old repertory with a spirit, an energy, *and* a technical command which were clearly of the thirties, reflecting the advances made in the years since the music was first created. It was not a group in which subtlety or orchestral refinement—or any kind of progressive adventurousness—had a place. It was a "hot" jazz band but—anomalously—solidly conservative in its outlook. It was not even, considering its consistent emphasis on up-tempo Dixieland jazz material, a proper dance band, except perhaps for jitterbugging. It *was* more of a true jazz orchestra than most, and it had a degree of musical integrity far beyond most Swing Era bands, black or white. Indeed, considering how popularly successful the band was—measurable in one respect by the fact that it appeared in the recording studios about four or five times a month—it is amazing how much genuine jazz it managed to perform. And for that, we can almost forgive the band for virtually never playing less than f.

21. Phil Moore was an interesting figure on the periphery of jazz. Although a pioneer of the block-chord style of piano and a fine song composer, Moore drifted increasingly into arranging for radio and films, arranging for and coaching popular singers (most notably Lena Horne, Dorothy Dandridge, and Martha Raye).

The Crosby band's view of jazz may have been a limited one, but it espoused that view with such conviction and authority, that we cannot but fail to honor its role in the history of jazz of the Swing Era. From the early *Royal Garden Blues* to the late *Sugar Foot Stomp* it kept the flame of a certain important lineage of jazz alive.

PAUL WHITEMAN

Whatever jazz qualities the Paul Whiteman orchestra had attained by the late twenties—with the arrival of Bix Beiderbecke and Frankie Trumbauer as well as the arranging talents of Bill Challis, William Grant Still, Lennie Hayton—these were unfortunately more or less dissipated in the thirties. In that decade the Whiteman band's work can only be described as erratic and diffuse. Even the relatively brief tenure of Bunny Berigan—from mid-1933 to November of that year—did little to elevate the band's overall creativity. Jazz fared a little better in the Whiteman band when the two Teagarden brothers joined it for a few years, but all in all the thirties were years during which the orchestra, technically very proficient and versatile, vacillated between too many stylistic directions: pop songs, novelty numbers, semi-classical works (including many of the major concert works of Grofé and Gershwin), some attempts at Dixieland reviving—and, occasionally, some spirited jazz.

The problem was one of leadership, both on Whiteman's part and his arrangers, themselves quite diverse in *their* talents and stylistic tendencies: Fud Livingston, Toots Camarata, Joe Mooney, and the eminent classical composer Adolph Deutsch.[22] What evolved on average was a skillful dance and show band.

With the orchestra's large instrumentation, still always including a small string section, the tendency was to over-arrange the simple dance and pop tunes. But even its more pretentious scores now lacked the virtue of any stylistic focus or individuality. They were randomly eclectic, often in a rather banal way, and rigidly played. Although the band could swing—one of the key players who *always* tried to see to that was bassist Art Miller—too often the more overblown scores collapsed under their own weight. At other times the results were merely "peppy" and stiffly vertical. Charlie Teagarden on trumpet seemed most able to ignore his confusing surroundings and play excellent, consistent straight-ahead jazz. But one or two players do not a jazz orchestra make, and when the Teagardens left in 1939 the relatively sporadic glimpses of jazz faded to nothingness.

Whiteman's attempts at reviving some degree of creative spontaneity met with some success in 1939 in his special instrumental groups: the Bouncing Brass (featuring not only Charlie Teagarden but trombonists Miff Mole and Buddy Morrow and drummer George Wettling), the Sax Octette (featuring four saxes, three flutes, an oboe, and a two-guitar rhythm section),[23] and his Swing Wing.

22. Adolph Deutsch, a London-born composer, is most famous for his excellent Hollywood film scores, notably *High Sierra*, *The Maltese Falcon*, *The Mask of Dimitrios*, and *Some Like It Hot*.
23. I suspect this group was a model for some of the early Alec Wilder Octets and Eddie Sauter woodwindy arrangements for Mildred Bailey in 1939 and 1940.

But the problem too often was repertory, the shoddy material with which the musicians and arrangers had to work (e.g. *Three Little Fishies, I Kiss Your Hand, Madame*). Still, an occasional glimmer of creativity and spontaneity did emerge. *Blue Skies* (with the Sax Octette) and *Heat Wave* and *I've Found a New Baby* (with the Bouncing Brass) have much to offer and were in any case superbly played.

This last fling with a *kind* of jazz came too late and too little. In effect, swing and more advanced forms of jazz had passed Whiteman by. Whether it was the intrinsically jazz-rooted music of the Lunceford band or Fletcher Henderson's work for Goodman or Eddie Sauter's advanced scores for Goodman—not to mention Ellington and Basie—all this music achieved more directly and imaginatively the quality, the challenging demands Whiteman in the thirties always talked about, claimed to aspire to, but only too rarely realized.

History was to repeat itself some fifteen to twenty years later when a man named Stan Kenton pursued some of the same goals with not too dissimilar results.[24]

PART 2

GLENN MILLER

The phenomenal popular success of Glenn Miller and his orchestra, beginning in 1939, became one of the great legends of American popular cultural history. In terms of statistical record-breaking, the band's popularity was unprecedented, shattering attendance and sales records that in some cases had stood for decades, breaking even the more recently established ones of Benny Goodman and Kay Kyser.[1] Miller's tragic death in 1944, after enlisting and then leading an outstanding forty-two-piece Air Force orchestra for several years, only served to fan the legend, and for millions of now older Americans his name and music still carry an undiminished aura of nostalgia and fondest musical memories.

Miller's music represented a vital social moment in the vast majority of young and middle-aged Americans' lives, and the distinctive sound of his orchestra is indelibly etched into the American consciousness. Its famous reed section sound was a musical phenomenon for which one is hard put to find many parallels, certainly in Western music. For while all great composers have their special sound—an amalgam of specific harmonic usages, voice-leading and instrumentation—it is hard to think of anyone with a sound quite so unique, quite so mesmerizing—and, more astonishingly, so resistant to becoming tedious. One

---

24. Stan Kenton and his orchestra will be dealt with in detail in Volume III of this History.

1. Kyser's band gained enormous popularity through its Kollege of Musical Knowledge radio program (from 1938 through the late 1940s). Kyser, although he played no instrument, always maintained a fine orchestra, playing essentially in the late-thirties' Glenn Miller style, featuring good musicians and a stable of good pop and novelty singers, most of whom were superior technically to many of the more highly touted dance-band vocalists. The Kyser band had a remarkable blend and balance and could, when required, play with an infectious rhythmic swing, especially with the long-time Glenn Miller drummer, Maurice Purtill, driving it.

has to go outside Western culture to Japanese *Gagaku* or Hindu music to find a sound so singularly distilled and unvariedly consistent in its use (although, needless to say, in the latter regard, Miller's few decades are no match for the others' millennia).

But to keep this discourse in perspective, we must remind ourselves that Glenn Miller's "sound" is only that: a sound, a sonority mixture. It is not a style, a language, an idiom, nor even a musical concept—at least not a large one. It is perhaps not much more than a dialect. But for all its lack of scope, it was nevertheless very special and able to penetrate our collective awareness in a way that few other sounds have, even those by musical masters infinitely more creative than Miller.

Ironically, Miller's rather sudden success in 1939 must be counted as one of the great musical/social surprises of the decade, matched only by Goodman's equally tide-turning sudden success at the Palomar Ballroom four years earlier. And like Goodman, who had struggled for nearly a decade in the popular music field, Miller had been at it as an arranger and trombonist for even longer. Indeed, Miller and Goodman had traveled much of the same professional routes. The reader will recall that Goodman and the five-year-older Miller first worked together in Ben Pollack's band in California in 1925. Miller, along with Tommy Dorsey, was a sideman with Goodman on hundreds of recording dates and dance jobs in the late twenties and early thirties. That both of their efforts to establish bands and to create a distinctive orchestral style were thwarted for many years may seem, in view of their later extraordinary successes, rather odd. But a closer look at the circumstances yields at least some possible explanations.

I believe that for bands like Goodman's or Miller's or Dorsey's to succeed in the particular way they did, a whole interrelated series of events and influences had to merge into a unique constellation. These developments, highly complex in their myriad details, can be winnowed down to the following major points: Armstrong's creation of a distinctive rhythmic language of jazz, along with the simultaneous development of several related orchestral and ensemble concepts which were able to incorporate the improvisatory nature of jazz into written/ arranged/memorized forms, set the stage for jazz to become among other things the primary American entertainment and dance music. Its proliferation, fed in turn, by the enormous growth of the American popular song and the parallel technological developments of radio, recordings, and film, attracted an extraordinary influx of gifted musicians, skilled craftsmen in their own rights, who readily assimilated the lessons of Armstrong and Henderson, and thus created a whole new professional environment for the developing music. Once the skilled white musicians had assimilated the primary ingredients of jazz from their black mentors and colleagues, they were ready to purvey the new music in styles that in turn found a previously untapped public. This public did not know that its white musical idols, bandleaders or instrumentalists, had acquired their jazz and swing conceptions from the blacks. But once that racial threshold had been crossed, jazz in its new form, now labeled "swing," was not only acceptable to large masses of new audiences but became in itself a self-generating and quickly proliferating new entertainment industry. At that point the constellation was set which would allow Goodman and then Miller, in essence emulating Goodman's example—with Dorsey and Shaw and many others in between—to create their own more commercially successful jazz and at the same time, because a *market* now existed, generate such astounding financial successes.

The kind of mass success Miller had can only be achieved with a music which is both simple and single-mindedly distinctive, reduced to an easily recognizable formula. And this—eventually—Miller accomplished to a T, whether fully consciously or in part inadvertently, is hard to say. But then the processes of invention and creativity in the arts are not entirely rationally explicable. They remain mysterious and defy exact analysis. And for their most hidden aspects we reserve the word "inspiration."

It seems clear, however, that in some dim and groping way Miller had been looking for "the sound" for a long, long time. Miller's early career is interesting from the point of view that it clearly prepared him for the kind of eclectic direction with which his music eventually triumphed. He was a versatile musician who, both as a far from outstanding trombonist and a constantly explorative arranger, could work on both sides of the stylistic fence: either in a kind of semi-improvised jazz, as with the various future-star-studded Ben Pollack bands, the Red Nichols groups, and the Dorsey Brothers orchestra, or in more commercial but still jazz-related settings of Broadway shows (like Gershwin's *Strike Up the Band* and *Girl Crazy*). By 1932 Miller was arranger and musical director for a band led by the very popular singer Smith Ballew.[2] In early 1935, Miller organized and arranged for Ray Noble's very successful American orchestra, playing trombone with the band as well.[3] It is significant that its sophisticated arrangements, fashioned by Noble and Miller, ranging from pseudo-Chicago-style jazz to fancily dressed-up jazz standards and sweet ballads, are in concept very similar to those of Miller's Air Force orchestra. Since the latter embodied Miller's musical ideals, again aligned to a massive public appeal, more even than his famous civilian band, it became clear where Miller's real predilections as arranger lay all along. The consistent contact with the commercial worlds of Broadway, Hollywood, and the Brill Building—all far, far removed from the mainstream of (black) jazz—obviously took hold of Miller. But by 1935 swing was in; and Miller, though at first reluctantly, began to assimilate a compromise formula which was essentially in the Goodman-via-Henderson swing camp, while still retaining its close ties to the world of popular music. Though it may sound shocking at first, it turns out that Miller's fabulously famous 1939–42 band actually represented a stylistic detour, which ironically World War II allowed him to "correct" with his Air Force orchestra.

2. Ballew was later to claim that Miller's first recordings as a leader in 1935 used *his* band. But evidently Ballew's memory was somewhat hazy since, although Miller used Ballew as vocalist on two of the four 1935 sides, that band consisted of sidemen from Ray Noble's orchestra with a few other non-Ballew musicians, temporarily working in New York, added.
3. It was also during this period that Miller studied with Joseph Schillinger (1895–1943), a Russian-born composer and theorist well-known for his posthumously published the *Schillinger System of Musical Composition*. Among Schillinger's many famous students were George Gershwin and (also Russian-born) Vladimir Dukelsky, better known on Broadway as Vernon Duke and the composer of *I Can't Get Started* and *April in Paris*.

Miller's early recordings of 1935 are eclectic in the extreme. Very prominently featuring a string quartet, as well as fine jazz soloists of the calibre of Bunny Berigan, Charley Spivak, clarinetist Johnny Mince, tenor-man Eddie Miller, and drummer Ray Bauduc, these performances are a veritable kaleidoscope of all known styles and effects in jazz and popular music (or even outside this realm as, for example, the direct lift from Tchaikovsky's *Romeo and Juliet* in A *Blues Serenade*). These musical mosaics at least show Miller's extraordinary versatility as an arranger, although it also becomes clear why these records had little success, especially against the by now well-coalesced Henderson arranging style, spreading like wildfire through the land. Evidently Miller was not aware of this in his Broadway and Rainbow Grill world, or simply didn't believe in it. And Miller, unlike Goodman, had no John Hammond to steer him in the right direction.

By January 1937, after arranging stints with Glen Gray and the likes of Ozzie Nelson and Vincent Lopez, Miller was determined to form a full-time swing band of his own. The six sides cut for Decca in March 1937, though again brilliantly played and arranged, were another miscalculation, featuring as they did primarily vocals in vintage material by early ragtime composers Percy Wenrich and Max Kortlander and old-time song-writer Fred Fisher in the 1913 *Peg O' My Heart*. A second date, this time for Brunswick, hit closer to the mark. Featuring a sterling trumpet section of Spivak, Manny Klein, and Sterling Bose (by then already a veteran of the Dorsey, Noble, and Goodman bands), reedmen Hal Mcintyre and Jerry Jerome (both bandleaders in their own right later in the 40s), the formidable Dick McDonough on guitar and Eak Kenyon on drums, the band recorded more up-to-date material including Gershwin's *I Got Rhythm* and even a Miller original called *Community Swing*. Not only were the arrangements more in a jazz or swing vein, but the then current major stylistic soloist conceptions were well represented: Hawkins (by Jerome), Armstrong (by Klein), Goodman (by McIntyre), and the incoming "sweet" trombone style of Tommy Dorsey (by Miller himself). Miller had by now understood that an essential ingredient of swing was a steady 4/4 beat, and that the old two-beat jazz was more or less a thing of the past.[4] He also exercised his well-known zest for thorough rehearsing, already achieving in these 1937 sides excitingly played and startlingly clean virtuoso performances. The four sides cut on June 9, 1937, are especially interesting for in them we can hear, at least in embryo, the essential ingredients of Miller's later style. Most firmly set is the sound of the six-man brass section with its biting, sharply etched, slightly piercing timbre. It is heard to particularly clear advantage on *Sleepy Time Gal*. The sax (or reed) sound is less settled. Miller and his fellow arranger (on *Time on my Hands*), Carl Biesecker, were experimenting with a great variety of reed ensemble combinations. On *Sleepy Time Gal* there is a three-part voicing for one alto and two tenors with the melody in the *lowest* voice, played by the second tenor. This effect, not uncommon in jazz and, as I have mentioned elsewhere, going all the way back

4. Only Lunceford was able to maintain a good swinging and thoroughly modern two-beat rhythm style well into the late thirties.

to "barbershop" harmonizations around the turn of the century, required that the "lead" (lowest) voice be played at a significantly louder dynamic level than the two top voices. A similar effect is used by Biesecker in *Time on My Hands*, but now in a four-way voicing with two altos and one tenor above the low "lead" second tenor.

On *Community Swing* Miller experiments with a rich somewhat sombre four-part sax ensemble in the low register, alternating this with bright brass. I suspect that Miller quickly traded in this low-register sax section effect for a higher-registered one, already much favored by Goodman, which, under McIntyre's and Skip Martin's luminous lead altos in later years, became one of the three memorable immediately identifying reed ensemble sounds of the Miller band. We hear him experimenting with it in *Sleepy Time Gal* in the second chorus behind the brass section.

Another typical Miller reed sound, that of two clarinets and two tenors, each pair in thirds an octave apart (well known from *Sunrise Serenade*), makes an early appearance here in the opening chorus of *I Got Rhythm*. Miller gives this effect considerable prominence, inventing a running eighth-note passage which by its rhythmic activity and well-projected dynamic level pushes Gershwin's actual theme, played in staccato brass punctuations, into the background.

Both arrangers, but especially Miller, were in top creative form. Among the many felicitous moments one would like to point out is the striking abrupt use of silence in the latter half of *I Got Rhythm* and the excellent ensemble-writing of the last twenty-six bars. Indeed, here Miller recomposes Gershwin's tune, fashioning a brand new coda (following Kenyon's drum solo). The last of the coda's three stanzas takes up Henderson's old call-and-response brass-and-reed exchanges idea in an entirely new way. Instead of the usual 2-bar or 1-bar alternations of choirs, Miller has the choirs only one *beat* apart (Ex. 1). This creates

Ex. 1

a marvelously whirling contrapuntal effect, made all the more exciting by the brasses' slight accenting of the second and fourth beats. The brass being also the more powerful of the two sections, the result is a delicious, subtle shifting of the beat (to four and two), anchored down only by the intensely driving 4/4 of the rhythm section.

Biesecker's arrangement of *Time on My Hands* is also first-rate. However, he did exactly what Miller was learning not to do, namely, exploring a more experimental approach. For example, Biesecker really takes Vincent Youmans's fine "changes" way out in chromatic alterations. As admirable as this may have been from a purely creative point of view, Miller, who had done his share of experimenting through the years, knew that such an approach would not lead to wide public acclaim. And such acclaim was now definitely his exclusive aim.

Despite its innovative ideas, Miller's *basic* orchestral conception on these June 1937 sides is still much beholden to the prevailing Goodman style. And Miller knew that his band's style was still too close to Goodman's to be able to compete with it. While to musicians and discriminating listeners the differences between Miller's and Goodman's styles were already perceptible, Miller knew that that was not enough. To the large untutored public there would be no discernible audible difference. And so his search went on.

The next year and a half was not easy. Bookings for the band were sporadic; so were recordings. In fact, if Miller hadn't had good connections at the Hotel Roosevelt in New Orleans (where his former boss Smith Ballew had had many successful residencies) or at the Raymor Ballroom in Boston, it is doubtful that the Glenn Miller Orchestra would have survived. Indeed, in 1937 and 1938 it was his New England bookings and the financial support from Charlie Scribman, the owner of a number of New England ballrooms, that enabled Miller to keep going. Two more recording dates in November and December 1937, though, met with little success, partly because Miller, with poor booking, was having trouble hanging on to his better sidemen. Instability of personnel is the one problem a leader fears most, and it is certainly not conducive to developing a cohesive distinctive style. Moreover the late 1937 recordings did not come out until early 1938, by which time Miller, having lost (reputedly) more than $18,000 during 1937, had disbanded.

But by April 1938, Miller had organized and rehearsed a new band, with an expanded five-man saxophone section and two personnel additions crucial to Miller's future: Tex Beneke and Wilbur Schwartz. Beneke, as the most featured soloist and sometime vocalist with Miller during the band's heyday, was to become world-famous. But Wilbur Schwartz has been little recognized for his unique contribution to Miller's success, even though it was Schwartz's warmly pulsating lead-clarinet sound over the four saxes that established Miller's fame with both musicians and the public. Miller had found "the sound," but it was the twenty-year-old Schwartz, a remarkably consistent and musical player, who had put it across.

Although bookings were now more plentiful—mainly, as mentioned, in New England (through Scribman's help)—the band was not yet catching on in a big way. A recording contract with RCA Victor for their thirty-five cents Bluebird label was obviously a prestigious prize for the struggling orchestra, but initially it produced only one session in September 1938, with nearly five months elapsing before the next one. The big breakthrough finally came, however, with an engagement in May 1939 at the famed Glen Island Casino in New Rochelle, New York. Whereupon the Casino's rival in New Jersey, the Meadowbrook Ballroom, hired Miller for seven weeks *prior* to the Glen Island opening. This double-whammy booking—Miller's Palomar, so to speak—tied in with nightly broadcasts, put Miller on the map once and for all. And now the Victor recording studios went to work, and out rolled the first big hits: *Moonlight Serenade* (Miller's own composition and theme), Frankie Carle's *Sunrise Serenade*, and *Little Brown Jug*.

To all appearances the sudden popularity of Miller's recordings in mid-1939, combined with the Meadowbrook and Glen Island openings (the latter to a record-breaking opening night crowd of 1800), seemed to signal an overnight success. After so many years of struggle, what had changed the tide so dramatically? (See Fig. 1.) Certainly not the recordings released in early 1939, which had only modest sales. Once again, as with Goodman, it appears to have been radio, that medium that the popular music industry of the 1930s was just beginning to learn to exploit effectively. Miller's late-night broadcasts from the Roseland State Ballroom in Boston, the Paradise Restaurant in New York, and the Meadowbrook itself (starting in March) were spreading the message of his new-sounding orchestra, linked to a popular repertory of golden oldies mixed with new novelty and swing numbers.

In part Miller was clinging to standard Goodman swing repertory: Henderson-style pieces like *King Porter Stomp, Wrappin' It Up, Down South Camp Meeting*, and even older staples like the *Bugle Call Rag* and *Tiger Rag*. But these were already being transformed to some degree, cut to Miller's own stylistic cloth. More than these, however, it was the novel lyric instrumentals, like

Fig. 1

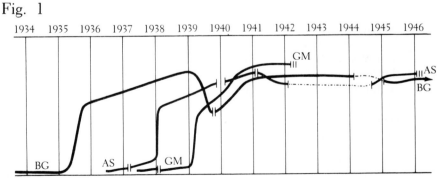

A graph depicting the relative popularity of three leading bands of the late 30s, early 40s.
BG = Benny Goodman, AS = Artie Shaw, GM = Glenn Miller
||=signifies changes in personnel; |||=termination of band; |·······|=temporary disbandment

Moonlight and *Sunrise*, virtually a new genre created by Miller,[5] with their distinctive clarinet and saxophone sound, that were attracting wide attention. Indeed, the opening of *Moonlight Serenade* is as irresistibly magical today as it was forty-five years ago. It is *sui generis*, and used as Miller's signature theme, opening and closing every broadcast and every dance, it quickly began to exert its awesome attraction.

Of course, in early 1939 that famous reed sound was not yet fully refined. Nor were the other "sounds" that Miller was developing in the other orchestra choirs. As mentioned, the tightly muted brass section was already set in 1937, but there were things to be done with the trombones, Miller's own instrument, and, above all, the rhythm section.

That was the section that gave him the most trouble, and its sound was the last to be stabilized. But I am convinced that Miller knew in his mind and inner ear exactly what he wanted to hear in a rhythm section. It had to swing, of course, and in a "modern" 4/4 manner. But it also had to have a fully integrated unified sound—not unlike Basie's. His problem instruments here were the guitar and drums. For a while Miller had been forced for economic reasons to work without a guitar. But he soon realized that a guitarless section would never provide the necessary "binding" in the rhythm section, or the much-needed harmonic underpinning for the relatively sparse and uncluttered instrumental textures he had in mind. After trying out a succession of guitarists, and borrowing Allan Reuss from Les Brown (for recording sessions only)—Reuss had been the rock-solid guitarist of Goodman's orchestra for nearly three years—Miller settled on Richard Fisher in mid-1939. His excellent but unsung work can be heard on nearly a hundred sides cut during his one year with the band.

But the most crucial player in a rhythm section is the drummer, obviously. And here Miller was fortunate to get a twenty-two-year-old drummer, fresh from working with Tommy Dorsey, by the name of Maurice "Moe" Purtill. Influenced both by Krupa and Jo Jones, Purtill had the kind of control of dynamics and sonority Miller was looking for—someone who could make the band swing in the clean, disciplined, well-behaved way he envisioned. Purtill filled this role to perfection. The rhythm section, with Bundock's steady bass already firmly ensconced, really began to jell in mid-1939 as evidenced by such sides as *The Day We Meet Again*, *Johnson Rag* (a much better piece than the title might suggest), *It Was Written in the Stars*, *The Changing World*, and *Say Si Si*. Especially in some of the latter titles, we can hear a rhythm section to which can be rightfully ascribed the approbation "homogenized." It is really an indivisible unit, fashioning from the three instruments (piano was rarely involved) a new organic *single* sound.

To appreciate Miller's approach to jazz—via the dance band, to be sure—we

---

5. Ellington had set the example much earlier with pieces like *Mood Indigo* and *Sophisticated Lady*, the latter initially performed as an instrumental; and Gene Gifford had followed with *Smoke Rings* in 1932. But most of the white public had never heard any Duke Ellington, and with the Casa Lomans the young college crowd preferred the razzle-dazzle "flag-wavers" like *Casa Loma Stomp*.

must understand his musical ideology and accept it on its own special narrow terms. We start with his unconditional determination to make a commercial, financial success with his music. And to accomplish that, Miller knew you had to attract not thousands but millions of listeners. And to achieve that, in turn, he knew—learning by trial and error in his earlier arranging and playing activities—that you had to pare down your music to something both simple and unique. Miller's genius, if you will, lay in correctly estimating the listening (and dancing) capacities of the average young-ish white American, and then inventing a music of considerable taste, performed with impeccable polish and skill, to satisfy the mass appetite. He refined that philosophy even further, constantly emphasizing in the band's arrangements three elemental points: 1) smoothness—of rhythm, of arrangements; 2) uncomplicated nature, for he realized that his listener's musical mind was slow and lazy; 3) contrast, especially of textures, so as not to induce boredom. In effect, the essence of Miller's formula was a kind of smoothed-out jazz: reliable, consistent, sufficiently predictable not to disturb but colorful enough to retain a mild element of surprise, and, above all, not too emotional or deeply expressive, i.e. an attractive patina rather than the real thing.

This was not a new formula in music, of course. Leopold Stokowski and Arthur Fiedler, for example, both in differing ways and contexts, pursued and achieved similar goals: a unique sense of sound combined with a direct uncomplicated, at times simplistic, interpretation of the music. Nor was this formula unknown to men like André Kostelanetz, David Rose, or Mantovani. And if these men's contributions to music are sometimes sneered at by purists, then theirs is in no way an absolute verdict; it is merely an opinion based on certain premises. So was Miller's music. And while one would never wish to argue that it represented the highest achievements of jazz—indeed, often enough Miller's band is connected to jazz by only the slimmest thread—it was often a music of considerable beauty and, unlike so much popular commercial music, never offensive.

The paring-down process on which Miller embarked took about two or three years. But when it was finished, it was in its way a thing of perfection, fail-safe and often magical. How raw in sonority and stiff in rhythm the early band could sound at first can be heard as late as early 1939 on such inanities as *Shut Eye* and *Cuckoo in the Clock*. Choice of repertory was then also still a severe problem. Arrangements of classics like Debussy's *Reverie* and Lieurance's popular *By the Waters of Minnetonka* (by way of Larry Clinton) came out pallid and inept. And why Miller let Tex Beneke, a terrible clarinetist, play a whole chorus on that instrument when he had Schwartz available is beyond reasonable comprehension. We know, of course, that for Miller, Beneke could do no wrong. But rigidly to limit solos to a few trusted friends like Beneke was surely a strange lapse of judgment in a man striving so determinedly for a certain kind of perfection. The same question might be asked regarding his singer Ray Eberle. The truth is that Eberle had no voice at all. He had never sung when Miller asked him to join his band as vocalist. Eberle's lumpy, sexless vocalizing dragged down many an otherwise passable performance. Miller eventually fired him—much too late, and then not for musical reasons.

Another liability in the early days of the band was Miller's own playing. Miller was never an outstanding trombonist, and his harsh, thin tone and poor intonation spoiled many a 1938 and 1939 side. I believe that Miller had no grand illusions about his playing, especially with men like Tommy Dorsey, Jack Jenney and Will Bradley around—not to mention the many extraordinary black trombonists. And so after a while he circumvented his weaknesses as a player by rarely attempting to play an open-horn jazz solo, and limiting his role to variously muted lyric solos and lead trombone. The mutes covered a multitude of sins, and these more limited assignments he actually handled with great stylishness and sonoric sensitivity.

Intonation problems plagued the band for some time, even on highly successful pieces like *Sunrise Serenade* and *In the Mood*. Listen to Aronson's flat alto and the out-of-tune trombone trio on the former title. More amazing is the slightly at odds intonation on *In the Mood*, with the saxes consistently slightly flat and the brass slightly sharp. This flaw was not enough to spoil an otherwise remarkable recording, even for sensitive ears; and, of course, most ears were hardly capable of discerning (or caring about) minor intonational deficiencies.

Retracing Miller's path to success through his recordings, we can hear the famous "Miller sounds" being gradually assembled. Although at first he preferred the somewhat steely sound of straight mutes in brass—he never explored the warm brass colors that Ellington's men, for example, developed—we can hear some progress towards mellowing the brass sonority from, say, a piece like *My Last Goodbye* (April 1939) to Eddie Durham's *Wham Re-Bop-Boom-Bam* four months later. But basically Miller stayed with the biting muted brass sound throughout the years of his civilian life, for he saw it as the necessary major contrasting sonority to the warm reed sounds.

The reed sounds took a while to perfect. Although the *concept* of the two distinctive reed section sounds (see Ex. 2 and 3) had been set for some time, the players could not at first always guarantee its realization. One of its first full flowerings appears on *Sunrise Serenade* (Ex. 2), the other on *And the Angels Sing* (April 1939) (Ex. 3a) and, of course, on the stunning *Moonlight Serenade* (Ex. 3b), recorded the same session, but which the band had already been playing for an entire year.

Another part of the sonoric assemblage was the soft muted trombone choir. Miller went to eight brass (four trumpets, four trombones) in the fall of 1939.

Ex. 2

Ex. 3a

Ex. 3b

This not only gave him a fuller harmonic pallette in the brass but enabled him to separate trumpets and trombones more easily into discrete choirs. The four-trombone-choir sound made its Miller debut on *Last Night*, open horn. But most frequently it was used with a variety of mutes, producing a gorgeous velvety sound and texture, never heard before in or out of jazz.[6] Fine early examples of this most important "Miller sound" can be heard on *Faithful Forever*—ravishingly—and in the extremely popular *Danny Boy*. It was the ultimate "romantic" sound, and when set in a slow tempo, as it invariably was, it was seductive and irresistible.

What evolved out of these sonoric experiments by late 1939 was a sound world that was unprecedented in the history of music—and unique (except by imitation). The half-dozen or so "Miller sounds"—the several brass and reed sounds and the rhythm section's—were henceforth used with masterful control, both in performance and arrangement. Indeed, it was a master stroke (though one need not necessarily agree with it or assume that it was the only or the best sound around) to *stay* with those half-dozen sonorities, rigorously to limit the band's playing (and the arrangers) to those specific timbres. These were clear, precise, predictable—and eminently satisfying. They worked. They provided that distinc-

6. Ellington had come close to it in *Blue Light* and *Subtle Lament*, but not with *four* trombones. Dorsey had begun to use four-trombone choirs in late 1938, the first to do so, but always open.

tive quality, instantly recognizable and very memorable, which Miller had known to be the key to the *kind* of success he strove for.

Miller was like a great painter who had decided to reduce his palette to a limited and precisely selected choice of colors. Whether three or four colors (as in *Speaking of Heaven*) or six or seven (as in *It Was Written in the Stars* or *On a Little Street in Singapore*), whether mostly muted or brightly open (as on *Ooh, What You Said*, one of Marion Hutton's least silly songs), the colors were always sharply etched. They became aesthetic absolutes, or were certainly used as such. Though they tended, given the largely "romantic," pop-ish repertory, towards pastel colors, lilacs and grays—almost never solid deep reds, for example—they were marvelously clearly differentiated. And to delineate these colorations even more so that even the laziest ears could get the effect, Miller used dynamics as almost no one ever had before. Each color had its own dynamic level, a few had two. These correlations were virtually inviolate and, like a great chef working with limited ingredients, Miller and his arrangers just mixed these colors and dynamic levels in constantly changing juxtapositions. This was most frequently applied in short strokes, brief 2- or 4- or at most 8-bar phrases. Sometimes, as in *Moonlight Serenade*, the muted brass would finish the last two bars of an otherwise reed-colored phrase. What is remarkable is that despite this coloristic, often almost mosaic approach, the arrangements are rarely cluttered. Despite the constantly changing colors and contrasts, there is a tremendous feeling of *line* in the Miller band's playing. Each piece is a self-contained unit, seamless and consistent on the surface, varied and contrasting underneath. The players, as they became familiar with the idiom—and they could do so relatively quickly because of the limited number of variables—could *feel* the sonoric links, the contrasts, as parts of a larger totality.

Of course, one of the great long-line-producing elements in the Miller band concept was the famous reed sound, especially in the lead-clarinet version. Not only was it a ravishing sound, but it was designed to give the long line to a piece. With all its precision, it was elastic; and it invariably created the illusion of an endless melody—almost Wagnerian in that sense. One had the feeling that the five reed players never had to breathe. Indeed, they accomplished what no other reed section ever had before: the closest equivalent to a string section without actually resorting to one. Here again Wilbur Schwartz—and, when the lead was in the alto, Hal McIntyre (and later Skip Martin)—must be given much of the credit. While the lead player can't make the whole section-sound by himself, he certainly dominates and controls it. The famous clarinet-lead is also an uncanny updated replication of the earlier style violin-lead in thousands of 1920s' dance bands.

All this was so firmly set by late 1939 that it made little difference who the arrangers were. It was understood by them that they were to work with the given "Miller sounds" and not their own. Minor variations were possible here and there, but they were seen as subtle manipulations *within*, never deviations *from*. Eddie Durham, who handled many of the jazzier instrumentals, was allowed to heat things up a little bit with, of course, the jitter-bugging younger crowd in mind. And when arrangers like Joe Lippman (*Blue Evening*), Charlie Dixon (*We Can Live on Love*), and the great Bill Challis (*Guess I'll Go Back Home*) added their own distinctive touch, it was either within the Miller concept or not allowed to roam very far afield. It also comes as no surprise that these more explorative arrangers were infrequently used and that the recordings of their efforts for the band, in most cases, did not sell very well.

The two arrangers who, besides Miller himself, did most of the work were Bill Finegan (later half of the team that led the Sauter-Finegan band) and Jerry Gray, the latter beginning in 1940. Finegan helped to create the Miller sound world, also adapting some of the swingier numbers (like Horace Henderson's *Rug Cutter's Swing*) to the band's prevailing style; and Jerry Gray perpetuated it—religiously.

The Miller band was not strong in soloists. It kept a semblance of a link with jazz as an improvised music by a sprinkling of solos on almost all recordings (a little more on dance dates as opposed to recordings). But it was never Miller's intention to build a great *jazz* band. Thus Miller kept a drill sergeant's control of his soloist corps, Beneke, as mentioned, receiving the lion's share. Beneke fitted Miller's "smooth-it-out" philosophy to a T. He played a smoothed-out Coleman Hawkins, with all the guts, graininess—and even dirt—of the originator cut out. It was a kind of pablum version of Hawkins, to which Beneke in due course added mild dehydrated doses of Chu Berry and Lester Young. But he was a consistent player, reliable within his limitations, and never really embarrassing. Good players like Al Klink and the brash, more experimentally inclined Jimmy Abato (who later played bass clarinet with the New York Philharmonic) were only exceptionally permitted by the captain to intrude a solo. Mysteriously, too, little Wilbur Schwartz was rarely used as a soloist. Undoubtedly not a great creative soloist—he certainly was not given a chance to prove it one way or the other—Schwartz's special clarinet sound and liquid style would have added some welcome solo variety.

In the trumpets Miller generally had good soloists—none in the trombones after he himself gave up on his Dixieland semi-hot soloing—although here again no innovations or great creativity were sought. Clyde Hurley and Johnny Best (and later Billy May) all worked well within established tradition, twice removed from the fountainhead, Louis Armstrong—in Hurley's case via Harry James and in Best's via Bunny Berigan.

As with all bands—this recurring refrain again—the vast majority of Miller's recordings were vocals: ballads or novelty songs, all unbelievably baby-ish in sentiment and in what passed for humor,[7] but always cleverly set in readily

---

7. It is, nearly fifty years later, totally incomprehensible to a reasonably intelligent mind how such infantile lyric drivel as was relentlessly pumped at American audiences by literally hundreds of bands in the thirties and forties, could be so unanimously accepted. That we could rise from this state of immaturity as a nation and rescue Europe from the Nazis is, I suppose, one of the triumphant possibilities—and attributes—of a democracy. It is also somehow a comforting thought that bands like Miller's and Dorsey's—and for that matter most of the black bands, too—could make these intellectually unpalatable inanities musically halfway bearable.

danceable tempos. Like Jimmie Lunceford, whom Miller admired greatly, Miller zeroed in on one primary medium dance tempo (about $\mathbf{\downarrow} = 90$), to which count-less recordings set in it can attest. There was, of course, a faster dance tempo for the jitterbuggers, and a very slow one for the dreamy lights-low, hugging-close dance numbers.

But it was Miller's clever management of his repertory, by sprinkling it liber-ally with jazz or quasi-jazz instrumentals, that places him above the ranks of the ordinary hotel or dance band. He successfully trod a fine line between captivat-ing the really young kids with up-tempo instrumentals and holding onto the older crowd by the moderate-tempoed ballads and dance numbers. History tells us, however, that we remember Miller today for *In the Mood, Tuxedo Junction, Pennsylvania Six Five Thousand*. Indeed, such pieces (and Goodman's most popular up-tempo hits) represent the Swing Era for millions of people to this day.

These pieces need not detain us too much in the context of a *jazz* history. But they do represent a type of jazz that not only epitomized the era for vast numbers of Americans—probably their only real contact with any form of jazz—but that represents a high order of craftsmanship. (The line between art and craft is often a thin one and, near the borderline between the two, distinctions are easily blurred and subjective.)

In the Mood should serve well as the ultimate Miller style swing-instrumental model. It also has an interesting history. A riff tune, built on blues changes, it was composed by the black reed instrumentalist and arranger Joe Garland. But as is so often the case in riff pieces, it was based on a motive that had kicked around a long time and was simply assembled, notated, and put by Garland in a specific copyrightable form. It appears that the trumpeter Wingy Manone first used the basic *In the Mood* lick in 1930 on a Chicago-style recording called *Tar Paper Stomp*. He recorded it again, rechristened as *Jumpy Nerves*, in 1939, just four months *before* Miller's *In the Mood* recording. But by that time Joe Garland had picked the riff up and had used it in his 1935 composition and arrangement of *There's Rhythm in Harlem* for the Mills Blue Rhythm Band. But long before that (March 1931) Horace Henderson had incorporated the riff as the second strain in his *Hot and Anxious*, recorded by both his brother Fletcher's band and Don Redman's.

Joe Garland took his 1935 arrangement with him when he left the Blue Rhythm Band along with Edgar Hayes, and recorded it as *In the Mood* for Hayes in early 1938. Next he offered it to Artie Shaw, who played but never recorded it, on the one hand thinking the simplistic riff a little beneath his own musical ambi-tions and on the other hand finding Garland's arrangement too long to fit on a ten-inch disc.

When Garland offered *In the Mood* to Miller, who was undoubtedly looking for strong new numbers for his Glen Island Casino booking, Miller grabbed the piece. With the precise skills of a first-rate surgeon Miller trimmed Garland's arrangement down to essentials, retaining the two initial strains, building in two solo sections (a saxophone exchange between Beneke and Klink, and a Hurley

16-bar trumpet solo over an A♭ pedal point) to the famous fade-away ending with its riff repeated three times at ever softer dynamic levels, then suddenly roaring in *ff* a fourth time for the final climax. At this point a trumpet-trio coda was added, climbing from the low register to a high A♭-chord (Ex. 4).

Ex. 4

As the example shows, this is a harmonically relatively complex passage, of the kind of modernity that Miller had by now ruled out. But here, after the somewhat static preceding material—the circular riff (heard already six times before the final coda), the trumpet solo pedal point—the zigzagging chromaticism of the trumpet trio, rising inexorably to the final climax, was an uncannily perfect touch. For their time these eight bars were not all that easy to play and to hear—and it took the trumpet section quite a while to play them really well. (On the recording they are still somewhat ragged.)

Part of the excitement of the whole coda derives from the exquisite sense of suspended animation created in the diminishing riff repetitions by the surprising elongation—it is surprising even after the 1000th listening—of the low unison A♭ pedal-note in the trombones, thereby yielding an unexpected 14-bar phrase length, rather than the traditional twelve.

No official word has ever been offered as to how the arranger's credits are to read. Two things are clear, however, from the aural evidence itself: 1) that Miller oversaw the construction of the arrangement, tailoring its components to his concept of the piece, and 2) that at least four hands contributed to the final result. Miller's pianist, Chummy MacGregor, seems to have laid claim to the final trumpet coda. My guess is that Eddie Durham did the actual transferring of Garland's original arrangement, as pruned by Miller, and that Durham is also responsible for the trombone pedals towards the end. He was a trombonist, of course, and had used similar effects for years with the Lunceford band.

It is ironic but in the nature of the popular music business, that Miller became a millionaire on *In the Mood* alone, unlike his three arranger helpmates—Garland, Durham, and MacGregor—who did not share in the financial rewards. Durham reputedly received all of *five dollars* for his contribution.

Glenn Miller is reputed to have flatly asked John Hammond, after the latter had written a scathing review of Miller, why he judged him *as a musician;* "All I'm interested in is making money." That unbelievable admission—surely taken somewhat baldly out of context—may be an exaggeration. On the other hand, Miller assuredly did become a hard-nosed businessman bandleader, as success piled on top of success. But his success was also aligned with a continuing need— a veritable obsession—to improve his product. As well as certain players had already served him, Miller always sought to strengthen the band whenever the occasion for a change in personnel occurred. Thus he acquired three fine players in 1940: the trumpet player and arranger Billy May, the Mexican clarinetist Ernie Caceres (on second alto), and an energetic young bass player, Herman "Trigger" Alpert.[8] But an even more important addition (in January 1941), certainly from the point of view of filling the already overflowing Miller coffers, were the Modernaires. They provided the band with a number of gigantic hits: *Juke Box Saturday Night*, *I Got a Gal in Kalamazoo*, and *Chattanooga Choo Choo*, the last-named selling a million records in the first six months of being issued, eventually becoming one of the few multimillion sellers in pre-rock-era times.[9] The Modernaires' smooth, superbly blended and well-tuned non-vibrato style, with Paula Kelly or Marion Hutton singing lead, was another example of Miller's ability to turn a musical concept, performed with consummate craft and taste, into a major commercial asset.

It is a strange anomaly that Miller, so commercially ambitious, should decide to enlist in the army, disbanding his orchestra, at a time when he was earning about $100,000 a month just from recordings. It was a precipitous action— Miller enlisted in September 1942—breaking numerous engagements and contracts. It left the music world stunned.

Miller's war years—until his mysterious and untimely death in December 1944— were dedicated to forming an all-star Army Air Force Band. It was really a forty-two-piece concert orchestra with, among other assets, a nineteen-man jazz or dance band similar to Miller's civilian group, one French horn, and a twenty-piece string ensemble. It was a magnificent orchestra, filled with first-rate musicians both from the jazz and "classical" sides. But its relationship to jazz was remote and intermittent. Miller saw it strictly as an entertainment unit, which could play a variety of popular music in a tasteful, instrumentally sophisticated fashion. And that, once again, he achieved.

Working with very fine arrangers, including Jerry Gray, Mel Powell, and Norman Leyden—Miller's Army Air Force orchestra was the non-civilian counterpart to André Kostelanetz's remarkable CBS orchestra of the early 1940s, featured nationwide on the famous Coca-Cola radio hour (right after the New York

---

8. The fine lyric cornetist Bobby Hackett also joined Miller in 1941 but played mostly guitar. Rarely featured as a cornet soloist on records (hear his *Rhapsody in Blue*), Hackett's Beiderbecke-inspired playing was reserved by Miller for special numbers, mostly on location and radio broadcasts, Miller evidently feeling that Hackett's softer style would not fit in with the solid powerhouse playing of his regular four-man trumpet section—an eminently correct decision. Nonetheless, Hackett occasionally contributed fine cornet solos to the Miller band, especially his glowing lyric solo on *String of Pearls*.
9. Gene Austin had had a multimillion seller way back in 1927 with a recording of *My Blue Heaven*. Miller's *Chattanooga Choo Choo* came next fourteen years later, but that was then topped by Bing Crosby's *White Christmas*.

Philharmonic broadcast). Miller's orchestra could fill almost any musical assignment, and with Trigger Alpert, guitarist Carmen Mastren from Dorsey's orchestra, and the fine swing drummer Ray McKinley, it had a more than capable foundation for a superb swing-dance band. Oddly enough Miller played very little of his own civilian band repertory, picking up instead jazz numbers like Mel Powell's *Mission to Moscow* and Lionel Hampton's *Flying Home*.

As I have suggested earlier, this Air Force orchestra was the kind of versatile ensemble he really loved and believed in. His arranger's mind envisioned a wide variety of repertory, stylishly arranged, impeccably performed, dressed up to the nines. I personally believe that Miller, had he lived, would never have returned to merely a dance band. The old ideal of Paul Whiteman's versatile orchestra—not necessarily Whiteman's "symphonic jazz" philosophy, however—lived on in Glenn Miller, reinterpreted in an extended format in his Air Force Band. How much further his musical and financial ambitions might have carried him must remain forever conjectural. That it would have been significant, whatever form(s) it might have taken, is not unlikely.

Whatever our individual final verdict may be on Glenn Miller, we must concede at least that it was he and Goodman and a half a dozen other white swing bands that brought an unprecedented and since then never equaled number of Americans as close to jazz as they were ever to be.

TOMMY DORSEY

The parallels between Glenn Miller and Tommy Dorsey are numerous. Both were, of course, trombonists and emerged as bandleaders during the same general period, the late 1930s. Both had led parallel careers as freelancers in the New York studios in the late twenties and early thirties, many times playing side by side in the same recording units or shows, both with a decided Dixieland or Chicago-style bent to their playing. They were not only colleagues and good friends, but many a time one would help the other in some professional situation, even to the extent of lending each other musicians from their respective orchestras. Miller was the beneficiary of Dorsey's helpfulness on numerous crucial occasions.

Both men looked somewhat alike in general facial features and wore similar small thin-rimmed glasses, heightening an air of disciplined fastidiousness, even primness. Both were also untiring taskmasters, constantly striving for musical perfection and for neatly dressed bandstand behavior. They were mostly regarded as martinets by their players, although both men had curious streaks of generosity. And finally both, though in different ways, were enormously successful businessmen-musicians.

There were also some important and striking dissimilarities. Whereas Miller was at best a proficient trombonist, mostly limiting himself to written-out lead work in his band, Dorsey was one of the greatest trombonists of all time—in any field. Miller was a superior arranger, whereas Dorsey, except for a few hilariously abortive attempts at arranging, had no inclinations in that direction. Even more important were their totally different stylistic conceptions of orchestral jazz and swing. Miller from the outset believed in and insisted on a solid four-beats-to-the-bar type of swing, eschewing the two-beat style of almost all other 1930s' bands (even many black orchestras). In Miller's band this was exemplified by a totally cohesive balanced three-man rhythm section of guitar, bass, and drums. Even pop songs, ballads, and novelty tunes were performed (with rare exceptions) with a 4/4 swing. Dorsey, on the other hand, did not adopt the four-beat feeling until late 1939 and early 1940, and then only intermittently. And even that would not have happened but for the virtually about-face stylistic influence of Sy Oliver. Before that (and even in non-Oliver arrangements during Oliver's tenure with the band) Dorsey clung almost religiously to his essentially Dixieland two-beat rhythmic approach.

Similarly, Miller from the very beginning pursued the ideal of a totally distinctive, even unique orchestral sound and style, whereas Dorsey was actively opposed to such an approach. For reasons that are not entirely clear, Dorsey was resolved to avoid a clear stylistic identity. Certainly the recorded aural evidence—until Sy Oliver's arrival, some 335 sides later—confirms that. One can only conjecture at this late date as to Dorsey's reasons for adopting such a non-style. One reason might be that he considered his already unique lyric trombone style (by 1935) to be identity enough. Indeed he may not have wanted any orchestral conception to interfere or compete with that. Secondly, his concept of the band was tied primarily to popular song and ballad repertory, first and foremost a dance band. And for Dorsey—following Lunceford's example—that meant a comfortable medium-tempo, two-beat bounce. His idea was to get the people out on the dance floor, and he knew from a hundred rival examples how that was best to be done. He had at that time virtually no conception of jazz (except in its Dixieland manifestation) or for that matter of swing—and certainly no inkling of black jazz music. And Dorsey had no John Hammond to steer him in that direction. Considering the enormous influence of Benny Goodman, beginning in 1935, it is startling to realize that he had none on Dorsey. Dorsey evolved into a swing band only very, very gradually and seemingly quite reluctantly.

Indeed, for the first four years of the band's existence Dorsey had a neatly separatist policy in which jazz—in its Dixieland guise—was segregated to a small group within the band, called the Clambake Seven. There was no crossing of lines, and the big band was limited to pop songs from Broadway musicals and Hollywood films, arrangements of light classics, a few trombone solo features (like Dorsey's famous *I'm Getting Sentimental over You*), and—very rarely—a Dixieland-in-swing-clothing instrumental.

But there is a curious contradiction in all this in that Dorsey's eschewal of a distinctive style led by sheer redundancy precisely to just that: a distinctive style, although it was a totally innocuous one, more non-style than style. Because Dorsey permitted virtually no deviation from his enunciated musical/aesthetic course, the result was only very remotely related to jazz.

There is further irony in the fact that, while Glenn Miller with his more innovative approach had to struggle for two and a half years before attaining his first successes (which then were of unprecedented magnitude), Dorsey had considerable and consistent success right from the beginning. Dorsey had engagements rather immediately at the Glen Island Casino and Meadowbrook and other major dance emporia, and found favor with Victor Records directly upon organizing his first band, while Miller had to struggle through almost two and a half years of one-nighters and intermittent layoffs before being accepted in the major venues of the day. And RCA Victor kept Miller for many years on their cheaper Bluebird label, whereas Dorsey was part of the higher priced Victor catalogue.

Part of Dorsey's relatively easy climb to fame can be attributed to the prior success, at least commercially, of the Dorsey Brothers' Orchestra, in existence on recordings with brother Jimmy as co-leader since 1928 but a permanently functioning orchestra only from the spring of 1934—incidentally with friend Glenn Miller almost always as second trombone and chief arranger. The legendary squabbling and feuding between the two Dorsey brothers eventually led to Tommy's walking off the stand during an engagement at the Glen Island Casino in May 1935. Within months, almost as if by pre-arrangement, Tommy took over the band of arranger-leader Joe Haymes, which with a few personel changes became the first Tommy Dorsey Orchestra.

How far apart in concept and style from, say, Goodman—let alone Ellington or Chick Webb, or even the Casa Loma band—Dorsey was in those mid-1930s' years can be heard on the hundreds of Dorsey recordings of that period. For, apart from an occasional solo by a Bunny Berigan or a Bud Freeman, there is very little that relates to jazz. But this early Dorsey period does deserve some comment, if only for the fact that Dorsey is generally treated much more kindly in jazz-writing than Miller—who often is not even mentioned—an imbalanced judgment which I find groundless. Recording almost exclusively vocals, literally *hundreds* of them, the format of these performances devised by Dorsey and his arrangers persists with numbing redundancy: Tommy's lyric trombone to state the theme, followed by the vocal, and to conclude, a slightly "hotter" final full or half-chorus which might feature frustratingly brief solos. The material was mostly lightweight in content and arranged in a lightweight manner, mostly in the prevailing dance or sweet styles, often dangerously close to or well within what musicians derisively call a "Mickey Mouse" style. The emphasis instrumentationally was primarily on clarinets, including almost always a bass clarinet (played for years by Fred Stulce), occasionally a flute, all set in a pleasant danceable two-beat-bounce tempo.

The one redeeming feature, however, on almost every piece was Tommy's trombone. Not a jazz player,[10] Dorsey could at best render a sort of mechanical,

10. Both Dorsey and Miller were very modest and honest about their shortcomings as jazz players. Both on various occasions declined to perform in the presence of or compete with their betters, Miller always deferring to Dorsey, while the latter idolized Jack Teagarden. Both Dorsey and Miller displayed their integrity in this regard: when by way of popular polls they were voted into All-Star bands, they politely declined to solo.

not very inspired, though technically facile Dixieland trombone. But as a lyric player and romantic balladeer Dorsey had no equal. Indeed he virtually invented the genre. His best emulator was the very gifted Bobby Byrne, who took Tommy's place in Jimmy Dorsey's band, playing all of Dorsey's high register lyric solos (as well as the "hot" jazz parts). But Dorsey was clearly the creator and master of this smooth "singing" trombone style, so seemingly effortless, largely because of his virtually flawless breath control, the ultimate foundation of all great wind playing. As good as Dorsey already was in the early and mid-1930s, he kept somehow miraculously improving to the point where some of his recorded solos of the early forties are almost beyond belief.

Tommy began developing his smooth lyric manner in his studio work, which often called for a sweet-style solo, and with the Brothers orchestra. His father—who taught him on a number of brass and wind instruments[11]—gave him a secure technical foundation and disciplined approach. It was that training, combined with his own great talent, that helped him become the top trombonist in New York. His perfect breath support, clean attack, and impeccably neat slide work enabled him to sing on the trombone's high register with unparalleled ease. It became his trademark and his ticket to popular stardom.

Dorsey was a shrewd player, never pushing his luck in the high range too far. His favorite highest note was D♭ (or C♯, enharmonically the same), and only rarely did he venture beyond that. (Only once did he assay high F, the Mount Everest of trombone-playing in those years, and that was on a misbegotten arrangement of Johann Strauss's *Blue Danube*; the Fs were splendid, though). Dorsey arrangers knew that the highest note in the opening theme statement, almost always played by Dorsey himself, would have to be that high D♭ or C♯. That is why so many of the Dorsey pieces started off in (for jazz) odd keys like A major (his *Star Dust*, for example), or E major (C♯ being then the third or sixth respectively) or G♭ major (with D♭ the fifth). Oddly enough this high note had an uncanny way of sounding higher with Dorsey than with other trombonists. Perhaps it was that his sound, though pure, was light, and that he played a tiny bit on the upper side of a pitch, giving his tone a certain extra brilliance. Of the literally *hundreds* of impeccable lyric solos Dorsey recorded, some of the most beautiful are *If My Heart Could Only Talk* (1937), *More Than Ever*, and *Annie Laurie* (1938), his bucket-mute solo on *Tea for Two* (1939), *Say It* (1940), *Violets for Your Furs* (1941), *Take Me*, and *Somewhere a Voice Is Calling* (1942) and almost any other solo from 1941 and 1942.

There is one other trombonist who in my estimation was Dorsey's equal as a lyric trombonist: Lawrence Brown, although in a quite different style. Indeed, Brown was a great admirer of Dorsey—as any trombonist would have to be—a fact not only audible in the aural evidence of Brown's playing in the late thirties and early forties but confirmed by him many times in personal conversations

---

11. Tommy played the trumpet rather well, and can be hard on that instrument in a splendidly spirited and quite advanced Armstrong-styled 1928 *Tiger Rag* recording, accompanied only by guitar (Eddie Lang), bass, and drums. He can also be heard to good effect on a 1939 performance of *Back to Back* with his orchestra.

with the author. The fact remains, though, that Brown was actually three trombonists rolled into one: a superb original lyric stylist, a first-rate section leader and viruoso technician, and on many occasions a highly original jazz trombonist—something that Dorsey was not.

It is always interesting—and indeed of paramount importance to the historian—to study the early formative efforts of an artist. For there one will find the clues, the early signs, of the talent one observes later in full flowering and maturity. Dorsey was by no means a beginner trombonist or bandleader in September 1935, but nonetheless it is instructive to hear his first recordings for Victor. For it becomes obvious that recording director Eli Oberstein had quite different plans for the Dorsey band than Tommy himself. Evidently Dorsey had in mind a two-pronged approach, featuring on the one hand his lyric trombone (as a higher quality of "sweet" style) and on the other a kind of "hot" big-band Chicago-Dixieland music: brash, bright, and jazzy. The latter can be heard on the band's flashy and wonderfully spirited rendition of ragtime composer Artie Matthews's old standard *Weary Blues*. This was performed in a typically driving, no-holds-barred arrangement by Spud Murphy (who, we will recall, was doing fine work for the young Benny Goodman band at that time). Even *Santa Claus Is Coming to Town* retains enough jazzy energy to be headed in the right general direction. *Take Me Back to My Boots and Saddle* was one of those compromise "commercial" numbers which every white band, no matter what its stylistic persuasion, was obliged to record if it wanted to survive. In this, Dorsey simply took a piece that, with its melodic trombone solo, loping bass clarinet accompaniment, and clippety-clop temple blocks, more or less plagiarized *On the Trail*, Ferde Grofé's big hit from the *Grand Canyon Suite*.

Interestingly, Tommy's best solo, his theme and a piece for which he became justifiedly world famous, *I'm Getting Sentimental over You*, was left to the last on that first 1935 record date. Even Dorsey's invincible embouchure was tired by this time. After many attempts and two official takes with about a dozen fluffs, Tommy had to give up and postpone the recording of that piece to another time. The splendid performance we all know was take 3, made almost a month later.

One can only suspect that Mr. Oberstein took over at this point, for Spud Murphy never arranged for Dorsey again and the sparky *Weary Blues* type of performance and arrangement was never heard of again. Instead came an endless series of novelty tunes and pop songs, arranged in the most insipid manner. The compromise that was obviously reached in respect to jazz was to relegate it to a small group (that would not contaminate the big band and spoil its image), called the Clambake Seven. (With Tommy and singer Edythe Wright—who, to undercut incongruously the potential *jazz* image of the Clambake band, sang on almost every one of their numbers—the personnel was actually *nine*.)

By the fourth Dorsey record date (two and three were given over to the tap-dancing movie star Eleanor Powell), the band was well ensconced in its near-Mickey Mouse non-style, as any number of recordings will attest. (Try *It's Written in the Stars* and *One Umbrella for Two* for size.) One begins to discern a mild improvement in late 1935–early 1936 in the arrangements of Paul Weston, whom Dorsey had inherited from the Haymes band, and whose arrangements in increasing measure added a modicum of instrumental distinction and a semblance of swing to the Dorsey book.[12] Perversely his arrangement of *Let It Be Me* (December 1935), the best in months of recordings, remained unissued despite an excellent performance. It featured quite incidentally a trombone trio. It is odd that Dorsey never made much of the trombone choir potential. Except for a very occasional trio or (later) quartet, Dorsey left this idea for Glenn Miller to develop. Dorsey and Weston seem also to have stumbled upon Miller's famous reed sound—long before Miller presented it in full-fledged form—as can be heard briefly on *Robins and Roses* and *Will I Ever Know It?* But they evidently didn't see anything special in it. It was certainly not pursued and developed, remaining relegated to isolated instances.

That excellent swing drummer, Davey Tough, who musically rescued many a band in his time, was a fine addition to Dorsey's orchestra in the spring of 1936. He and clarinetist Joe Dixon and trumpeter Max Kaminsky can all be heard to excellent effect on one of the Clambake Seven sides from this period, *Rhythm Saved the World*. Weston's progress as an arranger can be measured in Dorsey's highly successful recording of *Star Dust*, on which in the final half-chorus Weston more or less recomposes Carmichael's song in a most creative way, a fascinating precursor of the kind of thing that Gil Evans was to do so well twenty-five years later.

It is only in these mid-1936 Dorsey recordings that one begins to sense any awareness on his and the band's part of the Goodman-Henderson influence. Hesitantly and intermittently, a 4/4 swing à la Goodman begins to creep into the band's arranging and playing, oddly enough at first on such unexpected titles as *Mary Had a Little Lamb* and *On the Beach at Bali Bali*. (Other manifestations of a swing influence came, albeit several times removed, in the form of pseudo-riff pieces which were near-plagiarizations of Edgar Sampson's *Stompin' at the Savoy*, first recorded by Chick Webb in 1934).[13]

Another type of musical lifting brought Dorsey fame and fortune: the "swing classics," adaptations of popular classical melodies. The first of these were Anton Rubinstein's *Melody in F* and Rimsky-Korsakov's *Song of India* (originally from the opera *Sadko*), to be followed later by a half a dozen others (like Mendelssohn's *Spring Song* and Dvořák's *Humoresque* and *Goin' Home*). A gullible public readily swallowed these artistic subterfuges, flattered by the association with (allegedly) classical music.

---

12. Paul Weston later became one of the outstanding arrangers of mood music, consistently set with impeccable taste and often featuring top jazz players.

13. *Stompin' at the Savoy*, almost a kind of national anthem of the Swing Era, especially after Goodman's hit recording of late 1936, was beginning to infiltrate the repertories of even the most strait-laced bands. Once swing had been declared a safe and saleable commodity, even bands like Ozzie Nelson and Gene Kardos gave it a whirl, either by making their own arrangement of it or by recording the dozens of imitations being churned out by Tin Pan Alley songwriters.

But an even bigger hit for Dorsey—and a quite unexpected one—was *Marie*, the first of a series of pieces in which the band sang interpolated jivey answers, sung in unison, to the vocal soloist's lead.[14] *Marie*'s success unleashed a whole cycle of similar pieces, which did not end until *East of the Sun* with Frank Sinatra in 1940.

The two great moments on *Marie*, of course, belonged to Dorsey in his incomparable theme statement and to Bunny Berigan, who delivered one of his finest, most sweepingly authoritative solos. While one can always find traces of Louis Armstrong's influence in even the most original of 1930s' trumpeters, Berigan in his best playing (as on *Marie*) is quite his own man. It is a perfectly "composed" solo, a major statement in its own right, and as fine an example as one needs to find of how a jazz improvisation may transform fairly innocuous song material into highly creative art. Example 5 presents Berigan's solo in no-

Ex. 5

14. The general public did not know—and probably didn't much care—that Dorsey had taken the idea for the *Marie* arrangement from a little known black band, Ace Harris's (later Doc Wheeler's) Royal Sunset Serenaders, who in turn had appropriated the idea of the whole band singing from Don Redman, who began doing this sort of thing with his band in 1932. Wheeler's band, incidentally, never recorded until 1941 when, as a kind of early jump or rhythm-and-blues band, it had among its personnel trumpeters Reunald Jones and Cat Anderson, tenor-man Sam Taylor, and pianist Raymond Tunia.

tation,[15] showing how Berigan is constantly aware not only of the underlying changes but the melody as well, and his need to embellish and recompose it in response to it.[16] Notice, too, how, despite the basic two-beat feeling of the first half of the piece, Tough manages to create a semblance of 4/4 swing just by the way he emphasizes and fills in sonorically his second and fourth beats.

Another fine addition to the Dorsey band at this time was clarinetist and saxophonist Johnny Mince, who remained with Dorsey over four years. Mince, a brilliant and most reliable player, contributed dozens of well-structured fluent solos and with his liquid, bright sound added a distinctive color to the band, the reed counterpart to Dorsey's trombone. (Hear especially Mince's 1938 *I Never Knew* and *Chinatown, My Chinatown*.)

Dorsey's band was famous for its constant turnover of personnel. Someone once estimated that about 250 players passed through the band in the eleven years of its existence. Firings and hirings occurred almost weekly, and Dorsey's infamous Irish temper caused many a player to simply pack up and leave, just as Dorsey himself had done with his brother Jimmy. As a result of this instability, the sections in the Dorsey band and the orchestra as a whole never developed permanently cohesive ensembles. As soon as a particular section was beginning to jell in terms of style, sonority, and intonation, somebody would quit or get fired, and the process would have to begin all over again. That explains why as late as 1937 and 1938 (on occasion even later) the brass sound is often unbalanced and ordinary, the saxophone ensembles unblended and not well tuned (*My Old Flame, You and I Know*, etc.).

As a result of the unremitting stream of pop vocals, the band remained locked in its essentially "Mickey Mouse" stance.[17] Most of these vocals were sung by Jack Leonard, who had leaped to fame with the *Marie* recording but was basically a very bland singer, unable to conquer his tendency to sing flat. In this veritable avalanche of pop trivia, an occasional instrumental would crop up. By 1938 two or three—and once even a daring *four*—instrumentals might be cut on a given recording session. Unfortunately some of these were Larry Clinton's near-plagiarizations of Horace Henderson-type riff tunes. Most of Dorsey's audiences would not have approved of the Henderson originals, but they readily accepted Clinton's domesticated variety.

But gradually Paul Weston's sure and improving hand as an arranger could be felt ever more pervasively. Under his persistent ministrations, the band began to swing more and more, adopting increasingly an outright 4/4 beat (even if

15. It is little known that Irving Berlin's *Marie* was originally a sedate sentimental waltz. (Our musical example is in the 4/4 version). That waltzes did not always translate well into swing numbers was proven by Dorsey's adaptation of Strauss's *Blue Danube*, a small musical disaster.
16. In the 1950s Dorsey had his entire trumpet section play Berigan's original solo chorus in harmony.
17. It is even more devastating for the historian to find the Dorsey band recording—as late as 1937!—a 1905 coon song, *If the Man in the Moon Were a Coon* (see Glossary). And note the politely correct subjunctive.

reversions to two-beat were to occur right into the 40s). Weston's 'Deed I Do (February 1938) is a fine example of his craft at this time, offering also some fairly blistery-hot Dorsey trombone, and a flamboyant Bud Freeman solo, as well as sharply etched background drumming by Maurice Purtill (later Glenn Miller's drummer).[18]

To bolster the swing side of things, Dorsey brought in arranger Dean Kincaide, who had already done yeoman work for Goodman and the Bob Crosby bands. Kincaide's fine scores (*Panama, Washboard Blues* are typical examples) helped to break the Dorsey band's commercial stylistic mold by pushing it a few more degress in the Goodman direction. Another stylistic lift was given the band by two Benny Carter arrangements, one his own *Symphony in Riffs*, the other *Carolina Moon*, the former offering a superior solo by trumpeter Pee Wee Erwin, who had succeeded Berigan.

Erwin's successor in turn was Yank Lawson, an often inspired big-toned soloist who also performed the first plunger-muted solos for Dorsey. He can be heard to excellent advantage on *Old Black Joe, Down Home Rag, Sweet Sue, Hawaiian War Chant* (Lawson's playing is better than the last title and this *Sing, Sing, Sing*-type of piece might suggest), and *Tin Roof Blues*, actually the first blues piece Dorsey recorded in three years and 250 sides. Kincaide's arrangement serves the old 1920s' razzle-dazzle standard well by setting it in a slow-ish tempo, turning it into a brand-new piece. Hear the drama of Lawson's plunger solo against the beautiful organ-like sustained harmonies of the saxophones, or the heavily blues-inflected brass wailings behind Babe Russin's thrusting, squirmy tenor solo.

It is around this time that Dorsey expanded to a four-man trombone section (including himself) and began to use the rich trombone-choir sound, open on *Sweet Sue*, muted on *A Room with a View*—a sound which Glenn Miller was to turn into one of *his* band's aural specialties.

Another one of Miller's specialties, the tightly knit rhythm section, also begins to make intermittent tentative appearances in the Dorsey band now, as on *Blue Moon* and *Tea for Two* (early 1939). With these final stylistic moves and the acquisition in 1939 of drummer Buddy Rich, arrangers Bill Finegan and, above all, Sy Oliver, the stage was set for Dorsey's full entry into the Swing Era, belated and reluctant though it was. When in 1940, after Jack Leonard's long tenure as Dorsey's male vocalist finally ended, the twenty-four-year-old Frank Sinatra came over from Harry James's band, Dorsey acquired one of the greatest vocal stylists of our time. Sinatra and Oliver drove a deep wedge into the Dorsey stylistic mold, splitting the band into two clearly delineated species. If Dorsey's idea had always been to separate out, as a sort of tangential offshoot, the Clambake Seven's traditional jazz from the big band's primary pop-song dance-orchestra's function, this stylistic partition was now dramatized with the arrival of Sy Oliver

18. At this point Miller was just organizing his *second* band, while Dorsey had already cut over 200 sides in two and a half years.

Fig. 2

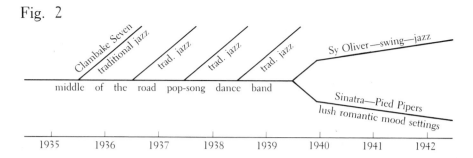

and the coming out of Axel Stordahl[19] as a major arranger. This development could be graphically depicted as in Fig. 2.

Sy Oliver finally gave Dorsey in late 1939 what he had never had (and claimed not to have wanted), and what his friend and rival Glenn Miller had already achieved: a distinctive jazz-oriented sound and style. Oliver's great talent, honed and perfected over the years with Lunceford, burst upon the Dorsey band like a series of grand musical detonations, most of which became major hits with war-time audiences starving for entertainment and relief from those years' pressures. But these new orientations were not merely greater commercial successes; they raised the Dorsey orchestra output—and performance—to an altogether new and higher level. Musical ideas, sounds, forms—all were more focused, more clearly and definitively articulated. Indeed in my entire years as a listener and student of jazz, I have never encountered as dramatic an overnight impact on an orchestra by just one individual as in the case of Sy Oliver with Tommy Dorsey's orchestra. Even within a single record date, the change of the band's playing, going from another arranger's work to Oliver's, is startling and leaves one slightly incredulous. Instantly, under Oliver's leadership, the band plays with a deep open-spaced swing and beat, feeling rather than reading the music. And the instrumental colors are now strong prime colors, blues-saturated. This applies not only to his best instrumentals (*Opus No 1, Swanee River, Another One of Them Things, Well, Git It*) but as well to Oliver's vocal accompaniments like *The One I Love, For You,* and *How Do You Do Without Me?*, among others.

Oliver made one crucial instrumentational change, which added a much-needed depth and fullness to the band's sound. Whereas Dorsey had *never* used a baritone saxophone, preferring the more soft-spoken bass clarinet (used on several hundred recordings), Oliver insisted on a baritone. With the bass notes

19. Stordahl had been with Dorsey as a staff arranger since the early days of the band but only began to assert himself as a significant arranger voice in 1940 with the arrival of Sinatra and the vocal quartet called the Pied Pipers. Stordahl stayed with Sinatra when the latter left Dorsey in late 1942, becoming his chief arranger and musical adviser through 1949.

now more powerfully rooted, the superstructure of brass could now also be augmented sonically.[20]

One must add that Oliver was much aided in this musical transformation by two other players, Buddy Rich and Ziggy Elman, the one helping to lead the band from the bottom (the rhythm section), as it were, the other from the top as style-setting lead trumpet. Although Elman was best known for his more strident and ostentatious solos with Goodman (which, as such things go, naturally became his big hits with the general public), he *could* play with taste and style as many of his performances with his own 1939 nine-piece band demonstrate. It took Elman a while to settle in tonally with the Dorsey band, but once he did he contributed impressively to the orchestra's quality. He dominated the brass sound, even more than Dorsey, and yet he played with ensemble restraint when such was required. His solo on *Swanee River* is exemplary: clear, simple, and effective. On the other stylistic side, as lead trumpet Elman could add an expressive vitality to a lush arrangement like *In the Blue of Evening*. Finally, as one of the most technically daring and secure trumpet players of that period, Elman could overwhelm with his self-assured brilliance in virtuoso pieces like *Well, Git It* and *Blue Skies*.

Buddy Rich was (and is) another master technician. From the very outset a manually exceptionally gifted percussionist, Rich, with his extrovert personality and tremendous nervous energy, added a powerhouse dimension to the Dorsey band it had never enjoyed before, and which was the perfect complement to Elman's trumpet-playing. As with Elman, when Rich lost control of musical discipline, the results could be vulgar and destructive. And that did happen. But when his energies and talents were appropriately channeled, Rich could add immensely to an orchestra's effectiveness of interpretation.

One of the band's most spectacular efforts, combining the talents of Sy Oliver, Elman, Rich, and Elman's trumpet sidekick Chuck Peterson was *Well, Git It*. Set at a good up-tempo clip, this Sy Oliver piece goes a few steps beyond the earlier big band "killer-dillers" in that it is more a full-fledged original, albeit with many solos. But these are carefully selected as to contrasts of dynamics and colors, and integrated into the total work in ways that only Ellington had succeeded in doing. Thus, though Elman is prominently featured, one does not have a sense of his mercilessly dominating the performance at the expense of the overall work. Other well-integrated and stylistically matching solos are by Heinie Beau (with a scintillating clarinet solo), Don Lodice (a simple roughhewn "from-

20. A striking demonstration of Oliver's impact on the band's performances exists in side-by-side recordings made in the same session within minutes of each other: *For You* and *Without a Song*, both vocals, one with Jo Stafford, the other with Sinatra. The former is a rich powerful arrangement by Oliver, using superb contrasts of dynamics and timbres, and featuring one of Ziggy Elman's more ecstatic solos. Oddly enough the main soloist, Jo Stafford, remains relatively impervious to the accompaniment, rather cooly delivering the song in a clear-toned voice. *Without a Song*, on the other hand, is a dull listless affair that must have bored the band to tears (especially its drummer). Hearing these two performances back to back, unidentified, one would never believe that they came from the same orchestra, let alone the same recording session.

the-belly" tenor solo), and Milt Raskin's light-limbed Basie-ish piano solo. But it is the composed and stunningly played two-trumpet coda (Elman and Peterson) that is the work's crowning glory. It was the sort of thing that arrangers and trumpet players had often assayed[21] but never as brilliantly as on *Well, Git It*. In its own boisterous extrovert way, *Well, Git It* was a triumph in combining simple idiomatic swing-riff material with the ultimate in instrumental virtuosity.

When Dorsey added a ten-piece string section and harp in April 1942, Sy Oliver took this well in stride. *On Blue Blazes*, set at a breakneck speed of $\downarrow = 320$ and again featuring Elman and Peterson—this time in back-to-back solos—Oliver resorted to the kind of jazzy virtuoso string-writing (all in eighth notes) which Morton Gould had been featuring for several years on radio and recordings with his popular concert orchestra. Even more effective, however, was the simple *Cherokee*-like countermelody given the strings in Oliver's *Opus No. 1*, one of the last end-stations of the swing-riff tune that had come to jazz a decade earlier from the Midwest and Southwest.

So much for that half, the swing/jazz half, of the Dorsey band. Although it tried, it could never balance, let alone compete, with the other even more popularly successful side, featuring the romantic ballads and mood pieces of Sinatra and the Pied Pipers. Their popular success was so great that it not only created the stylistic rift within the band I mentioned earlier but seriously threatened to take over the complete musical output of the Dorsey orchestra. Indeed, the effect of Sinatra's phenomenal success, replete with screaming bobby soxers and sold-out Paramount theatres and the like, was such that singers everywhere began to dominate popular music, even more than before, until eventually most big bands became strictly accompanimental and secondary to the vocalists. This development in turn was one of the main contributing factors leading to the demise of the big bands in the postwar period. The thirteen-and-a-half-month recording ban in 1942 exacerbated the situation, for singers *were* allowed to record, and did, while instrumentalists could not. When the ban and World War II were over, the band business wore a new look: the singers had taken over, and with wartime and postwar prosperity everyone was trying for "the big popular hit"— via the singers. As a result jazz—and even its most popular manifestation, swing— were driven to the sidelines or stifled altogether. But jazz is a hardy strain, and in this early-to-mid-forties situation it evolved, partly in self-defense, an entirely new language and new modes of expression: be-bop and the small combos—*and no singers*.

But that is getting ahead of our story. For those dramatic developments could not yet be foreseen in early 1940 when Sinatra, after singing successfully with Harry James for about half a year, joined Tommy Dorsey. From the outset it was clear that here was an entirely new breed of singer. Already somewhat jazz-influenced, Sinatra brought a new type of free and natural phrasing to songs,

---

21. On the assumption that two or three high-note trumpets make a more climactic finish than one, this idea had been put to the test many times, in earlier days by the Missourians on any number of tunes, on Claude Hopkins's version of *King Porter Stomp* and on Ellington's *Tootin' Through the Roof*, but more recently (three years earlier) on Miller's *In the Mood*.

which even Bing Crosby could not match in sensitivity and interpretive imagination. Subtle jazz inflections and a fine beat, even in slow ballads, characterized his singing. Like his boss, Tommy Dorsey, he had what musicians call
"natural time," very little to do with metronomic time, but rather just a "perfect
feeling." Unlike many singers and pseudo-singers of the time, Sinatra had remarkably good intonation. And again it wasn't a studied, learned intonation; he
had a "natural ear" for it.

But perhaps the newest feature of his singing was the sheer quality of the voice
itself. After decades of colorless, lightweight, expressionless male voices—mostly
effeminate-sounding crooning tenors—Sinatra's virile earthy baritone, with a rich
bottom voice, was a startling departure from the popular norm.

Sinatra's original way with a phrase could be heard immediately on his first
performance with Dorsey (and, of course, before that with Harry James as, for
example, on *All or Nothing at All*). On *The Sky Fell Down, Too Romantic*, and
Shake Down The Stars—his initial recordings with Dorsey—Sinatra is understandably still a bit shaky and not as poised as he was to be in later years, but
his basic talents shine through unequivocally, most importantly in his innate
ability to spin and hold a musical line, thereby making a musical totality of a
song rather than a series of vaguely connected phrases. Like Dorsey in his trombone solos, Sinatra would carry phrases across bar lines or phrase joinings, balancing out weak points in songs or dramatizing their best structural elements.

Sinatra learned much from Dorsey's playing, especially in regard to breath
control and musical line. On the other hand, it is undoubtedly those very talents
in Sinatra—in raw form, to be sure—that Dorsey found attractive in the first
place. Sinatra's "horn"-like approach was the perfect complement to Dorsey's
highly *vocal* approach to the trombone.

But even a talent like Sinatra's takes time to develop and mature. Uneven
though his singing was at first, albeit never less than musical, there were enough
standout performances to be the envy of any popular singer. In time he learned
how to use dynamics and subtle timbral shadings (*Fools Rush In*, March 1940),
or to swing in that unique relaxed lilting way of his, that he perfected later in
his 1950s' recordings (*Where Do You Keep Your Heart?*, May 1940).

He also learned to stretch slow tempos almost beyond the point of emotional
endurance. Songs like *I'll Never Smile Again* and *This Love of Mine* were not
only big million-seller hits—jukeboxes in millions of bars and restaurants were
a major factor here—but were remarkable musical breakthroughs, instantly imitated by hordes of other singers and vocal groups—mostly with disastrous results.
For an abnormally slow tempo can be carried off only by a singer with perfect
breath control and an exceptional sense of musical line; and these were talents
only a handful of singers commanded. In time, of course, singers worthy and
capable of imitating Sinatra did come along—one thinks of Vic Damone or
Steve Lawrence, for example—but even such were rare.

Many of Sinatra's Dorsey recordings were made with the Pied Pipers, an originally eight-member vocal group (seven male, one female) reduced by Dorsey to
four for reasons of economy. In contrast to Glenn Miller's Modernaires, which

specialized in swing numbers, the Pied Pipers concentrated on tantalizingly slow-paced mood pieces, which were extremely hard to sing. Adjusting from eight to only four voices—Sinatra was often a fifth voice—was not easy, and their first twenty-five recordings or so were all flawed by minor intonational problems, especially a tendency towards flatness on the part of Jo Stafford.[22] But no one in popular music had ever tried to sing at such slow tempos, and it took some time to learn how, technically and musically, to accomplish that. Even so, many of the Pied Pipers' records with Sinatra were in their special way laudable achievements, hauntingly romantic performances—and great commercial successes to boot: *Star Dust, I Guess I'll Have To Dream the Rest*, and perhaps their most compelling (though imperfect) performance, *The Night We Called It a Day*. The ultimate in romantic nostalgic balladry, Matt Dennis's beautiful tune was perfectly suited to the Pied Pipers' "*Mood Indigo*" sound—for we must remember that this all started with Ellington and Arthur Whetsol in the 1930 *Mood Indigo* (originally entitled *Dreamy Blues*). Dreamy and blue was the Pied Pipers' approach, perfectly aided and abetted here by Ziggy Elman's muted trumpet, four clarinets and a bass clarinet, and a whispering rhythm section. Although here the ties to jazz are tenuous and fragile, the fact remains that in *The Night* the Pied Pipers and Dorsey's musicians created a magical aura that will forever personify an era—at least a part of it.

These romantic outpourings required of the Dorsey band a whole new timbral palette. At first, cup-muted brass, limpid clarinets and bass clarinets, dulcet trombone choirs could suffice; and Stordahl, Weston, and Oliver became masterful at supplying the pastel-colored scores. But in time the arrangements reached such a degree of sumptuousness (hear the larger-than-life sound of the orchestra, still only 17 pieces, on such late 1941 recordings as *How About You?* or *Poor You*) that the only logical next step was to add strings. In April 1942, following Harry James's and Artie Shaw's examples, Dorsey added a ten-man string section (seven violins, two violas, and a cello) plus harp to his orchestra.[23] Even Sy Oliver's swing arrangements were now pushed aside, at least on recordings—on dance and theatre dates the instrumentals remained prominently featured—and as the band rushed to record everything it could before the August 1 recording ban, it concentrated on the lush string arrangements with their enormous commercial potential. And once again, in this particular genre, Dorsey, Stordahl, Sinatra, and occasionally the Pied Pipers created a number of perfectly crafted masterpieces of a kind. D'Artega's *In the Blue of Evening* and Grofé's *Daybreak* are hauntingly beautiful pieces, consummately performed—note the special opulence given these arrangements by the telling use of the harp. As such they represented in the field of luxurious popular "mood"-arranging the ultimate state

---

22. Jo Stafford went on to sing many fine vocals with the Dorsey band, later taking up a distinguished career as a single. She is also well known for her hilarious originally pseudonymous 1957 hit recording, made with her husband, Paul Weston, satirizing bad singers and accompanists: *The Piano Artistry of Jonathan Edwards*.

23. It is interesting to note that with his civilian band, Glenn Miller never succumbed to the "strings temptation," but made up for it with a vengeance in his Air Force orchestra.

of the art. (Only Kostelanetz, with even greater orchestral resources—and without a traveling orchestra to worry about—was to do better, if more coloristic orchestration and greater sumptuousness of sound is to be called "better").

The recording ban of 1942–43 in many ways delineated the end of an era and the beginning of another. New musical undercurrents, though still mostly submerged in those years were forming, and soon new musical impulses from black musicians would dramatically reshape the world of jazz and popular music. Within very few years the big bands, especially the expensive string-laden orchestras, were to become victims of both these musical and other extra-musical (largely economic) pressures. But even before that ultimate denouément, Dorsey's orchestra had reached its artistic and commercial zenith. Both Sinatra and the Pied Pipers left shortly after the onset of the recording ban. Elman and Rich went into the armed services, and the orchestra was decimated by other personnel losses. Although Rich came back in 1944, and Dorsey was able to acquire the long-time services of Charlie Shavers, the first black musician in his orchestra, the Dorsey band was never able to recapture its former brilliance and glory. It had its small successes, of course—even an "all-time hit"—in 1943 with *Boogie Woogie*. But the odd thing about that was that this record, first cut in 1938 and then a bouncing non-success, became a hit only when reissued during the recording ban. By then the tender sensibilities of white audiences could accept Dorsey's well-fumigated version of Pinetop Smith's boogie woogie (first recorded by the latter in the 1920s). And 1944 saw several other first-rate recordings, including the already mentioned *Opus No. 1* and a superb version of *On the Sunny Side of the Street*.

By the end of 1946 Dorsey—along with seven other top bandleaders—was forced to disband his orchestra, but, unlike most of the others, he reorganized two years later. Somehow with his Irish stubbornness and with significant help from Jackie Gleason (who featured the band on his early 1950s television show for several seasons), Dorsey maintained his orchestra until his untimely death in 1956.

Good examples of the band's postwar work abound, although these are rarely innovative or highly creative. The few white big bands that existed in the 1950s—many only for recording purposes—were all remarkable performing groups, regardless of their repertory or musical style, having access to a whole new generation of superior craftsmen and instrumental technicians. But the big bands, considered musical dinosaurs by many, were hardly the ideal arena for exploring the new developments in modern jazz. Except for Woody Herman and Stan Kenton, most surviving white bands spent their energies trying to revive in one way or another the late Swing Era—Dorsey included. Always a traditionalist, Dorsey would in his last years permit a Neal Hefti to bring a more modern orchestral and phrasing style to his band, or allow a Bill Finegan to introduce a few bitonal harmonies and modern chord substitutions. But these were essentially cosmetic changes, never affecting the Dorsey orchestra's basic traditional stance. Ultimately this was primarily a matter of repertory, for Dorsey (and hundreds of his white colleagues) never understood the fundamental truth that jazz is first and foremost a creative music. Dorsey could never think of jazz in creative terms or as instantaneous creative composing, equating it instead narrowly with Dixieland, already an essentially anachronistic style when Dorsey *started* his orchestra.

Except for Sy Oliver's work in the 1940s, Dorsey never came in contact with jazz *as* jazz or in terms of a jazz repertory, but was quite content to linger forever in a world of popular songs dressed in semi-jazz attire. Jazz standards for Dorsey meant things like *Milenberg Joys* or *Tin Roof Blues*. He, for example, never performed or recorded *Stompin' at the Savoy, One O'Clock Jump, Take the A Train*, or any number of other later jazz standards. In Dorsey's canon the arrangement reigned supreme; composition and creativity in the jazz sense were foreign to him and—as to many of his colleagues—of little concern.

Many fine players were privileged to play with Dorsey in those later years. The list might include drummer Louis Bellson, the fine clarinetist Walt Lewinsky, trumpeters Ray Wetzel and the young Doc Severinson, the modern pianist Gene Kutch, saxophonist Boomie Richman, and Dorsey's old friend, Lee Castle, who led the band after Dorsey's death. A selected list of distinctive recordings from the postwar period might include *It's Delovely, I Get a Kick Out of You, The Honey Dripper, Puddle Whump, Again, Farewell to Arms*, and *Rest Stop*.

With all the difficulties, personal and professional, of Dorsey's late years, he maintained his trombone-playing at an uncommonly high level to the very end. And although he could not make the transition to the modern era, his superb trombone-playing, in itself an artistic statement, will be remembered and cherished for generations to come. Dorsey was, after all, that sentimental and memorable gentleman of swing.

ARTIE SHAW

If there ever was a profoundly enigmatic and contradictory figure in jazz, it was Arthur Arshawsky, known to the world as Artie Shaw. Although Shaw is still alive and well at this writing, it is proper to use the past tense "was," since he left the field of music thirty years ago, in 1955.[24] The anomalies in Shaw's public career, fully justifying the terms "enigmatic" and "contradictory," are so numerous and complex as to make objective evaluation of his work as a musical artist a formidable task. Shaw's own explications of the more dramatic twists and turns of his career in his autobiography, *The Trouble with Cinderella*, have not been helpful. In fact, Shaw, possessor of a brilliant intellect and penetrating mind, has skillfully managed in his book to obscure with rationalizing smokescreens some of the more controversial episodes in his musical career.

The many mysteries and enigmas that thread and twist throughout his public life begin with the most basic of all: namely, how the rather mediocre clarinet player that Shaw was in the early 1930s as a studio freelancer in New York could

---

24. Shaw's return to music in 1985 is only partial, limited to organizing a replica of his swing bands but not actually performing himself.

become one of the two or three most outstanding clarinetists in all of jazz—some would say *the* greatest of them all. Shaw's often inept, stiff, squeaky playing in his early days—sample his work with Red Norvo's Swing Septet in 1934, for instance—provides no hint that within a few years he would give even Benny Goodman a run for his money, and would eventually (to many ears) topple from his throne the King of Swing as well as the King of the Clarinet. Here Shaw in his autobiography does provide the only logical explanation: once he had embarked upon a career as a bandleader, he lived and slept the clarinet, day and night, practicing seven and eight hours a day—what musicians call "paying your dues," that intensive "woodshedding" period without which even the most natural talents cannot reach the pinnacle of their profession and their craft.

By 1939 Shaw had progressed from a proficient imitator of Benny Goodman to a real master of the clarinet, virtually incomparable in the beauty of his tone and unique in his flawless control of the instrument's highest register. Moreover, he had developed into a highly individual improviser who, when really inspired, had not only an abundance of creative ideas but more than enough technique to summon them instantly and unerringly from his clarinet. Primarily a lyric player, Shaw excelled in his peak years in the long, flowing, seamless soaring line. Although he eventually learned to play with considerable rhythmic verve, swing was not his forte. Indeed, it was his weakness in the early years, and an element of his playing which at best was variable, dependent a great deal on the swing capabilities of his rhythm sections.

Similarly, although Shaw had technique to burn, he was not by inclination a virtuoso player. Technical feats as such interested him very little, and it must be said that he probably resisted more successfully than any other clarinetist the temptations to dazzle with superficial bravura exhibitions, temptations that are always near at hand with the technique-prone clarinet. Shaw was, in his best years, an uncompromising searcher for the lofty and the expressive, for real musical substance, not only in his own playing but in the styles and concepts of his bands. That he paradoxically so often failed to achieve these commendable goals will be among the more interesting aspects of the following chronicle of Shaw's work.

For to say that Shaw was a searcher for quality and substance—and individuality—is not to say that he necessarily always found it, at least not in the measure that he sometimes thought he had. The hard evidence of his actual work—his recordings and the airchecks that have survived—when disentangled from all the post-facto rationalizations, self-analyses and protestations of one kind or another that seemed always to be a part of Shaw's life—reveal that Shaw was seldom an accurate judge of his bands' merits—or demerits. He was also apt to misjudge the nature of and reasons for his popular successes as well as for his failures. Moreover, the evidence shows that he found it difficult to distinguish between his arrangers' contributions to his successes (and failures) and his own. He often took credit for achievements that belonged, at least to significant extents, to others—or, as in the case of some of his bigger commercial "hits," to luck and chance as well.

It is true that he, like Glenn Miller and to some extent Benny Goodman, had a hand, often significantly so, in the final shaping of an arrangement and its performance, by editing, subtracting, and adding. And that was a bandleader's prerogative, and the more articulate among them, like Shaw, certainly availed themselves of that leadership privilege.

The fact that Shaw had at least eight different bands between 1936 and 1955, when he withdrew from an active life in music—ten, if you count his Navy band and one other civilian transformation—is symptomatic of both his searching and his confusion, and ultimately of his inability to find what he was looking for. (Perhaps there are also parallels in Shaw's private life, particularly in his multiple marriages.) The first of these many orchestras lasted less than a year. It was a curious group in that it included a string quartet, essentially a nine-piece band plus four strings.[25] That was enough of an oddity in the early heyday of big swing bands to be a matter of considerable curiosity, if not controversy. Shaw promptly blamed his fledgling orchestra's lack of success on the audience's ignorance in not appreciating the validity and originality of such an instrumentation, and he chastised the public for preferring the louder, more straightahead swing of Goodman, Barnet, Berigan, and the two Dorseys with their brass and reed sections. (Shaw's rationalization also fails to take into account that there were *innumerable* fine pieces and performances by Ellington and Lunceford that were not all loud or, in fact, not loud at all.)

But this—the first of such Shaw misjudgements—is by no means the whole story. Contrary to such a simplistic rationalization, the evidence of the recordings from 1936 and early 1937 shows that the band suffered from a number of weaknesses, the most serious of which was that it played with almost no swing at all. Its rhythm, essentially two-beat, was generally very stiffly projected, and whatever momentum the band could occasionally gather was usually undercut and interrupted by the string quartet in cloying, slushy interludes, modulations, transitions, introductions, and codas. At the same time the playing of the five "horns" was often ragged and thin sounding. When one compares what Eddie Sauter was able to do with even fewer instruments in Red Norvo's 1936 band,[26] it becomes clear that Shaw and Joe Lippman—both reputedly responsible for the arrangements, either singly or jointly—did not approach this problem with much ingenuity or imagination. Most of the material was fairly tawdry to begin with, inconsequential pop and dance tunes of the period. The overall effect then was that of a band without a style: unsettled, eclectic, directionless. It offered an impression of restlessness and fragmentation, of searching and not finding.

As for the use of the string quartet, I'm sure that Shaw felt that he was integrating the strings—or at least trying to—into a jazz context. And on the face of it, why not? The idea of a jazz orchestra that contains both winds and strings is

25. Shaw liked to create the impression that the use of a string quartet in a "jazz" context was original with him. But the reader of this chapter will recall that Glenn Miller had in fact already experimented with this specific idea (i.e. not strings in general but a standard string quartet) in 1935, one year before Shaw. The concept was the same: a string quartet integrated into a small jazz group, consisting of a sextet of "horns" and a rhythm section.
26. See above, Chapter 6, part 2.

not inherently faulty—as most jazz writers seem to think. The problem is not—
and never has been—with the strings themselves, but rather how they are almost
always used. The moments in jazz when strings were used contrapuntally, for
example, or in fast moving passages—something strings happen to be able to do
extremely well—can probably be counted on one hand. The usual rudimentary
block writing, alternating with lush melodic lines, all played in a tasteless style
using excessive vibratos, slides, scoops, and other similarly banal effects, is *bound*
to produce a soggy, syrupy result. And, *of course*, such writing has nothing to
do with jazz.

But to blame that on the string instruments *per se* is unfair and absurd. The
most convincing proof that strings do not need to sound "soggy and syrupy"—
and in fact do not—can be found in several 100,000 classical symphonic pieces
from Corelli to the present, none of which—even those by, say, Rachmaninov,
Ravel, Delius and the like—sound remotely like any of their latter-day popular/
jazz/commercial counterparts.[27] Having a string quartet play half and whole notes
in close parallel harmony underneath an Artie Shaw clarinet solo was bound to
weigh down the overall sound with a blanket of acoustical sludge, and automatically reduce the possibility of swing to about nil. It is difficult to comprehend
how an intelligent musician like Shaw could so completely misjudge not only
what he was pretending to produce but its actual results as well. Nor is it possible
to understand how he could tolerate, let alone be responsible for and justify,
such mediocre results as are heard on, say, *No More Tears* (February 1937) and
the quite dreadful *There's Something in the Air* (October 1936). To blame the
public then for failing to recognize his orchestra's "superiority" is a measure of
Shaw's considerable lack of artistic objectivity and lack of self-criticism. For all
his serious-mindedness about art and the nature of the music business, Shaw
could also seemingly misjudge the quality and nature of his own art.

All in all, Shaw's first effort at producing and leading a jazz orchestra must
be counted as rather pathetic, judged by any serious standards of creativity—
especially considering the superb models that were all around him (Ellington,
Lunceford, Webb, Norvo, not to mention Shaw's arch rival and nemesis, Goodman).

Every bit of enthusiasm Shaw had previously brought to his first orchestra he
now lavished on the second installment, a standard fourteen-piece string-less
band, rather pretentiously called "Artie Shaw and His New Music." From the
outset this band was a marked improvement over the earlier one. With a better
rhythm section (Al Avola, Ben Guinsberg, and Cliff Leeman on guitar, bass,

27. That the saccharine effect produced by strings in popular music derives to a large extent from
the *manner* of playing is easily demonstrated by hundreds of examples in which arrangers of dance
or jazz orchestras have lifted, literally, passages by composers like Ravel—always a favorite object of
plagiarism. I can assure the reader that no symphony orchestra in the world would ever make these
Ravel passages sound the way they do on non-classical recordings. In this connection it is ironic that
such radio orchestra leaders in the 1940s as Morton Gould and André Kostelanetz, generally disregarded or maligned by jazz critics, not only favored a much purer string sound but also exploited
the strings to their full technical, idiomatic, and expressive potential—a fact for which, to my knowledge, they have never been given any credit.

and drums respectively), the band could begin to play with some sense of swing, although a few of the 1937 sides are still played in a vertical, ploddingly rhythmic manner that has almost nothing to do with jazz (*Someday Sweetheart*, for example). Shaw's own playing was now improving markedly, not only in the development of his tone but in the inventiveness of his improvisations and their technical execution. Although the band's brass tended at first to play with an unpleasant stridency and lack of internal balance, they did gradually improve in this respect, playing not only with more precision but with more linearity. The arrangements by Avola and trombonist Harry Rogers helped considerably in at least pointing the band in the right direction. Even so, in listening to many of these 1937 sides, it is hard to comprehend how two years after Palomar (Goodman's great breakthrough success) the Shaw band could still be so relatively far behind, in style, in execution, in its rhythmic drive and sound concept.

And then there were Tony Pastor's old-fashioned "hotel-band" saxophone solos and awful singers like Nita Bradley to contend with. On the plus side, more solidly in a jazz posture, at least in intent, were trumpeter Johnny Best (later an important member of the Glenn Miller band), George Arus, a severely limited but at least well-intentioned trombonist playing in a simplified Dixieland style, and novelty-and-scat singer Leo Watson (who was soon to have a direct influence on bassist Slam Stewart and his novelty/scat-singing cohort Slim Gaillard).

But above all, Shaw himself was coming into his own as an often splendid improvising soloist and a superior clarinetist. Though he still tended to sound at times like his rival Benny Goodman, a personal Shaw style was increasingly discernible. *All God's Children* and *It Goes to Your Feet* are exemplary breakthrough performances of Shaw pulling away from the Goodman influence. This new individuality could be heard especially in Shaw's tone—considerably warmer than Goodman's perfect-but-cool sonority—and above all in Shaw's development of the upper octave of the clarinet range and beyond. Whereas most of the best clarinetists—Goodman, Barney Bigard, Woody Herman, Johnny Mince, later Heinie Beau and Skip Martin—could manage high Fs and Gs (concert pitch) easily enough, they tended to limit such high notes to special climactic moments in solos and, generally speaking, did not linger much in that upper register. Nor did they venture much higher than that accepted note ceiling, whereas Shaw was continually exploring the *entire* upper range for its expressive, i.e. melodic potential, eventually extending the range right up to the high B♭, the first time—at least on Shaw's recordings—in *Meade Lux Special* (February 15, 1938). Goodman was to follow Shaw into this stratospheric region, but never with the consistency, ease, and commanding ability of incorporating this newly gained ground into fully melodic and technical expressions. [28]

At the same time, while Shaw talked a great deal about "emotion" and "ex-

---

28. To a large extent clarinetists were driven to extend the upper range of their instruments by the trumpet players. Since Armstrong and Eldridge had by the middle-late 30s established high F as a relatively comfortable norm for the upper range of the trumpet—very soon to be followed by younger players with Gs and A♭s—the clarinetists, playing an intrinsically higher-ranged instrument, were almost embarrassed into trying to out-distance their brass colleagues.

pressivity," reproving other clarinetists for "just showcasing technique," much of *his* playing in this 1937 period was emotionally remote and technique-minded. On the other hand, he was undeniably trying to climb out of the Goodman stylistic box and to search for a greater and deeper range of expression.

The band too was becoming at once more relaxed and more cohesive in its ensemble work, increasingly adopting the predominant Goodman-via-Fletcher Henderson idioms. Riff tunes, virtually banished in the earlier Shaw band, began to crop up in the repertory with some regularity (*Let 'Er Go, Non-Stop Flight, S.O.S.*), playing with much greater fluency in (aptly titled) pieces like *Free Wheeling* and *Free for All*. Still, the band's progress was by no means in a straight upward line. Pop ephemera (Shaw even recorded *Sweet Adeline*), pallid dance numbers, awful fake-voodoo-atmosphere-invoking pieces like *The Chant*[29] abound. There was certainly little sense of jazz as a *creative music*.

An interesting nuance here is Shaw's apparent inability to grasp the high quality of Jerry Gray's arranging talent. Gray had played first violin in Shaw's string-quartet band and by 1937, on a freelance basis, had begun to contribute some fairly interesting arrangements to the Shaw book (*Blue Skies*, for example). These were generally more complex than the simplistic efforts Shaw and his other arrangers were producing. Gray's arrangements were marked by at least a counterpoint of musical ideas; several lines or patterns going on simultaneously, ensemble interplay; and, above all, his arrangements swung more. And yet Shaw seems not to have followed up on Gray's fledgling initiatives—until, of course, the great commercial breakthrough of his *Begin the Beguine* arrangement.

Also worth noting is a temporary phase in Shaw's search for a style or an identity, of waking up to the pre-eminence of black composers, arrangers, and bandleaders—an inclination which by the way he steadfastly disavowed and regularly accused Goodman and Miller of pursuing to excess. I suspect that this was a much-delayed reaction to a similar (but considerably more genuine) realization on Charlie Barnet's part as early as 1933 and 1934 of the relative superiority of such black creative innovators as Benny Carter, Fletcher and Horace Henderson, and later, of course, Duke Ellington. In any case by late 1937 and early 1938 Shaw had discovered not only Basie but Carter, Ellington, even Edgar Sampson and Luis Russell (recording the last's famous *Call of the Freaks*). Carter was represented by his *Lost in the Shuffle* and *Symphony in Riffs* (a title which Shaw, with his ever-present but now momentarily dormant symphonic fascinations, must have loved).

This movement in the direction of the right, or at least, better sources and

29. Shaw's career-long fascination with this genre of music, usually meaning sinuous, sinister, pseudo-jungleistic fantasies over "exotic" tomtom beatings, is one of the greatest anomalies in the work of a man with such high intellectual ambitions. How he could chastise fellow musicians for being intellectual pygmies, for not knowing and reading Shakespeare, Balzac, and Joyce, or not listening to Beethoven string quartets, and at the same time consistently produce such trashy numbers as *The Chant, Nightmare, Ubangi,* and *Hindustan* (the last as late as 1942)—which the more gullible public in its need for exotica, of course, loved and turned into commercial hits for Shaw—is again one of those confounding contradictions in Shaw's personality.

models was abruptly arrested with the unexpected popular and commercial/financial success in the summer of 1938 of *Begin the Beguine*, Shaw's first major hit. Shaw had by this time developed a real ability to spin long, elegant, vibrant, seamless lines, almost as if he was trying to capture on his clarinet what a violin, without the need to breathe, could do so naturally and effectively.[30] Gray's arrangement, too, offered a pleasant interchange of textures, ensembles (interspersed with solos—even Tony Pastor captured a certain lyric quality), and harmonic variations of Cole Porter's tune (a remarkable *108-bar* structure, by the way).[31]

Much has been written, mostly by Shaw but also others, of how the success of *Beguine* changed his life, producing, allegedly, the great schism between his artistic ambitions and the oppressive pressures of popular success, with its multitude of jitterbugging hysterical fans, autograph hunters, suddenly interested press agents, public relations people, and other "parasites" of the music business. While any sincere, uncompromising artist would share Shaw's concern about these matters, it is worth noting that, despite all his verbal protestations, there is little actual evidence that Shaw tried very hard to elude such "bad" influences—until some years later, it must be admitted. There is a strong element of intellectual snobbism in Shaw's comments on the subject, and one cannot help but paraphrase a truism of Shakespeare, "me thinks he protesteth too much." In fact for the rest of 1938 the repertory continued to favor forgettable pop tunes—gone was the interest in black composers—offered in arrangements that occasionally matched what Goodman had been able to accomplish in popular swing style, but never surpassed it. The average, the passable, the mediocre stand right alongside the admirable, the skillful, the effective, in a confusing, still seemingly directionless mélange. A straightahead Henderson-style *What Is This Thing Called Love?* vies for the same attention as the by-then old-fashioned, relentlessly driven Casa Loma-style arrangement of *Copenhagen*, admittedly well performed, though. The ersatz primitivism of the opening of *Jungle Drums*—you guessed it: clarinet over tomtoms!—stands side by side, literally (recorded on the same day) with the lovely clarinet-and-saxes ending of *A Room with a View*, in which Shaw's finely sculpted soaring clarinet lines already predict the beautiful things to come in his great *Star Dust* performance of two years hence. Most of the arrangements are set in ordinary dance tempos and also seem to be totally unaware of the instrumental colors available in a jazz orchestra, something Duke Ellington had been showing the world for at least ten years. The instrumental choirs are assigned with unimaginative regularity their standard roles and registers—something Jerry Gray was soon to change—and even the great variety of brass mutes available by 1938 seem to be used only rarely and almost accidentally.

Ironically, Shaw spoke a great deal about each piece finding its own essence,

30. Shaw was hypercritical of almost all other living musicians, but his admiration for the great Jascha Heifetz was simply boundless.

31. I am indebted to Martin Williams for this revelation, Martin being one of the most avid tune-structure and chord-progression analyzers around. I must confess that, probably because *Beguine* was since my teens always a big "commercial hit," I never paid much attention to it and its structure until recently.

at the same time lambasting Goodman and Miller for trying to impose a single specific style on everything. Shaw spoke of "discerning" or "analyzing" a tune's character and then letting *that* "define the style in which it should be played." Brave words, these, and arguably well-advised ones, but unfortunately for the moment bearing little relevance to the actual results produced by Shaw's orchestra. Most of the arrangements in the 1937–38 period sound numbingly alike, and there is precious little, except on the most minimal creative scale, that differentiates the "essence" of one piece from another's. In the midst of all this one may hear a fresh voice, like young George Auld's brief Prez-like solo on *It Had To Be You*—Pastor had by now been banished to just the ballad-type romantic solos—or Ted Vesley's relatively "hot" and swinging trombone.

Then there *was*, however, the very young Helen Forrest—eighteen at the time—already an outstanding vocal and musical talent, notwithstanding the fact that at this time the twin influences of Mildred Bailey and Billie Holiday were still clearly audible in her work. Shaw's and the others' arrangements did not do much for her, however—they more or less ran parallel to her singing as it were. But she nevertheless, as much as Shaw himself, contributed substantially to the band's popular success, mainly by the sincerity and unmannered communicative directness with which she could deliver a song, even a mediocre one.

But the Shaw enigmas and contradictions continue in endless profusion. How does one reconcile the decision to record, say, *Indian Love Call* or an ordinary pop trifle like *I Have Eyes* with the decision to hire Billie Holiday as the band's singer, thereby engaging one of the greatest singing artists of all time, while simultaneously breaking the then still harshly maintained color line in the band business? Billie's singing on *Any Old Time* (July 1938), her only recorded vocal with Shaw (a telling fact?), is like a breath of fresh air in the welter of mediocre to average offerings Shaw was still generally dispensing. Though *Any Old Time* was by no means Billie's very best and some of her vocal mannerisms were beginning to clutter her style, she was clearly in a class by herself and a true jazz musician. Her one song with Shaw strikingly brings into focus how far Shaw himself was still removed from the essence of jazz.

But there was other help on the way—for whose contributions, once again, Shaw himself took the credit. It came in the form of two powerfully influential additions to the band: one, the acquisition of the extremely talented and versatile drummer Buddy Rich, then only twenty years old; and the full-time engagement of Jerry Gray as Shaw's primary arranger. These two musicians virtually transformed the band overnight. With *Lover Come Back to Me* (January 1939) and other performances from that period, the Shaw orchestra suddenly reached a new plateau, from which it was then able to begin the final assault upon the throne of the Kingdom of Swing, in order to topple the King himself, Benny Goodman.[32]

32. My dramatic description of this sudden-seeming stylistic, artistic breakthrough may surprise most readers, and will undoubtedly be regarded with great suspicion by a number of jazz "authorities." But to savor and absorb this stunning quantum qualitative leap, one must have listened to Shaw's recordings sequentially, systematically—a premise on which, incidentally, *all* of my listening to some 30,000 jazz recordings in the writing of this book has been based.

Gray's arrangements, now much less (if at all) under his leader's sway, gave the band a whole new tone and air. They were more spacious, less cluttered and fragmented than Shaw's and his other arrangers' earlier ones had been. They were more of a piece, focusing on a particular mood or idea or technique, just as Shaw had proposed but rarely previously carried out. Gray's arrangements were full of contrasts of color, of texture, of dynamics, breaking up old formularized arranging roles into new and different ensemble combinations. Gray took the trumpets, for example, out of the top-of-the-staff upper range, using them instead in all kinds of registers, mutings, dynamic levels, and timbral mixtures. The saxes, too, began to use dynamics and alluring phrase inflections, bent notes and the like; and instead of being relegated to the middle alto and tenor range, they suddenly found themselves a great deal of the time in their more luminous upper range. I am convinced that in much of his sax writing Gray, the violinist, was trying to capture some of the warmth, brilliance, and lyricism that fine string writing can so readily achieve.

Now the Shaw orchestra's performances *did* capture the mood and character of the Broadway show tunes he appropriated in his repertory. There was a sense, especially in his own playing, of each song being respected for its essence, rather than being buried under the façade of a particular arranging style. To a remarkable extent each song now received the kind of treatment its mood and lyrics seemed to indicate—a far cry from the formula-like arranging styles of most late-thirties' swing bands.

Finally, Gray's arrangements lent themselves to a more *swinging* performance style, more exciting and interesting musically, and at the same time more suited to the type of swing dancing that had spread like wildfire throughout the country in the wake of the Goodman-inspired swing craze. To be sure, none of what Gray was writing was in any profound sense new; it had all been done before by any number of major bands (Ellington, Lunceford, Henderson). But in the world of white bands—and especially Shaw's—these adaptations of already proven techniques loomed like major discoveries and revelations.

The timing of Buddy Rich's arrival in the band, coinciding as it did with Gray's breakthrough into a higher creative realm, was most fortuitous. Rich, immensely gifted, technically as well as imaginatively, and blessed with boundless energy and enthusiasm, seized upon the new spirit in Gray's arrangements and provided the band with the kind of uplifting drive it had never enjoyed before. That is something that probably only a drummer can give a band (or possibly a pianist of the formidable forcefulness of an Ellington), but not a clarinetist bent upon a primarily lyric and expressive approach, like Shaw. Moreover, Rich added significantly to the color palette of the Shaw band, extracting all manner of percussion sonorities available from his drum set—not to mention his shouted exhortations to the band, audible, for example, even on commercial recordings like *Traffic Jam* and on many on-location airchecks. Occasionally Rich, in bursts of youthful exuberance, would overdo things, play too much or too loud. But that was a relatively rare problem, compared for example with most of his playing in later years (an era of loud drummers in any case).

The musical and emotional excitement Shaw and his orchestra could generate on location was quite extraordinary. Many bands were known to perform better (or at least differently) in ballrooms and theatres than in the recording studio, with its bare walls, "inhuman" microphones, and audience-less ambiance. Shaw was no exception, judging by some of the 1938–39 air checks made available some years ago on Victor LPT-6000. Clearly, audience and orchestra fed on each other's well-stimulated energies. These performances are generally a revelation in the looser drive and collective spirit with which the band played, especially when Buddy Rich was aboard. The interplay between Shaw and his other soloists was often inspired, but the most astounding discovery for one who has only known Shaw through his official recordings is his own solo playing on these air shots. His performance of *Non-Stop Flight* (December 1, 1938) is nothing short of astonishing in its fusion of imaginative ideas with impeccable execution.

Rich brought to the Shaw band the musical energy and drive that he had gleaned from Chick Webb, Jo Jones, Sid Catlett, and other major black big-band drummers. This elemental force in turn stimulated Shaw to ever greater heights, not only as soloist but even as an arranger. His arrangement of *Rose Room*, for example, structurally well-balanced, incorporating contrasting instrumental colors, allows the rhythm section to function with perfect swing, and in turn frees the band to play in a more relaxed manner and with a fuller, richer sound. Shaw's own playing in this period (1939) was at an extraordinarily high level, both figuratively and literally. His awesome command of the highest register is amply displayed on *I'm Coming Virginia*, *Pastel Blue*, and many other sides. His playing at this time was also consistently musical and expressive, largely justifying his claims that it "unlike Goodman's grew from the music rather than from the instrument." I am not sure that the *caveat* about Goodman applies as strictly as Shaw intended it, but, comparisons aside, Shaw really could deliver what he boasted.

But that presents another irony. For the recorded evidence shows clearly that what Shaw always claimed *he* was teaching and extracting from his earlier bands— quality music and uncompromising creative energy—he had in fact rarely gotten. But conversely, it was the 1939 band, as sparked by Gray and Rich (as well as Auld and trumpeter Bernie Privin), that wrung from *him* a musical and technical excellence that he had rarely reached before. In effect, what Artie Shaw couldn't get out of his two first bands, the second one, at mid-juncture, *got out of him*.

Shaw's greatest success, both popular and critical, came at the very time (mid-1939) when Goodman had slipped down from the high crest of his initial popularity, reaching a temporary nadir, and in fact disbanding for a while, but reorganizing a few months later with an entirely new band. This left Shaw suddenly on top of the popularity polls[33] with no competition—at least for a few months, when Glenn Miller's sudden unprecedented success in the spring of

---

33. The popularity polls in the trade journals, like *Downbeat* and *Metronome*, were quite meaningless in any serious critical or artistic terms, since they reflected practically no reaction to the great black orchestras, which in turn were virtually unknown to white audiences.

1939 changed the whole picture. Shaw was still producing at high level (for example, *One Foot in the Groove*, a fine Wen d'Aury arrangement, or *Out of Nowhere*, with its superb, perfectly executed saxophone ensemble). And in *Traffic Jam*, composed and arranged by the young black tenor player Ted McRae, the Shaw band finally arrived at the level of virtuoso excitement and collective drive that Bennie Moten had already attained in 1932 on *Toby*, from which piece, by the way, the Shaw-McRae effort seems to have borrowed copiously. On *I Surrender Dear*, Shaw produces a marvel of a side-ending cadenza (parts of which, again, were recapitulated in his 1940 *Star Dust* hit).

But some ominous storm clouds were beginning to appear on Shaw's musical horizon. In September 1938 the high-strung Shaw had the first of several nervous breakdowns on the bandstand. Another alarming sign was the number of takes required to complete the recordings on two June 1939 sessions. *Comes Love* took seventeen *(sic!)* takes, and most of the other near-dozen sides required from four to eleven takes (the norm being one, or at most, two or three). More disturbingly, Shaw's own playing could suddenly falter badly, as on *All the Things You Are*, where his tone is surprisingly hard and cold, rather tubby in the middle register. Finally, as is almost inevitable, given the burdensome talent-exhausting demands a popular public career makes upon its leading talents (we see the same problem today with the lack of staying power of rock groups or television series), the band's arrangements wrote themselves increasingly into a formularized corner. A certain degree of creative burn-out had begun to take its toll. Also Shaw's personal aloofness as a leader, his inability to relate humanly, socially to his men, and the rigid maintenance of his impenetrable intellectual façade, all led to a serious erosion of the band's spirit.

The end came suddenly when Shaw, after a second and more serious physical collapse, returned to the band briefly, but in late November 1939 announced the immediate disbanding of his orchestra. Buddy Rich, sensing the impending demise, had already jumped ship, transferring over to Tommy Dorsey. Under Georgie Auld's leadership the Shaw band tried to carry on, but in three months it was all over. The second Shaw orchestra had entered the history books.

But only three and a half months and one Mexican vacation later, Shaw was back in the recording studios in Hollywood with a brand-new orchestra, pursuing his original dream of a string-rich ensemble. He had initially hoped to establish a sixty-five-piece (!) orchestra, but was dissuaded from doing so when he realized that almost no theatres or bandstands would hold such a large group, and settled for thirty-two players—a fifteen-piece jazz complement plus thirteen strings and a wind quartet of flute, oboe, bass clarinet, and horn.[34]

Yet another enigma: Shaw's luck held out, as the orchestra's very first recording, a rather eclectic and mostly commercial arrangement of a Mexican popular tune Shaw had heard on his recuperative vacation, became an immediate and overwhelming hit. Commercial hits are at best hard to explain, let alone predict.

34. It is interesting to note that both Shaw and Stan Kenton to some extent harbored quite similar ambitions: over-sized ensembles with quasi-symphonic pretentions and basically misconceived notions of "improving" or "bettering" jazz.

Frenesi is no exception. Only minimally and sporadically related to anything one could call jazz, the performance sports a superbly played melodic solo by trumpeter Mannie Klein and a pleasant horn solo by Jack Cave (who was later to become the first permanently employed horn player in a "jazz" orchestra, in Harry James's 1941 band). Indeed the *Frenesi* orchestra was not a jazz orchestra at all; it had no real jazz soloists of any consequence, and was heavily populated by Hollywood studio musicians. Moreover, Shaw's idea of engaging the black oboist and composer William Grant Still (who had arranged for Paul Whiteman in the late twenties and before that had been the oboist in Eubie Blake's pit band for his Broadway musical hit *Shuffle Along*) to arrange all six tunes on that first 1940 date, was perhaps a noble and generous thought but musically a mistake. Still's arrangements—*Frenesi* was by far the best—were mostly trite, formless, eclectic in the extreme—and, incidentally, quite jazz-less.[35]

When Shaw decided to take his new "dream band" on the road, he had to reorganize it with a permanent touring personnel. The high-paid studio musicians would not leave Hollywood, so Shaw was forced to revert to bona-fide jazz musicians (except for the strings, now reduced to nine): musicians like trumpeter Billy Butterfield, trombonist Jack Jenney, tenorman Jerry Jerome, and drummer Nick Fatool. These were by no means the best *jazz* musicians, white or black, that money could buy in 1940, and their selection (along with pianist Johnny Guarnieri, bassist Jud De Naut, and guitarist Al Hendrickson, and others) is either revealing of Shaw's real intentions or ascribable to arbitrariness and chance. As with Dorsey's relegating the "true" jazz to his Clambake Seven, thus leaving the big band to pursue more commercial interests, so Shaw now formed the Gramercy Five, a sextet (counting himself), that was the "jazz" nucleus of the full twenty-three-piece ensemble. The Gramercy Five's gimmick was the inclusion of a harpsichord, played stiffly by Guarnieri.[36] A stylistic amalgam of borrowings from Goodman's and John Kirby's sextets, and various boogie-woogie recordings, the Gramercy Five's fare was mildly interesting as jazz, although again popularly successful. With a technique similar to that of Charlie Shavers (in Kirby's group), Butterfield could dazzle the public with his fleet-fingered

35. An orchestration by Still of one of Shaw's favorite piano pieces, a brief composition by the American turn-of-the-century composer Edward MacDowell, called A *Deserted Farm*, was rejected at the time of making and not issued until 1978. It would have been better left in the Victor vaults, for in Still's turgid transcription it sounds like a fourth-rate out-of-tune symphony orchestra, the naively touching romanticism of the piano original mired in a morass of sentimentality.

Still (1895–1978), the dean of black classical composers, was a distinguished musician who wrote much fine music during his long productive career. But the here-mentioned spate of arrangements for Shaw was (except perhaps for *Frenesi*) a disappointing failure.

36. It was Alec Wilder who had first used the harpsichord in his Octets, starting in 1938, possibly at the suggestion of his longtime friend and oboist (later recording producer) Mitch Miller. There the harpsichord seems to me well-integrated and sonically appropriate to the character of these delightful musical vignettes. Although Shaw must have been aware of Wilder's Octets, it is more likely that for him the impetus to use a harpsichord came from a kind of "sleeper" hit recording by the American harpsichordist Sylvia Marlowe of Meade Lux Lewis's *Honky Tonk Train Blues* in 1940, the year in which that boogie-woogie opus (first recorded by Lewis in 1927) became the popular rage and was widely recorded, even on electric organ (by Milt Herth).

ensemble work in *Special Delivery Stomp*. But his work could also be quite mannered and synthetic, as in a blues called *Summit Ridge Drive* (named after the street in Hollywood on which Shaw's house was located). Shaw's playing in the Gramercy Five has often been singled out as being outstanding—and, granted, some of the later sides are effective, especially *The Gentle Grifter*. But on *Summit Ridge* Shaw's blues solo is more like a ballad, a long way from the kind of solo Barney Bigard or Woody Herman could regularly produce on a blues. The rhythm on *Cross Your Heart* was overly chunky, virtually devoid of swing. In tolerating such playing, one has to wonder whether Shaw knew the difference.

With the big band things did not fare much better—with one fortunate glorious exception. On *If It's You, Chantez Les Bas, This Is Romance,* and a number of other sides the strings formed an oppressive glutinous blanket of musical taffy—again it was the specific writing and playing, not the use of strings itself. And *Marinella* and *Danza Lucumi,* trite Latin numbers both, had nothing to do with jazz at all. But the performance of Lennie Hayton's arrangement of *Star Dust* was near perfect. Butterfield, Shaw, and Jenney were the soloists; and even the string writing was apposite, adding substantially to the special atmosphere and mood of the piece. For me the most memorable moment of the performance has always been Jack Jenney's magnificent trombone solo, considered in its day, for all its romantic cast, a major breakthrough statement, both in technical and expressive terms. The (for that time) extraordinary octave leap to high F (see Example 6) was admired far and wide by musicians and sophisticated audiences, not only for the ease with which Jenney managed the deed, but for

Ex. 6

his elegance and sensitivity of phrasing. It must be remembered that few trombonists had ventured into that uppermost range of the instrument—Dorsey went above his favorite high note, D♭, only once in his recording career—and if someone like Bobby Byrne or Trummy Young occasionally tackled a high F, it was almost always by a step-wise approach, never head-on in such a difficult, dare-devil octave leap. Jenney's rich, full-bodied sound added to the emotional appeal of the passage.

Shaw too played magnificently, not only topping his effort with a stunning high A but "singing" the whole solo with a loving, warm lyric feeling that no other clarinetist of the time could have matched.

Star Dust was another major hit for Shaw. (I remember being on tour in 1943 as a young horn player and hearing Shaw's *Star Dust* on every jukebox in every restaurant—*three years* after the record was issued.) But it, too, perpetuates the succession of enigmas and artistic puzzles scattered throughout Shaw's musical career. For how can one reconcile its excellence with the mediocrity that surrounded it?

One of the more undistinguished items, for example, recorded around this time was Shaw's *Concerto for Clarinet*. Anything but a true concerto, it was a pastiche thrown together out of some boogie-woogie blues, clarinet-over-tomtom interludes, a commonplace riff build-up towards the end, all encased in opening and closing virtuoso cadenzas for the leader's clarinet. It was exactly the kind of flimsy stylistic hodge-podge Hollywood film producers loved to feature in their musicals—*Concerto* was thrown together, as Shaw says, for a film biography of his life called *Second Chorus*—and even Shaw could not understand why the public made such a fuss over it.[37]

Again Shaw grew restless and in the spring of 1941 disbanded—only to form still another group. Presumably still searching for some elusive artistic goal, Shaw this time, in another surprise move, surrounded singer Lena Horne and seven outstanding black jazzmen, among them Henry "Red" Allen, J.C. Higginbotham, and Benny Carter, with thirteen strings and a harp. This was yet another and different edition of Shaw's ambivalent fascinations with jazz and symphonic music, but surely one of his more interesting conceptions. It was in essence the same idea that prompted his first orchestra in 1936: a small group of jazz players integrated with a string section. Only this time the jazz musicians were of major stature. Perhaps the idea had great potential. But after one recording date—four interesting but by no means fully cohesive sides were cut—Shaw abandoned the project, and in another about-face returned to a large quasi-symphonic format, comprising a regular fifteen-man big band, plus a sizable complement of strings. The orchestra was billed as "Artie Shaw and His Symphonic Swing." It included some first-rate musicians, including drummer Dave Tough and the black trumpet player "Hot Lips" Page, a great blues player. But perhaps the most crucial addition was, as we shall see, the trombonist and arranger Ray Conniff. For it was he who almost single-handedly *finally* brought "Artie Shaw and his Orchestra" in one fell swoop into jazz, late-swing, and modern jazz.

That was not to happen, however, for another three to four years. In the meantime (still in 1941), Shaw continued his searching, ecumenically trying many different categories of pieces, ranging from ordinary pop tunes and plain for-dancing numbers to advanced and sometimes commissioned compositions. He also hired a sizable number of diversely oriented arrangers, encompassing a wide range of talents from Bill Challis and Lennie Hayton to black arranger Fred

---

37. Some musicians were also impressed. The Trinidadian clarinetist Carl Barriteau, working in England, actually re-recorded the piece for Decca on two sides of a 12-inch 78 with a London freelance studio symphony orchestra around 1941. (Barriteau had played with the Bert Ambrose and Lew Stone orchestras as well as Ken "Snake Hips" Johnson's band, and was in 1941 the musical director of the First English Public Jam Session.) Shaw's *Concerto for Clarinet* was published and seriously studied by clarinetists and classical musical teachers, and it is still played nowadays by high-school and college orchestras, trying to show their "progressiveness."

Norman (who for years had been Claude Hopkins's prime arranger) to much younger men and women like Paul Jordan, Ray Conniff, and Margie Gibson.

The results were bound to be varied and uneven. But one thing all the resultant works had in common was a consistent attempt to deal with the strings more effectively, partly by integrating them more thoroughly with the jazz units. Whether this overall direction came from Shaw or whether these arrangers all had had enough of saccharine overbearing string sections is hard to say. But in one way or another they managed a noticeable degree of integration. Jerry Sears in Thomas Griselle's[38] *Nocturne* accomplished it by using the strings not alone and not in the upper sugary range but blended in with the saxes in the strings' lowest registers. Fred Norman used the strings on his *Solid Sam* in fast-moving energetic sixteenth-note passages. If the strings here did not yet swing, they also did not impede the swing of the rhythm section and the jazz soloists (Shaw and a very Webster-ish Auld). Ray Conniff in *Just Kiddin' Around* used the strings more or less in the integrative fashion Sy Oliver had pioneered a year earlier with Dorsey. Margie Gibson actually tried to make the strings swing on *Deuces Wild*—and almost succeeded.

But undoubtedly the most successful solution to the string problem was offered by composer Paul Jordan, whose advanced extended compositions recorded on the "classier" 12-inch 78s, were the most ambitious compositional efforts Shaw had yet undertaken to perform and record. Jordan (b. 1916) was a young composer from Chicago whom Shaw discovered and sponsored on records. Shaw's relationship to Jordan was similar to Kenton's with Bob Graettinger, although of much shorter duration. Little is known of Jordan today except that he moved to Denver, Colorado, in the early sixties, working there as a pianist and arranger until 1975, when an illness forced him temporarily into semi-retirement. (He is still living and working in Denver as of this writing, and he is not black as some recent Bluebird liner notes have suggested.) Jordan's only real claim to fame are the few recordings made under Shaw's aegis.

Jordan's *Evensong* and *Suite No.8* were real "compositions", strongly influenced by classical forms and techniques, though at the same time thoroughly grounded in certain jazz traditions (Ellington) and sound concepts. These pieces were far removed from the world of "arrangements" and dance numbers and pop tunes. They were in effect very early examples of Third Stream music, perhaps *the* earliest recorded by a major more-or-less standard jazz orchestra—and more importantly, of unusually high quality.[39]

38. Griselle (1891–1955), now an obscure minor American composer, who had studied with both Nadia Boulanger and Arnold Schönberg, acquired considerable but fleeting fame when he won a $10,000 prize in 1928—at that time an incredible amount of money—offered by the Victor Talking Machine Company for a composition by an American composer. The prize-winning work, which was also recorded by Victor, was *Two American Sketches*, one of which was entitled *Nocturne*.

39. It has always seemed to me that, given Shaw's propensities for a broad-ranging definition of jazz and his deep admiration for classical composers, he and some of his early 1940s' orchestras would have been the ideal candidates for commissioning and performing Stravinsky's *Ebony Concerto*. But my guess is that "the old man" preferred the un-bridled string-less excitement of *Caldonia* to the more sedate musical essays of Paul Jordan (or the pretensions of *Concerto for Clarinet*).

These two pieces stand in relation to Shaw's orchestra much as Ralph Burns's *Summer Sequence* stands to Woody Herman's 1946 Herd. Indeed Jordan's works are a direct precursor of Burns's opus (although I am not thereby implying that Burns knew, let alone emulated, Jordan's pieces). What is curious then is that, while *Summer Sequence* is well-known and remembered, Jordan's work languishes in oblivion. Since jazz-writing has so unjustly neglected—indeed to my knowledge totally ignored—these far from negligible pieces, they deserve some detailed discussion.

Evensong is a little gem. Essentially an "Aria" for clarinet and orchestra, serene in its twilight mood, it affords Shaw an excellent opportunity to display his supremely beautiful tone. The piece is cast in a simple ABA form. An introductory section, built on G-minor eleventh chord , leads to the main theme in F, a lovely song-like melody set over simple I-IV-V progressions. The theme's A A B A structure divides into 6 + 6 + 4 + 6-bar phrases. Jordan effectively uses chromatic alterations, especially ingeniously exploiting the harmonies' various major and minor shadings to keep the slow-paced harmonic progressions fluid and interesting (Ex. 7). The major seventh E, firmly ensconced in the

Ex. 7

melody, is used to link the two basic harmonic stations of this section: I-IV, i.e. Fm$^{6(7)}$-Bb^{-5} (Ex. 7b). The six-bar A phrases actually divide into 4- and 2-bar segments: four bars of solo clarinet and two bars of ensemble response, almost a kind of blues structure (which would be 2-and 2-bar segments). The song's 4-bar bridge is built upon the lovely and unusual progression of (Example 8):

Ex. 8

The main middle section, orchestrated in various soft reed and brass mixtures, blended judiciously with strings, is vaguely anchored in the key of A. However, it is so chromatically rich and constantly modulating that its tonal centering is soon completely undermined, and the shift back to F for the recapitulation of the initial song-section occurs almost imperceptibly. In this middle part one is frequently reminded, both in its instrumental colors and roving harmonies, of certain Ellington works, particularly *Reminiscing in Tempo*. The return to the final A section, varied and foreshortened, functions simultaneously as the coda of the piece.

As mentioned, the integration here of the strings with the full ensemble is quite successful; one is rarely aware of them as a foreign element. Jordan accomplishes this rather simply by several means: 1) using the strings in pedal points, accompanimental tremolos, and other such idiomatic string devices, in use for centuries in classical string-writing; 2) mixing the strings in with the winds, rather than continually isolating them from them; 3) asking the string players to play with a minimal, tasty, controlled vibrato, in lieu of the usual exaggerated fake-sensual kind, so in vogue in popular music.[40]

Jordan's *Evensong* is an evocative mood piece whose claims to jazz are modest: a quietly pulsating beat, some advanced "jazz" harmonies, the colors and inflections used by jazz players, and an overall relaxed looseness endemic to good jazz. Still, the jazz elements were subdued and introspective. In *Suite No. 8*, on the other hand, Jordan allows the jazz elements to project much more overtly. Here an introduction in the strings[41], again set in slow-motion roving chromatic harmonies, gradually evolves a brief *leitmotif* (Ex. 9a), which subsequently is subjected to various thematic, harmonic, and rhythmic variations. Its first transformation occurs in a short, vigorous but rather school-bookish *fugato* (Ex. 9b), which leads directly into the main "jazz section'—in fast 4/4 swing. Examples 9c and d, the former in the saxes, the latter in the brass, show two further variants of the *leitmotif.* This episode is set over a pedal point on G, which

Ex. 9a

Ex. 9b

---

40. Shaw was to achieve the ultimate integration of strings some years later in some little-known recordings for Columbia of two works by the composer/arranger and cellist Alan Shulman. In that session the "strings" consisted of a string quartet, Shaw coming full circle in returning to his first love, his 1936 experiments with a string-quartet-centered ensemble.

I am also reminded of Bill Russo's excellent *Image of Man* (1958), featuring altoist Lee Konitz, in which Russo required the string quartet to play completely *without* vibrato. Because the resultant "horn"-like sonorities fitted readily into a jazz context, the effect was quite startling and beautiful and a fine match for Konitz's lean-warm tone.

41. It should be pointed out that Jordan uses not only the violins effectively but violas, cellos, and a single double bass as well. The "classical" bass player on these recordings, incidentally, was Fred Zimmerman, later an important member of the New York Philharmonic's bass section and a leading teacher in New York. In that connection, it is interesting to note that Charles Mingus studied with Zimmerman and had him play the extremely difficult bowed part in the 1957 recording of his extended-form masterpiece *Revelations*.

Ex. 9c

prepares the improvised "choruses" in the key of C, using I—IV—V changes very similar to those of *Evensong*. The three soloists—Shaw, Auld, and "Hot Lips" Page—carry their assignments out well.

It might be argued (with some justification) that Auld's and Page's improvisations—the former in a booting Webster-ish mold, the latter a growly blueish plunger-mute solo—are stylistically extraneous to the work. It is true that both players played essentially *what they knew how to play* and paid little mind to Jordan's basic materials, thematic or otherwise. For them it was simply a sort of "Blues in C." This is, of course, the ancient problem of Third Stream efforts: how to integrate highly individual (or perhaps even limited) soloists into a more ambitious and specific compositional framework. On the other side of the argument, however, it is quite clear that both Auld and Page brought a native vitality to the piece, that without their solo contributions it would not have had. To which one can only add that Shaw comes off best among the three soloists. Though he plays brilliantly and with fine swing energy, he seems to have sensed that any soloistic extravagance would not be appropriate, confining himself therefore to a relatively controlled improvisation which would not break the bounds of Jordan's compositional frame.

One more transformation of the *leitmotif* (Ex. 9e), in brass, set over strings-and-saxes-in-unison trills, brings the piece to a strong and well-timed climax,

Ex. 9e

with Shaw adding to the bustling excitement with a spectacular ride-in over the

entire band on an *altissimo* B♭!

Jordan's *Evensong* and *Suite* may not be of the very highest masterpiece calibre—say, on a par with the best of Ellington's or Mingus's more "formal" extended compositions. But they surely do not deserve the total neglect they have inherited. They are at least as valuable and valid as any number of Swing Era pieces—one thinks, for example, of Larry Clinton's *Study in Brown* series or Raymond Scott's *In an 18th-Century Drawing Room*, Thornhill's *Snowfall*, Burns's *Summer Sequence*, or, for that matter, Shaw's own *Concerto for Clarinet*—that have been highly touted through the years and continue to be written about and praised. Recording and performing Jordan's works was one of Shaw's most felic-itous—and generous—undertakings, for which we owe him much respect and gratitude.

But seemingly unrelated to his orchestra's success or failure or mixed recep-tion, Shaw's erratic conduct as bandleader continued apace. A month after re-cording Jordan's works, Shaw disbanded once again, this time to enlist in April 1942 in the United States Navy. And as expected, when he returned to civilian life two years later, he formed yet another orchestra—this the sixth edition.

Roy Eldridge was its star soloist and Ray Conniff its chief arranger; and it had no strings. The rhythm section—as a team it was Shaw's best yet—consisted of drummer Lou Fromm, bassist Morris Rayman (both very underrated players), guitarist Barney Kessel, and the nineteen-year-old pianist, Dodo Marmarosa. With these talents as the focal point of the band's new direction, it became in short order the most consistent and innovative of Shaw's many orchestras. Un-like other Shaw aggregations, which either lagged critically behind the fold or tried to be too far ahead of all the others, the 1944 band was right in step with the times, even though quite definitely in the vanguard. This was due not so much to Shaw's day-to-day leadership or even his own playing as it was to the splendid arranging skills of Ray Conniff and a formidable array of guest arrangers, like Buster Harding, Eddie Sauter, Jimmy Mundy, and Bobby Sherwood. Though they all had their own individual stylistic characteristics and trademarks, they also had many qualities in common. These related mostly to the musical revo-lution that was taking place within jazz, the first revelations of which were be-ginning to appear on recordings of Gillespie and Parker as well as the young rarin'-to-go Woody Herman and Charlie Barnet bands. The incipient bop mes-sage was spreading rapidly, and within months young arrangers who readily adopted the new idiom—harmonically, rhythmically, thematically—had cropped up everywhere.

Shaw's main standard-bearer of the new language was Conniff, who produced an entire series of superior arrangements (as he also did for Harry James a few years later), which were perhaps not yet in the full pure bop idiom, but none-theless projected a very fresh modern concept and orchestration. Conniff's work can be sampled most rewardingly on such Shaw sides as *Jumpin' On the Merry-Go-Round*, *S'Wonderful*, *September Song*, and *Lucky Number*. Conniff had first worked for Shaw in 1941, producing at least one outstanding composition/arrangement at that time, *To a Broadway Rose*, in some ways far ahead of its time. In the latter half of *Rose*, Conniff sets up a long rhythmic pedal point on the hi-hat cymbal (played impeccably by Dave Tough), over which he then scatters a "tone-color-melody" of asymmetrically placed chords, setting the or-chestra's different choirs off against each other in different registers, colors, har-monic, densities, dynamics, etc. The passage clearly demonstrated Conniff's fer-tile orchestral imagination and considerable practical skill in manipulating such an "advanced" orchestral concept. But Shaw was either more involved with Paul Jordan at the time or simply failed to recognize Conniff's talent. In any case

Shaw, as we have seen, disbanded shortly thereafter, and a follow-up to *Rose* was thereby precluded.

Whether Conniff's engagement as trombonist/arranger with Shaw in 1944 occurred because Shaw recalled Conniff's talent or because it was a chance hiring of a fine player who happened to be available, I cannot say. What is certain is that this time Shaw appreciated his work and allowed it to prevail as the band's basic style. Conniff's arrangements were characterized by a deep, rich orchestral sound, finely balanced, set in spicily chromatic harmonies and voicings, and above all by a structural clarity that consistently avoided congestion and permitted soloists and sections to develop a deep, spacious, laid-back swing. Moreover, his arrangements revealed a keen sense of the need for a balanced variety. Conniff's work was filled with surprises (hear *S'Wonderful*, or sample the extraordinary harmonization of the bridge of *Lucky Number*, or Conniff's many superior trombone quartets), and was rarely repetitious or redundant.

During the same period Eddie Sauter contributed two outstanding works to the Shaw library, an unusual treatment of Gershwin's *Summertime* and an original called *Maid with the Flaccid Air* (a take-off—in the title only—on Debussy's *Maid with the Flaxen Hair*). *Maid* is one of those typically low-keyed, melodically/harmonically original Sauter compositions which in the subtlety and intelligence of its musical discourse was far removed from the standard swing-band traditions, particularly in their ever more frenetic war-years approach. It was a true jazz composition, not a mere arrangement of a tune; and although it emulated the concept of *composition* as pioneered, say, by Duke Ellington, it in no way imitated that master stylistically. Sauter was very much his own man in *Maid*, a quality which Shaw recognized and, temporarily anyway, appreciated. The Shaw orchestra's performance of this unusual work was excellent, with Shaw himself beautifully capturing the lyric essence of the piece, aided and abetted wonderfully at certain points by Chuck Gentry's elegant baritone counterlines.

But perhaps the most strikingly unified arrangements and/or compositions were those of Buster Harding: *Bedford Drive, The Glider, The Hornet, Little Jazz*, the latter a solo vehicle especially written for Roy Eldridge. Harding, like Conniff, concentrated on rich, gutsy, strongly harmonic voicings that could swing the whole band. In this respect alone they are simply masterful and demonstrate beyond any doubt how thoroughly and instantly a great arranger can transform a band. Although the Shaw band did not particularly ape Basie (as Barnet had done for years), *Bedford Drive* unequivocally gets that basic Basie feeling. And I am sure it was not because they rehearsed the piece for days on end to arrive at that feeling, but because that particular quality was contained in the writing: *there was no other way to play it.*

Harding's work, along with Conniff's and Sauter's, proves once again what Shaw, unlike most bandleaders, was reluctant to realize—or perhaps did realize intermittently but could not admit in public: namely, that the style of a band—good, bad, or indifferent—is determined unequivocally by the arranger, not the leader (unless the leader is also the style-setting arranger). Ellington, Goodman, Herman, Barnet, Miller, Norvo knew that—to name but a few; Armstrong,

Coleman Hawkins, Teddy Wilson did not. They thought that their leadership and their *soloistic abilities alone* would suffice to establish a band's style. They did not realize that it takes an imaginative, skillful arranger to translate a soloist's conception into an orchestral style.

Shaw's 1944–45 band, despite Eldridge's solo presence, for a while was not a jazz soloists' band; it was an ensemble orchestra, an *arranger's* band. Even Shaw's role as solo clarinet was secondary to the band's over-all style and ensemble work. What is surprising is that Shaw gave very few solo opportunities to his gifted pianist Dodo Marmarosa, and none in the 1945 Musicraft sides. Did Shaw not recognize Marmarosa's gift? And had he not heard of his amazing *The Moose* performance with Barnet?

For whatever reasons, Shaw's heart seems not to have been in this band very much, and his lack of commitment showed in his playing, which became listless and redundant. Again an irony: either the best or the second-best band Shaw ever had, and he couldn't or wouldn't keep the relationship going. Not unexpectedly now, another abrupt turnabout resulted: by early 1946 the huge string section with harp plus a large woodwind group, including horns, had returned. *I've Got You Under My Skin* is typical of Shaw's intentions here: strictly commercial. The arrangement, hardly distinguishable from any Kostelanetz or Jackie Gleason-type of arrangement, features an abundance of "romantic" written solos for English horn, for flute, for two horns, flute and bassoon duet, "heart-tugging" violin solos, surging string and harp passages—indeed all the *accoutrements* of that genre of music, well-done and beautifully performed. It is relevant to mention these facts only because Shaw would never admit his commercial temptations, while constantly talking about jazz, pure music, new music, etc. In any case, this type of lush romantic writing was certainly no longer new in 1946, having been created in some instances ten years earlier by the three great pioneers of "symphonic" treatments of popular and show tunes: André Kostelanetz, Morton Gould, and David Rose.

Any allusions to jazz were once again suppressed. They paradoxically surfaced more in Mel Torme's and the Mel-Tones' singing than in any of the instrumental playing. Torme, a remarkably gifted musician who often fashioned his own very sophisticated arrangements, had (still has) a unique voice with a tawny veiled quality that soon earned him an affectionately tendered nickname, "The Velvet Fog." In style he represented the first interesting extension of Sinatra's style, embodied here in a tenor rather than a baritone voice, and urged always in a more jazz-oriented direction.

The 1944–45 band was to constitute Shaw's final substantial contribution to the Big Band or Swing Era. A new orchestra, formed in 1949, featuring modern players like Zoot Sims, Al Cohn, Don Fagerquist, Sonny Russo—*and no strings*—lasted only a short time. A fine well-disciplined group, it nevertheless was not individual enough to survive, artistically and economically.

One more episode in Shaw's musical career requires chronicling here; and once again it constituted a bold about-face. In 1949 he returned to his original concept of performing with a string quartet, and recorded four sides: two consisting of specially composed works by Alan Shulman for clarinet, string quartet, and harp; two others for an enlarged string ensemble, winds and rhythm section in quasi-symphonic and somewhat effete arrangements of *The Man I Love* and *I Concentrate on You*. Shaw's playing in these two pieces is rather mannered and meandering, being content to embellish the melodies with lower- and upper-neighbor paraphrasings. It is as if the act of creating such an ensemble and getting it commercially recorded was more important to him than *how* he contributed to the effort.

On the other hand, Shulman's two works, *Mood in Question* and *Rendezvous for Clarinet and Strings*, are effective pieces with definite leanings in the direction of the French impressionist school and very little connection with jazz— although *Rendezvous* has a lively, catchy jazzy theme that enjoyed, as I recall, a certain popularity among musicians in the early 1950s. If Shulman's pieces, in some ways forerunners of Jimmy Giuffre's works with solo clarinet and strings a decade or so later, can be technically called Third Stream, they do not probe very deeply musically—in either stream. Nonetheless, they offer an attractive light blend of diverse elements, and achieve a musical cohesion which, for example, Shaw's *Concerto for Clarinet* never approached.

But the most striking aspect of these recordings is their superlative performances by Shaw and the New Music Quartet. This ensemble was a seminal group founded in 1947 and passionately dedicated to the performance of the most advanced contemporary classical literature—Bartók (at a time when his quartets were still rarely performed), Schönberg, Webern, Babbitt, and other younger Americans. It played this music with a degree of technical perfection and high musical intuition that few quartets have been able to match, let alone surpass. What is important, however, in *this* context is that the New Music's playing proves unequivocally that strings can swing, can be fully integrated and artistically contributive to a jazz or quasi-jazz effort, can play with impeccable taste, and need not be related to the cloying, sniffling sentimentalism that is intended to sell a record to a mindless mass public.

Around the same time (1949) Shaw embarked on yet another even more ambitious venture, clearly outside the field of jazz: the recording of eight short classical pieces by twentieth-century composers ranging from Ravel and Debussy to Shostakovitch and Kabalevsky, adapted for clarinet and symphony orchestra by arranger Hershey Kay and (in one instance) the Belgian composer Arthur Hoerée. These remarkable recordings, extremely rare collectors' items now, were beautifully performed by Shaw and an orchestra conducted by Walter Hendl, and showed a side of Shaw's talent—namely, his classical playing—that he had previously only touched lightly, easily demonstrating that he could hold his own with any clarinetist in the world, classical or otherwise, including his nemesis, Benny Goodman.[42]

42. How it must have rankled Shaw to see Goodman engaged by the major symphony orchestras and leading string quartets to perform the works of the great classical masters: Mozart, Weber, Debussy, Bartók, Milhaud, Copland! Shaw was obliged to hire his own free-lance orchestra for the 1949 Columbia recordings.

Whether Shaw *really* appreciated the integrative potential the New Music Quartet had demonstrated, and whether he *really* valued the remarkable nature of his efforts in classical music is not known. For once again Shaw abandoned these enterprises too—another zigzag turn in the road, and another career dead-end.

This then has been the complex chronicle of Artie Shaw's tortured role in this particular period of American musical history. Although Shaw remained in music another five years, sporadically performing with small groups, even mounting one more short-lived large band in 1953 (another commercially oriented Jackie Gleason-type of affair), essentially the trail of enigmas and contradictions, of failures and triumphs, ended there—perhaps to be continued in his other interests and professions. Undoubtedly Artie Shaw—movie producer, author, farmer, gun expert—failed to find in music-making the rewards and intellectual stimuli he required. At times too serious-minded, at others too indiscriminate, Shaw remained a frenzied searcher for his musical identity, his musical "truth." A brilliant, restless, driven man, Shaw was compelled with an all-consuming obsession to prove that he could play the clarinet better than anyone else. Jazz may have played an important role in his life at times, but it was a tenuous relationship, which could be broken at will. At times, jazz seemed to be for Shaw merely the *vehicle* by which he could dominate the music field and acquire the very fame which he then so disdainfully decried in public.

It is obviously not a prerequisite that a musician see jazz as his singular, exclusive commitment. But the tragedy of Shaw's musical life has been that, like the moth impelled towards the flame, Shaw could rarely resist the temptations to commercialize his talents, thereby consistently undermining the best that was in him as a creative musician. For all his intellectual and elitist idealism, Shaw was at heart a populist, one who not only felt he had to educate the public "to better things," but who did everything to always make and argue a point—*his* point, of coure.

But perhaps of all the enigmas Shaw's life poses, the most profoundly perplexing one is how a true musician of his remarkable talents could so unconditionally leave music.

It is not necessarily the cultural historian's role to judge the man; it is, however, his proper role to judge his works—an uncommonly complex task in the case of Shaw. In the final analysis we are compelled, as we are with all artists of any importance, to remember him by his best works. That Shaw was able in his *finest* accomplishments to sweep us along in his searching and discoveries and at one point (1939) represent the best the Swing Era had to offer, we can hold forever in highest esteem. In one of his later interviews with *Metronome* editor Barry Ulanov, being questioned about "style," Artie Shaw expansively replied: "I'll try anything." And so he did.

CHARLIE BARNET

There are some interesting parallels between Artie Shaw's and Charlie Barnet's lives and careers—apart from their multiple marriages (eleven(!) for Barnet, only eight for Shaw). They both formed numerous bands, although Barnet's were much more consistent stylistically than Shaw's. Both got the *Wanderlust* as young men, early on pursuing a musical life against family wishes: Barnet working on transatlantic oceanliners, playing his tenor sax; Shaw starting to play professionally at age fifteen and leaving home a year later to work in Cleveland, also playing tenor sax. Both men ended up freelancing in New York in the early thirties (and even played together on a Red Norvo date in 1934). Both left music temporarily early on: Shaw in 1934 to try farming in Pennsylvania, Barnet in 1936 to try an acting career in Hollywood (he actually appeared in two feature films).

There the parallels stop. For the two men had quite different orchestral conceptions—as we have seen, Shaw alone had *several*—and in their careers as bandleaders developed quite dissimilar styles. Moreover, whereas Shaw was a restlessly inveterate searcher for an individual identity, steadfastly opposed to modeling his band after other prevalent jazz modes, Barnet spent a good part of his career enthusiastically imitating and re-creating the music of Duke Ellington and Count Basie. As a saxophonist, Barnet's unabashedly overt models were Coleman Hawkins and Johnny Hodges. Interestingly, Barnet managed consistently to keep these twin influences discrete, the one reserved for his tenor playing, the other for his alto and soprano saxophones. Moreover, Barnet regularly populated his orchestras with players who could accurately re-create various prominent solo styles, particularly those of leading black players. A case in point is trumpeter Robert Burnet, who was as adept in simulating Cootie Williams's plunger-and-growl style (or for that matter Rex Stewart or Roy Eldridge) as Barnet was in reproducing Hodges. The eclectically gifted Bill Miller, long-time pianist with Barnet, could re-create quite readily two so divergent piano styles as Duke Ellington's and Count Basie's.

To ensure stylistic authenticity in the orchestral and ensemble realm, Barnet either used scores he bought directly from Ellington (as well as from Benny Carter, the Henderson brothers, and Don Redman) or had transcribed by Andy Gibson, a talented black arranger, who had earned his trumpet-playing spurs with such bands as Zack Whyte, McKinney's Cotton Pickers, and Lucky Millinder and had actually done some arranging work for Ellington.

Barnet's very earliest bands had little identity of their own. They were essentially hotel-style bands (Barnet worked many of the top hotels in New York), venturing occasionally into a "hot," more jazz-oriented dance style. Curiously, some of the Benny Carter compositions/arrangements Barnet acquired—*Nagasaki* and *On a Holiday* (1935), for example—leaned very much in the direction of the Casa Loma band; or perhaps their vertical staccato-mannerisms were more a matter of Barnet's *interpretation* of Carter's scores.

When Barnet organized his second band, following his Hollywood acting interlude, an appreciable expansion of jazz spirit became noticeable in the band's repertory. It had progressed from such dubious jazz material as *The Swing Waltz* and *I'm an Old Cowhand* (in 1936) to such 1939 jump-swing pieces as *Jump Session, Swing Street Strut, Midweek Function,* and quite explicit Ellington evocations like *Echoes of Harlem, Jubilesta,*[43] *Merry-Go-Round,* and *Rockin' in Rhythm.*

And yet, if one can describe certain orchestras and musicians as "coming into their own" at a certain point (say, Ellington and Lunceford in the early-to-mid 1930s, or Woody Herman in 1945), it is impossible to do so in the case of Barnet, since what he and his band "came into" was not "their own" style but that of Ellington and Basie, alternatingly, and a wide assortment of other then-current fashions. Significantly, even these latter influences were in the main black. And even such breakthrough popular hits for Barnet as his famous *Cherokee* of 1939 owed more to black musical influences than to any of the leading white bands of the time, i.e. Goodman and Shaw.

And yet, while we may admire Barnet for his excellent taste in picking such superior models to emulate, and respect him for so genuinely wishing to bring an awareness of true jazz to his largely white audiences—Barnet had a strong following amongst blacks, and was the first white band to play the Apollo Theatre in Harlem, the musical mecca for all black musicians—when judged at the highest levels, his accomplishments constitute a kind of phyrric victory. For, ironically, Barnet—like Shaw—believed that he was avoiding the kind of excessive stylization with which he charged Goodman and Miller (also Shaw's favorite targets). Little did Barnet realize that he too had arrived at a definite stylization, only it wasn't a self-created one as in the case of Glenn Miller, but one borrowed from two other creators, Ellington and Basie.

In a sense the issue under discussion here is not so much one of style but of repertory: that is, is there, can there be, should there be such a thing as a jazz "repertory," much in the sense that there is a classical repertory (which now stretches from the twelfth century to the present)? My answer would be a resounding *yes, as long as* we recognize that certain types of jazz (totally, spontaneously improvised) or certain major jazz figures simply cannot be re-created— or should not be, because it would be pointless: a Louis Armstrong, a Tatum, a Parker. And we must differentiate here on the one hand between a specific, conscious re-creation/imitation for its own sake and, on the other hand, a deep, probably unavoidable influence of one artist upon another in the way that, say, Taft Jordan, Oscar Peterson, and Sonny Stitt relate to the three above-mentioned artists respectively. Predominantly orchestral or ensemble jazz, with or without intermittent "improvised" solos, lends itself very well to re-creation, to re-interpretation, through hands other than the original creator's. As for solos, it is a matter of two viable options: one, whether to re-create literally the originally improvised elements of a performance, or, two, to re-interpret them in an at

---

43. *Jubilesta* was one of those "rhythmically torrid" pseudo-junglistic pieces that had a great vogue in the thirties. In Ellington's band the piece was also known under the titles of *Puerto Rican Chaos* or *Moonlight Fiesta.* But when Barnet recorded it in 1937 it was called *Emperor Jones.*

least stylistically authentic and respectful manner. The choice would depend upon the nature of the original material *and* the abilities, both creative and re-creative, of the reinterpreting musician. The range from slavish imitation to complete re-interpretation affords a wide latitude of interesting possibilities. Here judgment, taste, and sheer ability to accomplish whatever the task at hand, must be the final arbiter.

Charlie Barnet was undoubtedly the first well-known jazz figure consistently to perform other major jazz composers' repertories. And he did so not in the name of plagiarism or exploitation of others' materials for his own self-aggrandizement, but as a genuine tribute to their greater talent and an honest desire to make such repertory more widely known. Indeed, one could argue that Barnet suppressed his own individuality in order to serve the "higher" cause of proselytizing the works of those he considered the real masters of his field.

It needs to be said, however, that at times Barnet's re-creations and borrowings fell short of their mark. Occasionally, as on *Echoes of Harlem*, the performances miscarried because the players could not in all cases produce the appropriate Ellington "sound"; they just didn't have those particular instrumental sonorities fully at hand. Or, as on *Rockin' in Rhythm*, the band could not quite duplicate the joyous relaxed rhythm and articulation that the Ellington band could give this piece. Various other compositional or stylistic subtleties would often escape the Barnet players. Sometimes performances would be marred by indiscriminate eclectic mixing of styles, possibly inadvertent or heedless, as on *In a Mizz*, where wildly Ellington-ish moments must suddenly compete with Lombardo-style passages. It was not unusual to find shades of Ellington, Lunceford, Eld-ridge, Hawkins—with bits of Larry Clinton thrown in for good measure—all jostling for stylistic priority in a single piece (try *Midweek Function*).

In general, Barnet was at first more consistently successful in emulating Basie and capturing the Basie sound than Ellington's. This is undoubtedly attributable to the fact that the Basie sound is simply more imitable to begin with, less subtle and less wide-ranging than Ellington's. Still, both *The Count's Idea* and *The Duke's Idea* generally capture the spirit of the objects of their affection. Curi-ously, while the *solo* passages on *Duke's Idea* come respectably close to their mentors' styles (Barnet/Hodges; Burnet/Cootie) and the *ensembles* lack some of the Ellington band's richness of sonority and harmonic depth, the reverse is true of *Count's Idea*. Here the soloists do not capture the (probably uncapturable) subtleties of their idol's ways, while the ensemble passages come much closer.

Of course, with the passage of time, the Barnet band assimilated even Duke's style and sound to such a point that the "disciple" could hardly be distinguished from the "master." There are numerous such passages in *Wings over Manhat-tan*, a remarkable six-and-a-half minute suite in several tempos and varying moods (written by Billy May for performance at the 1939–40 New York World's Fair). The work itself is reminiscent of *Reminiscing in Tempo* and *Symphony in Black* (especially the latter's *Hymn of Sorrow* section), Ellington's two earliest extended-form works. Other startlingly authentic Ellington material can be found on Bar-net's *Mother Fuzzy, Murder at Peyton Hall, Blue Juice* among others, all from

1941. (The last title features a fine solo by the guitarist Bus Etri, one of the earliest and most gifted disciples of Charlie Christian, who like Christian died a premature death, killed in a car crash at age twenty-four.)

However one may feel about these matters, what seems incontestable is that, taken in its entirety, Barnet's *oeuvre*, as represented through his recordings, is the most consistently jazz-committed of any of the major white bandleaders.

If Barnet's career had ceased in 1941, he would have already earned a much respected place in jazz history. One would, however, have felt compelled to qualify his accomplishments with the *caveat* that the real Charlie Barnet remained musically *incognito*. Surprisingly, the next half-dozen years were to reveal another Barnet and, more importantly, another Barnet orchestra. Its distinctions were discernible on three fronts: the band acquired a much greater individual/collective identity; it was at times in the very vanguard of new developments in orchestral jazz; and in that role it helped propose and solidify a modern style of big-band jazz that set new standards of performing, arranging, and composing.

To be sure, the Barnet band was not alone in its vanguard position; at various times in those transitional years, Herman, Shaw, James, Hines, and Eckstine experimented with a more advanced idiom, with Herman's First Herd eventually taking a clear front-running lead in 1944. And Barnet's, like all those forties' bands, was the beneficiary of a brand-new generation of technically astonishingly well-equipped and creatively gifted musicians. Long before the full ascendancy of bop demanded new musical and technical standards of jazz musicians, the influence of Armstrong and Eldridge, of Hawkins and Young, of Lawrence Brown and Jack Teagarden had already brought forth a whole new *breed* of musicians, capable of tackling all manner of fresh technical and musical challenges.

Starting with Barnet's *I Like To Riff, Shady Lady, Smiles*, all from early 1942 (and all little known and written about), we can hear the dramatic conversion to an at once more individual and more modern, linear style. The transformation derives clearly from the work of arranger Andy Gibson, especially notable on *Shady Lady*. Here we hear for almost the first time new instrumental textures, particularly in the harmonizations and voicings of the saxophones, both in their brilliant singing upper range and their richer darker low registers. (The rendering of these new arranging concepts seems all the more remarkable for the fact that Barnet's saxophone section consisted of a group of relative unknowns—little touted even to this day.) Rhythmically we encounter modern pre-bop double-time figures in the ensembles, all the more striking for being set in a slow "down" tempo which most bands had not yet learned to play with swing. Drummer Cliff Leeman had quite a bit to do with this more modern linear feeling, as the lessons of Basie, Jo Jones, Walter Page, and Freddie Green were beginning to proliferate throughout the white jazz world.

Even though we have no recorded proof, this new stylistic direction (and independence) must have been further pursued by Barnet during the recording ban, for when his orchestra entered the studios again in October 1943, it had not only consolidated its previous gains but produced in *The Moose* a veritable masterpiece. This remarkable work and performance introduced both Ralph Burns, the arranger, and Dodo Marmarosa, the pianist; and it seems to me that here, in a trice, modern big-band jazz was born, or at least baptized. Essentially a solo vehicle for Marmarosa, composed and arranged by Burns, *The Moose* presents the then-only-seventeen-year-old pianist in a bright new stylistic amalgam of incipient bop and basic Basie-isms, in what may be his best recorded solo. Marmarosa commanded a technique, well grounded in the most challenging classical literature, which almost equaled Art Tatum's and which enabled him to execute virtually any idea that came to his mind.[44] Three brief excerpts may suffice to present a glimpse of his talent at this time (Ex. 10).

Ex. 10

But if Marmarosa's startlingly precocious solo-playing were all that could be admired on *The Moose*—as was so often the case in virtuoso solo vehicles by, say, Armstrong or Hines or Hawkins or Shaw—it would not warrant our further attention. But it is Ralph Burns's remarkable *concertante* setting for Marmarosa's pianistic exploits that make this one of the most important efforts of its kind in this entire period. To begin with there is none of the pretentiousness—grandiose introductions, high-flying cadenzas, ostentatious modulations—which so often

44. Unfortunately Marmarosa's later career was marked not only by a vagrant eclecticism, permitting very little self-identity, but also prolonged absences from the music profession.

afflicted these concerto-like productions (even Ellington was not entirely immune to such temptations, and certainly Kenton almost never was). What Burns—and Marmarosa—had in mind was something at once much simpler and grander, and much more pure jazz. The orchestral sections and solo passages flow into one another effortlessly, seamlessly, producing in the aggregate a single, unified, coherent work.

Perhaps even more interesting, certainly from a historical point of view, is the fact that in Burns's *The Moose* we hear full-blown for the first time the new orchestral jazz language that we know better from Woody Herman's mid-1940s' band and which was to characterize large-ensemble jazz for years to come. Already fully present is the rhythmic excitement of Burns's style, its inner drive and energy; and also the new virtuosity, especially as expressed in the Barnet brass, where Burns had the services of two outstanding trumpet players, Al Killian and Peanuts Holland.[45] Above all, this drive and virtuosity were expressed in a brand-new faster tempo on *The Moose*.

I don't think Burns has been given sufficient credit for this aspect of his work. While it is certainly true that Parker and Gillespie were the real harbingers of that rhythmic revolution that eventually irreversibly transformed jazz under the name of bop with its razor-sharp rhythmic distinctions and blazingly fast tempos, Burns's role as a translator of these new intimations into an orchestral conception should not be underestimated. That the nineteen-year-old Burns understood the true nature of the changes jazz was undergoing both well and *early* is amply demonstrated in *The Moose* and his many exceptional later scores for Herman.

What is also central to these developments, in particular the question of faster tempos, is the fact that in pieces like *The Moose, Apple Honey, Caldonia*—and Dizzy Gillespie's and Gil Fuller's *Things to Come* (which did not come along until 1946)—these composers and the bands for whom they wrote were clearly moving away from the realm of dance, i.e. jazz *as dance music* (in other words swing music)—into the realm of jazz as *composition*, as absolute music to be heard and listened to on its own merits and *not* (necessarily) as a music serving some other primary function, like dancing. This was after all the essence of the break between the Swing Era and Modern Jazz, as jazz moved away from the dancers and singers (with their sentimental tales of woe and bliss) to a primarily instrumental emphasis of jazz.

The new rapid tempos—not just medium tempos played with fast embellishments, but *inherently* faster tempos—were a crucial part of the move from swing

---

45. Al Killian was without a doubt the greatest of the late-Swing-Era high-note lead trumpeters. Not necessarily an outstanding jazz soloist, Killian specialized in stratospheric trumpeting which was totally consistent and often defied belief. His death in Los Angeles at the hands of a crazed landlord in 1950 was a stunning loss to jazz.

Peanuts Holland in his Barnet years was already an old veteran of the jazz scene. Readers of *Early Jazz* will recall meeting him in connection with the Alphonse Trent band, that most remarkable of black 1920s' orchestras. Always a bit of a musical eccentric, with a fine comic bent (often expressed in his scat-singing and novelty vocals), Holland was a strong musical and comedic asset in Barnet's 1940s' band. Holland emigrated to Europe in 1946 and died in 1979 in Sweden.

to modern jazz, and it is fascinating to discover that for a while—and rather early in the game—Charlie Barnet was a principal figure in these developments (*through*, however, the work of Burns and Marmarosa). The irony, of course, is that had Barnet kept Burns on as an arranger it would be he, Barnet, who might now be celebrated for the Herman Herd breakthroughs.

In point of fact, Burns left Barnet to go with Herman in the late spring of 1944, but not before he had contributed at least two more excellent scores to Barnet's library, both Ellingtonia. *Cotton Tail* suffers by comparison with Ellington's original, lacking in particular Ben Webster's great solo, for which one of Barnet's trombonists, Tommy Pederson, was no match. In some parts of the score Burns follows Ellington's performance very closely, but he puts his own stamp on the work at mid-point when he inserts one of his own driving full-ensemble passages, which in turn was reused verbatim as the introduction to *Apple Honey* (particularly appropriate since both *Cotton Tail* and *Apple Honey* are based on *I Got Rhythm* changes). Decidedly more his own is Burns's transformation of *Drop Me Off in Harlem*, featuring some excellent Roy Eldridge (who was temporarily sojourning in Barnet's band), a fine, fluent off-and-running Marmarosa piano solo, stunning brass ensembles scattered throughout, and one "lick" which is an almost exact retrograde-inversion of the *Apple Honey* (via *Cotton Tail*) introduction. Again, what we all think of as the Herman First Herd style is here fully present. Even the feel of the rhythm section—Burns takes Ellington's piece at an appreciably faster bop tempo than Ellington's original—is exactly that of the later Billy Bauer–Chubby Jackson–Don Lamond team.[46]

Gulf Coast Blues, Clarence Williams's old tune, receives an excitingly modern treatment at the hands of Ralph Flanagan and Andy Gibson, with a full array of advanced bitonal and tritone-oriented harmonies (hear particularly the ingenious introduction).

By late 1944 Barnet had another jazz hit on his hands, his famous *Skyliner*, which together with the other side of this 78, *West End Blues*, made quite a stunning jazz pairing. In some ways *Skyliner* was a follow up to Barnet's 1939 *Cherokee*, particularly in the way that the melody once again consisted of long sustained notes set over a fast tempo. The contrasts between two parts moving at vastly different speeds is always a most captivating effect, one that was known to musicians and composers as far back as the early Renaissance, and incidentally an effect well known to the musicians of the pure collective improvisational style of New Orleans. The same sort of contrasting effect is achieved here on *Skyliner* with the high-flying melodic line set against a four-times-as-fast beat and a swiftly moving riff theme in the brass. A comparison of the first eight bars of *Skyliner* and *Cherokee* (Ex. 11) will make the point even clearer.

West End Blues not only was a successful updating of Armstrong's famous 1928 classic, turned here into a vehicle for Barnet's strongly Hodges-beholden alto, but it also offered a measure of the enormous advances that had taken place

---

46. It was Chubby Jackson, by the way—who had been with Barnet briefly—who, after joining Herman, enticed Ralph Burns over to Woody's band (see Part 3, below).

Ex. 11

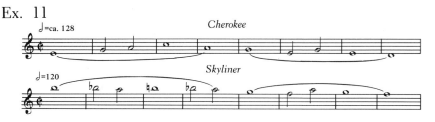

in brass playing since Louis's famous breakthrough recording. For in those years only Louis and perhaps one or two other players (like Jabbo Smith or Henry "Red" Allen—on a *good* day) could have played the opening trumpet cadenza. But here, sixteen years later, the entire Barnet brass section could play the cadenza in unison, and with ease. The whole performance is outstanding, featuring, besides Barnet's alto, many bop-oriented unison brass lines and a fine duet between Killian (open) and Holland) (muted), perhaps a subtle tribute to Armstrong and King Oliver in their classic duets of the early 1920s.

By 1945 Barnet had had to cede his front-running position to Woody Herman, although his commitment to a modern form of orchestral jazz was as strong as ever. It was simply that by 1945 the field was getting very crowded (as the chart on pp. 852–53 clearly shows), and several advanced styles were beginning to vie for priority. When Marmarosa left to go with Artie Shaw, Barnet replaced him with Al Haig, one of the fine early modern pianists who had already earned his stripes on small combo recordings with Parker and Gillespie. Haig contributed significantly on such pieces as *Xango, Surprise Party,* and *E Bob O Lee Bob*. Also in 1945 Barnet engaged a young singer, Fran Warren, who was later to make history with Claude Thornhill and arranger Charles Naylor on *Sunday Kinda Love,* but who in her debut at age nineteen with Barnet already gave a clear indication of her immense talent. *Just a Little Fond Affection* and *You'd Be So Nice To Come Home To* are fine examples of her work at this time. She was one of the few singers who could sustain a slow tempo, as on the last title, and still "open up" vocally and emotionally when the music required it.

In the ensuing years when many a big band decided to call it quits—one period, late 1946, alone witnessed the demise of Goodman's, Dorsey's, Herman's, James's and Teagarden's orchestras—Barnet kept right on going—and swinging. Continually sparked by Killian's amazing trumpet feats—full, round, fat altissimo B♭s and As were a commonplace for him—and driven by a never-say-die rhythm section, Barnet's was clearly one of the most exciting bands (along with Gillespie, Kenton) that made that postwar period so musically memorable. I can still vividly recall hearing the Barnet band night after night at the Aquarium in New York in the wild ensembles at the climax of *Things Ain't What They Used To Be,* thrilling to the perfectly rendered brass pyramids on *Skyliner,* never tiring of the riotous parodying of bad old-time musicians on *Darktown Strutters' Ball,* and marveling at Killian's ability on *East Side, West Side* to *never* miss what is undoubtedly the most spectacular high-note trumpet break ever played (Ex. 12).

Ex. 12

Eventually in 1948 Barnet, too, was forced to disband his orchestra. But a year later, at the height of the bop craze—Bop City and Birdland were now the two most successful New York jazz emporia—Barnet was persuaded to try another big band. Like Shaw's and Goodman's 1949 bands, this too was a short-lived venture, and not altogether successful artistically. Though Barnet hired excellent arrangers like Gil Fuller, Manny Albam, Pete Rugolo, all well-versed in the bop language, somehow their efforts lacked real substance. It was as if they and the band's soloists (like the young Doc Severinson, trombonist Dick Kenny, pianist Claude Williamson, tenorman Dick Hofer) could not penetrate beneath the frenetic exterior mannerisms of bop—or what they *regarded* as bop. Doc Severinson's solos, for example, though undoubtedly played with sincerity and conviction, sound now with nearly thirty-five years hindsight like a caricature of bebop. And even though Barnet himself learned to incorporate a great deal of the standard bop vocabulary in his own playing, it too remained a somewhat superficial and mechanical exercise. Perhaps Barnet's commitment to bop was not as profound as Capitol Records, which had just lost Kenton and whom they hoped to replace with Barnet, had expected. One can only hope that Barnet's devastatingly kitschy Kentonesque travesty of Gershwin's *Rhapsody in Blue* was done tongue-in-cheek. By contrast, one is all the more grateful for the excellent jazz the band could occasionally still dish up contained on *Really!*, a Kai Winding line not too dissimilar from Mel Powell's *Mission to Moscow* and originally entitled *Bop City*.[47]

In any case, while Barnet's and Shaw's bands were holding forth at Bop City, the antidote to their febrile, over-heated, scrambling brand of bop was already appearing up the street at Birdland in the cool, collected, emotionally balanced music of the Miles Davis Nonet (later to be dubbed "The Birth of the Cool").

Another Barnet band in 1958, with soloists of the calibre of Clark Terry, Charlie Shavers, Billy Byers, also did not fare much better. Its efforts were largely artificial and derivative, a fact one can measure rather tellingly by contemplating what, for example, Gil Evans was already creating by 1958 with (or without) Miles Davis (*Sketches of Spain, Porgy and Bess, New Bottle/Old Wine*).

Success and failure, artistic and/or commercial, constantly live side by side in jazz history. This book is filled with such chronicles. So there is no great shame in some of Barnet's later non-successes. What ultimately matters is that Barnet's commitment to jazz, successful or not—and sometimes, as we have seen, it was *very* successful, both artistically and commercially—was unswerving and unconditional.

---

47. This fine tune—then entitled *Dishwater*—received its ultimate treatment by the late great trumpeter Lee Morgan in one of the finest recordings of the 1950s.

GENE KRUPA

If we measure the remaining white orchestras to be discussed in terms of their true commitment to jazz—defined as a primarily improvised *creative* music—as well as their ability to play with swing, Gene Krupa's orchestra must rate second only to Barnet's. For, whatever his artistic lapses as a showman drummer, Krupa's commitment to jazz was sincere and unassailable. He was even more of a jazz fan than his thousands of admirers, with an almost childlike, inexhaustible enthusiasm for the music and a clear appreciation of that which was genuine. His relation to jazz was primarily emotional and instinctual, uncomplicated. He loved the spontaneous energy of jazz—and supplied a great deal of it in his drumming—and thrived on that rhythmic feeling that separates jazz, in his case in the form of swing music, from most other forms of music.

At first his orchestra, formed right after his abrupt departure from Goodman in 1938, sounded inevitably much like that of his former leader. Krupa certainly did not strike out in any new conceptual directions. His was a very much youth-oriented dance orchestra in the prevailing late 30s' swing-band style whose performance standards were high, whose musicianship was generally excellent, and which maintained a fine roster of jazz soloists, foremost among them tenor saxophonist Sam Donahue, clarinetist Sam Musiker, trumpeters Corky Cornelius and Dave Schultz. In addition Krupa featured Leo Watson, that irrepressibly energetic pre-bop scat singer, and the quite capable Irene Daye, a disciple of Mildred Bailey.[48]

Many of the pieces, of course, featured Krupa in solos (on tom-toms or snare drum) that more often than not contributed little to the overall musical continuity. Indeed, his solos, though technically invariably well played, were often the aesthetic low points of otherwise well-executed, brightly swinging performances[49] in arrangements by fine black arrangers like Jimmy Mundy, Chappie Willett, Fred Norman, Benny Carter—and even Ellington *(Hodge-Podge, The Sergeant Was Shy)*. A revealing example of how well the band played and swung can be heard on Willett's seven-minute composition, *Blue Rhythm Fantasy*, like several other early Krupa recordings *(Prelude to a Stomp, Rhythm Jam,*

48. Krupa featured another female singer during the first few months of his band's existence, Jerry Kruger, who, though little remembered today, seems to me to have been the link between Billie Holiday and Anita O'Day. Kruger, an ardent admirer of Billie's, was one of the first white singers to try to emulate Lady Day, interestingly not so much in the latter's vocal mannerisms as in the minimal use of vibrato and her pared-down simplified vocal lines. Anita O'Day's style of singing in its even sleeker "instrumental" and vibrato-less approach carried this concept of singing to even more original lengths.

49. Extended drum solos in the context of an orchestral performance are always at some disadvantage in that they are performed on a limited number of instruments (Krupa concentrated almost entirely on snare drum and two tom-toms), and they must perforce do without pitch, harmony, and melody. Great master drummers of later periods, like Max Roach—hear him in his completely absorbing extended solo on Sonny Rollins's *Blue Seven* (1958)—learned to compensate for these intrinsic shortcomings in a variety of ways. But in Krupa's day, very few drummers—Chick Webb was a notable exception—could hold a sophisticated listener's attention in a long *a capella* drum solo.

and *Jungle Madness*) originally written by Willett for the Mills Blue Rhythm Band. Throughout the performance of *Fantasy* one can hear virtually perfect orchestral and section balance, remarkable timbral blending, and impeccable intonation—all a tribute to Krupa as a bandleader and a caring musician (and rehearser).

Like any band of the period, Krupa's orchestra had to record its heavy share of pop vocals. But even these were tastefully sung by Irene Daye and set in lively tempos and arrangements that never let jazz out of sight for very long. And, though the band never achieved any outstandingly distinctive identity during this early period, it could be counted on to play with clear (well-rehearsed) execution, fine intonation, good swing, and a positive buoyant spirit. Elton Hill's *Manhattan Transfer* and Jimmy Mundy's *Don't Be Surprised* are but two of the happier examples one might cite.

The addition within months (in early 1941) of both Anita O'Day and Roy Eldridge gave the Krupa band not only further major jazz talents but two musicians with great popular appeal. Anita's "hip" new style was even more startling in its uniqueness than Eldridge's playing[50]. The latter's work was relatively well-known and, in any case, any number of talented Armstrong-influenced trumpet players, both white and black, had been on the scene for some years. But Anita's singing was something quite new, representing a radical break from the basic prevailing concept. Even among the best singers—Mildred Bailey, Ivie Anderson, Jimmy Rushing, Frank Sinatra, Mel Torme—singing was *interpretation of a lyric*, of a melody and words, of a story, via traditional vocal techniques. For Anita singing was a quasi-instrumental creative expression, in which words and text would become secondary and indeed at times would be eliminated altogether. It was a whole new way of thinking about singing—about using the voice—that derived from jazz as an *instrumentalist's* art, rather than the vocalist's art of communicating words and stories.

Even more economical than Billie Holiday's, Anita's style was less prone to mannerisms, although it was also not as rich or as deeply expressive as Billie's could be. There is a certain abstractness, an emotional aloofness in Anita's singing that at once saves it from ever becoming sentimental but also prevents it from probing very deeply. It is like a finely polished, hard-finished veneer that will permit no stains but also no penetration.

Anita's singing at first confused audiences, but she was soon able to win them over by concentrating in her repertory on sophisticated, often humorous novelty songs, many of which she sang in duet with Roy Eldridge, an updated version of the hokum and vaudeville routines of 1920s' jazz.

That kind of material in due course ensured Anita's *popular* success. On the artistic side she proved her abilities as soon as she arrived in the Krupa band on such sides as *Georgia on My Mind, Alreet, Fool Am I*. The influence of Billie Holiday is clearly audible but transformed into something highly personal and even more "instrumentalized." There are no frills, no extraneous vocalisms. The

---

50. Eldridge's work in the 1941 Krupa band is discussed in Chapter 6, above.

little scoops and bends that Billie invented for herself became with Anita an *integral* part of the style; they were no longer mere embellishment. The individuality of Anita's style was greatly enhanced by the uniqueness of her voice's timbre, with its distinctive and captivating huskiness, and by the virtual absence of vibrato. When vibrato occurred, usually only on long-note values, it was finely calibrated, used as a musically controlled, appropriate *affect*, rather than as merely an immutable aspect of the voice.

Also notable in a refreshingly new way was Anita's diction and articulation of words and syllables, all at the service of greater rhythmic drive and swing. Her skill in this area can be well appraised on the delightfully wordy *Massachusetts* (lyrics by Andy Razaf), and *Thanks for the Boogie Ride*, or her superb 1945 *Opus No. 1*.

Although the Krupa band in 1941 generally still played in the light airy swing manner of the late-1930s' Goodman band, it could on occasion develop a more modern and vigorous hard-swinging style (as, for example, on the excellent *Stop! The Red Light's On* and *The Walls Keep Talking*).

But in early 1943 Krupa was forced to disband his orchestra after being criminally indicted on a charge of "possession of marijuana," a charge which was later withdrawn. In late 1944, after a brief stint with Tommy Dorsey, Krupa organized his second band featuring a decidedly more modern style, in arrangements primarily by Eddie Finckel, Gerry Mulligan, and George Williams. And like so many bands of the late-war and postwar period, when countless players who had come into the ranks in the late thirties were still in the armed services, Krupa's also benefited from a whole new generation of technically advanced younger players, most of whom were already listening to Gillespie and Parker and favoring a newer chromatically enriched harmonic language. Trumpeters Don Fagerquist and Red Rodney, saxophonists Charlie Kennedy and Buddy Wise, trombonist Dick Taylor (later Frank Rossolino and Urbie Green) were some of the fine players that added a new virtuosic dimension to the Krupa band. Rodney was an especially promising talent at the time, as can be heard to good advantage on *Back Home in Indiana*, *Ain't Nowhere*, and *I Hear You Screaming*. And for the public there was tenor player Charlie Ventura, featuring a swashbuckling, often overbearingly romantic style, an amalgam of the Hawkins/Webster tenor axis and goodly doses of Johnny Hodges.

The new tone was set in pieces like *Leave Us Leap* (by Eddie Finckel) and *What's This?*, the latter with a clever scat bop vocal duet by Buddy Stewart and Dave Lambert.[51]

Finckel's work for Krupa, as exemplified by pieces like *Leave Us Leap.* and *Up an' Atom*, was more genuinely in a jazz vein than his later work for Boyd Raeburn, which often tended to classically influenced pretentiousness and bombast. *Leap*, with its stunning use of silence in the final chorus, is typical of the clean, incisive, swinging scores Finckel produced for Krupa. But two other ar-

---

51. Lambert, a pioneering bop vocalist and skillful arranger, came to great fame as a member of the Lambert-Hendricks-Ross trio of the late fifties. Buddy Stewart, a gifted ballad singer in the Sinatra style as well as a good scat singer—a rare combination of talents—died in 1950 in an auto accident at the age of twenty-eight.

rangers, George Williams and Gerry Mulligan, were even more instrumental in bringing the Krupa band into the modern era. Williams stayed with Krupa for four years (1945–49) and created a wide variety of outstanding scores in a style strongly reminiscent of Sy Oliver, ranging from inventive recastings of older material like *Dear Old Southland* and *Tea for Two* (the latter with a captivatingly hip interpretation by Anita O'Day) to *Ain't Nowhere, Gene's Boogie,* and his 1952 extended work *American Bolero,* not recorded by Krupa until 1961.

Krupa also did not record Gerry Mulligan's early work (1946–47) until a dozen years later with a star-studded specially assembled band for Norman Granz's Verve label. Krupa may simply have considered Mulligan's work too risky commercially—he *did* take a chance on two of his more "conservative" scores, *Disc Jockey Jump* (1947) and *How High the Moon* (1946)—notwithstanding his genuine commitment to the newer jazz styles, which he staunchly maintained into the early fifties and even sporadically beyond that. Indeed by 1949, the year the bop movement finally achieved wide public recognition, Krupa's orchestra had developed into a full-fledged modern ensemble. George Williams was still the chief arranger, turning out such fine scores as *Bop Boogie*[52] and *Lemon Drop* (the latter piece virtually the national anthem of bebop). Furthermore the Krupa band was as good as any around at the time and could do full justice to these more demanding scores. The band was, as were all of Krupa's orchestras, not only highly disciplined technically, but it played with an enthusiasm and energy often lacking in the other bands (like Goodman and Shaw) who temporarily jumped back on the big-band wagon in order to exploit the sudden popularity of bop. It is also to Krupa's credit that, for the most part, his own work as drummer-leader kept apace of the new modern jazz idiom and rarely seems at odds with either the arrangements or the other soloists' styles (Rodney, Fagerquist, Rossolino, Wise).

Ironically, the player who had considerable trouble adapting to the new bop style was Roy Eldridge, who had returned to Krupa in 1949. Eldridge was too much an individualist—and himself an earlier major style-setter—simply to abandon his identity in order to suit some newly prevailing conception, even if that conception was developed by his own disciple Gillespie. Eldridge's style was too emotional, too beholden to Armstrong and the "romantic" era of jazz—and, to be honest about it, a bit too undisciplined—to submit to the cooler, sleeker lines of bop. It is a little sad to hear him—on pieces like *G-Bop, The Gone Side*—debasing his art with collections of the standard bop trumpet clichés of the day. In this respect it is fascinating to compare Eldridge and his section mate Fagerquist, for example on *G-Bop* (Roy) and *To Be or Not To Be-Bop* (Fagerquist), Eldridge struggling with a strange language, Fagerquist at home in the new idiom, in full control of both technique and ideas. When Eldridge played himself, as on *Bop Boogie,*—a strong, expansive, well-focused solo—he fitted

---

52. For some reason Krupa had always had luck and a benign touch with boogie-woogie material. Often handled very vulgarly and primitively by white bands, boogie-woogie was for some reason always approached by Krupa with a certain sensitivity, extrapolating the best out of this limited style. The list of Krupa boogie pieces includes *Drum Boogie* (1941), *Boogie Blues* (1945), *Gene's Boogie* (1947), *Bop Boogie* (1949), all well worth hearing.

into George Williams's arrangement much better than when he tried to beat the younger players at *their* game.

By 1950, as with so many bandleaders who began at the height of the Swing Era, Krupa could no longer maintain the innovative drive of his earlier years. Except for sporadic attempts to recapture past glories with especially assembled studio bands—for example, those that recorded Mulligan's scores (as mentioned) and earlier Krupa hits, from *Rockin' Chair* to *Drummin' Man* (in 1956)—Krupa led small combos and worked with Granz's Jazz at the Philharmonic, often in staged drum battles with Buddy Rich. But below Krupa's often exasperating public image as a gum-chewing, tousled-haired showman drummer, there was a serious side which manifested itself in a variety of ways, such as his ongoing life-long study of percussion techniques, the founding of a drum school in New York (with Cozy Cole), and his unwavering commitment, whether in small or large groups, to true jazz.

It is also interesting to observe that, by and large, Krupa was a much better behaved, less ostentatious drummer in his own band than he was with Goodman's. In his commitment to real jazz, even in its more advanced bop manifestation, Krupa, with his fame, brought first-rate modern jazz to untold numbers of listeners who would otherwise never have had contact with it. He and his bands consistently aspired to the best and could always be relied upon to play with high discipline, enthusiasm, and an exuberant swing. Given the vagaries of the commercial world in which jazz has always had to fight for its survival, clearly this was no small achievement.

PART 3

WOODY HERMAN

If it is true that perception often is more "real" then reality, then the discrepancy between perception and reality—especially as it affects the lives and assessments of artists—ought to be a fascinating subject for the cultural historian. In that complex of feelings, opinions, assumptions, assertions—and, alas, prejudices—from which human judgments are constructed, reality can easily be suppressed or altered to suit certain preconceptions. And in these respects Woody Herman's place in jazz history, particularly as viewed by most critics and jazz historians, does not seem to square with the reality of his many remarkable achievements.

For Woody has rarely been accorded appropriate recognition for his consistently fine work as a clarinetist, as an alto saxophonist, and as a singer—he is generally dismissed as beneath discussion in these three areas—and even the many fine orchestras Woody has led through the years, his First Herd included, have been treated—at least until recently—rather casually by most jazz historians. Somehow his accomplishments are not deemed quite central to the main tradition(s) of jazz and therefore of minor consequence.

The fact that Herman is an excellent, at times superior clarinetist/saxophonist/singer—certainly never less than professional—and that his 1944–46 band was as exciting and influential an orchestra as jazz has seen is generally ignored or suppressed. Had Herman and his orchestra been black, the verdict would be quite different. For it is Woody's dilemma that, being white but knowing and deeply feeling that all the important innovative and creative impulses in jazz have derived from black musicians and sources, he has received little appreciation for striving to pay tribute to those sources, whether it was the blues or the emerging bebop of the early 1940s, or individuals like Webster or Hodges or Gillespie.

And it seems to me that what Woody has embraced he has always treated with a certain humility and integrity, and without self-aggrandizement. Nor has he merely taken and imitated without giving something back; his (and his arrangers') adaptations of their influences of others have always been assimilated, digested, and adopted with a significant amount of personal creativity.[1] To say this is not

Fig. 1

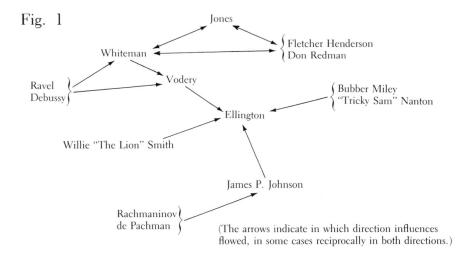

(The arrows indicate in which direction influences flowed, in some cases reciprocally in both directions.)

1. The questions of what *is* black and what *is* white in jazz, and what influences affected which musicians and when, are enormously complex ones, generally defying detailed, precise answers— that is, beyond the uncontestable reality that jazz originated with black Americans and that all of its major developments and innovations have derived from them. It is when one probes beneath that general truth that one may encounter vexing and virtually unanswerable questions of artistic pedigree and authorship. To what extent cross-fertilizing influences may be considered on the one hand as constructive, creative, genuine, honest, or on the other hand as simply derivative, spurious, parasitic, and merely commercially motivated is a question constantly before us, as crucial today as it ever was in the past. Inevitably, in a music which from its outset was a cultural hybrid, fused from both African and European stylistic/formal elements, artistic pedigree is hard to prove. The infinitely complex network of influences that connects, for example, the work of just the following almost randomly chosen collection of names—Duke Ellington, Will Vodery, Paul Whiteman, Isham Jones, Don Redman, Bubber Miley, Joe Nanton, Fletcher Henderson, Ravel, Debussy, Willie "The Lion" Smith, James P. Johnson, de Pachman, and Rachmaninov—every one of these names links up with one or more of the others in significant ways—offers a tiny glimpse of the futility of assigning unequivocal artistic precedence and superiority in these matters. Fig. 1, above, illustrates these relationships graphically, a microcosm of influences, which shows that no one develops in a cultural vacuum and without leaning in some way on someone else's talents or work.

to argue that Woody belongs in that pantheon of original creative artists of the calibre of Armstrong, Ellington, or Parker; nor even to argue that he is a virtuoso performer at the level of a Hines, an Eldridge, a Benny Goodman, or a Red Norvo. But it is to suggest that Woody Herman ought to be given credit where it is due (and in the measure it is due) as an outstanding figure in jazz, whose contributions to the music have often been important and never less than honest.

Herman belongs to that category of musicians who are not creative in the largest sense, who are not capable of being "unique" or "original", but who nevertheless succeed at very high levels of technical perfection, taste, and musical integrity. And if Woody based some aspects of his work as a performer and bandleader on other models, he always chose the best ones to emulate, through them aspiring to the highest ideals of perfection and craftmanship.

Certainly, he derived the essentials of his clarinet style from Goodman and one of Goodman's own major influences, Jimmy Noone. And yet Herman's clarinet playing is immediately identifiable as *his*, by the warmth and expressivity of his tone, by the distinctive turns-of-phrase he favors, and by the modest role he assigns himself in any orchestral or ensemble context.

Similarly, Herman's adulation of Johnny Hodges can be heard in all of his alto work. And yet there is an intensity and personal warmth beneath the outward manner in Woody's alto-playing that is undeniably his own.

His work as a singer is perhaps the least appreciated of his performing roles. This is all the more surprising since Woody really sings remarkably well, indeed better than the vast majority of those who think of themselves as professional singers. Again, Woody makes no pretenses as a vocalist, but the fact remains that in three particular vocal idioms—ballads, blues, and novelty songs—Woody has few equals. Listening to his ballad-singing on records, especially in the 1930s and 1940s, one is constantly surprised to find that we aren't listening to some famous established singer but simply to Woody Herman. His control of pitch, timbre, diction, and phrasing is never less than commensurate to the assignment at hand, and often times quite inspired and original. One tends to forget that before becoming a bandleader Woody had had a long career as a successful vaudeville singer and performer, going back to his teens; and that he was hired by that arch perfectionist of dance music, Isham Jones, primarily as a singer.

But clearly Herman's greatest contributions to jazz are as an orchestra leader, in 1945 producing one of the finest orchestras jazz has ever known and through it causing the creation of a body of works that stand to this day as classics of the post-Swing Era. Woody has also been an uncannily successful spotter of major talent, as the personnels of his various orchestras through the decades clearly demonstrate—from Neil Reid and Bill Harris to Urbie Green, from Stan Getz and Zoot Sims to Sal Nistico, from Joe Bishop to Ralph Burns and Neal Hefti.

In many respects the standards of excellence and professionalism Woody has maintained throughout his career were instilled in him in his early years in vaudeville and with the bands of Tom Gerun and Isham Jones. The latter especially was a major influence, not only in that Woody inherited the nucleus of

Jones's fine band (when disbanded in 1936) but that Jones's skills as an orchestral leader and his zeal for musical perfection were impressed upon Herman at a formative stage of his career. We tend to forget that Woody was barely twenty-three when he took over the leadership of the Isham Jones band, and that he inherited along with some of its personnel many of its best qualities of musicianship and discipline. These were still influentially formative years in Herman's career, and it is to his credit—and typical of his whole approach to band-leading—that he not only preserved the high standards of musicianship that Isham Jones had established but did so whilst accepting the band's titular leadership in the context of a "cooperative" orchestra. Herman has always been exceptional among bandleaders in appreciatively acknowledging the contributions of his sidemen.

For a better understanding of Woody Herman's early development we must digress briefly to examine the work of one of the most remarkable musicians to grace the American popular music scene, Isham Jones.[2]

Isham Jones, like his contemporary Paul Whiteman, led one of the finest dance bands of all time—some would argue *the* finest—for some seventeen years (from 1919 to 1936). Jones managed to combine the highest musicianship with a desire to present the best popular repertory in the most pleasurably danceable form. To that end, like Woody Herman after him, he always surrounded himself with the finest musicians available, thereby according dance music a professionalism and class it rarely enjoyed, especially in the 1920s. Jones was also a highly successful songwriter, the author of several hundred songs, a good two dozen of which were major hits and became standards that are still heard to this day—*It Had To Be You, I'll See You in My Dreams, No Greater Love, Swinging Down the Lane.*

Jones was, in addition, a first-rate arranger, as witness his outstanding work with his early 1920s' band. From the very outset Jones brought a sophisticated sense of variety (of orchestration, timbre, texture, and dynamics) to his dance band, literally unheard of in those days. One can listen to virtually any of the two hundred-odd sides Jones recorded, for example, between 1920 and 1927, and scarcely discover any repetition of instrumental combinations and devices. Unlike other bandleaders, both then and later, who searched for a formula or gimmick and then rigidly held on to it for the rest of their days, Jones eschewed formularization. His first criterion—that a piece be perfect for dancing—was combined with a high degree of creativity and resourcefulness in exploiting the necessarily limited instrumentation at his command (originally ten players, then enlarged to eleven and in the 1930s to fifteen and sixteen).

Indeed, Isham Jones was, along with Art Hickman and Paul Whiteman, one of the three prime innovators in determining the basic instrumentation and character of the modern American dance orchestra. But whereas Whiteman continually enlarged his orchestra and increased the number of doubling instruments,

2. I confess that while writing *Early Jazz* I was not quite aware of Isham Jones's outstanding accomplishments, or of his remarkable influence. Though he led a "dance band" rather than a jazz orchestra, I should have included mention of his pioneering work.

striving for "symphonic" proportions, Jones found ingenious ways of using his mere half-dozen melodic instruments to maximum varietal effect. He was particularly inventive in the use of his band's three reed instruments: soprano saxophone; alto saxophone doubling clarinet; and himself, in the early days mostly on C-melody sax, doubling occasionally on tenor, and by the mid-twenties switching more and more to tenor. By constantly varying ways of combining the reeds in duets and trios and in turn combining them, singly or collectively, with his two (later three) brass instruments and a violin (played by the excellent Leo Murphy), Jones was able to create an astonishing diversity of timbres and textures that no other bandleader in 1921 or 1922 even dreamt of, let alone realized. *Virginia Blues, High Brown Blues, Farewell Blues, My Honey's Lovin' Arms* (all from 1922) may serve as excellent examples of Jones's resourcefulness, matched perhaps only by Jelly Roll Morton in his 1926 Red Hot Peppers recordings (with only seven players!). *My Honey's Lovin' Arms* is typical of Jones's approach, as shown schematically in Figure 2.

Jones's recording of *Farewell Blues* is even more startling in its innovative use of instrumentation, dynamics, and contrasts of texture and mood. Aside from requiring unusual expressive swells in the theme statement ($\prec$ sfz $\succ$) and a (for the time) uncommon low-register clarinet solo, followed by a sobbing brass trio (led by Louis Panico, Jones's star trumpeter), Jones builds the last several choruses to a climactic ending by the triple device of a) a well-paced continuous crescendo, b) adding more and more instruments,

Fig. 2

Intro	A Vln/cornet lead (in 8ves) 3 saxes accomp. in harmony trb counterlines	B Reed trio (clar, sop, C-mel) w/intermittent obblig. of tpt and trb
8	16	32

B¹
Cornet lead (var. of
   B theme)
clar high reg. obblig.
trb counterlines (incl.
Tiger Rag interpolations)
	A¹
	Repeat of A
		B²
		Vln duet (arr'd)
		1. Vln and pno var. of
		   B theme
		2. Vln in harmony
		   (no tuba, bjo, drums)

32	16	32

B³ Full collect. ens. vln high obblig. clar high lead sop/C-mel improvise   harmonic counterlines tpt/trb obblig. counterlines
32

c) in increasingly higher registers—similar to the techniques used, for example, by Maurice Ravel in his 1928 *Bolero*. These final stanzas of *Farewell Blues* are also notable for their amazing swing, years ahead of others' capabilities in this regard, especially if one takes into account that it was never Isham Jones's intention to create a *jazz* orchestra, merely a superior *dance* band.

Just as astonishing is Jones's ability to adapt, as early as 1920, the often frenzied and inane collective improvisational style of groups like the Original Dixieland Jazz Band and Louisiana Five to a more musical and balanced conception. In this Jones was no doubt much influenced by King Oliver's Creole Jazz Band and the New Orleans Rhythm Kings, the former the finest jazz and dance orchestra in Chicago, the very city in which Jones formed his band in 1919.

Notable, too, is Jones's copious inclusion of blues or blues-like pieces in his repertory, hardly typical for a white dance orchestra in the 1920s. This is especially significant in view of the fact that Woody Herman's early band, as mentioned a direct descendant of the Jones orchestra, had a heavy component of blues in *its* repertory, and was in fact known as "the band that plays the blues." Many of Jones's early 1920s' blues were, of course, more ragtime than blues, or at least retained many of the rhythmic and stylistic characteristics of late ragtime. But here again Jones was a master at blending these two style elements with his own adaptations of the New Orleans collective improvisational idioms, all assimilated into an unerringly successful dance music.

And dance music is what Jones called it, even though much of it is clearly jazz or leans heavily in a jazz direction. It is, in fact, for the most part, truer to the spirit and rhythmic energy of jazz than many of the self-proclaimed jazz bands of the period, both black and white. (There is no question, for example, that the Isham Jones band of the early and mid-1920s swung much more than Fletcher Henderson's or Duke Ellington's bands in *their* early years. And that wasn't because Jones wanted to play jazz, but rather because he wanted to provide the ultimate in rhythmic dance music, music that would simply compel people get on the dance floor and dance.)

Later, when Jones felt obliged to give up playing and arranging and just lead his orchestra, he engaged two excellent composer-arrangers, Joe Bishop and Gordon Jenkins, to maintain the previous high levels of creativity, along with outstanding players like trumpeter Johnny Carlson, trombonist Jack Jenney, reedman Milt Yaner—and in 1934 Woody Herman.

In the thirties, Jones was able to maintain a striking balance between old and new, combining traditional elements with some of the more advanced directions of the period, especially in his highly effective blending of both a two-beat and 4/4 rhythmic pulse.[3] One simple device Jones used to produce a strong rhythmic

---

3. Jones's retention of the tuba well into the mid-1930s should not, however, be construed as evidence of a conservative penchant on his part, or of a longing to maintain an "old-fashioned" rhythmic feeling. On the contrary, it was Jones's desire to strengthen the bass lines by using *both* tuba and string bass (pizzicato) in order to provide a stronger harmonic foundation and rhythmic pulse, as well as a depth of sonority which orchestras like Tommy Dorsey's, for example, didn't discover until the very late 1930s, but which Whiteman on the other hand had already pioneered in the twenties and maintained well into the Swing Era.

momentum was maintaining a constant four-beats-to-the-bar accompaniment on the guitar (played expertly by Jack Blanchette), regardless of whether the rest of the rhythm section was in two or in four. With its emphasis of a steady swinging beat, Jones's orchestra could even make a waltz swing compellingly, as witness their 1932 *I'll Never Have To Dream Again*. (Other outstanding at times strongly swinging Jones performances are *Sentimental Gentleman from Georgia* (1932) and *Georgia Jubilee* and *Blue Room* (both from 1934.)

But to return to Woody Herman, the years 1936 to 1944 were for the Herman band a lengthy (and often economically precarious) period of growth and search for stylistic identity. Ironically, it was the orchestra's exceptional versatility that hindered it in readily finding a large sustaining audience. It excelled in not one but a number of stylistic areas and was unwilling to abandon any one of them, thereby undoubtedly fragmenting its potential audience. "The band that played the blues" also did very well with romantic ballads (especially those by the excellent songwriter-arranger-pianist Gordon Jenkins), also with dance numbers, Dixieland-style instrumentals, even "novelty" tunes, on which Herman and the band lavished a high degree of musical skill and entertainment know-how—again the twin legacy of his own vaudeville background and Isham Jones's philosophy of treating all manner of material with respect and high craft. In all of these eclectic endeavors Herman managed to keep commercialism to a minimum, more so than most bands of the period, including many black ones. Even Herman's solitary commercial and popular success, a 1939 hit called *Woodchoppers' Ball*, was in essence a jazz piece: an "original" and an instrumental, featuring Woody's blues clarinet, Neil Reid's swing trombone, Steady Nelson's Cootie Williams-style trumpet, and some nicely swinging riff-ensemble choruses.

The transformation into the orchestra that startled the music world in 1945, known as the First Herd, was very gradual, almost imperceptible. Some of the effects of these changes could be heard as early as 1941 in Lowell Martin's excellent (but too short) *Woodsheddin' with Woody*, his *Ten Day Furlough*, Robert Hartsell's *Hot Chestnuts*—all hard-swinging jazz instrumentals that not only matched the best that other leaders in the field, like Benny Goodman, Shaw, and Barnet were turning out, but already captured some of the drive and excitement of the 1945 *Apple Honey*, *Caldonia* and *Northwest Passage*. Starting with a fairly strong rhythm section of Hy White (guitar), Walt Yoder (bass), and Frank Carlson (drums) and such players as trumpeters Ray Linn and Cappy Lewis, tenor saxophonist Herbie Haymer—only transitionally in the band—Herman, by 1943, was hiring Ellington sidemen such as Ben Webster, Johnny Hodges, and Ray Nance to sit in on his record dates (as well as performing and/or recording, in 1942, two of Dizzy Gillespie's earliest compositions and arrangements). Ben Webster's richly florid solos can be heard to good advantage on such Herman recordings as *The Music Stopped* (also notable for being singer Frances Wayne's first recording with Herman), *Do Nothing Till You Hear from Me*, and *Who Dat Up There*. But even speedier and more dramatic changes were in the offing.

Between late 1943 and late 1944—a period when the recording ban was still partly in force—Dave Tough joined the rhythm section, the remarkable trombonist Bill Harris came over from Bob Chester's band, tenor saxophonist Flip Phillips (playing in a manner that combined all three major tenor styles: Hawkins, Webster, and Young) joined up; and arrangers Ralph Burns and Neal Hefti began revolutionizing the Herman band's style by moving it firmly forward in the direction of the new bop frontier, the first major white band to do so unequivocally and consistently.

But perhaps the most influential addition to the Herman band was bassist Chubby Jackson in 1943, not necessarily as an all-that-outstanding bass player (although by adding a fifth string to his bass, pitched at high C, a fourth above the usual upper G-string of the bass, he explored some new frontiers of his own in his walking bass lines and solos), but as an energetic catalytic force in the rhythm section, and—perhaps even more important—as a kind of self-proclaimed associate-leader to Woody, ferreting out new young talent and maintaining a lively contact with all that was new in jazz at the time.

What is so remarkable about the Herman band's stylistic transformation, from an eclectic all-purpose ensemble to the best "bop" or "modern jazz" orchestra in the land, is that this metamorphosis resulted from a thorough fusion of several specific early-1940s' style ingredients: the feel and swing of Basie's rhythm section; the fresh streamlined and linear virtuoso conception of brass-writing already articulated by Dizzy Gillespie[4]; and the new harmonic language previously explored by Ellington, Eddie Sauter, Sy Oliver, Buster Harding, and Ray Conniff. The primary synergistic agent in all this was the new post-Swing-Era technical skills possessed by the best young players, relentlessly energetic and virtuosic. This made possible a level of sheer instrumental excitement that was simply not available earlier, except in isolated instances.

These new qualities were effectively captured on a surprisingly large number of Herman recordings, starting with the up-tempo *Apple Honey* and *Caldonia* (1945), on through *Northwest Passage*, *Bijou*, *Blowing Up a Storm* (although in the last title the Carnegie Hall performance of March 25, 1946, is superior to the commercial recording in all respects), and *Your Father's Moustache*, *Wild Root*, *Fan It*, *Back Talk*, *Non-Alcoholic*, and finally to Ralph Burns's 1946 four-movement orchestral suite *Summer Sequence*.

On the lyric and ballad side there were also major contributions to the genre, invariably arranged by Ralph Burns: notably David Raksin's superb *Laura* (how well Woody plays and sings on this!); *I Surrender Dear*, a fine vehicle for Red Norvo's creative artistry[5]; *Panacea*; Bill Harris's lyric masterpiece *Everywhere*; and, above all, *Happiness Is Just a Thing Called Joe*, with Frances Wayne's sublime singing, surely one of the dozen most memorable vocals of the entire

---

4. We can hear such lines as early as 1942 on Herman's recordings of Gillespie's *Down Under*:

5. See Chapter 6, part 2, above, for a discussion of this performance.

Big Band and Swing Era. The singer captured the haunting bittersweet quality of Harold Arlen's song with a maturity, vocal imagination, and taste that avoids all cloying sentimentality—even in her copious use of *portamenti*—and that belies the fact that she was only twenty at the time. Ralph Burns's sensitive arrangement, subdued in pastel-colored muted brass and soft saxes (except for one dramatic 4-bar double-time outburst), provides a well-nigh perfect underscoring.

This extensive repertory, primarily the creation of Burns and Hefti—there was more, of course, some of it at not quite as high a level, and some of it not recorded commercially at all—has hardly dated in retrospect. It is as fresh and exciting now—even when played today by younger orchestras as "older repertory"—as it was then, over forty years ago. The reasons are obvious: the Burns/Hefti pieces were *really* new and original at the time, a striking amalgam of first-rate jazz solos (by the likes of Bill Harris, Flip Phillips, trumpeter Sonny Berman,[6] and Red Norvo, supported by a dynamic and indefatigable rhythm section), and orchestral writing derived from these very same fresh improvisatory styles. Secondly, the musicians played this material, night after night, with an infectious exuberance, an almost physically palpable excitement and a never-say-die energy. As I say, this partially represented the sheer pleasure of frolicking in such high-level instrumental virtuosity. But the band also played with a sense of pride in its individual and collective accomplishments. And it appreciated, indeed relished the newness of their style's harmonic and melodic language, the rich advanced harmonies, the lean, sleek bop lines. The musicians also knew they were playing for a leader who deeply appreciated their talents and their contributions to the cooperative whole.

Some four decades later we tend to forget *how* new this all was. As a result of the constant recycling since the late 1940s of that genre of big-band style by dozens of orchestras, we tend to take much of it for granted today. We should not forget, however, that there has been very little substantively new in big-band styling since Woody's First Herd, and that the ultimate perpetuation of that style during the last thirty years fell to Count Basie (for whom Hefti arranged for many years).

On the other hand, lest I appear to be overstating the case for the importance and influence of the Herman band, two points should be clarified. It was not in the full sense of the term a true bop band. Though Hefti, Sonny Berman, and Chubby Jackson were enthusiastic disciples of Gillespie and Parker and brought much of the new bop concepts into the Herman band, other players like Phillips, Harris, and Tough (and of course Woody himself) could not be readily aligned with the bop movement. They were "modern jazz" players with roots firmly ensconced in the late-thirties' swing styles. Thus the 1945 Herman band was only intermittently and/or somewhat exteriorly in a genuine bop mold. The distance between it and the pure bop-styled orchestras—Billy Eckstine's of 1944, Dizzy Gillespie's of 1946, and Oscar Pettiford's short-lived eighteen-piece band of early 1945—can be measured by comparing Herman's *Apple Honey, Cal-*

---

6. Berman, one of the earliest Dizzy Gillespie disciples, was developing into an important soloist of increasing originality when his career was cut short in a fatal auto accident at the age of twenty-two.

donia, or *Back Talk* with such pieces as Gillespie's *Things to Come* and *Emanon*, Pettiford's *Something for You*, Eckstine's *I Stay in the Mood for You* or *Blowing the Blues Away*.

But as the chart on p. 852 demonstrates, the Herman band was not only an early innovator in the new bop or bop-tinged orchestral style, but it committed itself to it with a perseverence and consistent quality not equaled by any other white band of the time. This was due in large measure, as we shall see, to Ralph Burns's arrangements and compositions, and the fortuitous coming together of a young, dynamic, exceptionally talented group of players. Although all the other major white bands of the 1940s—Barnet, James, Shaw, Kenton, Raeburn, and to a lesser extent Goodman—also drew on a whole fresh generation of arrangers and players, they all adopted the new modern jazz language well *after* the Herman band had made the change-over. Barnet, James, Shaw, and Raeburn were the first to follow suit, with Kenton and Les Brown trailing by a year or more. Moreover, except for Herman—and James with his 1945–46 band—all those orchestras retained a high proportion of pop and purely dance repertory. Their conversion and commitment to the idiom was not as deep as Herman's and his Herd.

As to the question of who got there first, clearly Eckstine's recording of *I Stay in the Mood*, with its exciting unison bop lines in the brass and Dizzy's concluding solo, takes precedence chronologically; it was recorded in April 1944 when Dizzy was just organizing the Eckstine band. On the other hand, the Herman band's *Apple Honey* (Ex. 1) and *Caldonia* (Ex. 2), basically head arrangements with some of their bop-ish brass figures supplied by Ralph Burns and Neal Hefti, were performed as early as the summer of 1944 (but not recorded until February 1945). Unquestionably, Gillespie and Eckstine's arranger Gerry Valentine inaugurated the new style *on records* (already explored with the Hines band in 1943, however not recorded—presumably because of the 1942–43 ban). But Woody Herman, with Jackson's and Hefti's ears close to the ground, picking

Ex. 1

Ex. 2

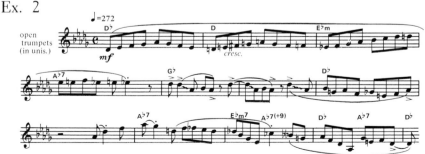

up the new vibrations from Harlem and Minton's was certainly not far behind. It is also a fair assumption that Herman's enormous commercial success with Columbia Records in 1945—along with Eckstine's—helped pave the way for the establishment in 1945 of Dizzy's prophetic band (it however did not record until mid-1946).

I have mentioned Herman's appreciativeness of his musicians' talents. But Herman was also a consistently accurate critical judge of talent, and allowed only his most creative players to solo. None was more gifted than Bill Harris, probably the most astonishingly original trombonist of the early modern-jazz era. Blessed with a seemingly unlimited technique, range, and endurance, Harris was at all times completely unpredictable, relentlessly original creatively. Yet he could always be relied upon to capture the essential mood or character of any given work or arrangement. A typical Harris solo could be passionate (*Northwest Passage*), eccentric (the 1946 *Woodchoppers' Ball*), quirky (*Nero's Conception*), suave (*Bijou*), intensely lyrical (*Everywhere*), fantastical (*Fan It*), and bop-ishly driving (*Apple Honey*). Harris's solos were like recitatives, based on some private scenario of his own invention, which at the same time provided his personal commentary—occasionally a mite garrulous—on the work in question. In all of his playing there was an underlying hard-edged humor, a sharp wit which could instantly break out in the most startling utterances. His seemingly unmoving, tough, taciturn outward expression—surely a mask hiding a highly complex and serious persona—kept Harris from ever descending to mere sentimentality—save perhaps to parody it. Even Harris's most extravagant musical expressions can usually be grasped in the light of his strange sense of humor and his penchant for the caustic and the sardonic. His control of musical content was as awesome as his control of technique. His often outrageous use of vibrato, for example, was by no means an uncontrolled aberration. It was on the contrary a finely calibrated, specifically embellishmental, expressive technique, always at the precise service of his musical intentions. It could cover the entire continuum from a searingly intense straight tone (no vibrato) to various extremes of vibrato (in both speed and pitch variance) and all gradations in between.[7] Harris also adapted with great effect the so-called "terminal vibrato" (André Hodeir's term), first developed by Louis Armstrong and trombonists like Jimmy Harrison and Dickie Wells. Harris often carried this effect one step further by stopping notes with an abrupt "ripped" kind of release, thereby adding powerful rhythmic punctuations to his phrases that heightened their sense of swing.[8]

Ralph Burns's always outstanding contributions to the Herman book were climaxed in 1946 with an ambitious four-movement twelve-minute work entitled *Summer Sequence*. Given the precedent in 1943 of Ellington's breakthrough extended-form suite *Black, Brown and Beige* and Burns's deep admiration for

7. I know of only one other artist who has such consummate control of vibrato, and that is Sarah Vaughan—more precisely the Sarah Vaughan of 1987 and the last fifteen years or so.
8. Harris's countless imaginative solos really defy notation and therefore do not appear here in musical examples. They must be heard to be appreciated fully. The relatively "simple" *Apple Honey* solo and the dazzlingly "extravagant" one on *Fan It* are two examples of Harris's art, suggested for the further-interested reader/listener.

Ellington's art, it was perhaps inevitable that, with his composer's (as opposed to arranger's) creative imagination, Burns would be inspired to try his hand at a similar large-scale work.

Summer Sequence was mostly composed in the summer of 1946 while on a Long Island vacation sojourn. Its four movements (played without pause) comprise a lively scherzo-like second movement, a quieter lyrical third movement, both enclosed by two outer movements whose central portions use an attractive rhapsodic 32-bar ballad theme. First stated by the guitar (Chuck Wayne) and further proclaimed by Bill Harris's trombone, this more or less traditional symmetrically formed theme contrasts strikingly with the two inner movements' many "asymmetrical" phrase structures (many of them an uncommon seven bars in duration). In addition, these latter sections abound with a constantly varied instrumentation, resulting in an unusual degree of textural and timbral variety. In these respects Burns was further surveying territory previously explored only by Ellington, Eddie Sauter, and (occasionally) Sy Oliver. In turn *Summer Sequence*, although never a large popular success—until, that is, its last movement was re-worked into *Early Autumn*, featuring Stan Getz's famous solo—exerted a considerable influence, in differing ways, to be sure, on such bands as Kenton's and Raeburn's, through their composer-arrangers Pete Rugolo, George Handy, and Eddie Finkel.

Summer Sequence is not without flaws. Some of its transitional passages are commonplace and seem stuck together out of extraneous material not intrinsic to the work; and its ending is weak indeed. But at its best, the work amply displays the potential for extended-form composition of the modern jazz orchestra, beyond the requisites of dance music.

The other work that radically broke through the confines of the traditional jazz-orchestral repertory, Herman's as well as any other, was Igor Stravinsky's *Ebony Concerto*, premiered by the Herman orchestra in Carnegie Hall, on March 25, 1946, and recorded by them with Stravinsky conducting, in August of that year. The work was scored for Woody's eighteen-piece orchestra plus horn and harp, in effect in a wind-ensemble piece.

Ebony Concerto, like Stravinsky's earlier "ragtime" pieces, remains one of the master's more elusive scores, partly because it occupies a no-man's land halfway between jazz and Stravinsky's mid-period neo-classic style; and partly because, due to its stylistic ambiguousness, it is rarely performed convincingly or with much understanding of its special performance needs. Indeed, it may well be that its fundamental performance problems have yet to be resolved, since even to this day players who can meet the technical demands of this work and at the same time infuse it with the jazz feeling and rhythmic vitality the work cries for—which Stravinsky undoubtedly heard in *Bijou*, *Goosey Gander*, and *Caldonia*—are still extremely rare. They are even more rarely assembled *in one place* to perform the work.[9]

9. In some respects the finest performance of *Ebony Concerto* I can recall to date, *including* my own attempts as a conductor of the work, was one given in the mid-fifties by Kurt Edelhagen and his orchestra of the South West German Radio (an orchestra, incidentally, which was later led for several years by Eddie Sauter).

Certainly the Herman orchestra was not quite equal to the task, typically becoming very tight and inexpressive when, as in this case, the composition seemed to eliminate the basic explicit beat and standard jazz feeling. Woody, with his characteristic honesty and modesty, stated on numerous occasions that the Herman band was not ready for this performing assignment. "We had no more right to play it than the man in the moon," he said.

The critics have never dealt fairly with Stravinsky's *Ebony Concerto*. Most jazz critics at the time of the premiere and recording were incapable of comprehending the work, casually dismissing it with comments of "not jazz" (or "inept jazz") and other profoundly intellectual pronouncements, never realizing that what they heard was not Stravinsky's *Ebony Concerto* at all but rather a poor performance of it. The classical critics, too, for the most part belittled the work as minor Stravinsky fare, generally unable, it seems, to savor its jazz allusions and at the same time apparently even incapable of appreciating its impeccable craftsmanship. (This seems to be the usual critical fate of category or style hybrids.) *Ebony Concerto* certainly does not deserve the status of an inconsequential trifle which most writers have accorded it. Nor could one argue that it ranks with Stravinsky's major works, like *Petrushka*, *The Rite of Spring*, *Symphony of Psalms*, and *The Rake's Progress*.

It is beyond the scope of this study to attempt to assign the work its ultimate "resting place"; let history and the future render that final verdict. What is relevant here, however, is that Stravinsky, with his usual unerringly sharp ear, composed a work which relates precisely to the more experimental, progressive side of the Herman band's mid-1940s' repertory, albeit in unmistakably Stravinskian terms. I am referring primarily to his consistent use of a) major-minor harmonies and melodies—an integral part of Stravinsky's musical language since around 1905—and b) of cross-rhythms and asymmetrical rhythmic patterns. The major-minor ambivalence relates quite naturally to the blue-note tradition of jazz and some of its more modern harmonic expressions, such as "raised ninth" chords or bitonal harmonies, especially the tritonally related ones.[10] This was one aspect of Stravinsky's *Ebony Concerto* the Herman musicians could hear—or at least should have been able to identify with. I cite but five brief excerpts exemplifying Stravinsky's application of this harmonic usage (Ex. 3a, b, c, d, e).

Ex. 3a

Stravinsky — Ebony Concerto (first movement)

(The same passage occurs earlier in the key of G)

10. For a full discussion of this development, see Chapter 5, part 2, above. For the moment I will just remind the lay reader that a "raised ninth" chord is actually a dominant seventh with a flat or "blue" third on top.

Ex. 3b

Stravinsky — Ebony Concerto (second movement)

Ex. 3c

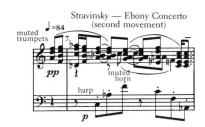

Stravinsky — Ebony Concerto (second movement)

Ex. 3d

Ex. 3e

On the face of it, the second passage (Ex. 3b) would appear to be clearly in F minor. And yet it has about it an aura of "major" and a distinctly blues-ish major-minor feeling. At the end of m. 7 (Ex. 3c) it becomes clear why this is so: the theme resolves clearly into F major, with only the harp still clinging to the minor tonality. In the third movement it should be noted that D minor and $B\flat^7$, here (Ex. 3d) combined in a bitonal harmony, are the two predominant (alternating) tonalities of the second movement. When this "cadence" recurs, the $B\flat$ chord (now in the piano) is combined with a G major chord in the trumpets (Ex. 3e). This latter tonality (G) has not only made a brief appearance in the opening measures (in the trumpets) but has crept increasingly into the continuity of the movement as it progresses, functioning in part as the subdominant of D major, the key to which the entire piece ultimately resolves in the brilliant closing coda.

As forward-looking as the *Ebony Concerto* is harmonically, rhythmically it tends to look back towards the period of Stravinsky's youth. For—and this is one of the *Concerto*'s anomalies (and one of its special performance problems)—the work relates much more to ragtime than to 1940s' swing. Stravinsky apparently never overcame his early fascination with ragtime and adhered to its simple syncopations and cross-accented patterns throughout his life, when dealing in any way with "jazz" elements. The opening of the *Concerto*, with its straight eighth-note patterns (Ex. 3f) is typical of Stravinsky's rhythmic language here. Clearly, it relates very little to the modern swing idiom.

Ex. 3f

In *Ebony Concerto*, as in other jazz-related works by Copland and Milhaud, Stravinsky was more interested in some of the music's externals, i.e. the *sounds* of jazz—its sonorities, the fascinating mutes (harmons, plungers) and the "effects" jazz musicians could get with them—than its substantive essence and rhythmic spontaneity. It was Stravinsky's loyalty to ragtime that undoubtedly influenced, for example, his life-long inability to understand that jazz was primarily an improvisatory art (ragtime being non-improvised). Nor did he ever fully comprehend that swing, freedom of rhythmic inflection, and rhythmic spontaneity were all keyed to the creation of a steady underlying beat and pulse. I suspect that Stravinsky in *Ebony Concerto* abstracted, and used only those, aspects of jazz *performance* that fascinated him. Nevertheless I am convinced that he also felt the drive and rhythmic energy in the Herman recordings he had heard, and that he would dearly have loved to incorporate those elements in his work. But he realized, I am sure, that these are precisely what cannot be captured in our notation, and which—I might add—must be supplied in performances of Stravinsky's *Ebony Concerto* before we can fully appreciate and assess this unique work.

Much more in the central tradition of evolving modern jazz was the work of Herman's small group, The Woodchoppers, formed in 1946, to a large extent to accommodate the talents of Red Norvo, who had just left the Goodman Sextet. Indeed, Herman appointed Norvo as his associate leader of the First Herd band, and put him musically in charge of the Woodchoppers. The group recorded ten sides, of which three were composed by Norvo (in colloboration with Shorty Rogers) and all arranged by him and Rogers. Rogers had worked with Norvo before in his 1945 Nonet and apparently was an ideal creative partner for Norvo, judging by the excellence of the Woodchopper recordings. The Woodchoppers were everything the Kirby Sextet was not[11]: progressive in outlook, aware of advances in both recent jazz and contemporary classical music (especially the works of Stravinsky) without fawning over it, capable of superior and—in the case of Bill Harris—outrageously inventive solo work, all in a true chamber ensemble conception.

The best sides, compositionally, are *Steps, Igor, Nero's Conception*, and in terms of performance the hilarious *Fan It* and *I Surrender Dear*, the latter a major solo vehicle for Norvo's vibraphone. Although virtually all the solos in the entire set are, as mentioned, of a high order and, more importantly, neatly integrated into the compositions, Harris is clearly the most provocative soloist. He contributes imaginatively on every track, endlessly inventive, full of surprises and protean versatility, obviously inspired by the freedom the small-group format provided. Among the many startling, yet effective contributions, perhaps the most daring occurs near the end of *Fan It*. Coming after a solo which Harris begins with a *four*-octave (sic!) upward leap, then continuing in a mad-gallop of running eight notes—*Fan It* is played at a breakneck speed of about $\sqrt{} = 270$—the final ensemble chorus breaks into fast-moving bop-ish riff figures. But Harris, unpredictable as ever, breaks through the ensemble mold, zanily braying out long-held notes in atonal dissonant opposition to the rest of the band. As the ensemble ritards and comes to a musical standstill, Harris lets out one more slithering two-octave yelp, punctuated by Don Lamond's final drum "bomb." It is hard to know what Harris was thinking, but it makes for one of the most hilarious yet musically valid endings in all of jazz.

Both Rogers and Berman play exceedingly well in their various assignments, albeit in a considerably more orthodox manner than Harris. Herman pays moving tributes to three of his reed idols: Barney Bigard (on *Steps*), Jimmy Noone (on *Nero's Conception*), and Johnny Hodges (on *Pam*).

Beyond that, except for guitarist Billy Bauer's struggling solos, all hands contributed handsomely to these sides. In their youthful exuberance, musical sophistication and taste, they were a bright spot in the early development of combo jazz, forming a bridge between such groups as the Goodman and Kirby Sextets and the new in-coming bop combos.

But by late 1946 the Herman Herd's popular success was so immense that, inevitably, the commercial interests began to move in on this potentially lucra-

11. See below, Chapter 9, for a discussion of the Kirby Sextet.

tive target. Recording executives, agents, managers, and sponsors pressed Herman to broaden his appeal to gain an even larger audience. Temporarily succumbing to some of these pressures, Herman began to play more pop tunes, even adding a vocal group. But some higher instinct told him that that was not a way for him to go. In December 1946 he disbanded his great orchestra, planning to take a long rest after more than twenty years of virtually uninterrupted, vacation-less toil.

But Herman's "retirement" lasted less than a year. By the end of 1947 he had organized another orchestra, soon to be known as the Second Herd or the "Four Brothers" orchestra, referring, of course, to one of the most conspicuous successes of the modern jazz era, Jimmy Giuffre's *Four Brothers*, featuring a saxophone quartet (in ensemble and solos) of three tenors and baritone. With this and other works like *Keen and Peachy* (an updated re-working of an earlier Herman recording, *Fine and Dandy*), Chubby Jackson's and George Wallington's *Lemon Drop*, Shorty Rogers's *Keeper of the Flame*, Herman rekindled the flame of orchestral jazz at a time when the big band was otherwise a virtually extinct institution.

Herman has continued to lead successive Herds through the years since the end of the big-band era, and is active to this day.* While his orchestras have not been in the importantly creative forefront since the 1950s, Herman has nonetheless remained a vital force in music, not only by remaining true to the spirit and essence of jazz, but by providing in effect a kind of "traveling conservatory" in which untold numbers of fine musicians have been able to acquire their advanced professional training. The list of Herman alumni reads like a *Who's Who* of modern jazz. Few have not been touched by Woody's musical/professional integrity and benign leadership.

Now and then there are such things.

HARRY JAMES

It is probably difficult for most jazz aficionados to think of the late Harry James as a major jazz figure. And perhaps one is justified in considering his right for a place in the jazz pantheon a controversial and qualified one. But if one looks at the full life-long record and chooses not to remember *only* the period of his greatest public popularity—the early 1940s—then one discovers a musician who devoted the greater part of his career to the cause of jazz. For the truth is that, in its baldest outlines, his life was involved almost continuously with jazz, certainly in his early days with Ben Pollack and Goodman, but also later, though less in the limelight, as leader of his own band for nearly thirty-five years, featuring outstanding jazz soloists such as Willie Smith, Ray Sims, Corky Corcoran, Buddy Rich, Red Kelly, and Jack Perciful and hard-swinging progressive arrangements by Ray Conniff and (in later years) Neal Hefti and Ernie Wilkins—all with a minimum of commercial intrusions.

James was undoubtedly the most technically assured and prodigiously talented

---

* Woody Herman died in late 1987, while this book was in production.

white trumpet player of the late Swing Era and early postwar years, both as an improvising jazz and blues player and as a richly expressive ballad performer. He was, unlike many other Armstrong disciples, a creative musician, unwilling to merely imitate the master. Indeed, James extended Armstrong's melodic and rhythmic conception in two dramatically divergent and quite personal directions: the one as a brilliant, often brash virtuoso soloist equipped with unlimited technique, accuracy and endurance; the other as a romantic popular song balladeer, at times carrying Armstrong's melodic style to its ultimate commercial extreme.

Yet, one can only speculate why a fine jazz player like James felt that he could fulfill his band-leading ambitions only via the most commercial of routes. Perhaps he wanted to ensure financial success and stability for himself and his orchestra first, before devoting himself to more progressive forms of jazz. Or perhaps, deep down, he realized that his eclectic talents were not sufficient to create a new and deeply original style which could survive as, for example, that of Armstrong or Gillespie or Hawkins or Ellington.

In any case James's orchestra was from the very outset commercially oriented, in striking contrast to the excellent jazz credentials he had already garnered, not only in his years with Goodman but with a variety of small groups featuring variously a nucleus of Basie musicians in 1937 and 1938 (Buck Clayton, Herschel Evans, Walter Page, Jo Jones) or his 1939 Boogie Woogie Trio with Pete Johnson and Albert Ammons (hear James's fine blues trumpet on *Home James*), or with Teddy Wilson (*Just a Mood*) and Lionel Hampton (1938). With such numbers as the schmaltzy *Chiribiribin*, the empty virtuosity of *Flight of the Bumble Bee*, and the mercilessly pretentious pastiche, *Concerto for Trumpet*, James set his band on an entirely different path from, say, the one Krupa had chosen a year earlier. Even bona fide jazz pieces like *King Porter Stomp*, *Two O'Clock Jump* and *Feet Draggin' Blues* were either cheapened (with the boogie-woogie intrusions on *Two O'Clock*) or listlessly, unswingingly performed (as on *Feet Draggin'*). In any case, the "jazz" instrumentals were hardly distinctive, being lesser imitations of the Goodman-via-Henderson manner, occasionally mildly "updated" by James's tenorman, Dave Matthews. It is possible—and has been so reported (by George Simon)—that James played a healthy sampling of "sensationally swinging" numbers on dance and ballroom dates, but certainly the recordings made for Brunswick between February and November 1939 do not indicate any such predilection.

The arrival of Frank Sinatra, to be replaced a half-year later by Dick Haymes (when Sinatra joined Tommy Dorsey), may have tipped James's approach even more in a populist direction. Though Sinatra's big success came with Dorsey, there is no question that James had discovered a major singing and musical talent, and that his presence had a more than casual impact on his band's popularity. Of these early nine Sinatra sides *All or Nothing at All* is the most impressive, showing the then twenty-three-year-old singer as already the possessor of a rich, warm baritone voice with a relatively straight unembellished delivery. He also barely got through the long high F at the end of the song. A moderate commercial success, the record became a big hit a few years later when rereleased by Columbia and when Sinatra was already firmly established as one of the top popular singers of the land, even threatening Bing Crosby in his number one position.

It is interesting to note that in these early recordings James is trying to be more crooningly "vocal" in his trumpet-playing than Sinatra in his singing; he abandons virtually all taste and standards in his emphasis on an exaggeratedly saccharine, cheap vibrato—something that undoubtedly impressed a musically illiterate audience, but which was technically the easiest thing to do and a gross aberration of both Armstrong's and the old classical cornet soloists' lyric style. (James knew this latter tradition well, for his father, who taught young Harry trumpet, was a conductor of traveling circus bands, where much of that earlier turn-of-the-century cornet-style survived well into the thirties and forties.)

After one year with the Varsity label, for whom James recorded a series of unimpressive, stiffly played sides and whose distribution was so poor in any case that the recordings would have had no impact, James returned to Columbia in early 1941. One of Columbia's producers, Morty Palitz, who had had some success with using woodwinds in recordings with Mildred Bailey and Eddie Sauter, as well as Alec Wilder's 1939–40 Octets, suggested that James add woodwinds and a string quartet. Harry opted for the strings, sensing that here his commercial hold on a larger audience could best be expanded. And to everyone's surprise—and to the jazz critics' utter dismay—James succeeded where others, like Shaw and Miller, had previously failed.

While James clung to a jazz approach—just barely—with such swing numbers as *Strictly Instrumental, Record Session, Sharp as a Tack, Jeffries' Blues*, and *Crazy Rhythm*, the big successes were his absolutely non-jazz-related "hat trick" of recordings of *Eli-Eli*, Rimsky Korsakov's *Flight of the Bumble Bee*, and the old cornet-solo favorite, *Carnival of Venice*, as well as the crooning vocals of Dick Haymes enveloped in strings (like *You Made Me Love You, My Silent Love*). Oddly enough, these ballads were in their own way quite effective, the strings adding some contrasting color and, I suppose, for many casual listeners "a bit of class." But it was James's own playing, totally convincing and authoritative, that made these recordings popularly successful. It wasn't the first time—nor the last—that an offering of questionable aesthetic taste would succeed with a large segment of the public by virtue of its irresistible combination of technical mastery and novelty of conception. For the fact remains that James's radiantly brassy tone, combined with an overbearing vibrato, was totally original and *instantly recognizable*. No one had ever dared to go that far—even James's section-mate in the Goodman band, Ziggy Elman—and, on purely commercial terms, it is that kind of nervy authority, technical perfection, and unequivocal recognizability that succeeds. It succeeds because it is clearly identifiable, therefore precisely labelable and therefore, in turn, marketable. James had stumbled onto a powerful formula for success, knowing incidentally, whatever his inclinations as a *jazz musician* may have been, that to compete directly with Glenn Miller or Count Basie or Goodman was folly, and would not garner him "a place in the sun." The formula he chose turned out to be irresistible: a star instrumentalist, technically invincible, romantic ballad singers (Sinatra, Haymes, Helen Forrest), and heady arrangements using strings, all superimposed on the vestiges of a jazz orchestra.

If the formula had had considerable commercial success with Dick Haymes—incidentally a first-rate musician, masterful in his phrasing—it was to turn into an incredible bonanza when James acquired Helen Forrest, who left Goodman's employ abruptly in late 1941, as the band's singer. (Haymes left James around the same time, attaining even greater acclaim with both Goodman and Dorsey.) The point about Helen Forrest's success with James was not so much how well she sang—she always had done that—but how effectively the James orchestra and its arrangers supported her singing, enhancing it, and drawing from her many truly magical performances. James was the first (except for Ellington) to exploit and capitalize fully on the presence of a band singer by creating special musical frameworks for that singing talent, tailor-made, so to speak, at the same time craftily exploiting the need during the tense wartime years for the comforting reassurance of sentimental ballads. Previously, band singers simply got up and delivered their songs in whatever fashion their talent permitted—as I have said elsewhere, singing, as it were, in parallel to the band but not really *with* it or *in* it. (This was not true, to be sure, of a few of the major vocal artists, like Jimmy Rushing with Basie, or Billie Holiday with Teddy Wilson, or Mildred Bailey with Eddie Sauter.) "Boy" and "girl" singers were simply a necessary appurtenance of a dance band in a realm where crooned "love and moon-in-June" lyrics were deemed to be an absolute trade prerequisite.

James saw that a singer of Helen Forrest's potential could achieve much more than that, could in fact be a dominant force in the popular success of an orchestra, in effect a co-leader. Of course, James did not foresee how such a development would affect the future course of jazz. But the results were soon fully audible and visible: as other bands, especially Dorsey (with Sinatra) copied the formula, singers took over the popular music field, jazz as swing was more or less driven out—certainly as a *leading* force. In turn a new form of jazz, namely bop, primarily instrumental and represented by smaller combos was to take over. By the end of the decade the split between the instrumental and vocal factions of jazz was irreparable, and eventually it would lead to a further separation in the form of the rock phenomenon, again a primarily vocal form of popular music.

While it is fashionable for jazz writers to pick out the relatively few "pure jazz" sides in the more commercially successful bands, using either the paucity or plenitude of such evidence to respectively condemn or praise their subject, it is a quite unrealistic approach and ultimately inaccurate. A discriminating historian cannot avoid looking at the *totality* of an artist's creativity; he must look at all facets of his work. And if we look at the James band's full recorded output in its first peak period (late 1941 through 1942), we discover not only a more balanced selection of its three repertory elements—ballad vocals, novelty vocals, and jazz instrumentals—but a considerable improvement in all three areas, especially in the quality of the jazz instrumentals. In such pieces as *Strictly In-*

strumental (originally written by Edgar Battle for the Lunceford band), *The Clipper*, *Crazy Rhythm*, James's own *Let Me Up*, and especially *The Mole*, the band developed an interesting synthesis of the lyrical-vocal and swinging jazz. The link between the two tendencies was the string section, integrated at its best in a way that no other band (even Shaw, who certainly tried) had ever succeeded in doing. It was to become a formula much imitated in those war years, especially successfully by Sy Oliver and Tommy Dorsey. In this way James found a new middle ground where strings and bona fide jazz instruments could coexist in friendly partnership. The results of this fusion were particularly effective on *The Mole*, where the strings seem to be no longer an intrusive element but rather one of the co-equal choirs of the orchestra. Particularly effective is the use of high floating violin harmonics, a device all but unknown to early jazz arrangers, in the final chorus (Ex. 4). Equally fetching is the superbly played muted trumpet quartet, an idea James had first developed when still in the Goodman band (Ex. 5).[12]

Ex. 4

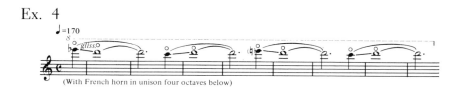

(With French horn in unison four octaves below)

Ex. 5

Just as the use of strings—and by mid-1942 a French horn—in a generally lyrical approach affected the way the James band played jazz in those years, so, too, conversely jazz in the form of swing often affected the treatment of ballads.

12. It is likely that James got the idea for such flashy trumpet trios from the earlier solo cornet literature, which abounded with such pieces. Two of the most famous and popular of these were Herbert Clarke's *Three Aces* and Walter Smith's *Three Kings*.

There were, of course, those outright lushly sentimental ballads like *But Not for Me*, *I Had the Craziest Dream*, and *By The Sleepy Lagoon* (the latter filching the entire introduction to Ravel's *Daphnis and Chloe*, Suite No. 2). But there were also songs like *I've Heard That Song Before*, a fine Helen Forrest vocal, played with a bouncy "rockin' chair" beat and swing that very few, if any, white bands had as yet achieved (and certainly not in ballads), and which was a fine precursor of the broadly swinging beat and style of James's superb 1944 *I'm Beginning To See the Light*.

Another development worth noting is the gradually increased integration of James's solos into the overall framework or arrangement. Whereas James had begun his band-leading career by appropriating all the solo space he could—with a few exceptions, like Vido Musso's extended solos on *Jeffries' Blues*—he had by early 1942 returned to a more modest policy. Listen to how beautifully James's solo on *Crazy Rhythm*, for example, is assimilated into the ensemble.

The two arrangers who managed this wide range of assignments for James in those years were Dave Matthews and Leroy Holmes. Matthews was a great admirer and student of Duke Ellington and brought some of the master's tone colors and voicings to the James band, notably on *Let Me Up* and *I'm Beginning To See the Light*. Notice how Matthews uses Ellington's old *Mood Indigo* trio of muted trumpet and trombone plus low-register clarinet in the former title, not this time in a sustained song-like theme, but in a jauntily moving jump/riff tune. The Duke-ish harmonization and voicing of the last eight bars of *I'm Beginning* are particularly fetching (Ex. 6), as is Alan Reuss's guitar coda with its fade-away blues-ish single-note line and final chord in harmonics (Ex. 7). *I'm Beginning* seems to me to attain the kind of admirable synthesis I spoke of earlier: it is a song, a vocal (sung well by Kitty Kallen), it uses strings (quite idiomatically), yet it is unquestionably a jazz performance.

Ex. 6

Ex. 7

Leroy Holmes composed and arranged such brilliant scores as *Prince Charming* and *The Mole*, well-made swing-riff tunes, smartly arranged, that did much to keep the jazz flame alive in James's band.

By the time the recording ban had run its course in 1944, James had revamped his personnel extensively; he had brought in Willie Smith and Corky Corcoran, the fine band pianist Arnold Ross and two superior rhythm section members, Alan Reuss and Ed Mihelich, a strong driving bass player who had already done wonders for the Krupa rhythm section. With the further addition of outstanding arranging talent in the persons of Johnny Thompson and Ray Conniff, the James band moved unqualifiedly into a leading position as one of the finest performing ensembles of the mid- and late-1940s, while perpetuating a harmonically, rhythmically advanced swing/dance-band style. Its singers—like Kitty Kallen, Ginnie Powell, and Buddy DeVito, all representing a new breed of vocalist who had been weaned on Anita O'Day, Peggy Lee, and Frank Sinatra—continued the trend of a more instrumentalized type of singing, with at least an awareness of jazz as a strongly *rhythmic* language. But above all the band concentrated in its repertory on a substantial amount of jazz instrumentals, mostly created by Ray Conniff, who had already contributed so importantly to Artie Shaw's 1944 band. *Friar Rock, Easy, I've Never Forgotten, 9:20 Special, Tuxedo Junction, What Am I Gonna Do?, Moten Swing, Vine Street Blues* are all striking examples of the kind of exuberant swing and blistering drive the James band could produce during this period. James's own playing had lost none of its assurance; his solo work poured out of his horn—as it was to throughout his career—with a sense of inevitability that no other trumpeter could equal with such consistency. In a long and truly remarkable career as a trumpet player James hardly ever missed a note. He played extraordinarily well almost until the day he died, an astonishing achievement for a brass player. His brilliant bravura solo on *Friar Rock* is but one typical example of his extraordinary facility and flawless execution (Ex. 8).

As I pointed out earlier, Harry James reverted increasingly in the ensuing years to a primarily jazz policy, albeit basically in what one might call a "progressive swing" idiom. In this respect James's career reverses the much more common pattern: tracing a gradual decline from high idealism (and even experimentalism) through various stages of compromise to commercial accommodation and ultimate artistic demise. James started at the other end; he sowed his commercial oats during his band's youthful years, achieving a security and fame early on which permitted him in later years to more or less play the kind of jazz-as-dance-music he knew best, always with an adequate measure of musical spontaneity and freedom, to keep his improvisatory and virtuosic skills well honed.

To his credit, James succumbed to a bop influence in his own playing only fleetingly, the Gillespie model being always a temptation for most trumpet players. In James's case these were minor flirtations that never deterred him from being his own man, instrumentally and creatively. Nor did he in the heyday years of bop, the late forties, like so many others turn his band into a bop ensemble. He had always admired Basie from his earliest days in New York, and

Ex. 8

it was perhaps inevitable that James's post-1950 bands were built upon the Basie model, especially since two of Basie's top arrangers, Ernie Wilkins and Neal Hefti, were responsible for most of the James book in the last three decades.[13]

It is also significant that by the early 1950s James had been cured of his initial conspicuous reliance on singers, and that during this entire later period—with but a few exceptions to re-create revivals of earlier successes—James worked entirely without singers—and no strings!

13. This period will be considered in appropriate detail in Volume III of this History.

LARRY CLINTON

Of the many bands that flourished during the Swing Era, one of the most popular for a while was Larry Clinton's, and, although certainly not one of the great creative ensembles of the period, it represented a *reductio ad minimum* of the essence of swing as a style. Clinton's influence as an arranger and composer was considerable, not only as the composer of catchy riff tunes (with even catchier titles) written for other bandleaders, and the development in his pieces of a simplified riff style which almost any band could adopt, but also because he was very adept at adopting popular classical pieces to dance music as ballads or swing numbers. These classics, as we have seen, became a vogue in the late thirties, spawning bands that specialized exclusively in such material, either original or adopted, and broadening the repertory of standard jazz/swing orchestras by the inclusion of these transformed classics. This was certainly not, in retrospect, a very important trend creatively, although in a superficial way it did represent one example of a modestly increasing sophistication on the part of audiences, many of whom had been previously unaware of either jazz *or* any form of classical music.

But of more importance, even if short-lived—Clinton's own band only survived four years (1937–41)—was his influence as a composer and as the leader of one of the more polished swing bands of the late thirties. He was himself an accomplished instrumentalist, playing quite capably trumpet, trombone and clarinet, and knew the value of fine disciplined musicianship. His band always featured skillful sidemen and could boast from time to time of fairly impressive soloists. Outstanding among these were three tenormen, Tony Zimmers (a woefully underrated musician), his successor George Berg, and later Don Hammond (hear the last on *Dig Me Honey*); trumpeter Walter Smith (who also doubled on the then very rare mellophone), trombonist Ford Leary, and two full-toned clarinetists, Ben Feman and Hank d'Amico.

Zimmers had worked with Wingy Manone, Artie Shaw, and various 52nd Street combos before joining Clinton in 1937. His clean "modern" style, anticipating later Prez-influenced players like Stan Getz and Lee Konitz, can be heard to good account on *How Am I To Know*, *Chant of the Jungle*, and *Dodging the Dean*. It was not exactly common to enter on a solo break in D♭ in the following manner (Ex. 9, from *Dodging*):

Ex. 9

The Clinton band was also typical of the late Swing Era (and its limitations) in that it almost always played with a comfortable, bouncy swing—typical is *My Buddy*—which made it an ideal band for dancing. The underside of this feature was that almost their entire repertory was restricted to the same perfect-for-dancing tempo: ballads, swing tunes, classics—it didn't matter—with, of course, a resultant redundancy that from a creative point of view was stultifying.

Redundancy was also a factor in Clinton's arranging and composing. After his early successes with *Dipsy Doodle* and *Satan Takes a Holiday* (both written by him for Tommy Dorsey) and *Study in Brown*, innocuous riff tunes but catchy enough with fellow musicians and the public, Clinton produced dozens of similar pieces, all stamped out of the same mold and formula. (This mold was in the first instance one which Clinton borrowed more or less intact from Horace Henderson, from pieces like *Hot and Anxious*.) The *Study* series went through all the colors—*Study in Blue, In Green, In Red, In Scarlet*, also *A Study in Modernism* and *Study in Surrealism*—but the problem was that the titles, though essentially meaningless, were more imaginative than the music. As a matter of fact the pieces all used the same pale, inoffensive instrumental colors, regardless of title.

Clinton also introduced to swing the upbeat trombone-trio glissando:

 . It not only appeared, often several times, in virtually every

one of his arrangements, but it became a favorite cliché with literally dozens of other swing bands. He also first used the long fade-out false ending followed by a renewed burst of energy, a device Glenn Miller turned into a gold mine a year or so later *(In the Mood)*.

Clinton was certainly not a major figure of the calibre of an Ellington or even a Glenn Miller, but he did contribute influentially for better *and* worse to the phenomenon that swing was. A first-class bandleader who appreciated impeccable musicianship[14] and sensitive treatment of musical materials, Clinton represented all that was typical—and problematic—of the Swing Era.

BOB CHESTER

Another excellent but underrated band of the late thirties and early forties was that of Bob Chester. Initially sponsored by Tommy Dorsey and brought to the attention of Eli Oberstein at Victor Records, the band was set up in mid-1939 as a rival and imitator of Glenn Miller, featuring especially Miller's by then famous reed-section sound. However, to Chester's credit, he soon abandoned this pointless policy and evolved a tasteful, effective "sweet-swing-dance" style that mixed the usual *de rigueur* pop tune vocals and ballads with swing instrumentals. During its first year the band was sparked by the brilliant, propulsively swinging lead trumpet of Alec Fila. (Fila, who was then enticed away to do similar work for Benny Goodman, was in turn replaced by Louis Mucci, that superb trumpeter who helped so much to set the tone, literally and figuratively, of the great 1948 Claude Thornhill orchestra.)

The three main early soloists in Chester's band—good capable players all—were cornetist Garner Clark, trombonist John Reynolds, and Chester himself on tenor saxophone. A fine singer by the name of Dolores O'Neill also contributed

14. An interesting confirmation of the skill of Clinton's orchestra is that, out of some 214 sides it recorded between 1937 and 1941, only eleven required more than a first take.

tasteful above-average vocals during the band's first year of existence. Later soloists (in 1943–44) were John La Porta, alto sax, and the great trombonist Bill Harris (both later with Woody Herman's First Herd). Contributing significantly to the band's fine dance beat and swing was bassist Ray Leatherwood, who was even featured in a solo on *57th Street Drag* in 1939, at a time when bass solos were still a remarkable rarity.

The most accurate way to summarize the Chester band's best work is to say that it was thoroughly professional (its ensemble and section blends, for example, were impeccable and often extraordinary), performed everything in style and good taste, and certainly aspired to play, when permitted to do so, a kind of mentals. During its first year the band was sparked by the brilliant, propulsively Harmonically/melodically unadventurous, its main interest lay in a kind of hard-swinging jazz that, like the Harlem bands at the Savoy, got the dancers out on the floor. That's the way it was in those war and prewar years, and in retrospect it is well to remember that the late thirties and early forties represent an era when our American dance, entertainment, and popular musics were in large measure contained within the overall realm of jazz.

The Chester band was at its best in pieces like Sy Oliver's *Easy Does It,* Edgar Battle's *Strictly Instrumental* or *Waterloo Bridge,* and Dave Rose's two contributions, *From Maine to California* and *Harlem Confusion* (the latter featuring for the time good "hot" swing trombone solos by John Reynolds) (Ex. 10). Gar-

Ex. 10

ner Clark, one of the few trumpeters to cling to the cornet (Armstrong's and all the early New Orleans players' original instrument), was a thoroughly consistent reliable soloist on any number of titles, although never particularly adventurous or searching. Cy Baker, one of his successors, was a more spectacular player and can be heard most effectively on *When You and I Were Young* and *Tanning Dr. Jekyll's Hyde.*

Among the hundreds of bands that populated the swing landscape of the late thirties to early forties, Bob Chester's band can easily be singled out as one of the more polished, thoroughly professional, eminently listenable, and committed to jazz with a high degree of musical integrity.

CLAUDE THORNHILL

One of the most outstanding and unusual bands of the late Swing Era—that is, the early forties—was that of Claude Thornhill—even more important, however, for its postwar (1946–48) work. There were in effect three different Thornhill bands between 1937 and 1948, the first of these a small group with various personnels, ranging between a sextet and a nonet, accompanying singer Maxine Sullivan. (Indeed, on most occasions the band was more or less that of John Kirby's Sextet, but at one point consisted of a woodwind group that in a slightly different incarnation became the Alec Wilder Octet.)

Thornhill's second band[15] was formed in 1940 and achieved surprisingly sudden popular success in early 1941, primarily as a result of a residency at the Glen Island Casino, the famous ballroom known as "the cradle of name bands," that had been the debut setting by then for so many swing and dance bands, most notably Glenn Miller's in 1939. It is during this early 1940s' period that Thornhill (with the help of arrangers Bill Borden, Andy Phillips, and by late 1941 Gil Evans) developed a unique style, which in its more advanced form in the postwar years made major contributions to bop and modern jazz, and in a smaller variant unit led to the historic Miles Davis Nonet, recordings made in 1949-50 which came later to be known as the "The Birth of the Cool."[16] Two factors determined the style and future course of the band. One was Thornhill's clear recognition that what the world needed in 1940 was *not* another riff-tune swing band in the image of Goodman or Miller. Second, an ASCAP ban which prevented the use of all copyrighted ASCAP material on radio forced big bands to search for repertory material in the public domain. Once again, as in the mid-1930s, the popular works of classical composers like Tchaikovsky, Grieg, Dvořák, Sinding and traditional tunes like *Auld Lang Syne, Londonderry Air,* and *Stack of Barley* were recruited and transformed into dance arrangements. Thornhill went about this with a vengeance and—it must be said—with more taste and skill than most. At the same time his own compositions, often classically oriented[17]—like the hypnotic, impressionistic tone "poemlet," *Snowfall*—answered to this trend and need.

15. Thornhill's third orchestra, featuring the important arrangements of Gil Evans (especially those on Charlie Parker's *Anthropology* and *Donna Lee*), will be discussed in detail in Volume III of this History.

16. The relationship of the Davis Nonet to the 1948 Thornhill band is manifold, but resides essentially 1) in the primary role played by Gil Evans in the very formation of the Nonet and providing many of its most characteristic arrangements; 2) the similarity of instrumentation and to some extent of personnel (Lee Konitz on alto, Joe Schulman, bass, Bill Barber, tuba, Sandy Siegelstein, horn). In effect, with the emphasis on horn and tuba colorations and generally middle-to-low register instruments (trombone, baritone saxophone)—even Davis's fluegelhorn-like sound corresponded to the trumpet sonority Thornhill featured in the lead trumpet work of players like Louis Mucci—the Miles Davis group was the Thornhill big band reduced to a nonet.

17. I have always felt that Thornhill secretly wished to have been a classical concert pianist. Not only do this performances (in rearranged versions) of the Grieg and the "Warsaw" Piano Concertos suggest this, but all his playing showed the refined touch, beauty of tone, and technical discipline of classical piano literature. His crystal-clear arpeggios or the pearly four-octave runs in thirds with which he loved to end pieces are some of the more obvious examples of his classical pianisms.

Although the treatment of some of these pieces, like Dvořák's *Humoresque* and Schumann's *Träumerei*, was corny and effete in the extreme—falling ineptly between jazz and classical music—Thornhill's own originals were often extraordinarily effective and beautiful in their unique way. Indeed, some of the opaque orchestral textures and blends, rich harmonizations and dense voicings, were completely novel, never having been heard before in either jazz *or* classical music. They emphasized clarinet and horn sonorities—the horns beginning in mid-1941 when Dick Hall and Vinny Jacobs joined the orchestra—usually set in sustained backgrounds in the middle and low registers in slow tempos: a soft carpet of sound over which Thornhill could weave his famous "one-finger" melodies and spell-binding embroideries. It was an irresistible sonoric combination—the pure, finely etched clarity of the piano over the velvety sound textures below—and its effect was often quite magical. No wonder people referred to these Thornhill pieces as a "musical aphrodisiacs." It was often questioned by fans of a more raucous, robust type of music how much this had to do with jazz, but pieces like *Sleepy Serenade, Love Tales, Autumn Nocturne, Lullaby of the Rain, Where or When* and his theme *Snowfall*—in effect a whole new genre of instrumental pieces—were much admired by the more sedate dancing crowd and audience and critics alike (Ex. 11).

These lush impressionistic mood pieces—reminiscent Ellington's *Mood Indigo*—were alternated, of course, with more lively up-tempo swing pieces, for which the Basie and Miller bands were surely the closest models. Lead trumpet Conrad Gozzo's powerful style energized the whole brass section, while Irving Fazola on clarinet and Dusty Dedrick on trumpet provided the jazz relief. In Bill Borden's arrangements of *O Sole Mio* and *Isn't It Wonderful*, or Gil Evans's *Buster's Last Stand*, the band showed that it could swing with the best of them, although always with that certain plush "cat's paw" approach.

Besides the sound of horns, Thornhill loved the clarinet, and at one point in 1941 had seven *(sic)* clarinets in his band, including Fazola and the outstanding bass clarinetist Jimmy Abato. The clarinet choir was used in subdued pastel-shaded backgrounds and low-register countermelodies, but just as often in brilliant high-flying virtuosic passages for all the clarinets in unison—a fine idea except for the fact that it is extraordinarily difficult to get six or seven clarinets to play really in tune (as every high school band director knows). It was a minor miscalculation on Thornhill's part, and a certain stridency of clashing intonation—probably unavoidable—mars many of these clarinet-dominated sides. I think that Thornhill secretly always wanted to have a string section—he used violins (very poorly, one must add) in his 1937 band—and to him the agile clarinets were a kind of jazzier substitute for violins. It was the band's only upper-register instrument (except his piano), and he used the brighter clarinet sound as a contrast to the darker-hued brass, horns and tuba.

When the wartime draft decimated the ranks of Thornhill's band—as it did with so many orchestras during 1941 and 1942—it became even more difficult to maintain a high quality ensemble capable of the subtle instrumental command the band's repertory required. Ironically, the Thornhill band's popularity,

Ex. 11

and reputation, rose so dramatically at this time that it almost climbed—at least among white bands—to the number one spot, recently vacated by Glenn Miller. But then Thornhill himself was inducted in the fall of 1942, joining Artie Shaw's Navy band, and that particular Thornhill orchestra was forced to break up.

It would be four years before Thornhill could return to civilian life and music. His new orchestra, formed in 1946, continued where the earlier one had left off, with Gil Evans now the band's chief musical architect. His sublime arrangements for Thornhill and his illustrious work in succeeding years in bringing not only jazz *per se* but jazz in its new form, bop, into a central position in the band's repertory are a matter of record and represent some of the more glorious moments in jazz history.

LES BROWN

Of the many hundreds of bands that swarmed onto the swing scene by the early 1940s, Les Brown's had become by the end of the war one of the most popular and successful. Indeed, it was one of the few orchestras to survive the decline of the big bands a few years later, although primarily through its long associations on radio and television with Bob Hope and Steve Allen. It comes as a surprise then to realize that the Brown band in its early incarnations did not offer much promise musically or even commercially. What eventually evolved into a good jazz-swing-dance band (that could with some justification use the tag line "Les Brown and His Band of Renown") was originally decidedly inferior, and thus represents one of the more startling artistic/stylistic transformations in jazz history—an ungainly cocoon into a quite beautiful butterfly.

Brown's earliest recordings from 1936, and even those of his second band formed in 1938, drably arranged (by Brown himself), stiffly played, at best a weak imitation of Benny Goodman, do not suggest in the slightest the level of fine musicianship, technical polish, and healthy swing energy the band could muster ten years later. And once again, as we have noted before in other instances, the difference was made by the arranger. In Brown's case there were several excellent arrangers involved in the band's transformation, but it was Frank Comstock in particular who, beginning in 1942, turned the Brown band into a crack modern-styled ensemble.

The first intimations of better things to come occur by 1939–40. One hears a considerable improvement over the earlier thumpy-rhythmed, pinch-toned, and often out of tune performances, in Mary Lou Williams's arrangement of her own *Walkin' and Swingin'* (1940) and such pieces as *Perisphere Shuffle* and *Trylon Stomp*, both written and arranged by Brown for the 1939–40 New York World's Fair (where Brown's band had one of its earliest long-term engagements). But a real breakthrough came in Ben Homer's clean, incisive *Joltin' Joe DiMaggio* of 1941, superbly played by the band with a fine two-beat Lunceford swing. There followed such fine scores as *Bizet Has His Day* (one of the few interesting, in this case even witty, transformations of classical material from that era); *Nothin'* from Ellington's *Jump for Joy*, in a clean, lean, swinging arrangement that anticipates the latter's *I'm Beginning To See the Light* of three years later; *Sunday* and *Out of Nowhere* in beautifully crafted arrangements featuring trumpeter Billy Butterfield in excellent extended solos.

After the 1942–43 recording ban was lifted, the Les Brown band moved even more successfully into the big-time category, evolving a tasteful modern postswing style that maintained its artistic validity and integrity for decades. From its earlier stylistic allegiance to Lunceford, the band now switched to a more Basie-like conception, the Basie of Buster Harding.[18] The two main architects of the Brown band's stylistic transformation were the aforementioned Frank Comstock

18. See above, Chapter 4.

and trumpeter Bob Higgins. But it was not long before Brown's entire arranging staff—including Ben Homer, Skip Martin (the latter had already worked for Basie in the late 30s), and guest arrangers like Ed Finckel, Joe Lippman, and Glenn Osser—perfected this style, all the while listening closely to what the other modern-oriented orchestras were doing (e.g. Eckstine, Gillespie, Barnet, Shaw, and especially Woody Herman's 1945–46 band). The fruits of these efforts, well worth hearing even today, can be found on innumerable recordings, of which one might single out Comstock's *I Got the Sun in the Morning, Flip Lid,* the extraordinary express tempo *12:55 Express,* Bob Higgins's outstanding sophisticated, hard driving *High on a Windy Trumpet* and the svelte *Lover's Leap,* Lippman's *It Couldn't Be True,* Homer's *Just One of Those Things.* Although this was primarily an "arrangers' band," considerable room was left for the orchestra's several expert soloists: Ted Nash in countless well-conceived, technically astonishing solos,[19] Jimmy Zito, the often startlingly gifted trumpet player (hear him on the spectacular high-flying *High on a Windy Trumpet*); trombonists Kenny Meisel and, later, Ray Sims (older brother of Zoot Sims); and a fine technically adept bass player, Bob Leininger (well featured on the Ellington-ish *Ready to Go Steady* and *It Couldn't Be True*).

Of course, it didn't hurt the Brown band—except in the eyes of jazz purists—to have several major popular hits, such as the famous wartime *Sentimental Journey,* and after the war the swinging *I've Got My Love To Keep Me Warm,* sung handsomely by Doris Day in her pre-Hollywood days. Nor was there any harm in the popularity of Butch Stone's many humorous novelty vocals, delivered in a hip insider's Harlem-influenced manner, and always tastefully arranged and played.

I find it astonishing that jazz histories have so far ignored the Les Brown band and its fine arrangers and soloists, especially since so many ensembles of much lesser quality or consistency are treated with much greater respect. It would seem that to become financially secure and popular with a wider public is still a great liability in jazz circles. But the facts are that Les Brown and his orchestra, once over its shaky beginnings, played more jazz than most and at least as much as many other highly touted ones. Like Basie, Brown evolved a stylistic formula that was broad-gauged enough to allow for variety, that was fresh and modern, yet not complex. Brown's recordings rarely sound stale or dated. Such formularization also has one interesting virtue: it promotes and allows for consistency. And it is in that sense, allied with a notable degree of taste, integrity, and com-

19. For reasons beyond my knowledge, Brown always featured in his band tenor saxophone soloists who had the most remarkable control of the instrument's upper range—and beyond. Indeed, an inattentive listener might easily assume the instrument being played was an alto or even a soprano saxophone. Wolffe Tayne, Brown's tenorman from 1938 to 1943, had that kind of exceptional high range (although his solo-playing was also often rather convoluted and undisciplined), and so did Ted Nash, Tayne's successor. Nash was one of that young generation of tenor players—Stan Getz was another—who adopted the lean linear style and light sound of Lester Young with a vengeance. Nash's complete control of the third and fourth octaves of the tenor saxophone's upper register, enabled him to expand dramatically the instrument's expressive range.

mitment to jazz, that the Les Brown band deserves an honorable niche in the history of jazz.

HAL MCINTYRE

The benign influence of Duke Ellington's music manifested itself in the styles of a number of white swing bands—the case of Charlie Barnet has already been discussed—but none more effectively and productively than in Hal McIntyre's orchestra. Formed in 1941 with the help and financial backing of Glenn Miller,[20] the orchestra's Ellington-influenced style was set by Dave Matthews, an ardent admirer of Ellington and, as a tenor saxophonist, a devotee of Ben Webster. It is interesting to note that a whole succession of tenor players in McIntyre's band—men like Ted Goddard and Johnny Hayes—had all thoroughly mastered Webster's personal style, both in up-tempo jazz and ballad solos. Similarly, though the Ellington approach was eventually diversified with other more orthodox swing conceptions, all of the McIntyre band's successive arrangers, including himself—Danny Hurd, Howard Gibeling, Sid Schwartz—were well versed in the subtleties of the "Ellington effect" (Strayhorn's term). What is important is that McIntyre and many of his soloists were not content merely to ape Ellington's music—they rarely played any of Ellington's compositions, as Barnet, for example, constantly did—but chose to apply the ingredients of Ellington's concept to their own music and, more admirably, in many cases develop them further. This is a not inconsiderable achievement, and it is once again astonishing to the jazz historian with a broadly comprehensive view of jazz that the McIntyre orchestra is never mentioned in any jazz histories or reference sources (except in the remarkable Roger Kinkle Encyclopedia).

Much more than routine imitators, McIntyre and his carefully chosen players reflected in their playing a deep love and respect for Ellington and really, unlike any other group, made a serious effort to modestly expand Ellington's universe in several interesting directions. In this respect the talents of two soloists in the McIntyre band—besides Hayes and Goddard—played crucial roles, most notably bassist Eddie Safranski, obviously a disciple of Jimmy Blanton and particularly of Ellington's bass feature *Jack the Bear*,[21] and trombonist Jimmy Emert, who, more than any other white player of the time, had mastered "Tricky Sam" Nanton's patented plunger style. Perhaps Emert made more creative use of *his* mentor's conception than Safranski did of Blanton's. Safranski expanded upon Blanton's work both by imitation—the latter's *Jack the Bear* solos are a fairly recurrent refrain in Safranski's playing—and further innovation. Emert, who had considerably more technical facility and greater range than Nanton, applied these extra dimensions to Nanton's style in original ways—one of the few players, black or white, to see alternative creative expressions in Nanton's concept. Emert's achievements can be heard to excellent effect on *Song of the Bayou, Apple Shiner, Sheik of Araby, Belzah Blues* (outstanding there), and *When Buddha Smiles* (Ex.

---

20. Hal McIntyre had achieved considerable fame as Glenn Miller's lead alto, adding crucially to that orchestra's special celebrated reed sound.
21. See above, Chapter 2. Safranski, with McIntyre for four years, became one of the stars of Stan Kenton's band (1945–48).

12). Emert's versatility extended also to his first-rate work as a lead trombone and an occasional solo in a Lawrence Brown manner, again not mere imitation of but original contribution to.

Ex. 12

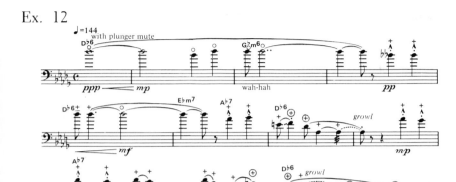

○ =half open;   ⊕ = ¾ closed;   + = tightly closed

McIntyre's orchestra played more jazz—and more consistently so—than any number of more famous and critically acclaimed orchestras (for example, Dorsey, Shaw, James), one clear manifestation of that being the great amount of solo space provided in its arrangements. Nowhere is that more evident than in the solo work of Safranski, who, at a time when bass solos were still a great rarity, was constantly featured. His impeccable clean style, small but firm tone, and his remarkable ability in the highest range of the bass constituted a significant breakthrough in the bass revolution that Blanton, Hinton, Haggart, and Page had started. Besides Safranski's own composition, *Concerto for Bass* of 1944— still greatly indebted to *Jack the Bear*—it is very much worth hearing his solo work on *Available Jones, Swinging on a Grapevine, Rockin' and Ridin', Cool as a Fool in a Pool, Strange Mood*—to name but a few. Even more interesting are Safranski's exciting, fine-swinging walking bass lines on, say, *St. Louis Blues* and *Who's Got the Ball* (Ex. 13), or his expressive background contributions— in walking eighth-notes, triplets and sixteenths—on *Mood Indigo* and *Swanee River* (Ex. 14).

The McIntyre soloists' contributions—Hayes's and Goddard's Webster-ish excursions and McIntyre's own beautiful alto work, much indebted to Johnny Hodges—should not be overlooked; and they were given more relevance by the manner in which the band's arrangers integrated solo into ensemble, provided varied and superbly swinging vehicles for the soloists. When so many late-Swing-Era bands were mired down in riff-tune formulas and endless call-and-response patterns, the McIntyre band retained a fresh outlook, always searching for new solutions to the problems of form and continuity, rarely succumbing to formulaic temptations. Interestingly, too, all four major arrangers held to a general unified style distinctive enough to be easily recognizable—even in its post-El-

Ex. 13

Ex. 14

lington phase—and yet one in which each arranger could develop a degree of individuality—again a resistance to formularizarion and stylistic atrophy. Moreover, the McIntyre band played more jazz instrumentals than most—even their relatively few vocals and popular songs were definitely couched in jazz terms (listen to *I Was Here When You Left Me*)—and it consistently swung more than most. Safranski and drummer Ralph Tilkin saw to that. Of the many first-rate advanced swing-style instrumentals which are well worth hearing I would especially single out Danny Hurd's *Available Jones, Apple Shiner, Sheik of Araby, Rockin' and Ridin', Strange Mood*; Howard Gibeling's *Who's Got the Ball, T'Ain't Me; Sherman Sherbet, Scarlet and Amber, King Porter Stomp, Sweet and Low* (arranger's credits of the last four-named not known to me). I would also recommend Sid Schwartz's heady, rich-textured *Swanee River* and, what I assume to be his impressive treatment of *Mood Indigo*.

This then was one of the truly fine bands of the era. Its excellence is attested to by its ability to survive the decline of big bands, working well into the 1950s (McIntyre died tragically in his California apartment in a cigarette-generated fire in 1959). On the other hand it cannot be said that the McIntyre band achieved top level popularity or the critical acclaim it surely deserved. For that it was too musicianly, played too tastefully, resisted commercialization too stubbornly, and recorded too few pop songs.

OTHER WHITE BANDS

The number of white big bands that flourished in the Swing Era was enormous—during its peak, the war years, probably some 450 name bands, not to mention the several hundred more "name"-less bands that populated American ballrooms and hotels in those years. The category "big band" could cover, of course, a multitude of musical sins, a diversity of styles and approaches, of which most had little or nothing to do with jazz—that is, jazz as a creative improvisatory art. The vast majority of these bands were interested only in popular success, measured commercially in numbers of records sold, in attendance numbers at ballrooms, dances, and night clubs, and in fan mail. Each catered to various lesser levels of audience tastes; and there developed, beginning already in the late 1920s but "perfected" to a high degree of refinement in the late 1930s, a number of distinct *categories* of bands: "sweet" bands, "dance" bands, "hotel" bands, "society" orchestras, "Mickey Mouse" bands, "novelty" bands. Of these a precious few changed to a more deliberate jazz style during the height of the Swing Era (the early 1940s), but in most cases these experiments—what was euphemistically called "adopting a jazz policy"—were tentative and short-lived.

Among the hundreds of bands, a handful not so far discussed deserve—in the context of this *jazz* history—at least an honorable mention, a footnote to the Swing Era. Most of them did not survive the big band era; but some evolved fairly distinctive styles, while others, less prominent creatively, were nonetheless important training grounds for the bright young instrumental talents coming up in the postwar era; some changed styles as jazz tastes changed in order to survive; others succumbed to commercial pressures of one kind or another; and, alas, a few of these bandleaders died and in most cases their bands with them. But a brief account of their achievements is nonetheless appropriate at this juncture.

Will Bradley and Ray McKinley led a pair of interesting bands that had at one time been a single orchestra, co-led by both men. Bradley, a superb virtuoso trombonist in the Tommy Dorsey vein, and McKinley, a fine imaginative, tasteful drummer, joined forces in 1939 to form their orchestra (with Bradley as front man and official leader). The arrangements (mostly by Leonard Whitney and Hugo Winterhalter) placed the emphasis squarely on swing without, however, evolving a distinctive style of their own—it was a light, easy-going amalgam of Goodman and Basie—and oddly enough never developed a completely successful ballad style, virtually de rigueur in those days of band singers and instrumental ballads. It lacked the warmth and languid tempos the best dance bands could purvey. But one of the Bradley band's hits, *Celery Stalks at Midnight*, provides a good measure of their collective ability as a jazz ensemble: an easy, crisp swing riding on Delmar Kaplan's fine walking bass and McKinleys' drums, more than capable solos, clear-textured ensembles, and a sophisticated arrangement making splendid use of dynamics.

In 1942 Bradley and McKinley, like the Dorsey brothers seven years earlier, came to a parting of the ways, largely over stylistic conceptual differences. McKinley had discovered boogie-woogie (belatedly), and when the band had a big commercial success with an inane novelty tune called *Beat Me, Daddy, Eight to the Bar*, followed by *Rock-a-Bye Boogie* and *Down the Road a Piece*, McKinley wanted to turn the band into a boogie-woogie unit. Bradley, on the other hand, was interested in preserving the orthodox swing-plus-ballad policy along with pursuing a more serious progressive approach,[22] a goal he achieved with his own newly revamped band, which had in it such outstanding young creative musicians as drummer Shelly Manne (then a youthful twenty-two years of age), master trombonist Bill Harris, and trumpeter Shorty Rogers (who replaced Pete Candoli). Unfortunately the band could not record during the union ban, and by 1943 its ranks had been completely decimated by the wartime draft. Bradley eventually returned to the New York studios, playing for a while also in the "Tonight Show" orchestra. But his outstanding playing on such pieces as *Celery Stalks, Jimtown Blues, Basin Street Boogie, It's a Square But It Rocks*—a remarkable blend of Teagarden, Dorsey and Higginbotham—and the best of his orchestra's Columbia sides constitute a reminder of the high quality of which even the less creative ensembles were sometimes capable. Even so, it is disappointing that much of the Bradley band's most impressive work never was put on record.

---

22. Will Bradley eventually turned completely to contemporary classical composing and, at a time when Alban Berg's music (except for the *Violin Concerto*) was virtually unknown in America, began a serious study of that composer's work. Unfortunately Bradley's many well-crafted atonal compositions, some for multiple-trombone choirs, are little known today. It is ironic that in later years it was McKinley, not Bradley, who eventually ended up with the more progressive band, featuring Eddie Sauter's abstract atonal scores.

McKinley's band also was short-lived—less than a year—but in that short period, miraculously dropping its boogie-woogie bias, played quite respectable jazz, featuring the fine clarinetist Mahlon Clark, the inventive pianist Lou Stein, the trombonist Brad Gowans, and a remarkable tuba player, Joe Parks, who was one of the first to play swinging melodic ensemble lines with the brass, rather than the usual oompah accompaniments of former years, thereby adding an uncommonly rich sonority to the McKinley brass.

McKinley spent the late war years in Glenn Miller's Air Force Band, but upon his return to civilian life formed a new band featuring this time the advanced arrangements and compositions of Eddie Sauter, as well as excellent young musicians like trumpeter Nick Travis, guitarist Mundell Lowe, and trombonist Vern Friley. Sauter's brilliant modern scores—*Sandstorm*, *Tumblebug*, *Borderline*, and, above all, the outstanding *Hangover Square*—unfortunately poorly recorded on the Majestic label, will be discussed in detail in the subsequent volume of this History.

Among those bands that changed styles from a sweet, strictly dance approach to a jazzier more modern idiom, the two Jans—Savitt and Garber (both violinists)—are worth mentioning. The Philadelphia-based orchestra of Jan Savitt and His Top Hatters developed early on a successful individual style through their hard-driving "shuffle rhythm,"[23] but also achieved a great popularity by featuring a very musical, clear-voiced black singer known as Bon Bon (real name George Tunnell), the first black singer openly, permanently hired by a white band.

Bon Bon's modern scat vocals on *Vol Vistu Gaily Star* and *Paper Picker* (sounding like an early Jon Hendricks) and such swing originals as Johnny Watson's *720 in the Books*, Jack Pleis's *Horizon*, Eddie Durham's *Blues in the Groove* and *It's Time to Jump and Shout* are still well worth hearing for their forceful hard-driving ensemble swing. Savitt's band played with such consistently impeccable ensemble and propulsive swing that it kept even its famous shuffle rhythm, constantly energized rhythmically, from becoming a stale cliché. Indeed, the Savitt band had achieved by early 1939 a 4/4 swing amalgam that was an interesting cross between Lunceford and Basie, the shuffle rhythm simple folded into it. The band's powerful swing can be heard at its best on the 1939 *That's a Plenty*, (surprisingly) on *Rose of the Rio Grande* and *Alla en El Rancho Grande*, the 1938 *Sugar Foot Stomp* and—in a more relaxed vein—the Horace Henderson-like *Big Beaver* from 1941. Contributing never less than capably, often brilliantly as jazz soloists were the dynamic trumpet star Johnny Austin,[24] tenor soloist Eddie Clausen (later replaced by the twenty-year-old Georgie Auld), and Austin's counterpart on trombone, the versatile Al Leopold. Austin is well worth

23. Jan Savitt, Russian-born and by all accounts a brilliant violin prodigy, after studies at the renowned Curtis Institute in Philadelphia and graduating, as the youngest member ever, directly into the Philadelphia Orchestra, under Leopold Stokowski.

24. Austin had already brought considerable jazz excitement to the Glenn Miller band in 1938 and early 1939, but did his most brilliant work with Savitt. His intense, hard-swinging, brash style—a kind of wild Harry James—not without a touch of the vulgar, made him the band's most compelling soloist.

hearing on *That's a Plenty, Kansas City Moods, Green Goon Jive,* and many other sides.

Savitt's famous hit recording, *Quaker City Jazz,* was actually one of the band's least accomplishments, being little more than a rigid emulation of jazz in the early 1930s' Casa Loma vein. It was natural for Savitt, with his classical background, to delve into the light classical repertory, which he and his arrangers Ted Daune, Billy Moore, and Jack Pleis did with more taste and skill than most. Moore's swing arrangement of Saint-Saëns' *My Heart at Thy Sweet Voice* (featuring a good Auld solo) is quite fetching, and even more unusual is Pleis's virtuosic treatment of Paul Dukas's *Sorcerer's Apprentice.*

But still more impressive was Savitt's adoption in 1942 of a small string section of six (including himself as lead violin), showing how well strings could be tastefully integrated into a basic jazz style. Unfortunately (because of the recording ban) only four sides—and not very representative ones—by this band were recorded.

Savitt continued leading excellent orchestras until his death from a cerebral hemorrhage in 1948 at age thirty-five.

Jan Garber's band was another that, to everyone's surprise, shifted to a "jazz policy" around 1942. Sensing that swing's popularity was now such that it was a safe style to pursue, he hired the fine arranger, Gray Rains, and a number of young musicians (among them Lenny Sims, Jack Kelliher, Gene de Paul). Garber had been—along with Isham Jones—one of the "hotter" dance bands as early as the beginning 1920s, but under the influence of Guy Lombardo's phenomenal popular success switched to a sweet dance style. Then, when Garber converted to a livelier, quite advanced jazzier swing idiom in 1942, his public was confused, while most musicians and critics were astounded. The recording ban prevented this Garber band from recording extensively, but its performances of those years were proof that a modicum of jazz and swing was within reach of any of the white bands of the time, if only their leaders and recording executives permitted it. In such a piece as *Clodhopper* we can hear the band play with a clean, bright, albeit somewhat polite swing and excellent ensemble balance. Garber's flirtation with jazz, however, was short-lived, for when the results were commercially less than spectacular, Garber returned to his earlier sweet style.

In some respects the most unusual band of the early 1940s was that led by Shep Fields—again a changeling. It was a 13-piece orchestra formed entirely of woodwinds and saxophones (except for the rhythm section)—an idea first suggested and realized by Paul Whiteman in his 1938 Sax Octette. Fields carried the idea several steps farther by having arrangers Lew Harris, Glenn Osser, Freddy Noble, and Sid Schwartz create scores using as many as thirty-four different instruments, including at various times four alto saxophones, six tenors, one baritone, one bass saxophone (not simultaneously, of course), nine flutes, nine clarinets, three bass clarinets, and all manner of combinations thereof—all this achieved with only nine reed players, who obviously had to be multitalented doublers. They included Ray Eckstrand, Al Freistat, Tommy Lucas, Romeo Penque, and Bob Lawson, and one of Fields's saxophonists for a while was Sid Caesar.

This unusual and original instrumentation with its great potential for a wide range of tone colors was used in such a versatile and effective way that one rarely felt the absence of brass, and indeed by juxtaposing saxophones and pure wood-winds, or high reeds and low reeds, the Fields band could easily approximate the rich varied sounds of a normal full band. The group's ensemble playing—much of it without vibrato—was quite extraordinary in terms of balance, blend, and impeccable intonation. Nor was the band lacking in a number of good soloists: Tommy Lucas, a Hodges devotee; Tommy Kaye, a fine guitarist who obviously admired both Django Reinhardt and Oscar Moore; and a tenor player (I can't identify) who loved the raspy, gutsy sounds of early-1940s Ben Webster. All these elements and talents come together extremely well in pieces like *Little Pink Elephants, Lover's Lament, 1600 by the Clock,* the very fast hard-swinging *Sheik of Araby,* the harmonically for the time very advanced *Sophisticated Lady* and *Things Ain't What They Used to Be* (the latter two both by Ellington).

The surprise here was that Fields had for many years featured a style billed as his "rippling rhythm," a corny amalgam of elements borrowed from such bands as Wayne King, Eddie Duchin, Hal Kemp, and Ted Fio Rito. Fields's "rippling rhythm" had been to his band what the "shuffling rhythm" had been to Savitt. But Fields, despite the fantastic popular success of his "Mickey Mouse" staccato-triplets-cum-temple-block mannerisms, sought to create a more musical sound in an orthodox jazz vein: hence the transformation in 1941. And the results were startlingly good.

But as the big bands disappeared one by one in the late forties and jazz evolved irreversibly into bop and small combo jazz, Fields's "idealism gave way to commercial realism," as writer George Simon once put it, and in 1947 Fields returned to his bubble music. *Sic transit gloria!*

Even more anomalous in other ways was the orchestra and career of Alvino Rey, beginning with the fact that the Latino-named leader Rey's real name was *Scotch-Irish* (Al McBurney) and that he specialized in electrified *Hawaiian* steel guitar sounds. Still stranger is the fact that, despite Rey's considerable popular success, right from the start in 1938, his band's Bluebird records have never been reissued on LP. All that is currently available of this very interesting orchestra is a collection of radio transcriptions and some air checks from 1942–46. I recall hearing the band frequently in those years and, even though my first allegiance was to Ellington and Basie, to Eckstine, Gillespie and Herman, I remember being very impressed by its often quite advanced, exciting arrangements and by Rey's modern guitar stylings. I was not then aware of who Rey's arrangers or soloists were, but I knew—just as I did in hearing the 1943 Hines band—that some new and impressive music was being made there. I learned much later that the young unknowns on his arranging staff were Ray Coniff, Neal Hefti, Johnny Mandel, Billy May, Frank de Vol, and, a little later, Nelson Riddle and

George Handy—all to play important roles in the development of modern orchestral jazz. I also learned much later that Rey's impressive roster of musicians
included Hal McKusick, Skeets Herfurt, Zoot Sims, Kai Winding, Milt Raskin,
Gene Traxler, and Joe Mondragon, and that the reason his rhythm section sounded
so good was that he had as drummers a whole string of exceptional talents: Nick
Fatool, Don Lamond, Mel Lewis, Bunny Shawker, and even the incomparable
Davey Tough. Nor can I forget Rey's beautifully voiced, modern guitar chordings, which gave the Hawaiian guitar a class and creative potential no other
player seemed to be able to extract from that instrument.

Among the titles to hear I would cite *The Major and the Minor*, the superbly
swinging Billy May arrangements of *April in Paris* and *Should I?*, the moody
Thornhill-ish *We'll Gather Lilacs*, and the captivating, broadly swinging *Sepul-
veda* and *Cement Mixer* (the last featuring a fine tenor solo by the twenty-year-
old Herbie Steward).

Once again the 1942-43 recording ban prevented, as it did with so many
young transitional bands, the perpetuation on wax of some of the better big-band
jazz of the period. And when Rey entered the Navy in early 1944, his band
broke up, to be reorganized in late 1945, but then lasting only a year or two.

Alvino Rey may not be much remembered today, a situation not likely to
change much since there are very few recordings of his orchestra reissued and
readily available. But for those of us of an age and fortunate enough to have
heard Rey and his fine orchestra, the sounds of his music linger on in our
memories as among the more exciting. In the meantime the 1946 transcriptions
issued on Hindsight Records will have to suffice as a faint remembrance of the
artistry of Alvino Rey.

To the extent that Charlie Spivak is remembered at all today, he is remembered—not altogether accurately—as that somewhat banal, sweet trumpet stylist
who was always vying with Harry James, Randy Brooks, and Ray Anthony for
top ratings in the *Downbeat* and *Metronome* magazine popularity poles. But
Spivak and his band (1940–47) were on occasion much more than that. A musician of great talent and integrity—he had contributed impressively to the bands
of the Dorsey Brothers, Ray Noble, Bob Crosby, and Tommy Dorsey before
forming his own band in 1940—Spivak was not always the swaggering, arrogant
trumpet-playing leader he was most often made out to be. Indeed, one of his
major career miscalculations—in a burst of modesty and reticence—was to virtually abandon for a while his brilliant open-horn-playing—in which Harry James
was garnering all the laurels at the time—and resort to a delicate, intimate,
always muted styling that was, alas, too subtle for the average dance-band fan.
But with the help of a fine bassist, Jimmy Middleton, and drummer Davey
Tough, as well as altoist Willie Smith (from Lunceford's band), Spivak's orchestra could swing with the best of them—especially when Spivak resorted to his
beautiful-toned open-horn-playing. On the other hand, without a truly distinctive orchestral style to build upon, the Spivak band ultimately deteriorated by

1945 to a fairly run-of-the-mill sweet band, producing pretty sounds, but little that contributed anything relevant to further developments in jazz.[25]

The white big bands of the Swing Era have usually received short shrift in jazz histories and reference books, leaving the general impression that as a lot they contributed little or nothing to the mainstream evolution of jazz. But the facts are otherwise, for the best of them—and there were quite a few of those, as we have seen—played as crucial a role in the gradually proliferating effusion of jazz as most of the leading black bands.[26] The white bands often codified and expanded upon the innovations of their black counterparts. But they also brought jazz—at least a certain style of jazz—to millions of whites who otherwise would never have heard any jazz at all. And if it is fair game, as it has been so often in the past, to celebrate black creativity while supressing relevant documentation about black bandleaders' and musicians' inability to resist commercial temptations, then it may be equally fair to point out that many of the white swing bands had a deep, sincere commitment to jazz, and that in their different individual ways they refined and extended jazz concepts and techniques in ways that ultimately contributed significantly to the development and dissemination of the music.

25. The five most interesting big-band latecomers—George Paxton, Elliot Lawrence, and Boyd Raeburn (orchestras formed in 1944), Georgie Auld (in 1943), and Randy Brooks (1945)—belong more to the modern post-swing period and will be dealt with in Volume III of this History.

26. I personally abhor the polarization of jazz and its evolution into black and white lineages, and if I have in some chapters of this book succumbed to a similar dichotomization, it is only in response, indeed in counterargument to 1) the prevailing biases maintained in most critical jazz circles; and 2) to the undeniable fact that, during the period covered in this volume, all major developments were originated by blacks, thus justifying from a strictly historical and chronological point of view some degree of separate treatment. Beyond that somewhat technical (though important) point, dividing jazz into its black and white traditions has little to commend it, for as we have seen time and time again, the cross references between black and white jazz conceptions were numerous and constant. What derived from where is not always so easy to discern, and at a certain higher level the lines between black and white jazz are more blurred than most jazz historians have been willing to admit.

8

The Territory Bands

A history of the Swing Era would not be complete without a discussion of the so-called black "territory bands,"[1] a particular phenomenon of 1930s' jazz history, distinct in many respects from the major name-band developments concentrated in New York and the Eastern seaboard. Many of these territory bands unfortunately never recorded. Others did record, but either in such meager quantity or with such unrepresentative material that a fair appraisal of their work through recordings is highly problematic. Most of these bands did not survive the thirties or early forties, and a few that did could do so only by converting to rhythm-and-blues.

These orchestras, from whatever region of the country, had several elements in common. One, they typically were led and peopled by musicians born at the turn of the century or its first decade, and thus in many cases developed musically when jazz, as a distinct musical style, did not yet exist or was barely assimilated into one. Such musicians often had their early training in classical music and their first professional experiences in various types of bands (circus, minstrel, carnival, school) or in ragtime groups. Although small "territory bands"—they were rarely larger than trios, quartets, and quintets—began to develop in the late years of the second decade of this century, territory bands as a more or less established, relatively pervasive institution did not come into existence until the early twenties. They were as much the product of a sociological revolution in the United States as a musical one. I am referring to the dramatically altered social climate of the twenties, now remembered as the Roaring Twenties, and in particular the major changes in the recreational and dance habits of Americans. These were profoundly influenced by the enormous success of the dance

1. Territory bands by definition were black. There were, of course, many white bands in the "territories" and hinterlands, but they tended to have the more lucrative and permanent jobs and therefore were not required to travel as much as the black bands. A few of the better white orchestras that fall within the scope of this history will be briefly mentioned in this chapter.

team of Irene and Vernon Castle who, along with their musical director James Europe, virtually revolutionized social dancing (at least among the younger generations) by creating new styles of popular dances, like the fox trot and the turkey trot, which were in turn greatly influenced by Afro-American dancing. In the wake of the Castles' success, public dance halls and ballrooms—all practically nonexistent before—proliferated in great numbers in major urban centers throughout the land. With the absorption of ragtime into jazz and the demise of most of the dances associated with ragtime, the incoming jazz idiom emerged as the perfect music for this kind of dancing, leaving the waltzes, polkas, and tangos to the older generations. And as the twenties developed, even the smaller cities and towns began to manifest a demand for dancing to jazz. But since many smaller communities still could not afford a permanent dance hall—even less a permanent orchestra to provide the music—the traveling territory bands came into existence in full force. One should also note that a major surge in the technological development of faster and more economical cars and buses in the 1920s, plus a burgeoning network of paved roads and highways, played a crucial role in the evolution of the territory bands.

Gradually most of the earlier smaller territory groups, playing mainly in traveling minstrel and carnival shows, switched to jazz as that music became the prevailing popular idiom and therefore a potential means of employment. This was true of bands as diverse, both in style and geographic location, as Bennie Moten (Kansas City, originating in ragtime), Curtis Mosby (Los Angeles, ragtime and early country-fiddle dance music), and Red Perkins (Omaha, minstrel shows and brass bands). Other bands of slightly later vintage took off from the early New Orleans polyphonic style, especially as put forward by King Oliver or Jelly Roll Morton: Fatty Martin (Houston) from the former, the Ross De Luxe Syncopaters (Miami and Savannah) from Morton—or Mosby again. Bands of still later origin, of course, received their initial inspiration to a lesser or greater extent from Louis Armstrong or early Duke Ellington or, in many instances, the Casa Loma band. Nor was the influence of Paul Whiteman or even Guy Lombardo ever far away.

What is interesting, however, is that many of the territory bands developed their own styles not so much by imitation of the Eastern bands as by their own natural talents and resources, and a blending of what were often very distinct regional styles, frequently influenced by particular ethnic traditions and social conditions. In other instances, territory bands in the twenties developed a conglomerate style from a variety of regional idioms which, when its various elements were merged, was to all intents and purposes similar to the prevailing Henderson-Redman orchestral style. What I am suggesting is that many of these bands did not *directly* imitate their big-name Eastern peers but arrived at similar styles by essentially the same kind of experimentation as some of those Eastern bands had.[2]

2. Two examples of such orchestras are Sonny Clay's (in California) and the St. Louis-based riverboat bands, such as Fate Marable's.

In this connection it should be noted that, just as there are no true Americans—we are all immigrants in one way or another (even the Indians came from Asia originally)—so in the early days there were no truly indigenous New York (or Chicago) bands—with one exception: Fletcher Henderson's orchestra. It was formed in New York, developed and remained there until well into the thirties, and began to travel extensively only then. Another way to put it is that virtually all jazz orchestras were at one time territory orchestras, at least of territory origin. Many of them—the Missourians, for example, from St. Louis, or Jimmie Lunceford, who started out in Nashville and Memphis—moved on to New York early in their careers. The early Ellington and Chick Webb bands came in from Washington and Baltimore, respectively.[3] Many others, of course, stayed in the territories, venturing east only sporadically, while still others, as we shall see, never came to New York at all.

Those bands that stayed in the territories—at least the best of them—played an enormously crucial role in the development of jazz, particularly swing, since it is they who tended to develop a distinctive regional style which then, in many cases, was eventually exported east to New York and there established itself in what would become in turn a *national* style. One has only to think of the far-reaching influence of the Basie and Lunceford orchestras, both originally "territory bands," and that of the Southwestern saxophone schools (both of the Ben Webster-Herschel Evans–Budd Johnson *and* Lester Young varieties) to realize the veracity of that statement. Indeed, it is easily arguable that these regional styles—say, Kansas City or Texas—were critically important because they were the seedbeds in which many of the most important innovators would grow and later on contribute decisively to the development of jazz in the thirties and forties. Lester Young, Charlie Christian, Jimmy Blanton, Jack Teagarden, Charlie Parker are just a few that come to mind.

These roaming nomadic territory bands were obviously critical also to offering important job and training opportunities to musicians, especially the young ones. And, as we shall see, these orchestras were versatile and eclectic, serving a wide variety of musical tastes. But a few were able to develop highly individual styles, comparable in originality and quality to many of the more famous Eastern big-name orchestras. And this may very well have included a few of them for whom unfortunately no recordings exist, like Speed Webb and Tommy Douglas.

The second point, common to most of these orchestras, is that they served vast areas of the country as traveling "music conservatories": training organizations, where young players could learn their craft, develop their skills as players or arrangers, and in general mature musically and professionally. Countless musicians of later "big-name" fame were alumni of these roving jazz conservatories. One problematic by-product of this state of affairs was that many of the territory bands experienced constant personnel losses and changes. And, whereas such circumstances might be a boon for individual players, for the leader, in his

3. Even New Orleans jazz was originally a "territory" style in the early days, which eventually spread through the South and Southwest, up the Mississippi River and on to Chicago, and even to New York by 1917, albeit in a diminished form, via the Original Dixieland Jazz Band.

attempts to keep a band together in order to forge a *particular orchestral* identity, it often prevented stabilization of an ensemble style, let alone the capacity for further development. As a result of this situation the territory bands' rosters (in a given region) show frequent overlapping of personnel; nor was it unknown that more prominently placed bandleaders would steal musicians from their rivals, or in some cases even take over entire bands.

As far as one can judge from the relatively slim evidence of recordings and hearsay, each major region had at least one outstanding orchestra, during particularly rich periods perhaps even several rival groups. Reports of first-rate musicians in every instrumental category who for one reason or another "never came East" abound among musicians. Indeed the notion that there were other Louis Armstrongs or Coleman Hawkinses out there in the hinterlands occurs with such frequency in musicians' chroniclings, that one must ascribe some degree of truth to these attestations. It is more than likely, on the other hand, that what was being admired by these fellow musicians was often some particular technical skill: a trumpet player's tone or range, or absolute note security, or a saxophone player's improvisational inventiveness. It is not likely that any major *innovator* of the calibre of an Armstrong or a Parker or an Ellington remained undiscovered—although statistically such a possibility does exist. In many, many cases very fine musicians who could easily have made it in the "big-time" chose not to venture forth but preferred for personal or economic reasons to stay closer to home. Buster Smith, the alto saxophonist, trombonist Ashford Hardee, trumpeter Nat Bates, the Texas pianist Peck Kelley are a few musicians of this calibre that come readily to mind.

The map in Figure 1 shows the geographic spread of the black territory bands. Among these Sonny Clay, Curtis Mosby, and Paul Howard on the West Coast; Bennie Moten, Alphonse Trent, Boots and His Buddies, the Jay McShann and Harlan Leonard bands in the Missouri-Texas region; Zack Whyte, Nat Towles, and Speed Webb in the Midwest, Alonzo Ross's De Luxe Syncopators in the Southeast, and the riverboat bands that plied the Mississippi and Ohio rivers, were in all likelihood the most important, and worthy of consideration here.[4]

For the unitiated reader-listener these orchestras will in fact provide some startling surprises. In some ways the most unexpected of these are to be found in the work of the Ross De Luxe Syncopators, all the more surprising for the fact that their recordings were made quite early (1927) and in a region, the Deep South, not exactly known for producing a great deal of advanced orchestral jazz. The South, with its relatively few large metropolitan urban areas, adhered much more tenaciously than any other region to older rural musical traditions, such as country blues as practiced by itinerant guitarists and/or singers—in any case rarely was there ensemble music of any magnitude. But Alonzo Ross's Miami-based ten-piece orchestra—short-lived though it was (it seems to have disbanded

---

4. The recordings of Alphonse Trent, Jesse Stone, Troy Floyd, Terrence Holder, Bennie Moten, Zack Whyte, Lloyd Hunter's Serenaders, Walter Page's Blue Devils, Grant Moore, the Missourians, and Neal Montgomery were all dealt with in some detail in *Early Jazz.*

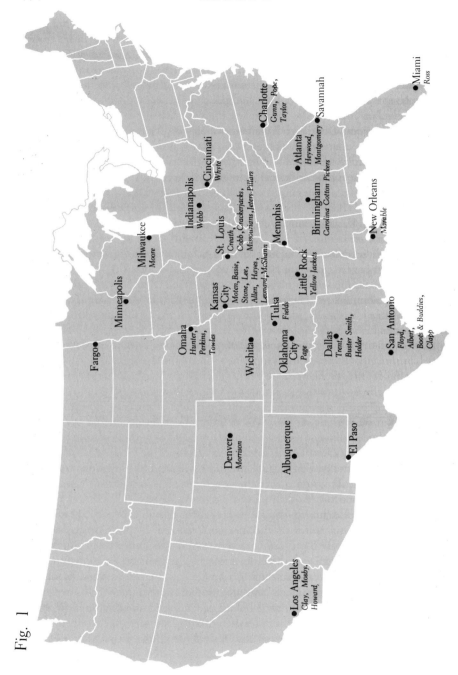

Fig. 1

already in 1928)—managed to produce some quite sophisticated ensemble jazz. Judging by the evidence of eight recorded sides, Ross himself was a very imaginative skillful arranger with access to some uncommonly strong players, including trumpeter Melvin Herbert, reedman Edmond Hall, the amazing banjoist Casker Towie, and tuba player Richard Fullbright (*and* Cootie Williams who, however, happened to be on leave from the band when they recorded in Savannah, Georgia, in 1927).

It was characteristic of the Ross orchestra to play the "head" of the tune in some relatively conservative or popular fashion—allusions to Whiteman or some of the more famous sweet dance bands—and then let the soloists and stylish ensembles loose for the remainder of the performance. There are on these eight recordings any number of saxophone ensembles, led by Ed Hall, which seem quite ahead of their time in conception and execution—and incidentally ahead of Benny Carter as well. Likewise, the coloristic and textural exploitation of the small ensemble seems quite remarkable for its time. One is led to conjecture that Ross and his orchestra must, in that respect at least, have listened well to Morton's Red Hot Peppers recordings. They seem equally well rehearsed, for most of their ensemble-playing and intonation (with the exception of one title, *Believe Me, Dear*) is virtually impeccable. And yet it is playing with a spunky rhythmic drive—as Morton would have put it: "with plenty rhythm!"

Apart from the many superb saxophone ensembles—exemplary on *Baby, Stop Teasing Me* and *Lady Mine*—there is Towie's spectacular banjo work, both in crisply articulated solos and breaks as well as strong rhythmic backing. A few bucolic tuba solos by Fullbright (he played later with the Teddy Hill band and Zutty Singleton) alternate with teasingly slidy ones by trombonist Eddie Cooper.

The best soloist is undoubtedly Ed Hall, fiery and volatile at every opportunity. Whether on alto or soprano or baritone sax—very little clarinet on these sides (his main instrument in later years)—he charges into each solo with a power and drive which in 1927 probably only Hawkins and Bechet could summon.

But it is the trumpet work in the Syncopators which in some ways fascinates the most. Robert Mason and the aforementioned Melvin Herbert had perfected the two-trumpet breaks (always muted) à la King Oliver and Louis Armstrong. These performances abound with them, flawlessly rendered. Additionally, the two players could change into a variety of stylistic guises. Although my solo identification must, alas, be conjectural, I believe it is Mason who plays the marvelously huge-toned ringing melodic solo on *Skad-O-Lee*, as well as the classically straight (in Bohemian cornet style à la Bohumir Kryl) hauntingly intoned solo on *Believe Me, Dear*. By contrast it is Herbert (presumably) who is given the extemporized jazz solos: fluent, secure, and technically advanced for the time.

Harmonically, too, the Syncopators were an interesting Band. Ross knew how to exploit the unusual changes in a pop song like *Mary Bell*, or to keep things harmonically lively through his expert modulations (there are quite a few on *Florida Rhythm*). Even more startling in this respect is the beautiful trumpet-trombone sequence in *Skad-O-Lee*. Notice how ingeniously Ross varies the advanced changes of the song in the fifth through eighth bars of each 8-bar phrase (Ex. 1). It is hard to think of a band in 1927 that could have managed anything quite as fascinating—even Ellington's.

Another quite outstanding orchestra, based in Charlotte, North Carolina, but of much later vintage, was Jimmy Gunn's Dixie Serenaders.[5] Unlike its prede-

Ex. 1

5. Gunn's Dixie Serenaders seems most certainly to have been a successor to an early band named Taylor's Dixie Serenaders. In fact, half of the Gunn band is identical with Taylor's group. Gunn was the pianist with Taylor and, as so often happened in the territory bands, probably took over the leadership from Taylor. Gunn seems to have improved the band dramatically, for Taylor's recordings, made in 1931, are for the most part very poor. The ensemble work is uniformly ragged, rough, and out of tune, and sounds very much—as one researcher has indicated—like that of high school and college students. The only soloists worth noting are Ernest Parham, a tenor saxophonist with a gutsy tone à la early Hawkins and a florid busy style, and Skeets Tolbert, an eloquent, poised alto player, who later recorded some forty sides in New York between 1939 and 1941 with his own band.

Tolbert's Gentlemen of Swing was not strictly speaking a territory band, although most of its six-

cessor, Gunn's group played with an easy relaxed "modern" swing, with a fine lilting beat provided by an unidentified drummer (as, for example, on *Slats' Shuffle* and *The Operator Special*). Tolbert contributed a number of elegant, fluent alto solos, but the outstanding musician seems to have been a trombonist known only as "Slats", playing in a highly virtuosic and inventive style not unlike Benny Morton's

The only other black band of some distinction in the Southeast (until Erskine Hawkins came along in 1936) was the Carolina Cotton Pickers, in existence between 1929 and 1944. They recorded fourteen sides in 1937 in Birmingham, Alabama, of which only six were released. Not nearly as disciplined as Ross's Syncopators, despite a decade of intervening developments in orchestral jazz, the Carolina band's recordings are primarily notable for Cat Anderson's (later Hampton's and Ellington's high-note trumpet star) youthful, searching solo work on *'Deed I Do*. Judging by its few recordings, the band was limited to a kind of chunky-rhythmed beat and sentimentally "soulful," slightly out-of-tune ensemble work—a functional provincial band at best.

A rather impressive white orchestra led by trumpeter Bob Pope also deserves mention, especially since the standard reference books on jazz and even George Simon's *The Big Bands* (which lists and comments on well over 500 bands!) ignore Pope completely. The band recorded some thirty-seven sides in 1936 and 1937 in Charlotte, N.C., and Birmingham, for the Bluebird label, many of them first-rate in the then prevailing swing idiom. Along with the mandatory pop songs and crooning vocals, Pope managed to record good jazz instrumentals, such as Jimmy Mundy's *Madhouse*, Claude Hopkins's *Washington Squabble*, Hal Mooney's *Swamp Fire*, also Henderson's *Blue Skies*, and *On Your Toes*, always rendered authentically and unabridged. Moreover the band played in a smooth, disciplined 4/4 swing style, made good use of dynamic and textural contrasts, and featured a fine trombonist (identity unknown) and Pope himself as soloists. All in all it was an above-average orchestra, hardly deserving to be so roundly ignored as it has been until now.

On the other side of the continent, in Los Angeles, several bands vied for attention early on, in particular Sonny Clay's Plantation Orchestra, Curtis Mosby and his Dixieland Blue Blowers, and Paul Howard[6] (a band that later came under the leadership of Les Hite and recorded with Louis Armstrong).

---

man personnel came from North Carolina or Kansas City (as in the case of trumpeter Carl "Tatti" Smith). It was a quite successful group playing many of the better white night clubs in New York, a well-disciplined clean-playing jump band, an eclectic group that could encompass Louis Jordan's blues-and-boogie riff style as well as novelty vocal material such as the King Cole Trio was purveying in the early 40s. Tolbert's own playing was an amalgam of Johnny Hodges, Willie Smith and Louis Jordan, always handsomely presented. Tolbert also did most of the arranging, creating simple unpretentious functional charts which were always cleanly executed. Among the band's more fetching numbers are *Those Draftin' Blues Bugle Blues*, *Big Fat Butterfly* and *Lazy Gal Blues*.

6. The Paul Howard orchestra has been dealt with in connection with Lionel Hampton (q.v.), who was Howard's drummer.

Sonny Clay, a multi-instrumentalist originally from Arizona, was one of the earliest black jazz musicians to settle in Los Angeles (around 1916). In the last years of the decade he played drums with Jelly Roll Morton and subsequently played with both Reb Spikes's Famous Syncopated Band and George Morrison's Denver-based band.[7] By the end of 1922 Clay had formed his own orchestra, an eight-piece group. It recorded sometime in 1923 or 1924 as the California Poppies, Clay presenting himself now as a pianist. Ernest Coycault (trumpet) was the major soloist—as he had been Bunk Johnson's replacement in 1910 in the Superior Band in New Orleans—albeit playing in a simple, limited style that even in 1924 could be considered ancient. Certainly these early sides reveal a band that in the solos and arranged ensembles played in a very stiff, labored, thumpy style. The only time the band can be said to come alive was in its final choruses when it traditionally moved into a polyphonic collective improvisation in New Orleans style, via the Original Dixieland Jazz Band, however, replete with novelty effects and barnyard yelps.

Clay recorded a few more times in Los Angeles in the mid-twenties (as, for example, with the Stompin' Six, their best efforts), in a style that is a pleasant but at times uneasy amalgam of ragtime, jazz (as filtered through the Original Dixieland Jazz Band and King Oliver's Creole Band), and primitive early instrumental blues. Except for the outstanding trombonist W. B. Woodman, who plays with an easy fluency rare for that time (and a subtle sense of humor), the players generally perform in an implacably rigid style and rhythm that must have seemed old-fashioned even at that time. And by 1928—well after Morton's, Armstrong's, and Hines's initial revolutionary recordings—the Clay band was still mired in a backward looking, stiff, polyphonic style which most bands had outgrown by then. Their "collective" concept was sometimes carried to considerable lengths, as when in *In My Dreams* a trio of two baritone saxes and tuba engage in grumbly low-register polyphonic interplay.

By 1931 Clay, now recording under a new band name, Dixie Serenaders, had advanced to a more homophonic (but still heavily stomping) orchestral style, and had acquired at least one fine, versatile soloist, trumpeter James "King" Porter, heard to good effect on *Cho-King* and *River, Stay 'Way from My Door*.

But to be fair, it is perhaps too much to expect a band like this, isolated from the mainstream, to have developed much of an orchestral conception or style so early in the history of jazz. Indeed, comparison with the earlier Henderson band of 1923 or 1924 (except after Armstrong's arrival) reveals that it, too, played more or less in the same stiff, staccato, slap-tongue style one hears on Clay's recordings. (On the other hand, an even earlier recording by Kid Ory's Sunshine Orchestra with true New Orleans musicians shows how free and spontaneous— even swinging—jazz *could* sound very early on (1922),[8] especially in the hands of a gifted cornetist like Mutt Carey.)

It needs also to be said (as suggested earlier) that Clay in all likelihood arrived

7. See *Early Jazz* for an account of George Morrison's fascinating career, Appendix, p. 359.
8. See *Early Jazz*, p. 74.

at this style—whatever its transitional merits—on his own, rather than in direct imitation of Henderson. I doubt that Henderson's Club Alabam Orchestra recordings were known to Clay, and in any case they would have been of such recent vintage as to preclude having already induced a lasting effect on Clay.

But by 1926 we can hear the difference between a Henderson and a Clay. For by 1926 Henderson was stunning the jazz world with such "advanced" pieces as *Stampede* and *Henderson Stomp*, while Clay was still clinging to his strange mixture of unswinging ensembles and once-removed New Orleans polyphony.

Mosby's band, on the other hand, certainly seemed to have learned well the lessons of Jelly Roll Morton, if not yet of Henderson. Indeed, since Morton had sojourned in Los Angeles between 1917 and 1923, and Mosby arrived there around 1918, it is likely that the two men knew each other and conceivably even worked together, although I cannot offer positive proof to that effect. In any case, Mosby's Blue Blowers band by 1927 featured a great diversity of solos on each track, peppered with frequent solo breaks and "plenty rhythm"—quite a bit of humor, too. This was an exuberant, extrovert band, much like the Missourians or the Savoy Bearcats, playing a mixture of stomp, fast blues, country fiddle (in the violin solos by Attwell Rose), and updated ragtime—occasionally also unafraid to blend these with a Lombardo-ish sweet style. Mosby's band could swing pretty hard—even in 1927 (hear them on *Tiger Stomp*). Its ensemble playing could be stunning (as on *Louisiana BoBo*). As for the soloists, trombonist Ashford Hardee was especially skillful, fluctuating between wildly extravagant breaks, sometimes covering two and a half octaves (as on *In My Dreams. and Tiger Stomp*), and highly fluent improvisations in a bouncy staccato style which many of the early trombonists favored. (Claude Jones, Miff Mole, and Snub Mosely are three trombonists who had that kind of technical agility, one that, I believe, derives in concept, as then jazzified in the 1920s, from the highly developed virtuoso style of the concert band soloists, like Arthur Pryor and Jiroslav Cimera.) Hardee is every bit as good as Jones, Mole, or Mosely, and typifies the kind of talent that musicians talk about when they refer to players who "never went East," "never got into name bands," but who were as good or better than the musicians who happened to become famous and enter the history books and discographies.

Trumpeter James Porter was also a reliable soloist and section leader, but clearly the outstanding player in the Mosby band's 1928 recordings was its tuba player, whose identity is unfortunately not known. In all of my years of listening to early jazz, when the tuba was the predominent bass instrument, I have never heard anything quite like this man (who happens to have been also superbly recorded). His tone was simply magnificent, not even matched by such tuba stalwarts as Ralph Escudero, Bass Edwards, John Kirby, Joe Tarto. But even more amazing is his "time," not only flawlessly accurate but with a pulse and implicit musical line—even in slow tempos like *Blue Blower Blues*—that is to my ears years ahead of the then prevailing state of the art. There is a grandeur in his playing that lifts the music (and the band) in a way that seems to me to be either unique or extremely rare for that period.

If we define the Midwest as an area comprising Kansas City, northward towards Nebraska and the Dakotas, thence eastward to Ohio and back around to St. Louis (and excluding for the present purposes the cities of Chicago and Detroit), then this region sported over the period under consideration nearly two dozen various-sized orchestras, many of them reputedly of very high musical calibre. Figure 2 gives an overview of these bands, including their specific geographic concentration and years of existence (in more or less chronological order). Asterisks indicate those that never recorded. The brackets indicate more or less the same band taken over by a different leader.

Fig. 2

Kansas City

	George E. Lee	1918?–32
*	Paul Banks	1918–42
	Jesse Stone	1920–28; 1934–40*
		(* in Chicago/New York)
	Bennie Moten	1922–35
*	Clarence Love	1925–48
	Walter Page's Blue Devils	1925–31
*	Jap Allen	1928–31
*	Tommy Douglas	1930–50 †
{ *	Thamon Hayes	1931–33
{	Harlan Leonard	1934–36; 1937–45
	Jay Mc Shann	1938–44; 1945–50s

Arkansas

Original Yellow Jackets	1932?–38?
Three-Fifteen and His Squares	1937
Fats Smith and His Rhythm Kings	1937

Omaha

	Red Perkins and His Dixie Ramblers	1923–41
	Hunter's Serenaders	1923–42
(*)	Nat Towles	1936–50 ††

Milwaukee

*	Eli Rice	1925–38
	Grant Moore	1926–38?

Indiana/Ohio

*	Speed Webb and His Hoosier Melody Lads	1925–38
	Zack Whyte	1924–late 1930s
*	Frank Terry	1925?–39

St. Louis

	Charlie Creath	1921–28
	Dewey Jackson	1932–1934
⎧	Wilson Robinson	1924–25
⎨	Cotton Club Orchestra	1925–28
⎩	The Missourians	1928–30 †††
⎧	Oliver Cobb	1928?–31
⎨	Eddie Johnson's Crackerjacks	1932–1934
	Winfield Baker's Crackerjacks	1934–35
⎩	Original St. Louis Crackerjacks	1935–38
	Jeters-Pillars Club Plantation Orchestra	1933–46

† Tommy Douglas led only small groups since the 1950s and died in 1965.
†† Nat Towles never recorded under his own name, but a majority of his band made four outstanding recordings in 1940 under Horace Henderson's titular leadership (see below, later this chapter).
††† The Missourians in 1930 came under the leadership of Cab Calloway and remained headquartered in New York.

Some of the best of these Midwest orchestras have either already been discussed in *Early Jazz* or did not record, thus leaving no hard analyzable evidence. Considering the favorable geographic location and venerable pre-jazz history of St. Louis, it is surprising that so little jazz of important quality developed there. The center of ragtime around the turn of the century and well into the second decade, St. Louis had the further advantage of being located on the Mississippi, halfway between New Orleans and Chicago. It became an important way-station on the trek north in the post-World War I migration of blacks to the northern industrial centers, soon followed by musicians seeking better employment in the new, fast-growing, black urban communities of the North. But curiously, except for the Missourians, a St. Louis-based orchestra that had made it big in New York by the mid-twenties, the "gateway to the West" did not produce a noteworthy orchestral tradition, as for example other major cities, including even Los Angeles and Dallas, did. What St. Louis *did* produce was a major school of trumpet players which early on, inspired by King Oliver's recordings, experimented with various techniques and mutes (including the lowly bathroom plunger), soon to be tagged by musicians as the "freak style." The early St. Louis-born-and-bred trumpet stars are legion, beginning with Charlie Creath, Dewey Jackson, Leonard Davis, Roger Dickerson, Oliver Cobb, Irving Randolph, Joe Thomas, Bob Shoffner and Harold Baker. One can account for this concentration of trumpet talent by the coming together of several compelling influences: on the one hand the spell cast by King Oliver's playing in the teens and early 1920s; on the other the chance presence in the St. Louis area of several highly talented black teachers and band directors, Major McElroy and Professor P. B. Lankford. Most of the above-named were their pupils. In addition there flourished in St. Louis and environs a brass band tradition, resulting from a high concentration of German emigrants to the area in the latter half of the nineteenth century, many of whom avocationally played in brass bands (and singing societies).

The Missourians, with their roustabout, rough and ready blues, and "Tiger Rag" style (see the Cab Calloway chapter) were a potent example of how this brass tradition—it included, of course, strong trombonists and tubists—manifested itself in black popular terms. Trumpeter Oliver Cobb (discussed in *Early Jazz*) was a charter member of this brass fraternity. Aside from the two boisterous band sides he recorded in 1929—both with risqué double-entendre lyrics typical of the period, and an example of what record companies often preferred in the way of novelty repertory—Cobb was accorded (for black instrumentalists) a rare opportunity of recording an extended solo on 78 records, in his case even two sides. Cobb's nine-minute *Cornet Pleading Blues* is a combination of simple but expressive cornet-blues-playing, strongly influenced by Louis Armstrong, alternating with lusty, growly blues-shouting (almost to the point of textual incoherence), again deeply indebted to Armstrong's vocalisms.

Cobb died in a drowning accident in 1931. His orchestra was taken over by pianist Eddie Johnson and, as the chart in Figure 2 shows, continued in two further incarnations until, as the Original St. Louis Crackerjacks, it disbanded in 1938. Although Johnson had brought in the eighteen-year-old trumpeter Harold Baker, already a fine soloist in the Armstrong manner, for the 1932 record date, the Crackerjacks never developed any clear orchestral identity under any of their three leaders. Baker was with the band only briefly, then he joined Don Redman in the mid-thirties and, of course, later Duke Ellington. The 1936 recordings by the Original St. Louis Crackerjacks, despite an occasional creditable solo, suffer from a thumpy, heavy-footed rhythm, ragged overbearing ensembles, and at times terrible intonation—not to mention some nauseating vocals. It may be unfair to judge this St. Louis band by its one day in the recording studio, but on the other hand there is no other evidence to indicate that it was more than a well-intentioned minor-league ensemble. It did not survive the Swing Era.

Probably the best and liveliest of the early St. Louis bands was Charlie Creath's Jazz-O-Maniacs. The leader was a strong, versatile trumpeter, equipped with a warm, powerfully expressive tone, skilled in the "freak" mute styles as well as collective improvisation and the blues. Judging by the twelve sides it recorded between late 1924 and mid-1927, the band played in a virile, blues-based, deeply felt style that must have been quite overpowering in person. During the period it recorded it was stylistically in a transition phase, caught halfway between New Orleans collective jazz and a more modern solo-oriented arranged style, leaning perhaps slightly more to the former. In its uncompromising way it did justice to both stylistic lineages. Except for *Way Down in Lover's Lane*, a sobbingly sentimental torch song, the Jazz-O-Maniacs' recordings are pure hard-driving, elemental jazz, with Creath clearly the main galvanizing force. But the band was strong in all departments. Thornton Blue was a vigorous, technically fluent clarinet soloist who could play intricate obbligatos or ride in high wails over the band in a collective final chorus. Trombonist Sonny Lee, while the author of an infamously slavering solo on *Way Down*, could also pump up any collective ensemble with his vigorous, unabashed hot style (hear him in the last chorus of the 1925 *Grandpa's Spells*).[9] Cranston Hamilton, a virtually unremembered pianist, had a formidable, clean technique and a remarkable ear for advanced harmonic accompaniments, even in blues songs (hear him on *Cold in Hand* behind Campbell). Pete Patterson, the banjoist, must have been one of the best, judging by the aural evidence of these recordings, playing with a wonderfully swinging, rocking, steady rolling beat. At first the Jazz-o-Maniacs lacked a bass, either string or brass, which gave the band a slight registral top-heaviness. But that problem was more than remedied when a tuba player named Cecil White joined the band in 1926, a player with a huge bursting tone, clean attack, and a marvelous sense of rhythmic momentum. Listen to his spectacular work on *Crazy Quilt*.

Still, Creath must have been the star of the band, as leader, lead trumpet, and all-around soloist. He is best heard on the early *Pleasure Mad*, the 1925 *King Porter Stomp*, *My Daddy Rocks Me*, *Grandpa's Spells* and *Butter Finger Blues*.[10]

Tuberculosis forced Creath to retire from trumpet playing in the late 1920s. He turned to the accordion and the saxophone, but was often inactive musically, until his death in 1951 after a prolonged final illness.

Trumpeter Dewey Jackson became St. Louis's leading player after Creath's semi-retirement, not only continuing Creath's tradition but taking on some of his players (like clarinetist Thornton Blue and drummer-singer Floyd Campbell). The four sides Jackson recorded in St. Louis on June 21, 1926, are quite representative of Jackson's Peacock Orchestra, which worked on the riverboat S.S. *Capitol*, hence *Capitol Blues*, their finest performance featuring excellent expressive Jackson and Blue. The ten-piece band featured, besides these, two other fine players like New Orleans bassist Pops Foster (mostly on tuba here) and a

---

9. One of several interesting curiosities regarding the black Creath band is that it recorded with the *white* trombonist Sonny Lee, who performed otherwise with the legendary Peck Kelley as well as Isham Jones, Charlie Barnet, Bunny Berigan, and Artie Shaw. Another even more fascinating discovery is the voice of Floyd Campbell, Creath's regular drummer. Campbell was, by the evidence of his several vocals (*Market Street Blues*, *I Woke Up Cold in Hand*, *Everyman*), not only a superior singer, primarily in the blues idiom, but one who sounds exactly like Jimmy Rushing! One is tempted to think that Rushing must have been influenced by Campbell, the similarity in style, timbre, vocal inflection, and diction being astonishing. (My surmise that the influence went from Campbell to Rushing is based only on the fact that Campbell was two years the elder of Rushing, and Campbell recorded as early as 1924, whereas Rushing's first vocal was in 1929, with Walter Page's Blue Devils. Of course, the reverse could be true since Rushing began singing in the Midwest around 1923–24. But even if one *did* influence the other, it still would not explain the remarkable coincidence of the two singers' almost identical and very unusual high-pitched voice and timbre.)

10. The Jazz-O-Maniacs' repertory was better than most bands. Not only *Market Street Blues* and *Market Street Stomp*, famous St. Louis tunes named after the city's main street, but Jelly Roll Morton's *King Porter Stomp* and *Grandpa's Spells* were an intrinsic part of their programming. Indeed, Creath's band was the *only* band besides Morton's Red Hot Peppers to record *Grandpa's*, one of Morton's finest ragtime pieces, written in 1923. Of the many *King Porter Stomp* recordings, Creath's is one of the very earliest issued, the fifth one in fact. It is ironic that, apart from Morton's own solo recording and his duet with King Oliver, it was two *commercial dance bands* that first took on *King Porter*: Al Turk's Princess Orchestra and the Benson Orchestra of Chicago!

clean-playing reliable pianist, Burroughs Lovingood, as well as trumpeter Albert Snaer, who later became Claude Hopkins's lead trumpet.

Jackson's playing was more ornate than Creath's, and indeed often threatened to become all ornamentation, beginning with an almost disturbingly intense and fast twittery vibrato. But it had that innate singing quality that is a hallmark (by way of New Orleans) of the St. Louis trumpet school and that has, now in retrospect, its own peculiar period charm, so different from Louis Armstrong's broader and more all-embracing conception. Jackson's Peacock Orchestra was perhaps best in its collective ensemble-playing. Here the players hit their full stride, with a grand pendulant swing—the quintessential 1920s New Orleans orchestral style and feeling—and a wonderfully dense and complex polyphonic sonic tapestry (as in *She's Crying for Me* or *Capitol Blues*).

The last and, by all evidence, the least of the St. Louis-based territory bands was the Jeter-Pillars Club Plantation Orchestra. It is a band quite difficult to assess fairly, for it recorded only four sides which, considering their appalling quality, make one hope fervently that these are not representative of their general work. Paradoxically, the orchestra could boast at various times of having in its ranks such outstanding talents as trumpeter Harry Edison, bassist Walter Page (both men later with Basie for many years), also bassist Jimmy Blanton (of Ellington fame), drummers Sid Catlett and Kenny Clarke, guitarist-arranger René Hall, and many fine lesser-known players. Furthermore, both James Jeter and Hayes Pillars had been long-standing members of the great Alphonse Trent orchestra.

But the Jeter-Pillars two recording dates in August 1937 produced nothing even remotely of quality commensurate with such levels of talent. One is reluctant to believe that the dreadful twittery falsetto vocals (in a manner revived some years back by Tiny Tim), Pillars's own lifeless hotel-style tenor, and the band's overall listlessly stiff playing represented its normal standards and capabilities.

There is one other type of territory band, particularly associated with the St. Louis area: the riverboat bands that plied the Mississippi between St. Louis and New Orleans, both on excursions and regularly scheduled runs. The most prominent among leaders of these bands were pianist Fate Marable and trumpeters Charlie Creath and Dewey Jackson. Marable, a Kentuckian from Paducah, began working on the river as early as 1907, and in 1917 was asked by the Streckfuss brothers, owners of the major steamship line in St. Louis, to form a band to tour the river. According to accounts by Marable himself[11] that first band was essentially a ragtime group. But two years later, evidently riding on the incoming tide of interest in jazz as the "new thing"—and a corresponding indifference to ragtime, the "old"—Marable organized a new orchestra, made up entirely of New Orleans musicians. This band, virtually a legend in jazz lore, included Louis Armstrong, Sam Dutrey (clarinet), Johnny St. Cyr (banjo), George "Pops" Foster (bass), Warren "Baby" Dodds (drums), and a mellophonist named Davey Jones (who incidentally was the one who taught Armstrong to read music). Arm-

11. *Downbeat*, June 1938, p. 8; *Jazz Journal*, December 1950, p. 1.

strong played with Marable for nearly three years, from 1918 to 1921, before going to Chicago to play second trumpet for King Oliver.

Joining Marable's band was considered by the New Orleans musicians like "going to the conservatory".[12] Marable was himself a well-trained musician who kept a tight control over his players. Indeed he was chosen by the Streckfuss brothers precisely because he could organize and lead a band that could read arrangements, play in a disciplined, well-rehearsed manner, and in general delight the customers with a basically genteel repertory of waltzes, polkas, tangos, and reels, with just enough "hot" jazz thrown in to keep things novel and exciting.

Marable's was the first band to record when the Okeh Company initially brought its recording equipment to New Orleans (in 1924). By that time Armstrong had been replaced by Sidney Desvignes, and Dodds, St. Cyr, Pops Foster and some of the other New Orleans men had also moved on to Chicago or St. Louis. Saxophonist Walter "Foots" Thomas (later Calloway's chief arranger and baritonist for many years) had joined Marable, as had Zutty Singleton—his first record date—replacing Dodds.

The 1924 personnel reveals that Marable's formerly all-New-Orleans orchestra had now been penetrated by a number of St. Louis musicians. As a consequence Marable's recordings, *Frankie and Johnny* and *Pianoflage*—alas, the only two—represent a classic example of the interpenetration not only of two different regional styles, New Orleans and St. Louis, but also of an early arranged dance-band idiom merged with the swing and lilt and relative freedom of a modified New Orleans style—ultimately a result which conceptually does not sound very different from Henderson's 1924 recordings. Indeed St. Cyr, in his recollections of the early days on the riverboats, pointed out that the Marable band's playing at that time sounded much like the old Fletcher Henderson recording of *Mandy, Make Up Your Mind*. "The ensemble part of this number sounded about like we did."[13] Interestingly enough, *Mandy* was recorded by Henderson several months *after* Marable's date; and indeed Henderson only developed his nine-or ten-piece orchestra in early 1924. There is little likelihood that Marable would have heard such Henderson records by March 1924, learned to imitate them, *and* record them in as fine a form as he did. It is much more likely that Marable's orchestra represents another example of a regional ensemble arriving *independently* at an amalgam of styles which coincidentally sounded like Henderson/Redman's early big-band jazz.

Frankie and *Pianoflage* (Roy Bargy's composition)[14] still exhibit that curious period mixture of straight ragtime and the "jerky" rhythms of early jazz, especially in the saxes. But one can hear through the old acoustic recording that this was a disciplined, well-led band that played consistently with a rhythmic drive

---

12. Quoted by drummer Zutty Singleton in *Hear Me Talkin' to Ya* (New York, 1955), p. 76.

13. *Jazz Journal*, November 1966, pp. 6–7.

14. Roy Bargy, an early pianist/musical director of the much recorded Benson Orchestra, also composed novelty piano pieces in the manner of Zez Confrey (*Pianoflage, Knice and Knifty*). But he is best known for his work in the late twenties with Paul Whiteman and performing the solo part in the first recording of Gershwin's *Concerto in F*.

and energy somewhat akin to swing. The band was hired by the riverboat owners to keep the customers happy and dancing, and one can tell how well they must have succeeded in that, for the music literally leaps out of these ancient acoustic recording grooves.

In Indiana, Speed Webb's Hoosier Melody Lads recorded four sides in 1926, but these were never released. They did perform, however, in a number of MGM films in 1928 during a sojourn in California. A measure of Webb's reputation among musicians and, in all likelihood, a fair indication of the quality of his bands through the years, can be gained from the list of outstanding musicians who at one time or another worked for him: trumpeters Roy Eldridge, Reunald Jones, John Nesbitt; trombonists Vic Dickenson, Gus Wilson; saxophonists Leonard Gay, Joe Eldridge, Jimmy Mundy; and pianist Teddy Wilson. As for its style, the jazz historian Albert McCarthy reports that, according to Teddy Wilson, a man not given to exaggerated claims, Webb's 1931 orchestra was comparable to Count Basie's early band.

Over in Nebraska three rather outstanding orchestras held sway during the period covered in this volume. But again recorded evidence of their work is scant. Hunter's Serenaders recorded in April 1931 (discussed in *Early Jazz*), while Red Perkins's Dixie Ramblers made it into the studios on two successive days a month later. Perkins and his musicians reflect the already mentioned transitional character of some of the territory bands. Perkins was born in 1890 and as a young man played in minstrel shows and worked as a bandmaster, playing on the side in traditional brass bands. By the time the Perkins group, actually an octet, recorded in 1931, it had acquired the ability to play with a peppy hard-driving energy, and it had learned the value of rehearsing to achieve well-drilled ensemble effects. At the same time, vestiges of a rather old-fashioned, straight marching-band idiom survive (for example, on *Hard Times Stomp*). Its stylistic vintage emphasizes on-the-beat playing, with jazzy syncopations coming off quite hard and stiff. *Old Man Blues* is, as might be expected, rather indebted to Ellington's 1930 opus of the same name, although it cannot match it in virtuosity and stylistic integrity. *Minor Blues* features some very fetching lyrical soprano saxophone-playing, which I take to be by Perkins himself and which reveals the unmistakable influence of Sidney Bechet.

One aspect of Perkins's Dixie Ramblers is indeed very unusual, especially for a black group. Three out of the four "horn" men doubled on brass and reeds. Thus, by quick switching of instruments, this little eight-piece band could produce a great variety of instrumental colors, and could as easily deliver a four-man brass section as a saxophone trio. A photograph dating from 1925 shows the group, then only a sextet, with at least fifteen different instruments (not counting various percussion), including a cello, a violin, and a French horn. An even greater oddity is the use on *Hard Times Stomp* of what I assume must be a sopranino clarinet, playing the following altissimo passage:

There can be little doubt that the finest territory band of all, at least since the days of Alphonse Trent, was one led by Nat Towles. Indeed the Towles orchestra by all evidence, limited and circumstantial though it is, must have been in many respects the equal of any orchestra of that time. Its arrangers may have lacked the ultimate creativity of Ellington, but in its performance quality—both in terms of its soloists and its ensemble-playing—I believe it could match the Ellington orchestra in its heyday, surpass Lunceford as well, and considerably outplay the early Basie band.

There is substantial verbal testimony to that effect, not only from musicians like Buddy Tate and trumpeter Harold Johnson but also from the fact that Horace Henderson took over four-fifths of the Towles band for a 1940 recording date. And this provides us with perhaps the most reliable testimony: those recordings, four sides in all.

The reader may well ask, if the Towles orchestra was so outstanding, why did it not record under its own name? Why was it not brought to New York, as Andy Kirk and Count Basie were, for example? At this late date[15] the full answer to these questions can perhaps never be known. But some of the factors involved seem to have been the following: Towles, who knew he had a great orchestra, (1) was evidently reluctant to leave the Midwest, fearful of losing his best players to the big Eastern name-bands; (2) seems not to have been very interested in national recognition; (3) John Hammond, who "discovered" the Basie and Ernie Fields bands, happened not to have caught up with Towles, although, according to Tate, he was alerted to the existence and remarkable quality of the band; (4) when Hammond got to Kansas City, Basie was in town (also on the radio), while Towles, as luck would have it, was on the road in small Missouri towns (with no radio outlets).

Towles's fear of his orchestra being raided by Eastern bandleaders was born out when Horace Henderson did just that, retaining only three of his own men for the 1940 recordings.[16] The irony, of course, is that, if Henderson had not done so, we would have *no* actual evidence of the Towles band's quality. As it is, the sides recorded in October 1940 give ample proof of the band's high calibre. And although one cannot *automatically* assume that these recorded sides offer the Towles band at its most representative, it is even harder to imagine that music-making of such a high order would have occurred only once on one day

15. Nat Towles died in 1963. Born in New Orleans in 1905, he took up the string bass as a teenager after studying guitar and violin. (Unusual is the fact that Towles never played the tuba, but this must be seen in the light of the fact that the tuba as a bass instrument was not nearly as popular in New Orleans as elsewhere.) Towles, after working with a variety of groups in New Orleans and the Southwest, spent the early 1930s in Jackson, Mississippi, and moved on to Dallas in 1935. In 1936 he moved to Omaha, which then became the center of his operations, and brought with him the nucleus of a college band he had taken over earlier in Austin, Texas.

His orchestra's most successful years, artistically and financially, were from the late 1930s to the mid-1940s. In 1950 Towles was forced to give up his big band, and nine years later he retired from music.

16. Not only did Horace "borrow" the Towles band for the October 1940 recording date, he actually appropriated it and led it until the end of that year.

in October 1940. This kind of ensemble-playing, of arranging and integrating solos so successfully within the overall performance—in short, such unity of conception and execution—cannot be achieved overnight, and must have been the result of months and years of hard work, of conscientious rehearsing—and of much collective talent.

You Don't Mean Me No Good is exemplary in all respects. A blues arranged by the band's tenor player, Bob Dorsey, the piece offers excellent, stylistically integrated solos, superior ensemble work, and a fetching vocal by drummer Debo Mills. Nat Bates begins and ends the performance with wonderfully lithe swinging trumpet statements, lean and clear in sound in the way that other new trumpet players of the day—Eldridge, Gillespie, McGhee, for example—were also suggesting. C.Q. Price follows with a fluent, somewhat florid alto sax solo which manages to suggest contrast to Bates's solo without disrupting the overall continuity, rhythmic flow, and springy beat. There follows a trombone solo by Archie Brown, I believe, which, though under-recorded by the Okeh engineers, offers abundant evidence that Towles had something quite beyond the typically limited territory band trombone section. (Trombones were generally the weakest area in territory bands.) Indeed, Brown seems to my ears to be not only a master of the plunger "talking" technique developed by "Tricky Sam" Nanton and virtually on a par with the latter, but altogether a remarkably versatile and compleat trombonist. On a casual listening one might assume there to be two trombonists involved in the *You Don't Mean Me No Good* solo, but it is actually one, playing one 12-bar chorus open, the other very tightly muted.

After the vocal by Debo Mills (from Dallas, Texas, and a veteran of the Lloyd Hunter and several other territory bands), delivered in a wonderfully casual mixture of Texas blues-shouting (with a pinch of nasal twang) and the kind of humorous vocals Woody Herman used to do in the late thirties and forties, arranger Dorsey sets up four relentlessly building choruses of full ensembles. Swinging brass block-chords are sustained over a captivatingly simple riff in unison saxophones, the effect being not unlike the final chorus of Ellington's masterful *Ko-Ko*. This kind of layering of texture by dividing brasses and saxes had, of course, been tried hundreds of times by 1940. But what is new here is that a third component—a third layer of counterpoint—is added by drummer Mills. And what is special about that is the way Mills integrates his drum interjections (using the whole drum set) into the prevailing texture and musical structure. Though excitingly rhythmic, the effect is almost melodic: another contrapuntal line added to and meshed with the saxes and brass.[17] Nat Bates closes out the side with his wonderfully understated, plaintive recapitulation of the opening chorus—almost vocal in its effect, and a fine contrast to the preceding rousing full-band ensembles.

17. Debo Mills, as far as I can ascertain, recorded only four times in his entire career—the four Henderson-led Towles sides under discussion here—but from this admittedly limited evidence one would have to assume that he was a first-rate musician, creatively and technically comparable to any of the more famous name-band drummers of the time.

Another quite outstanding side is "Sir" Charles Thompson's *Smooth Sailing*. Thompson was the Towles band's regular pianist and one of its chief arrangers. Since Horace was a pianist and now leading the Towles band, Thompson had to sit out the recording session, but he was asked to contribute on arrangement. *Smooth Sailing* is a youthful effort of the then twenty-two-year-old Thompson, and, although the performance sounds a trifle under-rehearsed in spots, it is nonetheless an impressive achievement. In style a cross between Lunceford and Basie, the score also has a number of modern touches that forecast things to come: the many unharmonized bop-ish unison lines that were so much a staple of the mid-forties, the penchant for a much more linear, melodic conception, and a more economical phrase construction. I believe the trumpet soloist is the equally young Harold "Money" Johnson (in later years a member of Ellington's orchestra), here on his first recording date. If somewhat youthfully brash and unsubtle, Johnson's solo nonetheless shows an already technically assured player, and like Thompson's arrangement of a more modern linear persuasion. Price and tenor-man Dorsey also contribute brief searching, unconventional solos.

Fats Waller's *Ain't Misbehavin'* receives a rather unusual treatment (in an arrangement that I judge to be Horace Henderson's) in that it is done in a lazy slow-ish tempo, almost in the manner of a ballad. Low sombre saxes accompany the two main soloists here: Emmet Berry—in an expansive, expressively wide-ranging improvisation, including a harmonically, for the time quite explorative *a capella* closing cadenza—and Archie Brown, in a delightfully relaxed, drawly solo in muted, slightly buzzy burnt-ochre tones.

The final side, *I'll Always Be in Love with You*, is perhaps the most conventional of the four but still has many felicitous moments, in particular another clear-headed authoritative solo by Berry.

All in all, these Towles/Henderson sides provide a chance glimpse of one of the most remarkable but least celebrated orchestras of the Swing Era. They certainly whet one's appetite to hear the sides Towles is reputed to have recorded in 1943 with a re-assembled big band, but which have, as far as I can ascertain, never been issued.

The Original Yellow Jackets, out of Little Rock, Arkansas, have often been singled out in jazz histories and discographies. However, their importance never carried beyond a local following. Their six issued recorded sides from 1937 present a band whose swing and rhythmic unity was somewhat inconsistent and whose soloists were of average talent. *Cross Street Swing* is perhaps their best recording. It features good ensemble work, a degree of harmonic inventiveness, and rhythmic drive. Whether these recordings are representative of their work is impossible to say with certainty at this late date.

Over in Hot Springs, Arkansas, two quite remarkable small jazz bands were recorded in March 1937 by the American Record Company: Three-Fifteen and His Squares and Fats Smith and His Rhythm Kings.[18] Smith was a singer who

---

18. Most of the seventeen days of ARC Vocalion recording in Hot Springs were devoted to a variety of other popular musics, such as white country, black gospel, blues singers, and a few white dance bands. I have not been able to discover where the Squares and the Rhythm Kings actually came

here delivers two near-novelty songs, *Music Makes Me Feel That Way* and *If I Had You In My Arms*, in a blues-ish, rough-hewn Louis Armstrong manner. What makes the sides interesting, though, from a jazz point of view are the two very capable trumpet soloists and a robust-sounding tenorman (all playing in a simple uncomplicated blues style) and the strong earthy rhythm section. Smith's incessant jive-talking over the soloists' work is annoying and rather mars these sides, but nonetheless they are, I suspect, a representative example of the kind of rustic, unpretentious, still folk-like jazz one could hear in the thirties in some of the more remote territories.

Three-Fifteen and His Squares is an even more interesting blues band, featuring (besides vocalist Dave Blunton) another excellent blues trumpeter, a surprisingly good pianist (in the general florid Kansas City blues style of a Pete Johnson), and a fine unidentified guitarist, weaving deftly placed single-note countermelodies in three-way counterpoint with the trumpet and tenor. And again the bass and drums provide that typical unmistakably stomping, heavy beat that one associates with Texas blues bands.

Of the four sides the Squares recorded on March 2, 1937, *Three-Fifteen Blues* and *Mollie Mae Blues* are played with affection and sensitivity: typical plaintive, tragic, yet unsentimental blues. *Drop My Stuff* is a rousing, swinging number dominated by the band's trumpeter, in a style not unlike Harry Edison's (with Basie), simpler perhaps and less sophisticated, but with a wonderfully fat rich tone. The tenor player also manages several energetically hustling choruses throughout these sides.

Smith's Rhythm Kings and Three-Fifteen may not have been the most sophisticated territory groups, but they worked very well within their limited capacities, and produced an honest, down-to-earth kind of jazz that is still a pleasure to hear.

The greatest concentration of outstanding musical talent was unquestionably centered in Kansas City and environs. As has been often noted, jazz prospered in Kansas City (during the thirties under the permissive political/social climate of the notorious Prendergast regime) to a degree that even New York could almost not match. In any case, bands, orchestras, ensembles of all sizes flourished there in rich abundance, with Count Basie's orchestra being only the most visible and durable of all those spawned there in the late twenties and thirties.

Many of these groups unfortunately did not have a chance to record commercially. Of those that did, not previously discussed in *Early Jazz*, there remain only Harlan Leonard's Rockets and Jay McShann, surely the last of the territory bands (which among other contributions brought the young Charlie Parker to New York). Both were what came to be known as "jump bands," with the emphasis in McShann's group more heavily on the blues, but both orchestras were well ensconced in the mainstream Kansas City tradition.

---

from. Nor do we know any of the personnel of these groups, except the two leader-singers involved. All we know is that they were recorded in Hot Springs because that is where ARC decided to set up its recording sessions, and one assumes from that that the two bands in question were from somewhere in the Arkansas-Northern Texas-Oklahoma territory.

Leonard's Rockets (as the chart in Fig. 2 shows) originally developed out of Thamon Hayes's Kansas City Rockets, which itself was a 1931 offshoot of the Bennie Moten band. When the Hayes Rockets folded in 1936, Leonard a year later took over another reputedly first-rate Kansas City band, founded and led by the fine altoist (and colleague of Charlie Parker) Tommy Douglas.

The name Rockets is catchy enough in its original "explosive" connotation, but it also referred to the group's repertory and style, with a strong emphasis on a southwestern rockin' rhythm, reflected in turn in titles like *Rock and Ride*, *Keep Rockin'*, and *Rockin' with the Rockets*. By the time the Rockets recorded in 1940 they had acquired a number of excellent soloists, most notably Henry Bridges (tenor saxophone), Fred Beckett (trombone), two interesting although not entirely consistent trumpet players, William H. Smith and James Ross, as well as one of the best Kansas City blues-shouters, Ernest Williams. In addition, Leonard drew on a host of good arrangers, among them Jesse Stone, Eddie Durham, Buster Smith and the then twenty-three-year-old Tadd Dameron.

A comparison with the early Count Basie band is perhaps unavoidable— Leonard's Rockets replaced Basie in Kansas City in several important jazz clubs when the latter left for New York. Perhaps the early Rockets were also somewhat looser in their stylistic and rhythmic approach, although Leonard's penchant for a more arranged style would seem to indicate otherwise. And, as is so often claimed by musicians and earlier jazz scholars, many 1930s' bands played in a more unfettered manner when on club or ballroom dates than in the recording studios, where they tended to be more "precise" and arrangement-conscious.

In any event, the evidence of the Rockets' only recordings—made in 1940— reveal an orchestra not so much of outstanding quality or particular identity as one of high musical integrity, unpretentious and uncompromising in its adherence to a certain mainstream Kansas City idiom. Its outstanding soloist certainly was Bridges, energetic and imaginative, in a style that combined essentials of Lester Young and Herschel Evans, the two great rival soloists in the Basie organization. Bridges can be heard to excellent advantage on his solo vehicle, *A la Bridges* (note especially the wonderfully expressive side-ending cadenza), but also on *Take 'Em* (in a Young vein) and *My Gal Sal*. A more *original* soloist in the band was Beckett, who in the 1930s had already evolved a certain linear fluency which presages the kind of bop-ish lines trumpeters and trombonists were to develop into a distinct style some years later.[19] I hear in Beckett's playing the influence of Trummy Young (his agility) and Jack Jenney (his tone and elegance) and both of these players' ease in the high register. But Beckett had an unfortunate tendency to play sharp, which mars some of his work. Still, his solos on *Skee*, *A La Bridges*, *400 Swing* (he ends the side on a beautifully clear ringing high G), and especially on *My Gal Sal*, reveal a player already fully at ease in a newly fluent, advanced style.

Intonation problems seem to have plagued the band fairly consistently—at

19. It is worth noting in this connection that J.J. Johnson, the great "modern jazz" trombonist, when asked who his major influences were, cited (besides Dizzy Gillespie) most prominently Fred Beckett.

least on these recordings—and quite a few sides are marred by out-of-tune section work (a particularly depressing example is Jesse Stone's otherwise wonderfully blues-ish moody *Snaky Feeling*.) There is also a certain ensemble insensitivity, especially in the brass (as, for example, on Buster Smith's arrangement of *Ride My Blues Away*). Fortunately these technical problems do not spill over too often into the work of the two trumpet soloists, Smith and Ross (the latter also one of the band's more effective arrangers). Ross seems the more adventurous of the two (hear him on *Parade of the Stompers* and *Mistreated*), although Smith contributed brilliantly to *Keep Rockin'*. Noteworthy, also, is a chorus of exchanges of "fours" by the two trumpeters, forming a seamless whole which many a single trumpet player would have been hard put to construct so cohesively.

Tadd Dameron's arrangements, in their denser, more chromatic harmonies and occasional fluent unison lines with their "modern" twists and turns, offer hints of his later ground-breaking work for Gillespie.

Harlan Leonard's Rockets, despite a considerable campaign on the part of its bookers (the Music Corporation of America) to promote the band, never really caught on in New York and cannot, in retrospect, be considered on a par with the major black orchestras of the time. But undoubtedly they were more appreciated in their home environs, and in any case offer us an example of the type of creditable jazz many of the non-eastern bands could deliver. Leonard disbanded in 1945 in Los Angeles and left music, eventually ending up in the employ of the Internal Revenue Service there.

Jay McShann's band, founded in 1938, was a latecomer as territory bands go. But it quickly became the most successful group in the Kansas City area, particularly as its only potential rivals, Basie's band and Leonard's Rockets, had already left for the East by then. McShann himself was (still is) an outstanding pianist, technically adept beyond the level of most of his contemporaries (with the exception of Hines, Wilson, Tatum, and Cole), who had earlier created a considerable local reputation as a solo and trio pianist. His style was greatly inspired by Hines—which is to say a full two-handed piano style, jumping octaves, dazzling runs, and left-hand punctuations—which, however, also managed to incorporate in a very personal way the blues and boogie-woogie tradition, so widespread in Kansas City in those days. His was a remarkable stylistic amalgam, which, when not reduced to its lowest rhythm-and-blues common denominator (as in McShann's later years), could be refreshingly original.

McShann also drew on the wide assortment of instrumental talent available in Kansas City, featuring at various times trumpeter Orville Minor, tenor Bob Mabane, drummer Gus Johnson, blues-shouter Walter Brown, and two outstanding altoists, John Jackson and Charlie Parker.

Although the band did not record commercially until April 1941 (in Dallas, Texas) that session caught the group more or less at its peak. But some slightly earlier broadcast transcriptions of members of McShann's band (fortunately including Parker), recorded in late 1940 in Wichita, Kansas, were released in the late 1970s on LP (Onyx 221). These are indeed the earliest performances by

Parker captured by recording equipment. They present unequivocal evidence of the originality and uniqueness of Parker's work, both in conception and execution, at a time when he was barely twenty. Indeed, one hears in Parker's playing on these transcriptions an authoritativeness and creative self-assurance which have nothing tentative or merely exploratory about them. This can only mean that Parker had reached an analogous level of stylistic individuality some considerable time earlier, I would guess no later than 1939. In that year Parker first visited New York and began experimenting in jam sessions with harmonic/melodic substitutions and a more advanced chromatic as well as rhythmic language.

These transcriptions also offer considerable evidence that Parker was well in advance of Gillespie as regards musical consistency, technical poise, and cohesiveness of conception—even though Gillespie was three years his senior. Parker was, of course, himself not yet entirely consistent in his execution nor fully in command of his ideas. But the newness and freshness of conception are indisputably in evidence. Nothing quite like it had ever been heard before on the saxophone, and for that matter, in jazz. Hear especially Parker's solo on *Honeysuckle Rose* and *Moten Swing* on the Wichita transcriptions; then think across the 1940 performing spectrum and see if you can find anything even remotely as fresh, daring, *and* substantial as Parker's playing. It is, in fact, remarkable in retrospect that, given Parker's precocious originality, virtually nobody took notice of him until years later, say, in 1945. Certainly Parker's solos on the McShann records were ignored by the critics or rejected in incomprehension, while his playing at Monroe's and Minton's in Harlem in 1942 was appreciated by only a small minority of admirers, including an occasional major visitor like Ben Webster. But I suspect that even these adherents stood before Parker's youthful art somewhat uncomprehendingly.

By the time of its 1941 commercial recordings, the McShann band had developed a clear stylistic identity, playing mostly blues, with a firm yet relaxed swinging style in simple, effective arrangements that gave ample room to the major soloists as well as, of course, Walter Brown. The 1941 arrangements were by William Scott, a tenor player with McShann, who at the time of the Dallas date was on leave with the U.S. Army. *Dexter Blues* is a Scott composition dedicated to Dave Dexter, who, as a *Downbeat* magazine editor, had done much to make the jazz world aware of Kansas City and McShann in particular. It features excellent growl trumpet by Orville Minor in the Cootie Williams manner, as well as a superbly expressive blues chorus by John Jackson. Because Jackson's section mate, Parker, was soon to make history—albeit Bird's work on the McShann recordings went virtually unnoticed, garnering only confused apathy at the time—Jackson's contribution to the McShann band has been, even in retrospect, sorely neglected. He was, to begin with, a remarkable lead alto who through his warm, intense, flowing sound gave McShann's saxophone section a coloration all its own. Second, *Dexter Blues*, one of his only two solos on the McShann dates, shows he was a far from ordinary soloist. It is a beautifully constructed statement, concise yet highly expressive, beyond mere technique, delivered in a rich pure tone that has in it the "wail and cry of the blues." Listen to his high F in the ninth bar of his all-too-brief solo and you will hear the essence of South/Midwest blues: that basically vocal tradition translated here into the instrumental realm.[20]

By comparison the younger Parker, still only twenty, seems a little uncertain of his ideas, especially at the end of his solo on *Swingmatism*, where he is stymied by the somewhat ambiguous and admittedly ill-advised diminished chord—although he fares much better on Hootie Blues. Parker is more self-assured on the next recording date a year later in mid-1942 (*Jumpin' Blues, Lonely Boy Blues, Sepian Bounce*). Although the "cool" timbre and linearization of musical ideas of Lester Young are clearly the base of his inspiration, he is also beginning to be very much his own man. *Lonely Boy* has the most traditional of the three Parker solos, plaintively expressive, holding close to the basic blues form. His three 4-bar phrases, all anchored to a high G♭ as their "head-note", clearly exploit the full blue-note potential, harmonically and melodically: in the key of E♭ the minor third, in A♭ the minor seventh, in B♭ the minor sixth (or enharmonically the augmented fifth) (Ex. 2).

 Ex. 2

Parker's *Jumpin' Blues* and *Sepian Bounce* solos are in a more modern vein, though very much out of Prez, His playing here is already all of a single concept: the leaner yet expressive tone, the reduced vibrato, the smoother melodic lines, the light airy ornamentations, the subtler rhythmic inflections—all coalesce into a new language different from anything ever heard before in jazz.[21]

The quality of McShann's own playing can be well assessed on several sides, including *Swingmatism* and *Sepian Bounce*. Although in a simplified Hines style, these performances retain some of the bite and drive of Hines' right hand, the rhythmic/harmonic invention of his left, all—as noted—united in a distinctive, playful, bluesish manner.

That the McShann orchestra could swing with the best of them (meaning, for example, Basie in that department) is clearly demonstrated on the 1942 sides, much aided and abetted here by Archie Hall's well-crafted arrangements. But by December 1943, in its next and last record date, the McShann band had lost some of its original character. It had also lost Charlie Parker.[22] Although the

20. Little is known about Jackson and his later career, the standard reference books taking no notice of him.
21. Dizzy Gillespie, in effect, met Parker musically through the latter's *Sepian Bounce*. Both musicians were at the time (early 1943) in Earl Hines's orchestra, but oddly enough did not particularly relate to each other. Trumpeter Benny Harris, also in the band, had transcribed Parker's *Sepian* solo and one night played it on trumpet for Gillespie, who, very impressed, listened to Parker thereafter with a new respect and affinity.
22. The recently issued so-called Red Cross recordings (on Stash St-260), privately recorded in a Chicago hotel room in 1943 with Parker on tenor, are an astonishing revelation. For here we have unequivocal proof that, only seven months after his last McShann recordings, Parker had completed the transition from Lester Young and Buster Smith (and even some latent influences of Coleman

orchestra was now expanded to 16 players, the seven-man brass section tended to have intonation and balance problems, Hall's arrangements had become more formularized, and the band's swing had become somewhat listless. Above all, it had lost its special Kansas City sound, undoubtedly due to the influx of Chicago- and New York-based musicians who replaced the band's original Kansians as the wartime draft began to take its toll. McShann is still active today, but since the mid-40s he has been leading small groups, mostly in a rhythm-and-blues format.

For a brief moment of history McShann and his orchestra, with the fortuitous momentary presence of Charlie Parker, represented an eloquent form of blues- oriented jazz, a fitting flourishing of the territory band tradition.

One of the most remarkable and moving recorded performances in all of jazz is *Piney Brown Blues* by Joe Turner and His Fly Cats, recorded in New York, November 11, 1940. The band is hard to classify, being neither a genuine small group—it was rather, like so many Kansas City bands, a small big band, in this case built around the duo team of pianist Pete Johnson and blues-shouter Joe Turner—nor a true territory band, for it rarely traveled and was in more or less permanent residence in Kansas City during much of the thirties (although it recorded exclusively in New York). Its nebulous classification notwithstanding, *Piney Brown* is here singled out as a uniquely memorable performance of ex- traordinary expressive power. Performed by a sextet (counting singer Joe Turner, known as "The Boss of the Blues"), *Piney Brown* is a blues dedicated to the memory of Piney Brown, a Kansas City club owner whose Sunset Café was home to countless jazz musicians and whose generosity and hospitality were legendary throughout the city's black district.

This performance is more than a fine rendition of a popular song; it transcends even the higher forms of standard blues. It is a poignant lament, a heartfelt jeremiad, a profound musical snapshot and document of a man, a time, and a place central to the history of jazz.

It is to know the cry of the blues in all of its pain and anguish to hear Joe Turner's virile voice break with sorrow at the death of his departed friend: "I dreamed I was standing on 18th and Vine; I shook hands with Piney Brown, and I could hardly keep from cryin'." Turner in his narrative blues had a re- markable ability to inject emotion and drama into his singing—what a great operatic baritone he could have been!—and nowhere is his singing more moving and expressive than on *Piney Brown*. The effect, however, is made even more overwhelming by Pete Johnson's astonishing piano embellishments and "Hot Lips" Page's muted trumpet obbligatos. The two instrumentalists create a con- stant counterpoint of secondary supportive ideas that pushes the music to the bearable limits of expression. Johnson's dense web of blue-note tremolos, trills, and runs, mostly in sixty-fourth notes, underscores the urgency of Turner's sing-

---

Hawkins) to his own full-blown distinctive idiom. These performances will require much further study to unravel the complex mix of past influences (especially Young on *Sweet Georgia Brown*, but also Hawkins on *Embraceable You*) hovering just beneath the surface of his now firmly asserted personal language, proffering a new speed (of mind and fingers) and a previously unheard of tech- nical command of the instrument.

ing and forms a kind of parallel commentary of musical tones to Turner's words. All this is fittingly supported by Abe Bolar and A.G. Godley, bass and drums respectively, one of the best rhythm teams in Kansas City. The same group, enlarged by three saxophonists—Don Stovall, Eddie Barefield, and Don Byas, but without Turner—also recorded *627 Stomp*, named after the Kansas City musicians local. A sturdy but unremarkable riff tune, the performance is noteworthy only for a brief solo by Stovall and the rhythm section's good swing.

Much more interesting are four sides recorded a year and a half earlier under Pete Johnson's leadership (as by his Boogie Woogie Boys), with blues vocals by Joe Turner. The outstanding sides here are *Cherry Red* and *Baby, Look at You*, both featuring beautiful and prophetic solos by Buster Smith. Smith's influence on Charlie Parker is clearly discernible here, not only in the warmth and depth of tone but in the choice of notes, clean fluent lines, and easy swing. Especially characteristic and "modern" are the sleek downward runs in *Baby* (Ex. 3) and the bold gestures in bar 5 and 6 of Buster's chorus on *Cherry* (Ex. 4).

Ex. 3

Ex. 4

Baby features fleeter-than-usual, almost elegant, finely swinging boogie-woogie piano by Johnson, while Page contributes a searingly "hot-lipped" growly solo on *Cherry*. And once again bassist Abe Bolar, this time in the company of drummer Eddie Dougherty, is superb in his earthy swing and economically constructed walking bass lines on *Cherry*. Bolar's playing here is as perfect a demonstration of the feel and meaning of Kansas City swing as one can ever hope to hear.

Some of the most distinctive and exciting territory bands were those that roamed the great Southwest—Texas, Oklahoma, New Mexico. And for some reason San Antonio was home base for quite a number of fine groups, among them Troy Floyd,[23] Don Albert, Boots and his Buddies, Joe Kennedy, and banjoist John Henry Braggs (or Briggs). The earliest San Antonio bands were those of Troy Floyd and Fatty Martin. Martin's ten-piece orchestra recorded in 1925 in Houston in a bracing style that was an odd mixture of two major popular, lingering influences of the time: the Original Dixieland Jazz Band and King Oliver's Creole Jazz Band. Trumpet duets à la Oliver, slap-tongue saxophones, and a typical peppy fast dance music all merge together in innocent confusion.

Like Terrence Holder, Don Albert was an outstanding trumpet player, and from 1926 to 1929, although a mere teenager, a leading member of Troy Floyd's orchestra. He formed his own band in New Orleans in late 1929, consisting mainly of younger New Orleanians. Don Albert and His Ten Pals (as the band was first known) played in a polyphonic collective improvisation style, probably not too dissimilar from Sam Morgan's fine New Orleans orchestra.[24] Albert resettled in San Antonio and his band became, with the breakup of Floyd's orchestra in 1932, the leading musical organization in that city. He eventually recorded eight sides for the Vocalion label in late 1936, by which time the band, now known somewhat pretentiously as "Don Albert and His Music, America's Greatest Swing Band" (and with that the first band to use the word "swing" in its name), had long ago dropped its New Orleans heritage and had turned into a rather coarse, hard-swinging outfit, typical of mid-1930s Texas provincial jazz. The arrangements, mostly by pianist Lloyd Glenn, were often cluttered and played in a heavy, chunkily swinging manner. The band also had serious intonation problems (for example on *Rockin' and Swingin'* and *On the Sunny Side of the Street*). Occasionally its soloists—trumpeters Billy Douglas and Alvin Alcorn, trombonist James "Geechy" Robinson, clarinetist Louis Cottrell (later active with New Orleans revival groups), altoist Harold "Dink" Taylor, baritonist Herb Hall (brother of Ed Hall)—were able partially to redeem a given side by spirited solo contributions (especially the energetic Douglas). But even then such isolated forays were derivative of some already previously established style (Douglas of

---

23. Troy Floyd's recordings were discussed in *Early Jazz*, pp. 291–93.
24. See *Early Jazz*, pp. 75–77.

Armstrong, Taylor of Hodges, etc.). Similarly, while the Albert band had no really distinctive style of its own, on two of its eight sides, *Deep Blue Melody* and *Rockin' and Swingin'*, it went all out to emulate Ellington, even—one would have to add—in a near-plagiaristic fashion. *Melody* is much beholden to Ellington's *Black Beauty*, while *Rockin'* is thematically indebted to *Rockin' in Rhythm*.

Around the time Troy Floyd's band broke up and Don Albert's orchestra was more and more on the road, the field was left open for another San Antonio band, known as Boots and His Buddies, led by drummer Clifford "Boots" Douglas, and for a while one of the best of all the southwestern territory bands in the 1930s. The qualification "for a while" stems from the fact that the band deteriorated badly over the years that it recorded (1935–38), and ultimately left a very mixed impression, its poorest sides being shockingly bad.[25]

In its best days Boots and His Buddies played in a manner at once disciplined and excitingly uninhibited. A certain earthy southwestern roughness was also part of their style, whether by default or intent, who can say? Douglas seems to have been a very capable drummer who, at his best—a kind of western Chick Webb—musically carried and drove the band, generating good swing and hard-edged balanced ensembles. But it is therefore all the more disheartening to hear his rhythmically listless work on some recordings—*The Vamp, Sleepy Gal, Coquette*, even *Blues of Avalon*, not to mention the later ones like *The Raggle Taggle, Lonely Moments, Lonesome Road Stomp*. It is as if he were *following* the band rather than *leading* it. At such times the Boots band reminds one of a middling baseball team with one or two star players but otherwise average players and a mediocre manager. While Douglas, as chief arranger and leader, must have seen to it initially that such matters as intonation, orchestral balance, rhythmic ensemble were well attended to, the recorded evidence of the later sessions,

25. Studying the recorded output of Boots and His Buddies was a sobering object lesson for me (as jazz researcher and historian) in how drastically one can err in assessing an orchestra's (or a player's) worth if that assessment is based on incomplete evidence. My first very favorable impressions of the Boots band some thirty years ago were based on hearing their 1937 *Blues of Avalon* through the good offices of that foremost Kansas City and Territory Band historian, Frank Driggs (to whom all jazz research in this area is forever indebted).

An even better impression was gained upon hearing a further selection of some of the best (mostly early) Boots sides, such as *Rose Room, Riffs, How Long, Georgia*, and *Ain't Misbehavin'*. Based on those performances, I was ready to conclude that the Boots band was one of the most exciting and spirited of the mid-1930s. It was not until I heard, more recently, their entire recorded output, that I realized that the band made many absolutely atrocious sides and that it had begun to deteriorate badly by 1937 and its recording career terminated in late 1938. Had I rested my evaluation of the band on only those first-heard best sides, I would surely have blundered into a quite faulty assessment of its overall work.

This thought also provides a compelling reminder of the uncertainty and risks involved in evaluating bands (and players) who only recorded once or very rarely—as, for example, the Original St. Louis Crackerjacks or George Lee or Hunter's Serenaders or Walter Page's Blue Devils. Can we be sure—indeed, how can we really know—that their one day in the recording studio accurately represented their work? How can we know whether a band recorded before its prime—or for that matter well after it? How can we know whether the material recorded on a single session was representative of that band's most characteristic work, or whether it was simply what the *recording director* determined would be recorded and released?

revealing glaring deficiencies in those respects, suggests that Douglas—for whatever reasons—seemed no longer to care or was simply unaware of the band's obvious problems. Indeed, the rather horrendous intonation on pieces like *Marie*, *The Weep*, *Lonely Moments*, and *Chubby* is hard to explain on any terms except perhaps a complete demoralization of the entire band. (I can think of no other example of an orchestra with the high potential of Boots and His Buddies playing so poorly on a recording, as on those last-named sides.)[26]

While at its best the Boots band could be a very exciting group, resplendent with a number of outstanding soloists and espousing a relatively sophisticated modern style (as good as that, say, of Andy Kirk or Claude Hopkins), when one listens to all forty-two sides the band recorded between 1935 and 1938, one realizes that it was actually an orchestra that never did find its own style. Indeed, one suspects that the reason for the Bluebird label's unusual generosity in recording the Boots band as voluminously as it did lay in the fact that it was willing to accommodate eclectically to a wide variety of tastes, including the frankly commercial. At its swingingest and jazziest the band showed a strong influence of the Casa Loma band and of the best of Bennie Moten's masterful 1932 recordings *(Toby, Prince of Wails)*. And it could transform such stylistic leanings into a fairly personal, regionally slanted expression. But it also was quite amenable to mimicking the sweetest and corniest of white commercial dance bands, as in the exaggeratedly "sweet" *Wild Cherry* (really a take-off on Don Redman's popular *Cherry*), or on *Marie*, here imitating the Doc Wheeler Sunset Orchestra's *Marie* (a year *before* Tommy Dorsey stole it from the latter and had an enormous popular hit with it). On *Coquette* we are given Hal Kemp's muted clipped-note brass style, and on *Swanee River Blues* we are treated to the full-blown Lombardo sax-section sound, while, finally, *Careless Love* parades ineptly as a Dixieland number (presumably trying to cash in on the Bob Crosby band's big successes).

Boots's wide-ranging eclecticism asserted itself in another interesting—and rather annoying—manifestation: the band recorded a dozen or so pieces under false titles, presumably to avoid paying royalties. Apart from the aforementioned *Wild Cherry* (which was the band's theme song), *San Antonio Tamales* was actually the Brunies brothers' 1925 song hit, *Angry*; *The Weep* was really Ann Ronnell's *Willow Weep for Me*; *The Vamp* was Will Hudson's *Nitwit Serenade*; and *The Somebody* Gershwin's *Somebody Loves Me* (to mention only a few).

But with all this, at times there was a certain class in this band when left to its own best intentions. Even if the players didn't manage consistently to achieve their best on records, one can hear that they knew what that "best" was. They achieved it most naturally through their leading soloists: tenor saxophonist Baker Millian, trumpeters Charles Anderson and L.D. Harris, and altoist Alva Brooks. Millian was certainly an impressive if not entirely consistent soloist in the grand, full-toned, energetic southwestern tradition, offering a personal but somewhat

26. It may also be significant that not once in the forty-two recorded sides did the recording director allow the Boots band to try more than one take per side, so he was obviously trying to cram as much recorded material, regardless of quality, onto wax during his rare visits to San Antonio.

cooler blend of Herschel Evans and Coleman Hawkins (later the influence of Lester Young also became discernible). Millian can be heard to excellent advantage on *The Goo, The Sad, Rose Room,* and *Blues of Avalon.*

Perhaps even more remarkable, in terms of daring and originality, were the band's two trumpet soloists, Anderson and Harris. The former can be heard in remarkably advanced solos on *The Goo* (see Ex. 5), *Riffs,* and *Rhythmic Rhapsody.* Technically clean, tonally lithe, secure and cohesive in execution, Ander-

Ex. 5

son played with a modern feel very much akin to the young Roy Eldridge and (even younger) Dizzy Gillespie of those years. The point is that Anderson was *not necessarily* following Eldridge's lead, since he was recording with Boots's Buddies around the same time Eldridge was making *his* first recordings, and had been playing with Douglas's band since around 1934.[27]

Another fine trumpet display occurs on *Ain't Misbehavin'* in a rambunctious exchange of "eights" between Harris and Anderson. Equally impressive is Harris's full 32-bar chorus on *The Sad,* unusual not only for sounding like Rex Stewart in his distinctive late thirties–early 1940s' Ellington style but for its astonishingly poised and modern double-time approach. Harris improvises in sixteenths virtually throughout (see Ex. 6), however, not as ornaments or passing tones on the underlying slow-ballad quarter-note beats, but as "eighth notes" in an implied, fast doubled-up tempo, in other words two rhythmic levels up from the base tempo.

27. There is a strong similarity in general character, newness of style, and tonal conception between a player like Anderson and Towles's Nat Bates, for example. It suggests that the best of these young territory trumpeters were as influenced and competitively inspired by *each other* as they were by the more famous Eastern soloists.

Ex. 6

Another aspect of the Boots band's versatility when playing well was its fine ensemble sense, especially in the saxophone section—with the exceptions as previously noted—generally supported and inspired by Douglas's hard-driving, controlling, tasteful drumming. Finally, one should mention A.J. Johnson, a better than average band-pianist, playing in an updated stride style. His solos, more than the usual wandering anonymous fill-ins, were cleanly structured, individual musical statements that led cohesively to the next ensemble or solo—perhaps a modest accomplishment when measured against the Wilsons and Tatums of the era, but rare enough in the world of 1930s' big bands. Johnson seems even to have been sensitive to the compositions' and arrangements' character, for he intelligently picked up in his solos from the previous chorus and then developed his own solo and passed it back to the band. In this way his solos were never an interruption, an intrusion, but rather they furthered the basic continuity and thematic flow of the piece.

In 1929 Sunny Clapp and his Band O' Sunshine, a white band, recorded several sides in San Antonio. It generally provided comfortable two-beat dance music with an occasional foray into jazz. Its clarinetist Sidney Arodin (later with Louis Prima and Wingy Manone) could weave a fine obbligato around any soloist, vocal or instrumental, and was himself a capable soloist. Tom Howell was a more than average trumpeter in what would now be called a Dixieland style, then, in 1929, of course, relatively new. *Very* new is the startlingly modern, "atonal" clustery introduction to *Bundle of Southern Sunshine* (Ex. 7). Odd, too, that the band sported a frequently featured bass saxophone soloist (could this have been Arodin?), whose lumbering, even oafish solos add a strange, inadvertently droll element to these performances.

Ex. 7

The last San Antonio band to be organized and recorded in the mid-1930s was John Henry Bragg (or Briggs) and His Rhythm Five. Judging by the four sides it recorded, it was a lively hard-swinging group in the western idiom. As a quintet consisting of an alto and four rhythm—its personnel is not known, although Bragg surely is the banjoist—the group had no need for arrangements. It played in a busy unedited improvisatory manner—hear it on *Ethiopian Stomp* and *Pleading*—featuring an especially fluent and virtuosic pianist (who I suspect is Al Freeman, Don Albert's pianist in the early 1930's).[28]

Over in Dallas, of course, the Alphonse Trent band reigned supreme in the 1920s; and when it went on the road and eventually disbanded, Terrence Holder, like Don Albert, one of the region's star trumpet soloists, became pre-eminent in that city.[29]

One of the very best of the Southwestern territory bands was Ernie Fields's orchestra, which was formed in 1930 and remained active through various transformations well into the 1950s. From their home base of Tulsa, Oklahoma, Fields and his band roamed the entire region of Texas, Oklahoma, Kansas, often foraying north to states like Idaho and the Dakotas. In 1939 Fields was "discovered" by John Hammond, brought to New York—where he recorded nine sides—and was promised a build-up by manager Willard Alexander along the lines the

28. Jack Sharpe's KXYZ Novelty Band (a misnomer, for it was musically more than that) and Joe Kennedy's Orchestra, both from Houston, were among the best of the white territory bands headquartered in that city, although they recorded in San Antonio in 1935. Their prime interest today lies in the playing of the "horn" men: trumpeter Joe Lube, reedman Jimmy Bruton with Kennedy; Kit Reid (trumpet), Joe Barbee (tenor sax) with KXYZ. Especially interesting is Lube (rhymes with "ruby"), whose playing has a remarkable "modern" fluency, particularly when he uses his harmon mute (still rare in solos in those pre-Gillespie days), and whose tendency to feel in double-time rhythms puts him stylistically much closer to bebop than to, say, Armstrong. Unfortunately the rhythm sections of both bands greatly constrict their soloist potential, pounding away insensitively in relentless "oompah" accompaniments.

29. The Trent orchestra was discussed in *Early Jazz*, 299–303. Terrence Holder's band never recorded under Holder's name, but did so years later when it had become Andy Kirk and His Clouds of Joy (see above, Chapter 5, Part 2).

latter had given Basie. But this did not materialize, and, although Fields recorded sporadically on several other occasions in the forties and fifties, his band
never caught on in the big time, and Fields was eventually forced to turn to
rhythm-and-blues.

Some sense of the quality the Fields band had achieved by the late thirties
can be gained from its recordings of 1939. In arrangements by René Hall—like
Eddie Durham a triple-threat trombonist-guitarist-arranger—the band produced
a full rich sound with a wonderfully loose swing, rather like the Basie band. Its
ensemble work was highly disciplined, beautifully balanced. Its soloists, though
not of the first creative rank, were nonetheless imaginative and often inspired
improvisers. Trumpeter Amos Woodruff, for example, took pleasure in crossing
the styles of Cootie Williams and Rex Stewart into a personal amalgam, as tenor
Roy Douglas did with Herschel Evans (his sound) and Lester Young (his notes).
Luther West was a first-rate altoist in the Hodges manner who, as lead alto, also
gave the sax section its warm vibrant cast. Clarence Dixon was a fine, clean
drummer, one of the most experienced of the territory band percussionists.

T-Town Blues and *Lard Stomp* are probably the band's best sides out of the
nine recorded in the fall of 1939. Woodruff and Douglas give a good account of
their work, as does the whole band, leaving little doubt that it was one of the
most poised and professional ensembles to come out of Kansas City. It did not
have the range of first-calibre soloists Basie could draw upon, and perhaps—
partially as a result of that—it relied too much on riffing and riff build-ups for
its structure and continuity. But in terms of its medium-tempo relaxed swing
and, in general, a wonderful sense of rhythmic well-being, the band was hard
to match, let alone beat.

Despite the commonalities among the widely scattered territory bands, there
is one group of bands that stands out as more distinctive and unified in conception and style than any other. That is the collection of bands that ranged through
the Southwest, from Texas to Kansas City (such bands as Trent, Floyd, Moten
and Walter Page.) What makes this region stand apart from the others is that it
was the only one to develop a major original, broad-based (rather than regional)
orchestral concept. Interestingly enough, that concept evolved out of elements
which, with the exception of the New Orleans style, *were entirely indigenous to
the region*. And what bound that style and that region together was the blues.
Whatever individual characteristics a band or group (or player) might possess,
they were invariably founded on the bedrock of the blues: its mood, its tone, its
feeling, its throb, and its rootedness in everyday life. By the time this style was
exported to New York, through Basie, for example, and a little later in a different
guise through Charlie Parker, it was so strong and unique that it could to a large
extent assert itself as a "national" style.

Ironically, in a sense that sounded the death knell of the territory bands. Once
a major regional style had taken on national status and had been redisseminated
to the territories, the need for developing further regional styles seemed to have
passed. This coincided with another development: the increased expansion of

touring by the major bands, many of whom—like Ellington, Lunceford, and Calloway—had not traveled as much in earlier years because they had enjoyed long residencies in either New York or Los Angeles (Hollywood). Once these leading orchestras began to travel extensively, using trains and eventually, in the late thirties, even planes, regularly penetrating the former "territories," the need for local bands was greatly diminished. Moreover, if a person could hear Duke Ellington or Count Basie or Andy Kirk in the local theatre or ballroom, why would he want to hear some lesser (or at least less famous) local band? But while it lasted, the territory band tradition was an important one and in balance, a glorious one.

In retrospect, the regional bands in their heyday served several vital functions, for they offered excellent music to areas where the big name-bands rarely or never penetrated, and provided experience and training for younger musicians in an era when music schools and conservatories were still quite oblivious of jazz. It was an era in which musicians learned their craft on the road, in hundreds of one-nighters, exhausting bus trips, playing in clubs and dance halls, in competitive band battles and after-hours jam sessions. The territory bands were an integral and most important part of the Swing Era—indeed, unique to it. Their demise was a great loss to jazz, and it is not at all clear that their modern-day counterparts—the thousands of university, college, and high school jazz ensembles—play as crucial a role in furthering and developing the music. The best of the territory bands were at the cutting edge of jazz; they were the fertile fields on which new musical seeds could grow. Today's educational counterparts are too rarely in the forefront of jazz, content to purvey the commercial derivatives of jazz and re-creations of the past.

9

Small Groups

In an era when most jazz is performed by small groups, consisting generally of from three to six players, and when the big fifteen-piece orchestras of the Swing Era are but a relic of the distant past, it is hard to realize that small-band jazz—"combo jazz" as it became known in the 1940s—was at one time the exception rather than the rule. When the big swing bands roamed the land, small groups were quite rare and were considered, as in the case of the Goodman Trio, the John Kirby Sextet, or the Nat King Cole Trio, a refreshing novelty. Such groups offered a distinctive type of chamber-music jazz, often in direct reaction to the ever-expanding, louder orchestral forces so overwhelmingly favored in the late Swing Era.

Other small groups existed as well—indeed by the hundreds—but they were small by default rather than by design. These were miniature big-bands in effect, cut to size by economics—especially in the depth of the Depression—or other practical considerations. Their music was orchestral in intent and conception, and though their ensembles may not have numbered more than seven or eight, they tried—and often ingeniously succeeded—in sounding as ample as the bigger bands.

Eventually, of course, by the mid-to-late forties, with the demise of the big bands and the introduction of an entire new language of jazz in the form of bop, the combo became the primary pervasive performing unit, a condition which has not changed significantly to this day.

Historically, of course, jazz started with small groups. In the early years, except for the parade bands of New Orleans and the larger ragtime ensembles of the teens, the latter sometimes expanded to twelve or fifteen players in the richer and larger venues, jazz ensembles rarely exceeded the quintet size. The big orchestras such as Henderson's and Ellington's did not come along until the mid-1920s. Even commercially more successful dance bands, like Paul Whiteman's or Isham Jones's, did not grow to full size until the end of the decade.

The larger the group, the more its music had to be organized or arranged; and so it wasn't until pioneer arrangers like Don Redman, Duke Ellington, Jesse Stone, Bill Challis, Fud Livingston, and Isham Jones had learned how to deal with larger instrumental forces that a real *orchestral* tradition could be launched. The history of the early jazz and dance orchestras is inevitably one of physical expansion, from trios, quartets, and quintets gradually to nine or ten players and eventually, around 1930–31, to fourteen- and fifteen-piece ensembles. Henderson's first real "orchestra" in 1924 numbered only ten players, as did King Oliver's Creole Jazz Band in Chicago in 1926. Even so, these were the exceptions, and the full flowering of what one could accurately call orchestral jazz did not occur until the dawn of the Swing Era in the early 1930s. But, as noted, even some of the small units, though limited in physical numbers, often tried to emulate the orchestral concepts initiated by Henderson or Ellington or Moten—*and* Whiteman.

Before that initial development of large orchestras in the 1920s, jazz was obviously played perforce by very small ensembles, typified by such early groups as the Original Dixieland Jazz Band (a quintet), the New Orleans Rhythm Kings, the Original Memphis Five, the Wolverines, Red Nichols' Five Pennies, and the various other Nichols or Miff Mole-led groups, Joe Venuti's Blue Four and, above all, Louis Armstrong's Hot Five. Armstrong expanded to the Hot Seven in 1927; and, of course Jelly Roll Morton's memorable Red Hot Peppers recordings of 1926 also featured seven players: a "front line" of three horns and a four-man rhythm section. Except for Morton, who *thought orchestrally* (even though his forces were numerically limited), and to some extent the Nichols' Five Pennies, all these small group players used their formats as vehicles for their individual soloistic expression. There was little sense of developing a chamber music (small ensemble conception) per se. The Hot Five and Hot Seven, Venuti's Blue Four, Bix and Tram, the Austin High School Gang, the McKenzie and Condon Chicagoans—all were vehicles for the projection of the solo talents of Armstrong, Hines, Venuti, Lang, Beiderbecke, Trumbauer, McPartland, Teschemacher, Muggsy Spanier, Bud Freeman, and the like. It is worth noting that most of such groups were not permanently organized units but specially convened solely for purposes of recording. Only in the case of Morton's Red Hot Peppers and Nichols's various groups was there any attempt to integrate solo virtuosity into larger compositional (or arranging) frameworks and to assimilate them into a collective performing whole. The best work of the Nichols' Five Pennies and Charleston Chasers, for example, is much more concerned with extending the confines of small-ensemble jazz *qua* chamber jazz than exploiting the solo virtuoso talents—considerable though they were—of the group's individual players.

Unfortunately I neglected to mention the various Red Nichols groups in *Early Jazz*, a fact of which I was rather pointedly apprised by countless admirers of traditional jazz. By way of some amends (although the best work of the Five Pennies, Charleston Chasers, Arkansas Travelers et al. lies outside the time period covered in this volume), I have no hesitancy in suggesting that these groups at their best constituted one of the glories of late 1920s' jazz, and that their recordings—some two to three hundred of them—exerted a tremendous influence in their day, much as the Casa Loma Orchestra did a few years later in the orchestral realm, and aroused as much excitement, especially among musicians as the Goodman Trio and Quartet did in 1935 and the Miles Davis Quintet in 1955–56.

RED NICHOLS

The importance of the Red Nichols group lay not so much in their soloistic capabilities as in their ensemble spirit. Their performances on records were very much a shared collective enterprise: chamber music in the truest sense. Although Nichols and trombonist Miff Mole could be quite outstanding as soloists, they did not make that an issue of their performances, as Louis Armstrong, Jabbo Smith, and Coleman Hawkins, for example, did. In that sense Nichols and Mole retained the true spirit of New Orleans *collective* jazz—at least until the various groups they led ceased to exist, or turned commercial, or converted into big bands (as in the case of Nichols, whose "Five Pennies" had grown to twelve and fifteen by 1929, at one point, with four strings added, even to nineteen). They also exemplified the notion, fast losing ground in the late 1920s, that the ideal jazz could be created only in a small-band context.

What is perhaps most remarkable about the Nichols/Mole-led groups is (a) that, despite the free-wheeling spontaneity they espoused in their recordings, they perfected and maintained a level of ensemble-playing unheard of previously, and (b) that they managed to resist, for a couple of years at least, the pressures to commercialize their music through the intrusion of pop tunes and vocals, which were almost always imposed on jazz groups by profit-minded recording directors. Evidently, Nichols and company had an unusually free hand in their choice of repertory, as a result of which they recorded not only trifles like *The Harbor of My Heart* or *A Cup of Coffee, A Sandwich and You*, but jazz standards like *Davenport Blues, Farewell Blues, After You've Gone, Darktown Strutters' Ball, That's a-Plenty, Ja Da*, and some of the newer jazz instrumentals like *Imagination, Delirium, Feelin' No Pain, Five Pennies*, and Hoagy Carmichael's complex *Washboard Blues*. As for the quality of their ensemble (i.e. chamber) playing, it is truly astonishing for its time. And although the worked-out (or arranged) ensembles are mostly quite sophisticated and technically tricky of execution, there is hardly a performance which is less than faultless.

Wonderful, too, is the variety that these groups packed into their performances—variety in many respects: instrumentational, formal, textural, harmonic, even dynamic. And though their recordings represent a specific and well-defined collective style, *within* that style there is to be found an amazing amount of personal liberty and diversity. This also occurred at the individual level: a player like percussionist Vic Berton, despite his relatively limited set of instruments, seems never to have been at a loss to create such diversity, even while providing a constantly energizing underlying beat.

As noted, the Nichols groups were not bands to which one listened only for their great solo contributions. Indeed, some of these players—Jimmy Dorsey, Eddie Lang, for example—were rather limited as soloists, especially in regard to rhythm and swing. Others, like Pee Wee Russell or Leo McConville, frequent guests of the group, were unpredictable and inconsistent, nonetheless occasionally turning out splendid work. The four mainstays, however—Nichols, Mole, pianist Arthur Schutt, and Berton—were not only astonishingly consistent, considering the staggering number of recordings they produced, but they matched each other in style, in skill levels, in attitude, in energy, and inventiveness. A lot of that was sheer talent, fortuitously matched by happenstance for a few years in one ensemble; the rest was hard work and a love for what they were doing. This unanimity of style and skill ensured both a coherent continuity of solos and a consistency of ensemble, hardly matched in any other small group of the time.

Red Nichols has not been treated kindly in jazz histories. Stigmatized by some as a mere Bix Beiderbecke imitator, and chastised for eventually going the easy-money route (even to the extent of conducting radio commercials for major corporations), his actual contribution to jazz in his heyday has been unjustly minimized and obscured. The profound influence of Beiderbecke on Nichols is, of course, indisputable; but that is not to deny him the ability to forge his own musical personality. Nor should his amazing technical assurance be held against him. His ringing tone and springy, punchy rhythmic drive, both derived from Beiderbecke but then, individualized, provided the stylistic spark plug for his early bands. His succinct, uncomplicated solo style, maintained with remarkable consistency, enhanced the majority of his 1926–28 recordings. He may not have had the soul of Armstrong or Beiderbecke; he may have tried to be too "clever" at times (and some of that was just a healthy sense of humor); he may not have plumbed the depths of music the way Berigan could. But he was a dazzling perfectionist in his way and believed intensely in the intrinsic beauty and validity of improvised jazz—"hot music," as they called it then.

Miff Mole was, if anything, an even more extraordinary musician. A pioneer trombonist who, beginning in 1921 and 1922, set standards of playing for years to come—indeed beyond the ability of many to equal or to accomplish—Mole possessed a technical brilliance and flexibility that remained uniquely his for at least a decade. His range was phenomenal, his slide work impeccably clean, his intonation flawless, his tonguing and rhythm lithe. He made everything sound easy, at a time when most trombonists could barely struggle to play some inane tailgate lick in tune and on time. And, again, the image of a robot-like technical wonder may be raised by such a description. And if he too—like his friend Nichols—lacked the depth of a Jack Teagarden, the soul of a Jimmy Harrison, or the breadth and warmth of a Lawrence Brown, he was nevertheless a complete master of his instrument whose work was marked by taste, a remarkable harmonic ear, and a clearly etched, unmistakable musical personality.

Both Schutt and Berton were eclectically gifted musicians with, again, enormous technical skills and sophistication. Other than the solo pianists like Morton, Johnson, Hines, and Waller, Schutt was one of the very first band pianists to play extended solos in a full two-fisted romping style which managed to merge ragtime, stride, blues, and classical techniques. Berton for his part was a master on all manner of percussion equipment (including the timpani, on which he was fond of playing entire melodies or bass lines). He brought to the Nichols ensembles a fertile imagination and an indefatigable rhythmic energy. There can also be little doubt that Berton's flashy talent allowed for a greater integration of "the drums" into ensemble jazz than had theretofore been possible.

One other musician must be singled out, whose contribution to many Nichols-Mole sessions has never been fully appreciated: Fud Livingston. He not only composed some of the most advanced numbers in the groups' repertories (like *Humpty Dumpty, Imagination, Feelin' No Pain*) but was an astonishingly gifted arranger, an ideal creative partner to Nichols in both extending the ensembles' musical horizons and preserving their chamber-music integrity.

The Nichols and Mole groups, in all their various guises, personnels, and pseudonyms, eventually succumbed to the commercial pressures of the marketplace. But for a few glorious years, they produced a happy, unwaveringly positive, often witty and humor-edged music that, as a coherent unified body of work comprising hundreds of performances, was undoubtedly unique in its time. They strove for and achieved a new kind of ensemble sophistication, developed out of a *collective instinct* rather than a *single composer's imagination*. In that respect they were conservatives, harking back to the rarified beauty of a pure New Orleans ensemble tradition. But in the most important way they were modern men of (or ahead of) their time: although they probably did not think of themselves as "artists," they had created a music that was clearly intended by them not for dancing and casual background entertaining, but for listening.[1]

But the experiments of the Nichols and Red Hot Peppers groups left little

1. The reader will undoubtedly find his own favorites among the many Nichols and Mole-led combos. However, given the bewildering size of their recorded catalogue, I have taken the liberty of listing below in chronological order a relatively small selection of outstanding performances, indicating, where applicable, especially felicitous solo or ensemble or arranging contributions.

Alabama Stomp (Redheads)—Mole, Nichols, ensembles
Buddy's Habits (Five Pennies)—Mole, Berton
After You've Gone (Charleston Chasers)—Nichols, ensemble
Bugle Call Rag (Five Pennies)—Venuti, Berton
Back Beats (Five Pennies)—Lang, Venuti, Berton
Sensation (Arkansas Travelers)—Nichols
Delirium (Charleston Chasers)—Schutt
My Gal Sal (Miff Mole's Little Molers)—Nichols, Mole, Rollini
Honolulu Blues (Miff Mole's Little Molers)—Pee Wee Russell, Nichols
Imagination (Charleston Chasers)—Intro, arrangement (Livingston)
Feelin' No Pain (Charleston Chasers)—Russell, ensemble, trombone-guitar-washboard trio, celesta-guitar duet, two-cornet break
A Good Man Is Hard to Find (Redheads)—Mole
Mississippi Mud (Charleston Chasers)—ensemble, arrangement (Livingston)
Crazy Rhythm (Miff Mole's Little Molers)—Mole, trombone-mellophone duet, ending
That's A Plenty (Miff Mole's Little Molers)—Nichols, Mole, Berton
Moanin' Low (Charleston Chasers)—Eva Taylor
After You've Gone (Miff Mole's Little Molers)—Berton, chromatic breaks, Mole

long-range imprint on chamber jazz developments of the time, their potential impact swept away by the rise of the big bands in the early 1930s. Thus little in the way of significant change or expansion of a true chamber-jazz concept occurred until the arrival of the Goodman Trio. And *its* birth was virtually accidental, the result of an informal get-together one evening at singer Mildred Bailey's home where Goodman and Wilson were by chance invited guests.

The instantaneous success of the Goodman Trio (soon to be expanded to a quartet) had two major consequences: 1) it reaffirmed the viability, both artistically and commercially, of a true chamber-jazz concept, fundamentally different from an orchestral one; and 2) it inaugurated the notion—tried only once before (by Ben's Bad Boys, drawn from the larger Ben Pollack band)—of extracting a small group from a larger orchestra. Within a very short time the "band-within-a-band" idea proliferated throughout the field, spawning Dorsey's Clambake Seven, Bob Crosby's Bob Cats, Shaw's Gramercy Five, Basie's Kansas City Six and Seven, Ellington's various small groups, and more.

Even Armstrong, the most famous soloist fronting a big band, was eventually persuaded to try—in his case it was a return to his New Orleans musical roots— a small-ensemble format in 1940. Many of these small groups were created to serve various secondary functions. For example, Dorsey's Clambake Seven purveyed a more traditional, conservative type of jazz, leaving the parent orchestra to pursue its more commercial swing-oriented goals. In the case of Crosby, the distinctions between his Bob Cats and his big band were fairly blurred, since the latter already evoked the style and spirit of an augmented Dixieland combo, a compromise and concession to both the young swing enthusiasts (the large band) and the traditionalist purists (the small group). Shaw's Gramercy Five arose out of even more conflicting impulses. On the one hand, Shaw, true chamber musician at heart—his first ensemble was a small band containing a string quartet— must have welcomed the opportunity to express himself in a more intimate musical format. On the other hand, there was also the need to try and better his arch rival Goodman in an area where the latter had lately become pre-eminently successful: small group jazz. And, lastly, Shaw had by then already tried every conceivable kind and size of instrumental format. Why not now a five-piece combo—with a *harpsichord*, the ultimate chamber instrument?

Another branch of this chamber trend was the series of small-band explorations—again for recording purposes only—by Teddy Wilson and Billie Holiday, and then Lionel Hampton in the late 1930s. And although they produced much memorable music and espoused to some extent the spontaneous interaction between a select group of players (and one singer) on a more intimate basis than was probable in a large band, they, too, ultimately expressed an orchestral conception in miniature. This was also (and especially) true of the several Ellington small groups, variously led by Hodges, Bigard, Williams, and Stewart: Ellington's orchestra reduced to its inner nucleus. As with the big band, these performances—again for recording purposes only—were mostly dominated by the composer Ellington. The music was arranged and well prepared, and little was left to spontaneous interaction of the players. It was the Ellington band in miniature, which produced, of course, considering the high creative plateau it occupied, a host of superior performances.[2]

JOHN KIRBY

Leaving the Goodman small combos aside, the first two and, in different ways, most provocative Swing Era groups to investigate the small group format for its intrinsic chamber, i.e. non-orchestral potentiality, were the John Kirby Sextet and the Nat "King" Cole Trio. Both ensembles came into existence in 1937 and achieved considerable popular success—Kirby right away, Cole somewhat later but more lastingly. As we shall see, each went rather immediately in quite divergent stylistic directions: the one (Kirby) into a stifling artificiality that soon led completely away from jazz, leaving no trace of its existence; the other (Cole) developing a fresh modern playing (and singing) style, whose influence was enormous and could be felt for years in various pianists and singers.

The Kirby Sextet was born, so to speak, on New York's famed 52nd Street, originally recording under clarinetist Buster Bailey's name and leadership. That early group, a septet—Kirby later reduced it to a sextet by dropping the guitar—comprised an ill-matched group including Frankie Newton (trumpet), Bailey, Pete Brown (alto sax), Don Frye (piano)—ill-matched at least for its avowed musical intentions: a kind of polite, refined, classically biased chamber music that might capture that audience which was put off by the unpredictable spontaneity and alleged "roughness" of most jazz. Newton and Brown were both quite individualistic, spontaneously creative swing musicians, hardly cut out to subject themselves to the kinds of controlled, often non-jazz intentions Bailey and Kirby had in mind. It was not until the greatly gifted, technically very facile Charlie Shavers and the more malleable Russell Procope (who later spent twenty-eight years as Ellington's lead alto) replaced Newton and Brown, that Kirby had found a match for Bailey and thereby a "front-line" of soloists who could fulfill the group's aesthetic goals. Although Kirby would probably never have admitted it, these were, apart from the objectives mentioned above, to capture at least a part of that new audience market that had been created a few years earlier by Raymond Scott's Quintette (note the pretentious spelling), with its classically oriented and cleverly titled novelty repertory.

The titles, in both instances, already tell a good part of the story, although we again have to remind ourselves that titles in jazz, more so then than perhaps now, often had no relationship to the content of the music. So, even though the titles were witty, appealing to a broad popular and generally naive mentality, they in most cases told you nothing about the music. Whereas Scott had his *Reckless Night on Board an Ocean Liner, Dinner Music for a Pack of Hungry*

2. Among the most memorable small-group Ellingtonia are: under Bigard, *Lament for a Lost Love*; under Hodges, *Squatty Roo, Passion Flower, Jitterbug's Lullaby*; under Rex Stewart, *Linger Awhile, Mobile Bay, Subtle Slough*, and, above all, the four sides recorded in Paris in 1939 as Rex Stewart's Big Four (*Solid Rock, Low Cotton*, etc.), discussed in detail later in this chapter.

Cannibals, Bumpy Weather over Newark, Careful Conversation at a Diplomatic Function, and *Siberian Sleigh Ride,* Kirby had his *Rehearsin' for a Nervous Breakdown, Zooming at the Zombie, Beethoven Riffs On, Afternoon in Africa,* and answered Scott's *In an 18th-Century Drawing Room* with Shavers's *In a 20th Century Closet.*

But even leaving aside the zany titles, evoking long dead memories of Zez Confrey and his novelty pieces *(Kitten on the Keys, Greenwich Witch, Parade of the Jumping Beans),* there were severe problems with the music the Kirby group produced, and it is difficult now, more than fifty years later, to imagine what prompted the Sextet's considerable popularity. Undoubtedly much of their repertory was created to wow the tourist customers who flocked to 52nd Street on their one visit to New York, to hear "some o' that crazy new jazz." Little did they know that the Kirby version was hardly jazz at all. But leaving labels aside, it wasn't very good or important music, by whatever name. What is surprising is that, for a while anyway, sophisticated jazz fans and even some musicians took this music seriously. One must assume that a great part of the fascination lay in the well-rehearsed, disciplined playing of the group, especially Shavers's (for the time) rather spectacular technical wizardry on the trumpet.

Shavers was certainly *the* outstanding musician in the group, commanding a virtually flawless technique, unusual speed, and remarkable dynamic control. Indeed, the Kirby Sextet could not have prevailed (after its shaky start with Newton) if Shavers or someone like him hadn't come along. That other "someone" hardly existed, for Shavers represented a brand new breed of trumpet player, in the vanguard technically and conceptually, of which only a handful existed at the time: himself, Gillespie, and perhaps players like Nat Bates and Charles Anderson out in the Midwest. They were all inspired by the breakthroughs in trumpet-playing achieved by Roy Eldridge, but in the case of Shavers there seems also to have been a strong influence of high quality classical trumpet-playing, exemplified by a fine tone, smooth legato, clean tonguing, and an even control of range. Shavers and Gillespie, almost identical in age, had known each other since 1936, when both played in the Frankie Fairfax band of Philadelphia. Gillespie, in fact, admits that there he "learned all of Roy's solos from Charlie."

The similarities in Gillespie's and Shavers's playing, especially technically, are most striking. But whereas Gillespie played with more fire and eventually contributed most significantly to the creation of a whole new jazz idiom, Shavers lacked that creative fire but had, even early on, more control and technical fluency. Though their talents overlapped, Shavers leaned more to the side of execution, while Gillespie veered more to the creative side, bringing the necessary execution along as needed. Another way of articulating the difference between Shavers and Gillespie in the late thirties is to suggest that at that time Gillespie could not have played the Kirby book. He lacked the control and reading skill, and it is hard to think of anyone but Shavers at the time who could have managed the particular virtuoso challenges and finesse required. In the end, however, Shavers's playing was more decorative and technique-oriented than intrinsically expressive. Although he can be regarded in some respects as one of the earliest boppers, his relation to bop lies more in its speed and rhythmic fluency, the technical razzle-dazzle of bop, than in its essence as a melodically/harmonically/rhythmically reconstituted (or in any case much amended) language of jazz.

Shavers's talents lay not only in his trumpet work. He was in effect the chief architect of the Kirby Sextet's style and repertory, composing most of the pieces and doing most of the arranging. Though one may in the end question the quality of this product, there can be no doubt of Shavers's skill. If ultimately his lightweight riff pieces became alarmingly redundant, and his voicings of the three "horns" became completely predictable and routinized, he still showed at age twenty an above average talent in momentarily suggesting a way out from the polyphonic practices of the New Orleans past—espoused by, say, Bob Crosby's bands (small and large)—and the omnipresent call-and-response routines of the Henderson-oriented formulas. Shavers did not foresee that his "neo-classic" approach was bound to lead to an aesthetic dead end. Nor did he sense the new directions in which the jazz language was drifting, to a large extent propelled there by his old friend Dizzy Gillespie. It is significant, too, that Shavers left Kirby in 1944—to join, of all people, his arch rival and far inferior musical *jargonneur*, Raymond Scott.

Shavers was also unquestionably the most compelling soloist in the Kirby Sextet. He considerably outshone and outplayed his colleagues, except perhaps on occasion Billy Kyle, a tastefully swinging pianist whose harmonic adventurousness and relaxed, poised, bouncy individual manner—an attractive amalgam of Hines, Wilson, and Basie—fitted the group's style handsomely. Shavers could be brilliant and exciting, as a sampling of his solos on *Front and Center*, *Tweed Me*, *Fifi's Rhapsody*, *No Blues at All*, and *St. Louis Blues* (take 1) will readily show. By comparison, Bailey and Procope do not come off nearly as well. Bailey was never an imaginative jazz artist, at best a fluent, technically well-equipped functional player. His work always smacked of being worked-out, slightly mechanical, and devoid of the spontaneity one associates with major jazz figures. His solos with Kirby, mostly stiff and rigid in execution, could have been played as well by any gifted and slightly flexible classical player. Procope, too, was never a major soloist, although I find his work with the Kirby Sextet often below his own par, ill at ease or perhaps even stifled by the limited opportunities for extended improvisation. In self-defense Procope often resorted to merely "running the changes," as musicians call it, mostly in arpeggios and other melodic clichés. *It's Only a Paper Moon* and *Tweed Me* show him at his worst, while *St. Louis Blues* and *From A-Flat to C* present him in a much more effective light. Both Bailey and Procope were, of course, excellent readers and had the discipline, still rare in those years, to cope with the intricate and technically sophisticated arranged ensembles in which the Kirby Sextet indulged.

O'Neil Spencer was a good drummer for the group, exhibiting the necessary control and refinement for such chamber-sized ensemble-playing. He often gave the performances a much needed rhythmic buoyancy and variety. Kirby, although the group's titular leader, played in a subdued, polite manner that under-

lined the effeteness of much of the music. His intonation was also often questionable, and his few walking solo choruses (*Paper Moon, No Blues at All* for
example) are sometimes embarrassing. He was also frequently under-recorded,
giving the whole ensemble a bottomless, top-heavy sound with little of the rhythmic drive and lift a strong bass player can give a group. This all in marked
contrast to his fine earlier work with Henderson's and Webb's orchestras.

Its solo work limited, both in quantity and quality, the Kirby Sextet's case rests
on its compositions and ensemble skills. And when it is possible to admire the
group for its remarkable, at times even flawless, renditions of Shavers's (or Kyle's)
arranged ensembles, a jazz group's worth cannot stand on its ensemble virtues
alone, no matter how impeccable. And here, of course, we come to the crux of
the problem. The Kirby Sextet, whatever it thought it was doing, can in balance
barely be considered in the realm of jazz. One does not even have to invoke
their "jazzing of the classics" to make such a statement, pitiful and naive as
these attempts at bridging the two fields of music were. (Although Kirby and his
men can almost be forgiven, since by 1938 almost everyone in Swing Land was
raping the popular classics—but only the lighter ones, to be sure.) There was in
this trend to identify with the classics a mixture of admiration and envy (at their
status) as well as mockery and disdain. But even worse were such misdirected
efforts, listlessly performed, as Lou Singer's *Night Whispers* or *Beethoven Riffs
On*— in which vulgar plunger growls on Shavers's trumpet are mindlessly pitted
against a mechanical rendition of excerpts from the second movement of Beethoven's Seventh Symphony—or *Temptations* and *I Love You Truly*. Singer's
Bugler's Dilemma at least has the light-hearted charm of some delightful bitonal
harmonies and catchy bugle fanfares of the kind that Leroy Anderson would turn
into a best seller for the Boston Pops a decade later. The idea of performing
Thomas Griselle's lovely, moody *Nocturne* was, I am sure, born of the noblest
of impulses and a desire to break down the barriers between jazz and classical
music. But even its nicely played performance was bound to fall between the
jazz and classical stools, for it was neither classical music of much import or
originality nor identifiable in the slightest way with jazz. (Performing an elegant
poignant mood piece by Ellington—like *Blue Light* or *Subtle Lament*—might
have been much more to the point.) And what are we to make of such travel-
ogue items as *Down on the Desert* and *Arabian Nightmare?* A bunch of carous-
ing 52nd Street tourists may have found such musical excursions elevating, but
they can hardly be taken seriously by an even mildly discriminating listener.

As noted earlier, the Kirby Sextet's popularity began to wane after 1942. Kirby
managed to keep the ensemble going through the war. Later, after the group
had eventually broken up, Kirby tried to revive it in the late forties, but this time
could not find an audience. The "Biggest Little Band" faded into history without
leaving a trace of an influence.

Even in their best pieces like *Sweet Georgia Brown*,[3] *Front and Center, Royal*

3. Dizzy Gillespie claims to have invented the catchy riff with which his and Kenny Clarke's *Salt
Peanuts* begins and points to his early use of the phrase in his recording of *Little John Special* with
Lucky Millinder's band on July 29, 1942. However, it can be found on Shavers' arrangement of

Garden Blues, although well-conceived and brilliantly executed, the inherent limitations of the group's conception and instrumentation are apparent. Even without Shaver's insistence on constantly giving the trumpet the lead line, the instrumentation of clarinet, alto, and trumpet, when deprived (by choice) of any polyphonic options and locked into more or less homophonic block-chordal, close-harmony ensembles, was bound to lead to a deadening redundancy. Nor could this mini-ensemble—perhaps *did* is a more accurate word—ever achieve a truly dynamic climax. Here, of course, the basic conception of an eminently polite music that would not offend genteel tastes and ears was primarily at fault.

Similarly, the arrangements' format, reproduced with assembly-line precision and regularity, became stifling of any formal creativity. The preordained need to give at least four of the group's players a solo, preceded and succeeded by the opening-closing "head," thereby quickly filling every three-minute side, made the Shavers arrangements totally predictable in form and content. In the long run, no degree of performance dexterity could hide the creative paucity imposed by these constraints, nor could all the aesthetic pretension, exemplified by a flimsy alliance with pseudo-classical music, disguise the effeteness of the results or the commercial impulses that motivated their conception. Sadly, the talent and invention embodied in the group was essentially misdirected. And in that respect the Kirby Sextet reflected the least, i.e. the confusions, of that time.

The Sextet was momentarily fortunate in finding an audience naive enough to find their music acceptable and entertaining—a new kind of "jazz," so they thought. But in the confusion of the era, the audience could not know that all they had in the Kirby Sextet was a somewhat elevated pop music. For it was an era when that which was jazz—true jazz—and that which wasn't, was not really very clear to the majority of Americans.

KING COLE

That is precisely why success for the Nat "King" Cole Trio came discouragingly slowly. Though the group was formed in 1937, the same year as the Kirby group, the Cole Trio had to wait six years to achieve its first major popular success—with the recording of *Straighten Up and Fly Right*, released on Capitol Records in early 1944—even though it was attracting the admiring attention of fellow musicians and jazz enthusiasts almost from the start. The magnitude of Cole's talent as a pianist, an improvising creative musician, an early modernist, and then somewhat later as a singer, was apparent to discerning ears almost immediately. However, in the commercial marketplace of the Swing Era big

---

Sweet Georgia Brown recorded by the Kirby Sextet *three* years earlier (on May 19, 1939). Of course, it is possible that Shavers stole the lick from Gillespie, who might have fooled around with some such riff pattern even before 1939—although I doubt this. Players, of course, stole and borrowed from each other all the time, and we'll probably never be able to know the actual origin of many of these pet phrases. Nor would I be much surprised if the *Salt Peanuts* lick is found to have been accidentally used by some other player years earlier.

bands, a tiny trio of piano, bass, and guitar—black musicians at that—had some difficulty in being heard and appreciated.

After a long residency at the Swannee Inn in Los Angeles, where incidentally Cole first turned to singing (in response to audience requests), this essentially instrumental trio was given its first opportunity to record in December 1940.[4]

As fine an improvising pianist as Cole was—and by 1940 he had simplified his Hines-oriented style with a generous leavening of Teddy Wilson—the magic of the King Cole Trio was just as dependent on the remarkable work of its guitarist Oscar Moore and the subtle interplay between the two musicians. Moore was one of the earliest to adopt the electric guitar, and by the time he recorded in 1940 had developed a mature personal style, delicately poised between and capable of both imaginative, beautifully shaped solos and sensitive accompaniments of great variety: freely chordal, single-line, and, of course, when needed, rhythm guitar.

Since Cole became in the last seven years of his life world-renowned as a singer, it is little remembered today that he was in his earlier career not only one of the most outstanding jazz pianists of his day but stylistically one of the most advanced. He has been given little recognition in the available histories of jazz for his innovative harmonic/melodic approach, as early as 1940, far ahead of any of his contemporaries (except for Tatum and, as always, Ellington). Indeed, it needs to be said that Cole and Moore were already in the earliest forties—and for all one knows, perhaps even before—consistently using advanced voicings and harmonic substitutions of a kind and quality that some of the early boppers, even Parker, were using only sporadically or tentatively at the time. In the case of Cole and Moore, such innovative ideas were an integral part of their playing, as even the earliest pre-Capitol records show. *Sweet Lorraine* (from 1940) and *Scotchin' with the Soda* (from 1941), especially the last chorus, are but two examples that offer abundant proof of their innovative procociousness. *Sweet Lorraine* in a subsequent remake was one of the Trio's big hits of 1944, and it is interesting to note that the group found little reason to update their earlier (1940) rendition; the performance is in all pertinent respects essentially the same— and quite marvelous.

There are really three aspects of the King Cole Trio's work that deserve closer scrutiny. One is the aforementioned individuality and freshness of their musical language, what others might call their style. (I prefer language because it was more than a mere style that they created.) Another is Cole's extraordinarily sensitive and unique vocal stylings, and his use of text and enunciation in what

4. Cole's debut on records had occurred four and a half years earlier with his brother Eddie Cole's Solid Swingers, a sextet of three horns and three rhythm. Nat, aged nineteen, composed all four titles and appears to be on these sides a pianist as yet in search of a style, Although Cole worshiped his idol, Earl Hines, he had not yet in 1936 absorbed the master's influence sufficiently to have worked through to a personal style. While *Stompin' at the Panama*, in a meaninglessly complex solo, reveals some of Cole's youthful confusion, his work on *Honey Hush* already reveals glimpses of his later charmingly bouncy style and sensitive piano touch. On the other hand, his playing on the ballad *Bedtime*, with its unison melody two octaves apart, seems to emulate the limited single-line stylings of someone like Eddie Duchin.

was—except for Sinatra's equally original approach evolved around the same time—the only new vocal conception by a male singer in a decade or so. Lastly, there is the novelty song, the often humorous side of the Trio's output, with its introduction of a three-way unison singing manner, at once a consummate technical achievement (in its fine control of intonation and vocal timbre) and delightfully entertaining.

Taking the Trio's linguistic talents first—I am here using the term "linguistic" as distinct from and not to be confused with the vocal aspects of their work, although the latter also overlap with and are part of their overall language—one must emphasize the group's historical precedency in this regard, at least in 1940 and 1941. Admittedly, by 1943 and 1944 the new harmonic innovations, while not yet commonplace, had begun to be used by increased numbers of younger players coming into jazz at that time.[5] But a sampling of the 1940 *Sweet Lorraine* and *This Will Make You Laugh* from August 1941 (to isolate only two of the more outstanding examples) will reveal any number of remarkable harmonic/melodic felicities (see Exs. 1 and 2) that, moreover, do not appear to be brought in as some unusual reaching-out effect, but are clearly a natural, spontaneous, and inseparable part of the whole.[6]

Ex. 1

5. For a further examination of these developments the reader may be interested in reviewing the discussion thereof above, in Chapter 7, especially in regard to the bands of Charlie Barnet and Woody Herman.

6. One oddity of the four Decca sessions (comprising sixteen titles in all) is the fact that on two of these dates the Trio is augmented to a quartet: a second rhythm-only guitar is added on the first date (Dec. 6, 1940) and a drummer (probably Lee Young?) is added on the third date. These additions were not publicly acknowledged by either Decca or the Trio, nor have I ever seen this fact mentioned in any writing on the subject or the recordings' liner notes.

Ex. 2

Other memorable passages occur in *I'm Lost, I Can't See for Lookin'* (sample the second highly chromatic bridge), and *My Lips Remember Your Kisses*. But the Trio's zenith was reached in a whole string of perfect recordings in late 1943 and early 1944: most notably *Gee, Baby Ain't I Good to You, Embraceable You, The Man I Love,* and *Body and Soul*. These performances sound as fresh and captivating today as they did then, forty years ago.

Apart from the individual contributions of the three players—bassist Johnny Miller had by now replaced the rather too subdued Wesley Prince—these four sides are outstanding for the superb integration of all three instruments: harmonically, rhythmically, contrapuntally, timbrally, and dynamically. One has to wait for the remarkable Lennie Tristano Trio of 1946 and the early Modern Jazz Quartet of a decade later to hear such sensitively integrated playing again.

Moreover, this linguistic integration was achieved not in terms of any stylistic restraints on the players, much less a conservative holding back in order to find easier coordination, but rather on terms that allowed the players, especially the two principal ones, Cole and Moore, the utmost individual freedom on the linguistic cutting edge of the music.

Among the superior *individual* contributions, one must single out Cole's triplety, and for its time, unusually configurated solo on *Gee, Baby*, his brightly colored solo in luminous high register thirds on *Embraceable* and his solo, certainly a composition in itself, on *Body and Soul*, probably the most memorable invention of his pianistic career (Ex. 3).

Aside from Cole's superb choice of notes and harmonic taste, what elevates this entire chorus to an even higher plane is the degree of invention with which he manipulates the given rhythmic elements. Building on Moore's magnificent preceding chorus, which intermittently implies double-time feelings, Cole fulfills those implications by moving from his favorite eighth-note triplets through decorative sixteenths to an extended full-fledged, swinging double-time passage in the second "eight," which one can only describe with the word "grandeur."

Ex. 3

Stated in beautifully balanced high-register block chords, with just the slightest thematic allusion to Grieg's *Hall of the Mountain King*—Cole uses the near-quotation, rather than (as so often with Swing Era musicians) *it using him*—he develops and spins out the double-time figure in sovereign control, manipulating the harmonies so as to fit Johnny Green's original "changes," at the same time causing the most delicious, spicy, harmonic entanglements with Moore's chordings. Like the first sixteen bars of Cole's solo, the entire chorus teeters on the edge of double-time, now leaning one way (towards triplets in single-time), then leaning fully into swing sixteenths over an implied doubled-up eighth-note beat, or sometimes teasingly hovering in between, uncommitted to either side.

The prolonged passages in right-hand thirds heard on *Embraceable You* became a hallmark of Cole's playing around 1943, and although the idea may sound tawdry in bald verbal description, Cole used it with such exquisite taste that it usually illuminates his solos. Perhaps his most distinctive contribution as a melodic improviser, however, was his unique and at the time unprecedented way of incorporating eighth-note triplet passages in his solos and accompaniments. If they were not totally original with Cole (which I am almost prepared to argue except for the existence of certain Art Tatum passages), they were a singular feature of his language and style, made all the more distinctive by Cole's unique piano touch and buoyant rhythmic feel.

Moore is so intimately partnered with Cole that all that one may say about the latter can be applied to the former, except in guitaristic terms. As mentioned, his solo on *Body and Soul* (Ex. 4) is outstanding, at times even sublime. But his solos on *Gee, Baby* and *My Lips Remember*, or his beautiful counterlines on *I'm Lost*, are equally fascinating, not the least because of Moore's superb, clear, but warm amplified guitar sound. He was a master of the sensuous slide or moan— hear him on *The Man I Love, That Ain't Right*—and used this effect with great taste for the purpose of a certain kind of poignant expression (rather than sentimental indulgence, as was the case with so many pseudo-Hawaiian guitarists of the Swing Era and such players as Alvino Rey).[7] It may be overstating the case a little, but I never heard Oscar Moore play a bad or uninteresting solo, and by that I mean to include the many, many times I heard him in person in the King Cole Trio in the mid-1940s. And let us not overlook his superb rhythm playing (as, for example, on *F.S.T.*).

If I have concentrated thus far on the Trio's slow pieces and/or ballad performances, it is because I am certain that these represent the group's most important and serious work. And part of the beauty of these performances resides unquestionably in Nat Cole's fine singing. Turning into a vocalist almost by accident, he discovered that he had, in addition to a superb ear, a distinctive voice —a baritone in range with a tenor quality—with a warm velvety timbre which projected an aura of intimacy. In all of Nat Cole's best ballad-singing one cannot escape the impression that he is singing directly to you—and for you alone.

I believe his vocal style was wholly his own, although one can hear in his almost vibrato-less singing and certain ornamental inflections subtle traces of an early influence by Billie Holiday. Cole's diction was superb, and songs were enunciated with a mildly broad southern vowelization that was extremely appealing, but which, alas, in the waning days of the Trio he turned into an unvarying mannerism.[8]

---

7. Although Alvino Rey was a fine musician with an excellent harmonic ear, he sometimes exploited the guitar's glissando effects to intolerable degrees, thereby gaining, however, a certain popular/commercial success in the early forties. (See Chapter 7, Part 3, for more on Rey.)

8. Interestingly, Cole abandoned these phonetic mannerisms during his subsequent career as a solo singer.

Ex. 4

Another unusual element of his singing style, paradoxically, was an intermittent and ever so slight tendency to sing certain middle-register notes flat. I believe this was not an affectation but the by-product of an untrained voice, particularly insufficient breath support. Strangely, this imperfection, as sublimated by Cole's superior musicianship and as used innately in the service of a deeper expression, had its own peculiar charm. (It is an effect not unknown amongst singers and even some instrumentalists, though, curiously, it only works if a pitch is flattened, not if it is sharpened). In some odd way, with Cole it heightened the sense of intimacy and gave him a touch of vulnerability which, again, was especially appealing to the ladies.

By contrast, the numerous novelty vocals recorded by the Trio present an entirely different side of its work. Although the term "novelty vocals" may immediately conjure up the most fearful of images—and, God knows, the Swing Era saw tens of thousands of such inanities committed under the guise of "novelty"—here again the taste and sheer skill with which the King Cole Trio handled such material was of such high order that they all but turned it into a new art form. What was new was the Trio's singing in unison—while simultaneously playing their instruments, of course. This they did to catchy, jivey lyrics in a bouncy swinging manner that was quite irresistible. Although all professional ensemble-singing is expected to be in tune, singing in a three-way unison presents its own special intonational challenges. Nor is the absolute *timbral* blending of voices the King Cole Trio achieved to such perfection easy to come by. Examples of this highly entertaining aspect of the Trio's work abound, starting with *Gone with the Draft* (1940) right through *Call the Police, Straighten Up and Fly Right* to *Route 66* (1946). It was not long before other small groups imitated this technique, most notably the Page Cavanaugh Trio and the Joe Mooney Quartet (see below).

As so often happens in the popular and jazz fields, where with seeming inevitability groups and individuals decline after reaching some form of artistic peak, so, too, the King Cole Trio fell prey to such tendencies. Although by far not the worst example of artistic decline, the Trio's work did begin as of 1945 to suffer from a degree of routinization, the adoption of certain stylistic mannerisms, and a general disinclination to experiment, to advance, to grow musically. By the sheer size of their basic talents, however, the group's decline was modest and, if measured against much of the surrounding mediocrity and even some of their imitators, the King Cole Trio still has to rank quite high in the scheme of things. Even in the most critical assessment of their work, say, as "lightweight entertainment music," the King Cole Trio always operated at high levels of taste and skill and imagination. How far we are from that today in our popular music!

As Nat Cole's singing matured in depth of expression, its effect, especially on the opposite sex, was quite devastating. And one can well understand why it was almost inevitable that Cole would turn his talents to a solo singing career. Indeed, the immense success of *Nature Boy*[9] in 1948 sealed his fate in that respect. Recording more and more in a solo setting with lush string and woodwind orchestras, Cole dropped the Trio in 1951 and pursued the solo career until his death in 1965.

9. *Nature Boy* is a curiosity in American popular music history. Composed by a long-bearded, barefoot, Christ-like hermit by the name of Eben Ahbez, the song fell into Cole's hands and, as arranged by Frank De Vol, became an overnight million-seller hit. Despite its astonishing commercial success, the performance is also an artistic success in its field and a credit to all participants, not least of all Cole, who sang with an unforgettable poignancy and warmth.

The natural descendants of the Cole Trio were Johnny Moore's Three Blazers, the Page Cavanaugh, the Art Tatum, Errol Garner and Oscar Peterson trios, the latter three without benefit of vocal participation. Each of these, of course, developed its own style and musical personality, although Cavanaugh's group was the closest in conception to Cole's, and eventually even more commercially oriented. Dozens of other excellent piano-led trios and quartets emerged in the mid-1940s, including those led by Dardanelle Breckenridge, Barbara Carroll, Beryl Booker, and a trio led by bassist Vivien Garry. But none were more outstanding than the Joe Mooney Quartet and Lennie Tristano's short-lived trio of 1946.

JOE MOONEY

Joe Mooney, active as an organist in later years in Miami until his death in 1975, is now little remembered, even though his quartet of 1943–49 was one of the most popular of small combos and much admired by fellow musicians. Featuring the improbable combination of accordion (Mooney), clarinet (Andy Fitzgerald), guitar (Jack Hotop), and bass (Gate Frega), the group nevertheless achieved a remarkable degree of sonoric, textural integration.[10] Its relaxed, sensitive, and intricate ensemble-playing was a treat to hear in those postwar years, when the last of the big bands still thought the route to popular survival lay in playing louder and faster. As someone who heard the Mooney Quartet frequently in those years, I can well recall its effect on listeners, as they were drawn into its mood of hushed intimacy and disarming warmth, qualities that unfortunately did not register as well on the group's recordings as they did in live performances. In some ways the Mooney Quartet's music was too subtle to be fully captured on wax; it needed the intimate personal interrelation with a listening audience to make its point. Nonetheless, the more than a dozen sides Mooney recorded in 1946–47 are much worth hearing as an example of a certain kind of refined chamber jazz, not heard again until the Modern Jazz Quartet of the 1950s.

The Mooney Quartet began recording in November 1946 with a song every singer seemed to have rediscovered that year: Kurt Weill's 1938 classic *September Song*. Dozens of recordings were made in 1946, but none as unusual and tasteful as Mooney's. Blind from birth,[11] Joe Mooney brought to his singing a sen-

10. An equally improbable instrumental combination, also remarkably well integrated, can be heard on six splendid small group sides made by the Emilio Caceres Trio in 1937. Consisting of violin (Emilio), brother Ernie on clarinet and baritone sax, and guitar, it is astonishing how the violin and clarinet blended and, even more surprisingly, how Ernie's gutty, burly baritone functioned so successfully with the violin. The answer lies in the fact that the two brothers were superb musicians, with excellent tone on their respective instruments—a prerequisite for intelligent ensemble-blending. The rhythm guitar acted as a bridge and unifier between the string and reed instruments.

11. Joe Mooney (1911–75) began singing professionally in his teens, first appearing on radio and then recording 1929–31 with his brother Dan as The Sunshine Boys. These very rare recordings reveal the eighteen-year-old Mooney's multiple talents—as pianist, arranger and singer—at an early yet already very sophisticated stage. The arrangements are enormously skillful and witty, exploiting

sitivity typical of the sightless, which in his case sounded like a blend of Bunny Berigan's singing (as on *I Can't Get Started*) and Nat King Cole's. Mooney's phrasing is well-nigh perfect on *September*, so gently nuanced, so poignant in timbre, with a touch of nostalgia very appropriate to this song. The accompaniment is no less ideal, blending graceful clarinet interjections and sensitive guitar chordings with his own accordion backgrounds.

Two things are remarkable about the Mooney Quartet's ensemble settings: Mooney's accordion never sounded raw and raucous in tone, as accordions so often do; and his arrangements had a wonderful sense of airiness, of lightness. They were never dense, really more contrapuntal in conception than homophonic. Very occasionally the constant alternation of instruments led to an excess of fragmentation, but generally the four musicians were so sensitive to each other's tone and attack that they could carry the line of the music across the many instrumental linkups, as in some extended *Klangfarbenmelodie*,[12] creating a delicate web-like texture.

Mooney's arrangements were initially made for the quartet's club appearances, and usually had to be cut for recording purposes to fit the 10-inch duration limit. On slow pieces, like *September Song*, this meant that the purely instrumental middle section of a performance had to be eliminated or at least drastically abridged. It also meant that the improvisations heard in the club rarely got onto the quartet's recordings. Sometimes Mooney would write a new shorter "bridge" especially for the record date (as in *September Song* and *Prelude to a Kiss*), but these expediencies did detract somewhat from the original more extended versions.

The flip side of *September Song, Just a Gigolo*, showed another aspect of the quartet's work: its rollicking, easy humor set in light, bouncy, swing-riff tunes. Except for the two brief instrumental interludes, which are beautifully concerted, *Gigolo* is even sparser in its backgrounds to Mooney's vocals. Taking a leaf from the King Cole Trio's book, the quartet sings the tune mostly in unison

---

the limited resources of two light tenor voices (Joe and Dan), piano (Joe Mooney), violin (Joe Venuti), and guitar (Dick McDonough or Eddie Lang) to maximum results. (On some recordings Joe and Dan are accompanied alternately by Tommy Dorsey or Mannie Klein and guitar.) Bright tempos and good swing, catchy lyrics, clever scat duets, tricky modulations, abrupt tempo changes and (for 1929) very "modern", clean harmonizations all combine to create in these intricate musical vignettes entertaining yet highly musical, tasteful performances. Especially interesting is the March, 1929 *My Troubles Are Over*, in which the two singers not only manage to create at one point the illusion of a five-note *(sic)* harmonic "pyramid", but also sneak in an appropriately felicitious quote from Walter Donaldson's *Changes*, a favorite song of Whiteman's Rhythm Boys whose lyrics celebrate, among other things, fancifully chromatic harmonic changes. The influence of the Rhythm Boys is certainly discernible in the two Mooney boys's singing and arranging—a not unreasonable expectation in two 18-year olds—but in turn, there can be little question that the Boswell Sisters, who began recording in 1931, a year and a half *after* the Sunshine Boys, learned much from Joe Mooney's arrangements, especially in terms of unusual tempo changes and modulations.

After another stint on radio (in Cincinnati at WLW), Mooney turned to arranging for various bands (Buddy Rogers, Frank Dailey, Paul Whiteman, Russ Morgan, and Les Brown), and subsequently formed his first quartet in 1943.

12. Tone-color melody, i.e. a melodic line which several tone colors (instruments) share and pass around.

lines, accompanied only by walking bass, and scattered accordion punctuations. At times Fitzgerald and Hotop vocalize a wordless sustained counter-melody against Mooney's foreground singing. Occasionally Mooney intersperses some bop-ish scatting (Ex. 5), much like Dave Lambert and Buddy Stewart had done with Gene Krupa's band in early 1945 (in *What's This?*) and anticipating the Lambert-Hendricks-Ross bop vocals of a decade later.

Ex. 5

Although *Gigolo* is stylistically beholden to the Cole Trio (of *Route 66* and *Straighten Up and Fly Right*), it is no mere imitation. It has its own personality, shyer and more restrained than Cole, deromanticized, cleaner, and more linear in conception, less of Hines and Tatum and more of pure bop.

Even Mooney's ballads tend to have the clean sparse lines of bop, also the tendency to imply and often feature explicitly a constant underlying double-time feeling, sometimes even the double of that. The time continuum here hovers as if on a tempo fulcrum, seesawing easily—almost unnoticeably—between single and double-time. This rhythmic diversity gives the quartet's work a flexible, spontaneous, off-the-cuff buoyancy that belies the group's painstaking rehearsing. Good examples of this wonderfully light and transparent ballad style are *Nancy with the Laughing Face, Warm Kiss and Cold Heart, You Go to My Head,* and Ellington's *Prelude to a Kiss.*

Nancy also contains one of those marvelous instrumental bridges that Mooney could shake out of his sleeve so easily. It is only four bars long, but is an exquisite example of Mooney's artful way with harmony, texture, timbre, and musical line (Ex. 6)—its sly allusion to Billy Strayhorn's *Chelsea Bridge* notwithstanding.

Ex. 6

Another beautiful six-bar instrumental episode can be found on *Prelude to a Kiss* (Ex. 7). Apart from its gently swaying harmonies, it also exemplifies Mooney's aforementioned penchant for three-layered rhythmic structuring. As the notated example reveals, m. 1 is split between a subtle quadruple-time in clarinet and guitar and single-time in the bass. Measure 2 drops down to single-time with eighth-note triplets in the latter half (triplets being as rare in Mooney's language as they are common in Cole's). Measure 3 is basically in single-time, while in the latter half of m. 4 double-time sneaks in. Measures 5 and 6 revel in no less than three discrete layers: a combination of quadruple- and double-time in clarinet and guitar, a combination of double- and single-time in the bass, against sustained organ-like *half notes*—in effect "half-time"—in the accordion. It all meshes together in a wonderful rhythmic/melodic/harmonic polyphony.

This instrumental interlude is also typical of the method used by Mooney to condense his slow-tempo arrangements so as to fit on a 10-inch disc, to my knowledge an idea unique to Mooney. Whereas common practice was to cut at

Ex. 7

the end of the first 32-bar song structure to the next 8-bar bridge, either purely instrumentally or vocally repeating the text of the bridge. Mooney uses the instruments alone for *six* bars, bringing in the text in bars 7 and 8—in this case with the words "a Schubert tune with a Gershwin touch"—and continuing on to the last eight. By this means he has the best of both worlds: he preserves a brief instrumental segment as well as a touch of the bridge text, which then links them up with the last stanza of the song.

The Mooney Quartet's lively up-tempo novelty numbers are no less intriguing and tasteful than their ballads. The best of these, besides *Just a Gigolo*, are *A Man with a Million Dollars*, *Tea for Two*, *From Monday On*, and Peggy Lee's song *What More Can a Woman Do?*. Full of wonderful inventions, buoyant rhythms, these pieces are transformed by Mooney from (in some cases) silly pop novelty tunes into fascinating miniature compositions. *Million Dollars* has two particularly outstanding instrumental interludes, two made possible by the fast tempo. The first episode, of which Example 8 shows mm. 5–16, features some ingenious bitonal canonic repartee between the four instruments. In the next interlude Mooney scats along in octave unison with his accordion, in effect adding a fifth "instrument" to the ensemble in a wonderfully arching phrase (Ex. 9).

From Monday On is the liveliest, hardest swinging, most virtuosic of the entire Mooney collection. It is a real *tour de force* of a performance, virtually

Ex. 8

Ex. 9

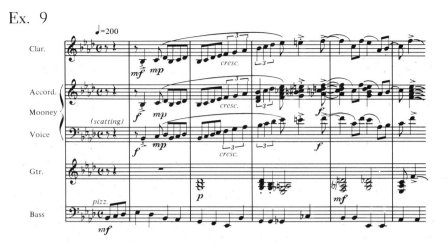

perfect in conception and execution, a tribute to these four musicians' technical skills and ensemble sensitivity.

What More, with Mooney now on piano instead of accordion, is even more intricate in structure. Besides being entirely instrumental, it is quite complex contrapuntally and on the verge of atonality, much like Lennie Tristano's Trio sides of 1946 (see below). *What More* is also largely improvised, and again richly embellished with double- and quadruple-time effects. It features Fitzgerald quite extensively, and, in fact, the last third of the performance turns effectively into a concerto for clarinet and three accompanying instruments. It is all quite masterful, played with watch-like precision, and all in all a brilliant demonstration of the Mooney Quartet's collective ability to turn a popular song into a challenging, complex, yet listenable "composition."

Perhaps the Quartet's most fetching performance—and Mooney's most ingenious arrangement—is *Tea for Two*, recorded December 30, 1946. It is both a spoof on the Youmans tune (which by the late 1930s had been virtually relegated to a mere vehicle for tap dancers) and a hilarious reinvention of the famous piece.

A wonderfully "hip" introduction—one of Mooney's rare intros (as explained below)—sets the tone for the entire piece, serving also to introduce some of Mooney's impish new lyrics (Ex. 10). The initial chorus, more or less straight, is delivered with infectious swing. Then, after a full instrumental chorus of playfully inventive ensemble, which features in the final eight the marvelous cluster effect of Example 11, Mooney updates Irving Caesar's original 1925 lyrics, imagining his *Tea for Two* couple blissfully survived to 1983:

Flash! 1983
Scene: chick's still on his knee.
She goes for he,
But he's up to his eyeballs

Ex. 10

Ex. 11

In teaballs.
And there's been nobody near 'em,
To see 'em or hear 'em,
No relations
Or weekend vacations.
They've never been known
To answer that telephone.
Bada looba dabop
Be lab dat.
Dawn breaks,
She wakes,
Still bakes those knocked-out cakes.
They've never been tasted,
But they're not wasted;
They're so pretty to see.
They started to raise a family
But the kids left home at the age of three,
Singing: "Oolong,
Too much o' that Oolong."
And now since the kids departed
The family's right where it started:
Back to Tea for Two.

Like Mary Lou Williams's *Land of Oobladee,* Timmie Rogers's *Flagalapa,* Sonny Burke's *Black Coffee,* Mooney's spoof on *Tea for Two* is wonderfully witty entertainment, impeccably served up with sophisticated musical taste.

Another interesting aspect of Mooney's work is that he usually dispenses with introductions entirely. On most pieces he will go right to the top of the song, often *a capella*—something only a *very good secure* musician can do.

A word should be said about clarinetist Andy Fitzgerald. Although I admit to some concern for Fitzgerald always being cooped up in Mooney's soft-spoken refined arrangements, delimited both in improvisation opportunities and dynamic levels, the man managed this extraordinarily confining task remarkably well, especially in his consummate dynamic and tonal control of the upper register. Never being able to bust out must have been rather frustrating, but he never protruded unmusically, and his warm, elegant tone suited all of the quartet's needs, whether to dominate momentarily or to delineate a counter melody, or to subside into the background as a harmonic fill-in. In this connection we should note that Fitzgerald would often play slurred tremolos—an easy natural effect on the clarinet—filling out some missing notes in the harmonies and almost creating the illusion of *two* clarinets in the ensemble. Most arrangers would have simply put such "missing" notes in the accordion or guitar, but Mooney resisted that obvious temptation and, by putting such notes in a clarinet tremolo, not only filled out the harmony as needed but, as a bonus, acquired a sense of subtle forward motion which a fast-moving tremolo tends to give.

Ultimately the charm of Mooney's work with his quartet lies in what Alec Wilder once called Mooney's "childlike simplicity" combined with "absolutely spell-binding intricacy." I would add that Mooney all his life was in his music-making wry yet romantic, *both* in a non-obvious way. Indeed, the history of jazz has had little to offer in the way of such a rarefied blending of refined taste, sophisticated musical invention, disciplined execution, and lighthearted unpretentious humor. The quartet's whisper-soft performances *made* you listen concentratedly—its music was not for casual listening—and even though the recordings do not capture the full magic of the live performances, they are well worth hearing. It is most regrettable that Mooney's Quartet work has been virtually forgotten in the intervening years.

REX STEWART

Among the all-time gems of small group jazz, virtually in a class by itself, is a quartet of sides recorded in Paris in April 1939 by the great French guitarist, Django Reinhardt, and three members of Duke Ellington's orchestra: Rex Stewart, Barney Bigard, and Billy Taylor.[13]

These four performances are masterpieces of "chamber jazz," yet in no way lightweight or effete as that term often tends to connote. Rooted essentially in the blues and a sophisticated modern, earthy mainstream jazz, it is extraordinary how much soulful music these four instrumentalists produce—most of the time there are, actually, only three or two playing—and how beautifully Reinhardt's near-classical acoustic guitar style blends into the three Ellington musicians' conception.

Each of the four pieces is crammed with an array of ravishing details, beautiful, ingenious, sensitive, seemingly simple but in fact resulting from a most complex subtle interrelationship of the four players. Filled with melodic beauty, harmonic invention, a refined yet earthy swing, superb counterpoint between the instruments (in duet, trio or quartet), these performances can be counted amongst the finest achievements of jazz, and are worthy of close study and wide dissemination, not the incomprehensible neglect they have suffered.

It is difficult to single out any one of the four pieces above the others, or indeed separate individual solos from their surrounding context. Perfect in form and continuity, ideas flowing organically one into the other, a subtle amalgam of solo and ensemble, any singling out of this or that passage can give only a very limited idea of the quality of these sublime creations. And transcription into notation cannot begin to give a sense of the rich tone colors these four instruments produce here and the refined, controlled, completely natural jazz inflections which grace these performances. Nonetheless, a few brief musical examples must suffice to present at least a surface impression of the music (and some reference for my comments).

Low Cotton begins with a magisterial upward-spiraling arpeggio played by Rex

---

13. These four sides were originally recorded under Rex Stewart's leadership by the French Swing label and released in the United States in the early forties on the HRS label as by Rex Stewart's Big Four. Three of the original titles—*Montmartre, Finesse,* and *Solid Old Man*—were changed on the HRS reissues to *Django's Jump, Night Wind,* and *Solid Rock,* respectively. The fourth title is *Low Cotton.*

Ex. 12

Stewart alone (Ex. 12), leading directly into a warmly blues-ish low-register clarinet solo by Bigard. A Django solo chorus follows—Stewart gets the bridge—accompanied only by Taylor's softly walking bass. Django's ideas here (Ex. 13) are rich and imaginative, both melodically and harmonically, making exquisite counterpoint with Taylor's bass, and at the same time exploiting some delicate timbres unique to the guitar. The full quartet ends the side with a low-key, beautifully poised collective ensemble.

Ex. 13

Finesse (Night Wind), composer-credited to Billy Taylor, is, if anything, even more remarkable in its effect, considering the simplicity of means employed. Four simple guitar chords, ingenious in their juxtaposition (Ex. 14), introduce a quietly impassioned Stewart theme statement, glowing in tone and embellished

Ex. 14

here and there with the most wondrous half-valve timbral colorations.[14] Richly chordal guitar and bass figures provide the perfect accompaniment. Bigard now enters with one of his more flamboyant inventions, tailored here, however, to the small-group context. A *sotto voce*, delicate 2-bar guitar break leads into Django's solo, a single-line (mostly) statement—against an ultra-simple bass part (see Ex. 15)—so flawless in its composition that we are not even aware as we listen, that the original 16-bar theme has been foreshortened to fourteen bars. The entire performance is rendered in Example 15.

Another instance of impeccable two-part counterpoint—we must remember that this is spontaneously improvised music, not laboriously calculated—opens *Solid Rock*, a simple medium-tempo 12-bar blues. Stewart's theme, following the introductory guitar-bass duet, is recapitulated at the end, in between encasing three superb solo statements by Stewart, Reinhardt, and Bigard in sequence. Stewart is especially in his element here, ornamenting his plaintive blues with strangely expressive trills, a variety of vibratos and note slides, and poignantly mournful between-the-cracks half-valve moans. In twelve brief measures Stewart says more here than most trumpet players can manage in a month of solos.

Reinhardt's solo is gently songful, bending his notes towards the end almost as if in response to Stewart. Bigard[15] follows with a more intense "argumentive" statement, but note how tastefully Reinhardt here breaks his rhythm accompaniment for three measures to add a slightly ominous, rustling chordal tremolo at the harmonic high point of the phrase. An almost joyful reprise of Stewart's theme, set in a strong shuffle rhythm in the guitar forms

the "climax" of the performance. Neither fast nor loud—the loudest dynamic on all four pieces is a *mf*—the sense of climax is achieved by the simplest means: a four-way collective of all the instruments (in contrast to the preceding duet and trio combinations) and an intensification of the inner rhythmic movement, along with a slight increase in dynamic level.

Django's Jump is only slightly less interesting than the other performances, because it has fewer special moments and is marred by a minusculely insignificant note mistake by Reinhardt. Still, it is an effervescent joyous romp that contrasts beautifully with the more introspective *Low Cotton*, with *Night Wind's*

14. Fellow trumpet players always marveled at Rex Stewart's ability not only to play virtually any note with any fingering but to alter his sound at will to almost any timbre, thereby practically obviating the need to resort to different tone-altering mutes.
15. Bigard also plays some tasteful drums (with brushes) on this side when not playing the clarinet.

Ex. 15

evocation of human nocturnal loneliness, and the heart-felt restrained joy of *Solid Rock*.

Whenever jazz might be called upon to demonstrate to its skeptics that it need not be and *is not necessarily* a loud, raucous, banal music—such accusations have followed jazz throughout its history—these tasteful "classic" performances provide perfect irrefutable proof. Though little known, they are gemstones of jazz that should be heard by every appreciator of good music—of whatever ideological persuasion.

LENNIE TRISTANO

It is no more than fitting that we close this chapter on small group jazz with a brief preview—a glimpse into the future as it were—afforded by one of the most prophetic recordings in all jazz history: the Lennie Tristano Trio's 1946 rendition of *I Can't Get Started*.[16] If one were to construct a list of the dozen or so major stations in the development of jazz in the twenty years between 1926 and 1946, including such historic breakthrough creations as Armstrong's *West End Blues*, Henderson's *The Stampede* and *King Porter Stomp*, a half-dozen Duke Ellington works like *Mood Indigo, Reminiscing in Tempo, Diminuendo and Crescendo In Blue, Cotton Tail*, Lester Young's 1936 *Lady Be Good*, Hawkins's *Body and Soul*, Tatum's *Aunt Hagar's Blues*, Gillespie and Parker's *Shaw Nuff*, Herman's *Apple Honey*—pieces, compositions, improvisations, performances that in some crucial way moved jazz dramatically forward—then I would happily include Tristano's *I Can't Get Started*. Each such piece made its impact in one or (at most) two realms of music: *West End* in rhythm, *Mood Indigo* in tone color and harmony, *Reminiscing* in form, *Diminuendo* in the variation principle, *Body and Soul* in melodic improvisation, and so on. Tristano's breakthrough was primarily in the realm of harmony and in a return to polyphony.

Very few radical innovations in jazz have broken new ground on *all* fronts: melody, harmony, rhythm, timbre, dynamics, form, and structure etc. Those that have come closest to this ideal are the Henderson pieces, Parker's and Gillespie's collaborations, *Cotton Tail*, and, if there is one element that shows up more consistently than any other in these innovatory pieces, even if only partially or in a moderate form, then it is rhythm—perhaps the most quintessential jazz element and driving force and its most characteristic attribute. This is precisely where Tristano's creativity was most lacking; and it accounts, I am sure, for a large part of the rejection and apathy with which these Tristano sides were met. They didn't swing the way all jazz by then was supposed to do. That may make them less important in the overall picture than some total and unqualified masterpiece, but it does not make them irrelevant or unworthy of consideration.

I promised a brief glimpse into the future, as it appeared then in the mid-

16. Recorded on October 8, 1946, this and two other sides were released in early 1947 by the then new, small Keynote label. Although these records found little public resonance and tepid critical acclaim (except for *Metronome* magazine's Barry Ulanov), they did create quite a stir among the more "advanced" musicians of the time, including many on the "classical" side.

forties, the years of my youth. And a glimpse it shall have to be. A thorough analysis of all of Tristano's early work[17] will be forthcoming in the next volume of this History. For the moment then only a few insights into *I Can't Get Started* to close out this chapter and send us on our way to the modern era of jazz.

The amazing series of densely chromatic chords with which the performance begins immediately heralds that something remarkable is about to happen here. And so it does. *Started* is transformed into a completely new composition by Tristano's harmonic ministrations and manipulations of it. The original song is the merest pretext for a whole new concept of jazz in which tonality and atonality, harmony and counterpoint, meet on common ground, in brand new fusions. This is accomplished almost entirely by Tristano alone, his two trio partners—Billy Bauer on guitar and Clyde Lombardi on bass—performing their traditional and limited roles: Bauer in single-line melodic statements, Lombardi in a simple, rather inertly plodding bass line, outlining the song's basic chordal scheme. On this unextraordinary foundation Tristano builds a remarkable improvised superstructure of great harmonic, melodic, and even to some extent rhythmic invention. Tristano literally envelops Bauer's simple *tonal* lines in *atonal* constructions and gestures, weaving criss-crossing counterpoints, metric cross-rhythms, and alternatingly dense and lightweight textures (Ex. 16). Miraculously these atonal constructions always relate nonetheless to the *tonal* roots of the song, and therefore provide an excellent introduction for the novice in atonality to such music. As "far out" as Tristano's chordal blocks may be if taken separately, they are always anchored in the song's root progressions. As I say, his playing sits on the cusp of tonality and atonality. Technically, many of these harmonic constructions might be called "bitonal," while others are so near the border of atonality that a clear distinction is no longer possible—and in a larger sense, academic—an achievement that in 1946 could only be accomplished by a harmonic ear of genius calibre.

Ex. 16

17. Besides the Trio sides of 1946 and '47, Tristano recorded with the Earl Swope Sextet in 1945, as well as in some remarkably precocious and advanced solo piano performances of the same year.

Tristano also reconstructs *Started* in rhythmic and metric terms. For example, the song's first two measures—after the solo piano introduction—are stated in single-time, with Bauer's guitar in the lead. But already in bar 3 the piano and guitar (not the bass) flip into double-time, and a bar later into *double* double-time (Ex. 16). Having broken through these rhythmic barriers this early on, the two players (guitar and piano) are now at liberty to maneuver freely between and among these three tempo tracks (eighth-note triplets are also brought in later as well), sometimes simultaneously, sometimes independently of each other. This remarkable interplay is maintained throughout the performance, with Tristano being most consistently the initiator, the inspirer.

Later on the song is even more drastically rhythmically—and now metrically—altered. The entire performance consists of one and a half choruses of the song. The "half" begins with the bridge, with Bauer again in the melodic lead. But this time the bridge is cut (reduced) to three and a half 4/4 bars plus five 3/4 bars and one 2/4 bar—thirty-one beats in all, one short of the expected thirty-two. The final "eight" is transformed into six 4/4 bars, plus a performance-ending tag-vamp in a 3/8 pattern (Ex. 17) overlayered on the fundamental 4/4 meter—a rhythmic configuration that feels all the more natural and expected for having been used several times earlier in the performance.

Ex. 17

There is much more to be said about this astonishing performance, but, as indicated, further analysis will be left to a future time. Stylistically/chronologically Tristano's *I Can't Get Started* belongs with the modern period (and Volume III). It had the misfortune of being too far ahead of its time, and so it functions effectively as a transition, a springboard to the modern era of small group jazz. Hence its brief appearance here.

It was often said of Tristano that he was a "cold" "mechanical" player, that his music was "too intellectual." That may occasionally have been true in his later years, but even then it may be arguable that his "intellectualism" was an unintentional surface manifestation. However that may be, Tristano's early work pulsates with the vitality of invention, luxuriates in warm sensuous harmonies, revels in a richly varied pianistic touch, and pleasures in the contrapuntal independence of his two hands. If that be mere "intellectualism," so be it, although it is much more likely that it is only so in the ear of the beholder.

10

Things to Come

To read most of the histories and reference books on jazz is to gain the impression that jazz died around 1942. This notion is furthered, by implication, in those writings that use the recording ban of 1942–43 as a convenient cut-off point for the further discussion of developments in jazz. Others, by more explicit emphasis, leave the impression that there *may* have been jazz after World War II but that its greatest period occurred before that, and that the real masterworks and essence of true jazz can be found only between the late 1920s and 1945. Still others, of course, are quite unequivocal about proclaiming the final "demise of jazz" to have occurred in the postwar era, and that modern jazz or bop and what followed in the further innovations of the sixties and seventies are all rather a "corruption of jazz," not upholding its original "true values and spirit."

None of these rationales, implicit or explicit, is valid, of course, and arguments on behalf of one or the other of the theories are ultimately untenable. For jazz, like any other artistic/cultural/social expression, is the product of an organic continuity, an evolutionary process, that appears in many forms and takes on constantly changing stylistic characteristics. The history of jazz does not stop or begin at some convenient chronological point and at the observer's pleasure; it does not even always lend itself to a chronological delineation into decade partitions, measured in round numbers, except as the most convenient (and superficial) of time frames.

And above all, we should recognize that many musicians' lives and careers simply do not fit into predetermined stylistic and generational time divisions. Coleman Hawkins, Henry "Red" Allen, and Pee Wee Russell—to name just three important players—never stopped developing and growing; and, even though they began working in the 1920s, they remained vitally active well into the modern era, and certainly did not reach some artistic/creative impasse in the mid-1940s just because there was a recording ban or because big bands went into decline. Conversely, some players, while contributing importantly for a while, for one reason or another lost their creative momentum and in many cases did not even last through the era into which they were born—again defying easy pigeonholing into neat little time slots divisible by decades.

I certainly do not wish to leave any impression in this History that the years from 1932 to the late forties represent some especially sacred period in jazz, better and more vital than others. That the Swing Era was an incredibly rich and exciting period is undeniable, and surely the reader, if he was not already aware of it, will have come to realize and savor what was rare and good and special about the Swing and Big Band Era. For it was a unique time—as I suppose all large time periods ultimately are—unique in our cultural history, and unique in our social-political history, uniquely bounded as it happens on one side by a devastating economic depression and on the other by a global war. And we might as well realize that just as a time can never come back, so it is futile to wish that it and its music will return—except in our memories and nostalgic reflections.

As I look back over the period covered thus far in the two volumes of this History and resort for the moment to those convenient time-frame classifications, I see the years from, say, 1923 to 1932—the years of Armstrong and Hawkins and Bessie Smith, of late Morton and early Ellington—as an age of restless curiosity, of forging ahead unwaveringly into the unknown, and the development in effect of a new art form. I see the next period, from 1932 to 1945, as the establishment in jazz of a system of order, of a sense of unity, which allowed great things to be achieved, nonetheless all resting on the foundations laid in the late 1920s.

The next period, from 1945 on, as I see it, constitutes a gigantic tugging and pulling and shoving, wrenching jazz apart and then fundamentally and excitingly reshaping it, putting it together again. In those burgeoning years there was a spring and tension in early bop, a drive, at times a rough energy that eventually became refined, that was followed by an increase in subtlety and sophistication as manifested by the artistry of, say, the Miles Davis Nonet, the Modern Jazz Quartet, the work of Sonny Rollins and Theolonious Monk, of Charlie Mingus and Max Roach and Clifford Brown and Eric Dolphy, and many others.

Thus each period eventually exemplifies and defines itself, even if sometimes its deciphering cannot be accomplished in its own time and must await retrospective interpretation. And yet as individual as each era may ultimately be, it cannot be entirely separated from its connections to the past and its links to the future. It is in this sense that I have tried at all times to resist the temptation to totally isolate the Swing Era from its antecedents as well as its heirs. That is why I have so often reached back into the 1920s to show the origin of certain concepts or developments, and have frequently even referred the reader to the preceding volume in this History. On the other hand, I have also gone ahead into the modern era in such cases where the achievements of an artist's career warranted it. And certainly Volume III will pick up threads first introduced in the present book, cross-referencing them with the past and the future, as well as dealing intrinsically with the postwar modern era and the most recent present-day jazz developments.

From all three volumes it will be abundantly clear that jazz is a grand historical continuum,[1] that a) jazz does not exist in some isolated musical, cultural vacuum; b) that jazz is a diverse and many-splendored musical expression; c) that it comprises a complex network of both individualistic and general styles, hardly satisfactorily explained by such other popular notions as the "jazz-moved-up-the-river" theory or its unqualified chronological division into "classic–swing–modern" periods; and, above all, d) that it cannot be *rationally* argued that some of those periods represent true jazz and that others do not.

To understand how the bop revolution was inevitable, we must recognize several factors with profound implications. The stylistic pulling and tugging I referred to earlier was, again, not an isolated musical phenomenon occurring in a social vacuum. The whole world was torn asunder by a global conflict, surely a political pulling and tugging of major proportions. The war disrupted not only peoples and nations but a way of life. The comfortable stability jazz had at last achieved in the waning years of the 1930s, embraced in fact as America's single and unique popular music, was quite suddenly shattered, never to come together again in quite the same way.

Moreover, swing in that environment of stability began increasingly to concern itself with its own self-perpetuation. Swing, as represented by the average dance band, existed as we have seen only for the present and *in* the present. It became in far too many instances a static music that never looked outside or beyond itself. Anxious only to hold onto its own order and stability, it was bound to petrify.

But true jazz by its very nature cannot be held to a formula or be based on some stationary perfection. Indeed, the greatness of jazz lies in the fact that it never ceases to develop and change. In so far as swing ultimately tried to impede that process (and progress), it was doomed to die of its own internal inertia.

These thoughts come to mind as one contemplates the grand transition that occurred—as it happened—in the 1940s, and moved jazz from one idiom (called swing) to another (first called rebop or bebop, then later just bop, and finally modern or progressive jazz). For what happened then was as much evolution as it was revolution, and the similarities and commonalities between the two eras are as great as the dissimilarities. Indeed, these developments extended over a substantial period of time—almost a decade, reaching back into the late thirties and not really consummated in some clearly discernible manner until 1946 or 1947. Hundreds of individual contributions, both small and large, helped to shape this intricate process,[2] which, looked at closely in its day-to-day developments, was slow and painstaking—and met with considerable resistance.

It is of some significance that the initial evolvement of bop in the early 1940s occurred at precisely the same time as the advent of the New Orleans Revival. More than that, the jazz mainstream suddenly split asunder into several splinter

1. It is a sad fact that, if jazz nowadays plays any role at all in the average American's life, it is limited to "Dixieland" and the simplistic, cliché-ridden, rather crude entertainments that mostly pass for early jazz nowadays.
2. This is analogous to the process scientists call "phase transition": water when heated turning into steam, when frozen turning into ice; or as when rain changes to sleet and eventually to snow.

directions: bop moving forward and breaking off into its own stylistic worlds; Dixieland and the New Orleans Revival retrogressing in the opposite direction; some of the major bands holding on unswervingly to the swing mainstream; and most crucially, singers beginning to dominate the band business and popular music altogether. In that four-way refraction, jazz experienced the first serious dispersion of its audience—and its musicians—in different and opposing directions. It was in a way the first aesthetic crisis jazz had had to face, all prior developments having moved forward in a more or less broadly accepted straight line and single direction.

Some writers have tried to suggest that the recording ban broke the momentum of jazz's progress. It is tragic, of course, that many exceptional young bands and musicians went unrecorded in their early peak years. (How wonderful it would be to hear recordings of the young Parker and Gillespie in Earl Hines's 1942–43 band, or the outstanding Charlie Barnet band of those years, or the young Thelonious Monk, Bud Powell, and Errol Garner.) But the recording ban did not stop musicians from playing, from developing, or searching for newer forms of expression: it only stopped them from *recording*. In fact it is possible that the recording ban in a peculiar way favored the advancement of jazz in the form of bop, because it did not have to contend in its fragile and formative years with a booming record industry, which surely would have rejected it or tried to muzzle it creatively. It was not until new small record companies sprang up in the mid-1940s, companies either willing to take some risks or actually supportive of the new jazz, that bop found a friendly haven in the recording field. And by then bop was strong and ready for its unrestrained diffusion.

Indeed, it is remarkable that the recording ban had so little negative effect on jazz, except in a financial way. In fact, the ban helped some aspects of jazz quite profoundly. For example, record companies began to reissue earlier records from their catalogues, which was not only a boon to jazz record collectors but created an awareness among many music lovers that jazz *did* have a venerable history to be taken seriously and appreciated, at the same time reminding listeners of the deeper values in the pre-Swing Era jazz, values which had been in many cases dissipated and abandoned.

But perhaps the recording ban's most profound (and in the short term largely negative) influence resulted from the record industry's total embrace of singers. Musicians/instrumentalists were not allowed to record during the ban, while singers could; and before the ban was over singers like Frank Sinatra, Bing Crosby, Dick Haymes, Doris Day, Dinah Shore, Perry Como, and hundreds of much lesser talents were recording prolifically, using vocal ensembles as backgrounds. Many of these vocal recordings became commercial hits, virtually by default for lack of instrumental competition, and many singers acquired the status of stars almost overnight, an advantage over instrumentalists they were never to relinquish.

For it was this fateful forward lunge of singers in the popular market that helped to seal the fate of big bands and drove a permanent wedge between themselves and jazz. Jazz was to all intents and purposes *driven* to bop by the dominance of singers in the popular market, almost none of them "jazz" singers (by any reasonable definition of the term "jazz"). That market had at one time been unified in its acceptance of jazz, in the form of swing. But now it was severely fragmented, catering to a commercially and stylistically divided audience which was unable to reconcile the easy attractions of popular singers with the ever more demanding challenges of the young boppers, ready to reform and "advance" jazz. Trying to stay on safe ground somewhere in the middle were the die-hard swing bands, hoping not to lose their audience to *either* the renegade boppers *or* the solo singers. For the steadfast conservatives, there were the reissues and the early jazz to rejoice in and the New Orleans revivalists and neo-Dixielanders. Thus, not only was the house of jazz divided, but so were its occupants.

I have frequently referred to the gradual atrophying of swing: atrophy by repetition, formularization, the reduction of improvisation and, thereby, loss of spontaneity of creation. By the time bop came in, most big bands had become so creatively restrictive and inflexible and so entrapped by their own popularity and commercial success, that they could not really deal with the faster moving, technically more demanding, lighter, airier expressions of bop, not to mention the spectre of perhaps losing what audience they had left. Some orchestras did make the transition to modern jazz, of course—Woody Herman, Charlie Barnet, Boyd Raeburn, Stan Kenton, Billy Eckstine—but most bands floundered on these new craggy musical and economic reefs.

Inevitably jazz turned to the small combo: quartets and quintets, occasionally ranging to octets and nonets. Here the fresh ideas and exploratory thrust of bop— its greater technical agility, new clarity of lines, more advanced harmonies and melodic constructions—had at last found a flexible, versatile medium, the ideal vehicle for these new forms of expression. Interestingly, in this respect jazz had come full circle and returned to the smaller ensembles of its early New Orleans and Chicago years. But, most important of all, jazz (bop) had found its way back to improvisation. By 1945 and '46 the cutting edge of jazz was now a more "abstract" kind of musical expression and language; it was less narrative, less impressionistic, less descriptive.

The thrust now was once again towards individual and spontaneous creativity, and in the direction of solo virtuosic prowess—again, in a way like classic New Orleans jazz, except that the latter was more ensemble-oriented, technically more limited, and harmonically less advanced. But the individual creative freedom was the same, perhaps even more so now, since bop was a much more solo-oriented music.

The arranger was now also de-emphasized, demoted from his primary role in the swing bands. What was there to arrange for a quintet of two horns and three rhythm, when in all likelihood at least two of the players were the composer-leaders of the group (e.g., Parker and Gillespie, Monk and Milt Jackson, Clifford Brown and Max Roach)? What was there to arrange when the music was going to be primarily improvised and, in any case, brief ensemble passages could be put together in an instant in a "head" arrangement?

With this new music challenging the primacy of the big bands, with the postwar period now dominated by singers and the whole field experiencing dramatic economic changes, the end of the Big Band Era was in sight. By the late 1940s and early 1950s many leaders of the prewar period could no longer sustain their earlier popularity; nor could most of them come to terms with bop and compete with the extraordinary influx of new innovating talent.

The demise of swing and the big bands signaled the end of an era, the end of a remarkable two decades of music, years filled—as we have seen—with great performances and recordings, inspired by an extraordinary range of talents, and ennobled by the finest period in the history of American popular songs, many of which became the basis for a whole new world of improvised jazz, and which endure to this day.

But in human history every ending is also a new beginning. And so it is with jazz. As pointed out already, jazz was merely in phase-transition, evolving from one mode of expression to another, with the basic root concept and structure intact. At its best, the Swing Era was, as chronicled in this volume, a most glorious period in the history of American music, but it certainly was not the final chapter of the story. What followed was in many ways even more exciting and, if the truth be told, given to a purer, more personalized form of individual expression. Ever more America's own art music and ever less America's entertainment and popular music, jazz has since the Swing Era experienced its share of struggle to endure and survive. And with the combined emergence in the 1960s of rock and the (in many cases) increased complexity and intellectualization of jazz, its very survival was for a while threatened. But jazz is a hardy strain, stronger in the end than any of its offspring and derivatives which periodically try to subdue and stifle it.

Volume III of this History will chronicle the exciting development of jazz in the postwar years: the full flowering of modern jazz, the rich and unprecedented effusion of talent that marks the most recent three or four decades of this music. Although the present volume, as a practical consideration, ends essentially in the mid-1940s, it should not be taken to imply some inherent qualitative demarcation on my part. Another glowing chapter in American music is yet to come. Tune in again in a few years.

Appendix I

	Barnet	Herman	Eckstine	Raeburn	James
1943					
Oct	The Moose				
Nov		Do Nothin'			
Dec					
1944					
Jan		Under My Skin			
Feb	Cotton Tail	I'll Get By			
	Drop Me Off				
March	Gulf Coast	Milkman			
April			I Stay in the Mood		
May			Good Jelly		
June		Apple Honey			
July		(V-Disk)			
Aug	Skyliner				
Sept		Happiness			
Oct	West End	(V-Disc)			
Nov					Beginning
Dec		I Ain't Got	Blowin' the Blues		
		Nothing			
1945					
Jan				March of Boyds	
Feb		Caldonia			
		Apple Honey			
		Happiness			
March		NW Passage			
April					
May					
June					
July					
Aug		Good Earth			
Sept		Bijou			
Oct				Forgetful	
Nov					
Dec					Friar Rock
					Who's Sor
					Now
1946					
Jan					
Feb					Easy
March					
April					
May		Fan It		Boyd Meets	
				Stravinsky	
June					
July					
Aug	Cherokee				
Sept	No. 2	Summer Sequence			
		Everywhere			
Oct					
Nov					
Dec		Woodchopper's			
		Ball			

⋅w	Krupa	Kenton	Gillespie	Brown	
					1943
					Oct
					Nov
					Dec
					1944
					Jan
					Feb
					March
					April
					May
					June
					July
					Aug
					Sept
					Oct
⋅pin on					Nov
⋅erry-Go-Round					Dec
					1945
Vonderful	What's This				Jan
ford Drive|	Leave Us Leap				
⋅'t Help Lovin'					Feb
					March
⋅e Jazz					April
⋅nmertime		Tampico			May
⋅ky Number					June
					July
					Aug
					Sept
	Tea for Two	Artistry Jumps			Oct
					Nov
		Artistry in Rhythm			Dec
					1946
	I Hear You	Intermission Riff			Jan
				Lover's Leap	Feb
					March
					April
	Ain't Nowhere				May
			Our Delight		June
		Artistry in Perc.	Things To Come		July
		Willow Weep			Aug
					Sept
	Southland				Oct
			Emanon		Nov
					Dec

Appendix II

As suggested in Chapter IV (p. 225), I thought it would be instructive to illustrate the element of swing in visualized terms, with the important advantage that such visualizations are more unequivocally accurate and precise than any verbal description. They are thus representations which hardly permit arbitrary or variable interpretations.

The illustrations depicted here show the *envelope* of the sound in each example, indicating the relative level or volume of the sound. The envelope can be used to examine such characteristics as the attack and decay and fluctuations of a tone. The illustrations were developed from computer analyses of recorded performances of the four musical excerpts. The "original" performances by Louis Armstrong and Ray Brown were put on tape, and then paired with the exact same excerpts, rendered on tape by Bo Winiker (trumpeter) and Richard Sarpola (bassist) respectively. Winiker and Sarpola were instructed to play the excerpts in a non-swinging, technically correct manner, but identical to the original models in respect to tempo and dynamic levels.

The rather dramatic differences between playing which swings and playing which doesn't can be clearly seen in these graphic illustrations, most particularly in the difference in the decay patterns of the notes. Note, for example, the visibly long durations in Ray Brown's walking bass line (Fig. 1a), as compared with the much shorter and more quickly thinning-out patterns produced by the non-swinging bass notes of Richard Sarpola (Fig. 1b). Indeed, Brown's notes almost link up with each other in a continuous musical line, while Sarpola's notes show considerable interruptions between individual notes, clearly indicating a lack of line and a lack of swing.

Similar differentiations can be seen by comparing the two swinging examples of Louis Armstrong (Figs. 2a, 3a) and the same excerpts played in a non-swinging manner by Bo Winiker (Figs. 2b, 3b).

Apart from visually depicting the difference between swinging and non-swinging playing, the illustrations reveal some other aspects of performance. Winiker's classically oriented playing shows sameness of note production: controlled and clean, accurately placed in the time continuum. It is akin to what in computer language is called "synthetic speech." Armstrong's playing on the

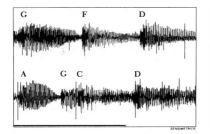

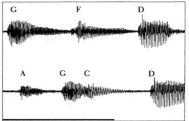

Figure 1a. *How High the Moon*, played by Ray Brown from the LP "The Oscar Peterson Trio at the Stratford Shakespearean Festival"; Verve MGV-8024 (1962). The seven notes of the excerpt occur in the fifth bar after Ray Brown's solo. (If anyone wants to learn what swing is and how it sounds, the Peterson Trio's recording of *How High the Moon* provides the ultimate lesson. It is not possible to listen to this performance without wanting to move one's feet, hand, body in time to the beat.)

Figure 1b. *How High the Moon*, recorded on tape by Richard Sarpola in 1986.

(Sectors plotted—256; sectors per line—128; sampling rate—20 kHz; time compression—64:1; line duration—1.63 seconds; indicated time unit (black line parallel to bottom frame)—1 second; vertical reduction for 1a—200:1; for 1b—300:1)

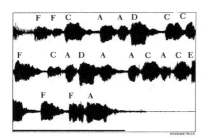

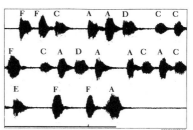

Figure 2a. *Home*, played by Louis Armstrong, recorded originally on Okeh 41552 (1932), reissued on Epic EE-22019. The excerpt is part of a series of double-time solo breaks near the end of the performance.

Figure 2b. *Home*, recorded on tape by Bo Winiker in 1986.

(Sectors plotted—384; sectors per line—128; sampling rate—20 kHz; time compression—64:1; line duration—1.63 seconds; indicated time unit (black line parallel to bottom frame)—1 second; vertical reduction for 2a—600:1; for 2b—250:1)

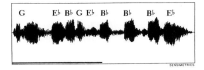

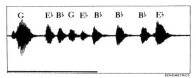

Figure 3a. *Mahagony Hall Stomp*, played by Louis Armstrong, recorded originally on Victor 24232 (1933), reissued on Victor LPM-2322. The excerpt is a solo break near the end of the performance.

Figure 3b. *Mahagony Hall Stomp*, recorded on tape by Bo Winiker in 1986.

(Sectors plotted—384; sectors per line—160; sampling rate—20 kHz; time compression—80:1; line duration—2.04 seconds; indicated time unit (black line parallel to bottom frame)—1 second; vertical reduction for 3a—600:1; for 3b—250:1)

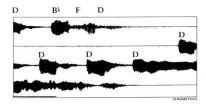

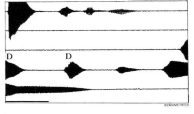

Figure 4a. *Laughing Louie*, played by Louis Armstrong, recorded originally on Bluebird B-5363 (1933), reissued on Victor LPM-2322.

Figure 4b. *Laughing Louie*, recorded on tape by Bo Winiker in 1986.

(Sectors plotted—1080; sampling rate—15.15 kHz; time compression—32:1; line duration—1.08 seconds; indicated time unit (black line parallel to bottom frame)—.25 seconds; vertical reduction for 4a—800:1; for 4b—200:1)

other hand is looser, exhibits full attacks and full durations, and above all, enormous variety. This is more akin to what in computer language is called "connected speech," that is, human speech. Similarly, Ray Brown's attacks are firm and full (shown by the very dense black tracings at the beginning of each note), followed by a strong sustained resonance. Sarpola's classically oriented pizzicato attacks are less full, much more varied in their structure and—obviously—drier, less resonant in duration.

TECHNICAL INFORMATION

Each musical example was, as mentioned, copied onto tape and then played into a computer where it was s3Bdigitized, that is, converted to a stream of numbers. The numbers are obtained by measuring the level of the signal repeatedly and rapidly, in this case 20,000 times per second. This process is the first step in digital recording. The numbers are then stored on the recording tape in a code of magnetic dots. In preparing the envelope traces, the stream of numbers was recorded on the computer's internal magnetic storage device.

The stored numbers can be used by the computer to reconstitute the original signal as a picture, as shown on pp. 856–57, by controlling the position of a pen moving across paper. In the case of these illustrations, a laser beam controlled by the computer made the envelope traces.

Ex. 1 (used in Fig. 1)

Ex. 2 (used in Fig. 2)

Ex. 3 (used in Fig. 3)

Ex. 4 (used in Fig. 4)

If drawn on a scale that allows each individual measurement to be seen, a single second of music would occupy a chart more than sixteen feet long. The information here has been compressed into slightly more than three inches by performing certain mathematical operations on the data. Such operations are made possible by the storage of the signal in the form of numbers, since computers can add, subtract, compare, and average numbers at high speed. The enormous compression of the recorded information normally makes the elementary vibrations of the recorded sound waves invisible. However, at low frequencies that occur in some parts of the pizzicato bass examples, the individual vibrations of the strings (the waveforms) can be seen.

Although separated into horizontal lines for convenience in drawing and printing, each trace is actually a continuous record of the corresponding musical excerpt. A trace begins at the left side and proceeds, as time advances, to the right and down to the next line, just as one reads a printed page. The vertical scale in each plot is arbitrary, and no conclusions can be drawn from the relative heights of the envelopes in different recordings. In fact, the heights have been adjusted to compensate for differences in the recordings used as source material. The differing vertical reductions in these eight illustrations were applied to make the two trumpeters' and two bassists' playing—recorded in the first instance over fifty years apart, in the second twenty-five years apart, on different recording equipment and in different acoustical environments—appear visually similar in order to make comparison easier.

Envelope traces allow precise visual comparison of the attack, decay, and fluctuation in the level of a tone. However, the envelope tracings do not directly show the spectral characteristics of a sound, which largely determine its timbre. Nevertheless, the envelope does show some information relevant to timbre. Tones with an envelope that begins with a steep, precipitous rise sound characteristically "hard" as they begin. Notes that show an envelope that starts gradually have a softer, springier, pure-sounding start. Notes that display an irregular envelope outline are likely to sound raspy or rough; where the envelope is smooth, the tones generally have a correspondingly smooth, uniform sound.

Glossary

Note: In addition to the use of roman numerals for the various degrees of the scale, the following signs occur in the musical notations:

o = diminished chord
ø = half-diminished chord (reading upwards, two minor thirds and one major third)

aug = augmented chord
m = minor chord
− = minor (i.e. −9 or ♭9)
+ = major (i.e. +9)

All other chords not modified by one of the above signs are assumed to be major chords.

˘ = unstressed or unweighted notes.
´ = stressed or weighted notes.

ACCELERANDO   Speeding up in tempo.
ALTERNATE-FINGERING   An effect produced on valve or keyed instruments when alternate or "false" fingering is used to produce a note.
ANTIPHONY   A form of musical response, as of one choir answering another; a music characterized by the alternation of two or more different parts.
ARPEGGIO   The production of the tones in a chord in rapid succession, i.e. not simultaneously.
ATONALITY   Absence of tonality; a music characterized by a method of organization without reference to a key or tonal center, one using the tones of the chromatic scale impartially and autonomously. See *Chromaticism*.
BIMETRIC   A term applied to the use of two different meters simultaneously. See *Polymetric*.
BINARY TIME   A metric or rhythmic structure characterized by units of two, such as 2/4 or 2/8.
BITONALITY   The simultaneous use of two different tonalities or keys.

861

BLOCK CHORDS   Large, many-voiced chords, which move in parallel motion.

BLUE NOTE   A microtonal variant, usually flatted from the pure intonation of the
note. It is associated almost exclusively with the third, fifth, and seventh
degrees of the scale. It is freely used in *Blues* and jazz.

BLUES   A form of folk music developed by the Negro slaves in the United States
during the nineteenth century. Blues were notated, harmonized, and published beginning in the second decade of the twentieth century. The typical blues text has a stanza of three lines, the second of which is a repetition
of the first. It usually tells of moods of depression, natural disasters, or the
loss of a loved one. As the blues became urbanized, the subject matter
became broader, including eventually the evocation of happier moods. In
a corollary development, the blues form crystallized into a specific chord
and measure pattern. The most common form is the twelve-bar blues set
in the following chord progression: I-IV-I-V-I. Eight-bar and sixteen-bar
blues are also relatively common. Today blues can refer to a vocal blues
song, or simply to the twelve-bar blues structure, the most basic musical
form in jazz.

BOMBS   Colloquial for strong, off-the-beat accents used by drummers; a device
that became very common during the bop and modern jazz eras, but was
not unknown to drummers before that time.

BOOGIE-WOOGIE   A "primitive" manner of playing the blues on the piano. It is
characterized by a steady, repetitive *ostinato* figure in the left hand or bass.

BOOK   The term used to describe the library of a band or combo.

BOP   The name given to a period in jazz, and to the music characteristic of that
period (*ca.* 1943–53). Also known as bebop or (less familiarly) rebop.

BREAK   A short rhythmic-melodic *cadenza* interpolated by an instrumentalist (or
singer) between ensemble passages.

BRIDGE   The name given to the third eight-bar section in a thirty-two-bar song
form; i.e. the *B* part of an *A A B A* song form. Synonymous with RELEASE
and CHANNEL.

BROKEN TENTH   The interval of the tenth or a chord spanning this interval played
not simultaneously but in rapid succession. Left-hand patterns using a
series of broken tenths to fill out a chord progression came into use in the
1920s. They may have been initiated originally by pianists whose hands
were not large enough to reach a tenth on the keyboard.

CADENZA   An extemporized section in a composition, particularly a concerto,
providing a soloist with an opportunity to display his virtuosity.

CALL-AND-RESPONSE PATTERN   A musical form common to much jazz and African music in which a "call," usually by a solo singer or instrumentalist, is
answered by a "response," usually by an ensemble or (in African music)
the assembled participants in a ritual; a pattern found in religious cere-
monies in which the congregation responds to the "call" of the preacher.

CANON, CANONIC   A musical form or technique in which a second (or third, fourth,
etc.) part imitates a first part or melodic line. Canonic imitation is frequently used in contrapuntal works.

CHALUMEAU   An obsolete forerunner of the clarinet; also, by inference, the lowest register of the clarinet.

CHANGES   See *Chord changes*.

CHANNEL   See BRIDGE.

CHORD CHANGES   Another term for a chord progression. In jazz, the term "changes" is commonly used alone, as in "the changes of a tune."

CHORD PROGRESSION   A series of successive chords.

CHORUS   A musical form in jazz delineating a chord structure or progression which in its totality forms the basis for an improvisation, such as a "blues chorus"; the term is also used by jazz musicians to denote an improvised solo. To play such a solo is to "take a chorus." Also the main body of a popular song, as distinct from the prefatory *Verse*.

CHROMATICISM   The use of chromatic intervals and of chords altered by chromatic means. The term "chromatic" in music refers to tones foreign to a given key and to the free utilization of altered notes and the half-steps of the chromatic (12-note) scale.

CLAM   A mistake or missed note. See also *Fluff*.

CODA   A distinct and clearly demarcated closing section, from the Italian word for "tail."

CONCERTANTE   Concerto-like.

COMPING   An abbreviated term synonymous with "accompanying." It is most frequently applied to the harmonic backgrounds of piano or guitar.

CONTRAPUNTAL   See *Counterpoint*.

COON SONG   A song associated with "coons," a colloquial, derogatory, and now obsolete term for blacks. Coon songs developed in the days of minstrel shows through the latter part of the nineteenth century, and survived into the early days of recording. Stylistically they were a vocal relative of piano ragtime.

COUNTERMELODY   A secondary melody accompanying a primary voice or musical idea.

COUNTERPOINT   Music in several independent yet related parts. See *Polyphony*.

CROSS-ACCENTS   See *Cross-rhythms*.

CROSS-RHYTHMS   The use of two or more rhythmic patterns in such a manner as to produce counter-rhythms or non-simultaneous accentuation; the placing of stressed notes or accents against one another.

CUTTING CONTEST   A term for *Jam sessions* or dances at which various bands or— less commonly—individual players try to "cut" each other, i.e. battle for first place.

DERBY   A derby-shaped mute used on brass instruments.

DESCANT LINE   The term "descant" has had many meanings through the centuries. Here it is used in the sense of an improvised line played in a higher register than the other instruments are playing.

DIATONIC   Pertaining to the standard major and minor scales and to the tonality derived from these scales.

DICTY   Slang for "elegant," "high-class."

DOMINANT   The fifth degree of the diatonic scale; the triad on the fifth degree.

DOUBLE-STOPS   Two notes played simultaneously on one stringed instrument. (The strings are "stopped" by the fingers.)

DOUBLE-TIME   A term applied to doubling a tempo so that it becomes twice as fast as the original. In a 4/4 meter, the playing of eight eighth-notes as if they constituted two bars of twice-as-fast quarter notes is an example of double-time.

EIGHT   Usually one of the three eight-bar phrases in the typical 32-bar AABA popular song structure.

EMBELLISHMENT   Ornamentation.

EMBOUCHURE   Originally French, but widely used in English; signifies the shaping and holding of the lips against the mouthpiece in order to produce a musical tone on a wind instrument.

ENHARMONIC   An adjective referring to two different notations for the same tone, as, for example, *f* sharp and *g* flat; therefore, the interchangeable spelling of the same note.

FERMATA   A pause or holding of a note (or chord).

FLAG-WAVER   A term used to denote a fast, climactic band arrangement or composition. Every well-known swing band had "flag-wavers," often used in competitions with other bands.

FLATTED FIFTH   The flat variant of the fifth degree; the interval formed by the lowered fifth degree and the tonic. In the key of C, *g* flat is the flatted fifth (see *Tritone*).

FLUFF   A mistake or missed note. See also *Clam*.

FOURS   A term applied to the alternating or trading of four-bar improvisations between instruments or sections.

GHOST NOTES   Notes more implied than actually played. They are used consistently in jazz on all instruments, but particularly wind instruments, and are most often associated with subsidiary or passing notes.

GLISSANDO   A sliding effect between two notes, usually with the implication that the entire distance is covered in an ascending or descending slide, as on a trombone or violin.

GROWL   A raspy, rough effect used on wind instruments, particularly the brass. It is often used in conjunction with the plunger mute.

HEAD ARRANGEMENTS   Arrangements improvised or worked out collectively by an entire band or group; usually not written down, but memorized "in the head."

HI-HAT CYMBAL   An essential part of a jazz drummer's equipment: two small cymbals that can be struck together by operating a foot pedal.

HOMOPHONIC   Music in which a primary melodic line is accompanied by subsidiary harmony parts; the opposite of *Polyphony*. Generally applied to chordal writing in music.

HORIZONTAL RELATIONSHIPS   The melodic, or linear, aspects of a musical structure as differentiated from the harmonic, or chordal. Relationships notated and read horizontally, i.e. across the page from left to right, in musical notation. See V*ertical relationships.*

"HORN"   In jazz parlance any wind or blown instrument.

IMPROVISATION   A manner of playing extemporaneously, i.e. without benefit of written music. Improvisation, if it is not absolutely essential to jazz, is considered to be the heart and soul of jazz by most jazz musicians and authorities. It is equatable with composing on the spur of the moment.

INFLECTION   In jazz, inflection connotes the entire gamut of individual phrasing idiosyncrasies developed by jazz artists, such as accenting, attacking, holding, bending, flattening of notes, and the manifold combinations thereof. The inflections peculiar to jazz are an essential requisite of *Swing.*

JAM SESSION   An informal gathering of musicians, playing on their own time and improvising, often exhaustively, on one or two numbers. Jam sessions began as a spontaneous after-hours diversion for jazz musicians who felt musically constrained during professional engagements. In the late thirties pseudo-jam sessions were organized by entrepreneurs who engaged musicians specifically to "jam." In the 1950s and '60s, jam sessions became a rarity.

JIVE   A slang expression denoting glib or foolish talk; the jargon of jazz musicians (now slightly obsolete).

JUNGLE MUSIC   A term applied to certain pieces (and a style derived therefrom) by the Duke Ellington band in the late 1920s; named after the jungle-like sounds and imitations particularly of the brass instruments.

KEY CENTER   See *Tonic.*

KLANGFARBEN   German for tone color or timbre.

KLANGFARBEN MELODY   A tone color melody in which segments of a melody or theme are distributed among several instruments.

LEAD   The top or leading voice in a section, most frequently applied to the first trumpet in a band, as in "lead trumpet."

LICK   A short phrase or passage; often with the connotation of a commonly used phrase or a cliché.

MICROTONE, MICROTONAL   An interval smaller than a half-tone, for example, a quarter-tone or a sixth-tone.

MINSTREL SHOWS   A form of entertainment developed in the nineteenth century by black entertainers; a forerunner of vaudeville.

MODULATION   The process of changing from one key or tonality to another.

OBBLIGATO   An accompanimental or semi-independent melody; an embellishment of a melody.

OUT-CHORUS   A final chorus; in a band, usually a climactic full-ensemble chorus.

PARAPHRASE   A form of improvising that allows the original melody improvised upon to be readily recognized, i.e. a melodically ornamental form of improvisation.

PASSING TONE   A non-harmonic note (or notes) between two harmonic notes of successive chords.

PEDAL POINT   A sustained note held, usually in the bass, under a series of moving chords or melodic lines.

PEDAL-POINT BREAK   A *Break* executed over a harmonic *Pedal point*.

PENTATONIC   Consisting of five notes; a five-note scale.

PITCH   The identification of a musical tone as determined by the frequency of vibrations of the sound waves. In Western notation pitches are given a letter name from the alphabet and are represented by a particular degree in the musical staff. Pitch is a more precise term for note or musical tone.

PIZZICATO   Italian for "plucked," primarily used in connection with string instruments.

PLUNGER   A common rubber toilet plunger used as a muting device by trumpet and trombone players.

POLYMETRIC   Applied to the use of three or more meters simultaneously.

POLYPHONY   A term, from the Greek "many-voiced," denoting a musical structure characterized by the independence of its parts. "Polyphony" can be applied to the simultaneous use of several melodies or contrapuntal lines.

POLYRHYTHM   The use of three or more rhythms simultaneously in different parts.

POP TUNES   Popular tunes.

RACE RECORDINGS   A term applied in the 1920s to the recordings made specifically for the Negro market.

RAGTIME   A music characterized by syncopated melody over a regularly accented rhythmic accompaniment. In its strictest sense ragtime refers to a music style developed on the piano in the late nineteenth century.

RELEASE   See BRIDGE.

RIDE CYMBAL   A suspended cymbal used since the 1930s to delineate the main "time" patterns of jazz drummers.

RING-SHOUT   A song-dance in which dancers move counter-clockwise in a ring, singing in a leader-chorus, i.e. *Call-and-response*, form.

RIP   A rapid upward figure on brass instruments, usually produced by tightening the embouchure without using correct fingerings, i.e. playing basically on the harmonic overtone series.

RITARDANDO   Slowing up in the tempo.

RUBATO   Free in tempo.

SCAT-SINGING   A manner of singing employing nonsense syllables.

SHAKE   An instrumental effect sounding like a trill, but usually encompassing a wider intervallic range. It is produced by literally "shaking" the mouthpiece against the lips in a lateral motion. Generally speaking, valves are not used; the shake therefore uses the tones of the brass instruments' harmonic series.

SHOUT   A style of singing the blues in a forceful, "shouting" manner. The term was also applied to instrumentalists who played in a similar manner, such as the "shout pianists" James P. Johnson and Fats Waller.

SIDEMAN   A player in a jazz or dance band, as differentiated from the leader.

STANDARD TUNES, STANDARDS   Familiar, well-established popular songs or instrumental compositions, used by jazz musicians as a basis for improvisation.

STOCK ARRANGEMENT   A published commercial arrangement, usually simplified and standardized; the term is derived from arrangements that are in stock as opposed to especially written arrangements. Compare *Head Arrangements*.

STOMP   A term synonymous with "blues"; it has an extra connotation of a heavy or strongly marked beat.

STOP-TIME   A type of discontinuous rhythm used to accompany tap dancers and, by extension, instrumentalists and singers; a typical example of stop-time jazz is the playing of only the first beat in every two bars.

SUBDOMINANT   The fourth degree of the diatonic scale; the triad on the fourth degree.

SWING   1. A rhythmic element and a manner of playing (inflecting) rhythms peculiar to jazz.
2. A period in the development of jazz (1935–1945) characterized by the emergence and national popularity of "swing" bands; the Swing Era.

SYNCOPATION   A temporary shifting or displacement of a regular metrical accent; the emphasis on a weak or unaccented note so as to displace the regular meter.

TAG-ENDING   A colloquial expression used by musicians to indicate an added, or "tagged-on," ending to a composition or performance.

TERMINAL VIBRATO   A vibrato used at the end of a held tone.

TESSITURA   The general range of a melody, melodic line, or voice part; that part of the compass in which most of the tones of a melody lie.

THIRD STREAM   A term applied in its widest sense to a music or style which combines the essential characteristics and techniques of both jazz and "classical" music; by extension the creative fusion of any folk or vernacular musics with "classical" traditions.

TIMBRE   The tone quality that differentiates one instrument from another; the acoustical properties of an instrument defining its "tone color" (German: *Klangfarbe*). Synonymous also with "sonority."

TONAL CENTER   Identical with *Tonic*.

TONIC   The first degree of the scale; the triad on the first degree, and in tonality the key identified with it.

TRITONE   The interval of the augmented fourth. In the tempered tuning of the piano, it is identical as well to the flatted fifth.

TURNBACK   A jazz musicians' term for that part of an improvised chorus during which the chord progression returns to the initial chord of the piece or the tonic. A turnback usually occurs at the last two bars of an eight- or twelve-bar structure. Most jazz musicians have a number of "improvised" turnback phrases at their command for various turnback chord progressions that are standard in jazz tunes.

UNISON   Two or more instruments or voices sounding on one pitch; the interval of a perfect prime.

VERSE   The introductory section of a popular song or ballad, as distinguished from the *Chorus*. The latter consists most commonly of thirty-two bars while the verse may have an irregular number of bars and may be sung or played in a free tempo.

VERTICAL RELATIONSHIPS   The harmonic, or chordal, aspects of a musical structure as differentiated from the melodic, or linear. Relationships notated and read vertically, i.e. up and down the page, in musical notation. Also, the rhythmic aspects of a musical structure. For example, a rhythmic simultaneity, i.e. a chord, will appear vertically aligned in musical notation, whereas non-simultaneous rhythmic elements will appear vertically unaligned. (See *Horizontal relationships.*)

VIBRATO   The artificial wavering of a note, consisting of slight, rapidly recurring fluctuations of pitch.

VOICE-LEADING, VOICING   A term referring to the manner in which the various voices in a harmonic progression are placed by the arranger or composer or, in a *head arrangement*, by the individual players. The term is commonly used in all music.

WALKING BASS   A term applied to a pizzicato (plucked) bass line that moves in a steady quarter-note rhythm and in scalar or intervallic patterns not limited to the chord tones; i.e. including *passing tones*.

"WEAK" NOTES   Rhythmically unstressed notes.

Index

Note: **Boldface** indicates extended discussion. Dates, when not provided, are unavailable.